Lecture Notes in Computer Science 12922

More information about this subseries at http://www.springer.com/series/7409

Andreas Hotho · Eva Blomqvist · Stefan Dietze ·
Achille Fokoue · Ying Ding · Payam Barnaghi ·
Armin Haller · Mauro Dragoni ·
Harith Alani (Eds.)

The Semantic Web –
ISWC 2021

20th International Semantic Web Conference, ISWC 2021
Virtual Event, October 24–28, 2021
Proceedings

 Springer

Editors
Andreas Hotho (iD)
University of Würzburg
Würzburg, Germany

Stefan Dietze
University of Düsseldorf
Düsseldorf, Germany

Ying Ding
University of Texas
Austin, TX, USA

Armin Haller
Australian National University
Canberra, ACT, Australia

Harith Alani (iD)
The Open University Walton Hall
Milton Keynes, UK

Eva Blomqvist (iD)
Linköping University
Linköping, Sweden

Achille Fokoue
IBM Research - Thomas J. Watson Research
Hawthorne, CA, USA

Payam Barnaghi
Imperial College
London, UK

Mauro Dragoni
Fondazione Bruno Kessler
Povo, Trento, Italy

ISSN 0302-9743   ISSN 1611-3349 (electronic)
Lecture Notes in Computer Science
ISBN 978-3-030-88360-7   ISBN 978-3-030-88361-4 (eBook)
https://doi.org/10.1007/978-3-030-88361-4

LNCS Sublibrary: SL3 – Information Systems and Applications, incl. Internet/Web, and HCI

This Springer imprint is published by the registered company Springer Nature Switzerland AG
The registered company address is: Gewerbestrasse 11, 6330 Cham, Switzerland

Preface

How often does it happen that no one at a big international conference complains about coffee, food, wifi, cramped rooms, and long queues everywhere? This has now happened, for the second year in a row, at the International Semantic Web Conference (ISWC). These are some of the advantages of organizing a virtual conference. It is true that virtual conferences are challenging and unsatisfying in many ways, but they force us all to rethink how to run conferences that are far more accessible to those with physical disabilities, visa restrictions, family constraints, or insufficient research and travel funds. Virtual conferences are also more friendly towards the environment, which does not normally appreciate our habit of flying around the world to attend endless conferences. Having said that, most of us desperately miss the best parts of a conference: the social and scientific buzz, the networking, and the late bar sessions where the greatest and stupidest ideas are sometimes born!

It is my honour to introduce the proceedings of ISWC 2021, and to be the general chair for this conference which celebrates its 20th birthday this year. My most important task as the general chair was to assemble the team that would actually drive the conference and lead it to success. I am so delighted and humbled by the brilliant organization committee, the Senior Program Committee (SPC), and the small army of over 460 Program Committee (PC) members who produced 1032 peer reviews.

This has not been a typical year by any stretch of the imagination, but it was thrilling to realize that ISWC is resilient to pandemics, where 1066 authors from 41 countries collaborated during difficult circumstances to make a total of 364 submissions to the various tracks of the conference. I am extremely thankful to all these brave authors, for without them this conference would have not even existed.

The Research Track, chaired by Eva Blomqvist and Andreas Hotho, received 133 full paper submissions, out of which 24 were accepted, resulting in an acceptance rate of 18%. This track is dedicated to novel and significant research contributions addressing theoretical, analytical, and empirical aspects of the Semantic Web and its intersection with other disciplines. As was the case last year, this track adopted a double-blind approach, where the authors and reviewers remain anonymous. One addition to this track this year was the introduction of a reproducibility checklist for the authors to complete at submission time, in an attempt to encourage them to pay close attention to this important issue. This track was supported by 238 PCs and 24 SPCs, in addition to many external reviewers.

The In-Use Track this year was chaired by Payam Barnaghi and Ying Ding, and continued with the tradition of taking submissions describing applied and validated applications and solutions that benefit from the use of Semantic Web technologies. This track had 45 PC members, received 31 submissions, and accepted 7 with a 23% acceptance rate. The Resources Track, chaired by Stefan Dietze and Achille Fokoue, promoted the sharing of resources which support, enable, or utilize Semantic Web research, including datasets, ontologies, software, and benchmarks. This Track received 38 papers, and accepted 11, thus yielding a 29% acceptance rate. The Resources Track was aided by 8 SPCs and 38 PCs.

Aspects of innovative commercial and industry-strength knowledge graphs and semantic technologies were covered as usual by the Industry Track, This track was chaired by Juan Sequeda and Lorena Etcheverry, and received 20 submissions that are currently under review by 12 PCs. The Doctoral Consortium (DC) gave PhD students the opportunity to present their work and receive constructive feedback from senior members of the Semantic Web community. The DC Track was chaired by Valentina Tamma, Miriam Fernandez, and María Poveda Villalón, and received 16 submissions which were reviewed by 16 PC members who accepted 6 papers, thus giving an acceptance rate of 38%.

The Posters, Demos, and Lightning Talks Track was chaired by Catia Pesquita and Oshani Seneviratne. This track complements the paper tracks of the conference by offering an opportunity to present late-breaking research results, on-going projects, and speculative or innovative work in progress. The track received 102 poster and demo submissions, which were reviewed by 65 PC members who accepted 74 of them with an acceptance rate of 73%. The Lightning Talks part of this track opened a few weeks before ISWC 2021 took place.

Laura Hollink and Mayank Kejriwal chaired the Workshop and Tutorials Track of ISWC this year. Workshops are the primary venues for the exploration of emerging ideas as well as for the discussion of novel aspects of established research topics. Tutorials aim to deliver focused training to Semantic Web researchers and practitioners on key topics and latest work and technologies. Out of the 13 workshop and 4 tutorial proposals submitted, 12 and 3 were accepted respectively. The Semantic Web Challenges Track, chaired by Ernesto Jiménez-Ruiz, Jianyan Chen, and Despoina Magka, accepted 7 challenges this year. This track has a great record in advancing the state of the art in various Semantic Web areas through popular open competitions.

One new addition we came up with this year is the Missions Track. This track was partly inspired by the Vision Track that was included last year, and partly by the need to set up Missions to tackle big and persistent challenges. This year, the mission was Reproducibility. The track was chaired by Raphaël Troncy, and a few prominent scientists were invited to give short talks about their views, work, aspirations, and recommendations towards reproducibility in the Semantic Web.

My thanks also go to the local chair, Kathy Fontaine, and the rest of the local organization team for competently managing the conference, for developing and maintaining the conference website, and for taking care of all the digital logistics associated with running a virtual conference. The sponsorship and publicity chairs, Rafael Gonçalves and Anastasia Dimou, did a superb job in raising sponsorship for the conference in this particularly challenging climate and widely publicizing the conference and its program on the web and social media. I am also in gratitude to the proceedings and metadata chairs, Armin Haller and Mauro Dragoni, who skilfully navigated us through the challenging tasks of generating these proceedings, and of capturing and publicly sharing the conference data in a reusable and open format.

To reduce the ever expanding organization committee of ISWC, and to increase efficiency, we merged highly overlapping tracks and duties that are normally assigned to different chairs. To this end, we combined publicity with sponsorship, DC with student mentoring, posters and demos with lightning talks, and proceedings with metadata. Hence, many of the members of the organization committee took on extra tasks compared to their predecessors from previous ISWC conference, for which I am very grateful.

Finally, my special thanks go to the Semantic Web Science Association (SWSA) for taking such good care of this conference for over 20 long years.

Harith Alani, ISWC 2021 General Chair, on behalf of all the editors.

September 2021

Andreas Hotho
Eva Blomqvist
Stefan Dietze
Achille Fokoue
Ying Ding
Payam Barnaghi
Armin Haller
Mauro Dragoni
Harith Alani

Organization

Organization Committee

General Chair

Harith Alani   Knowledge Media Institute, The Open University, UK

Local Chair

Kathy Fontaine   Rensselaer Polytechnic Institute, USA

Research Track Chairs

Andreas Hotho   University of Würzburg, Germany
Eva Blomqvist   Linköping University, Sweden

In-Use Applications Track Chairs

Ying Ding   University of Texas at Austin, USA
Payam Barnaghi   Imperial College London, UK

Industry Track Chairs

Juan Sequeda   data.world, USA
Lorena Etcheverry   Universidad de la República, Uruguay

Resources Track Chairs

Stefan Dietze   GESIS Leibniz Institute for the Social Sciences and
            Heinrich-Heine-University Düsseldorf, Germany
Achille Fokoue   IBM Research AI, Yorktown Heights, USA

Poster, Demos and Lightning Talk Track Chairs

Catia Pesquita   Universidade de Lisboa, Portugal
Oshani Seneviratne   Rensselaer Polytechnic Institute, USA

Doctoral Consortium Chairs

Valentina Tamma   University of Liverpool, UK
Miriam Fernandez   The Open University, UK
María Poveda Villalón   Universidad Politécnica de Madrid, Spain

Workshop and Tutorial Chairs

Laura Hollink   Centrum Wiskunde & Informatica, The Netherlands
Mayank Kejriwal   University of Southern California, USA

Mission Track Chair

Rafaël Troncy   EURECOM, France

Sponsorship and Publicity Chairs

Rafael Gonçalves   Stanford University, USA
Anastasia Dimou   Ghent University and imec, Belgium

Proceedings and Metadata Chairs

Armin Haller   Australian National University, Australia
Mauro Dragoni   Fondazione Bruno Kessler, Italy

Semantic Web Challenges Track Chairs

Ernesto Jiménez-Ruiz   City University of London, UK, and University of
                                   Oslo, Norway
Jianyan Chen   University of Oxford, UK
Despoina Magka   Facebook AI Research, UK

Research Track Senior Program Committee

Michael Cochez   Vrije Universiteit Amsterdam, The Netherlands
Oscar Corcho   Universidad Politécnica de Madrid, Spain
Claudia D'Amato   University of Bari Aldo Moro, Italy
Gianluca Demartini   The University of Queensland, Australia
Mauro Dragoni   Fondazione Bruno Kessler, Italy
Paul Groth   University of Amsterdam, The Netherlands
Peter Haase   metaphacts, Germany
Olaf Hartig   Linköping University, Sweden
Aidan Hogan   Universidad de Chile, Chile
Laura Hollink   Centrum Wiskunde & Informatica, The Netherlands
Katja Hose   Aalborg University, Denmark
Wei Hu   Nanjing University, China
Sabrina Kirrane   Vienna University of Economics and Business,
                                   Austria
Markus Luczak-Roesch   Victoria University of Wellington, New Zealand
Boris Motik   University of Oxford, UK
Francesco Osborne   The Open University, UK
Jeff Z. Pan   University of Edinburgh, UK

Axel Polleres   Vienna University of Economics and Business,
                                     Austria
Achim Rettinger   Trier University, Germany
Harald Sack   FIZ Karlsruhe – Leibniz Institute for Information
                                     Infrastructure and Karlsruhe Institute of
                                     Technology, Germany
Elena Simperl   King's College London, UK
Martin G. Skjæveland   University of Oslo, Norway
Valentina Tamma   University of Liverpool, UK
Maria Esther Vidal   TIB Leibniz Information Center for Science and
                                     Technology, Germany

Research Track Program Committee

Achille Fokoue   IBM, USA
Adila A. Krisnadhi   Universitas Indonesia, Indonesia
Adrián Soto   Universidad Adolfo Ibáñez, Chile
Agnieszka Lawrynowicz   Poznan University of Technology, Poland
Alasdair Gray   Heriot-Watt University, UK
Alba Fernandez-Izquierdo   Universidad Politécnica de Madrid, Spain
Albert Meroño-Peñuela   King's College London, UK
Alessandro Bozzon   Delft University of Technology, The Netherlands
Alessandro Faraotti   IBM, Italy
Alessandro Piscopo   BBC, UK
Alex Borgida   Rutgers University, USA
Alexandre Rademaker   IBM Research and EMAp/FGV, Brazil
Alina Petrova   University of Oxford, UK
Ana Iglesias-Molina   Universidad Politécnica de Madrid, Spain
Anastasia Dimou   Ghent University, Belgium
Andreas Harth   University of Erlangen-Nuremberg and Fraunhofer
                                     IIS-SCS, Germany
Andreas Thalhammer   F. Hoffmann-La Roche AG, Switzerland
Andrés García-Silva   ExpertSystem, Spain
Andriy Nikolov   AstraZeneca, Germany
Anisa Rula   University of Brescia, Italy
Ankur Padia   Philips Research North America, USA
Antoine Zimmermann   École des Mines de Saint-Étienne, France
Armando Stellato   University of Rome Tor Vergata, Italy
Axel-Cyrille Ngonga Ngomo   Paderborn University, Germany
Aya Zoghby   Mansoura University, Egypt
Bernardo Pereira Nunes   Australian National University, Australia
Bernhard Haslhofer   Austrian Institute of Technology, Austria
Bijan Parsia   University of Manchester, UK
C. Maria Keet   University of Cape Town, South Africa
Carlos Badenes-Olmedo   Universidad Politécnica de Madrid, Spain

Carlos Bobed	University of Zaragoza, Spain
Carlos Buil Aranda	Universidad Técnica Federico Santa María, Chile
Carsten Lutz	University of Bremen, Germany
Catia Pesquita	Universidade de Lisboa, Portugal
Christian Bizer	University of Mannheim, Germany
Claudio Gutierrez	Universidad de Chile, Chile
Cogan Shimizu	Kansas State University, USA
Cuong Xuan Chu	Max Planck Institute for Informatics, Germany
Dagmar Gromann	University of Vienna, Austria
Danh Le Phuoc	Technical University of Berlin, Germany
Daniel Garijo	Information Sciences Institute, Spain
Daniel Miranker	University of Texas at Austin, USA
Daniela Oliveira	Universidade de Lisboa, Portugal
Daniele Dell'Aglio	Aalborg University, Denmark
David Chaves-Fraga	Universidad Politécnica de Madrid, Spain
David Ratcliffe	Defence, Australia
David Tena Cucala	University of Oxford, UK
David Toman	University of Waterloo, Canada
Davide Buscaldi	LIPN, Université Paris 13, France
Dejing Dou	University of Oregon, USA
Deshendran Moodley	University of Cape Town and CAIR, South Africa
Domagoj Vrgoc	Pontificia Universidad Católica de Chile, Chile
Dumitru Roman	SINTEF, Norway
Dunja Mladenic	Jozef Stefan Institute, Slovenia
Egor V. Kostylev	University of Oslo, Norway
Elena Demidova	Bonn University, Germany
Ernesto Jiménez-Ruiz	City, University of London, UK
Essam Mansour	Concordia University, Canada
Fabien Gandon	Inria, France
Fabrizio Orlandi	Trinity College Dublin, Ireland
Fadi Zaraket	American University of Beirut, Lebanon
Frank Wolter	University of Liverpool, UK
Gabriela Montoya	Aalborg University, Denmark
Gerd Stumme	University of Kassel, Germany
Giovanni Casini	ISTI – CNR, Italy
Giuseppe Pirrò	Sapienza University of Rome, Italy
Giuseppe Rizzo	LINKS Foundation, Italy
Gong Cheng	Nanjing University, China
Grigoris Antoniou	University of Huddersfield, UK
Grit Denker	SRI International, USA
Guilin Qi	Southeast University, China
Guillermo Vega-Gorgojo	Universidad de Valladolid, Spain
Guohui Xiao	Free University of Bozen-Bolzano, Italy
Hai Wan	Sun Yat-sen University, China
Hala Skaf-Molli	University of Nantes, France
Haofen Wang	Tongji University, China

Henry Rosales-Méndez	University of Chile, Chile
Hiba Arnaout	Max Planck Institute for Informatics, Germany
Hideaki Takeda	National Institute of Informatics, Japan
Honghan Wu	University College London, UK
Huan Gao	Microsoft, China
Hubert Naacke	Sorbonne Université, UPMC, LIP6, France
Ibrahim Abdelaziz	IBM, USA
Ikuya Yamada	Studio Ousia Inc., Japan
Ilkcan Keles	Aalborg University, Denmark, and Turkcell, Turkey
Isabel Cruz	University of Illinois Chicago, USA
Jacco van Ossenbruggen	CWI and Vrije Universiteit Amsterdam, The Netherlands
Jacopo Urbani	Vrije Universiteit Amsterdam, The Netherlands
Javier D. Fernández	F. Hoffmann-La Roche AG, Switzerland
Jean-Paul Calbimonte	University of Applied Sciences and Arts Western Switzerland, Switzerland
Jianfeng Du	Guangdong University of Foreign Studies, China
Jiaoyan Chen	University of Oxford, UK
Jorge Gracia	University of Zaragoza, Spain
Jose Emilio Labra Gayo	Universidad de Oviedo, Spain
José Luis Ambite	University of Southern California, USA
Jose Manuel Gomez-Perez	expert.ai, Spain
Josiane Xavier Parreira	Siemens AG Österreich, Austria
Juan F. Sequeda	data.world, USA
Julian Padget	University of Bath, UK
Kai-Uwe Sattler	TU Ilmenau, Germany
Kalpa Gunaratna	Samsung Research, USA
Kavitha Srinivas	IBM, USA
Ken Kaneiwa	The University of Electro-Communications, Japan
Kenny Zhu	Shanghai Jiao Tong University, China
Kewen Wang	Griffith University, Australia
Konstantin Schekotihin	Alpen-Adria Universität Klagenfurt, Austria
Krishnaprasad Thirunarayan	Wright State University, USA
Kuldeep Singh	Cerence GmbH and Zerotha Research, Germany
Lei Hou	Tsinghua University, China
Linmei Hu	Beijing University of Posts and Telecommunications, China
Lorena Etcheverry	Universidad de la República, Uruguay
Lu Zhou	Kansas State University, USA
Lucie-Aimée Kaffee	University of Southampton, Germany
Luigi Asprino	University of Bologna and STLab (ISTC-CNR), Italy
Luis Galárraga	Inria, France
Luis Ibanez-Gonzalez	University of Southampton, UK
Magdalena Ortiz	Vienna University of Technology, Austria
Manas Gaur	Wright State University, USA
María Poveda-Villalón	Universidad Politécnica de Madrid, Spain

Marco Luca Sbodio	IBM Research, Ireland
Marco Rospocher	Università degli Studi di Verona, Italy
Mariano Consens	University of Toronto, Canada
Mariano Rico	Universidad Politécnica de Madrid, Spain
Mariano Rodríguez Muro	Google, USA
Maribel Acosta	Ruhr University Bochum, Germany
Markus Krötzsch	TU Dresden, Germany
Marta Sabou	Vienna University of Technology, Austria
Martin Giese	University of Oslo, Norway
Martin Rezkx	Google, USA
Matteo Palmonari	University of Milano-Bicocca, Italy
Matthias Klusch	DFKI, Germany
Maulik R. Kamdar	Elsevier Inc., USA
Maurizio Lenzerini	Sapienza University of Rome, Italy
Maxime Lefrançois	MINES Saint-Etienne, France
Mayank Kejriwal	Information Sciences Institute, USA
Md. Rezaul Karim	Fraunhofer FIT, Germany
Mehwish Alam	FIZ Karlsruhe - Leibniz Institute for Information Infrastructure, Germany
Meng Wang	Southeast University, China
Michael Färber	Karlsruhe Institute of Technology, Germany
Mohad-Saïd Hacid	Université Lyon 1, France
Mounira Harzallah	LS2N, University of Nantes, France
Muhammad Saleem	AKSW, University of Leizpig, Germany
Mustafa Jarrar	Birzeit University, Palestine
Nadine Steinmetz	TU Ilmenau, Germany
Nandana Mihindukulasooriya	IBM Research, USA
Naoki Fukuta	Shizuoka University, Japan
Nathalie Aussenac-Gilles	IRIT CNRS, France
Oktie Hassanzadeh	IBM, USA
Olivier Corby	Inria, France
Oscar Romero	Universitat Politécnica de Catalunya, Spain
Pan Hu	University of Oxford, UK
Panos Alexopoulos	Textkernel B.V., The Netherlands
Paolo Bouquet	University of Trento and OKKAM, Italy
Pascal Molli	LS2N, University of Nantes, France
Pasquale Minervini	University College London, UK
Patrick Philipp	FZI Research Center for Information Technology, Germany
Pedro Szekely	USC Information Sciences Institute, USA
Peng Wang	Southeast University, China
Petar Ristoski	eBay Inc., USA
Peter Bloem	Vrije Universiteit Amsterdam, The Netherlands
Peter Patel-Schneider	Xerox PARC, USA
Philipp Cimiano	Bielefeld University, Germany
Philippe Cudre-Mauroux	University of Fribourg, Switzerland

Pierpaolo Basile	University of Bari, Italy
Pieter Colpaert	Ghent University and imec, Belgium
Pouya Ghiasnezhad Omran	Australian National University, Australia
Prateek Jain	LivePerson Inc., USA
Rafael Peñaloza	University of Milano-Bicocca, Italy
Raghava Mutharaju	IIIT-Delhi, India
Ralf Möller	University of Luebeck, Germany
Ralf Schenkel	Trier University, Germany
Raúl García-Castro	Universidad Politécnica de Madrid, Spain
Renzo Angles	Universidad de Talca, Chile
Riccardo Tommasini	University of Tartu, Italy
Rinke Hoekstra	Elsevier Inc., The Netherlands
Roman Kontchakov	Birkbeck, University of London, UK
Ronald Denaux	Karlsruhe Institute of Technology, Germany
Ruben Verborgh	Ghent University and imec, Belgium
Ruijie Wang	University of Zurich, Switzerland
Ryutaro Ichise	National Institute of Informatics, Japan
Sebastián Ferrada	Universidad de Chile, Chile
Sebastian Rudolph	TU Dresden, Germany
Sebastian Skritek	TU Wien, Austria
Serena Villata	I3S, CNRS, France
Shinichi Nagano	Toshiba Corporation, Japan
Shrestha Ghosh	Max Planck Institute for Informatics, Germany
Shusaku Egami	National Institute of Advanced Industrial Science and Technology, Japan
Simon Werner	University of Trier, Germany
Stasinos Konstantopoulos	NCSR Demokritos, Greece
Stefan Dietze	GESIS - Leibniz Institute for the Social Sciences, Germany
Stefan Schlobach	Vrije Universiteit Amsterdam, The Netherlands
Steffen Thoma	FZI Research Center for Information Technology, Germany
Sumit Bhatia	IBM, India
Summaya Mumtaz	University of Oslo, Norway
Takahiro Kawamura	National Agriculture and Food Research Organization, Japan
Takanori Ugai	Fujitsu Laboratories Ltd., Japan
Terry Payne	University of Liverpool, UK
Thomas Meyer	University of Cape Town and CAIR, South Africa
Tobias Käfer	Karlsruhe Institute of Technology, Germany
Tobias Kuhn	Vrije Universiteit Amsterdam, The Netherlands
Tom Hanika	University of Kassel, Germany
Tomi Kauppinen	Aalto University School of Science, Finland
Ujwal Gadiraju	Delft University of Technology, The Netherlands
Uli Sattler	University of Manchester, UK
Umberto Straccia	ISTI-CNR, Italy

Valentina Presutti	University of Bologna
Valeria Fionda	University of Calabria, Italy
Valerio Basile	University of Turin, Italy
Varish Mulwad	GE Research, USA
Victor de Boer	Vrije Universiteit Amsterdam, The Netherlands
Vinay Chaudhri	Stanford University, USA
Vincent Lully	Sorbonne University, France
Vinh Nguyen	National Library of Medicine, USA
Weiqing Wang	Monash University, Australia
Werner Nutt	Free University of Bozen-Bolzano, Italy
Xander Wilcke	Vrije Universiteit Amsterdam, The Netherlands
Xiaowang Zhang	Tianjin University, China
Xin Wang	Tianjin University, China
Yanghua Xiao	Fudan University, China
Yuan-Fang Li	Monash University, Australia
Yuanzhe Zhang	Institute of Automation, Chinese Academy of Sciences, China
Yuzhong Qu	Nanjing University, China
Zequn Sun	Nanjing University, China
Zhe Wang	Griffith University, Australia
Zied Bouraoui	CRIL-CNRS and University of Artois, France

Research Track Additional Reviewers

Anais Ollagnier	Université Côte d'Azur, CNRS, Inria, I3S, France
Bastian Schäfermeier	L3S Research Center, Germany
Blerina Spahiu	L'Università di Milano-Bicocca, Italy
Cristian Camilo Berrío Aroca	expert.ai, Spain
Daniel Schraudner	Friedrich-Alexander-Universität Erlangen-Nürnberg, Germany
David Purcell	Amazon, Japan
Endri Kacupaj	University of Bonn, Germany
Frederic Bartscherer	Karlsruhe Institute of Technology, Germany
Gabriel Amaral	King's College London, UK
Gunjan Singh	Indraprastha Institute of Information Technology and IIIT Delhi, India
Hang Dong	University of Liverpool, UK
Huayu Zhang	University of Edinburgh, UK
Jiaoyan Chen	University of Oxford, UK
Joshua Schwartz	Kansas State University, USA
Kristian Noullet	Karlsruhe Institute of Technology, Germany
Lucia Siciliani	University of Bari Aldo Moro, Italy
Matteo Antonio Senese	Politecnico di Torino, Italy
Matthias Baumgartner	University of Zurich, Switzerland
Maximilian Stubbemann	L3S Research Center, Germany

Mina Schütz   Austrian Institute of Technology, Austria
Monika Jain   Manipal University, India
Nicolas Tempelmeier   L3S Research Center, Germany
Oleksandra Vsesviatska   FIZ Karlsruhe – Leibniz Institute for Information
                            Infrastructure, Germany
Roberto Avogadro   L'Università di Milano-Bicocca, Italy
Romana Pernisch   University of Zurich, Switzerland
Russa Biswas   FIZ Karlsruhe – Leibniz Institute for Information
                            Infrastructure and Karlsruhe Institute of
                            Technology, Germany
Sotiris Batsakis   University of Huddersfield, UK
Sven Schlarb   Austrian Institute of Technology, Austria
Tabea Tietz   FIZ Karlsruhe – Leibniz Institute for Information
                            Infrastructure, Germany
Thorben Funke   L3S Research Center, Germany
Valentina Anita Carriero   University of Bologna, Italy
Yiyi Chen   FIZ Karlsruhe – Leibniz Institute for Information
                            Infrastructure, Germany

Resources Track Senior Program Committee

Irene Celino   Cefriel, Italy
Elena Demidova   University of Bonn, Germany
Dimitar Dimitrov   GESIS - Leibniz Institute for the Social Sciences,
                            Germany
Anna Lisa Gentile   IBM Research, USA
Aidan Hogan   Universidad de Chile, Chile
Christoph Lange   Fraunhofer FIT and RWTH Aachen University,
                            Germany
Matteo Palmonari   University of Milano-Bicocca, Italy
Heiko Paulheim   University of Mannheim, Germany

Resources Track Program Committee

Katarina Boland   GESIS - Leibniz Institute for the Social Sciences,
                            Germany
Elena Cabrio   Université Côte d'Azur, CNRS, Inria, I3S, France
Francesco Corcoglioniti   Free University of Bozen-Bolzano, Italy
Olivier Curé   Université Paris-Est, LIGM, France
Enrico Daga   The Open University, UK
Jérôme David   Inria, France
Daniele Dell'Aglio   Aalborg University, Denmark
Anastasia Dimou   Ghent University, Belgium
Nicola Fanizzi   Università degli Studi di Bari Aldo Moro, Italy
Tudor Groza   Pryzm Health, Australia

Christophe Guéret	Accenture Labs, Ireland
Peter Haase	metaphacts, Germany
Antoine Isaac	Europeana and Vrije Universiteit Amsterdam, The Netherlands
Elmar Kiesling	Vienna University of Economics and Business, Austria
Tomas Kliegr	Prague University of Economics and Business, Czech Republic
Adila A. Krisnadhi	Universitas Indonesia, Indonesia
Paea LePendu	University of California, Riverside, USA
Maria Maleshkova	University of Siegen, Germany
Albert Meroño-Peñuela	King's College London, UK
Pascal Molli	LS2N, University of Nantes, France
Lionel Médini	LIRIS, University of Lyon, France
Alina Petrova	University of Oxford, UK
Rafael Peñaloza	University of Milano-Bicocca, Italy
Giuseppe Pirró	Sapienza University of Rome, Italy
María Poveda-Villalón	Universidad Politécnica de Madrid, Spain
Maria Del Mar Roldan-Garcia	Universidad de Malaga, Spain
Harald Sack	FIZ Karlsruhe – Leibniz Institute for Information Infrastructure and Karslruhe Institute of Technology, Germany
Mark Schildhauer	NCEAS, USA
Stefan Schlobach	Vrije Universiteit Amsterdam, Germany
Patricia Serrano Alvarado	LS2N, University of Nantes, France
Cogan Shimizu	Kansas State University, USA
Blerina Spahiu	University of Milano-Bicocca, Italy
Kavitha Srinivas	IBM Research, USA
Vojtěch Svátek	University of Economics, Prague, Czech Republic
Ruben Taelman	Ghent University and imec, Belgium
Maria Esther Vidal	TIB Leibniz Information Center for Science and Technology and Leibniz University of Hannover, Germany
Tobias Weller	Karlsruhe Institute of Technology, Germany
Ziqi Zhang	SUniversity of Sheffield, UK

Resources Track Additional Reviewers

Oleksandra Bruns	FIZ Karlsruhe – Leibniz Institute for Information Infrastructure, Germany
Endri Kacupaj	University of Bonn, Germany
Anaïs Ollagnier	Université Côte d'Azur, CNRS, Inria, I3S, France
Joshua Schwartz	Kansas State University, USA
Tabea Tietz	FIZ Karlsruhe – Leibniz Institute for Information Infrastructure, Germany

In-Use Track Program Committee

Aidan Hogan	Universidad de Chile, Germany
Alexander O'Connor	Autodesk, Inc., Germany
Andriy Nikolov	AstraZeneca, USA
Anna Lisa Gentile	IBM Research, USA
Artem Revenko	Semantic Web Company GmbH, Austria
Beatrice Markhoff	University of Tours, France
Carlos Buil Aranda	Universidad Técnica Federico Santa María, Chile
Christophe Debruyne	Trinity College Dublin, Ireland
Cong Yu	Google, USA
Craig Knoblock	USC Information Sciences Institute, USA
Declan O'Sullivan	Trinity College Dublin, Ireland
Damien Graux	Inria, France
Daniel Garijo	Universidad Politécnica de Madrid, Spain
Daniel Gruhl	IBM Almaden Research Center, USA
Dezhao Song	Thomson Reuters, Canada
Djellel Difallah	NYU, USA
Dumitru Roman	SINTEF, Norway
Fabrizio Orlandi	Trinity College Dublin, Ireland
Farahnaz Akrami	University of Texas at Arlington, USA
Francesco Osborne	The Open University, UK
Jose Manuel Gomez-Perez	expert.ai, Spain
Josiane Xavier Parreira	Siemens AG Österreich, Austria
Kerry Taylor	Australian National University, Australia, and University of Surrey, UK
Maria Bermudez-Edo	University of Granada, Spain
Mariano Rico	Universidad Politécnica de Madrid, Spain
Martin Bauer	NEC Laboratories Europe, Germany
Matteo Palmonari	University of Milano-Bicocca, Italy
Matthäus Zloch	GESIS - Leibniz Institute for the Social Sciences, Germany
Maxime Lefrançois	MINES Saint-Etienne, France
Mayank Kejriwal	USC Information Sciences Institute, USA
Michael Luggen	University of Fribourg, Switzerland
Nicolas Heist	University of Mannheim, Germany
Oscar Corcho	Universidad Politécnica de Madrid, Spain
Petar Ristoski	IBM Almaden Research Center, USA
Peter Haase	metaphacts, Germany
Philippe Cudre-Mauroux	University of Fribourg, Switzerland
Renzo Angles	Universidad de Talca, Chile
Sonia Bergamaschi	Universita' di Modena e Reggio Emilia, Italy
Stefan Bischof	Siemens AG Österreich, Austria
Tobias Käfer	Karlsruhe Institute of Technology, Germany
Tomi Kauppinen	Aalto University School of Science, Finland
Vanessa Lopez	IBM Research, USA
Xuezhi Wang	Google, USA

Sponsors

Gold Sponsors

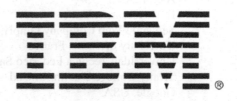

http://www.ibm.com

Google

https://google.com

metaphacts

https://www.metaphacts.com

https://www.oracle.com/goto/rdfgraph

Silver Sponsors

https://franz.com/

https://www.ebay.com/

https://www.ugent.be/ea/idlab/en

Contents

In-Use Track

Research Track

PCSG: Pattern-Coverage Snippet Generation for RDF Datasets

Xiaxia Wang[1], Gong Cheng[1(✉)], Tengteng Lin[1], Jing Xu[1], Jeff Z. Pan[2],
Evgeny Kharlamov[3,4], and Yuzhong Qu[1]

[1] State Key Laboratory for Novel Software Technology,
Nanjing University, Nanjing, China
{xxwang,tengtenglin,jingxu}@smail.nju.edu.cn, {gcheng,yzqu}@nju.edu.cn
[2] School of Informatics, University of Edinburgh, Edinburgh, UK
[3] Bosch Center for Artificial Intelligence, Robert Bosch GmbH, Gerlingen, Germany
[4] Department of Informatics, University of Oslo, Oslo, Norway
evgeny.kharlamov@de.bosch.com
https://knowledge-representation.org/j.z.pan/

Abstract. For reusing an RDF dataset, understanding its content is a prerequisite. To support the comprehension of its large and complex structure, existing methods mainly generate an abridged version of an RDF dataset by extracting representative data patterns as a summary. As a complement, recent attempts extract a representative subset of concrete data as a snippet. We extend this line of research by injecting the strength of summary into snippet. We propose to generate a pattern-coverage snippet that best exemplifies the patterns of entity descriptions and links in an RDF dataset. Our approach incorporates formulations of group Steiner tree and set cover problems to generate compact snippets. This extensible approach is also capable of modeling query relevance to be used with dataset search. Experiments on thousands of real RDF datasets demonstrate the effectiveness and practicability of our approach.

Keywords: RDF data · Snippet · Data pattern · Dataset search

1 Introduction

We have witnessed increasingly many RDF datasets published on the Semantic Web, but understanding the content of a large RDF dataset is still a challenge. Fruitful efforts have been made to compute and present an abridged version of an RDF dataset by extracting representative data patterns to form a *summary* [2]. Summaries are typically composed of schema-level elements, i.e., classes and properties [7,14,24,28,29]. Complementary to the aggregate nature of summaries, a recent line of research extracts a representative subset of instance-level triples to form a compact *snippet* exemplifying concrete data in an RDF dataset [6,15]. We follow this trend to generate snippets that can be incorporated into RDF dataset search engines and profiling tools used by human users.

© Springer Nature Switzerland AG 2021
A. Hotho et al. (Eds.): ISWC 2021, LNCS 12922, pp. 3–20, 2021.
https://doi.org/10.1007/978-3-030-88361-4_1

Research Questions. Existing methods [6,15] generate a snippet by extracting a compact connected RDF subgraph that covers the most important classes and properties in an RDF dataset. There are three limitations of these methods, which pose three research questions (RQs) accordingly. Firstly, these methods aim at covering representative schema-level elements, but they are not powerful enough to attend to combinations of these elements in entity descriptions, i.e., patterns which have been extensively studied in summary generation [7,14,24,28,29]. **RQ1:** How can we generate compact pattern-coverage snippets for RDF datasets? Secondly, while a snippet being a connected RDF subgraph might benefit users' understanding, if the original RDF dataset comprises multiple components, however, connectivity will force existing methods [6,15] to extract a snippet from only one component but ignore the content of all other components. Alternatively, if we extract a sub-snippet from each component and merge all sub-snippets, we will be likely to suffer from redundancy and inefficiency. **RQ2:** How can we jointly consider all components to generate a compact snippet? Thirdly, dataset search [3] is a major downstream application of snippets, and it is often triggered by a query which cannot be exploited by the above methods [6,15]. Query-dependent snippets may help users better determine the relevance of retrieved RDF datasets. **RQ3:** How can we extend snippet generation to be biased toward a given query?

Research Contributions. To answer the above RQs, we inject the strength of summarization (i.e., pattern) into snippet generation and combine the two lines of research. We propose to generate compact *pattern-coverage snippets* for RDF datasets. We answer the three RQs with the following research contributions.

- **For RQ1:** We present an algorithm Basic for generating a compact snippet covering all the patterns of entity descriptions and links in an RDF dataset. Basic achieves compactness by solving a group Steiner tree problem.
- **For RQ2:** Using Basic as a subroutine, we present an algorithm PCSG which handles disconnectivity by generating a compact pattern-coverage snippet that merges the smallest number of sub-snippets extracted from different components. PCSG achieves compactness by solving a set cover problem.
- **For RQ3:** We present an algorithm QPCSG which extends PCSG to generate a query-biased pattern-coverage snippet. QPCSG covers each query keyword as a pseudo-pattern of its matching entity descriptions and links.

Outline. The remainder of the paper is organized as follows. We discuss related work in Sect. 2. We describe Basic in Sect. 3. We describe its extensions PCSG and QPCSG in Sect. 4, and we evaluate these algorithms in Sect. 5 and Sect. 6, respectively. We empirically compare snippet with summary in Sect. 7. We conclude the paper with future work in Sect. 8.

2   Related Work

Given a piece of RDF data [18], a snippet is a subset of triples. Various kinds of snippets have been generated to facilitate different downstream tasks.

RDF Dataset Snippet. To compactly exemplify the content of a large RDF dataset, IlluSnip [6] generates a snippet by formulating a maximum-weight-and-coverage connected graph problem. It aims at extracting an optimum subset of k triples represented as a connected RDF graph that covers the most frequent classes, properties, and the most central entities in the RDF dataset. An approximation algorithm is designed for this NP-hard problem. In [15], a more scalable anytime version of IlluSnip is presented and it can generate snippets for RDF datasets accessible via SPARQL endpoints. Different from IlluSnip, KSD [6] formulates a weighted maximum coverage problem where it removes the constraint on connectivity. Its objective of optimization further aims at covering the most keywords in a keyword query so that it is suitable for RDF dataset search engines. To evaluate these snippets, in [26] a set of metrics are defined to measure how many important classes, properties, entities, and keywords are covered in a snippet. Compared with IlluSnip and KSD, while our approach also aims at covering schema-level elements, we focus on patterns of entity descriptions and links which are *combinations* of classes and properties. Patterns can provide a "higher-order" preview of data than *separate* classes and properties.

RDF Dataset Sample. To efficiently answer SPARQL queries over an RDF dataset, SampLD [20] creates a sample to replace the original RDF dataset. It extracts central triples from the RDF dataset as they are considered to frequently appear in the answers to common queries. GLIMPSE [21] has a similar goal but its ranking of triples is personalized, i.e., biased toward a user's query history. In [12], a sample is created to capture the structural and statistical features of an RDF dataset to benefit query plan optimization. Compared with our dataset snippets which are generated to be read by *human users*, dataset samples are created to be used by *machines* in SPARQL query processing. The two problems and their solutions are fundamentally different.

Entity Summary. The research on entity summarization aims at generating a representative snippet called an entity summary for RDF data that describes *a specified entity* to show its main features [16]. Methods addressing this problem compute a ranking of triples but they cannot apply to an RDF dataset containing *many and various entities* studied in our work.

RDF Dataset Summary. A summary of an RDF dataset usually refers to a set of patterns in the data [2]. Patterns are combinations of classes and properties [7,14,24,28,29], or more complex path-based patterns [1,23]. Snippet and summary provide *complementary views* of an RDF dataset: snippets containing representative *instance-level* triples; summaries comprising representative *schema-level* patterns. They are both important features of a dataset profile [8]. Our approach *combines their strengths* by generating a pattern-coverage snippet. Different from our focus, there are also dataset summaries that can be used for optimizing distributed query answering [10,11] or vocabulary reduction [25].

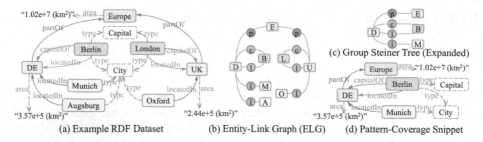

Fig. 1. An RDF dataset and its pattern-coverage snippet generated by `Basic`.

3   Snippet Generation: A Basic Approach

3.1   Problem Formulation

RDF data is a set of subject-predicate-object triples and can be represented as an RDF graph. An example RDF dataset is shown in Fig. 1(a).

Snippet. Given an RDF dataset D which is a set of triples, a *snippet* S of D is a subset of triples represented as a connected RDF graph [6,15]. Connectivity indicates that S describes a set of interlinked entities and exhibits cohesion which is beneficial to users' understanding [6]. In this section we follow this definition.

However, if D itself is represented as a disconnected RDF graph, a snippet defined as above can only be generated from one component and will have to ignore the data in other components. To overcome this limitation, while in this section we assume D is represented as a connected RDF graph, in Sect. 4.1 we will cope with disconnectivity in our full approach.

Pattern. Given a set of triples T, an instance-level entity e is described by a subset of triples where e is the subject or the object. The schema-level elements in these triples form the *entity description pattern* (EDP) of e, consisting of sets of classes (`C`), forward properties (`FP`), and backward properties (`BP`):

$$
\begin{aligned}
\texttt{edp}(e, T) &= \langle \texttt{C}(e, T),\ \texttt{FP}(e, T),\ \texttt{BP}(e, T) \rangle, \\
\texttt{C}(e, T) &= \{c : \exists \langle e,\ \texttt{rdf:type},\ c \rangle \in T\}, \\
\texttt{FP}(e, T) &= \{p : \exists \langle e,\ p,\ o \rangle \in T\} \setminus \{\texttt{rdf:type}\}, \\
\texttt{BP}(e, T) &= \{p : \exists \langle s,\ p,\ e \rangle \in T\}.
\end{aligned}
\tag{1}
$$

A triple where the object is an entity is of particular interest as it represents a link between two entities. The predicate and the EDPs of the two entities in such a triple $\langle e_i,\ p,\ e_j \rangle$ form the *link pattern* (LP) of this triple:

$$
\texttt{lp}(\langle e_i,\ p,\ e_j \rangle, T) = \langle \texttt{edp}(e_i, T),\ p,\ \texttt{edp}(e_j, T) \rangle.
\tag{2}
$$

For example, given T comprising all the triples in Fig. 1(a), we use different colors to show entities and links in Fig. 1 having different patterns such as

$$
\texttt{edp}(\text{Berlin}, T) = \texttt{edp}(\text{London}, T) = p_1 = \langle \{\texttt{Capital}, \texttt{City}\}, \{\texttt{capitalOf}, \texttt{locatedIn}\}, \emptyset \rangle
$$
$$
\texttt{edp}(\text{DE}, T) = \texttt{edp}(\text{UK}, T) = p_2 = \langle \emptyset, \{\texttt{partOf}, \texttt{area}\}, \{\texttt{capitalOf}, \texttt{locatedIn}\} \rangle
$$
$$
\texttt{lp}(\langle \text{Berlin}, \texttt{locatedIn}, \text{DE} \rangle, T) = \texttt{lp}(\langle \text{London}, \texttt{locatedIn}, \text{UK} \rangle, T) = \langle p_1, \texttt{locatedIn}, p_2 \rangle.
$$

By iterating over all entities and links in T, we obtain the set of all EDPs and the set of all LPs in T, denoted by $\mathtt{EDP}(T)$ and $\mathtt{LP}(T)$, respectively.

Pattern-Coverage Snippet. Given an RDF dataset D, a *pattern-coverage snippet* S of D is a snippet that covers all the EDPs and LPs in D:

$$\mathtt{EDP}(D) = \mathtt{EDP}(S) \quad \text{and} \quad \mathtt{LP}(D) = \mathtt{LP}(S). \tag{3}$$

For example, Fig. 1(d) shows a pattern-coverage snippet of the RDF dataset in Fig. 1(a). Observe that S may not be unique. For example, $S = D$ is a trivial pattern-coverage snippet. We aim at finding a compact S of the *smallest size* in terms of the number of triples. We refer to this optimization problem as the *pattern-coverage snippet problem* (PCSP). We will present a solution to PCSP in Sect. 3.2.

Note that if the heterogeneity of D is very high containing many different EDPs and LPs, S covering all patterns can hardly be very compact. In Sect. 4.2 we will extend our approach to cope with high heterogeneity.

3.2   Algorithm Basic

We solve PCSP by Algorithm Basic. Its three steps are outlined in Algorithm 1. We illustrate the output of each step in Fig. 1(b), Fig. 1(c), and Fig. 1(d).

Step 1. We firstly represent an RDF dataset D as an undirected graph where nodes and edges represent entities and entity links in D, respectively. Each node is labeled with its EDP, and each edge is labeled with its LP. Then we convert labeled edges into labeled nodes by subdividing each edge. The subdivision is referred to as the *entity-link graph* representation of D, denoted by $\mathtt{ELG}(D)$, as illustrated by Fig. 1(b) where different labels are represented by different colors.

Step 2. Observe that PCSP essentially looks for a smallest connected subgraph of $\mathtt{ELG}(D)$ whose node labels cover $\mathtt{EDP}(D)$ and $\mathtt{LP}(D)$. It would be straightforward to reduce PCSP to an unweighted version of the well-known *group Steiner tree problem* (GSTP): all nodes having the same label form a group. GSTP requires finding a smallest tree that connects at least one node from each group and hence it covers all distinct labels. GSTP is NP-hard, and we solve it using KeyKG+ [22], a state-of-the-art approximation algorithm for GSTP. Note that for each leaf in the computed tree representing an entity link, we expand the tree to contain both entities it links, as illustrated by the dotted edge in Fig. 1(c).

Step 3. From the computed subgraph of $\mathtt{ELG}(D)$ we derive a pattern-coverage snippet S as follows. For each node in the subgraph representing an entity e, from the triples describing e in D: we choose all triples describing e's classes, and for each property in $\mathtt{edp}(e, D)$ we choose an arbitrary triple describing e using this property. For each node in the subgraph representing an entity link: we choose its corresponding triple from D. All the chosen triples form S, as illustrated by Fig. 1(d).

Algorithm 1: Basic	**Algorithm 2:** PCSG
Input: An RDF dataset D. **Output:** A pattern-coverage snippet S. 1 Construct ELG(D); 2 Compute a group Steiner tree in ELG(D); 3 Derive S from the computed subgraph; 4 **return** S;	**Input:** An RDF dataset D. **Output:** A pattern-coverage snippet S. 1 $\mathcal{D} \leftarrow$ Components(D); 2 $P \leftarrow$ EDP(D) $\cup$ LP(D); 3 $S \leftarrow \emptyset$; 4 **while** $P \neq \emptyset$ **do** 5 $\quad$ $D_i \leftarrow$ $\underset{D_j \in \mathcal{D}}{\arg\max} |(EDP(D_j) \cup$ LP$(D_j)) \cap P|$; 6 $\quad$ $S \leftarrow S \cup$ Basic (D_i); 7 $\quad$ $P \leftarrow P \setminus (EDP(D_i) \cup$ LP$(D_i))$; 8 **return** S;

Time Complexity. The run-time of Basic is dominated by KeyKG+ in Step 2. KeyKG+ runs in $O(n^2 g + ng^3)$ time [22], where $n \leq 3|D|$ is the number of nodes in ELG(D), and $g = |$EDP(D) $\cup$ LP(D)$|$ is the number of groups. Thanks to the efficiency of KeyKG+ [22], Basic is also efficient and practical as we will see in the experimental results in Sects. 5 and 6.

4 Snippet Generation: Extended Approaches

In this section, we extend Basic to accommodate more general settings.

4.1 Extension to Disconnectivity: Algorithm PCSG

Basic assumes the connectivity of D. We use it as a subroutine to be called by our main algorithm PCSG which is extended to handle disconnectivity as follows.

A straightforward idea is to generate a pattern-coverage *sub-snippet* for each component of D and then merge all sub-snippets. However, different components may contain common patterns. It may be unnecessary to generate and merge sub-snippets for all components to form a pattern-coverage snippet S of D. To improve the compactness of S and the efficiency of its generation, we aim at finding a smallest subset of components that cover all the patterns in D. It is an instance of the well-known *set cover problem* (SCP) where EDP(D) $\cup$ LP(D) is the universe and for each component D_j, EDP(D_j) $\cup$ LP(D_j) $\subseteq$ EDP(D) $\cup$ LP(D) is a set. SCP requires finding the smallest number of sets whose union equals the universe. SCP is NP-hard, and we solve it using a standard greedy algorithm [9].

The extended algorithm PCSG, standing for *pattern-coverage snippet generation*, is presented in Algorithm 2. Let $\mathcal{D}$ be the set of all components of D (line 1). P denotes the universe (line 2). Initially S is empty (line 3). Then iteratively until P is fully covered (line 4), we greedily choose a component D_i that contains the largest number of uncovered patterns (line 5). We use Basic to generate a pattern-coverage sub-snippet of D_i and add its triples to S (line 6). Finally we update P for the next iteration (line 7).

Moreover, we modify Basic to generate a possibly smaller sub-snippet of D_i. Observe that the sub-snippet only needs to cover (EDP(D_i) $\cup$ LP(D_i)) $\cap P$ rather than $\text{EDP}(D_i) \cup \text{LP}(D_i)$. In Basic, when formulating GSTP we ignore the groups that correspond to the patterns in $(\text{EDP}(D_i) \cup \text{LP}(D_i)) \setminus P$.

PCSG has the same time complexity as Basic.

4.2 Extension to High Heterogeneity: Algorithm PCSG-τ

PCSG requires a snippet S to cover all the patterns in D. If D is highly hetero-geneous and contains many different patterns, S will inevitably be very large. Below we extend PCSG to achieve a trade-off between pattern coverage and snip-pet size to handle high heterogeneity.

We modify PCSG to generate a possibly smaller snippet that only covers the most important patterns in D. Observe that patterns are not equally important. We define the *relative frequency* of an EDP as the proportion of entities that have this EDP in D. The relative frequency of an LP is defined analogously. More frequent patterns are considered more important. We separately rank all EDPs and all LPs in descending order of relative frequency. In PCSG, we restrict the universe P to only contain top-ranked EDPs and LPs whose total relative fre-quency of EDP and total relative frequency of LP exceed τ which is a parameter describing a percentage. The extended algorithm is referred to as PCSG-τ.

4.3 Extension to Query Relevance: Algorithm QPCSG(-τ)

Below we extend PCSG and PCSG-τ to generate *query-biased snippets* to be pre-sented in dataset search to help users determine the relevance of RDF datasets.

Consider a keyword query Q. We modify PCSG and PCSG-τ to generate a pattern-coverage snippet S that matches all the keywords in Q. Specifically, we view each keyword $q \in Q$ as a *pseudo-pattern*. Each entity or entity link in D is extended to have a set of patterns consisting of: its EDP or LP, and all the pseudo patterns it matches (computed by an off-the-shelf matcher). Accordingly, when formulating GSTP in Basic, for each pseudo-pattern $q \in Q$ we add a group consisting of all entities and entity links that match q. In PCSG and PCSG-τ, we add all the pseudo-patterns in Q to the universe P, and we refer to the extended algorithms as QPCSG and QPCSG-τ, respectively.

Regarding the matcher, we adopt the following simple implementation for our experiments. An entity e matches $q \in Q$ if q appears in any triple describing e in D. An entity link $\langle e_i, p, e_j \rangle$ matches q if q appears in the textual form of p.

5 Evaluation of PCSG(-τ)

We firstly carried out experiments to verify two research hypotheses (RHs) about the *effectiveness* (RH1) and *practicability* (RH2) of our approach PCSG(-τ).

– **RH1:** PCSG(-τ) generates better snippets than [6,15].
– **RH2:** PCSG(-τ) efficiently generates compact snippets.

All our experiments presented in the paper were serially conducted on an Intel Xeon E7-4820 (2GHz) with 80GB memory for JVM. Source code, experimental data, and example snippets are online: https://github.com/nju-websoft/PCSG.

Table 1. Statistics about RDF datasets.

Portal	#RDF Datasets	#triples		#classes		#properties		#EDPs		#LPs	
		Median	Max	Median	Max	Median	Max	Median	Max	Median	Max
DataHub.io	311	1,272	20,968,879	3	2,030	16	3,982	15	270,224	27	156,722
Data.gov	9,233	4,000	6,343,524	1	2	13	545	3	500	2	1,103
Overall	9,544	4,000	20,968,879	1	2,030	14	3,982	3	270,224	2	156,722

5.1   RDF Datasets

We retrieved all datasets with RDF dumps from two data portals: `DataHub.io` and `Data.gov`. We successfully downloaded and used Apache Jena 3.9.0 to parse 9,544 RDF datasets. Their statistics are shown in Table 1. Observe that many entities in datasets from Data.gov are untyped and are described by uniform patterns, probably converted from tabular data.

5.2   Participating Methods

Ours. We implemented three variants: `PCSG`, `PCSG-90%`, `PCSG-80%`.

Baseline. IlluSnip [6,15] represented the state of the art in snippet generation for RDF datasets. Its original version [6] could not scale to large RDF datasets. We used its anytime version [15] and allowed two hours for computing a snippet. We followed [15] to set its parameters. IlluSnip generated size-bounded snippets containing at most k triples. For a fair comparison, for each RDF dataset we set k to the number of triples in the snippet generated by our approach. Accordingly, there were three variants: IlluSnip, IlluSnip-90%, IlluSnip-80%.

5.3   Experiment 1: Coverage of Schema

$PCSG(-\tau)$ and IlluSnip both aimed at schema coverage. To verify RH1, we compared their effectiveness in this aspect.

Metrics. We assessed a snippet's capability of covering four kinds of schema-level elements: class, property, EDP, and LP. For each kind, we measured a snippet's *schema coverage rate* by calculating the total relative frequency (defined in Sect. 4.2) of all the schema-level elements of this kind covered in the snippet. It represented the weighted proportion of covered schema-level elements which were weighted by their numbers of instances. Note that for class and property, their schema coverage rates had been used for evaluating the quality of a snippet in [26] (called `coSkm`). We basically extended it to EDP and LP.

Results. For each approach we calculated its schema coverage rates on each of the 9,544 RDF datasets. The results are summarized in Table 2. All the participating methods achieved (near) perfect schema coverage rates for class and property. It was not surprising: IlluSnip directly optimizes these rates; $PCSG(-\tau)$ indirectly boosts these rates via pattern coverage. However, IlluSnip was unaware of patterns and exhibited considerably lower schema coverage rates for EDP and LP than $PCSG(-\tau)$. Indeed, for $PCSG-\tau$ these rates were guaranteed to exceed τ,

Table 2. Schema coverage rates (mean ± SD).

	Class	Property	EDP	LP
PCSG	1.000 ± 0.000	1.000 ± 0.000	1.000 ± 0.000	1.000 ± 0.000
IlluSnip	0.993 ± 0.079	0.999 ± 0.011	0.822 ± 0.285	0.790 ± 0.320
PCSG-90%	0.999 ± 0.019	0.999 ± 0.006	0.981 ± 0.030	0.976 ± 0.035
IlluSnip-90%	0.991 ± 0.092	0.999 ± 0.013	0.794 ± 0.310	0.762 ± 0.344
PCSG-80%	0.999 ± 0.025	0.998 ± 0.010	0.957 ± 0.061	0.947 ± 0.071
IlluSnip-80%	0.982 ± 0.131	0.998 ± 0.017	0.784 ± 0.317	0.751 ± 0.353

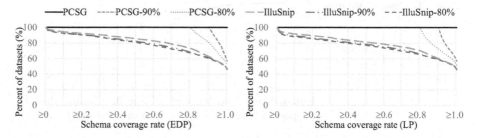

Fig. 2. Cumulative distributions of schema coverage rate.

as illustrated by their cumulative distributions over all RDF datasets in Fig. 2. The results supported RH1 in terms of schema coverage.

5.4 Experiment 2: User Preference

Besides schema coverage rates, to verify RH1, we conducted a user study to compare the quality of snippets generated by different methods. We recruited 20 students majoring in computer science from a university via a mailing list, all having the necessary knowledge about RDF and paid to participate.

Procedure and Metrics. We followed the experimental design for snippet comparison described in [6]. Specifically, each participant was randomly assigned ten RDF datasets. For each RDF dataset, the participant could obtain an overview by accessing its metadata and top-twenty most frequent schema-level elements of each kind: class, property, EDP, and LP, each associated with its frequency (i.e., number of instances). Two snippets of this RDF dataset generated by PCSG-80% and IlluSnip-80% were presented in random order to avoid position bias. Each snippet was visualized as a node-link diagram. Its *quality* was to be rated in the range from 1 to 5 indicating how well it exemplified the content of the RDF dataset. The participant was encouraged to briefly explain the rating.

Results. The results of user-rated quality on 200 RDF datasets are summarized in Table 3. Paired two-sample t-test showed that PCSG-80% generated significantly ($p < 0.01$) better snippets than IlluSnip-80%. PCSG-80% was rated ≥ 4 on most RDF datasets (80%), while for IlluSnip-80% this proportion was only 39%,

Table 3. User-rated quality.

	Mean ± SD
PCSG-80%	4.09 ± 0.97
IlluSnip-80%	3.24 ± 1.12
	Proportion
PCSG-80% > IlluSnip-80%	59.00%
PCSG-80% = IlluSnip-80%	24.50%
PCSG-80% < IlluSnip-80%	16.50%

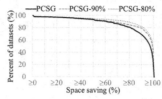
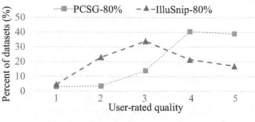

Fig. 3. Distributions of quality.

Table 4. Space savings (mean ± SD).

PCSG	87.02% ± 21.42%
PCSG-90%	89.62% ± 20.98%
PCSG-80%	91.45% ± 19.22%

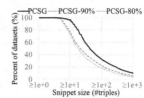

Fig. 4. Cum. distributions of space saving.

Fig. 5. Cum. distributions of snippet size.

according to the distributions in Fig. 3. On 59% of all RDF datasets PCSG-80% was thought to generate better snippets. Participants in their explanations of PCSG-80%'s ratings were satisfied with the comprehensive classes and properties included in each entity description which facilitated the comprehension of data content and structure. The results supported RH1 in terms of user preference. However, on 17% of all RDF datasets IlluSnip-80% was thought to generate better snippets. In fact, participants' explanations were mainly concerned about visualization: snippets generated by PCSG-80% were often denser and hence their node-link diagram visualizations appeared more complex. It inspires us to study presentation methods that are more suitable for EDPs and LPs in future work.

5.5   Experiment 3: Space Saving and Run-Time

To verify RH2, we measured the space saving and run-time of our approach.

Metrics. We measured the *space saving* of our approach on an RDF dataset:

$$\text{space saving} = 1 - \frac{\text{number of triples in the generated snippet}}{\text{number of triples in the RDF dataset}}, \qquad (4)$$

and we reported the *size* of a snippet in terms of the number of triples. Recall that IlluSnip was configured to generate snippets of the same size as ours, thereby having the same space saving and size. We also reported the *run-time* of each approach on an RDF dataset (excluding the time for parsing RDF dumps).

Results. We calculated the space saving of our approach on each of the 9,544 RDF datasets. The results are summarized in Table 4. Our approach substantially reduced the size of an RDF dataset by an average of about 90%. The

Table 5. Run-time in milliseconds (mean ± SD).

PCSG	2,806 ± 95,310
IlluSnip	856,446 ± 2,103,072
PCSG-90%	1,336 ± 70,896
IlluSnip-90%	572,099 ± 1,722,136
PCSG-80%	981 ± 47,325
IlluSnip-80%	446,110 ± 1,516,651

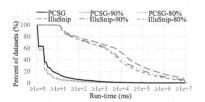

Fig. 6. Cum. distributions of run-time.

space savings of PCSG, PCSG-90%, and PCSG-80% were above 95% on 57%, 69%, and 72% of all RDF datasets, respectively, as illustrated by the cumulative distributions in Fig. 4. The median numbers of triples in their generated snippets were only 41, 20, and 17, respectively, as illustrated by the cumulative distributions in Fig. 5. These numbers were comparable to the size constraints on compact snippets ($k = 40$ or $k = 20$) proposed in previous research [6,15,26]. The results supported the compactness part of RH2. However, we observed a small proportion of snippets containing more than 1,000 triples for highly heterogeneous RDF datasets using diverse combinations of hundreds of properties to describe entities. Their browsing could be facilitated by an interface for filtering as in [17].

For each approach we recorded its run-time on each of the 9,544 RDF datasets. The results are summarized in Table 5. PCSG(-τ) was more than two orders of magnitude faster than IlluSnip. The run-time of PCSG, PCSG-90%, and PCSG-80% was below one second on 98%, 98%, and 99% of all RDF datasets, respectively, as illustrated by the cumulative distributions in Fig. 6. The results supported the efficiency part of RH2. However, for several highly heterogeneous datasets containing thousands of EDPs and LPs, PCSG(-τ) used more than an hour. Though still faster than IlluSnip and acceptable as offline computation, it suggested room for further improving the performance of our approach.

6   Evaluation of QPCSG(-τ)

We also carried out experiments to verify two research hypotheses (RHs) about the *effectiveness* (RH3) and *practicability* (RH4) of our approach QPCSG(-τ).

- **RH3:** QPCSG(-τ) generates better query-biased snippets than [27].
- **RH4:** QPCSG(-τ) efficiently generates compact query-biased snippets.

6.1   Queries and RDF Datasets

From three published research datasets [4,5,13] we collected 2,067 keyword queries representing real-world data needs. In our experiments, since keywords were to be matched with the content of an RDF dataset rather than its metadata, we followed an existing annotation scheme [4] to manually annotate each

Table 6. Statistics about queries.

Source	#queries	#filtered queries	#words in a filtered query		
			Min	Median	Max
Ref. [13]	449	399	1	3	12
Ref. [4]	1,498	843	1	3	15
Ref. [5]	120	114	3	6	15

Table 7. Statistics about RDF datasets in Q-D pairs.

	#Q-D pairs	#triples		#classes		#properties		#EDPs		#LPs	
		Median	Max	Median	Max	Median	Max	Median	Max	Median	Max
Overall	13,429	9,049	10,733,302	1	2,030	20	3,982	11	270,224	10	156,722

query and removed keywords that were to be matched with metadata (e.g., data format, license). We also removed stop words and filtered out empty queries. For the remaining 1,356 filtered queries, their statistics are shown in Table 6.

To match queries with the 9,544 RDF datasets described in Sect. 5.1, we employed Apache Lucene 7.5.0 to index the content of each RDF dataset as a pseudo document by transforming each triple into a sentence concatenating its subject, predicate, and object in their textual forms (e.g., `rdfs:label`, local name, lexical form). We used the default document retrieval model provided by Lucene and kept ten top-ranked RDF datasets for each query. As a result we obtained 13,429 query-dataset pairs, or Q-D pairs for short. For the RDF datasets in these Q-D pairs, their statistics are shown in Table 7.

6.2 Participating Methods

Ours. We implemented three variants: QPCSG, QPCSG-90%, QPCSG-80%.

Baseline. KSD [27] represented the state of the art in query-biased snippet generation for RDF datasets. We followed [27] to set its parameters. KSD generated size-bounded snippets containing k triples. For a fair comparison, for each RDF dataset we set k to the number of triples in the snippet generated by our approach. Accordingly, there were three variants: KSD, KSD-90%, KSD-80%.

6.3 Experiment 4: Coverage of Query and Schema

QPCSG(-τ) and KSD both aimed at query coverage and schema coverage. To verify RH3, we compared their effectiveness in these two aspects.

Metrics. Given a set of keywords in a query, we used two metrics [26] to assess a snippet's capability of covering the query: coKyw calculating the proportion of keywords covered in the snippet; coCnx calculating the proportion of keyword

Table 8. coKyw, coCnx, and schema coverage rates (mean ± SD).

	coKyw	coCnx	Class	Property	EDP	LP
QPCSG	0.948 ± 0.124	0.841 ± 0.308	1.000 ± 0.000	1.000 ± 0.000	1.000 ± 0.000	1.000 ± 0.000
KSD	0.895 ± 0.239	0.489 ± 0.443	0.944 ± 0.207	0.916 ± 0.219	0.222 ± 0.316	0.070 ± 0.190
QPCSG-90%	0.948 ± 0.124	0.839 ± 0.307	0.998 ± 0.013	0.998 ± 0.009	0.947 ± 0.041	0.943 ± 0.042
KSD-90%	0.888 ± 0.248	0.455 ± 0.442	0.905 ± 0.262	0.867 ± 0.261	0.190 ± 0.307	0.047 ± 0.168
QPCSG-80%	0.948 ± 0.124	0.836 ± 0.309	0.996 ± 0.020	0.981 ± 0.080	0.890 ± 0.081	0.883 ± 0.082
KSD-80%	0.884 ± 0.253	0.438 ± 0.440	0.892 ± 0.284	0.842 ± 0.281	0.174 ± 0.296	0.037 ± 0.153

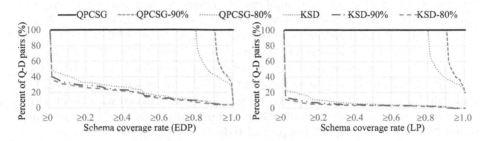

Fig. 7. Cum. distributions of schema coverage rate.

Table 9. Space savings (mean ± SD).

QPCSG	88.07% ± 20.78%
QPCSG-90%	90.90% ± 19.87%
QPCSG-80%	92.38% ± 18.36%

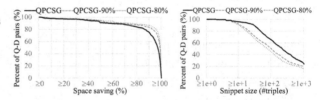

Fig. 8. Cum. distributions of space saving.

Fig. 9. Cum. distributions of snippet size.

pairs connected by a path in the RDF graph representation of the snippet. For schema coverage we reused *schema coverage rate* defined in Sect. 5.3.

Results. For each approach we calculated its coKyw, coCnx, and schema coverage rates on each of the 13,429 Q-D pairs. The results are summarized in Table 8. All the participating methods achieved satisfying coKyw and schema coverage rates for class and property, which was not surprising since they directly or indirectly optimize these metrics. However, QPCSG(-τ) achieved noticeably higher coCnx than KSD which did not attend to connectivity. KSD was also unaware of patterns and exhibited considerably lower schema coverage rates for EDP and LP than QPCSG(-τ). Observe that for QPCSG-τ these rates were guaranteed to exceed τ, as illustrated by their cumulative distributions over all Q-D pairs in Fig. 7. The results supported RH3 in terms of query and schema coverage.

6.4   Experiment 5: Space Saving and Run-Time

To verify RH4, we measured the space saving and run-time of our approach.

Metrics. We reused *space saving*, *size*, and *run-time* defined in Sect. 5.5.

Results. We calculated the space saving of our approach on each of the 13,429 Q-D pairs. The results are summarized in Table 9. Our approach substantially reduced the size of an RDF dataset by an average of about 90%. The space savings of QPCSG, QPCSG-90%, and QPCSG-80% were above 95% on 59%, 76%, and 81% of all Q-D pairs, respectively, as illustrated by the cumulative distributions in Fig. 8. The median numbers of triples in their generated snippets were 215, 101, and 77, respectively, as illustrated by the cumulative distributions in Fig. 9. These numbers appeared larger than those of PCSG(-τ) reported in Sect. 5.5 because their scopes of statistics were different: the RDF datasets in Q-D pairs here were much larger and more heterogeneous (medians: 9,049 triples, 11 EDPs, 10 LPs in Table 7) than those in Sect. 5 (medians: 4,000 triples, 3 EDPs, 2 LPs in Table 1) so that many keyword queries were matched with them. However, *on the same RDF dataset*, QPCSG(-τ) did not output noticeably more triples than PCSG(-τ). The compactness part of RH4 was still supported.

Table 10. Run-time in milliseconds (mean ± SD).

QPCSG	39,301 ± 268,090
KSD	89,516 ± 718,355
QPCSG-90%	14,215 ± 131,611
KSD-90%	55,458 ± 473,939
QPCSG-80%	13,369 ± 126,801
KSD-80%	44,757 ± 384,312

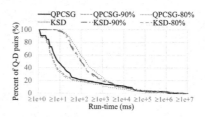

Fig. 10. Cum. distributions of run-time.

For each approach we recorded its run-time on each of the 13,429 Q-D pairs. The results are summarized in Table 10. QPCSG(-τ) was more than twice as fast as KSD. The run-time of QPCSG, QPCSG-90%, and QPCSG-80% was below one second on 85%, 88%, and 91% of all Q-D pairs, though above ten seconds on 11%, 7%, and 4%, respectively, as illustrated by the cumulative distributions in Fig. 10. Again, QPCSG(-τ) actually did not use noticeably more time than PCSG(-τ) *on the same RDF dataset*. The efficiency part of RH4 was also supported.

7   Empirical Comparison with Summary

Since PCSG(-τ) injects the strength of summary (i.e., pattern) into snippet, it would be desirable to empirically compare them. We conducted a user study to compare their usefulness for performing the task of SPARQL query completion [24]. We recruited 30 students majoring in computer science from a university, all having the necessary knowledge about SPARQL and paid to participate.

RDF Dataset. For this experiment we used DBpedia 2016-10.

Participating Methods. We compared PCSG-80% with ABSTAT [24], a popular summarization method. We used ABSTAT to compute a summary containing all the ontologically minimal patterns of triples in DBpedia, and we reproduced its tabular interface for presenting and filtering patterns with autocomplete [17]. For a fair comparison, we implemented a similar interface for PCSG-80%: entity descriptions in the snippet were grouped by EDP and then were presented in a tabular interface for presenting and filtering EDPs with autocomplete.

Procedure and Metrics. We followed the experimental design for SPARQL query completion described in [24]. Firstly, each participant performed two *simple tasks*: one using the snippet generated by PCSG-80% and the other using the summary computed by ABSTAT, performed in random order to avoid position bias. Each simple task asked the participant to rely on PCSG-80% or ABSTAT to convert a natural language query into a SPARQL query consisting of two triple patterns. The participant was given an incomplete SPARQL query where a predicate was left blank to type in a property. Next, in the same way the participant performed two *complex tasks*: completing a SPARQL query consisting of four triple patterns where two predicates and one object were left blank to type in two properties and one class, respectively. Before all tasks the participant was given a tutorial on the two interfaces with a warm-up task. After all tasks the participant rated each method in the range from 1 to 5 indicating its *usefulness*. The participant was encouraged to briefly explain the rating. We also reported the binary *accuracy* of a completed SPARQL query by comparing it with the gold standard, and reported the *time* for completing a SPARQL query.

Table 11. Accuracy and time (mean $\pm$ SD) for completing a SPARQL query.

	Accuracy			Time (seconds)		
	Simple task	Complex task	Overall	Simple task	Complex task	Overall
PCSG-80%	0.900 $\pm$ 0.300	0.900 $\pm$ 0.300	0.900 $\pm$ 0.300	85.9 $\pm$ 39.0	164.0 $\pm$ 84.6	124.9 $\pm$ 76.6
ABSTAT	0.933 $\pm$ 0.249	0.833 $\pm$ 0.373	0.883 $\pm$ 0.321	117.6 $\pm$ 51.1	214.3 $\pm$ 154.1	166.0 $\pm$ 124.6

Results. The results of accuracy and time for completing 120 SPARQL queries are summarized in Table 11. While paired two-sample t-test showed that the difference between the accuracy using PCSG-80% and the accuracy using ABSTAT was not statistically significant ($p > 0.05$), participants spent 25% less time using PCSG-80% and this difference was statistically significant ($p < 0.01$). The results of user-rated usefulness are summarized in Table 12. Paired two-sample t-test showed that PCSG-80% was significantly ($p < 0.01$) more useful than ABSTAT. PCSG-80% was rated ≥ 4 by most participants (93%), while for ABSTAT this

Table 12. User-rated usefulness.

	Mean ± SD
PCSG-80%	4.47 ± 0.62
ABSTAT	3.60 ± 0.95
	Proportion
PCSG-80% > ABSTAT	66.67%
PCSG-80% = ABSTAT	26.67%
PCSG-80% < ABSTAT	6.67%

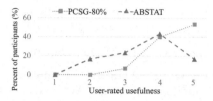

Fig. 11. Distributions of usefulness.

proportion was 60%, according to the distributions in Fig. 11. By 66.67% of all participants PCSG-80% was thought to be more useful than ABSTAT. Participants in their explanations of ratings preferred PCSG-80% because it helped participants find all the needed classes and properties in one entity description, while using ABSTAT they had to find multiple patterns of triples. Besides, compared with abstract patterns in the summary, concrete entity descriptions in the snippet exemplified the use of classes and properties and improved participants' confidence. However, by 6.67% of all participants ABSTAT was thought to be more useful than PCSG-80%. The explanations were concerned about complexity: participants were overloaded by some large entity descriptions in the snippet.

8   Conclusion and Future Work

We presented novel methods PCSG(-τ) and QPCSG(-τ) for generating pattern-coverage snippets for RDF datasets. They effectively generated better snippets than existing methods in terms of schema coverage, query coverage, and user preference, and their space savings and run-time demonstrated practicability. In the future, we plan to optimize PCSG(-τ) and QPCSG(-τ) to address some shortcomings observed in the experiments. Firstly, we observed a few large snippets even with $\tau = 80\%$. To solve this problem, we plan to adapt our approach to generating a size-bounded snippet that covers the most frequent patterns in an RDF dataset. We will also consider merging similar EDPs [28] or mining common sub-EDPs to reduce snippet size. However, such a snippet may not precisely reflect how entities are described in the dataset. Secondly, to address participants' concerns about visualization in the user study, we will investigate presentation methods [19] that are more suitable for showing patterns.

Combining the strengths of snippet and summary, our snippet appeared more useful than the summary computed by ABSTAT in assisting SPARQL query completion over DBpedia. However, based on a single downstream task and a comparison with a single method, one shall not draw a general conclusion that our snippets can be substituted for all summaries in all tasks. Rather, we believe they are complementary. In future work we will carry out experiments to comprehensively evaluate various summarization and snippet generation methods.

Acknowledgements. This work was supported by the NSFC (62072224).

References

1. Campinas, S., Delbru, R., Tummarello, G.: Efficiency and precision trade-offs in graph summary algorithms. In: IDEAS 2013, pp. 38–47 (2013)
2. Čebirić, Š., et al.: Summarizing semantic graphs: a survey. VLDB J. **28**(3), 295–327 (2018). https://doi.org/10.1007/s00778-018-0528-3
3. Chapman, A., et al.: Dataset search: a survey. VLDB J. **29**(1), 251–272 (2019). https://doi.org/10.1007/s00778-019-00564-x
4. Chen, J., Wang, X., Cheng, G., Kharlamov, E., Qu, Y.: Towards more usable dataset search: from query characterization to snippet generation. In: CIKM 2019, pp. 2445–2448 (2019)
5. Chen, Z., Jia, H., Heflin, J., Davison, B.D.: Leveraging schema labels to enhance dataset search. In: Jose, J.M., et al. (eds.) ECIR 2020. LNCS, vol. 12035, pp. 267–280. Springer, Cham (2020). https://doi.org/10.1007/978-3-030-45439-5_18
6. Cheng, G., Jin, C., Ding, W., Xu, D., Qu, Y.: Generating illustrative snippets for open data on the web. WSDM **2017**, 151–159 (2017)
7. Cheng, G., Jin, C., Qu, Y.: HIEDS: a generic and efficient approach to hierarchical dataset summarization. In: IJCAI 2016, pp. 3705–3711 (2016)
8. Ellefi, M.B., et al.: RDF dataset profiling - a survey of features, methods, vocabularies and applications. Semant. Web **9**(5), 677–705 (2018)
9. Feige, U.: A threshold of ln n for approximating set cover. J. ACM **45**(4), 634–652 (1998)
10. Fokoue, A., Meneguzzi, F., Sensoy, M., Pan, J.Z.: Querying linked ontological data through distributed summarization. In: AAAI 2012 (2012)
11. Harth, A., Hose, K., Karnstedt, M., Polleres, A., Sattler, K., Umbrich, J.: Data summaries for on-demand queries over linked data. In: WWW 2010 (2010)
12. Heling, L., Acosta, M.: Estimating characteristic sets for RDF dataset profiles based on sampling. In: Harth, A., et al. (eds.) ESWC 2020. LNCS, vol. 12123, pp. 157–175. Springer, Cham (2020). https://doi.org/10.1007/978-3-030-49461-2_10
13. Kacprzak, E., Koesten, L., Tennison, J., Simperl, E.: Characterising dataset search queries. In: WWW 2018, pp. 1485–1488 (2018)
14. Khatchadourian, S., Consens, M.P.: ExpLOD: summary-based exploration of interlinking and RDF usage in the linked open data cloud. In: Aroyo, L., et al. (eds.) ESWC 2010. LNCS, vol. 6089, pp. 272–287. Springer, Heidelberg (2010). https://doi.org/10.1007/978-3-642-13489-0_19
15. Liu, D., Cheng, G., Liu, Q., Qu, Y.: Fast and practical snippet generation for RDF datasets. ACM Trans. Web **13**(4), 19:1–19:38 (2019)
16. Liu, Q., Cheng, G., Gunaratna, K., Qu, Y.: Entity summarization: State of the art and future challenges. CoRR abs/1910.08252 (2019)
17. Palmonari, M., Rula, A., Porrini, R., Maurino, A., Spahiu, B., Ferme, V.: ABSTAT: linked data summaries with abstraction and statistics. In: ESWC 2015 Satellite Events, pp. 128–132 (2015)
18. Pan, J.Z.: Resource description framework. In: Staab, S., Studer, R. (eds.) Handbook on Ontologies. IHIS, pp. 71–90. Springer, Heidelberg (2009). https://doi.org/10.1007/978-3-540-92673-3_3
19. Parvizi, A., Mellish, C., van Deemter, K., Ren, Y., Pan, J.Z.: Selecting ontology entailments for presentation to users. In: KEOD 2014, pp. 382–387 (2014)

20. Rietveld, L., Hoekstra, R., Schlobach, S., Guéret, C.: Structural properties as proxy for semantic relevance in RDF graph sampling. In: Mika, P., et al. (eds.) ISWC 2014. LNCS, vol. 8797, pp. 81–96. Springer, Cham (2014). https://doi.org/10.1007/978-3-319-11915-1_6
21. Safavi, T., Belth, C., Faber, L., Mottin, D., Müller, E., Koutra, D.: Personalized knowledge graph summarization: from the cloud to your pocket. In: ICDM 2019, pp. 528–537 (2019)
22. Shi, Y., Cheng, G., Kharlamov, E.: Keyword search over knowledge graphs via static and dynamic hub labelings. In: WWW 2020, pp. 235–245 (2020)
23. Song, Q., Wu, Y., Lin, P., Dong, X., Sun, H.: Mining summaries for knowledge graph search. IEEE Trans. Knowl. Data Eng. 30(10), 1887–1900 (2018)
24. Spahiu, B., Porrini, R., Palmonari, M., Rula, A., Maurino, A.: ABSTAT: ontology-driven linked data summaries with pattern minimalization. In: Sack, H., Rizzo, G., Steinmetz, N., Mladenić, D., Auer, S., Lange, C. (eds.) ESWC 2016. LNCS, vol. 9989, pp. 381–395. Springer, Cham (2016). https://doi.org/10.1007/978-3-319-47602-5_51
25. Wang, K., Wang, Z., Topor, R.W., Pan, J.Z., Antoniou, G.: Eliminating concepts and roles from ontologies in expressive descriptive logics. Comput. Intell. 30(2), 205–232 (2014)
26. Wang, X., et al.: A framework for evaluating snippet generation for dataset search. In: Ghidini, C., et al. (eds.) ISWC 2019. LNCS, vol. 11778, pp. 680–697. Springer, Cham (2019). https://doi.org/10.1007/978-3-030-30793-6_39
27. Wang, X., Cheng, G., Kharlamov, E.: Towards multi-facet snippets for dataset search. In: PROFLILES & SemEx 2019, pp. 1–6 (2019)
28. Zneika, M., Lucchese, C., Vodislav, D., Kotzinos, D.: Summarizing linked data RDF graphs using approximate graph pattern mining. In: EDBT 2016, pp. 684–685 (2016)
29. Zneika, M., Vodislav, D., Kotzinos, D.: Quality metrics for RDF graph summarization. Semant. Web 10(3), 555–584 (2019)

A Source-to-Target Constraint Rewriting for Direct Mapping

Ratan Bahadur Thapa and Martin Giese[✉]

Department of Informatics, University of Oslo, Oslo, Norway
{ratanbt,martingi}@ifi.uio.no

Abstract. Most of the existing structured digital information today is still stored in relational databases. That's why it is important for the Semantic Web effort to expose the information in relational databases as RDF, or allow to query it using SPARQL. Direct mapping is a fully automated approach for converting well-structured relational data to RDF that does not require formulating explicit mapping rules [2,8]. Along with the mapped RDF data, it is desirable to have a description of that data. Previous work [3,8] has attempted to describe the RDF graph in terms of OWL axioms, which is problematic, partly due to the open world semantics of OWL. We start from the direct mapping suggested by Sequeda et al. [8], which integrates and extends the functionalities of proposal [10] and the W3C recommendation [2], and present a source-to-target semantics preserving rewriting of constraints in an SQL database schema to equivalent SHACL [7] constraints on the RDF graph. We thus provide a SHACL description of the RDF data generated by the direct mapping without the need to perform a costly validation of those constraints on the generated data. Following the approach of [8], we define the rewriting from SQL constraints to SHACL by a set of Datalog rules. We prove that our source-to-target rewriting of constraints is constraint preserving and weakly semantics preserving.

1 Introduction

Relational *constraints*, also known as *integrity constraints* in relational database theory [1], have traditionally been used to restrict the data in the database to those considered meaningful to the application at hand. Constraints are stated when a relational schema is defined and checked when the stored data is modified or new data is inserted. When relational data is mapped into RDF [4], using Direct Mapping [2] or R2RML [5], the constraints on the original relational data imply certain constraints on the RDF graph, but existing tools do not make these constraints explicit, and the theory behind such constraints on the output of the mapping is not well explored. However, the integrity of the data that is being stored or represented in the RDF graph is a critical piece of information in practice, both to detect problems in the RDF dataset and provide data quality guarantees for the purpose of RDF data exchange and interoperability.

Previous work has attempted to capture the properties of the RDF graph resulting from direct mapping using OWL [8] or as DL-Lite$_{\text{RDFS}}$ axioms with

© Springer Nature Switzerland AG 2021
A. Hotho et al. (Eds.): ISWC 2021, LNCS 12922, pp. 21–38, 2021.
https://doi.org/10.1007/978-3-030-88361-4_2

identification constraints [3]. However, as Sequeda et al. [8, Theorem 3] established, OWL axioms alone cannot provide a mapping that has both of the desirable properties of being *monotone*, i.e., an insertion of new data to the database does not require the alteration of already computed RDF triples, and *semantics preserving*, i.e., one-to-one correspondence between legal relational data and RDF graph satisfying OWL axioms. This is due to (1) DL semantics following the Open World Assumption, and (2) OWL not adopting the Unique Name Assumption (UNA). In our work, we transform integrity constraints on the source data into integrity constraints on the RDF graph, expressed in SHACL, the Shapes Constraint Language [7]. SHACL, as opposed to OWL, subscribes to the Closed World Assumption and is based on the UNA, which makes it a more suitable candidate than OWL for expressing integrity constraints on an RDF graph.

Our work is based on the direct mapping of [8] which is similar to that of the W3C recommendation [2], but has a better treatment of SQL tables that correspond to many-to-many binary relations. The transformation of both the SQL schema and the database instance is described as a set of Datalog rules in [8], which we exploit by describing our generation of SHACL constraints also in terms of Datalog rules, on the same vocabulary. We preserve the original properties of the mapping [8], such as *information preservation*, i.e., the original relational data can be reconstructed from the mapped RDF, and *query preservation*, i.e., SQL queries over source relational data can be rewritten to equivalent SPARQL queries over the mapped RDF.

Our transformation takes into account data types, primary and foreign key constraints, as well as not null and uniqueness constraints in an SQL Schema definition. Under certain reasonable assumptions such that all relations in the relational schema have a primary key and database instances satisfy their primary and foreign key constraints, our proposed SHACL constraint rewriting for direct mapping is *constraint preserving*, i.e., all the original SQL constraints of source database can be reconstructed from the output SHACL constraints, and *weakly semantics preserving*, which means that it exhibits all of the desirable properties proposed in [8].

In Sect. 2, we review central notions of relational databases, SQL constraints, RDF, SHACL and Direct mapping. Section 3 introduces the central notion of constraint rewriting and the properties: constraint preservation and semantics preservation. In Sect. 4, we give the Datalog rules for the proposed rewriting. Section 5 states the properties of the proposed rewriting. Section 6 discusses shortcoming of the rewriting and Sect. 7 concludes the paper.

2   Preliminaries

In this section, we fix notions and notations fundamental to the definition of direct mapping [8] and SHACL constraints [7].

Databases. Let Δ be a countably infinite set of constants, including the reserved symbol null. A *relational schema* $\mathcal{R}$ is a finite set of relation names, known as *relation schemas*. We associate with each relation schema $R \in \mathcal{R}$ a finite, non-empty *set of named attributes*, denoted by att(R). An *instance* $\mathcal{D}$ of $\mathcal{R}$ assigns to each relation schema $R \in \mathcal{R}$ a finite set of tuples $R^{\mathcal{D}}$, where each *tuple* $t \in R^{\mathcal{D}}$ is a function that assigns to each attribute in $\text{att}(R)$ a value from the domain Δ. We write $\bar{X}$ as shorthand for a sequence $X_1, \ldots X_n$ of attributes for some $n > 0$, and $X \in \bar{X}$ to say that X is one of the elements of the sequence. $|\bar{X}| = n$ denotes the length of the sequence. Further, we write $\bar{X} \lhd R$ to denote that $\bar{X}$ is a non-empty sequence of attributes of R, i.e. $\emptyset \subsetneq \{X_1, \ldots, X_n\} \subseteq \text{att}(R)$. We write $t(\bar{X})$ to denote the restriction of a tuple $t \in R^{\mathcal{D}}$ to a sequence $\bar{X} \lhd R$ of attributes. Finally, a *database* is a pair $(\mathcal{R}, \mathcal{D})$, where $\mathcal{R}$ is a relational schema and $\mathcal{D}$ is an instance of $\mathcal{R}$.

SQL Constraints. We now define constraints on a relational schema, similarly to the SQL Data Definition Language. The direct mapping of [8] considers only *primary key* (PK) and *foreign key* (FK) constraints, which they refer to as *key constraints*. In addition to these key constraints, we also take account of *not null* (NN) and *unique* (UNQ) entity integrity constraints, as well as *SQL data types*, on a relational schema $\mathcal{R}$, which we refer to as *data constraints*. We write δ for sets of data constraints and σ for sets of key constraints. When there is no risk of confusion, we will often write $\Sigma = \sigma \cup \delta$ to say that Σ is a set of constraints, consisting of key constraints σ and data constraints δ.

A NN constraint on a relational schema $\mathcal{R}$ is an expression of the form $\text{NN}(X, R)$ for any $X \in \text{att}(R)$ with $R \in \mathcal{R}$. Similarly, a UNQ or PK constraint on a relational schema $\mathcal{R}$ is an expression of the form $\text{UNQ}(\bar{X}, R)$ or $\text{PK}(\bar{X}, R)$, respectively, for any $\bar{X} \lhd R$ with $R \in \mathcal{R}$. An instance $\mathcal{D}$ of $\mathcal{R}$ satisfies:

- $\text{NN}(X, R)$ if for every $t \in R^{\mathcal{D}}$, $t(X) \neq \text{null}$.
- $\text{UNQ}(\bar{X}, R)$ if for every $t, t' \in R^{\mathcal{D}}$, if $t(X) = t'(X) \neq \text{null}$ for every $X \in \bar{X}$, then $t = t'$.
- $\text{PK}(\bar{X}, R)$ if (1) for every $t \in R^{\mathcal{D}}$ and $X \in \bar{X}$, $t(X) \neq \text{null}$, and (2) for every $t, t' \in R^{\mathcal{D}}$, if $t(\bar{X}) = t'(\bar{X})$, then $t = t'$.

An FK constraint on $\mathcal{R}$ is an expression of the form $\text{FK}(\bar{X}, R, \bar{Y}, S)$ for any $\bar{X} \lhd R$ and $\bar{Y} \lhd S$ with $|\bar{X}| = |\bar{Y}|$ and $R, S \in \mathcal{R}$. An instance $\mathcal{D}$ of $\mathcal{R}$ satisfies $\text{FK}(\bar{X}, R, \bar{Y}, S)$ if for every $t \in R^{\mathcal{D}}$: either (1) $t(X) = \text{null}$ for some $X \in \bar{X}$, or (2) there is a tuple $t' \in S^{\mathcal{D}}$ such that $t(\bar{X}) = t'(\bar{Y})$. Next, to handle SQL data types, let the domain of each data type T be given as a subset $\Delta_T \subseteq \Delta$ with null $\in \Delta_T$. An SQL data type declaration on $\mathcal{R}$ is an expression of the form $\text{TYPE}(X, R, T)$ for an attribute $X \in \text{att}(R)$ with $R \in \mathcal{R}$, where T is an SQL data type. An instance $\mathcal{D}$ of $\mathcal{R}$ satisfies $\text{TYPE}(X, R, T)$ on $X \in \text{att}(R)$, if $t(X) \in \Delta_T$ for every $t \in R^{\mathcal{D}}$. Given an instance $\mathcal{D}$ of a relational schema $\mathcal{R}$ and a constraint C on $\mathcal{R}$, we write $\mathcal{D} \vDash C$ to denote that $\mathcal{D}$ satisfies C.

A *relational schema $\mathcal{R}$ with constraints Σ* consists of a relational schema $\mathcal{R}$ and a set of constraints $\Sigma = \sigma \cup \delta$ on $\mathcal{R}$, such that (1) σ contains exactly one primary key declaration $\text{PK}(\bar{X}, R)$ for each $R \in \mathcal{R}$, and (2) $\text{UNQ}(\bar{Y}, S) \in \delta$ for all $\text{FK}(\bar{X}, R, \bar{Y}, S) \in \sigma$, as usual in all SQL implementations. W.l.o.g., we also assume that (3) for every $\text{PK}(\bar{X}, R) \in \sigma$, $\text{UNQ}(\bar{X}, R) \in \delta$ and $\text{NN}(X, R) \in \delta$ for every $X \in \bar{X}$. These data constraints are clearly implied by the PK constraint, but making them explicit will simplify the presentation. Given a relational schema $\mathcal{R}$ with constraints Σ and an instance $\mathcal{D}$ of $\mathcal{R}$, we call $\mathcal{D}$ a *legal instance* of $\mathcal{R}$ with Σ denoted by $\mathcal{D} \vDash \Sigma$, if $\mathcal{D}$ satisfies all constraints in Σ.

Example 1. *For a running example, consider a relational database consisting of relation schemas:* `Emp` *for employees,* `Acc` *for expense accounts,* `Prj` *for research projects, as well as* `Asg` *for the m:n relation that assigns employees to projects:*

```
create table Emp (E_id integer primary key, Name varchar not null,
                  Post varchar);
create table Acc (A_id integer primary key, Name varchar unique);
create table Prj (P_id integer primary key, Name varchar not null,
         ToAcc integer not null unique foreign key references Acc(A_id));
create table Asg (ToEmp integer foreign key references Emp(E_id),
                  ToPrj integer foreign key references Prj(P_id),
                  primary key (ToEmp,ToPrj));
```

RDF Graph. Assume that $\mathcal{I}, \mathcal{B}$ and $\mathcal{L}$ are countably infinite disjoint sets of *Internationalized Resource Identifiers* (IRIs), *blank nodes* and *literals*, respectively. An *RDF triple* is defined as a triple $\langle s, p, o \rangle$, where $s \in \mathcal{I} \cup \mathcal{B}$ is called the subject, $p \in \mathcal{I}$ is called the predicate and $o \in \mathcal{I} \cup \mathcal{B} \cup \mathcal{L}$ is called the object. An *RDF graph* $G \subset (\mathcal{I} \cup \mathcal{B}) \times \mathcal{I} \times (\mathcal{I} \cup \mathcal{B} \cup \mathcal{L})$ is a finite set of RDF triples.

Definition 1 (Nodes). *The set of* nodes *of an RDF graph G is the set of subjects and objects of triples in the graph, i.e.* $\{s, o \mid \langle s, p, o \rangle \in G\}$.

SHACL Constraints. SHACL [7] is a language to describe a set of syntactic conditions on RDF graphs. A SHACL document is a set of shapes, called the *shape graph*. When we validate an RDF graph with respect to a shape graph, we call the former the *data graph*.

For the purpose of this paper, each shape in a shape graph S can be expressed as a triple $\langle s, \tau, \phi \rangle$ consisting of a shape IRI s, a *target definition* τ, and a *constraint definition* ϕ. The τ and ϕ are expressions that determine for every data graph G and node n of G, whether n is a target of the shape, $G \models \tau(n)$, resp., whether n satisfies the constraint, $G \models \phi(n)$. All shapes generated by our transformation have an 'implicit target class,' which means that s is also the IRI of a class and $G \models \tau(n)$ iff n is a SHACL instance of class s.[1]

A data graph G validates against a shape $\langle s, \tau, \phi \rangle$ if for all nodes n of G, if $G \models \tau(n)$, then $G \models \phi(n)$. A data graph G validates against a shape graph S, written $G \vDash S$, iff G validates against all shapes in S.

In addition to the *core constraint components* of SHACL (namespace `sh:`), we introduce a SPARQL-based constraint component `uq:uniqueValuesForClass` in Sect. 4, p. 10 to translate UNQ constraints equivalent SHACL constraints.

Example 2. *Consider the following SHACL node shape (left) and RDF graph (right):*

---

[1] https://www.w3.org/TR/shacl/#implicit-targetClass.

```
:Employee a sh:NodeShape, rdfs:Class;
  sh:property [ sh:path :hasID;              :Julie a :Employee;
               sh:nodeKind sh:Literal;         :hasID "001"^^xsd:int.
               sh:maxCount 1; sh:minCount 1;  :Magnus a :Employee;
               sh:datatype xsd:int ];          :hasID "002"^^xsd:int.
  uq:uniqueValuesForClass [ uq:unqProp :hasID;
               uq:unqForClass :Employee ].
```

The shape for :Employee has (1) an implicit class target declaration, meaning that all the members of the :Employee class are target nodes of the node shape, (2) a property shape that declares that all employees must have exactly one ID with data type xsd:int, and (3) a uq:uniqueValuesForClass *constraint that declares that there is no other employee with the same ID. An instance of :Employee validates against the node shape if it satisfies both constraints. The data graph on the right validates against the shape, but can be made invalid by changing the ID of Julie to "002"^^xsd:int.*

Direct Mapping. We now briefly review the direct mapping $\mathcal{DM}$ as defined by Sequeda et al. [8], which integrates and extends the functionalities of the proposal of [10] and the W3C recommendation [2]. The input of $\mathcal{DM}$ consists of a relational schema $\mathcal{R}$, a set σ of PK and FK constraints on $\mathcal{R}$, as well as an instance $\mathcal{D}$ of $\mathcal{R}$. The output is an RDF graph with OWL axioms. $\mathcal{DM}$ is described as a set of Datalog rules. Section 4.1 of [8] defines the following Datalog predicates to represent $\mathcal{R}$, σ and $\mathcal{D}$.

1. $\text{REL}(R)$: Indicates that R is a *relation schema* in $\mathcal{R}$.
2. $\text{ATTR}_n(\bar{X}, R)$: Indicates that $\bar{X} \lhd R$, with $|\bar{X}| = n$.
3. $\text{PK}_n(\bar{X}, R)$ and $\text{FK}_n(\bar{X}, R, \bar{Y}, S)$ represent key constraints, as introduced previously, with $|X| = |\bar{Y}| = n$.
4. $\text{VALUE}(V, X, t, R)$: V is the value of $X \in \text{att}(R)$ in a tuple with identifier t in $R^{\mathcal{D}}$.

As is usual in Datalog, subscripts are added to predicate symbols to distinguish variants with different arities.

Section 4.2 of [8] gives rules that determine the RDFS classes and properties to be generated, as well as their ranges and domains, from the relational schema: If a relation $R \in \mathcal{R}$ is *not* identified as representing a binary many-to-many relation,[2] it is translated to a class, i.e., $\text{CLASS}(R)$. Each foreign key reference of R is translated to an object property, represented by an OP_{2n} fact, and each attribute $X \in \text{att}(R)$ to a datatype property, i.e., a DTP fact. If a relation $Q \in \mathcal{R}$ *is* identified as a binary relation $\text{BINREL}(Q)$, i.e., $\text{att}(Q) = \{X,Y\}$ with $\text{PK}_2(X, Y, Q)$ such that X and Y are foreign key references to tables R and T, then the translation will be an object property between R and T.

Section 4.3.1 of [8] gives rules that generate the IRIs for the classes and properties determined by the previous mapping rules: It generates facts with

---

[2] This identification of binary relations is the main technical difference between the direct mapping of Sequeda et al. [8] and the W3C recommendation [2].

the predicates CLASSIRI for the classes, OP_IRI$_1$ for object properties from binary relations, OP_IRI$_{2n}$ for the other object properties and DTP_IRI for the datatype properties. Figure 1 gives a summary of the predicates and their arguments.

Section 4.3.2 of [8] gives rules that output OWL axioms as OWL/RDF triples from IRIs for classes and properties. We will ignore these and generate SHACL constraints instead. The rules in Sect. 4.4 of [8] generate RDF triples from the instance $\mathcal{D}$ (encoded as VALUE facts), based on the previously determined classes and properties, and the rules in Sect. 6 generate unsatisfiable OWL axioms in the case where the database instance violates its key constraints.

In our work, we generate SHACL constraints instead of OWL axioms, so we ignore the rules of [8] that output OWL axioms. The remaining rules of [8] can be divided into (1) the set $\mathcal{M}^s$ of rules that generate the classes and properties and their IRIs from the relational schema $\mathcal{R}$ and the set σ of PK and FK constraints, and (2) the set $\mathcal{M}^i$ of rules that transform an instance $\mathcal{D}$ of $\mathcal{R}$ into an RDF graph based on the facts produced by $\mathcal{M}^s$, as well as the constraints σ.

BINREL(Q, X, Y, R, X', T, Y')	REL(Q) is a binary schema, i.e.,att(Q)={X,Y} with PK$_2$(X, Y, Q), FK$_1$(X, Q, X', R) and FK$_1$(Y, Q, Y', T)
CLASS(R)	REL(R) is a non-binary schema
OP$_{2n}$($\bar{X}, \bar{Y}, R, T$)	Non-binary schema REL(R) has FK$_n$($\bar{X}, R, \bar{Y}, T$) consisting of $n \geq 1$ attributes, i.e., $|\bar{X}| = |\bar{Y}| = n$.
DTP(X, R)	Non-binary schema REL(R) has $X \in$ att(R)
CLASSIRI(R, R^{IRI})	R^{IRI} is the IRI of the class generated for CLASS(R)
DTP_IRI(X, R, X^{IRI})	X^{IRI} is the IRI of the datatype property for DTP(X, R)
OP_IRI$_1$($Q, X, Y, R, X', T, Y', Q^{\text{IRI}}$)	Q^{IRI} is the IRI of the object property for the binary schema BINREL(Q, X, Y, R, X', T, Y')
OP_IRI$_{2n}$($\bar{X}, \bar{Y}, R, T, W^{\text{IRI}}$)	W^{IRI} is the IRI of the obj. prop. OP$_{2n}$($\bar{X}, \bar{Y}, R, T$) generated from FK$_n$($\bar{X}, R, \bar{Y}, T$) of REL(R), $|\bar{X}| = n \geq 1$

Fig. 1. The Datalog predicates used to represent classes and properties in [8].

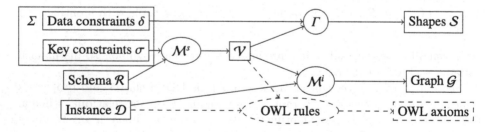

Fig. 2. An overview of direct mapping $\mathcal{M}$. The $\mathcal{DM}$ rules for OWL axioms are not relevant to our work. Γ is the constraint rewriting to be defined in Sect. 4.

Definition 2 (Directly mapped schema). *We denote by $\mathcal{V} = \mathcal{M}^s(\mathcal{R}, \sigma)$ the set of all facts with predicates* CLASS, BINREL, OP$_{2n}$, DTP, CLASSIRI, OP_IRI$_1$, OP_IRI$_{2n}$ *and* DTP_IRI *that result from (a) representing $\mathcal{R}$ and σ as Datalog facts, and (b) applying the rules in $\mathcal{M}^s$ exhaustively. We call $\mathcal{V}$ the directly mapped schema given by the direct mapping.*

For illustration, Fig. 3 gives $\mathcal{V}$ for the relational schema of Example 1.

Predicates for schema	Class and property predicates	IRI predicates
Rel(Emp)	Class(Emp)	ClassIRI(Emp, :Emp)
Attr₁(Emp, E_id)	DTP(E_id, Emp)	DTP_IRI(E_id, Emp, :Emp#E_id)
Attr₁(Emp, Name)	DTP(Name, Emp)	DTP_IRI(Name, Emp, :Emp#Name)
Attr₁(Emp, Post)	DTP(Post, Emp)	DTP_IRI(Post, Emp, :Emp#Post)
Rel(Prj)	Class(Prj)	ClassIRI(Prj, :Prj)
Attr₁(Prj, P_id)	DTP(P_id, Prj)	DTP_IRI(P_id, Prj, :Prj#P_id)
Attr₁(Prj, Name)	DTP(Name, Prj)	DTP_IRI(Name, Prj, :Prj#Name)
Attr₁(Prj, ToAcc)	DTP(ToAcc, Prj)	DTP_IRI(ToAcc, Prj, :Prj#ToAcc)
FK₁(ToAcc, Prj, A_id, Acc)	OP₂(ToAcc, A_id, Prj, Acc)	OP_IRI₂(ToAcc, A_id, Prj, Acc, :Prj, Acc#ToAcc, A_id)
Rel(Acc)	Class(Acc)	ClassIRI(Acc, :Acc)
Attr₁(Acc, A_id)	DTP(A_id, Acc)	DTP_IRI(A_id, Acc, :Acc#A_id)
Attr₁(Acc, Name)	DTP(Name, Acc)	DTP_IRI(Name, Acc, :Acc#Name)
Rel(Asg)	BinRel(Asg,ToEmp,ToPrj, Emp,E_id,Prj,P_id)	OP_IRI₁(Asg,ToEmp,ToPrj,Emp,E_id,Prj,P_id, :Asg#ToEmp, ToPrj, E_id, P_id)

Fig. 3. The directly mapped schema $\mathcal{V}$ for the relational schema in Example 1. We use QNames, i.e., abbreviations starting with a colon, such as ':Emp #E_id', for the IRIs generated by the mappings $\mathcal{M}^s$.

Definition 3 (Directly mapped RDF graph). *We denote by* $\mathcal{G} = \mathcal{M}^i(\mathcal{V}, \sigma, \mathcal{D})$ *the RDF graph that contains one triple* $\langle s, p, o \rangle$ *for each fact* TRIPLE(s, p, o) *generated by (a) representing* $\mathcal{D}$ *and* σ *as Datalog facts, (b) applying the rules in* $\mathcal{M}^i$ *exhaustively to these facts and the ones in* $\mathcal{V}$. *We call* $\mathcal{G}$ *the directly mapped RDF graph.*

See Fig. 2 for an overview of the different components of the direct mapping. We will write $\mathcal{M}$ for the entire direct mapping defined by applying first $\mathcal{M}^s$ and then $\mathcal{M}^i$. Note that [8, Sect. 4.4.1] contains a rule to generate *blank nodes* for the tuples of relation schemas not having a primary key. This is not needed in our setting since we have assumed that σ contains a PK constraint for every relation $R \in \mathcal{R}$. Finally, note that $\mathcal{M}$ does not interfere with the RDF generation process of $\mathcal{DM}$ except ignoring the rules that generate OWL axioms. Therefore, all the properties [8, Theorem 1 and 2] of $\mathcal{DM}$, except the semantics preservation, are transferable to the $\mathcal{M}$, i.e., $\mathcal{M}$ is information preserving, query preserving and monotonic.

3 Constraint Rewriting: Definition and Properties

We will define a source-to-target constraint rewriting for the direct mapping $\mathcal{M}$ described above. The input of this rewriting is the directly mapped schema $\mathcal{V}$ of a relational database and the set δ of SQL data constraints declared on the schema $\mathcal{R}$ of the database. The output is a set of SHACL shapes.

Let $\mathbb{S}$ be the set of all SHACL shapes and $\mathbb{G}$ the set of all pairs of the form $(\mathcal{V}, \delta)$ such that $\mathcal{V} = \mathcal{M}^s(\mathcal{R}, \sigma)$ is a directly mapped schema of a relational schema $\mathcal{R}$ with constraints $\Sigma = \sigma \cup \delta$, i.e., a set of key constraints σ and data constraints δ.

Definition 4 (Constraint rewriting). *A constraint rewriting is a function* $\mathcal{T} : \mathbb{G} \to \mathcal{P}(\mathbb{S})$.

We are now ready to introduce two fundamental properties of a constraint rewriting: *constraint preservation* and *semantics preservation*.

Definition 5 (Constraint preservation). *A constraint rewriting $\mathcal{T}$ is con-straint preserving if there is a computable mapping $\mathcal{N} : \mathcal{P}(\mathbb{S}) \to \mathbb{G}$ such that for every directly mapped schema $\mathcal{V} = \mathcal{M}^s(\mathcal{R}, \sigma)$ of any relational schema $\mathcal{R}$ with constraints $\Sigma = \sigma \cup \delta$, $\mathcal{N}(\mathcal{T}(\mathcal{V}, \delta)) = (\mathcal{V}, \delta)$.*

The monotonicity [8, Definition 4] property of direct mapping $\mathcal{M}$ ensures that a re-computation of the entire RDF graph from the database is not required when the database is updated after the mapping. Here, it is straightforward to see that a constraint rewriting according to Definition 4 is independent of the database instance, hence, any updates in the database instance do not influence the rewriting of SHACL constraints for the $\mathcal{M}$. This is in contrast to [8], where the rules in Sect. 6.1 have to produce OWL axioms based on the database *instance* to ensure semantics preservation while contradicting the monotonicity property [8, Theorem 3]. Therefore, when we state the additional properties of a constraint rewriting $\mathcal{T}$ for $\mathcal{M}$ that generates a desired one-to-one correspondence between relational databases and the directly mapped RDF graphs with the SHACL constraints, we preserve all the properties of $\mathcal{M}$.

Definition 6 (Semantics preservation). *A constraint rewriting $\mathcal{T}$ is seman-tics preserving if for every relational schema $\mathcal{R}$ with constraints $\Sigma = \sigma \cup \delta$ and arbitrary instance $\mathcal{D}$ of $\mathcal{R}$:*

$$\mathcal{D} \vDash \Sigma \iff \mathcal{G} \vDash \mathcal{S},$$

where $\mathcal{V} = \mathcal{M}^s(\mathcal{R}, \sigma)$, $\mathcal{G} = \mathcal{M}^i(\mathcal{V}, \sigma, \mathcal{D})$ is the directly mapped RDF graph and $\mathcal{S} = \mathcal{T}(\mathcal{V}, \delta)$ is the set of SHACL shapes.

We recall that the direct mapping $\mathcal{M}$ relies on primary keys to generate IRIs for the tuples [8, Sect. 4.4.1] of relation schemas being translated into RDF, and on foreign key references for object properties. The semantics preservation does not hold if these key constraints are violated in the relational database. Sequeda et al. circumvent this problem in [8, Sect. 6.1] by taking the database instance as an extra argument of the rewriting and generating an unsatisfiable OWL axiom if key constraints are violated. To avoid making the generated constraints depend on the instance, we restrict the notion of semantics preservation to database instances that satisfy the key constraints:

Definition 7 (Weak semantics preservation). *A constraint rewriting $\mathcal{T}$ is weakly semantics preserving if for every relational schema $\mathcal{R}$ with constraints $\Sigma = \sigma \cup \delta$ and arbitrary instance $\mathcal{D}_\sigma$ of $\mathcal{R}$ that satisfies the key constraints σ of $\mathcal{R}$:*

$$\mathcal{D}_\sigma \vDash \Sigma \iff \mathcal{G} \vDash \mathcal{S},$$

where $\mathcal{V} = \mathcal{M}^s(\mathcal{R}, \sigma)$, $\mathcal{G} = \mathcal{M}^i(\mathcal{V}, \sigma, \mathcal{D}_\sigma)$ is the directly mapped RDF graph and $\mathcal{S} = \mathcal{T}(\mathcal{V}, \delta)$ is the set of SHACL constraints.

Constraint and semantics preservation are two independent properties of a constraint rewriting $\mathcal{T}$: the former is a syntactic property and the latter is semantic. It is possible to define a constraint rewriting that is constraint preserving and not semantics preserving, and vice versa. In the following section, we will define a concrete constraint rewriting Γ that is both constraint preserving and weakly semantics preserving.

4 The Constraint Rewriting Γ

We now define a concrete constraint rewriting Γ. According to Definition 4, Γ takes a directly mapped schema $\mathcal{V} = \mathcal{M}^s(\mathcal{R}, \sigma)$ and a set of data constraints δ and produces a set of SHACL shapes. In order to keep our definitions tightly linked to the definition of $\mathcal{M}$, we define Γ in terms of Datalog rules based on the Datalog facts in $\mathcal{V}$ generated by the rules of $\mathcal{M}^s$, as well as a set of Datalog facts representing the constraints in δ. We will first define the predicates used to represent relational schemata and SHACL constraints, and then give the Datalog rules that define Γ.

4.1 Datalog Predicates

Predicates for relational schemata. To represent a relational schema $\mathcal{R}$ with constraints $\Sigma = \sigma \cup \delta$, we reuse the Datalog representation from [8] as introduced in Sect. 2, i.e., REL(R), ATTR$_n$($\bar{X}, R$), PK$_n$($\bar{X}, R$) and FK$_n$($\bar{X}, R, \bar{Y}, S$). Since [8] only uses key constraints, we additionally need the following predicates to represent data constraints.

1. TYPE(X, R, T) indicates that ATTR$_1$(X, R) has an SQL data type T.
2. NN$_1$(X, R) and UNQ$_n$($\bar{X}, R$) represent not null and unique constraints (see Sect. 2).
3. TYPEXML(X, R, T) indicates that ATTR$_1$(X, R) has XML Schema datatype T, e.g., xsd:string, xsd:integer. These have to be generated from the TYPE(X, R, T) constraints of the database to map SQL data types to XML datatypes; we omit the details.

Predicates for SHACL Syntax. We introduce a number of predicates to express SHACL shapes. A general vocabulary to encode SHACL shapes would have to take the recursive syntax into account, but this is not needed in our rewriting setting: we only require a limited number of different SHACL constraint components, that are easily represented by a few Datalog predicates.

– We generate exactly one shape for each class in $\mathcal{V}$ mapped by $\mathcal{M}^s$. In fact, we use the class IRI to identify the shape, i.e., *sh:NodeShape*, as is done with implicit target classes in SHACL. This means that the *sh:targetClass* declaration is implicit, i.e., also the class IRI.
– For each class, we generate a number of simple property and node shapes, based on the RDF vocabulary in $\mathcal{V}$ corresponding to each class IRI and the SQL constraints in the relational schema.

We use the following predicates to represent SHACL shapes:

1. $\text{SHAPE}(R)$: Indicates that the IRI R designates a node shape with implicit class target, i.e.,

$$R \text{ a sh:NodeShape, rdfs:Class.}$$

Note that our transformation uses the same IRI to identify node shape and the class target as is done with implicit target class.

2. $\text{PROP}(R, P, S)$: Indicates that the node shape R has a property shape that requires the values of the predicate with IRI P to be instances of the *rdfs:Class* identified by the IRI S, i.e.,

$$\text{sh:property [sh:path } P; \quad \text{sh:nodeKind sh:IRI;} \quad \text{sh:class } S \text{].}$$

3. $\text{DATA}(R, P, T)$: Indicates that the node shape R has a property shape that requires the values of predicate P to be literals with XML Schema datatype T, i.e.,

$$\text{sh:property [sh:path } P; \quad \text{sh:nodeKind sh:Literal;} \quad \text{sh:datatype } T].$$

4. $\text{MAXPROP}(R, P, S)$: Indicates that the node shape R has a property shape that requires the predicate P to have at most one value, which belongs to the class S, i.e.,

$$\text{sh:property [sh:path } P; \quad \text{sh:nodeKind sh:IRI;} \quad \text{sh:maxCount 1;} \quad \text{sh:class } S].$$

5. $\text{CRDPROP}(R, P, S)$: Indicates that the node shape R has a property shape that requires the predicate P to have exactly one value, which belongs to the class S, i.e.,

$$\text{sh:property [sh:path } P; \quad \text{sh:nodeKind sh:IRI;} \quad \text{sh:minCount 1;} \quad \text{sh:maxCount 1;} \quad \text{sh:class } S].$$

6. $\text{INVPROP}(R, P, S)$: Like $\text{PROP}(R, P, S)$ but for the inverse path of P:

$$\text{sh:property [sh:path [sh:inversePath } P]; \quad \text{sh:nodeKind sh:IRI;} \quad \text{sh:class } S].$$

7. $\text{INVMAXPROP}(R, P, S)$: Like $\text{MAXPROP}(R, P, S)$ but for the inverse path of P:

$$\text{sh:property [sh:path [sh:inversePath } P]; \quad \text{sh:nodeKind sh:IRI;} \quad \text{sh:maxCount 1 sh:class } S].$$

8. $\text{MAXDATA}(R, P, T)$ and $\text{CRDDATA}(R, P, T)$:   Like   the   predicate $\text{DATA}(R, P, T)$ with maximum-one and exactly-one cardinality restrictions, respectively. For instance, predicate $\text{MAXDATA}(R, P, T)$:

$$\text{sh:property [sh:path } P; \quad \text{sh:nodeKind sh:Literal;} \quad \text{sh:maxCount 1;} \quad \text{sh:datatype } T].$$

9. $\text{UNQTUPLE}_n(R, \bar{P})$: Indicates that the node shape R has a constraint that requires the combination of values of the predicates $\bar{P}$ to be unique among all the members of the class R. This cannot be expressed using the core SHACL constraint components, so we define a SHACL-SPARQL constraint

component for the purpose.[3] A Datalog fact $\text{UNQTUPLE}_n(R, P_1, \ldots, P_n)$ then translates to a node shape

uq:uniqueValuesForClass [uq:unqProp $P_1, \ldots, P_n$;   uq:unqForClass R].

The uq:uniqueValuesForClass component is defined as follows:

@prefix uq: <http://sirius−labs.no/shapes/unique#>
uq:UniqueValuesConstraintComponent a sh:ConstraintComponent ;
   sh:parameter [sh:path uq:uniqueValuesForClass] ;
   sh:nodeValidator [a sh:SPARQLSelectValidator ;
      sh:select """SELECT $this ?other WHERE {
         FILTER NOT EXISTS {
            GRAPH $shapesGraph {$uniqueValuesForClass uq:unqProp ?prop}
            $this ?prop ?thisVal .
            ?other ?prop ?otherVal .
            FILTER (?thisVal != ?otherVal)
         }
         FILTER (?other != $this)
         GRAPH $shapesGraph {$uniqueValuesForClass uq:unqForClass ?class}
         ?other rdf:type $class .
      }"""] .

As per the definition of SHACL-SPARQL, the object of the shape triple with predicate :uniqueValuesForClass is accessible in the SPARQL query as $uniqueValuesForClass, and the :unqProp parameters can be accessed using "GRAPH $shapesGraph". The sh:select SPARQL query will be evaluated with $this bound to each target node in turn. What it does is to search for ?other!=$this resources that do not (FILTER NOT EXISTS) disagree (?thisVal != ?otherVal) on any of the :unqProp properties $P_1, \ldots, P_n$ given by the shape. Note that this uses the pre-bound variable $shapesGraph, which is an optional feature for SHACL-SPARQL processors.[4]

4.2 The Constraint Rewriting Γ Rules

The following set of Datalog rules for Γ act on the directly mapped schema $\mathcal{V}$ produced by $\mathcal{M}^s \subset \mathcal{M}$ together with the set δ of data constraints expressed as Datalog facts, and generates SHACL shapes by using the shape predicates defined in Sect. 4.1.

First, the rule (1) is used to generate SHACL shapes for all the CLASSIRI vocabularies produced by $\mathcal{M}^s$.

$$\text{SHAPE}(R^{\text{IRI}}) \longleftarrow \text{CLASSIRI}(R, R^{\text{IRI}}) \qquad (1)$$

For example, SHACL predicates $\text{SHAPE}(\textit{:Emp})$, $\text{SHAPE}(\textit{:Prj})$ and $\text{SHAPE}(\textit{:Acc})$ hold in our Example 1, assuming that $\textit{:Emp}$, etc., are the IRIs generated by the mappings $\mathcal{M}^s$ from the relation schema names, $\text{CLASSIRI}(\text{Emp}, \textit{:Emp})$, etc.

---

[3] For $n = 1$ the same requirement could be expressed using dash:uniqueValueForClass from http://datashapes.org/constraints.html, but not for larger n.

[4] See https://www.w3.org/TR/shacl/#sparql-constraints-prebound.

Second, the rules (2) to (5) are used to generate SHACL property shapes for the case where the direct mapping identifies a relation schema Q as binary, therefore mapping it to an object property, as opposed to an RDFS class and one property per attribute. In this case, the directly mapped schema $\mathcal{V}$ contains a fact $\text{OP\_IRI}_1(Q, X, Y, R, X', T, Y', Q^{\text{IRI}})$, which expresses that

- $Q(X, Y)$ is a relation schema with exactly two attributes X and Y, and $\text{PK}_2(X, Y, R)$,
- X is a foreign key reference to attribute X' of R,
- Y is a foreign key reference to attribute Y' of T, and
- Q^{IRI} is the IRI of the property generated from Q.

There will also be facts $\text{CLASSIRI}(R, R^{\text{IRI}})$ and $\text{CLASSIRI}(T, T^{\text{IRI}})$ that give the IRIs of the classes generated from R and T. For instance, for the relation schema 'Asg' in Example 1, the directly mapped schema $\mathcal{V}$ in Fig. 3 contains facts $\text{CLASSIRI}(\text{Emp}, :Emp)$, $\text{CLASSIRI}(\text{Prj}, :Prj)$ and

$$\text{OP\_IRI}_1(\text{Asg}, \text{ToEmp}, \text{ToPrj}, \text{Emp}, \text{E\_id}, \text{Prj}, \text{P\_id}, :Asg\#ToEmp, ToPrj, E\_id, P\_id).$$

In general, since Q^{IRI} is a many-to-many relation, the only constraints that can be guaranteed on the directly mapped RDF concern the type of the involved nodes. However, if there is a UNQ constraint on X, we can conclude that elements of R^{IRI} can participate in at most one Q^{IRI} triple, and similarly if there is a UNQ constraint for Y. The following two rules generate a property shape for Q^{IRI} with or without maximum cardinality 1, depending on whether is a UNQ constraint on X of Q or not:

$$\text{MAXPROP}(R^{\text{IRI}}, Q^{\text{IRI}}, T^{\text{IRI}}) \longleftarrow \text{UNQ}_1(X, Q), \text{OP\_IRI}_1(Q, X, Y, R, X', T, Y', Q^{\text{IRI}}), \quad (2)$$
$$\text{CLASSIRI}(R, R^{\text{IRI}}), \text{CLASSIRI}(T, T^{\text{IRI}})$$

$$\text{PROP}(R^{\text{IRI}}, Q^{\text{IRI}}, T^{\text{IRI}}) \longleftarrow \neg\text{UNQ}_1(X, Q), \text{OP\_IRI}_1(Q, X, Y, R, X', T, Y', Q^{\text{IRI}}), \quad (3)$$
$$\text{CLASSIRI}(R, R^{\text{IRI}}), \text{CLASSIRI}(T, T^{\text{IRI}})$$

Note that some of our rules use negated atoms: e.g., $\neg\text{UNQ}_1(X, Q)$ indicates that there is *no* unique constraint for the attribute $X \lhd Q$. The next rules do the same for the inverse direction of Q^{IRI}:

$$\text{INVMAXPROP}(T^{\text{IRI}}, Q^{\text{IRI}}, R^{\text{IRI}}) \longleftarrow \text{UNQ}_1(Y, Q), \text{OP\_IRI}_1(Q, X, Y, R, X', T, Y', Q^{\text{IRI}}), \quad (4)$$
$$\text{CLASSIRI}(R, R^{\text{IRI}}), \text{CLASSIRI}(T, T^{\text{IRI}})$$

$$\text{INVPROP}(T^{\text{IRI}}, Q^{\text{IRI}}, R^{\text{IRI}}) \longleftarrow \neg\text{UNQ}_1(Y, Q), \text{OP\_IRI}_1(Q, X, Y, R, X', T, Y', Q^{\text{IRI}}), \quad (5)$$
$$\text{CLASSIRI}(R, R^{\text{IRI}}), \text{CLASSIRI}(T, T^{\text{IRI}})$$

Third, the rules (6) to (9) are used to generate the SHACL property shapes for the object properties that stem from foreign key references in relations that were not identified as binary. For these, $\mathcal{M}^s$ generates Datalog facts $\text{OP\_IRI}_{2n}(\bar{X}, \bar{Y}, R, T, W^{\text{IRI}})$ where

- $\bar{X}$ are some attributes of R and $\bar{Y}$ are some attributes of T,
- There is a foreign key constraint $\mathrm{FK}_n(\bar{X}, R, \bar{Y}, T)$ from R to T, and
- W^{IRI} is the IRI constructed for this object property.

E.g., a Datalog fact $\mathrm{OP\_IRI}_2(\texttt{ToAcc}, \texttt{A\_id}, \texttt{Prj}, \texttt{Acc}, \textit{:Prj}, \textit{Acc}\#\textit{ToAcc}, \textit{A\_id})$ is generated for the foreign key reference of schema 'Prj' in Fig. 3.

Since the direct mapping produces one resource per tuple in an instance of R, and a W^{IRI} triple only for non-null attribute values, the property W^{IRI} will have a cardinality of 'at most 1.' If there is additionally a non-null constraint for the attributes $\bar{X}$, the cardinality will be 'exactly 1.' We use the notation $\overline{\mathrm{NN}}(\bar{X}, R)$ in a rule to mean that $\mathrm{NN}_1(X, R)$ is present for all $X \in \bar{X}$. The following rules generate property paths with a maximum cardinality, and with or without a minimum cardinality depending on the presence of NN constraints:

$$\mathrm{CRDPROP}(R^{\mathrm{IRI}}, W^{\mathrm{IRI}}, T^{\mathrm{IRI}}) \longleftarrow \overline{\mathrm{NN}}(\bar{X}, R), \mathrm{OP\_IRI}_{2n}(\bar{X}, \bar{Y}, R, T, W^{\mathrm{IRI}}), \qquad (6)$$
$$\mathrm{CLASSIRI}(R, R^{\mathrm{IRI}}), \mathrm{CLASSIRI}(T, T^{\mathrm{IRI}})$$

$$\mathrm{MAXPROP}(R^{\mathrm{IRI}}, W^{\mathrm{IRI}}, T^{\mathrm{IRI}}) \longleftarrow \neg\overline{\mathrm{NN}}(\bar{X}, R), \mathrm{OP\_IRI}_{2n}(\bar{X}, \bar{Y}, R, T, W^{\mathrm{IRI}}), \qquad (7)$$
$$\mathrm{CLASSIRI}(R, R^{\mathrm{IRI}}), \mathrm{CLASSIRI}(T, T^{\mathrm{IRI}})$$

The following two rules are for the inverse direction from relation schema T to R. The crucial observation here is that if there is a constraint $\mathrm{UNQ}_n(\bar{X}, R)$, then the inverse property of W^{IRI} has a maximum cardinality of '1'. Otherwise, the typing is the only guarantee we have on the inverse.

$$\mathrm{INVMAXPROP}(T^{\mathrm{IRI}}, W^{\mathrm{IRI}}, R^{\mathrm{IRI}}) \longleftarrow \mathrm{UNQ}_n(\bar{X}, R), \mathrm{OP\_IRI}_{2n}(\bar{X}, \bar{Y}, R, T, W^{\mathrm{IRI}}), \qquad (8)$$
$$\mathrm{CLASSIRI}(R, R^{\mathrm{IRI}}), \mathrm{CLASSIRI}(T, T^{\mathrm{IRI}})$$

$$\mathrm{INVPROP}(T^{\mathrm{IRI}}, W^{\mathrm{IRI}}, R^{\mathrm{IRI}}) \longleftarrow \neg\mathrm{UNQ}_n(\bar{X}, R), \mathrm{OP\_IRI}_{2n}(\bar{X}, \bar{Y}, R, T, W^{\mathrm{IRI}}), \qquad (9)$$
$$\mathrm{CLASSIRI}(R, R^{\mathrm{IRI}}), \mathrm{CLASSIRI}(T, T^{\mathrm{IRI}})$$

Fourth, the rules (10) and (11) handle the datatype properties that are generated by $\mathcal{M}^s$ for every attribute of a non-binary relation schema. A fact $\mathrm{DTP\_IRI}(X, R, X^{\mathrm{IRI}})$ in $\mathcal{V}$ denotes mapping of an attribute $X \in \mathrm{att}(R)$ to a datatype property with IRI X^{IRI}. For instance, we have facts like $\mathrm{DTP\_IRI}(\texttt{Name}, \texttt{Emp}, \textit{:Emp}\#\textit{Name})$, etc., for Example 1 in Fig. 3. The following rules treat the case with and without an NN constraint on an attribute X.

$$\mathrm{MAXDATA}(R^{\mathrm{IRI}}, X^{\mathrm{IRI}}, T) \longleftarrow \neg\mathrm{NN}_1(X, R), \mathrm{DTP\_IRI}(X, R, X^{\mathrm{IRI}}), \qquad (10)$$
$$\mathrm{TYPEXML}(X, R, T), \mathrm{CLASSIRI}(R, R^{\mathrm{IRI}})$$

$$\mathrm{CRDDATA}(R^{\mathrm{IRI}}, X^{\mathrm{IRI}}, T) \longleftarrow \mathrm{NN}_1(X, R), \mathrm{DTP\_IRI}(X, R, X^{\mathrm{IRI}}), \qquad (11)$$
$$\mathrm{TYPEXML}(X, R, T), \mathrm{CLASSIRI}(R, R^{\mathrm{IRI}})$$

Finally, rule (12) generates node shapes that reflect UNQ constraints on (combinations of) attributes. For all $n \geq 1$:

$$\text{UNQTUPLE}_n(R^{\text{IRI}}, X_1^{\text{IRI}}, \dots, X_n^{\text{IRI}}) \longleftarrow \text{UNQ}_n(\bar{X}, R), \tag{12}$$
$$\text{DTP\_IRI}(X_1, R, X_1^{\text{IRI}}), \dots, \text{DTP\_IRI}(X_n, R, X_n^{\text{IRI}}),$$
$$\text{CLASSIRI}(R, R^{\text{IRI}})$$

Example 3. *The following SHACL predicates result from the application of rewriting rules (1)–(12) on the relations schemas stated in Example 1.*

SHAPE(:*Emp*)	*by Γ rule 1*
CRDDATA(:*Emp*, :*Emp#E_id*, *xsd:integer*);	*by Γ rule 11*
UNQTUPLE$_1$(:*Emp*, :*Emp#E_id*);	*by Γ rule 12*
CRDDATA(:*Emp*, :*Emp#Name*, *xsd:string*);	*by Γ rule 11*
MAXDATA(:*Emp*, :*Emp#Post*, *xsd:string*);	*by Γ rule 10*
PROP(:*Emp*, :*Asg#ToEmp,ToPrj,E_id,P_id*, :*Prj*).	*by Γ rule 3*
SHAPE(:*Prj*)	*by Γ rule 1*
CRDDATA(:*Prj*, :*Prj#P_id*, *xsd:integer*);	*by Γ rule 11*
UNQTUPLE$_1$(:*Prj*, :*Prj#P_id*);	*by Γ rule 12*
CRDDATA(:*Prj*, :*Prj#Name*, *xsd:string*);	*by Γ rule 11*
CRDDATA(:*Prj*, :*Prj#ToAcc*, *xsd:integer*);	*by Γ rule 11*
UNQTUPLE$_1$(:*Prj*, :*Prj#ToAcc*);	*by Γ rule 12*
CRDPROP(:*Prj*, :*Prj,Acc#ToAcc,A_id*, :*Acc*);	*by Γ rule 6*
INVPROP(:*Prj*, :*Asg#ToEmp,ToPrj,E_id,P_id*, :*Emp*).	*by Γ rule 5*
SHAPE(:*Acc*)	*by Γ rule 1*
CRDDATA(:*Acc*, :*Acc#A_id*, *xsd:integer*);	*by Γ rule 11*
UNQTUPLE$_1$(:*Acc*, :*Acc#A_id*);	*by Γ rule 12*
MAXDATA(:*Acc*, :*Acc#Name*, *xsd:string*);	*by Γ rule 10*
INVMAXPROP(:*Acc*, :*Prj,Acc#ToAcc,A_id*, :*Prj*);	*by Γ rule 8*

We refer to our technical report [9, Appendix C.4] for the complete translation of these SHACL predicates into the SHACL document.

5   Properties of the Constraint Rewriting Γ

We now study the properties of our constraint rewriting Γ for the direct mapping $\mathcal{M}$: constraint preservation and semantics preservation, defined in Sect. 3.

First, we show that the constraint rewriting Γ does not lose any SQL data constraints of the relational database that is being translated into the RDF graph:

Theorem 1. *The constraint rewriting Γ is constraint preserving.*

Proof Outline: We explicitly define an inverse mapping $\mathcal{N} : \mathcal{P}(\mathbb{S}) \to \mathbb{G}$ of Γ. Then, letting $(\mathcal{V}', \delta') = \mathcal{N}(\Gamma(\mathcal{V}, \delta))$, we show that $\mathcal{V}' = \mathcal{V}$ and $\delta' = \delta$, using a case distinction over all facts in $\mathcal{V}$ and δ and all possible shapes in $\Gamma(\mathcal{V}, \delta)$. We refer to our technical report [9, Appendix B.1] for the complete proof.

Second, we establish that the constraint rewriting Γ for direct mapping $\mathcal{M}$ is not semantics preserving. For that, we first recall that mapping $\mathcal{M}$ does not generate: (1) an IRI from a null value, (2) distinct IRIs for the repeated tuples of the relation schema. These facts can be used to construct a counterexample to show that mapping $\mathcal{M}$ generates a consistent RDF graph w.r.t. the generated SHACL constraints when the primary keys of input database are violated. Observe that in Example 4, an obstacle to obtain a semantic-preserving constraint rewriting Γ for $\mathcal{M}$ is the semantics of direct mapping $\mathcal{M}$ w.r.t. the PKs of relation schemas.

Example 4. *Consider a relation schema "create table User (id integer primary key);" with three tuples: $t_1.id = 1$, $t_2.id = 1$ and $t_3.id = $ null, respectively, violating the primary key constraint of the schema definition. It is straightforward to see that the directly mapped RDF triples of the tuples of schema 'User' (on the right) validate against the SHACL shape generated from the schema definition of 'User' (on the left), which leads to a contradiction w.r.t. the Definition 6.*

SHAPE($:User$)	$:User/id=1$ rdf:type $:User.$
CRDDATA($:User, :User\#id, xsd:integer$)	$:User/id=1$ $:User\#id$ $1.$
UNQTUPLE$_1$($:User, :User\#id$).	

Proposition 1. *The constraint rewriting Γ is not semantics preserving.*

Finally, we study the weak semantics preservation property of Γ.

Example 5. *Consider a database instance such as: Emp(011, Ida, PhD), Prj(021, PeTWIN, 034), Acc(034, NFR) and Asg(012, 022), of the relational schema given in Example 1, violating the foreign keys ToEmp and ToPrj of the relation schema Asg. Then, $\mathcal{M}$ generates the following RDF triples:*

$:Emp/E\_id=011$ rdf:type $:Emp;$	$:Prj/P\_id=021$ rdf:type $:Prj;$	$:Acc/A\_id=034$ rdf:type $:Acc;$
$:Emp\#E\_id$ $011;$	$:Prj\#P\_id$ $021;$ $:Prj\#Name$ $"PeTWIN";$	$:Acc\#A\_id$ $034;$
$:Emp\#Name$ $"Ida";$	$:Prj\#ToAcc$ $034;$	$:Acc\#Name$ $"NFR".$
$:Emp\#Post$ $"PhD".$	$:Prj,Acc\#ToAcc,A\_id$ $:Acc/A\_id=034.$	

satisfying the SHACL shapes given by the SHACL predicates produced by the rewriting Γ in Example 3.

Observe that in Example 5, the SHACL shapes resulted by the Γ in Example 3 fail to detect the violation of foreign keys of the relation schema Asg, essentially because the rewriting Γ for $\mathcal{M}$ does not generate SHACL constraints for the binary schema. The main reason behind this flaw is that the direct mapping $\mathcal{M}$ does not generate a class for the binary schema, and hence, the rewriting Γ does not produce a SHACL shape for the schema Asg to capture the violations of ToEmp and ToPrj foreign keys. Likewise, observe that if we change the Prj tuple in Example 5 to Prj(021, PeTWIN, 031), violating the foreign key ToAcc, and we remove the NN constraint on ToAcc from the schema Prj then the node ':Prj/P_id=021' validates the generated SHAPE(:Prj). That means that only the 'not null' SQL data constraints on FKs is sufficient for the constraint rewriting Γ to detect the violation of FKs on the relational schema.

In summary, we observe: (1) The direct mapping $\mathcal{M}$ as defined by Sequeda et al., including the W3C recommendation [2], generates one resource per tuple of a database instance (for non-binary relation schemata) and the IRI of this tuple is generated from the relation's primary key. This approach breaks down if the PK constraint is violated, which explains why semantics preservation does not hold as stated. (2) The binary relations 'BINREL' rule as defined by the direct mapping $\mathcal{M}$ of Sequeda et al., but not in the W3C recommendation, are not suitable for the SHACL constraint rewriting Γ since the mapping $\mathcal{M}$ does not generate a class for these binary schemas in the relational database. (3) Not all data constraints on FKs are strong enough to guarantee the semantics of FKs on relation schema in the SHACL constraint rewriting Γ. However, if we restrict our attention to the database instances $\mathcal{D}_\sigma$ that satisfy their PKs and FKs constraints, then the semantics preservation is restored.

Theorem 2. *The constraint rewriting Γ is weakly semantics preserving.*

Proof Outline: First, we show that the direct mapping $\mathcal{G}$ of a legal instance $\mathcal{D}$ of the relational schema with constraints satisfies all shapes generated by Γ, by a case distinction over the possible shapes. This involves a detailed analysis of the directly mapped triples and the semantics of the SHACL shapes. For the other direction, we show that every possible violation of a data constraint in a database instance $\mathcal{D}$ that satisfies the key constraints entails that $\mathcal{G}$ fails to validate at least one of the SHACL constraints generated by Γ. This requires a case distinction over the data constraints δ and their role for the direct mapping. We refer to our technical report [9, Appendix B.1] for the complete proof.

Finally, in summary, the constraint rewriting Γ defined in Sect. 4 is both constraint preserving and weakly semantics preserving.

6   Discussion

We have extended the direct mapping $\mathcal{M}$ from relational data to RDF, proposed in [8], with SHACL constraints by using the SQL data constraints, including data types which were missing from both previous extensions of direct mappings [3,8]. All of the good properties of the original extension of direct mapping [8] apply to our extension. Contrary to previous work, our extension describes the mapped data using SHACL constraints instead of OWL axioms. This is what makes our mapping (weakly) semantic preserving.

We note that our constraint rewriting Γ, specified in Sect. 4.2, is not semantics preserving if: (1) relation schemas without PKs are considered. This is because $\mathcal{M}$ produces blank nodes for the tuples of relation schemas without PKs, which are problematic for core SHACL but could be handled by extensions to the core;[5] and (2) relational databases violating the PKs and FKs constraints

---

[5] e.g., using SPARQL-based Target Types in https://www.w3.org/TR/shacl-af/.

are considered for the constraint rewriting Γ, because the mapping $\mathcal{M}$ often produces an RDF graph that is consistent w.r.t. the generated SHACL shapes even if the PKs and FKs are violated in the source database. This cannot easily be fixed, since $\mathcal{M}$ relies on the uniqueness of PKs to generate distinct RDF resources.

The interest of database instances that might violate their primary or foreign key constraints lies purely in the formulation of the 'completeness' direction (right to left) of semantics preservation. Stating that every database constraint violation entails a violation of a shape on the RDF graph means that the shapes are 'strong enough,' they give the strongest possible guarantee on the shape of RDF graphs produced by $\mathcal{M}$. We have seen in the discussion following Example 4 and 5 that the 'semantics preservation' approach does not work well with key constraints unless the database instance is explicitly included in the constraint rewriting, similar to the work of Sequeda et al., to trigger the unsatisfiability of the directly mapped graph whenever keys are violated in the source database. However, Sequeda et al. [8, Theorem 3] established that the desirable condition of direct mapping being monotone is an obstacle to obtain a semantics preserving even if the database instance is explicitly included in the constraint rewriting. Therefore, we believe that, instead of relying on the database instance, a more useful formulation of the completeness of constraint rewriting for direct mapping can be found, such as maximally implied SHACL constraints, i.e., completeness meaning that any other SHACL constraints are either not implied by the source constraints, or subsumed by the maximally implied SHACL constraints.

Further, we observe that our constraint rewriting could be extended for relation schemas without PKs in combination with OWL axioms, in a similar manner as shown for the combination of DL-Lite_{RDFS} axioms and tree-based identification constraints in [3], where the relation schemas without PKs could be used to generate OWL axioms if there exists no foreign key referential integrity constraint between the schemas with and without PKs. However, the presence of referential integrity constraints between schemas with and without PKs might be an obstacle to generate a semantic-preserving constraint rewriting in this setting, therefore, we leave this transformation as an open question.

7 Conclusion

In this paper, we have proposed an extension of direct mapping with the constraint rewriting. The constraint rewriting transfers the semantic information of SQL constraints from the relational database to the RDF graph while keeping intact all the good properties of the direct mapping [8], i.e., information preserving, query preserving and monotonic. In contrast to previous work, we have studied the extension of direct mapping with SHACL constraints instead of the OWL axioms. Finally, we have shown that our constraint rewriting extends the original form of direct mapping of relational databases to an RDF graph while guaranteeing constraint and weak semantics preservation.

The SHACL descriptions of a directly mapped RDF graph could be useful for the semantic optimization of SPARQL queries, analogous to the database constraints that can be used for efficient query answering in an *Ontology-Based Data Access* platform [11]. Further, any ontology alignments that follow the W3C direct mapping directives to connect the ontological vocabulary to the relational database, such as BootOX [6], could be improved by extending bootstrapping with the SHACL description of source data that fits more closely with RDF/OWL representation.

In future work, we would like to concentrate on the more intuitive interpretation of constraint rewriting for the direct mapping specified in denotational semantics [2]. We also aim to extend our constraint rewriting from direct mapping to the interrelated and complementary W3C standard: R2RML [5].

Acknowledgements. This work was supported by the Norwegian Research Council via the SIRIUS Centre for Research Based Innovation, Grant Nr. 237898. We thank Evgeny Kharlamov and Egor Kostylev for many fruitful discussions, Holger Knublauch for help with SHACL-SPARQL, and Roman Kontchakov for invaluable assistance in preparing the final version.

References

1. Abiteboul, S., Hull, R., Vianu, V.: Foundations of Databases, vol. 8. Addison-Wesley, Reading (1995)
2. Arenas, M., Bertails, A., Prud'hommeaux, E., Sequeda, J.: A direct mapping of relational data to RDF. W3C recommendation, W3C, September 2012
3. Calvanese, D., Fischl, W., Pichler, R., Sallinger, E., Simkus, M.: Capturing relational schemas and functional dependencies in RDFS. In: Twenty-Eighth AAAI Conference on Artificial Intelligence (2014)
4. Cyganiak, R., Wood, D., Lanthaler, M.: RDF 1.1 concepts and abstract syntax. W3C recommendation, W3C, February 2014
5. Das, S., Sundara, S., Cyganiak, R.: R2RML: RDB to RDF mapping language, W3C recommendation, W3C (2012)
6. Jiménez-Ruiz, E., et al.: BootOX: practical mapping of RDBs to OWL 2. In: Arena, M., et al. (eds.) ISWC 2015. LNCS, vol. 9367, pp. 113–132. Springer, Cham (2015). https://doi.org/10.1007/978-3-319-25010-6_7
7. Knublauch, H., Kontokostas, D.: Shapes constraint language (SHACL). W3C recommendation, W3C, July 2017
8. Sequeda, J.F., Arenas, M., Miranker, D.P.: On directly mapping relational databases to RDF and OWL. In: Proceedings of 21st International Conference on World Wide Web, pp. 649–658. ACM (2012)
9. Thapa, R.B., Giese, M.: A source-to-target constraint rewriting for direct mapping. Technical report Nr 498, Department of Informatics, University of Oslo, July 2021
10. Tirmizi, S.H., Sequeda, J., Miranker, D.: Translating SQL applications to the semantic web. In: Bhowmick, S.S., Küng, J., Wagner, R. (eds.) DEXA 2008. LNCS, vol. 5181, pp. 450–464. Springer, Heidelberg (2008). https://doi.org/10.1007/978-3-540-85654-2_40
11. Xiao, G., Calvanese, D., Kontchakov, R., et al.: Ontology-based data access: a survey. In: Proceedings of International Joint Conference on Artificial Intelligence. Survey Track, pp. 5511–5519. IJCAI Organization (2018)

Learning to Predict the Departure Dynamics of Wikidata Editors

Guangyuan Piao[1(✉)] and Weipeng Huang[2]

[1] Department of Computer Science, Maynooth University, Maynooth, Ireland
guangyuan.piao@mu.ie
[2] Insight Centre for Data Analytics, University College Dublin, Dublin, Ireland
weipeng.huang@insight-centre.org

Abstract. Wikidata as one of the largest open collaborative knowledge bases has drawn much attention from researchers and practitioners since its launch in 2012. As it is collaboratively developed and maintained by a community of a great number of volunteer editors, understanding and predicting the departure dynamics of those editors are crucial but have not been studied extensively in previous works. In this paper, we investigate the synergistic effect of two different types of features: statistical and pattern-based ones with DeepFM as our classification model which has not been explored in a similar context and problem for predicting whether a Wikidata editor will *stay* or *leave* the platform. Our experimental results show that using the two sets of features with DeepFM provides the best performance regarding *AUROC* (0.9561) and *F1* score (0.8843), and achieves substantial improvement compared to using either of the sets of features and over a wide range of baselines.

Keywords: Wikidata editors · Crowdsourcing dynamics · Classification

1 Introduction

Wikidata [28] is a community-driven knowledge base with its initial primary goal to be a central knowledge base to serve all Wikimedia projects. Since its launch in late 2012, it has become one of the most active projects of the Wikimedia Foundation in terms of contributors [13]. As one of the largest open, free, multilingual knowledge bases, Wikidata has contributed significantly to the Linked Open Data Cloud[1,2] and our research community along with DBpedia [11]. Wikidata currently contains over 90M items and over 1.3B edits have been made since the project launch[3], and has been widely used in various domains such as natural language processing [10], recommender systems [23], and life sciences [29].

As a community effort, editors on open collaborative knowledge bases such as Wikidata and Wikipedia add and edit information collaboratively and play a crucial role in the growth of those platforms. Therefore, in the context of

---

[1] https://lod-cloud.net/.
[2] https://bit.ly/2O1KZAV.
[3] https://www.wikidata.org/wiki/Wikidata:Statistics/en.

© Springer Nature Switzerland AG 2021
A. Hotho et al. (Eds.): ISWC 2021, LNCS 12922, pp. 39–55, 2021.
https://doi.org/10.1007/978-3-030-88361-4_3

Wikipedia, there have been many studies on predicting the editing dynamics of users[4] such as how many contributions an editor will make or whether the editor will stay on or leave the platform [2,31]. Similar to Wikipedia, editors on Wikidata platform are critical to its success and understanding editing dynamics such as whether an editor will leave the platform is important but little attention has been given in the context of Wikidata [24], which is our focus of this study.

We seek answers to questions such as (1) what types of features are useful for predicting the departure dynamics of Wikidata editors, (2) what types of machine learning (ML) approaches perform well for the prediction, and (3) how well those approaches applied to Wikipedia can perform in the context of Wikidata. To this end, we investigate different types of features and investigate a wide range of ML approaches including best-performing ones adapted from previous studies in the context of Wikipedia, and investigate a new approach adopted from the recommender system domain which has not been explored in previous studies for predicting whether an editor will stay on or leave Wikidata. In summary, our contributions are: (1) We investigate two sets of features – statistical and pattern-based ones – for predicting inactive editors on Wikidata (Sect. 3). We show the synergistic effect on using both sets of features in Sect. 6, which has not been used together in a similar context; (2) We adopt DeepFM model [9] as our classification approach, which is exploited for the prediction task in the context of Wikidata for the first time to our best knowledge, and show its effectiveness by comparing a wide range of classification models in Sect. 6 including those applied to Wikipedia; (3) Our source code and the processed Wikidata dataset can be found here[5]. The dataset includes more than 0.5B edits by 371,068 users (Sect. 4), which can be a good resource for studying different problems such as recommending Wikidata items.

2   Related Work

In the context of Wikipedia, many studies have been conducted regarding the departure dynamics of Wikipedia editors in the literature. For example, Gandica et al. [7] defined a function of edit probability and showed that the editing behavior of Wikipedia editors is far from random and the number of previous edits is a good indicator of their future edits. Zhang et al. [31] proposed a ML approach with a set of statistical features extracted from different periods of each user's edit history for predicting the future edit volume of Wikipedia editors where they showed that GBT (Gradient Boosted Trees) and kNN (k-Nearest Neighbors) provide the best performance. Instead of *statistical* features, Arelli et al. [1,2] proposed leveraging *pattern-based* features with respect to consecutive edited pages, and constructed Boolean features regarding a set of frequent patterns for predicting whether a Wikipedia user might leave or stay on the platform. In addition to predicting activeness or edit volume of users, other aspects regarding edit behaviors such as quality, edit sessions on the platform,

---

[4] We use the words *editors* and *users* interchangeably in this rest of the paper.
[5] https://bit.ly/3yyJhZj.

and the difference between Wikipedians and non-Wikipedian editors have been studied as well [4,8,16]. In contrast to the popularity of previous studies regarding different aspects on Wikipedia, less studies have been explored in the context of Wikidata, which is our focus in this study for classifying potential inactive Wikidata editors.

Recently, Mora-Cantallops et al. [14] conducted a literature review of research on Wikidata and revealed the main research topics on Wikidata such as users and their editing practices, knowledge organization, external references, and the language of editors [10,19,21]. We focus on the first topic (users and their editing practices), which is most relevant to our work. Piscopo et al. [20] studied different types of editors such as bots, human editors, registered, anonymous editors to understand how those editors influence the quality of items on Wikidata. In [3,15] the authors performed a cluster analysis of the editing activities of Wikidata editors to compare them with typical roles found in peer-production and collaborative ontology engineering projects, and studied the dynamic participation patterns across those characterized roles of Wikidata editors. More recently, Sarasua et al. [24] conducted a large-scale longitudinal data analysis for Wikidata edit history over around four years until 2016 to study the evolution of different types of Wikidata editors. Their study revealed many interesting findings such as the number of new editors joining the Wikidata has been increasing over time, and the majority of contribution has been made by a few editors with a skewed distribution of contributions. We observe that similar trends have continued in our Wikidata dataset with edit history until 2020 (Sect. 4). The authors [24] also investigated the edit volume and the lifespan (i.e., short or long) of editors during their active time on Wikidata where their focus is on *gone* editors.

Compared with those works, we focus on the problem of predicting the activeness of registered editors in the future on Wikidata in this work, investigate the synergistic effect of considering both statistical and pattern-based features, and exploit DeepFM model for the first time for the problem.

3   Proposed Approach

This section provides a formal definition of the Wikidata user classification task, followed by the description of the proposed approach.

Problem Formulation. Our goal is to learn a binary classifier $f(\mathbf{x}_u) \rightarrow y_u$ where $\mathbf{x}_u$ denotes a set of features based on the edit history of a user u, and y_u is the class label indicating activeness of u with 1 for inactive and 0 for active.

Overview of Our Approach. The approach for the classification task of Wikidata editors consists of (1) statistical and/or pattern-based features, and (2) a DeepFM classification model where those features are used as an input.

3.1   Statistical Features

Here we discuss the set of statistical features used in our model. These features utilize the edit history of Wikidata editors. All of these features try to capture users' editing behavior on Wikidata from different perspectives.

1. *Total # of edits* ($N_{total\cdot edit\cdot ent}$) indicates the total number of edits have been made by an editor on Wikidata.
2. *Distinct # of edited entities* ($N_{dist\cdot edit}$). The *total # of edits* does not distinguish edited entities. This feature aims to capture the number of distinct entities have been edited by a user.
3. *Diversity of edit actions* ($Div_{edit\cdot act}$). To capture the diversity of different types of edit actions (see Sect. 4), we use the Shannon-Entropy [25] of different edit actions in the same manner as in [24] as: $H(T) = -\sum_{i=1}^{n} P(t_i) \cdot \log P(t_i)$ where T indicates different types of edit actions, and $|T| = n$.
4. *Diversity of entities* (Div_{ent}). We measure the diversity of edited entities of a user using the Shannon-Entropy. The intuition is that the diversity of edited entities of a user could also be different across active and inactive editors.
5. *The # of days between first and last edits* (T_{edit}) refers to the time difference between a user's first and last edits during a certain period.
6. *Diversity of day of week* (Div_{day}). This measures the diversity of day of the week based on the edit history of each user using the Shannon-Entropy.
7. *The # of days between first edit and prediction time* ($L_{first\cdot pred}$). This indicates the time difference between a user's first edit on Wikidata and the prediction time to predict whether a user will become inactive or not.
8. *The # of days between the last edit and prediction time* ($L_{last\cdot pred}$) indicates the time difference between a user's last edit and the predicted time.

For the first six features, we extract those in the last p months from the prediction time using 10 different time periods $p \in P = \{\frac{1}{16}, \frac{1}{8}, \frac{1}{4}, \frac{1}{2}, 1, 2, 4, 12, 36, 108\}$ to capture the editing behavior over different time periods, which has been inspired by [31] in the context of Wikipedia for predicting the edit volume of users. For instance, we extract the set of features based on the edit history from the last 12 months from the prediction time when $p = 12$. Here, 108 months in our Wikidata dataset (see Sect. 4) cover the whole edit history of each editor. As a result, there are $6 \times 10 + 2 = 62$ statistical features in total. As one might expect, some of those features can be skewed and we apply a logarithmic scale, $x_{after} = \log(x_{before} + 1)$, to them before feeding those into any ML approach.

3.2   Pattern-Based Features

In contrast to *statistical* features such as the above-mentioned ones, *pattern-based* features have been explored in the context of Wikipedia for predicting the departure dynamics of editors [1]. To investigate which type of features performs better or the synergistic effect of combining those two sets of features for our classification task on Wikidata, we investigate those statistical and pattern-based features – separately and together – in our experiments in Sect. 5. In the following paragraphs, we describe the set of pattern-based features used.

To start with, the edit history of each user is considered as a chronological sequence of each consecutive pair (i_1, i_2) of edited entities. For each pair (i_1, i_2), the following information is extracted for describing each pair:

- **r/n**: Whether i_2 is an entity that has already been edited by the user before, i.e., **r** if i_2 is a re-edit, and **n** otherwise.
- **m/n**: Whether i_2 is a *normal entity* (**n**) or others such as *properties* (**m**). On Wikidata, each entity is identified by a unique entity ID, which is a number prefixed by a letter (Q, L, P)[6]. Here we consider an entity which starts with "Q" as a *normal entity*.
- If i_2 is a re-edit – **c/n**: Whether i_1 is the same as i_2, i.e., these are two consecutive edits (**c**) on the same entity or not (**n**).
  Otherwise (i_2 is a new edit) – **z/o/u**: Common classes (via the property *instance of*) between entity i_1 and i_2: **z** for zero classes in common, **o** for at least one class in common, and **u** for information is not available.
- **v/f/s**: Time difference between the two edits where **v** indicates *very fast* edit (less than three minutes), **f** refers to *fast* edit (less than 15 min), and **s** for *slow* edit (more than 15 min).

For example, **rncv** for a pair of entities (i_1, i_2) indicates that i_2 is a re-edit (**r**) and is a normal entity (**n**) which is the same as i_1 (**c**), and the time difference between the two consecutive edits is less than three minutes (**v**). Given this representation of edit history, pattern-based features can be extracted with the following two main steps [1].

First, frequent patterns from the *active* and *inactive* user edit histories in the training set are extracted separately using PrefixSpan [18] algorithm, which is one of the fastest sequential pattern mining algorithm. Those pattern-based features are extracted using SPFM data mining library [6]. Each pattern contains a sequence of pairs of entities consecutively edited by an editor where each pair is described using above-mentioned features (e.g., **rncv**). Afterwards, the frequency of each pattern f is calculated for both the *active* and *inactive* classes.

Next, two sets of patterns are extracted where the first one contains top frequent patterns that appear in both classes based on the absolute frequency difference between the two classes, and the second set contains top frequent patterns only appear for active class[7]. Finally, we select the set of top k patterns of length l that appear for both classes and for active editors only. We used the same setting as in [1] where $k = 13$ and $l \in \{1, 2, 3\}$, which results in a total of 78 Boolean features for any classifier as an input with 1 indicates a pattern appears in the edit history of an editor, 0 otherwise.

3.3 DeepFM as the Classification Model

On top of above-mentioned features, we adopt a DeepFM-based classification model which was proposed in [9] for recommender systems. To the best of our knowledge, this is the first attempt of utilizing the DeepFM model for user classification tasks on Wikidata. DeepFM was designed to automatically capture

---

[6] https://www.wikidata.org/wiki/Wikidata:Identifiers: items are prefixed with Q, properties are prefixed by P, lexemes are prefixed by L.

[7] Similar to the observation in [1], there is no pattern only appears for inactive editors.

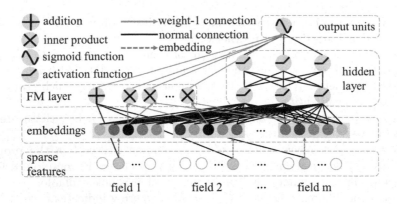

Fig. 1. DeepFM architecture from [9], which consists of two main components: FM part on the left and DNN part on the right.

feature interactions by modeling low-order feature interactions through Factorization Machines (FM) and high-order feature interactions via Deep Neural Networks (DNN). Intuitively, modeling different types of interactions via DeepFM plays a crucial role in capturing the temporal dynamics of editing behaviors.

The model consists of two main components: an FM component and DNN component as illustrated in Fig. 1. Moreover, the model has the ability of memorizing low- and high-order feature interactions and generalizing feature combinations by jointly training the FM and DNN components for the combined prediction model:

$$\hat{y} = \sigma(\hat{y}_{FM} + \hat{y}_{DNN}) \tag{1}$$

where $\hat{y}_{FM}$ indicates the output from the FM part, $\hat{y}_{DNN}$ indicates the output from the DNN part of DeepFM, and σ is the *sigmoid* function. In the following, we briefly introduce the FM component and Deep component separately.

The *FM component* of DeepFM is a factorization machine introduced by Rendle et al. [22] to learn feature interactions for recommender systems. It consists of two parts with the first one considers linear interactions among features, and the second one with pairwise feature interactions as inner product of respective feature latent vectors as follows.

$$\hat{y}_{FM} = \langle \mathbf{w}, \mathbf{x} \rangle + \sum_{i=1}^{d} \sum_{j=i+1}^{d} \langle \mathbf{v}_i, \mathbf{v}_j \rangle x_i x_j \tag{2}$$

where $\mathbf{w}, \mathbf{x} \in \mathbb{R}^d$, $\mathbf{v}_i \in \mathbb{R}^k$, and d and k indicate the number of features and the dimension of a feature's latent factor, respectively. And $\langle \cdot, \cdot \rangle$ is the dot product of two vectors.

The *DNN component* is a feed-forward neural network which aims to learn high-order feature interactions. The first layer $\mathbf{a}^{(0)}$ in Eq. 3 is an embedding layer which compresses the input field vectors to the embedding vectors: $[\mathbf{e_1}, \mathbf{e_2}, \ldots, \mathbf{e_m}]$ for sparse/categorical features where for dense/numerical features the embedding layer will be ignored. DeepFM reuses the latent feature vectors in the FM component as network weights which are learned and used for this compression, and the FM and DNN components share the same feature embeddings.

$$\mathbf{a}^{(0)} = [\mathbf{e_1}, \mathbf{e_2}, \dots, \mathbf{e_m}], \quad \mathbf{a}^{(l+1)} = \sigma(\mathbf{W}^{(l)}\mathbf{a}^{(l)} + \mathbf{b}^{(l)}) \tag{3}$$

$$\hat{y}_{DNN} = \mathbf{W}^{|H|+1}\mathbf{a}^{|H|} + \mathbf{b}^{|H|+1} \tag{4}$$

where $\mathbf{a}^{(l)}$, $\mathbf{W}^{(l)}$, and $\mathbf{b}^{(l)}$ refer to the output, weights, and bias of l-th layer, and $|H|$ is the total number of hidden layers.

Training Details. We use the cross-entropy loss (or log loss) as our loss function, and the objective is to minimize the loss over all N training examples.

$$\mathcal{L} = -\frac{1}{N} \sum_{i=1}^{N} [y_i \cdot \log \hat{y}_i + (1 - y_i) \cdot \log(1 - \hat{y}_i)] \tag{5}$$

where y_i and $\hat{y}_i$ denote the ground truth and the predicted probability of class 1 for i-th instance, respectively. To resolve the overfitting problem, we use 20% of the training data as our validation set to adopt an early stopping strategy. We run up to 1,000 epochs for training, but the early stopping strategy stops the training if there is no improvement of $AUROC$ (Area Under the Receiver Operating Characteristics) on the validation set.

4 Wikidata Dataset

In this section, we discuss the Wikidata dataset for our study and provide exploratory analysis with respect to edit history of Wikidata users in Sect. 4.1. We use the Wikidata dump of 2020-12-01[8] with respect to edit history for our study. As we are interested in ordinary human editors who are registered on Wikidata, we further excluded edits from anonymous users (who we only know an IP address), bot accounts and administrators of Wikidata based on the open bot list[9] and admin list[10]. After filtering, the dataset contains 371,068 users with 519,121,793 edits in total for our analysis and experiments. The raw data includes crucial edit information for each edit such as:

- *Username* which indicates unique username who made an edit.
- *Time* with respect to the edit.
- *Entity* which refers to the unique entity ID such as Q13580495.
- *Edit action type* which denotes an automatic comment such as wbcreateredirect (Creates entity redirects) generated by the Wikidata's backend[11]. We choose top 50 edit action types which covers 99.9% of the whole data and treat the rest as "others".

We explore the filtered Wikidata dataset in detail in the following.

---

[8] https://dumps.wikimedia.org/wikidatawiki/20201201/.
[9] https://www.wikidata.org/wiki/Wikidata:Bots.
[10] https://www.wikidata.org/wiki/Wikidata:Administrators.
[11] Registered actions in Wikidata's backend: https://bit.ly/39NsrMh.

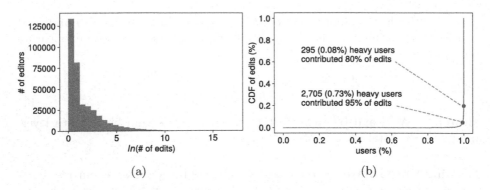

Fig. 2. (a) Histogram of editors in terms of the number of edits, and (b) CDF of edits for those editors on Wikidata until 2020-12-01.

4.1 Exploratory Analysis of the Dataset

First, we look at the distribution of edit volume on Wikidata. Figure 2a shows the histogram of the number of edits of all users. The figure illustrates that there are a lot of users making a low number of edits while a small number of *heavy users* making a high number of edits. The CDF (Cumulative Distribution Function) plot of edits in Fig. 2b further illustrates this phenomenon. More specifically, the green dot in the figure refers to a point that 295 out of 371,068 users (0.08%) contributed 80% of the total edits. In addition, the blue dot indicates that 2,705 (0.73%) users contributed 95% of all edits, which again shows that a small number of users have contributed the majority of the edits.

Next, we look at the lifespan of those editors, i.e., the duration between a user's first and last edits in days. The histogram of Wikidata users' lifespan is shown in Fig. 3a, where the lifespan of each user is scaled logarithmically using natural logarithm. As we can see from the figure, there are three distinct areas where the first two areas on the left correspond to occasional users who stopped editing Wikidata entities after the first few edits or newly joined editors, while the right area corresponds to editors with deeper interests in staying in the community and keeping editing Wikidata entities until they lose interest because of some reason. The separation point between the first two areas and the last one is 6.54 h. This is shorter than the observation on editors' lifespan on Wikipedia [31] where the point for separation is around 8 h.

Finally, we analyze the number of users who started or stopped editing Wikidata as well as that of users who started and stopped editing for each year from 2012 to 2020. On top of the same analysis done for the period between 2012 and 2016 in [24], our analysis including recent years could provide some insights on the trends the number of editors who started or stopped. Figure 3b shows an increasing trend over the years regarding the number of users in three aspects (i.e., who started, stopped, started and stopped). The numbers of stopped (as well as started and stopped) for 2020 are excluded in the figure as we have no clue about the last edits of users in 2020 are indeed their last edits. Hence, we

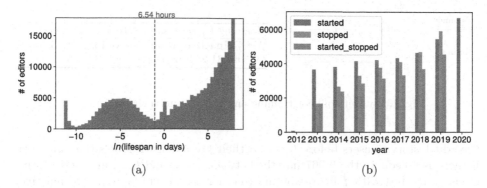

Fig. 3. (a) Histogram of editors in terms of their lifespan in days, and (b) the number of editors started and stopped using Wikidata from 2012 to 2020.

cannot consider them as stopped. The figure illustrates that although the number of newcomers is increasing, the number of users who stopped contributing to Wikidata is also increasing, which again shows the importance of predicting leaving editors and additional efforts might be needed to keep those users, e.g., recommending entities of their interests to edit.

5   Experimental Setup

In this section, we discuss our experimental setup including datasets for training and testing our user classification approaches (Sect. 5.1), a set of methods for comparison and evaluation (Sect. 6.1), and evaluation metrics (Sect. 5.3).

Instead of defining a new threshold for determining an editor as inactive based on his/her activity, we adopt the definition of a recent study from Sarasua et al. [24] for deriving the ground truth labels of editors. According to [24], if a user has not been editing any entity for 9.967 months (299 days), we consider the user as an *inactive* user (who stopped using Wikidata)[12].

5.1   Dataset

Similar to previous studies, we further limit users with more than one edit for training and testing different approaches including ours. Figure 4 illustrates how the dataset is divided into training and testing sets, which aims to resemble a real-world scenario. In the figure, t_{test} indicates the timestamp which is 9.967 months before the last edit time in our dataset, and t_{train} refers to the timestamp which is 9.967 months before t_{test}. We train a classification model f based on

---

[12] The threshold should make the majority of user labels (active or inactive) stable, e.g., the majority of inactive users decided based on their activities until a timestamp t and the predefined threshold should remain inactive after t. This suggests a higher value for the threshold is desirable, e.g., 9.967 months is better than 3 months, and we observe that the majority of inactive users do not visit the platform afterwards.

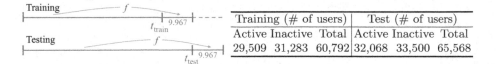

Training (# of users)			Test (# of users)		
Active	Inactive	Total	Active	Inactive	Total
29,509	31,283	60,792	32,068	33,500	65,568

Fig. 4. Dataset split for training and testing and their statistics.

the edit history of users before t_{test} and their ground truth labels (i.e., inactive if there is no edit in the 9.967 months between t_{train} and t_{test}, and active otherwise), and test with f for predicting whether a user will be active or inactive after t_{test}. For both training and testing, we limit users who are *active* before t_{train} and t_{test} to predict whether those active users will remain active or become inactive. Take testing as an example, we limit active users based on their activity between t_{train} and t_{test}, i.e., those inactive users during the time between t_{train} and t_{test} by our definition are already "gone" and therefore excluded for testing. As summarized in Fig. 4, there are 60,792 editors with 29,509 active and 31,283 inactive ones in the training set, and 65,568 editors in total with 32,068 active and 33,500 inactive ones in the test set for evaluation.

5.2   Compared Methods

Due to the difference between our task and the tasks of previous studies discussed in Sect. 2, and the difference between the Wikidata and Wikipedia datasets, those approaches from previous works could not apply to our problem directly. Nevertheless, we tried our best to adapt five previous approaches proposed in the context of Wikipedia or different tasks for our task in the context of Wikidata in addition to using DeepFM to investigate the classification performance. We use a naming convention of [ML model]-[the first two characters of the main author] in the following to distinguish those methods adapted for comparison, and provide their details.

GBT-Zh [31] uses Gradient Boosted Trees with three features such as the number of edits, the number of edited entities, and the length between the first and the last edit extracted from each of the 10 periods in P for each user in the same manner as ours. We tuned the max depth hyper-parameter with a grid search over $\{2, 4, 6, 8, 10\}$ using a 3-fold cross validation. The *drift* feature which measures the average number of edits of all editors in [31] is the same for all examples and is not important for our classification task although it is important for predicting the number of edits of users by capturing the overall changes of edit volume over time. Therefore, this feature is excluded in this adapted method.

kNN-Zh [31] leverages the same set of features as GBT-Zh but uses kNN as the classification model. The number of neighbors k is drawn from 200 to 3,000 in step of 200 using a 3-fold cross validation.

RF-Sa [24] is adapted to our context using Random Forest with a set of features such as the number of total edits, the average number of edits per item, the number of distinct items edited, and the diversity of types of edits extracted from each of the last 10 consecutive months introduced in [24]. Similar to GBT-Zh, we tuned the max depth hyper-parameter with a grid search over $\{2, 4, 6, 8, 10\}$ using a 3-fold cross validation. The ML model used in [24] was designed to analyze the edit volume of each user during his/her lifetime on Wikidata before he/she becomes inactive (or leaves the platform), and cannot be directly applied in our context for several reasons. For example, it trains a RANSAC model [5] for *each* user with the aforementioned features, and uses the parameters of the RANSAC model for training a Random Forest model to classify high/low volume or long/short lifespan editors with the focus on "gone" users. As one might expect, this results in not only training a great number of RANSAC models but also requires a good number of edits for each user for fitting the corresponding RANSAC model. Therefore, we use the set of features with Random Forest directly here as our baseline.

LR-Sa [24] leverages the same set of features as RF-Sa but uses Logistic Regression for classification. We tuned the regularization strength with a grid search over $\{0.1, 1, 10, 100, 1000\}$ using a 3-fold cross validation.

SVM-Ar is adapted from [1] which utilizes the set of pattern-based features introduced in Sect. 3.2 with a Support Vector Machine (SVM) classifier for predicting inactive editors. We tuned the regularization strength and the kernel parameter (γ) of a non-linear Radial Basis Function (RBF) kernel of SVM with a grid search over $\{0.1, 1, 10, 100, 1000\}$ and $\{1, 0.1, 0.01, 0.001, 0.0001\}$ using a 3-fold cross validation.

DeepFM-Stat refers to the proposed approach using DeepFM with the set of statistical features introduced in Sect. 3.1. We implemented DeepFM-Stat with DeepCTR library [26]. After tuning parameters such as dropout, batch sizes, and the number of hidden layers using 20% of the training set for validation, we opt to use the default DeepFM architecture of DeepCTR, which uses two hidden layers both with 128 nodes for its DNN part, embedding size $k = 4$, without dropout [27] as there is no significant improvement compared to the default architecture.

DeepFM-Pattern uses the same architecture as DeepFM-Stat but uses the set of pattern-based features used for SVM-Ar and introduced in Sect. 3.2.

DeepFM-Stat+Pattern considers both the statistical features and pattern-based features, which has not been explored together before. We investigate the synergistic effect of those two sets of features in the context of DeepFM.

We implemented GBT-Zh, kNN-Zh, RF-Sa, LR-Sa, and SVM-Ar with scikit-learn [17]. For DeepFM with different sets of features such as Stat, we run five times and the results in Sect. 6 are based on the averages over the five runs. All experiments are run on a laptop with Intel(R) Core(TM) i5-3230M (@2.6 GHZ) processor and 8 GB RAM.

5.3   Evaluation Metrics

We use $AUROC/AUC$ (Area Under the Receiver Operating Characteristics), $F1$ (F1 score) to evaluate the classification performance of different methods introduced in Sect. 6.1. The $F1$ score: $F1 = 2 \cdot \frac{precision \cdot recall}{precision + recall}$ is the harmonic mean of precision and recall, where the precision is the number of true positive predictions divided by the number of total positive predictions, and the recall refers to the number of true positive predictions divided by the number of all instances should have been predicted as positive. Compared to $F1$ where classification is based on a single threshold 0.5 (one if the predicted probability is equal or higher than the threshold, and zero otherwise), $AUROC$ reflects the classification performance at various threshold settings by measuring the area under the ROC curve, which shows a trade-off between the true positive rate and false positive rate. We analyze the $F1$ score of *inactive* class and $AUROC$ as our focus here is predicting editors that would become inactive.

6   Results

In this section, we first investigate the classification performance of those methods introduced in Sect. 6.1, and analyze the usefulness of our statistical features introduced in Sect. 3.1 in detail.

6.1   Comparison with the Set of Different Methods

Here we discuss the results with respect to two questions mentioned in Sect. 1 such as what types of ML approaches perform well for the prediction, and how well those approaches applied to Wikipedia can perform in the context of Wikidata. Table 1 shows the overall classification results in terms of $AUROC$ and $F1$ with the set of methods compared. As shown in the table, for approaches using either *statistical* or *pattern-based* features, DeepFM-Stat achieves the best performance of $AUROC$ (0.8928) and $F1$ (0.8247) followed by GBT-Zh. Despite the fact that GBT-Zh is adapted from edit volume prediction on Wikipedia, we notice that the approach provides a strong performance with an $AUROC$ score of 0.8890 and an $F1$ score of 0.8205 for classifying inactive users on Wikidata as well. Similar to the observation for predicting edit volume on Wikipedia, the classification performance of kNN-Zh is worse than GBT-Zh with the same set of features. RF-Sa and LR-Sa, which are adapted from the method for analyzing the edit volume of a Wikidata editor during his/her lifetime on the platform, perform worse than other methods. Overall, DeepFM-Stat improves the $AUROC$ score 0.43%–16.75% and the $F1$ score 0.51%-6.15% compared to those non-DeepFM alternatives either using statistical features or pattern-based ones for classifying inactive editors on Wikidata.

Next, we investigate what types of features (e.g., statistical, pattern-based, or both of them) are useful in the context of DeepFM. We observe

Table 1. Classification performance of the set of methods compared in terms of *AUROC* and *F1* with the best-performing ones in **bold**.

Method	*AUROC*	*F1*
GBT-Zh	0.8890	0.8205
kNN-Zh	0.8731	0.7935
RF-Sa	0.7647	0.7769
LR-Sa	0.7656	0.7795
SVM-Ar	0.8396	0.8029
DeepFM-Pattern	0.8786 ± 0.0002	0.7992 ± 0.0028
DeepFM-Stat	0.8928 ± 0.0001	0.8247 ± 0.0006
DeepFM-Stat+Pattern	$\mathbf{0.9561 \pm 0.0005}$	$\mathbf{0.8843 \pm 0.0012}$

that DeepFM-Stat+Pattern, which considers both the statistical and pattern-based features together, further improves the performance significantly compared to using either statistical or pattern-based features alone. For example, DeepFM-Stat+Pattern achieves an *AUROC* score of 0.9561 and an *F1* score of 0.8843, which outperforms DeepFM-Stat (+7.09% of *AUROC*, +7.23% of *F1*) and DeepFM-Pattern (+8.82% of *AUROC*, +10.65% of *F1*). This shows that the two types of features – statistical and pattern-based ones – can complement each other and achieves the best classification performance on predicting inactive editors, which has not been explored in previous studies[13].

Finally, Fig. 5 illustrates the time required for training each of those methods where we observe all except SVM-Ar can be trained within 30 min. As one might expect, leveraging both statistical and pattern-based features (DeepFM-Stat+Pattern) results in increased training time compared to only using either of the sets of features. The training/fitting time for all methods is arguably reasonable, which can be updated periodically (e.g., every day or week) easily, and the time can be further improved with a better infrastructure.

6.2 Analysis of Statistical Features

In this section, we analyze the set of statistical features introduced in Sect. 3.1 to answer the following questions: (1) *Are those features improving the classification performance compared to the features adapted in previous studies when the same ML approach is applied?* (2) *How much improvement can we achieve by considering a greater number of periods in P?* (3) *Which statistical feature contributes the most to the performance with DeepFM?*

Contribution of Proposed Features. Here we investigate whether using our features improves the classification performance compared to using the set of

---

[13] Similar trends can be observed when we limit users with at least five edits instead of one. For example, DeepFM-Stat+Pattern provides the best performance and improves *AUROC* 10.7% and 11.5% compared to using GBT-Zh and kNN-Zh.

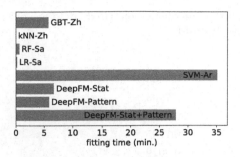

Fig. 5. Time required for training.

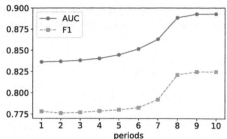

Fig. 6. Impact of the number of periods.

Table 2. Proposed features used with different classification approaches.*-Stat indicates * model with our statistical features introduced in Sect. 3.1.

	AUROC (Improvement)	F1 (Improvement)
GBT-Zh	0.8890	0.8205
GBT-Stat	**0.8918** (+0.32%)	**0.8225** (+0.24%)
kNN-Zh	0.8731	0.7935
kNN-Stat	**0.8898** (+1.91%)	**0.8172** (+2.99%)
SVM-Ar	0.8396	0.8029
SVM-Stat	**0.8640** (+2.91%)	**0.8040** (+0.14%)
DeepFM-Zh	0.8922 ± 0.0001	0.8223 ± 0.0029
DeepFM-Stat	**0.8928** $\pm$ **0.0001** (+0.07%)	**0.8247** $\pm$ **0.0006** (+0.29%)

features that are adapted from previous studies when the same ML approach is applied. Table 2 illustrates the performance in the context of four different methods such as GBT, kNN, SVM, and DeepFM. The results show that using our statistical features consistently achieves better *AUROC* and *F1* scores with those methods, which indicates the effectiveness of those features.

Contribution of Periods in P. Next, we demonstrate how the performance changes with the increasing number of periods considered to construct the set of statistical features. More specifically, we start from considering the shortest period ($\frac{1}{16}$ for p), and add the next period in P one by one for each experiment. The experimental results are shown in Fig. 6. It illustrates that taking more periods for extracting temporal dynamic features improves the performance for both *AUROC* and *F1* where the improvement gradually diminishes. In particular, the performance is improved significantly when the 8th period (12 months) is added where the *AUROC* improves from 0.8631 to 0.8885 (+2.94%), and the *F1* score improves from 0.7921 to 0.8211 (+3.66%).

Contribution of Each Feature. Finally, we investigate which feature contributes the most to the classification performance by removing each feature.

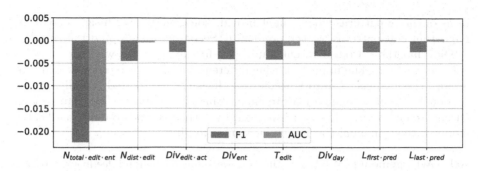

Fig. 7. Impact on `DeepFM-Stat` when each statistical feature is removed.

The results are illustrated in Fig. 7 where the performance is averaged over five runs when each feature is removed. The figure demonstrates that, $N_{total \cdot edit \cdot ent}$ – the number of total edits in the last $p \in P$ months – is a set of features that contribute the most in terms of both $AUROC$ and $F1$. This is in line with the findings from [7] which shows the number of edits before is a good indicator of the future edits of an editor on Wikipedia. We also notice that all other features contribute to a certain extent for $F1$ score while the contribution of other features except $N_{total \cdot edit \cdot ent}$ to $AUROC$ is lower than that to $F1$.

7 Conclusions

In this paper, we investigated a wide variety of classification approaches to predict Wikidata editors who will leave the platform. To the best of our knowledge, this is the first work on predicting inactive editors on Wikidata. To this end, we investigated a set of proposed statistical features together with a set of adapted pattern-based features and leveraged DeepFM as the classification method from recommender systems. In addition, we also built several adapted approaches from previous studies in the context of Wikipedia or different tasks, and investigated those approaches for our classification problem regarding Wikidata editors. We have shown, in the evaluation, that `DeepFM-Stat` achieves the best $AUROC$ and $F1$ performance compared to other adapted methods when using either set of features. In addition, we also showed that using both statistical and pattern-based features can improve the performance significantly and achieves the best $AUROC$ and $F1$ score. The promising results with DeepFM indicate that other alternative models invented for recommender systems [12,30] can be explored in the future for our problem. We also believe our Wikidata dataset containing the edit history over seven years will benefit the research community for studying other aspects related to Wikidata such as recommender systems for recommending entities of interest or understanding edit behavior difference between registered and anonymous editors etc.

Despite the promising performance, there are many interesting questions left unanswered. First, our work does not reveal the set of most influential patterns of the 78 patterns which might provide some interesting insights regarding important edit patterns for the prediction. Secondly, we adopted the threshold – 9.967 months – from a recent study [24] for determining whether an editor left the platform. The impact of using different threshold values for deriving the ground truth labels of editors needs to be further investigated. Finally, current approaches require manual feature engineering. In the future, we plan to focus on end-to-end approaches and investigate whether an end-to-end classification model without manual feature engineering is feasible.

Acknowledgements. We thank the reviewers for the helpful feedback. Weipeng Huang is supported by SFI under the grant SFI/12/RC/2289_P2.

References

1. Arelli, H., Spezzano, F.: Who will stop contributingf predicting inactive editors in Wikipedia. In: 2017 IEEE/ACM International Conference on Advances in Social Networks Analysis and Mining (ASONAM), pp. 355–358. IEEE (2017)
2. Arelli, H., Spezzano, F., Shrestha, A.: Editing behavior analysis for predicting active and inactive users in Wikipedia. In: Kaya, M., Alhajj, R. (eds.) ASONAM 2018. LNSN, pp. 127–147. Springer, Cham (2019). https://doi.org/10.1007/978-3-030-02592-2_7
3. Cuong, T.T., Müller-Birn, C.: Applicability of sequence analysis methods in analyzing peer-production systems: a case study in wikidata. In: Spiro, E., Ahn, Y.-Y. (eds.) SocInfo 2016. LNCS, vol. 10047, pp. 142–156. Springer, Cham (2016). https://doi.org/10.1007/978-3-319-47874-6_11
4. Druck, G., Miklau, G., McCallum, A.: Learning to predict the quality of contributions to wikipedia. WikiAI **8**, 7–12 (2008)
5. Fischler, M.A., Bolles, R.C.: Random sample consensus: a paradigm for model fitting with applications to image analysis and automated cartography. Commun. ACM **24**(6), 381–395 (1981)
6. Fournier-Viger, P., et al.: The SPMF open-source data mining library version 2. In: Berendt, B., et al. (eds.) ECML PKDD 2016. LNCS (LNAI), vol. 9853, pp. 36–40. Springer, Cham (2016). https://doi.org/10.1007/978-3-319-46131-1_8
7. Gandica, Y., Carvalho, J., Dos Aidos, F.S.: Wikipedia editing dynamics. Phys. Rev. E **91**(1), 012824 (2015)
8. Geiger, R.S., Halfaker, A.: Using edit sessions to measure participation in Wikipedia. In: CSCW, pp. 861–870 (2013)
9. Guo, H., Tang, R., Ye, Y., Li, Z., He, X.: Deepfm: a factorization-machine based neural network for CTR prediction. In: IJCAI (2017)
10. Kaffee, L.-A., et al.: Mind the (language) gap: generation of multilingual Wikipedia summaries from Wikidata for ArticlePlaceholders. In: Gangemi, A., et al. (eds.) ESWC 2018. LNCS, vol. 10843, pp. 319–334. Springer, Cham (2018). https://doi.org/10.1007/978-3-319-93417-4_21
11. Lehmann, J., et al.: Dbpedia-a large-scale, multilingual knowledge base extracted from Wikipedia. Semantic Web **6**(2), 167–195 (2015)
12. Lian, J., Zhou, X., Zhang, F., Chen, Z., Xie, X., Sun, G.: xDeepFM: combining explicit and implicit feature interactions for recommender systems. In: Proceedings of the 24th ACM SIGKDD International Conference on Knowledge Discovery & Data Mining, pp. 1754–1763 (2018)

13. Malyshev, S., Krötzsch, M., González, L., Gonsior, J., Bielefeldt, A.: Getting the most out of wikidata: semantic technology usage in Wikipedia's knowledge graph. In: Vrandečić, D., et al. (eds.) ISWC 2018. LNCS, vol. 11137, pp. 376–394. Springer, Cham (2018). https://doi.org/10.1007/978-3-030-00668-6_23
14. Mora-Cantallops, M., Sánchez-Alonso, S., García-Barriocanal, E.: A systematic literature review on wikidata. Data Technol. Appl. (2019)
15. Müller-Birn, C., Karran, B., Lehmann, J., Luczak-Rösch, M.: Peer-production system or collaborative ontology engineering effort: what is wikidata? In: Proceedings of the 11th International Symposium on Open Collaboration, pp. 1–10 (2015)
16. Panciera, K., Halfaker, A., Terveen, L.: Wikipedians are born, not made: a study of power editors on Wikipedia. In: CSCW, pp. 51–60 (2009)
17. Pedregosa, F., et al.: Scikit-learn: machine learning in python. JMLR **12**, 2825–2830 (2011)
18. Pei, J., et al.: Mining sequential patterns by pattern-growth: the prefixspan approach. IEEE Trans. Knowl. Data Eng. **16**(11), 1424–1440 (2004)
19. Pellissier Tanon, T., Kaffee, L.A.: Property label stability in wikidata: evolution and convergence of schemas in collaborative knowledge bases. In: Companion Proceedings of the Web Conference 2018, pp. 1801–1803 (2018)
20. Piscopo, A., Phethean, C., Simperl, E.: What makes a good collaborative knowledge graph: group composition and quality in wikidata. In: Ciampaglia, G.L., Mashhadi, A., Yasseri, T. (eds.) SocInfo 2017. LNCS, vol. 10539, pp. 305–322. Springer, Cham (2017). https://doi.org/10.1007/978-3-319-67217-5_19
21. Piscopo, A., Vougiouklis, P., Kaffee, L.A., Phethean, C., Hare, J., Simperl, E.: What do wikidata and wikipedia have in common? An analysis of their use of external references. In: Proceedings of the 13th International Symposium on Open Collaboration, pp. 1–10 (2017)
22. Rendle, S.: Factorization machines. In: 2010 IEEE International Conference on Data Mining, pp. 995–1000. IEEE (2010)
23. Ristoski, P., Paulheim, H.: RDF2Vec: RDF graph embeddings for data mining. In: Groth, P., et al. (eds.) ISWC 2016. LNCS, vol. 9981, pp. 498–514. Springer, Cham (2016). https://doi.org/10.1007/978-3-319-46523-4_30
24. Sarasua, C., Checco, A., Demartini, G., Difallah, D., Feldman, M., Pintscher, L.: The evolution of power and standard wikidata editors: comparing editing behavior over time to predict lifespan and volume of edits. CSCW **28**(5), 843–882 (2019)
25. Shannon, C.E.: A mathematical theory of communication. ACM SIGMOBILE MOB. Comput. Commun. Rev. **5**(1), 3–55 (2001)
26. Shen, W.: Deepctr: easy-to-use, modular and extendible package of deep-learning based CTR models (2017). https://github.com/shenweichen/deepctr
27. Srivastava, N., Hinton, G., Krizhevsky, A., Sutskever, I., Salakhutdinov, R.: Dropout: a simple way to prevent neural networks from overfitting. J. Mach. Learn. Res. **15**(1), 1929–1958 (2014)
28. Vrandečić, D., Krötzsch, M.: Wikidata: a free collaborative knowledgebase. Commun. ACM **57**(10), 78–85 (2014)
29. Waagmeester, A., et al.: Science forum: wikidata as a knowledge graph for the life sciences. Elife **9**, e52614 (2020)
30. Yang, Y., Xu, B., Shen, S., Shen, F., Zhao, J.: Operation-aware neural networks for user response prediction. Neural Netw. **121**, 161–168 (2020)
31. Zhang, D., Prior, K., Levene, M., Mao, R., van Liere, D.: Leave or stay: the departure dynamics of wikipedia editors. In: Zhou, S., Zhang, S., Karypis, G. (eds.) ADMA 2012. LNCS (LNAI), vol. 7713, pp. 1–14. Springer, Heidelberg (2012). https://doi.org/10.1007/978-3-642-35527-1_1

Towards Neural Schema Alignment for OpenStreetMap and Knowledge Graphs

Alishiba Dsouza[1]([✉])(iD), Nicolas Tempelmeier[2](iD), and Elena Demidova[1](iD)

[1] Data Science and Intelligent Systems (DSIS), University of Bonn, Bonn, Germany
{dsouza,elena.demidova}@cs.uni-bonn.de
[2] L3S Research Center, Leibniz Universität Hannover, Hannover, Germany
tempelmeier@L3S.de

Abstract. OpenStreetMap (OSM) is one of the richest, openly available sources of volunteered geographic information. Although OSM includes various geographical entities, their descriptions are highly heterogeneous, incomplete, and do not follow any well-defined ontology. Knowledge graphs can potentially provide valuable semantic information to enrich OSM entities. However, interlinking OSM entities with knowledge graphs is inherently difficult due to the large, heterogeneous, ambiguous, and flat OSM schema and the annotation sparsity. This paper tackles the alignment of OSM tags with the corresponding knowledge graph classes holistically by jointly considering the schema and instance layers. We propose a novel neural architecture that capitalizes upon a shared latent space for tag-to-class alignment created using linked entities in OSM and knowledge graphs. Our experiments aligning OSM datasets for several countries with two of the most prominent openly available knowledge graphs, namely, Wikidata and DBpedia, demonstrate that the proposed approach outperforms the state-of-the-art schema alignment baselines by up to 37% points F1-score. The resulting alignment facilitates new semantic annotations for over 10 million OSM entities worldwide, which is over a 400% increase compared to the existing annotations.

Keywords: OpenStreetMap · Knowledge graph · Neural schema alignment

1 Introduction

OpenStreetMap (OSM) has evolved as a critical source of openly available geographic information globally, including rich data from 188 countries. This information is contributed by a large community, currently counting over 1.5 million volunteers. OSM captures a vast and continuously growing number of geographic entities, currently counting more than 6.8 billion [15]. The descriptions of OSM entities consist of heterogeneous key-value pairs, so-called *tags*, and include over 80 thousand distinct keys. OSM keys and tags do not possess machine-readable semantics, such that OSM data is not directly accessible for semantic applications. Whereas knowledge graphs (KGs) can provide precise semantics for geographic entities, large publicly available general-purpose KGs like Wikidata [30],

© Springer Nature Switzerland AG 2021
A. Hotho et al. (Eds.): ISWC 2021, LNCS 12922, pp. 56–73, 2021.
https://doi.org/10.1007/978-3-030-88361-4_4

DBpedia [2], YAGO [26], and specialized KGs like EventKG [10], and Linked-GeoData [25] lack coverage of geographic entities. For instance, in June 2021, 931,574 entities with tag `amenity=restaurant` were present in OSM, whereas Wikidata included only 4,391 entities for the equivalent class "restaurant".

An alignment of OSM and knowledge graphs at the schema level can make a wide variety of geographic entities in OSM accessible through semantic technologies and applications. The automatic suggestions of alignment candidates can help to create accurate schema mappings in human-in-the-loop applications. Furthermore, alignment models can help OSM volunteers to map geographic entities in OSM and annotate these entities with KG classes.

The problem of schema alignment between OSM and KGs is particularly challenging due to several factors, most prominently including the heterogeneous representations of types and properties of geographic entities via OSM tags, unclear tag semantics, the large scale and flatness of the OSM schema, and the sparseness of the existing links. OSM does not limit the usage of keys and tags by any strict schema and provides only a set of guidelines[1]. As a result, the types and properties of OSM entities are represented via a variety of tags that do not possess precise semantics. Consider an excerpt from the representations of the entity "Zugspitze" (mountain in Germany) in Wikidata and OSM:

<table>
<tr><td colspan="3">Wikidata</td><td colspan="2">OpenStreetMap</td></tr>
<tr><td>**Subject**</td><td>**Predicate**</td><td>**Object**</td><td>**Key**</td><td>**Value**</td></tr>
<tr><td>*Q3375*</td><td>*label*</td><td>*Zugspitze*</td><td>*id*</td><td>*27384190*</td></tr>
<tr><td>*Q3375*</td><td>*coordinate*</td><td>$47°25'N, 10°59'E$</td><td>*name*</td><td>*Zugspitze*</td></tr>
<tr><td>*Q3375*</td><td>*parentpeak*</td><td>*Q15127*</td><td>*natural*</td><td>*peak*</td></tr>
<tr><td>*Q3375*</td><td>*instance of*</td><td>*mountain*</td><td>*summit:cross*</td><td>*yes*</td></tr>
</table>

In Wikidata, an entity type is typically represented using the `instance of` property. In this example, the statement "Q3375 `instance of` mountain" indicates the type "mountain" of the entity "Q3375". In OpenStreetMap, the type "mountain" of the same entity is indicated by the tag `natural=peak`. As OSM lacks a counterpart of the `instance of` property, it is unclear which particular tag represents an entity type and which tags refer to other properties. Furthermore, multiple OSM tags can refer to the same semantic concept. Finally, whereas the OSM schema with over 80 thousand distinct keys is extensive, the alignment between OSM and knowledge graphs at the schema level is almost nonexistent. For instance, as of April 2021, Wikidata contained 585 alignments between its properties and OSM keys, corresponding to only 0.7% of the distinct OSM keys. Overall, the flatness, heterogeneity, ambiguity, and the large scale of OSM schema, along with a lack of links, make the alignment particularly challenging.

Existing approaches for schema alignment operate at the schema and instance level and consider the similarity of schema elements, structural similarity, and instance similarity. As OSM schema is flat, ontology alignment methods that utilize hierarchical structures, such as [13,17], are not applicable. A transformation of OSM data into a tabular or relational format leads to highly sparse tables with

---

[1] OSM "How to map a": https://wiki.openstreetmap.org/wiki/How_to_map_a.

numerous columns. Therefore, approaches to syntactic or instance-based alignment for relational or tabular data, such as e.g., [6,32], or syntactic matching of schema element names [28] cannot yield good results for matching OSM tags with KG classes.

This paper takes the first important step to align OSM and knowledge graphs at the schema level using a novel neural method. In particular, we tackle tag-to-class alignment, i.e., we aim to identify OSM tags that convey class information and map them to the corresponding classes in the Wikidata knowledge graph and the DBpedia ontology. We present the Neural Class Alignment (NCA) model - a novel instance-based neural approach that aligns OSM tags with the corresponding semantic classes in a knowledge graph. NCA builds upon a novel shared latent space that aligns OSM tags and KG concepts and facilitates a seamless translation between them. To the best of our knowledge, NCA is the first approach to align OSM and KGs at the schema level with a neural method.

Our contributions are as follows:

- We present NCA – a novel approach for class alignment for OSM and KGs.
- We propose a novel shared latent space that fuses feature spaces from knowledge graphs and OSM in a joint model, enabling simultaneous training of the schema alignment model on heterogeneous semantic and geographic sources.
- We develop a novel, effective algorithm to extract tag-to-class alignments from the resulting model.
- The results of our evaluation demonstrate that the proposed NCA approach is highly effective and outperforms the baselines by up to 37% points F1-score.
- As a result of the proposed NCA alignment method, we provide semantic annotations with Wikidata and DBpedia classes for over 10 million OSM entities. This result corresponds to an over 400% increase compared to currently existing annotations.
- We make our code and datasets publicly available and provide a manually annotated ground truth for the tag-to-class alignment of OSM tags with Wikidata and DBpedia classes[2].

2   Problem Statement

In this section, we formalize the problem definition. First, we formally define the concepts of an OSM corpus and a knowledge graph. An OSM corpus contains nodes representing geographic entities. Each node is annotated with an identifier, a location, and a set of key-value pairs known as tags.

Definition 1. *An OSM corpus $C = (N, T)$ consists of a set of nodes N representing geographic entities, and a set of tags T. Each tag $t \in T$ is represented as a key-value pair, with the key $k \in K$ and a value $v \in V$: $t = \langle k, v \rangle$. A node $n \in N$, $n = \langle i, l, T_n \rangle$ is represented as a tuple containing an identifier i, a geographic location l, and a set of tags $T_n \subset T$.*

---

[2] GitHub repository: https://github.com/alishiba14/NCA-OSM-to-KGs.

A knowledge graph contains real-world entities, classes, properties, and relations.

Definition 2. *A knowledge graph $\mathcal{KG} = (E, C, P, L, F)$ consists of a set of entities E, a set of classes $C \subset E$, a set of properties P, a set of literals L, and a set of triples $F \subseteq E \times P \times (E \cup L)$.*

The entities in E represent real-world entities and semantic classes. The properties in P represent relations connecting two entities, or an entity and a literal value. An entity in a KG can belong to one or multiple classes. An entity is typically linked to its class using the `rdf:type`, or an equivalent property.

Definition 3. *A class of the entity $e \in E$ in the knowledge graph $\mathcal{KG} = (E, C, P, L, F)$ is denoted as: class(e) = $\{c \in C \mid (e, \textbf{rdf:type}, c) \in F\}$.*

An OSM node and a KG entity referring to the same real-world geographic entity and connected via an identity link are denoted linked entities.

Definition 4. *A linked entity $(n, e) \in E_L$ is a pair of an OSM node $n = \langle i, l, T_n \rangle$, $n \in N$, and a knowledge graph entity $e \in E$ that corresponds to the same real-world entity. In a knowledge graph, a linked entity is typically represented using a $(e, \textbf{owl:sameAs}, i)$ triple, where i is the node identifier. E_L denotes the set of all linked entities in a knowledge graph.*

This paper tackles the alignment of tags that describe node types in an OSM corpus to equivalent classes in a knowledge graph.

Definition 5. *Tag-to-class alignment: Given a knowledge graph $\mathcal{KG}$ and an OSM corpus $\mathcal{C}$, find a set of pairs tag_class $\subseteq (T \times C)$ of OSM tags T and the corresponding $\mathcal{KG}$ classes, such that for each pair $(t, c) \in$ tag_class OSM nodes with the tag t belong to the class c.*

3   Neural Class Alignment Approach

An alignment of an OSM corpus with a knowledge graph can include several dimensions, such as entity linking, node classification (i.e., aligning OSM nodes with the corresponding semantic classes in a knowledge graph), as well as alignment of schema elements such as keys/tags and the corresponding semantic classes. The alignments in these dimensions can reinforce each other. For example, linking OSM nodes with knowledge graph entities and classifying OSM nodes into knowledge graph classes can lead to new schema-level alignments and vice versa. Our proposed NCA approach systematically exploits the existing identity links between OSM nodes and knowledge graph entities based on this intuition. NCA builds an auxiliary classification model and utilizes this model to align OSM tags with the corresponding classes in a knowledge graph ontology.

NCA is an unsupervised two-step approach for tag-to-class alignment. Figure 1 presents an overview of the proposed NCA architecture. First, we build

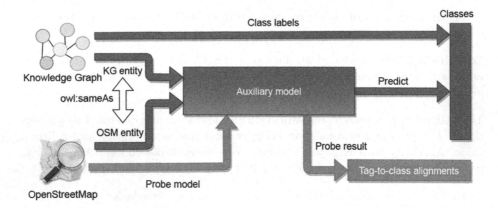

Fig. 1. Overview of the NCA architecture. The gray color indicates the first step (training of the auxiliary classification model). The orange color indicates the second step, i.e., the extraction of tag-to-class alignments. (Color figure online)

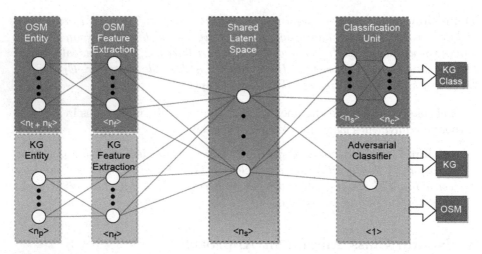

Fig. 2. The auxiliary classification model architecture. The blue color indicates the KG classification component, yellow marks the adversarial entity discrimination component. Parameters inside angular brackets denote the number of neurons in each layer, and lines denote the fully connected layers. (Color figure online)

an auxiliary neural classification model and train this model using linked entities in OSM and a KG. As a result, the model learns a novel shared latent space that aligns the feature spaces of OSM and a knowledge graph and implicitly captures tag-to-class alignments. Second, we systematically probe the resulting model to identify the captured alignments.

3.1   Auxiliary Neural Classification Model

In this step, we build a supervised auxiliary neural classification model for a dummy task of OSM node and KG entity classification. The model resulting from this step is later used for the tag-to-class alignment. Figure 2 presents the model architecture. The parameters n_t, n_k, n_p, n_c denote the number of OSM tags, number of OSM keys, number of KG properties, and number of KG classes, respectively. We experimentally select the number of neurons in the feature extraction layer (n_f) and the shared latent space layer (n_s). The auxiliary classification model architecture consists of several components described below.

OSM Node Representation. We represent an OSM node as a binary vector in an **O**-dimensional vector space. The space dimensions correspond to OSM tags or keys, and binary values represent whether the node includes the corresponding tag or key. The vector space dimensions serve as features for the classification model, such that we also refer to this space as the OSM feature space. To select the most descriptive tags to be included as dimensions in the OSM feature space, we filter out low-quality tags using OSM taginfo[3]. We include only the tags with an available description in the OSM wiki[4] having at least 50 occurrences within OSM. For tags with infrequent values (e.g., literals), we include only the keys as dimensions. We aim to align geographic concepts and not specific entities; thus, we do not include infrequent and node-specific values such as entity names or geographic coordinates in the representation. For instance, the concept of "mountain" is the same across different geographic regions, such that the geographic location of entities is not informative for the schema alignment.

KG Entity Representation. We represent a KG entity as a binary vector in a **V**-dimensional vector space. The space dimensions correspond to the KG properties. Binary values represent whether the entity includes the corresponding property. The vector space dimensions serve as features for the classification model, such that we also refer to this space as the KG feature space. To select the most descriptive properties to be included in the KG feature space, we rank the properties based on their selectivity concerning the class and the frequency of property usage (i.e., the number of statements in the KG that assign this property to an entity). Given a property p, we calculate its weight as: $weight(p, c) = n_{p,c} * log\frac{N}{c_p}$. Here, $n_{p,c}$ denotes the number of statements in which the property p is assigned to an entity of class c, N denotes the total number of classes in a knowledge graph, and c_p is the number of distinct classes that include the property p. For each class c, we select top-25 properties as features. These properties are included as dimensions in the KG feature space.

OSM & KG Feature Extraction. The KG and OSM feature representations serve as input to the specific fully connected feature extraction layers: OSM feature extraction and KG feature extraction. The purpose of these layers is to refine the vector representations obtained in the previous step.

---

[3] OSM taginfo: https://taginfo.openstreetmap.org/tags.
[4] OSM wiki: https://wiki.openstreetmap.org/wiki/.

Shared Latent Space & Adversarial Classifier. We introduce a novel *shared latent space* that fuses the initially disjoint feature spaces of OSM and KG such that entities from both data sources are represented in a joint space similarly. In addition to the training on OSM examples, shared latent space enables us to train our model on the KG examples. These examples provide the properties known to indicate class information [21]. The shared latent space component consists of a fully connected layer that receives the input from the OSM and KG feature extraction layers. Following recent domain adaption techniques [9], we use an adversarial classification layer to align latent representations of KG and OSM entities. The objective of the adversarial classifier is to discriminate whether the current training example is an OSM node or a KG entity, where the classification loss is measured as binary cross-entropy.

$$BinaryCrossEntropy = -\frac{1}{n}\sum_{i=1}^{n}[y_i \times \log(\hat{y}_i) + (1 - y_i) \times \log(1 - \hat{y}_i)],$$

where n is the total number of examples, y_i is the true class label, and $\hat{y}_i$ is the predicted class label. Intuitively, in a shared latent space, the classifier should not be able to distinguish whether a training example originates from OSM or a KG. To fuse the initially disjoint feature spaces, we reverse the gradients from the adversarial classification loss: $\mathcal{L}_{adverse} = -BinaryCrossEntropy_{adverse}$.

Classification Unit. To train the auxiliary classification model for the OSM nodes, we exploit linked entities. We label OSM nodes with semantic classes of equivalent KG entities. We use these class labels as supervision in the OSM node classification task. More formally, given a linked entity, $(n, e) \in E_L$, the training objective of the model is to predict *class(e)* from n. Analogously, the training objective for a KG entity e is to predict the class label *class(e)* of this entity.

We utilize a 2-layer feed-forward network as a classification model. In the last prediction layer of this network, each neuron corresponds to a class. As an entity can be assigned to multiple classes, we use a sigmoid activation function and a binary cross-entropy loss to achieve multi-label classification: $\mathcal{L}_{classifcation} = BinaryCrossEntropy_{classification}$. Finally, the joint loss function $\mathcal{L}$ of the network is given by $\mathcal{L} = \mathcal{L}_{classifcation} + \mathcal{L}_{adverse}$. In the training process, we alternate OSM and KG instances to avoid bias towards one data source.

3.2   Tag-to-Class Alignment

In this step, we systematically probe the trained auxiliary classification model to extract the tag-to-class alignment. The goal of this step is to obtain the corresponding KG class for a given OSM tag. Algorithm 1 details the extraction process. First, we load the pre-trained auxiliary model m (line 1) and initialize the result set (line 2). We then probe the model with a given list of OSM tags $\mathcal{T}$ (line 3). For a single tag $t \in \mathcal{T}$, we feed t to the OSM input layer of the auxiliary

Algorithm 1. Extract Tag-to-Class Alignment

Input:	m	Trained auxiliary model
	T	List of OSM tags
	th_a	Alignment threshold
Output:	$align \subseteq (T \times C)$	Extracted alignment of tags and classes

```
 1: load(m)
 2: align ⇐ ∅
 3: for all t ∈ T do
 4:    forward_propagation(t, m)
 5:    activations ⇐ extract_activations(m)
 6:    for all a ∈ activations do
 7:       if a > th_a then
 8:          align ⇐ align ∪ {(t, class(a))}
 9:       end if
10:    end for
11: end for
12: return align
```

model and compute the complete forward propagation of t within m (line 4). We then extract the activation of the neurons of the last layer of the classification model before the sigmoid nonlinearity (line 5). As the individual neurons in this layer directly correspond to KG classes, we expect that the activation of the specific neurons quantifies the likeliness that the tag t corresponds to the respective class. For each activation of a specific neuron a that is above the alignment threshold th_a (line 6–7), we extract the corresponding class c and add this class to the set of alignments (line 8). We determine the threshold value experimentally, as described later in Sect. 5.3. As an OSM tag can have multiple corresponding classes, we opt for all matches above the threshold value. Finally, the resulting set *align* constitutes the inferred tag-to-class alignments.

3.3 Illustrative Example

We illustrate the proposed NCA approach at the example of the "Zugspitze" mountain introduced in Sect. 1. We create the representation of the Wikidata object "Q3375" in the KG feature space by creating a binary vector that has ones in the dimensions that correspond to the properties that this entity contains, such as, **label**, **coordinate**, **parentpeak**, and zeros otherwise. Note that the **instance of** predicate is not included in the feature space, as this predicate represents the class label. Similarly, we encode the OSM node with the id "27384190" in the OSM feature space by creating a vector that includes **name**, **natural=peak**, **summit:cross** as ones, and zeros in all other dimensions. As described above, we use frequent key-value pairs such as **natural=peak** as features, whereas for the infrequent key-value pairs, such as **name=Zugspitze**, we use only the key (i.e., **name**) as a feature. The KG and OSM features spaces

are then aligned in the shared latent space. To form this space, we train the auxiliary classification model that learns to output the correct class labels, such as
"mountain". In the last prediction layer of this model, each neuron corresponds
to a class. After the training is completed, we probe the classification model
with a single tag, such as `natural=peak`. The activation of the neurons in the
prediction layer corresponds to the predicted tag-to-class mapping. We output
all classes with the activation values above the threshold th_a (here: "mountain").

4   Evaluation Setup

This section introduces the evaluation setup regarding datasets, ground truth
generation, baselines, and evaluation metrics. All experiments were conducted
on an AMD Opteron 8439 SE processor @ 2.7 GHz and 252 GB of memory,
whereas the execution of NCA required up to 16 GB of memory only.

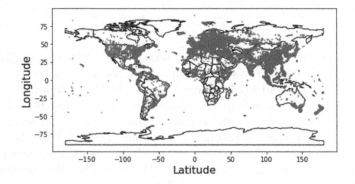

Fig. 3. OSM and Wikidata linked entities located on a world map.

4.1   Datasets

We carry out our experiments on OSM, Wikidata [30], and DBpedia [2] datasets.

Knowledge Graphs: A sufficient number of linked entities and distinct classes
is essential to train the proposed neural model and achieve a meaningful schema
alignment. As illustrated in Fig. 3, OSM to Wikidata links are highly frequent in
the European region. We systematically rank European countries according to
the number of linked entities between OSM and knowledge graphs. We choose
the top-4 countries having at least ten distinct classes in the linked entity set.
Based on these criteria, we select the Wikidata datasets for France, Germany,
Great Britain, and Russia as well as the DBpedia datasets for France, Germany,
Great Britain, and Spain. Although over 100,000 entity links between Russian
DBpedia and OSM exist, most entities belong to only two classes. Hence, we
omit Russian DBpedia from our analysis. Additionally, to understand the effect
of NCA in other parts of the world, we select the USA and Australia with a

moderate amount of KG links. In our experiments, we consider Wikidata and DBpedia snapshots from March 2021. We collect the data from knowledge graphs by querying their SPARQL endpoints. We only consider geographic entities, i.e., the entities with valid geographic coordinates.

OpenStreetMap: We extract OSM data for France, Germany, Great Britain, Spain, Russia, the USA, and Australia. To facilitate evaluation, we only consider OSM nodes which include links to knowledge graphs. The number of entities assigned to specific knowledge graph classes follows a power-law distribution. We select the classes with more than 100 entities (i.e., 3% of classes in Wikidata) to facilitate model training. Note that some KG entities are linked to more than one OSM node, such that the number of nodes and entities in the dataset differ.

4.2 Ground Truth Creation

For Wikidata, we start the creation of our ground truth based on the "Open-StreetMap tag or key" Wikidata property[5]. This property provides a link between a Wikidata class and the corresponding OSM tag. However, this dataset is incomplete and lacks some language-specific classes as well as superclass and subclass relationships based on our manual analysis. We manually extended the ground truth by checking all possible matches obtained by the proposed NCA approach and all baseline models used in the evaluation. We added all correct matches to our ground truth. For DBpedia, we constructed the ground truth manually by labeling all combinations $(T \times C)$ of OSM tags t and $\mathcal{KG}$ classes C in our dataset. For both KGs, we consider region-specific matches ("Ortsteil" vs. "District") and subclass/superclass relations (e.g., "locality" vs. "city/village").

4.3 Baselines

The schema alignment task of OSM and KG has not been addressed before, such that no task-specific baseline exists. For evaluation, we choose the state-of-the-art baselines from schema alignment for tabular data (Cupid [13], EmbDI [5], Similarity Flooding [14]), which is the closest representation to the OSM flat schema structure. Furthermore, we evaluate string similarity using Levenshtein distance, word embeddings-based cosine similarity, and SD-Type [21] - an established approach for type inference. To fit our data to the baselines, we convert our OSM (source) data and KG (target) data into a tabular format. For OSM, we use the tags and keys as columns and convert each node into a row. Similarly, for KGs, the properties and classes are converted into columns, and the entities form the rows. We evaluate our proposed method against the following baselines:

Cupid: Cupid [13] matches schema elements based on element names, structure, and data types. Cupid is a 2-phase approach. The first phase calculates the lexicographic similarity of names and data types. The second phase matches

---

[5] Wikidata "OpenStreetMap tag or key" property: https://www.wikidata.org/wiki/Property:P1282.

elements using the structural similarity based on the element proximity in the ontology hierarchy. As the OSM schema is flat, we consider a flat hierarchy, where the OSM table is the root and all columns are child nodes. The final Cupid score is the average similarity between the two phases.

Levenshtein Distance (LD): The Levenshtein distance (edit distance) is a string-based similarity measure used to match ontology elements lexicographically. The Levenshtein distance between two element names is calculated as the minimal number of edits needed to transform one element name to obtain the other. The modifications include addition, deletion, or replacement of characters [28]. We calculate the Levenshtein distance between all pairs of class names and tags and accept pairs with a distance lower than the threshold $th_l \in [0, 1]$.

EmbDi: EmbDi [5] is an algorithm for schema alignment and entity resolution. The algorithm maps table rows to a directed graph based on rows, columns, and cell values. EmbDi infers column embeddings by performing random walks on the graph. The random walks form sentences that constitute an input to a Word2Vec model. Finally, the similarity of the two columns is measured as the cosine similarity of the respective embeddings.

Similarity Flooding (SF): Similarity Flooding [14] transforms a data table into a directed labeled graph in which the nodes represent table columns. The weights of graph edges represent the node similarity, initialized using string similarity of the column names. The algorithm refines the weights by iteratively propagating similarity values along the edges. Each pair of nodes connected with a similarity value above the matching threshold forms an alignment.

SD-Type (SD): SD-Type [21] is an established approach for type inference. While SD-type was originally proposed to infer instance types based on conditional probabilities, we transfer the idea to infer class types. We calculate the conditional probability of a tag t given a class c as follows: $p(c|t) = \frac{\sum(t \cap c)}{\sum t}$. We accept all the matches with the probability values above threshold $th_l \in [0, 1]$.

Word Embedding Based Cosine Similarity (WECS): We use pre-trained word embeddings[6] trained using fastText [4] with 300 dimensions to obtain the word vectors of tag and class names. We calculate the cosine similarity between the word vectors of each tag-class pair. We accept all pairs with cosine similarity above the threshold $th_l \in [0, 1]$ as a match.

For LD, SD and WECS, we apply an exhaustive grid search to optimize the value of th_l for each dataset and report the highest resulting F1-scores. For the Cupid, EmbDi, and SF baseline implementation, we use the source code from the delftdata GitHub repository[7].

4.4 Metrics

The standard evaluation metrics for schema alignment are precision, recall, and F1-score computed against a reference alignment (i.e., ground truth). We eval-

---

[6] https://dl.fbaipublicfiles.com/fasttext/vectors-crawl/cc.en.300.bin.gz.
[7] Delftdata GitHub repository: https://github.com/delftdata/valentine.

uate the mappings as pairs, where each pair consists of one tag and one class (tag-to-class alignment). **Precision** is the fraction of correctly identified pairs among all identified pairs. **Recall** is the fraction of correctly identified pairs among all pairs in the reference alignment. **F1-score** is the harmonic mean of recall and precision. We consider the F1-score to be the most relevant metric since it reflects both precision and recall.

5   Evaluation

The evaluation aims to assess the performance of the proposed NCA approach for tag-to-class alignment in terms of precision, recall, and F1-score. Furthermore, we aim to analyze the influence of the confidence threshold and the impact of the shared latent space on the alignment performance. Note that we do not evaluate the artificial auxiliary classification task. Instead, we evaluate the utility of the auxiliary model in the overall schema alignment task. We train and evaluate the models for each country and knowledge graph separately.

5.1   Tag-to-Class Alignment Performance

Table 1 and 2 summarize the performance results of the baselines and our proposed NCA approach with respect to precision, recall and F1-score for tag-to-class alignment of OSM tags to Wikidata and DBpedia classes, respectively. As we can observe, the proposed NCA approach outperforms the baselines in terms of F1-score on all datasets. On Wikidata, we achieve up to 13% points F1-score improvement and ten percentage points on average compared to the best baseline. On DBpedia, we achieve up to 37% points F1-score improvement and 21% points on average. As OSM lacks a hierarchical structure, limiting structural comparison, most of the applicable baselines build on the name comparison. Here, the heterogeneity of OSM tags limits the precision of the baselines substantially. SD-Type obtains the highest F1-score amongst baselines. NCA uses the property, tags, and keys information from the shared latent space and achieves higher performance than the best performing SD-Type baseline. For other baselines, the absolute values achieved are relatively low. SF, WECS, and EmbDI obtain only low similarity values, resulting in low precision. An increase of the confidence threshold for these baselines leads to zero matches. The tag-class pairs vary significantly in terms of linguistic and semantic similarities. The correct pairs obtained using WECS do not obtain sufficiently high scores to discriminate from the wrong matches, making WECS one of the weakest baselines.

We observe performance variations across countries and knowledge graphs, with Australian Wikidata and French DBpedia achieving the highest F1-scores compared to other countries. These variations can be explained by the differences in the dataset characteristics, including the number of links, entities per class, and unique tags and classes per country. These characteristics vary significantly across the datasets. Furthermore, the number of classes per entity varies. On average, Wikidata indicates one class per entity (i.e., the most specific class).

Table 1. Tag-to-class alignment performance for OSM tags to Wikidata classes.

Name	France			Germany			Great Britain			Russia			USA			Australia			Average		
	P	R	F1	P	R	F1	P	R	F1	P	R	F1	P	R	F1	P	R	F1	P	R	F1
CUPID	0.06	1.00	0.12	0.03	0.70	0.06	0.07	1.00	0.14	0.08	0.80	0.15	0.06	1.00	0.11	0.25	1.00	0.38	0.09	0.91	0.16
LD	0.45	0.28	0.35	0.65	0.34	0.44	0.54	0.37	0.44	0.64	0.34	0.45	0.39	0.37	0.38	0.31	0.41	0.36	0.49	0.35	0.40
EMBDI	0.03	1.00	0.06	0.02	1.00	0.03	0.04	1.00	0.06	0.02	1.00	0.03	0.01	1.00	0.03	0.08	0.91	0.15	0.05	0.98	0.06
SF	0.03	1.00	0.06	0.02	1.00	0.03	0.01	1.00	0.03	0.02	1.00	0.03	0.01	1.00	0.03	0.08	1.00	0.16	0.04	1.00	0.06
WECS	0.35	0.09	0.14	0.23	0.16	0.19	0.10	0.28	0.14	0.25	0.29	0.26	0.23	0.06	0.09	0.13	0.53	0.21	0.22	0.23	0.16
SD	0.73	0.55	0.63	0.72	0.36	0.48	0.88	0.33	0.49	0.45	0.45	0.48	0.84	0.40	0.54	0.95	0.55	0.70	0.76	0.44	0.55
NCA	0.63	0.66	**0.65**	0.59	0.65	**0.61**	0.71	0.56	**0.63**	0.64	0.51	**0.58**	0.79	0.61	**0.69**	0.85	0.78	**0.82**	0.70	0.63	**0.66**

Table 2. Tag-to-class alignment performance for OSM tags to DBpedia classes.

Name	France			Germany			Great Britain			Spain			USA			Australia			Average		
	P	R	F1	P	R	F1	P	R	F1	P	R	F1	P	R	F1	P	R	F1	P	R	F1
CUPID	0.32	1.00	0.48	0.18	1.00	0.31	0.41	1.00	0.58	0.44	1.00	0.63	0.10	1.00	0.17	0.48	1.00	0.65	0.32	1.00	0.47
LD	0.31	0.57	0.41	0.32	0.37	0.34	0.73	0.46	0.57	0.34	0.94	0.50	0.42	0.97	0.59	0.58	0.62	0.60	0.45	0.65	0.50
EMBDI	0.16	1.00	0.28	0.09	1.00	0.17	0.29	1.00	0.45	0.24	1.00	0.38	0.33	1.00	0.51	0.32	1.00	0.50	0.24	1.00	0.38
SF	0.14	1.00	0.27	0.10	1.00	0.18	0.27	1.00	0.42	0.24	1.00	0.39	0.33	1.00	0.50	0.30	1.00	0.46	0.23	1.00	0.37
WECS	0.30	65	0.41	0.16	0.97	0.28	0.22	0.96	0.36	0.38	0.67	0.49	0.41	0.95	0.57	0.45	0.66	0.53	0.32	0.81	0.44
SD	0.92	0.57	0.70	0.34	0.98	0.50	0.57	0.88	0.69	0.83	0.58	0.69	0.70	0.47	0.58	0.95	0.55	0.70	0.71	0.67	0.64
NCA	0.95	0.90	**0.92**	0.96	0.79	**0.87**	0.81	0.84	**0.83**	1.00	0.84	**0.91**	0.70	0.70	**0.70**	0.95	0.76	**0.85**	0.90	0.81	**0.85**

Table 3. Example tag-to-class alignments obtained using the NCA approach.

Wikidata: France	Germany	Great Britain	Russia	USA	Australia
amenity=bicycle_rental: bicycle-sharing station	amenity=cinema: movie theater	railway=station: railway station	station=subway: metro station	landuse=reservoir: reservoir	amenity=library: public library
DBpedia: France	Germany	Great Britain	Spain	USA	Australia
railway=station: Place	place=municipality: Place	place=hamlet: Place	railway=station: ArchitecturalStructure	man_made=lighthouse: Location	public_transport=station: Infrastructure

In contrast, DBpedia indicates three classes per entity (i.e., the specialized and more generic classes at the higher levels of the DBpedia ontology). This property makes the model trained on the DBpedia knowledge graph more confident regarding the generic classes, such that generic classes obtain higher F1-scores than the specialized classes. Our observations indicate that it is desirable to obtain more training examples that align entities with more specific classes, such as in the Wikidata dataset. Table 3 illustrates the most confident tag-to-class alignments in terms of the obtained model activations using the NCA approach. As discussed above, Wikidata alignments with high confidence scores are more specific than those obtained on DBpedia.

5.2   Influence of the Shared Latent Space

Table 4 summarizes the performance of the proposed NCA approach and NCA without the shared latent space for tag-to-class alignment of OSM with Wikidata and DBpedia, respectively. We observe that the shared latent space helps to achieve an increase in F1-score of 34% points and 11% points for Wikidata and DBpedia, respectively. Compared to the Wikidata datasets, we observe smaller improvements on DBpedia datasets. DBpedia has an imbalance between the tags

Table 4. Tag-to-class alignment performance for Wikidata and DBpedia.

Approach	Avg. Wikidata			Avg. DBpedia		
	Precision	Recall	F1	Precision	Recall	F1
NCA w/o shared latent space	0.48	0.25	0.32	0.65	0.88	0.74
NCA	0.70	0.63	**0.66**	0.90	0.81	**0.85**

and classes, resulting in many-to-one alignments between tags and classes, where one class corresponds to several tags. For example, in all DBpedia datasets, the *place* and *populatedPlace* are frequently occurring classes for various tags such as `tourism=museum`, `place=village`, `place=town`. In such a case, DBpedia properties add less specific information to the matching process. Furthermore, we observe a high F1-score of the proposed NCA approach without the shared latent space on the DBpedia dataset. Intuitively, further improving these high scores is more difficult than improving the comparably low scores on Wikidata (e.g., 0.32 F1-score on Wikidata). In summary, the shared latent space improves the performance, with the highest improvements on Wikidata.

5.3 Confidence Threshold Tuning

We evaluate the influence of the confidence threshold value th_a on the precision, recall, and F1-score. The threshold th_a indicates the minimum similarity at which we align a tag to a class. Figure 4 and 5 present the alignment performance with respect to th_a for Wikidata and DBpedia. As expected, we observe a general trade-off between precision and recall, whereas higher values of th_a result in higher precision and lower recall. We select the confidence threshold of $th_a = 0.25$ and $th_a = 0.4$ for Wikidata and DBpedia, respectively, as these values allow balancing precision and recall. The threshold can be tuned for specific regions.

5.4 Alignment Impact

To assess the impact of NCA, we compare the number of OSM entities that can be annotated with semantic classes using the alignment discovery by NCA

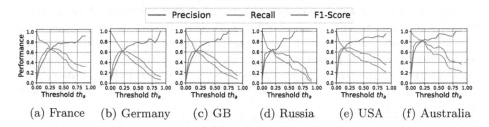

(a) France   (b) Germany   (c) GB   (d) Russia   (e) USA   (f) Australia

Fig. 4. Precision, recall, and F1-score vs. the confidence threshold for Wikidata. (Color figure online)

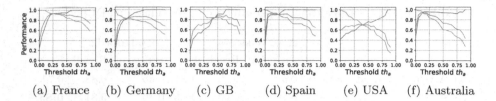

Fig. 5. Precision, recall, and F1-score vs. the confidence threshold for DBpedia. (Color figure online)

with the number of entities that are linked to a KG in the currently existing datasets. For Wikidata, we observe 2,004,510 linked OSM entities and 10,163,762 entities annotated with semantic classes using NCA. This result corresponds to an increase of 407.04% of entities with semantic class annotations. For DBpedia, we observe 1,396,378 linked OSM entities and 8,301,450 entities annotated with semantic classes using NCA. This result corresponds to an increase of 494.5% of entities with semantic class annotations. We provide the resulting annotations as a part of the WorldKG knowledge graph[8].

6   Related Work

This work is related to ontology alignment, alignment of tabular data, feature space alignment, and link discovery.

Ontology Alignment. Ontology alignment (also ontology matching) aims to establish correspondences between the elements of different ontologies. The efforts to interlink open semantic datasets and benchmark ontology alignment approaches have been driven by the W3C SWEO Linking Open Data community project[9] and the Ontology Alignment Evaluation Initiative (OAEI)[10] [1]. Ontology alignment is conducted at the element-level and structure-level [20]. The element-level alignment typically uses natural language descriptions of the ontology elements, such as labels and definitions. Element-level alignment adopts string similarity metrics such as, e.g., edit distance. Structure-level alignment exploits the similarity of the neighboring ontology elements, including the taxonomy structure, as well as shared instances [17]. Element-level and structure-level alignment have also been adopted to align ontologies with relational data [6] and tabular data [32]. Jiménez-Ruiz et al. [11] divided the alignment task into independent, smaller sub-tasks, aiming to scale up to very large ontologies. In machine learning approaches, such as the GLUE architecture [7], semantic mappings are learned in a semi-automatic way. In [19], a matching system integrates string-based and semantic similarity features. Recently, more complex

---

[8] WorldKG knowledge graph: http://www.worldkg.org.
[9] https://www.w3.org/wiki/SweoIG/TaskForces/CommunityProjects/
LinkingOpenData.
[10] OAEI evaluation campaigns: http://oaei.ontologymatching.org.

approaches using deep neural networks have been proposed for ontology alignment and schema matching [3,22,31]. The lack of a well-defined ontology in OSM hinders the application of ontology alignment approaches. In contrast, the instance-based NCA approach enables an effective alignment of tags to classes.

Tabular Data Alignment. Another branch of research investigated the schema alignment of tabular data [23]. EmbDi [5] approach uses random walks and embeddings to find similarities between schema elements. Cupid [13] matches schema elements based on element names, structure, and data types. Similarity Flooding [14] transforms a table into a directed labeled graph in which nodes represent columns to compute similarity values iteratively. We employ the EmbDi, Cupid, and Similarity Flooding algorithms as baselines for our evaluation. Although the conversion of OSM key-value-based data into a tabular form is possible in principle, the resulting tables are highly sparse. Therefore, as seen in Sect. 4.3, tabular data alignment approaches do not perform well on the alignment task addressed in this work.

Feature Space Alignment. Recently, various studies investigated the alignment of feature spaces extracted from different data sources. Application domains include computer vision [8] and machine translation [12]. Ganin et al. [9] proposed a neural domain adaptation algorithm that considers labeled data from a source domain and unlabeled data from a target domain. While this approach was originally used to align similar but different distributions of feature spaces, we adopt the gradient reversal layer proposed in [9] to fuse information from the disjoint features spaces of OSM and KGs, not attempted previously.

Link Discovery. Link Discovery is the task of identifying semantically equivalent resources in different data sources [16]. Nentwig et al. [16] provide a recent survey of link discovery frameworks with prominent examples, including Silk [29] and LIMES [18]. In particular, the Wombat algorithm, integrated within the LIMES framework [24], is a state-of-the-art approach for link discovery in knowledge graphs. Specialized approaches [27] focus on link discovery between OSM and knowledge graphs. We build on existing links between OSM and knowledge graphs to align knowledge graph classes to OSM tags in this work.

7 Conclusion

In this paper, we presented NCA – the first neural approach for tag-to-class alignment between OpenStreetMap and knowledge graphs. We proposed a novel shared latent space that seamlessly fuses features from knowledge graphs and OSM in a joint model and makes them simultaneously accessible for the schema alignment. Our model builds this space as the core part of neural architecture, incorporating an auxiliary classification model and an adversarial component. Furthermore, we proposed an effective algorithm that extracts tag-to-class alignments from the resulting shared latent space with high precision. Our evaluation results demonstrate that NCA is highly effective and outperforms the baselines by up to 37% points F1-score. We make our code and manually annotated ground truth data publicly available to facilitate further research. We believe that NCA is applicable to other geographic datasets having similar data structure as OSM; we leave such applications to future work.

Acknowledgements. This work was partially funded by DFG, German Research Foundation ("WorldKG", DE 2299/2-1), BMBF, Germany ("Simple-ML", 01IS18054) and BMWi, Germany ("d-E-mand", 01ME19009B).

References

1. Algergawy, A., et al.: Results of the ontology alignment evaluation initiative 2019. In: OM-2019. CEUR Workshop Proceedings, vol. 2536, pp. 46–85 (2019)
2. Auer, S., Bizer, C., Kobilarov, G., Lehmann, J., Cyganiak, R., Ives, Z.: DBpedia: a nucleus for a web of open data. In: Aberer, K., et al. (eds.) ASWC/ISWC -2007. LNCS, vol. 4825, pp. 722–735. Springer, Heidelberg (2007). https://doi.org/10.1007/978-3-540-76298-0_52
3. Bento, A., Zouaq, A., Gagnon, M.: Ontology matching using convolutional neural networks. In: LREC 2020, pp. 5648–5653. ELRA (2020)
4. Bojanowski, P., Grave, E., Joulin, A., Mikolov, T.: Enriching word vectors with subword information. Trans. Assoc. Comput. Linguist. **5**, 135–146 (2017)
5. Cappuzzo, R., Papotti, P., Thirumuruganathan, S.: Creating embeddings of heterogeneous relational datasets for data integration tasks. In: SIGMOD 2020, pp. 1335–1349. ACM (2020)
6. Demidova, E., Oelze, I., Nejdl, W.: Aligning freebase with the YAGO ontology. In: CIKM 2013, pp. 579–588. ACM (2013)
7. Doan, A., Madhavan, J., Domingos, P.M., Halevy, A.Y.: Ontology matching: a machine learning approach. In: Staab, S., Studer, R. (eds.) Handbook on Ontologies. International Handbooks on Information Systems, pp. 385–404. Springer, Heidelberg (2004). https://doi.org/10.1007/978-3-540-24750-0_19
8. Fernando, B., Habrard, A., Sebban, M., Tuytelaars, T.: Unsupervised visual domain adaptation using subspace alignment. In: ICCV 2013. IEEE (2013)
9. Ganin, Y., et al.: Domain-adversarial training of neural networks. J. Mach. Learn. Res. **17**, 59:1–59:35 (2016)
10. Gottschalk, S., Demidova, E.: EventKG - the hub of event knowledge on the web - and biographical timeline generation. Semantic Web **10**(6), 1039–1070 (2019)
11. Jiménez-Ruiz, E., Agibetov, A., Chen, J., Samwald, M., Cross, V.: Dividing the ontology alignment task with semantic embeddings and logic-based modules. In: ECAI 2020. FAIA, vol. 325, pp. 784–791. IOS Press (2020)
12. Lample, G., Conneau, A., Ranzato, M., Denoyer, L., Jégou, H.: Word translation without parallel data. In: ICLR 2018. OpenReview.net (2018)
13. Madhavan, J., Bernstein, P.A., Rahm, E.: Generic schema matching with cupid. In: VLDB 2001, pp. 49–58. Morgan Kaufmann (2001)
14. Melnik, S., Garcia-Molina, H., Rahm, E.: Similarity flooding: a versatile graph matching algorithm and its application to schema matching. In: ICDE 2002 (2002)
15. Neis, P.: OSMstats. https://osmstats.neis-one.org/. Accessed 10 Apr 2021
16. Nentwig, M., Hartung, M., Ngomo, A.N., Rahm, E.: A survey of current link discovery frameworks. Semantic Web **8**(3), 419–436 (2017)

17. Ngo, D.H., Bellahsene, Z., Todorov, K.: Opening the black box of ontology matching. In: Cimiano, P., Corcho, O., Presutti, V., Hollink, L., Rudolph, S. (eds.) ESWC 2013. LNCS, vol. 7882, pp. 16–30. Springer, Heidelberg (2013). https://doi.org/10.1007/978-3-642-38288-8_2

18. Ngomo, A.N., Auer, S.: LIMES - a time-efficient approach for large-scale link discovery on the web of data. In: IJCAI 2011, pp. 2312–2317. IJCAI/AAAI (2011)

19. Nkisi-Orji, I., Wiratunga, N., Massie, S., Hui, K., Heaven, R.: Ontology alignment based on word embedding and random forest classification. In: ECML PKDD (2018)

20. Otero-Cerdeira, L., Rodríguez-Martínez, F.J., Gómez-Rodríguez, A.: Ontology matching: a literature review. Expert Syst. Appl. **42**(2), 949–971 (2015)

21. Paulheim, H., Bizer, C.: Type inference on noisy RDF data. In: ISWC 2013 (2013)

22. Qiu, L., Yu, J., Pu, Q., Xiang, C.: Knowledge entity learning and representation for ontology matching based on deep neural networks. Clust. Comput. **20**, 969–977 (2017)

23. Rahm, E., Bernstein, P.A.: A survey of approaches to automatic schema matching. VLDB J. **10**(4), 334–350 (2001)

24. Sherif, M.A., Ngonga Ngomo, A.-C., Lehmann, J.: WOMBAT – a generalization approach for automatic link discovery. In: Blomqvist, E., Maynard, D., Gangemi, A., Hoekstra, R., Hitzler, P., Hartig, O. (eds.) ESWC 2017. LNCS, vol. 10249, pp. 103–119. Springer, Cham (2017). https://doi.org/10.1007/978-3-319-58068-5_7

25. Stadler, C., Lehmann, J., Höffner, K., Auer, S.: LinkedGeoData: a core for a web of spatial open data. Semantic Web **3**(4), 333–354 (2012)

26. Pellissier Tanon, T., Weikum, G., Suchanek, F.: YAGO 4: a reason-able knowledge base. In: Harth, A., et al. (eds.) ESWC 2020. LNCS, vol. 12123, pp. 583–596. Springer, Cham (2020). https://doi.org/10.1007/978-3-030-49461-2_34

27. Tempelmeier, N., Demidova, E.: Linking OpenStreetMap with knowledge graphs - link discovery for schema-agnostic volunteered geographic information. Future Gener. Comput. Syst. **116**, 349–364 (2021)

28. Unal, O., Afsarmanesh, H.: Using linguistic techniques for schema matching. In: ICSOFT 2006, pp. 115–120. INSTICC Press (2006)

29. Volz, J., Bizer, C., Gaedke, M., Kobilarov, G.: Silk - A link discovery framework for the web of data. In: LDOW 2009. CEUR, vol. 538. CEUR-WS.org (2009)

30. Vrandecic, D., Krötzsch, M.: Wikidata: a free collaborative knowledgebase. Commun. ACM **57**(10), 78–85 (2014)

31. Xiang, C., Jiang, T., Chang, B., Sui, Z.: ERSOM: a structural ontology matching approach using automatically learned entity representation. In: EMNLP (2015)

32. Zhang, S., Balog, K.: Web table extraction, retrieval, and augmentation: a survey. ACM Trans. Intell. Syst. Technol. **11**(2), 13:1–13:35 (2020)

Improving Inductive Link Prediction Using Hyper-relational Facts

Mehdi Ali[1,2(✉)], Max Berrendorf[3], Mikhail Galkin[4], Veronika Thost[5], Tengfei Ma[5], Volker Tresp[3,6], and Jens Lehmann[1,2]

[1] Smart Data Analytics Group, University of Bonn, Bonn, Germany
{mehdi.ali,jens.lehmann}@cs.uni-bonn.de
[2] Fraunhofer Institute for Intelligent Analysis and Information Systems (IAIS), Sankt Augustin, Dresden, Germany
{mehdi.ali,jens.lehmann}@iais.fraunhofer.de
[3] Ludwig-Maximilians-Universität München, Munich, Germany
{berrendorf,tresp}@dbs.ifi.lmu.de
[4] Mila, McGill University, Montreal, Canada
mikhail.galkin@mila.quebec
[5] IBM Research, MIT-IBM Watson AI Lab, Cambridge, USA
vth@zurich.ibm.com, tengfei.ma1@ibm.com
[6] Siemens AG, Munich, Germany
volker.tresp@siemens.com

Abstract. For many years, link prediction on knowledge graphs (KGs) has been a purely transductive task, not allowing for reasoning on unseen entities. Recently, increasing efforts are put into exploring semi- and fully inductive scenarios, enabling inference over unseen and emerging entities. Still, all these approaches only consider triple-based KGs, whereas their richer counterparts, hyper-relational KGs (e.g., Wikidata), have not yet been properly studied. In this work, we classify different inductive settings and study the benefits of employing hyper-relational KGs on a wide range of semi- and fully inductive link prediction tasks powered by recent advancements in graph neural networks. Our experiments on a novel set of benchmarks show that qualifiers over typed edges can lead to performance improvements of 6% of absolute gains (for the Hits@10 metric) compared to triple-only baselines. Our code is available at https://github.com/mali-git/hyper_relational_ilp.

1 Introduction

Knowledge graphs are notorious for their sparsity and incompleteness [16], so that predicting missing links has been one of the first applications of machine learning and embedding-based methods over KGs [9,22]. A flurry [2,20] of such algorithms has been developed over the years, and most of them share certain commonalities, i.e., they operate over *triple-based* KGs in the *transductive* setup, where all entities are known at training time. Such approaches can neither operate on unseen entities, which might emerge after updating the graph, nor

---

M. Ali and M. Berrendorf—Equal contribution.

© Springer Nature Switzerland AG 2021
A. Hotho et al. (Eds.): ISWC 2021, LNCS 12922, pp. 74–92, 2021.
https://doi.org/10.1007/978-3-030-88361-4_5

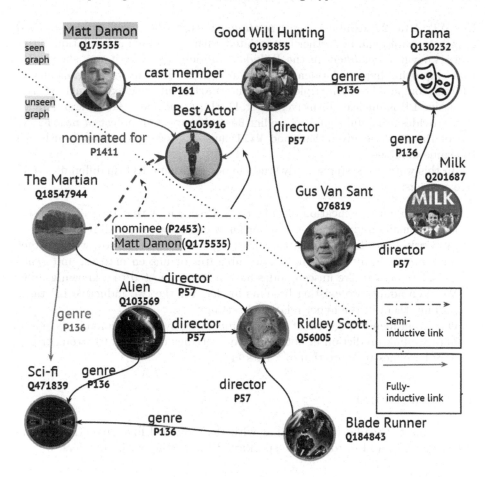

Fig. 1. Different types of inductive LP. Semi-inductive: the link between The Martian and Best Actor from the seen graph. Fully-inductive: the genre link between unseen entities given a new unseen subgraph *at inference time*. The qualifier (nominee: Matt Damon) over the original relation nominated for allows to better predict the semi-inductive link.

on new (sub-)graphs comprised of completely new entities. Those scenarios are often unified under the *inductive* link prediction (LP) setup. A variety of NLP tasks building upon KGs have inductive nature, for instance, entity linking or information extraction. Hence, being able to work in inductive settings becomes crucial for KG representation learning algorithms. For instance (cf. Fig. 1), the director-genre pattern from the seen graph allows to predict a missing genre link for The Martian in the unseen subgraph.

Several recent approaches [13,24] tackle an inductive LP task, but they usually focus on a specific inductive setting. Furthermore, their underlying KG structure is still based on triples. On the other hand, new, more expressive KGs like Wikidata [26] exhibit a *hyper-relational* nature where each triple (a typed edge in a graph) can be further instantiated with a set of explicit relation-entity pairs, known as *qualifiers* in the Wikidata model. Recently, it was shown [17] that employing hyper-relational KGs yields significant gains in the transductive LP task compared to their triple-only counterparts. But the effect of such KGs on inductive LP is unclear. Intuitively (Fig. 1), the (nominee: Matt Damon) qualifier provides a helpful signal to predict Best Actor as an object of nominated for of The Martian given that Good Will Hunting received such an award with the same nominee.

In this work, we systematically study hyper-relational KGs in different inductive settings:

– We propose a classification of inductive LP scenarios that describes the settings formally and, to the best of our knowledge, integrates all relevant existing works. Specifically, we distinguish *fully-inductive* scenarios, where target links are to be predicted in a new subgraph of unseen entities, and *semi-inductive* ones where unseen nodes have to be connected to a known graph.
– We then adapt two existing baseline models for the two inductive LP tasks probing them in the hyper-relational settings.
– Our experiments suggest that models supporting hyper-relational facts indeed improve link prediction in both inductive settings compared to strong triple-only baselines by more than 6% Hits@10.

2   Background

We assume the reader to be familiar with the standard link prediction setting (e.g. from [22]) and introduce the specifics of the setting with qualifiers.

2.1   Statements: Triples Plus Qualifiers

Let $G = (\mathcal{E}, \mathcal{R}, \mathcal{S})$ be a hyper-relational KG where $\mathcal{E}$ is a set of entities, $\mathcal{R}$ is a set of relations, and $\mathcal{S}$ a set of statements. Each statement can be formalized as a 4-tuple (h, r, t, q) of a head and tail entity[1] $h, t \in \mathcal{E}$, a relation $r \in \mathcal{R}$, and a set of qualifiers, which are relation-entity pairs $q \subseteq \mathfrak{P}(\mathcal{R} \times \mathcal{E})$ where $\mathfrak{P}$ denotes the power set. For example, Fig. 1 contains a statement (Good Will Hunting, nominated for, Best Actor, {(nominee, Matt Damon)}) where (nominee, Matt Damon) is a qualifier pair for the main triple. We define the set of all possible statements as set

$$\mathbb{S}(\mathcal{E}_H, \mathcal{R}, \mathcal{E}_T, \mathcal{E}_Q) = \mathcal{E}_H \times \mathcal{R} \times \mathcal{E}_T \times \mathfrak{P}(\mathcal{R} \times \mathcal{E}_Q)$$

with a set of relations $\mathcal{R}$, a set of head, tail and qualifier entities $\mathcal{E}_H, \mathcal{E}_T, \mathcal{E}_Q \subseteq \mathcal{E}$. Further, $\mathcal{S}_{train}$ is the set of training statements and $\mathcal{S}_{eval}$ are evaluation statements. We assume that we have a feature vector $\mathbf{x}_e \in \mathbb{R}^d$ associated with

---

[1] We use *entity* and *node* interchangeably.

each entity $e \in \mathcal{E}$. Such feature vectors can, for instance, be obtained from entity descriptions available in some KGs or represent topological features such as Laplacian eigenvectors [6] or regular graph substructures [10]. In this work, we focus on the setting with one fixed set of known relations. That is, we do not require $\mathbf{x}_r \in \mathbb{R}^d$ features for relations and rather learn relation embeddings during training.

2.2 Expressiveness

Models making use of qualifiers are strictly more expressive than those which do not: Consider the following example with two statements, $s_1 = (h, r, t, q_1)$ and $s_2 = (h, r, t, q_2)$, sharing the same triple components, but differing in their qualifiers, such that $s_1|q_1 = False$ and $s_2|q_2 = True$. For a model f_{NQ} not using qualifiers, i.e., only using the triple component (h, r, t), we have $f_{NQ}(s_1) = f_{NQ}(s_2)$. In contrast, a model f_Q using qualifiers can predict $f_Q(s_1) \neq f_Q(s_2)$, thus being strictly more expressive.

Table 1. Inductive LP in the literature, a discrepancy in terminology. The approaches differ in the kind of auxiliary statements $\mathcal{S}_{inf}$ used at inference time: in whether they contain entities seen during training E_{tr} and whether new entities E_{inf} are connected to seen ones (*k-shot* scenario), or (only) amongst each other, in a new graph. Note that the evaluation settings also vary.

Named scenario	$\mathcal{S}_{inf}$	Unseen ↔ Unseen	Unseen ↔ Seen	Scoring against	In our framework
Out-of-sample [1]	k-shot	–	✓	E_{tr}	SI
Unseen entities [12]	k-shot	–	✓	E_{tr}	SI
Inductive [8]	k-shot	–	✓	E_{tr}	SI
Inductive [24]	New graph	✓	–	E_{inf}	FI
Transfer [13]	New graph	✓	–	E_{inf}	FI
Dynamic [13]	k-shot + new graph	✓	✓	$E_{tr} \cup E_{inf}$	FI/SI
Out-of-graph [4]	k-shot + new graph	✓	✓	$E_{tr} \cup E_{inf}$	FI/SI
Inductive [27]	k-shot + new graph	✓	✓	$E_{tr} \cup E_{inf}$	FI/SI

3 Inductive Link Prediction

Recent works (cf. Table 1) have pointed out the practical relevance of different inductive LP scenarios. However, there exists a terminology gap as different authors employ different names for describing conceptually the same task or, conversely, use the same *inductive LP* term for practically different setups. We propose a unified framework that provides an overview of the area and describes the settings formally.

Let $\mathcal{E}_\bullet$ denote the set of entities occurring in the training statements $\mathcal{S}_{train}$ at any position (head, tail, or qualifier), and $\mathcal{E}_\circ \subseteq \mathcal{E} \setminus \mathcal{E}_\bullet$ denote a set of unseen entities. In the *transductive* setting, all entities in the evaluation statements are seen during training, i.e., $\mathcal{S}_{eval} \subseteq \mathbb{S}(\mathcal{E}_\bullet, \mathcal{R}, \mathcal{E}_\bullet, \mathcal{E}_\bullet)$. In contrast, in *inductive* settings, $\mathcal{S}_{eval}$, used in validation and testing, may contain unseen entities. In order to be able to learn representations for these entities at inference time, inductive approaches may consider an additional set $\mathcal{S}_{inf}$ of *inference statements* about (un)seen entities; of course $\mathcal{S}_{inf} \cap \mathcal{S}_{eval} = \emptyset$.

The *fully-inductive* setting (FI) is akin to transfer learning where link prediction is performed over a set of entities not seen before, i.e., $\mathcal{S}_{eval} \subseteq \mathbb{S}(\mathcal{E}_\circ, \mathcal{R}, \mathcal{E}_\circ, \mathcal{E}_\circ)$. This is made possible by providing an auxiliary inference graph $\mathcal{S}_{inf} \subseteq \mathbb{S}(\mathcal{E}_\circ, \mathcal{R}, \mathcal{E}_\circ, \mathcal{E}_\circ)$ containing statements about the unseen entities in $\mathcal{S}_{eval}$. For instance, in Fig. 1, the training graph is comprised of entities Matt Damon, Good Will Hunting, Best Actor, Gus Van Sant, Milk, Drama. The inference graph contains new entities The Martian, Alien, Ridley Scott, Blade Runner, Sci-fi with one missing link to be predicted. The fully-inductive setting is considered in [13,24].

In the *semi-inductive* setting (SI), new, unseen entities are to be connected to seen entities, i.e., $\mathcal{S}_{eval} \subseteq \mathbb{S}(\mathcal{E}_\bullet, \mathcal{R}, \mathcal{E}_\circ, \mathcal{E}_\bullet) \cup \mathbb{S}(\mathcal{E}_\circ, \mathcal{R}, \mathcal{E}_\bullet, \mathcal{E}_\bullet)$. Illustrating with Fig. 1, The Martian as the only unseen entity connecting to the seen graph, the semi-inductive statement connects The Martian to the seen Best Actor. Note that there are other practically relevant examples beyond KGs, such as predicting interaction links between a new drug and a graph containing existing proteins/drugs [5,18]. We hypothesize that, in most scenarios, we are not given any additional information about the new entity, and thus have $\mathcal{S}_{inf} = \emptyset$; we will focus on this case in this paper. However, the variation where $\mathcal{S}_{inf}$ may contain k statements connecting the unseen entity to seen ones has been considered too [1,8,12] and is known as *k-shot learning* scenario.

A mix of the fully- and semi-inductive settings where evaluation statements may contain two instead of just one unseen entity is studied in [4,13,27]. That is, unseen entities might be connected to the seen graph, i.e., $\mathcal{S}_{eval}$ may contain seen entities, and, at the same time, the unseen entities might be connected to each other; i.e., $\mathcal{S}_{inf} \neq \emptyset$.

Our framework is general enough to allow $\mathcal{S}_{eval}$ to contain new, unseen relations r having their features $\mathbf{x}_r$ at hand. Still, to the best of our knowledge, research so far has focused on the setting where all relations are seen in training; we will do so, too.

We hypothesize that qualifiers, being explicit attributes over typed edges, provide a strong inductive bias for LP tasks. In this work, for simplicity, we require both qualifier relations and entities to be seen in the training graph, i.e., $\mathcal{E}_Q \subseteq \mathcal{E}_\bullet$ and $\mathcal{R}_Q \subseteq \mathcal{R}$, although the framework accommodates a more general case of unseen qualifiers given their respective features.

4   Approach

Both semi- and fully-inductive tasks assume node features to be given. Recall that relation embeddings are learned and, often, to reduce the computational complexity, their dimensionality is smaller than that of node features.

4.1 Encoders

In the semi-inductive setting, an unseen entity arrives without any graph structure pointing to existing entities, i.e., $\mathcal{S}_{inf} = \emptyset$. This fact renders message passing approaches [19] less applicable, so we resort to a simple linear layer to project all entity features (including those of qualifiers) into the relation space: $\phi : \mathbb{R}^{d_f} \to \mathbb{R}^{d_r}$

In the fully inductive setting, we are given a non-empty inference graph $\mathcal{S}_{inf} \neq \emptyset$, and we probe two encoders: (i) the same linear projection of features as in the semi-inductive scenario which does not consider the graph structure; (ii) GNNs which can naturally work in the inductive settings [11]. However, the majority of existing GNN encoders for multi-relational KGs like CompGCN [25] are limited to only triple KG representation. To the best of our knowledge, only the recently proposed STARE [17] encoder supports hyper-relational KGs which we take as a basis for our inductive model. Its aggregation formula is:

$$\mathbf{x}'_v = f\left(\sum_{(u,r) \in \mathcal{N}(v)} \mathbf{W}_{\lambda(r)} \phi_r(\mathbf{x}_u, \gamma(\mathbf{x}_r, \mathbf{x}_q)_{vu}) \right) \tag{1}$$

where γ is a function that infuses the vector of aggregated qualifiers $\mathbf{x}_q$ into the vector of the main relation $\mathbf{x}_r$. The output of the GNN contains updated node and relation features based on the adjacency matrix A and qualifiers Q:

$$\mathbf{X}', \mathbf{R}' = \text{STARE}(A, \mathbf{X}, \mathbf{R}, Q)$$

Finally, in both inductive settings, we linearize an input statement in a sequence using a padding index where necessary: $[\mathbf{x}'_h, \mathbf{x}'_r, \mathbf{x}'_{q_1^r}, \mathbf{x}'_{q_1^e}, [\text{PAD}], \ldots]$. Note that statements can greatly vary in length depending on the amount of qualifier pairs, and padding mitigates this issue.

Table 2. Semi-inductive (SI) and fully-inductive (FI) datasets. $S_{ds}(Q\%)$ denotes the number of statements with the qualifiers ratio in train ($ds = tr$), validation ($ds = vl$), test ($ds = ts$), and inductive inference ($ds = inf$) splits. E_{ds} is the number of distinct entities. R_{ds} is the number of distinct relations. S_{inf} is a basic graph for vl and ts in the FI scenario.

Type	Name	Train			Validation			Test			Inference		
		S_{tr} (Q%)	E_{tr}	R_{tr}	S_{vl} (Q%)	E_{vl}	R_{vl}	S_{ts} (Q%)	E_{ts}	R_{ts}	S_{inf}(Q%)	E_{inf}	R_{inf}
SI	WD20K (25)	39,819 (30%)	17,014	362	4,252 (25%)	3544	194	3,453 (22%)	3028	198	–	–	–
SI	WD20K (33)	25,862 (37%)	9251	230	2,423 (31%)	1951	88	2,164 (28%)	1653	87	–	–	–
FI	WD20K (66) V1	9,020 (85%)	6522	179	910 (45%)	1516	111	1,113 (50%)	1796	110	6,949 (49%)	8313	152
FI	WD20K (66) V2	4,553 (65%)	4269	148	1,480 (66%)	2322	79	1,840 (65%)	2700	89	8,922 (58%)	9895	120
FI	WD20K (100) V1	7,785 (100%)	5783	92	295 (100%)	643	43	364 (100%)	775	43	2,667 (100%)	4218	75
FI	WD20K (100) V2	4,146 (100%)	3227	57	538 (100%)	973	43	678 (100%)	1212	42	4,274 (100%)	5573	54

4.2 Decoder

Given an encoded sequence, we use the same Transformer-based decoder for all settings:

$$f(h, r, t, q) = g(\mathbf{x}'_h, \mathbf{x}'_r, \mathbf{x}'_{q_1^r}, \mathbf{x}'_{q_1^e}, \ldots)^T \mathbf{x}'_t \text{ with}$$
$$g(\mathbf{x}'_1, \ldots, \mathbf{x}_k) = \text{Agg}(\text{Transformer}([\mathbf{x}'_1, \ldots, \mathbf{x}'_k]))$$

In this work, we evaluated several aggregation strategies and found a simple mean pooling over all non-padded sequence elements to be preferable. Interaction functions of the form $f(h, r, t, q) = f_1(h, r, q)^T f_2(t)$ are particularly well-suited for fast 1-N scoring for tail entities, since the first part only needs to be computed only once.

Here and below, we denote the linear encoder + Transformer decoder model as QBLP (that is, Qualifier-aware BLP, an extension of BLP [13]), and the STARE encoder + Transformer decoder, as STARE.

4.3 Training

In order to compare results with triple-only approaches, we train the models, as usual, on the subject and object prediction tasks. We use stochastic local closed world assumption (sLCWA) and the local closed world assumption (LCWA) commonly used in the KG embedding literature [2]. Particular details on sLCWA and LCWA are presented in Appendix A. Importantly, in the semi-inductive setting, the models score against all entities in the training graph E_{tr} in both training and inference stages. In the fully-inductive scenario, as we are predicting links over an unseen graph, the models score against all entities in E_{tr} during training and against unseen entities in the inference graph E_{inf} during inference.

5 Datasets

We take the original transductive splits of the WD50K [17] family of hyper-relational datasets as a leakage-free basis for sampling our semi- and fully-inductive datasets which we denote by WD20K.

5.1 Fully-Inductive Setting

We start with extracting *statement entities* $\mathcal{E}'$, and sample n entities and their k-hop neighbourhood to form the statements (h, r, t, q) of the transductive train graph S_{train}. From the remaining $\mathcal{E}' \setminus \mathcal{E}_{train}$ and $S \setminus S_{train}$ sets we sample m entities with their l-hop neighbourhood to form the statements S_{ind} of the inductive graph. The entities of S_{ind} are disjoint with those of the transductive train graph. Further, we filter out all statements in S_{ind} whose relations (main or qualifier) were not seen in S_{train}. Then, we randomly split S_{ind} with the ratio about 55%/20%/25% into inductive inference, validation, and test statements, respectively. The evaluated models are trained on the transductive train graph S_{train}. During inference, the models receive an unseen inductive inference graph from which they have to predict validation and test statements. Varying k and l, we sample two different splits: V1 has a larger training graph with more seen entities whereas V2 has a bigger inductive inference graph.

5.2 Semi-inductive Setting

Starting from all statements, we extract all entities occurring as head or tail entity in any statement, denoted by $\mathcal{E}'$ and named *statement entities*. Next, we split the set of statement entities into a train, validation and test set: $\mathcal{E}_{train}, \mathcal{E}_{validation}, \mathcal{E}_{test}$. We then proceed to extract statements $(h, r, t, q) \in S$ with one entity (h/t) in $\mathcal{E}_{train}$ and the other entity in the corresponding statement entity split. We furthermore filter the qualifiers to contain only pairs where the entity is in a set of allowed entities, formed by $\mathcal{A}_{split} = \mathcal{E}_{train} \cup \mathcal{E}_{split}$, with split being train/validation/test. Finally, since we do not assume relations to have any features, we do not allow unseen relations. We thus filter out relations which do not occur in the training statements.

5.3 Overview

To measure the effect of hyper-relational facts on both inductive LP tasks, we sample several datasets varying the ratio of statements with and without qualifiers. In order to obtain the initial node features we mine their English surface forms and descriptions available in Wikidata as `rdfs:label` and `schema:description` values. The surface forms and descriptions are concatenated into one string and passed through the Sentence BERT [23] encoder based on RoBERTa [21] to get 1024-dimensional vectors. The overall datasets statistics is presented in Table 2.

6 Experiments

We design our experiments to investigate whether the incorporation of qualifiers improves inductive link prediction. In particular, we investigate the fully-inductive setting (Sect. 6.2) and the semi-inductive setting (Sect. 6.3). We analyze the impact of the qualifier ratio (i.e., the number of statements with qualifiers) and the dataset's size on a model's performance.

Table 3. Results on FI WD20K (100) V1 & V2. #QP denotes the number of qualifier pairs used in each statement (including padded pairs). Best results **in bold**, second best underlined.

Model	#QP	WD20K (100) V1					WD20K (100) V2				
		AMR(%)	MRR(%)	H@1(%)	H@5(%)	H@10(%)	AMR(%)	MRR(%)	H@1(%)	H@5(%)	H@10(%)
BLP	0	22.78	5.73	1.92	8.22	12.33	36.71	3.99	1.47	4.87	9.22
CompGCN	0	37.02	10.42	5.75	15.07	18.36	74.00	2.55	0.74	3.39	5.31
QBLP	0	28.91	5.52	1.51	8.08	12.60	35.38	4.94	2.58	5.46	9.66
StarE	2	41.89	9.68	3.73	**16.57**	20.99	40.60	2.43	0.45	3.86	6.17
StarE	4	35.33	10.41	4.82	15.84	21.76	37.16	5.12	1.41	7.93	12.89
StarE	6	34.86	**11.27**	**6.18**	15.93	21.29	47.35	4.99	1.92	6.71	11.06
QBLP	2	**18.91**	10.45	3.73	16.02	22.65	**28.03**	**6.69**	**3.49**	8.47	12.04
QBLP	4	20.19	10.70	3.99	16.12	24.52	31.30	5.87	2.37	7.85	**13.93**
QBLP	6	23.65	7.87	2.75	10.44	17.86	34.35	6.53	2.95	**9.29**	13.13

Table 4. Results on the FI WD20K (66) V1 & V2. #QP denotes the number of qualifier pairs used in each statement (including padded pairs). Best results **in bold**, second best underlined.

Model	#QP	WD20K (66) V1					WD20K (66) V2				
		AMR(%)	MRR(%)	H@1(%)	H@5(%)	H@10(%)	AMR(%)	MRR(%)	H@1(%)	H@5(%)	H@10(%)
BLP	0	34.96	2.10	0.45	2.29	4.44	45.29	1.56	0.27	1.88	3.35
CompGCN	0	35.99	5.80	2.38	8.93	12.79	47.24	2.56	1.17	3.07	4.46
QBLP	0	35.30	3.69	1.30	4.85	7.14	42.48	0.94	0.08	0.79	1.82
StarE	2	37.72	**6.84**	**3.24**	**9.71**	13.44	52.78	2.62	0.74	3.55	5.78
StarE	4	38.91	6.40	2.83	8.94	13.39	51.93	**5.06**	**2.09**	7.34	9.82
StarE	6	38.20	6.87	3.46	8.98	**13.57**	47.01	4.42	2.04	5.73	8.97
QBLP	2	30.37	3.70	1.26	4.90	8.14	53.67	1.39	0.41	1.66	2.59
QBLP	4	30.84	3.20	0.90	4.00	7.14	**37.10**	2.08	0.38	2.20	4.92
QBLP	6	**26.34**	4.34	1.66	5.53	9.25	39.12	1.95	0.41	2.15	4.10

6.1 Experimental Setup

We implemented all approaches in Python building upon the open-source library **pykeen** [3] and make the code publicly available.[2] For each setting (i.e., dataset + number of qualifier pairs per triple), we performed a hyperparameter search using early stopping on the validation set and evaluated the final model on the test set. We used AMR, MRR, and Hits@k as evaluation metrics, where the Adjusted Mean Rank (AMR) [7] is a recently proposed metric which sets the mean rank into relation with the expected mean rank of a random scoring model. Its value ranges from 0%–200%, and a lower value corresponds to better model performance. Each model was trained at most 1000 epochs in the fully inductive setting, at most 600 epochs in the semi-inductive setting, and evaluated based on the early-stopping criterion with a frequency of 1, a patience of 200 epochs (in the semi-inductive setting, we performed all HPOs with a patience of 100 and 200 epochs), and a minimal improvement $\delta > 0.3\%$ optimizing the $hits@10$ metric. For both inductive settings, we evaluated the effect of incorporating 0, 2, 4, and 6 qualifier pairs per triple.

---

[2] https://github.com/mali-git/hyper_relational_ilp.

6.2   Fully-Inductive Setting

In the full inductive setting, we analyzed the effect of qualifiers for four different datasets (i.e., WD20K (100) V1 & V2 and WD20K (66) V1 & V2, which have different ratios of qualifying statements and are of different sizes (see Sect. 5). As triple-only baselines, we evaluated CompGCN [25] and BLP [13]. To evaluate the effect of qualifiers on the fully-inductive LP task, we evaluated StarE [17] and QBLP. It should be noted that StarE without the use of qualifiers is equivalent to CompGCN.

General Overview. Tables 3 and 4 show the results obtained for the four datasets. The main findings are that (i) for all datasets, the use of qualifiers leads to increased performance, and (ii) the ratio of statements with qualifiers and the size of the dataset has a major impact on the performance. CompGCN and StarE apply message-passing to obtain enriched entity representations while BLP and QBLP only apply a linear transformation. Consequently, CompGCN and StarE require $\mathcal{S}_{inf}$ to contain useful information in order to obtain the entity representations while BLP and QBLP are independent of $\mathcal{S}_{inf}$. In the following, we discuss the results for each dataset in detail.

Results on WD20K (100) FI V1 & V2. It can be observed that the performance gap between BLP/QBLP (0) and QBLP (2,4,6) is considerably larger than the gap between CompGCN and StarE. This might be explained by the fact that QBLP does not take into account the graph structure provided by $\mathcal{S}_{inf}$, therefore is heavily dependent on additional information, i.e. the qualifiers compensate for the missing graph information. The overall performance decrease observable between V1 and V2 could be explained by the datasets' composition (Table 2), in particular, in the composition of the training and inference graphs: $\mathcal{S}_{inf}$ of V2 comprises more entities than V1, so that each test triple is ranked against more entities, i.e., the ranking becomes more difficult. At the same time, the training graph of V1 is larger than that of V2, i.e., during training more entities (along their textual features) are seen which may improve generalization.

Results on WD20K (66) FI V1 & V2. Comparing StarE (2,4) to CompGCN (0), there is only a small improvement on this dataset. Also, the improvement of QBLP (2,4,6) compared to BLP and QBLP (0) is smaller than on the previous datasets. This can be connected to the decreased ratio of statements with qualifiers. Besides, the training graph also has fewer qualifier pairs, $\mathcal{S}_{inf}$ which is used by CompGCN and StarE for message passing consists of only 49% of statements with at least one qualifier pair, and only 50% of test statements have at least one qualifier pair which has an influence on all models. This observation supports why StarE outperforms QBLP as the amount of provided qualifier statements cannot compensate for the graph structure in $\mathcal{S}_{inf}$.

6.3 Semi-inductive Setting

In the semi-inductive setting, we evaluated BLP as a triple-only baseline and QBLP as a statement baseline (i.e., involving qualifiers) on the WD20K SI datasets. We did not evaluate CompGCN and StarE since message-passing-based approaches are not directly applicable in the absence of $\mathcal{S}_{inf}$. The results highlight that aggregating qualifier information improves the prediction of semi-inductive links despite the fact that the ratio of statements with qualifiers is not very large (37% for SI WD20K (33), and 30% for SI WD20K (25)). In the case of SI WD20K (33), the baselines are outperformed even by a large margin. Overall, the results might indicate that in semi-inductive settings, performance improvements can already be obtained with a decent amount of statements with qualifiers.

Table 5. Results on the WD20K SI datasets. #QP denotes the number of qualifier pairs used in each statement (including padded pairs).Best results **in bold**, second best underlined.

Model	#QP	WD20K (33) SI					WD20K (25) SI				
		AMR(%)	MRR(%)	H@1(%)	H@5(%)	H@10(%)	AMR(%)	MRR(%)	H@1(%)	H@5(%)	H@10(%)
BLP	0	**4.76**	13.95	7.37	17.28	24.65	6.01	12.45	5.98	17.29	23.43
QBLP	0	7.04	28.35	14.44	28.58	36.32	6.75	17.02	8.82	22.10	29.50
QBLP	2	11.51	**35.95**	**20.70**	**34.98**	**41.82**	<u>5.99</u>	<u>20.36</u>	<u>11.77</u>	**24.86**	**32.26**
QBLP	4	11.38	<u>34.35</u>	<u>19.41</u>	<u>33.90</u>	<u>40.20</u>	12.18	**21.05**	**12.32**	24.07	30.09
QBLP	6	<u>4.98</u>	25.94	15.20	30.06	38.70	**5.73**	19.50	11.14	<u>24.73</u>	<u>31.60</u>

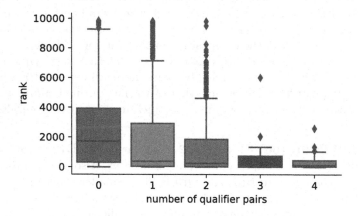

Fig. 2. Distribution of individual ranks for head/tail prediction with StarE on WD20K (66) V2. The statements are grouped by the number of qualifier pairs.

6.4 Qualitative Analysis

We obtain deeper insights on the impact of qualifiers by analyzing the StarE model on the fully-inductive WD20K (66) V2 dataset. In particular, we study individual ranks for head/tail prediction of statements with and without qualifiers (cf. Fig. 2) varying the model from zero to four pairs. First, we group the test statements by the number of available qualifier pairs. We observe generally smaller ranks which, in turn, correspond to better predictions when more qualifier pairs are available. In particular, just one qualifier pair is enough to significantly reduce the individual ranks. Note that we have less statements with many qualifiers, cf. Appendix D.

We then study how particular qualifiers affect ranking and predictions. For that, we measure ranks of predictions for distinct statements in the *test set* with and without masking the qualifier relation from the inference graph $\mathcal{S}_{inf}$. We then compute ΔMR and group them by used qualifier relations (Fig. 3). Interestingly, certain qualifiers, e.g., `convicted of` or `including`, deteriorate the performance which we attribute to the usage of rare, qualifier-only entities. Conversely, having qualifiers like `replaces` reduces the rank by about 4000 which greatly improves prediction accuracy. We hypothesize it is an effect of qualifier entities: helpful qualifiers employ well-connected nodes in the graph which benefit from message passing.

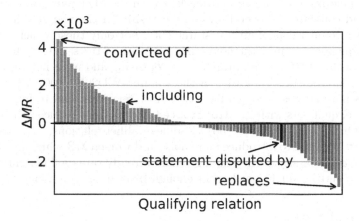

Fig. 3. Rank deviation when masking qualifier pairs containing a certain relation. Transparency is proportional to the occurrence frequency, bar height/color indicates difference in MR *for evaluation statements using this qualifying relation* if the pair is masked. More negative deltas correspond to better predictions.

Table 6. Top 3 worst and best qualifier relations affecting the overall mean rank (the last column). Negative ΔMR with larger absolute value correspond to better predictions.

WD20K (100) V1 FI		
Wikidata ID	relation name	ΔMR
P2868	subject has role	0.12
P463	member of	-0.04
P1552	has quality	-0.34
P2241	reason for deprecation	-26.44
P47	shares border with	-28.91
P750	distributed by	-29.12
WD20K (66) V2 FI		
P805	statement is subject of	13.11
P1012	including	5.95
P812	academic major	5.07
P17	country	-19.96
P1310	statement disputed by	-20.92
P1686	for work	-56.87

Finally, we study the average impact of qualifiers on the whole graph, i.e., we take the whole *inference graph* and mask out all qualifier pairs containing one relation and compare the overall evaluation result on the test set (in contrast to Fig. 3, we count ranks of all test statements, not only those which have that particular qualifier) against the non-masked version of the same graph. We then sort relations by ΔMR and find top 3 most confusing and most helpful relations across two datasets (cf. Table 6). On the smaller WD20K (100) V1 where all statements have at least one qualifier pair, most relations tend to improve MR. For instance, qualifiers with the `distributed by` relations reduce MR by about 29 points. On the larger WD20K (66) V2 some qualifier relations, e.g., `statement is subject of`, tend to introduce more noise and worsen MR which we attribute to the increased sparsity of the graph given an already rare qualifier entity. That is, such rare entities might not benefit enough from message passing.

7   Related Work

We focus on semi- and fully inductive link prediction approaches and disregard classical approaches that are fully transductive, which have been extensively studied in the literature [2,20].

In the domain of triple-only KGs, both settings have recently received a certain traction. One of the main challenges for realistic KG embedding is the impossibility of learning representations of unseen entities since they are not present in the train set.

In the semi-inductive setting, several methods alleviating the issue were proposed. When a new node arrives with a certain set of edges to known nodes, [1] enhanced the training procedure such that an embedding of an unseen node is a linear aggregation of neighbouring nodes. If there is no connection to the seen nodes, [27] propose to *densify* the graph with additional edges obtained from pairwise similarities of node features. Another approach applies a special meta-learning framework [4] when during training a meta-model has to learn representations decoupled from concrete training entities but transferable to unseen entities. Finally, reinforcement learning methods [8] were employed to learn relation paths between seen and unseen entities.

In the fully inductive setup, the evaluation graph is a separate subgraph disjoint with the training one, which makes trained entity embeddings even less useful. In such cases, the majority of existing methods [12,13,28,29] resort to pre-trained language models (LMs) (e.g., BERT [15]) as *universal featurizers*. That is, textual entity descriptions (often available in KGs at least in English) are passed through an LM to obtain initial semantic node features. Nevertheless, mining and employing structural graph features, e.g., shortest paths within sampled subgraphs, has been shown [24] to be beneficial as well. This work is independent from the origin of node features and is able to leverage both, although the new datasets employ Sentence BERT [23] for featurizing.

All the described approaches operate on triple-based KGs whereas our work studies inductive LP problems on enriched, hyper-relational KGs where we show that incorporating such hyper-relational information indeed leads to better performance.

8   Conclusion

In this work, we presented a study of the inductive link prediction problem over hyper-relational KGs. In particular, we proposed a theoretical framework to categorize various LP tasks to alleviate an existing terminology discrepancy pivoting on two settings, namely, semi- and fully-inductive LP. Then, we designed WD20K, a collection of hyper-relational benchmarks based on Wikidata for inductive LP with a diverse set of parameters and complexity. Probing statement-aware models against triple-only baselines, we demonstrated that hyper-relational facts indeed improve LP performance in both inductive settings by a considerable margin. Moreover, our qualitative analysis showed that the achieved gains are consistent across different setups and still interpretable.

Our findings open up interesting prospects for employing inductive LP and hyper-relational KGs along several axes, e.g., large-scale KGs of billions statements, new application domains including life sciences, drug discovery, and KG-based NLP applications like question answering or entity linking.

In the future, we plan to extend inductive LP to consider unseen relations and qualifiers; tackle the problem of suggesting best qualifiers for a statement; and provide more solid theoretical foundations of representation learning over hyper-relational KGs.

Acknowledgements. This work was funded by the German Federal Ministry of Education and Research (BMBF) under Grant No. 01IS18036A and Grant No. 01IS18050D (project "MLWin"). The authors of this work take full responsibilities for its content.

A   Training

In the sLCWA, negative training examples are created for each true fact $(h, r, t) \in KG$ by corrupting the head or tail entity resulting in the triples $(h', r, t)/(h, r, t')$. In the LCWA, for each triple $(h, r, t) \in KG$ all triples $(h, r, t') \notin KG$ are considered as non-existing, i.e., as negative examples.

Under the sLCWA, we trained the models using the margin ranking loss [9]:

$$L(f(t_i^+), f(t_i^-)) = \max(0, \lambda + f(t_i^-) - f(t_i^+)) \ , \tag{2}$$

where $f(t_i^+)$ denotes the model's score for a positive training example and $f(t_i^-)$ for a negative one.

For training under the LCWA, we used the binary cross entropy loss [14]:

$$\begin{aligned} L(f(t_i), l_i) = -\,(l_i \cdot \log(\sigma(f(t_i))) \\ + (1 - l_i) \cdot \log(1 - \sigma(f(t_i)))), \end{aligned} \tag{3}$$

where l_i corresponds to the label of the triple t_i.

B   Hyperparameter Ranges

The following tables summarizes the hyper-parameter ranges explored during hyper-parameter optimization. The best hyper-parameters for each of our 46 ablation studies will be available online upon publishing.

C   Infrastructure and Parameters

We train each model on machines running Ubuntu 18.04 equipped with a GeForce RTX 2080 Ti with 12 GB RAM. In total, we performed 46 individual hyperparameter optimizations (one for each dataset/model/number-of-qualifier combination). Depending on the exact configuration, the individual models have between 500k and 5M parameters and take up to 2 h for training.

D   Qualifier Ratio

Figure 4 shows the ratio of statements with a given number of available qualifier pairs for all datasets and splits. We generally observe that there are only few statements with a large number of qualifier pairs, while most of them have zero to two qualifier pairs.

Table 7. Hyperparameter ranges explored during hyper-parameter optimization. FI denotes the fully-inductive setting and SI the semi-inductive setting. For the sLCWA training approach, we trained the models with the margin ranking loss (MRL), and with the LCWA we used the BCEL (Binary Cross Entropy loss)

Hyper-parameter	Value
GCN layers	{2,3}
Embedding dim.	{32, 64, ... , 256 }
Transformer hid. dim.	{512, 576, ... , 1024 }
Num. attention heads	{2, 4}
Num. transformer heads	{2, 4}
Num. transformer layers	{2, 3, 4}
Qualifier aggr.	{sum, attention}
Qualifier weight	0.8
Dropout	{0.1, 0.2, ... , 0.5 }
Attention slope	{0.1, 0.2, 0.3, 0.4 }
Training approaches	{sLCWA, LCWA}
Loss fcts.	{MRL, BCEL}
Learning rate (log scale)	[0.0001, 1.0)
Label smoothing	{0.1, 0.15}
Batch size	{128, 192, ... , 1024}
Max Epochs FI setting	1000
Max Epochs SI setting	600

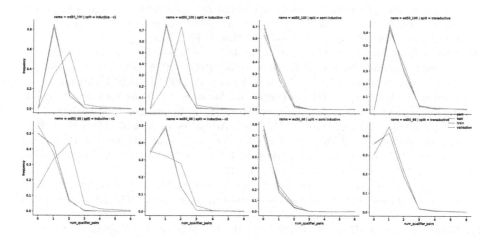

Fig. 4. Percentage of statements with the given number of available qualifier pairs for all datasets and splits.

References

1. Albooyeh, M., Goel, R., Kazemi, S.M.: Out-of-sample representation learning for knowledge graphs. In: Cohn, T., He, Y., Liu, Y. (eds.) Proceedings of the 2020 Conference on Empirical Methods in Natural Language Processing: Findings, EMNLP 2020, Online Event, 16–20 November 2020, pp. 2657–2666. Association for Computational Linguistics (2020)
2. Ali, M., et al.: Bringing light into the dark: a large-scale evaluation of knowledge graph embedding models under a unified framework. CoRR arXiv:2006.13365 (2020)
3. Ali, M., et al.: PyKEEN 1.0: a python library for training and evaluating knowledge graph embeddings. J. Mach. Learn. Res. **22**(82), 1–6 (2021). http://jmlr.org/papers/v22/20-825.html
4. Baek, J., Lee, D.B., Hwang, S.J.: Learning to extrapolate knowledge: Transductive few-shot out-of-graph link prediction. In: Larochelle, H., Ranzato, M., Hadsell, R., Balcan, M., Lin, H. (eds.) Advances in Neural Information Processing Systems 33: Annual Conference on Neural Information Processing Systems 2020, NeurIPS 2020, 6–12 December 2020 (2020). Virtual
5. Bagherian, M., Sabeti, E., Wang, K., Sartor, M.A., Nikolovska-Coleska, Z., Najarian, K.: Machine learning approaches and databases for prediction of drug-target interaction: a survey paper. Brief. Bioinform. **22**(1), 247–269 (2020). https://doi.org/10.1093/bib/bbz157
6. Belkin, M., Niyogi, P.: Laplacian eigenmaps and spectral techniques for embedding and clustering. In: Dietterich, T.G., Becker, S., Ghahramani, Z. (eds.) Advances in Neural Information Processing Systems 14 [Neural Information Processing Systems: Natural and Synthetic, NIPS 2001, Vancouver, British Columbia, Canada, 3–8 December 2001], pp. 585–591. MIT Press (2001)
7. Berrendorf, M., Faerman, E., Vermue, L., Tresp, V.: Interpretable and fair comparison of link prediction or entity alignment methods with adjusted mean rank. In: 2020 IEEE/WIC/ACM International Joint Conference on Web Intelligence and Intelligent Agent Technology (WI-IAT 2020). IEEE (2020)
8. Bhowmik, R., de Melo, G.: Explainable link prediction for emerging entities in knowledge graphs. In: Pan, J.Z., et al. (eds.) ISWC 2020. LNCS, vol. 12506, pp. 39–55. Springer, Cham (2020). https://doi.org/10.1007/978-3-030-62419-4_3
9. Bordes, A., Usunier, N., García-Durán, A., Weston, J., Yakhnenko, O.: Translating embeddings for modeling multi-relational data. In: Burges, C.J.C., Bottou, L., Ghahramani, Z., Weinberger, K.Q. (eds.) Advances in Neural Information Processing Systems 26: 27th Annual Conference on Neural Information Processing Systems 2013. Proceedings of a Meeting Held 5–8 December 2013, Lake Tahoe, Nevada, United States, pp. 2787–2795 (2013)
10. Bouritsas, G., Frasca, F., Zafeiriou, S., Bronstein, M.M.: Improving graph neural network expressivity via subgraph isomorphism counting. CoRR arXiv:2006.09252 (2020)
11. Chami, I., Abu-El-Haija, S., Perozzi, B., Ré, C., Murphy, K.: Machine learning on graphs: a model and comprehensive taxonomy. CoRR arXiv:2005.03675 (2020)
12. Clouatre, L., Trempe, P., Zouaq, A., Chandar, S.: MLMLM: link prediction with mean likelihood masked language model (2020)

13. Daza, D., Cochez, M., Groth, P.: Inductive entity representations from text via link prediction (2020)
14. Dettmers, T., Minervini, P., Stenetorp, P., Riedel, S.: Convolutional 2D knowledge graph embeddings. In: AAAI, pp. 1811–1818. AAAI Press (2018)
15. Devlin, J., Chang, M., Lee, K., Toutanova, K.: BERT: pre-training of deep bidirectional transformers for language understanding. In: Burstein, J., Doran, C., Solorio, T. (eds.) Proceedings of the 2019 Conference of the North American Chapter of the Association for Computational Linguistics: Human Language Technologies, NAACL-HLT 2019, Minneapolis, MN, USA, 2–7 June 2019, Volume 1 (Long and Short Papers), pp. 4171–4186. Association for Computational Linguistics (2019)
16. Dong, X., et al.: Knowledge vault: a web-scale approach to probabilistic knowledge fusion. In: Macskassy, S.A., Perlich, C., Leskovec, J., Wang, W., Ghani, R. (eds.) The 20th ACM SIGKDD International Conference on Knowledge Discovery and Data Mining, KDD 2014, New York, NY, USA, 24–27 August, 2014, pp. 601–610. ACM (2014)
17. Galkin, M., Trivedi, P., Maheshwari, G., Usbeck, R., Lehmann, J.: Message passing for hyper-relational knowledge graphs. In: Webber, B., Cohn, T., He, Y., Liu, Y. (eds.) Proceedings of the 2020 Conference on Empirical Methods in Natural Language Processing, EMNLP 2020, Online, 16–20 November 2020, pp. 7346–7359. Association for Computational Linguistics (2020)
18. Gaudelet, T., et al.: Utilising graph machine learning within drug discovery and development. CoRR arXiv:2012.05716 (2020)
19. Gilmer, J., Schoenholz, S.S., Riley, P.F., Vinyals, O., Dahl, G.E.: Neural message passing for quantum chemistry. In: Precup, D., Teh, Y.W. (eds.) Proceedings of the 34th International Conference on Machine Learning, ICML 2017, Sydney, NSW, Australia, 6–11 August 2017. Proceedings of Machine Learning Research, vol. 70, pp. 1263–1272. PMLR (2017)
20. Ji, S., Pan, S., Cambria, E., Marttinen, P., Yu, P.S.: A survey on knowledge graphs: representation, acquisition and applications. CoRR arXiv:2002.00388 (2020)
21. Liu, Y., et al.: RoBERTa: a robustly optimized BERT pretraining approach. CoRR arXiv:1907.11692 (2019)
22. Nickel, M., Tresp, V., Kriegel, H.: A three-way model for collective learning on multi-relational data. In: Getoor, L., Scheffer, T. (eds.) Proceedings of the 28th International Conference on Machine Learning, ICML 2011, Bellevue, Washington, USA, 28 June–2 July 2011, pp. 809–816. Omnipress (2011)
23. Reimers, N., Gurevych, I.: Sentence-BERT: sentence embeddings using Siamese BERT-networks. In: Proceedings of the 2019 Conference on Empirical Methods in Natural Language Processing. Association for Computational Linguistics (2019). https://arxiv.org/abs/1908.10084
24. Teru, K., Denis, E., Hamilton, W.: Inductive relation prediction by subgraph reasoning. In: Proceedings of the 37th International Conference on Machine Learning, ICML 2020, 13–18 July 2020, Virtual Event. Proceedings of Machine Learning Research, vol. 119, pp. 9448–9457. PMLR (2020)
25. Vashishth, S., Sanyal, S., Nitin, V., Talukdar, P.P.: Composition-based multi-relational graph convolutional networks. In: 8th International Conference on Learning Representations, ICLR 2020, Addis Ababa, Ethiopia, 26–30 April 2020. OpenReview.net (2020). https://openreview.net/forum?id=BylA_C4tPr
26. Vrandecic, D., Krötzsch, M.: Wikidata: a free collaborative knowledgebase. Commun. ACM 57(10), 78–85 (2014)
27. Wang, B., Wang, G., Huang, J., You, J., Leskovec, J., Kuo, C.J.: Inductive learning on commonsense knowledge graph completion. CoRR arXiv:2009.09263 (2020)

28. Yao, L., Mao, C., Luo, Y.: KG-BERT: BERT for knowledge graph completion (2019)
29. Zhang, Z., Liu, X., Zhang, Y., Su, Q., Sun, X., He, B.: Pretrain-KGE: learning knowledge representation from pretrained language models. In: Cohn, T., He, Y., Liu, Y. (eds.) Proceedings of the 2020 Conference on Empirical Methods in Natural Language Processing: Findings, EMNLP 2020, Online Event, 16–20 November 2020, pp. 259–266. Association for Computational Linguistics (2020)

Large-Scale Multi-granular Concept Extraction Based on Machine Reading Comprehension

Siyu Yuan[1], Deqing Yang[1](✉), Jiaqing Liang[2], Jilun Sun[2],
Jingyue Huang[1], Kaiyan Cao[1], Yanghua Xiao[2,3](✉), and Rui Xie[4]

[1] School of Data Science, Fudan University, Shanghai, China
{yuansy17,yangdeqing,jingyuehuang18,kycao20}@fudan.edu.cn
[2] School of Computer Science, Fudan University, Shanghai, China
{jlsun18,shawyh}@fudan.edu.cn
[3] Fudan-Aishu Cognitive Intelligence Joint Research Center, Shanghai, China
[4] Meituan, Beijing, China
rui.xie@meituan.com

Abstract. The concepts in knowledge graphs (KGs) enable machines to understand natural language, and thus play an indispensable role in many applications. However, existing KGs have the poor coverage of concepts, especially fine-grained concepts. In order to supply existing KGs with more fine-grained and new concepts, we propose a novel concept extraction framework, namely *MRC-CE*, to extract large-scale multi-granular concepts from the descriptive texts of entities. Specifically, MRC-CE is built with a machine reading comprehension model based on BERT, which can extract more fine-grained concepts with a pointer network. Furthermore, a random forest and rule-based pruning are also adopted to enhance MRC-CE's precision and recall simultaneously. Our experiments evaluated upon multilingual KGs, i.e., English *Probase* and Chinese *CN-DBpedia*, justify MRC-CE's superiority over the state-of-the-art extraction models in KG completion. Particularly, after running MRC-CE for each entity in CN-DBpedia, more than 7,053,900 new concepts (instanceOf relations) are supplied into the KG. The code and datasets have been released at https://github.com/fcihraeipnusnacwh/MRC-CE.

Keywords: Concept extraction · Knowledge graph · Machine reading comprehension · Multi-granular concept · Concept overlap

This work is supported by Science and Technology on Information Systems Engineering Laboratory at the 28th Research Institute of China Electronics Technology Group Corporation, Nanjing Jiangsu, China (No. 05202002), National Key Research and Development Project (No. 2020AAA0109302), Shanghai Science and Technology Innovation Action Plan (No. 19511120400) and Shanghai Municipal Science and Technology Major Project (No. 2021SHZDZX0103).

A. Hotho et al. (Eds.): ISWC 2021, LNCS 12922, pp. 93–110, 2021.
https://doi.org/10.1007/978-3-030-88361-4_6

1 Introduction

The concepts in knowledge graphs (KGs) [3,36,41] enable machines to better understand natural languages and thus play an increasingly significant role in many applications, such as question answering [7], personalized recommendation [32], commonsense reasoning [25], etc. Particularly, fine-grained concepts greatly promote the downstream applications. For example, if entity *Google* has 'technology company' and 'search engine company' as its concepts, a job recommender system would recommend Google rather than Wal-Mart to a graduate from computer science department based on such fine-grained concepts.

Although there have been a great number of efforts on constructing KGs in recent years, the concepts in existing KGs are still far from being complete, especially for fine-grained concepts. In the widely used Chinese KG *CN-DBpedia* [41], there are nearly 17 million entities but only 0.27 million concepts in total, and more than 20% entities even have no concepts. In general, fine-grained concepts contain more than one modifier, and thus have longer characters (words). However, the average character length of CN-DBpedia concepts is only 3.62, implying that most of them are coarse-grained.

The poor coverage of concepts, especially fine-grained concepts, in the existing KGs is due to their approaches' drawbacks. Most of the existing concept acquisition approaches are based on *generation* or *extraction* from texts. Generation methods often generate coarse-grained concepts from free texts since they are inclined to generate high-frequency words [2,34]. Extraction methods mainly have three types of models. Pattern-matching models [3,24,36,45] focus on extracting concepts from texts based on handcrafted patterns or rules, but the recall of concept extraction (CE) is low due to their limited generalization ability. Classification models [9,15,18,40] identify concepts through classifying a given entity into a predefined concept set based on text information, but can not find new concepts. Sequence labeling models [22,38] treat the CE problem as a sequence labeling task, but can not handle the problem of *concept overlap*. The concept overlap refers to the phenomenon that a concept term is the subsequence of another concept term. For example, in Fig. 1, once a sequence labeling model labels 'company' as Concept 1, it would not label 'multinational technology company' as a fine-grained concept, since it can not mark a token with different labels.

Machine reading comprehension (MRC) model can extract the answer from the contextual texts for a proposed question. Inspired by MRC model's excellent extraction capability, we handle CE problem as an MRC task in this paper, and propose a novel CE framework named *MRC-CE*, to implement large-scale multi-granular CE from the descriptive texts of given entities. MRC-CE can extract more multi-granular concepts than previous concept extraction models due to the following reasons. Firstly, MRC-CE is built with an MRC model based on BERT [8] (BERT-MRC), which can find abundant new concepts and handle the problem of *concept overlap* well with a pointer network [37]. Secondly, a random forest [30] and rule-based pruning are adopted to filter the candidate concepts output by BERT-MRC, which enhances MRC-CE's precision and recall

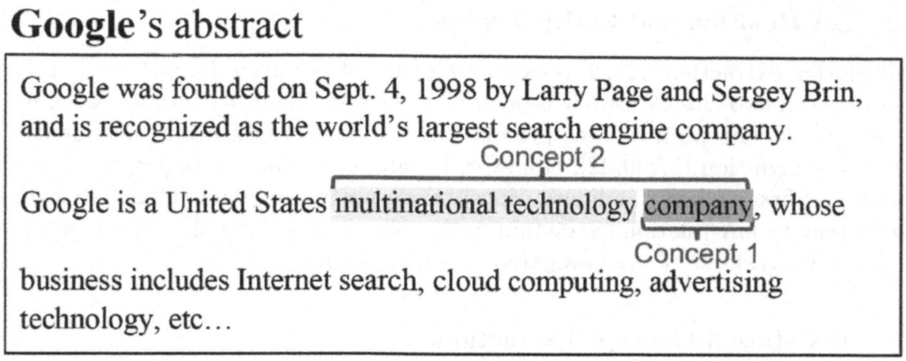

Google's abstract

Google was founded on Sept. 4, 1998 by Larry Page and Sergey Brin, and is recognized as the world's largest search engine company.

Concept 2

Google is a United States multinational technology company, whose

Concept 1

business includes Internet search, cloud computing, advertising technology, etc...

Fig. 1. The abstract text of entity *Google*. The problem of concept overlap in the text is challenging for traditional extraction models to extract multiple concepts from the same span.

simultaneously. Furthermore, MRC-CE has been proven capable of acquiring large-scale multi-granular concepts through our extensive experiments.

The major contributions of this paper can be summarized as follows:

1. To the best of our knowledge, this is the first work to employ MRC model in text-based CE for large-scale KG completion.
2. Through our experiments, more than 7,053,900 new concepts (instanceOf relations) were extracted by our MRC-CE for completing the large-scale Chinese KG *CN-DBpedia*. Furthermore, the online service of CE based on MRC-CE is released on http://kw.fudan.edu.cn.

The rest of this paper is organized as follows. Section 2 is the review of related works and Sect. 3 is the detailed introduction of our framework, respectively. We display our experiment results in Sect. 4 to justify the effectiveness and rationality of MRC-CE. We also display the CE results of applying our framework on CN-DBpedia and Meituan[1] in Sect. 5, and at last conclude our work in Sect. 6.

2   Related Work

In this section, we review some works related to concept acquisition.

2.1   Ontology Extension

Ontology [5] extension focuses more on identifying hypernym-hyponym relationships [23, 46, 47]. Unlike it, our goal is to acquire more new concepts, especially fine-grained concepts, to complete the existing KGs. Thus, we did not compare MRC-CE with these methods in our experiments.

---

[1] https://www.meituan.com.

2.2   IsA Relation and Entity Typing

IsA relation extraction [12,29] is extracting the subsumption (subClassOf) relation between two classes. Entity type aims to classify an entity into a predefined set of types (concepts), such as person, location and organization without new concept recognition [17,40,42]. However, in our setting in this paper, the entity is given at first and its candidate concepts are not pre-defined. Thus, our work is different to isA relation extraction and entity typing, and thus the methods of these two tasks were not compared in our experiments.

2.3   Text-Based Concept Extraction

In this paper, we only focus on extracting the concepts already existing in the texts rather than concept generation. Hence we pay attention to extraction models rather than generative models [2,34]. The existing CE methods can be divided into three categories.

Pattern-Matching Method. Pattern-matching methods [3,4,16,24,36,39,41, 45] try to extract concepts from free texts based on handcrafted patterns or rules. They can acquire accurate concepts, but only have low recall due to the poor generalization ability. Comparatively, our MRC-CE achieves CE task based on MRC model beyond the limitation of handcrafted patterns, and thus acquires more concepts.

Learning-Based Method. Classification models transform CE into classification [9,17,18,40] to determine which concept in a predefined set meets hypernym-hyponym relation with the given entity, but they can not acquire new concepts. Sequence labeling models have been proven effective on extraction tasks [1,21,22,38]. Given the extraction feature, sequence labeling models can also extract concepts from the texts describing entities as our MRC-CE. Recently, pre-trained contextual embeddings have been widely used in sequence labeling models [6,35,43,44] to gain good performance, but can not handle the problem of *concept overlap*.

Knowledge-Based Method. These methods [4,26,27] mainly use the external information from KGs to achieve extraction tasks, resulting in good CE. However, these models have poor generalization ability and only focus on a specific field.

2.4   Machine Reading Comprehension

MRC [19] is a task to seek the answer from contextual texts for a proposed question, which can be categorized into four classes according to answer format, i.e., cloze test, multiple choice, span extraction and free answering. The span extraction [31,33] is most related and similar to our task. The state-of-the-art pre-trained language models [8,20] are often applied in MRC tasks. More recently, many researchers have employed MRC model in accomplishing other NLP tasks, including nested NER [13] and RE [14]. Comparatively, our MRC-CE is the first attempt of employing MRC model in text-based CE.

3   Methodology

In this section, we introduce our CE framework in detail.

3.1   Task Definition

Our CE task can be formulated as follows. Given an entity e and its relevant descriptive text, denoted as a sequence of words $X = \{x_1, x_2, ..., x_n\}$ where $x_i (1 \leq i \leq n)$ is a word token, the CE task aims to find one or multiple spans from X as e's concept(s).

3.2   Data Construction

The descriptive text of high quality plays an important role in text-based CE. Since our task scenario is span extraction, the input text should contain the concept(s) of the given entity. We consider the given entity's abstract in encyclopedia since it is well structured and explicitly mentions the concept(s) of the given entity. In the following introduction, the input text is always referred to the abstract of a given entity. The construction details of our English and Chinese datasets will be introduced in Subsect. 4.1.

3.3   Summary

To employ MRC model for CE, we need to construct appropriate questions towards which the spans in the text are extracted. Since our target is to extract concepts from the abstract of a given entity, we set the question Q as 'What is the concept for [entity]?'. The pipeline of our MRC-CE is displayed in Fig. 2, which can be divided into three modules, i.e., the concept extractor, concept selector and concept pruner. The first module is BERT-MRC built with a pointer network [37], which receives the input text and extracts candidate multi-granular concepts from the text. The second module adopts a random forest [30] to select the desirable concepts from the candidates output by BERT-MRC. The third module prunes away the unsatisfactory concepts from the second module's outputs based on some pruning rules.

3.4   MRC-Based Concept Extractor

The BERT-MRC in our framework is built with a BERT [8] encoder and a pointer network to generate candidate spans along with their corresponding confidence scores of being concepts. We took each entity's concepts from the KG which also exist in the entity's abstract text as the real labels of one training sample.

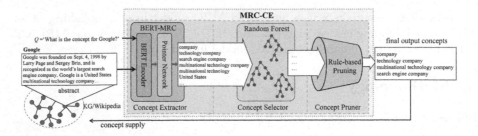

Fig. 2. The pipeline of our MRC-CE framework.

BERT Encoding. In this module, BERT is used as an encoder layer to generate an embedding for each input token, based on which the subsequent pointer network predicts the confidence score for each candidate extracted span. At first, the tokens of input X and the tokens of input X and the question Q are concatenated together as follows, to constitute the input of BERT encoder.

$$\{[CLS]q_1, q_2, ..., q_m[SEP]x_1, x_2, ..., x_n\}$$

where [CLS] and [SEP] are special tokens, and $q_i(1 \leq i \leq m)$ is a token of Q. Then, BERT encoder outputs the text token embedding matrix $\mathbf{E} \in \mathbb{R}^{n \times d}$, where d is the embedding dimension.

Generating Candidate Concepts by Pointer Network. With the token embeddings in $\mathbf{E}$, a pointer network is built to predict the probability of a token being the start position and end position of the answer, through a fully connected layer after the BERT encoder. Then, the confidence score of each span can be calculated as the sum of the probability of its start token and end token. One span can be output repeatedly as the same subsequence of multiple extracted concepts through an appropriate selection threshold. This strategy enables extracting multi-granular concepts. For example, in Fig. 3, 'company' is extracted for multiple times corresponding to three concepts of different granularity, if the confidence score threshold is set to 0.85.

Specifically, we use $\mathbf{p}^{start}, \mathbf{p}^{end} \in \mathbb{R}^n$ to denote the vectors storing each token's probability of being the start position and end position, respectively. They are calculated based on $\mathbf{E}$ as

$$[\mathbf{p}^{start}; \mathbf{p}^{end}] = softmax(\mathbf{EW} + \mathbf{B}) \tag{1}$$

where $\mathbf{W}, \mathbf{B} \in \mathbb{R}^{n \times 2}$ are both trainable parameters. Given a span with x_i and x_j as the start token and the end token, respectively, its confidence score $cs_{ij} \in \mathbb{R}$ can be calculated as

$$cs_{ij} = p_i^{start} + p_j^{end} \tag{2}$$

Then, BERT-MRC generates a ranking list of candidate concepts (spans) along with confidence scores, and outputs the concepts with the confidence scores larger than the selection threshold.

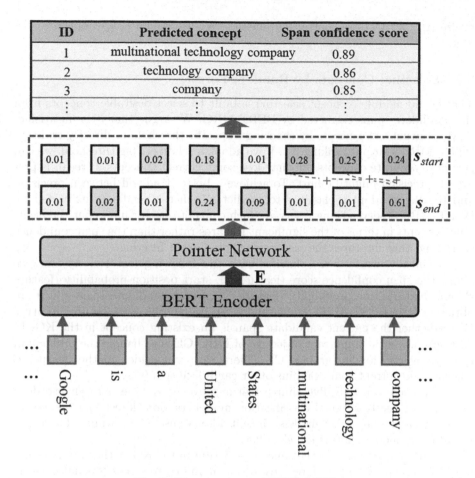

Fig. 3. The structure of BERT-MRC.

BERT-MRC Loss. We adopt cross entropy function $CrossEntropy(\cdot)$ as the loss function of BERT-MRC. Specifically, suppose the set $Y_{start} \in \mathbb{R}^n$ (or $Y_{end} \in \mathbb{R}^n$) contains the real label of an input token $x_i (1 \leq i \leq n)$ being the start (or end) position of a concept. And $Y_{span} \in \mathbb{R}^{C_n^2}$ contains the real label of a span $x_i x_j$ where x_i and x_j are the start position and end position of a concept, respectively. Then, we have the following three losses for the predictions of the three situations:

$$\mathcal{L}_{start} = CrossEntropy(\mathbf{p}^{start}, Y_{start})$$
$$\mathcal{L}_{end} = CrossEntropy(\mathbf{p}^{end}, Y_{end}) \tag{3}$$
$$\mathcal{L}_{span} = CrossEntropy(\mathbf{cs}, Y_{span})$$

Then, the comprehensive loss of training BERT-MRC is

$$\mathcal{L} = \alpha \mathcal{L}_{start} + \beta \mathcal{L}_{end} + (1 - \alpha - \beta) \mathcal{L}_{span} \tag{4}$$

where $\alpha, \beta \in (0, 1)$ are control parameters. We use Adam [10] to optimize the loss.

3.5 Selecting Concepts by Random Forest

The second module (concept selector) is built to select desirable concepts from the candidate spans extracted by BERT-MRC. We argue that it is unsatisfactory to output the concepts by choosing a specific threshold to directly truncate BERT-MRC's output ranking list. If we adopt a relatively big threshold, we can get more accurate concepts but may lose some correct concepts. If recall is preferred, precision might be hurt. To achieve a better trade-off between precision and recall, we adopt a classifier to predict whether a candidate extracted by BERT-MRC deserves being reserved. Such concept selector filters out the desirable concepts in terms of the significant features rather than the span confidence score, and thus improves the performance of concept filtering.

Specifically, we feed the classifer with the following features. At first, we adopt the span confidence score (feature A), start position probability (feature B) and end position probability (feature C) of each candidate span, which are obtained from BERT-MRC. Furthermore, we use another two features. Feature D is whether the current candidate span is an existing concept in the KG. In addition, the most important objective of MRC-CE is to handle the problem of concept overlap for fine-grained CE. Therefore, we consider another feature E whether the current span contains other candidate span(s).

Since there are only five simple features, we do not need to choose deep models. For the traditional classification model, random forest [30] has better accuracy than many other models, since it adopts ensemble learning. Therefore, we adopt random forest as the classifier.

We did not directly use the concepts existing in the KG as the training samples' real labels of random forest given that many correct concepts not existing in the KG can be extracted by BERT-MRC. Thus, we invited some volunteers to label the training samples manually. Specifically, we randomly sampled 1,000 results from BERT-MRC's outputs and requested the volunteers to label whether the result is a correct concept of the corresponding entity. Then, we saved the features and the labels of the results to constitute the training samples. The significance values of the five features obtained through training the random forest towards the Chinese corpus (CN-DBpedia) are listed in Table 1. From the table, we find that except for feature A, feature D is the most significant feature to select desirable concepts. It implies that referring to the existing concepts in KGs is very crucial to extract new concepts.

Table 1. The significance values of the five features in MRC-CE's random forest for Chinese KG *CN-DBpedia*.

Feature	A	B	C	D	E
Significance	0.34	0.20	0.16	0.25	0.05

3.6 Rule-Based Concept Pruning

There are still some wrong concepts being reserved after above concept selection. The errors can be roughly categorized into three classes as below.

1. The extracted concepts are semantically exclusive with each other. For example, both 'president' and 'vice president' could be extracted by BERT-MRC, but they are mutually exclusive in terms of conceptualization. Obviously, a president cannot be a vice president simultaneously.
2. The modifier of a concept is mistakenly extracted as another concept. For example, 'railway' and 'station' are both extracted as concepts from the span 'railway station'.
3. A correct concept is mistakenly mixed with a functional word. For example, both 'is ancient costume drama' and 'in high school' are wrong concepts, where 'is' and 'in' are the redundant tokens.

In this step, some pruning strategies are executed based on explicitly rules, since above errors can be easily recognized according to some pre-defined patterns. For example, for the class that the extracted concepts are mutually exclusive in semantics, we set our pruning rule case by case rather than setting a general rule.

4 Experiments

In this section, in order to justify our framework's CE capability for KG completion, we evaluate its performance upon a Chinese KG *CN-DBpedia* and an English KG *Probase*.

4.1 Datasets

Chinese Dataset. We obtained the latest data of CN-DBpedia from its open websites[2] and randomly selected 100,000 entities along with their concepts and abstract texts, as the sample pool. Then, we randomly selected 500 samples from the sample pool as the test set, and the rest samples were divided as the training and validation set according to 9:1, to learn the models. For BERT-MRC, we took each entity's concepts from the KG which also exist in the entity's abstract text as the real labels of one training sample. For training the random forest, we invited some volunteers to label whether the candidate concepts from BERT-MRC are the given entity' concepts since many correct concepts not existing in the KG can be extracted by BERT-MRC. When evaluating the models with the test samples, we invited some volunteers to assess whether the concepts extracted by the models are correct, given that many new concepts not existing in the KG may be extracted.

---

[2] http://kw.fudan.edu.cn/cndbpedia.

English Dataset. Probase[3] has the hypernym-hyponym relations between concepts and entities, but no abstract texts of entities. Hence, we first fetched the entities along with their concepts from Probase, and then crawled entities' abstract texts from Wikipedia.[4] Particularly, we totally sampled 50,000 entities with their concepts and abstract texts. Then, we constructed the training, validation and test set the same as the Chinese dataset.

4.2 Baselines

We compared our MRC-CE with the following five state-of-the-art models to justify MRC-CE's performance. Please note that, the models we selected are NER and Open IE models since NER and Open IE are extraction tasks which are mostly meet our task scenario. Besides, We also compare the pattern matching approaches.

We did not compare the methods for ontology extension and the generation models, since both of them do not meet our task scenario, i.e., text-based CE. The entity typing models and classification models were also not included because they can not meet the objective to complete existing KGs with new concepts. The knowledge-based methods were also excluded since most of them are only applicable to specific fields.

Hearst Patterns [28]. Hearst patterns are the basic and popular rules for extracting concepts from free texts. We totally designed 5 Hearst patterns to achieve concept extraction, which are listed in Table 2.[5] We allowed leading and following noun phrases to match limited modifiers to extract fine-grained concepts.

Table 2. The full set of Hearst patterns for *CN-DBpedia* and *Probase*.

CN-DBpedia	X is Y
	X is a type/a of Y...
	X is one of Y
	X belongs to Y
	Y is located/founded/ in...
Probase	X is a Y that/which/who
	X is one of Y
	X is a member/part/form... of Y
	X refers to Y
	As Y, X is ...

XLNet-NER [44]. With the capability of modeling bi-directional contexts, XLNet demonstrates an excellent sequence labeling model in many NLP tasks, such as NER and Open IE, which is also applicable to our task.

---

[3] https://www.microsoft.com/en-us/research/project/probase/.
[4] https://www.wikipedia.org/.
[5] We translate Chinese patterns for CN-DBpedia into English.

FLAIR [1]. FLAIR is a novel NLP framework combining different word and document embeddings to achieve excellent results. FLAIR can be employed in our CE task since it can extract spans from the text.

KVMN [22]. As a sequence labeling model, KVMN was proposed to handle NER by leveraging different types of syntactic information through attentive ensemble.

XLM-R [6]. It is a transformer-based multilingual masked language model incorporating XLM [11] and RoBERTa [20]. It can achieve CE task since it is also a sequential labeling model.

BERT-BiLSTM-CRF [35,43]. It is an advanced version of BERT built with BiL-STM and CRF. This language model is used to obtain optimal token embeddings, based on which the downstream tasks such as NER and Open IE, CE are well achieved.

4.3 Experiment Settings

In MRC-CE, we adopted a BERT-base with 12 layers, 12 self-attention heads and $H - 768$ as BERT-MRC's encoder. The training settings are: batch size = 4, learning rate = 3e−5, dropout rate = 0.1 and training epoch = 2. In addition, we set $\alpha = 0.3, \beta = 0.25$ in Eq. 4 based on parameter tuning. Besides, we chose 50 as the tree number of the random forest.

4.4 Experiment Results

CE Performance Comparison. We refer to an extracted concept of a given entity that already exists in the KG as an *EC* (existing concept), and refer to an extracted correct concept of a given entity that does not exist in the KG as a *NC* (new concept). NCs are more significant than ECs given that the primary objective of our work is KG completion, i.e., supplying new instanceOf relations. Please note that a NC in fact corresponds to a new instanceOf relation to a given entity rather than being a unique new concept, because the concept linked by this new instanceOf relation may already exist in the KG as another entity's concept.

All models' CE results of the Chinese dataset and the English dataset are listed in Table 3, where EC # and NC # are the number of existing concepts and new concepts (instanceOf relations) of the entities, respectively. From the table we find that, compared with other models, MRC-CE extracts more NCs. As we claimed before, our framework is capable of extracting fine-grained or long-tail concepts from the texts. To justify it, we counted the average number of characters (for Chinese) or words (for English) constituting ECs (EC length) and NCs (NC length). The larger NC length is, the more possible the NC is to be fine-grained/long-tail. Although Hearst Patterns's NC length is larger than MRC-CE's in the Chinese dataset, it ignores some coarse-grained concepts and thus it can not achieve multi-granular concept extraction. For example, as shown in Table 6, Hearst Patterns only regards 'the railway station of JR East Japan' as a whole concept, whereas MRC-CE can extract 'station', 'railway station' and 'the railway station of JR East Japan' simultaneously from the same span.

Table 3. CE performance comparisons of 500 test samples.

Dataset	Model	EC #	NC #	EC length	NC length	OC ratio	Prec.	R-Recall	R-F1
CN-DBpedia	Hearst Patterns	158	222	2.63	**7.1**	NA	95.24%	27.24%	42.36%
	XLNet-NER	391	46		2.61	NA	89.92%	5.64%	10.62%
	FLAIR	405	63		3.11	NA	**95.51%**	7.73%	14.30%
	KVMN	247	253		4.03	NA	64.27%	31.04%	41.86%
	XLM-R	89	250		5.35	NA	76.35%	30.67%	43.77%
	BERT-BiLSTM-CRF	411	25		4.32	NA	88.26%	3.07%	5.93%
	MRC-CE	**519**	**323**		4.91	**29.35%**	92.22%	**39.63%**	**55.44%**
Probase	Hearst Patterns	308	402	1.25	2.04	NA	**95.56%**	20.18%	33.32%
	XLNet-NER	534	398		1.42	NA	92.00%	19.98%	32.83%
	FLAIR	307	141		1.67	NA	84.69%	7.08%	13.06%
	KVMN	186	404		1.96	NA	47.50%	20.28%	28.43%
	XLM-R	**672**	322		1.48	NA	81.74%	16.16%	26.99%
	BERT-BiLSTM-CRF	191	154		1.68	NA	81.18%	7.73%	14.12%
	MRC-CE	636	**626**		**2.31**	**36.82%**	90.08%	**31.38%**	**46.54%**

To prove MRC-CE's capability of extracting overlapped concepts, we further recorded the ratio of overlapped concepts (one is another one's subsequence) to all extracted concepts, denoted as OC ratio in Table 3. The precision (Prec.) is the ratio of the correct concepts assessed by the volunteers to all concepts extracted by the model. FLAIR obtains the highest Prec. mainly due to its high precision of ECs, but it is howbeit meaningless to KG completion. The denominator of recall is the number of all new (correct) concepts in the input text. Since it is difficult to know all new concepts in the input text except for the costly human assessment, we report the relative recall (R-Recall) to measure the new concept extraction ability of the models. Specifically, the new concepts extracted by all models are regarded as the overall NCs. Then, the relative recall is calculated as NC # divided by the number of overall NCs. Accordingly, the relative F1 (R-F1) can also be calculated with Prec. and R-Recall. The results of Table 3 show that MRC-CE can gain satisfactory precision and recall simultaneously.

Ablation Study. We further display the results of ablation study on the Chinese dataset, to investigate the effectiveness of each module in MRC-CE. At first, we took the BERT-MRC with fixed threshold truncation (FTT) as one ablated variant of our framework [13], denoted as BERT-MRC+FTT. In this variant, we simply chose the spans output by BERT-MRC that have the confidence score higher than 0.8, as the extracted concepts. Furthermore, we respectively appended the rest two modules to BERT-MRC, to propose another two ablated variants, denoted as BERT-MRC+RF and BERT-MRC+RULE.

The comparison results of all variants and MRC-CE (BERT-MRC+RF+RULE) are listed in Table 4. The results show that Prec. drops 1.39% and 0.64% without RULE (BERT-MRC+RF vs. BERT-MRC+RF+RULE), as well as R-Recall drops 3.23% and 17.58% without RF (BERT-MRC+RULE vs. BERT-MRC+RF+RULE) in CN-DBpedia and Probase, respectively. It proves that

Table 4. CE results of ablation study.

Dataset	Model	EC #	NC #	Prec.	R-Recall	R-F1
CN-DBpedia	BERT-MRC+FTT	**522**	311	87.96%	83.83%	85.84%
	BERT-MRC+RF	519	**323**	90.83%	**87.06%**	88.91%
	BERT-MRC+RULE	**522**	311	91.84%	83.83%	87.65%
	BERT-MRC+RF+RULE	519	**323**	**92.22%**	**87.06%**	**89.57%**
Probase	BERT-MRC+FTT	**646**	502	79.56%	71.21%	75.15%
	BERT-MRC+RF	636	**626**	89.44%	**88.79%**	89.12%
	BERT-MRC+RULE	**646**	502	84.72%	71.21%	77.38%
	BERT-MRC+RF+RULE	636	**626**	**90.08%**	**88.79%**	**89.43%**

Table 5. Comparisons between RoBERTa and BERT in CN-DBpedia.

Encoder	Model	EC#	NC#	EC length	NC length	OC ratio	Prec.	R-Recall.	R-F1.
RoBERTa	+FTT	403	105	2.63	4.97	4.75%	92.87%	25.80%	40.38%
	+RF	404	119		4.92	6.69%	89.71%	29.24%	44.10%
	+RULE	403	105		4.91	4.73%	**95.31%**	25.80%	40.61%
	+RF+RULE	404	119		**5.01**	6.93%	94.92%	29.24%	44.71%
BERT	+FTT	**522**	311	2.63	4.72	27.74%	87.96%	76.41%	81.78%
	+RF	519	**323**		4.75	27.26%	90.83%	**79.36%**	84.71%
	+RULE	**522**	311		4.74	27.83%	91.84%	76.41%	83.42%
	+RF+RULE	519	**323**		4.91	**29.35%**	92.22%	**79.36%**	**85.31%**

MRC-CE can obtain better performance with RF and RULE since they are complementary to each other.

Meanwhile, we investigate different BERT-based encoders' influence on CE performance. To this end, we replaced BERT with RoBERTa [20] in Concept Extractor module. Then, RF and RULE were also adopted to filter out the candidate spans output by RoBERTa-MRC. The comparison results are shown in Table 5, showing that although the variants with RoBERTa gain higher Prec., they are inferior to the indicators with BERT on other metrics. It is possibly due to that, RoBERTa tends to extract the spans the same as the concepts existing in the KG from the texts, and thus it is easy to ignore the new concepts.

Case Study. We further delve into the concepts extracted by MRC-CE and baselines through some case studies. Table 6 lists the correct concepts extracted by the models along with the existing concepts of two entities.[6] It shows that MRC-CE extracts more fine-grained and overlapped concepts from the texts than the baselines.

---

[6] *Prince Station*'s abstract text and CE results were translated from Chinese.

Table 6. The CE results of two specific entities along with their existing concepts in the KG.

Dataset	Entity	Abstract text	Model	Correct extracted concept
CN- DBpedia	PrinceStation	Prince station is the railway station of JR East Japan and Tokyo Metro	Existing concepts	location, station
			XLNet-NER	station
			FLAIR	station
			KVMN	railway station
			XLM-R	railway station
			BERT-BiLSTM-CRF	station
			Hearst Patterns	the railway station of JR East Japan
			MRC-CE	station, railway station, the railway station of JR East Japan
Probase	Franklin Delano Roosevelt	Franklin Delano Roosevelt was an American politician who served as the 32nd president. He became a central figure in world events during the first half of the 20th century. As a dominant leader of his party. He built New Deal Coalition	Existing concepts	figure, president, leader, politician
			XLNet-NER	president,leader figure, politician
			FLAIR	politician
			KVMN	politician
			XLM-R	figure, president, leader, politician
			BERT-BiLSTM-CRF	politician
			Hearst Patterns	American politician
			MRC-CE	figure, politician, leader, president, American politician

Table 7. The statistics of extracted concepts for all entities in CN-DBpedia.

Data type	instanceOf relation #	Unique concept #	NC	Avg. NC # per entity	Avg. concept # per entity	Avg. character # per concept
Original	11,494,627	270,025	–	–	2.04	3.62
Extracted	9,021,805	894,689	7,053,900	3.16	5.20	4.92

5   Applications

We further demonstrate MRC-CE's advantages on the KG completion of some real applications.

5.1   KG Completion

After training MRC-CE, we ran it for all entities in CN-DBpedia to supply substantial new instanceOf relations including unique new concepts. Please note that the instanceOf relations only focus on the relations between the entity and concept. The related statistics of CE results are listed in Table 7. Please note that the extracted concepts counted in the table include some wrong concepts. According to the table, MRC-CE extracts more than 7,053,900 new instanceOf relations (NC #). In addition, the extracted concepts have more characters than the original concepts existing in CN-DBpeida. The results justify MRC-CE's capability of extracting large-scale multi-granular concepts for KG completion.

5.2 Domain Concept Acquisition

Our MRC-CE have achieved excellent results concept acquisition on the abstract texts of given entities. In order to verify MRC-CE's capability of acquiring concepts for a certain domain, we also employed MRC-CE in the domain of Meituan which is a famous Chinese e-business platform. Specifically, we collected 117,489 Food & Delight entities in Meituan along with their descriptive texts from CN-DBpedia. After running MRC-CE, we got 458,497 new instanceOf relations from the texts, and the CE precision is 78.0% based on human assessments on 100 samples, justifying that MRC-CE can be successfully applied to domain concept acquisition.

6 Conclusion

In this paper, we propose a concept extraction framework MRC-CE to achieve large-scale multi-granular concept completion for existing KGs. MRC-CE is capable of extracting massive multi-granular concepts from entities' descriptive texts. In our framework, a BERT-based MRC model with a pointer network is built to handle the problems of concept overlap. Meanwhile, a random forest and rule-based pruning are also employed to obtain satisfactory concept extraction (CE) precision and recall simultaneously. Our extensive experiments have justified that our MRC-CE not only has excellent CE performance, but also is competent to acquire large-scale concepts for multilingual KGs. Furthermore, MRC-CE makes a great contribution to supply sufficient concepts for the Chinese KG *CN-Dbpedia*.

References

1. Akbik, A., Bergmann, T., Blythe, D., Rasul, K., Schweter, S., Vollgraf, R.: FLAIR: an easy-to-use framework for state-of-the-art NLP. In: Proceedings of NAACL, pp. 54–59 (2019)
2. Alomari, S., Abdullah, S.: Improving an AI-based algorithm to automatically generate concept maps. Comput. Inf. Sci. **12**(4), 72 (2019)
3. Auer, S., Bizer, C., Kobilarov, G., Lehmann, J., Cyganiak, R., Ives, Z.: DBpedia: a nucleus for a web of open data. In: Aberer, K., et al. (eds.) ASWC/ISWC -2007. LNCS, vol. 4825, pp. 722–735. Springer, Heidelberg (2007). https://doi.org/10.1007/978-3-540-76298-0_52
4. Bai, H., Xing, F.Z., Cambria, E., Huang, W.B.: Business taxonomy construction using concept-level hierarchical clustering. arXiv preprint arXiv:1906.09694 (2019)
5. Budin, G.: Ontology-driven translation management. In: Knowledge Systems and Translation (2005)
6. Conneau, A., et al.: Unsupervised cross-lingual representation learning at scale. arXiv preprint arXiv:1911.02116 (2019)

7. Cui, W., Xiao, Y., Wang, W.: KBQA: an online template based question answering system over freebase. In: Proceedings of IJCAI (2016)
8. Devlin, J., Chang, M.W., Lee, K., Toutanova, K.: BERT: pre-training of deep bidirectional transformers for language understanding. arXiv preprint arXiv:1810.04805 (2018)
9. Ji, J., Chen, B., Jiang, H.: Fully-connected LSTM–CRF on medical concept extraction. Int. J. Mach. Learn. Cybern. **11**(9), 1971–1979 (2020). https://doi.org/10.1007/s13042-020-01087-6
10. Kingma, J., Ba, J.: Adam: a method for stochastic optimization. In: Proceedings of ICLR (2015)
11. Lample, G., Conneau, A.: Crosslingual language model pretraining. In: Proceedings of NeurIPS (2019)
12. Li, N., Tian, M., Lv, S.: Extracting hierarchical relations between the back-of-the-book index terms. In: Hong, J.-F., Zhang, Y., Liu, P. (eds.) CLSW 2019. LNCS (LNAI), vol. 11831, pp. 433–443. Springer, Cham (2020). https://doi.org/10.1007/978-3-030-38189-9_45
13. Li, X., Feng, J., Meng, Y., Han, Q., Wu, F., Li, J.: A unified MRC framework for named entity recognition. In: Proceedings of ACL (2020)
14. Li, X., et al.: Entity-relation extraction as multi-turn question answering. arXiv preprint arXiv:1905.05529 (2019)
15. Liang, J., Xiao, Y., Wang, H., Zhang, Y., Wang, W.: Probase+: inferring missing links in conceptual taxonomies. IEEE Trans. Knowl. Data Eng. **29**(6), 1281–1295 (2017)
16. Liang, J., Xiao, Y., Wang, H., Zhang, Y., Wang, W.: Probase+: inferring missing links in conceptual taxonomies. IEEE TKDE **29**(6), 1281–1295 (2017)
17. Liang, J., Zhang, Y., Xiao, Y., Wang, H., Wang, W., Zhu, P.: On the transitivity of hypernym-hyponym relations in data-driven lexical taxonomies. In: Proceedings of AAAI, vol. 31 (2017)
18. Liao, J., Sun, F., Gu, J.: Combining concept graph with improved neural networks for Chinese short text classification. In: Wang, X., Lisi, F.A., Xiao, G., Botoeva, E. (eds.) JIST 2019. CCIS, vol. 1157, pp. 205–212. Springer, Singapore (2020). https://doi.org/10.1007/978-981-15-3412-6_20
19. Liu, S., Zhang, X., Zhang, S., Wang, H., Zhang, W.: Neural machine reading comprehension: methods and trends. Appl. Sci. **9**(18), 3698 (2019)
20. Liu, Y., et al.: RoBERTa: a robustly optimized BERT pretraining approach. arXiv preprint arXiv:1907.11692 (2019)
21. Nguyen, A.D., Nguyen, K.H., Ngo, V.V.: Neural sequence labeling for Vietnamese POS tagging and NER. In: Proceedings of IEEE-RIVF, pp. 1–5. IEEE (2019)
22. Nie, Y., Tian, Y., Song, Y., Ao, X., Wan, X.: Improving named entity recognition with attentive ensemble of syntactic information. arXiv preprint arXiv:2010.15466 (2020)
23. Petrucci, G., Rospocher, M., Ghidini, C.: Expressive ontology learning as neural machine translation. JWS **52**, 66–82 (2018)
24. Ponzetto, S.P., Strube, M.: WikiTaxonomy: a large scale knowledge resource. In: Proceedings of ECAI, vol. 178, pp. 751–752. Citeseer (2008)
25. Poria, S., Hussain, A., Cambria, E.: EmoSenticSpace: dense concept-based affective features with common-sense knowledge. In: Multimodal Sentiment Analysis. SC, vol. 8, pp. 85–116. Springer, Cham (2018). https://doi.org/10.1007/978-3-319-95020-4_5

26. Preum, S.M., Shu, S., Alemzadeh, H., Stankovic, J.A.: EMSContExt: EMS protocol-driven concept extraction for cognitive assistance in emergency response. In: Proceedings of AAAI, pp. 13350–13355 (2020)
27. Qiu, J., Chai, Y., Tian, Z., Du, X., Guizani, M.: Automatic concept extraction based on semantic graphs from big data in smart city. IEEE Trans. Comput. Soc. Syst. **7**(1), 225–233 (2019)
28. Roller, S., Kiela, D., Nickel, M.: Hearst patterns revisited: automatic hypernym detection from large text corpora. In: Proceedings of ACL (2018)
29. Ruan, D.R., He, X.Y., Li, D.Y., Gao, K.: Modeling and extracting hyponymy relationships on Chinese electric power field content. In: 2016 8th International Conference on Modelling, Identification and Control (ICMIC), pp. 439–443. IEEE (2016)
30. Sammut, C., Webb, G.I. (eds.): Encyclopedia of Machine Learning and Data Mining. Springer, Boston (2017). https://doi.org/10.1007/978-1-4899-7687-1
31. Seo, M., Kembhavi, A., Farhadi, A., Hajishirzi, H.: Bidirectional attention flow for machine comprehension. arXiv preprint arXiv:1611.01603 (2016)
32. Sharma, R., Gopalani, D., Meena, Y.: Concept-based approach for research paper recommendation. In: Shankar, B.U., Ghosh, K., Mandal, D.P., Ray, S.S., Zhang, D., Pal, S.K. (eds.) PReMI 2017. LNCS, vol. 10597, pp. 687–692. Springer, Cham (2017). https://doi.org/10.1007/978-3-319-69900-4_87
33. Shen, Y., Huang, P.S., Gao, J., Chen, W.: ReasoNet: learning to stop reading in machine comprehension. In: Proceedings of ACM SIGKDD, pp. 1047–1055 (2017)
34. Shvets, A., Wanner, L.: Concept extraction using pointer-generator networks. arXiv preprint arXiv:2008.11295 (2020)
35. Song, Y., Tian, S., Yu, L.: A method for identifying local drug names in Xinjiang based on BERT-BiLSTM-CRF. Autom. Control Comput. Sci. **54**(3), 179–190 (2020). https://doi.org/10.3103/S0146411620030098
36. Suchanek, F.M., Kasneci, G., Weikum, G.: YAGO: a core of semantic knowledge. In: Proceedings of WWW (2007)
37. Vinyals, O., Fortunato, M., Jaitly, N.: Pointer networks. In: Proceedings of NIPS, pp. 2692–2700 (2015)
38. Wei, Z., Su, J., Wang, Y., Tian, Y., Chang, Y.: A novel hierarchical binary tagging framework for joint extraction of entities and relations. arXiv preprint arXiv:1909.03227 (2019)
39. Wu, W., Li, H., Wang, H., Zhu, K.Q.: Probase: a probabilistic taxonomy for text understanding. In: Proceedings of ACM SIGMOD, pp. 481–492 (2012)
40. Xu, B., et al.: METIC: multi-instance entity typing from corpus. In: Proceedings of CIKM, pp. 903–912 (2018)
41. Xu, B., et al.: CN-DBpedia: a never-ending Chinese knowledge extraction system. In: Benferhat, S., Tabia, K., Ali, M. (eds.) IEA/AIE 2017. LNCS (LNAI), vol. 10351, pp. 428–438. Springer, Cham (2017). https://doi.org/10.1007/978-3-319-60045-1_44
42. Xu, B., Zhang, Y., Liang, J., Xiao, Y., Hwang, S., Wang, W.: Cross-lingual type inference. In: Navathe, S.B., Wu, W., Shekhar, S., Du, X., Wang, X.S., Xiong, H. (eds.) DASFAA 2016. LNCS, vol. 9642, pp. 447–462. Springer, Cham (2016). https://doi.org/10.1007/978-3-319-32025-0_28
43. Yang, Y., Shen, X., Wang, Y.: BERT-BiLSTM-CRF for Chinese sensitive vocabulary recognition. In: Li, K., Li, W., Wang, H., Liu, Y. (eds.) ISICA 2019. CCIS, vol. 1205, pp. 257–268. Springer, Singapore (2020). https://doi.org/10.1007/978-981-15-5577-0_19

44. Yang, Z., Dai, Z., Yang, Y., Carbonell, J., Salakhutdinov, R.R., Le, Q.V.: XLNet: generalized autoregressive pretraining for language understanding. In: Proceedings of NIPS, pp. 5753–5763 (2019)
45. Yao, J., Cui, B., Cong, G., Huang, Y.: Evolutionary taxonomy construction from dynamic tag space. WWW **15**(5–6), 581–602 (2012). https://doi.org/10.1007/s11280-011-0150-4
46. Yilahun, H., Abdurahman, K., Imam, S., Hamdulla, A.: Automatic extraction of Uyghur domain concepts based on multi-feature for ontology extension. IET Netw. **9**(4), 200–205 (2020)
47. Zhao, G., Zhang, X.: Domain-specific ontology concept extraction and hierarchy extension. In: Proceedings of NLPIR, pp. 60–64 (2018)

Graphhopper: Multi-hop Scene Graph Reasoning for Visual Question Answering

Rajat Koner[1(✉)], Hang Li[1,2], Marcel Hildebrandt[1,2], Deepan Das[3], Volker Tresp[1,2], and Stephan Günnemann[3]

[1] Ludwig Maximilian University of Munich, Munich, Germany
koner@dbs.ifi.lmu.de
[2] Siemens AG, Munich, Germany
[3] Technical University of Munich, Munich, Germany

Abstract. Visual Question Answering (VQA) is concerned with answering free-form questions about an image. Since it requires a deep semantic and linguistic understanding of the question and the ability to associate it with various objects that are present in the image, it is an ambitious task and requires multi-modal reasoning from both computer vision and natural language processing. We propose Graphhopper, a novel method that approaches the task by integrating knowledge graph reasoning, computer vision, and natural language processing techniques. Concretely, our method is based on performing context-driven, sequential reasoning based on the scene entities and their semantic and spatial relationships. As a first step, we derive a scene graph that describes the objects in the image, as well as their attributes and their mutual relationships. Subsequently, a reinforcement learning agent is trained to autonomously navigate in a multi-hop manner over the extracted scene graph to generate reasoning paths, which are the basis for deriving answers. We conduct an experimental study on the challenging dataset GQA, based on both manually curated and automatically generated scene graphs. Our results show that we keep up with human performance on manually curated scene graphs. Moreover, we find that Graphhopper outperforms another state-of-the-art scene graph reasoning model on both manually curated and automatically generated scene graphs by a significant margin.

Keywords: Visual Question Answering (VQA) · Knowledge graph reasoning · Scene graph reasoning · Multi-modal reasoning · Reinforcement learning

1 Introduction

Visual Question Answering (VQA) is a challenging task that involves understanding and reasoning over two data modalities, i.e., images and natural lan-

---

R. Koner, H. Li and M. Hildebrandt—Equal contribution.

Electronic supplementary material The online version of this chapter (https:// doi.org/10.1007/978-3-030-88361-4_7) contains supplementary material, which is available to authorized users.

A. Hotho et al. (Eds.): ISWC 2021, LNCS 12922, pp. 111–127, 2021.
https://doi.org/10.1007/978-3-030-88361-4_7

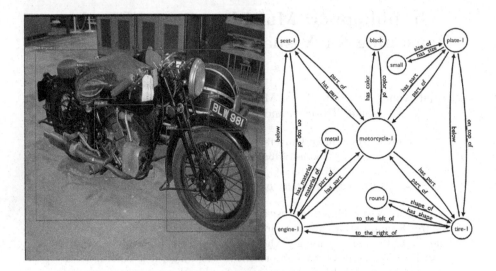

Fig. 1. Example of an image and the corresponding scene graph. Since the scene graph is a directed graph with typed edges, it resembles a knowledge graph and permits the application of knowledge-base completion techniques.

guage. Given an image and a free-form question which formulates a query about the presented scene—the issue is for the algorithm to find the correct answer.

VQA has been studied from the perspective of scene and knowledge graphs [6,33], as well as vision-language reasoning [1,10]. To study VQA, various real-world data sets, such as the *VQA* data set [4,24], have been generated. It has been argued that, in the *VQA* data set, many of the apparently challenging reasoning tasks can be solved by an algorithm through exploiting trivial prior knowledge, and thus by shortcuts to proper reasoning (e.g., clouds are white or doors are made of wood). To address these shortcomings, the *GQA* dataset [17] has been developed. Compared to other real-world datasets, *GQA* is more suitable for evaluating reasoning abilities since the images and questions are carefully filtered to make the data less prone to biases.

Plenty of VQA approaches are agnostic towards the explicit relational structure of the objects in the presented scene and rely on monolithic neural network architectures that process regional features of the image separately [2,39]. While these methods led to promising results on previous datasets, they lack explicit compositional reasoning abilities, which results in weaker performance on more challenging datasets such as *GQA*. Other works [15,31,34] perform reasoning on explicitly detected objects and interactive semantic and spatial relationships among them. These approaches are closely related to the scene graph representations [19] of an image, where detected objects are labeled as nodes and relationships between the objects are labeled as edges. In this work, we aim to combine VQA techniques with recent research advances in the area of statistical relation learning on knowledge graphs (KGs). KGs provide human-understandable, structured representations of knowledge about the real world via collections of factual statements. Inspired by multi-hop reasoning methods on KGs such as [8,12,38], we propose Graphhopper, a novel method that models the VQA task as a path-finding problem on scene graphs. The underlying idea can be summarized with the phrase: Learn to walk to the correct answer. More specifically, given an image, we consider a scene graph and train a reinforcement learning agent to conduct a policy-guided random walk on the scene graph until a conclusive infer-ence path is obtained. In contrast to purely embedding-based approaches, our method provides explicit reasoning chains that lead to the derived answers. To sum up, our major contributions are as follows.

- Graphhopper is the first VQA method that employs reinforcement learning for multi-hop reasoning on scene graphs.
- We conduct a thorough experimental study on the challenging VQA dataset named QGA to show the compositional and *interpretable* nature of our model.
- To analyze the reasoning capabilities of our method, we consider manually curated (ground truth) scene graphs. This setting isolates the noise asso-ciated with the visual perception task and focuses solely on the language understanding and reasoning task. Thereby, we can show that our method achieves human-like performance.
- Based on both the manually curated scene graphs and our own automatically generated scene graphs, we show that Graphhopper outperforms the Neural State Machine (NMS), a state-of-the-art scene graph reasoning model that operates in a setting, similar to Graphhopper.

Moreover, we are the first group to conduct experiments and publish the code on generated scene graphs for the GQA dataset.[1] The remainder of this work is organized as follows. We review related literature in the next section. Section 3 introduces the notation and describes the methodology of Graph-hopper. Section 4 and Sect. 5 detail an experimental study on the benchmark dataset GQA. Furthermore, through a rigorous study using both manually-curated ground-truth and generated scene graphs, we examine the reasoning capabilities of Graphhopper. We conclude in Sect. 6.

2   Related Work

Visual Question Answering: Various models have been proposed that perform VQA on both real-world [4,17] and artificial datasets [18]. Currently, leading VQA approaches can be categorized into two different branches: First, mono-lithic neural networks, which perform implicit reasoning on latent representations obtained from fusing the two data modalities. Second, multi-hop methods that form explicit symbolic reasoning chains on a structured representation of the data. Monolithic network architectures obtain visual features from the image either in the form of individual detected objects or by processing the whole

---

[1] Code is available at: https://github.com/rajatkoner08/Graphhopper.

image directly via convolutional neural networks (CNNs). The derived embeddings are usually scored against a fixed answer set along with the embedding of the question obtained from a sequence model. Moreover, co-attention mechanisms are frequently employed to couple the vision and the language models allowing for interactions between objects from both modalities [2,5,20,40,41]. Monolithic networks are among the dominant methods on previous real-world VQA datasets such as [4]. However, they suffer from the black-box problem and possess limited reasoning capabilities with respect to complex questions that require long reasoning chains (see [7] for a detailed discussion).

Explicit reasoning methods combine the sub-symbolic representation learning paradigm with symbolic reasoning approaches over structured representations of the image. Most of the popular explicit reasoning approaches follow the idea of neural module networks (NMNs) [3] which perform a sequence of reasoning steps realized by forward passes through specialized neural networks that each correspond to predefined reasoning subtasks. Thereby, NMNs construct functional programs by dynamically assembling the modules resulting in a question-specific neural network architecture. In contrast to the monolithic neural network architectures described above, these methods contain a natural transparency mechanism via functional programs. However, while NMN-related methods (e.g., [14,26]) exhibit good performance on synthetic datasets such as CLEVR [18], they require functional module layouts as additional supervision signals to obtain good results. Closely related to our method is the Neural State Machine (NSM) proposed by [16]. NSM's underlying idea consists of first constructing a scene graph from an image and treating it as a state machine. Concretely, the nodes correspond to states and edges to transitions. Then, conditioned on the question, a sequence of instructions is derived that indicates how to traverse the scene graph and arrive at the answer. In contrast to NSM, we treat path-finding as a decision problem in a reinforcement learning setting. Concretely, we outline in the next section how extracting predictive paths from scene graphs can be naturally formulated in terms of a goal-oriented random walk induced by a stochastic policy that allows the approach to balance between exploration and exploitation. Moreover, our framework integrates state-of-the-art techniques from graph representation learning and NLP. This paper only considers basic policy gradient methods, but more sophisticated reinforcement learning techniques will be employed in future works.

Statistical Relational Learning: Machine learning methods for KG reasoning aim at exploiting statistical regularities in observed connectivity patterns. These methods are studied under the umbrella of statistical relational learning (SRL) [27]. In recent years, KG embeddings have become the dominant approach in SRL. The underlying idea is that graph features that explain the connectivity pattern of KGs can be encoded in low-dimensional vector spaces. In the embedding spaces, the interactions among the embeddings for entities and relations can be efficiently modeled to produce scores that predict the validity of a triple. Despite achieving good results in KG reasoning tasks, most embedding-based methods have problems capturing the compositionality expressed by long reasoning chains. This often limits their applicability in complex reasoning tasks. Recently, multi-hop reasoning methods such as MINERVA [8] and DeepPath [38] were proposed. Both methods are based on the idea that a reinforcement learning agent is trained to perform a policy-guided random walk until the answer entity to a query is reached. Thereby, the path finding problem of the agent can be modeled in terms of a sequential decision making task framed as a Markov decision process (MDP). The method that we propose in this work follows a similar philosophy, in the sense that we train an RL agent to navigate on a scene graph to the correct answer node. However, a conceptual difference is that the agents in MINERVA and DeepPath perform walks on large-scale knowledge graphs exploiting repeating statistical patterns. Thereby, the policies implicitly incorporate approximate rules. In addition, instead of free-form processing questions, the query in the KG reasoning setting is structured as a pair of symbolic entities. That is why we propose a wide range of modifications to adjust our method to the challenging VQA setting.

3   Method

The task of VQA is framed as a scene graph traversal problem. Starting from a hub node that is connected to all other nodes, an agent sequentially samples transitions to neighboring nodes on the scene graph until the node corresponding to the answer is reached. In this way, by adding transitions to the current path, the reasoning chain is successively extended. Before describing the decision problem of the agent, we introduce the notation that we use throughout this work.

Notation: A scene graph is a directed multigraph where each node corresponds to a scene entity which is either an object associated with a bounding box or an attribute of an object. Each scene entity comes with a type that corresponds to the predicted object or attribute label. Typed edges specify how scene entities are related to each other. More formally, let $\mathcal{E}$ denote the set of scene entities and consider the set of binary relations $\mathcal{R}$. Then a scene graph $SG \subset \mathcal{E} \times \mathcal{R} \times \mathcal{E}$ is a collection of ordered triples (s, p, o) - subject, predicate, and object. For example, as shown in Fig. 1, the triple *(motorcycle-1, has_part, tire-1)* indicates that both a motorcycle (subject) and a tire (object) are detected in the image. The predicate *has_part* indicates the relation between the entities. Moreover, we denote with p^{-1} the inverse relation corresponding to the predicate p. For the remainder of this work, we impose completeness with respect to inverse relations in the sense that for every $(s, p, o) \in SG$ it is implied that $(o, p^{-1}, s) \in SG$.

Environment. The state space of the agent $\mathcal{S}$ is given by $\mathcal{E} \times \mathcal{Q}$ where $\mathcal{E}$ are the nodes of a scene graph SG and $\mathcal{Q}$ denotes the set of all questions. The state at time t is the entity e_t at which the agent is currently located and the question Q. Thus, a state $S_t \in \mathcal{S}$ for time $t \in \mathbb{N}$ is represented by $S_t = (e_t, Q)$. The set of available actions from a state S_t is denoted by $\mathcal{A}_{S_t}$. It contains all outgoing

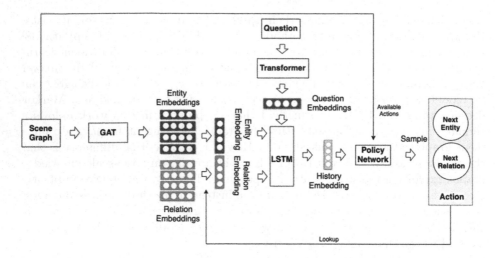

Fig. 2. The architecture of our scene graph reasoning module.

edges from the node e_t together with their corresponding object nodes. More formally, $\mathcal{A}_{S_t} = \{(r, e) \in \mathcal{R} \times \mathcal{E} : S_t = (e_t, Q) \wedge (e_t, r, e) \in \mathcal{SG}\}$. Moreover, we denote with $A_t \in \mathcal{A}_{S_t}$ the action that the agent performed at time t. We include self-loops for each node in $\mathcal{SG}$ that produce a *NO_OP*-label. These self-loops allow the agent to remain at the current location if it reaches the answer node. Furthermore, the introduction of inverse relations allows agent to transit freely in any direction between two nodes (Fig. 2).

The environments evolve deterministically by updating the state according to previous action. Formally, the transition function at time t is given by $\delta_t(S_t, A_t) := (e_{t+1}, Q)$ with $S_t = (e_t, Q)$ and $A_t = (r, e_{t+1})$.

Auxiliary Nodes: In addition to standard entity relation nodes present in a scene graph, we introduce a few auxiliary nodes (e.g. hub node). The underlying rationale for the inclusion of auxiliary nodes is that they facilitate the walk for the agent or help to frame the QA-task as a goal-oriented walk on the scene graph. These additional nodes are included during run-time graph traversal, but they are ignored during the compile time such as when computing node embedding. For example, we add a hub node (*hub*) to every scene graph which is connected to all other nodes. The agent then starts the scene graph traversal from a *hub* with global connectivity. Furthermore for a binary question, we add YES and NO nodes to the scene entities that correspond to the final location of the agent. The agent can then transition to either the YES or the NO node.

Question and Scene Graph Processing. We initialize words in Q with GloVe embeddings [29] with dimension $d = 300$. Similarly we initialize entities and relations in $\mathcal{SG}$ with the embeddings of their type labels. In the scene graph, the node embeddings are passed through a multi-layered graph attention network (GAT) [36]. Extending the idea from graph convolutional networks [22] with a self-attention mechanism, GATs mimic the convolution operator on regular grids where an entity embedding is formed by aggregating node features from its neighbors. Relations and inverse relations between nodes allows context to flow in both ways through GAT. Thus, the resulting embeddings are context-aware, which makes nodes with the same type, but different graph neighborhoods, distinguishable. To produce an embedding for the question Q, we first apply a Transformer [35], followed by a mean pooling operation.

Finally, since we added auxiliary *YES* and *NO* nodes to the scene graph for binary questions, we train a feedforward neural network to classify query-type (i.e., questions that query for an object in the depicted scene) and binary questions. This network consists of two fully connected layers with ReLU activation on the intermediate output. We find that it is easy to distinguish between query and binary questions (e.g., query questions usually begin with *What, Which, How*, etc., whereas binary questions usually begin with *Do, Is*, etc.). Since our classifier achieves 99.99% accuracy we will ignore the error in question classification in the following discussions.

Policy. We denote the agent's history until time t with the tuple $H_t = (H_{t-1}, A_{t-1})$ for $t \geq 1$ and $H_0 = hub$ along with $A_0 = \emptyset$ for $t = 0$. The history is encoded via a multilayered LSTM [13]

$$\mathbf{h}_t = \text{LSTM}\left(\mathbf{a}_{t-1}\right), \tag{1}$$

where $\mathbf{a}_{t-1} = [\mathbf{r}_{t-1}, \mathbf{e}_t] \in \mathbb{R}^{2d}$ corresponds to the embedding of the previous action with $\mathbf{r}_{t-1}$ and $\mathbf{e}_t$ denoting the embeddings of the edge and the target node into $\mathbb{R}^d$, respectively. The history-dependent action distribution is given by

$$\mathbf{d}_t = \text{softmax}\left(\mathbf{A}_t\left(\mathbf{W}_2\text{ReLU}\left(\mathbf{W}_1\left[\mathbf{h}_t, \mathbf{Q}\right]\right)\right)\right), \tag{2}$$

where the rows of $\mathbf{A}_t \in \mathbb{R}^{|\mathcal{A}_{S_t}| \times d}$ contain latent representations of all admissible actions. Moreover, $\mathbf{Q} \in \mathbb{R}^d$ encodes the question Q. The action $A_t = (r, e) \in \mathcal{A}_{S_t}$ is drawn according to categorical $(\mathbf{d}_t)$. Equations (1) and (2) induce a stochastic policy π_θ, where θ denotes the set of trainable parameters.

Rewards and Optimization. After sampling T transitions, a terminal reward is assigned according to

$$R = \begin{cases} 1 & \text{if } e_T \text{ is the answer to } Q, \\ 0 & \text{otherwise.} \end{cases} \tag{3}$$

We employ REINFORCE [37] to maximize the expected rewards. Thus, the agent's maximization problem is given by

$$\arg\max_\theta \mathbb{E}_{Q \sim \mathcal{T}} \mathbb{E}_{A_1, A_2, \ldots, A_N \sim \pi_\theta} \left[R \,\middle|\, e_c\right], \tag{4}$$

where $\mathcal{T}$ denote the set of training questions. During training the first expectation in Eq. (4) is substituted with the empirical average over the training set. The second expectation is approximated by the empirical average over multiple roll-outs. We also employ a moving average baseline to reduce the variance. Further, we use entropy regularization with parameter $\lambda \in \mathbb{R}_{\geq 0}$ to enforce exploration. During inference, we do not sample paths but perform a beam search with width 20 based on the transition probabilities given by Eq. (2).

Additional details on the model, the training and the inference procedure along with sketches of the algorithms, and a complexity analysis can be found in the supplementary material.

4   Dataset and Experimental Setup

In this section we introduce the dataset and detail the experimental protocol.

4.1   Dataset

The *GQA* dataset [17] has been introduced with the goal of addressing key short-comings of previous VQA datasets, such as *CLEVR* [18] or the *VQA* dataset [4]. *GQA* is more suitable for evaluating the reasoning and compositional abilities of a model in a realistic setting. It contains 113K images, and around 1.2M questions split into roughly 80%/10%/10% for the training, validation, and testing. The overall vocabulary size consists of 3097 words, including 1702 object classes, 310 relationships, and 610 object attributes.

Due to the large number of objects and relationships present in GQA, we used a pruned version of the dataset (see Sect. 5) for our generated scene graph. In this work, we have conducted two primary experiments. First, we report the results on manually curated scene graphs provided in the *GQA* dataset. In this setting, the true reasoning and language understanding capabilities of our model can be analyzed. Afterward, we evaluate the performance of our model with the generated scene graphs on pruned GQA dataset. It shows the performance of our model on noisy generated data. We have used state of the art Relation Transformer Network (RTN) [23] for the scene graph generation and DetectoRS [30] for object detection. We have conducted all the experiments on "test-dev" split of the GQA.

Question Types: The questions are designed to evaluate the reasoning abilities such as visual verification, relational reasoning, spatial reasoning, comparison, and logical reasoning. These questions can be categorized either according to structural or semantic criteria. An overview of the different question types is given in supplementary (see Table 4).

4.2   Experimental Setup

Scene Graph Reasoning: Regarding the model parameters, we apply 300 dimensional GloVe embeddings to both the questions and the graphs (i.e., edges and nodes). Moreover, we employ a two-layer GAT [36] model. The dropout [32] probability of each layer is set to 0.1. The first layer has eight attention heads.

Each head has eight latent features which are concatenated to form the output features of that layer. The output layer has eight attention heads with mean aggregation, so that the output also has 300-dimensional features. We apply dropout with $p = 0.1$ to the attention coefficients at each layer. This essentially means that each node is exposed to a stochastically sampled neighborhood during training. Moreover, we employ a two-layer Transformer [35] decoder model. The model dimension is set to 300, and the key and query dimensions are both set to 64 with dropout $p = 0.1$. The LSTM of the policy networks consists of a uni-directional layer with hidden size 300. Finally, the agent performs a fixed number of transitions. In question answering, most questions concern one subject to be explored within one reasoning path originated from the start node. Hence, we set the maximum number of steps to 4, without resetting. By contrast, the binary questions have 8 steps and a reset frequency of 4. In other words, the agent is prompted to the hub node after the fourth step.

Training the Graphhopper: In terms of the training procedure, the GAT, the Transformer, and the policy networks are initialized with Glorot [11] initialization. We train our model with data from the *val_balanced_questions* tier. We use a batch size of 64 and sample a batch of questions along with their associated graphs. We collect 20 stochastic rollouts for each question performed in a vectorized form to utilize parallel computation. For each batch, we collect the rewards when a complete forward pass is done. Then the gradients are approximated from the rewards and applied to update the weights. We employ the Adam optimizer [21] with a learning rate of 10^{-4} for all trainable weights. The coefficient for the action entropy, which balances exploration and exploitation, starts from 0.2 and decreases exponentially at each step with a factor 0.99.

Next to other standard Python libraries, we mainly employed PyTorch [28]. All experiments were conducted on a machine with one NVIDIA RTX 2080 Ti GPU and 64 GB RAM. Training the scene graph reasoner of Graphhopper for 40 epochs on GQA takes around 10 h, testing about 1 h.

4.3   Performance Metrics

Along with the accuracy (i.e., Hits@1) on open questions ("Open"), binary questions (yes/no) ("Binary"), and the overall accuracy ("Accuracy"), we also report the additional metric "Consistency" (answers should not contradict themselves), "Validity" (answers are in the range of a question; e.g., *red* is a valid answer when asked for the color of an object), "Plausibility" (answers should be reasonable; e.g., red is a reasonable color of an apple reasonable, blue is not), as proposed in [17].

5   Results and Discussion

As outlined before, VQA is a challenging task, and there is still a significant performance gap between state-of-the-art VQA methods and human performance on challenging, real-world datasets such as GQA (see [17]). Similar to other existing methods, our architecture involves multiple components, and it important to be able to analyse the performance of the different modules and processing steps in isolation. Therefore we first present the results of our experiments on manually curated, ground-truth scene graphs provided in the GQA dataset and compare the performance of Graphhopper against NSM and humans. This setting allows us to isolate the noise from the visual perception component and quantify our methods' reasoning capabilities. Subsequently, we present the results with our own generated scene graphs.

In addition, we also observed that the inclusion of auxiliary nodes helps the agent to achieve efficient performance. *Hub* node performs better compare to starting from any random nodes, as its facilitate easier forward and backtracking from a node. For binary question instead of YES or NO node, we experimented where the path of the agent was processed by another classifier (e.g., a logistic regression) and the classification logits were assigned as rewards. However, this led to inferior results; most likely due to the absence of a weight-sharing mechanism and due to the noisy reward signal produced by the classifier. These observations supports our assumption on the role of auxiliary nodes we have used in scene graph.

Reproducing NSM: [15] proposed the state of the art method named NSM for VQA. NSM is the conceptually most similar method, as it also exploits the scene graph reasoning for VQA. We consider NSM to be our baseline method for comparison. However, their approach to reasoning is different from ours. To compare the reasoning ability of our method with the same generated scene graph, we tried to reproduce NSM, as the code for NSM is not open-sourced. We have used the available parameters from [15] and the implementation from [9].

Table 1. A comparison of Graphhopper with human performance and NSM based on manually curated scene graphs.

Method	Binary	Open	Consistency	Validity	Plausibility	Accuracy
Human [17]	91.2	87.4	**98.4**	**98.9**	**97.2**	89.3
NSM [15]	51.03	18.79	81.36	83.69	79.12	34.5
Graphhopper	**92.18**	**92.40**	91.92	93.68	93.13	**92.30**

5.1   Results on Manually Curated Scene Graphs

In this section, we report on an experimental study with Graphhopper on the manually curated scene graphs provided along with the *GQA* dataset. Table 1 shows the performance of Graphhopper and compares it with the human performance reported in [17] and with the performance of NSM on the same underlying manually curated scene graphs. We find that Graphhopper strictly outperforms

NSM with respect to all performance measures. In particular, on the open questions, the performance gap is significant. Moreover, Graphhopper also slightly outperforms humans with respect to the accuracy on both types of questions. On the other hand, concerning the supplementary performance measures consistency, validity, and plausibility, Graphhopper is outperformed by humans but nevertheless consistently reaches high values. Overall, these results can be seen as a testament of the reasoning capabilities and establish an upper bound to the performance of Graphhopper.

5.2   Results on Automatically Generated Graph

The process of generating a graph representation for visual data is a costly and complex procedure. Although the scene graph generation is not the main focus of this work, it constituted one of the major challenges to create good scene graph for GQA due to the following facts:

- There is no open source code for GQA scene graph generation or object detection.
- A large number of instances and an uneven class distribution in GQA leads to a significant drop in the accuracy compared to existing scene graph datasets (see [24]).
- There is a lack of attribute prediction models in modern object detection frameworks.

In this work, we address all of these challenges as our model's performance is directly dependent on the quality of the scene graph. We will also open-source our code base for transparency and accelerate the development scene graph-based reasoning for VQA.

Generation of Scene Graph: To address these problems, first, we choose two state-of-the-art network, RTN [23] for scene graph generation, and DetectoRS [30] for object detection. The transformer [35] based architecture of RTN and its contextual scene graph embedding is most closely related to our architecture and for our future expansion. To make Graphhopper generic to any scene graph generator, we haven't use contextualized embedding from RTN, instead we rely on GAT for contextualization.

Pruning of GQA: GQA has more than 6 times the number of relationships compared to Visual Genome [24], which is the most used scene graph generation dataset, and contains more than 18 times the number of objects compared to the most common object detection dataset COCO [25]. Also, the class distribution is highly skewed which causes a significant drop in the accuracy for both the object detection and the scene graph generation task. To efficiently prune the number of instances, we take the first 800 classes, 170 relationships, and 200 attributes based on their frequency of occurrence in the training questions and answers. This pruning allows us to reduce more than 60% of the words while covering more than 96% of the combined answers in the training set.

  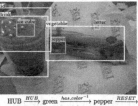

HUB $\xrightarrow{HUB}$ white $\xrightarrow{has\_color^{-1}}$ number $\xrightarrow{RESET}$
HUB $\xrightarrow{HUB}$ black $\xrightarrow{has\_color^{-1}}$ wristband → no

HUB $\xrightarrow{HUB}$ large $\xrightarrow{NO\_OP}$ large $\xrightarrow{has\_size^{-1}}$ refrigerator

HUB $\xrightarrow{HUB}$ green $\xrightarrow{has\_color^{-1}}$ pepper $\xrightarrow{RESET}$
HUB $\xrightarrow{HUB}$ green $\xrightarrow{has\_color^{-1}}$ vegetable → yes

(a) Question: Is the color of the number the same as that of the wristband? Answer: No.

(b) Question: What is the name of the appliance that is not small? Answer: Refrigerator.

(c) Do both the pepper and the vegetable to the right of the ice cube have green color? Answer: Yes.

Fig. 3. Three examples question and the corresponding images and paths.

Attribute Prediction: One of the shortcomings of existing scene graph generation and object detection networks is that they do not predict the attributes (e.g., the color or size of an object) of a detected object. Therefore, we have incorporated the attribute prediction for answering the question on GQA. Contextualized object embedding from RTN [23] is used for attribute prediction as

$$P_{attribute} = \sigma(W(Obj_{context}, P_{obj})), \qquad (5)$$

where W, $Obj_{context}$, P_{obj}, $P_{attribute}$ are the weight matrices of a linear layer, the contextual embedding of an object, the probability distribution over all objects and the probability distribution over the attributes. σ denotes the sigmoid function.

We have trained both the object detector and the scene graph generator on a pruned version of GQA with their respective default parameters after the prepossessing. This helps to increase the coverage of all the instances (e.g., objects, attributes, relationships) on training questions from 52% to 77% implying that our generated scene graph now covers 77% of all instances that represent answers to the training questions.

Table 2. A comparison of our method with NSM, based on generated scene graphs. Graphhopper (pr) indicates that we employed predicted relations from RTN [23].

Method	Binary	Open	Consistency	Validity	Plausibility	Accuracy
NSM [15]	51.88	19.83	82.01	86.28	81.75	35.34
Graphhopper	**69.48**	**44.69**	**83.64**	**89.42**	**85.13**	**56.69**
Graphhopper (pr)	85.84	77.27	92.98	92.26	89.50	81.41

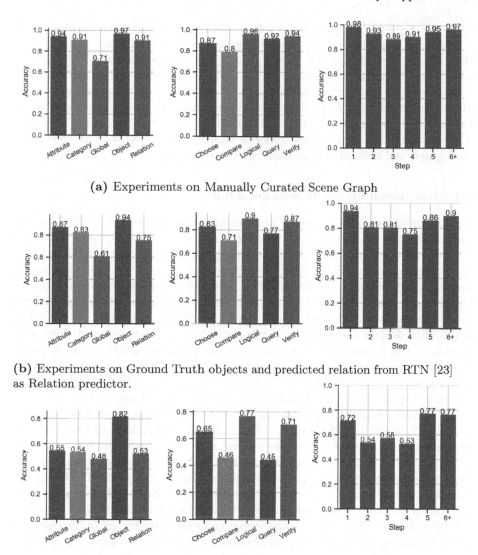

(a) Experiments on Manually Curated Scene Graph

(b) Experiments on Ground Truth objects and predicted relation from RTN [23] as Relation predictor.

(c) Experiments on Generated Scene Graph using DetectoRS [30] object detector and RTN [23] as Scene Graph generator.

Fig. 4. Comparison of the performance of our model on various Scene Graph generation settings, (left) accuracy across various semantic instances ("Attribute", "Global", "Relation" etc.) required to answer a question (middle) accuracy on multiple types of question category ("Choose", "Logical", "Verify" etc.) and (right) accuracy on minimum number of steps needed to reach the answer node.

Table 2, shows the performance of Graphhopper in two settings: First, with a generated graph where we predict the classes, the attributes, and relationships using our own pipeline. Second, where we only use the predicted relationships from RTN [23] (with ground truth objects and attributes). We find that Graphhopper consistently outperforms NSM [15] based on the generated graph. Moreover, in the "pr" or predicted relations setting, it achieves an even higher score as the graphs do not contain any misprediction from the object detector. These encouraging results show superior reasoning abilities both on the generated graph and generated relationships between objects.

5.3 Discussion on the Reasoning Ability

To further analyze the reasoning abilities of Graphhopper, Fig. 4 disentangles the results according to different types of questions: 5 semantic types (left) and 5 structural types (middle). Moreover, we report the performance of Graphhopper according to the length of the reasoning path (right) (see the supplementary material for additional information). Moreover, we show the performance of Graphhopper separately for each of the three scene graph settings that we considered in this work. Figure 4a shows performance on a manually curated scene graph that depicts the actual performance in an ideal environment. Figure 4b illustrates the performance based on only the predicted relationships between objects. This setting shows the performance of Graphhopper along with a scene graph generator. Finally, Fig. 4c depicts the performance based on the object detector, the scene graph generator, and Graphhopper. First and foremost, we find that Graphhopper consistently achieves high accuracy on all types of questions in every setting. Moreover, we find that the performance of Graphhopper does not suffer if answering the questions requires many reasoning steps. We conjecture that this is because high-complexity questions are harder to answer, but due to proper contextualization of the embeddings (e.g., via the GAT and the Transformer), the agent can extract the specific information that identifies the correct target node. The good performance on these high-complexity questions can be seen as evidence that Graphhopper can efficiently translate the question into a transition on the scene graph hopping until the correct answer is reached.

Examples of Reasoning Path: Figure 3 shows three examples of scene graph traversals of Graphhopper that lead to the correct answer. One can see in these examples that the sequential reasoning process over explicit scene graph entities makes the reasoning process more comprehensible. In the case of wrong predictions, the extracted path may offer insights into the mechanics of Graphhopper and facilitate debugging.

6 Conclusion

We have proposed Graphhopper, a novel method for visual question answering that integrates existing KG reasoning, computer vision, and natural language processing techniques. Concretely, an agent is trained to extract conclusive reasoning paths from scene graphs. To analyze the reasoning abilities of our method, we conducted a rigorous experimental study on both manually curated and generated scene graphs. Based on the manually curated scene graphs we showed that Graphhopper reaches human performance. Moreover, we find that, on our own automatically generated scene graph, Graphhopper outperform another state-of-the-art scene graph reasoning model with respect to all considered performance metrics. In future works, we plan to combine scene graphs with common sense knowledge graphs to further enhance the reasoning abilities of Graphhopper.

References

1. Abbasnejad, E., Teney, D., Parvaneh, A., Shi, J., Hengel, A.V.D.: Counterfactual vision and language learning. In: Proceedings of the IEEE/CVF Conference on Computer Vision and Pattern Recognition, pp. 10044–10054 (2020)
2. Anderson, P., et al.: Bottom-up and top-down attention for image captioning and visual question answering. In: Proceedings of the IEEE Conference on Computer Vision and Pattern Recognition, pp. 6077–6086 (2018)
3. Andreas, J., Rohrbach, M., Darrell, T., Klein, D.: Neural module networks. In: Proceedings of the IEEE Conference on Computer Vision and Pattern Recognition, pp. 39–48 (2016)
4. Antol, S., et al.: VQA: visual question answering. In: Proceedings of the IEEE International Conference on Computer Vision, pp. 2425–2433 (2015)
5. Cadene, R., Ben-Younes, H., Cord, M., Thome, N.: MUREL: multimodal relational reasoning for visual question answering. In: Proceedings of the IEEE Conference on Computer Vision and Pattern Recognition, pp. 1989–1998 (2019)
6. Chen, L., Zhang, H., Xiao, J., He, X., Pu, S., Chang, S.F.: Counterfactual critic multi-agent training for scene graph generation. In: Proceedings of the IEEE/CVF International Conference on Computer Vision, pp. 4613–4623 (2019)
7. Chen, W., Gan, Z., Li, L., Cheng, Y., Wang, W., Liu, J.: Meta module network for compositional visual reasoning. arXiv preprint arXiv:1910.03230 (2019)
8. Das, R., et al.: Go for a walk and arrive at the answer: reasoning over paths in knowledge bases using reinforcement learning. In: ICLR (2018)
9. Eyzaguirre, C.: NSM. https://github.com/charlespwd/project-title (2019)
10. Gan, Z., Chen, Y.C., Li, L., Zhu, C., Cheng, Y., Liu, J.: Large-scale adversarial training for vision-and-language representation learning. arXiv preprint arXiv:2006.06195 (2020)
11. Glorot, X., Bengio, Y.: Understanding the difficulty of training deep feedforward neural networks. In: Proceedings of the Thirteenth International Conference on Artificial Intelligence and Statistics, pp. 249–256 (2010)
12. Hildebrandt, M., Serna, J.A.Q., Ma, Y., Ringsquandl, M., Joblin, M., Tresp, V.: Reasoning on knowledge graphs with debate dynamics. arXiv preprint arXiv:2001.00461 (2020)
13. Hochreiter, S., Schmidhuber, J.: Long short-term memory. Neural Comput. 9(8), 1735–1780 (1997)
14. Hu, R., Andreas, J., Rohrbach, M., Darrell, T., Saenko, K.: Learning to reason: end-to-end module networks for visual question answering. In: Proceedings of the IEEE International Conference on Computer Vision, pp. 804–813 (2017)

15. Hudson, D., Manning, C.D.: Learning by abstraction: the neural state machine. In: Advances in Neural Information Processing Systems, pp. 5901–5914 (2019)
16. Hudson, D.A., Manning, C.D.: Compositional attention networks for machine reasoning. arXiv preprint arXiv:1803.03067 (2018)
17. Hudson, D.A., Manning, C.D.: GQA: a new dataset for real-world visual reasoning and compositional question answering. arXiv preprint arXiv:1902.09506 (2019)
18. Johnson, J., Hariharan, B., van der Maaten, L., Fei-Fei, L., Lawrence Zitnick, C., Girshick, R.: CLEVR: a diagnostic dataset for compositional language and elementary visual reasoning. In: Proceedings of the IEEE Conference on Computer Vision and Pattern Recognition, pp. 2901–2910 (2017)
19. Johnson, J., et al.: Image retrieval using scene graphs. In: Proceedings of the IEEE Conference on Computer Vision and Pattern Recognition, pp. 3668–3678 (2015)
20. Kim, J.H., Jun, J., Zhang, B.T.: Bilinear attention networks. In: Advances in Neural Information Processing Systems, pp. 1564–1574 (2018)
21. Kingma, D.P., Ba, J.: Adam: a method for stochastic optimization. arXiv preprint arXiv:1412.6980 (2014)
22. Kipf, T.N., Welling, M.: Semi-supervised classification with graph convolutional networks. arXiv preprint arXiv:1609.02907 (2016)
23. Koner, R., Sinhamahapatra, P., Tresp, V.: Relation transformer network. arXiv preprint arXiv:2004.06193 (2020)
24. Krishna, R., et al.: Visual genome: connecting language and vision using crowd-sourced dense image annotations. Int. J. Comput. Vis. **123**(1), 32–73 (2017)
25. Lin, T.Y., et al.: Microsoft COCO: common objects in context. In: Fleet, D., Pajdla, T., Schiele, B., Tuytelaars, T. (eds.) ECCV 2014. LNCS, vol. 8693, pp. 740–755. Springer, Cham (2014). https://doi.org/10.1007/978-3-319-10602-1_48
26. Mao, J., Gan, C., Kohli, P., Tenenbaum, J.B., Wu, J.: The neuro-symbolic concept learner: interpreting scenes, words, and sentences from natural supervision. arXiv preprint arXiv:1904.12584 (2019)
27. Nickel, M., Murphy, K., Tresp, V., Gabrilovich, E.: A review of relational machine learning for knowledge graphs. Proc. IEEE **104**(1), 11–33 (2015)
28. Paszke, A., et al.: Automatic differentiation in PyTorch (2017)
29. Pennington, J., Socher, R., Manning, C.D.: GloVe: global vectors for word representation. In: Empirical Methods in Natural Language Processing (EMNLP), pp. 1532–1543 (2014). http://www.aclweb.org/anthology/D14-1162
30. Qiao, S., Chen, L.C., Yuille, A.: DetectoRS: detecting objects with recursive feature pyramid and switchable Atrous convolution. arXiv preprint arXiv:2006.02334 (2020)
31. Shi, J., Zhang, H., Li, J.: Explainable and explicit visual reasoning over scene graphs. In: Proceedings of the IEEE Conference on Computer Vision and Pattern Recognition, pp. 8376–8384 (2019)
32. Srivastava, N., Hinton, G., Krizhevsky, A., Sutskever, I., Salakhutdinov, R.: Dropout: a simple way to prevent neural networks from overfitting. J. Mach. Learn. Res. **15**(1), 1929–1958 (2014)
33. Tang, K., Niu, Y., Huang, J., Shi, J., Zhang, H.: Unbiased scene graph generation from biased training. In: Proceedings of the IEEE/CVF Conference on Computer Vision and Pattern Recognition, pp. 3716–3725 (2020)
34. Teney, D., Liu, L., van Den Hengel, A.: Graph-structured representations for visual question answering. In: Proceedings of the IEEE Conference on Computer Vision and Pattern Recognition, pp. 1–9 (2017)
35. Vaswani, A, et al.: Attention is all you need. In: Advances in Neural Information Processing Systems, pp. 5998–6008 (2017)

36. Veličković, P., Cucurull, G., Casanova, A., Romero, A., Lio, P., Bengio, Y.: Graph attention networks. arXiv preprint arXiv:1710.10903 (2017)
37. Williams, R.J.: Simple statistical gradient-following algorithms for connectionist reinforcement learning. Mach. Learn. **8**(3–4), 229–256 (1992)
38. Xiong, W., Hoang, T., Wang, W.Y.: DeepPath: a reinforcement learning method for knowledge graph reasoning. In: Proceedings of the 2017 Conference on Empirical Methods in Natural Language Processing (EMNLP 2017), Copenhagen, Denmark. ACL (2017)
39. Yang, Z., He, X., Gao, J., Deng, L., Smola, A.: Stacked attention networks for image question answering. In: Proceedings of the IEEE Conference on Computer Vision and Pattern Recognition, pp. 21–29 (2016)
40. Yu, Z., Yu, J., Fan, J., Tao, D.: Multi-modal factorized bilinear pooling with co-attention learning for visual question answering. In: Proceedings of the IEEE International Conference on Computer Vision, pp. 1821–1830 (2017)
41. Zhu, C., Zhao, Y., Huang, S., Tu, K., Ma, Y.: Structured attentions for visual question answering. In: Proceedings of the IEEE International Conference on Computer Vision, pp. 1291–1300 (2017)

EDG-Based Question Decomposition for Complex Question Answering over Knowledge Bases

Xixin Hu, Yiheng Shu, Xiang Huang, and Yuzhong Qu[✉]

State Key Laboratory
for Novel Software Technology, Nanjing University, Nanjing, China
{xixinhu,yhshu,xianghuang}@smail.nju.edu.cn, yzqu@nju.edu.cn

Abstract. Knowledge base question answering (KBQA) aims at automatically answering factoid questions over knowledge bases (KBs). For complex questions that require multiple KB relations or constraints, KBQA faces many challenges including question understanding, component linking (e.g., entity, relation, and type linking), and query composition. In this paper, we propose a novel graph structure called Entity Description Graph (EDG) to represent the structure of complex questions, which can help alleviate the above issues. By leveraging the EDG structure of given questions, we implement a QA system over DBpedia, called **EDGQA**. Extensive experiments demonstrate that **EDGQA** outperforms state-of-the-art results on both LC-QuAD and QALD-9, and that EDG-based decomposition is a feasible way for complex question answering over KBs.

Keywords: Entity description graph · Question answering · Question decomposition

1 Introduction

Knowledge base question answering (KBQA) aims at answering factoid questions over knowledge bases (KBs) such as DBpedia, Freebase, and Wikidata. One of the widely used approaches of KBQA is semantic parsing, where natural language questions (NLQs) are transformed into formal queries on a KB [4]. Existing semantic-parsing-based approaches [2,26] have achieved promising results on simple questions that can be answered by matching a single relation (or path) in a KB [24].

However, answering complex questions that require retrieving multiple KB facts is still very challenging. For instance, the golden formal query shown in Fig. 1 (a) contains various components including a grounded entity, an intermediate variable, a variable for the final answer, and several KB predicates and type constraints. It requires accurate component linking and sub-query composition to build such a complicated formal query, which is not trivial. Several approaches enumerate possible relation paths and rank them all [1,4,13]. In this way, the search space grows exponentially with the length of relation paths, and the enumeration makes it difficult to find the precise query path.

© Springer Nature Switzerland AG 2021
A. Hotho et al. (Eds.): ISWC 2021, LNCS 12922, pp. 128–145, 2021.
https://doi.org/10.1007/978-3-030-88361-4_8

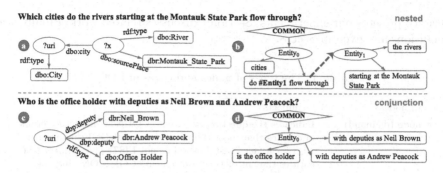

Fig. 1. SPARQL (a. and c.) and EDG (b. and d.) on two exemplar questions. The dashed line connects a description to an intermediate entity.

Question decomposition is a practical way of solving complex questions and has been used in recent researches. Existing approaches cast the decomposition problem as an instance of span prediction [15] or split point prediction [20] problem to generate sub-questions. However, multiple relations or constraints may still exist in sub-questions, making it difficult to be answered. Besides, they only define limited patterns of sub-question composition, which are inadequate for various scales of complex questions. In addition to sub-question generation, Abstract Meaning Representation (AMR) is also used to represent NLQs [11]. AMR helps to identify and compose the relations in NLQs but also brings granularity mismatch with KBs. To bridge the mismatch, complicated rules are designed. In general, the existing approaches have not yet reached a satisfactory level.

In this paper, we propose a novel graph structure called **Entity Description Graph** (EDG) to represent the structure of NLQs. Entities are at the center of how people represent and aggregate knowledge, which is the basic driving force of EDG. Examples of EDG are shown in Fig. 1 (b, d). The root, a diamond node, indicates the question type, e.g., "COMMON" means the question intends to find an entity or a set of entities. The entities in the EDG, oval nodes, are described by some verb phrases or noun phrases, indicated by rounded rectangles. In some cases, complex descriptions refer to intermediate entities, e.g., *"do #Entity1 flow through"* in Fig. 1 (b). By doing so, EDG can represent the graph structure of complex questions. Intuitively, EDG is an entity-centric graph, where phrase-level descriptions provide relational assertion or constraints about entities.

To generate EDG for a given question, we design some rules based on the constituency tree. We leverage EDG to generate sub-queries and integrate them based on the EDG structure. Furthermore, we implement a KBQA system based on EDG, called EDGQA[1]. Our experiments show that it outperforms state-of-the-art results on both LC-QuAD [22] and QALD-9 [23].

The remainder of the paper is organized as follows. Section 2 proposes the Entity Description Graph. Section 3 presents an overview of EDGQA. Section 4 details the EDG decomposition process, and Sect. 5 details the query generation.

---

[1] Source code is available at https://github.com/HXX97/EDGQA.

Section 6 presents our experiments. Section 7 discusses related work. Finally, the conclusions are given in Sect. 8.

Table 1. The types of nodes and edges in EDG

Type of nodes	Comments
Root node (diamond)	Indicates the question type, e.g., COUNT: count the number of entities that meet the requirements JUDGE: determine whether a fact is established or not LIST: give a full list of entities that meet the requirements COMMON: find the answer that completes the question into a declarative sentence
Entity node (oval)	A placeholder for an entity to be found in the KB
Description node (rounded rectangle)	A phrase that describes its corresponding entity node
Type of edges	Comments
Quest edge	Connects a root node to the target entity
Constraint edge	Connects an entity node to its corresponding description nodes
Reference edge	Connects a description node to an intermediate entity nested in the description

2 Entity Description Graph

In this paper, we use an RDF graph as a KB for question answering. An RDF graph $\mathcal{K}$ is a collection of triples in the form of (s, r, o), e.g., (dbr:Current_River, dbo:sourcePlace, dbr:Montauk_State_Park)[2], where s, r, o represent the subject, relation, and object, respectively. For a factoid question, the answer $\mathcal{A}$ is a subset of the entities in $\mathcal{K}$, or the result of a calculation such as aggregation (COUNT) and assertion (ASK). Hence, answering a question is to find the target *entities* in a KB that match the *descriptions* in the question, where the calculation is needed in some situations. For example, as indicated in Fig. 1 (d), *"is the office holder"*, *"with deputies as Neil Brown"* and *"with deputies as Andrew Peacock"* are descriptions about the target entities of the question, say $Entity_0$.

Conjunction and nesting are common forms of complex questions [3,10]. In the case of *nested* questions, a description of an entity may contain intermediate entities described by some sub-descriptions. For example, given a phrase *"do the rivers starting at the Montauk State Park flow through"*, we can extract an intermediate entity $Entity_1$ described by *"the rivers"* and *"starting at the Montauk State Park"*. The intermediate entity is crucial to finding the final answer to the question.

In the case of *conjunction* questions, the descriptions about the target entity usually come from different aspects. For question *"Who is the office holder with deputies as Neil Brown and Andrew Peacock"*, we can extract three different descriptions. *"is the office holder"* describes the occupation of the target entity, *"with deputies as Neil Brown"* and *"with deputies as Andrew Peacock"* describe the people associated with the target entity.

---

[2] dbr: http://dbpedia.org/resource, dbo: http://dbpedia.org/ontology.

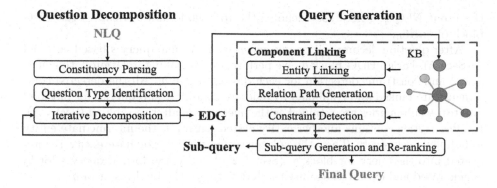

Fig. 2. EDGQA system overview: question decomposition phase and query generation phase.

By decomposing the question into the form of entities and their descriptions, we can have a straightforward view of the question structure, which indicates how the sub-queries should be integrated. Descriptions are at the phrase level, including verb phrases or noun phrases, etc.

Based on the above idea, we introduce the **Entity Description Graph** (EDG) to describe NLQs. An EDG is a rooted directed acyclic graph, consisting of three types of nodes and three types of edges, as shown in Table 1. The target entity is connected to the root node of an EDG. Several descriptions can be connected to an entity node. Intermediate entities can be referred to from some complicated descriptions. An entity and its descriptions form an **EDG block**, e.g., $Block_0$ and $Block_1$ in Fig. 3 (c). These two blocks are connected by a reference edge.

Representing NLQs by EDG brings the following benefits. 1) Candidate phrases are provided for component linking. 2) A structural basis for the sub-query composition of complex questions is provided. We will discuss these issues in Sect. 6.4.

3 Overview

Our proposed KBQA system EDGQA consists of two phases: question decomposition and query generation. The question decomposition phase generates an EDG for the NLQ, and the query generation phase generates and combines sub-queries based on the EDG. A system overview is illustrated in Fig. 2.

For an NLQ q, we first obtain a constituency parsing tree [5] of q, and then identify the question type according to the result of constituency parsing (Sect. 4.1). The generation process of EDG $\mathcal{G}$ is iterative (Sect. 4.2). Initially, the whole q is viewed as a single description of the target entity. Then the description is iteratively parsed until no additional entity nodes or description nodes are generated. Finally, the EDG $\mathcal{G} = \langle root, \{b_0, b_1, ..., b_L\} \rangle$ is generated to represent the input NLQ q, where *root* denotes the root node and b_i denotes the EDG block of *entity_i*.

After question decomposition, we generate the formal query s based on EDG $\mathcal{G}$ (Sect. 5). For an EDG block b_i, we perform entity linking, relation path generation, and constraint detection for each description in b_i. All the detected components are ranked and combined to generate candidate sub-queries for block b_i, and top-k sub-queries are retained as the query for b_i after re-ranking (Sect. 5.1). If a description contains another entity nested within it, the intermediate entity is handled recursively. Then the sub-query for the intermediate entity is integrated into the query for block b_i (Sect. 5.2). Finally, the formal query s for b_0 is generated and executed against the KB $\mathcal{K}$ to get the final result of q.

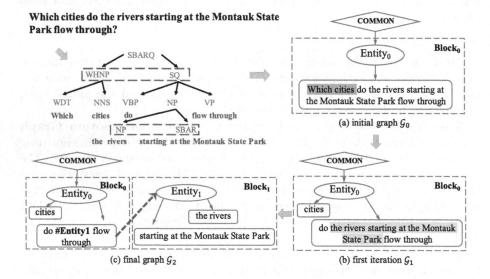

Fig. 3. Running example of question decomposition, spans identified by W-rule and A-rule are marked.

4   Question Decomposition

In this phase, we decompose a question into an EDG. Our method for question decomposition consists of 3 steps: 1) constituency parsing, 2) question type identification and 3) iterative decomposition. The decomposition process is illustrated in Algorithm 1, which is detailed as follows.

4.1   Constituency Parsing and Question Type Identification

Constituency parsing aims to extract a constituency-based parse tree from a sentence that represents its syntactic structure according to a phrase structure

Algorithm 1. QuestionDecomposition

Input: A natural language question q
Output: An EDG $\mathcal{G}$ for q

1: $\mathcal{T} \leftarrow$ ConstituencyParsing(q)
2: $\mathcal{G}_0, b_0 \leftarrow$ QuestionTypeIdentification($\mathcal{T}$)
3: $i \leftarrow 0$, $j \leftarrow 0$ // the number of iteration and the number of current block
4: **repeat**
5:     $\mathcal{G} \leftarrow \mathcal{G}_i$
6:     **for all** description d in b_j **do**
7:         **if** A-Rule($d, \mathcal{T}$) or N-Rule($d, \mathcal{T}$) is matched **then**
8:             $e_{j+1}, \bigcup_{k=1}^{h} d_{j+1,k} \leftarrow$ ExtractNewEntity(d) // extract a new entity from d
9:             $b_{j+1} \leftarrow \bigcup_{k=1}^{h} d_{j+1,k} \cup \{e_{j+1}\}$ // h is the number of description nodes for e_{j+1}.
10:            $\mathcal{G}_{i+1} \leftarrow \mathcal{G}_i \cup b_{j+1}$ // add the newly generated block
11:            $i \leftarrow i+1$
12:            $j \leftarrow j+1$
13:        **else if** W-Rule($d, \mathcal{T}$) or C-Rule($d, \mathcal{T}$) is matched **then**
14:            $d'_1, d'_2 \leftarrow$ SplitDescription(d) // split d into sub-descriptions
15:            $b_j \leftarrow b_j - \{d\}$
16:            $b_j \leftarrow b_j \cup \{d'_1, d'_2\}$ // replace d with sub-descriptions
17:            $i \leftarrow i+1$
18:        **end if**
19:    **end for**
20: **until** $\mathcal{G}$ equals $\mathcal{G}_i$
21: **return** $\mathcal{G}$

---

grammar. Since EDG is a phrase-level structural representation of the question, it is natural to generate EDG from the constituency parsing. We generate the constituency tree $\mathcal{T}$ based on Stanford CoreNLP Parser[3], which is shown in the upper left part of Fig. 3. Our decomposition is based on the phrase structure grammar of constituency parsing.

Typically, the root label of the constituency tree indicates the question type. For example, SBARQ denotes a direct question introduced by a *wh*-word and SQ denotes an inverted boolean question. We create a root node to represent the question type according to the root label. We have defined four question types: COUNT, JUDGE, LIST, and COMMON, detailed in Table 1. To identify the question type more precisely, we collect a set of trigger words based on co-occurrence frequency, e.g., "*count the number of*" usually indicates COUNT questions.

After question type identification, we create an entity node representing the target entity of the question, denoted by $entity_0$, and connect it to the root node with a quest edge. The whole question is viewed as a single description connected to the target entity before the following decomposition. The initial graph is denoted as $\mathcal{G}_0$, consisting of a root node and a block b_0, which is shown in Fig. 3(a).

---

[3] https://stanfordnlp.github.io/CoreNLP/.

4.2   Iterative Decomposition

After initial graph generation, we decompose the descriptions according to the
constituency tree iteratively. The decomposing module is a rule-based system
that detects the predefined phrase-structure patterns and then decomposes the
descriptions into several sub-descriptions. In general, this module consists of the
following rules:

W-Rule identifies wh-phrase labels, such as WHNP, WHPP, WHADJP. A wh-
phrase (e.g. *"Which cities"*) consists of a wh-word and a phrase that describes
an aspect of the target entity. Most type constraints are derived from the wh-
phrases and thus it is important to identify them at first. We split the original
description into two sub descriptions: the phrase introduced by the wh-word and
the others, shown in Fig. 3 (a).

C-Rule identifies coordinating conjunction tags, such as CC (e.g., *"and"*)
or RB (e.g., *"also"*). Conjunction is a regular form of complex questions, which
joins multiple constraints or relations. The clauses split by a conjunction word
usually introduce different constraints. Note that there may exist coordination
ambiguity in such sentences. For example, given a description *"with deputies as
Neil Brown and Andrew Peacock"*, we need to know that *"Andrew Peacock"* is
conjoined with *"Neil Brown"* instead of *"with deputies as Neil Brown"*. In this
case, we rewrite the description into two sub-descriptions: *"with deputies as Neil
Brown"* and *"with deputies as Andrew Peacock"*.

A-Rule identifies attributive clauses or adverbial clauses labeled by SBAR,
SBARQ or SQ. An attributive clause (e.g., *"the rivers starting at the Montauk State
Park"*) serves as an attribute to a noun or pronoun in the main clause. It usually
indicates the existence of an intermediate entity when such an attributive clause is
identified. We extract the clause (e.g., *"starting at the Montauk State Park"*) along
with the antecedent (e.g., *"the rivers"*) from the original description and create an
entity node representing this intermediate entity, as is shown in Fig. 3 (b).

N-Rule identifies compound noun phrases which contain prepositional
phrases (e.g., *"the daughter of Obama"*) labeled by PP or possessive phrases (e.g.,
"Obama's daughter") labeled by POS. Similar to attributive clauses, compound
noun phrases tend to include intermediate entities. We extract such compound
noun phrases and create an entity node referred from the original description.

In summary, W-Rule and C-Rule are designed to split a description into
several sub-descriptions (**SplitDescription** in Algorithm 1). A-Rule and N-
Rule are designed to extract intermediate entities from the original descriptions
(**ExtractNewEntity** in Algorithm 1).

At each iteration, we apply the above rules to each description in the block,
and then split the descriptions or generate new entity nodes according to the
matched rules. This process is repeated until no description is split or extracted.
As shown in Fig. 3, the graph after the first iteration is denoted as $\mathcal{G}_1$ and the
final graph is denoted as $\mathcal{G}_2$, which means the process is iterated twice. Finally,
$\mathcal{G}_2$ is returned as the EDG generated for the original question.

5   Query Generation

An EDG gives a hierarchical decomposition of an NLQ and provides a clear structure for sub-query generation and composition without the need to enumerate a large number of possible relation paths or sub-query combinations. The query generation starts from the EDG structure.

We denote the EDG as $\mathcal{G} = \langle root, \{b_0, b_1, ..., b_L\}\rangle$, where $root$ is the root node, b_0 is the block of the target entity asked by the question and b_i is the block of intermediate $entity_i$. Intuitively, a block is a structured representation for an entity, and thus we can map a block to a formal sub-query whose execution results are the answers for the entity. Note that a reference edge connects a block b_i to another block referred from b_i. In this way, the EDG blocks form a tree. We follow the trace of the block tree to generate sub-queries for each block recursively. If a block b_i refers to one or more blocks, we generate the sub-queries of its referred blocks and then merge them into the query for b_i. Figure 4 shows the process of query generation for the example in Fig. 3, which will be detailed below. The process of generating queries for each block is given in Algorithm 2. It is a recursive algorithm and the query generated for b_0 is viewed as the query for the full NLQ.

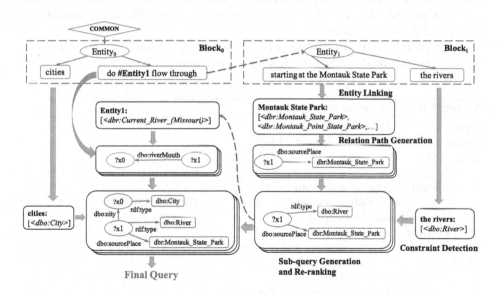

Fig. 4. Running example of sub-query generation and composition.

5.1   Block Query Generation

We generate the query for a block through a pipeline consisting of 4 modules: 1) entity linking, 2) relation path generation, 3) constraint detection, and 4) sub-query generation and re-ranking. The starting three modules form a phrase-level component linking module (line 4 in Algorithm 2) and the last module integrates the components to generate candidate sub-queries for this block (line 6 in Algorithm 2).

Entity Linking. We ensemble Dexter [21], EARL [8] and Falcon [18] as one entity retriever. We assume that a description contains at most one entity in the KB. For a description d_i in block b, the entity retriever gives a list of candidate entities denoted as E_i, e.g., dbr:Montauk_State_Park and dbr:Montauk_Point_State_Park in Fig. 4. Then we average distance-based string similarity metrics (Jaro distance, Dice coefficient, and Levenshtein distance) to measure the confidence score $p_{ent}(e)$ of each $e \in E_i$. To reduce the ambiguity brought by the retriever, we assume that the distance of candidate entities in a block should be relatively close in the KB [8]. If a candidate entity in a description is not reachable in 2 hops from any candidate in other descriptions in the KB, the entity is abandoned. In this way, EDG can help the entity disambiguation.

Relation Path Generation. We follow the work of [16] to generate candidate relations of E_i for each description d_i. The candidate relation list is denoted as R_i.

A major challenge is to properly rank these candidate relations according to their relevance to the question. Since EDG has already decomposed the question into phrase-level descriptions, there is no need to detect relation mentions. The description naturally provides mentions for relation linking. To select the accurate relation mapping to description d_i, we measure the similarity from both literal and semantic aspects.

For semantic similarity, we use a BERT-based [6] semantic matching model. Specifically, the model takes the text of d_i with entity-masked mention (e.g.,

---

Algorithm 2. BlockQueryGeneration

Input: An EDG block $b = \{d_i\}_{i=1}^h$
Output: A set of candidate queries Q for b

1: $Q \leftarrow \emptyset$
2: **if** b contains no reference edge **then**
3:    **for all** description d_i in b **do**
4:       $E_i \leftarrow$ EntityLinking(d_i), $R_i \leftarrow$ RelationLinking(d_i), $C_i \leftarrow$ ConstraintDetection(d_i)
5:    **end for**
6:    $Q \leftarrow$ Sub-query generation and re-ranking for b given $(\langle E_i, R_i, C_i \rangle)_{i=1}^h$
7: **else**
8:    **for all** description d_i in b **do**
9:       **if** exists b_j referred from d_i **then**
10:          $Q_j \leftarrow$ BlockQueryGeneration(b_j) // generate sub-query for b_j
11:          $d_i \leftarrow$ SubQueryIntegration(d_i, Q_j) // take the sub-query results
12:       **end if**
13:    **end for**
14:    $Q \leftarrow$ BlockQueryGeneration(b) // no reference edge in block b after the above loop
15: **end if**
16: **return** Q

"*starting at*") and the candidate relations in R_i (e.g., dbo:sourcePlace) as input. The output is the probability of the sentence-pair binary classification (related or not related), regarded as the semantic similarity sim_{sem} between the relation and the description. Due to the lack of training data, we collect distant supervision data from the training sets of QA datasets. More precisely, for a question and query pair in QA datasets, we mask the entity mentions in the original question. Then we extract all the relations from the golden query as positive cases, which means the relations can be inferred from the masked question. To collect negative cases, we randomly sample some relations associated with the grounded entities in the question.

For literal similarity, we use string similarity sim_{lit} in the same way as entity linking. We also use a paraphrase dictionary [25] to get the paraphrases of the relation and calculate the similarity sim_{dict} between the paraphrases and the descriptions. Finally, the relation confidence p_{rel} is calculated as Eq. 1.

$$p_{rel}(r) = \mu \; sim_{sem}(r, m) + (1 - \mu) \; \max(sim_{lit}(r, m), sim_{dict}(r, m))) \tag{1}$$

where r is the label of the relation and m stands for the mention (description with entity masked). The hyper-parameter μ is used to balance the importance of semantic score and literal score.

Constraint Detection. We mainly focus on type constraints and adopt DBpedia Ontology[4] as the type bank. For noun phrase descriptions (e.g., "*the rivers*" in Fig. 4) where no entities are spotted, we measure its string similarity to all the DBpedia types and reserve types with high similarity score (e.g., "dbo:River") as candidates. The list of all candidate types for description d_i is denoted as C_i.

Sub-query Generation and Re-ranking. When all the components are linked by previous modules, we generate the sub-query s for block b by compositing the candidate entities, relations, and constraints. More specifically, as shown in Fig. 4, we combine the triple patterns generated from descriptions into a query s for a block. The query s can be modeled as a set of triples $s = \{\langle ?x_b, r_i, e_i \rangle_{i=1}^{h} \}$, where $r_i \in R_i \cup \{\text{rdf:type}\}$, $e_i \in E_i \cup C_i$ and $?x_b$ denotes the answer of block b. To measure the quality of this query, we multiply the confidence scores of all the components in s to get the component-level score p_{comp}.

$$p_{comp}(s) = \prod_{i=1}^{h} p_{rel}(r_i) \cdot p_{ent}(e_i) \tag{2}$$

where h is the number of triples in s.

Besides the above component-level score $p_{comp}(s)$, we also take advantage of the context of this block by a block-level semantic matching model to estimate the quality of sub-query candidates. Specifically, we convert the block b and the query s to two sequences with additional special tokens, and then utilize a BERT-based semantic matching model to measure the correlation between the

---

[4] https://wiki.dbpedia.org/services-resources/ontology.

two sequences. Take the block b_1 in Fig. 4 as an example, we represent block b_1 as:

   [BLK] [DES] the rivers [DES] starting at the Montauk State Park

where [BLK] tags the start of a block and [DES] tags the start of a description. Similarly, we represent the candidate query as:

   [TRP] x1 type river [TRP] x1 source place Montauk State Park

where [TRP] denotes the start of a triple in the query. The semantic matching task is also modeled as a sentence-pair classification task here, and the score given by the model is denoted as p_{blk}. The final score of a sub-query is shown in Eq. 3 by combining the above two scores.

$$p_{query}(s) = \lambda\, p_{comp}(s) + (1 - \lambda)\, p_{blk}(s) \tag{3}$$

where λ is a hyper-parameter. Finally, a ranked list of candidate sub-queries for block b is generated. We select top-k sub-queries as the output of the block query generation.

5.2   Sub-query Integration

If an EDG block refers to one or more blocks, we recursively solve referred blocks beforehand and get a collection of candidate sub-queries. We execute the candidate sub-queries to get candidate intermediate entities, e.g., $\#Entity_1$ of block b_0 in Fig. 4. The candidate intermediate entities are viewed as the entity linking results of the descriptions referring to them, e.g., "do $\#Entity_1$ flow through" of block b_0 in Fig. 4. In this way, we can generate the query for this block. Finally, the formal query s_0 for b_0 is generated and executed against the KB to retrieve the answer to the question.

Instead of generating sub-queries separately [3,19,20], we consider them together, because the results of the sub-queries bring extra evidence for follow-up query generation. Take the block b_0 in Fig. 4 as an example, it is unlikely to select the correct relation dbo:city if we do not get the intermediate entity dbo:Current_River_(Missouri) at first. Besides, we avoid enumerating possible combinations of sub-queries as [19], since the composition of sub-queries is guided by the EDG structure.

6   Experiments

6.1   Experimental Setup

Datasets. We use two KBQA datasets to evaluate EDGQA.

- **LC-QuAD** [22] is the **L**arge-scale **C**omplex **Q**uestion **A**nswering **D**ataset over DBpedia (2016-04), with 4,000 training and 1,000 test questions. The average length of questions is 11.46 words.
- **QALD-9** [23] is an open-domain QA campaign over DBpedia (2016-10) with 408 training and 150 test questions. The average length of questions is 7.49 words.

All experiment results are reported on the LC-QuAD and QALD-9 test set. The training set is used for distant supervision for relation linking and sub-query re-ranking.

Metrics. For all the experiments, the metrics are precision (P), recall (R), and macro F1 (F) for both datasets. Macro-F1-QALD [23] (F-Q) is also included for QALD-9.

Comparative Approaches. We compare EDGQA with several methods including non-decomposition and decomposition approaches, as well as the graph-driven approach. All comparative approaches include the entity linking module.

1) **WDAqua** [7] is a KB agnostic QA system based on keyword extraction and query templates.
2) **QAmp** [24] uses unsupervised message passing, which propagates confidence scores obtained by parsing the NLQ and matching KB terms to possible answers.
3) **gAnswer** [9] generates the semantic query graph to model the query intention in the NLQ in a structural way.
4) **NSQA** [11] uses AMR to parse questions and performs logical queries via neural networks.

The results of WDAqua and QAmp for LC-QuAD 1.0 are from the official leaderboard[5], and the results of WDAqua and gAnswer for QALD-9 are from the QALD-9 official report [23].

Implementation Details. For the semantic matching model in relation path ranking and sub-query re-ranking, we fine-tune the BERT model[6] for the sentence-pair classification task with default hyper-parameters. For hyper-parameters of the weighted average in Eq. 1 and 3, we set μ to 0.45 and λ to 0.55. We set k to 2 for intermediate entities, which means we execute the top-2 ranked sub-queries and merge the results into a candidate set. For target entities of the question, we only reserve the top-1 ranked query.

6.2   Results and Discussion

As is shown in Table 2, EDGQA outperforms state-of-the-art results on both LC-QuAD and QALD-9. Both precision and recall of EDGQA are at a high level compared with competitors. It makes a significant improvement on LC-QuAD compared with the best competitor (39.5% improvement on F1). QALD-9 questions are more difficult to answer, but EDGQA still achieves competitive results. gAnswer with semantic query graph and NSQA with AMR parsing perform relatively well, and the latter one had the highest precision on QALD-9.

To compare EDGQA with other question decomposition methods, we generate sub-questions with the model from [20] and follow its original composition strategy to implement a comparative approach with existing linking tools. This model

---

[5] http://lc-quad.sda.tech/lcquad1.0.html.
[6] https://github.com/google-research/bert.

Table 2. QA performance on LC-QuAD and QALD-9

Approaches	LC-QuAD 1.0			QALD-9			
	P	R	F	P	R	F	F-Q
WDAqua [7]	0.22	0.38	0.28	0.261	0.267	0.250	0.289
QAmp [24]	0.25	0.50	0.33	–	–	–	–
gAnswer [9]	–	–	–	0.293	0.327	0.298	0.430
NSQA[11]	0.38	0.40	0.38	**0.314**	0.322	0.309	0.453
Pointer network* [20]	0.220	0.241	0.230	0.096	0.109	0.102	0.190
EDGQA	**0.505**	**0.560**	**0.531**	0.313	**0.403**	**0.320**	**0.461**

FQ: Macro-F1-QALD measure, *: our implementation

named **pointer network** [20] identifies split points in the NLQ and decomposes the NLQ into spans. In our implementation, if it outputs the empty set of answers for a sub-question, we solve it directly without decomposition. It is denoted as pointer network* in Table 2.

The decomposition of the pointer network does not present a significant advantage to the QA task. Since its decomposition is only a simple combination of spans and not entity-centric, there may still be multiple relations or constraints in a sub-question, and the entity to which they belong is not clear. In contrast, EDGQA composes individual sub-queries in an entity-centric manner, and their composition has a structure to follow.

6.3 Quality of Question Decomposition

Currently, it is hard to make a comprehensive criterion for evaluating the quality of question decomposition. We attempt to evaluate the quality of EDG generation in terms of question type identification and the number of EDG blocks.

Correct question type identification is the prerequisite for the QA task. The type of most questions are identified correctly on both datasets (type accuracy in Table 3).

In the ideal decomposition, an EDG block corresponds to an entity to be queried on the KB (Sect. 2), which is represented by a variable in a SPARQL query. We count the number of questions where the number of EDG blocks (#b) is equal to the number of SPARQL variables (#v) and the number of those questions where #b is not equal to #v, separately. The F1 measure of answering these two types of questions is shown in Table 3, respectively. The significant difference between them shows that the relationship between #b and #v for each question is a distinctive feature that influences the QA performance. Questions that meet this criterion (#b = #v) are answered significantly better than other questions. Thus, it can be regarded as one criterion to judge the quality of EDG generation since it is an objective criterion and highly related to QA.

We observe that most of the questions meet this criterion on both LC-QuAD and QALD-9 (79.4% and 73.3%). The EDG block representing an entity can

Table 3. Detailed comparison of EDGs with golden SPARQL queries

Datasets	Criterion	#question	Type accuracy	F
LC-QuAD	#b = #v	794	0.997	0.650
	#b ≠ #v	206	1.000	0.107
QALD-9	#b = #v	110	0.945	0.416
	#b ≠ #v	40	0.900	0.014

Table 4. Ablation study on EDGQA, EL: entity linking, RL: relation linking

Methods	LC-QuAD 1.0			QALD-9			
	P	R	F	P	R	F	F-Q
EDGQA	**0.505**	**0.560**	**0.531**	**0.313**	**0.403**	**0.320**	**0.461**
w/o decomposition	0.368	0.455	0.407	0.219	0.272	0.226	0.368
w/o phrase level RL	0.301	0.367	0.331	0.138	0.230	0.137	0.345
w/o phrase level EL & RL	0.284	0.350	0.314	0.138	0.230	0.137	0.345
w/o re-ranking	0.485	0.540	0.511	0.294	0.390	0.301	0.430

correspond well to the SPARQL variable. As an entity-centric decomposition, EDG gives an appropriate granularity.

6.4 Ablation Study

To illustrate the impact of EDG on component linking and query generation, we perform several ablation experiments as shown in Table 4.

W/o Decomposition. To verify the effect of decomposition on complex query generation, we solve the whole question as a single description directly. The F1 measure decreases by 23.35% and 29.37% on two datasets, respectively. It shows that only the linking and re-ranking (line 2–6 Algorithm 2) are not sufficient for complex questions. The split of descriptions and the recursive query generation (line 7–15 in Algorithm 2) brought by EDG are also necessary.

W/o Phrase Level Entity and Relation Linking. To verify the usefulness of the EDG decomposition for linking, we put the whole question into linking tools instead of these phrases, and still apply the recursive query generation. The F1 measure decreases by 40.87% and 57.19% on two datasets, respectively. It shows that complex questions remain a challenge for existing linking tools. The granularity of the EDG decomposition helps the correspondence of NLQ to entities or relations in the KB.

W/o Re-ranking. To verify the effect of the re-ranking method (Sect. 5.1) with EDG block information, we run QA without the re-ranking step. The F1 measure decreases by 3.77% and 5.94% on two datasets, respectively. While phrase-level component linking has worked well, the re-ranking method still aids the QA task.

It also shows that our query generation does not highly depend on a ranking model compared to the methods enumerating relation paths [4,12].

6.5 Error Analysis

We analyze all the questions answered incorrectly by EDGQA (F1 < 1.0). The major causes of errors are summarized as follows.

Relation Linking Error (38.63%). We observe that relation linking is a bottleneck of EDGQA. Although we leverage several semantic matching models, it is still difficult to select the correct relation from all the candidates. There are two main reasons for error relation linking: (1) indistinguishable relations, e.g., the golden query contains "dbp:founders"[7] while our system selects "dbp:founder"; (2) implicit relations with no explicit evidence, e.g., given a question *"Give me all animals that are extinct."*, the golden query contains a relation path ?uri dbo:conservationStatus ''EX'' to represent *"are extinct"* while EDGQA fails to identify this relation.

Entity Linking Error (37.03%). Some questions require complex reasoning and disambiguation for entity linking, which is challenging for existing entity linking tools. For example, dbr:Lee_Robinson_(American_football) is a desired entity URI in the question *"What city has the football team in which Lee Robinson debuted?"*. However, EDGQA links it to "dbr:Lee_Robinson_(footballer)".

Question Decomposition Error (11.29%). About 11.29% of questions are decomposed incorrectly due to constituency parsing errors and limited coverage of our decomposition rules. Since we generate the query based on EDG, an incorrect EDG usually results in an inaccurate query. For example, given a question *"Which monarchs of the United Kingdom were married to a German?"*, EDGQA decomposes the question into two descriptions: *"monarchs of the United Kingdom"* and *"were married to a German"*, where EDGQA fails to identify the intermediate entity represented by *"a German"*.

7 Related Work

Complex Question Answering Over KBs. Traditional KBQA researches [2,17] mainly focus on learning semantic parsers that translate questions into logical forms for simple questions. To address the challenges brought by complex questions, recent researches propose an alternative way by reducing semantic parsing to query graph generation [1,13,14,26]. They first identify the main relation path and then adds constraints to it. To select the correct query, they enumerate possible candidate query graphs and rank them by neural semantic matching models. As the number of candidates grows, it is more difficult to find accurate query graphs. To reduce the search space of candidate queries, existing works introduce constraints from various perspectives. Chen et al. [4] leverage

---

[7] http://dbpedia.org/property.

the structural to restrict candidates. Lan et al. [12] present a beam-search based method to generate the query graph iteratively. The main difference between our approach and previous ones is that we leverage EDG to generate sub-queries, and avoid exhaustive enumeration of query candidates.

Question Decomposition. There are mainly two directions for question decomposition: split-based and template-based methods. Talmor and Berant [20] use a pointer network to find split points for an NLQ. Zhang et al. [27] further utilize this decomposition for semantic parsing. Min et al. [15] decompose questions in a span prediction manner for machine reading comprehension task. These split-based decomposition methods take spans as sub-questions while a sub-question may still contain multiple relations and constraints. Another direction is template-based methods, which decompose the NLQ q by pre-collected templates. The basic idea is to calculate the similarity between sub-sentences of q and natural language patterns [28]. Shin et al. [19] build a question-query graph library to match sub-questions to sub-query graphs and then combine them into a complete query. Instead of collecting templates, EDG provides guidance on sub-query generation and integration, which helps to generate accurate complete queries.

8   Conclusions

In this paper, we studied the problem of decomposing complex questions for KBQA. The main contributions of this paper are summarized as follows.

- We propose a novel graph structure called Entity Description Graph (EDG) to represent complex questions, which is an entity-centric decomposition.
- We present a rule-based method to decompose a question into an EDG iteratively.
- We implement an EDG-based KBQA system called EDGQA. By leveraging the EDG structure, EDGQA recursively generates and integrates sub-queries effectively.
- Experiments show that EDGQA outperforms state-of-the-art results on both LC-QuAD and QALD-9. In particular, it makes significant improvements on LC-QuAD.

   In future work, we consider the use of neural networks to generate EDGs. Besides, we are going to apply EDG to answering complex questions on other KBs such as Freebase. Furthermore, it is also interesting to incorporate EDG with a retrieve-based method or template-based method for answering complex questions.

Acknowledgements. This work was supported by the National Natural Science Foundation of China under Grant 61772264. We would like to thank Xiaoyin Pan for her efforts in the early stages of this work.

References

1. Bao, J., Duan, N., Yan, Z., Zhou, M., Zhao, T.: Constraint-based question answering with knowledge graph. In: COLING, pp. 2503–2514 (2016)
2. Berant, J., Chou, A., Frostig, R., Liang, P.: Semantic parsing on Freebase from question-answer pairs. In: EMNLP, pp. 1533–1544 (2013)
3. Bhutani, N., Zheng, X., Jagadish, H.V.: Learning to answer complex questions over knowledge bases with query composition. In: CIKM, pp. 739–748 (2019)
4. Chen, Y., Li, H., Hua, Y., Qi, G.: Formal query building with query structure prediction for complex question answering over knowledge base. In: IJCAI, pp. 3751–3758 (2020)
5. De Marneffe, M.C., MacCartney, B., Manning, C.D., et al.: Generating typed dependency parses from phrase structure parses. In: LREC, vol. 6, pp. 449–454 (2006)
6. Devlin, J., Chang, M., Lee, K., Toutanova, K.: BERT: pre-training of deep bidirectional transformers for language understanding. In: NAACL-HLT, pp. 4171–4186 (2019)
7. Diefenbach, D., Singh, K., Maret, P.: WDAqua-core0: a question answering component for the research community. In: Dragoni, M., Solanki, M., Blomqvist, E. (eds.) SemWebEval 2017. CCIS, vol. 769, pp. 84–89. Springer, Cham (2017). https://doi.org/10.1007/978-3-319-69146-6_8
8. Dubey, M., Banerjee, D., Chaudhuri, D., Lehmann, J.: EARL: joint entity and relation linking for question answering over knowledge graphs. In: Vrandečić, D., et al. (eds.) ISWC 2018. LNCS, vol. 11136, pp. 108–126. Springer, Cham (2018). https://doi.org/10.1007/978-3-030-00671-6_7
9. Hu, S., Zou, L., Yu, J.X., Wang, H., Zhao, D.: Answering natural language questions by subgraph matching over knowledge graphs. TKDE **30**(5), 824–837 (2018)
10. Kalyanpur, A., Patwardhan, S., Boguraev, B., Lally, A., Chu-Carroll, J.: Fact-based question decomposition in deepQA. IBM J. Res. Dev. **56**(3.4), 13:1–13:11 (2012)
11. Kapanipathi, P., et al.: Question answering over knowledge bases by leveraging semantic parsing and neuro-symbolic reasoning. arXiv preprint arXiv:2012.01707 (2020)
12. Lan, Y., Jiang, J.: Query graph generation for answering multi-hop complex questions from knowledge bases. In: ACL, pp. 969–974 (2020)
13. Luo, K., Lin, F., Luo, X., Zhu, K.: Knowledge base question answering via encoding of complex query graphs. In: EMNLP, pp. 2185–2194 (2018)
14. Maheshwari, G., Trivedi, P., Lukovnikov, D., Chakraborty, N., Fischer, A., Lehmann, J.: Learning to rank query graphs for complex question answering over knowledge graphs. In: Ghidini, C., et al. (eds.) ISWC 2019. LNCS, vol. 11778, pp. 487–504. Springer, Cham (2019). https://doi.org/10.1007/978-3-030-30793-6_28
15. Min, S., Zhong, V., Zettlemoyer, L., Hajishirzi, H.: Multi-hop reading comprehension through question decomposition and rescoring. In: ACL, pp. 6097–6109 (2019)
16. Pan, J.Z., Zhang, M., Singh, K., Harmelen, F., Gu, J., Zhang, Z.: Entity enabled relation linking. In: Ghidini, C., et al. (eds.) ISWC 2019. LNCS, vol. 11778, pp. 523–538. Springer, Cham (2019). https://doi.org/10.1007/978-3-030-30793-6_30
17. Reddy, S., Lapata, M., Steedman, M.: Large-scale semantic parsing without question-answer pairs. TACL **2**, 377–392 (2014)

18. Sakor, A., et al.: Old is gold: linguistic driven approach for entity and relation linking of short text. In: NAACL, pp. 2336–2346 (2019)
19. Shin, S., Lee, K.H.: Processing knowledge graph-based complex questions through question decomposition and recomposition. Inf. Sci. **523**, 234–244 (2020)
20. Talmor, A., Berant, J.: The web as a knowledge-base for answering complex questions. In: NAACL HLT, vol. 1, pp. 641–651 (2018)
21. Trani, S., Ceccarelli, D., Lucchese, C., Orlando, S., Perego, R.: Dexter 2.0: an open source tool for semantically enriching data. In: ISWC, pp. 417–420 (2014)
22. Trivedi, P., Maheshwari, G., Dubey, M., Lehmann, J.: LC-QuAD: a corpus for complex question answering over knowledge graphs. In: d'Amato, C., et al. (eds.) ISWC 2017. LNCS, vol. 10588, pp. 210–218. Springer, Cham (2017). https://doi.org/10.1007/978-3-319-68204-4_22
23. Usbeck, R., Gusmita, R.H., Ngomo, A.C.N., Saleem, M.: 9th challenge on question answering over linked data (QALD-9) (invited paper). In: Semdeep/NLIWoD@ISWC (2018)
24. Vakulenko, S., Garcia, J.D.F., Polleres, A., de Rijke, M., Cochez, M.: Message passing for complex question answering over knowledge graphs. In: CIKM, pp. 1431–1440 (2019)
25. Xue, B., Hu, S., Zou, L., Cheng, J.: The value of paraphrase for knowledge base predicates. In: AAAI, pp. 9346–9353 (2020)
26. Yih, W.t., Chang, M.W., He, X., Gao, J.: Semantic parsing via staged query graph generation: question answering with knowledge base. In: ACL-IJCNLP, pp. 1321–1331 (2015)
27. Zhang, H., Cai, J., Xu, J., Wang, J.: Complex question decomposition for semantic parsing. In: ACL, pp. 4477–4486 (2019)
28. Zheng, W., Yu, J.X., Zou, L., Cheng, H.: Question answering over knowledge graphs: question understanding via template decomposition. In: Proceedings of the VLDB Endowment (2018)

Zero-Shot Visual Question Answering Using Knowledge Graph

Zhuo Chen[1,2], Jiaoyan Chen[3], Yuxia Geng[1,2], Jeff Z. Pan[4], Zonggang Yuan[5], and Huajun Chen[1,2(✉)]

[1] College of Computer Science and Hangzhou Innovation Center,
Zhejiang University, Hangzhou, China
{zhuo.chen,gengyx,huajunsir}@zju.edu.cn
[2] AZFT Joint Lab for Knowledge Engine, Hangzhou, China
[3] Department of Computer Science, University of Oxford, Oxford, UK
jiaoyan.chen@cs.ox.ac.uk
[4] School of Informatics, The University of Edinburgh, Edinburgh, UK
[5] NAIE CTO Office, Huawei Technologies Co., Ltd., Shenzhen, China
yuanzonggang@huawei.com
https://knowledge-representation.org/j.z.pan/

Abstract. Incorporating external knowledge to Visual Question Answering (VQA) has become a vital practical need. Existing methods mostly adopt pipeline approaches with different components for knowledge matching and extraction, feature learning, etc. However, such pipeline approaches suffer when some component does not perform well, which leads to error cascading and poor overall performance. Furthermore, the majority of existing approaches ignore the answer bias issue— many answers may have never appeared during training (i.e., unseen answers) in real-word application. To bridge these gaps, in this paper, we propose a Zero-shot VQA algorithm using knowledge graph and a mask-based learning mechanism for better incorporating external knowledge, and present new answer-based Zero-shot VQA splits for the F-VQA dataset. Experiments show that our method can achieve state-of-the-art performance in Zero-shot VQA with unseen answers, meanwhile dramatically augment existing end-to-end models on the normal F-VQA task.

Keywords: Visual Question Answering · Zero-shot learning · Knowledge graph

1 Introduction

Visual Question Answering (VQA) is to answer natural language questions according to given images. It plays an important role in many applications such as advertising and personal assistants to the visually impaired. It has been widely investigated with promising results achieved due to the development of image and natural language processing techniques. However, most of the current solutions still cannot address the open-world scene understanding where the answer

A. Hotho et al. (Eds.): ISWC 2021, LNCS 12922, pp. 146–162, 2021.
https://doi.org/10.1007/978-3-030-88361-4_9

is not directly contained in the image but comes from or relies on external knowledge. Considering the question "Q1: Normally you play this game with your?" in Fig. 1, some additional knowledge is indispensable since that the answer "*dog*" cannot be found out with the content in the image alone.

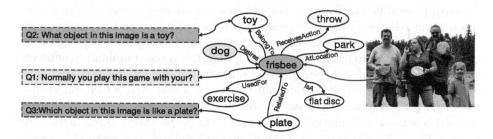

Fig. 1. VQA Examples. Q1: the answer is outside the image and question; Q2 and Q3: the answers are within the images or questions but require additional knowledge.

Some VQA methods have been developed to utilize external knowledge for open-world scene understanding. For example, Marino et al. [16] extensively utilize unstructured text information from the Web as external information but fail to address the noise (irrelevant information) in the text. Wang et al. [27] first extract visual concepts from images and then link them to an external knowledge graph (KG). The corresponding questions can then be transformed into a series of queries to the KG (e.g., SPARQL queries) to retrieve answers. Zhu et al. [31] instead construct a multi-modal heterogeneous graph by incorporating the spatial relationships and descriptive semantic relationships between visual concepts, as well as supporting facts retrieved from KGs, and then apply a modality-aware graph convolutional network to infer the answer. However, the performance of all these methods would be dramatically impacted if one module of the pipeline does not perform that well (a.k.a. error cascading [7]). Although some end-to-end models such as [2,13] have been proposed to avoid error cascading, they are still quite preliminary, especially on utilizing external knowledge, with worse performance than the pipeline methods on many VQA tasks.

Another important issue raised in VQA is the dependence on labeled training data, i.e., the model is trained by a dataset of (question, image, answer) tuples, and generalizes to answer questions about objects and situations that have already been presented in the training set. However, for new types of questions or answers, and objects newly emerge in images, there is a need for collecting labeled tuples and training the model from the scratch. Targeting such a limitation, Zero-shot VQA (ZS-VQA), which aims to predict with objects, questions or answers that have never appeared in training samples, has been proposed. Teney et al. [25] address questions that include new words; while [9,22] address images that contain new objects. However, all of these VQA methods still focus on the closed-world scene understanding without considering unseen answers and rarely make full use of KG. In this paper, we utilize KG to study VQA with open-world scene understanding, which requires external knowledge to answer the question, and ZS-VQA, especially the sub-task that addresses new answers.

In this paper, we present a ZS-VQA algorithm using KG and a mask-based learning mechanism, and at the same time propose a new Zero-shot Fact VQA (ZS-F-VQA) dataset which is to evaluate ZS-VQA for unseen answers. Firstly, we learn three different feature mapping spaces separately, which are semantic space about relations, object space about support entities, and knowledge space about answers. Each of them is used to align the joint embedding of image-question pair (I-Q pair) with corresponding target. Via the combination between all those chosen supporting entities and relations, masks are decided according to a mapping table which contains all triplets in a fact KG, which guides the alignment process of unseen answer prediction. Specially, the marks can be used as hard masks or soft masks, depending on the VQA tasks. Hard marks are used in ZS-VQA tasks; e.g., with the ZS-F-VQA dataset, our method achieves state-of-the-art performance and far superior (30–40%) to other methods. On the other hand, soft marks are used in standard VQA tasks; e.g., with the F-VQA dataset, our method achieves a stable improvement (6–9%) on baseline end-to-end method and well alleviates the error cascading problem of pipeline models. To sum up, the main contributions are summarized below:

- We propose a robust ZS-VQA algorithm using KGs,[1] which adjusts answer prediction score via masking based on the alignments between supporting entities/relations and fusion I-Q pairs in two feature spaces.
- We define a new ZS-VQA problem which requires external knowledge and considers unseen answers. Accordingly, we develop a ZS-F-VQA dataset for evaluation.
- Our KG-based ZS-VQA algorithm is quite flexible. It can successfully address both normal VQA tasks that rely on external knowledge and ZS-VQA tasks, and can be directly used to augment existing end-to-end models.

2 Related Work

2.1 Visual Question Answering

Traditional VQA Methods. Since proposed in 2015 by [3], a few VQA methods, which apply multi-modal feature fusion between question and image for final answer decision, have been proposed. Various attention mechanisms [2,29] are adopted to refine specific regions of the image for corresponding question meanwhile to make the prediction process interpretable. Graph-based approaches such as [6] combine multi-modal information and enhance the interaction among significant entities in texts and images.

Knowledge-Based VQA. Utilizing symbolic knowledge is a straight forward solution to augment VQA. To study incorporating external knowledge with VQA, datasets such as F-VQA [27], OK-VQA [16] and KVQA [23] have been

---

[1] Our code and data are available at https://github.com/China-UK-ZSL/ZS-F-VQA.

developed. Each question in F-VQA refers to a specific fact triple in relevant KG like ConceptNet. While OK-VQA is manually marked without a guided KG as reference which leads to its difficulty. KVQA targets at world knowledge where questions are about the relationship between characteristics.

To incorporate such external knowledge, [26,27] generate SPARQL queries for querying the constructed sub-KG according to I-Q pairs. [17,18,28,31] extract entities from image and question to get related concepts from KG for answer prediction. Marino et al. [16] take unstructured knowledge on the Web to enhance the semantic representation of I-Q joint feature. All of the above methods utilize pipeline approaches to narrow the answer scope, but they are often ad-hoc, which limits their deployment and generalization to new datasets. Most importantly, the errors will be magnified during running since each module usually has no ability to correct previous modules' errors. End-to-end model like [2,13] are more general and can avoid error cascading, but they are still preliminary, especially in addressing VQA problems which require external knowledge.

Different from these approaches, our proposed framework leverages the advantages of both end-to-end and pipeline approaches. We improve the model transferability meanwhile effectively avoid the error cascading (see our case study as illustrated in Fig. 5), making it quite general to different tasks and very robust with promising performance achieved.

2.2 Zero-Shot VQA

Machine learning often follows a closed world assumption where classes to predict all have training samples. However, the real-world is not completely closed and it is impractical to always annotate sufficient samples to re-train the model for new classes. Targeting such a limitation, zero-shot learning (ZSL) is proposed to handle these novel classes without seeing their training samples (i.e., unseen classes) [5,10]. Teney et al. [25] first propose Zero-shot VQA (ZS-VQA) and introduce novel concepts on language semantic side, where a test sample is regarded as unseen if there is at least one novel word in its question or answer. Ramakrishnan et al. [22] incorporate prior knowledge into model through pre-training with unstructured external data (from both visual and semantic level). Farazi et al. [9] reformulate ZS-VQA as a transfer learning task that applies closely seen instances (I-Q pairs) for reasoning about unseen concepts. A major limitation of these approaches is that they seldom consider the imbalance and low resources problem regarding the answer itself. Open-answer VQA requires models to select answer with the highest activation from fixed possible K answer categories, but the model cannot tackle unseen answers because answers are isolated with no specific meaning. Besides, VQA is defined as a classification problem without utilizing enough semantic information of the answer. Agrawal et al. [1] propose a new setting for VQA where the test question-answer pairs are compositionally novel compared to training question-answer pairs. Some methods [12,24] try to align answer with I-Q joint embedding through feature representation for realizing unseen answer prediction or simply for concatenating their representation as the input of a fully connected layer for score prediction [25]. However, all of them are powerless to answer those I-Q pairs that require external knowledge, and the relevance among answers are still not strong enough with insufficient external information. The ZS-VQA method proposed in this paper incorporates richer and more relevant knowledge by using KGs, through which the existing common sense is well utilized and more accurate answers are often given.

3   Preliminaries

Visual Question Answering (VQA) and Zero-Shot VQA. A VQA task is to provide a correct answer a given an image i paired with a question q. Following the open-answer VQA setting defined in [12], let a be a member of the answer pool $\mathcal{A} = \{a_1, ..., a_n\}$, the candidates of which are the top K (e.g. 500) most frequent answers of the whole dataset. A dataset is represented by a set of distinctive triplets $\mathcal{D} = \{(i, q, a) | i \in \mathcal{I}, q \in \mathcal{Q}, a \in \mathcal{A}\}$ where $\mathcal{I}$ and $\mathcal{Q}$ are respectively image and question sets. A testing dataset is denoted as $\mathcal{D}_{te}$ with each triplet (i, q, a) not belonging to training dataset $\mathcal{D}_{tr}$. We denote $\mathcal{D}_{tr}^{zsl} = \{(i, q, a) | i \in \mathcal{I}, q \in \mathcal{Q}, a \in \mathcal{A}_s\}$ and $\mathcal{D}_{te}^{zsl} = \{(i, q, a) | i \in \mathcal{I}, q \in \mathcal{Q}, a \in \mathcal{A}_u\}$, where $\mathcal{A}_s$ and $\mathcal{A}_u$ respectively denote the seen answer set and the unseen answer set with $\mathcal{A}_u \cap \mathcal{A}_s = \emptyset$. ZS-VQA is much harder than normal VQA, since information in the image and question is insufficient for answers that have never appeared in the training samples. Specifically, we study two settings at testing stage of ZS-VQA: one is the standard ZSL, where the candidates answers of a testing sample (i, q, a) are $\mathcal{A}_u$, while the other is the generalized ZSL (GZSL) with $\mathcal{A}_u \cup \mathcal{A}_s$ as candidates answers during testing. It should be noted that regular VQA only predicts with seen answers, while VQA under the GZSL setting predicts with both seen and unseen answers.

Knowledge Graph (KG). KGs have been widely used in knowledge representation and knowledge management [19,20]. The KG we used is a subset of three KGs (DBpedia, ConceptNet, WebChild) selected by Wang et al. [27] (in the form of RDF[2] triple). It is used to establish the prior knowledge connection, which includes a set of answer nodes and concept (tool) nodes to enrich the relationships among answers. Besides, different relations (edges) are applied to represent the fact graph (triples).

Taking Fig. 1 as an example, all (i, q) pairs could be divided into two categories according to their answer sources: 1) Those answers which are outside the images and questions. Such as the answer "dog" to question "Q1: Normally you play this game with your?", the data source of the answer here is the external KG which contains the triple <frisbee, BelongTo, toy> for QA support. 2) Those answers that can be found in images or questions. In this situation, there are often more than one object in image/question for screening through some implicit common sense relations (e.g., "Q2: Which object in this image is like a plate?" targets at finding the correct object related to plate). Then, one fact triple (e.g. <plate, RelatedTo, frisbee>) could play the role of answer guidance.

---

[2] https://www.w3.org/TR/2014/REC-rdf11-mt-20140225/.

4   Methodology

4.1   Main Idea

Our main idea is motivated by two deficiencies in current knowledge-based VQA approaches. Firstly, in those methods it is common to build intermediate models and involve KG queries in a pipeline way, which leads to error cascading and poor generalization. Secondly, most of them define VQA as a classification problem which does not utilize enough knowledge of the answers, and fails to predict unseen answers or to transfer across datasets whose candidate answers have little or no overlap. For example, as shown in Fig. 1, if concept "frisbee" has not appeared in training set, traditional VQA will fail to recognize it in testing phase for answer out-of-vocabulary (OOV) problem. While other method [12] which takes answer semantics into account has lost the relation information: "Desires" came from entity "dog", or "RelatedTo" came from entity "plate".

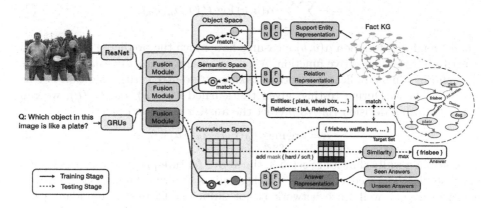

Fig. 2. An overview of our framework.

By utilizing semantics embedding feature as answer representation, we convert VQA from a classification task into a mapping task. After parameter learning, the distribution of the joint embedding between question and image can partly get close to answer's one with shadow knowledge included in. We call it the knowledge space about answers. Besides, we independently define two other feature spaces: semantic space about relations and object space about support entities. Semantic space aims to project (i, q) joint feature into a relation according to the semantic information in triplets, while object space targets at establishing relevant connection between (i, q) and a support entity (a.k.a. entity on KG). They play the role for answer guidance when combined together (see Sect. 4.2 for detail). In order to overcome those limitations proposed in Sect. 2.1, we provide a soft/hard mask method in this situation to effectively enhance alignment process meanwhile alleviating error cascading.

4.2 Establishment of Multiple Feature Spaces

Following [12], we establish connection between an answer and its corresponding (i, q) pair via projecting them into a common feature space and get close to each other. Firstly, a fusion feature extractor $F_\theta (i, q)$ between q and i is leveraged to combine multimodal information. Meanwhile, we define $G_\phi(a)$ as the representation of answer a. We follow the probabilistic model of compatibility (PMC) drawn from [12] and add loss temperature τ for better optimization:

$$P(a \mid i_n, q_n) = \frac{\exp \left(F_\theta (i_n, q_n)^\top G_\phi(a)/\tau \right)}{\sum_{a' \in \mathcal{A}} \exp \left(F_\theta (i_n, q_n)^\top G_\phi (a') /\tau \right)} \tag{1}$$

where $\mathcal{A}$ denotes $\mathcal{A}_u$ when the setting is standard ZSL else remain the same, and a is the correct answer of (i_n, q_n). For learning the parameters to maximize the likelihood in overall PMC model, we employ following loss function:

$$\ell_a = -\sum_n^N \sum_{b \in \mathcal{A}} \alpha(a, b) \log P (b \mid i_n, q_n) \tag{2}$$

where weighting function $\alpha(a, b)$ measures how much the predicted answer b can contribute to the objective function. A nature design is $\alpha(a, b) = \mathbb{I}[a = b]$, where $\mathbb{I}[.]$ denotes binary indicator function, taking value of 1 if the condition is true else 0 for false. During testing, given the learned $F_\theta (i, q)$ and $G_\phi(a)$, we can apply following decision rule to predict the answer $\hat{a}$ to (i, q) pair:

$$\hat{a} = \arg \max_{a \in \mathcal{A}} F_\theta(i, q)^\top G_\phi(a) \tag{3}$$

Like the results shown in Sect. 5.3, the above feature projection process could learn shallow knowledge in VQA which requires external knowledge. However, it performs not well since network is not sufficient to model abundant prior knowledge with small amount of training data (see data statistics in Table 1).

Matching the elements in images or questions to KG entities in an explicit [27] or implicit [9] way can augment the model with knowledge to well address the open-world scene understanding problem (see links in Fig. 1 toy example). In our method, the alignment between image/question and KG is implicitly done by multiple feature spaces rather than simply object detection. We leverage another two feature spaces for answer revising:

1) **Semantic space** focuses on the language information within (i, q), which works as a guidance toward the projection of triplet relations r in KG. In particular, the signal of q is more crucial than i in this part.
2) Compared with traditional image classification which identifies the correct category of a given image, the **object space** is more likely a feature space about support entity classifier which simultaneously observes images and texts for salient feature. Specifically, the alignment between support entity e embedding and (i, q) joint embedding avoids the direct learning of complex knowledge, meanwhile acts on the subsequent answer mask process together with the prediction relations r obtained in semantic space.

Similarly, we define their embedding function as $G_{\phi\star}(r)$, $G_{\phi\diamond}(e)$ and the corresponding (i, q) joint embedding function as $F_{\theta\star}(i, q)$, $F_{\theta\diamond}(i, q)$ for distinction. Other formulas and probability calculation methods remain the same as answer such as loss function ℓ_r and ℓ_e, which are model's overall optimization goal together with ℓ_a. The parameters in these three pairs of models are independent except for the frozen input embedding layers.

Pre-trained word vector contains the latent semantics in real-world natural language. In order to get the initialized representation of the answer, relation and support entity, we employ GloVe embedding [21] meanwhile compare other answer representation like KG embedding [4] or ConceptNet embedding [15] (see Sect. 5.4 for detail).

Besides, different surface forms (e.g., mice & mouse) should be considered for the same meaning. [12] takes advantage of the weighting function $\alpha(a, b)$ with WUPS score, which is reliant on semantic similarity scores between a and b. We find that it works well with singular and plural disambiguation (e.g. WUPS $(dog, dogs) \approx 0.929$), but fails in many cases of tense disambiguation (e.g., WUPS $(cook, cooking) \approx 0.125$, WUPS $(play, played) \approx 0.182$). So we apply NLTK tools (e.g., WordNetLemmatizer) to achieve more accurate word split and Minimum Edit Distance (MED) for concept disambiguation.

4.3 Answer Mask via Knowledge

Masking is widely used in language model pre-training for improving machine's understanding of the text. Two examples are masking part of the words in the training corpus (e.g. BERT [8]) and masking common sense concepts (e.g. AMS [30]). But they rarely consider the direct constraint of knowledge in prediction results, ignoring that human beings know how to make reasonable decision under the guidance of existing prior knowledge. Different from all these methods, we propose an answer masking strategy for VQA.

With the learned $F_{\theta\star}$ and $F_{\theta\diamond}$, we get the disjoint fusion embedding in two independent feature spaces, which are respectively taken as the basis for subsequent entity and relation matching: For a given (i, q) pair, vector similarity Sim is calculated via $F_{\theta\star}(i, q)^{\top} G_{\phi\star}(r_n)$ for relation, and $F_{\theta\diamond}(i, q)^{\top} G_{\phi\diamond}(e_n)$ for support entity. Those e and r, which correspond to the top-k Sim value, separately constitute the candidate set $\mathcal{C}_{ent}$ and $\mathcal{C}_{rel}$ where k is distinguished with k_r and k_e. Then target set $\mathcal{C}_{tar}$ is collected as follows:

$$\mathcal{C}_{tar} = \{t \mid (\exists(t, r, e) \vee \exists(e, r, t)) \wedge r \in \mathcal{C}_{rel} \wedge e \in \mathcal{C}_{ent}\} \tag{4}$$

$\mathcal{C}_{tar}$ contributes to the masking strategy on all answers $a_n \in \mathcal{A}$ via:

$$sim((i, q), a_n) = \begin{cases} (F_\theta(i, q)^{\top} G_\phi(a_n))/\tau & \text{if } a_n \in \mathcal{C}_{tar} \\ (F_\theta(i, q)^{\top} G_\phi(a_n))/\tau + s & \text{otherwise} \end{cases} \tag{5}$$

where s represents the score for masking which is the mainly distinction between hard mask and soft mask (see Sect. 5.4 for detail). Soft score greatly reduces the error cascading caused by the pipeline method through the whole model, which will be discussed in Sect. 5.5. Meanwhile, the significance of hard mask comes from its superior performance in ZSL setting as shown in Sect. 5.3. Finally, the predicted answer $\hat{a}$ to the (i, q) pair is identified as:

$$\hat{a} = \arg \max_{a \in \mathcal{A}} sim((i, q), a) \tag{6}$$

It should be noted that candidate targets cannot just be regarded as the candidate answers due to the existence of soft mask, which revises the answer probability rather than simply limits answer's range. Moreover, as mentioned in Sect. 5.4 and 5.4, k and s mentioned above are hyper parameters which can cause various influence toward the result.

5   Experiments

We validate our approach for both normal VQA and ZS-VQA with ZSL/GZSL settings. In addition to the overall results, we conduct ablation studies for analyzing the impact of: 1) different factors in answer embedding; 2) the mask score; and 3) different hyper parameters (e.g. k_e, k_r). Finally, we evaluate its advantage on data transferability and mitigating error cascading.

5.1   Datasets and Metrics

F-VQA. As a standard publicly available VQA benchmark which requires external knowledge, F-VQA [27] consists of $2,190$ images, $5,286$ questions and a KG of $193,449$ facts. Each (i, q, a) in this dataset is supported by a corresponding common sense fact triple extracted from public structured databases (e.g., ConceptNet, DBPedia, and WebChild). The KG has 101K entities and 1833 relations in total, 833 entities are used as answer nodes. In order to achieve parallel comparison, we maintain the coincide experiment setting with [18,27] to use standard dataset setting which contains 5 splits (by images), and prescribe candidate answers to the top-500 (%94.30 to entire as our check) for experiments. The over all data statistics after disambiguation are shown in Table 1.

ZS-F-VQA. The ZS-F-VQA dataset is a new split of the F-VQA dataset for zero-shot problem. Firstly we obtain the original train/test split of F-VQA dataset and combine them together to filter out the triples whose answers appear in top-500 according to its occurrence frequency. Next, we randomly divide this set of answers into new training split (a.k.a. seen) $\mathcal{A}_s$ and testing split (a.k.a. unseen) $\mathcal{A}_u$ at the ratio of 1:1. With reference to F-VQA standard dataset, the division process is repeated 5 times. For each (i, q, a) triplet in original F-VQA dataset, it is divided into training set if $a \in \mathcal{A}_s$. Else it is divided into testing set. The data statistics are shown in Table 1, where #class represents the number of data after deduplicated and #instance represents the number of samples. We denote "Overlap" as the intersection size of element sets within training and testing triples. Note that the overlap of answer instance between training and testing set in F-VQA are 2565 compared to 0 in ZS-F-VQA.

Table 1. The detailed data statistics. Average number of (i, q, a) in each train/test split in F-VQA is 2757/2735 compared to 2732/2760 of ZS-F-VQA.

#class	Images	Question	Answer	Support entity
	Train/Test/Overlap	Train/Test/Overlap	Train/Test/Overlap	Train/Test/Overlap
F-VQA	1059/1064/0	2431/2409/573	387/401/288	1695/1668.8/312
ZS-F-VQA	1297/1312/486	2384/2380/264	250/250/0	1578/1477/86
#instance	Overlap	Overlap	Overlap	Overlap
F-VQA	0	1372	2565	312
ZS-F-VQA	990	814	0	218

Evaluation Metrics. We measure the performance by accuracy and choose $Hit@1$, $Hit@3$, $Hit@10$ here together with MRR/MR to judge the comprehensive performance of model. $Hit@X$ indicates that the correct answer ranks in the top-k predicted answer sorted by probability. Mean Reciprocal Rank (MRR) measure the average reciprocal values of correct predicted answers compared to Mean Rank (MR). All the results we report are averaged across all splits.

5.2 Implementation Details

Fusion Model. We employ several models to parameterize the fusion function F_θ. We follow [12] to employ the Multi-layer Perceptron (MLP) and Stacked Attention Network (SAN) [29] as the representation of grid based visual fusion model. Meanwhile, we choose Up-Down (Bottom-Up and Top-Down Attention) [2] and Bilinear Attention Networks (BAN) [13] to measure the impact of bottom-up issue on external knowledge VQA problem. Moreover, we directly compare with [27] in some baselines like Qqmaping [27] Hie [14] under identical setting. Among all these methods, SAN is chosen as the base feature extractor F_θ of our framework for its better performance(see Fig. 2).

Visual Features. To get i_n, we extract visual features from the layer 4 output of ResNet-152 ($14 \times 14 \times 2048$ tensor) pre-trained on ImageNet. Meanwhile applying ResNet-101-based Faster R-CNN pre-trained on COCO dataset to get bottom-up image region features. The object number per image is fixed into 36 with 1024 output dimensional feature.

Text Features. Each word in question and answer is represented by its 300-dimension GloVe [21] vector. The sequence of embedded words in question (average length is 9.5) is then fed into Bi-GRU for each time step. We have also tried to embed answer with GRU but find that it mostly leads to overfitting since the training set is not huge enough and average answer length is merely 1.2. So we simply represent the answer by averaging its word embedding.

During training, we utilize Adam optimizer with the mini-batch size as 128. Dropout and batch normalization are adopted to stabilize the training. We use a gradual learning rate warm up ($2.5 \times (epoch + 1) \times 5 \times 10^{-4}$) for the first 7 epochs, decay it at the rate of 0.7 for every 3 epochs for epochs 14 to 47, and remain the same in rest epochs. Meanwhile, the loss temperature τ is set to 0.01 and early stopping is used where *patience* is equal to 30. The model is trained offline, and thus the training time usually does not impact the method's application. In prediction, we currently consider 500 candidate answers for each testing sample. This makes the computation for evaluation affordable.

5.3   Overall Results

Table 2. The overall results (% for *Hit@K*) on standard F-VQA datasets (TOP-500). [†] denotes that the model is modified under a mapping-based setting (i.e., remove the last classifier layer of the (i, q) fusion network), which contrasts with traditional classifier-based approach.

Methods	*Hit*@1	*Hit*@3	*Hit*@10	*MRR*	*MR*
Hie-Q+I [14]	33.70	50.00	64.08	–	–
MLP	34.12	52.26	69.11	–	–
Up-Down [2]	34.81	50.13	64.37	–	–
Up-Down[†]	40.91	57.47	72.74	–	–
SAN [29]	41.62	58.17	72.69	–	–
Hie-Q+I+Pre [14]	43.14	59.44	72.20	–	–
BAN [13]	44.02	58.92	71.34	–	–
BAN[†]	45.95	63.36	78.12	–	–
MLP[†]	47.55	66.76	<u>81.55</u>	–	–
SAN[†]	49.27	<u>67.30</u>	81.79	0.605	14.75
top-1-Qqmaping [27]	52.56	59.72	60.58	–	–
top-3-Qqmaping [27]	<u>56.91</u>	64.65	65.54	–	–
Our method (*soft mask score* = 10)					
$k_r = 3, \ k_e = 1$	**58.27**	75.2	86.4	0.683	11.72
$k_r = 3, \ k_e = 3$	57.42	**76.51**	87.53	**0.685**	10.51
$k_r = 3, \ k_e = 5$	53.84	74.88	**88.49**	0.661	9.58
$k_r = 5, \ k_e = 10$	54.02	74.53	88.03	0.660	**9.17**

Results on F-VQA. To demonstrate the effectiveness of our model under generalized VQA condition, we conduct experiments under standard F-VQA dataset. Results in Table 2 gives an overview of the comprehensive evaluation for some representative approaches over this datasets. It is interesting that the Up-Down and BAN behave worse than SAN, which may be caused by overfitting of the model due to more parameters and limited training data (less than 3000). But among all those settings, the results demonstrate that our models all outperform corresponding classifier-based or mapping-based models to varying degrees. The stable improvement (compare with SAN[†]) achieved by our model indicates that adding our method to other end-to-end framework under generalized knowledge VQA setting could also lead to stable performance improvement. Most importantly, our proposed KG-based framework is independent of fusion model, which makes it possible for multi-scene migration and multi-model replacement.

Results on ZS-F-VQA. We report the prediction results under the standard ZSL setting and GZSL setting in Table 3. Considering that the traditional classifier-based VQA model fail to work on ZS-VQA since there is no overlap of answer label between the testing set and training set (see Table 1 for detail), we simply skip these methods here. We set larger parameters k under ZSL/GZSL setting to mitigate the strong constraint on answer candidate caused by hard mask. From the overall view, the performance of our model has been significantly improved on the basis of SAN† model.

Most importantly, the models obtain the state-of-the-art performance under respective indicators with various parameter settings. Take the result in GZSL setting as an example, our method achieve 29.39% improvement for $hit@1$ (from 0.22% to 29.39%), 44.17% for $hit@3$ and 75.34% for $hit@3$. We have similar observations when the setting transforms into standard ZSL. To sum up, these observations demonstrate the effectiveness of the model in the ZSL/GZSL scenario, but it also reflects model's dependence on trade off between k_r and k_e (this will be discussed in Sect. 5.4).

Table 3. The overall results (% for $Hit@K$) on ZS-F-VQA datasets under the setting of ZSL/GZSL.

Methods	GZSL					ZSL				
	$Hit@1$	$Hit@3$	$Hit@10$	MRR	MR	$Hit@1$	$Hit@3$	$Hit@10$	MRR	MR
Up-Down†	0.00	2.67	16.48	–	–	13.88	25.87	45.15	–	–
BAN†	0.22	4.18	18.55	–	–	13.14	26.92	46.90	–	–
MLP†	0.07	4.07	27.40	–	–	18.84	37.85	59.88	–	–
SAN†	0.11	6.27	31.66	0.093	48.18	20.42	37.20	62.24	0.337	19.14
Our method (*hard mask score* = 100)										
$k_r = 25,\ k_e = 1$	**29.39**	43.71	62.17	**0.401**	29.52	46.87	62	78.14	0.572	12.22
$k_r = 15,\ k_e = 3$	12.22	**50.44**	73.10	0.339	22.2	**50.51**	70.44	84.24	**0.625**	9.27
$k_r = 15,\ k_e = 5$	6.69	42.91	**75.34**	0.293	20.61	49.11	**71.17**	86.06	0.622	8.6
$k_r = 25,\ k_e = 15$	1.96	24.8	72.85	0.208	18.72	40.21	67.04	**88.51**	0.563	7.68
$k_r = 25,\ k_e = 25$	1.19	18.81	66.97	0.180	**18.14**	35.87	61.86	88.09	0.528	**7.3**

5.4 Ablation Studies

Table 4. The impact of different answer embedding toward model performance (%) on standard F-VQA datasets (TOP-500). $x(a)$, $h(a)$ and $v(a)$ respectively denote KGE, ConceptNet embedding, and original GloVe embedding. CLS is classifier-based method.

Methods	$Hit@1$	$Hit@3$	$Hit@10$
CLS	38.64	54.87	69.38
$v(a)$	**46.32**	**63.96**	**78.44**
$x(a)$	44.13	59.94	71.94
$h(a)$	45.62	62.99	77.34
$v(a) + h(a)$	45.86	63.67	78.43
$v(a) + h(a) + x(a)$	45.18	62.95	77.14

Choice of Answer Embedding. To compare the influence of answer embedding in feature projection performance, we define $g_\phi(a) = g_\phi(\mathcal{C}[x(a); h(a); v(a)])$ in this part where $\mathcal{C}$ denotes simple concatenate function. Specially, $x(a)$, $h(a)$ and $v(a)$ respectively denotes KG embedding (KGE), ConceptNet embedding [15], and original GloVe embedding. This KGE technique can be used to complete the KG with missing entities or links, meanwhile produce the embedding of nodes and links as their representations. Specially, we adopt TransE [4] as $x(.)$ and train it on our KG. As for $h(a)$, we utilize the BERT-based node representations generated by a pre-trained common sense embedding model [15], which exploits the structural and semantic context of nodes within a large scale common sense KG. As the result shown in Table 4, when work independently, word2vec representation (78.44%) of answers exceed graph based methods (71.94% for KGE and 77.34% for ConceptNet Embedding in $Hit@10$) in performance even though they contain more information. We guess that when the size of the dataset is small, the complexity of neural network limits model's sensitivity to the input representation. So finally we simply choose GloVe as the initial representation of all inputs.

Impact of Mask Score. In this part we mainly discuss the effect of mask score on ZS-F-VQA and F-VQA which is reflected by $hit@1$ (Left), $hit@3$ (Middle) and $hit@10$ (Right) accuracy as shown in Fig. 3. Caused by the sparsity of high-dimensional space vector, the value of $F_{\theta\diamond}(i,q)^\top G_{\phi\diamond}(f_n))$ is quite small as we observing on experiment. This is also another reasons why we define τ for the scale-up of vector similarity (in addition to accelerating model convergence). Considering that $sim((i,q), a_n)$ distributes from 145 to 232, we simply take 100 as the dividing line of score between hard mask and soft mask which is big enough for correcting an incorrect answer into a correct one in testing stage. As shown in

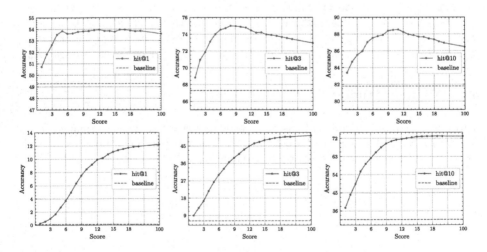

Fig. 3. Impact of mask score in standard F-VQA ($k_r = 3$, $k_e = 10$) under generalized setting (Up), and ZS-F-VQA ($k_r = 15$, $k_e = 3$) under GZSL setting (Down).

Fig. 3, the result gaps between soft mask (i.e., low score) and hard mask (i.e., high score) are completely different in ZSL and GZSL VQA scenarios. We consider following reasons: 1) Firstly, do not try to rely on network to model complex common sense knowledge when data is scarce: When applied to ZS-F-VQA, we notice that model merely learns prior shallow knowledge representation and poor transfer capabilities for unseen answers (see Sect. 5.5). In this case, the strong guiding capability of additional knowledge makes a great contribution to answer prediction. 2) Secondly, if the training samples are sufficient, the error cascading caused by pipeline mode may become the restriction of model performance: When applied to standard F-VQA, the model itself already has high confidence in correct answer and external knowledge should appropriately relax the constraint. We observe that overly strong guidance (i.e., hard mask) becomes a burden at this moment, so soft mask is in demand as a soft constraint. This reflects the necessity of defining different mask.

Impact of Support Entity and Relation. As shown in Fig. 4, we notice that $hit@1$ and $hit@10$ cannot simultaneously achieve the best, despite that the model can always exceed the baseline a lot with different k. This phenomenon is plausible since that the more restrictive target candidate set is, the more likely it succeed predicting answer in a smaller range, with the cost of missing some other true answers due to the error prediction of support entity/relation. The contrast between MRR and MR well reflects this view (see Table 3).

5.5 Interpretability

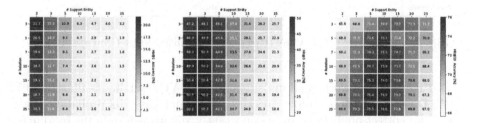

Fig. 4. Impact of #support entity (k_e) and #relation (k_r) on GZSL setting.

To further validate the effectiveness of our knowledge-based ZS-VQA model, we visualize the output and intermediate process of our method compared to best baseline model SAN[†] [12]. Figure 5 (Up) shows the detected support entities, relations, and answers for four examples in ZS-F-VQA dataset together with answer predicted by SAN[†] and the groudtruth one. It indicates that normal models tend to align answer directly with meaning content in question/image (e.g. bicycle in Case 3) or match the seen answers (e.g. airplane in case 4), which is a lazy way of learning accompanied by overfitting. To some extend, the difficult common sense knowledge stored in structured data is utilized to playing a guiding role here. Our method can also be generalized to predict multiple answers since the probabilistic model can calculate scores for all candidates to select the top-K answers (see answer "tv" in Case 2 of Fig. 5).

Question		What thing does the animal in this image have as a part?	Which object in this image could perform a screen	which object in this image is faster than bike?	Which object in this image is related to fly?
Image					
Our Model	Support Entity	zebra, elephant, zoo, giraffe	screen capture, screen, computer display, display image	fast than bicycle, bike, ride, fast than car	fly, catch fly, attempt to fly, learn to fly
	Relation	has a, part of, is a	capable of, used for, related to	slow, expensive, efficient	related to, belong to, specific
	Answer	stripe, horse, string ✓	computer, tv, keyboard ✓	car, bicycle, traffic light ✓	dragonfly, bird, airplane ✓
SAN†	Answer	string, water, ocean ✗	mouse, hand, lamp ✗	bicycle, traffic light, airplane ✗	airplane, kite, fly ✗
Ground Truth		stripe	computer	car	dragonfly

Question		Which object in this image is a cartilaginous fish?	Which object in this image is related to drive?	What is the place in this image used for?
Image				
Our Model	Support Entity	fish, eat fish, fish tank, carp, crab	drive, disk drive, drive on, drive lorry, drive only on track	ocean, sandy, lake, ocean beach, sand
	Relation	is a, belong to, related to	related to, specific, used for	used for, related to, capable of
	Answer	ray, jellyfish, lobster, turtle, sea, fish ✓	horse, cattle, car, cart, train, bicycle ✓	store boat, sail boat, swim, ski, swimming, life preserver ✓
SAN†	Answer	ray, turtle, fish, frog, jellyfish, lobster ✓	horse, cart, cow, sheep, cattle, camel ✓	life preserver, travel across water, sea, desert, ocean , store boat ✗
Ground Truth		grass	cattle	swim

Fig. 5. Cases under GZSL VQA (Up) and Generalized VQA (Down) setting.

Our method also works well under generalized VQA setting as illustrated in Fig. 5 (Down). For those simpler answers, it can increase the probability (e.g. Case 6) for correct prediction. More importantly, distinguish from the hard mask (dark shadows) in ZSL setting, the soft mask strategy here effectively alleviates error cascading which reduces the influence from previous model's error (e.g. failed prediction on support entity lead to the error mask on Case 5).

6   Conclusion

We propose a Zero-shot VQA model via knowledge graph for addressing the problem of exploiting external knowledge for Zero-shot VQA. The crucial factor to the success of our method is to consider both the knowledge contained in the answer itself and the external common sense knowledge from knowledge graphs. Meanwhile we convert VQA from a traditional classification task to a mapping-based alignment task for addressing unseen answer prediction. Experiments on multiple models support our claim that this method can not only achieve outstanding performance in zero-shot scenarios but also make steady progress at different end-to-end models on the general VQA task. Next we will further investigate KG construction and KG embedding methods for more robust but compact semantics for addressing ZS-VQA. Moreover, we will release and improve the ZS-VQA codes and data, in conjunction with K-ZSL [11].

Acknowledgments. This work is funded by 2018YFB1402800/NSFCU19B2027 /NSFC91846204. Jiaoyan Chen is founded by the SIRIUS Centre for Scalable Data Access (Research Council of Norway) and Samsung Research UK.

References

1. Agrawal, A., Kembhavi, A., Batra, D., Parikh, D.: C-VQA: a compositional split of the visual question answering (VQA) v1.0 dataset. CoRR arXiv:1704.08243 (2017)
2. Anderson, P., et al.: Bottom-up and top-down attention for image captioning and visual question answering. In: CVPR, pp. 6077–6086 (2018)
3. Antol, S., et al.: VQA: visual question answering. In: ICCV, pp. 2425–2433 (2015)
4. Bordes, A., Usunier, N., García-Durán, A., Weston, J., Yakhnenko, O.: Translating embeddings for modeling multi-relational data. In: NIPS, pp. 2787–2795 (2013)
5. Chen, J., Geng, Y., Chen, Z., Horrocks, I., Pan, J.Z., Chen, H.: Knowledge-aware zero-shot learning: survey and perspective. In: IJCAI Survey Track (2021)
6. Chen, L., Gan, Z., Cheng, Y., Li, L., Carin, L., Liu, J.: Graph optimal transport for cross-domain alignment. In: ICML, vol. 119, pp. 1542–1553 (2020)
7. Chen, W., Zha, H., Chen, Z., Xiong, W., Wang, H., Wang, W.Y.: HybridQA: a dataset of multi-hop question answering over tabular and textual data. In: EMNLP, pp. 1026–1036 (2020)
8. Devlin, J., Chang, M., Lee, K., Toutanova, K.: BERT: pre-training of deep bidirectional transformers for language understanding. In: NAACL, pp. 4171–4186 (2019)
9. Farazi, M.R., Khan, S.H., Barnes, N.: From known to the unknown: transferring knowledge to answer questions about novel visual and semantic concepts. Image Vis. Comput. **103**, 103985 (2020)
10. Geng, Y., et al.: OntoZSL: ontology-enhanced zero-shot learning. In: WWW, pp. 3325–3336 (2021)
11. Geng, Y., Chen, J., Chen, Z., Pan, J.Z., Yuan, Z., Chen, H.: K-ZSL: resources for knowledge-driven zero-shot learning. CoRR arXiv:2106.15047 (2021)
12. Hu, H., Chao, W., Sha, F.: Learning answer embeddings for visual question answering. In: CVPR, pp. 5428–5436 (2018)
13. Kim, J., Jun, J., Zhang, B.: Bilinear attention networks. In: NeurIPS, pp. 1571–1581 (2018)
14. Lu, J., Yang, J., Batra, D., Parikh, D.: Hierarchical question-image co-attention for visual question answering. In: NIPS, pp. 289–297 (2016)
15. Malaviya, C., Bhagavatula, C., Bosselut, A., Choi, Y.: Commonsense knowledge base completion with structural and semantic context. In: AAAI, pp. 2925–2933 (2020)
16. Marino, K., Rastegari, M., Farhadi, A., Mottaghi, R.: OK-VQA: A visual question answering benchmark requiring external knowledge. In: CVPR, pp. 3195–3204 (2019)

17. Narasimhan, M., Lazebnik, S., Schwing, A.G.: Out of the box: reasoning with graph convolution nets for factual visual question answering. In: NeurIPS, pp. 2659–2670 (2018)
18. Narasimhan, M., Schwing, A.G.: Straight to the facts: learning knowledge base retrieval for factual visual question answering. In: Ferrari, V., Hebert, M., Sminchisescu, C., Weiss, Y. (eds.) ECCV 2018. LNCS, vol. 11212, pp. 460–477. Springer, Cham (2018). https://doi.org/10.1007/978-3-030-01237-3_28
19. Pan, J., et al. (eds.): Reasoning Web: Logical Foundation of Knowledge Graph Construction and Querying Answering. Springer, Cham (2017). https://doi.org/10.1007/978-3-319-49493-7
20. Pan, J., Vetere, G., Gomez-Perez, J., Wu, H. (eds.): Exploiting Linked Data and Knowledge Graphs for Large Organisations. Springer, Cham (2017). https://doi.org/10.1007/978-3-319-45654-6
21. Pennington, J., Socher, R., Manning, C.D.: GloVe: global vectors for word representation. In: EMNLP, pp. 1532–1543 (2014)
22. Ramakrishnan, S.K., Pal, A., Sharma, G., Mittal, A.: An empirical evaluation of visual question answering for novel objects. In: CVPR, pp. 7312–7321 (2017)
23. Shah, S., Mishra, A., Yadati, N., Talukdar, P.P.: KVQA: knowledge-aware visual question answering. In: AAAI, pp. 8876–8884 (2019)
24. Shevchenko, V., Teney, D., Dick, A.R., van den Hengel, A.: Visual question answering with prior class semantics. CoRR arXiv:2005.01239 (2020)
25. Teney, D., van den Hengel, A.: Zero-shot visual question answering. CoRR arXiv:1611.05546 (2016)
26. Wang, P., Wu, Q., Shen, C., Dick, A.R., van den Hengel, A.: Explicit knowledge-based reasoning for visual question answering. In: IJCAI, pp. 1290–1296 (2017)
27. Wang, P., Wu, Q., Shen, C., Dick, A.R., van den Hengel, A.: FVQA: fact-based visual question answering. IEEE TPAMI **40**(10), 2413–2427 (2018)
28. Wu, Q., Wang, P., Shen, C., Dick, A.R., van den Hengel, A.: Ask me anything: free-form visual question answering based on knowledge from external sources. In: CVPR, pp. 4622–4630 (2016)
29. Yang, Z., He, X., Gao, J., Deng, L., Smola, A.J.: Stacked attention networks for image question answering. In: CVPR, pp. 21–29 (2016)
30. Ye, Z., Chen, Q., Wang, W., Ling, Z.: Align, mask and select: a simple method for incorporating commonsense knowledge into language representation models. CoRR arXiv:1908.06725 (2019)
31. Zhu, Z., Yu, J., Wang, Y., Sun, Y., Hu, Y., Wu, Q.: Mucko: multi-layer cross-modal knowledge reasoning for fact-based visual question answering. In: IJCAI, pp. 1097–1103 (2020)

Learning to Recommend Items
to Wikidata Editors

Kholoud AlGhamdi[✉], Miaojing Shi, and Elena Simperl

King's College London, London, UK
{kholoud.alghamdi,miaojing.shi,elena.simperl}@kcl.ac.uk

Abstract. Wikidata is an open knowledge graph built by a global community of volunteers. As it advances in scale, it faces substantial challenges around editor engagement. These challenges are in terms of both attracting new editors to keep up with the sheer amount of work, and retaining existing editors. Experience from other online communities and peer-production systems, including Wikipedia, suggests that personalised recommendations could help, especially newcomers, who are sometimes unsure about how to contribute best to an ongoing effort. For this reason, we propose a recommender system *WikidataRec* for Wikidata items. The system uses a hybrid of content-based and collaborative filtering techniques to rank items for editors relying on both item features and item-editor previous interaction. A neural network, named neural mixture of representations, is designed to learn fine weights for the combination of item-based representations and optimize them with editor-based representation by item-editor interaction. To facilitate further research in this space, we also create two benchmark datasets, a general-purpose one with 220,000 editors responsible for 14 million interactions with 4 million items, and a second one focusing on the contributions of more than 8,000 more active editors. We perform an offline evaluation of the system on both datasets with promising results. Our code and datasets are available at https://github.com/WikidataRec-developer/Wikidata_Recommender.

1 Introduction

Wikidata is an open knowledge graph built by a global community of volunteers [40]. Since its launch in 2012 it reached more than 90 million items and 24,000 active editors[1]. Manual contributions are core to Wikidata [40]: editors add new content, keep it up-to-date, model knowledge as graph items and properties, and decide on all rules of content creation and management. However, as Wikidata advances in scale, it faces substantial challenges around editor engagement [34].

Experience from other online communities and peer-production systems, including Wikipedia, Quora and others, suggests that one way to improve engagement is through *recommendations* [7,9,44]. This is especially true for editors who are relatively new to Wikidata, who need to overcome so-called 'legitimate peripheral participation' (LPP) effects to continue to engage [28]. According to LPP,

---

[1] www.wikidata.org/wiki/Wikidata:Statistics/en.

© Springer Nature Switzerland AG 2021
A. Hotho et al. (Eds.): ISWC 2021, LNCS 12922, pp. 163–181, 2021.
https://doi.org/10.1007/978-3-030-88361-4_10

newcomers are more likely to become members of a community if they are provided with suggestions of (typically lower-risk) tasks they could carry out to further the goals of the community [19].

At the moment, looking for relevant items to edit in Wikidata remains challenging because of the sheer number of options available [34]. The suggested and open tasks page[2] gives a useful but daunting overview of the various ways in which people could contribute to Wikidata. Many task lists are automatically generated, without taking into account aspects such as editor tenure, previous editing history or interests. This lack of focus is also said to prevent editors from developing reinforced editing habits, which increases the likelihood of dropouts [34]. Seasoned editors use tools such as *QuickStatements*[3] and *Watchlist*[4] to organise their work, but such tools become relevant only once editors have identified productive ways to contribute.

For these reasons, we propose *WikidataRec*, a recommender system for Wikidata items. The system uses content-based and collaborative filtering techniques to rank items for editors relying on both item features and item-editor previous interaction. Collaborative filtering is a representative approach to address recommendation task with implicit feedback, which learns item-centric and editor-centric edit representations using matrix factorization [17] from item-editor interaction data. We adopt it in this work and further facilitate it with additional information from item content and relations, where we learn these representations from by sentence embedding model ELMo [26] and graph embedding model TransR [20], respectively. To combine the multiple representations, we introduce the neural mixture of representations (NMoR), a neural network inspired by mixture of experts [13] that produces fine weights for different item-based representations. It is optimized over the editor-based representation to rank items to editors. The proposed *WikidataRec* demonstrates a large capacity of leveraging items' contents, relations, and edit history between editors and items into the recommender.

To facilitate further research in this space, we also create two benchmark datasets, a general-purpose one with 220,000 editors responsible for 14 million interactions with 4 million items, and a more focused one with contributions of more than 8,000 active editors with more than 200 edits each. We evaluate the system on these datasets against several baselines and analyse the impact of different features and levels of data sparsity on performance. The results are promising, though challenges remain because of unbalanced participation, sparse interaction data and little explicit information about editors' interests and feedback.

2   Background and Related Work

2.1   Wikidata Data Model

Wikidata consists of structured records stored in form of entities, where each entity is allocated a separate page and described by a set of terms and statements [40].

---

[2] www.wikidata.org/wiki/Wikidata:Contribute/Suggested_and_open_tasks.
[3] https://quickstatements.toolforge.org/#/.
[4] www.wikidata.org/wiki/Help:Watchlist.

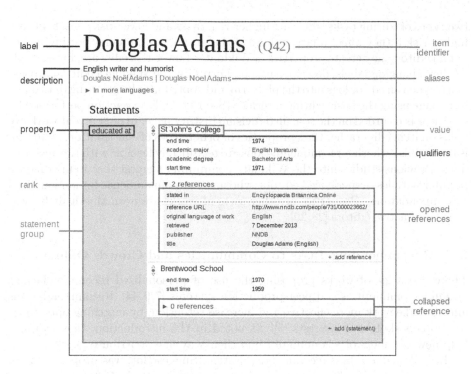

Fig. 1. The structure of an Wikidata item. Source: [42]

There are two types of entities, items and properties, situated in different namespaces. The namespaces are identified by URIs using numbers and letters, with the letter Q relating to items and the letter P to properties. Although there are other namespaces in Wikidata, we focus only on these two, as they are most relevant for our recommender system. Items and property pages have a similar interface, starting with labels, descriptions and aliases, which are language-specific, and then moving on to statements, which are language-agnostic. Each statement contains a set of triplet edges (head, relation, tail), capturing the different types of relations between entities in the world, e.g., London $\overrightarrow{\text{capital of}}$ United Kingdom. Pages also include sitelinks connecting to Wikipedia articles or other Wikimedia projects [24]. Each page is indexed by a unique identifier. Figure 1 shows an example of a Wikidata item page.

2.2   Editors and Editing in Wikidata

Anyone can edit Wikidata. The literature tends to distinguish between two types of contributions: manual ones, carried out by registered or anonymous editors, and bots. Bots are used for repetitive editing tasks, but do not contribute to discussions, modeling decisions, or rules for content creation, and management [24]. Human editors may get involved in any type of activities, though some require specific access rights or ontology engineering skills [28,29]. Furthermore, there are two types of editing tasks which are higher-risk tasks and lower-risk ones. Edits are higher-risk if they affect a larger share of the graph, e.g. property editing; hence not all editors may create properties in Wikidata. Lower-risk edits are, for example adding/changing labels, descriptions, etc. Formally, the Wikidata editing process starts when an editor logs into the platform and contributes by inserting data on an item page using the basic editing interface (See Fig. 1). Every action performed by an editor is recorded on the so-called revision history page. In our current work, we focus on item edits rather than properties or other types of contributions. Our aim is to establish whether recommendations are technically feasible with the available data. Previous studies into the Wikidata community suggest that item edits are popular with less experienced editors, who are the main audience for personalised recommendations. Properties or other sorts of works are normally dealt by seasoned and active editors [28,29].

2.3   Recommending Tasks to Communities and Crowds Online

There are a lot of works proposing the use of personalized recommendations in online communities and peer-production systems [7,9,44]. Recommendations aim to make work more effective and increase retention, by matching open tasks to people's skills and interests [5]. As noted in the introduction, they can also help new members of a community find their way and contribute [9,28].

In Wikipedia, a first recommender system, SuggestBot, was proposed in [5]. It used article titles, links, and co-editing patterns as main features to recommend articles to editors. A more recent recommender system by [23] represents Wikipedia articles using Graph Convolutional Networks. Both works aim to recommend items (Wikipedia articles) to editors based on features of items and editors. There is no explicit feedback that would confirm an editor's interest in an article. Equally, there is very little information about editors beyond what they have edited so far [23]. Our system is similar in spirit to [5] and [23], though our neural approach incorporates additional item-based features and a mix of representations.

In community question-answering (CQA), several papers develop recommender systems to route users to questions they might be interested in answering, hence improving their engagement on the platform and reducing question answering time [7,21,37,38]. [7,37] model recommendation as a classification problem, using different machine learning techniques. They implement a hybrid approach with content and collaborative knowledge to address the sparsity problem. [21,38] apply graph embedding techniques to tackle the same problem. Similarly, we mix item and relational representations with collaborative filtering to solve in a novel application context.

Another related area is online crowdsourcing, where the aim is to allocate tasks published by a requester to an online crowd. [18,33] employ a probabilistic matrix factorization (PMF) to recommend suitable tasks to crowdworkers based on their previous activities, performance, and preferences. They handle the cold start problem by utilizing predefined categories (e.g., sentiment analysis, translation, image labeling) as additional features to improve the recommendation accuracy.

2.4   Evaluating Recommender Systems

Evaluation Methodologies. To evaluate the performance of a recommender system, *precision@k* and *recall@k* are the most common metrics for top-k recommendations task with implicit data [36]. *Precision@k* measures the relevance of the recommended items list, whereas *recall@k* gives insight about how well the recommender is able to recall all the items the editor has rated positively (or interacted with) in the test set [36]. Moreover, there is a set of metrics that cares about where the relevant item appears in the recommended list. For instance, *mean average precision(MAP)* and *mean average recall (MAR)* are popular metric for search engines and are applied to the recommendation task [2]. In these metrics, the relevant items are required to be placed as high on the recommendation list as possible [36]. There is also a family of metrics such as *catalog coverage* and *diversity* that pays special attention to editor experience [2]. The *catalog coverage* evaluates whether the recommender algorithm can generate recommendations with a high proportion of items, and the *diversity* evaluates how diverse the set of proposed recommendations within a single recommended list [2].

Recommender Datasets. Recommender datasets are available for items such as movies (using MovieLens)[5] or products (using the Amazon dataset)[6]. In other tasks, such benchmarks are not widely available. The systems discussed in Sect. 2.3 are mostly evaluated on custom-built datasets derived from the platforms' activity logs. This is also the case with our system, which to the best of our knowledge is the first of its kind for Wikidata. To encourage further research in this space, we hence provide two new datasets for the community to reuse, specified in Sect. 3.

3   Wikidata Recommender Datasets

3.1   From Wikidata Dumps to Relational Tables

Wikidata dumps are readily available as JSON, RDF and XML[7]. In our work we use the JSON and XML ones from July 1, 2019. The JSON dump contains all Wikidata pages without their edit history, which is available as XML. We parse the JSON data to extract all Wikidata items along with their corresponding identifiers, labels, descriptions, and statements. For the text data (i.e. label and description), we fetch only the English language version and discard data for other languages, because English is the best covered language in Wikidata [15]. Also, we ignore items' metadata about aliases and sitelinks as we do not use them as features in our system. We transform the parsed data into CSV and import it into a PostgreSQL database (as a *Wikidata-items-content* table); further processed the raw data containing the items' statements (i.e. claims) in

---

[5] https://grouplens.org/datasets/movielens/.
[6] https://jmcauley.ucsd.edu/data/amazon/.
[7] https://dumps.wikimedia.org/wikidatawiki/.

similar way (as a *Wikidata-items-relations* PostgreSQL table). Next, we work on the XML dump to extract editing information for each individual editor. We only focus on edits that are performed on an item's namespace and ignore all other non-item-related actions, as we do not model this information in our system. For each edit, the following information is kept: who carried out the edit, the item being edited, the timestamps of the edit, and the comment indicating the specific action executed by the editor on the item. They are stored in PostgreSQL (as a *Wikidata-editors-edits* table).

3.2   Sampling and Cleaning

We randomly sample 14 million editing activities performed by 221, 353 editors who are human registered (i.e. non-bots). We sort these activities in ascending order based on timestamps. We refer to this as the *Wikidata-14M* dataset. We also want to test the system on a denser dataset that contains the editors who interacted with a larger number of items in their editing history and the items that received edits by a high number of editors. The *Wikidata-14M* dataset is filtered by keeping editors who edited at least 200 unique items during their tenure and items that have been edited by at least 5 different editors. We refer to it as the *Wikidata-Active-Editors* dataset. We then removed some outliers from both datasets - 2.14% of editors in *Wikidata-14M* and 5% in *Wikidata-Active-Editors* edited a very large number of items in a very short time relative to the size of their contributions. This is considered as the case for institutional accounts that publish their data via Wikidata [39]. We remove those accounts and their edits from the datasets, as they are not the main target editors for recommendations. We use both datasets to evaluate our system. The first one *Wikidata-14M* depicts the actual diversity of editing activities in Wikidata with a mix of active and more casual editors. The second one *Wikidata-Active-Editors* focuses on more active editors and items - we use it to understand the effects of data sparsity on recommender performance.

Table 1. Number of items, editors and interactions in the two Datasets.

Dataset	# editors	# items	# interactions
Wikidata-14M	221,353	4,881,720	14,045,523
Wikidata-Active-Editors	8,024	381,784	3,272,086

Table 2. Statistics of the distribution of editing activities among editors and items.

	Wikidata-14M			Wikidata-Active-Editors		
	Median	Mean	Std	Median	Mean	Std
# items/editor	1	72	534	900	1,244	2,197
# edits/editor	2	143	1,413	1,045	4,666	32,338
# editors/item	1	2	3.7	-	-	-

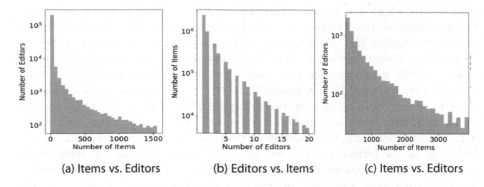

|(a) Items vs. Editors|(b) Editors vs. Items|(c) Items vs. Editors|

Fig. 2. Editing Activities Distribution in *Wikidata-14M* (a and b) and in *Wikidata-Active-Editors* (c).

3.3 Datasets Description

Table 1 reports some key descriptive statistics of the two datasets, *i.e.* number of editors, items and interactions. Figure 2a, 2b and 2c characterise the distribution of edits in the two datasets. For *Wikidata-14M*, Fig. 2a shows the number of items edited by each editor - most editors edited only a few items ($< 1,000$); while fewer than 100 editors (out of $221,353$) edited more than $1,500$ items. Table 2 illustrates this skewed distribution: the median values are much smaller than the mean values, both per editor and per item. It is in line with observations from previous studies in Wikidata and other large-scale community-driven knowledge engineering initiatives [16,29,34], which attest that a small core of contributors are responsible for a majority of the work. This also gives us an opportunity to increase retention in the long tail of editors (novice editors mostly) through recommendations. We also examine items that are edited by multiple editors, which is useful in collaborative filtering: Fig. 2b shows that most items have been edited only by small number of editors; the highest number of editors per item is 20. This implies the issue of cold-start for new items, we address it by mining item content and relation information for recommendation (see Sect. 4).

We observe similar, though less pronounced effects for *Wikidata-Active-Editors* (see Fig. 2c and Table 2): the interaction data between editors and items are denser, e.g. the mean and median of the number of items per editor is $1,244$ and 900, respectively, showing a less skewed distribution. Notice we do not have the corresponding Fig. 2b (Editors vs. Items) for *Wikidata-Active-Editors*, because all active editors are filtered and selected, making this statistic no longer meaningful.

4 Wikidata Recommender System

4.1 Problem Statement

Our problem is defined as follows: given a set of N editors, a set of M items, and an interaction matrix $A^{N \times M} = \{a_{ij}\}$, where each matrix entry a_{ij} is either 1 or

0 indicating whether editor i has edited item j. The task is learning to estimate the preference scores of editors to items so as to rank and recommend new items to editors. Solving this problem is not straightforward: as discussed in Sect. 3, there exists a high number of items but a low number of interactions between items and editors; many items have only a few edits. Standard approaches using collaborative filtering [35] rely primarily on the item-editor interaction data and do not perform well in our scenario. Intuitively, there are two ways to improve it: by including more information from either editors (e.g. their interests or activities) or items (e.g. their content or relations). In this paper we focus on the latter, as for the former, there is very little descriptive information available for Wikidata editors, a known issue also present in Wikipedia [5,23]. Of course one could try to collect additional information about editors from their activities in Wikidata discussions or contributions to other WikiProjects. This however is not the scope of this paper as we decide to steer away from it to avoid the potential ethical implications.

4.2 Approach

We introduce a Wikidata recommender system *WikidataRec* which is a hybrid model combining item content and relation information with collaborative filtering [17] by means of mixture of experts (MoE) [13] (Fig. 3). The matrix factorization (MF) decomposes the item-editor interaction matrix A into editor-centric and item-centric edit representations, denoted by e_i and v_j for editor i and item j respectively. Item content representation, denoted by c_j, is obtained by the sentence embedding model ELMo [26]; and item relation representation, denoted by r_j, is obtained by the graph embedding model TransR [20] building upon the Wikidata knowledge graph. To combine multiple item-based representations, we introduce a neural mixture of representations (NMoR) inspired by MoE, in which we utilize a soft-gating to assign different weights to each representation. More specifically, the network takes four inputs e_i, v_j, c_j and r_j, where v_j, c_j and r_j are added with weights (w_v, w_c, w_r) produced from a soft-gating branch whose input is the concatenation of v_j, c_j and r_j. The merged item representation is fed into an element-wise dot product layer together with e_i to predict the preference score x_{ij}. At the training stage, x_{ij} is optimized with the cross-entropy loss over the ground truth label in A; while at testing, it is used to recommend items to the editors. The whole process can be written as,

$$x_{ij} = e_i(w_v \cdot v_j + w_c \cdot c_j + w_r \cdot r_j)^\mathsf{T}. \tag{1}$$

Notice item and editor representations are used in the network as fixed representations (i.e., they are not updated during the training process). They are learned in advance by MF, ELMo, and TransR, respectively. We decide not to jointly tune these representations for efficiency and simplicity reasons, as it is not lightweight to integrate all the models in a whole. We will work on joint learning in our future work.

Below we first specify the generation of e_i, v_j, c_j and r_j and then introduce the neural mixture of representations for w_v, w_c and w_r.

4.3   Editor-Centric and Item-Centric Edit Representations

Editing activities are summarized in the interaction matrix A. Inspired by [17], we use matrix factorization to decompose A into the editor's latent representation matrix $E^{N \times Z}$ and the item's latent representation matrix $V^{M \times Z}$. This is achieved by approximating the target matrix A via the matrix product of two low-rank matrices E and V:

$$\widehat{A} = EV^{\mathsf{T}} \tag{2}$$

Each row e_i in E can be seen as a latent representation of editor i in terms of its edits. Similarly, each row v_j of V describes an item j with respect to its edits by different editors. Thus, the prediction formula from Eq. (2) can also be written as:

$$\widehat{a_{ij}} = e_i v_j^{\mathsf{T}} \tag{3}$$

In order to single out E, V from A, we utilize Bayesian Personalized Ranking (BPR) [32] to optimize $\widehat{A}$ over it. If we look at Eq. (1), $\widehat{a_{ij}}(e_i v_j^{\mathsf{T}})$ is its first term.

4.4   Item Content Representation

To generate item content representation c_j, we need an embedding model that can learn both semantic and syntactic representations from text. There are various embedding models that learn item representations from words, sentences, or paragraphs. Among them, word embedding models such as Word2Vec [22], GloVe [25] and FastText [14] are widely used for many recommendation tasks [8], but they have limitations: the order of words is ignored, which leads to the loss

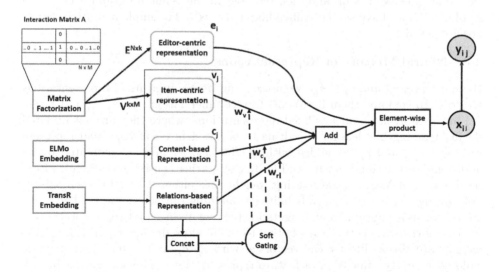

Fig. 3. The architecture of *WikidataRec*.

of the syntactic and semantic meaning in sentences [41]. We therefore considered two state-of-the-art sentence embedding models instead, specifically Embeddings from Language Models (ELMo) and Sentence-BERT. ELMo [26] employs a bi-directional deep LSTM network which takes an entire sentence as input, assigns representation to each word in the sentence, then takes the average of the vectors of words to output a Z-dimensional vector for the input sentence. Sentence-BERT [31] relies on a bi-directional Transformer network [31] which learns from fix-sized semantically meaningful sentences. We preferred ELMo to Sentence-BERT to generate c_j because of the high computational costs of the latter, particularly on large corpora [30]. Each item in Wikidata has a very short description which naturally serves as input sentence to ELMo. The implementation details are in Sect. 5.1.

4.5 Item Relational Representation

Item relational reprentations are built upon the Wikidata graph over items. We model item relations as a directed labeled graph, where it has a set of nodes to represent items, a set of edges (unweighted) to represent relations between items, and labels to capture the type of relations (see Sect. 2.1). Over different graph embedding models [3, 20, 43], we adopt the TransR [20], a representative approach for heterogeneous graphs, to learn low-dimensional (Z in this work) relational embedding of items, r_j. It builds entity and relation embeddings by regarding a relation as a translation from head entity to tail entity [20]. Different from other graph embedding methods [3, 43] which normally assume the embedding of entities and relations within the same space, TransR represents entities and relations in distinct spaces and projects entities from entity space to relation space via a projection matrix. For this reason, it is selected to model the heterogeneity of items and their relations in the Wikidata graph. Items with similar relations have similar embedding in TransR. The implementation details are in Sect. 5.1.

4.6 Neural Mixture of Representations

Having e_i, v_j, c_j, and r_j ready, we present our neural mixture of representations (NMoR) to combine them for Wikidata recommendation. e_i, v_j, c_j, and r_j are fed into NMoR in parallel as fixed representations, where they are not updated during training but learned in advance (as noted in Sect. 4.2). Item representations v_j, c_j and r_j are added with weights w_v, w_c and w_r generated by an additional soft-gating branch (see Fig. 3). Soft-gating is used to distinguish from hard-gating in MoE. In hard-gating, weights are either 0 or 1 for each expert. Soft-gating can be seen as probabilities combining different experts. The motivation for assigning different weights to different item-based representations is to control their respective contribution to the final prediction x_{ij} (Eq. 1). These weights are also Z-dimensional vectors as with v_j, c_j, and r_j such that they are tailored to every dimension of feature representations. The soft-gating branch takes the concatenation of v_j, c_j and r_j of size $1 \times Z \times 3$ (corresponding to rows, columns, and channels of the tensor) as input; three 1D convolutional layers (kernel size 1 × 1, filters 1024) followed by ReLu are applied to process the tensor along its channels; the number of their output channel remains 3. The output of the last convolutional layer is thus of size 1 × Z × 3, where each channel corresponds to the weight for certain item-based representation (w_v, w_c or w_r). At every column of the tensor, it is softmaxed over channels such that the three values at each column are summed to 1. The merged item representation $w_v \cdot v_j + w_v \cdot c_j + w_r \cdot r_j$ is passed through the element-wise dot product layer with e_i, their similarity value x_{ij} is hence computed. To optimize x_{ij}, we adopt the binary cross-entropy loss,

$$L = -(y_{ij} \log(\sigma(x_{ij})) + (1 - y_{ij}) \log(1 - \sigma(x_{ij}))), \tag{4}$$

where x_{ij} is transformed into a probability using the sigmoid activation function $\sigma(\cdot)$; y_{ij} is the ground truth label of either 0 or 1 in A indicating whether interaction between the item j and editor i has been observed (*i.e.* positive instances) or not (*i.e.* negative instances). Since A is sparse, we randomly select negative instances to make its number the same to that of positive instances. x_{ij} indicates how likely item j is relevant to editor i, we can use it to recommend items to editors at testing.

Traditional weight tuning approach like line search is only suitable for optimizing a limited number of weights, for instance, one parameter for each item-based representation. The proposed NMoR optimizes weights in a neural network which enables a refined weight steering on every dimension of the item-based representation.

5   Experiments

5.1   Experimental Setup and Implementation Details

We run experiments on the two datasets *Wikidata-14M* and *Wikidata-Active-Editors* introduced in Sect. 3. Both datasets are structured in an editor-item-edits format. For each dataset, similar to [11,12], we follow the hold-out strategy to select 80% items associated with each editor to constitute the training set and use the remaining 20% as the test set. Within the training set, we set aside 10% as validation data for hyper-parameter tuning. In *Wikidata-14M* dataset, 25% of the editors edited only between 2 to 6 different items during their editing tenure on the selected dates; these are cold-start editors. Therefore, we exclude these editors from the training set and include them only in the test set. We do this because the editing data for this type of editor are rather too sparse to be informative during training. However, we use this data in the test set, as we want to evaluate the performance of *WikidataRec* on cold-start editors. Z for feature representations is set to 1024.

NMoR: To learn NMoR, the batch size is set to 32. The model is learned with Adam optimizer with a learning rate of 0.001 for 100 epochs.

ELMo: To generate the item content representations, we start from the *Wikidata-items-content* table in our datasets, and then follow the following steps using Python's Spacy: 1) tokenize and normalize the content (label and description) of each item; 2) remove stopwords, punctuation and single-letter words; 3) use part-of-speech tagging and retained only nouns and adjectives. We pass the resulting corpus as input to the ELMo model. ELMo is pre-trained on the 1 Billion Word Benchmark that contains about $800M$ tokens of general-purpose data from WMT 2011 [4]. This is very comprehensive such that fine-tuning on Wikidata is no longer necessary. Following [10], we simply forward each Wikidata item descriptor to ELMo to obtain the item-content representation. Notice ELMo produces multi-scale output which we average them.

TransR: To generate the item relational representations, we first build the labeled directed graph $G(V, E, P)$ from the *Wikidata-items-relations* (Sect. 3.1), where V signifies Wikidata items (the head of the triplet), E inter-item relations (the tail of the triplet), and P relations' types (the relation of the triplet). We use the graph as input to train the TransR model. The original triplets in the graph are the positive instances. We sample a few of them to replace either their heads or tails with wrong components to create negative triplets. TransR is trained with both positive and negative triplets using binary cross-entropy loss. It is optimized with the SGD optimizer for 10 epochs; the batch size is 128 and learning rate is 0.01.

5.2 Evaluation Protocols

For evaluation, in order to simulate the practical recommendation scenario in Wikidata, we follow the spirit in [23] to carry out the test: for each editor i and the item-editor interaction matrix A in the test set, we 1) split the items of editor i into half-half where the editor-centric edit representation e_i along with the representations of item-centric edit, content, and relations v_j, c_j and r_j are obtained by excluding the second-half items in A in our model; 2) exclude the editor i from A to generate the representations of item-centric edits, item-content and item relations for the second half of items in our model; 3) randomly select 50 negative items that were not edited by editor i, where we can obtain their corresponding sub-matrix of A and obtain their item-based representations; 4) feed (e_i, v_j, c_j and r_j) obtained from step 1 to our NMoR along with the item-based representations obtained from steps 2 and 3 to obtain their ranking scores.

The evaluation criteria is to measure how well *WikidataRec* ranks the correct items against the negative items for a given editor. Therefore, we employ *Precision@k*, *Recall@k*, and *MAR@k* (see Sect. 2.4). We are also interested in the diversity of the recommended items, as editing a different set of items is a noted behavior in Wikidata community [27,34]. Having a diverse recommendation would allow the editors to discover a wide range of items for the editing.

Table 3. Precision@k and Recall@k results comparison between our model and state-of-the-art for *Wikidata-14M*.

	Precision @k		Recall @k		
	5	10	50	100	200
GMF	0.096	0.071	0.135	0.183	0.274
BPR-MF	0.050	0.043	0.093	0.135	0.190
eALS	0.048	0.027	0.087	0.112	0.154
YouTube-DNN	0.105	0.082	0.142	0.204	0.305
WikidataRec	**0.120**	**0.113**	**0.215**	**0.243**	**0.337**

5.3   Results on Wikidata-14M

Comparison to State of the Art. We compare *WikidataRec* against the following methods on *Wikidata-14M*: **BPR-MF** [32] is a representative collaborative filtering model that uses matrix factorization (MF) as the underlying predictor and is optimized with a pairwise ranking loss. It is suitable for recommendation scenarios with no explicit editor feedback and personalised ranked recommendation results. **eALS** [12] is also a MF-based method that is optimized with square loss. It treats all unobserved interactions as negative instances and weights them non-uniformly by the item's popularity. **GMF** [11] is a neural network-based collaborative filtering which implements MF with cross-entropy loss. It embeds each item and editor in the network and computes their element-wise dot product to predict the relevance score. **YouTube-DNN** [6] is a neural recommender for YouTube videos, using deep candidate generation and ranking networks. It uses a hybrid of users' activities and content information of users and items and directly learns their low dimensional representations. In this paper, we adapt YouTube-DNN with our item content and relational representations.

Table 3 shows the results: *WikidataRec* achieves the best performance over all with both accurate and diverse recommendations. First, it outperforms the collaborative-filtering (CF) methods GMF, eALS and BPR-MF by a large margin. CF methods only rely on the item-editor interactions data without taking into account the information of items themselves, whereas adding additional item content and relation information significantly improves the recommendation performance in our model (see Table 4). Our model also beats Youtube DNN. Youtube-DNN learns item's content and relational embedding in a neural network with random initialization while we employ additional state-of-the-art embedding models (i.e., ELMo and TransR) to generate them separately which yields superior performance.

Ablation Study. We ablate different components of *WikidataRec* on the *Wikidata-14M* to understand the effect of each one.

Item Contents and Relations. To justify the importance of item content and relations in *WikidataRec*, we start with the original collaborative filtering

Table 4. Ablation study of *WikidataRec* on *Wikidata-14M*.

	Precision @k		Recall @k			MAR@k		Diversity
	5	10	50	100	200	5	10	10
CF (BPR-MF)	0.050	0.043	0.093	0.135	0.190	0.069	0.107	0.252
+ item content	0.104	0.086	0.189	0.199	0.287	0.108	0.170	0.502
+ item relations	**0.120**	**0.113**	**0.215**	**0.243**	**0.337**	**0.133**	**0.224**	**0.567**
WikidataRec w/o NMoR	0.085	0.072	0.165	0.209	0.284	0.090	0.191	0.521
WikidataRec w/ NMoR	**0.120**	**0.113**	**0.215**	**0.243**	**0.337**	**0.133**	**0.224**	**0.567**

Table 5. Ablation study of embedding methods for item content on *Wikidata-14M*.

	Embedding model	Precision@5	Recall@50	**Recall@100**
BPR-MF +	Word2Vec	0.060	0.123	0.158
	FastText	0.029	0.069	0.115
	ELMo	**0.104**	**0.189**	**0.199**

(CF) technique, BPR-MF, and gradually add item content and relational representations using NMoR. The results are in Table 4 which show that values in every metric are increased by considering item content and relations. Particularly, item content representations provide rich information in terms of words and semantic meanings in items, which contribute more in performance increase; item relational representations in contrast contribute less. We can note each feature's contributions from the amount of increase when each of them is added. We suggest the reason as these relations are learned from the Wikidata graph, which is unevenly and sparingly connected, as discussed in [29].

Neural Mixture of Representations. To ablate the proposed NMoR, Table 4 further illustrates the results of *WikidataRec* with and without using it. For the latter, the item-based representations are added with no weights. WikidataRec with NMoR performs significantly better than WikidataRec without NMoR.

Embedding Models for Item Content. We compare the ELMo model with two text embedding models, Word2Vec [22] and FastText [14] to generate item content representations. Word2Vec and FastText are lightweight models which we train them from scratch using our Wikidata. The results are in Table 5: ELMo outperforms Word2Vec and FastText clearly. ELMo employs the deep bi-directional Language Model (biLM), which provides a very rich representation about the word tokens and captures the semantic and syntactic meaning of words. This is not the case in the Word2Vec and FastText who utilize shallow neural networks.

5.4   Results on Wikidata-Active-Editors

We ran another ablation study of our model on the second dataset, *Wikidata-Active-Editors*, introduced in Sect. 3.3. *Wikidata-Active-Editors* is a subset of

Table 6. Ablation study of *WikidataRec* on *Wikidata-Active-Editor*.

	Precision @k		Recall @k			MAR@k		Diversity
	5	10	50	100	200	5	10	10
CF (BPR-MF)	0.079	0.055	0.139	0.260	0.236	0.115	0.193	0.353
+ item content	0.143	0.109	0.253	0.302	0.349	0.157	0.251	0.565
+ item relations	**0.164**	**0.131**	**0.289**	**0.342**	**0.391**	**0.179**	**0.297**	**0.596**
WikidataRec w/o NMoR	0.132	0.073	0.196	0.295	0.323	0.134	0.245	0.553
WikidataRec w/ NMoR	**0.164**	**0.131**	**0.289**	**0.342**	**0.394**	**0.179**	**0.297**	**0.596**

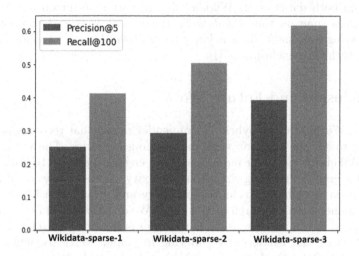

Fig. 4. *WikidataRec* with various sparsity levels.

Wikidata-14M, focusing on active editors and frequently edited items. The results are in Table 6, in which we note improved results on *WikidataRec* by adding item content and relations. In particular, content-based information contributed most towards the performance of the model. On the other hand, the contribution of relational information is less than that of content information. Furthermore, the results show that *WikidataRec* with NMoR performs better than *WikidataRec* without NMoR.

Dataset Sparsity. We further study the sparsity of the dataset in terms of its item-editor interaction data. Wikidata is very sparse in nature: a small number of interactions between items and editors are observed. *Wikidata-Active-Editors* is denser than *Wikidata-14M*, but its sparsity is still 99.90%, which means only 1% of interactions are observed over all the possible connections from every item to every editor in the dataset. To study the influence of the dataset sparsity, we extract three sub-datasets from *Wikidata-Active-Editors* with different sparsity yet roughly the same size (about 6000 editors and 10,000 items): *Wikidata-sparse-1* with 99.81% sparsity, *Wikidata-sparse-2* with 99.68% sparsity, and *Wikidata-sparse-3* with 99.27%. The editors in each dataset have edited more than 200 different items, and each item has edited by more than 16 different editors. Figure 4 show the Precision@5 and Recall@10 on the three subsets. It shows that when the sparsity decreases (from 99.81% to 99.27%, data gets denser), our model performance increases. This again verifies the conclusion in [1].

5.5   Discussion and Analysis of Results on both Datasets

Comparing the results of the two datasets (Table 4 and Table 6), we summarize that: 1) adding item content and relations with NMoR improves the performance on both datasets; 2) WikidataRec performs better on the *Wikidata-Active-Editors* than on the *Wikidata-14M*; the former is with denser editing data, so having less sparse data is likely to improve the results. This finding is consistent with the conclusion of [1].

6   Conclusion and Future Work

We present *WikidataRec*, a hybrid recommender model that recommends Wikidata items to editors based on their past editing activities. The work is motivated by Wikidata's quest for more (and more engaged) editors to keep up with a knowledge graph of growing size and complexity. As the first work of its kind, our focus is on establishing technical feasibility and providing a benchmark for future recommendation research in Wikidata. We do so with solid system implementation and benchmark datasets. Our model is informed by related research in content-based and collaborative filtering in similar verticals, which cannot rely upon explicit feedback for the recommendation task. It uses state-of-the-art models for representation learning and operates by means of a mixture of experts [13]. We employ ELMo [26] for items' content-based representations and TransR [20] for items' relations-based representations. The results, though far from perfect, are promising and could be considered a baseline for future Wikidata recommender work.

Based on our experiments, we make three claims for the recommendation task in Wikidata: 1) Collaborative filtering is not enough to recommend Wikidata items, as editing data is very sparse; however, adding item content and relational representations significantly enhances performance; 2) Not each item representation contributes to the final predictions equally. We show how to optimise the weights with NMoR; 3) While our model works better on the denser datasets extracted from *Wikidata-Active-Editors* data, showing that there is room for improvement.

We plan to extend the work in several directions. First, we plan to run editor studies, including interviews with more or less experienced editors to learn about their current ways to choose what they work on and perhaps uncover how existing technical affordances and interfaces influence such decisions. Second, we aim to experiment with other recommender models, particularly sequential learning and time-sensitive models that encode the temporal aspect and distinguish between older and more recent editor interests, as well as with ways to elicit more information about the editors in a responsible way. One option here would be to recruit new editors for a study in which they would explicitly consent to us collecting such information or would provide additional information about their interests themselves. Also, since the data of Wikidata can be represented as item-item relation graph and editor-item graph, exploring graph neural networks (GNNs) for a recommendation would be an interesting future direction. The advantages provided by the GNNs would provide great potential to advance our recommendation task. Third, topic-recommendation is another area that might interests the editors in Wikidata more than item recommendations. We plan to investigate this area. In addition, we are going to conducting an editor-centric evaluation would provide a space to examine and compare the feasibility and effectiveness of the two algorithms (topic vs. item recommendations).

References

1. Adomavicius, G., Zhang, J.: Impact of data characteristics on recommender systems performance. ACM Trans. Manag. Inf. Syst. (TMIS) (2012)
2. Aggarwal, C.C., et al.: Recommender systems (2016)
3. Bordes, A., Usunier, N., Garcia-Duran, A., Weston, J., Yakhnenko, O.: Translating embeddings for modeling multi-relational data. In: Neural Information Processing Systems (2013)
4. Chelba, C., et al.: One billion word benchmark for measuring progress in statistical language modeling. arXiv preprint arXiv:1312.3005 (2013)
5. Cosley, D., Frankowski, D., Terveen, L., Riedl, J.: SuggestBot: using intelligent task routing to help people find work in Wikipedia. In: International Conference on Intelligent User Interfaces (2007)
6. Covington, P., Adams, J., Sargin, E.: Deep neural networks for Youtube recommendations. In: ACM Conference on Recommender Systems (2016)
7. Dror, G., Koren, Y., Maarek, Y., Szpektor, I.: I want to answer; who has a question?: Yahoo! answers recommender system. In: ACM SIGKDD International Conference on Knowledge Discovery and Data Mining (2011)
8. Esmeli, R., Bader-El-Den, M., Abdullahi, H.: Using Word2Vec recommendation for improved purchase prediction. In: International Joint Conference on Neural Networks (2020)
9. Freyne, J., Jacovi, M., Guy, I., Geyer, W.: Increasing engagement through early recommender intervention. In: ACM Conference on Recommender Systems (2009)
10. Hassan, H.A.M., Sansonetti, G., Gasparetti, F., Micarelli, A., Beel, J.: BERT, ELMO, USE and InferSent sentence encoders: the panacea for research-paper recommendation? In: RecSys (Late-Breaking Results) (2019)
11. He, X., Liao, L., Zhang, H., Nie, L., Hu, X., Chua, T.S.: Neural collaborative filtering. In: The International Conference on World Wide Web (2017)
12. He, X., Zhang, H., Kan, M.Y., Chua, T.S.: Fast matrix factorization for online recommendation with implicit feedback. In: International ACM SIGIR Conference on Research and Development in Information Retrieval (2016)
13. Jacobs, R.A., Jordan, M.I., Nowlan, S.J., Hinton, G.E.: Adaptive mixtures of local experts. Neural Comput. (1991)

14. Joulin, A., Grave, E., Bojanowski, P., Mikolov, T.: Bag of tricks for efficient text classification. arXiv preprint arXiv:1607.01759 (2016)
15. Kaffee, L.A., Piscopo, A., Vougiouklis, P., Simperl, E., Carr, L., Pintscher, L.: A glimpse into babel: an analysis of multilinguality in Wikidata. In: Proceedings of the 13th International Symposium on Open Collaboration, pp. 1–5 (2017)
16. Kanza, S., Stolz, A., Hepp, M., Simperl, E.: What does an ontology engineering community look like? A systematic analysis of the schema.org community. In: Gangemi, A., et al. (eds.) ESWC 2018. LNCS, vol. 10843, pp. 335–350. Springer, Cham (2018). https://doi.org/10.1007/978-3-319-93417-4_22
17. Koren, Y., Bell, R., Volinsky, C.: Matrix factorization techniques for recommender systems. Computer (2009)
18. Kurup, A.R., Sajeev, G.: Task recommendation in reward-based crowdsourcing systems. In: International Conference on Advances in Computing, Communications and Informatics (2017)
19. Lave, J., Wenger, E.: Legitimate peripheral participation. Learning and Knowledge (1999)
20. Lin, Y., Liu, Z., Sun, M., Liu, Y., Zhu, X.: Learning entity and relation embeddings for knowledge graph completion. In: AAAI Conference on Artificial Intelligence (2015)
21. Liu, Z., Li, K., Qu, D.: Knowledge graph based question routing for community question answering. In: International Conference on Neural Information Processing (2017)
22. Mikolov, T., Chen, K., Corrado, G., Dean, J.: Efficient estimation of word representations in vector space. arXiv preprint arXiv:1301.3781 (2013)
23. Moskalenko, O., Parra, D., Saez-Trumper, D.: Scalable recommendation of Wikipedia articles to editors using representation learning. arXiv preprint arXiv:2009.11771 (2020)
24. Müller-Birn, C., Karran, B., Lehmann, J., Luczak-Rösch, M.: Peer-production system or collaborative ontology engineering effort: What is wikidata? In: International Symposium on Open Collaboration (2015)
25. Pennington, J., Socher, R., Manning, C.D.: Glove: Global vectors for word representation. In: Proceedings of the 2014 Conference on Empirical Methods in Natural Language Processing (EMNLP) (2014)
26. Peters, M.E., et al.: Deep contextualized word representations. arXiv preprint arXiv:1802.05365 (2018)
27. Piscopo, A., Phethean, C., Simperl, E.: What makes a good collaborative knowledge graph: group composition and quality in Wikidata. In: International Conference on Social Informatics (2017)
28. Piscopo, A., Phethean, C., Simperl, E.: Wikidatians are born: paths to full participation in a collaborative structured knowledge base (2017)
29. Piscopo, A., Simperl, E.: Who models the world?: Collaborative ontology creation and user roles in Wikidata. In: The ACM on Human-Computer Interaction (2018)
30. Polignano, M., de Gemmis, M., Semeraro, G.: Contextualized BERT sentence embeddings for author profiling: the cost of performances. In: Gervasi, O., et al. (eds.) ICCSA 2020. LNCS, vol. 12252, pp. 135–149. Springer, Cham (2020). https://doi.org/10.1007/978-3-030-58811-3_10
31. Reimers, N., Gurevych, I.: Sentence-BERT: sentence embeddings using Siamese BERT-networks. arXiv preprint arXiv:1908.10084 (2019)
32. Rendle, S., Freudenthaler, C., Gantner, Z., Schmidt-Thieme, L.: BPR: Bayesian personalized ranking from implicit feedback. arXiv preprint arXiv:1205.2618 (2012)

33. Safran, M., Che, D.: Efficient learning-based recommendation algorithms for top-N tasks and top-N workers in large-scale crowdsourcing systems. ACM Trans. Inf. Syst. (TOIS) **37**(1), 1–46 (2018)
34. Sarasua, C., Checco, A., Demartini, G., Difallah, D., Feldman, M., Pintscher, L.: The evolution of power and standard Wikidata editors: comparing editing behavior over time to predict lifespan and volume of edits. Comput. Support. Coop. Work (CSCW) (2019)
35. Schafer, J.B., Frankowski, D., Herlocker, J., Sen, S.: Collaborative filtering recommender systems. In: The Adaptive Web (2007)
36. Shani, G., Gunawardana, A.: Evaluating recommendation systems. In: Recommender Systems Handbook (2011)
37. Sun, J., Vishnu, A., Chakrabarti, A., Siegel, C., Parthasarathy, S.: ColdRoute: effective routing of cold questions in stack exchange sites. Data Mining Knowl. Discov. (2018)
38. Sun, J., Zhao, J., Sun, H., Parthasarathy, S.: An end-to-end framework for cold question routing in community question answering services. arXiv preprint arXiv:1911.11017 (2019)
39. Turki, H., et al.: Wikidata: a large-scale collaborative ontological medical database. J. Biomed. Inf. (2019)
40. Vrandečić, D., Krötzsch, M.: Wikidata: a free collaborative knowledge base (2014)
41. Wang, B., Wang, A., Chen, F., Wang, Y., Kuo, C.C.J.: Evaluating word embedding models: methods and experimental results. APSIPA Trans. Sig. Inf. Process. (2019)
42. Wikipedia: Wikidata (2021). https://en.wikipedia.org/wiki/Wikidata. Accessed 26 June 2021
43. Xiao, H., Huang, M., Hao, Y., Zhu, X.: TransA: an adaptive approach for knowledge graph embedding. arXiv preprint arXiv:1509.05490 (2015)
44. Yang, L., Amatriain, X.: Recommending the world's knowledge: application of recommender systems at Quora. In: ACM Conference on Recommender Systems (2016)

Graph-Boosted Active Learning for Multi-source Entity Resolution

Anna Primpeli$^{(\boxtimes)}$ and Christian Bizer

Data and Web Science Group, University of Mannheim, Mannheim, Germany
{anna,chris}@informatik.uni-mannheim.de

Abstract. Supervised entity resolution methods rely on labeled record pairs for learning matching patterns between two or more data sources. Active learning minimizes the labeling effort by selecting informative pairs for labeling. The existing active learning methods for entity resolution all target two-source matching scenarios and ignore signals that only exist in multi-source settings, such as the Web of Data. In this paper, we propose ALMSER, a graph-boosted active learning method for multi-source entity resolution. To the best of our knowledge, ALMSER is the first active learning-based entity resolution method that is especially tailored to the multi-source setting. ALMSER exploits the rich correspondence graph that exists in multi-source settings for selecting informative record pairs. In addition, the correspondence graph is used to derive complementary training data. We evaluate our method using five multi-source matching tasks having different profiling characteristics. The experimental evaluation shows that leveraging graph signals leads to improved results over active learning methods using margin-based and committee-based query strategies in terms of F1 score on all tasks.

Keywords: Entity resolution · Link discovery · Multi-source entity matching · Active learning

1 Introduction

Entity resolution, also referred as entity matching or link discovery, aims to identify records in one or multiple data sources which describe the same real-world entity [4,5]. Supervised entity resolution methods treat entity matching as a classification problem and rely on a labeled set of matching and non-matching record pairs for training [5,7]. Active learning aims to minimize the labeling effort by involving the annotator in the learning loop and selecting only the most informative pairs for labeling [27].

There has been quite some research on active learning for entity resolution [3, 9,12,17,26]. However, to the best of our knowledge, all of these works focus on active learning methods for matching records between two data sources, while signals that only exist in multi-source settings are not exploited to further reduce the number of record pairs that need to be labeled by the annotator. Exploiting

© Springer Nature Switzerland AG 2021
A. Hotho et al. (Eds.): ISWC 2021, LNCS 12922, pp. 182–199, 2021.
https://doi.org/10.1007/978-3-030-88361-4_11

such signals is for example beneficial for link discovery [16] in the context of the Web of Data [8], as link discovery efforts often target multiple data sources.

We fill in this gap and propose an active learning method for entity resolution that exploits additional signals that only exist in multi-source settings. We consider the multi-source entity resolution task as a combination of multiple two-source matching tasks between pairs of data sources having the same schema but different underlying matching patterns. Figure 1 shows an example of a multi-source entity resolution task consisting of four data sources describing mobile phones (Fig. 1a). The pairwise combinations of the four data sources constitute a multi-source matching task comprising of six two-source tasks (Fig. 1b). For each of these tasks different attributes can be relevant for matching, e.g. *name* and *brand* for task A-C and *name* and *price* for task A-D. The goal of multi-source entity resolution is to learn a matcher that correctly identifies correspondences between the records of all sources. These correspondences can be viewed as a correspondence graph with all distinct records being the nodes of the graph connected by edges indicating matching record pairs (Fig. 1c). The discovered correspondences are used afterwards to fuse data from multiple sources or are published as RDF links on the Web of Data [8].

Data set A			
ID	name	price	brand
A1	i-phone 4	200€	Apple
A2	htc one m9	220€	htc

Data set B			
ID	name	price	brand
B1	iphone 4	190€	apple
B2	one m9	210€	htc

Data set C			
ID	name	price	brand
C1	iphone 4		apple

Data set D			
ID	name	price	brand
D1	htc m9	220€	

Task	Record Pair	Label
TASK A-B	A1-B1	match
	A2-B2	match
	A1-B2	non-match
	A2-B1	non-match
TASK A-C	A1-C1	match
	A2-C1	non-match
TASK A-D	A1-D1	non-match
	A2-D1	match
TASK B-C	B1-C1	match
	B2-C1	non-match
TASK B-D	B1-D1	non-match
	B2-D1	match
TASK C-D	C1-D1	non-match

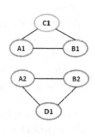

(a) Data sources   (b) Two-source matching tasks of the multi-ER task   (c) Correspondence graph

Fig. 1. Example of a multi-source entity resolution task.

This paper proposes *ALMSER*, a graph-boosted **A**ctive **L**earning method for **M**ulti-**S**ource **E**ntity **R**esolution which exploits the rich correspondence graph that the multi-source setting offers in two ways: First, to pick informative query candidates and second to boost the training of the learner with additional training data. Most active learning methods apply either a query-by-committee strategy [3, 26] or a margin-based strategy [13, 14] for picking informative candidates and use only the labeled set at each iteration for training the learner. Query-by-committee strategies measure the informativeness of the query candidates as the degree of disagreement among the predictions of a classifier ensemble, while margin-based strategies pick the instances that are closer to the decision boundary of a classifier. In contrast, our query strategy exploits graph signals such as graph transitivity and minimum cuts to discover potentially false negative and false positive record pairs among the predictions of the learner. We assume that focusing on the errors of the learner to derive informative pairs for labeling can lead to the faster discovery of relevant matching patterns in comparison to uncertainty-based query strategies. For boosting the training of the learner, we derive likely matching and non-matching record pairs from the clean components of the graph which we use as additional training data.

We evaluate ALMSER using five multi-source entity resolution tasks having different profiling characteristics. Our evaluation shows that graph signals lead to an overall improved performance over baseline methods which use a state-of-the-art committee-based query strategy and a margin-based query strategy.

The contributions of our work are summarized as follows:

- We are the first to tackle the problem of multi-source entity resolution with active learning.
- We propose an active learning method for multi-source entity resolution which uses the correspondence graph for query selection and training data augmentation.
- We evaluate our method on five multi-source entity resolution tasks and show that it consistently outperforms baseline methods that do not use graph signals in terms of F1 score. In terms of area under the F1 score curve, our method also performs better than methods that use graph signals for training data augmentation but not for query selection.

The remainder of the paper is organized as follows: Sect. 2 discusses related work on multi-source entity resolution and active learning. Section 3 explains our method. Section 4 presents the experimental setup and discusses the experimental results. Finally, Sect. 5 concludes the paper and summarizes our findings.

2   Related Work

Entity resolution is a central prerequisite for integrating data from multiple sources [4, 5, 19] as well as for setting RDF links in the context of the Web of Linked Data [8, 16]. Entity resolution has been extensively studied over decades [6, 16, 19]. Although there exist works on supervised and unsupervised multi-source entity resolution [1, 24, 28] as well as on active learning methods for the two-source matching task [3, 9, 13], there has been no work on multi-source entity resolution with active learning.

Multi-source Entity Resolution: There are two lines of research on multi-source entity resolution which either focus on solving the scalability issues of integrating data from multiple sources [28] or use graph signals in supervised [1] or unsupervised matching settings [25]. The supervised SOCCER method proposed by Shen et al. [28] defines an efficient order of pair-wise matching tasks in large multi-source settings. In the work of Bellare et al. on knowledge base synthesis [1], a supervised classifier is applied during the matching step and the matching results are refined using the connected components of the correspondence graph, similar to our work. Saeedi et al. compare different clustering methods for multi-source entity resolution [24] and propose CLIP [25] a clustering approach which requires hand-written domain specific rules for calculating the weighted edges of the graph. The CLIP method assumes duplicate-free sources, an assumption which is not necessary for our proposed method. JointBERT [20] applies deep learning techniques for multi-source entity resolution and treats the matching problem in parallel as a binary and multi-class classification task.

Active Learning for Entity Resolution: Active learning aims to minimize the human labeling effort involved in supervised tasks [27]. Active learning approaches with a specific focus on RDF link discovery [16] include EAGLE [17] and ActiveGenLink [9]. Meduri et al. compare various active learning methods for entity resolution on multiple benchmark data sets for two-source matching and show that random forest classifiers with learner-aware committee-based query strategies achieve fast convergence and close to perfect entity matching quality [13]. However, it is reported that for some tasks margin-based query strategies can perform equally well. Therefore, we compare ALMSER to both committee-based and margin-based active learning baselines. There have been many active learning methods for entity resolution which use committee-based query strategies for selecting informative candidates [3,9,26]. In the work of Chen et al. [3] it is shown that using a committee of heterogeneous classifiers is more effective in comparison to committees consisting of the same model with different parametrisations. Recent works on active learning for entity resolution have turned the focus to deep learning based methods tailored for low-resource settings [10,15]. Such methods rely on transfer learning [10] or large randomly sampled sets [15] for initializing the deep learning models and require a pre-labeled development set for hyperparameter optimization [10,15]. In comparison to the existing deep active learning works for entity matching, our suggested approach involves less annotation effort as it leverages unsupervised matching for initialization and does not require an additional development set for model learning.

Active Learning with Graph Signals: Using graph signals for boosting the query strategy of active learning methods, has been explored in related work for different applications [2,18] and has inspired our work on graph-boosted active learning for multi-source entity resolution. Nguyen et al. develop an active learning method for image classification which uses the k-medoid algorithm for clustering the data [18]. Different signals of the graph structure, such as the cluster representativeness and density are used for refining an uncertainty sam-

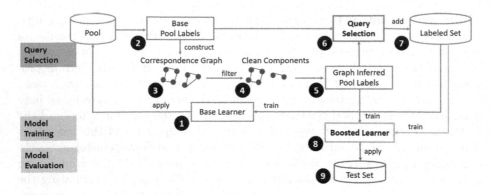

Fig. 2. Overview of the ALMSER algorithm.

pling query strategy. Similarly, Bilgic et al. propose an active learning method for multi-class classification which exploits graph signals for boosting an uncertainty sampling query selection strategy [2].

3   Methodology

In this section, we present our proposed active learning algorithm for multi-source entity resolution, which we abbreviate with ALMSER. This subsection summarizes the overall process that is executed by ALMSER. The following subsections detail each step in the process.

We consider a pool-based active learning setting in which a pool of unlabeled record pairs is available to the learner. This pool is typically the result of a preceding blocking step [5]. Figure 2 gives an overview of the ALMSER algorithm. We initialize ALMSER by bootstrapping the labeled set of record pairs (Artefact 7 in Fig. 2). After initialization, the following steps are executed: First, we train a base learner using the current labeled set (1) and get base predictions for all unlabeled record pairs of the pool (2) which together with the labeled set are used to construct a correspondence graph (3). Next, we derive the clean components of the graph (4) and assign graph-inferred labels to the record pairs of the pool which are part of the clean components (5). The query strategy picks the most informative record pair for labeling considering the disagreement between the predicted labels of the base learner and the graph-inferred labels (6). The selected record pair is annotated as *match* or *non-match* and is added to the labeled set (7). We exploit the graph-inferred labels to derive additional training data which together with the labeled set are used for training the boosted learner (8). In order to evaluate how the performance of the boosted learner develops during the active learning process, we apply the boosted learner to the test set after each iteration (9).

3.1   Initialization of ALMSER

The initialization of active learning is a non-trivial step which has been shown to suffer from the cold start problem [12,22]. This problem refers to the lack of labeled data from all classes in the early iterations which further hinders the training of the learner as well as of the classifiers used for query selection in the case of classification-based query strategies. To circumvent the cold start problem, we apply an unsupervised bootstrapping method which summarizes the feature vector of each record pair into an aggregated similarity score and selects as seeding pairs the ones with the lowest and highest scores. The details about this method are presented in [22]. We apply the approach for each two-source task of the multi-source setting and select two record pairs per task: one with the highest and one with the lowest aggregated score. Considering that in the very early active learning iterations the base model, which we use to construct the correspondence graph, is highly unstable, we perform the first 20 active learning iterations using the state-of-the-art committee based query-strategy HeALER [3]. Afterwards, we switch to the graph-based query strategy that we explain in Sect. 3.5.

3.2   Correspondence Graph Construction

After initializing the labeled set, the graph-boosted active learning cycle starts. In each active learning iteration we construct the correspondence graph of the multi-source task (steps 1–3 in Fig. 2) with the aim to obtain graph signals which we exploit in later steps of our methodology for query selection and model training. The correspondence graph contains all distinct records of the record pairs in the pool and the labeled set as nodes. We add an edge to the graph for every confirmed matching record pair in the labeled set, while we add no edge for every labeled non-matching pair.

Additionally, we use the pool predictions of a random forest classifier, which we refer to as base learner, for inferring potential matching pairs. More concretely, in each iteration the base learner is trained on all record pairs of the labeled set and applied to the record pairs of the pool. Each pool pair is assigned the predicted base label, *match* or *non-match* together with a confidence score, which is the predicted class probability of the base learner. We add an edge to the correspondence graph between the nodes of every pool record pair with a matching base label, while we add no edge if the base label is non-match.

Finally, we assign weights to the edges of the correspondence graph. Every edge that derives from the labeled set and is therefore confirmed to be true, receives the weight 100. The edges deriving from the base learner matching predictions are weighted according to their confidence score.

3.3   Correspondence Graph Cleansing

Exploiting the transitivity of the correspondence graph can lead to the discovery of false negative base learner predictions: e.g. given three record pairs (A-B), (B-C) and (A-C) which have been predicted by the base learner as *match*, *match*

Labeled Set	
A-B	match
B-C	match
D-E	match
D-F	match
D-H	non-match
I-K	match
I-J	match

(a) Example labeled set of current iteration

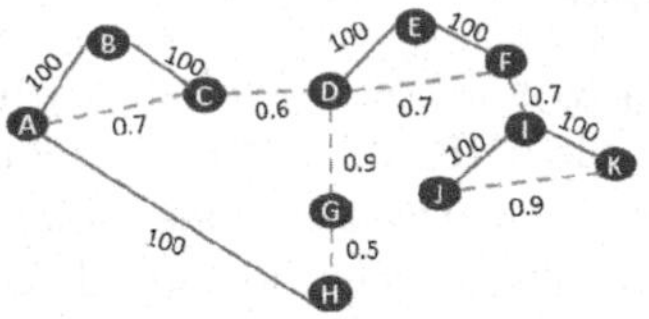

(b) Cor. graph given labeled set and base-model predictions

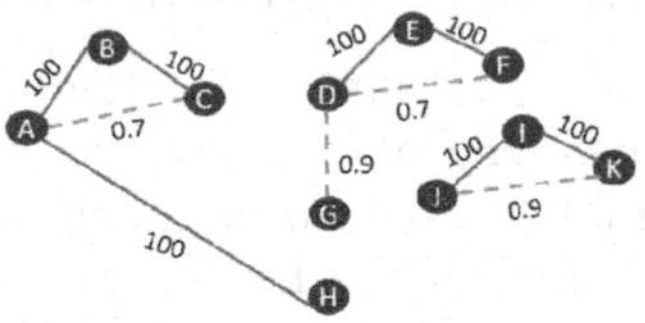

(c) Cor. graph after removal of minimum cuts (D-C & G-H) and bridges (F-I)

Fig. 3. Exploiting the graph to detect false positives - an example.

and *non-match* respectively, we can infer using graph transitivity that (A-C) is also a matching pair and that it is likely a false negative prediction of the base learner.

However, given that the edges of the correspondence graph deriving from the matching base learner predictions are subject to some noise, a wrongly assigned edge can lead to a series of false positive record pairs. Therefore, we need to discover likely wrong edges and remove them from the correspondence graph. The example in Fig. 3 demonstrates this problem. Figure 3b shows an example graph with 11 nodes and weighted edges. The solid edges connect nodes of matching record pairs found in the labeled set of Fig. 3a and are therefore assigned a weight of 100 while the dotted edges represent the base labels and are assigned their corresponding confidence weights. The resulting graph is connected and forms one connected component, i.e. there is a path from any node to any other node in the graph, indicating that all nodes refer to the same real-world entity. However, this cannot be the case as there is a confirmed non-matching pair $(D - H)$ in the labeled set of Fig. 3a. Therefore, the path between the nodes D and H needs to be cut. Given the edge weights, we calculate the minimum cut of the graph. The edges which should be removed in order to cut the path between D and H are the following: $(D - C)$ and $(G - H)$ as their total edge weight is less than any other cut alternative. We can additionally observe that the edge $(F - I)$, forms a bridge between the two components (E, D, F, G) and (I, J, K) and is a possible false positive. Figure 3c shows the graph after minimum cuts and bridges removal which reveals three connected components.

We rely on these observations and remove edges between nodes of potentially false positive record pairs using a two step procedure. First, we iterate over all non-matching pairs in the labeled set and for each pair we check if there is a path between the two nodes-records in the graph. In case we find a path, we calculate the minimum cut of the graph considering the weights of the edges. For the calculation of the minimum cuts, we use the *networkx* implementation.[1] As second step, we identify and remove bridge edges from the graph. In order to

---

[1] https://networkx.org/documentation/stable/reference/algorithms/generated/networkx.algorithms.flow.minimum_cut.html.

ensure that there is no unnecessary increase of many small-sized components, we only remove the bridge edges connecting nodes having more than two neighbours each.

3.4 Clean Components Filtering

After cleansing the correspondence graph, we filter its clean components and assign graph-inferred labels to a subset of the pool record pairs (steps 4–5 in Fig. 2) with the aim to get more accurate graph signals that can both identify wrong base learner predictions and lead to clean augmented training data.

In order to derive the clean components of the correspondence graph, we first compute all connected components. Considering that smaller components are cleaner than larger ones, we assume a component to be clean if its size is equal or smaller than the amount of data sources to be matched. Although this heuristic comes natural for deduplicated sources, we show during evaluation that it is also a good approximation for discovering the clean components of the graph in multi-source matching tasks with non-deduplicated data sources.

We use the correspondence graph and the clean connected components to assign graph-inferred labels to a subset of the pool record pairs. For record pairs belonging to the same clean component, we assign a matching graph-inferred label. If there is no path in the correspondence graph between the two records of the pair, then we assign a non-match graph-inferred label. Finally, for record pairs belonging to non-clean components, no graph-inferred label is assigned.

3.5 Query Selection

The query selection strategy of ALMSER evaluates as the most informative candidates the record pairs whose graph-inferred label is different from the base label and assigns binary informativeness scores to all record pairs in the pool: 1 if there is a conflict between the base and the graph-inferred labels otherwise 0 (Step 6 in Fig. 2). While margin-based and committee-based query strategies aim to select instances for which the learner or a committee of models produces non-confident predictions, our query strategy uses the clean components of the correspondence graph to pick instances that are most likely predicted wrong by the base learner. These disagreements between the graph and the base learner hint towards matching patterns that are not covered yet by the base learner and can occur under two conditions: First, if the record pair has been predicted by the base learner to be a non-match and due to graph transitivity the graph-inferred label is match. Second, if the record pair has been predicted as match by the base learner but the corresponding edge was found to be a bridge edge or was part of a minimum cut between confirmed non-matching pairs and therefore was removed during the cleansing step, as described in Sect. 3.3.

We illustrate the discovery of new matching patterns by graph transitivity with the simple example of Fig. 4 which presents three records from different data sources describing the same author (4a) and a subset of labeled pairs and base learner predictions (Fig. 4b) which are used to construct the correspondence graph (Fig. 4c). Given the matching pair (1a-2a) of the labeled set, the base learner might be trained to capture matching patterns based on the similarity of the *Lastname* and the *Works* attributes. However, it might wrongly predict the pair (1a-3a) as non-matching as it has not learned yet the pattern that high similarity of *Birthdate* and *Firstname* together also indicate a match. Based on the graph transitivity, the pair (1a-3a) is assigned a matching graph-inferred label and therefore receives an informativeness score of 1. Selecting this pair as a query candidate supports the model in learning the relevance of the *Birthdate* and *Firstname* attribute combination for matching.

Source - ID	Firstname	Lastname	Birthdate	Works
1-a	Kiki	Dimoula	06.06.1931	In absentia
2-a		Dimoula		In absentia
3-a	Kiki		06.06.1931	In absentia

(a)

Labeled Set (subset)	
(1a-2a)	match
Base Learner Predictions (subset)	
(1a-3a)	non-match
(2a-3a)	match

(b)

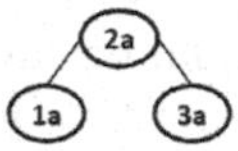

(c)

Fig. 4. Graph-boosted query selection strategy - an example.

In order to ensure that the query strategy selects equally likely false positives, i.e. pairs with a non-match graph inferred label, and likely false negative pairs, i.e. pairs with a match graph-inferred label, we assign selection probability weights to all record pairs with an informativeness score of 1. For example, given 10 likely false negatives and 1 likely false positive, we assign the selection probability weights 0.1 for each false negative and 1.0 for the false positive pair. Finally, given the selection probability scores, we perform weighted random selection over the candidate record pairs with an informativeness score of 1 and select one pair which is annotated and added to the labeled set (Step 7 in Fig. 2).

3.6   Boosted Learner Training

In a real-world active learning setting, we would learn one boosted model at the very last active learning iteration, as the boosted learner does not affect the query selection, i.e. the query strategy of ALMSER is agnostic towards the boosted learner. However, in order to be able to evaluate the boosted model along each active learning iteration, we train it and apply it to the test set as final step of each iteration (Steps 8 and 9 in Fig. 2). We perform training data augmentation with the aim to improve the training of the boosted learner. Similarly to the base learner, we use a random forest classifier as the boosted learner, assuming that a random forest model with a large number of estimators can expand to fit the matching patterns of all matching tasks in a multi-source entity resolution setting. For training the boosted learner we use both the record pairs of the labeled set, which contains the records pairs selected during initialization as explained in Sect. 3.1 and the manually validated record pairs, and the subset of

Table 1. Profiling information of evaluation matching tasks.

Multi-source task	# Data sources	# Pairs (in K)		Schema Complex.	Range of sparsity	Corner cases
		Matches	Non-matches			
MusicBrainz	5	16.1	369.7	[3–5]	[0.05–0.12]	[0.08–0.42]
MusicBrainz_mut	5	16.1	369.7	[3–6]	[0.05–0.23]	[0.06–0.62]
Computers	4	4.8	69.6	[3–4]	[0–0.05]	[0.02–0.30]
computers_mut	4	4.8	69.6	[3–6]	[0–0.18]	[0.24–0.50]
Restaurants	4	11.2	56.5	[4–7]	[0–0.08]	[0.05–0.19]

the pool record pairs which have been assigned a graph-inferred label, i.e. record pairs deriving from clean components of the correspondence graph of the current iteration.

4   Experimental Evaluation

We evaluate ALMSER using five multi-source matching tasks having different profiling characteristics. In this section, we first present the evaluation tasks. Afterwards, Sect. 4.3 compares ALMSER to two baseline active learning methods that do not use graph signals. Section 4.4 evaluates the distinct components of ALMSER that exploit graph signals and compares them to baseline methods using the graph signal only for training data augmentation. All data sets and code used for experimental evaluation are available for public download.[2]

4.1   Multi-source Matching Tasks

We use five multi-source matching tasks for our experimental evaluation. The tasks cover the domains music, products, and restaurants. Table 1 contains profiling information about the five tasks, including the amount of sources to be matched as well as the amount of matching and non-matching pairs per task. In our previous work on profiling entity matching tasks [21], we have defined a set of profiling dimensions for assessing the difficulty of entity matching tasks. The last three columns in Table 1 show the value ranges of the profiling dimensions schema complexity, sparsity, and corner cases for the two-source matching tasks that make up each multi-source task. Schema complexity refers to the amount of attributes that contribute to solving the matching task. Sparsity indicates the ratio of missing attribute values. The dimension corner cases approximates the fraction of difficult to match pairs within each task [21].

The MusicBrainz multi-source task has been used for the evaluation in [24, 25]. The task is based on song records from the MusicBrainz dataset. Each data source is a modified version of the original dataset and therefore the two-source matching tasks that make up the multi-source task have different underlying

---

[2] https://github.com/wbsg-uni-mannheim/ALMSER-GB.

patterns: while in five of the ten two-source tasks the attributes *album*, *length* and *title* are most relevant for matching, for the rest of the tasks different attributes reveal the underlying matching patterns such as *title* and *song number* or *title* and *artist*. Additionally to the original MusicBrainz multi-source task, we curate a modified version of it, abbreviated with *MusicBrainz_mut*, by increasing the attribute sparsity up to 30% per data source and adding noise in 50% of the attribute values which further results in an increase of corner cases in comparison to the original MusicBrainz task.

We exploit the WDC Training Corpus for Large-scale Product Matching[3] [23] and derive a subset of computer product records published in four e-commerce websites, for curating the product-related multi-source matching task, which we abbreviate with *computers*. Similarly to the MusicBrainz task, we curate a modified version of the computers task which we abbreviate with *computers_mut* and contains an increased schema complexity, sparsity and amount of corner cases. While the underlying matching patterns of the original task focus mostly on the combination of the *title* and *part number* attributes, the mutated version of the tasks requires additional attributes to be solved such as *category*, *capacity* and *generation*.

The restaurant related multi-source task derives from the Magellan repository[4] which provides a large number of two-source matching tasks. We retrieve four of the restaurant data sources that have been crawled from large restaurant aggregators and use the phone number as weak supervision in order to establish the complete mappings between all data source pairs. While three of the six two-source matching tasks have a low containment of corner cases ($<10\%$) and can be solved only with address related attributes, the rest of the two-source tasks require additional attributes such as *name*, *cuisine* and *website*.

We turn the records of all tasks into features vectors by calculating datatype specific similarity scores, similar to the Magellan entity matching system [11]. For string attributes, the following similarity scores are calculated: Levenshtein, Jaccard, Jaccard with inner Levenshtein, token overlap, and token containment. For numeric attributes the absolute difference is calculated and re-scaled to the range [0, 1]. In the case that a similarity score cannot be computed for an attribute combination because of missing values, we assign the out of range score -1. This allows any classifier to consider all record pairs without dropping or replacing the missing values.

The selected multi-source tasks cover two distinct scenarios: the first scenario includes matching tasks of duplicate free data sources and therefore their correspondence graph forms connected components of maximum size equal to the total amount of sources, which is the case of the MusicBrainz and MusicBrainz_mut tasks. The second scenario covers tasks of non-deduplicated data sources resulting in components that are larger than the total amount of sources, which happens for the computers, computers_mut, and restaurants tasks.

---

[3] http://webdatacommons.org/largescaleproductcorpus/v2/.
[4] https://sites.google.com/site/anhaidgroup/useful-stuff/data.

4.2 Experimental Setup

We split the multi-source tasks into two subsets: one for initializing the pool that is available for querying and one for testing. In order to ensure that there is no leakage by graph transitivity from the pool set to the test set, we split the record pairs to pool pairs and test pairs based on the connected components of the complete correspondence graph with a ratio 70%–30%.

We execute three runs for each active learning experiment and allow 200 iterations for each run. In each iteration, one record pair is selected for annotation, i.e. 200 record pairs have been labeled in total by the end of each experimental run. We report the mean F_1micro score per iteration as well as the standard deviation which measures the model stability among the different experimental runs. Additionally, we report the upper learning bound of passive learning for which all record pairs of the pool together with their respective labels are used for model learning. All experiments were run on a Linux server with Intel Xeon 2.4 GHz processors. Considering that ALMSER constructs in each iteration a correspondence graph, its runtime is larger in comparison to baseline methods which do not use graph signals, e.g. one baseline iteration for the computers task without graph signals takes 2.9–3.15 s while one ALMSER iteration takes 14.58–15.10 s.

4.3 Comparison to Baselines Without Graph Signals

We compare ALMSER to two baseline active learning methods using the two distinct types of classification-based query strategies: committee-based and margin-based [19] and no graph signals. The first baseline method, abbreviated with QHC, uses the state-of-the-art committee-based query strategy of the HeALER algorithm [3] which measures the informativeness of each candidate record pair as the disagreement of the predictions of a committee of heterogeneous classification models. Similar to their method, ALMSER also uses random forest classifiers as learners. The second baseline method which is a common margin-based baseline [13,14,27], abbreviated with MB is a learner agnostic method, i.e. the classification model used as part of the query strategy is different from the learner, and selects the query candidates with minimum distance to the decision hyperplane defined by a SVM classifier. The learners of the baseline methods do not use graph signals and therefore are trained only on the labeled set. In order to ensure a comparable start of the learning process for all methods, we apply the initialization step that we describe in Sect. 3.1 for all baseline methods.

Figure 5 shows the average F1 score curves of ALMSER and the two baseline methods for each multi-source matching task per iteration. Additionally, we show the standard deviation of the F1 scores per iteration with the light coloured area around the plotted curves and the upper learning bound of passive learning. We can observe that as the active learning process unfolds, ALMSER outperforms both baselines for all tasks. The sudden drops in F1 in the early iterations, e.g. iterations 25 to 50 for the setting computers_mut as shown in Fig. 5d, can be

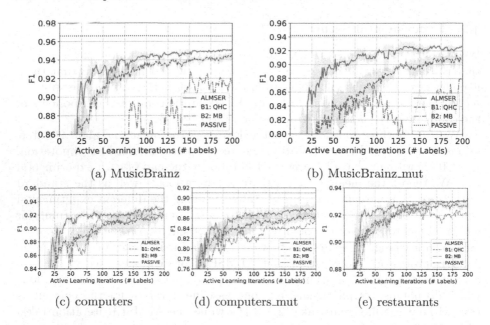

(a) MusicBrainz   (b) MusicBrainz_mut

(c) computers   (d) computers_mut   (e) restaurants

Fig. 5. Comparison of ALMSER to active learning baselines and passive learning.

attributed to the overfitting of the model on a small amount of clean data and is a common observation for active learning methods [3].

When 200 record pairs have been annotated, the ALMSER F1 scores for all tasks are by 0 to 0.032% points lower than the passive learning results that would be achieved by training a random forest classifier with all pairs from the pool as training data. The MB baseline underperforms the QHC baseline for all tasks while it fails to converge after 200 iterations for both the MusicBrainz and the MusicBrainz_mut tasks. Table 2 compares the F1 scores of the baseline methods MB and QHC to ALMSER at three points of the active learning process. We can observe that ALMSER achieves a quicker gain in F1 in the earlier iterations of the active learning process and outperforms the QHC and MB baselines by up to 5.5 and 13.4% points respectively at the 75th iteration. Although ALMSER outperforms the two baseline methods that use no graph signals even in the 200th active learning iteration, the gain in F1 is reduced to 1.9 and 4.8% points for the QHC and MB baselines respectively.

In order to evaluate in which kind of tasks ALMSER achieves the highest boost in comparison to the QHC baseline, which was shown to outperform the MB baseline, we measure the area between ALMSER's and QHC's F1 curves. The area between the F1 curves is the largest for the MusicBrainz_mut task which is the task having the largest containment in corner cases (up to 62%) as well as the highest sparsity (up to 23%) among all multi-source tasks used for the experiments. In contrast, the smallest area between ALMSER's and QHC's F1 curves is the one of the restaurants task, which contains the lowest amount of corner cases (up to 19%) of all tasks. This indicates that ALMSER is especially fitted for more difficult multi-source matching tasks which require the matcher to deal with different matching patterns.

Table 2. Evaluation of baselines with no or partial graph signals - F_1 and AUC.

Iteration	AL method	MusicBrainz	MusicBrainz_mut	Computers	Computers_mut	Restaurants
F_1 @ 75th	MB	0.805	0.836	0.881	0.833	0.915
	MB_boost_learner	0.877	0.833	0.889	0.827	0.914
	QHC	0.921	0.851	0.891	0.841	0.917
	QHC_boost_learner	0.891	0.891	0.894	0.843	0.924
	ALMSER_qs	0.912	0.841	0.919	0.842	0.916
	ALMSER	**0.939**	**0.906**	**0.921**	**0.862**	**0.926**
F_1 @ 125th	MB	0.890	0.817	0.912	0.840	0.919
	MB_boost_learner	0.866	0.856	0.910	0.846	0.917
	QHC	0.932	0.893	0.909	0.854	0.925
	QHC_boost_learner	0.914	0.914	0.901	0.865	**0.930**
	ALMSER_qs	0.924	0.884	**0.927**	0.868	0.923
	ALMSER	**0.946**	**0.920**	0.918	**0.873**	0.929
F_1 @ 200th	MB	0.914	0.879	0.925	0.854	0.920
	MB_boost_learner	0.903	0.872	0.922	0.859	0.924
	QHC	0.945	0.908	0.918	0.866	0.927
	QHC_boost_learner	0.926	0.926	0.916	0.871	**0.932**
	ALMSER_qs	0.934	0.896	**0.938**	**0.884**	0.926
	ALMSER	**0.951**	**0.927**	0.930	0.878	0.931
F1-AUC 50th-200th	MB	128.81	123.84	135.68	124.82	138.02
	MB_boost_learner	138.28	131.74	136.56	127.21	138.52
	QHC	140.07	132.43	135.62	127.66	138.51
	QHC_boost_learner	136.39	136.39	134.93	128.82	138.35
	ALMSER_qs	138.37	131.38	138.96	128.95	138.21
	ALMSER	**141.57**	**137.51**	**139.19**	**130.13**	**139.18**

4.4 Evaluation of the Graph-Boosted Components

In this part of our experimental analysis, we evaluate the two graph-boosted components of ALMSER, i.e. the query strategy and the model learning. We evaluate the following three setups that use partial graph signals and compare them to ALMSER: 1. ALMSER_qs, a variation of ALMSER which utilizes the graph signal only as part of the query strategy but not for boosting the learner with additional training data, 2. QHC_boost_learner which applies the QHC query strategy for selecting candidates and uses the graph signal for augmenting the training data and boosting the learner as described in Sect. 3.6, and 3. MB_boost_learner uses the MB query strategy together with augmenting the training data.

We present the F1 scores at three snapshots of the active learning process for all methods that use graph signals for data augmentation in Table 2. Additionally, we report the area under the F1 curve (F1-AUC) from iteration 50 to iteration 200 for all methods. We observe that the best performing methods for all tasks and snapshots use partial, e.g. ALMSER_qs at iteration 125 for the computers, or full graph signals, e.g. ALMSER at iteration 200 for the MusicBrainz_mut task. Although ALMSER underperforms its individual graph-boosted components for five snapshot-task combinations as shown in Table 2, the area under the F1 curve of ALMSER is the largest for all tasks, indicating that ALMSER achieves overall better results between iterations 50 and 200. Comparing the AUC scores of the approaches that partially utilize graph signals, we see that none of them consistently outperforms the other. For some tasks, e.g. MusicBrainz_mut, using graph signals for boosting the learner in combination with a QHC query strategy performs better than exploiting the graph only for selecting query candidates. This observation is reversed for other tasks, e.g. computers_mut.

Finally, we report the size and correctness of the augmented training set which results from the clean components of the correspondence graph, as explained in Sect. 3.4. Figure 6 presents the accuracy of the augmented training set in comparison to the accuracy of the complete correspondence graph for the MusicBrainz_mut and the restaurants tasks, in each active learning iteration. We observe that our heuristic for filtering clean components extracts a cleaner part of the correspondence graph, as the accuracy of the augmented training set exceeds the one of the complete graph in each iteration for multi-source tasks with both duplicate free (MusicBrainz_mut) and non-duplicate free (restaurants) data sources.

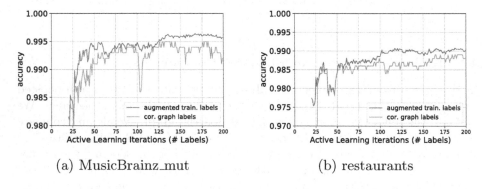

(a) MusicBrainz_mut   (b) restaurants

Fig. 6. Correctness of augmented training data vs graph labels.

Exploiting the record pairs from the clean components for training the boosted learner, results in large amounts of additional training pairs. However, only the subset of record pairs in the augmented training set with a graph-inferred label different from the base label can give additional matching information to the boosted learner. Table 3 shows the size of the augmented training set, the amount of record pairs in the training set with a disagreement between the graph-inferred and the base labels, as well as the ratio of correct graph-inferred labels to all record pairs with a disagreement in three active learning snapshots. Although the size of the augmented training set is much larger in comparison to the clean labeled data, there is only a relatively small amount of disagreements between the predictions of the base learner trained on the labeled set and the graph-inferred labels. Considering that for the majority of those disagreements the graph-inferred label is correct (78.8–96.7% as shown in Table 3), we can conclude that the additional matching information that the boosted learner derives from the clean components of the graph, is subject only to a small amount of noise and can successfully support the discovery of additional matching patterns which are not covered yet by the record pairs in the labeled set.

Table 3. Augmented training data in three AL snapshots.

Iteration	Musicbrainz_mut			Restaurants		
	#Train pairs (K)	#Disagr.	% Correct graph	#Train pairs (K)	#Disagr.	% Correct graph
75th	256.5	1,476	0.966	42.8	73	0.821
125th	256.4	1,506	0.967	42.5	52	0.788
200th	254.7	1,009	0.874	42.6	27	0.814

5 Conclusion

This paper presented ALMSER, the first active learning method for multi-source entity resolution. ALMSER exploits the correspondence graph that is available in multi-source entity resolution settings to improve two components of the active learning workflow: the query strategy and the training of the learner. Our evaluation on five multi-source tasks showed that ALMSER outperforms two baseline active learning methods including the state-of-the art committee-based query strategy which use no graph signals in terms of F1 score on all tasks. We evaluated the distinct graph-boosted components of the ALMSER algorithm and showed that utilizing graph signals as part of both the query selection and the model training achieve an increased overall performance.

References

1. Bellare, K., Curino, C., Machanavajihala, A., Mika, P., Rahurkar, M., Sane, A.: WOO: a scalable and multi-tenant platform for continuous knowledge base synthesis. PVLDB **6**(11), 1114–1125 (2013)
2. Bilgic, M., Mihalkova, L., Getoor, L.: Active learning for networked data. In: Proceedings of ICML (2010)

3. Chen, X., Xu, Y., Broneske, D., Durand, G.C., Zoun, R., Saake, G.: Heterogeneous committee-based active learning for entity resolution (HeALER). In: Welzer, T., Eder, J., Podgorelec, V., Kamišalić Latifić, A. (eds.) ADBIS 2019. LNCS, vol. 11695, pp. 69–85. Springer, Cham (2019). https://doi.org/10.1007/978-3-030-28730-6_5

4. Christen, P.: Data Matching: Concepts and Techniques for Record Linkage, Entity Resolution, and Duplicate Detection. Data-Centric Systems and Applications. Springer, Heidelberg (2012). https://doi.org/10.1007/978-3-642-31164-2

5. Christophides, V., Efthymiou, V., Palpanas, T., Papadakis, G., Stefanidis, K.: An overview of end-to-end entity resolution for big data. ACM Comput. Surv. (CSUR) **53**(6), 1–42 (2020)

6. Fellegi, I.P., Sunter, A.B.: A theory for record linkage. J. Am. Stat. Assoc. **64**(328), 1183–1210 (1969)

7. Halevy, A., Rajaraman, A., Ordille, J.: Data integration: the teenage years. In: Proc. VLDB, 9–16 (2006)

8. Heath, T., Bizer, C.: Linked Data: Evolving the Web into a Global Data Space. Synthesis Lectures on the Semantic Web. Morgan & Claypool Publishers (2011)

9. Isele, R., Bizer, C.: Active learning of expressive linkage rules using genetic programming. Web Semant. **23**, 2–15 (2013)

10. Kasai, J., Qian, K., Gurajada, S., Li, Y., Popa, L.: Low-resource deep entity resolution with transfer and active learning. In: Proceedings of ACL (2019)

11. Konda, P., et al.: Magellan: toward building entity matching management systems over data science stacks. PVLDB **9**(13), 1581–1584 (2016)

12. Konyushkova, K., Sznitman, R., Fua, P.: Learning active learning from data. In: Proceedings of Advances in Neural Information Processing Systems (2017)

13. Meduri, V., Popa, L., Sen, P., Sarwat, M.: A comprehensive benchmark framework for active learning methods in entity matching. In: Proceedings of SIGMOD (2020)

14. Mozafari, B., Sarkar, P., Franklin, M., Jordan, M., Madden, S.: Scaling up crowdsourcing to very large datasets: a case for active learning. PVLDB **8**(2), 125–136 (2014)

15. Nafa, Y., et al.: Active deep learning on entity resolution by risk sampling. arXiv preprint arXiv:2012.12960 (2020)

16. Nentwig, M., Hartung, M., Ngonga Ngomo, A.C., Rahm, E.: A survey of current link discovery frameworks. Semant. Web **8**(3), 419–436 (2017)

17. Ngonga Ngomo, A.-C., Lyko, K.: EAGLE: efficient active learning of link specifications using genetic programming. In: Simperl, E., Cimiano, P., Polleres, A., Corcho, O., Presutti, V. (eds.) ESWC 2012. LNCS, vol. 7295, pp. 149–163. Springer, Heidelberg (2012). https://doi.org/10.1007/978-3-642-30284-8_17

18. Nguyen, H.T., Smeulders, A.: Active learning using pre-clustering. In: Proceedings of ICML (2004)

19. Papadakis, G., Ioannou, E., Thanos, E., Palpanas, T.: The Four Generations of Entity Resolution. Synth. Lect. Data Manag. **16**(2), 1–170 (2021)

20. Peeters, R., Bizer, C.: Dual-objective fine-tuning of BERT for entity matching. PVLDB **14**(10) (2021)

21. Primpeli, A., Bizer, C.: Profiling entity matching benchmark tasks. In: Proceedings of CIKM (2020)

22. Primpeli, A., Bizer, C., Keuper, M.: Unsupervised bootstrapping of active learning for entity resolution. In: Harth, A., et al. (eds.) ESWC 2020. LNCS, vol. 12123, pp. 215–231. Springer, Cham (2020). https://doi.org/10.1007/978-3-030-49461-2_13

23. Primpeli, A., Peeters, R., Bizer, C.: The WDC training dataset and gold standard for large-scale product matching. In: Companion Proceedings of WWW (2019)

24. Saeedi, A., Peukert, E., Rahm, E.: Comparative evaluation of distributed clustering schemes for multi-source entity resolution. In: Kirikova, M., Nørvåg, K., Papadopoulos, G.A. (eds.) ADBIS 2017. LNCS, vol. 10509, pp. 278–293. Springer, Cham (2017). https://doi.org/10.1007/978-3-319-66917-5_19
25. Saeedi, A., Peukert, E., Rahm, E.: Using link features for entity clustering in knowledge graphs. In: Gangemi, A., et al. (eds.) ESWC 2018. LNCS, vol. 10843, pp. 576–592. Springer, Cham (2018). https://doi.org/10.1007/978-3-319-93417-4_37
26. Sarawagi, S., Bhamidipaty, A.: Interactive deduplication using active learning. In: Proceedings of SIGKDD (2002)
27. Settles, B.: Active Learning: Synthesis Lectures on Artificial Intelligence and Machine Learning. Morgan & Claypool Publishers (2012)
28. Shen, W., DeRose, P., Vu, L., Doan, A., Ramakrishnan, R.: Source-aware entity matching: a compositional approach. In: Proceedings of ICDE (2007)

Computing CQ Lower-Bounds over OWL 2 Through Approximation to RSA

Federico Igne[ORCID], Stefano Germano[(✉)][ORCID], and Ian Horrocks[ORCID]

Department of Computer Science, University of Oxford, Oxford, UK
{federico.igne,stefano.germano,ian.horrocks}@cs.ox.ac.uk

Abstract. Conjunctive query (CQ) answering over knowledge bases is an important reasoning task. However, with expressive ontology languages such as OWL, query answering is computationally very expensive. The PAGOdA system addresses this issue by using a tractable reasoner to compute lower and upper-bound approximations, falling back to a fully-fledged OWL reasoner only when these bounds don't coincide. The effectiveness of this approach critically depends on the quality of the approximations, and in this paper we explore a technique for computing closer approximations via RSA, an ontology language that subsumes all the OWL 2 profiles while still maintaining tractability. We present a novel approximation of OWL 2 ontologies into RSA, and an algorithm to compute a closer (than PAGOdA) lower bound approximation using the RSA combined approach. We have implemented these algorithms in a prototypical CQ answering system, and we present a preliminary evaluation of our system that shows significant performance improvements w.r.t. PAGOdA.

Keywords: CQ answering · Combined approach · Ontology approximation · RSA

1 Introduction

Conjunctive query (CQ) answering is one of the primary reasoning tasks over knowledge bases for many applications. However, when considering expressive description logic languages, query answering is computationally very expensive, even when considering only complexity w.r.t. the size of the data (*data complexity*). Fully-fledged reasoners oriented towards CQ answering over unrestricted OWL 2 ontologies exist but, although heavily optimised, they are only effective on small to medium datasets. In order to achieve tractability and scalability for the problem, two main approaches are often used: either the expressive power of the input ontology or the completeness of the computed answers is sacrificed.

This work was supported by the AIDA project (Alan Turing Institute), the SIRIUS Centre for Scalable Data Access (Research Council of Norway, project no.: 237889), Samsung Research UK, Siemens AG, and the EPSRC projects AnaLOG (EP/P025943/1), OASIS (EP/S032347/1) and UK FIRES (EP/S019111/1).

A. Hotho et al. (Eds.): ISWC 2021, LNCS 12922, pp. 200–216, 2021.
https://doi.org/10.1007/978-3-030-88361-4_12

Using the first approach, query answering procedures have been developed for several fragments of OWL 2 for which CQ answering is tractable with respect to data complexity [1]. Three such fragments have been standardised as *OWL 2 profiles*, and CQ answering techniques for these fragments have been shown to be highly scalable at the expense of expressive power [2,11,12,17–19]. Using the second approach, several algorithms have been proposed to compute an approximation of the set of answers to a given CQ. This usually results in computing *a sound subset* of the answers, sacrificing completeness. One such technique is to approximate the input ontology to a tractable fragment, e.g., by dropping all those axioms outside the fragment; a tractable algorithm can then be used to answer CQs over the approximated ontology. This process is clearly sound but possibly incomplete, and hence provides a *lower-bound* answer to any given query.

A particularly interesting approach to CQ answering over unrestricted OWL 2 ontologies, using a combination of the aforementioned techniques, is adopted by PAGOdA [21]. Its "pay-as-you-go" approach allows us to use a Datalog reasoner to handle the bulk of the computation, computing lower and upper approximations of the answers to a query, while relying on a fully-fledged OWL 2 reasoner like HermiT only as necessary to fully answer the query.

While PAGOdA is able to avoid the use of a fully-fledged OWL 2 reasoner in some cases, its performance rapidly deteriorates when the input query requires (extensive) use of the underlying OWL 2 reasoner. Results from our tests show that whenever PAGOdA relies on HermiT to compute the bulk of the answers to a query, computation time is usually prohibitive and sometimes unfeasible. The computation of lower and upper bounds is achieved by under- and over-approximating the ontology into OWL 2 RL so that a tractable reasoner can be used for CQ answering. The tractability of OWL 2 RL is achieved in part by avoiding problematic interactions between axioms that can cause an exponential blow-up of the computation (so-called *and-branching*). As it turns out, this elimination of problematic interactions between axioms is rather coarse, and PAGOdA often ends up falling back to the underlying OWL 2 reasoner even when it is not really needed.

This work expands on this "pay-as-you-go" technique; it aims to improve the lower-bound approximation in PAGOdA, tightening the gap between lower and upper bounds and minimising the use of HermiT. We achieve this by (soundly) approximating the input ontology into RSA [3], an ontology language that subsumes all the OWL 2 profiles, for which CQ answering is still tractable, and for which a CQ answering algorithm based on the *combined approach* has been proposed in [5]. We present a novel algorithm for approximating the input ontology into RSA, and an implementation [10] of the combined approach CQ answering algorithm adapted to the use of RDFox [13–16] as a backend Datalog reasoner; this includes the design of an improved version of the filtering step for the combined approach, optimised for RDFox. In addition, we streamline the execution of the combined approach by factoring out those steps in the combined approach that are *query independent* to make answering multiple queries over the same knowledge base more efficient. To summarise (Fig. 1), given an OWL 2 ontology, we propose an algorithm to approximate it down to RSA, and compute its canonical model as part of the combined approach algorithm for RSA; we then derive an improved filtering program from the input query that, combined with the canonical model produces a lower-bound of the answers to the query over the original ontology.

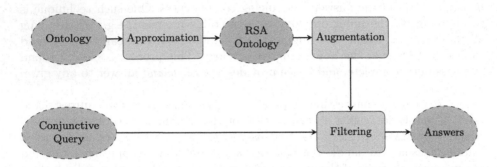

Fig. 1. RSAComb Architecture.

We have integrated our improved lower bound computation into PAGOdA and carried out a preliminary evaluation to assess its effectiveness. Our experimental results show that the new technique yields significant performance improvements in several important application scenarios.

2   Preliminaries

PAGOdA is a reasoner for sound and complete conjunctive query answering over OWL 2 knowledge bases, adopting a "pay-as-you-go" approach to compute the certain answers to a given query. It uses a combination of a *Datalog reasoner* and a *fully-fledged OWL 2 reasoner*; PAGOdA treats the two systems as black boxes and tries to offload the bulk of the computation to the former and relies on the latter only when necessary.[1]

To achieve this, PAGOdA exploits the Datalog reasoner to compute a lower and upper bound to the certain answers to the input query. If these bounds match, then the query has been fully answered; otherwise the answers in the "gap" between the bounds are further processed and verified against the fully-fledged reasoner. Lower and upper bounds are computed by approximating the input ontology to a logic program and answering the query over the approximations.

---

[1] The capabilities, performance, and scalability of PAGOdA inherently depend on the ability of the fully-fledged OWL 2 reasoner in use, and the ability to delegate the workload to a given Datalog reasoner. In the best scenario, with an OWL 2 DL reasoner, PAGOdA is able to answer *internalisable queries* [8].

In the following we provide a brief description of the computation of the lower bound, since some details will be useful later on. See [21] for a more in-depth description of the algorithm and heuristics in use.

Given an *ontology* $\mathcal{O}$ and a CQ q, the *disjunctive Datalog* subset of the input ontology is computed, denoted $\mathcal{O}^{DD}$, by dropping any axiom that does not correspond to a disjunctive Datalog rule. Using a variant of *shifting* [4], $\mathcal{O}^{DD}$ is polynomially transformed in order to eliminate disjunction in the head. The resulting Datalog program $\mathtt{shift}(\mathcal{O}^{DD})$ is sound but not necessarily complete for CQ answering. A first materialisation is performed, and the resulting facts are added to the input ontology to obtain $\mathcal{O}'$. Next, the $\mathcal{ELHO}_{\perp}^{r}$ [18] subset of $\mathcal{O}'$ is computed[2], denoted $\mathcal{O}'_{\mathcal{EL}}$, by dropping any axiom that is not in $\mathcal{ELHO}_{\perp}^{r}$; the final lower bound is then computed by applying the *combined approach* for $\mathcal{ELHO}_{\perp}^{r}$ [12,19] to q over $\mathcal{O}'_{\mathcal{EL}}$.

While PAGOdA performs really well on simpler queries over complex OWL 2 ontologies, it can struggle when addressing more complex queries that actually make use of the complexity and expressivity of the underlying ontology language.

To improve PAGOdA's performance and compute a tighter lower-bound we approximate the input ontology to RSA, a tractable ontology language (more expressive than $\mathcal{ELHO}_{\perp}^{r}$) based on the Horn-$\mathcal{ALCHOIQ}$ language with additional global restrictions on role interaction. To perform this approximation, we proceed similarly to PAGOdA, by dropping any axiom in the input ontology that is not part of a particular target DL language ($\mathcal{ALCHOIQ}$ in our case) and remove any disjunction in the axioms by means of a shifting step. Finally, we introduce a novel algorithm to approximate the resulting Horn-$\mathcal{ALCHOIQ}$ ontology into RSA by weakening axioms as needed to ensure that the global restrictions on role interactions are satisfied.

Logic Programs. We assume familiarity with standard concepts of first-order logic (FO) such as term, variable, constant, predicate, atom, literal, logic rule, (stratified) programs. See [5] and the extended version of this paper [9, Appendix A], for a formal introduction to these concepts.

We will call a rule *definite* without negation in its body, and *Datalog* a function-free definite rule. A Datalog rule is *disjunctive* if it admits disjunction in the head. A *fact* is a Datalog rule with an empty body. Given a stratified program $\mathcal{P}$, we denote its *least Herbrand model* (LHM) as $M[\mathcal{P}]$, and define $\mathcal{P}^{\approx,\top}$ the program extended with axiomatisation rules for equality ($\approx$) and truth value ($\top$) in a standard way [5].

Ontologies and Conjunctive Query Answering. We define Horn-$\mathcal{ALCHOIQ}$ as the set of axioms that are allowed in the language and specify its semantics by means of translation to definite programs. The definition will fix a *normal form* for this ontology language [5], and w.l.o.g. we assume any input ontology in Horn-$\mathcal{ALCHOIQ}$ contains only these types of axioms.

---

[2] $\mathcal{ELHO}_{\perp}^{r}$ is an OWL 2 EL fragment, for which CQ answering is tractable.

Table 1. Normalised Horn-$\mathcal{ALCHOIQ}$ axioms and their translation in definite rules.

Axioms α	Definite rules $\pi(\alpha)$
(R1) R^-	$R(x,y) \to R^-(y,x); R^-(y,x) \to R(x,y)$
(R2) $R \sqsubseteq S$	$R(x,y) \to S(x,y)$
(T1) $\prod_{i=1}^{n} A_i \sqsubseteq B$	$\bigwedge_{i=1}^{n} A_i(x) \to B(x)$
(T2) $A \sqsubseteq \{a\}$	$A(x) \to x \approx a$
(T3) $\exists R.A \sqsubseteq B$	$R(x,y) \wedge A(y) \to B(x)$
(T4) $A \sqsubseteq\, \leq 1R.B$	$A(x) \wedge R(x,y) \wedge B(y) \wedge R(x,z) \wedge B(z) \to y \approx z$
(T5) $A \sqsubseteq \exists R.B$	$A(x) \to R(x, f_{R,B}^{A}(x)) \wedge B(f_{R,B}^{A}(x))$
(A1) $A(a)$	$\to A(a)$
(A2) $R(a,b)$	$\to R(a,b)$

Let N_C, N_R, N_I be countable disjoint sets of concepts names, role names and individuals respectively. We define a *role* as an element of $N_R \cup \{R^- \mid R \in N_R\}$, where R^- is called *inverse role*. We also introduce a function $Inv(\cdot)$ closed for roles s.t. $\forall R \in N_R : Inv(R) = R^-, Inv(R^-) = R$. An *RBox* $\mathcal{R}$ is a finite set of axioms of type (R2) in Table 1 where R, S are roles. We denote $\sqsubseteq^*_\mathcal{R}$ as a minimal relation over roles closed by reflexivity and transitivity s.t. $R \sqsubseteq^*_\mathcal{R} S$, $Inv(R) \sqsubseteq^*_\mathcal{R} Inv(S)$ hold if $R \sqsubseteq S \in \mathcal{R}$. A *TBox* $\mathcal{T}$ is a set of axioms of type (T1-5) where $A, B \in N_C$, $a \in N_I$ and R is a role. An *ABox* $\mathcal{A}$ is a finite set of axiom of type (A1-2) with $A \in N_C$, $a, b \in N_I$ and $R \in N_R$. An *ontology* is a set of axioms $\mathcal{O} = \mathcal{A} \cup \mathcal{T} \cup \mathcal{R}$. Finally, if we consider $\mathcal{ALCHOIQ}$, the TBox is further extended with an additional axiom type $A \sqsubseteq \bigsqcup_{i=1}^{n} B_i$ allowing disjunction on the right-hand side.

A *conjunctive query (CQ)* q is a formula $\exists \vec{y}.\psi(\vec{x}, \vec{y})$ with $\psi(\vec{x}, \vec{y})$ a *conjunction* of function–free atoms over $\vec{x} \cup \vec{y}$, and $\vec{x}$, $\vec{y}$ are called *answer variables* and *bounded variables* respectively. Queries with an empty set of answer variables are called *boolean conjunctive queries (BCQ)*. Let π be the translation of axioms into definite rules defined in Table 1; by extension we write $\pi(\mathcal{O}) = \{\pi(\alpha) \mid \alpha \in \mathcal{O}\}$. An ontology $\mathcal{O}$ is satisfiable if $\pi(\mathcal{O}^{\approx,\top}) \not\models \exists y.\bot(y)$. A tuple of constants $\vec{c}$ is an *answer* to q if $\mathcal{O}$ is *unsatisfiable* or $\pi(\mathcal{O}^{\approx,\top}) \models \exists \vec{y}.\psi(\vec{c}, \vec{y})$. The set of answers to a query q is written $cert(q, \mathcal{O})$.

3   Combined Approach for CQ Answering in RSA

RSA (*role safety acyclic*) ontologies and their combined approach for conjunctive query answering were originally presented in [3,5]. In this section we recapitulate a minimal set of definitions and theorems that will make the paper more self-contained and help the reader better understand our contribution.

RSA is a class of ontology languages designed to subsume all OWL 2 profiles, while maintaining tractability of standard reasoning tasks like CQ answering. The RSA ontology language is designed to avoid interactions between axioms that can result in the ontology being satisfied only by exponentially large (and potentially infinite) models. This problem is often called *and-branching* and can be caused by interactions between axioms of type (T5) with either axioms (T3) and (R1), or axioms (T4), in Table 1.

RSA includes all axioms in Table 1, restricting their interaction to ensure a polynomial bound on model size [3].

Definition 1. *A role R in $\mathcal{O}$ is* unsafe *if it occurs in axioms (T5), and there is a role S s.t. either of the following holds:*

1. *$R \sqsubseteq_{\mathcal{R}}^* Inv(S)$ and S occurs in an axiom (T3) with left-hand side concept $\exists S.A$ where $A \neq \top$;*
2. *S is in an axiom (T4) and $R \sqsubseteq_{\mathcal{R}}^* S$ or $R \sqsubseteq_{\mathcal{R}}^* Inv(S)$.*

A role R in $\mathcal{O}$ is safe *if it is not unsafe.*

Note that, by definition all OWL 2 profiles ($\mathcal{RL}$, $\mathcal{EL}$ and $\mathcal{QL}$) contain only *safe* roles.

Definition 2. *Let PE and E be fresh binary predicates, let U be a fresh unary predicate, and let $u_{R,B}^A$ be a fresh constant for each concept $A, B \in N_C$ and each role $R \in N_R$. A function π_{RSA} maps each (T5) axiom $\alpha \in \mathcal{O}$ to $A(x) \rightarrow R(x, u_{R,B}^A) \wedge B(u_{R,B}^A) \wedge PE(x, u_{R,B}^A)$ and $\pi(\alpha)$ otherwise. The program $\mathcal{P}_{RSA}$ consists of $\pi_{RSA}(\alpha)$ for each $\alpha \in \mathcal{O}$, rule $U(x) \wedge PE(x, y) \wedge U(y) \rightarrow E(x, y)$ and facts $U(u_{R,B}^A)$ for each $u_{R,B}^A$, with R unsafe.*

Let M_{RSA} be the LHM of $\mathcal{P}_{RSA}^{\approx, \top}$. Then, $G_{\mathcal{O}}$ is the digraph with an edge (c, d) for each $E(c, d)$ in M_{RSA}. Ontology $\mathcal{O}$ is equality-safe *if for each pair of atoms $w \approx t$ (with w and y distinct) and $R(t, u_{R,B}^A)$ in M_{RSA} and each role S s.t. $R \sqsubseteq Inv(S)$, it holds that S does not occur in an axiom (T4) and for each pair of atoms $R(a, u_{R,B}^A), S(u_{R,B}^A, a)$ in M_{RSA} with $a \in N_I$, there is no role T such that both $R \sqsubseteq_{\mathcal{R}}^* T$ and $S \sqsubseteq_{\mathcal{R}}^* Inv(T)$ hold.*

We say that $\mathcal{O}$ is RSA *if it is equality-safe and $G_{\mathcal{O}}$ is an oriented forest.*

The fact that $G_{\mathcal{O}}$ is a DAG ensures that the LIIM $M[\mathcal{P}_{\mathcal{O}}]$ is finite, whereas the lack of "diamond-shaped" subgraphs in $G_{\mathcal{O}}$ guarantees polynomiality of $M[\mathcal{P}_{\mathcal{O}}]$. The definition gives us a programmatic procedure to determine whether an Horn-$\mathcal{ALCHOIQ}$ ontology is RSA.

Theorem 1 ([5], **Theorem** *2*). *If $\mathcal{O}$ is RSA, then the size of $M[\mathcal{P}_{\mathcal{O}}]$ is polynomial in the size of $\mathcal{O}$.*

3.1   RSA Combined Approach

Following is a summary of the combined approach (with filtration) for conjunctive query answering for RSA presented in [5]. This consists of two main steps to be offloaded to a Datalog reasoner able to handle *negation* and *function symbols*.

The first step computes the canonical model of an RSA ontology over an extended signature (introduced to deal with *inverse roles* and *directionality* of newly generated binary atoms). The computed canonical model is not universal and, as such, might lead to spurious answers in the evaluation of CQs.

The second step of the computation performs a filtration of the computed answers to identify only the *certain answers* to the input query.

Canonical Model Computation. The computation of the canonical model for an ontology $\mathcal{O}$ is performed by computing the LHM of a translation of the ontology into definite rules. The translation for each axiom type is given in [5] and is an enhanced version of the translation given in Table 1 where axioms of type (T5) are *skolemised* if the role involved is unsafe, and *constant skolemised* otherwise[3]. We call this translation $E_\mathcal{O}$ and denote the computed canonical model as $M[E_\mathcal{O}]$. $M[E_\mathcal{O}]$ is polynomial in $|\mathcal{O}|$ and if $\mathcal{O}$ is satisfiable; $\mathcal{O} \models A(c)$ iff $A(c) \in M[E_\mathcal{O}]$ (see [5, Theorem 3]).

Filtering Spurious Answers. For the filtering step, a *query dependent* logic program $\mathcal{P}_q$ is introduced to filter out all spurious answers to an input query q over the extended canonical model $M[E_\mathcal{O}]$ computed in the previous section.

The program identifies and discards any match that cannot be enforced by a TBox alone and hence correspond to spurious answers induced by the canonical model. For more details on the construction of $\mathcal{P}_q$, please refer to [9, Appendix B], and [5, Section 4].

Let $\mathcal{P}_q$ be the filtering program for q, and $\mathcal{P}_{\mathcal{O},q} = E_\mathcal{O} \cup \mathcal{P}_q$, then we know that $M[\mathcal{P}_{\mathcal{O},q}]$ is polynomial in $|\mathcal{O}|$ and exponential in $|q|$ (see [5, Theorem 4]). We obtain a "guess and check" algorithm that leads to an NP-completeness result for BCQs [5]. The algorithm first materialises $E_\mathcal{O}$ in polynomial time and then guesses a match σ to q over the materialisation; finally it materialises $(\mathcal{P}_{\mathcal{O},q})\sigma$.

Theorem 2 ([5], Theorem 5). *Checking whether $\mathcal{O} \models q$ with $\mathcal{O}$ an RSA ontology and q a BCQ is NP-complete in combined complexity.*

3.2 Improvements to the Combined Approach

In the following we give an overview of the improvements introduced in the RSA combined approach, built on top of the original theory presented in the previous sections.

RDFox Adoption. One first technical difference from the original work on the RSA combined approach is the adoption of RDFox as a Datalog reasoner instead of DLV. RDFox provides support for *stratified negation* but it does not provide direct support for *function symbols*. We simulate function symbols using the built-in Skolemisation feature, making it possible to associate a fresh term to a unique tuple of terms. While doing so, we keep somewhat closer to the realm of description logics since RDF triples are a first-class citizen and only atoms with arity ≤ 2 are allowed.

Improved Filtering Program. RDFox is primarily an RDF reasoner and its ability to handle Datalog (with a set of useful extension) makes it able to capture the entire $\mathcal{RL}$ profile. We were able to partially rewrite and simplify the filtering

---

[3] A more detailed description of this step is provided in [9, Appendix B].

step in the RSA combined approach: a first rewriting step gets rid of all atoms with arity greater than 2; filtering rules are then greatly simplified by making extensive use of the Skolemisation function provided by RDFox, hence avoiding some expensive *joins* that would slow down the computation (see [5, Section 5], especially the results for query q_1).

Example 1. We show rule (3c) in the original filtering program (w.r.t. a query $q(\vec{x}) = \psi(\vec{x}, \vec{y})$ where $\vec{x} = x_1, \ldots, x_m$, $\vec{y} = y_1, \ldots, y_n$), along with its simplification steps. Rule (3c) computes the transitive closure of a predicate *id*, keeping track of identity between anonymous terms w.r.t. a specific match for the input query.

$$id(\vec{x}, \vec{y}, u, v), id(\vec{x}, \vec{y}, v, w) \rightarrow id(\vec{x}, \vec{y}, u, w) \tag{1}$$

Provided we have access to a function KEY to compute a new term that uniquely identifies a tuple of terms, we can *reify* any n-ary atom into a set of n atoms of arity 2. E.g., an atom $P(x, y, z)$ becomes $P_1(k, x), P_2(k, y), P_3(k, z)$, where $k = \text{KEY}(x, y, z)$ and P_n, for $1 \leq n \leq arity(P)$, are fresh predicates of arity 2. Rule (1) then becomes

$$\begin{aligned}
id_1(k, x_1), \ldots, &id_{m+n}(k, y_n), id_{m+n+1}(k, u), id_{m+n+2}(k, v), \\
id_1(j, x_1), \ldots, &id_{m+n}(j, y_n), id_{m+n+1}(j, v), id_{m+n+2}(j, w), \\
l := \text{KEY}(\vec{x}, \vec{y}, u, w) &\rightarrow id_1(l, x_1), \ldots, id_{m+n}(l, y_n), \\
&id_{m+n+1}(l, v), id_{m+n+2}(l, w)
\end{aligned} \tag{2}$$

Using the SKOLEM functionality[4] in RDFox, we are able to reduce the arity of a predicate P (see predicate *id* in Rule (3)) without having to introduce $arity(P)$ fresh predicates. Also note how joins over multiple terms (*id* joining over $(\vec{x}, \vec{y})$ in (1)) can now be rewritten into simpler joins (*id* joining over a single term k)[5].

$$\begin{aligned}
id(k, j), \text{SKOLEM}(\vec{x}, \vec{y}, u, v, j), id(k, l), \text{SKOLEM}(\vec{x}, \vec{y}, v, w, l), \\
\text{SKOLEM}(\vec{x}, \vec{y}, u, w, t) \rightarrow id(k, t)
\end{aligned} \tag{3}$$

□

Query Independent Computation. One of the main features of the combined approach for conjunctive query answering over knowledge bases is its two-stage process. The first step, i.e., the computation of the canonical model, is notably dependent solely on the input knowledge base; similarly the filtration step is only dependent on the query.

The two-stage nature of the approach can be implemented directly in RDFox using different *named graphs* to store the materialisation of the combined approach and the filtering step respectively. Assigning different named graphs (here

---

[4] https://docs.oxfordsemantic.tech/tuple-tables.html#rdfox-skolem.

[5] Rule 3 showcases how the SKOLEM function can be used in both directions: given a sequence of terms, we can *pack* them into a single fresh term; give a previously skolemised term, we can *unpack* it to retrieve the corresponding sequence of terms.

essentially used as *namespaces*) to different parts of the computation allows us to treat them independently, managing partial results of a computation, dropping or preserving them. This means that for every new query over the same knowledge base we only need to perform the filtering step. Once the answers to a particular query are computed we can simply drop the named graph corresponding to the filtering step for that query and start fresh for the next one.

Note that RDFox supports parallel computation as well, and since the filtering steps for a set of queries are independent of each other we can execute multiple filtering steps in parallel to take advantage of hardware parallelisation (see Sect. 7).

Top and Equality Axiomatisation. RDFox has built-in support for $\top$ (*top*, *truth* or `owl:Thing`) and *equality* (`owl:sameAs`), so that $\top$ automatically *subsumes* any new class introduced within an RDF triple, and equality between terms is always consistent with its semantics.

In both cases we are not able to use these features directly: in the case of top axiomatisation, we import axioms as Datalog rules, which are not taken into consideration when RDFox derives new $\top$ subsumptions; in the case of equality axiomatisation, the feature cannot be enabled along other features like *aggregates* and *negation-as-failure*, which are extensively used in our system.

To work around this, we introduce the axiomatisation for both predicates explicitly. For more details on the set of rules used for this, we refer the reader to [9, Appendix C].

3.3   Additional Fixes

Our work also includes a few clarifications on theoretical definitions and their implementation.

In the canonical model computation in [5], the `notIn` predicate is introduced to simulate the semantics of set membership and in particular the meaning of `notIn[a, b]` is "a is not in set b". During the computation of the canonical model program we have complete knowledge of any set that might be used in a `notIn` atom. For each such set S, and for each element $a \in S$, we introduce the fact `in[a,S]` in the canonical model. We then replace any occurrence of `notIn[?X, ?Y]` in the original program E_O with `NOT in[?X, ?Y]`, where `NOT` is the operator for *negation-as-failure* in RDFox.

A similar approach has been used to redefine and implement predicate NI, representing the set of *non-anonymous* terms in the materialised canonical model. We enumerate the elements of this set introducing the following rule:

```
NI[?Y] :- named[?X], owl:sameAs[?X, ?Y] .
```

where `named` is a predicate representing the set of constants in the original ontology.

A final improvement has been made on the computation of the `cycle` function during the canonical model computation. The original definition involved a search over all possible triples (A, R, B) where $A, B \in N_C$, $R \in N_R$ in the original ontology. We realised that traversing the whole space would significantly slow down the computation, and is *not* necessary; we instead restrict our search over all (A, R, B) triples that appear in a (T5) axiom $A \sqsubseteq \exists R.B$ in the original normalised ontology.

4 Integration of RSA into PAGOdA

As described in Sect. 2 and in [21], the process of computing the lower-bound of the answers to an input query involves (1) approximating the input ontology to *disjunctive Datalog* and further processing the rules to obtain a Datalog program; (2) approximating the input ontology to $\mathcal{ELHO}_\perp^r$ and applying the corresponding combined approach presented in [18].

These two approximations are handled independently, by means of materialisation in the first case, and the combined approach in the second; this allows PAGOdA to avoid having to deal with *and-branching* and the resulting intractability of most reasoning problems (see Definition 1). The RL and $\mathcal{ELHO}_\perp^r$ approximations used by PAGOdA eliminate *all* interactions between axioms (T5) and either axioms (T4) or axioms (T3) and (R1)[6]. However, not all such interactions cause an exponential jump in complexity, and PAGOdA's filtering of such cases is unnecessarily coarse. In RSA, interactions between these types of axioms are allowed but limited, and the filtering of those cases that may lead to and-branching is based on a fine-grained analysis of *role safety*; hence the lower-bound produced by the RSA combined approach is often larger than the one computed by PAGOdA.

In the following we show how to integrate the aforementioned combined approach for RSA into the lower-bound computation procedure.

4.1 Lower-Bound Computation

We take different steps depending on how the input ontology can be classified. We assume w.l.o.g. that the input ontology is consistent and normalised.

If the input ontology is inside one of the OWL 2 profiles, we simply use the standard PAGOdA algorithm to compute the answers to the query. Note that this check is purely syntactic over the normalised ontology.

If the first check fails (i.e., the ontology is not in any of the profiles), we check whether the ontology is in RSA. This can be done using the polynomial algorithm presented in [5] and reimplemented in our system (Sect. 3). If the input ontology is inside RSA we are able to apply the combined approach for query answering directly and collect the sound and complete set of answers to the input query. Efficiency of the RSA combined approach, compared to PAGOdA, mainly depends on the input ontology and the type of query; as explained earlier, this

---

[6] Note that OWL 2 RL does not allow axioms (T5) and OWL 2 EL (which contains $\mathcal{ELHO}_\perp^r$) does not allow axioms (T4) or inverse roles (R1).

new approach is particularly effective when query answers depend on interactions between axioms that belong to different profiles. Based on our tests (see Sect. 6 for more details), if PAGOdA is not able to compute the complete set of answers by means of computing its lower and upper-bounds and instead relies on HermiT to finalise the computation, then the RSA approach can be up to 2 orders of magnitude faster in returning the complete set of answers.

If the input ontology is not RSA, we approximate it to $\mathcal{ALCHOIQ}$. The approximation is carried out by removing any axiom in the normalised ontology that is not part of $\mathcal{ALCHOIQ}$. We then eliminate any axiom involving *disjunction* on the right-hand side using a *program shifting* technique. Note that this approach is the same used by PAGOdA to handle disjunctive rules in the original lower-bound computation. This procedure guarantees to produce a sound (but not necessarily complete) approximation w.r.t. CQ answering. The resulting ontology is in Horn-$\mathcal{ALCHOIQ}$.

The next step involves the approximation from Horn-$\mathcal{ALCHOIQ}$ to RSA. We achieve this using a novel algorithm to approximate an Horn-$\mathcal{ALCHOIQ}$ ontology to RSA in polynomial time (Sect. 5). Then, we can apply the RSA combined approach to the resulting approximated ontology.

We can then summarise the overall procedure in the following steps:

1. If the input ontology is inside one of the OWL 2 profiles, we run the standard PAGOdA algorithm. In this scenario, PAGOdA is able to compute complete query answers using a tractable procedure for the relevant profile.
2. If the input ontology is in RSA, we run the combined approach algorithm described in Sect. 3.1. This will return the complete set of answers to the input query.
3. If the ontology is not RSA we substitute the lower-bound computation process in PAGOdA with the following steps:
   (a) We approximate the input ontology to Horn-$\mathcal{ALCHOIQ}$ by first discarding any non-$\mathcal{ALCHOIQ}$ axioms, and then using a *shifting technique* to eliminate disjunction on the right-hand side of axioms.
   (b) We use a novel algorithm to approximate the Horn-$\mathcal{ALCHOIQ}$ ontology to RSA (see Sect. 5).
   (c) We apply the RSA combined approach to obtain a lower-bound of the answers to the query.
   (d) We continue with the standard PAGOdA procedure to compute the complete set of answers.

The approximation algorithm guarantees that the combined approach applied over the approximated RSA ontology will return a subset (lower-bound) of the answers to the query over the original ontology, i.e., $cert(q, \mathcal{O}_{RSA}) \subseteq cert(q, \mathcal{O})$, where q is the input CQ, $\mathcal{O}$ is the original ontology and $\mathcal{O}_{RSA}$ is its RSA approximation. Let ℓ_P be the lower-bound computed by PAGOdA, and ℓ_R be the lower-bound computed by our procedure; then we have in general that $l_P \subseteq l_R$.

5 Horn-$\mathcal{ALCHOIQ}$ to RSA Approximation

One of the steps involved in the process of integrating the RSA combined approach in PAGOdA is the approximation of the input ontology to RSA. In the
original algorithm, PAGOdA would approximate the ontology by removing most
of the out-of-profile axioms and deal in a more fine-grained manner with *existential quantification* and *union*.

Note that we can't directly apply this approach to the new system since the
definition of RSA is not purely syntactical and an approximation to RSA by
removing out-of-language axioms is not possible. Instead, we propose an algorithm that first approximates the input ontology to an Horn-$\mathcal{ALCHOIQ}$ ontology $\mathcal{O}$ and then further approximates $\mathcal{O}$ to RSA using a novel technique acting
on the custom dependency graph $G_{\mathcal{O}}$ presented in Definition 2.

In the following we provide a description of the algorithm to approxi-
mate a Horn-$\mathcal{ALCHOIQ}$ ontology $\mathcal{O}_S$ into an RSA ontology $\mathcal{O}_T$ such that
$cert(q, \mathcal{O}_T) \subseteq cert(q, \mathcal{O}_S)$.

Given an Horn-$\mathcal{ALCHOIQ}$ ontology $\mathcal{O}$, checking if $\mathcal{O}$ is RSA consists of:

1. checking whether $G_{\mathcal{O}}$ is an *oriented forest*;
2. checking whether $\mathcal{O}$ is *equality safe*.

We first consider (1). If $\mathcal{O}$ is not RSA, then it presents at least one cycle
in $G_{\mathcal{O}}$. The idea is to disconnect the graph and propagate the changes into the
original ontology. A way of doing this is to delete some nodes $u_{R,B}^A$ from the
graph to break the cycles. By definition of $u_{R,B}^A$, the node uniquely identifies
an axiom $A \sqsubseteq \exists R.B$ of type (T5) in $\mathcal{O}$ and hence, removing the axiom will
break the cycle in $G_{\mathcal{O}}$. We can gather a possible set of nodes that disconnect
the graph by using a slightly modified version of a BFS visit. The action of
deleting the nodes from the graph can be then propagated to the ontology by
removing the corresponding T5 axioms. Due to monotonicity of first order logic,
deleting axioms from the ontology clearly produces a lower-bound approximation
of the ontology w.r.t. conjunctive query answering. We summarise this process
in Algorithm 1.

Next, we need to deal with *equality safety* (2). The following step can be
performed to ensure this property:

- delete any T4 axiom that involves a role S such that there exists $w \approx t$ (with
  w and y distinct) and $R(t, u_{R,B}^A)$ in M_{RSA} and $R \sqsubseteq Inv(S)$;
- if there is a pair of atoms $R(a, u_{R,B}^A), S(u_{R,B}^A, a)$ in M_{RSA} with $a \in N_I$ and
  a role T such that both $R \sqsubseteq_{\mathcal{R}}^* T$ and $S \sqsubseteq_{\mathcal{R}}^* Inv(T)$ hold, then remove some
  axiom (R2) to break the derivation chain that deduces either $R \sqsubseteq_{\mathcal{R}}^* T$ or
  $S \sqsubseteq_{\mathcal{R}}^* Inv(T)$.

Note that the set of nodes that are computed by the graph visit to disconnect
all cycles in a graph is not, in general, unique, and hence might not guarantee
the tightest lower-bound on the answers to a given query. On the other hand
this gives us a simple way of determining whether the approximation will affect

---

Algorithm 1: Approximate an Horn-$\mathcal{ALCHOIQ}$ ontology to RSA

   Input: Ontology dependency graph G
1   let N be the set of nodes in G;
2   let C be an empty set;
3   **foreach** *node* n *in* N **do**
4   **if** n *is not* discovered **then**
5   let S be an empty stack;
6   push n in S;
7   **while** S *is not* empty **do**
8   pop v from S;
9   **if** v *is not* discovered **then**
10   label v as *discovered*;
11   let *adj* be the set of nodes adjacent to v;
12   **if** *any node in adj is* discovered **then**
13   push v in C;
14   **else**
15   **foreach** *node* w *in adj* **do**
16   push w in S;

17 remove C from G;

---

the resulting answer computation. It is easy to see that if the deleted axioms are not involved in the computation of the answers to the input query, the set of answers will be left unaltered and will correspond to the set of answers to the query w.r.t. to the original ontology.

With reference to the PAGOdA approach, $cert(q, O_P) \subseteq cert(q, O_T)$ for both approximations O_P to Datalog and $\mathcal{ELHO}_\perp^r$ used by PAGOdA for the lower-bound computation.

6 Evaluation

Implementation Details. As part of this work, we introduce RSAComb, a new and improved implementation of the combined approach algorithm for RSA, released as free and open source software [10]. On the one hand, the implementation presented in [5] is not available, and on the other hand we wanted to take advantage of a tight integration with RDFox and simplify the subsequent integration in PAGOdA.

Our implementation is written in Scala and uses RDFox[7] as the underlying Datalog reasoner. At the time of writing, development and testing have been carried out using Scala v2.13.5 and RDFox v4.1. Scala allows us to easily interface with Java libraries and in particular the OWLAPI [7] for easy ontology manipulation. We communicate with RDFox through the Java wrapper API provided with the distribution.

---

[7] https://www.oxfordsemantic.tech/product.

Testing Environment. All experiments were performed on an Intel(R) Xeon(R) CPU E5-2640 v3 @ 2.60 GHz with 16 real cores, extended via hyper-threading to 32 virtual cores, 512 GB of RAM and running Fedora 33, kernel version 5.8.17–300.fc33.x86_64. While PAGOdA is inherently single core, we were able to make use of the multicore CPU and distribute the computation across cores, especially for intensive tasks offloaded to RDFox.

Comparison with PAGOdA. To compare our system against PAGOdA, we performed our tests on the LUBM ontology [6], for which the PAGOdA distribution offers pre-generated datasets[8]. We performed our tests on three different queries for which PAGOdA does require HermiT to complete the computation (i.e., the query is classified as "FullReasoning"); the first two (31 and 34) were used as they originally shipped with the PAGOdA distribution, while query 36 was chosen to show that even a simple query can be problematic for PAGOdA and how our improved approach is able to solve the problem. In fact, we were able to identify a whole class of queries for which PAGOdA does not perform well, and query 36 can be seen as a minimal example from this class. We provide all queries in [9, Appendix D].

LUBM is not in Horn-$\mathcal{ALCHOIQ}$ (because of some *role transitivity* axiom) but contains only safe roles. Datasets from the PAGOdA distribution are automatically generated with the LUBM data generator[9], with the parameter indicating the number of universities ranging from 100 up to 800, with steps of 100.

For queries where PAGOdA does not require HermiT, the performance of PAGOdA and RSAComb are very similar. In Table 2, we show the results for our three queries. For each query we provide in order: the size of the ABox, the number of answers to the query, preprocessing and answering time in PAGOdA, preprocessing time in our system (including approximation to RSA and computation of the canonical model), answering time for RSAComb (including filtering program computation and filtering step, answers gathering). Execution time had a timeout set to 10 h and timed-out computation is indicated in the tables with a hyphen "-".

The results clearly show how our system is able to compute the complete set of answers to the queries in considerably less time and without the need of a fully-fledged reasoner like HermiT. For larger datasets, the introduction of our system makes the difference between feasibility and unfeasibility. Focusing on query 36, we are able to limit the impact that a high number of answers to a query has on performance.

Another important aspect shown here is that, even when factoring out the preprocessing time for both systems (we can argue that this step can be pre-computed offline when the ontology is fixed), we still achieve considerably faster results, especially when it comes to datasets of larger size.

---

[8] https://www.cs.ox.ac.uk/isg/tools/PAGOdA/.
[9] http://swat.cse.lehigh.edu/projects/lubm/uba1.7.zip.

Table 2. Comparison of answering time for PAGOdA and our system with multiple queries over LUBM. Timed-out computations are indicated with a hyphen "-".

ABox Size	Query ID	Answers	PAGOdA Preprocessing (s)	PAGOdA Answering (s)	RSAComb Preprocessing (s)	RSAComb Answering (s)
100	34	4	196	109	41	2
	31	18		159		3
	36	72927		219		154
200	34	4	461	2303	78	5
	31	18		7535		5
	36	145279		-		613
300	34	4	824	10563	112	7
	31	18		23309		7
	36	217375		-		1227
400	34	4	1023	14527	153	10
	31	18		-		11
	36	290516		-		2593
500	34	4	1317	23855	206	12
	31	18		-		13
	36	363890		-		4174
600	34	4	1738	33322	210	16
	31	18		-		15
	36	436961		-		4302
700	34	4	2390	-	252	19
	31	18		-		21
	36	509401		-		4667
800	34	4	3619	-	260	22
	31	18		-		21
	36	582658		-		6105

7   Discussion and Future Work

We presented a novel algorithm to approximate an OWL 2 ontology into RSA, and an algorithm to compute a lower-bound approximation of the answers to a CQ using the RSA combined approach. We showed that this lower-bound is stricter than the one computed by PAGOdA and provided an implementation of the algorithms in a prototypical CQ answering system.

We are already working on additional improvements to the approximation algorithm to RSA; the current visit of the dependency graph to detect the axioms to delete might be improved with different heuristics and might in some cases take into account the input query (deleting axioms that are not necessarily involved in the computation of the answers). A similar approach could be introduced to integrate RSA in the upper-bound of the answers to a query, with the ultimate goal of improving this step in PAGOdA as well.

On a different note, we hope to obtain additional improvements in performance in the current implementation of the RSA combined approach by introducing parallel execution of filtering steps for different input queries, using the *named graph* functionality provided by RDFox. This was partially motivated by the promising results recently shown in [20], where parallelisation techniques are applied to the *tableau algorithm* to improve its performance on expressive ontology languages.

Finally, we would like to explore the possibility to avoid the conversion of axioms into Datalog overall and come up with a different encoding of the RSA combined approach that would make use of the built-in support for OWL 2 $\mathcal{RL}$ currently present in RDFox.

References

1. Calvanese, D., De Giacomo, G., Lembo, D., Lenzerini, M., Rosati, R.: Data complexity of query answering in description logics. In: Proceedings, Tenth International Conference on Principles of Knowledge Representation and Reasoning, Lake District of the United Kingdom, 2–5 June 2006, pp. 260–270. AAAI Press (2006)
2. Calvanese, D., De Giacomo, G., Lembo, D., Lenzerini, M., Rosati, R.: Tractable reasoning and efficient query answering in description logics: the DL-lite family. J. Autom. Reasoning **39**(3), 385–429 (2007). https://doi.org/10.1007/s10817-007-9078-x
3. Carral, D., Feier, C., Grau, B.C., Hitzler, P., Horrocks, I.: Pushing the boundaries of tractable ontology reasoning. In: Mika, P., et al. (eds.) ISWC 2014. LNCS, vol. 8797, pp. 148–163. Springer, Cham (2014). https://doi.org/10.1007/978-3-319-11915-1_10
4. Eiter, T., Fink, M., Tompits, H., Woltran, S.: On eliminating disjunctions in stable logic programming. In: Dubois, D., Welty, C.A., Williams, M. (eds.) Principles of Knowledge Representation and Reasoning: Proceedings of the Ninth International Conference (KR2004), Whistler, Canada, 2–5 June 2004, pp. 447–458. AAAI Press (2004). http://www.aaai.org/Library/KR/2004/kr04-047.php
5. Feier, C., Carral, D., Stefanoni, G., Cuenca Grau, B., Horrocks, I.: The combined approach to query answering beyond the OWL 2 profiles. In: Proceedings of the Twenty-Fourth International Joint Conference on Artificial Intelligence, IJCAI 2015, Buenos Aires, Argentina, 25–31 July 2015, pp. 2971–2977. AAAI Press (2015)
6. Guo, Y., Pan, Z., Heflin, J.: LUBM: a benchmark for OWL knowledge base systems. J. Web Semant. **3**(2–3), 158–182 (2005). https://doi.org/10.1016/j.websem.2005.06.005
7. Horridge, M., Bechhofer, S.: The OWL API: a java API for OWL ontologies. Semantic Web **2**(1), 11–21 (2011). https://doi.org/10.3233/SW-2011-0025
8. Horrocks, I., Tessaris, S.: A conjunctive query language for description logic aboxes. In: Kautz, H.A., Porter, B.W. (eds.) Proceedings of the Seventeenth National Conference on Artificial Intelligence and Twelfth Conference on on Innovative Applications of Artificial Intelligence, Austin, Texas, USA, 30 July–3 August 2000, pp. 399–404. AAAI Press/The MIT Press (2000). http://www.aaai.org/Library/AAAI/2000/aaai00-061.php
9. Igne, F., Germano, S., Horrocks, I.: Computing CQ lower-bounds over OWL 2 through approximation to RSA - extended version (2021). https://arxiv.org/abs/2107.00369

10. Igne, F., Germano, S., Horrocks, I.: RSAComb - combined approach for conjunctive query answering in RSA, June 2021. https://doi.org/10.5281/zenodo.5047811
11. Kontchakov, R., Lutz, C., Toman, D., Wolter, F., Zakharyaschev, M.: The combined approach to query answering in DL-Lite. In: Principles of Knowledge Representation and Reasoning: Proceedings of the Twelfth International Conference, KR 2010, Toronto, Ontario, Canada, 9–13 May 2010. AAAI Press (2010)
12. Lutz, C., Toman, D., Wolter, F.: Conjunctive query answering in the description logic EL using a relational database system. In: Boutilier, C. (ed.) IJCAI 2009, Proceedings of the 21st International Joint Conference on Artificial Intelligence, Pasadena, California, USA, 11–17 July 2009, pp. 2070–2075 (2009). http://ijcai.org/Proceedings/09/Papers/341.pdf
13. Motik, B., Nenov, Y., Piro, R., Horrocks, I.: Handling owl: Sameas via rewriting. In: Proceedings of the Twenty-Ninth AAAI Conference on Artificial Intelligence, Austin, Texas, USA, 25–30 January 2015, pp. 231–237. AAAI Press (2015)
14. Motik, B., Nenov, Y., Piro, R., Horrocks, I.: Incremental update of datalog materialisation: the backward/forward algorithm. In: Proceedings of the Twenty-Ninth AAAI Conference on Artificial Intelligence, Austin, Texas, USA, 25–30 January 2015, pp. 1560–1568. AAAI Press (2015)
15. Motik, B., Nenov, Y., Piro, R., Horrocks, I., Olteanu, D.: Parallel materialisation of datalog programs in centralised, main-memory RDF systems. In: Proceedings of the Twenty-Eighth AAAI Conference on Artificial Intelligence, Québec City, Québec, Canada, 27–31 July 2014, pp. 129–137. AAAI Press (2014)
16. Nenov, Y., Piro, R., Motik, B., Horrocks, I., Wu, Z., Banerjee, J.: RDFox: a highly-scalable RDF store. In: Arenas, M., et al. (eds.) ISWC 2015. LNCS, vol. 9367, pp. 3–20. Springer, Cham (2015). https://doi.org/10.1007/978-3-319-25010-6_1
17. Ren, Y., Pan, J.Z., Guclu, I., Kollingbaum, M.: A combined approach to incremental reasoning for EL ontologies. In: Ortiz, M., Schlobach, S. (eds.) RR 2016. LNCS, vol. 9898, pp. 167–183. Springer, Cham (2016). https://doi.org/10.1007/978-3-319-45276-0_13
18. Stefanoni, G., Motik, B.: Answering conjunctive queries over EL knowledge bases with transitive and reflexive roles. CoRR abs/1411.2516 (2014)
19. Stefanoni, G., Motik, B., Horrocks, I.: Introducing nominals to the combined query answering approaches for EL. In: desJardins, M., Littman, M.L. (eds.) Proceedings of the Twenty-Seventh AAAI Conference on Artificial Intelligence, 14–18 July 2013, Bellevue, Washington, USA. AAAI Press (2013). http://www.aaai.org/ocs/index.php/AAAI/AAAI13/paper/view/6156
20. Steigmiller, A., Glimm, B.: Parallelised ABox reasoning and query answering with expressive description logics. In: Verborgh, R., et al. (eds.) ESWC 2021. LNCS, vol. 12731, pp. 23–39. Springer, Cham (2021). https://doi.org/10.1007/978-3-030-77385-4_2
21. Zhou, Y., Cuenca Grau, B., Nenov, Y., Kaminski, M., Horrocks, I.: Pagoda: pay-as-you-go ontology query answering using a datalog reasoner. J. Artif. Intell. Res. 54, 309–367 (2015)

Fast ObjectRank for Large Knowledge Databases

Hiroaki Shiokawa(✉) [ID]

Center for Computational Sciences, University of Tsukuba, Tsukuba, Japan
shiokawa@cs.tsukuba.ac.jp

Abstract. ObjectRank is an essential tool to evaluate an importance of nodes for a user-specified query in heterogeneous graphs. However, existing methods are not applicable to massive graphs because they iteratively compute all nodes and edges. This paper proposes SchemaRank, which detects the exact top-k important nodes for a given query within a short running time. SchemaRank dynamically excludes unpromising nodes and edges, ensuring that it detects the same top-k important nodes as ObjectRank. Our extensive evaluations demonstrate that the running time of SchemaRank outperforms existing methods by up to two orders of magnitude.

Keywords: Heterogeneous graph · Search algorithm · Big data

1 Introduction

ObjectRank [9] is an essential tool to analyze heterogeneous graphs composed of *multiple node-types*. It evaluates an importance of nodes in a graph for a user-specified query by performing *random walk with restarts* (RWR). Unlike traditional graph similarities [26], ObjectRank captures not only (1) the structural closeness but also (2) the relationships among multiple node-types in the graph. Because heterogeneous graphs are currently the most common data model to represent various knowledge resources (*e.g.,* knowledge graphs), ObjectRank is employed in various Semantic Web applications due to its effectiveness.

For instance, ObjectRank plays important roles in question-answering tasks [2] and representation learning tasks [4]. To improve the accuracy, these tasks must capture the relationships among data entities in their learning models (*e.g.,* deep neural networks). However, understanding how strongly entities affect each other is not a trivial task since various data resources such as QA sites and knowledge bases are formed as heterogeneous graphs [16,27]. To address this issue, recent approaches have employed the random-walk analysis such as ObjectRank [13]. By evaluating the importance with respect to query entities, these approaches successfully capture representative relationships to improve their models.

Similarly, ObjectRank is also applicable for Semantic Web search [3]. For example, Serene [3] applied ObjectRank to ranking entities of knowledge graphs

© Springer Nature Switzerland AG 2021
A. Hotho et al. (Eds.): ISWC 2021, LNCS 12922, pp. 217–234, 2021.
https://doi.org/10.1007/978-3-030-88361-4_13

based on ontology by using heuristic weight assignments. It first converts user-specified query-keywords into query nodes of ObjectRank by picking up nodes having a subset of the keywords. Then, Serene performs ObjectRank and returns top-k entities to users, each of which is likely relevant to the query-keywords. Analogously, ObjectRank can be applicable in other recent applications such as recommendation [12], sentiment analysis [30], and bioinformatics [29].

Although it is effective in many applications, ObjectRank is computationally expensive because all nodes and edges are computed iteratively. If $|V|$ and $|E|$ are the number of nodes and edges, respectively, ObjectRank requires $O((|V|+|E|)t)$ time, where t is the number of iterations. In the mid-2000s, ObjectRank was applied to small graphs such as user query logs, which had a few thousand nodes at most. By contrast, recent Semantic Web applications must handle large knowledge graphs with a few million nodes [15,21–23]. That is, the applications suffer from a long computation time due to the expensive costs of ObjectRank.

1.1   Existing Works and Challenges

The expensive cost in ObjectRank has led to various efficient approaches. *Indexing methods* are the most successful to date [1,10]. Instead of just-in-time importance computations, these methods pre-compute the node-importance for several query patterns. After receiving a query, the methods approximately compute the node-importance utilizing the pre-computed results according to the query patterns. By employing indexing approaches, the expensive cost is successfully moderated. However, [20] recently pointed out that indexing methods require a long runtime for pre-computation. For instance, in our evaluations, the methods required more than 17 h for pre-computing 1.5 million nodes.

Recently, *pruning methods* have become popular to reduce the large runtime for various RWR-based algorithms [5,7]. The main idea is to remove nodes with a low importance during iterative computations for a given query. For example, Fujiwara *et al.* proposed a fast top-k algorithm, *SimMat* [7], for SimRank [11]. SimMat reduces the graph by pruning nodes with a low importance through SVD. Hence, it can efficiently find top-k important nodes for a given query.

However, SimMat and its variants [5,6] are not applicable to ObjectRank for two reasons. First, they require high costs to estimate nodes with a low importance because their SVD-based method incurs $\Omega(|V|^3)$ time [8]. Second, their pruning approaches degrade the accuracy of ObjectRank. Since they are designed for homogeneous graphs, they do not guarantee the accuracy of the node-importance on heterogeneous graphs. For example, Sato *et al.* proposed a fast ObjectRank algorithm called *FORank* [20] by extending the pruning methods [6]. However, as shown in [20], FORank cannot find the same top-k nodes as ObjectRank. Thus, a fast and exact algorithm for ObjectRank remains elusive.

1.2   Our Approaches and Contributions

We present a novel fast ObjectRank algorithm called *SchemaRank*. Given a user-specified query, SchemaRank efficiently detects the same top-k important nodes as ObjectRank. SchemaRank is based on the property of real-world graphs in which the distribution of node-importance is highly skewed [24]. That is, the vast majority of nodes have a low importance in real-world graphs.

Based on the above property, SchemaRank dynamically excludes unpromising nodes that cannot become the top-k important nodes. To determine which nodes to exclude, SchemaRank employs the following two-step RWRs: First, *coarse-grained RWR* estimates the distribution of importance at the node-type level. If specific node-types yield a low importance, SchemaRank prunes all nodes with those node-types in the second step. Second, *fine-grained RWR* prunes unpromising nodes by incrementally refining the estimated distribution at the node level. Once a node outputs a lower importance than the k-th highest node-importance, SchemaRank incrementally removes the node from the graph. This leads to the following characteristics:

- **Fast:** SchemaRank is faster than the state-of-the-art algorithms proposed in the last few years (Sect. 4.1). In our experiments, the running time of SchemaRank outperforms them by up to two orders of magnitude (Table 3).
- **Exact:** We theoretically guarantee that SchemaRank always outputs the same top-k nodes as ObjectRank (Theorem 2), although it prunes nodes with a low importance. We experimentally verified that it returns the same top-k ranking importance as ObjectRank (Fig. 4).
- **Easy to deploy:** SchemaRank does not require pre-computations (Algorithm 1); given a query, it quickly outputs top-k nodes on the fly.

SchemaRank is the first solution that achieves a fast and exact top-k importance evaluation on massive heterogeneous graphs. For instance, SchemaRank returns the exact top-k nodes within three seconds on a DBLP graph with 1.5 million nodes. Although ObjectRank effectively enhances the quality of Semantic Web applications, it is difficult to apply to massive graphs. By providing our fast and exact algorithm, SchemaRank will enhance many applications.

2   Preliminary

Here, we briefly introduce the background. Table 1 lists the main symbols and their definitions.

2.1   Data Model

ObjectRank transforms the given data entities into a heterogeneous graph for importance evaluation [9]. The generated graph is two-fold: *schema-graph* and *data-graph*.

Schema-Graph: A schema-graph is a *user-specified* graph that defines the relationships among entity-types (node-types). We denote a schema-graph as $G_S = (V_S, E_S, W_S)$, where V_S, E_S, and W_S are sets of nodes, edges, and edge-weights, respectively. V_S represents node-types, and E_S models their relationships. For each edge $e \in E_S$, an edge-weight $w_S(e) \in W_S$ must be defined such that $w_S(e) \in [0, 1]$ to emphasize the relevance between two node-types.

Table 1. Definitions of symbols.

Symbol	Definition
G_S	Schema-graph
V_S	Set of nodes in a schema-graph G_S
E_S	Set of edges in a schema-graph G_S
W_S	Set of edge-weights in a schema-graph G_S
$w_S(e)$	Edge-weight of $e \in E_S$.
G_D	Data-graph
V_D	Set of nodes in a data-graph G_D
$V_D(i)$	Set of nodes having a node-type i in V_D
E_D	Set of edges in a data-graph G_D
W_D	Set of edge-weights in a data-graph G_D
$w_D(e)$	Edge-weight of $e \in E_D$.
V_q	Set of query nodes $s.t.\ V_q \subseteq V_D$
$V_q(i)$	Set of query nodes having a node-type i in V_q
$\mathbf{r}$	Importance vector of G_D
$\mathbf{q}$	Query vector of G_D
$\mathbf{A}$	Transition matrix of G_D
α	Dumping factor $s.t.\ \alpha \in [0,1]$
$\mathbf{r}_S$	Importance vector of G_S in Definition 2
$\mathbf{q}_S$	Query vector of G_D in Definition 1
$\mathbf{S}$	Transition matrix of G_D in Definition 2
$\underline{r}_i^{(t)}$	Lower bound of r_i in the t-th iteration
$\overline{r}_i^{(t)}$	Upper bound of r_i in the t-th iteration
$\epsilon^{(t)}$	k-th highest lower bound in the t-th iteration.

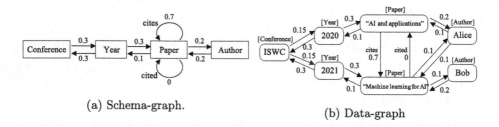

(a) Schema-graph.

(b) Data-graph

Fig. 1. A schema-graph and its corresponding data-graph.

Figure 1 (a) depicts a schema-graph example for bibliographic entities. The graph consists of four node-types (Conference, Year, Paper, and Author). Because "cites" has the largest edge-weight in W_S, herein the importance evaluation emphasizes paper-citation relationships.

Data-Graph: ObjectRank generates a data-graph $G_D = (V_D, E_D, W_D)$ from a schema-graph to materialize actual entity relationships, where V_D, E_D, and W_D are sets of nodes, edges, and edge-weights, respectively. V_D represents entities, each of which has a node-type defined in the schema-graph. We denote $V_D(i)$ as a set of nodes with node-type i in V_D. ObjectRank links pairs of nodes u and v with node-types i and j, respectively, if the schema-graph has an edge between node-types i and j. For each edge $e_{u,v}$ linking u to v, it assigns an edge-weight, $w_D(e_{u,v}) \in W_D$, which is equal to the edge-weight $w_S(e_{i,j})$ divided by the number of nodes in $V_D(j)$ connected from node u.

Figure 1 (b) shows an example of a data-graph instantiated from the schema-graph in Fig. 1 (a), where each node represents an actual entity (*e.g.*, paper title and author name, associated with the corresponding node-type). In Fig. 1 (b), Alice has an edge-weight of 0.1 for each Paper node because (1) the edge-weight between Author and Paper is 0.2 in the schema-graph and (2) Alice is adjacent to two Paper nodes.

2.2 Importance Evaluation

ObjectRank computes the importance of nodes on the data-graph. Given a set of query nodes $V_q \subseteq V_D$, it returns an importance vector $\mathbf{r} = (r_1, r_2, \ldots, r_{|V_D|})^{\mathrm{T}}$, where $r_i \in \mathbb{R}$ is the importance of node $i \in V_D$. By letting $\alpha \in [0, 1]$ and $r_i = 1/|V_D|$, $\mathbf{r}$ can be obtained by iteratively applying the following equation until $\mathbf{r}$ converges:

$$\mathbf{r} = \alpha \mathbf{A} \mathbf{r} + (1 - \alpha)\mathbf{q}, \tag{1}$$

where $\mathbf{A} \in \mathbb{R}^{|V_D| \times |V_D|}$ is a transition matrix of G_D, whose (i, j)-th element A_{ij} is equal to $w_D(e_{i,j}) \in W_D$. Additionally, $\mathbf{q} \in \mathbb{R}^{|V_D|}$ is a query vector, whose i-th element q_i is $1/|V_q|$ if node $i \in V_q$. Otherwise $q_i = 0$. Although the convergence of Eq. (1) is guaranteed [14], it requires $O((|V_D| + |E_D|)t)$ time until it converges, where t is the number of iterations.[1]

3 Proposed Method: SchemaRank

We present SchemaRank that efficiently detects exact top-k important nodes for a query. First, we overview the ideas and then give a full description.

3.1 Basic Ideas

Our goal is to efficiently find the same top-k important nodes as ObjectRank. ObjectRank iteratively computes all nodes in a data-graph until $\mathbf{r}$ converges. By contrast, SchemaRank dynamically prunes unpromising nodes that cannot become the top-k nodes after convergence. As discussed by Sun *et al.*, real-world

---

[1] ObjectRank can easily handle updates of graphs (*e.g.*, nodes/edges insertion or deletion, and changes of weights) by using the Gauss-Southwell algorithm. Thus, this work does not consider such updates.

graphs have a highly skewed importance distribution [24]. The vast majority of nodes practically yield a low importance. Hence, we design SchemaRank to prune such unpromising nodes using a two-step approach: *coarse-grained RWR* and *fine-grained RWR*. First, the coarse-grained RWR roughly estimates the importance distribution at the node-type level. Then the fine-grained RWR prunes unpromising nodes by incrementally refining the distribution at the node level. Once a specific node-type yields a low importance, all nodes with that node-type are removed from the data-graph. Instead of computing all nodes, SchemaRank computes only essential nodes that are likely to become the top-k nodes.

Our approach has several advantages. (1) SchemaRank finds the top-k nodes with a short running time on real-world graphs. Our approach successfully handles the skewness of the importance distribution in real-world graphs [24] because SchemaRank increases its performance if a lot of nodes output a low importance. This leads to computation efficiency. (2) SchemaRank finds the same top-k nodes as ObjectRank. We theoretically demonstrated that SchemaRank safely discards unpromising nodes. Thus, SchemaRank does not sacrifice the quality of ObjectRank. (3) Because SchemaRank does not require any pre-computations, it can efficiently find the exact top-k nodes as ObjectRank on the fly. Hence, SchemaRank provides users with a simple solution using ObjectRank.

3.2   Coarse-Grained RWR

As the first step, SchemaRank roughly estimates the importance distribution at the node-type level. To estimate the importance for each node-type, SchemaRank performs RWR on the schema-graph G_S. Recall that the schema-graph represents the relationships among node-types. By performing RWR on G_S, our algorithm detects node-types with a low importance in the importance evaluation.

To estimate the importance distribution at the node-type level, SchemaRank first constructs the following vector:

Definition 1 (Query vector q_S). *Let $V_q(i)$ be a set of query nodes with a node-type $i \in V_S$. $q_S \in \mathbb{R}^{|V_S|}$ is a query vector whose i-th element is $q_{S,i} = |V_q(i)|/|V_q|$.*

To illustrate an example of q_S, let's say $V_q = \{Alice, ISWC\}$ is a set of user-specified query nodes selected from the data-graph in Fig. 1. We clearly have $|V_q(Author)| = 1$ from the corresponding schema-graph. Thus, $q_{S,Author} = 0.5$. SchemaRank then estimates the distribution as follows:

Definition 2 (Importance vector of G_S). *SchemaRank computes the following importance vector $r_S \in \mathbb{R}^{|V_S|}$:*

$$r_S = \alpha S r_S + (1 - \alpha) q_S, \tag{2}$$

where $\alpha \in [0,1]$, and $S \in \mathbb{R}^{|V_S| \times |V_S|}$ is a transition matrix of G_S, whose (i,j)-th element $S_{ij} = w_S(e_{i,j})$ in W_S.

In Definition 2, SchemaRank estimates the importance distribution at the node-type level by performing RWR on the schema-graph G_S. Definition 2 has the following property:

Lemma 1. *Let $V_D(i)$ be a set of nodes in V_D with a node-type $i \in V_S$. $r_{S,i} = \sum_{u \in V_D(i)} r_u$ always holds, where $r_{S,i}$ is the i-th element of r_S.*

Proof: From Eq. (2), we have the following

$$r_{S,i} = \alpha \sum_{j \in V_S} S_{ij} r_{S,j} + (1 - \alpha) q_{S,i}. \tag{3}$$

From Definition 1, $q_{S,i} = \sum_{u \in V_D(i)} q_u$. Also, from Sect. 2.1, $\sum_{j \in V_S} S_{ij} r_{S,j} = \sum_{u \in V_D(i)} \sum_{v \in V_D} A_{uv} r_v$. Therefore, we have the following equation:

$$\text{Eq. (3)} = \sum_{u \in V_D(i)} \left\{ \alpha \sum_{v \in V_D} A_{uv} r_v + (1 - \alpha) q_u \right\}. \tag{4}$$

Thus, $r_{S,i} = \sum_{u \in V_D(i)} r_u$ always holds.   □

Lemma 1 implies that Definition 2 effectively estimates the distribution of node-type level importance obtained by ObjectRank. Additionally, from Lemma 1, $r_u \leq r_{S,i}$ holds for any $u \in V_D(i)$. That is, nodes with a node-type i should be unpromising in ObjectRank if $r_{S,i}$ yields a low importance. By following this property, SchemaRank prunes such nodes in subsequent steps.

3.3   Fine-Grained RWR

Next, SchemaRank detects the top-k important nodes from the importance vector r_S estimated in the previous step. SchemaRank iterates (1) *upper and lower bounds estimation* and (2) *incremental pruning* until convergence.

Upper and Lower Bounds Estimation: In this step, SchemaRank estimates the bounds of node-importance in the data-graph by using the query vector q and the importance vector r_S estimated in the previous step.

Suppose that node $i \in V_D$ has a node-type $u \in V_S$. As we proved in Lemma 1, the importance r_i should be smaller than $r_{S,u}$. That is, $r_{S,u}$ plays a good upper bound of the importance r_i. To leverage this property, SchemaRank first constructs a vector $b^{(0)} \in \mathbb{R}^{|V_D|}$ from r_S, whose i-th element is initialized as $b_i^{(0)} = r_{S,u}/\|b^{(0)}\|$. Afterward, it estimates the following upper and lower bounds of node-importance from $b^{(0)}$ and q, respectively.

Definition 3 (Upper and lower bounds). *In the t-th iteration, the lower bound* $\underline{r}_i^{(t)}$ *and the upper bound* $\overline{r}_i^{(t)}$ *of node i are defined as*

$$\underline{r}_i^{(t)} = \begin{cases} (1-\alpha)q_i & (t=0) \\ \underline{r}_i^{(t-1)} + (1-\alpha)\alpha^t p_i^{(t)} & (t>0) \end{cases}, \tag{5}$$

$$\overline{r}_i^{(t)} = \begin{cases} b_i^{(0)} + \frac{\alpha}{1-\alpha}\overline{A}_i & (t=0) \\ \underline{r}_i^{(t-1)} + \alpha^t b_i^{(t)} + \frac{\alpha^{t+1}}{1-\alpha}\Delta^{(t)}\overline{A}_i & (t>0) \end{cases}, \tag{6}$$

where $\overline{A}_i = \max\{A_{ij} | j \in V_D\}$, $\Delta^{(t)} = \sum_{u \in V_D} \max\{b_u^{(t)} - b_u^{(t-1)}, 0\}$, *and* $p_i^{(t)}$ *and* $b_i^{(t)}$ *are the i-the elements of* $\mathbf{p}^{(t)} = \mathbf{A}^t\mathbf{q}$ *and* $\mathbf{b}^{(t)} = \mathbf{A}^t\mathbf{b}^{(0)}$, *respectively.*

Definition 3 estimates the importance of each node after convergence. Based on the following properties, Definition 3 can more precisely estimate the importance of each node by recursively updating $\overline{r}_i^{(t)}$ and $\underline{r}_i^{(t)}$.

Lemma 2. *By Definition 3,* $\underline{r}_i^{(t)} \le r_i \le \overline{r}_i^{(t)}$ *holds.*

Proof: We first prove $\underline{r}_i^{(t)} \le r_i$. From Eq. (1),

$$\mathbf{r}^{(t)} = \alpha^t \mathbf{A}^t \mathbf{r}^{(0)} + (1-\alpha)\sum_{j=0}^{t-1} \alpha^j \mathbf{A}^j \mathbf{q}. \tag{7}$$

If $t \to \infty$, $\mathbf{r} = \mathbf{r}^{(\infty)}$. Thus, assuming the number of iterations t goes to ∞, the following condition can be derived

$$r_i = (1-\alpha)\sum_{j=0}^{\infty} \alpha^j p_i^{(j)} \ge (1-\alpha)\sum_{j=0}^{t} \alpha^j p_i^{(j)} = \underline{r}_i^{(t)}. \tag{8}$$

We then prove $r_i \le \overline{r}_i^{(t)}$. If $t \to \infty$, a Markov chain converges to the stationary distribution regardless of where it begins [28]. That is, $p_i^{(t)} \approx b_i^{(t)}$ holds for a large t. Thus, from Eq. (1), we have the following condition

$$r_i \approx \quad (1-\alpha)\sum_{j=0}^{t} \alpha^j b_i^{(j)} + (1-\alpha)\sum_{j=1}^{\infty} \alpha^{t+j} b_i^{(t+j)}$$

$$\le (1-\alpha)\sum_{j=0}^{t} \alpha^j b_i^{(j)} + \alpha^t b_i^{(t)} + \frac{\alpha^{t+1}}{1-\alpha}\Delta^{(t)}\overline{A}_i = \overline{r}_i^{(t)}. \tag{9}$$

Therefore, from Eqs. (8) and (9), $\underline{r}_i^{(t)} \le r_i \le \overline{r}_i^{(t)}$ holds. □

Lemma 3. *If* $t = \infty$, $\underline{r}_i^{(\infty)} = \overline{r}_i^{(\infty)} = r_i$ *always holds.*

Proof: From Eqs. (8) and (9), $\underline{r}_i^{(t)} \to r_i$ and $\overline{r}_i^{(t)} \to r_i$ if $t \to \infty$ since $\alpha^\infty = 0$ and $\frac{\alpha^\infty}{1-\alpha} = 0$. Thus, from Lemma 2, $\underline{r}_i^{(\infty)} = \overline{r}_i^{(\infty)} = r_i$ holds. □

Lemmas 2 and 3 indicate that the exact importance r_i can be obtained by continuously updating $\overline{r}_i^{(t)}$ and $\underline{r}_i^{(t)}$. Based on this property, SchemaRank incrementally prunes unpromising nodes in the following procedure.

Algorithm 1. Proposed method: SchemaRank

Input: G_S: schema-graph, G_V: data-graph, **q**: query vector, and k: # of results
Output: T: a set of top-k nodes
  1: $t \leftarrow 0$;
  2: Construct $\mathbf{q}_S$ by Definition 1;
  3: **while** $\mathbf{r}_S^{(t)}$ does not converge **do**
  4:     $\mathbf{r}_S^{(t+1)} \leftarrow \alpha \mathbf{Sr}_S^{(t)} + (1 - \alpha)\mathbf{q}_S$;
  5:     $t \leftarrow t + 1$;
  6: Construct $\mathbf{b}^{(0)}$, $t \leftarrow 0$, and $T \leftarrow V_D$;
  7: **while** $\underline{r}_i^{(t)}$ and $\overline{r}_i^{(t)}$ do not converge for $\forall i \in T$ **do**
  8:     **for each** $i \in T$ **do**
  9:         Update $\underline{r}_i^{(t)}$ and $\overline{r}_i^{(t)}$ by Definition 3;
10:     **If** $T > k$ **then** $T \leftarrow V_D^{(t)}$ by Definition 4;
11:     $t \leftarrow t + 1$;
12: **return** T;

Incremental Node Pruning: Using the upper and lower bounds, SchemaRank incrementally prunes unpromising nodes that cannot become the top-k important nodes. Let $\epsilon^{(t-1)}$ be the k-th highest lower bound obtained in $(t-1)$-th iteration. In each iteration, SchemaRank constructs the following subset by incrementally pruning unpromising nodes.

Definition 4 (Incremental pruning). *In the t-th iteration, SchemaRank constructs a subset of V_D defined as $V_D^{(t)} = \{i \in V_D^{(t-1)} | \overline{r}_i^{(t-1)} \geq \epsilon^{(t-1)}\}$.*

Definition 4 indicates that SchemaRank incrementally prunes a node if its upper bound $\overline{r}_i^{(t-1)}$ is smaller than $\epsilon^{(t-1)}$. This leads the following property.

Lemma 4. *If $i \notin V_D^{(t)}$, node i never becomes a top-k node.*

Proof: Suppose node i has been pruned in the t-th iteration, *i.e.*, $\overline{r}_i^{(t)} < \epsilon^{(t)}$. From Lemmas 2 and 3, the bounds become tighter as the number of iteration t increases. That is, we hold $r_i = \overline{r}_i^{(\infty)} \leq \cdots \leq \overline{r}_i^{(t+1)} \leq \overline{r}_i^{(t)}$, and $\epsilon^{(t)} \leq \epsilon^{(t+1)} \leq \cdots \leq \epsilon^{(\infty)}$. Thus, once $i \notin V_D^{(t)}$ holds, $r_i < \epsilon^{(\infty)}$, which completes the proof. $\square$

From Lemma 4, SchemaRank can safely remove unpromising nodes during the iterative computations.

3.4   Algorithm

Algorithm 1 gives a full description of SchemaRank. First, SchemaRank performs the coarse-grained RWR (Sect. 3.2) on the schema-graph G_S (lines 2–5). It iterates RWR on G_S until the importance vector $\mathbf{r}_S$ converges. Afterward, SchemaRank starts the fine-grained RWR (Sect. 3.3) on the data-graph G_D (lines 6–12). To estimate the importance of nodes, it constructs vector $\mathbf{b}^{(0)}$ from

r_S obtained in the previous step (line 6). Then it estimates the upper and the lower bounds of each node from Definition 3 (lines 8–9), and it prunes unpromising nodes by following Definition 4 (line 10). SchemaRank iterates (1) the recursive bounds updated by Definition 3 and (2) the incremental node pruning by Definition 4 until T reaches k. Once the top-k importance nodes are specified, SchemaRank performs only the bound updates (lines 8–9) to obtain converged node importance by following Lemma 3 (line 7).

Unlike existing methods, SchemaRank does not require pre-computations. Hence, it is a simple solution to find the same top-k nodes as ObjectRank.

Next we discuss the theoretical aspects of SchemaRank. Let c and d be the average sizes of $V_D^{(t)}$ and degree, respectively. We have the following properties:

Theorem 1. *SchemaRank requires $O((|V_S|+|E_S|)t_S+(cd+\log c \log k)t_D)$ time, where t_S and t_D are the numbers of iterations on G_S and G_D, respectively.*

Proof: From Definition 2, the coarse-grained RWR incurs $O((|V_S| + |E_S|)t_S)$ time. In the fine-grained RWR, it explores the top-k nodes by performing the incremental pruning. In each iteration, SchemaRank estimates the upper and the lower bounds for all nodes in $V_D^{(t)}$. This procedure incurs $O(cd)$ time because $b_i^{(t)}$ and the bounds are obtained in $O(d)$ time and $O(1)$ time, respectively. SchemaRank then updates $V_D^{(t)}$ by Definition 4. The k-th highest lower bound $\epsilon^{(t)}$ can be found in $O(\log c \log k)$ time using Fibonacci heaps. Thus, SchemaRank needs $O((|V_S| + |E_S|)t_S + (cd + \log c \log k)t_D)$ time.   □

In practice, $|V_S| \ll c \le |V_D|$, and $|E_S| \ll cd \le |E_D|$ because the schema-graph consists of only the node-types. Hence, the practical time complexity is $O((|V_S|+|E_S|)t_S + (cd + \log c \log k)t_D) \approx O((cd + \log c \log k)t_D)$. Consequently, the running costs of SchemaRank is dramatically lower than ObjectRank, which requires $O((|V_D| + |E_D|)t_D)$ time until convergence.

Theorem 2. *SchemaRank outputs the same top-k nodes as ObjectRank.*

Proof: From Lemma 3, we have $\underline{r}_i^{(\infty)} = \bar{r}_i^{(\infty)} = r_i$. Thus, SchemaRank can detect the same k-th highest important nodes as ObjectRank by increasing the number of iterations. From Lemma 4, once node $i \notin V_D^{(t)}$, it cannot become the top-k important nodes. Thus, Theorem 2 holds.   □

Theorem 2 indicates that SchemaRank efficiently detects the top-k nodes without sacrificing the accuracy of ObjectRank.

4   Evaluation

Here, we experimentally discuss the efficiency and the exactness of SchemaRank. **Methods:** We compared SchemaRank with the following algorithms.

– **ObjectRank:** The baseline method [9].

Table 2. Statistics of real-world datasets.

Name	$|V_D|$	$|E_D|$	Source
ACM (small)	629 K	632 K	Citation-network V1
DBLP (small)	1.51 M	2.08 M	DBLP-Citation-network V4
ACM (large)	2.38 M	10.4 M	ACM-Citation-network V8
DBLP (large)	4.10 M	36.6 M	DBLP-Citation-network V11

- **BinRank:** The indexing algorithm for ObjectRank [10]. It runs ObjectRank for several clustered queries in advance. Then it indexes nodes whose importance is higher than a threshold. Given a query, BinRank performs RWR on the indexed nodes.
- **LORank:** The pruning method for ObjectRank [19]. It prunes nodes whose importance is lower than the user-specified threshold.
- **SimMat:** The top-k pruning algorithm for RWR [7]. SimMat estimates low important nodes through SVD-based pre-computation. Given a query, it incrementally prunes nodes with a low importance.
- **FORank:** The state-of-the-art pruning-based top-k algorithm for ObjectRank [20]. This is an extension of fast RWR algorithms, F-Rank [6] and Castanet [5]. It incrementally estimates the importance, and it prunes unpromising nodes by using a user-specified threshold.

We set $\alpha = 0.85$, which is the same as [9], and the maximum number of iterations is 10,000. For all competitors, we used the parameter settings recommended by their papers. We conducted all experiments on a server with Intel Xeon CPU 2.60 GHz and 128 GiB RAM. We implemented all methods in C++ as a single-threaded program with the entire graph held in the main memory.

Datasets: We used four public real-world graphs published by AMiner [25].[2] Table 2 shows their statistics. The graphs are extracted from ACM digital library or DBLP bibliographic database. They are composed of four node-types: authors, papers, conferences, and years.

Schema-Graph: In the experimental evaluations, we tested the following schema-graphs with different edge-weight distributions.

- **Skewed:** The schema-graph shown in Fig. 1 (a), which has skewed edge-weights as same as [10].
- **Uniform:** A schema-graph that assigns uniform edge-weights to the graph in Fig. 1 (a). We assigned an edge-weight 0.5 for all edges in Fig. 1 (a).

Query Nodes: For each dataset, we randomly selected 100 nodes from the data-graph, and tested each algorithm using the query nodes. We reported the average results with the standard deviation when testing each query 50 times.

---

[2] All datasets are publickly available at https://aminer.org/citation.

Table 3. Running time (± standard deviation) on real-world datasets.

(a) ACM (small)

Methods	Skewed	Uniform	Pre-comp.
SchemaRank ($k = 10^2$)	**0.82** (±0.002) s	**1.21** (±0.002) s	—
SchemaRank ($k = 10^3$)	**1.01** (±0.003) s	**1.45** (±0.001) s	—
ObjectRank	4.51 (±0.007) s	4.41 (±0.009) s	—
BinRank	3.33 (±0.005) s	3.05 (±0.001) s	10.1 h
LORank	2.59 (±0.004) s	3.42 (±0.005) s	—
SimMat ($k = 10^2$)	2.21 (±0.009) s	2.34 (±0.007) s	14.4 h
SimMat ($k = 10^3$)	3.12 (±0.009) s	3.22 (±0.008) s	14.4 h
FORank ($k = 10^2$)	1.75 (±0.003) s	1.94 (±0.001) s	—
FORank ($k = 10^3$)	2.25 (±0.002) s	2.33 (±0.002) s	—

(b) DBLP (small)

Methods	Skewed	Uniform	Pre-comp.
SchemaRank ($k = 10^2$)	**1.91** (±0.003) s	**2.54** (±0.003) s	—
SchemaRank ($k = 10^3$)	**2.08** (±0.002) s	**2.63** (±0.003) s	—
ObjectRank	22.8 (±0.011) s	22.7 (±0.009) s	—
BinRank	6.42 (±0.009) s	7.22 (±0.011) s	17.9 h
LORank	16.4 (±0.008) s	17.2 (±0.008) s	—
SimMat ($k = 10^2$)	N/A	N/A	>24 h
SimMat ($k = 10^3$)	N/A	N/A	>24 h
FORank ($k = 10^2$)	6.77 (±0.002) s	7.45 (±0.003) s	—
FORank ($k = 10^3$)	8.68 (±0.003) s	9.03 (±0.004) s	—

(c) ACM (large)

Methods	Skewed	Uniform	Pre-comp.
SchemaRank ($k = 10^2$)	**41.1** (±0.056) s	**55.3** (±0.064) s	—
SchemaRank ($k = 10^3$)	**56.3** (±0.066) s	**68.6** (±0.072) s	—
ObjectRank	24,122 (±1.41) s	24,306 (±1.67) s	—
BinRank	N/A	N/A	>24 h
LORank	22,068 (±4.43) s	23,328 (±5.09) s	—
SimMat ($k = 10^2$)	N/A	N/A	>24 h
SimMat ($k = 10^3$)	N/A	N/A	>24 h
FORank ($k = 10^2$)	320 (±0.224) s	347 (±0.206) s	—
FORank ($k = 10^3$)	381 (±0.258) s	423 (±0.211) s	—

(d) DBLP (large)

Methods	Skewed	Uniform	Pre-comp.
SchemaRank ($k = 10^2$)	**134** (±0.195) s	**169** (±0.106) s	—
SchemaRank ($k = 10^3$)	**168** (±0.173) s	**241** (±0.122) s	—
ObjectRank	>24 h	>24 h	—
BinRank	N/A	N/A	>24 h
LORank	>24 h	>24 h	—
SimMat ($k = 10^2$)	N/A	N/A	>24 h
SimMat ($k = 10^3$)	N/A	N/A	>24 h
FORank ($k = 10^2$)	2,209 (±1.908) s	2,677 (±1.966) s	—
FORank ($k = 10^3$)	2,431 (±1.912) s	3,137 (±1.903) s	—

4.1   Efficiency

We evaluated the running time of each algorithm on real-world graphs. Table 3 shows the results for the two types of schema-graphs. For the top-k algorithms (*i.e.,* SchemaRank, SimMat, and FORank), we varied the size of k as 10^2 and 10^3. Since BinRank and SimMat require pre-computations, we also assessed their pre-computation time.

Overall Results: Table 3 demonstrates that SchemaRank outperforms the other algorithms. SchemaRank is up to 644.7 times and 16.5 times faster than ObjectRank and the state-of-the-art algorithm FORank, respectively. As described in Sect. 2.2, ObjectRank incurs $O((|V_D| + |E_D|)t)$ time since it iteratively computes all nodes and edges. By contrast, SchemaRank computes only the essential nodes and edges through the coarse-grained RWR and the fine-grained RWR. As shown in Fig. 1 (a), the schema-graphs are very small ($|V_S| = 4$ and $|E_S| = 8$). Thus, the computation cost for the coarse-grained RWR should be low. For instance, in this evaluation, the coarse-grained RWR consumed 10 microseconds at most. Hence, as we proved in Theorem 1, SchemaRank practically shows $O((|V_S| + |E_S|)t_S + (cd + \log c \log k)t_D) \approx O(cd + \log c \log k)$ time. Because this is a nearly linear time against c, which is the average size of the nodes computed in each iteration, our approach is faster than the other methods.

Skewed v.s. Uniform Schema-Graph: We then assessed the impact of the schema-graph types: Skewed and Uniform. Table 3 shows that Skewed requires a shorter running time than Uniform. These results imply that SchemaRank effectively handles the skewness of node-importance in the real-world datasets [24]. The coarse-grained RWR finds many node-types with a low importance if the edge-weights are highly skewed. Thus, in the Skewed schema-graph, it can prune a large portion of nodes earlier.

Pre-computation Time: Although BinRank and SimMat successfully reduced the running time on small graphs, they require long pre-computation time as shown in Table 3. As a result, they cannot compute large graphs, *i.e.,* ACM (large) and DBLP (large), since the pre-computation is not complete within 24 h. In contrast, SchemaRank does not require the pre-computation. Thus, our proposal can find the top-k nodes on the fly.

4.2   Effectiveness

Here, we discuss the effectiveness of the coarse-grained RWR. In Fig. 2, we compared the running time of SchemaRank with its variant, which excludes the coarse-grained RWR, and two baselines (FORank and ObjectRank). SchemaRank-w/o-CR represents SchemaRank without the coarse-grained RWR that replaces $\mathbf{b}^{(t)}$ with $\mathbf{p}^{(t)}$ in Eq. (6). Figure 2 demonstrates that SchemaRank is up to 12.5 times faster than SchemaRank-w/o-CR. By contrast, SchemaRank-w/o-CR is competitive or slightly faster than the state-of-the-art algorithm FORank. Thus, our coarse-grained RWR improves the efficiency without high

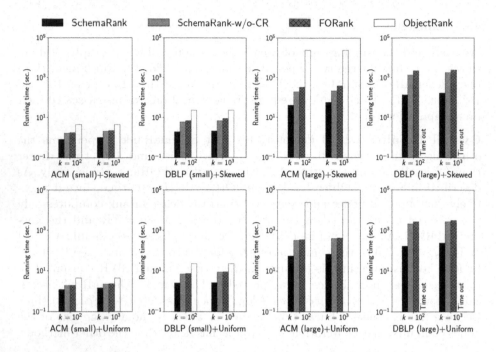

Fig. 2. Effectiveness of coarse-grained RWR

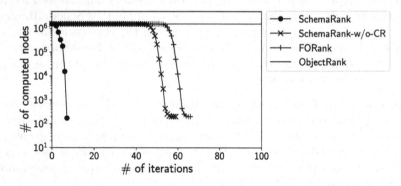

Fig. 3. # of computed nodes on DBLP (small).

pre-computation costs. Because it reveals the importance distribution at the node-type level, SchemaRank can quickly exclude unpromising nodes with a low importance.

To further discuss how the coarse-grained RWR effectively works, Fig. 3 plots the number of nodes computed by each algorithm in each iteration. In this evaluation, we used DBLP (small) with the schema-graph (Skewed), and we set $k = 10^2$. SchemaRank removes more than 97.9% nodes of the graph after a few iterations, whereas the other ones compute more significant numbers of nodes

and iterations. These results demonstrate that the coarse-grained RWR successfully reduces the computation costs and terminates the iterations earlier. In
real-world graphs, the vast majority of nodes should have a low importance. By
capturing this skewness through the coarse-grained RWR, SchemaRank successfully reduces the size of computed nodes c within a few iterations.

4.3 Exactness

A major advantage of SchemaRank is that it finds the same top-k important
nodes as ObjectRank, while dynamically pruning unpromising nodes. To verify
the exactness of SchemaRank, we compared the top-k nodes obtained by each
algorithm against those obtained by ObjectRank. We used *average precision* [18]
to measure the accuracy of top-k ranking importance compared with ObjectRank. The average precision is the mean score of precision@n [17] ($1 \leq n \leq k$).
If an average precision is one, the top-k ranking importance is identical to ObjectRank. We tested $k = 10^2$ and $k = 10^3$ on all datasets except for DBLP (large).

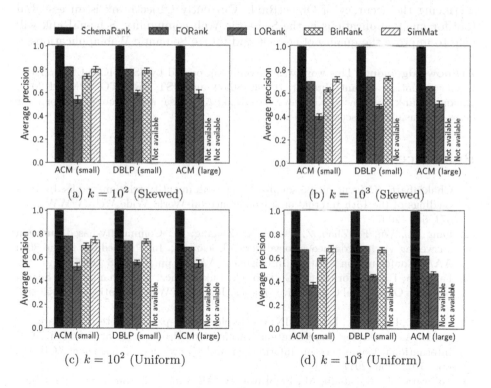

Fig. 4. Average precision of top-k ranking.

Figure 4 shows the average precision of each algorithm. SchemaRank is always
one, whereas FORank, LORank, BinRank, and SimMat plateau at lower average

precision values. Hence, SchemaRank always outputs the same top-k results and ranking as ObjectRank. On the other hand, the other methods fail to reproduce the results of ObjectRank, although they reduce the runtime. As we proved in Theorem 2, SchemaRank guarantees that the same top-k nodes as ObjectRank are found. In addition, as discussed in Lemma 3, the upper and lower bounds converge to the same node importance as ObjectRank as the number of iterations increases. Therefore, SchemaRank can inherit the importance evaluation quality of ObjectRank, although it drastically reduces the running time.

5   Conclusion

We proposed SchemaRank, which is an efficient algorithm that detects exact top-k important nodes from massive heterogeneous graphs (*e.g.*, knowledge graphs). SchemaRank estimates the node-importance distribution at the node-type level, and it prunes unpromising nodes by a two-step RWR approach. In the experiments, SchemaRank offers an improved efficiency for massive graphs without sacrificing the accuracy of ObjectRank. Currently ObjectRank is an essential tool for many applications in the Semantic Web community. SchemaRank will help to improve the quality of current and future Semantic Web applications.

Acknowledgement. This work was partially supported by JSPS KAKENHI Early-Career Scientists (Grant Number JP18K18057) and JST PRESTO JPMJPR2033, Japan. I thank to Hiroyuki Kitagawa, Toshiyuki Amagasa, and Tomoki Sato for their helps and insightful discussions.

References

1. Chakrabarti, S.: Dynamic personalized pagerank in entity-relation graphs. In: Proceedings of the 16th International Conference on World Wide Web (WWW), pp. 571–580 (2007)
2. Fang, H., Wu, F., Zhao, Z., Duan, X., Zhuang, Y.: Community-based question answering via heterogeneous social network learning. In: Proceedings of the 30th AAAI Conference on Artificial Intelligence (AAAI), pp. 122–128 (2016)
3. Fazzinga, B., Gianforme, G., Gottlob, G., Lukasiewicz, T.: Semantic Web Search based on Ontological Conjunctive Queries. Journal of Web Semantics **9**(4), 453–473 (2011)
4. Fu, T.Y., Lee, W.C., Lei, Z.: HIN2Vec: explore meta-paths in heterogeneous information networks for representation learning. In: Proceedings of the 26th ACM International Conference on Information and Knowledge Management (CIKM), pp. 1797–1806 (2017)
5. Fujiwara, Y., Nakatsuji, M., Shiokawa, H., Mishima, T., Onizuka, M.: Efficient ad-hoc search for personalized PageRank. In: Proceedings of the ACM SIGMOD International Conference on Management of Data (SIGMOD), pp. 445–456 (2013)
6. Fujiwara, Y., Nakatsuji, M., Shiokawa, H., Mishima, T., Onizuka, M.: Fast and exact top-k algorithm for PageRank. In: Proceedings of the 27th AAAI Conference on Artificial Intelligence (AAAI 2013), pp. 1106–1112 (2013)

7. Fujiwara, Y., Nakatsuji, M., Shiokawa, H., Onizuka, M.: Efficient search algorithm for SimRank. In: Proceedings of the 29th IEEE International Conference on Data Engineering (ICDE), pp. 589–600 (2013)
8. Golub, G., Van Loan, C.: Matrix Computations, 4th edn. Johns Hopkins University Press, Baltimore (2012)
9. Hristidis, V., Hwang, H., Papakonstantinou, Y.: Authority-based keyword search in databases. ACM Trans. Database Syst. **33**(1) (2008)
10. Hwang, H., Balmin, A., Reinwald, B., Nijkamp, E.: BinRank: scaling dynamic authority-based search using materialized subgraphs. IEEE Trans. Knowl. Data Eng. **22**(8), 1176–1190 (2010)
11. Jeh, G., Widom, J.: SimRank: a measure of structural-context similarity. In: Proceedings of the 18th ACM SIGKDD Conference on Knowledge Discovery and Data Mining (KDD), pp. 538–543 (2002)
12. Jiang, Z., Liu, H., Fu, B., Wu, Z., Zhang, T.: Recommendation in heterogeneous information networks based on generalized random walk model and Bayesian personalized ranking. In: Proceedings of the 11th ACM International Conference on Web Search and Data Mining (WSDM), pp. 288–296 (2018)
13. Komamizu, T.: Learning interpretable entity representation in linked data. In: Hartmann, S., Ma, H., Hameurlain, A., Pernul, G., Wagner, R.R. (eds.) DEXA 2018. LNCS, vol. 11029, pp. 153–168. Springer, Cham (2018). https://doi.org/10. 1007/978-3-319-98809-2_10
14. Langville, A.N., Meyer, C.D.: Google's PageRank and Beyond: The Science of Search Engine Rankings. Princeton University Press (2012)
15. Lehmann, J., et al.: DBpedia-a large-scale, multilingual knowledge base extracted from Wikipedia. Semantic Web **6**(2), 167–195 (2015)
16. Li, B., King, I.: Routing questions to appropriate answerers in community question answering services. In: Proceedings of the 19th ACM International Conference on Information and Knowledge Management (CIKM), pp. 1585–1588 (2010)
17. Manning, C.D., Raghavan, P., Schütze, H.: Introduction to Information Retrieval. Cambridge University Press, New York (2008)
18. Robertson, S.: A New Interpretation of Average Precision. In: Proceedings of the 31st Annual International ACM SIGIR Conference (SIGIR), pp. 689–690 (2008)
19. Sakakura, Y., Yamaguchi, Y., Amagasa, T., Kitagawa, H.: A local method for ObjectRank estimation. In: Proceedings of the 15th International Conference on Information Integration and Web-based Applications and Services (iiWAS), pp. 92:92–92:101 (2013)
20. Sato, T., Shiokawa, H., Yamaguchi, Y., Kitagawa, H.: FORank: fast ObjectRank for large heterogeneous graphs. In: Companion Proceedings of The Web Conference (WWW), pp. 103–104 (2018)
21. Shiokawa, H.: Scalable affinity propagation for massive datasets. In: Proceedings of the AAAI Conference on Artificial Intelligence (AAAI 2021), vol. 35, no. (11), pp. 9639–9646, May 2021
22. Shiokawa, H., Amagasa, T., Kitagawa, H.: Scaling fine-grained modularity clustering for massive graphs. In: Proceedings of the 28th International Joint Conference on Artificial Intelligence (IJCAI), pp. 4597–4604 (2019)
23. Suchanek, F.M., Kasneci, G., Weikum, G.: YAGO: a core of semantic knowledge. In: Proceedings of the 16th International Conference on World Wide Web (WWW), pp. 697–706 (2007)
24. Sun, J., Qu, H., Chakrabarti, D., Faloutsos, C.: Neighborhood formation and anomaly detection in bipartite graphs. In: Proceedings of the 5th IEEE International Conference on Data Mining (ICDM), pp. 418–425 (2005)

25. Tang, J., Zhang, J., Yao, L., Li, J., Zhang, L., Su, Z.: ArnetMiner: extraction and mining of academic social networks. In: Proceedings of the 14th ACM SIGKDD International Conference on Knowledge Discovery and Data Mining (KDD), pp. 990–998 (2008)
26. Tong, H., Faloutsos, C.: Center-piece subgraphs: problem definition and fast solutions. In: Proceedings of the 12th ACM SIGKDD International Conference on Knowledge Discovery and Data Mining (KDD), pp. 404–413 (2006)
27. Tsitsulin, A., Mottin, D., Karras, P., Müller, E.: VERSE: versatile graph embeddings from similarity measures. In: Proceedings of the 2018 World Wide Web Conference (WWW), pp. 539–548 (2018)
28. Wan, L., Lou, W., Abner, E., Kryscio, R.J.: A comparison of time-homogeneous Markov chain and Markov process multi-state models. Commun. Stat. Case Stud. Data Anal. Appl. 2(3–4), 92–100 (2016)
29. Yu, D.L., Ma, Y.L., Yu, Z.G.: Inferring MicroRNA-disease association by hybrid recommendation algorithm and unbalanced bi-random walk on heterogeneous network. Sci. Rep. 9(2474) (2019)
30. Zhao, Z., Lu, H., Cai, D., He, X., Zhuang, Y.: Microblog sentiment classification via recurrent random walk network learning. In: Proceedings of the 26th International Joint Conference on Artificial Intelligence (IJCAI), pp. 3532–3538 (2017)

Open Domain Question Answering over Knowledge Graphs Using Keyword Search, Answer Type Prediction, SPARQL and Pre-trained Neural Models

Christos Nikas[1,2], Pavlos Fafalios[1(✉)] (iD), and Yannis Tzitzikas[1,2] (iD)

[1] Information Systems Laboratory, FORTH-ICS, Heraklion, Greece
{cnikas,fafalios,tzitzik}@ics.forth.gr
[2] Computer Science Department, University of Crete, Heraklion, Greece

Abstract. Question Answering (QA) in vague or complex open domain information needs is hard to be adequate, satisfying and pleasing for end users. In this paper we investigate an approach where QA *complements* a general purpose interactive keyword search system over RDF. We describe the role of QA in that context, and we detail and evaluate a pipeline for QA that involves a general purpose entity search service over RDF, answer type prediction, entity enrichment through SPARQL, and pre-trained neural models. The fact that we start from a general purpose keyword search over RDF, makes the proposed pipeline widely applicable and realistic, in the sense that it does not pre-suppose the availability of knowledge graph-specific training dataset. We evaluate various aspects of the pipeline, including the effect of answer type prediction, as well as the performance of QA over existing benchmarks. The results show that, even by using different data sources for training, the proposed pipeline achieves a satisfactory performance. Moreover we show that the ranking of entities for QA can improve the entity ranking.

Keywords: Open domain question answering · Knowledge graphs · Keyword search · Answer type prediction

1 Introduction

Question answering over knowledge bases (KBQA) is an important NLP task because of the rapid growth of knowledge bases (KBs) on the web and the commercial value they bring for real-world applications [18]. In knowledge bases, where data is represented as a graph, e.g. using the Resource Description Framework (RDF), methods relying on Graph Processing and SPARQL Query Generation are adopted in order to extract the desired information [5]. At the same time, neural network-based (NN-based) Question Answering (QA) methods have received increasing attention in recent years and have already achieved very good results [1]. Although such methods require large amounts of training data, pre-trained language models [4] have become available, that can be fine-tuned on

© Springer Nature Switzerland AG 2021
A. Hotho et al. (Eds.): ISWC 2021, LNCS 12922, pp. 235–251, 2021.
https://doi.org/10.1007/978-3-030-88361-4_14

specific data to obtain high quality results for various tasks, such as sequence classification and extractive QA.

Nevertheless in vague or complex open domain information needs and questions, that require considering and joining facts, QA methods are not that good [19]. At the same time, there is not a single QA component per QA task that is perfect, and the performance of a QA component varies based on questions with different features; see the detailed analysis in [24]. Indeed, all the 12 baseline approaches evaluated over the QALD-2 dataset (containing natural language questions) of the DBpedia-Entity benchmark [7] achieve NDCG@10 (Normalized Discounted Cumulative Gain at rank 10) less than 0.37.[1]

Since we are interested in a general purpose and widely applicable method for open domain QA, in this paper we investigate an approach where at its core has a *keyword search* service. This allows exploiting the wealth of techniques related to text pre-processing, retrieval and language models, thus tackling some of the weaknesses of current components, like those identified in [24], related to the upper/lowercase of named entities, the implicit entity names (that NER tools usually fail to identify due to the various morphological variations), the abbreviations in named entities, and others. In addition, not all question intentions can be identified and mapped to the correct SPARQL statement (e.g. questions that can be answered by the textual descriptions in the `rdfs:comment`), therefore the exploitation of IR and NLP techniques is indispensable. In brief keyword search can provide relevant hits for any kind of information need, and there are already scalable and effective approaches for keyword search over RDF [10].

Fig. 1. Open domain QA over knowledge graphs as part of an interactive keyword search system over RDF.

As application context, we consider a *multi-perspective* keyword search over RDF, like the one presented in [17], that provides perspectives (tabs) that show the more relevant triples, the more relevant entities, graphical visualizations that show how the top-ranked triples are connected, and schema-based filterings. In such a context, the QA tab (as depicted in Fig. 1) is expected to provide a short

---

[1] https://github.com/iai-group/DBpedia-Entity.

and concise answer, if that is feasible. We could therefore say that we investigate an approach for open-domain QA over Knowledge Bases that could complement general purpose interactive keyword search over RDF. In such a dynamic context, we cannot expect that a training dataset is available for the knowledge base, and especially when the same approach needs to be deployed over another knowledge base.

We present a QA approach that relies on: (i) an entity search system to retrieve unstructured textual descriptions for entities, (ii) a Semantic Answer Type prediction component to predict the answer type, (iii) SPARQL to retrieve structured information that matches the predicted answer type, (iv) an entity enrichment component to expand the textual description with the information retrieved from the triplestore, and (v) a powerful language model fine-tuned for QA to extract the final answers.

In brief, given a natural language question, we first retrieve the top-k entities and their textual descriptions (through keyword search), then we get the triples only of these entities that have the predicted answer type, then we generate natural language sentences and we apply extractive QA using a pre-trained neural model, as illustrated in Fig. 2.

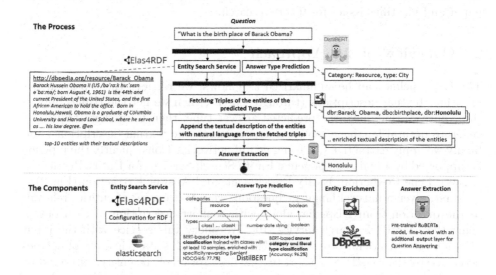

Fig. 2. The considered QA process and components.

Related research questions are: (a) How good can the QA pipeline over DBpedia be, in comparison to approaches and benchmarks over a different knowledge graph (in our case Freebase)? (b) How does Answer Type Prediction affect the quality of QA? (c) How can answers from this QA pipeline contribute to the entity retrieval task over DBpedia-Entity dataset [7], and entity ranking in general?

The results of our evaluation indicate that the answers generated by this approach provide additional value for entity search when combined with the initial entities retrieved by the search service used. Our approach can also perform well on difficult QA datasets ($>$ 52% Accuracy), without having been trained on the specific datasets, but relying on the structured and unstructured information retrieval methods that we use. In brief, the main contribution of this work are: (a) we investigate a process for QA in the context of an keyword search access paradigm, (b) we detail the QA pipeline that comprises components for Entity Retrieval, Answer Type Prediction, Entity Enrichment, and Answer Extraction, (c) we evaluate the pipeline over multiple datasets, showcasing the value added by our approach. To the best of our knowledge, no previous work uses KBQA within an interactive search system over RDF where QA complements the other perspectives (and thus consistency with the input that feeds all perspectives is required), nor evaluated the effect of Query Answer Type prediction. The source code of our implementation and a running demo are publicly accessible.[2]

The rest of this paper is organized as follows: Sect. 2 provides an overview of the approach, Sect. 3 describes Answer Type Prediction, Sect. 4 describes Entity Retrieval and Extraction, Sect. 5 describes Answer Extraction, Sect. 6 focuses on evaluation, Sect. 7 describes related work, and finally, Sect. 8 concludes the paper and identifies issues for future research.

2   Overview of the Approach

The QA pipeline can be summarized as follows: we retrieve the top-k entities and their textual descriptions (through search), then we get the triples only of these entities that have the predicted answer type, then from these triples we generate natural language sentences for enriching the textual descriptions, and finally we apply extractive QA using neural networks. Consequently the pipeline is supported by 4 main components: Entity Search Service (for Entity Retrieval), Answer Type Prediction, Entity Enrichment, and Answer Extraction (Fig. 2).

First, given a natural language question, we retrieve a set of entities relevant to the question from DBpedia, along with a short description of each entity, using the Elas4RDF search service [10]. We query this service with the input question after removing stop words. The output of this stage is a list of entities described by their URI and a short textual description of the entity, extracted by a descriptive (for the entity) property, in our case `rdfs:comment`. The number of retrieved entities is set to 10, but it can be adjusted. A higher number of entities could yield more useful answers, but will require more time to be processed.

In parallel, we predict the answer type of the input natural language question by extending and improving a previous work on Answer Type Prediction [16] (this step is detailed in Sect. 3).

---

[2] Source code: https://github.com/isl/elas4rdfdemo, Demo: https://demos.isl.ics.forth.gr/elas4rdf/.

Then we expand the description of each entity with information from RDF nodes matching the predicted answer type by running SPARQL queries at real-time (this step is described in Sect. 4).

Finally, we use a RoBERTa [11] model fine-tuned on the SQuAD-2 dataset [20] to perform extractive QA for the input question using the extended description of each entity. Therefore, we obtain an natural language answer from each retrieved entity. Finally, we rank the answers using the score from the output of the model and present them on the user interface of the keyword search system (more in Sect. 5).

3 Answer Type Prediction

Here we describe how we perform Answer Type Prediction, i.e. how we predict the type of the answer of a natural language question, given the question. In comparison to [16], in our work we use two classifiers (instead of three) by integrating the *literal type prediction* classifier and the *category prediction* classifier. With this change, we simplify the approach, and reduce memory footprint (more in Sect. 3.2). Given the real-time context of out approach, we also use DistilBERT instead of BERT to achieve better response time and efficiency while maintaining high performance (more in Sect. 3.5).

3.1 Overview

The task is split in two stages: *Category prediction* and *Type prediction*. In particular, we model the problem as a two-stage classification task: in the first step the task is to predict the general category of the answer (*resource, literal,* or *boolean*), while in the second step the task is to predict the particular answer type (*number, date, string,* or a particular *resource class* from a target ontology).

We use the two datasets provided by SMART Task [14], one using the DBpedia ontology and the other using the Wikidata ontology. Both follow the below structure: Each question has (a) a question id, (b) a question text in natural language, (c) an answer category (*resource/literal/boolean*), and (d) an answer type (which depends on the answer category). If the category is *resource*, answer types are ontology classes from either the DBpedia ontology (~760 classes) or the Wikidata ontology (~50K classes). If the category is *literal*, answer types are either *number, date,* or *string*. Finally, if the category is *boolean*, answer type is always *boolean*. An excerpt from this dataset is shown below:

```
[ {
  "id": "dbpedia_14427",
  "question": "What is the name of the opera based on Twelfth Night?",
  "category": "resource",
  "type": ["dbo:Opera", "dbo:MusicalWork", "dbo:Work" ]
},{
  "id": "dbpedia_23480",
  "question": "Do Prince Harry and Prince William have the same parents?",
```

```
"category": "boolean",
"type": ["boolean"]
} ]
```

With respect to the size of the datasets, the DBpedia dataset contains 21,964 questions (train: 17,571, test: 4,393) and Wikidata 22,822 questions (train: 18,251, test: 4,571). The DBpedia training set consists of 9,584 resource, 2,799 boolean, and 5,188 literal questions. The Wikidata training set consists of 11,683 resource, 2,139 boolean, and 4,429 literal questions.

For question category and type prediction we use two DistilBERT sequence classification models. We choose DistilBERT instead of BERT to reduce memory footprint and time required to answer a question.

3.2 Question Category and Literal Type Prediction

A question can belong to one of the following three categories: (1) boolean, (2) literal, (3) resource. *Boolean questions* (also referred to as Confirmation questions) only have 'yes' or 'no' as an answer (e.g. *"Does the Owyhee river flow into Oregon?"*). Thus, there is no further classification for this category of questions. *Resource questions* have a specific fact as an answer (e.g. *"What is the highest mountain in Italy?"*) that can be described by a class in an ontology (e.g. http://dbpedia.org/ontology/Mountain). *Literal questions* have a literal value as answer, which can be a *number, string,* or *date* (e.g. *"Which is the cruise speed of the airbus A340?"*).

To detect question categories, we fine-tune a DistilBERT model using the Huggingface PyTorch implementation.[3] We choose a BERT-based model because we approach answer type prediction as a classification problem where each question is a sequence of words.

Since we only use three types to classify literal questions, we integrate literal type prediction into the same classifier with category prediction, following the approach of [22]. By doing this, we save computing requirements and reduce memory footprint because we avoid using a different BERT classifier for literal type prediction. Therefore, this model classifies each question in one of the following five classes: 1) boolean, 2) literal date, 3) literal number, 4) literal string, 5) resource.

To fine tune the model we used the training datasets provided for the SMART task. Specifically, we used questions from both the DBpedia and the Wikidata dataset. Since the data is imbalanced for categories (13.7% boolean, 26.6% literal, 59.4% resource), we randomly sampled questions for each class so that all classes had the same number of samples.

As we will see below, this model achieves 97.7% accuracy on our test set in this prediction task.

---

[3] https://huggingface.co/transformers/.

3.3   Resource Answer Type Prediction

The prediction of the answer type of questions in the *resource* category is a more fine-grained (and thus more challenging) classification problem, because of the large number of types a question can be classified to ($\sim$760 classes on DBpedia and $\sim$50K classes on Wikidata). Therefore, it is not effective to train a classifier on all the ontology classes, especially for open-domain tasks.

To reduce the number of possible types for classification, we selected a subset (C) of all ontology classes, based on the number of samples of each class in the training set. This subset C contains classes that have at least k occurrences in the training set. We set $k = 10$ as this number provides a good trade-off between number of classes and performance. The choice of this parameter is described more extensively in Sect. 3.4. The final number of classes in C is 88. Since we chose to train the system on a subset of all the classes, our classifier cannot handle questions with labels that are not included in this subset. To tackle this problem, we replace their labels with the labels of super classes that belong in C. Then we fine tune a DistilBERT model on them.

Since most questions in the dataset have several answer types ordered by specificity, according to the semantic hierarchy formed in the ontology, in the fine tuning stage we use these questions multiple times, one with each of the provided types as the label. The goal is to find an answer type that is as specific as possible for the question. However, the model may classify a question to a more general answer type in the ontology. To tackle this problem, we 'reward' (inspired by [3]) the predictions of the classes that lie below the top class. The reward of a class c is measured by the depth of the class in the hierarchy, specifically, $reward(c) = depth(c)/depth_{Max}$, where $depth(c)$ is the depth of c in its hierarchy, while $depth_{Max}$ is the maximum depth of the ontology (6 for DBpedia). This means that, after applying normalization and adding the rewards on the output of the model, the top class can be a sub-class that was originally ranked below a more general class. For example, for the question *"What is the television show whose company is Playtone and written by Erik Jendresen?"* the top 5 classes that the classifier predicts are: 1) Work, 2) TelevisionShow, 3) Film, 4) MusicalWork, 5) WrittenWork. Then rewards are applied to classes that are a subclass of Work. After applying the rewards, the top 5 classes are: 1) TelevisionShow, 2) Work, 3) Film, 4) Book, 5) MusicalWork. We can see that TelevisionShow is now the top prediction, which is both correct and more specific than the previous top prediction (Work).

3.4   Tuning of the k Parameter

To find the optimal value for the parameter k, which is the minimum sample size required to include a class in the subset of classes included in the classifier, we evaluated our system using 4 different values: 5, 10, 30 and 50. Table 1 shows the number of classes included in the classifier for each different value of k and the corresponding performance. We notice that the best results are obtained using k = 10, while the results for all other cases are slightly worse.

Table 1. Performance of *Resource Answer Type Prediction* for different values of k.

Value	Classes	NDCG@5	NDCG@10
5	180	0.775	0.765
10	151	0.786	0.778
30	79	0.785	0.772
50	55	0.785	0.748

3.5   Model Selection

DistilBERT [21] is a smaller general-purpose language representation model based on BERT [4]. A DistilBERT model can be 40% smaller in size than an equivalent BERT model, while retaining 97% of its language understanding capabilities and being 60% faster. We chose this model for category classification and answer type classification because the compromise in the language understanding capabilities is not significant for us, since our models perform well enough for the required tasks. At the same time, answer type prediction is part of a QA system that runs as part of a keyword search Web application, therefore answer time speed and memory footprint are important in this context.

4   Entity Enrichment

For *Resource* and *Literal* questions, as predicted by the Answer Type Prediction step, we exploit the SPARQL endpoint of the underlying KB to find facts about the retrieved entities that match the predicted answer type. In our case, since the entity retrieval stage works over DBpedia, we selected DBpedia, however any KB could be used. Then, we generate natural language sentences from these facts and append the sentences to the entity description.

For *Resource* questions, for each entity, we retrieve all RDF triples where the subject is the entity, and the object has an RDF type that matches the top type returned by the Answer Type Prediction component, or an equivalent class, using the following query:

```
select distinct str(?pl) as ?pLabel ?a where {
    <entity uri> ?p ?a .
    ?p rdfs:label ?pl .
    <answer type> owl:equivalentClass ?eq .
    ?a rdf:type ?eq .
        FILTER(lang(?pl) = 'en' || lang(?pl) = '') }
```

For *Literal Date* questions we retrieve triples where the property that connects the entity with the candidate answer has an rdfs:range equal to xsd:date.

For *Literal Number* and *String* questions we retrieve all triples where the subject is the entity and the object is a literal. Then we check programmatically if the object is numeric or a string depending on the answer type. We follow this process because not all literal RDF Nodes have an XSD Schema data type.

From the retrieved triples we use the label of the corresponding entity, the object which is a candidate answer, and the label of the property that connects the entity with this answer. Then we generate a sentence of the form *"entity_label + property_label + object"* and append it to the textual description of the entity.

5 Answer Extraction

This stage receives a list of entity URIs and their expanded textual descriptions. For each entity in the list, we generate an answer from the expanded entity description using a RoBERTa model for extractive QA from the *huggingface* transformers library[4]. Then, we sort the answers by their score and display them on the QA perspective of the web application, along with the answer category and type.

The model that we use is fine-tuned on the SQuAD dataset provided by `deepset.ai`[5]. RoBERTa (Robustly optimized BERT approach) is a retraining of BERT with improved training methodology, using 10 times more data and compute power. We chose this model over BERT because of the increased difficulty of the extractive QA task.

A few indicative examples of Q-A pairs follow: (Q: Who did Mozart write his four horn concertos for? A: Joseph Leutgeb), (Q: What things did Martin Luther King do? A: human rights advocate and community activist), (Q: When did Charles Goodyear invent rubber? A: 1839) (Q: Who is the father of Queen Elizabeth II? A: King George VI).

6 Evaluation

In Sect. 6.1 we evaluate our approach over WebQuestions [2], a benchmark consisting of popular questions asked on the web that are answerable by Freebase, a different knowledge base than DBpedia, which our system retrieves information from, so essentially we evaluate how good our approach for open domain QA is while retrieving information from a *different source* and without having been previously trained over this specific dataset. In Sect. 6.2 we investigate how the task of Answer Type Prediction affects the effectiveness of QA. In Sect. 6.3 we evaluate the performance of our approach as a standalone QA system over the DBpedia-Entity collection [7]. In Sect. 6.4 we evaluate how answers from our QA pipeline can contribute to the entity retrieval task over the DBpedia-Entity dataset, and entity ranking in general. In Sect. 6.5 we discuss the efficiency of the system and in Sect. 6.6 we provide a summary of the evaluation results.

6.1 Experiment 1: Webquestions

WebQuestions [2] is a popular dataset for benchmarking QA engines, especially ones that work on structured knowledge bases. It is a dataset of question-answer

---
[4] https://huggingface.co/transformers/.
[5] https://huggingface.co/deepset/roberta-base-squad2.

pairs obtained from non-experts. It contains 6,642 questions collected using the Google Suggest API to obtain questions that begin with a wh-word and contain exactly one entity. Answers were generated using Amazon Mechanical Turk. The AMT task requested that workers answer the question using only the Freebase page of the question's entity. An example of a question-answer pair is the following:

```
Question: "What countries are part of the UK?"
Answers: "Scotland","England","Wales","Northern Ireland"
```

To evaluate our approach over this benchmark, we obtained answers from our system for all 2,032 questions in the test collection. Then, we compute the following metrics:

- *Precision*: The percentage of terms retrieved as answers by our system, that are included in the correct answers, averaged over all questions
- *Recall*: The percentage of terms in the correct answers, that are also retrieved as answers by our system, averaged over all questions
- *F1*: The harmonic mean of precision and recall
- *Accuracy*: The percentage of questions that received at least one correct answer

For reasons of performance, we limit the number of facts returned by the SPARQL endpoint to 20 (more in Sect. 6.5). We compute the evaluation scores for different sets of answers of varying confidence by considering only answers that have a score above a specific threshold t and trying different values for t. The results are displayed in Table 2.

Table 2. Evaluation results over WebQuestions.

Threshold	0.0	0.1	0.2	0.3	0.4	0.5	0.6	0.7	0.8	0.9
Precision	7.007	16.170	18.607	21.290	23.710	25.261	28.101	31.185	37.543	**43.363**
Recall	31.263	27.712	29.016	27.894	29.078	30.882	31.279	33.465	34.506	**40.477**
F1	9.710	16.957	19.074	19.695	21.664	23.224	25.039	28.356	31.443	**39.200**
Accuracy	**53.759**	47.597	47.570	46.893	47.697	48.031	47.867	48.765	52.380	52.174

We can see that a threshold value of 0.9 yields the best values for Precision, Recall and F1. Accuracy is higher for a threshold value of 0 because (as expected) including all answers (score $>= 0$) leads to a higher probability that at least one correct answer will be included, however the 0.9 threshold gives a close to the optimal accuracy. Overall, our system has a satisfactory performance even though it has not been previously trained on this specific dataset, such as the systems in codalab[6] (e.g., [9]), or end-to-end neural-based models (e.g., [13]).

---

[6] https://worksheets.codalab.org/worksheets/0xba659fe363cb46e7a505c5b6a774dc8a.

6.2   Without Answer Type Prediction

To examine the value that is added to this QA pipeline by the answer type prediction component, we evaluate our system over the same dataset and metrics as in Sect. 6.1, but without using the answer type prediction component.

Therefore, in this case, the text provided to the extractive QA model is the textual description of each entity retrieved by the entity search system, without being expanded with facts matching the answer type, as described in Sects. 3 and 4. We report the following results using the best value for the answer score threshold (0.9) determined in Experiment 1: Precision: 37.356, Recall: 32.966, F1: 32.181, Accuracy: 48.122. We see that results are lower by 4–8 percentage points, suggesting the positive effect of answer type prediction.

6.3   Experiment 2: DBpedia Entity: QA

DBpedia-Entity is a standard test collection for entity search over DBpedia [7]. It is meant for evaluating retrieval systems that return a ranked list of entities (DBpedia URIs) in response to a free text user query. This dataset contains named entity queries, keyword queries, list queries and QA queries. We consider the subset of QA queries, which contains 140 queries from the QALD-2 challenge (Question Answering over Linked Data) [12]. These are natural language questions that can be answered by DBpedia entities, for example, "Who is the mayor of Berlin? Each entity/answer is accompanied by a score in 3-point relevance scale: *highly relevant (2)* (the entity is a direct answer to the query), *relevant (1)* (the entity can be shown as an answer to the query, but not among the top results), *irrelevant (0)*.

Other systems that report results over this benchmark use the NDCG@10 and NDCG@100 metrics because they focus on entity search. In our case, since we use this benchmark for QA, we consider Precision scores, in order to find out whether the top answers returned by our system are relevant to the query.

We evaluate the performance of our approach as a standalone QA system for the task of entity search. To do this we compute the Precision scores at the values 1, 3 and 5. The results obtained for varying values of answer score threshold are given in Table 3.

Table 3. Precision @1, @3, @5 for varying answer score threshold over DBpedia-Entity.

Threshold	0	0.1	0.2	0.3	0.4	0.5	0.6	0.7	0.8	0.9
P@1	33.573	49.331	55.432	55.641	55.938	56.190	58.857	57.241	57.273	**69.444**
P@3	27.840	42.006	48.265	47.951	46.595	50.813	52.905	51.207	52.348	**69.444**
P@5	24.543	41.008	47.147	46.836	45.768	49.716	51.905	51.207	52.348	**69.444**

The results are good in the sense that more than 69% of answers are relevant to their corresponding questions. Below (in Sect. 6.4) we also explore how this component can improve the performance of a dedicated Entity Search system by adding the set of answers to the set of entities retrieved by the search system.

6.4   Experiment 3: DBpedia Entity: QA+RANKING

We use the DBpedia Entity dataset [7] to evaluate the performance of Elas4RDF as an entity retrieval system for QA. Our goal for this experiment is to find out how the answers retrieved using this work affect the performance of Elas4RDF for QA tasks. Therefore, we use the group of queries from the DBpedia Entity collection that are Natural Language Questions (e.g. "Who is the mayor of Berlin?"). This group contains 140 of the 467 total queries in the benchmark. Over this group of queries, we compute the NDCG scores (@10 and @100) for:

- Entities retrieved by the Elas4RDF search service [10]
- Entities retrieved by the Elas4RDF search service *combined* with high scoring answers from the QA tab

To fuse the set of answers from the QA tab with the set of entities from the search service, we retrieve all entities from the search service, then we select a number (a) of answers from the QA tab and add them to the list of entities. Each entity has a score computed by the search service and each answer a score computed by the QA component. All scores are in the range scale of 0 to 1. We try two approaches to compute these scores:

I Keep the score from each entity and answer as computed by the entity search system and the QA component.
II Sum scores for entities in both rankings.

Finally, we sort the list of combined entities and answers by these scores, and we keep the top 10 or 100 results, depending on the NDCG metric that we wish to compute.

The results are displayed in Tables 4 and 5. The first row (baseline) corresponds to results for the entities returned by the QA component when no additional answers have been added. The next rows correspond to results for varying number of top answers from the QA component added to the baseline. We can see that including answers from the QA tab improves the NDCG score in all cases. The highest improvement in almost all cases occurs when the top-5 answers are added to the list of entities.

Table 4. NDCG scores over Natural Language Questions of the DBpedia Entity collection for approach I: Keep Initial Scores

	NDCG@100		NDCG@10	
Answers added	Score	Difference	Score	Difference
0 (baseline)	0.325	0	0.325	0
1	0.352	0.027	0.352	0.027
3	0.372	0.047	0.353	0.028
5	**0.384**	**0.059**	**0.354**	**0.029**
10	0.382	0.057	0.353	0.028

Table 5. NDCG scores over Natural Language Questions of the DBpedia Entity collection for approach II: Sum Scores

	NDCG@100		NDCG@10	
Answers added	Score	Difference	Score	Difference
0 (baseline)	0.325	0	0.325	0
1	0.355	0.03	0.355	0.03
3	0.375	0.05	**0.358**	**0.033**
5	**0.387**	**0.062**	0.357	0.032
10	0.386	0.061	0.356	0.031

As regards the comparison of approaches I and II, we can see that approach II obtains better results with a small difference (0.003 improvement of NDCG@100 using 5 answers). The reason for this is that approach II handles cases were an answer is returned by both the entity search system and the QA component.

Overall we can say that our QA pipeline could be considered as a method for ranking entities in the context of entity search. In comparison to a "plain" entity search, our pipeline is computationally more expensive because of the memory and time requirements added by the answer type prediction, entity enrichment and answer extraction components (see Sect. 6.5), but it can give better results in certain cases. Specifically, it can improve NDCG@100 by 6.2% points.

6.5   Efficiency

While running, the system's memory footprint is approximately 1.4 GB, and it takes up 511 MB of space to store all required models. To evaluate the time required to answer a question, we record times for each step of the pipeline as well as the overall time required to provide the final answers for all (2,032) questions in the Webquestions dataset (Sect. 6.1) and compute their average. This experiment was performed on a machine with 6 physical cores running Debian Linux. We found that the average time for the Answer Type Prediction stage is 0.1 s, for the Entity Enrichment stage 3.9 s, for the Answer Extraction stage 4.3 s and the overall average time required to provide the final answers is 8.3 s. We can see that answer type prediction is the fastest stage, because it uses a lighter language model (DistilBERT) while the other 2 stages are quite slower, because of the response time of the SPARQL queries for Entity Enrichment and the larger language model used for Answer Extraction (Table 6).

Table 6. Average time cost for each stage of the pipeline

Answer type prediction	Entity enrichment	Answer extraction
0.1 s (1.2%)	3.9 s (47%)	4.3 s (51.8%)

One could highly improve the efficiency by using a locally hosted triplestore that would provide a faster response time. Moreover one could speed up the answer extraction stage by using the RoBERTa model on a GPU. Finally, the number of returned facts could also be limited by setting a maximum response size, or using more strict SPARQL queries (e.g., by ignoring the equivalent classes), or using equivalence-aware indexes like those described in [15].

6.6 Executive Summary

We summarize the evaluation results as follows: We have shown that our approach for open domain QA can obtain satisfactory results, i.e. 54% accuracy, 39% F1 over popular QA benchmarks, something that is very interesting because it does not follow a supervised end-to-end approach trained on the same knowledge base, but makes use of different information sources than those intended by the benchmarks. We have also showed that the answer type prediction and entity enrichment stages improve Precision by 6%, Recall by 7% and F1 score by 7% (over WebQuestions). In addition we have shown that our approach can be used in combination with an entity search system to improve entity search tasks by 6% NDCG@100 (over DBpedia Entity dataset).

7 Related Work

For a survey of QA approaches over knowledge bases see [5]. In general, systems have converged to two major approaches: (i) Semantic Parsing (SP), and (ii) Information Extraction (IE); the former focuses on question understanding and therefore attempts to convert sentences into their semantic representation, such as logical forms, while the latter (IE) approach aims at identifying topic (focus) entities in the input question and then, via pre-defined templates, map the question to the KB predicates, and finally, explore the KG neighborhood of the matched entities. Our approach cannot be classified to any of these two extremes: although it starts from keyword search (that has an IE flavor), in parallel it performs Answer Type Prediction (that has a SP flavor), it enriches the textual description with SPARQL-fetched triples of the entities of the predicted type (SP and IE-flavors), and then it exploits pre-trained Neural Networks for the extraction of the final answer.

In comparison to related work, e.g. see [24] for a recent overview of QA approaches over DBpedia, the most related works are: [8] which converts the natural language question into two subqueries: SPARQL query and keyword search. That work uses a keyword index for special keywords rather than a whole knowledge graph for keyword search and produces the final answer using an algorithm to combine SPARQL results and keyword search results. Another work regarding QA and Keyword Search is SINA [23]. That system performs query preprocessing to tokenize, remove stopwords and lemmatize terms in the query, then groups keywords into segments and generates conjunctive federated SPARQL queries to retrieve answers. In contrast to our approach, that work relies fully on a SPARQL endpoint instead of using a dataset-specific index for keyword search. However, from our experience, and as stated in [8], not all query intentions can be identified and mapped to the correct SPARQL statement.

Finally, we should note that the effect of Answer Type Prediction has been investigated in entity search ([6] shows that it improves significantly NDCG@10), however, to the best of our knowledge, no other work has investigated how it affects QA over knowledge graphs. Moreover, as mentioned in the introductory section, to our knowledge no previous work uses KBQA within an interactive search system over RDF where QA complements the other perspectives (and thus consistency with the input that feeds all perspectives is required).

8 Concluding Remarks

Since QA over knowledge graphs is hard to be adequate, satisfying and pleasing for end users, in this paper we have investigated an approach for QA in a more realistic context, i.e. in the context of an interactive search system over RDF where QA complements the other perspectives that are given to the users. We start from the entity ranking that is offered by the keyword search system, and we build on top a pipeline for QA that involves SPARQL, semantic answer type prediction, and pre-trained neural networks. We have evaluated our approach over two different datasets and showcased the value it provides for QA and entity search tasks. We have shown that for open domain QA this approach achieves satisfactory results, i.e. 54% accuracy and 39% F1 over a popular QA benchmark (WebQuestions), even if (a) no training has been performed over this particular benchmark, and (b) the method uses a different information source (DBpedia) than the one intended by the benchmark (FreeBase).

We have also showed how the Answer Type Prediction and Entity Enrichment stages, do improve Precision by 6%, Recall by 7% and F1 score by 7% (over WebQuestions). Finally, we have shown that our approach can be used in combination with an entity search system to improve entity search tasks by 6% NDCG@100 (over DBpedia Entity dataset).

Overall, the proposed pipeline can be applied over large knowledge graphs, since the process starts from an efficient and effective keyword search system, while the next steps exploit pre-trained neural network models.

As regards future research, it is worth investigating more questions from the DBpedia Entity dataset (not only QA-related), to see whether the entity ranking is improved in all cases, and to investigate methods for further improving the effectiveness of the approach without limiting its applicability.

References

1. Abbasiantaeb, Z., Momtazi, S.: Text-based question answering from information retrieval and deep neural network perspectives: a survey (2020)
2. Berant, J., Chou, A., Frostig, R., Liang, P.: Semantic parsing on Freebase from question-answer pairs. In: Proceedings of the 2013 Conference on Empirical Methods in Natural Language Processing, pp. 1533–1544 (Oct 2013)

3. Deng, J., Krause, J., Berg, A.C., Fei-Fei, L.: Hedging your bets: optimizing accuracy-specificity trade-offs in large scale visual recognition. In: 2012 IEEE Conference on Computer Vision and Pattern Recognition, pp. 3450–3457. IEEE (2012)
4. Devlin, J., Chang, M.W., Lee, K., Toutanova, K.: BERT: pre-training of deep bidirectional transformers for language understanding (2018)
5. Dimitrakis, E., Sgontzos, K., Tzitzikas, Y.: A survey on question answering systems over linked data and documents. J. Intell. Inf. Syst., 1–27 (2019)
6. Garigliotti, D., Hasibi, F., Balog, K.: Identifying and exploiting target entity type information for ad hoc entity retrieval. Inf. Retrieval J. **22**(3), 285–323 (2019)
7. Hasibi, F., et al.: DBpedia-entity v2: A test collection for entity search. In: Proceedings of the 40th International ACM SIGIR Conference on Research and Development in Information Retrieval, pp. 1265–1268 (2017)
8. Hu, X., Duan, J., Dang, D.: Natural language question answering over knowledge graph: the marriage of SPARQL query and keyword search. Knowl. Inf. Syst. (2021). https://doi.org/10.1007/s10115-020-01534-4
9. Jain, S.: Question answering over knowledge base using factual memory networks. In: Procs of the NAACL Student Research Workshop. Association for Computational Linguistics, San Diego, California, June 2016
10. Kadilierakis, G., Fafalios, P., Papadakos, P., Tzitzikas, Y.: Keyword search over RDF using document-centric information retrieval systems. In: Harth, A., et al. (eds.) ESWC 2020. LNCS, vol. 12123, pp. 121–137. Springer, Cham (2020). https://doi.org/10.1007/978-3-030-49461-2_8
11. Liu, Y., et al.: RoBERTa: a robustly optimized BERT pretraining approach (2019)
12. Lopez, V., Unger, C., Cimiano, P., Motta, E.: Evaluating question answering over linked data. Web Semant. **21**, 3–13 (2013)
13. Lukovnikov, D., Fischer, A., Lehmann, J., Auer, S.: Neural network-based question answering over knowledge graphs on word and character level. In: Proceedings of the 26th International Conference on World Wide Web, pp. 1211–1220 (2017)
14. Mihindukulasooriya, N., Dubey, M., Gliozzo, A., Lehmann, J., Ngomo, A.C.N., Usbeck, R.: SeMantic AnsweR Type prediction task (SMART) at ISWC 2020 Semantic Web Challenge. CoRR/arXiv abs/2012.00555 (2020)
15. Mountantonakis, M., Tzitzikas, Y.: Content-based union and complement metrics for dataset search over RDF knowledge graphs. J. Data Inf. Q. (JDIQ) **12**(2), 1–31 (2020)
16. Nikas, C., Fafalios, P., Tzitzikas, Y.: Two-stage semantic answer type prediction for question answering using BERT and class-specificity rewarding. In: Proceedings of the SeMantic AnsweR Type prediction task (SMART) at ISWC 2020, pp. 19–28 (2020)
17. Nikas, C., Kadilierakis, G., Fafalios, P., Tzitzikas, Y.: Keyword search over RDF: is a single perspective enough? Big Data Cogn. Comput. **4**(3), 22 (2020)
18. Noy, N., Gao, Y., Jain, A., Narayanan, A., Patterson, A., Taylor, J.: Industry-scale knowledge graphs: lessons and challenges. Queue **17**(2), 48–75 (2019)
19. Qi, P., Lee, H., Sido, O.T., Manning, C.D.: Retrieve, rerank, read, then iterate: answering open-domain questions of arbitrary complexity from text (2020)
20. Rajpurkar, P., Jia, R., Liang, P.: Know what you don't know: unanswerable questions for squad. In: Proceedings of the 56th Annual Meeting of the Association for Computational Linguistics (Volume 2: Short Papers), pp. 784–789 (2018)
21. Sanh, V., Debut, L., Chaumond, J., Wolf, T.: DistilBERT, a distilled version of BERT: smaller, faster, cheaper and lighter. arXiv preprint arXiv:1910.01108 (2019)

22. Setty, V., Balog, K.: Semantic answer type prediction using BERT. In: Procs of the SeMantic AnsweR Type prediction task (SMART) at ISWC 2020 Semantic Web Challenge, vol. 2774, pp. 10–18 (2020). CEUR-WS.org
23. Shekarpour, S., Marx, E., Ngonga Ngomo, A.C., Auer, S.: SINA: semantic interpretation of user queries for question answering on interlinked data. J. Web Semant. **30**, 39–51 (2015)
24. Singh, K., Lytra, I., Radhakrishna, A.S., Shekarpour, S., Vidal, M.E., Lehmann, J.: No one is perfect: analysing the performance of question answering components over the DBpedia knowledge graph. J. Web Semant. **65**, 100594 (2020)

Automatically Extracting OWL Versions of FOL Ontologies

Torsten Hahmann[(✉)] and Robert W. Powell II

School of Computing and Information Sciences, University of Maine,
Orono, ME 04469, USA
{torsten.hahmann,robert.powell}@maine.edu

Abstract. While OWL and RDF are by far the most popular logic-based languages for Semantic Web Ontologies, some well-designed ontologies are only available in languages with a much richer expressivity, such as first-order logic (FOL) or the ISO standard Common Logic. This inhibits reuse of these ontologies by the wider Semantic Web Community. While converting OWL ontologies to FOL is straightforward, the reverse problem of finding the closest OWL approximation of an FOL ontology is undecidable. However, for most practical purposes, a "good enough" OWL approximation need not be perfect to enable wider reuse by the Semantic Web Community.

This paper outlines such a conversion approach by first normalizing FOL sentences into a function-free prenex conjunctive normal (FF-PCNF) that strips away minor syntactic differences and then applying a pattern-based approach to identify common OWL axioms. It is tested on the over 2,000 FOL ontologies from the Common Logic Ontology Repository.

Keywords: Ontology translation · Common Logic · First-order logic · Web Ontology Language (OWL) · Prenex Normal Form (PNF)

1 Introduction

Ontologies make knowledge about our world explicit, with uses in a variety of settings, ranging from conceptual modeling and knowledge management, to the dissemination of the semantics of data on the web, and to automated reasoning that supports knowledge querying, discovery, and integration. Ontologies amendable to automated reasoning must be specified in a language with machine-interpretable formal semantics, such as various description logics including the Web Ontology Language, OWL2 [12,17], first-order logic or Common Logic [13], or rule languages like SWRL (https://www.w3.org/Submission/SWRL/). The specific choice of ontology language depends on a number of factors, including the complexity of the domain that is modeled, the amount of detail that needs to be expressed (including what kind of relations need to be modeled), the kind and

This material is based in part upon work supported by The National Science Foundation under grants OIA-1937099, OIA-2033607, and III-1565811.

complexity of the reasoning that needs to be supported (e.g., verification of the ontology's internal consistency or its consistency with large data sets, querying of data, or only classification tasks), and the required reasoning efficiency. In the choice of language we make a trade-off between expressivity and tractability [4]. Description logics (see, e.g., [1]) sacrifice some expressivity for decidability or even tractability while first-order logic and more expressive languages sacrifice decidability for increased expressivity.

The OWL and OWL2 families of ontology languages [12,17] have become de-facto standards for representing semantic knowledge to be used for lightweight reasoning such as classification tasks and consistency checking of a taxonomy. However, more expressive language, such as full first-order logic (FOL), are beneficial in settings when greater expressivity or flexibility in how knowledge is captured are paramount. For example, FOL permits use of functions and relations of arbitrary arity, which are critical for modeling spatio-temporal phenomena (which often add a temporal parameter to relations), and supports axiomatizing the interaction between relations in more detail. FOL has found a variety of uses, including for the specification of foundational ontologies such as DOLCE, BFO or GFO, for mid-level/generic ontologies (e.g., about spatial and/or temporal aspects or processes), and for domain reference ontologies such as the Hydro Foundational Ontology [11]. In many cases, the developed first-order ontologies primarily serve as reference representations (reference ontologies in the sense of [11,14]) that guide integration of ontologies across domains or help extract lightweight versions for specific purposes (e.g. DOLCE-Lite). But currently, these lightweight versions must be crafted by hand (see, e.g., [2]) which is not only costly but is further inhibited by many Semantic Web or domain experts being less familiar or less confident in working with FOL. Another issue with manually crafted OWL versions of FOL ontologies is the overhead of having to simultaneously maintain an OWL and a FOL version of an ontology and any potential discrepancies that may result. This motivates the work presented here: we want to develop an approach to automatically produce OWL versions from existing FOL ontologies. This will help leverage the significant resources that have already been invested in developing rigorous, densely axiomatized first-order logic ontologies and will make them accessible to a broader community of domain scientists who are more familiar with the OWL notation. It also would make the knowledge encoded in the FOL ontologies amendable to automated reasoning tasks that need to scale by magnitudes beyond what first-order reasoners currently can accomplish [20].

Because of the undecidability of FOL, computing a maximal OWL approximation of an FOL ontology is an intractable task that would require reasoning over its possibly infinite set of theorems. That is why instead of aiming for the elusive maximal approximation, we more pragmatically aim to efficiently produce "good enough" approximations. A "good enough" OWL2 ontology only needs to contain the kind of knowledge that an average OWL2 developer would have included in a hand-crafted, "native" OWL ontology, i.e. one that has been originally developed in OWL, for the same domain and scope.

2   Approach

Approximating a first order logic (FOL) ontology into a set of web ontology language (OWL) expressions presents multiple issues. The fact that the complexity of some FOL statements exceeds OWL's expressivity is not addressed here as it may require significant ontology re-engineering efforts. But a related issue is which OWL constructs to actually look for. This is addressed in Sect. 2.1 that identifies FOL templates of common OWL constructs. The additional issues of how to identify the portions of a FOL axiom that can be expressed via the available OWL expressions and how to deal with FOL's syntactic flexibility in encoding the same semantic content are tackled in Sect. 2.2, which develops a suitable normal form as basis for comparing FOL sentences against the templates. But even after normalization, matching of FOL sentences against the templates is rather expensive as discussed in Sect. 2.4. We develop a first-pass filtering approach described in Sect. 2.3. Figure 1 outlines our overall approach.

2.1   Common OWL Constructs as FOL Sentences

FOL provides a very small and generic set of logical connectives, but does not prescribe or constrain how to logically capture the semantic relationships between a set of non-logical symbols (i.e., the vocabulary of the domain) [11]. In contrast, OWL provides a large set of constructs, which are by design closely aligned with the kind of knowledge that people most commonly want to capture and which guide how to semantically relate a domain vocabulary. Consider as example the definition of the class **Father** from the OWL Primer [12]:

> **Father SubClassOf IntersectionOf(Man Parent)**

In FOL, this could be expressed in multiple ways, for example[1]:

$$\forall x[Father(x) \rightarrow Man(x) \wedge Parent(x)]$$
$$\Leftrightarrow \forall x[\neg Man(x) \vee \neg Parent(x) \rightarrow \neg Father(x)]$$
$$\Leftrightarrow \forall x[\neg Father(x) \vee (Man(x) \wedge Parent(x))]$$
$$\Leftrightarrow \forall x[(\neg Father(x) \vee Man(x)) \wedge (\neg Father(x) \vee Parent(x))]$$
$$\Leftrightarrow \neg \exists x[Father(x) \wedge (\neg Man(x) \vee \neg Parent(x))]$$
$$\Leftarrow \forall x[Father(x) \leftrightarrow Man(x) \wedge Parent(x)]$$

In comparison, OWL ontologies are less syntactically variable and heavily rely on simple cases of the available constructs. We mostly find taxonomic knowledge about classes and relations, domain and range restrictions on relations and classes, and simple properties of relations (reflexivity, symmetry, etc.) while more complex, nested class and property expressions are used sparingly even when permitted. A study of 518 OWL ontologies [7] has found that over 90% of class axioms are simple, meaning that they contain at most three class or property names. This observation informs our approach. It suggests starting with the

---

[1] The last sentence is not logically equivalent but still contains the same subclass relationship as one direction of the biconditional.

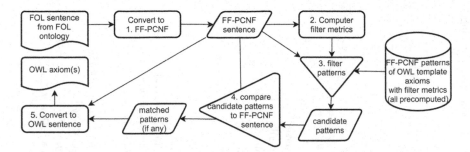

Fig. 1. Overview of our approach: Sentences are read from a FOL ontology and then converted to FF-PCNF (1). Once converted, metrics are computed (2) to filter the FF-PCNF for candidate templates (3) based on pre-computed template metrics. The sentences are then tested for exact matches against the templates' FF-PCNF (4). The matching ones produce OWL axioms (5).

OWL constructs and translating them to FOL rather than building an inventory of all the possible ways one could encode an OWL construct in FOL.

As summarized in Table 1, all Class and Object Property Axioms[2] from the OWL 2 Structural Specification [17] are supported[3]. But Class and Property Expressions therein are restricted as follows:

- Class expressions can make use of at most one propositional connective/-operation (`IntersectionOf`, `UnionOf`, or `ComplementOf`). Because our example definition of `Father` contains only one connective (an intersection) in its superclass expression, it is translated.
  Object property expressions may make use of one `InverseOf` expression.
- The Object Property Restrictions Existential Quantification, Universal Quantification, and Self-Restriction are supported but class expressions therein are also limited to a maximum of one propositional connective.
- Object Property Cardinality Restrictions are not supported as they are cumbersome to express in FOL and rarely, if at all, used in FOL.
- Class expressions involving Individuals (namely Enumeration of Individuals or Individual Value Restrictions) are not supported because individuals are not commonly included in FOL ontologies[4].

These templates still cover 97.4% of the simple class axioms from [7] and many additional role and complex class axioms not further broken down in [7]. Moreover, our restrictions are of no consequence for those OWL2 profiles that impose more stringent limits in the use of propositional connectives and inverses.

2.2   FF-PCNF for Dealing with Syntactic Variations in FOL

A specific challenge we have to overcome is that FOL is much less syntactically restricted than OWL as demonstrated by the Father construct. In order to

---

[2] Data Properties are indistinguishable from Object Properties in FOL and not used.
[3] Their exact FOL encoding does not really matter after the normalization step.
[4] All Individuals encountered during parsing are declared as such in the OWL output.

Table 1. OWL constructs with equivalent FOL sentences and FF-PCNF sentences that serve as templates for filtering and matching.

OWL	Representative FOL sentence	FF-PCNF template
Class expression axioms		
1 SubClassOf(C D)	$\forall x[C(x) \to D(x)]$	$\forall x[\neg C(x) \vee D(x)]$
1a EquivalentClasses(C D)	Inferred from SubClassOf axioms	
2 DisjointClasses(C D)	$\forall x[C(x) \to \neg D(x)]$	$\forall x[\neg C(x) \vee \neg D(x)]$
2a DisjointUnionOf(C D E $\cdots$)	Inferred from SubClassOf and DisjointClasses axioms	
Object property axioms		
3 SubObjectPropertyOf(R S)	$\forall x,y[R(x,y) \to S(x,y)]$	$\forall x,y[\neg R(x,y) \vee S(x,y)]$
3a EquivalentObjectProperties(R S)	Inferred from SubObjectPropertyOf axioms	
3b InverseObjectProperties(R S)	inferred from SubObjectPropertyOf axioms (involving an inverse)	
4 DisjointObjectProperties(R S)	$\forall x,y[R(x,y) \to \neg S(x,y)]$	$\forall x,y[\neg R(x,y) \vee \neg S(x,y)]$
5 ObjectPropertyDomain(R C)	$\forall x,y[R(x,y) \to C(x)]$	$\forall x,y[\neg R(x,y) \vee C(x)]$
6 ObjectPropertyRange(R C)	$\forall x,y[R(x,y) \to C(y)]$	$\forall x,y[\neg R(x,y) \vee C(y)]$
7 ReflexiveObjectProperty(R)	$\forall x[R(x,x)]$	$\forall x[R(x,x)]$
8 IrreflexiveObjectProperty(R)	$\forall x[\neg R(x,x)]$	$\forall x[\neg R(x,x)]$
9 SymmetricObjectProperty(R)	$\forall x,y[R(x,y) \to R(y,x)]$	$\forall x,y[\neg R(x,y) \vee R(y,x)]$
10 AsymmetricObjectProperty(R)	$\forall x,y[R(x,y) \to \neg R(y,x)]$	$\forall x,y[\neg R(x,y) \vee \neg R(y,x)]$
11 TransitiveObjectProperty(R)	$\forall x,y,z[R(x,y) \to [R(y,z) \to R(x,z)]]$	$\forall x,y,z[\neg R(x,y) \vee \neg R(y,z) \vee R(x,z)]$
12 FunctionalObjectProperty(R)	$\forall x,y,z[R(x,y) \to [R(x,z) \to y=z]]$	$\forall x,y,z[\neg R(x,y) \vee \neg R(x,z) \vee\, = (y,z)]$
13 InverseFunctionalObjectProperty(R)	$\forall x,y,z[R(x,y) \to [R(z,y) \to x=z]]$	$\forall x,y,z[\neg R(x,y) \vee \neg R(z,y) \vee\, = (x,z)]$
Class axioms with existential or universal quantification or self-reference		
14 SubClassOf(C ObjectSomeValuesFrom(R D))	$\forall x\exists y[C(x) \to R(x,y) \wedge D(y)]$	$\forall x\exists y[[\neg C(x) \vee R(x,y)] \wedge [\neg C(x) \vee D(y))]]$
15 SubClassOf(ObjectSomeValuesFrom(R D) C)	$\forall x\exists y[R(x,y) \wedge D(y) \to C(x)]$	$\forall x\exists y[\neg R(x,y) \vee \neg D(x) \vee C(y)]$
16 SubClassOf(C ObjectAllValuesFrom(R D))	$\forall x,y[C(x) \wedge R(x,y) \to D(y)]$	$\forall x,y[\neg C(x) \vee \neg R(x,y) \vee D(y)]$
17 SubClassOf(ObjectAllValuesFrom(R D) C)	$\forall x,y[R(x,y) \to D(y) \to C(x)]$	$\forall x,y[[R(x,y) \vee C(x)] \wedge [\neg D(y) \vee C(x)]]$
18 SubClassOf(C ObjectHasSelf(R))	$\forall x[C(x) \to R(x,x)]$	$\forall x[\neg C(x) \vee R(x,x)]$
19 SubClassOf(ObjectHasSelf(R) C)	$\forall x[R(x,x) \to C(x)]$	$\forall x[\neg R(x,x) \vee C(x)]$

$$\forall x[A(x) \rightarrow \exists y[\neg(B(x,y) \vee \neg D(y))]] \tag{1a}$$

$$\equiv \forall x[\neg A(x) \vee \exists y[\neg(B(x,y) \vee \neg D(y))]] \tag{1b}$$

$$\equiv \forall x[\neg A(x) \vee \exists y[B(x,y) \wedge D(y)]] \tag{1c}$$

$$\equiv \forall x \exists y[\neg A(x) \vee (B(x,y) \wedge D(y))] \tag{1d}$$

$$\equiv \forall x \exists y[(\neg A(x) \vee B(x,y)) \wedge (\neg A(x) \vee D(y))] \tag{1e: FF-PCNF}$$

$$\equiv \forall x \exists y[\neg A(x) \vee (B(x,y) \wedge D(y))] \tag{PNF; same as 1d}$$

$$\approx \forall x[(\neg A(x) \vee B(x,f(x)) \wedge (\neg A(x) \vee D(y))] \tag{CNF}$$

Fig. 2. Conversion of an example FOL sentence into FF-PCNF. The PNF and CNF conversions are included for comparison as the last two lines. Sentence (d) is where the prenex is formed and (e) is the result of distributing disjunctions over conjunctive terms. The final sentence (e) matches the FF-PCNF template 14.

identify certain OWL constructs, we have to manage this syntactic flexibility. We will do so using a normal form. Normal forms constrain the structure of an expression to enable more streamlined sentence processing for automated reasoning tasks. A normal form for easily comparing FOL expressions to the OWL constructs in Table 1 must fulfill three requirements: 1) make it easy to compare entire FOL sentences or portions thereof to the OWL constructs, 2) maintain existential quantification in order to identify `ObjectSomeValuesFrom` expressions, and 3) remove any function symbols.

Conjunctive normal form (CNF) is probably the most widely used normal form in knowledge representation. It represents a FOL sentence as a universally quantified sentence comprised of a single conjunction over several disjunctive terms. Such conjunctions over disjunctive terms are attractive for our purposes because the FOL versions of our OWL templates, with the exceptions of 14 and 17, only contain disjunctions. Thus by breaking a sentence into one big universally quantified conjunction over a set of disjunctions (the latter are commonly called "clauses") we can check each disjunction individually against the OWL templates. However, conversion to CNF (see, e.g., [4]) removes existential quantifiers during the Skolemization step and renders standard CNF unsuitable for our purposes. Prenex normal forms (PNF), on the other hand, maintain existential quantification by pulling out all quantifiers to the very front of the sentence, called the prenex (e.g. the $\forall x \exists y$ portion in Fig. 2(e)), followed by a quantifier-free portion called the matrix (e.g. the $(\neg A(x) \vee B(x,y)) \wedge (\neg A(x) \vee D(y))$ portion). To meet our needs, we alter the standard CNF conversion by replacing the Skolemization step by a prenex-forming step that moves both universal and existential quantifiers to the front. During this step, quantifiers are also heuristically coalesced to reduce the overall number of quantifiers as explained further down. Because OWL does not know function symbols, we re-encode them as predicates in a step before prenex construction. As explained further down, we substitute function symbols of arity n by new $(n+1)$-ary predicates with a new existentially quantified variable. Because of how we combine aspects of CNF and PNF and remove all functions, we call the result *function-free prenex conjunctive normal form* (FF-PCNF). Note that just like in the standard conversion to CNF, the final distribution step may exponentially increase the length and, thus, the number of FF-PCNF sentences because universally quantified conjunctions form separate sentences for the subsequent steps.

Function Substitution. Within the matrix, all n-ary functions are substituted by new (n+1)-ary predicates. Any occurrence of the function symbol in an atom is replaced by a conjunction over two terms: (1) the old atom with the functional term substituted by a new universally quantified variable and (2) the new (n+1)-ary predicate over the function's nested terms and the newly introduced variable. To maintain satisfiability two new sentences need to be added to ensure that the new (n+1)-ary predicates are indeed functional in their behaviour: (a) $\forall \overrightarrow{x} \exists y P_f(\overrightarrow{x}, y)$ (there is some result for every combination of inputs of the function) and (b) $\forall \overrightarrow{x}, y, z[P_f(\overrightarrow{x}, y) \wedge P_f(\overrightarrow{x}, z) \rightarrow y = z]$ (there is at most one result for any combination of inputs of the function). Note that these sentences do not need to be explicitly added to our FF-PCNF sentences; instead we can immediately add a `FunctionalObjectProperty` axiom on the newly introduced predicate P_f. Note further that function removal only yields OWL axioms for unary functions, because all other result in predicates of arity three or greater that are currently not converted to OWL.

Quantifier Coalescing. During prenex creation, there is an opportunity to shorten the final prenexes. Depending on variable placement in the sentence, like quantifiers and their variabes can be merged ("coalesced") into a single quantified variable, which will increase the chances that a sentence matches one of the FF-PCNF templates later on. Quantifier coalescing applies standard logical rules:

$$\forall x[A(x)] \wedge \forall y[B(y)] \iff \forall z[A(z) \wedge B(z)]$$

$$\exists x[A(x)] \vee \exists y[B(y)] \iff \exists z[A(z) \vee B(z)]$$

To leverage this potential without sacrificing efficiency we apply a greedy heuristic with a single look-ahead when deciding which quantifier to coalesce when there are multiple choices. If the parent term is a conjunction then universal quantifiers are coalesced, otherwise existential quantifiers are coalesced. In the case where the parent is a quantifier itself, it absorbs children with like quantifiers before applying the look-ahead for the merged quantifier again.

2.3   Filtering FF-PCNF Sentences by Templates

To utilize FF-PCNF as a normal form to identify the presence of OWL axioms within FOL axioms, we have converted the "representative" FOL translation of each OWL axiom templates from Table 1 into an FF-PCNF template as shown in column 4. To identify whether a particular sentence from an FOL ontology contains any OWL axioms, we convert the FOL sentence to FF-PCNF (step 1 in our approach) and then need an efficient way to compare the result against the stored FF-PCNF templates (step 3). This comparison can be extremely expensive: It is not a simple string comparison because of the variations in variable

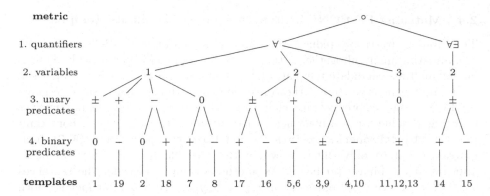

Fig. 3. Decision tree (implemented as set filters) of the four filtering metrics to identify potential OWL axioms in a FF-PCNF sentence. The leafs are the candidate templates from Table 1. Criteria 3 and 4 distinguish between presence or absence of positive and/or negative unary (criteria 3) and binary (criteria 4) predicates. In criteria 3 a "0" indicates the absence of unary predicates, + and −, respectively, the presence of only positive or only negated unary predicates, and ± the presence of both positive and negated unary predicates. Analogously for binary predicates in criteria 4. For example, template 16 requires two universally quantified variables, both positive and negated unary predicates (at least one of each), and only negated binary predicates. Combinations not in the decision tree lead to outright rejection of a sentence.

and predicate names or variations in the number of predicates. For example, the class $D(x)$ in template 1 could be named differently or be any anonymous union of classes. To keep the number of costly comparisons to a minimum, a filtering method first eliminates all obvious mismatches. Four efficiently computable filtering metrics (step 3) are suggested by the templates' syntactic structure:

1. the type of quantifiers found in the prenex,
2. the number of quantified variables,
3. the presence of unary or binary predicates in the matrix,
4. and the signs of the predicates (positive, negated or a mix).

Applied in that order, these metrics create the fourteen groups of sentences shown in Fig. 3, with ten groups leading to a unique template. Thus, in many cases a FF-PCNF sentence needs to be compared against only one template.

As a final filtering step, the number of atoms (i.e. the number of predicate instances) and the number of distinct predicates are used to further reduce the number of clauses that must be inspected closer for a match against some of the object property templates. Reflexive, irreflexive, symmetric, asymmetric, or transitive axioms can only be present if exactly one distinct predicate name is used. The number of atoms is also fixed: 1 for a reflexive or irreflexive property, 2 for a symmetric or asymmetric one, and 3 for a transitive one. Likewise, a functional or inverse functional axiom requires exactly two distinct predicate names, one of which must be the equals predicate.

2.4   Matching FF-PCNF Sentences Against Candidate Templates

The filtering drastically reduces the number of candidate FF-PCNF sentences – eliminating many altogether – that must be compared more closely against one or multiple candidate templates (step 4 in our approach). This comparison – the most expensive step of the conversion algorithm – then tests whether a FF-PCNF sentence precisely matches a candidate template. It typically involves checking variable use and placement across atoms within the clause. For example, the `ObjectPropertyDomain(R C)` and `ObjectPropertyRange(R C)` templates (5 and 6) only differ in where the variable in the unary predicate appears in the binary predicate. As another example, consider the sentences $\forall xy[\neg R(x,y) \vee S(x,y)]$ and $\forall xy[\neg R(x,y) \vee S(y,x)]$. By the filter metrics both match the templates for `SubObjectProperty(R S)`: they have two universally quantified variables and no unary predicates and a mix of positive and negated binary predicates. Thus filtering leaves templates 3 and 9 as candidates, but 9 is later ruled out because it is restricted to a single named predicate. Subsequently, the first sentence can be matched to the template. The second sentence, however, would not yet be a precise match because the variables in the predicate S are inverted. To create a precise match, the `InverseOf` needs to be added to the predicate S, resulting in the OWL axiom `SubObjectProperty(R InverseOf(S))`. When no match is established the FF-PCNF sentence is discarded.

2.5   Ensuring Adherence to OWL2 Global Restrictions

To guarantee decidability, OWL2 makes some global restrictions on the use of properties. Two restrictions on object properties are relevant to our translations. (1) The *simple role restriction* disallows use of complex object properties (roles) in constructs such as `FunctionalObjectProperty` or `DisjointObject-Properties`. To enforce it, we track all properties that are used in such constructs. At the end, we discard all axioms that would make these properties non-simply, namely transitive declarations (template 11) and axioms that use them within an `ObjectPropertyChain` construct. (2) Violations of the *property hierarchy restriction* only occur in the presence of multiple `ObjectPropertyChains` involving the same property. But these are quite rare in our translations: Only seven ontologies in our test set contain two or more `ObjectPropertyChains` and only one[5] actually violates the restriction. Thus, we defer to the `OWL API profile checker` tool[6] to identify such violations after producing OWL2 files and leave it up to human experts to resolve non-compliance.

Finally, we also allow choosing a target *OWL2 profile* [21]: Full (default), DL, EL, QL, or RL. To achieve this, disallowed object property axioms (e.g. FunctionalObjectProperty in EL and QL) and axioms wherein certain complex expressions are disallowed (e.g. `InverseOf` in EL; or `UnionOf` inside domain or range restriction axioms in EL, QL or RL) are discarded at the end.

---

[5] http://colore.oor.net/bipartite_incidence/owl/interval_incidence.all.owl.
[6] https://github.com/stain/profilechecker.

3   Implementation

The approach is implemented in Python 3 as part of the open-source project macleod[7]. The implementation utilizes an internal object structure to encode a FOL ontology, a parser to construct the internal object structure from CLIF files, methods for each type of object that support conversion into FF-PCNF, and methods for writing OWL axioms.

The internal object structure (see `src/macleod/logical/`) represents an ontology as a tree, each node encoding a logical or non-logical entity from a FOL ontology. Logical objects are: `Ontology`, sentences (`Axiom`), quantified formula (`Quantifier` with specializations `Existential` and `Universal`), connective formulas (`Connective` with specializations `Disjunction` and `Conjunction`), and negated formula (`Negation`). Atoms are represented as `Predicates` and may contain functional terms, denoted as `Functions`. The various object types provide methods that support conversion to FF-PCNF. E.g., a `Negation` supports pushing negation inwards, a `Function` supports rewriting as a `Predicate`, and a `Conjunctive` supports distribution of disjunctions over conjunctions.

The parser (`src/macleod/parsing/parser.py`) utilizes a Backus-Naur grammar of a portion of the CLIF notation of Common Logic [13]. A lexer (an advanced tokenizer) and parser are built using Python's PLY library[8] to implement the grammar, to tokenize the CLIF files, and to finally parse them. Parsing substitutes implications and biconditionals by CNF sentences. It results in representing each CLIF file as an `Ontology` object, which contains the axioms and keeps track of all imported CLIF files, which are recursively parsed into separate `Ontology` objects. During parsing, additional information, such as lists of all predicate and function symbols and their arities, and variables names are saved for each `Ontology` and each `Axiom` for later use.

Python's ElementTree XML API[9] is used to write the axioms in OWL/XML format. For completeness, declaration axioms for all encountered predicates of arity two or less, i.e. all classes and object properties, are automatically included regardless of whether they appear in any resulting OWL axiom.

4   Experimental Results

4.1   Materials

We have tested the approach on ontologies from the Common Logic Ontology Repository (COLORE: http://colore.oor.net), which currently contains over 2,700 files with sentences in the CLIF syntax of the Common Logic standard [13]. Some do not specify ontologies per se, but rather theorems, mappings between ontologies, partial models, or serve archival purposes. Of the 2,283 files that do represent ontologies or modules thereof (like individual definitions), 2,102

---

[7] https://github.com/thahmann/macleod.
[8] PLY is a Python port of the standard Unix tools Lex and Yacc.
[9] https://docs.python.org/3/library/xml.etree.elementtree.html; the Owlready2 module was another option but writing axioms was not as straightforward.

(92%) were successfully parsed; others either contain syntax errors or make use of unsupported Common Logic constructs that go beyond standard FOL. Our first evaluation uses all FOL sentences from the 2,102 successfully parsed files. Our second evaluation uses entire ontologies – i.e. CLIF files recursively closed under the `cl:imports` construct – rather than individual files. For 1,965 ontologies all imported modules can be parsed correctly. Of those, we select the 302 that contain a minimum of 15 predicates (unary or binary ones) and 15 axioms. Many smaller ontologies do not meet the predicate threshold; they primarily serve as modules of larger ontologies or are theories of common mathematical structures used as tools for verifying other ontologies. The 302 utilized ontologies range from 15 to 128 unary and binary predicates (median of 24) and 18 to 246 axioms (median of 69). While these may still be small compared to OWL ontologies, they are quite sizable for FOL ontologies.

To avoid distorting our results by many fairly similar ontologies, we group them by hierarchy. A hierarchy shares a signature and often a substantial set of imports (and, thus, axioms) [10]. The utilized ontologies span 33 hierarchies, 11 of which reside in a hierarchy of their own (listed first in Fig. 4)[10]. Of the remaining 22 hierarchies (bottom of Fig. 4) 17 contain 2 to 11 ontologies, and five are larger hierarchies with 20 to 76 ontologies.

4.2   Results

All tests are conducted using Python 3.7 on a Windows 10 laptop (i5-8350, 4 cores at 1.7 GHz base frequency, 8 GB RAM). The reported times are wall times that include parsing the CLIF file and its import closure.

The first experiment translates all 2,102 parseable CLIF files individually[11]. Altogether, they contain 4,257 FOL sentences, but only 3,387 (78%) of them use only predicates of arity one or two and can reasonably be expected to yield translations. They yielded 7,941 FF-PCNF sentences[12]. Filtering identified 5,957 FF-PCNF sentence-template pairs (on average 0.75 per FF-PCNF sentence and 1.76 per FOL sentence). 2,241 of these candidates produced OWL axioms, which amounts on average to 0.66 OWL axioms per FOL sentence. The whole experiment (including parsing, filtering and matching) finished in 151s apart from one ontology, namely `periods/periods_over_rationals.clif`, that increased exponentially in length and whose conversion and filtering/matching took 265s alone but did not yield any OWL axioms. Table 2 summarizes the axiom distribution: they are almost equally divided between class and object property axioms. 28.3% are subclass axioms, with the majority (540; 24.1% of total) being simple while 95 (4.2% of total) are complex. Among object property axioms, domain and range restrictions (18.5%) are most prevalent, followed by subproperty axioms

---

[10] For the `gwml2` and the `simple_features` we only work with the complete ontologies because the submodules are not particularly meaningful on their own.

[11] Full results are available from https://github.com/thahmann/macleod/blob/master/research/ISWC2021-experimental-data.xlsx and the OWL2 outputs are provided in https://colore.oor.net/ in the `owl` subfolder of each ontology hierarchy.

[12] Recall that universally quantified conjunctions are split into separate sentences.

Table 2. Summary of the OWL axioms obtained from all parseable CLIF modules.

FOL axioms		FF-PCNF	candidate	# OWL2	Prop. Class	Inverses	Property
total	arity≤ 2	sentences	templates	Axioms	Operations		Chains
4,257	3,387	7,941	5,957	2,241	236	158	30

total #	Class Axioms: *53%*			ObjectProperty Axioms: *47%*			
OWL2 Axioms	SubClass	SomeValuesFrom/ AllValuesFrom	Disjoint Classes	Sub Properties	Disjoint Property	Domain/ Range R.	Other
2,241	635	310	194	249	61	414	336
	28.3%	*13.8%*	*8.7%*	*11.1%*	*2.7%*	*18.5%*	*15.0%*

(11.1%). The remainder are property disjointness (2.7%) and various property descriptors such as (ir)reflexivity, (a)symmetry, or functional properties. Even with the imposed limitation on unions, intersections, and complements, we produced 236 such operations in class expressions. Inverses and property chains were used 158 and 30 times, respectively.

The results from our second experiment on 302 ontologies with at least 15 axioms and 15 predicates of arity $\leq$ 2 are summarized in Fig. 4. It took on average 3.6s to convert these ontologies, though with some larger ontologies taking a bit longer: `molecular_graph/definitions/most_elements.clif` with 246 axioms and 128 predicates took over 23s, while the larger ontologies in the `multidim_space_physcont` hierarchy also took up to 14s.

One measure of efficacy is the number of OWL axioms produced per FOL sentence: It ranges from 0.4 to 1.33 across hierarchies (with a max. of 2.42 for individual ontologies), though most fall within 0.73 ± 0.23 OWL axioms (median + standard deviation). However, this is a purely statistical measure and does not capture how much of the semantics are preserved: It neither measures how many FOL axioms are *fully* translated nor does it normalize by the length, density or complexity of the source FOL axioms. A better way to judge the quality of the produced ontologies is by comparing them to "native" OWL2 ontologies. One established criteria for comparing the quality of ontologies is their semantic richness (or "axiom density") [8,19] that captures how tightly classes are constrained. It is typically measured in terms of the axiom-class ratio, for which we obtain a median of 4.00 across hierarchies. But the FOL ontologies in our experiments contain more properties (a median of 14.3) than classes (median of 11.0) which is not typical for OWL ontologies[13]. Thus, an axiom-concept ratio that divides the number of axioms by the total number of classes *and* properties is a more appropriate metric. We obtain a mean of 1.62 across the hierarchies, though with a fairly wide spread (0.40 to 2.21). Nevertheless, all but 3 hierarchies (`location_varzi`, `vision_cardworld`, `financial`) have an average ratio of one or more axioms per concepts.

5   Discussion

The results demonstrate that our approach is able to quickly extract OWL2 versions even from sizable FOL ontologies. It is expected to scale well because

---

[13] The 514 ontologies in [7] contain 618,260 classes but only 22,046 properties.

	# Ont.	# FOL sentences	# FOL sentences of arity ≤2	# Predicates of arity ≤2 (unary/binary) - higher arity predicates	PCNF sentences	candidate patterns	# of OWL	OWL axioms per FOL sentence	axioms per concept (i.e. predicates of arity ≤2)	axiom per class	subclass	disjoint classes	someValuesFrom/ allValuesFrom	subproperty	disjoint properties	domain / range restrictions	other property axioms	Average Conversion Time in s
\simple_features\sfc_fol.clif		110	110	59 (35/24) - 0	307	292	130	1.18	2.20	3.71	51	15	6	24	7	19	8	4.70
\mapsee\mapsee.clif		39	39	25 (13/12) - 0	74	112	52	1.33	2.08	4.00	16	6	7	6	0	23	8	0.79
\ciro\ciro-core.clif		115	81	41 (20/21) - 11	229	192	81	1.00	1.98	4.05	22	6	17	3	0	25	8	5.29
\chains_process\chains_state.clif		54	46	21 (9/12) - 3	111	116	40	0.87	1.90	4.44	4	6	5	1	0	18	6	1.58
\cyclic_process\cyclic_state.clif		51	43	21 (9/12) - 3	101	116	40	0.93	1.90	4.44	4	6	5	1	0	18	6	1.42
\process_specification_language\psl_outercore.clif		104	72	31 (11/20) - 11	199	151	52	0.72	1.68	4.73	8	6	5	3	0	23	7	3.77
\combined_time\combined_time_def.clif		22	20	15 (4/11) - 2	73	142	23	1.15	1.53	5.75	0	1	4	0	0	16	2	2.40
\gwml2\gwml2_full.clif		81	81	66 (49/17) - 0	136	189	88	1.09	1.33	1.80	52	14	14	0	0	3	5	3.57
\velocity\speed.clif		56	56	26 (11/15) - 0	106	95	32	0.57	1.23	2.91	2	6	1	10	3	4	6	1.06
\molecular_graph\definitions\most_elements.clif		246	246	128 (126/2) - 0	359	143	129	0.52	1.01	1.02	129	0	0	0	1	0	0	23.47
\location_var\\region_location.clif		23	20	20 (3/17) - 2	65	37	8	0.40	0.40	2.67	0	0	2	3	1	0	2	0.89

the following numbers (except the number of ontologies) are all averages over all ontologies in each hierarchy that have 15 or more axioms and predicates

	# Ont.	# FOL sentences	# FOL sentences of arity ≤2	# Predicates of arity ≤2 (unary/binary) - higher arity predicates	PCNF sentences	candidate patterns	# of OWL	OWL axioms per FOL sentence	axioms per concept (i.e. predicates of arity ≤2)	axiom per class	subclass	disjoint classes	someValuesFrom/ allValuesFrom	subproperty	disjoint properties	domain / range restrictions	other property axioms	Average Conversion Time in s
\multidim_space_space\ & \multidim_space_spch\	5	102	95	33 (15/18) - 1	202	198	73	0.78	2.21	4.82	14.0	9.0	4.0	16.0	4.0	18.0	9.0	9.01
\multidim_space_voids\	8	155	146	46 (21/25) - 1	296	401	101	0.70	2.19	4.76	22.0	9.0	6.5	22.3	4.3	23.8	13.4	6.70
\multidim_space_physcont\	32	185	176	59 (21/37) - 1	351	503	127	0.72	2.18	5.91	22.0	9.0	7.3	33.6	5.6	32.4	16.7	9.92
\multidim_space_codi(b)\	59	57	57	59 (21/37) - 1	133	102	46	0.83	1.86	5.26	9.7	4.7	1.9	1.0	3.2	6.7	5.4	1.75
\direct_quality_process\	2	57	49	23 (10/13) - 3	164	151	41	0.84	1.83	4.14	4.0	6.0	5.0	1.0	0.0	18.0	7.0	2.95
\injection_bipartite_process\	2	57	49	23 (10/13) - 3	164	151	41	0.84	1.83	4.14	4.0	6.0	5.0	1.0	0.0	18.0	7.0	3.35
\onto_stit\	2	41	37	19 (6/14) - 1	77	75	35	0.93	1.81	6.27	0.0	11.5	5.0	4.0	0.0	11.0	3.0	0.74
\weak_bipartite_process\	2	55	47	23 (11/13) - 3	116	134	41	0.88	1.80	3.99	4.0	6.0	5.0	1.0	0.0	18.0	7.0	1.47
\multidim_occupy\	5	120	96	37 (17/20) - 4	236	149	66	0.70	1.78	3.91	6.0	16.6	13.4	10.0	3.0	7.2	9.6	2.43
\mcg_process\	2	58	50	24 (11/13) - 3	124	137	41	0.82	1.76	3.85	4.0	6.0	5.0	1.0	0.0	18.0	7.0	1.89
\rcc_continuous_process\	4	76	68	24 (11/13) - 3	286	157	41	0.60	1.74	3.85	4.0	6.0	5.0	1.0	0.0	18.0	7.0	7.27
\dolce\ and \dolce_XYZ\	20	72	64	47 (39/8) - 3	145	123	77	1.21	1.71	2.03	48.0	25.0	3.5	13.5	0.0	0.5	0.0	1.77
\multidim_mereotopology_codi(b)\	76	67	67	23 (8/16) - 0	128	108	40	0.61	1.68	5.59	3.3	4.4	0.8	0.8	3.6	5.5	8.5	1.66
\mor\	3	59	36	19 (13/5) - 8	207	96	34	0.88	1.64	2.40	9.5	6.0	6.5	10.0	2.0	8.0	0.0	4.13
\size\	6	92	79	33 (15/18) - 3	181	155	53	0.66	1.59	3.76	4.0	11.5	10.0	10.0	3.0	11.0	8.5	2.46
\psl_XYZ\	11	64	53	25 (10/14) - 4	110	106	38	0.72	1.54	3.68	6.8	5.7	6.7	1.7	2.0	11.0	5.8	1.57
\tripartite_incidence\	29	35	32	18 (8/10) - 3	97	53	27	0.86	1.51	3.41	3.0	3.0	2.3	2.0	2.0	12.0	1.0	1.46
\multidim_mereotopology_omt(b)\	8	79	69	23 (8/15) - 2	158	97	35	0.50	1.50	4.46	3.4	4.0	0.4	12.0	3.3	4.5	7.3	2.03
\owltime\ and \owltime_XYZ\	6	34	32	16 (5/11) - 1	51	71	25	0.84	1.47	5.25	4.0	1.0	0.0	4.0	0.8	13.7	1.0	0.50
\bipartite_incidence\	2	21	18	18 (5/13) - 4	62	41	21	1.19	1.16	4.20	4.0	3.0	0.0	0.0	2.0	8.0	1.0	1.15
\vision_cardworld\	5	53	39	22 (6/16) - 6	128	80	19	0.52	0.91	3.14	4.0	3.0	3.0	1.6	0.8	6.0	1.0	3.47
\financial\	2	99	99	91 (53/38) - 0	113	94	57	0.56	0.61	1.04	35.5	18.5	18.5	12.0	0.0	6.0	0.0	1.33
Totals:	302	2537	2270	(89.5%)														
					per FOL sentence				mean % of total OWL axioms:		29%	13%	10%	12%	3%	24%	10%	
MEAN		77	69	35	2.6	2.3	53.1	0.82	1.62	3.92	15.4	6.8	5.5	6.2	1.5	12.5	5.3	3.57
MEDIAN		59	56	24	2.4	2.3	41.0	0.83	1.71	4.00	6.0	6.0	5.0	2.0	0.0	12.0	6.0	2.03
MIN		21	18	15	1.1	0.6	8.0	0.40	0.40	1.02	0.0	0.0	0.0	0.0	0.0	0.0	0.0	0.50
MAX		246	246	128	5.8	7.1	130.0	1.33	2.21	6.27	129.0	25.0	18.5	33.6	7.0	32.4	16.7	23.47
STD DEVIATION		47	46	24	0.9	1.0	31.2	0.23	0.43	1.27	24.7	5.1	4.5	8.1	1.9	8.3	4.0	4.21

Fig. 4. Results from converting 302 ontologies from COLORE that contain at least 15 unary or binary predicates and at least 15 axioms.

the sentence by sentence conversion makes the time needed mainly dependent upon the number of candidates that need to be matched after filtering, which is linearly related to the number of FOL sentences.

The most critical evaluation aspect is the correctness of the resulting OWL2 ontologies. We have checked all 302 ontologies for syntactic correctness and conformance with OWL2-Full using the OWL API profile checker, while spot-checking adherence to more restricted OWL2 profiles when selected. The produced ontologies can also be successfully loaded in the Protege ontology development environment and be used for reasoning, such as classification, with off-the-shelf OWL2 reasoners such as Hermit.

To evaluate the quality of the produced ontologies, we primarily rely on the axiom-concept ratio as an indicator for their semantic richness in comparison to "native" OWL ontologies, which were originally developed in OWL. While our average axiom-concept ratio of 1.62 (over hierarchies) is lower than the average of 2.05 over the 518 native OWL ontologies (with over 1.7M axioms) from [7], our median of 1.71 is actually higher than theirs (1.62). That means more than half of our ontologies – which are essentially produced for free now – are already semantically richer than half of the existing OWL ontologies. The much lower variance (indicated by the standard deviation of 0.45) compared to that of 2.25 in [7] is evidence that we can consistently deliver OWL ontologies of high quality across domains – likely because of the higher quality of the FOL ontologies. With a few exceptions, such as /location_varzi/region_location.clif and the /financial/ hierarchy, this can be taken as evidence that our OWL2 outputs are already "good enough" to be usable for many practical purposes.

The generated axioms also exhibit more diversity than the native OWL ontologies. The analyzed OWL ontologies in [7] consist of 55% simple subclass axioms (varying between 41 and 62% for different benchmark sets) and 24% subclass axioms with existential quantification (someValuesFrom), while property axioms make up only 5.2% (2.4% being domain and range restrictions). Not a single disjointness axiom was found among the native OWL ontologies. These numbers confirm the perception that native OWL ontologies often leave properties underdeveloped. The stark differences in use of property axioms (over 47% of all axioms in our results) underline that translating FOL ontologies can yield OWL ontologies that may often be richer – especially in the axiomatization of properties – than native OWL ontologies.

An initially *unanticipated* side benefit is the increase in intelligibility of FOL ontologies via translations. It provides developers of FOL ontologies access to a wealth of OWL development tools. Protege's (albeit) simple taxonomic and graphical visualizations of the resulting (inferred) class and property hierarchies, especially in combination with the integrated reasoners (e.g. Hermit), allowed us to spot axiomatization errors in FOL ontologies. Identifying these issues directly from the CLIF source was non-trivial because they were the result of axioms being combined across multiple CLIF files. With the help of the OWL reasoners' justifications and the log of the OWL axioms FOL sources, we could trace the errors to the originating FOL files and specific axioms.

Limitations. As initially discussed, an ontology's theory can be axiomatized in dramatically different ways, up to entirely disjoint sets of axioms [10]. This means that some knowledge that would be relevant to an OWL version may not be explicitly represented, but only inferred. Our template-based approach currently does not aim to infer such knowledge. It would require a *semantic translation* approach that can add to the OWL ontology by strategically or systematically guessing additional axioms (e.g. predicted subclass relationships or disjointness of sibling classes) that can be added after successful proving by an FOL theorem prover. Because of the intractability of FOL reasoning, such an approach will be limited in practice. But the potential benefits can be glimpsed at through one specific example:`/multidim_mereotopology_codi/codi_with_theorems.clif` is logically equivalent to `/multidim_mereotopology_codi/codi.clif` but explicitly adds (successfully proved) theorems that, for example, establish disjointness of properties. The difference in the outcome is striking: the number of OWL axioms increases from 32 to 52, raising the axiom-to-concept ratio from a mediocre 1.42 to 2.42, the highest among all translated ontologies and landing within the top quartile of native OWL2 ontologies.

6 Related Work

The idea of translating knowledge between different knowledge representation formalisms has been studied previously, for example in the Ontolingua [9], Onto-Morph [5], and OntoMerge [6] systems and the distributed ontology language (DOL) [15], all of who aim to combine knowledge from ontologies represented in different languages. Ontolingua employs an intermediary language for which syntactic translations are defined to each knowledge representation language. OntoMorph employs direct syntactic translations between pairs of languages while also sketching the idea of semantic translations. OntoMerge also employs an internal language that is the result of syntactic translations of a source language, but then performs reasoning on the internal language before syntactically translating inferences. The DOL [15] provides a meta-language for specifying relationships between ontologies that are specified in different logical languages. However, reasoning with such heterogeneous sets of ontologies is expensive and intractable as it involves meta-reasoning over multiple logics. Moreover, as is the case with CLIF, reasoning support is limited. Currently, the heterogeneous toolset (HETS) [16] is the only tool that supports the DOL language and many available off-the-shelf reasoners for FOL and OWL cannot be reused. In contrast, our work on translation from FOL to OWL is more narrowly concerned with overcoming syntactic, semantic, and pragmatic differences between these two specific languages in order to make existing FOL more widely accessible and leverage the wider tool availability for OWL ontologies.

The theoretical basis of description logics [1] serve as foundations for bridging different ontologies languages, specifically propositional, description and first-order logic. Borgida [3] in particular provides formal translations to FOL for the syntactic constructs found in DL, the formal underpinning of OWL. These translations are leveraged here to express OWL axioms as semantically equivalent FOL sentences that serve as extraction templates.

The tool ROWLTab [18], also uses a PNF to translate from the rule-base language SWRL to OWL. But it differs in its overall goal, aiming to support domain experts in developing *new* OWL ontologies. We focus instead on creating OWL versions of *existing* FOL ontologies to increase accessibility and reuse. An example is the work by [2], who painstakingly translated a single ontology. We aim instead for less detailed but fast, cheap and fully automated translations.

7   Summary

Unrestricted usage of FOL results in an undecidable ontology [4] that effectively curbs the ontology's utilization where tractable reasoning is required. At the same time, the expressive capabilities of FOL, its flexibility, and its established formal underpinnings, still speak in favor of FOL as a representation language for reference ontologies. But existing FOL ontologies – which are the result of countless hours of ontology development and verification – are largely inaccessible to many knowledge engineers who are unfamiliar or uncomfortable with FOL. Moreover, there is a dearth of tools available to support the development, extension, or adoption of FOL ontologies. To widen the accessibility and usability of those FOL ontology, we have proposed a pragmatic ontology engineering approach to automatically extract OWL2 approximations from FOL ontologies that conform to specific desired OWL2 profiles. This essentially produces high-quality OWL2 ontologies for free now. These OWL ontologies can be inspected, extended, and used as the foundation for future development and can benefit from all available OWL tooling, such as for ontology visualization and evaluation. This helps to verify, evolve, and reuse the source FOL ontologies. More importantly, it avoids redundant ontology engineering efforts or maintaining copies of the ontologies in two languages with different expressivity (FOL and OWL).

We proposed FF-PCNF as an intermediate representation to more easily identify OWL patterns from FOL sentences despite FOL's syntactic flexibility. We demonstrated the practical usability and scalability of the approach by generating 2,241 OWL axioms from 3,387 FOL sentences in 150 s using a single core of a modern CPU and a negligible amount of memory. While the resulting ontologies make heaviest use of five OWL constructs (subclasses, domain and range restrictions, disjoint classes, subproperties), all 19 axiom templates are used to some extent.

Future Work needs to apply a broader set of ontology metrics (see e.g. [8,19]) to evaluate the produced ontologies and to identify better measures of the amount of semantics that are preserved by the translation. We further hope that our results can serve as baseline for continuous improvement of FOL-to-OWL translations. Potential avenues for improvement include tackling predicates of higher arities or inferring additional OWL axioms using FOL theorem proving.

Acknowledgment. We thank the four anonymous reviewers for their comments and suggestions that helped improve the final version.

References

1. Baader, F., Horrocks, I., Sattler, U.: Description logics. In: Staab, S., Studer, R. (eds.) Handbook on Ontologies. IHIS, pp. 21–43. Springer, Heidelberg (2009). https://doi.org/10.1007/978-3-540-92673-3_1
2. Benevides, A.B., Bourguet, J.R., Guizzardi, G., Peñaloza, R., Almeida, J.: Representing a reference foundational ontology of events in SROIQ. Appl. Ontol. **14**(3), 293–334 (2019). https://doi.org/10.3233/AO-190214
3. Borgida, A.: On the relative expressiveness of description logics and predicate logics. Artif. Intell. **82**(1–2), 353–367 (1996). https://doi.org/10.1016/0004-3702(96)00004-5
4. Brachman, R.J., Levesque, H.J.: Knowledge Representation and Reasoning. Elsevier (2004)
5. Chalupsky, H.: OntoMorph: a translation system for symbolic knowledge. In: KR 2000, pp. 471–482. Morgan Kaufmann (2000)
6. Dou, D., McDermott, D., Qi, P.: Ontology translation on the semantic web. In: Spaccapietra, S., Bertino, E., Jajodia, S., King, R., McLeod, D., Orlowska, M.E., Strous, L. (eds.) Journal on Data Semantics II. LNCS, vol. 3360, pp. 35–57. Springer, Heidelberg (2005). https://doi.org/10.1007/978-3-540-30567-5_2
7. Eberhart, A., Shimizu, C., Chowdhury, S., Sarker, M.K., Hitzler, P.: Expressibility of OWL axioms with patterns. In: Verborgh, R., et al. (eds.) ESWC 2021. LNCS, vol. 12731, pp. 230–245. Springer, Cham (2021). https://doi.org/10.1007/978-3-030-77385-4_14
8. García, J., García-Peñalvo, F.J., Therón, R.: A survey on ontology metrics. In: Lytras, M.D., Ordonez De Pablos, P., Ziderman, A., Roulstone, A., Maurer, H., Imber, J.B. (eds.) WSKS 2010. CCIS, vol. 111, pp. 22–27. Springer, Heidelberg (2010). https://doi.org/10.1007/978-3-642-16318-0_4
9. Gruber, T.R.: A translation approach to portable ontology specifications. Knowl. Acquis. **5**(2), 199–220 (1993)
10. Grüninger, M., Hahmann, T., Hashemi, A., Ong, D., Ozgovde, A.: Modular first-order ontologies via repositories. Appl. Ontol. **7**(2), 169–209 (2012). https://doi.org/10.3233/AO-2012-0106
11. Hahmann, T., Stephen, S.: Using a hydro-reference ontology to provide improved computer-interpretable semantics for the groundwater markup language (GWML2). Int. J. Geogr. Inf. Sci. **32**(6), 1138–1171 (2018). https://doi.org/10.1080/13658816.2018.1443751
12. Hitzler, P., Parsia, B., Patel-Schneider, P., Rudolph, S.: OWL 2 Web Ontology Language Primer (Second Edition) (2012). https://www.w3.org/TR/owl2-primer/
13. ISO 24707:2018 Common Logic (CL): a framework for a family of logic-based languages (2018). https://www.iso.org/standard/66249.html
14. Menzel, C.: Reference Ontologies - Application Ontologies: Either/Or or Both/And? In: WS on Reference and Application Ontologies at KI-03 (2003)
15. Mossakowski, T., Codescu, M., Neuhaus, F., Kutz, O.: The distributed ontology, modeling and specification language – DOL. In: Koslow, A., Buchsbaum, A. (eds.) The Road to Universal Logic. SUL, pp. 489–520. Springer, Cham (2015). https://doi.org/10.1007/978-3-319-15368-1_21

16. Mossakowski, T., Maeder, C., Lüttich, K.: The heterogeneous tool set, HETS. In: Grumberg, O., Huth, M. (eds.) TACAS 2007. LNCS, vol. 4424, pp. 519–522. Springer, Heidelberg (2007). https://doi.org/10.1007/978-3-540-71209-1_40
17. Motik, B., Patel-Schneider, P., Parsia, B.: OWL 2 Web Ontology Language Structural Specification and Functional-Style Syntax (Second Edition) (2012). https://www.w3.org/TR/owl2-syntax/
18. Sarker, M.K., Krisnadhi, A., Carral, D., Hitzler, P.: Rule-based OWL modeling with ROWLTab Protégé plugin. In: Blomqvist, E., Maynard, D., Gangemi, A., Hoekstra, R., Hitzler, P., Hartig, O. (eds.) ESWC 2017. LNCS, vol. 10249, pp. 419–433. Springer, Cham (2017). https://doi.org/10.1007/978-3-319-58068-5_26
19. Sicilia, M., Rodríguez, D., García-Barriocanal, E., Sánchez-Alonso, S.: Empirical findings on ontology metrics. Expert Syst. Appl. **39**(8), 6706–6711 (2012). https://doi.org/10.1016/j.eswa.2011.11.094
20. Stephen, S., Hahmann, T.: Model-finding for externally verifying FOL ontologies: a study of spatial ontologies. In: International Conference on Formal Ontologies in Information Systems (FOIS 2020), pp. 233–248. IOS Press (2020). https://doi.org/10.3233/FAIA200675
21. Wu, Z., Fokoue, A., Grau, B., Horrocks, I., Motik, B.: OWL 2 Web Ontology Language Profiles (Second Edition) (2012). https://www.w3.org/TR/owl2-profiles/

Using Compositional Embeddings for Fact Checking

Ana Alexandra Morim da Silva⬤, Michael Röder(✉)⬤,
and Axel-Cyrille Ngonga Ngomo⬤

DICE Group, Department of Computer Science, Paderborn University, Paderborn, Germany
{michael.roeder,axel.ngonga}@uni-paderborn.de

Abstract. Unsupervised fact checking approaches for knowledge graphs commonly combine path search and scoring to predict the likelihood of assertions being true. Current approaches search for said metapaths in the discrete search space spanned by the input knowledge graph and make no use of continuous representations of knowledge graphs. We hypothesize that augmenting existing approaches with information from continuous knowledge graph representations has the potential to improve their performance. Our approach ESTHER searches for metapaths in compositional embedding spaces instead of the graph itself. By being able to explore longer metapaths, it can detect supplementary evidence for assertions being true that can be exploited by existing fact checking approaches. We evaluate ESTHER by combining it with 10 other approaches in an ensemble learning setting. Our results agree with our hypothesis and suggest that all other approaches can benefit from being combined with ESTHER by 20.65% AUC-ROC on average. Our code is open-source and can be found at https://github.com/dice-group/esther.

1 Introduction

Large knowledge graphs (KGs) such as the Google Knowledge Graph [23], DBpedia [3], and WikiData [18] are now of the backend of a growing number of data-driven applications including Web search [23], community-support systems [2] and personal assistants [18] with several billion users in total. Ensuring the veracity of the assertions in such KGs has hence become mission-critical for the KG community. However, the sheer size of most KGs makes a manual verification difficult. Consequently, automated methods for ensuring the veracity of the assertions found in knowledge graphs (called *fact validation* [21] or *fact checking* [9]) are becoming indispensable.

Unsupervised fact checking approaches for KGs commonly combine path search and scoring to predict the likelihood of assertions being true [28]. To achieve this goal, several approaches rely on identifying metapaths [13,25,33] or corroborative paths [28] that are correlated with the predicate of the assertion to check. State-of-the-art approaches search for paths in the discrete search space spanned by the input KG graph and make no use of continuous representations, i.e., embeddings of KGs [4,7,16,24,31]. We hypothesize that *augmenting existing approaches with embeddings has the potential to improve their performance*. Our approach ESTHER searches for metapaths by exploiting a compositional embedding of the input KG instead of

© Springer Nature Switzerland AG 2021
A. Hotho et al. (Eds.): ISWC 2021, LNCS 12922, pp. 270–286, 2021.
https://doi.org/10.1007/978-3-030-88361-4_16

the discrete representation of the graph. By being able to explore longer metapaths, it can detect supplementary evidence for assertions being true that can be exploited by existing fact checking approaches. We evaluate ESTHER by combining it with 10 other approaches in an ensemble learning setting. The results we obtained on the benchmark datasets FB15k-237 and WN18RR corroborate our hypothesis and suggest that nearly all other approaches benefit from being combined with ESTHER by 20.65% AUC-ROC on average.

The rest of this paper is structured as follows. In the next section, related work is described. Section 3 describes preliminaries for our approach, which is presented in Sect. 4. Section 5 describes our evaluation and presents our results, which are further discussed in Sect. 6. Section 7 concludes the paper.

2   Related Work

Fact checking approaches can be divided into (1) approaches that rely on unstructured *textual* sources [9,14,27] and (2) approaches that use *structured* reference knowledge [4,21,22,24]. In this work, we focus on the second category of approaches—especially on those approaches that use a knowledge graph as reference. Path-based approaches regard a given KG as a labeled directed graph with entities as nodes and relations as edges connecting these nodes. Given an assertion in the form of a triple (s, p, o), Ciampaglia et al. [6] propose to search within the reference KG for the shortest paths up to length k that (1) connect s and o, and (2) are semantically similar to p. Their Knowledge Linker (KL) system measures this similarity based on the specificity of the path, i.e., the degree of intermediate nodes of the path. Shiralkar et al. [22] extend this idea by using the co-occurrence of properties to calculate their similarity. They propose KL-Rel as an extension of KL and Knowledge Stream (KS), which relies on multiple paths and the maximum flow between s and o. They compare their approaches with other approaches to rank paths proposed by Jeh et al. [10], Katz [12] and Xu et al. [32], and approaches that measure the similarity between two entities proposed by Adamic et al. [1], Liben-Nowell et al. [15] and Shi et al. [20]. Syed et al. [28] propose the usage of RDF Schema information, i.e., the domain and range of p. Their approach COPAAL identifies metapaths between s and o and uses the domain and range information of p to identify the set of possible subjects and objects for p in the knowledge graph. Based on this information, it approximates the normalized pointwise mutual information between the metapaths and p to identify paths that corroborate the given fact.

In contrast to these unsupervised approaches, several supervised approaches relying on metapaths have been proposed [13,25,33]. For example, Lao et al. [13] present PRA, which searches for metapaths in the knowledge graph and extracts features with these paths to train a classifier. While these metapaths have to be extracted manually by experts, Shi et al. [21] propose a method to automatically extract metapaths—called *anchored predicate* paths—given a set of labeled examples. Their approach PredPath relies on the rdf:type information contained in the input knowledge graph. All these path-based approaches are limited to shorter paths. Most of them have not been evaluated beyond a length of 3 predicates. This is caused by the large amount of longer paths that exist between s and o which lead to very high run times. Li et al. [14] propose Facty that combines evidence from different sources. Facty searches for single triples within the reference knowledge graph that contain s and o but may have a different predicate. These triples are used as pieces of evidence. In contrast to the previously mentioned approaches, Facty takes also textual sources into account. The extracted triples are combined with evidence from other sources like web searches, query logs and web tables. The authors propose a knowledge fusion algorithm that takes the pieces of evidence and information about their sources as input to calculate a final veracity score.

A related field of research which already makes use of knowledge graph embeddings is the area of link prediction [4, 16, 24, 31]. However, the problems of link prediction and fact checking are different. In link prediction, the goal is to compute how likely it is that any assertion whose subject, predicate and object belong to the input graph $\mathcal{G}$ should belong to a complete version of $\mathcal{G}$ [19]. Fact checking focuses on checking a single, given assertion based on the given graph [9, 22, 27, 28]. Key difference between these two fields also include their runtimes and applications. Fact checking algorithms are typically used in online scenarios while link prediction algorithms are used offline [28].

3 Preliminaries

This section introduces concepts that are necessary to understand our approach. It covers the definitions of RDF knowledge graphs, corroborative paths [28] and knowledge graph embeddings [4, 17, 26].

Definition 1 (RDF knowledge graph). *Let* $\mathbb{E}, \mathbb{B}, \mathbb{P}, \mathbb{L}$ *be the sets of all RDF resources, blank nodes, RDF predicates, and literals, respectively. Let* $\mathbb{E}, \mathbb{B}$ *and* $\mathbb{L}$ *be mutually disjoint and* $\mathbb{P} \subset \mathbb{E}$. *An RDF KG* $\mathcal{G}$ *is defined as a set of RDF triples of the form* (s, p, o) *with* $\mathcal{G} \subset (\mathbb{E} \cup \mathbb{B}) \times \mathbb{P} \times (\mathbb{E} \cup \mathbb{B} \cup \mathbb{L})$.

$\mathcal{G}$ can be regarded as a labeled directed graph, with triples being directed edges labeled with the property p, with the nodes s as head and o as tail. We define inverted edges by means of the inverse property p^{-1} for an existing property p as follows: $(s, p, o) \Leftrightarrow (o, p^{-1}, s)$.

3.1 Corroborative Paths

Definition 2 (Path). *A path of length* k *in a knowledge graph* $\mathcal{G}$ *is a sequence of triples from* $\mathcal{G}$ *of the form* $(v_0, p_1, v_1), (v_1, p_2, v_2), ..., (v_{k-1}, p_k, v_k)$ *[28].*

Several paths can exist between two nodes v_0 and v_k. We use $\pi^l(v_0, v_k)$ to denote these paths. Following [28], we define γ as a function from $\mathbb{E} \cup \mathbb{P} \cup \mathbb{B} \cup \mathbb{L}$ to the set of all RDFS classes, where $\gamma(v)$ is the set of all RDFS classes that v is an instance of. For example, if the RDFS classes (also called *types*) that could be inferred from a given graph $\mathcal{G}$ for the entity BarackObama using RDFS semantics were exactly Person, Politician and OfficeHolder, we would write $\gamma($BarackObama$) =$ { Person, Politician, OfficeHolder}. Let λ be a function that maps a given set of types t_x to a set of resources that are instances of at least one element of t_x by virtue of RDFS semantics.

Definition 3 (Typed paths). *The set of typed paths* $\Pi^k_{(t_x,t_y)}$ *of length k between vertices of types* t_x *and* t_y *in a knowledge graph* $\mathcal{G}$ *are defined as follows [28]:*

$$\Pi^k_{(t_x,t_y)} = \{\pi^k(v_0, v_k) \mid t_x \subseteq \gamma(v_0) \wedge t_y \subseteq \gamma(v_k)\}. \tag{1}$$

These paths can be further restricted by using a vector of properties $\vec{q} = q_1, \ldots, q_k$:

Definition 4 ($\vec{q}$-restricted typed paths). *The set of* $\vec{q}$-restricted typed paths $\Pi^k_{(t_x,t_y),\vec{q}} \subseteq \Pi^k_{(t_x,t_y)}$ *is defined as follows [28]:*

$$\Pi^k_{(t_x,t_y),\vec{q}} = \{\pi^k(v_0, v_k) \mid \pi^k(v_0, v_k) \in \Pi^k_{(t_x,t_y)}, \\ \forall i \in [0, k-1] : (v_i, p_{i+1}, v_{i+1}) \in \pi^k(v_0, v_k) \rightarrow p_{i+1} = q_{i+1}\}. \tag{2}$$

This is the set of typed paths that have exactly the properties of $\vec{q}$ as predicates of the sequence of triples the paths consist of. These paths are used by Syed et al. [28] to identify paths that corroborate the correctness of the given fact (s, p, o). To define the set of corroborative paths, we use $R(p)$ to denote the set of all types t so that p rdfs:range t can be inferred from the input knowledge graph using RDFS semantics. We also account for the practical use of our approach by considering the set $R'(p)$, which we defined as the set of classes such that the assertion p rdfs:range t is explicitly stated in the input knowledge graph. $D(p)$ and $D'(p)$ are defined analogously for rdfs:domain.

Definition 5 (Corroborative paths). *The* corroborative paths *for a predicate p are defined as follows [28]:*

$$\Pi^k(p) = \bigcup_{j=1}^{k} \Pi^j_{(D(p),R(p))}. \tag{3}$$

3.2 Knowledge Graph Embeddings

KGs are a discrete representation of knowledge. They can be embedded into a continuous space via a knowledge graph embedding (KGE). Various algorithms have been proposed to generate KGEs. Because our approach assumes that a KGE has already been generated and due to the limited space, we focus on the features of the generated KGEs and refrain from presenting much details on the single algorithms that generate them.[1] Each KGE used in this paper comes with a number of dimensions in the embedding space (n) and a mapping function $e(\cdot)$ that maps an RDF resource of $\mathcal{G}$ to a vector representation within the embedding space.

Definition 6 (Compositional KGE). *Let* p_1, p_2 *and* p_3 *be properties and* x, y, z *be nodes in the KG. A KGE is compositional if the following holds:*

$$(x, p_1, y) \wedge (y, p_2, z) \Rightarrow (x, p_3, z) \quad (\forall x, y, z) \\ \Leftrightarrow \quad e(p_1) \oplus e(p_2) \approx e(p_3) \tag{4}$$

where $\oplus$ *is an operator that combines the embedding vectors of two properties.*

---

[1] We refer to [30] for a survey of KGE techniques.

Table 1. Summary of the KGE related operations used by ESTHER and their implementation in TransE, RotatE and DensE. ∘ denotes the Hadamard product, ⊗ the Hamilton product, $\overline{e}$ the complex conjugate and $e(p)^{-1}$ the inverse of a quaternion.

ESTHER	Mapping function	Composition	Inversion
	$e(\cdot)$	$e(p_1) \oplus e(p_2)$	$e(p^{-1})$
TransE	$\mathbb{E} \to \mathbb{R}^n$	$e(p_1) + e(p_2)$	$-e(p)$
RotatE	$\mathbb{E} \to \mathbb{C}^n$	$e(p_1) \circ e(p_2)$	$\overline{e(p)}$
DensE	$\mathbb{E} \to \mathbb{H}^n$	$e(p_1) \otimes e(p_2)$	$e(p)^{-1}$

We base our search for paths in an embedding space on the compositionality assumption. Hence, we work with the following compositional KGE algorithms: TransE [4], RotatE [26], DensE [17] (Table 1).

TransE represents the property p in an assertion (s, p, o) as a translation from s to o. This is accomplished through the minimization of the L1 or L2 norm between the $e(s) + e(p)$ and $e(o)$ [4]. The model attempts to maximize the score function

$$\delta_{\text{TransE}} = -||e(s) + e(p) - e(o)||. \tag{5}$$

RotatE models the predicate p in an assertion (s, p, o) as a rotation. The predicates are represented as complex numbers. Like TransE, RotatE also aims to approximate the subject and predicate vector with the object entity's vector. $\overline{e}$ the complex conjugate.

$$\delta_{\text{RotatE}} = -||e(s) \circ e(p) - e(o)|| \tag{6}$$

$$||e(\cdot)|| = \sum_i^n ||e(\cdot)_i|| = \sum_i^n \left| \sqrt{e(\cdot)_i \overline{e(\cdot)_i}} \right| \tag{7}$$

DensE also represents predicates as rotations from the subject to the object entity. However, it does so by considering 3D rotations followed by a scaling factor on the subject entity. The predicates are therefore represented by quaternions. The quaternion modelling allows for non-abelian composition patterns, dependent on the operation direction. The dissimilarity function used is the L2-norm. $\mathcal{O}(\cdot)$ denotes the transformation applied on the entity such that $e(o)_i = \mathcal{O}(e(p)_i)e(s)_i$.

$$\delta_{\text{DensE}} = -\frac{1}{2} \left(||\mathcal{O}(e(p))e(s) - e(o)|| + ||\mathcal{O}(e(p)^{-1})e(o) - e(s)|| \right) \tag{8}$$

4   Approach

4.1   Intuition

ESTHER is built on the assumption that existing paths between s and o can corroborate the existence of the triple (s, p, o). Hence, it searches for corroborative paths $\Pi^k(p)$ as suggested by Syed et al. [28]. However, in contrast to the state of the art, ESTHER performs this search in a continuous space. There, the embedding of corroborative paths have a similar direction and length as the embedding of p. ESTHER identifies candidates for corroborative paths by utilizing the A* search algorithm. In a second step, the identified paths are scored based on their statistical co-occurrence with p. Paths that corroborate the occurrence of p are used as corroborative paths in the third step. This final step checks whether the given subject s and object o are connected with these paths. In the following, we describe the three steps in more detail.

4.2 Combining Properties to Paths

ESTHER's main objective is to assess the veracity of a given triple (s, p, o) by leveraging a compositional embedding model of the reference graph to find corroborative paths for the property p. These paths are searched in the embedding space. A good candidate for a corroborative path is a q-restricted path that (1) connects the domain and range of p and (2) has an embedding that is similar to the embedding of p. The embedding of the path is computed by combining the embeddings of the properties in $\vec{q}$:

$$\bigoplus_{i=1}^{|\vec{q}|} e(q_i) \approx e(p) \tag{9}$$

Previous approaches showed that it is beneficial for the path search to be able to use the directed edges between two vertices in both directions [22,28]. ESTHER leverages this idea by considering inverse properties for all p with $\forall(s, p, o) \in G, \exists(o, p^{-1}, s)$. As such, a set of inverse properties is defined as $\mathbb{P}_G^{-1} = \{p^{-1} \forall p \in \mathbb{P}_G\}$ and the joint set $\mathbb{P}_G^* = \mathbb{P}_G \cup \mathbb{P}_G^{-1}$ to aid in bidirectional path-finding.

When concatenating properties to create paths, the schema of the knowledge graph has to be taken into account since not all properties can be freely combined with each other. We defined an extended $|\mathbb{P}_G^*| \times |\mathbb{P}_G^*|$ property-adjacency matrix $\mathcal{M}$ that indicates whether two properties can be adjacent in a path. Since $\mathcal{G}$ is a directed graph, the pair of properties (p_i, p_j) are adjacent if the range of the first property, $R(p_i)$, fits to the domain of the second, $D(p_j)$. The matrix expresses this as follows:

$$\mathcal{M}_{i,j} = \begin{cases} 1, & \text{if properties } p_i \text{ and } p_j \text{ can be adjacent} \\ 0, & \text{otherwise.} \end{cases} \tag{10}$$

ESTHER implements five different modes to decide whether two properties fit to each other with respect to their domain and range. They are defined as follows:

Strict equality (S) : $\mathcal{M}_{i,j} = 1 \Leftrightarrow R'(p_i) = D'(p_j)$ $\qquad(11)$

Subsumed (SU) : $\mathcal{M}_{i,j} = 1 \Leftrightarrow R(p_i) \supseteq D(p_j)$ $\qquad(12)$

Non-disjoint (ND) : $\mathcal{M}_{i,j} = 1 \Leftrightarrow R'(p_i) \cap D'(p_j) \neq \emptyset$ $\qquad(13)$

Non-disjoint subsumption (NDS) : $\mathcal{M}_{i,j} = 1 \Leftrightarrow R(p_i) \cap D(p_j) \neq \emptyset$ $\qquad(14)$

Irrelevant (I) : $\forall p_i, p_j \in \mathbb{P}_G^*, \mathcal{M}_{i,j} = 1$ $\qquad(15)$

It can be seen that all modes rely on the range and domain of the properties except the I mode, which allows the combination of all properties.

Algorithm 1: ESTHER's path search algorithm

Input: $p, N, k, e(\cdot), \mathbb{P}_\mathcal{G}, \mathcal{M}, \mathcal{G}$
Output: A set of corroborative paths $\Pi^k(p)$

1   $\Pi^k(p) \leftarrow \{\}$;
2   $Q \leftarrow \{\}$;
3   **for** $i = 1$ *to* $|\mathbb{P}_\mathcal{G}|$ **do**
4   // Add properties with a domain that matches the domain of p according to $\mathcal{M}$
5   **if** $D(p_i) = D(p)$ **then**
6   // the queue takes two values: a path and its priority (i.e., its distance to p)
7         $Q.\text{add}(\{p_i\}, -||e(p_i) - e(p)||)$;
8   **end**
9   **end**
10 **while** $(|Q| > 0)$ && $(|\Pi^k(p)| < N)$ **do**
11      $\vec{q} \leftarrow Q.poll()$;
12   **if** $|\vec{q}| <= k$ **then**
13   // If the range of the last property in the path equals p's range
14   **if** $R(\vec{q}_{|\vec{q}|-1}) = R(p)$ **then**
15           $P.\text{add}(path)$;
16   **end**
17   **end**
18   **if** $|\vec{q}| < k$ **then**
19   // Extend this path
20   **for** $i = 1$ *to* $|\mathcal{M}|$ **do**
21   **if** $\mathcal{M}_{\vec{q}_{|\vec{q}|-1}, p_i} = 1$ **then**
22              $Q.\text{add}(\vec{q} \cup p_i, -||e(\vec{q}) - e(p)||)$;
23   **end**
24   **end**
25   **end**
26 **end**
27 **return** $\Pi^k(p)$;

Syed et al. [28] exclude paths with a loop in their search, i.e., while exploring the graph, the search algorithm is not allowed to visit a node twice. However, we aimed to quantify the effect of loops on our approach. Hence, ESTHER can be configured to allow or disallow loops. If loops are not allowed, the property p_i can not be added to $\vec{q}$ when extending a path if $\vec{q}$ already contain its opposite p_i^{-1}.

4.3 Path Search

ESTHER uses the A* search algorithm to find the N best corroborative path candidates for a given property p. Let d be a distance measure in the embedding space. The A* search is configured to search for paths with a length up to k that minimize the distance to the property embedding. To this end, the A* search should minimize the error ε:

$$\min(\varepsilon) = \min(d(e(\vec{q}), e(p)) + \eta|\vec{q}|) \tag{16}$$

Table 2. Example paths for the predicate `nationality` found in the FB15k-237 dataset.

q-restricted path	ε	$\zeta_{p,\vec{q}}$
`place_of_birth` $\longrightarrow$ `marriage.location_of_ceremony` $\longleftarrow$ `nationality` $\longrightarrow$	7.87	0.47
`people.place_lived.location` $\longrightarrow$ `place_of_birth` $\longleftarrow$ `sibling` $\longrightarrow$ `nationality` $\longrightarrow$	9.30	0.27
`languages` $\longrightarrow$ `countries_spoken_in` $\longrightarrow$	10.88	0.07

where η is a weight that allows to penalize longer paths. Algorithm 1 shows the pseudo code for the path search. A priority queue is used to sort the incomplete path candidates according to their error ε. The queue is initialized with all properties that share the same domain as p. In each step, the best incomplete path from the queue is selected and combined with new properties based on $\mathcal{M}$. A new corroborative path is found when the newly added property has the same range as p. The search stops as soon as N corroborative paths have been found or all possible paths with length k have been checked. Table 2 shows example corroborative paths that have been identified by the search algorithm for the predicate `nationality` in the FB15k-237 dataset (see Sect. 5). The paths show that ESTHER will make use of information like (1) the nationality of other people that married in the place of birth of the subject, (2) the nationality of siblings of people that were born in places at which the subject lived, and (3) the countries in which the language of a subject is spoken.

4.4 Path Scoring

The result of the previous step is a set of corroborative paths $\Pi^k(p)$. The second step scores these paths by measuring their cooccurrence with p within $\mathcal{G}$. Previous works [28] point out that deriving the necessary path counts is computationally expensive and provide a heuristic to compute the normalized pointwise mutual information for a q-restricted path and p. We reuse the heuristics for ESTHER but make use of the positive NPMI (PNPMI) for the path scores. Preliminary results showed that most negative NPMI values (1) were very small and, hence, statistically not reliable, and (2) reduced the performance of ESTHER. Let $\mathcal{P}(p)$ be the probability that a random triple has the property p as predicate and let $\hat{\mathcal{P}}$ denote approximated probabilities. We calculate the probability of a q-restricted path, the probability of the cooccurrence of a q-restricted path and p, and the approximation of the PNPMI as follows:

$$\hat{\mathcal{P}}\left(\Pi^k_{(t_x,t_y),\vec{q}}\right) = \frac{|\Pi^k_{(t_x,t_y),\vec{q}}|}{|\lambda(t_x)| \cdot |\lambda(t_y)|} \tag{17}$$

$$\hat{\mathcal{P}}\left(\Pi^k_{(t_x,t_y),\vec{q}},p\right) = \frac{|\{\pi^k(a,b) \in \Pi^k_{(t_x,t_y),\vec{q}} : (a,p,b) \in \mathcal{G}\}|}{|\lambda(t_x)| \cdot |\lambda(t_y)|} \tag{18}$$

$$\widehat{\mathrm{PNPMI}}(\Pi^k_{(t_x,t_y),\vec{q}},p) = \max\left(\frac{\log\left(\frac{\hat{\mathcal{P}}\left(\Pi^k_{(t_x,t_y),\vec{q}},p\right)}{\hat{\mathcal{P}}\left(\Pi^k_{(t_x,t_y)}\right)\mathcal{P}(p)}\right)}{-\log\left(\hat{\mathcal{P}}\left(\Pi^k_{(t_x,t_y),\vec{q}},p\right)\right)}, 0\right). \tag{19}$$

The calculation has to handle outliers which can be caused by the approximation. To this end, we define the score of the path $\Pi^k_{(D(p),R(p)),\vec{q}}$ dubbed $\zeta_{p,\vec{q}}$ as follows:

$$\zeta_{p,\vec{q}} = \min\left(1, \widehat{\text{PNPMI}}(\Pi^k_{(D(p),R(p)),\vec{q}}, p)\right) \tag{20}$$

Table 2 shows the scores for the three example paths.

4.5 Veracity Calculation

The veracity calculation of a single fact (s, p, o) is done by checking whether the subject s and object o of the fact are connected by corroborative paths of the previously determined set $\Pi^k(p)$. Let Z be the set of the path scores $\zeta_{p,\vec{q}}$ of all corroborative paths $\Pi^k_{(D(p),R(p)),\vec{q}} \in \Pi^k(p)$ that connect s and o at least once. The final truth score τ is calculated as the cubic mean of the scores in Z.[2] In the special case, that no corroborative paths could be identified for p 0.0 is returned. If corroborative paths have been found but none of them exists between s and o -1 is returned.

$$\tau = \begin{cases} 0.0 & \text{if } \Pi^k(p) = \emptyset \\ -1 & \text{if } (\Pi^k(p) \neq \emptyset) \wedge (Z = \emptyset) \\ \sqrt[3]{\frac{1}{|Z|} \sum_{\zeta_{p,\vec{q}} \in Z} \zeta^3_{p,\vec{q}}} & \text{else} \end{cases} \tag{21}$$

It is worth noticing that only the last step of ESTHER relies on the fact to be checked. In a fact checking scenario, the search for corroborative paths and their scoring can be done in a pre-processing step. The service that checks the single facts only has to perform the veracity calculation step. This is different to approaches other approaches like KL [6], KS [22] and COPAAL [28] that have to perform their search for paths based on the given fact.

4.6 Complexity Analysis

The complexity of ESTHER can be derived by determining the complexity of (1) the generation of the property-adjacency matrix, (2) the path finding algorithm and (3) the calculation of the PNPMI values for the top-N paths for each of the predicates. The first step is a pairwise comparison of properties and has a time and a space complexity of $O(|\mathbb{P}_\mathcal{G}|^2)$. The second step is based on the A* algorithm, which has a time complexity of $O(|\mathbb{P}_\mathcal{G}|^k)$. A single PNPMI value relies on the number of paths, the number of predicates and the number of pairs which are connected by both. Deriving the counts for the paths and the pairs that both have in common is the expensive part which grows linearly with respect to the length of the paths k. This has to be done for all N top paths for each predicate that ESTHER should support in the fact checking step. This leads to a time and space complexity of $O(kN|\mathbb{P}_\mathcal{G}|)$. Hence, the setup of ESTHER for a given knowledge graph has a time and a space complexity of

---

[2] Preliminary tests showed a good performance for the cubic mean in comparison to the arithmetic mean and the quadratic mean.

Table 3. Data statistics of FB15k-237 and WN18RR

	FB15k-237	WN18RR
Entities	14 541	40 943
Relations	237	11
Triples	289 650	89 869

$O(|\mathbb{P}_\mathcal{G}|^k + |\mathbb{P}_\mathcal{G}|^2 + kN|\mathbb{P}_\mathcal{G}|) = O(|\mathbb{P}_\mathcal{G}|^k + kN|\mathbb{P}_\mathcal{G}|)$. It should be noted that the generation of the KGE is not part of the complexity as we assume the embedding as given.

To check a single fact, the previously identified paths for p are used. In the worst case N corroborative paths have to be checked. ESTHER checks whether these paths exist between s and o of the given fact. Hence, this check has a complexity of $O(kN)$.

5 Evaluation

5.1 Datasets

We use the datasets FB15k-237 [29] and WN18RR [8]. These datasets have a size that permits the computation of embeddings in a reasonable time and, hence, have a widespread usage in works related to KGE. Table 3 gives statistical information about the datasets. Both datasets are divided in a training, validation and test split. We generate embeddings based on the training and validation data and extend the test data to be used for fact checking. We extend the two knowledge graphs with their respective ontologies (incl. type information) to ensure that the fact checking approaches can make use of them.[3] A class hierarchy is required to make use of the SU and NDS modes of ESTHER. For WN18RR, the class hierarchy is present in its ontology. However, since Freebase does not support a class hierarchy [5], we inferred the hierarchy from the existing data in FB15k-237. Given two types t_x and t_y, we consider t_x to be a subclass of t_y if all instances of t_x are instances of t_y, i.e., $\lambda(t_x) \subseteq \lambda(t_y)$.

Each dataset's test split is a set of true facts. For a fact checking experiment, a set of false facts is needed. We adopt the approach in [9] and randomly sample 750 triples, which we then corrupt to create false triples. The false triples are generated by corrupting the subject, the object and both the subject and object, each $\frac{1}{3}$ of the time. Entities are replaced with random entities of the same type as the original entities.[4]

5.2 Setup

We evaluate ESTHER in three experiments. In all experiments, the effectiveness of each fact checking approach is measured using the area under ROC (AUC-ROC), the area

---

[3] The ontology for FB15k-237 is available at https://github.com/knowledgegraph/schema. The ontology for WN18RR was adapted from https://www.w3.org/2006/03/wn/wn20/. The added information is not taken into account while generating the embeddings.

[4] The extended datasets can be found at https://hobbitdata.informatik.uni-leipzig.de/esther/.

Table 4. Hyper-parameters used to generate TransE, RotatE and DensE embeddings.

	FB15k-237			WN18RR		
	TransE	RotatE	DensE	TransE	RotatE	DensE
Dimensions	1000	1000	500	500	500	200
Learning rate	0.00005	0.00005	0.0001	0.00005	0.00005	0.0001
Batch size	1024	256	512	512	128	256
Iterations	100 000	100 000	100 000	80 000	80 000	100 000
Margin	9.0	9.0	9.0	6.0	6.0	12.0
Adversarial temperature	1.0	1.0	1.0	0.5	0.5	0.3
Neg. sample size	256	256	256	1024	512	1024

under precision recall curve (AUC-PR) and the F1-measure. The latter needs a threshold to separate positive and negative classes. We use a threshold that maximizes each approach's F1-measure.

In our first experiment, we evaluate different configurations of ESTHER on both datasets. Current surveys present over 40 different KGE approaches [11]. We have to choose a subset of the available algorithms due to limited resources. We use TransE, RotatE and DensE because they (1) are compositional embeddings, (2) represent diverse embedding spaces (real numbers, complex numbers and quaternions) and (3) are well cited.[5] The parameters used for the generation of the embeddings are listed in Table 4 and are taken from the respective publications since they were suggested for the two datasets. Only the batch size was reduced to make the embeddings work on our GPU. For each KGE, we run ESTHER with all different modes, a varying maximum length of paths $k = [1, 6]$ and different numbers of top paths $N = \{10, 20, 50, 100, 200, 500\}$. All runs are executed twice—with and without allowing loops in the paths. In all runs, the penalty for long paths η is set to 1.

In our second experiment, we compare the best performing mode of ESTHER with 10 other approaches that have been used for fact checking, namely: COPAAL [28], KS [22], Katz [12], Pathent [32], Simrank [10], AdamicAdar [1], Jaccard [15], Degree product [20], PredPath [21] and PRA [13].[6] The first 8 approaches are unsupervised while PredPath and PRA are supervised. For the supervised approaches, we perform a 10-fold cross validation to get results for all facts. In addition to the effectiveness, we measure the runtime of the single systems to evaluate their efficiency.[7]

---

[5] We use the implementation for TransE and RotatE of https://github.com/DeepGraphLearning/KnowledgeGraphEmbedding and the DensE implementation of https://github.com/anonymous-dense-submission/DensE.

[6] For our experiments, we used the source code provided by Shiralkar et al. [22] in the version of October 31st 2018 (see https://github.com/shiralkarprashant/knowledgestream). However, The source code of KL [6] and KL-Rel [22] did not work for us. Hence, a comparison with these approaches was not possible.

[7] The runtime experiments were conducted on a system with an Intel®Core™i5-7500 CPU @ 3.40GHz, 16 GB RAM and Ubuntu 20.04.2 LTS.

Table 5. Configurations of ESTHER that yield the best AUC-ROC values with the different KGEs. AUC-ROC, AUC-PR and F1-measure are shown as percentages.

	KGE	Mode	Loops	k	N	AUC-ROC	AUC-PR	F1-measure
FB15k-237	TransE	S	Y	4	200	82.53	75.79	85.50
	RotatE	S	Y	4	200	**83.07**	85.54	76.61
	DensE	S	Y	3	200	81.82	84.48	76.60
WNRR18	TransE	I	Y	3	500	**77.55**	88.61	71.06
	RotatE	I	Y	5	500	73.15	85.25	66.67
	DensE	I	Y	2	500	71.19	85.45	66.67

The third experiments combines each of the compared approaches with ESTHER. Let $\mathcal{A}$ be one of the approaches and let $\tau_{(s,p,o),\mathcal{A}}$ be the veracity score that it returns for a given fact (s, p, o). Let $\tau_{(s,p,o),\mathcal{E}}$ be the veracity score returned by ESTHER for the same fact. We collect these values for each fact and use them as input for a meta-algorithm. As meta-algorithm, we use different classifiers (Random Forest and SVM) and regression algorithms (REPTree, SMO and REPTree with bagging) which return a classification or a veracity score, respectively.[8] The meta-algorithm is evaluated in a 10-fold cross validation.

5.3   Results

The first experiment gives a large amount of results. Due to the limited space, we focus on those results that give us a good insight into ESTHER's performance. The results of the modes S, SU, ND and NDS are comparable in nearly all configurations. Moreover, ESTHER achieves better results if loops are allowed. Hence, we only report results for the modes S and I with loops. Table 5 shows the configurations of ESTHER that achieve the highest AUC-ROC values for the different KGEs and datasets. The influence of N and k is visualized in Fig. 1. For FB15k-237, the S mode achieves better results while the I mode yields better results for WN18RR. ESTHER performs better when using TransE or RotatE embeddings than using DensE embeddings.

The second experiment compares the performance of ESTHER with 10 other fact checking approaches. The left half of Tables 6 and 7 show the results. It can be seen that ESTHER performs better than most of the other approaches on both datasets. However, it is outperformed by KS on FB15k-237 and KS, Pathent and PrePath on WN18RR with respect to the AUC-ROC. The results of the runtime comparison are in Fig. 2.

The third series of experiments evaluates the combinations of ESTHER with each of the other fact checking approaches. All meta-algorithms led to an increase of the average performance. Random Forest, SVM, SMO and REPTree led to an average improvement of the AUC-ROC of 18.5%, 13.4%, 18.8% and 20.2%. REPTree combined with Bagging led to the highest average improvement of 20.65%. Because of the limited space, only the results of this meta-algorithm are reported in detail in the right half of Tables 6 and 7 for the two datasets, respectively.

---

[8] We use WEKA for all meta-algorithms. https://www.cs.waikato.ac.nz/~ml/weka/.

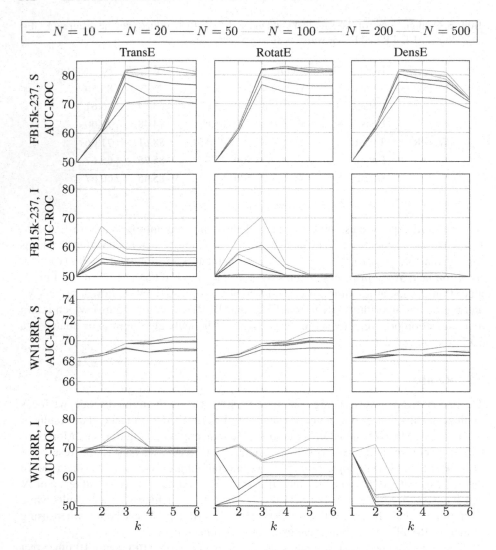

Fig. 1. AUC-ROC (in %) results for ESTHER (loops allowed) for both datasets and both modes on different embedding models and varying values for k and N.

6 Discussion

The experimental results presented in the previous Section led us to several insights. Figure 1 shows that the S mode is more stable than the I mode with respect to the increase of path lengths. Even with a k that is higher than the optimum, the performance remains high for TransE and RotatE models and high values of N. ESTHER also shows a robust behavior with high N values, i.e., the performance might decrease only slightly if N is increased while k remains the same. It can be concluded that ESTHER's scoring and veracity calculation are able to filter noisy paths that have been identified

Table 6. Performance of other fact checking approaches on FB15k-237 and their performance if they are combined with ESTHER. The number in brackets shows the performance difference.

Approach	Without ESTHER			With ESTHER		
	AUC-ROC	AUC-PR	F1-score	AUC-ROC	AUC-PR	F1-score
COPAAL	77.42	70.13	66.67	87.12 (+09.70)	85.53 (+15.40)	81.40 (+14.73)
KS	**87.59**	**83.29**	**82.75**	89.97 (+02.38)	89.08 (+05.79)	83.67 (+00.92)
Katz	82.80	80.43	78.01	86.30 (+03.50)	85.62 (+05.19)	78.98 (+00.97)
Pathent	73.46	63.87	74.68	84.75 (+11.29)	84.72 (+20.85)	77.53 (+02.85)
Simrank	40.07	44.29	66.76	81.60 (+41.53)	82.41 (+38.12)	75.55 (+08.79)
AdamicAdar	72.12	72.57	70.22	85.36 (+13.24)	85.29 (+12.72)	78.16 (+07.94)
Jaccard	38.56	46.04	66.67	82.91 (+44.35)	82.48 (+36.44)	76.24 (+09.57)
Degree product	77.11	76.20	72.87	83.28 (+06.17)	83.54 (+07.34)	78.33 (+05.46)
PredPath	69.87	77.25	68.30	83.76 (+13.89)	84.33 (+07.08)	76.95 (+08.65)
PRA	08.53	36.56	66.67	**97.44** (+88.91)	**98.09** (+61.53)	**93.44** (+26.77)

Table 7. Comparison of other fact checking approaches with and without ESTHER on WN18RR

Approach	Without ESTHER			With ESTHER		
	AUC-ROC	AUC-PR	F1-score	AUC-ROC	AUC-PR	F1-score
COPAAL	68.11	83.68	66.67	79.38 (+11.27)	86.14 (+02.46)	77.99 (+11.32)
KS	**86.44**	**90.85**	**82.96**	**94.92** (+08.48)	**96.17** (+05.32)	**89.75** (+06.79)
Katz	69.96	73.19	67.97	86.22 (+16.26)	83.19 (+10.00)	79.97 (+12.00)
Pathent	79.98	82.67	75.66	86.94 (+06.96)	90.43 (+07.76)	82.30 (+06.64)
Simrank	44.15	46.09	66.67	82.47 (+38.32)	87.25 (+41.16)	75.77 (+09.10)
AdamicAdar	59.86	64.79	66.67	84.22 (+24.36)	87.78 (+22.99)	76.40 (+09.73)
Jaccard	42.34	47.96	66.67	87.18 (+44.84)	90.26 (+42.30)	80.03 (+13.36)
Degree product	65.57	67.80	66.67	87.43 (+21.86)	90.39 (+22.59)	80.39 (+13.72)
PredPath	80.20	85.95	78.59	82.20 (+02.00)	87.43 (+01.48)	79.43 (+00.84)
PRA	71.80	85.90	66.67	75.35 (+03.55)	82.81 (−03.09)	71.06 (+04.39)

by the search but are not helpful for the fact checking task. The I mode shows in most configurations a peak. This is a hint that ignoring the domain and range gives the search algorithm the ability to find a large amount of paths that are close the given property but do not exist in practice. These paths can fill the top N in cases with longer k and replace meaningful paths that have been identified with shorter values for k. Another hint for this behavior is that the I mode works better on the dataset that contains less properties. This behavior may lead to problems in practice since it will be hard to identify the correct configuration for this peak without training data. Another insight is that ESTHER works more reliable on TransE and RotatE than on DensE models. With respect to the path length, the results on FB15k-237 show that paths of length 4 can lead to better results than shorter paths. This might be an interesting result for similar approaches like COPAAL or KS. The SU, ND and NDS modes have nearly no difference to the S mode. This is caused by the ontologies of both datasets. The SU and NDS mode would show

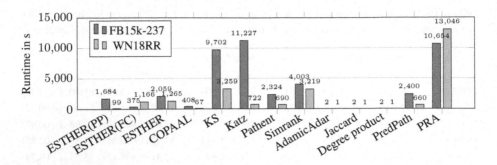

Fig. 2. Runtimes of the different approaches in seconds. For ESTHER, we report the runtime of the best performing configurations separated into pre-processing (PP), fact checking (FC) and the complete runtime.

an effect if a class is used as the range of one property and has a subclass that is used as the domain of another property. The ND and NDS mode would show different results for domain and range definitions that comprise more than a single class. Non of the situations occur in WN18RR. In FB15K-237, the S mode allows 667 property combinations while the SU mode alles 1089. This difference does not seem to have an impact on the performance and is small compared to the I mode which allows 56169 combinations. The ND and NDS modes do not add any new combinations in comparison to the S and SU mode, respectively.

The comparison of ESTHER with other approaches shows that it is able to outperform most other approaches—including COPAAL which is based on corroborative paths as well (see Tables 6 and 7). It also shows that KS performs best while Syed et al. [28] found COPAAL to perform better than KS on a DBpedia-based dataset. This underlines that FB15k-237 and WN18RR that have been used intensively in the knowledge graph embedding research area might have different features than a DBpedia or other, larger knowledge graphs. The runtime comparison shows that ESTHER has a better efficiency on FB15k-237 than most other approaches including the better performing KS and PredPath. AdamicAdar, Jaccard and Degree product are faster than ESTHER because they only compare the direct neighbors of s and o, i.e., they only take paths of length 2 into account. On WN18RR, the higher k and N values of the best performing ESTHER configuration lead to a higher runtime than most of the other approaches.

The result of the third experiment clearly show that the solution space explored by ESTHER is complementary to that explored by solutions based on discrete data. This claim is supported by the significant increase of performance for all approaches when they are combined with ESTHER.[9] Hence, a combination of approaches that are based on a discrete representation of a knowledge graph with an approach that relies on a continuous representation clearly leads to better fact checking results.

---

[9] We use a Wilcoxon signed rank test with $\alpha = 0.01$.

7 Conclusion

The goal of this paper was to measure whether the combination of information contained in continuous and discrete representations of knowledge graphs can improve state-of-the-art methods for fact checking. We presented ESTHER, the first path-based fact checking approach that makes use of a continuous graph representation by using knowledge graph embeddings. Our results suggest that ESTHER is complementary to existing approaches on the fact checking problem. In particular, ESTHER improves the performance of all other fact checking approaches if they are combined with ESTHER using a decision tree. Natural continuations of our work include using ensemble learning to combine the 11 approaches considered in this paper. Corresponding experiments will be carried out in future works. In addition, we plan to run ESTHER on larger knowledge graphs with more complex ontologies, e.g., DBpedia. However, this step depends on the development of scalable knowledge graph embedding algorithms to generate the compositional embeddings.

Acknowledgements. This work has been supported by the German Federal Ministry of Education and Research (BMBF) within the EuroStars project E!113314 FROCKG under the grant no 01QE19418. This work has been supported by the European Union's Horizon 2020 research and innovation programme under the Marie Skłodowska-Curie grant agreement No 860801.

References

1. Adamic, L.A., Adar, E.: Friends and neighbors on the web. Soc. Netw. **25**(3), 211–230 (2003)
2. Athreya, R.G., Ngonga Ngomo, A.C., Usbeck, R.: Enhancing community interactions with data-driven chatbots-the dbpedia chatbot. In: Companion of the Web Conference 2018 on the Web Conference 2018, pp. 143–146 (2018)
3. Auer, S., Bizer, C., Kobilarov, G., Lehmann, J., Cyganiak, R., Ives, Z.: DBpedia: a nucleus for a web of open data. In: Aberer, K., et al. (eds.) ASWC/ISWC -2007. LNCS, vol. 4825, pp. 722–735. Springer, Heidelberg (2007). https://doi.org/10.1007/978-3-540-76298-0_52
4. Bordes, A., Usunier, N., Garcia-Duran, A., Weston, J., Yakhnenko, O.: Translating embeddings for modeling multi-relational data. In: Advances in Neural Information Processing Systems, pp. 2787–2795 (2013)
5. Chah, N.: OK google, what is your ontology? or: exploring freebase classification to understand Google's knowledge graph. CoRR abs/1805.03885 (2018)
6. Ciampaglia, G.L., Shiralkar, P., Rocha, L.M., Bollen, J., Menczer, F., Flammini, A.: Computational fact checking from knowledge networks. PLoS ONE **10**(6), e0128193 (2015)
7. Demir, C., Ngonga Ngomo, A.C.: Convolutional complex knowledge graph embeddings. In: Proceedings of the Extended Semantic Web Conference (2020)
8. Dettmers, T., Minervini, P., Stenetorp, P., Riedel, S.: Convolutional 2D knowledge graph embeddings. CoRR abs/1707.01476 (2017)
9. Gerber, D., et al.: DeFacto–temporal and multilingual deep fact validation. Web Semantics **35**, 85–101 (2015)
10. Jeh, G., Widom, J.: Simrank: a measure of structural-context similarity. In: Proceedings of the Eighth ACM SIGKDD International Conference on Knowledge Discovery and Data Mining (2002)
11. Ji, S., Pan, S., Cambria, E., Marttinen, P., Yu, P.S.: A survey on knowledge graphs: representation, acquisition, and applications. IEEE Trans. Neural Netw. Learn. Syst. 1–21 (2021)

12. Katz, L.: A new status index derived from sociometric analysis. Psychometrika **18**(1), 39–43 (1953)
13. Lao, N., Cohen, W.W.: Relational retrieval using a combination of path-constrained random walks. Mach. Learn. **81**(1), 53–67 (2010)
14. Li, F., Dong, X.L., Langen, A., Li, Y.: Knowledge verification for long-tail verticals. Proc. VLDB Endow. **10**(11), 1370–1381 (2017)
15. Liben-Nowell, D., Kleinberg, J.: The link prediction problem for social networks. In: Proceedings of the Twelfth International Conference on Information and Knowledge Management (2003)
16. Lin, Y., Liu, Z., Sun, M., Liu, Y., Zhu, X.: Learning entity and relation embeddings for knowledge graph completion. In: Twenty-Ninth AAAI Conference on Artificial Intelligence (2015)
17. Lu, H., Hu, H.: Dense: an enhanced non-abelian group representation for knowledge graph embedding (2020)
18. Malyshev, S., Krötzsch, M., González, L., Gonsior, J., Bielefeldt, A.: Getting the most out of wikidata: semantic technology usage in wikipedia's knowledge graph. In: Vrandečić, D., et al. (eds.) ISWC 2018. LNCS, vol. 11137, pp. 376–394. Springer, Cham (2018). https://doi.org/10.1007/978-3-030-00668-6_23
19. Nickel, M., Tresp, V., Kriegel, H.P.: Factorizing yago: scalable machine learning for linked data. In: Proceedings of the 21st International Conference on World Wide Web (2012)
20. Shi, B., Weninger, T.: Fact checking in large knowledge graphs - a discriminative predicate path mining approach. CoRR abs/1510.05911 (2015)
21. Shi, B., Weninger, T.: Discriminative predicate path mining for fact checking in knowledge graphs. Knowl.-Based Syst. **104**, 123–133 (2016)
22. Shiralkar, P., Flammini, A., Menczer, F., Ciampaglia, G.L.: Finding streams in knowledge graphs to support fact checking. In: 2017 IEEE International Conference on Data Mining (ICDM), pp. 859–864. IEEE (2017)
23. Singhal, A.: Introducing the knowledge graph: things, not strings. Official google blog, May 2012. https://www.blog.google/products/search/introducing-knowledge-graph-things-not/
24. Socher, R., Chen, D., Manning, C.D., Ng, A.: Reasoning with neural tensor networks for knowledge base completion. In: Advances in Neural Information Processing Systems (2013)
25. Sun, Y., Han, J., Yan, X., Yu, P.S., Wu, T.: Pathsim: meta path-based top-k similarity search in heterogeneous information networks. Proc. VLDB Endow. **4**(11), 992–1003 (2011)
26. Sun, Z., Deng, Z., Nie, J., Tang, J.: Rotate: knowledge graph embedding by relational rotation in complex space. CoRR abs/1902.10197 (2019)
27. Syed, Z.H., Röder, M., Ngonga Ngomo, A.C.: Factcheck: validating RDF triples using textual evidence. In: Proceedings of the 27th ACM International Conference on Information and Knowledge Management, pp. 1599–1602. ACM (2018)
28. Syed, Z.H., Röder, M., Ngomo, A.-C.N.: Unsupervised discovery of corroborative paths for fact validation. In: Ghidini, C., et al. (eds.) ISWC 2019. LNCS, vol. 11778, pp. 630–646. Springer, Cham (2019). https://doi.org/10.1007/978-3-030-30793-6_36
29. Toutanova, K., Chen, D., Pantel, P., Poon, H., Choudhury, P., Gamon, M.: Representing text for joint embedding of text and knowledge bases. In: Proceedings of the 2015 Conference on Empirical Methods in Natural Language Processing, pp. 1499–1509, September 2015
30. Wang, Q., Mao, Z., Wang, B., Guo, L.: Knowledge graph embedding: a survey of approaches and applications. IEEE Trans. Knowl. Data Eng. **29**(12), 2724–2743 (2017)
31. Wang, Z., Zhang, J., Feng, J., Chen, Z.: Knowledge graph embedding by translating on hyperplanes. In: Twenty-Eighth AAAI Conference on Artificial Intelligence (2014)
32. Xu, Z., Pu, C., Yang, J.: Link prediction based on path entropy. Phys. A **456**, 294–301 (2016)
33. Zhao, M., Chow, T.W., Zhang, Z., Li, B.: Automatic image annotation via compact graph based semi-supervised learning. Knowl.-Based Syst. **76**, 148–165 (2015)

Background Knowledge in Schema Matching: Strategy vs. Data

Jan Portisch[1,2](✉) [ID], Michael Hladik[3] [ID], and Heiko Paulheim[1] [ID]

[1] Data and Web Science Group, University of Mannheim, Mannheim, Germany
{jan,heiko}@informatik.uni-mannheim.de
[2] SAP SE Business Technology Platform — One Domain Model, Walldorf, Germany
jan.portisch@sap.com
[3] SAP SE Business Process Intelligence, Walldorf, Germany
michael.hladik@sap.com

Abstract. The use of external background knowledge can be beneficial for the task of matching schemas or ontologies automatically. In this paper, we exploit six general-purpose knowledge graphs as sources of background knowledge for the matching task. The background sources are evaluated by applying three different exploitation strategies. We find that explicit strategies still outperform latent ones and that the choice of the strategy has a greater impact on the final alignment than the actual background dataset on which the strategy is applied. While we could not identify a universally superior resource, BabelNet achieved consistently good results. Our best matcher configuration with BabelNet performs very competitively when compared to other matching systems even though no dataset-specific optimizations were made.

Keywords: Schema matching · Ontology matching · Background knowledge · Knowledge graphs · Knowledge graph embeddings · Data integration

1 Introduction

Ontology matching or *schema matching* is the non-trivial task of finding correspondences between entities of two or more given ontologies or schemas. The matching can be performed manually or through the use of an automated matching system. In both cases, the context is very important and concept knowledge is required. Therefore, automated matching systems require background knowledge to excel at the schema matching task. In most cases, *WordNet* is used as a form of general concept knowledge with a plain synonym lookup strategy. However, over the last decade many other sources of background knowledge that are much larger and also contain instance data have emerged. In addition, strategies to exploit structured knowledge, such as knowledge graph embedding models, have been developed but are rarely used in ontology matching. Exploiting background knowledge for ontology matching is still one of multiple challenges that is yet to be solved [39].

© Springer Nature Switzerland AG 2021
A. Hotho et al. (Eds.): ISWC 2021, LNCS 12922, pp. 287–303, 2021.
https://doi.org/10.1007/978-3-030-88361-4_17

In this paper, we compare the performance of six different background datasets of varying size and characteristics for the task of schema matching. For each dataset, three different strategies are exploited. Besides an in-depth evaluation of the matching performance, we strive to test the following hypotheses:

H1 The strategy is more important than the resource.
H2 The resource is more important than the strategy.
H3 There is a superior resource.
H4 There is a superior strategy.

The remainder of this paper is structured as follows: In the next section, we present an overview on related work. Section 3 describes the general evaluation architecture that is used, as well as the generic matching process that was implemented for this paper. The background datasets and the strategies that are explored are presented in Sects. 4 and 5, respectively. The strategies on the background knowledge datasets are evaluated on four different gold standards in Sect. 6. The paper closes with a summary and an outlook on future work.

2   Related Work

Ontology and schema matching systems are evaluated by the *Ontology Alignment Evaluation Initiative (OAEI)*[1] every year since 2005. While, to our knowledge, there is no large comparison of different general knowledge background sources or exploitation strategies, many individual matching systems exist that make use of external background knowledge. In 2013, Euzenat and Shvaiko [5] counted more than 80 schema matching systems that exploit *WordNet*. Besides WordNet, few other general background data sources are used: The *WikiMatch* [12] system exploits the *Wikipedia* search API by determining concept similarity through the overlap of returned Wikipedia articles for a search term. *WeSeE Match* [29] queries search APIs and determines similarity based on TF-IDF scores on the returned Web site titles and excerpts. A synonymy and translation lookup strategy based on *Wiktionary* is used in [34] for monolingual and multilingual matching. Lin and Krizhanovsky [22] exploit *Wiktionary* for translation lookups within a larger matching system.

In the biomedical and life science domain, specialized external background knowledge is broadly available and heavily exploited for ontology matching. Chen et al. [4] extend the LogMap matching system to use *BioPortal*, a portal containing multiple ontologies, alignments, and synonyms, by (i) applying an overlap based approach as well as by (ii) selecting a suitable ontology automatically and using it as mediating ontology. As mappings between biomedical ontologies are available, those are used as well: Groß et al. [9] exploit existing mappings to third ontologies, so called *intermediate ontologies*, to derive mappings. This approach is extended by Annane et al. [1] who use BioPortal by exploiting existing alignments between the ontologies found there for matching through a path-based approach: By linking source and target concepts into the global mapping graph,

---

[1] http://oaei.ontologymatching.org/.

the paths that connect the concepts in that graph are used to derive new mappings. In the same domain, research has also been conducted on background knowledge selection. Faria et al. [7] propose the usage of a metric, called *Mapping Gain (MG)*, which is based on the number of additional correspondences found given a baseline alignment. Quix et al. [35] use a keyword-based vector similarity approach to identify suitable background knowledge sources. Similarly, Hartung et al. [10] introduce a metric, called *effectiveness*, that is based on the mapping overlap between the ontologies to be matched. While in the biomedical domain, many specialized resources are available and data schemas are heavily interlinked, this is not the case for other domains. As a consequence, such methods cannot be easily translated and applied.

Background knowledge sources are also used for multilingual matching tasks. Here, translation APIs are often used such as *Microsoft Bing Translator* by *KEPLER* [17] or *Google Translator* by *LogMap*.

Approaches that exploit vector representations of concepts are rarely found in the ontology or schema matching domain. The *DOME* [14] matching system employs a *doc2vec* [20] approach to concepts within the ontologies to be mapped. Similarly, *AnyGraphMatcher* [23] attempts to embed the ontologies to be mapped at runtime but achieves very low results in the OAEI 2019. *DESKMatcher* [27] applies a knowledge graph embedding approach on external knowledge but did not perform competitively in the OAEI 2020 either. *WebIsALod* is exploited as external background knowledge in [31] through a combined string matching and graph embedding strategy.

These examples show that there is a larger body of works exploiting background knowledge with various strategies; however, they are always used in the context of a larger matching system. Ablation studies and therefore statements about the utility of a particular source and/or strategy are not available.

3 General Approach

To close this gap, we propose a simple, generic matching process that can work with different sources of background knowledge and exploitation strategies. Our aim is *not* to build a top-performing matching system, but to provide a testbed for a fair comparison of different background knowledge sets and strategies.

3.1 Overview

Figure 1 depicts the architectural evaluation setting: A generic *matcher* accepts two ontologies and outputs an alignment. Thereby, it applies a *strategy* that can be exchanged independently of other matcher settings. Given labels, the matcher can ask a generic *linker* whether a concept is available in a background knowledge source. Depending on the request type, the linker returns one or more corresponding concepts from the background knowledge. For *Wiktionary*, for instance, the matcher can ask for concept European Union and the linker would return dbnary-eng:European_Union. This linking process is also known as *anchoring* or *contextualization* [6]. Now that the matcher knows the representation in the background knowledge set, it can request further information through a generic *resource wrapper* (such as similarities between concepts). Therefore, a *resource* and a corresponding *linking process* (that is wrapped by the *linker*) have to be set. The implementation allows to change the *resource* and the *linking process* independently of other matcher settings such as the *strategy*.

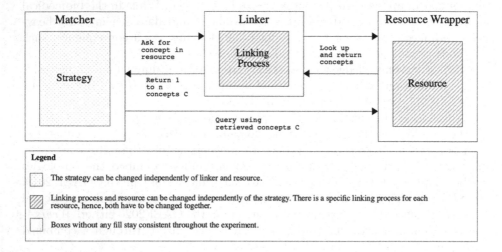

Fig. 1. Architectural setting to evaluate different background datasets exploiting different strategies.

3.2 Matching Process

The matching process can be divided into two parts: linking and matching. The linking operation is implemented as a three step process: (i) *Full Label Linking*, (ii) *Longest Token Linking*, and (iii) *Token Linking*. Later linking steps are only performed when the previous step was not able to link the label. In step (i), the full, i.e. unchanged, label is linked to a concept in the background knowledge source. Often, labels are composite concepts that do not appear in the knowledge source as a whole but in parts. To cover this case, step (ii) tokenizes labels and truncates them from the right. Linked parts are removed and the process is repeated to check for further concepts. This allows to detect long sub-concepts even if the full string cannot be found. Label *conference banquet*, for example, cannot be linked to the Wiktionary background dataset using the full label. However, by applying right-to-left truncation, the label can be linked to two concepts, namely *conference* and *banquet*, and in the following also be matched to concept *conference dinner* which is linked in the same fashion. The last fallback strategy is token linking (iii) which tokenizes each label (using spaces, underscores, and camel case recognition) and links the individual tokens to the background dataset.

After completion of the linking process, the match operation is performed. Multiple strategies are implemented here (see Sect. 5) which operate on the links. For the synonymy strategy, a match would be, for instance, annotated for *(person, individual)* given that the two labels are synonymous according to the background dataset employed. If there are multiple links (linking steps (ii) and (iii)), a match requires that every link has a matching partner (according to the strategy applied) in the set of links of the other label. In order to obtain a one-to-one alignment, the Hungarian extraction method [19] is applied.

The overall matching runtime performance is improved by adding string matches directly to the final alignment. This step runs independently of the strategy or the background dataset used. It does not skew the outcome because all strategies under consideration in this paper are purely label-based. Hence, the same label used for two entities would always lead to a match.

Overall, the matching process scales with $O(nm)$ where n is the number of elements in one ontology and m is the number of elements in the other ontology.[2] It is important to note that the scalability can be improved by adding a candidate pre-selection/blocking component. However, since scalability is not the main concern of this paper, we decided against complicating the matching pipeline.

The matcher is implemented using the *Matching EvaLuation Toolkit* [15,16] *(MELT)*[3], an open-source Java framework for matcher development, tuning, evaluation, and packaging recommended by the OAEI. The matcher is implemented so that it is possible to use different sources of background knowledge and different strategies within the matching process. The implementation of this paper (linker, background sources, significance evaluation) has been unit tested, documented, and contributed to the framework so that other researchers can use the matching parts of the implementation (e.g. to easily use Wikidata synonyms/hypernyms through an API) for their matching system.[4]

4   Background Datasets

For this paper, six knowledge graphs are exploited as background knowledge within the matching process. They are quickly introduced in the following:

BabelNet [28] is a large multilingual knowledge graph that integrates (originally) Wikipedia and WordNet. Later, additional resources such as Wiktionary were added. The integration between the resources is performed in an automated manner. The dataset does not just contain lemma-based knowledge but also instance data (named entities) such as the singer and songwriter *Trent Reznor*.

---

[2] The size of the external resource is not relevant within the matching process since all similarity functions applied here are lookup-based. When training an embedding with the external resource, the size of the resource affects scalability; however, the training is a one-time process – once the vectors are available, they can be reused in all other matching tasks.

[3] https://github.com/dwslab/melt/.

[4] https://dwslab.github.io/melt/matcher-development/with-background-knowledge.

For the embedding strategy, the RDF version of BabelNet 3.6 was used[5], for the other strategies, the BabelNet 4.1 indices.

Wiktionary is a "collaborative project run by the Wikimedia Foundation to produce a free and complete dictionary in every language"[6]. The project is organized similarly to Wikipedia: Everybody can contribute and edit the dictionary. The content is reviewed in a community process. Like Wikipedia, Wiktionary is available in many languages.

DBnary [38] is an RDF version of Wiktionary that is publicly available.[7] The DBnary dataset makes use of an extended *LEMON* model [24] to describe the data. For this work, a recent download from March 2021 of the English Wiktionary has been used.

WebIsALOD is a large hypernymy graph based on the *WebIsA* database [37]. The latter is a dataset which consists of hypernymy relations extracted from the *Common Crawl*, a large set of crawled Web pages. The extraction was performed in an automatic manner through Hearst-like [11] lexico-syntactic patterns. For example, from the sentence "[...] added that the country has favourable economic agreements with major economic powers, including the European Union.", the fact isA(european_union, major_economic_power) is extracted.[8] *WebIsA-LOD* [13] is the Linked Open Data endpoint which allows to query the data in SPARQL.[9] In addition to the endpoint, machine learning was used to assign confidence scores to the extracted triples. For this work, a confidence threshold of 0.5 for hypernymy relations was chosen. The dataset of the endpoint is filtered, i.e. it contains a subset of the original *WebIsA* database, to ensure a higher data quality. The knowledge graph contains instances as well as more abstract concepts that can also be found in a dictionary.

WordNet [8] is a well-known and heavily used database of English words that are grouped in sets which represent one particular meaning, so called *synsets*. The resource is strictly authored. *WordNet* is publicly available, included in many natural language processing frameworks, and often used in research. An RDF version of the database is also available for download and was used for this work.[10]

Wikidata [40] is a collaboratively built knowledge base containing more than 93 million data items. Like Wikipedia and Wiktionary, the project is run by the Wikimedia Foundation. It is publicly available[11] and under a permissive license. For this work, a download from March 2021 has been used.

---

[5] Unfortunately, there is no RDF version of the latest BabelNet version.
[6] https://web.archive.org/web/20190806080601/https://en.wiktionary.org/wiki/Wiktionary/.
[7] http://kaiko.getalp.org/about-dbnary/download/.
[8] http://webisa.webdatacommons.org/417880315.
[9] http://webisa.webdatacommons.org/.
[10] http://wordnet-rdf.princeton.edu/about/.
[11] https://www.wikidata.org/wiki/Wikidata:Main_Page.

DBpedia [21] is a knowledge graph that is extracted from Wikipedia infoboxes. The underlying RDF files are available for download. For this work, the latest available files as of March 2021 have been downloaded via the DBpedia Databus[12] (rather than the 2016-10 version of DBpedia that is often used).

5 Strategies

In the following, the exploitation strategies applied on the datasets outlined in the previous section are introduced.

5.1 Synonymy

The synonymy strategy exploits existing synonymy relations in the datasets. On *Wiktionary*, for instance, *tired* is explicitly named as a synonym for *sleepy*. Given two entities $e_1 \in O_1$ and $e_2 \in O_2$ of two ontologies O_1 and O_2, a match is annotated if the synonymy relation holds between at least one pair of their labels l_{e_1} and l_{e_2} according to the background dataset B that is used. This is depicted in Eq. 1.

$$isMatch_B(e_1, e_2) = isSynonymous_B(l_{e_1}, l_{e_2}) \tag{1}$$

The WebIsALOD dataset does not contain explicitly stated synonyms. Here, a synonym is assumed if both labels l_{e_1} and l_{e_2} appear as hypernyms of each other as shown in Eq. 2. This occurs more often than one might assume due to the automatic extraction process that is applied to create this knowledge graph.[13] The intuition behind the assumption here is that two things X and Y are describing the same thing if it was stated on the Web that X is a Y and that Y is an X.

$$isMatch_{\text{WebIsALOD}}(e_1, e_2) = isHypernymous(l_{e_1}, l_{e_2}) \wedge isHypernymous(l_{e_2}, l_{e_1}) \tag{2}$$

For DBpedia, the properties `rdfs:label`, `foaf:name`, `dbo:alias`, `dbp:name`, and `dbp:otherNames` are used to obtain labels, and two entities are considered synonymous if they have at least one label in common. On Wikidata, we use `rdfs:label` and `skos:altLabel` to obtain labels, and determine synonymy with the same mechanism.

5.2 Synonymy and Hypernymy

The synonymy and hypernymy strategy exploits the synonymy relations in the background datasets and, in addition, the hypernymy relations. Given two labels

---

[12] https://databus.dbpedia.org/.

[13] For example, *symposium* and *conference* are mutual hypernyms of each other in WebIsALOD.

l_{e_1} and l_{e_2} of two entities e_1 and e_2, a match is annotated if one of the semantic relations holds between the two labels as depicted in Eq. 3.

$$isMatch_B(e_1, e_2) = isSynonymous_B(l_{e_1}, l_{e_2})$$
$$\vee\ isHypernym_B(l_{e_1}, l_{e_2}) \ \vee \ isHypernym_B(l_{e_2}, l_{e_1}) \tag{3}$$

For DBpedia, the properties `rdf:type` and `dbo:type` are used to obtain hypernyms. On Wikidata, we use `wdt:P31` (instance of) and `wdt:P279` (subclass of).

5.3 Knowledge Graph Embeddings

Knowledge graph embeddings, i.e. the vector-based representation of the elements within a knowledge graph, are a very active research area in recent years. Many such methods are known [18]. For this paper, we exploit the *RDF2Vec* [36] approach: Random walks through the knowledge graph are generated starting from each node. The walks include the named edges of the graph. After the walk generation, the *word2vec* [25] algorithm is applied. Thereby, a vector representation for each node and each edge is obtained. This embedding approach has been chosen due to its simplicity, its good performance on a multitude of tasks (rather than being developed for only one task, RDF2Vec is task agnostic), its previous usage in ontology matching, and its scalability. It is important to note that the background knowledge source is transformed into a vector space – not the ontologies that are to be matched.

Two entities $e_1 \in O_1$ and $e_2 \in O_2$ of two different ontologies O_1 and O_2 are matched if their labels l_{e_1} and l_{e_2} can be mapped to a vector $v_{l_{e_1}}$ and $v_{l_{e_2}}$ in the background knowledge dataset B and the cosine similarity sim between the two vectors is larger than a predefined threshold t. Hence:

$$isMatch_B(e_1, e_2) = sim(v_{l_{e_1}}, v_{l_{e_2}}) > t \tag{4}$$

For WebIsALOD and WordNet, the pre-trained models from *KGvec2go*[14] [32] were used. The models were trained with the same configuration and, therefore, allow for comparability. Embeddings for the other three graphs are not available for download and were trained specifically for this paper.

Despite good scalability behavior of the embedding approach, vector representations for BabelNet, Wikidata, and DBpedia could not be calculated within 10 days. Therefore, *RDF2Vec Light* [33] was used for those very large knowledge graphs. The variant is based on the notion that, given a concrete task, only a small set of nodes within a knowledge graph are of actual interest. For example, given the matching task within the anatomy domain, a vector representation of *Year Zero*, a music album by the industrial rock band *Nine Inch Nails*, is not of particular interest. Therefore, a set of nodes of interest is defined in advance and walks are only generated for those. For ontology matching, the set of nodes of interest is known through the linking operation. Experiments showed that the performance of the light variant yields good results on various machine learning

---

[14] http://kgvec2go.org/.

tasks compared to the classic variant [33]. For this work, the following parameters have been used: 500 walks per node, $depth = 4$ (i.e., 4 node hops), SG variant, $window = 5$, and $dimension = 200$. For the matcher configuration, a threshold of $t = 0.7$ was used.

5.4   Combination of Sources

The combination strategy exploits all datasets at the same time with the strategies mentioned above. For the synonymy strategy, a match is annotated if any background dataset finds evidence for a synonymy relation. The same logic is also applied in the synonymy and hypernymy strategy and the embedding strategy.

6   Evaluation

We evaluate all combinations of the strategies presented in Sect. 5 and background datasets presented in Sect. 4 on four evaluation datasets: (i) *OAEI Anatomy* [2], (ii) *OAEI Conference* [3], (iii) *SAP FS* [30], and (iv) *LargeBio*. The experiments were performed on a 24 core server (à 2.6 GHz) with 386 Gb of RAM running Debian 10.

6.1   Evaluation Datasets

Dataset (i) consists of two anatomical ontologies where the human anatomy has to be mapped to the anatomy of a mouse. The *Conference* dataset (ii) consists of 16 ontologies from the conference domain and 120 alignment tasks between them. Out of those, 21 reference alignments are publicly available. The results reported in this paper refer to the available alignments. In order to allow for comparability with other matching systems, micro averages are reported; those are also reported by the *OAEI Conference* track organizers. The *SAP FS* dataset (iii) is a proprietary evaluation dataset from the banking and insurance industry consisting of 5 matching tasks. The ontologies in that dataset have been derived from conceptual data models. The dataset has been provided to the authors of this paper for research purposes by *SAP SE Financial Services*. In order to allow for comparability with the numbers reported in the original paper, macro averages are reported here. From the LargeBio track (iv), the FMA/NCI small test case is used for the evaluation here. Overall, 21 matching system variants are evaluated on four tracks with a total of 28 test cases.

6.2   Evaluation Metrics

The alignments are evaluated using precision, recall, and F_1 which is the harmonic mean of the latter two. In addition, it is evaluated whether the alignments obtained by the different strategy-source combinations are significantly different. Therefore, a significance metric is required. For this work, we use McNemar's significance test as proposed by Majid et al. [26]: Be R the reference alignment and

A_1, A_2 two system alignments. We can now calculate the two relevant elements from the contingency table as follows:

$$n_{01} = |(A_2 \cap R) - A_1| + |A_1 - A_2 - R|$$
$$n_{10} = |(A_1 \cap R) - A_2| + |A_2 - A_1 - R|$$

(5)

The significance can then be determined using McNemar's asymptotic test with continuity correction:

$$\chi^2 = \frac{(|n_{01} - n_{10}| - 1)^2}{n_{01} + n_{10}}$$

(6)

For a small sample size ($n = n_{01} + n_{10}$; $n < 25$), McNemar's exact test has to be used to obtain the p value:

$$p = \sum_{x=n_{01}}^{n} (\binom{n}{x})(\frac{1}{2})^2$$

(7)

For this paper, a significance level alpha of $\alpha = 0.05$ was chosen. As a side contribution of this work, the evaluation code for significance testing has been contributed to the MELT framework [15] to facilitate reuse by other researchers.

6.3   Results

The performance results in terms of precision, recall, and F_1 are presented in Table 1. The number of significantly different test case alignments is given in Fig. 2. More detailed performance and significance statistics as well as all alignments are available for download.[15] It can be seen that the synonymy strategy consistently achieves the highest precision throughout all background knowledge resources. In terms of F_1, the synonymy strategy performs best in most cases when evaluating the strategy on each background source separately. The only area where the synonymy strategy falls short is recall. The significance tests show that despite similar scores, the alignments within this strategy group are significantly different in 285 out of 588 cases. This is also visible in Fig. 2 which shows the number of significantly different alignments (given two matching systems). From the figure, it can be seen, for instance, that there are 22 significantly different alignments between DBpedia and Wiktionary using the synonymy strategy but only 5 different alignments between DBpedia and the combination approach using the synonymy strategy.

With the exception of BabelNet, the addition of hypernyms increases recall.[16] However, a drop in precision leads to overall lower F_1 scores (with the exception of DBpedia on SAP FS and Wikidata on FMA/NCI). The results indicate that hypernyms could be used in more complex matching strategies, e.g. as part of candidate generation. Nonetheless, a naïve merge of synonymy and hypernymy

---

[15] https://github.com/janothan/bk-strategy-vs-data-supplements/.

[16] This may seem odd at first. However, lower recall values are due to the Hungarian optimization method to obtain a 1:1 alignment, which, in that case, extracts more false positives.

Table 1. Evaluation results of six different background knowledge datasets exploiting three different strategies on four different gold standards. Note that for the *Conference* task, micro averages are used while for the *SAP FS* task, macro averages are reported. Baselines are given as reported by the OAEI organizers (FMA/NCI baselines are not provided).

Knowledge graph	Strategy	Anatomy			Conference			SAP FS			FMA/NCI (small)		
		P	R	F1	P	R	F1	P	R	F1	P	R	F1
BabelNet	SYN	0.946843	0.75197889	**0.838**	0.67711	0.565895	**0.617**	0.40352626	0.15272657	0.2215869	0.909340659	0.3696947	0.52567496
	SYN + HYP	0.9346405	0.754617	0.83503649	0.56206896	0.534426	0.5478991159	0.3358366758	0.15268351	0.214134	0.86925795	0.366344	0.515453
	RDF2Vec (light)	0.51411879259	0.6965692208	0.59159663	0.3311879	0.26880119	0.28874225	0.2061385478	0.137710	0.16511569	0.311879	0.2650811	0.28874251
WebIsALOD	SYN	0.96682027	0.6919525	0.80066128	0.6593886	0.4950819	0.56554307	0.467575	0.143885038	0.20005382	**0.979**	0.26507818	0.417228
	SYN + HYP	0.91493055	0.695290659	0.790104947	0.457642	0.5372355	0.4942554	0.349247	0.14640464	0.2063198	0.86739659	0.265450483	0.4064994
	RDF2Vec	0.7888575667	0.7011187335	0.742318435	0.26872964	0.5409836	0.3590859	0.26074486	0.13992453405	0.1821158	0.63668430	0.2688011	0.37801047
Wiktionary	SYN	0.968	0.711741	0.820220	0.690677966	0.534426	0.6025878	0.4589141	0.145607	0.2210721	0.97677419	0.281831	0.43744582
	SYN + HYP	0.9668755	0.7124011055	0.820357	0.674897119	0.5377049	0.5985401.5	0.4587493	0.145607834	0.2210530	0.97179487	0.28204	0.4373918061
	RDF2Vec	0.644016837	0.706464379	0.67337967	0.24888335.5	0.52459016	0.3375527	0.28574	0.14272146	0.19036204	0.47678795	0.282948622	0.3551401869
WordNet	SYN	0.9635555	0.7150395	0.8209011	**0.722**	0.527868	0.6098484	0.415209	0.148036455	0.2182567	0.96325	0.32204	0.48270089285714
	SYN + HYP	0.92875318	0.72222955	0.81126159	0.61363636	0.5311475	0.569420	0.3741607	0.151498959	0.2156717	0.87740628	0.3224125093	0.471549
	RDF2Vec	0.733287858	0.70910290	0.7209926	0.504672867	0.5311475	0.5311475	0.3801157542875	0.1389549784	0.203513597	0.6257621951	0.30565897	0.41070535
DBpedia	SYN	0.935569285	0.699208	0.800302	0.70892	0.49508196	0.5830115583	0.4972262675	0.14222	0.2211920	0.9165067	0.35555	0.512339
	SYN + HYP	0.935569	0.699208	0.800302	0.70892	0.49508196	0.583011583	**0.537**	0.156059908	**0.242**	0.9165067	0.35555	0.512339
	RDF2Vec (light)	0.593905817	0.707124	0.645588678	0.15437561455526	0.514754098	0.22375189	0.2224630890	0.1519484469	0.1812755	0.467644	0.343782570	0.39665523
Wikidata	SYN	0.924342105	0.7414248	0.8228404	0.636015	0.54426229	0.58657	0.44657	0.16317916	0.2390206	0.8941176	0.339538	0.4921748515
	SYN + HYP	0.9243421	0.74142	0.8228404	0.63601	0.544262295	0.58657	0.446360	0.163136	0.238943	0.89422135	0.3399106	0.4925816
	RDF2Vec (light)	0.5464720194	0.74076517	0.62895547	0.124531133278	0.544262295508	0.20268	0.2037966	0.1471509	0.17090225	0.354004	0.3209233	0.33665299
Combinations	SYN	0.881918819	0.788258	0.832462	0.49577464	0.57704918	0.53333	0.37601	0.1777831	0.24141958	0.8290155	0.476545	**0.605**
	SYN + HYP	0.81509177	**0.791**	0.8028	0.338951	0.5934426	0.4314660	0.30123	0.17875	0.22436515	0.727477	**0.481**	0.5791125
	RDF2Vec	0.24105	0.78627	0.36898	0.04960	**0.620**	0.24183006	0.13893309	**0.194**	0.162076	0.160778	0.4184661	0.2523033
Baseline	-	0.997	0.622	0.766	0.76	0.41	0.53	0.52	0.15	0.23	-	-	-

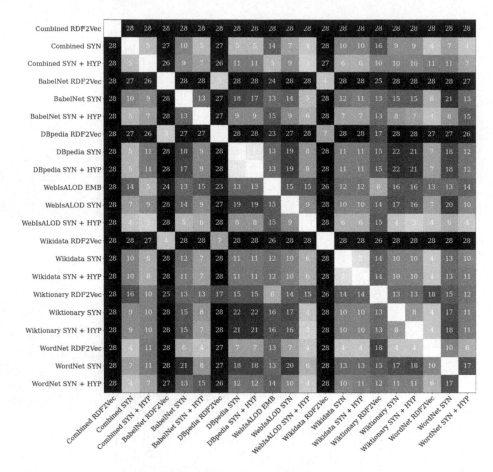

Fig. 2. Matrix with the number of significantly different test case alignments given two matcher configurations. A higher total number of significantly different test case alignments has a darker shading in the figure. In total, there are 28 test cases.

sets as main strategy is not generally suitable for precise matching on the given evaluation datasets.

The embedding-based approach falls short of performing competitively. While the recall can be increased in some cases, the method generally scores a significantly lower precision leading to an overall low F_1 score. One likely reason for the bad performance of the embeddings is that the RDF2Vec vector similarity seems to be an indicator for relatedness rather than actual concept similarity – an observation that has also been made earlier [32]. More promising usage scenarios for the embedding models exploited in this paper are likely candidate selection and hybrid strategies. Concerning significance testing, the embedding strategies produce the most significantly different alignments of all strategies evaluated in this paper. In addition, it was observed that embedding large background knowledge datasets is computationally very expensive which does not apply to the matching run time after the models were trained.

Concerning the choice of background knowledge, WordNet, Wiktionary, and BabelNet are similar in the sense that they are focused on lexical facts. Babel-Net, the largest of the three, scores the overall best F_1 score on Anatomy and Conference. On the remaining two tracks, the performance is competitive.

Despite its small size, WordNet also achieves competitive results compared to Wiktionary on Anatomy, Conference, and SAP FS and outperforms the latter significantly on the LargeBio task. Nevertheless, unlike WordNet, Wiktionary and BabelNet are constantly growing over time due to a community-driven creation process and might outperform WordNet in the long run.

DBpedia performs in the mid-range in terms of F_1. The recall is lower than that of the better performing systems (BabelNet, Wiktionary, WordNet). The most likely explanation is a lower concept coverage since DBpedia contains rather instances than class concepts. Interestingly, the addition of hypernyms has rarely any effect on this particular background source.

Wikidata performed similarly to DBpedia. Like the latter dataset, the addition of hypernyms does not change the results significantly.

The WebIsALOD dataset achieves the lowest overall results. The most likely reason is that the dataset is not authored but automatically built leading to a lot of noise contained in the dataset (wrong hypernyms). The comparatively bad performance of the synonymy strategy may be grounded in the fact that WebIsALOD is the only graph evaluated here that does not explicitly state synonyms – but instead those are derived, as outlined before, which is less precise.

The combination of different background knowledge sources increases the recall in all cases. Except on the LargeBio dataset, the drop in precision cannot make up for increases in recall.

When comparing the performance numbers on evaluation dataset level, it can be seen that the *Anatomy* matching task achieves the best results – this is likely due to a high textual overlap of the labels. On the *Conference* task, the matchers achieve a lower precision and recall score. These observations are in line with those at *OAEI* campaigns. On the domain specific *SAP FS* dataset, it can be seen that recall and precision scores are low. Likely explanations here are a domain specific vocabulary, low explicitness of knowledge (many semantic details are hidden in lengthy descriptions) as well as a complex many-to-many matching problem (see [30] for details).

It is important to note that the work presented here is not intended to be a full-scale matching system but rather a comparison of different background knowledge datasets and exploitation strategies. Nonetheless, the performance of the best matching results achieved here on *Anatomy* and *Conference* are comparable to *OAEI* matching results reported in the most recent 2020 campaign. A comparison in terms of F_1 is depicted in Fig. 3. It can be seen, that the best configuration of this paper performs in both cases above the median of the systems submitted in 2020. On Anatomy, it is noteworthy, that the first three systems (AML, Lily, and LogMapBio) use domain-specific resources leading to an advantage over the general-purpose resources exploited in this work.

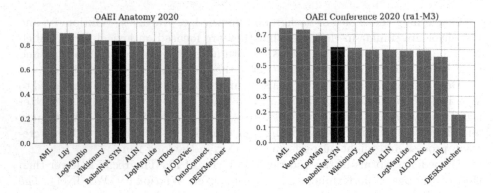

Fig. 3. Performance in terms of F_1 on the OAEI Anatomy and Conference tracks of 2020.

Hypotheses. In order to evaluate hypotheses 1 and 2, we averaged the relative share of significantly different alignments on all test cases (i) while keeping the background source constant and changing the strategy (Eq. 8) and (ii) while keeping the strategy constant and changing the background source (Eq. 9):

$$impact_{strategy} = \frac{\sum_{bk \in BK} \frac{\sum_{tc \in TC} \sum_{s_1 \in S} \sum_{s_2 \in S} sig(m(bk,s_1),m(bk,s_2))}{|TC|*|S|^2-|TC|*|S|}}{|BK|} \tag{8}$$

$$impact_{source} = \frac{\sum_{s \in S} \frac{\sum_{tc \in TC} \sum_{bk_1 \in BK} \sum_{bk_2 \in BK} sig(m(bk_1,s),m(bk_2,s))}{|TC|*|BK|^2-|BK|*|S|}}{|S|} \tag{9}$$

where S is the set of strategies, BK is the set of background sources, $sig(align$-$ment_1, alignment_2)$ is the significance function which will return 1 if the two provided alignments are significantly different and else 0, and $m(bk, s)$ is the matching function which returns the alignment by using the specified background knowledge source bk and strategy s.

While keeping the background knowledge source constant and changing the strategy, we observed on average 57.5% significantly different alignments with a standard deviation of $\sigma = 0.163$. On the other hand, while keeping the strategy constant and changing the background knowledge source, we obtained on average 51.76% significantly different alignments with a standard deviation of $\sigma = 0.181$. Given our experimental setup, we hence accept H1 and reject H2 since a variation in the strategic component has a higher impact on the alignments than a variation of the background sources under consideration in this study. It is noteworthy that both components lead on average to more than 50% significantly different alignments. Since our results do not indicate that there is a superior resource over all test sets, we can reject H3. However, it is noteworthy that BabelNet achieves consistently good (on two tracks the best) results in terms of F_1 when using the synonymy strategy. Similarly, we do not find a superior strategy over each and every single test case and reject H4 – but yet, the synonymy strategy achieved the best F_1 score on 3 out of 4 tracks and consistently performed very well compared to the other strategies.

7   Summary and Future Work

In this paper, we evaluated three different matching strategies using six different general purpose knowledge graphs on various evaluation datasets. We find that the strategy influences the final alignment more than the underlying dataset. Given the strategies evaluated here, those exploiting explicitly stated knowledge outperform a latent strategy. However, the exploitation of graph embeddings for data integration and schema matching is novel and its performance is still very low. While no superior general knowledge dataset could be identified, BabelNet produced consistently good or the best results. The humanly verified datasets outperformed the automatic generated one. Concerning the level of authoring between the datasets, the results indicate no clear superiority of expert-validated knowledge graphs over those created and validated by an open community.

In the future, we plan to exploit further embedding strategies, such as translational approaches, for schema matching as well as graph-based and dataset specific strategies. We further plan to examine more domain-specific matching tasks such as the *SAP FS* dataset.

References

1. Annane, A., Bellahsene, Z., Azouaou, F., Jonquet, C.: Selection and combination of heterogeneous mappings to enhance biomedical ontology matching. In: Blomqvist, E., Ciancarini, P., Poggi, F., Vitali, F. (eds.) EKAW 2016. LNCS (LNAI), vol. 10024, pp. 19–33. Springer, Cham (2016). https://doi.org/10.1007/978-3-319-49004-5_2
2. Bodenreider, O., Hayamizu, T.F., Ringwald, M., de Coronado, S., Zhang, S.: Of mice and men: aligning mouse and human anatomies. In: AMIA 2005 (2005)
3. Cheatham, M., Hitzler, P.: Conference v2.0: an uncertain version of the OAEI conference benchmark. In: Mika, P., et al. (eds.) ISWC 2014. LNCS, vol. 8797, pp. 33–48. Springer, Cham (2014). https://doi.org/10.1007/978-3-319-11915-1_3
4. Chen, X., Xia, W., Jiménez-Ruiz, E., Cross, V.V.: Extending an ontology alignment system with bioportal: a preliminary analysis. In: ISWC 2014 Posters & Demonstrations Track. CEUR Workshop Proceedings, vol. 1272, pp. 313–316 (2014)
5. Euzenat, J.: Ontology Matching, 2nd edn. Springer, New York (2013). https://doi.org/10.1007/978-3-642-38721-0
6. Euzenat, J., Shvaiko, P.: Matching strategies. In: Ontology Matching, pp. 149–197. Springer, Heidelberg (2013). https://doi.org/10.1007/978-3-642-38721-0_7
7. Faria, D., Pesquita, C., Santos, E., Cruz, I.F., Couto, F.M.: Automatic background knowledge selection for matching biomedical ontologies. PloS One **9**(11) (2014)
8. Fellbaum, C. (ed.): WordNet: An Electronic Lexical Database. Language, Speech, and Communication. MIT Press, Cambridge (1998)

9. Groß, A., Hartung, M., Kirsten, T., Rahm, E.: Mapping composition for matching large life science ontologies. In: Proceedings of the 2nd International Conference on Biomedical Ontology. CEUR Workshop Proceedings, vol. 833 (2011)

10. Hartung, M., Gross, A., Kirsten, T., Rahm, E.: Effective composition of mappings for matching biomedical ontologies. In: Simperl, E., et al. (eds.) ESWC 2012. LNCS, vol. 7540, pp. 176–190. Springer, Heidelberg (2015). https://doi.org/10.1007/978-3-662-46641-4_13

11. Hearst, M.A.: Automatic acquisition of hyponyms from large text corpora. In: 14th International Conference on Computational Linguistics, COLING 1992, Nantes, France, 23–28 August 1992, pp. 539–545 (1992)

12. Hertling, S., Paulheim, H.: WikiMatch - Using Wikipedia for ontology matching. In: OM@ISWC 2012, vol. 946, pp. 37–48 (2012)

13. Hertling, S., Paulheim, H.: WebIsALOD: providing hypernymy relations extracted from the web as linked open data. In: d'Amato, C., et al. (eds.) ISWC 2017. LNCS, vol. 10588, pp. 111–119. Springer, Cham (2017). https://doi.org/10.1007/978-3-319-68204-4_11

14. Hertling, S., Paulheim, H.: DOME results for OAEI 2018. In: OM@ISWC 2018, pp. 144–151 (2018)

15. Hertling, S., Portisch, J., Paulheim, H.: MELT - matching EvaLuation toolkit. In: Acosta, M., Cudré-Mauroux, P., Maleshkova, M., Pellegrini, T., Sack, H., Sure-Vetter, Y. (eds.) SEMANTiCS 2019. LNCS, vol. 11702, pp. 231–245. Springer, Cham (2019). https://doi.org/10.1007/978-3-030-33220-4_17

16. Hertling, S., Portisch, J., Paulheim, H.: Supervised ontology and instance matching with MELT. In: OM@ISWC 2020. CEUR Workshop Proceedings, vol. 2788, pp. 60–71 (2020). CEUR-WS.org

17. Kachroudi, M., Diallo, G., Yahia, S.B.: KEPLER at OAEI 2018. In: OM@ISWC 2018, pp. 173–178 (2018)

18. Kazemi, S.M., et al.: Relational representation learning for dynamic (knowledge) graphs: a survey. CoRR abs/1905.11485 (2019)

19. Kuhn, H.W.: The Hungarian method for the assignment problem. Naval Res. Logistics Q. 2(1–2), 83–97 (1955)

20. Le, Q.V., Mikolov, T.: Distributed representations of sentences and documents. In: Proceedings of the 31th International Conference on Machine Learning (ICML), pp. 1188–1196 (2014)

21. Lehmann, J., et al.: DBpedia - a large-scale, multilingual knowledge base extracted from Wikipedia. Semant. Web 6(2), 167–195 (2015)

22. Lin, F., Krizhanovsky, A.: Multilingual ontology matching based on Wiktionary data accessible via SPARQL endpoint. In: RCDL 2011. CEUR Workshop Proceedings, vol. 803, pp. 1–8 (2011)

23. Lütke, A.: AnyGraphMatcher submission to the OAEI knowledge graph challenge 2019. In: OM@ISWC 2019 (2019)

24. McCrae, J., et al.: Interchanging lexical resources on the Semantic Web. Lang. Resour. Eval. 46(4), 701–719 (2012)

25. Mikolov, T., Sutskever, I., Chen, K., Corrado, G.S., Dean, J.: Distributed representations of words and phrases and their compositionality. In: 27th Annual Conference on Neural Information Processing Systems 2013, pp. 3111–3119 (2013)

26. Mohammadi, M., Atashin, A.A., Hofman, W., Tan, Y.: Comparison of ontology alignment systems across single matching task via the Mcnemar's test. ACM Trans. Knowl. Discov. Data 12(4), 51:1–51:18 (2018)

27. Monych, M., Portisch, J., Hladik, M., Paulheim, H.: DESKMatcher. In: OM@ISWC 2020. CEUR Workshop Proceedings, vol. 2788, pp. 181–186 (2020)

28. Navigli, R., Ponzetto, S.P.: BabelNet: the automatic construction, evaluation and application of a wide-coverage multilingual semantic network. Artif. Intell. **193**, 217–250 (2012)
29. Paulheim, H.: WeSeE-match results for OEAI 2012. In: OM@ISWC 2012 (2012)
30. Portisch, J., Hladik, M., Paulheim, H.: Evaluating ontology matchers on real-world financial services data models. In: Posters & Demos of SEMANTiCS 2019 (2019)
31. Portisch, J., Hladik, M., Paulheim, H.: Alod2vec matcher results for OAEI 2020. In: Shvaiko, P., Euzenat, J., Jiménez-Ruiz, E., Hassanzadeh, O., Trojahn, C. (eds.) OM@ISWC 2020. CEUR Workshop Proceedings, vol. 2788, pp. 147–153 (2020)
32. Portisch, J., Hladik, M., Paulheim, H.: KGvec2go - knowledge graph embeddings as a service. In: Proceedings of the International Conference on Language Resources and Evaluation (LREC), Marseille, France (2020)
33. Portisch, J., Hladik, M., Paulheim, H.: Rdf2Vec light - a lightweight approach for knowledge graph embeddings. In: ISWC 2020 Demos and Industry Tracks. CEUR Workshop Proceedings, vol. 2721, pp. 79–84 (2020)
34. Portisch, J., Paulheim, H.: Wiktionary matcher results for OAEI 2020. In: OM@ISWC 2020. CEUR Workshop Proceedings, vol. 2788, pp. 225–232 (2020)
35. Quix, C., Roy, P., Kensche, D.: Automatic selection of background knowledge for ontology matching. In: SWIM 2011, p. 5. ACM (2011)
36. Ristoski, P., Rosati, J., Noia, T.D., Leone, R.D., Paulheim, H.: Rdf2vec: RDF graph embeddings and their applications. Semant. Web **10**(4), 721–752 (2019)
37. Seitner, J., et al.: A large database of hypernymy relations extracted from the web. In: LREC 2016 (2016)
38. Sérasset, G.: DBnary: Wiktionary as a lemon-based multilingual lexical resource in RDF. Semant. Web **6**(4), 355–361 (2015)
39. Shvaiko, P., Euzenat, J.: Ontology matching: state of the art and future challenges. IEEE Trans. Knowl. Data Eng. **25**(1), 158–176 (2013)
40. Vrandečić, D., Krötzsch, M.: Wikidata: a free collaborative knowledgebase. Commun. ACM **57**(10), 78–85 (2014)

A Graph-Based Approach for Inferring Semantic Descriptions of Wikipedia Tables

Binh Vu[(✉)], Craig A. Knoblock, Pedro Szekely, Minh Pham, and Jay Pujara

USC Information Sciences Institute, Marina Del Rey, CA 90292, USA
{binhvu,knoblock,pszekely,minhpham,jpujara}@isi.edu

Abstract. There are millions of high-quality tables available in Wikipedia. These tables cover many domains and contain useful information. To make use of these tables for data discovery or data integration, we need precise descriptions of the concepts and relationships in the data, known as semantic descriptions. However, creating semantic descriptions is a complex process requiring considerable manual effort and can be error prone. In this paper, we present a novel probabilistic approach for automatically building semantic descriptions of Wikipedia tables. Our approach leverages hyperlinks in a Wikipedia table and existing knowledge in Wikidata to construct a graph of possible relationships in the table and its context, and then it uses collective inference to distinguish genuine and spurious relationships to form the final semantic description. In contrast to existing methods, our solution can handle tables that require complex semantic descriptions of n-ary relations (e.g., the population of a country in a particular year) or implicit contextual values to describe the data accurately. In our empirical evaluation, our approach outperforms state-of-the-art systems on the SemTab2020 dataset and outperforms those systems by as much as 28% in F1 score on a large set of Wikipedia tables.

Keywords: Semantic models · Semantic descriptions · Knowledge graphs · Probabilistic soft logic · Semantic web · Linked data · Ontology

1 Introduction

Wikipedia is one of the largest encyclopedias in the world. Extracting and integrating the structured data from Wikipedia to knowledge graphs (KGs) can bring great benefits to many applications. DBpedia, a popular KG, has shown the success and impact of such a strategy, but only uses infoboxes. Besides these infoboxes, Wikipedia also has millions of high-quality tables covering a wide range of domains. Leveraging these tables can potentially help to add or keep the knowledge in KGs up-to-date. For example, in an evaluation dataset collected from Wikipedia (Sect. 4.1), we found that approximately 64% of the relationships in the data in these tables are not present in Wikidata. However, it is challenging to make use of these tables on a large scale as they are stored in different schemas. The task of building semantic descriptions of tables (also

© Springer Nature Switzerland AG 2021
A. Hotho et al. (Eds.): ISWC 2021, LNCS 12922, pp. 304–320, 2021.
https://doi.org/10.1007/978-3-030-88361-4_18

called semantic modeling [19, 20]) addresses this challenge by precisely describing concepts and relationships contained in the data in a machine-readable form. A semantic description of a table is a graph where each node represents either an ontology class, a column, an entity, or a literal (e.g., number, text, or date), and each edge represents an ontology property encoding a relationship between the two nodes (Fig. 1). From the semantic description, we can automatically generate mapping rules of mapping languages such as RML [4] or D-REPR [21] to convert the table data to RDF triples to import into KGs.

Since creating semantic descriptions requires significant effort and expertise [9], there are many studies to address this problem. Generally, they can be placed into two groups. The first group is supervised methods trained on a set of known semantic descriptions with given domain ontologies [19, 20]. These methods are difficult to apply to the Wikipedia tables as there is little training data available. The second group is methods that utilize KGs such as DBpedia [3, 16] or Wikidata [13, 18] to integrate data from tables. The intuition of these approaches is that the overlap between entities in a table with entities in KGs can be used to recover the semantic description of the table. Specifically, by matching the property values of the overlapped entities with other cells in the table, they can predict binary relationships between two columns based on the matched properties and column types using the types of the entitites.

Approaches in the second group can be applied to map the Wikipedia tables and generally do not require retraining their systems when the KG ontology is updated. However, they have two main limitations. First, their methods only consider values inside the tables but not values in the surrounding context. We found in many tables that the implicit contextual values are critical to understanding the semantics of a table. For example, a table about cast members of a movie and their roles typically does not have the movie in the table data as it is mentioned in the context. Second, they do not deal with n-ary relations needed to accurately and fully represent knowledge in the tables. Examples of n-ary relations are a politician elected to an office position from an electoral district or sales of a company reported in a particular year.

To address these issues, we present a new approach for semantic modeling that uses graphs to represent possible (n-ary) relationships in the tables and collective inference to eliminate spurious relationships on the graphs. Specifically, we construct a candidate graph containing relationships between table columns and its context values by leveraging possible connections between data in the table and existing knowledge in Wikidata. Then, incorrect relationships in the candidate graph are detected and removed using a Probabilistic Soft Logic (PSL) [1] model. Through collective inference, the PSL model favors links with high confidence, more informative, and consistent with constraints in the ontology and existing knowledge in Wikidata. To assess the effectiveness of our method, we evaluate our method on a real-world dataset for mapping tables to Wikidata and on the dataset from the SemTab2020 challenge [6]. These experiments show that our method outperforms the state-of-the-art systems on all datasets, with an improvement of 28% F_1 score on the real-world dataset.

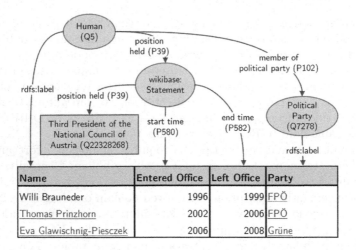

Fig. 1. A table of third presidents of the National Council of Austria with its semantic description on top. The node `wikibase:Statement` is used to represent an n-ary relationship of a position (Third President) and its start and end time. The position is not in the table but is introduced via an entity (the green node). (Color figure online)

The contribution of this paper is a novel graph-based method for semantic modeling that collectively determines correct relationships between two or more columns and implicit contextual values using PSL. Our solution offers two key technologies: (i) an algorithm to construct a graph of plausible semantic descriptions of tables using external knowledge from Wikidata and (ii) a probabilistic model that utilizes features from external knowledge and related relationships in the graph for robust relationship prediction.

2   Motivating Example

In this section, we explain the problem by giving an example of mapping a real table about the third presidents of the National Council of Austria to Wikidata. This example is also used throughout the paper to illustrate the steps of our approach. We also interchangeably refer to Wikidata entities, classes (Qnodes), and properties (Pnodes) either by their labels and ids (e.g., `Human (Q5)`) or just by their ids (e.g., `Q5`).

Figure 1 shows a snippet of the table at the bottom and its semantic description on the top. In the figure, yellow nodes represent ontology classes, green nodes represent entities or literals, and edges are ontology properties. For example, the link `rdfs:label` between the node `Human (Q5)` and the first column depicts that each cell in the column is a person whose name is specified in the value of that cell. Similarly, the link `P102` between the class `Human (Q5)` and `Political Party (Q7278)` states that each person is a member of the corresponding political party. The property `position held (P39)` connects the node `Q5` to an entity `Q22328268` and columns `Entered Office` and `Left Office` to describe the time each person holds the third president position. This is an n-ary relationship and is represented by an intermediate `wikibase:Statement` node. Note that in Wikidata every claim is represented as a statement, so there is a statement node for the relationship P102 of node Q5 and node Q7278. However, since this is a binary relationship, we have omitted the statement node for conciseness.

In the table, some cells are linked to Wikipedia articles such as Eva Glawischnig-Piesczek (3rd row, 1st column). By querying Wikidata to obtain a Qnode associated with the `Eva Glawischnig-Piesczek` article, we know that she was the `third president of the National Council of Austria` (Q22328268) from 2006 to 2008. As the information appears in the same row of the 2nd and 3rd columns, this suggests that `start time` (P580) and `end time` (P582) could be the relationships between those columns and of an n-ary relationship `position held` (P39) of Q22328268. Following this process, we may discover in the second row that `Thomas Prinzhorn` was a second president, and he left the office in 2002, while there may be no suggestions from data in the 1st row as `Wilhelm Brauneder` does not link to any Qnode.

From this example, we observe that matching table data to KGs can suggest correct semantic descriptions. Yet, predictions solely relying on data matching can be imprecise. To go beyond simple data matching, we develop a graph-based approach that uses a probabilistic graphical model to combine evidence from external knowledge and related possible matched relationships to predict the most probable semantic description.

3   Building Semantic Descriptions of Tables

The problem of finding semantic descriptions of Wikipedia tables is defined as follows. Let T be a linked relational table, in which a cell $c_{i,j}$ of row i, column j may link to entities in a target KG, $C = \{v_1, v_2, ..., v_n\}$ be a set of values (literals or entities in KG) found in the surrounding context of T. We want to find the semantic description $sm(T, C)$ of T with respect to its context C.

Our approach consists of two main steps. The first step is to build a candidate graph of relationships between columns and context values. Then, we use collective inference to identify correct relationships and correct types of columns containing entities (called entity columns) to create a final semantic description.

Preprocessing. Since we use Wikidata as the target KG, the semantic description will be described in terms of the Wikidata ontology. Classes of the ontology are all Qnodes participating in the `subclass of` (P279) relationship, and properties of the ontology are all Wikidata properties and the `rdfs:label` property. Also, cells in the Wikipedia tables are not directly linked to Wikidata entities but have hyperlinks to Wikipedia articles. Thus, we apply a preprocessing step to automatically convert the hyperlinks to Wikipedia articles to Wikidata entities using Wikidata sitelinks.

3.1   Constructing Candidate Graphs

To create a candidate graph, we first create a data graph of all possible relationships between table cells and table context. Then, we summarize the data

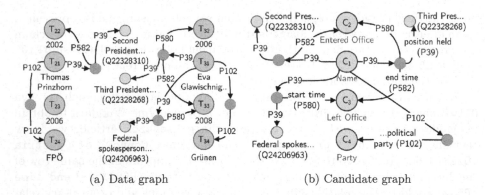

(a) Data graph   (b) Candidate graph

Fig. 2. Excerpts of a data graph and a candidate graph built from the data graph for the table in Fig. 1. Some edges are displayed without their full labels for readability. Grey, blue, yellow, and green nodes are statements, table cells, table columns, and entities, respectively.

graph to obtain relationships between columns and table context. This approach makes it easy to handle n-ary relations and infer missing links.

Constructing Data Graphs. Algorithm 1 outlines the process of building a data graph. To begin with, we add cells of T and items in C as nodes to an empty graph G_d (line 1–5). Then, we find paths in Wikidata that connect two nodes in G_d using two functions FindEnt2EntPaths and FindEnt2LiteralPaths (lines 8–11). The former function simply returns paths between two entities in Wikidata. The latter function returns paths from an entity to a literal. Since literals in the table are not always matched exactly with the corresponding values in the KG, we "fuzzy" match literals depending on their types. For example, numbers are matched if they are within a 5% range; dates are matched if they are equal or their years are equal (when the literals only have years); strings are matched if they are the same. The function FindEnt2EntPaths has an extra parameter max_hop controlling the length of discovered paths. If the maximum hop is two, a path can reach a target literal or entity via an intermediate entity in Wikidata. If the target entity or literal is found in qualifiers of statements, we also return extra paths from the source entity to the statements' values in order to comply with the Wikidata data model. Note that we only need to find paths between pairs of nodes that can be linked (line 7). Two nodes are linkable when they are cells of the same record (i.e., in the same row), or one node is a cell and the other node is a value in the context.

The discovered paths will then be added to G_d such that the original identifiers of Wikidata statements and entities are preserved (line 12). This allows paths of n-ary relationships to be connected automatically as they share the same Wikidata statements. Figure 2a shows an excerpt of the data graph for the table in the motivating example after this step.

Algorithm 1: CONSTRUCT DATA GRAPH

Input: Input table T, Input context $\mathcal{C} = \{v_1, ..., v_n\}$, Max hop max_hop
Output: the data graph G_d

1   $G_d \leftarrow$ empty graph
2   add cells in the table ($c_{i,j} \in T$.cells) as nodes to G_d
3   add values in the context ($v_i \in \mathcal{C}$) as nodes to G_d
4   newPaths $\leftarrow []$
5   **for** $n_i \leftarrow G_d$.nodes **do**
6   **for** $n_j \leftarrow G_d$.nodes **do**
7   **if** CanLink (n_i, n_j) **then**
8   **for** $e_i \leftarrow n_i$.linkedEntities **do**
9   **for** $e_j \leftarrow n_j$.linkedEntities **do**
10   add FindEnt2EntPaths (e_i, e_j, max_hop) to newPaths
11   add FindEnt2LiteralPaths (e_i, n_j) to newPaths

12 AddPaths $(G_d,$ newPaths$)$
13 InferMissingLinks (G_d)
14 **return** G_d

Finally, we run inference on G_d to complete missing links based on logical rules specified in the Wikidata ontology. Specifically, our ad-hoc rule-based reasoner uses sub-property, inverse, and transitive rules. The intuition is that the final graph G_d after inference should be the same as if we run inference on the KG, then build the data graph G_d.

Constructing Candidate Graphs. With the data graph G_d built from the previous step, we will summarize it to create a super graph of plausible semantic descriptions. The step is similar to a reversion of the process that generates an RDF graph from the semantic description of the table. Specifically, relationships of cells of two columns or of cells of a column and a context value are consolidated if they are of the same property. For example, in Fig. 2b, relationships P102 between cells of columns 1 and 2 are grouped to be represented as one edge P102 between these columns in the graph.

This idea is implemented in Algorithm 2. It starts by adding columns in the tables (line 1–2) as nodes to G_s. Then, we add literal or entities nodes in G_d to G_s keeping their original id (line 3). Next, for each pair of nodes (u_d and v_d) in G_d in which v_d is the value of a property e of u_d specified by statement node stmt_d (lines 4–7), we find the corresponding nodes of u_d and v_d in G_s called u_s and v_s, respectively (line 8). If u_d is a cell node, then its corresponding node u_s in G_s will be the column node; otherwise, u_s will be the node of the same id. Next, we add a new statement node stmt_s of the relationship e between u_s and v_s if it does not exist (lines 9–11). After that, we add new qualifiers to stmt_s based on qualifiers of stmt_d with a similar manner (line 13–16).

Algorithm 2: CONSTRUCT CANDIDATE GRAPH

    Input: A data graph G_d, Input table T
    Output: the candidate graph G_s
1 $G_s \leftarrow$ empty graph
2 add columns in the table T as nodes to G_s
3 add literal or entity nodes in G_d as nodes to G_s, keeping their original id
4 **for** $u_d \leftarrow G_d$.nodes **do**
5   **for** $v_d \leftarrow G_d$.nodes **do**
6   **if** v_d is value of a property e of u_d **then**
7             $\text{stmt}_d \leftarrow$ statement of property e linking u_d and v_d
8             $u_s, v_s \leftarrow$ corresponding node of u_d, v_d in G_s, respectively
9             $\text{stmt}_s \leftarrow$ statement of property e linking u_s and v_s
10   **if** stmt_s does not exist **then**
11               $\lfloor$ add stmt_s to G_s and link u_s to v_s: $u_s \xrightarrow{e} \text{stmt}_s \xrightarrow{e} v_s$
12   **for** qualifier q of stmt_d **do**
13             $t_d \leftarrow$ target node of q of stmt_d in G_d
14             $t_s \leftarrow$ corresponding node of t_d in G_s
15   **if** the qualifier $\text{stmt}_s \xrightarrow{q} t_s$ does not exist **then**
16               $\lfloor$ add qualifier $\text{stmt}_s \xrightarrow{q} t_s$ to G_s

17 **return** G_s

3.2 Predicting Correct Relationships Using PSL

The candidate graph obtained from the previous step can contain spurious relationships. To identify correct relationships, we use PSL [1]. PSL is a machine learning framework for developing probabilistic graphical models using first-order logic. A PSL model consists of predicates and rules (logic or arithmetic) constructed from those predicates. An example of a PSL rule is as follow:

$$w : \text{CLOSEFRIEND}(A, B) \wedge \text{CLOSEFRIEND}(B, C) \Rightarrow \text{FRIEND}(A, C)$$

where w is weight of the rule, CLOSEFRIEND, FRIEND are predicates, A, B, C are variables. The example rule can be read as "if A and B are close friends and B and C are close friends, then A and C should be friends". If a rule in PSL does not have weight, it will be considered as a hard constraint. Given a set of predicates' values called observations, PSL substitutes (or grounds) predicates in the rules with the observations and performs convex optimization to infer values of the unobserved predicates.

PSL Model. Table 1 shows the list of main predicates in our PSL model. CORRECTREL(N_1, N_2, P) and CORRECTTYPE(N, T) are the target predicates that we want PSL to infer the values. With these predicates, we design the following PSL rules.

$$\neg \text{CORRECTREL}(N_1, N_2, P_1) \tag{1}$$

$$\neg\textsc{CorrectType}(N, T) \tag{2}$$

$$\textsc{CanRel}(N_1, N_2, P) \wedge \textsc{PosRelFeat}_i(N_1, N_2, P) \Rightarrow \textsc{CorrectRel}(N_1, N_2, P) \tag{3}$$

$$\textsc{CanRel}(N_1, N_2, P) \wedge \textsc{NegRelFeat}_i(N_1, N_2, P) \Rightarrow \neg\textsc{CorrectRel}(N_1, N_2, P) \tag{4}$$

$$\textsc{CanType}(N, T) \wedge \textsc{PosTypeFeat}_i(N, T) \Rightarrow \textsc{CorrectType}(N, T) \tag{5}$$

$$\textsc{CanRel}(N_0, S, P) \wedge \textsc{Statement}(S) \wedge \textsc{CanRel}(S, N_1, P) \wedge \textsc{CanRel}(S, N_2, Q)$$
$$\wedge\, N_1 \neq N_2 \wedge \neg\textsc{CorrectRel}(S, N_1, P) \Rightarrow \neg\textsc{CorrectRel}(S, N_2, Q) \tag{6}$$

$$\textsc{CanRel}(N_1, S_1, P_1) \wedge \textsc{Statement}(S_1) \wedge \textsc{CanRel}(S_1, N_2, P_1)$$
$$\wedge\, \textsc{CanRel}(N_1, S_2, P_2) \wedge \textsc{Statement}(S_2) \wedge \textsc{CanRel}(S_2, N_2, P_2) \tag{7}$$
$$\wedge\, \text{SubProp}(P_1, P_2) \Rightarrow \neg\textsc{CorrectRel}(N_1, S_2, P_2)$$

$$\textsc{CanRel}(N_1, S_1, P_1) \wedge \textsc{Statement}(S_1) \wedge \textsc{CanRel}(S_1, N_2, P_1)$$
$$\wedge\, \textsc{CanRel}(N_1, S_2, P_2) \wedge \textsc{Statement}(S_2) \wedge \textsc{CanRel}(S_2, N_2, P_2) \tag{8}$$
$$\wedge\, \text{SubProp}(P_1, P_2) \Rightarrow \neg\textsc{CorrectRel}(S_2, N_2, P_2)$$

$$\textsc{CanRel}(N_1, N_2, P_1) \wedge \textsc{CanRel}(N_2, N_3, P_2) \wedge \textsc{CorrectRel}(N_2, N_3, P_2)$$
$$\wedge\, \textsc{OneToMany}(N_2, N_3) \Rightarrow \neg\textsc{CorrectRel}(N_1, N_2, P_2) \tag{9}$$

Rules 1 and 2 are default negative priors indicating that usually there is no relationship between two nodes and no type of column, respectively. Rules 3 and 4 state that if there is a link (N_1, N_2, P) between two nodes in G_s and there is a feature supporting or opposing the link, then the relationship (N_1, N_2, P) should be correct or incorrect, respectively. The supporting and opposing features of (N_1, N_2, P) are computed based on the number of rows in which we discover the relationship (N_1, N_2, P) (denoted as $match(N_1, N_2, P)$), and the number of rows in which existing data of the relationship in Wikidata is different from the data in the table (denoted as $difference(N_1, N_2, P)$). The two numbers are normalized in various ways: divided by the number of rows, number of rows that have entities, or by $\sum_p match(N_1, N_2, p) + difference(N_1, N_2, p)$ resulting in different features. Similar to rule 3, rule 5 also uses features to predict if T is a correct type of column N. Currently, it uses one feature which is the percentage of rows containing entities of type T.

Table 1. Predicates in the PSL model

Predicates	Meaning
$\textsc{CanRel}(N_1, N_2, P)$	A candidate relationship P between nodes N_1 and N_2
$\textsc{CorrectRel}(N_1, N_2, P)$	Denoting if a relationship (N_1, N_2, P) is correct
$\textsc{CanType}(N, T)$	A candidate type T of column N
$\textsc{CorrectType}(N, T)$	Denoting if the type column N is T
$\text{SubProp}(P_1, P_2)$	Property P_1 is a subproperty of P_2
$\textsc{Statement}(N)$	Node N in the candidate graph is a statement node
$\textsc{PosRelFeat}_i(N_1, N_2, P)$	Value of feature i backing the relationship (N_1, N_2, P)
$\textsc{NegRelFeat}_i(N_1, N_2, P)$	Value of feature i opposing the relationship (N_1, N_2, P)
$\textsc{PosTypeFeat}_i(N, T)$	Value of feature i backing the column type (N, T)
$\textsc{OneToMany}(N_1, N_2)$	A value in column N_1 is associated with multiple values in column N_2

Different from the previous rules, rules 6, 7, 8, 9 are applied to a group of relationships. They are used to enforce consistency of the descriptions with the Wikidata data model as well as to introduce inductive bias or prior knowledge of the desired semantic descriptions. Specifically, rule 6 states that if a property of a statement is inferred to be false, then the statement's qualifiers should also be false. Rules 7 and 8 favor fine-grain properties. Finally, rule 9 prefers that properties' values of non-subject entities should have a one-to-one correspondence to the entities. The non-subject entities are defined as entities with incoming relationships from other entities in the table (i.e., not the main entities that the table is about).

We use the same weight ($w = 2$) for all rules, except that the default negative priors (rules 1 and 2) should have less weight as instructed in PSL tutorial ($w = 1$); rules that introduce preferences should have very small weights (rules 7 and 8 have $w = 0.1$); and rules that act as constraints should have very high weights (rule 9 has $w = 100$).

Inference and Post-processing. From G_s, we extract values of all predicates in the PSL model except the CORRECTREL and CORRECTTYPE predicates. Then, we run PSL inference to determine the values of the two predicates which represent the probabilities of links between nodes in G_s and types of columns, respectively. Values that have probabilities lower than a chosen threshold (0.5) are considered incorrect and are removed.

After running inference, there could be more than one correct link between two nodes. For instance, the PSL model predicts that `capital` (P36), `capital of` (P1376), or `located in...`(P131) are correct relationships for `Capital City` and `Country`. Thus, we run a post-processing step that selects only one path between two nodes such that it maximizes the sum of probabilities of relationships in the final semantic description while maintaining the tree structure of the description.

4   Evaluation

4.1   Datasets for Semantic Modeling

Our objective is to assess the ability of our method to infer correct semantic descriptions of linked tables. There are several standard datasets for benchmarking this problem, such as T2D [17] or Limaye [10]. However, these datasets are not linked to Wikidata; they are relatively simple and do not capture the complexity of the semantic modeling problem in Wikipedia tables. Therefore, we introduce a new dataset of 250 Wikipedia tables, called 250 WT, with their semantic descriptions built using the Wikidata ontology.

The new dataset's tables are selected from a pool of 2 million relational Wikipedia tables with the following procedure to ensure good coverage over multiple domains and produce high-quality unambiguous annotations. First, we filter to keep tables with at least one relationship between columns and have at least one column with at least 8 links[1]. Each table is then assigned to a

---

[1] This requirement is to help reduce ambiguity and speed up the annotation process.

Table 2. Details of the 250 WT dataset. New data is the data that is extracted from tables but is not in Wikidata.

Average number of rows	46.34
Average number of columns	5.536
% new relationships	(21235/33336) 63.7%
% new entities	(3717/21007) 17.7%
% missing entities' type	(996/21007) 4.7%
(sampled) % new relationships (after fixing entity linking (FEL))	(1464/2241) 65.3%
(sampled) % new relationships (before FEL)	(1560/2241) 69.6%
(sampled) % incorrect relationships (after FEL)	(3/2241) 0.13%
(sampled) % new or missing type entities (after FEL)	(214/1393) 15.4%
(sampled) % new or missing type entities (before FEL)	(260/1393) 18.7%

category for stratified sampling to select a maximum of 30 tables per category. The category is the most popular ontology class of the QNode's classes associated with the Wikipedia article of the table. For example, tables in Wikipedia list articles will be assigned to category `Wikimedia list article (Q13406463)`. We initially drew a sample size of 500, then two annotators annotated tables in each category one at a time (ordered by category size) until they agreed on the same semantic descriptions. However, we stopped the manual annotation process when we reached 250 tables as the cost exceeded our budget.

Table 2 shows the details of the 250 WT dataset. If we extract data from the tables using their semantic descriptions, we obtain 33,336 new relationships and 21,007 new entities or entities' types. By comparing the extracted data with Wikidata's data, we found that 63.7% and 17.7% of relationships and entities are not in Wikidata, respectively. As the comparison is computed automatically, the new data may include data that is already in Wikidata (due to errors in entity linking) or is incorrect. Therefore, we sampled 10% (24/237) of the tables that have new data to manually check and fix the linked entities, then verified the extracted relationships. We found that there are 46 (3.3%) incorrectly linked or not linked entities and only 3 (0.13%) incorrect relationships in the tables. This result shows that Wikipedia tables contain new knowledge and can be very useful to enhance Wikidata.

Finally, to compared with other systems that match tables to Wikidata, we also use a synthetic dataset from the final round of the SemTab 2020 Challenge [6]. This dataset contains approximately 22 thousand tables generated automatically from Wikidata. This dataset also comes with a list of target columns for which we need to predict the types and a list of target columns' pairs for which we need to predict the relationships. However, there are some entity columns or columns' pairs in the tables that should be annotated but are not due to not being in the target lists. Thus, for this dataset, we follow the SemTab2020 evaluation protocol to only evaluate the predictions on the items of the two lists.

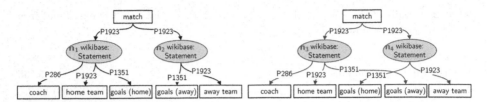

Fig. 3. Example for CPA metric (left is ground truth and right is prediction). Green and red edges are correct and incorrect, respectively. (Color figure online)

4.2   Experiment Settings

Evaluation Metrics. We assess the predicted semantic descriptions' quality in two different tasks: assigning an ontology class to a column (called an entity column) and predicting relationships in the table.

The first task is the Column-Type Annotation (CTA) task in the SemTab 2020 Challenge and is evaluated using the same metrics: approximations of precision, recall, and F_1 score. The difference between the approximate metric with its original version is the use of a scoring function, score($\cdot$), to calculate the correctness of an annotation. Let $d(x)$ be the shortest distance of the predicted class to the ground truth (GT) class. $d(x)$ is 0, 1 if the predicted class is equal to GT, or parent or child of GT, respectively. Then, score$(x) = 0.8^{d(x)}$ if $d(x) \leq 5$ and x is a correct annotation or an ancestor of GT; score$(x) = 0.7^{d(x)}$ if $d(x) \leq 3$ and x is a descendent of GT; otherwise, score$(x) = 0$.

The second task is slightly different from the Column-Property Annotation (CPA) task in the SemTab 2020 challenge due to n-ary relationships. As shown in Fig. 3, despite the fact that the relationship (P1923, P1351) between `match` and `goals (home)` is the same as in the ground truth, it is not the correct relationship as it belongs to a different team. Inspired by the idea in [19], we find the best mapping between statement nodes in a predicted description to statement nodes in the ground truth description that maximizes the number of overlapping edges between them. Then, we measure the approximate precision, recall, and F_1 of edges as in the CTA task. For example, in Fig. 3, the best mapping is $\{n_3 \rightarrow n_1, n_4 \rightarrow n_2\}$ as it returns 5 overlapping edges. We have two incorrect edges: $\langle n_3, \text{P1351}, \text{goals (away)} \rangle$ and $\langle n_4, \text{P1351}, \text{goals (home)} \rangle$. Hence, the approximate precision and recall are $\frac{2}{7}$.

Baselines. We compare our method, named GRAMS, with two state-of-the-art (SOTA) systems: MantisTable [3] and BBW [18] in mapping tables to Wikidata. MantisTable achieves SOTA results on several gold-standard benchmark datasets on mapping to DBpedia. BBW is among the top-3 winners[2] of the SemTab 2020 challenge and finished in second place in the final round (within 0.1–0.2% average F1 score from the top performer). To ensure a fair assessment, we modify the

---

[2] We could not evaluate the other winning systems as we were unable to get access to their code and the papers do not describe them precisely.

Table 3. Performance comparison with baseline systems on CPA and CTA tasks. MantisTable* and BBW* are given correct tables' subject column.

Dataset	Method	CPA			CTA		
		Precision	Recall	F_1	Precision	Recall	F_1
250 WT	MantisTable	0.535	0.442	0.484	0.928	0.331	0.488
	MantisTable*	0.559	0.569	0.564	**0.940**	0.394	0.556
	BBW	0.796	0.123	0.214	0.850	0.233	0.367
	BBW*	0.740	0.559	0.638	0.759	0.777	0.768
	GRAMS-ST	0.526	**0.681**	0.594	–	–	–
	GRAMS	**0.824**	0.650	**0.726**	0.819	**0.813**	**0.816**
SemTab2020	MantisTable	0.985	0.976	0.981	0.977	0.800	0.880
	BBW	**0.996**	**0.995**	**0.995**	0.980	0.980	0.980
	GRAMS-ST	0.990	0.989	0.990	–	–	–
	GRAMS	**0.996**	0.994	**0.995**	**0.982**	**0.981**	**0.982**

inputs of the SOTA systems to use linked relational tables (i.e., tables' cells are already linked to entities in Wikidata) instead of plain relational tables.

In addition, we also develop another baseline, named GRAMS-ST, for comparison on the CPA task in which we replace the PSL inference with a Steiner Tree algorithm [19]. The idea of using the Steiner Tree algorithm is to find a semantic description of a table such that the total weight of relationships is minimized. The weight of a relationship is defined as the inverse of the number of rows in which we discover the relationship using Wikidata's data. Hence, it is similar to choosing the most popular relationship.

The evaluated datasets and our source code are available on Github[3].

4.3 Performance Evaluation

Table 3 shows that GRAMS outperforms the baseline systems on all tasks in all datasets, except on the CPA task of SemTab2020, where we have similar result to BBW. We report GRAMS's performance as the average of 5 independent runs (standard deviations less than 0.001) since our PSL model is a probabilistic model. In the 250 WT dataset, GRAMS exceeds the SOTA baselines by 24.2% and 32.8% of F_1 score on the CPA and CTA tasks, respectively. GRAMS also surpasses our alternative version (GRAMS-ST) by 13.2% F_1 score on the CPA task. This demonstrates that the PSL model, which takes into account both likelihood of the candidate predictions and contradicting evidence, is more robust than a model based on selecting the most frequent relationship.

The superior performance of GRAMS over the SOTA baselines on the 250 WT dataset comes from two main sources. First, MantisTable and BBW needs to identify a subject column from which we find relationships to other

---

[3] https://github.com/usc-isi-i2/GRAMS/releases/tag/iswc-2021.

Table 4. Average running time (seconds) per table of GRAMS in comparison with baseline systems.

Dataset	GRAMS	MantisTable	BBW
250 WT	1.155	0.627	2.674
SemTab2020	0.273	0.136	0.550

columns. Hence, their performance is significantly affected if the results of the subject column detection step are incorrect. If we give MantisTable and BBW the correct subject columns, we observe an increase in their F_1 scores on the CPA task by 8% and 42.4%, and on the CTA task by 6.8 and 40.1%, respectively. Second, tables in the 250 WT dataset are more challenging. Many tables are denormalized tables, which include more than one type of entities, require n-ary relationships or context values to model their data. Thanks to the candidate graph and the PSL model, GRAMS outperforms the SOTA baselines by 8.8% F_1 score even when they receive the correct subject columns of the tables.

However, GRAMS and the baselines do not perform well on tables that have little overlapping with Wikidata's data. For example, GRAMS can not predict correct semantic description of a table in 250 WT dataset about athletics participating in a Summer Universiade and their ranking since Wikidata do not have data of the Universiade's participation. This explains the significant gap between the F_1 score on the SemTab2020 dataset and the 250 WT dataset.

4.4 Running Time Evaluation

In this experiment, we evaluate GRAMS's running time against the baseline systems: MantisTable and BBW. The experiment is run on a single machine with Intel E5-2620v4 and 32GB RAM. We use a local key-value database to store Wikidata to avoid the network overhead in our experiment. The results are reported in Table 4. MantisTable is the fastest system and BBW is the slowest system among the three. Although our system is more complex than the baselines and is not well optimized, it has a reasonable running time especially on the SemTab2020 dataset, which contains 22127 tables. This demonstrates that our system can handle large datasets.

5 Related Work

Understanding semantics of data sources is an important task for data integration [5] and has attracted much research over the years. There are several problem formulations to address this task such as the schema matching [15] problem, which finds a correspondence between the current schema of a data source and the target schema, or semantic labeling [7,14], which assigns each attribute in a data source with one of the predefined semantic types or concepts. However, these problems are fundamentally different from the semantic modeling problem as they do not describe relationships of source attributes explicitly. Hence in the rest of this section, we will only discuss previous work that annotates both concepts and relationships of source attributes.

In general, there are two lines of research in semantic modeling, which target two different use cases. The first use case is for users who have an ontology suitable for their own problem and want to normalize their data sources according to the ontology. Methods in this line of research often take two inputs: a target ontology and a training set of known semantic descriptions. Taheriyan et al. [19] build a semantic description by finding a Steiner Tree that connects the data source's attributes, in which the Steiner Tree is a subgraph of the graph created by integrating known semantic descriptions in the training set. As the Steiner Tree problem is NP-hard, they use an approximation algorithm to find the tree that has high frequency relationships, fewer nodes (concise), and highly overlapped with existing semantic descriptions (coherence). Vu et al. [20] developed a probabilistic graphical model (PGM) for computing the likelihood of a semantic description of a data source and use it as a scoring function to search for the most probable semantic description of a target data source. To distinguish between good and bad semantic descriptions, the PGM exploits relationships within the data and structural patterns to enforce concepts consistent with the semantic description. Despite being flexible on choosing a target ontology, these approaches suffer from the cold start problem: users need to label enough data sources before the systems can achieve good performance. This issue is more profound with a large ontology as they would need lots of training data. Thus, making these methods difficult to apply to Wikipedia tables that span many different domains.

The second use case is for harvesting structure information from millions of public web tables to publish to a knowledge graph (KG) for people to use. Generally, approaches in this line of research leverage existing knowledge in the target KG, so they are less hungry for training data. Their common methodology is to identify KG entities in a table (Entity Linking - EL) and match the properties of entities with values in the table to find column types (CTA) and binary relationships between columns (CPA). As the three tasks (EL, CTA, and CPA) are interdependent, Limaye et al. [10] use a probabilistic graphical model to solve them jointly. Yet, the graphical model is expensive as the number of variables in the models increases linearly with the size of the table, making it difficult to converge on an optimal solution. Mulwad et al. [11] improve it by presenting a new approximate inference algorithm named semantic message passing. However, their methods do not produce a complete semantic description as they ignore non-entity columns in the tables. Comparing to their graphical models, the size of our PSL model is not proportional to the number of rows of the tables. Our PSL model goes beyond selecting semantic description that maximizes matching scores; it incorporates structural patterns and penalizes relationships that are inconsistent with constraints in the ontology and existing knowledge in the KG. Also, PSL performs inference by solving a convex optimization problem while their approaches rely on approximate message passing algorithms.

Later work expands the problem setting to include literal columns. Ritze et al. [17] first identify a subject column of a table and candidate entities in the column, then find the candidate relationships between the subject column with other columns in the table. They iteratively update the candidate entities and candidate relationships until there is no additional change in the entity matching score with the relationship matching score. Zhang et al. [22] also use an iterative approach to refine entity linking results to be consistent with the annotated column types and the table's domain, estimated using a bag-of-words method, and then predict column relationships. Nguyen et al. [12], winner of the SemTab 2019 challenge, also recalibrate the results of three tasks (EL, CTA, and CPA) after their first initial prediction. Current state-of-the-art results on the T2Dv2 and Liyame2000 standard datasets are achieved by Cremaschi et al. [3], which combine and extend features from previous work to improve the accuracy of subject column detection, and the three tasks.

Wikidata, although being popular in the Semantic Web and AI communities, is not used for the semantic modeling problem prior to the SemTab 2020 challenge. However, they do not leverage Wikidata to its full extent (e.g., qualifiers are excluded from the evaluation). New techniques used in the winning systems [2,8,13,18] of the challenge mainly depend on scoring functions to rank the matched results or fuzzy search methods to retrieve better candidate entities. In comparison to our work, most of the aforementioned methods [2,3,8,13,17,18,22] make an assumption about the table structure: a table has only one subject column, and all relationships in the table are between the subject column and other columns. This limits the ability to predict relationships between non-subject columns, which are often found in denormalized tables (e.g., two tables about books and authors are merged into one). As our approach does not make this assumption, not only can we detect relationships between non-subject columns but we also avoid the cascaded error from the subject column detection phase. Furthermore, we broaden the scope of the problem to build semantic descriptions containing n-ary relationships and implicit contextual values. Instead of using an iterative approach to solve the CTA and CPA tasks, our solution using PSL enables us to express complex dependencies between columns and their relationships and solve the tasks jointly through convex optimization. Therefore, we were able to obtain better performance than previous state-of-the-art methods.

One limitation of our approach is that it is unable to build the semantic description of a table in which each row of the table has a different property. For example, a table about awards and nominees of films has a "result" column describing whether a film won the award or not. The property award received (P166) should be used when the film won; otherwise, we should use the property nominated for (P1411). Currently, none of the previous work on the semantic modeling problem can address this problem.

6   Conclusion and Future Work

In this paper, we present a novel graph-based approach for building semantic descriptions of Wikipedia Tables using Wikidata. Our approach constructs a candidate graph of possible relationships between columns in the table and uses collective inference to identify correct relationships and types. The evaluation shows that by using graphs to represent relationships and collective inference, our approach is robust compared to state-of-the-art systems and can handle tables with complex descriptions.

This work focuses on Wikipedia relational tables, in which we leverage existing hyperlinks. As many Web tables do not have links, we plan to extend our method to incorporate an entity disambiguation module to link cells in tables to entities in Wikidata. Another future direction of our work is to support non-relational tables by detecting layout and extracting the table data to a relational format.

We also plan to use our approach to help address the cold start problem of supervised semantic modeling systems. Specifically, we can apply our method to annotate millions of Wikipedia tables to create a large labeled dataset. This dataset can be used for weakly supervised training of semantic modeling systems on custom domain ontologies provided by the users.

Acknowledgments. This research was sponsored by the Army Research Office and the Defense Advance Research Projects Agency and was accomplished under Grant Number W911NF-18-1-0027. The views and conclusions contained in this document are those of the authors and should not be interpreted as representing the official policies, either expressed or implied, of the Army Research Office and Defense Advance Research Projects Agency or the U.S. Government. The U.S. Government is authorized to reproduce and distribute reprints for Government purposes notwithstanding any copyright notation herein.

References

1. Bach, S.H., Broechcler, M., Huang, B., Getoor, L.: Hinge-loss markov random fields and probabilistic soft logic. J. Mach. Learn. Res. **18**(1), 3846–3912 (2017)
2. Chen, S., et al.: Linkingpark: an integrated approach for semantic table interpretation. In: Semantic Web Challenge on Tabular Data to Knowledge Graph Matching (SemTab). CEUR-WS. org (2020)
3. Cremaschi, M., De Paoli, F., Rula, A., Spahiu, B.: A fully automated approach to a complete semantic table interpretation. Future Gener. Comput. Syst. **112**, 478–500 (2020)
4. Dimou, A., Sande, M.V., Colpaert, P., Verborgh, R., Mannens, E., de Walle, R.V.: Rml: a generic language for integrated rdf mappings of heterogeneous data. In: 7th Workshop on Linked Data on the Web, Proceedings, vol. 184 (2014)
5. Doan, A., Halevy, A., Ives, Z.: Principles of Data Integration. Elsevier, Edinburgh (2012)
6. Hassanzadeh, O., Efthymiou, V., Chen, J., Jiménez-Ruiz, E., Srinivas, K.: SemTab 2020: Semantic Web Challenge on Tabular Data to Knowledge Graph Matching Data Sets (2020)
7. Hulsebos, M., et al.: Sherlock: a deep learning approach to semantic data type detection. In: Proceedings of the 25th ACM SIGKDD International Conference on Knowledge Discovery & Data Mining, pp. 1500–1508. KDD '19, Association for Computing Machinery, New York, NY, USA (2019)

8. Huynh, V.P., Liu, J., Chabot, Y., Labbé, T., Monnin, P., Troncy, R.: Dagobah: enhanced scoring algorithms for scalable annotations of tabular data. In: Semantic Web Challenge on Tabular Data to Knowledge Graph Matching (SemTab). CEUR-WS. org (2020)

9. Knoblock, C.A., et al.: Lessons learned in building linked data for the american art collaborative. In: ISWC 2017–16th International Semantic Web Conference (2017)

10. Limaye, G., Sarawagi, S., Chakrabarti, S.: Annotating and searching web tables using entities, types and relationships. Proc. VLDB Endow. **3**(1–2), 1338–1347 (2010)

11. Mulwad, V., Finin, T., Joshi, A.: Semantic message passing for generating linked data from tables. In: Alani, H., et al. (eds.) ISWC 2013. LNCS, vol. 8218, pp. 363–378. Springer, Heidelberg (2013). https://doi.org/10.1007/978-3-642-41335-3_23

12. Nguyen, P., Kertkeidkachorn, N., Ichise, R., Takeda, H.: Mtab: Matching tabular data to knowledge graph using probability models. CoRR abs/1910.00246 (2019)

13. Nguyen, P., Yamada, I., Kertkeidkachorn, N., Ichise, R., Takeda, H.: Mtab4wikidata at semtab 2020: tabular data annotation with wikidata. In: Semantic Web Challenge on Tabular Data to Knowledge Graph Matching (SemTab). CEUR-WS. org (2020)

14. Pham, M., Alse, S., Knoblock, C.A., Szekely, P.: Semantic labeling: a domain-independent approach. In: Groth, P., et al. (eds.) ISWC 2016. LNCS, vol. 9981, pp. 446–462. Springer, Cham (2016). https://doi.org/10.1007/978-3-319-46523-4_27

15. Rahm, E., Bernstein, P.A.: A survey of approaches to automatic schema matching. VLDB J. **10**(4), 334–350 (2001)

16. Ritze, D., Bizer, C.: Matching web tables to dbpedia-a feature utility study. Context **42**(41), 19–31 (2017)

17. Ritze, D., Lehmberg, O., Bizer, C.: Matching html tables to dbpedia. In: Proceedings of the 5th International Conference on Web Intelligence, Mining and Semantics, pp. 1–6 (2015)

18. Shigapov, R., Zumstein, P., Kamlah, J., Oberländer, L., Mechnich, J., Schumm, I.: bbw: Matching csv to wikidata via meta-lookup. In: CEUR Workshop Proceedings, vol. 2775, pp. 17–26. RWTH (2020)

19. Taheriyan, M., Knoblock, C.A., Szekely, P., Ambite, J.L.: Learning the semantics of structured data sources. J. Web Semant. **37–38**, 152–169 (2016)

20. Vu, B., Knoblock, C., Pujara, J.: Learning semantic models of data sources using probabilistic graphical models. In: The World Wide Web Conference, pp. 1944–1953. WWW '19, ACM, New York, NY, USA (2019)

21. Vu, B., Pujara, J., Knoblock, C.A.: D-repr: a language for describing and mapping diversely-structured data sources to rdf. In: Proceedings of the 10th International Conference on Knowledge Capture, pp. 189–196 (2019)

22. Zhang, Z.: Effective and efficient semantic table interpretation using tableminer+. Semant. Web **8**(6), 921–957 (2017)

Generative Relation Linking for Question Answering over Knowledge Bases

Gaetano Rossiello, Nandana Mihindukulasooriya$^{(\boxtimes)}$, Ibrahim Abdelaziz,
Mihaela Bornea, Alfio Gliozzo, Tahira Naseem, and Pavan Kapanipathi

IBM Research, T.J. Watson Research Center, Yorktown Heights, NY, USA
{gaetano.rossiello,nandana.m,ibrahim.abdelaziz1}@ibm.com,
{mabornea,gliozzo,tnaseem,kapanipa}@us.ibm.com

Abstract. Relation linking is essential to enable question answering over knowledge bases. Although there are various efforts to improve relation linking performance, the current state-of-the-art methods do not achieve optimal results, therefore, negatively impacting the overall end-to-end question answering performance. In this work, we propose a novel approach for relation linking framing it as a generative problem facilitating the use of pre-trained sequence-to-sequence models. We extend such sequence-to-sequence models with the idea of infusing structured data from the target knowledge base, primarily to enable these models to handle the nuances of the knowledge base. Moreover, we train the model with the aim to generate a structured output consisting of a list of argument-relation pairs, enabling a knowledge validation step. We compared our method against the existing relation linking systems on four different datasets derived from DBpedia and Wikidata. Our method reports large improvements over the state-of-the-art while using a much simpler model that can be easily adapted to different knowledge bases.

Keywords: Relation linking · Question answering · Knowledge bases

1 Introduction

The goal of Knowledge Base Question Answering (KBQA) systems is to transform natural language questions into SPARQL queries that are then used to retrieve answer(s) from the target Knowledge Base (KB). Relation linking is a crucial component in building KBQA systems. It identifies the relations expressed in the question and maps them to the corresponding KB relations. For example, in Fig. 1, to translate the question *"What is the owning organization of the Ford Kansas City Assembly Plant and also the builder of the Ford Y-block engine?"* into its corresponding SPARQL query, it is necessary to determine the two KB relations: *dbo:owningOrganisation*, *dbo:manufacturer*.

Relation linking has proven to be a challenging problem, with state-of-the-art approaches performing less than 50% F1 on the majority of the datasets [11, 14, 18],

---

G. Rossiello and N. Mihindukulasooriya—Equal contributions.

© Springer Nature Switzerland AG 2021
A. Hotho et al. (Eds.): ISWC 2021, LNCS 12922, pp. 321–337, 2021.
https://doi.org/10.1007/978-3-030-88361-4_19

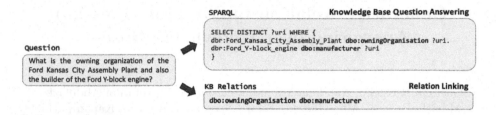

Fig. 1. An example taken from LC-QuAD 1.0 showing the difference between KBQA and RL tasks. Knowledge Base Question Answering (on the top): given the question, predict the gold SPARQL query. Relation Linking (on the bottom): given the question, predict the KB relations *dbo:owningOrganisation, dbo:manufacturer*.

thus making it a bottleneck for the overall performance of KBQA systems. The challenges primarily arise from the following factors: 1) relations in text and the KB are often lexicalized differently (implicit mentions); 2) questions with multiple relations and 3) training data is often limited. While past approaches have tried to tackle these issues by either creating hand-coded rules [19], or by using semantic parsing [14], these challenges can be naturally addressed using the latest advances in auto-regressive sequence-to-sequence models (seq2seq) which have been shown to perform surprisingly well on tasks such as question answering [10], slot filling [17] or entity linking [2], in a generative fashion. However, seq2seq models have not yet been explored for relation linking, particularly in the context of KBQA. In this work, we introduce GenRL, a novel generative approach for relation linking that capitalises on pre-trained seq2seq models.

A simple seq2seq model for relation linking can be trained using just the question text to generate a sequence of relations. However, such models, trained on only the question text, are unable to deal with the nuances of the knowledge bases when determining and linking relations from text. Therefore, we further extend this model by introducing knowledge integration and validation mechanisms. Knowledge integration enhances the encoder representation by infusing structured data from the KB, consisting of a set of relation candidates connected with the entities pre-identified in the questions. Such knowledge integration can have a two-fold advantage: (a) enhancing the performance of the relation linking model when there is a lack of training data by using information from the knowledge graph; (b) ability to deal with unseen relations since it is transformed into a re-ranking task.

The main contributions of this work are as follows:

- a novel generative model for relation linking in the context of KBQA;
- a knowledge integration that enhances the model with information from the knowledge base to handle unseen relations and a knowledge validation module to further filter, disambiguate and re-rank the relations generated by the seq2seq model;
- an extensive experimental evaluation on four KBQA datasets showing large improvements over the state-of-the-art. We obtain an F1 increase between

Input: Question

What is the owning organization
of the Ford Kansas City Assembly
Plant and also the builder of the
Ford Y-block engine?

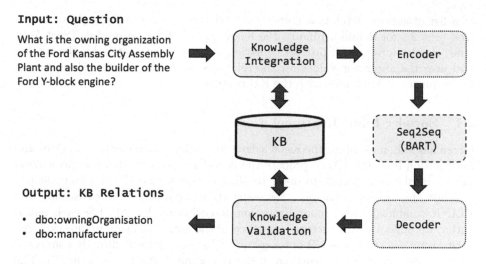

Output: KB Relations

- dbo:owningOrganisation
- dbo:manufacturer

Fig. 2. GenRL framework

9%–59% over the state-of-the-art on different datasets derived from knowledge
bases such as DBpedia and Wikidata.

2   GenRL: Generative Relation Linking

In this section, we describe GenRL, our generative method for relation linking. Our approach is based on an encoder-decoder paradigm where a model
is trained to transform a sequence of input tokens into a sequence of target
tokens. Formally, let us define $S = [s_1, ..., s_N]$ as the source sequence given
as input to the encoder, and $T = [t_1, ..., t_M]$ as the target sequence generated by the decoder. The probability of the target sequence is defined as:
$P(T|S) = \prod_{k=1}^{M}(P(t_k|t_{<k}, S))$. The probability of generating the token t_k at
step k is conditioned on the entire source sequence as well as the tokens that
have been generated so far by the decoder on the target side. In a straight forward application of seq2seq models for relation liking, the input would be the
question text and the output would be a sequence of KB relations. In GenRL, we
adopt BART [9], a pre-trained seq2seq language model based on the transformer
[22] architecture, with two main components: a bi-directional encoder and a left-
to-right decoder. BART achieves remarkable performance when fine-tuned on
sequence generation tasks, making it a good candidate for our problem.

Figure 2 shows a high-level overview of the GenRL architecture. The system
takes a natural language question as input. A necessary first step in our approach
is to recognise the entities in the question and link them to the target KB using
an entity linking system. The Knowledge Integration module (Sect. 2.1) aims to
query the KB, enrich the question with a list of candidate relations according
to the detected entities, and prepare the encoder representation for the seq2seq
model. The decoder of seq2seq model generates a structured sequence consisting

of a list of argument-relation pairs, based on the enriched input representation (see Sect. 2.2 for details). Finally, the Knowledge Validation module (Sect. 2.3), analyses the top-k most probable relation sequences generated by the model, and uses the argument values for the relations in the sequence to determine if the sequence is consistent with the KB content.

2.1   Encoder Input Representation

Given a question as input, the Knowledge Integration module extracts additional information from the KB to prepare the encoder representation for the seq2seq model, as shown in Fig. 3. In order to allow access to the KB, we first identify and link the entities in the question using an entity linker. In our case, we used BLINK combined with a neural mention detection model [24]. For each linked entity, we build a text structure comprised of the entity mention in question, the entity type defined in the KB ontology and a list of relations[1] directly connected with the entity: [Entity mention | Entity type | Rel1, ..., RelN]. The entity structure for all entities in the question is concatenated with the natural language question. When an entity is typed with multiple classes, we use the class hierarchy information to find the most specific type that will prune all the generic types. If there are more than one classes after pruning, the class with most instances in the KG is used.

Encoder Input Representation

```
• What is the owning organization of the Ford Kansas City Assembly Plant and also the builder
  of the Ford Y-block engine?

• [Ford Kansas City Assembly Plant | Building | owningOrganisation, assembly, latD, region,
  longD, owner, country, free, freeType, website, ...]

• [Ford Y-block engine | AutomobileEngine | engine, configuration, production,
  productionEndYear, productionStartYear, date, similar, manufacturer ...]
```

Decoder Output Representation

```
1. [Ford Kansas City Assembly Plant | owningOrganisation] [Ford Y-block engine | manufacturer]
2. [Ford Kansas City Assembly Plant | owningOrganisation] [Ford Y-block engine | builder]
3. [Ford Kansas City Assembly Plant | owningOrganisation] [Ford Y-block engine | engine]
4. [Ford Kansas City Assembly Plant | owningOrganisation] [Ford Y-block engine | automobile]
5. ...
```

Fig. 3. Input-Output representations for the sequence-to-sequence model

This new representation has three advantages: 1) it provides detected entities explicitly to the model; 2) enriches the encoder with local information about

---

[1] In the encoder-decoder representations, we consider only the relation names or labels by removing the URIs and namespaces for DBpedia and converting the property ID to the corresponding relation label for Wikidata. The knowledge validation module converts the relation labels back to URIs.

the entities in the question, such as their types; 3) it provides a pre-built list of relations used as possible candidates. With this enriched representation, we observe an increased generalisation capability of the seq2seq model showing better performance. Moreover, this representation assists the model in generating relations that have not been seen during training by exposing the model to a list of candidate relations from the KB. This is helpful especially for those relation type labels which have a lexical gap with the text in the question.

However, BART's encoder can handle only a limited number of tokens (i.e. 512) and the entity data structures may exceed this limit when there is a high number of distinct relations connected to the entities. In order to address this issue, we pre-rank the relations for each entity in the question using the word embedding similarity technique between the question and the relation labels similar to the lexical similarity approach described in [14].

2.2 Decoder Output Representation

We design the target sequence for the decoder using a data structure formatted as follows: [Arg1 | Rel1], ..., [ArgN | RelN]. For each predicted relation, the model also generates one of its arguments. The relation arguments can be KB entities that appear in the question, or placeholders for answer variable or unbound intermediate variables for multi-hop relations in the query. In the first case, we train the seq2seq model in order to generate the entities recognised in the question paired with the corresponding KB relations. In the example in Fig. 3, the model generated entity *Ford Kansas City Assembly Plant* as an argument for the relation *owningOrganisation* and the entity *Ford Y-block engine* as an argument for the relation *manufacturer*.

In the second case, the model generates placeholders for unbound variables. We show such an example in see Fig. 5, where the relation *dbo:owner* is not directly connected with any entities in the question. Our strategy is to pair these multi-hop relations with the question Wh terms (i.e. *Who*) used as a placeholder. We use the gold SPARQL queries in the training set to generate this output for training the model.

2.3 Knowledge Validation

During knowledge validation the system analyses each candidate output sequence produced by the decoder. In this phase we map the arguments (entity mentions or Wh terms) back to entity URIs or variables, use them to validate candidate outputs and convert the relation labels into URIs in the KB ontology with the correct namespaces.

We collect all the argument-relation pairs for a given output sequence and build all possible graphs that are subsequently used to query the KB. If one of the resulting graphs is matched in the KB then we consider the predicted sequence is valid. We discard the sequences that the model produces in cases when none of the graphs is matched in the KB. Building all possible graphs based on the argument-relation pair uses the following set of heuristics:

```
Candidate Graphs:
• dbr:Ford_Kansas_City_Assembly_Plant dbo:owningOrganisation ?x .
  dbr:Ford_Y-block_engine dbo:manufacturer   ?x.
• ?x dbo:owningOrganisation dbr:Ford_Kansas_City_Assembly_Plant .
  dbr:Ford_Y-block_engine dbo:manufacturer   ?x .
KB Triples:
  dbr:Ford_Kansas_City_Assembly_Plant dbo:owningOrganisation dbr:Ford_Motor_Company
  dbr:Ford_Y-block_engine dbo:manufacturer dbr:Ford_Motor_Company
```

Fig. 4. Knowledge validation example for a sequence of entity-relation pairs. This shows how the first decoder output sequence from Fig. 3 is validated.

Entity-Relation Heuristics. We expand each entity-relation pair into triples by first considering the possible namespaces for the predicted relation labels. For the case of DBpedia, the namespaces are *dbo:*[2] and *dbp:*[3]. Next, we consider two triples where the entity is either in the subject or object position. To complete the triple, we use an unbound variable $?x$ to indicate the missing argument. To create a single connected graph, entity-relation pairs in the same candidate sequence use the same unbound variable $?x$ across all triples. Each entity-relation pair creates four triples and cartesian product of triples from each entity-relation pair creates all possible candidate graphs. In order to make this process efficient, we prune the invalid single triples first before expanding with product to create candidate graphs. Furthermore, it follows decoder ranking and stops as soon as the first valid candidate graph is found. Finally in Fig. 4 we show two possible candidate graphs for a given model output. The first graph has a match in the KB which validates the sequence produced by the model. The KB triples that match the first graph are shown at the bottom of Fig. 4. In the example in Fig. 3, we validate the decoder sequence on the first position. In cases where the first generated relation sequence can not be validated against the KB (because none of its graphs is matched), we proceed to the next generated sequence and the process stops as soon as the first valid sequence is found.

Placeholder-Relation Heuristics. We expand each placeholder-relation pair into triples similarly to entity-relation pairs. In this case, the placeholder is replaced with a new unbound variable $?y$ to represent the *unknown* or the *answer*. We complete the triple with the unbound variable $?x$ similar to the previous case to connect the triples to each other and create a set of candidate graphs.

In the example in Fig. 5 we show two possible graphs for the first sequence generated by the model, with one placeholder-relation pair. The first graph is matched by the KB content and we show the matching triples in the figure. Since at least one of the graphs we produced for the output sequence has been matched, the output system is valid and relation labels can be converted to their corresponding URIs. It is worth noting though that this process of only using

---

[2] http://dbpedia.org/ontology/.
[3] http://dbpedia.org/property/.

```
Question: Who owns the newspaper which was founded by Nehru ?
Gold Relations: dbp:founder, dbo:owner
Model Output: [Nehru | founder ] [Who | owner]
              [Nehru | foundedBy ] [Who | owner]
Candidate Graphs:
• ?x dbp:founder dbr:Jawaharlal_Nehru
  ?x dbo:owner ?y
• dbr:Jawaharlal_Nehru dbo:founder ?x
  ?x dbo:owner ?y
KB Triples:
  dbr:The_National_Herald_(India) dbp:founder dbp:Jawaharlal_Nehru
  dbr:The_National_Herald_(India) dbo:owner dbr:Indian_National_Congress
```

Fig. 5. Knowledge validation example for a sequence of entity-relation and placeholder-relation pairs

two unbound variables does not scale well to arbitrarily long questions with a large number of triples and we plan to investigate it as our future work.

We validate the top N query candidates according to the ranking order of the decoder sequentially ($N = 50$ in our experiments). The KG validation phase stops once we find a valid candidate query graph with matching triples in the KB. Thus, if there are other valid graphs with lower confidence at lower ranks in the decoder, they will be automatically ignored.

In the previous example we explained the process using DBpedia as the KB. As for Wikidata, we have followed a similar process but due to complexities of the Wikidata model, it requires handing reified statements and qualifier properties using several other patterns. In contrast to DBpedia, relations can be either connected to entities directly ($wdt{:}$[4]) or through reified statements ($p{:}$[5],$ps{:}$[6], $pq{:}$[7]). For example, qualifier relations are only associated with statements and some specific relations such as "*instance of (P31)*" or "*subclass of (P279)*" is only attached to entities and not statements. Once all SPARQL query variations are generated according to the Wikidata model, the validation process is similar to one described for DBpedia.

KBQA datasets contain *ASK* questions that have to be treated differently because, by design, when the expected answer is false such as "Was Barack Obama president of Canada?", these questions contain triple patterns that are not present in the KG. We handle this by using two simple heuristics (a) Identify ASK questions using the question tokens, and (b) train the decoder argument pairs for *ASK* to be "[E1 - RelA] [E2 - RelA]".

Once an *ASK* query is detected, GenRL relaxes the KV to adapt to possible *false ASK* questions using the following strategy. In particular, we first try to validate top N decoder outputs (N=10, in our experiments) assuming it's an ASK question with a True answer (*i.e.*, a valid triple in the KB). Generally, as ASK triples have both entities bounded, a positive validation gives a stronger

---

[4] http://www.wikidata.org/prop/direct/.
[5] http://www.wikidata.org/prop/.
[6] http://www.wikidata.org/prop/statement/.
[7] http://www.wikidata.org/prop/qualifier/.

signal. If none of the top n candidates are validated with KG, we return the top decoder output assuming it's an ASK question with a NO (False) answer.

3 Evaluation

In this section, we detail our experimental setup and evaluate our approach against the state-of-the-art KBQA relation linking approaches. We adopt standard evaluation metrics such as precision, recall, and F1 on DBpedia and Wikidata based KBQA datasets.

3.1 Experimental Setup

Benchmarks. We perform experiments on four datasets targeting two popular KBs, DBpedia and Wikidata. Each question in these datasets comes with its corresponding SPARQL query, annotated with gold relations. In particular, we used the following datasets:

- **QALD-9** [21]: is a dataset based on the DBpedia (2016-04 version) with 408 training questions and 150 test questions in natural language. The questions and the gold SPARQL queries are manually created.
- **LC-QuAD 1.0** [20]: is another dataset based on DBpedia (2016-10 version) with a total of 5,000 questions (4,000 train and 1,000 test) based on templates and then paraphrased.
- **LC-QuAD 2.0** [5]: A large dataset based on Wikidata with 6,046 test questions and around 24k training questions. Questions in this dataset have a good variety and complexity levels such as multi-fact questions, temporal questions and questions that utilise qualifier information.
- **SimpleQuestions-WD** [4]: A version of the popular SimpleQuestions dataset mapped to Wikidata. It comprises of 5,622 test questions, and around 19K training questions. This is a subset of the original dataset on Freebase which contained 108K questions. As the name implies, all questions in this dataset are simple with queries encompassing a single triple in the KB.

Baselines. For the DBpedia-based benchmarks, we compare GenRL with Falcon [18] and SLING [14]. As for Wikidata-based benchmarks, we compare against Falcon 2.0 [19] and KB-Pearl [11]. We did not directly compare with the other systems on SimpleQuestions (Freebase) such as Lukovnikov et al. [12] (F1: 0.83) because SimpleQuestions(Wikidata) is on a different KG and is a smaller subset. Finally, we provide a seq2seq baseline (GenRL wo/KB) by fine-tuning BART having only the question as a source and the list of relations as a target.

Model Settings. We trained our seq2seq model using BART-large on the training data provided for each dataset and set the encoder size to 512 tokens. We used 2 NVIDIA V100 GPUs to train the models over 10 epochs with a batch size of 4. With this setup, the models generally do not require long training time. For example, on LC-QuAD 2.0, the largest dataset, the training requires 12hrs. On QALD-9, with a few hundred examples, the train runtime is only 9 min. During inference, we expanded the beam search up to 50 beams in order to generate the top-50 list of entity-relation pairs ranked by their probabilities.

3.2 Results

Tables 1 and 2 show the results of GenRL in comparison to other state-of-the-art approaches on DBpedia and Wikidata based datasets. These results evidently show that GenRL outperforms all the existing approaches by a large margin, i.e. achieving a higher F1 score between 9 points (compared to SLING on QALD) and 59 points (compared to Falcon on Simple Questions-WD).

The results, particularly for BART, show that vanilla seq2seq models in most cases perform better than the state-of-the-art relation linking approaches such as SLING, Falcon, and KBPearl. This clearly demonstrates that the challenges with relation linking can be naturally addressed using simple seq2seq models. Furthermore, our model GenRL is using knowledge integration and performs better than the baseline seq2seq model on all the datasets. These results show the positive impact of the KB integration in GenRL, which we further demonstrate with extensive analysis and ablation study in the next sections.

Table 1. Relation linking results on DBpedia based datasets. GenRL wo/KB refers to our model without Knowledge Integration and Knowledge Validation.

	LC-QuAD 1.0			QALD-9		
	P	R	F1	P	R	F1
Falcon 1.0 [18]	0.42	0.44	0.43[a]	0.23	0.23	0.23[a]
SLING [14]	0.41	0.55	0.47[a]	0.39	0.50	0.44[a]
GenRL wo/KB	0.47	0.50	0.48	**0.51**	0.43	0.47
GenRL	**0.54**	**0.74**	**0.60**	0.49	**0.61**	**0.53**

[a]These numbers differ from the cited paper because we only performed evaluation on the test set in this experiment setup. The cited papers used both training and test set for their evaluation. We reevaluated them only for test set.

3.3 Detailed Analysis

Accuracy of Predicting the Number of Relations. In order to evaluate the system's ability to predict the correct number of relations, we have calculated the percentages of questions where (a) predicted number of relations is same as the number of gold relations, (b) predicted number of relations is larger than the

Table 2. Relation linking results on Wikidata based datasets. LC-QuAD 2.0_{1942} is the subset used by KBPearl [11].

	LC-QuAD 2.0			LC-QuAD 2.0_{1942}			SimpleQ WD		
	P	R	F1	P	R	F1	P	R	F1
Falcon 2.0 [19]	0.44	0.37	0.40	0.43	0.32	0.36^a	0.35	0.44	0.39
KBPearl [11]	-	-	-	0.57	0.48	0.52^b	-	-	-
GenRL wo/KB	0.81	0.81	0.81	0.87	**0.86**	0.87	0.96	0.96	0.96
GenRL	**0.88**	**0.82**	**0.84**	**0.89**	0.85	**0.87**	**0.98**	**0.98**	**0.98**

[a]We calculated the results for the subset using the file at https://github.com/SDM-TIB/falcon2.0/blob/master/datasets/results/test_api/falcon_lcquad2.csv

[b]The KBPearl paper reports F1 of 0.41 due to a typo but its authors confirmed the correct F1 to be 0.52.

gold relations and (c) the predicted number of relations is smaller than the number of gold relations. This experiment checks only the accuracy of predicting the correct number of relations, without considering if relations themselves are correct. Table 3 indicates that seq2seq models are stronger in predicting the correct number of relations from text compared to rule-based systems such as Falcon 1.0 and 2.0. GenRL wo/KB model has slightly better performance in predicting the correct number of relations. In our analysis, the slight decrease was mainly influenced by the entity linking error propagation during KI. Furthermore, we can see that all systems perform better on template-based datasets (LC-QuAD 1.0/2.0) than manually constructed datasets (QALD-9).

Table 3. A comparison of the predicted number of relations vs the number of gold relations in the LC-QuAD 2.0 dataset.

Dataset	QALD - 9			LC-QuAD 1.0			LC-QuAD 2.0		
Num of rels	pred = gold	pred > gold	pred < gold	pred = gold	pred > gold	pred < gold	pred = gold	pred > gold	pred < gold
Falcon 1/2	26%	23%	51%	43%	34%	23%	31%	16%	54%
GenRL wo/KB	70%	9%	21%	93%	1%	6%	94%	1%	5%
GenRL	69%	7%	24%	87%	1%	12%	92%	1%	7%

Entity Linking Error Propagation. In order to understand the impact of entity linking which is used by both knowledge integration and validation steps, we performed an experiment on LC-QuAD 1.0 using gold standard entities similar to EERL [16]. EERL reported an F1 of 0.55 with a precision of 0.53 and a recall of 0.58. With gold entities, GenRL resulted in an F1 of 0.68 with a precision of 0.60 and a recall of 0.83 compared to the 0.60 F1 with machine entity linking. Gold entities help to align the questions better with KG in both Knowledge Integration (improving recall) and Knowledge Validation (improving precision).

Impact on End-to-end KBQA Performance. In order to check the impact on KBQA, we have used the state-of-the-art KBQA system by [8] and replaced its relation linking module with GenRL. For LC-QuAD 1.0, it results in a ~15% point increase in Macro F1 from 44.45 to 59.63. We intend to investigate this further and expand it to other datasets in the future.

3.4 Error Analysis

LC-QuAD 1.0. While analysing the low precision of our results in LC-QuAD 1.0 dataset, we noticed that the dataset used for this benchmark, that is, DBpedia 2014-04 version has an issue of redundancy in relations. For example, *Ben Ysursa* and *Gonzaga University* are connected using both *dbo:almaMater* and *dbp:almaMater* relations. In such cases, the gold standard query can contain either one of them. It is not possible for relation linking systems to produce the exact relation in terms of *dbo:/dbp:* variant as in the gold standard since both of them are equally valid (in terms of retrieving the same exact answer from the KB). For example, Table 4 shows a question with its gold relation set compared to three other equally valid relation sets where each one of them gets a different F1 score according to how much it matches the specific set of gold relations.

Table 4. An example query from LC-QuAD 1.0 training set

Gold Standard Query	Relations yielding the same answer	Rel Prediction F1
In which state is the alma mater of Ben Ysursa located?	dbp:almaMater dbo:state	1.0
	dbo:almaMater dbo:state	0.5
SELECT DISTINCT ?uri WHERE { dbr:Ben_Ysursa dbp:almaMater ?x . ?x dbo:state ?uri . }	dbp:almaMater dbp:state	0.5
	dbo:almaMater dbp:state	0.0

In order to understand the significance of the problem, we have analysed the 4,000 training questions in LC-QuAD 1.0 and found 2,623 (66%) of them had other variations of valid queries (queries that will generate non-empty results) only by changing the namespace (e.g., *dbo:state* vs *dbp:state*). In 1,587 variations, they produced the exact same list of answers as the query in the gold standard and in 881 cases they produced a partial match with the gold answer, and in 155 cases they produced a different answer. If we create all valid SPARQL query variations based on the answer set overlap and re-evaluated our system allowing any of those equivalent combination to be the gold query, GenRL gets an F1 of 0.73 (P: 0.72 and R: 0.76) compared to the standard evaluation of 0.60 F1. This provides evidence that the precision of GenRL on LC-QuAD 1.0 in Table 1 is affected by this issue of the DBpedia KB.

QALD-9 This dataset contains complex queries that sometimes contain several unions to fit exactly to the question that is being asked and the KB content as shown in Fig. 6. Predicting relations for such complex queries is challenging for all relation linking systems.

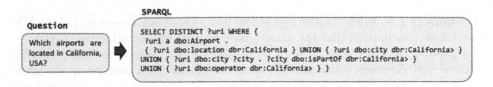

Fig. 6. A SPARQL query using UNIONs from QALD-9 dataset. Here the single relation *located in* is mapped to four KB relations: *location, city, isPartOf* and *operator*.

LC-QuAD 2.0 We noticed that gold SPARQL queries contained some relations that are deleted[8] such as *P134*, *P727*, and *P1112*. In LC-QuAD 2.0 training data, we counted 20 such relations. Our evaluation was run on a snapshot of April, 2021 version of the KB and Wikidata has evolved significantly since 2019, the time LC-QuAD 2.0 was created. Nevertheless, we assume that most facts in questions might not have changed and the negative impact of this on reported numbers to be minimal. Furthermore, we have noticed that some of the questions do not match with their SPARQL queries. For example, there were some questions with text such as "What is it?" or "How is it".

Finally, we observed some unnatural questions due to the use of templates, e.g., "Who is the country for head of state of Mahmoud Abbas?". Despite these issues, GenRL was able to outperform all existing systems and achieves a promising performance across all datasets. This indicates that GenRL is tolerant to these types of questions.

4 Discussion

4.1 Qualitative Analysis

In this experiment, we took a random 10% of LC-QuAD 1.0 training data as a training subset and another 10% as a validation set with the number of unseen relations in the validation set being 114 relations. Table 5 shows a number of examples from the validation dataset. GenRL could predict relations where there is a lexical gap between the question text and the relations itself such as *settlementType* and *placeOfBurial*. It was also able to predict multiple explicit (e.g. *network, sire*), implicit (e.g. *honours, starring*), and even unseen relations (e.g.

---

[8] https://www.wikidata.org/wiki/Wikidata:Requests_for_deletions/Archive/2019/ Properties/1.

instrument and cpu) thanks to its knowledge integration and validation steps. However, implicit relation and relations with lexical gap still pose a challenge on GenRL and on all existing relation linking approaches. In particular, for the question *Name the rivers who originate from Essex?*, the question text does not imply why a model would prefer "mouthPlace" (gold) over *sourceRegion* (predicted). Similarly, in the question *Who acted in the movies whose music is composed by Walter Scharf?*, again the text for "acted" is actually closer to the predicted relation "starring" than to the gold "artist". We intend to investigate further on how to use KB knowledge to handle such cases in our future work.

Table 5. Qualitative Analysis of GenRL predictions from LC-QuAD-1 dataset

Question	Gold	Predicted	Correct
Single relation:			
What are the towns who have Thesaban system?	settlementType	settlementType	✓
Where is the grave of Ivan III of Russia?	placeOfBurial	placeOfBurial	✓
Multiple relations:			
In which sitcom did Jeff Conaway acted and had TNT as its network?	starring, network	starring, network	✓
Which awards have been given to the horse who sired Triplicate?	sire, honours	sire, honours	✓
Unseen relations:			
What famous musicians play the remo?	instrument	instrument	✓
Which appliance's CPU is Cell (microprocessor) and predecessor is PlayStation 2?	cpu, predecessor	cpu, predecessor	✓
Wrong predictions:			
Name the rivers who originate from Essex?	mouthPlace	sourceRegion	✗
Who acted in the movies whose music is composed by Walter Scharf?	musicComposer, artist	musicComposer, starring	✗

4.2   Generative Structured Output Evaluation

Table 6. Results for the structured output generated by the seq2seq model

	n. train	P	R	F1
QALD-9	398	0.65	0.63	0.63
LC-QuAD 1.0	4,000	0.73	0.76	0.74
LC-QuAD 2.0	24,000	0.85	0.86	0.85
SimpleQ WD	19,235	0.98	0.98	0.98

Table 6 shows the results computed only considering the output from the seq2seq model using the argument-relation representation as the gold standard. On DBpedia-based datasets, we observe higher numbers compared to the results of GenRL showed in Table 1 (+10 F1 on QALD-9, +14 F1 on LC-QuAD 1.0). In this case the seq2seq model has been trained on relation labels without URIs.

The difference in performance can be explained by the challenge of disambiguating the appropriate namespaces (*dbo* vs *dbp*) as discussed in Sect. 3.4. It is worth noticing the performance achieved on QALD-9 despite the fact that the model has been fine-tuned only on 398 examples. On both Wikidata-based datasets, we observe very high numbers mainly due to the availability of larger training sets. In particular, the seq2seq model pushes the boundaries on SimpleQuestions-WD obtaining an F1 of around 98% solving the task for this dataset.

4.3   Training with Less Data

In this section, we study the performance of the system on LC-QuAD 1.0, as we vary the size of the training set. We hold out a subset of randomly selected 400 questions from the training set that we use as a development set. We create different training splitting on the remaining part.

Table 7. Training with less data study on LC-QuAD 1.0, GenRL trained on a percentage of training data and tested on a development set of 400 questions

Train (%)	P	R	F1
1%	0.53	0.47	0.48
10%	0.64	0.66	0.63
20%	0.68	0.72	0.69
40%	0.73	0.78	0.74
60%	0.75	0.80	0.77
80%	0.77	0.82	0.78

Table 7 reports the results of this study. Each row shows the performance of GenRL trained on different portions of the original training set. Surprisingly, the model trained only on 1% of the training set (i.e. 40 examples) obtains 48% F1. In addition, with the 20% the model achieves performance close to that obtained by a fully trained model.

5   Related Work

Knowledge base question answering has become a popular task due to its relevance to many real-world applications. The recent KBQA systems, particularly on knowledge bases such as DBpedia [1] and Wikidata [23] can be categorized into rule-based, unsupervised systems [7,8] and end-to-end trained models [3,13,25]. Rule-based approaches [7,8] use semantic/dependency parses and have shown to be highly effective for KBQA. Among supervised approaches pretrained language models have been popularly used for answering questions over a knowledge base. In both of these categories of KBQA systems, the performance of transforming natural language question text to SPARQL is impacted by entity and relation linking components [8]. In particular, relation linking has shown to be the primary error propagation module and needs to be significantly improved.

Existing relation linking approaches can be broadly categorised into rule-based, distantly supervised and strictly supervised methods. Several rule-based systems have been proposed recently for relation linking [6,15,16,18,19]. Among those, Falcon [18] jointly links entities and relations in a question to DBpedia using a sequence of steps including POS tagging, n-gram tiling and compounding. Falcon 2.0 [19] is the recent version of Falcon that performs linking to Wikidata knowledge base. Similarly, Entity Enabled Relation Linking (EERL) [16] investigated the use of questions' entities to support relation linking task over DBpedia KB. KBPearl [11] is another system that performs joint entity and relation linking to Wikidata. It first creates a semantic graph of text using OpenIE and maps both entities and relations to a given KB. SLING [14] is an example of a distantly supervised system. It leverages semantic parsing techniques for better question understanding and builds an ensemble of approaches (e.g., statistical mapping, word embedding) to achieve state-of-the-art performance on various DBPedia datasets. Among those components, a BERT-based distantly supervised relation extraction system is trained using sentences automatically collected from Wikipedia. Compared to these approaches, GenRL has the important advantage of not being KB-specific, which enables easy domain portability across different KBs. In addition, GenRL does not require the use of NLP components such as semantic parsing that helps reduce error propagation in the overall approach.

6   Conclusions and Future Work

In this work, we show that relation linking can be formulated as a sequence generation problem leveraging recent advancements in auto-regressive sequence-to-sequence models. This simple yet powerful approach is shown to largely outperform all existing relation linking systems that apply sophisticated heuristics over several datasets. To further improve this model, we proposed the knowledge integration and validation strategies which infuse the structure of the underlying knowledge base into the neural model. In our experiments, we show that this strategy helps the model to better generalise especially on relations not previously seen during training. The knowledge integration and validation steps resulted in absolute improvements of up to 12% on F1 score compared to the simple seq2seq model. In our research agenda, we plan to investigate generative models with knowledge integration to model the end-to-end KBQA setup.

References

1. Auer, S., Bizer, C., Kobilarov, G., Lehmann, J., Cyganiak, R., Ives, Z.: DBpedia: a nucleus for a web of open data. In: The Semantic Web, pp. 722–735 (2007)
2. Cao, N.D., Izacard, G., Riedel, S., Petroni, F.: Autoregressive entity retrieval. CoRR abs/2010.00904 (2020)

3. Chen, Y., Li, H., Hua, Y., Qi, G.: Formal query building with query structure prediction for complex question answering over knowledge base. In: International Joint Conference on Artificial Intelligence (IJCAI) (2020)
4. Diefenbach, D., Tanon, T.P., Singh, K.D., Maret, P.: Question answering benchmarks for wikidata. In: Proceedings of the ISWC 2017 Posters and Demonstrations and Industry Tracks Co-located with 16th International Semantic Web Conference (ISWC 2017), Vienna, Austria, 23–25 October 2017 (2017). http://ceur-ws.org/Vol-1963/paper555.pdf
5. Dubey, M., Banerjee, D., Abdelkawi, A., Lehmann, J.: LC-QuAD 2.0: a large dataset for complex question answering over Wikidata and DBpedia. In: Ghidini, C., et al. (eds.) ISWC 2019. LNCS, vol. 11779, pp. 69–78. Springer, Cham (2019). https://doi.org/10.1007/978-3-030-30796-7_5
6. Dubey, M., Banerjee, D., Chaudhuri, D., Lehmann, J.: EARL: joint entity and relation linking for question answering over knowledge graphs. In: Vrandečić, D., et al. (eds.) ISWC 2018. LNCS, vol. 11136, pp. 108–126. Springer, Cham (2018). https://doi.org/10.1007/978-3-030-00671-6_7
7. Hu, S., Zou, L., Yu, J.X., Wang, H., Zhao, D.: Answering natural language questions by subgraph matching over knowledge graphs. IEEE Trans. Knowl. Data Eng. 30(5), 824–837 (2017)
8. Kapanipathi, P., et al.: Leveraging abstract meaning representation for knowledge base question answering. Findings of the Association for Computational Linguistics: ACL (2021)
9. Lewis, M., et al.: BART: denoising sequence-to-sequence pre-training for natural language generation, translation, and comprehension. In: ACL, pp. 7871–7880. Association for Computational Linguistics (2020)
10. Lewis, P.S.H., et al.: Retrieval-augmented generation for knowledge-intensive NLP tasks. In: NeurIPS (2020)
11. Lin, X., Li, H., Xin, H., Li, Z., Chen, L.: KBPearl: a knowledge base population system supported by joint entity and relation linking. Proc. VLDB Endow. 13(7), 1035–1049 (2020)
12. Lukovnikov, D., Fischer, A., Lehmann, J.: Pretrained transformers for simple question answering over knowledge graphs. In: Ghidini, C., et al. (eds.) ISWC 2019. LNCS, vol. 11778, pp. 470–486. Springer, Cham (2019). https://doi.org/10.1007/978-3-030-30793-6_27
13. Maheshwari, G., Trivedi, P., Lukovnikov, D., Chakraborty, N., Fischer, A., Lehmann, J.: Learning to rank query graphs for complex question answering over knowledge graphs. In: Ghidini, C., et al. (eds.) ISWC 2019. LNCS, vol. 11778, pp. 487–504. Springer, Cham (2019). https://doi.org/10.1007/978-3-030-30793-6_28
14. Mihindukulasooriya, N., et al.: Leveraging semantic parsing for relation linking over knowledge bases. In: Pan, J.Z., et al. (eds.) ISWC 2020. LNCS, vol. 12506, pp. 402–419. Springer, Cham (2020). https://doi.org/10.1007/978-3-030-62419-4_23
15. Mulang, I.O., Singh, K., Orlandi, F.: Matching natural language relations to knowledge graph properties for question answering. SEMANTiCS 2017, 89–96 (2017)
16. Pan, J.Z., Zhang, M., Singh, K., Harmelen, F., Gu, J., Zhang, Z.: Entity enabled relation linking. In: Ghidini, C., et al. (eds.) ISWC 2019. LNCS, vol. 11778, pp. 523–538. Springer, Cham (2019). https://doi.org/10.1007/978-3-030-30793-6_30
17. Petroni, F., et al.: KILT: a benchmark for knowledge intensive language tasks. CoRR abs/2009.02252 (2020)
18. Sakor, A., et al.: Old is gold: linguistic driven approach for entity and relation linking of short text. In: NAACL: HLT 2019, pp. 2336–2346 (2019)

19. Sakor, A., Singh, K., Patel, A., Vidal, M.E.: Falcon 2.0: An entity and relation linking tool over wikidata. In: Proceedings of the 29th ACM International Conference on Information & Knowledge Management, pp. 3141–3148 (2020)
20. Trivedi, P., Maheshwari, G., Dubey, M., Lehmann, J.: LC-quad: a corpus for complex question answering over knowledge graphs. ISWC **2017**, 210–218 (2017)
21. Usbeck, R., Gusmita, R.H., Ngomo, A.N., Saleem, M.: 9th challenge on question answering over linked data (QALD-9) (invited paper). In: Semdeep/NLIWoD@ISWC. CEUR Workshop Proceedings, vol. 2241, pp. 58–64 (2018). CEUR-WS.org
22. Vaswani, A., et al.: Attention is all you need. In: NIPS, pp. 5998–6008 (2017)
23. Vrandečić, D., Krötzsch, M.: Wikidata: a free collaborative knowledgebase. Commun. ACM **57**(10), 78–85 (2014)
24. Wu, L., Petroni, F., Josifoski, M., Riedel, S., Zettlemoyer, L.: Scalable zero-shot entity linking with dense entity retrieval. In: Proceedings of the 2020 Conference on Empirical Methods in Natural Language Processing (EMNLP), pp. 6397–6407. Association for Computational Linguistics, November 2020
25. Yu, M., Yin, W., Hasan, K.S., dos Santos, C.N., Xiang, B., Zhou, B.: Improved neural relation detection for knowledge base question answering. ACL **2017**, 571–581 (2017)

Dataset or Not? A Study on the Veracity of Semantic Markup for Dataset Pages

Tarfah Alrashed[1], Dimitris Paparas[2($\boxtimes$)], Omar Benjelloun[2], Ying Sheng[2], and Natasha Noy[2]

[1] CSAIL, MIT, Cambridge, USA
`tarfah@mit.edu`
[2] Google Research, Google, New York, USA
`{dpaparas,benjello,yingsheng,noy}@google.com`

Abstract. Semantic markup, such as `Schema.org`, allows providers on the Web to describe content using a shared controlled vocabulary. This markup is invaluable in enabling a broad range of applications, from vertical search engines, to rich snippets in search results, to actions on emails, to many others. In this paper, we focus on semantic markup for datasets, specifically in the context of developing a vertical search engine for datasets on the Web, Google's Dataset Search. Dataset Search relies on `Schema.org` to identify pages that describe datasets. While `Schema.org` was the core enabling technology for this vertical search, we also discovered that we need to address the following problem: pages from 61% of internet hosts that provide `Schema.org/Dataset` markup do not actually describe datasets. We analyze the veracity of dataset markup for Dataset Search's Web-scale corpus and categorize pages where this markup is not reliable. We then propose a way to drastically increase the quality of the dataset metadata corpus by developing a deep neural-network classifier that identifies whether or not a page with `Schema.org/Dataset` markup is a dataset page. Our classifier achieves 96.7% recall at the 95% precision point. This level of precision enables Dataset Search to circumvent the noise in semantic markup and to use the metadata to provide high quality results to users.

Keywords: Datasets · Dataset search · Semantic markup

1 Introduction

As the Web has grown in size and complexity, finding specialized information has become more challenging. Generalist search engines such as Google and Bing do well on common queries, but start to reach their limits when users are looking for content of a specific type or in a specific domain [3]. Vertical search engines have filled that niche by targeting domain-specific content and enabling users to explore it in a more structured way [24]. To illustrate, contrast the standard "10 blue links" Web search results with the experience offered by Pinterest for images, by Amazon

© The Author(s) 2021
A. Hotho et al. (Eds.): ISWC 2021, LNCS 12922, pp. 338–356, 2021.
https://doi.org/10.1007/978-3-030-88361-4_20

for products, or by Google Scholar for publications. Generalist search engines are catching up by offering vertical-specific experiences for certain domains by showing, for example, custom results for jobs, recipes, or events.

Datasets are an important category of such specialized content [4]. With the adoption of open data in governments at all levels and with the scientific community encouraging data publication best practices [8], there is now a treasure trove of public datasets to help us understand the world, advance science, inform decision making, and enable social change. However, as the number of datasets continues to grow, it has become increasingly difficult to find relevant datasets using traditional search engines [15]. There are now thousands of dataset repositories on the Web with tens of millions of datasets [2]. Our team built Dataset Search [20], a tool that provides a single entry point for users to find datasets across all these repositories. Dataset Search is an interface over metadata of datasets from these different repositories and individual pages describing datasets. It relies on semantic markup in `Schema.org` and DCAT[1] to identify pages that describe datasets and their salient features of a given dataset, such as its name, description, license, and spatial and temporal coverage.[2]

`Schema.org` has become prevalent on the Web as a way to express the semantics of Web page content: it is present on more than 30% of Web pages [10]. It has enabled a wide range of applications and is indispensable for many search engines. However, in building Dataset Search, we discovered that we cannot always take `Schema.org/Dataset` markup at face value: pages may include this markup erroneously or for the purposes of search-engine optimization [2]. This problem is likely exacerbated by many, often vague, definitions of what constitutes a dataset. For example, Renear and colleagues analyzed the similarities and differences among dataset definitions in scientific literature [23].

In this paper, we analyze the scale of the problem, focusing in particular on whether pages with `Schema.org/Dataset` markup actually describe datasets. We then develop a method to mitigate the effect of misrepresented semantics by training a model to identify "true" dataset pages automatically. `Schema.org` is an important signal in interpreting Web pages, but we may need additional processing to ensure that markup that designates dataset pages is reliable.

The task of identifying dataset pages automatically presents unique challenges. First, datasets can cover any subject matter from core sciences to art, to real estate, to politics—or anything else. Therefore, for datasets the subject itself is not a distinguishing characteristic, and we cannot rely on domain-specific terminology either to include or to exclude a page. Second, the presence of terms such as "dataset" or "data" is not unique to pages that describe a dataset. For instance, there are thousands of tutorials and online courses for data scientists that discuss how to work with data and are not dataset pages. Third, there are no definitive structural cues for pages that describe datasets: a page with a table or a link to a CSV file may or may not represent a dataset.

---

[1] https://www.w3.org/TR/vocab-dcat-2/.

[2] We use "semantic markup" to refer to the `Schema.org` metadata embedded in Web pages. The data representation may not technically be in a markup format, such as RDFa or Microdata, but could be embedded JSON-LD instead.

These difficulties are not unique to datasets. Other types of creative work, such as blogs and instructional materials, can cover any subject matter. The approaches that we discuss should be applicable to these verticals too.

Specifically, in this paper we make the following contributions:

- We motivate the need to address the veracity of semantic markup for datasets by analyzing cases where it does not correspond to the content of a page.
- We present a deep neural network that identifies whether a Web page with Schema.org/Dataset is a dataset page. To the best of our knowledge, this is the first model to focus on dataset pages.
- We demonstrate that our model outperforms the state-of-the-art classifiers for vertical and functional classification when those are used for dataset pages.
- We publish the following artifacts resulting from this research[3]:
  - A dataset of 223K URLs of pages with Schema.org/Dataset markup from 4.5K hosts, labeled as describing a dataset or not.
  - Source code with model configurations that can be used to retrain them.

2   Datasets and Dataset Pages: Problem Definition

The key to our work is the definition of what constitutes a *dataset* and a *dataset page*. Schema.org, for example, defines a dataset as a "A body of structured information describing some topic(s) of interest." This definition is fairly general, and a likely culprit in the lack of clarity among metadata authors on what constitutes a dataset (cf. Section 4). The dataset definition in DCAT is similarly general.

We use the following definitions to clarify the scope in the context of datasets on the Web:

- A **dataset** is a collection of data items reflecting the results of such activities as measuring, reporting, collecting, analyzing, or observing.
- A **data item** itself can be an image, a number, a sentence, a structured object, another dataset. This list of types of data items is not exhaustive.
- A **dataset page** is a Web page that describes a dataset.

For example, a dataset can be a collection of values from a sensor, a set of labeled images, a set of sentences annotated with entities, or a set of survey responses. At the same time, an individual data item, such as a single measurement value, is not (usually) itself a dataset. Similarly, a collection of data items that can be derived computationally from first principles (i.e., a table of prime numbers or a table converting measurements) is not a dataset. A page that both describes and analyzes a dataset and provides links to a dataset download is a dataset page. A similar page where the dataset is embedded in the page as a table is also a dataset page. However, a page that has only a table, with no description of the table and no metadata, is not a dataset page.

Finally, we can informally think of a dataset page as any Web page that a user of a vertical dataset-search engine, such as Google's Dataset Search [20], might expect to see in the results.

---

[3] Available at www.doi.org/10.34740/kaggle/dsv/2407935.

Note that this definition does not require the page to have any semantic markup identifying it as a dataset.

Classification Problem. Let W be the set of all Web pages. Each Web page w is represented as a tuple $w = (u, c, m)$ where u is its URL, c its content, and m its (possibly empty) semantic markup. Let D be the set of all dataset pages. The *dataset-classification problem* is: given w, determine whether $w \in D$.

In this paper we restrict our attention to the set M of all Web pages with Schema.org/Dataset markup and we study the following problem (Fig. 1): Given a page with markup, $w \in M$ (i.e., m is not empty), determine whether $w \in D$ (i.e., whether w is a dataset page).

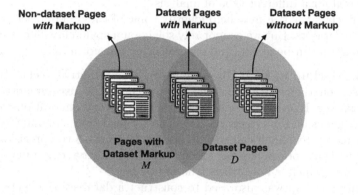

Fig. 1. Dataset pages and pages with Schema.org/Dataset markup on the Web. Not all pages with Schema.org/Dataset markup are dataset pages. Our goal is to identify the set w, where $w \in M \cap D$, as accurately as possible.

3 Related Work

Earlier analyses of the quality of linked open data and Schema.org highlighted common errors and ways to address them. For instance, Meusel and Paulheim proposed ways to fix errors automatically based on schema definitions [18]. The work on Pedantic Web discussed ways to use syntactic validation or reasoning to improve metadata [12]. The problem that we focus on is essentially that of a wrong assignment of semantic type, which these approaches do not address.

We can look to other research areas for approaches to identify the type of content on the page: Web page classification and leveraging semantic markup in classification applications.

Web Page Classification. The key relevant approaches to classifying Web pages are topic classification, functional classification, and spam classification [22].

Topic classification categorizes Web pages based on their topic or subject (e.g., whether a page is about "news" or a "movie") for topic-specific search engines and Web content management [22]. Approaches to topic classification range from using only the URL [1,11], to using the page content [5,27], to including the structure as well as the content [14].

Functional classification determines the role that a Web page plays (e.g., a page can be a "course page" or a "faculty page"). Choudhury and colleagues used both textual content and hyperlinks to determine the role of a page [5]. Baykan and colleagues [1] devised a URL-based classifier for university pages, and argued that URL-based classification is preferable to content-based classification when Web pages need to be classified before they are fetched.

Datasets on the Web can cover any topic and be part of a page that plays any role (e.g., a dataset in a course page). Thus, neither topic nor functional classification applies directly for this domain; that is, a classifier that relies on specific features of a vertical or a function might not work as well on identifying dataset pages. Others have also demonstrated that these types of classifiers might not work well for a different type of analysis [21].

A spam classifier [19] may help identify some of the non-dataset pages that claim to be datasets. But we cannot rely solely on a spam classifier: a page with dataset markup can be a valid (non-spam) page, but not a dataset page.

Semantic Markup in Web Classification. An alternative to classifying Web pages based on their URL, content, or structure is to use semantic markup like `Schema.org`. Krutil and colleagues used `Schema.org` annotations to classify pages into genres and micro-genres [16]. They argued that assigning Web pages to one or more predefined category labels would increase the precision of Web search. But their work makes the assumption that `Schema.org` annotations are used correctly, which is not always true in practice.

Semantic markup was also used to construct a database of events from the Web [25]. In this work, authors recognized that they cannot trust all event annotations as describing actual events. To address this problem, they manually identified large websites that use semantic markup incorrectly and removed them from their training set. Dataset pages have much more diverse structure than event pages. Thus, we can create similar training data by including pages that have semantic markup and excluding sites with known incorrect markup, but our features and model will be quite different than those for events.

4   The Veracity Problem for Datasets

We performed a manual analysis of whether or not pages with `Schema.org/Dataset` markup were dataset pages, in the context of building and maintaining Dataset Search's corpus. To ensure the quality of search results, we regularly monitor sites that produce a large number of new pages with `Schema.org/Dataset` (our threshold was several hundred new such pages in a week) and verify whether or not these pages are dataset pages (cf. Section 2). We also enabled Dataset Search users to report pages that are not datasets. We verify such reports and, if warranted, exclude these pages or sites from the corpus. From this analysis, we collect a list of regular expressions that captures the URLs that are not dataset pages, a "denylist". As of today, this list captures hundreds of internet hosts.

Sometimes, the decision is straightforward (e.g., a page describing a gadget is not a dataset page); sometimes it is more of a judgement call driven by what we believed users expect to see in the search results (e.g., a real estate listing that has a table with tax history for a property).

The following are categories of pages with Schema.org/Dataset markup that were not dataset pages. This list is not exhaustive; rather, these categories are the types of pages that we have encountered multiple times in our corpus analysis:

Product pages: pages that describe a product or a collection of products, ranging from books to industrial supplies to real estate.

Data points: individual data points rather than datasets, such as stock price for a specific stock on a specific date; weather on a specific date in a location; lottery results for a specific date.

Information about items: pages describing a company or a medical practice.

Conversion tables: conversion between measurement systems or currencies.

Lists of terms: a collection of synonyms for a word.

Class exercises: pages with exercises and solutions for a class.

Explanations of an item: pages that provide a definition of an item or a tutorial on how to use it, such as a page describing the uses of a specific file extension (this particular example surprisingly prevalent).

The incorrect use of semantic markup in these cases is not necessarily malicious or intentionally misleading. "Dataset" is such a general term that providers may feel that it can apply to almost anything—making the task of creating a useful dataset search engine that much harder.

The process that we described in this Section clearly does not scale because it requires regular manual inspection of pages. It is also not comprehensive: we were able to examine only hosts with many new datasets; smaller sites could still appear in search results and make user experience worse. Thus, we built a classifier for dataset pages that enabled continuous comprehensive analysis and quality checks. It also provided a quantitative measure of the scale of the problem (see Sect. 6.4 for the results).

5   Dataset Classifier

We now discuss (1) the feature selection, (2) the creation of labeled data for training, testing, and evaluation, and (3) the details of the classifier. At a high level, we used a manual analysis to create a set of labeled data, experimented with a variety of structured and unstructured page features, and used an internal AutoML implementation to select and train a suitable model.

5.1   Feature Selection

Dataset pages come in various shapes. Figure 2 (left) shows three examples of dataset pages. The first page consists of a description and a list of files, while the other two represent datasets using tables or charts. Some repositories like data.gov, have a consistent layout and structure for all their dataset pages. Other dataset pages, like the ones on GitHub, do not have a standard structure.

We trained our classifier on a combination of features extracted from both the HTML content and the semantic markup of Web pages.

URL and HTML Content Features

Early work on Web page classification [1,11] considered only properties related to URLs. While URL-based classification does not provide ideal accuracy, this approach eliminates the need to analyze the page itself.

Repositories often add their dataset pages under a /dataset or a /catalog path and URLs may have terms indicating that the page is about a dataset (dataset, opendata, etc.). We capture the URL in tokenized form after pre-processing it to drop the domain. We exclude the domain because the number of distinct domains in our training set is orders of magnitude smaller than the number of pages, thus including it will overfit the model for specific domains.

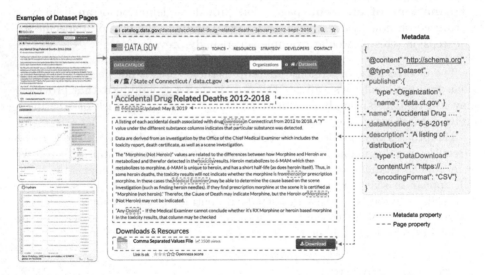

Fig. 2. An example of a dataset page, with highlighted page and metadata properties, and a few additional examples of dataset pages of varying structures.

To build a robust model that can handle a wide variety of dataset page structures, we need a representation of the page contents that does not depend on the page structure. We use a keyword extractor for Web pages to generate a vector of *prominent terms* and used them as features. Prominent terms are a collection of terms (unigrams/bigrams) with associated weights in the [0,1] scale. Each weight represents how relevant a term is for the page in question. To compute the weight of each term appearing in the document, we use a proprietary scoring model similar to the one proposed by Xiong and colleges [26]. Prominent terms consist of the top 100 terms resulting from that scoring.

Metadata Features

We used our observations from the manual analysis (Sect. 4) and the frequency of properties in the corpus [2] to select the `Schema.org` properties to use as features. Table 1 summarizes those properties. It also captures whether we used the values of a property (Sect. 5.4 discusses how we processed them) or simply the presence of the property in the metadata. For example, `name` and `description`[4] are required for every dataset and their content was the most useful source of information. Presence of download information through `distribution`, `encodingFormat` and `fileFormat` were likely to be a signal of high quality metadata, and thus, a valid dataset page. Similarly, the content of the provider or creator properties provided additional features.

We trained classifiers on two sets of features: a lightweight classifier (denoted DC-L) that used only `name` and `description` as metadata features and a full classifier (DC-F) that used all the features from Table 1. We found that both DC-F and DC-L achieved the same very high accuracy (Sect. 6), indicating that `name` and `description` together with prominent terms contain enough information to correctly classify a page.

Table 1. The features that we used for the two classifiers. For metadata features, the table captures whether we used the value of the property or just its presence (bool).

	Property value	$DC-L$	$DC-F$
Non metadata features			
URL (without domain)			✓
Prominent Terms		✓	✓
`Schema.org` features			
`name`	value	✓	✓
`description`	value	✓	✓
`distribution`	bool		✓
`encodingFormat, fileFormat`	bool		✓
`provider, publisher`	value		✓
`author, creator`	value		✓
`doi`	value		✓
`catalog`	bool		✓
`dateCreated`	bool		✓
`dateModified`	bool		✓
`datePublished`	bool		✓

5.2   Labeled Data

We created an annotated dataset by sampling Dataset Search's corpus `Schema.org/Dataset` markup, which included millions of pages from thousands of domains [2]. We then labeled the data as either a dataset page or not.

---

[4] Unqualified property names such as `name` belong to the `Schema.org` namespace.

We made the following assumption when labeling the data: If a host had pages with Schema.org/Dataset then either *all* of those pages were dataset pages or *none* of them were. Therefore, it was sufficient to sample a few pages from a site with semantic markup to label all pages from that site as positive or negative examples. Our earlier analysis showed that this assumption was almost always true: If website editors added Schema.org/Dataset to their pages, they either uniformly added it correctly or uniformly misused it.

Labeling Process. All samples from our "denylist" (Sect. 4) were labeled as non-datasets. Additions to the denylist take place regularly and two team members, a proposer and an approver, must agree with the addition; and thus transitively, with the "not-dataset" label too.

For the remaining samples, we followed an in-house data-labeling approach. We formed a team of 7 raters —some of the authors of the paper and other colleagues— that reviewed the definition from Sect. 2 and together analyzed a number of positive and negative examples in order to align our ratings. We then grouped the samples by host and partitioned them in 7 batches. We assigned each batch to a rater who labeled all hosts in it as "dataset", "not-dataset", or "unclear". We then had a follow up session where we discussed all "unclear" hosts, eventually labeling them as "dataset" or "not-dataset".

Sampling Process. We used three sources of labeled pages. First, we randomly sampled pages that we had previously added manually to our denylist. Second, we sampled pages from the top 50 hosts in terms of the number of pages with Schema.org/Dataset. Finally, we obtained a random sample of about 1000 hosts from our corpus. Our labeled set had 223K pages, split almost equally between positive and negative examples.

We split the data into training, validation, and test sets with a rough ratio of 70:15:15, respectively. We now discuss the approaches that we used to ensure that the labeled set as a whole and the distribution between these subsets was balanced and diverse.

Balanced Host Representation. Because some hosts have millions of dataset pages and some have only a handful, we balanced the number of pages from each host in the labeled sample to avoid overfitting for a specific host. If a host had fewer than 100 pages with Schema.org/Dataset, we included all of them. For hosts with 101 to 2500 pages, we used a sampling rate of $10/\sqrt{\text{pages in host}}$, and for hosts with more than 2500 such pages we used a sampling rate of $500/\text{pages in host}$. Thus, the number of samples from a host is increasing with the number of pages in the host and capped at 500.

Balance in Test vs Training Set. Pages from the same data repository usually look similar because they are generated by the same code from a data catalog or a database. Thus, if we train a model on a subset of pages from a repository R and then use pages from R in our test data, it will be too easy for the model to identify them. To prevent the effects of memorization [14], we ensured that pages from the same host were either all in the training or all in the test set.

Pages in Different Languages. Dataset Search's corpus has pages in almost 100 languages. However, it was not practical for us to create a labeled set with balanced number of positive and negative examples in all languages. Indeed, our initial random sample contained a small number of pages in a specific language only as negative examples, causing the model to learn that all pages in that language are not datasets. In our final labeled set, we included pages in the five most frequently used languages (English, Chinese, Spanish, German, French). For other languages, we used the Google Translate API to translate the content of the relevant features (Table 1) into English and treated them as English pages.

5.3   Classifier Details

We trained multiple classifiers, starting with a rich set including all features in Table 1 (DC-F) and then experimenting with gradually smaller feature sets. The end result of this process was a lightweight classifier trained on only three features: `name`, `description`, and prominent terms (DC-L).

To pick an optimal model and to tune hyperparameters, we used a version of AdaNet [6], a framework to analyze and learn neural networks (NNs), to search over the space of Ensemble Estimators combining DNNs and Linear Estimators. We obtained the following models:

DC-L Model. An ensemble estimator combining:

1. A feed-forward NN with one fully connected layer of 186 hidden units, implemented using TensorFlow DNNEstimator.[5] The architecture uses a Scaled Exponential Linear Unit (SeLU) activation function,[6] a dropout rate of 0.28673, and has Batch Normalization enabled.
2. A Linear estimator implemented using TensorFlow LinearEstimator.[7]

For ensembling we used AutoEnsemble[8] and optimized for sigmoid cross entropy loss[9] using the Adam Optimizer [13] with learning rate $= 0.00677$, $\beta_1 = .9$, $\beta_2 = .999$, and gradients clipped using a clip norm of 0.00037. We used a batch size of 128 and trained to convergence (45k steps) using a custom trainer built on TensorFlow Extended.[10]

---

[5] https://www.tensorflow.org/api_docs/python/tf/estimator/DNNEstimator.

[6] https://www.tensorflow.org/api_docs/python/tf/keras/activations/selu.

[7] https://www.tensorflow.org/api_docs/python/tf/estimator/LinearEstimator.

[8] https://adanet.readthedocs.io/en/v0.9.0/_modules/adanet/autoensemble/estimator.html.

[9] https://www.tensorflow.org/api_docs/python/tf/nn/sigmoid_cross_entropy_with_logits.

[10] https://www.tensorflow.org/tfx.

DC-F Model. An ensemble estimator combining:

1. A feed-forward NN with three fully connected layers of 329, 351, and 292 hidden units respectively. Dropout rate is 0.08277 and Batch Normalization is disabled. The rest of the details are the same as for DC-L.
2. A Linear estimator implemented using TensorFlow LinearEstimator.

For ensembling we followed the same approach as for DC-L but with a learning rate of 0.00076 and a clip norm of 0.25035.

5.4 Feature Processing

To process the values for text features in Table 1, we tokenized on white-space and punctuation and then combined words into unigrams and bigrams, presented to the model as a bag of words. This approach considers occurrences of words in isolation, as well as pairs of words. We selected tokens to retain in a vocabulary based on adjusted mutual information between each token and the label. This filtering reduced the vocabulary size to 3–4% of the original. We used two out-of-vocabulary hash buckets for any tokens that are not in the vocabulary. For the DNN sub-graph, the tokens were embedded using a learned embedding of size proportional to the log of the vocabulary size. To create a fixed dimensional input vector, the variable length bags of tokens were combined using the weighted sum of the embedding weights, divided by the square root of the sum of the squares of the weights[11].

6 Dataset Classifier: Evaluation and Results

Our experiments measure the accuracy of the dataset classifiers, DC-F and DC-L. We also compare them to three state-of-the-art Web page classifiers, which we implemented as our baseline methods.

6.1 Baseline Methods

Section 3 presented a number of approaches to Web page classification. Vertical and functional classifications are two of the main types that researchers have studied extensively [22]. We applied three state-of-the-art methods to classify dataset pages: One functional classifier and two vertical classifiers (content-based and content and structure based). We trained all three models on the labeled data described in Sect. 5.2. We evaluated our dataset classifier against classifiers developed for different purposes because, to the best of our knowledge, no classifiers have been developed specifically for datasets.

Functional Classifiers (Content-Based). Choudhury et al. [5] evaluated numerous methods for categorizing Web pages based on their role by using the content and the hyperlink text on the page. They used the WebKB dataset [7] to

---

[11] https://www.tensorflow.org/api_docs/python/tf/nn/embedding_lookup_sparse.

train and test a number of models, mainly Multinomial Naive Bayes (NB) and Support Vector Machine (SVM) to classify Web pages from computer science departments of several universities into multiple categories: project, course, faculty, department. We implemented their approach by training the SVM and NB models on the content and hyperlink text. We chose to apply this method because SVMs have worked well for text classification, due to the large dimensionality of the feature space, and the sparsity of feature vectors [5]. In addition, SVM and NB have been used as baselines for many content-based Web classification [22].

Vertical Classifier (Content-Based). The second baseline method that we use is inspired by the work from Zhao et al. [27]. They proposed a network-classification model based on deep learning that takes the title and description ("short text"), and the textual content of the Web page ("long text") as features. They classified pages from Web portals, like Sina and NetEase, into a number of vertical categories (entertainment, art, etc.). Instead of considering the whole content text as their only input feature, the authors argued that considering the title and description of the page yielded a better classification accuracy [9]. Following their approach, we trained three variants of the model: Using the title and description (short text), using only the content text (long text), and using the title, description and the content text (short/long text).

Vertical Classifier (Content- and Structure-Based). As an alternative to classification based only on content, we also considered RiSER [14], a model that incorporates both the structure and content of pages to classify machine-generated emails into verticals (hotel, bill, etc.). Such emails are typically short, and have rich HTML structure. Instead of considering the whole document content as a feature, RiSER extracts the first 200 textual terms from the DOM-tree, with the XPaths that lead to them. RiSER authors trained their model on a large corpus of anonymized emails received by users of Gmail and evaluated it on two different classification tasks. To retrain RiSER, we used the html extracted from the data presented in Sect. 5.2. However, unlike emails, the assumption that the first 200 words will contain a useful signal is not true for webpages. To address this, we pre-processed all html and removed text with tags that are frequently irrelevant, such as buttons (e.g., "login") and menus (e.g., "home"). We then trained and tested Riser using the results of this cleanup.

6.2 Metrics

We compare the two variants of our dataset classifier, namely DC-F and DC-L, with the three baseline methods using the area under the precision-recall curve (AUC-PR). Classifiers are often evaluated using area under the receiver operating characteristic curve (AUC-ROC). However, ROC curves may provide an excessively optimistic view of the performance for highly skewed domains [14]. The AUC-PR is similar to AUC-ROC in that it summarizes the curve with a range of threshold values as a single score. The score can then be a point of comparison between different models on a binary classification problem where a score of 1.0 represents a model with perfect skill. AUC-PR alone is insufficient to evaluate our models because applications like dataset search require very high precision. Indeed, returning non-dataset pages to users searching for datasets would be a poor user experience. Therefore, we evaluate our models based on their recall at a fixed level of high precision, specifically at a precision equal to 95% (@P95). In addition to the AUC-PR and recall @P95 metrics, we report the F1-score @P95 (in both Table 2 and Fig. 3) for the dataset classifier variants and baseline models. F1-score is the weighted average of precision and recall. Thus, comparing the models based on their F1-score should be the same as comparing them using the recall @P95 metric.

We trained multiple classifiers using different combinations of features and from this process we concluded that name, description, and prominent terms are the most important ones for the classification.

6.3 Results

Table 2 shows the results for the three baseline methods. For the functional classifiers, SVM performed slightly better than the Multinomial NB, with an AUC-PR of 77, but a low recall @P95. Classifiers tailored to identify the role of a page are not suitable to identify pages that contain datasets.

Vertical classifiers performed better than the functional ones. RiSER achieved a higher AUC-PR than all other baselines, however, it was still only able to correctly identify 66% of dataset pages at @P95.

Table 2. The performance of DC-L, DC-F, and baseline classifiers.

Type of classifier	Model	AUC-PR	R@P95	F1@P95
Functional (content based)	Multinomial NB	0.67	0.22	0.35
	SVM	**0.77**	**0.24**	**0.38**
Vertical (content based)	DNN (Short)	0.85	0.49	0.63
	DNN (long)	**0.90**	**0.56**	**0.69**
	DNN (short/long)	0.88	0.55	0.68
Vertical (content & structure based)	**RiSER**	**0.96**	**0.66**	**0.77**
Dataset (content & metadata based)	**DC-L**	**0.99**	**0.97**	**0.96**
	DC-F	**0.99**	**0.96**	**0.96**

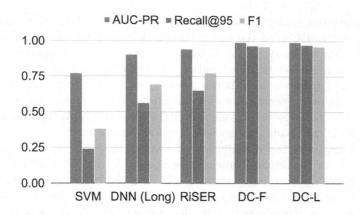

Fig. 3. Performance (AUC-PR, Recall and F1 score at Precision=95) comparisons between our dataset classifier variants (DC-F and DC-L) and the baseline methods.

Figure 3 shows the results for DC-F and DC-L, compared to the best model for each baseline method from Table 2: Content and link based SVM, content based (long text) DNN, and RiSER. DC-L outperforms the functional SVM classifier by an additive factor of 73%, the vertical DNN classifier by 41%, and RiSER by 31% on recall @$P95$. The results show that using both metadata properties and page properties as features provides performance gains over using only page properties.

The AUC-PR metric is also improved for the DC-F and DC-L variants compared to the baseline models. DC-L outperforms the SVM classifier by 22%, the vertical DNN classifier by 9%, and the RiSER model by 3%.

We manually inspected the 1% of web pages that the classifier predicted incorrectly. We found that some of these pages are information pages that describe a company, a product, a place, or a person, others are online web page translators, climate web pages, and pages about scientific papers or stock data. Some of these pages are tricky to label, such as the stock data and the climate pages. Others are obvious non-dataset pages, like the info pages.

6.4 Corpus-Level Analysis

We used DC-L to evaluate the veracity of dataset markup in our entire corpus of more than 600M pages on the Web with the minimal `Schema.org/Dataset` markup (at least name and description). For pages in a language other than the five that we trained the classifier on, we first translated their features to English. We used the @$P95$ prediction threshold t for which our experiments achieved the highest recall and precision (Fig. 3). We aggregated the results at the host level and classified hosts into those with more than half of their pages scoring above t (dataset hosts) and the rest (non-dataset hosts). We then assigned each page the same label as its host, regardless of its individual classification score. This majority-vote smearing of the score ensured robustness against outliers.

To validate our majority-vote approach, we performed an additional evaluation of applying DC-L to the entire corpus. We randomly sampled 250 hosts classified by our majority-vote method as dataset hosts and another 250 hosts classified as non-dataset hosts, excluding hosts that were already in the labeled data. We again followed an in-house labeling approach (Sect. 5.2). We labeled these 500 hosts and determined recall and precision to be 99% and 96% respectively. The recall at host level is slightly higher than for individual pages, likely because the majority-vote aggregation accounts for outliers.

Figure 4 captures the distribution of dataset and non-dataset pages and hosts for the entire corpus. These numbers exclude the 10 largest hosts with `Schema.org/Dataset` on non-dataset pages as those hosts account for 40% of non-dataset pages and are true outliers. For comparison, the next 10 largest hosts by number of non-dataset pages account for only 7% of these pages. The results show that the majority of hosts (61%) and pages (84%) are non-dataset pages.

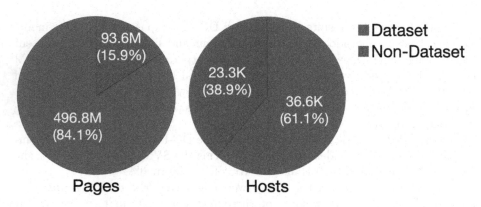

Fig. 4. Dataset vs non-dataset pages and hosts in the Web corpus with `Schema.org/Dataset` markup (excluding 10 largest non-dataset hosts).

7   Discussion and Future Work

In this paper, we analyzed the basic premise of whether semantic markup can be taken at face value. For datasets at least, this premise does not always hold true (Sect. 4). The difficulty of defining what a dataset is likely contributes to the problem. Having `Schema.org` define a dataset more precisely (similar to what we proposed in Sect. 2) may significantly alleviate the problem. However, it may be useful to evaluate more deeply how prevalent this problem is in other verticals, such as recipes, jobs, events, and so on.

7.1   Understanding Classification Results

Our classifiers outperformed the baseline classifiers (Sect. 6) because the dataset classification task cannot be reduced to one of the problem classes for which existing classifiers were designed. The functional classifiers, SVM and the Multi-nomial NB, aimed to identify the role of pages. The vertical classifier DNN was designed to identify the vertical or the topic of pages. Finally, RiSER focused on classifying highly structured, short business-to-consumer emails. Dataset pages can serve multiple functions, may belong to many verticals, and are not uniform in size and structure.

Our results show that using only `name` and `description` as metadata features achieves essentially the same accuracy as using other properties or URL-based features. That is, knowing that the page is marked up with `Schema.org/Dataset` and seeing the value for name and description properties is often sufficient to determine whether it is a dataset page. Other properties, however, can provide important information about the quality of the page. Presence of download information through the `distribution`, `encodingFormat` and `fileFormat` properties may be a signal of high quality metadata. We also noticed that dataset pages often contain more complete metadata: they have 5.2 properties on average, whereas non-dataset pages have 2.57.

7.2   Quality Versus Coverage

Our work focused on the problem of *quality* in the context of dataset search: identifying whether or not a page that has `Schema.org/Dataset` is a dataset page. For this problem, high recall and precision are essential. A dataset page with `Schema.org/Dataset` markup comes from a content provider who put in the effort to describe semantics of the page. Mis-classifying such a page as "not a dataset" will be both unfair to the content provider and detrimental to the quality of search results. Thus, we need high recall. At the same time, a page with dataset metadata that is not a dataset page would not be useful to a user searching for datasets. If there was a small number of such pages, we could simply ignore the problem because these pages would rarely show up in search results. However, it turns out that there are tens of millions of pages that contain semantic markup without actually describing a dataset. Thus, high precision is crucial to achieve high quality of search results: We want to ensure that non-dataset pages are unlikely to show up among results that contain predominantly true dataset pages. With AUC-PR of 99 (Table 2), the model we proposed is sufficiently accurate to decide automatically what pages to include in a dataset search engine.

There is a complementary problem to the problem of quality, that of *coverage* (Fig. 1): given a Web page without `Schema.org/Dataset` metadata, decide whether this page is a dataset page. We did not address the problem of coverage in this paper, however, future work may address how we can use URL and content features to classify pages in this domain. Even if such a classifier does not have high recall, it can be useful to identify key data repositories that do not have `Schema.org` markup, and inform an outreach strategy towards influencers and repositories, as described by Noy and colleagues [20].

In this work, we focused on the veracity of the type of entity a Web page is about (i.e., `Schema.org/Dataset`), not on specific property values [17]. Just like type information, property values also cannot be taken at face value. It would be useful to explore the space where the property values are set incorrectly, intentionally or not, in order to continue improving the quality of applications that rely on semantic markup.

8   Conclusions

The goal of semantic markup such as `Schema.org` is to provide a machine-readable interpretation of the contents of a Web page. This markup has enabled a myriad of applications. However, as these applications begin to cover domains with ambiguous and more general artifacts, such as datasets, the markup becomes more noisy and less reliable. Specifically, we showed that providers often misunderstand when a page should be typed as a dataset page, which is an example of such general category. We propose a way to remedy the problem automatically by using semantic markup as an important signal but also considering other features to support it. Our work enables high quality results based on `Schema.org`, making use of the rich semantics, even in a domain where the markup is unreliable.

Acknowledgments. We are grateful to Amy Skerry-Ryan, Katrina Sostek, Marc Najork, and Shiyu Chen for discussions on this work.

Data and Code Availability. We have made both the dataset discussed in Sect. 5.2 and code to train the models from Table 1 available through www.doi.org/10.34740/ kaggle/dsv/2407935. However, we had to remove the *prominent terms* column from the dataset because the scoring model we used to obtain it is not publicly available. Interested users can replicate this scoring using the model by Xiong and colleagues [26].

References

1. Baykan, E., Henzinger, M., Marian, L., Weber, I.: Purely URL-based topic classification. In: 18th International Conference on World Wide Web. WWW 2009, pp. 1109–1110 (2009). https://doi.org/10.1145/1526709.1526880
2. Benjelloun, O., Chen, S., Noy, N.: Google dataset search by the numbers. In: International Semantic Web Conference (2020)
3. Bozzon, A., Brambilla, M., Ceri, S., Fraternali, P.: Liquid query: multi-domain exploratory search on the web. In: 19th International Conference on World Wide Web. WWW 2010, pp. 161–170 (2010). https://doi.org/10.1145/1772690.1772708
4. Chapman, A., et al.: Dataset search: a survey. VLDB J. **29**(1), 251–272 (2019). https://doi.org/10.1007/s00778-019-00564-x
5. Choudhury, S., Batra, T., Hughes, C.: Content-based and link-based methods for categorical webpage classification (2016)
6. Cortes, C., Gonzalvo, X., Kuznetsov, V., Mohri, M., Yang, S.: AdaNet: adaptive structural learning of artificial neural networks. In: International Conference on Machine Learning, pp. 874–883 (2017)

7. Craven, M., McCallum, A., PiPasquo, D., Mitchell, T., Freitag, D.: Learning to extract symbolic knowledge from the world wide web, Tech. Rep. Carnegie-mellon univ pittsburgh pa school of computer Science (1998)
8. Fenner, M., Crosas, M., et al.: A data citation roadmap for scholarly data repositories. Sci. Data **6**(1), 1–9 (2019). https://doi.org/10.1038/s41597-019-0031-8
9. Golub, K., Ardö, A.: Importance of HTML structural elements and metadata in automated subject classification. In: Rauber, A., Christodoulakis, S., Tjoa, A.M. (eds.) ECDL 2005. LNCS, vol. 3652, pp. 368–378. Springer, Heidelberg (2005). https://doi.org/10.1007/11551362_33
10. Guha, R.V., Brickley, D., Macbeth, S.: Schema.org: evolution of structured data on the web. Commun. ACM **59**(2), 44–51 (2016)
11. Hernández, I., Rivero, C.R., Ruiz, D., Corchuelo, R.: A statistical approach to URL-based web page clustering. In: 21st International Conference on World Wide Web. WWW 2012 Companion, pp. 525–526 (2012). https://doi.org/10.1145/2187980.2188109
12. Hogan, A., Harth, A., Passant, A., Decker, S., Polleres, A.: Weaving the pedantic web. LDOW **628**, 26 (2010)
13. Kingma, D.P., Ba, J.: Adam: a method for stochastic optimization. arXiv preprint arXiv:1412.6980 (2014)
14. Kocayusufoglu, F., et al.: Riser: learning better representations for richly structured emails. In: The Web Conference, WWW 2019, pp. 886–895 (2019). https://doi.org/10.1145/3308558.3313720
15. Koesten, L.M., Kacprzak, E., Tennison, J.F.A., Simperl, E.: The trials and tribulations of working with structured data: -a study on information seeking behaviour. In: CHI 2017 (2017). https://doi.org/10.1145/3025453.3025838
16. Krutil, J., Kudĕka, M., Snášel, V.: Web page classification based on schema.org collection. In: 2012 Fourth International Conference on Computational Aspects of Social Networks (CASoN), pp. 356–360 (2012)
17. Lin, B.Y., Sheng, Y., Vo, N., Tata, S.: FreeDOM: a transferable neural architecture for structured information extraction on web documents. In: ACM KDD, pp. 1092–1102 (2020). https://doi.org/10.1145/3394486.3403153
18. Meusel, R., Paulheim, H.: Heuristics for fixing common errors in deployed *schema.org* microdata. In: Gandon, F., Sabou, M., Sack, H., d'Amato, C., Cudré-Mauroux, P., Zimmermann, A. (eds.) ESWC 2015. LNCS, vol. 9088, pp. 152–168. Springer, Cham (2015). https://doi.org/10.1007/978-3-319-18818-8_10
19. Najork, M.: Web spam detection encyclopedia of database systems (2009)
20. Noy, N., Brickley, D., Burgess, M.: Google dataset search: building a search engine for datasets in an open web ecosystem. In: The Web Conference, WWW 2019 (2019). https://doi.org/10.1145/3308558.3313685
21. Pang, B., Lee, L., Vaithyanathan, S.: Thumbs up? Sentiment classification using machine learning techniques. In: A Empirical Methods in Natural Language Processing, EMNLP, USA, pp. 79–86 (2002). https://doi.org/10.3115/1118693.1118704
22. Qi, X., Davison, B.D.: Web page classification: Features and algorithms. ACM Comput. Surv. **41**(2) (2009). https://doi.org/10.1145/1459352.1459357
23. Renear, A.H., Sacchi, S., Wickett, K.M.: Definitions of dataset in the scientific and technical literature. Am. Soc. Inf. Sci. Technol. **47**(1), 1–4 (2010). https://doi.org/10.1002/meet.14504701240
24. Shettar, R., Bhuptani, R.: A vertical search engine-based on domain classifier. Int. J. Comp. Sci. Secur. **2**(4), 18–27 (2007)

25. Wang, Q., Kanagal, B., Garg, V., Sivakumar, D.: Constructing a comprehensive events database from the web. In: 28th ACM CIKM (2019). https://doi.org/10.1145/3357384.3357986
26. Xiong, C., Liu, Z., Callan, J., Liu, T.Y.: Towards better text understanding and retrieval through kernel entity salience modeling. In: 41st ACM SIGIR (2018)
27. Zhao, Q., Yang, W., Hua, R.: Design and research of composite web page classification network based on deep learning. In: 2019 IEEE 31st International Conference on Tools with Artificial Intelligence (ICTAI), pp. 1531–1535. IEEE (2019)

Learning Visual Models Using a Knowledge Graph as a Trainer

Sebastian Monka[1,2]([✉]), Lavdim Halilaj[1], Stefan Schmid[1],
and Achim Rettinger[2]

[1] Bosch Research, Renningen, Germany
{sebastian.monka,lavdim.halilaj,stefan.schmid}@de.bosch.com
[2] Trier University, Trier, Germany
rettinger@uni-trier.de

Abstract. Traditional computer vision approaches, based on neural networks (NN), are typically trained on a large amount of image data. By minimizing the cross-entropy loss between a prediction and a given class label, the NN and its visual embedding space are learned to fulfill a given task. However, due to the sole dependence on the image data distribution of the training domain, these models tend to fail when applied to a target domain that differs from their source domain. To learn a more robust NN to domain shifts, we propose the *knowledge graph neural network* (KG-NN), a neuro-symbolic approach that supervises the training using image-data-invariant auxiliary knowledge. The auxiliary knowledge is first encoded in a knowledge graph with respective concepts and their relationships, which is then transformed into a dense vector representation via an embedding method. Using a contrastive loss function, KG-NN learns to adapt its visual embedding space and thus its weights according to the image-data invariant knowledge graph embedding space. We evaluate KG-NN on visual transfer learning tasks for classification using the mini-ImageNet dataset and its derivatives, as well as road sign recognition datasets from Germany and China. The results show that a visual model trained with a knowledge graph as a trainer outperforms a model trained with cross-entropy in all experiments, in particular when the domain gap increases. Besides better performance and stronger robustness to domain shifts, these KG-NN adapts to multiple datasets and classes without suffering heavily from catastrophic forgetting.

Keywords: Neuro-symbolic · Knowledge graph · Transfer learning

1 Introduction

Deep neural networks (NNs) are widely used in computer vision (CV). Their main strength lies in their ability to find complex underlying features in images. A common method for training an NN is to minimize the cross-entropy loss, which is equivalent to maximizing the negative log-likelihood between the empirical distribution of the training set and the probability distribution defined by the model. This relies on the independent and identically distributed (i.i.d.)

© Springer Nature Switzerland AG 2021
A. Hotho et al. (Eds.): ISWC 2021, LNCS 12922, pp. 357–373, 2021.
https://doi.org/10.1007/978-3-030-88361-4_21

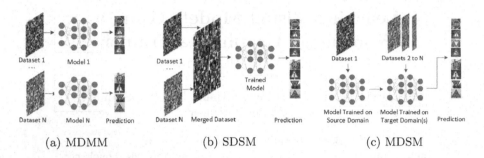

(a) MDMM	(b) SDSM	(c) MDSM

Fig. 1. Categorization of domain adaptation approaches: a) Multiple Domains Multiple Models (MDMM); b) Single Domain Single Model (SDSM); and c) Multiple Domains Single Model (MDSM).

assumptions as underlying rules of basic machine learning, which state that the examples in each dataset are independent of each other, that train and test set are identically distributed and drawn from the same probability distribution [12]. However, if the train and test domains follow different image distributions the i.i.d. assumptions are violated, and deep learning leads to unpredictable and poor results [44]. This has been demonstrated by using adversarially constructed examples [13] or variations in the test images such as noise, blur, and JPEG compression [19]. Authors in [7] even claim that any standard NN suffers from such an unpredictable distribution shift when it is deployed in the real world.

Transfer learning approaches that deal with such distribution shifts can be grouped into three main categories as depicted in Fig. 1: a) *Multiple Domains Multiple Models (MDMM)*; b) *Single Domain Single Model (SDSM)*; and c) *Multiple Domains Single Model (MDSM)*. MDMM approaches treat all datasets as independent and train a respective model for each of them. Therefore, these approaches are very costly to train, and learned knowledge cannot be transferred between datasets. SDSM approaches train a single model on a large dataset merged from many smaller ones. However, it is difficult to create a balanced dataset required by the NN to learn a general representation suitable for all domains. MDSM approaches train a single model on various datasets at different stages, and can therefore transfer learned knowledge to new domains. However, if trained with the standard cross entropy these models suffer from an unpredictable and error-prone knowledge transfer and *catastrophic forgetting*, where learned knowledge from previous datasets tends to be forgotten after training on the current dataset.

To reduce the high dependency on the training domain, pre-training methods that generate rich embedding spaces seem to be a promising research direction for CV and natural language processing (NLP). Exploring these embedding spaces, it is found that NNs encode visually similar classes close to each other when sufficient training data is available. Recently, the idea of training an NN with an image-independent embedding space in form of language embeddings has also been proven to be beneficial for CV tasks [22, 36, 54].

In this paper, we introduce the *knowledge graph neural network* (KG-NN), a novel approach to learn a visual model using a knowledge graph (KG) and its knowledge graph embedding h_{KG} as a trainer. More concretely, a domain-invariant embedding space using a KG and an appropriate KG embedding algorithm is constructed. We then train KG-NN with a contrastive loss function to adapt its visual embedding to h_{KG} given by the KG. KG-NN, therefore, learns the relevant features of the images by connecting semantically similar classes and distinguishing them from different ones. The benefit is two-fold. First, KG-NN will be more robust to distribution shifts since the embedding space is independent of the dataset distribution, and second, it is enriched with additional semantic data in a controlled manner.

To investigate the generalization and adaption of KG-NN in real-world scenarios, the task of visual transfer learning provides a suitable testing environment. Transfer learning tasks consist of a source and a target dataset, differing in terms of their underlying distribution, e.g. sensors, environments, countries. A domain generalization task has only access to labeled source data, whereas the domain adaptation task contains a small amount of additional labeled target data. For domain generalization - *Scenario 1*, we performed two experiments: 1) object classification, where the NN is trained on the mini-ImageNet [47] dataset and evaluated on derivatives; 2) road sign recognition, where the NN is trained on the German Traffic Signs Dataset (GTSRB) [43] and evaluate on the Chinese Traffic Signs Dataset (CTSD) [52]. For domain adaptation - *Scenario 2*, we train the NN on GTSRB and additional labeled target data from CTSD. In both scenarios, the respective KGs are developed in Resource Description Framework (RDF) representation. RDF provides the necessary means for an easy and flexible extension of the defined schemas and allows for enriching and interlinking entities in the KGs with complementary information from other sources.

The generality of our approach becomes apparent in the fact that it can be assigned to any of the three categories illustrated in Fig. 1 since we provide an alternative and enriched training method for NNs. While in this paper, we only compare with approaches from the third category, our results indicate that KG-NN is significantly more accurate compared to a conventional approach based on the cross-entropy loss in any domain-changing scenario. Our main contributions of this paper are summarized as follows:

- We introduce KG-NN, a neuro-symbolic approach that uses prior domain-invariant knowledge captured by a KG to train an NN.
- We adapt a contrastive loss function to combine knowledge graph embeddings with the visual embeddings learned by the NN.
- We evaluate the KG-NN approach in domain generalization and domain adaptation tasks on two different scenarios with respective image datasets.

The paper starts with the definition of preliminaries in Sect. 2. Section 3 presents a detailed description of KG-NN where a KG is used as a trainer. Section 4 provides an evaluation on two datasets in a domain generalization and domain adaptation task. Related work is outlined in Sect. 5. We conclude the paper and provide an outlook on future directions in Sect. 6.

2 Preliminaries

Knowledge Graph. We adopt the definition given by Hogan et al. [21] where a knowledge graph is *a graph of data aiming to accumulate and convey real-world knowledge, where entities are represented by nodes and relationships between entities are represented by edges.* In its most basic form, a KG is a set of triples $G = H, R, T$, where H is a set of entities, $T \subseteq E \times L$, is a set of entities or literal values and R, a set of relationships which connects H and T.

Knowledge Graph Embedding. A knowledge graph embedding h_{KG} is a representation of entities and edges of a KG in a high-dimensional vector space while preserving its latent structure [21]. Related to language embeddings, we count h_{KG} as a form of a semantic embedding h_s. The h_{KG} is learned by a knowledge graph embedding method $KGE(\cdot)$ using entities and relations encoded in the KG. Individual vectors, corresponding to the entities from the KG represented in h_{KG} are denoted as $h_{KG,a}$ with dimensionality d_P.

Visual Embedding. An *encoder network* $E(\cdot)$ is part of the NN and maps images x to a visual embedding $h_v = E(x) \in \mathbb{R}^{d_E}$, where the activations of the final pooling layer and thus the representation layer have a dimensionality d_E, where d_E depends on the encoder network that is used. If the encoder network is learned using a semantic embedding, we define it as $h_{v(s)}$. If the semantic embedding is given by a KG we further denote the visual-semantic embedding as $h_{v(KG)}$.

Visual Projection. A *projection network* $P(\cdot)$ maps the normalized embedding vectors h_v into a visual projection $z = P(h_v) \in \mathbb{R}^{d_P}$ in which it is compared with the class-label representation of the h_{KG}. For the projection network $P(\cdot)$, we use a multi-layer perceptron [15] with a single hidden layer, an input dimensionality d_E, and output vector of size d_P to match the dimensionality of h_{KG}.

Transfer Learning. A formal definition of transfer learning is presented in [38] as follows: *Given a source domain D_S with input data X_S, a corresponding source task T_S with labels Y_S, as well as a target domain D_T with input data X_T and a target task T_T with labels Y_T, the objective of transfer learning is to learn the target conditional probability distribution $P_T(Y_T|X_T)$ with the information gained from D_S and T_S where $D_S \neq D_T$ or $T_S \neq T_T$.* Transfer learning with no target data at training is referred to as domain generalization, whereas supervised domain adaptation has access to a small amount of labeled target data.

3 Knowledge Graph as a Trainer

In this section, we define the basic terminology of the KG-NN approach as well as the underlying pipeline for the realization of a transfer learning task.

The main objective of KG-NN is incorporating prior knowledge into the deep learning pipeline using a knowledge graph as a trainer. As depicted in Fig. 2a, the

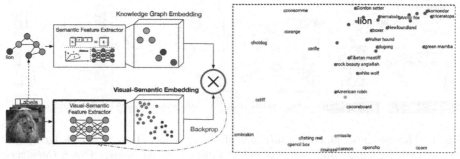

(a) Training abstraction of $h_{v(KG)}$.   (b) Knowledge graph embedding h_{KG}.

Fig. 2. KG-NN Approach: a) the main building blocks for learning a visual-semantic embedding space $h_{v(KG)}$ using a knowledge graph as a trainer; b) the 2D projection of the semantic-embedding h_{KG} represented in a knowledge graph.

class labels of a given dataset are infused to the NN in form of a high-dimensional vector of the knowledge graph embedding space h_{KG}, instead of using the standard one-hot encoded vectors. This h_{KG} shown in Fig. 2b is generated from a KG using a knowledge graph embedding method $KGE(\cdot)$. It incorporates domain-invariant relations to other classes inside or outside the dataset and therefore enriches the NN with auxiliary knowledge in an indirect manner. To guide the adaption of the NN to the h_{KG} space, we use the *contrastive knowledge graph embedding loss*. It compares the respective outputs from the visual feature extractor with the class label vectors of the h_{KG} forming a visual-sematic embedding space $h_{v(KG)}$. As a result, the learned NN projects respective images close to their representations given by the h_{KG}.

Contrastive Knowledge Graph Embedding Loss. We derive the contrastive knowledge graph embedding loss from the supervised contrastive loss [4,23] which extend the multi-class N-pair loss [41] or InfoNCE loss [33] with class label information. Instead of contrasting images in the batch against an anchor image, we adapt the loss to contrast images of the batch against the class label representation of the h_{KG}. A batch consists of 2N training samples, two augmented versions for each of the N training images. Within a batch, an anchor $i \in \{1...2N\}$ is selected that corresponds to a specific class label y_i and therefore assigns a specific embedding vector of the h_{KG}, $h_{KG,i}$. Positive samples are all samples that correspond to the same class label as the anchor i. The numerator in the loss function computes a similarity score between the anchor vector of the h_{KG}, $h_{KG,i}$, and the visual projection vector of a positive sample in the batch, z_j. The denominator computes the similarity score between the anchor vector of the h_{KG} and the visual projection vector of all other samples z_k in the batch. We choose the cosine similarity as the distance measure in the high-dimensional space. For each anchor i, there can be many positive samples, which contribute

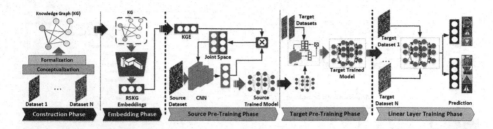

Fig. 3. The designed pipeline consisting of five phases where a knowledge graph acts as a trainer supporting adaption and generalization: *Knowledge Graph Construction*; *Knowledge Graph Embedding*; *Source Domain Pre-Training*; *Target Domain Pre-Training*; and *Linear Layer Training*.

to the final loss, where N_{y_i} is their total number. The KG-based contrastive loss function is then given by:

$$\mathcal{L}_{KG} = \sum_{i=1}^{2N} \mathcal{L}_{KG,i} \tag{1}$$

with

$$\mathcal{L}_{KG,i} = \frac{-1}{2N_{y_i} - 1} \sum_{j=1}^{2N} \mathbb{1}_{i \neq j} \cdot \mathbb{1}_{y_i = y_j} \cdot \log \frac{\exp\left(\boldsymbol{h}_{KG,i} \cdot \boldsymbol{z}_j / \tau\right)}{\sum_{k=1}^{2N} \mathbb{1}_{i \neq k} \exp\left(\boldsymbol{h}_{KG,i} \cdot \boldsymbol{z}_k / \tau\right)} \tag{2}$$

where $\boldsymbol{z}_l = P(E(\boldsymbol{x}))$, $\mathbb{1}_{k \neq i} \in \{0, 1\}$ is an indicator function that returns 1 iff $k \neq i$ evaluates as true, and $\tau > 0$ is a predefined scalar temperature parameter. During optimization of the loss function $\mathcal{L}_{KG}$, the NN learns its weights by mapping its projection $\boldsymbol{z}_l$ to the $\boldsymbol{h}_{KG}$ space.

3.1   Adaptation to a Labeled Target Domain

Training robust NNs is crucial in real-world scenarios as deployment domains typically differ from the training ones. The knowledge graph as a trainer can influence how an NN should behave in different environments by providing a stable embedding space. However, if the domain gap is quite large, it is beneficial to fine-tune the NN on labeled data of the target domain. We design a training pipeline to support a transfer learning scenario where a small amount of labeled target data exists. An overview of this pipeline comprised of five consecutive phases is shown in Fig. 3.

Knowledge Graph Construction. Knowledge graphs can represent prior knowledge encoded with rich semantics in a graph structure. Based on the selected scenario, underlying knowledge of one or multiple domains is conceptualized and formalized into a KG. Since KGs are manually curated by human experts, it is possible to define an underlying schema comprising multiple classes from different domains. This joint representation of domains enables inferring relations between classes, which can then be transferred into high-dimensional vector space.

Knowledge Graph Embedding. The KG is transformed into a knowledge graph embedding space h_{KG} via a knowledge graph embedding method $KGE(\cdot)$. There are various approaches to generate these dense vectors that encode all entities and relations within the KG [8,30,31]. Note that KG-NN can operate on any h_{KG} generated by any $KGE(\cdot)$, as an h_{KG} only reflects similarities between entities by distances and positions in the vector space. Thus, if entities share many properties in the KG, they are closely located in space.

Source Domain Pre-training. We train KG-NN from scratch using the KG as a trainer and do not initialize the NN with pre-trained weights from ImageNet [39] As the $h_{v(KG)}$ space of KG-NN depends on the KG instead of the source dataset, KG-NN can be applied to other domains following the same semantic relations given by the KG. This property is shown on the domain generalization task.

Target Domain Pre-training. Small amounts of labeled target data can usually be gathered with manageable effort. However, just fine-tuning an NN with additional target domain data using the cross-entropy loss leads to catastrophic forgetting and thus poor accuracy. We assume that this happens because the NN tries to find a new h_v that fits the target domain, but differs from the embedding obtained from the source domain. In contrast, NNs optimized on the source domain using a KG as a trainer, can simply be enriched with additional target data using the same training method. Therefore, KG-NN pre-trained on the source domain, is retrained on the target dataset using the same h_{KG}.

Linear Layer Training. For adaption to a downstream task like classification, we add a randomly-initialized linear fully-connected layer to the trained encoder network. The size of the output vector depends on the number of classes. This linear layer is trained with the default cross-entropy loss, while the parameters of the encoder network remain unchanged.

4   Experiment

We conduct experiments on two different scenarios with multiple datasets to demonstrate the benefit of training an NN using a knowledge graph as a trainer, which leads to more accurate and more robust models in terms of the distribution shift. We compare KG-NN with two baselines: 1) CE, which trains the NN using the supervised cross-entropy loss; and 2) SupCon, which trains the NN with the (self-)supervised contrastive loss [23]. We chose CE, as it is typically used for training NNs, as well as SupCon, as this approach utilizes a similar contrastive loss function, however without the incorporation of prior knowledge and supervision. CE and SupCon learn an embedding layer based on the data distribution of the source dataset, whereas KG-NN relies on the embedding given by the knowledge graph. To qualitatively evaluate the influence of the knowledge graph embedding we further compare against GloVe, a variation of KG-NN that uses a GloVe [35] language embedding instead of h_{KG}. All approaches use the same ResNet-50 [17] backend as encoder network and only differ in their method how this encoder network is trained.

Two different scenarios are defined to analyze our approach to concrete transfer learning tasks. *Scenario 1* - we investigate the sensitivity to distribution shifts using a domain generalization task. Therefore, we train: a) KG-NN, CE, Sup-Con, and GloVe from scratch on mini-ImageNet and evaluate on its derivatives, ImageNetV2 [37], ImageNet-R [18], ImageNet-Sketch [48] and ImageNet-A [20]; b) KG-NN, CE, and SupCon from scratch on GTSRB, and evaluate on CTSD. *Scenario 2* - we focus on supervised domain adaptation, a more practical scenario where KG-NN, CE, and SupCon are trained on GTSRB and fully retrained on CTSD with a small amount of target data. Note that we exclude GloVe when using GTSRB/CTSD since the language embedding does not contain a specific representation for each roadsign class and therefore can not be applied straight forward.

4.1   Scenario 1 - Domain Generalization

Domain generalization describes the task of learning generalized models on a source domain so that they can be used on unseen target domains. Therefore, KG-NN is used without the target domain pre-training phase.

Experiment 1 - Wordnet-Subset with Mini-ImageNet

Dataset Settings. As source domain, we use mini-ImageNet, a derivative of the ImageNet dataset, consisting of 60K color images of size 84×84 with 100 classes, each having 600 examples. Compared to ImageNet, this dataset fits in memory on modern machines, making it very convenient for rapid prototyping and experimentation. For the evaluation, we use the target domains: ImageNetV2, which contains 10 new test images per class and closely follows the original labeling protocol; ImageNet-R, which has art, cartoons, deviantart, etc. renditions of 200 ImageNet classes resulting in 30,000 images; ImageNet-Sketch comprising 50,000 images, 50 images for each of the 1000 ImageNet classes; and ImageNet-A, which contains real-world, unmodified, and naturally occurring examples that cause machine learning model's performance to significantly degrade.

Knowledge Graph and KG Embedding Space. WordNet is a lexical database containing nouns, verbs, adjectives, and adverbs of the English language structured into respective synsets [28,46]. Each synset is an underlying concept consisting of a collection of synonyms as well as its relations to other synsets. The *Mini Word-Net Knowledge Graph* (MWKG) is created by extracting the respective synsets of each label from the mini-ImageNet dataset from [2] into RDF representation. These synsets are grouped based on the lexical domain they pertain to, e.g. *animal*, *artifact*, or *food*. They are represented as classes and further described with relations such as: *hypernym*, *meronym*, *synset-member*. Additionally, a shallow taxonomy is established by extracting the parents of each synset including their relationships and attributes. In total, MWKG contains 198 classes with 8

	CE	SupCon	GloVe	KG-NN
Mini-ImageNet	64.5 +1.7%	56.2 +10.0%	64.7 +1.5%	**66.2**
ImageNetV2	49.3 +3.2%	43.8 +8.7%	49.5 +3.0%	**52.5**
ImageNet-R	20.6 +9.4%	26.0 +4.0%	27.4 +2.6%	**30.0**
ImageNet-Sketch	12.3 +15.4%	22.3 +5.4%	24.3 +3.4%	**27.7**
ImageNet-A	4.3 +1.0%	4.2 +1.1%	5.0 +0.3%	**5.3**

Fig. 4. Accuracy of the domain generalization task using mini-ImageNet as source and multiple derivatives as target domains. We compare KG-NN with the standard CE, SupCon, a version of our loss without auxiliary knowledge of a KG, and GloVe, a version of KG-NN using a language embedding instead of a h_{KG}.

annotation properties. We transfer MWKG into a 300-dimensional h_{KG} using the MRGCN [51], which exploits the literal information in addition to classes and their relationships. To realize that, we use the MRGCN's node classification feature to build the h_{KG} that explicitly clusters the six lexical domains: animal, artifact, communication, food, object, and plant.

Training Details. All models use a ResNet-50 backend and are pre-trained with a batch size of 1024 on the mini-ImageNet dataset. We resize the images to 32 × 32 for fast prototyping. KG-NN and SupCon are trained for 1000 epochs using their respective contrastive loss function, stochastic gradient descent (SGD) with a learning rate of 0.5, cosine annealing, and a temperature of $\tau = 0.5$. CE is trained for 500 epochs with the cross-entropy loss and SGD with a learning rate of 0.8. For the *linear-layer phase*, we train an *one-layer* MLP on top of the frozen encoder networks of KG-NN, SupCon, and CE, with an adam optimizer and a learning rate of 0.0004.

Evaluation. We evaluate the models on ImageNetV2, ImageNet-R, ImageNet-Sketch, and ImageNet-A. KG-NN outperforms CE, SupCon, and GloVe on the trained source as well as on unknown target domains as shown in Fig. 4. This means that KG-NN makes use of the additional semantic information. It can be seen that CE fails particularly when the domain gap increases. We assume that this happens due to its high specialization on the source domain. SupCon cannot reach the performance of CE on the source dataset, however, it outperforms CE on more general target tasks. We see that pre-training on a more generic self-supervised task helps the NN to extract more general features. GloVe, the version of KG-NN that relies on a language embedding instead of a KG, is also outperformed by KG-NN. We see that the performance of KG-NN depends on the quality of the embedding space, which we can control manually using different KGs or $KGE(\cdot)$s.

Experiment 2 - RoadSign KG with GTSRB and CTSD

Dataset Settings. The German Traffic Sign Dataset (GTSRB), which contains 51,970 images of 43 road signs, is used as the source domain, and the Chinese Traffic Sign Dataset (CTSD), which contains 6,164 images of 58 road signs, as the target domain. We resize all images to a uniform size of 32 × 32 pixels. Note that we do not cut out the road signs, but take the whole image for classification. Both datasets contain a domain shift as they were recorded with different cameras in different countries and hence have different appearances.

Knowledge Graph and KG Embedding Space. First, we construct a small knowledge graph for traffic sign recognition (RSKG) that contains all classes of both datasets incorporated in an underlying domain ontology. To encode the formal semantics of road signs from different countries and standards, we first develop the *RoadSign* ontology. It contains classes (e.g. RoadSign, Shape, Icon, Color), relationships (e.g. hasShape, hasIcon, hasColor) and attributes (e.g. label, textWithinSign, etc.). The actual road signs that exist within given datasets are represented as concrete *individuals*. Note that this information is extracted from externally available road-sign standards, without accessing the datasets. Currently, RSKG contains 18 classes, 11 object properties, 2 datatype properties, and 101 individuals. It is important to mention that the knowledge graph can be further populated with concrete road signs instances from other countries. This would enrich RSKG and could help to find inter-relations between the domains. We transfer RSKG into a 300-dimensional h_{KG} by using MRGCN [51] as we also want to exploit its literal information. Therefore, we use MRGCN in the node classification task to build a h_{KG} that explicitly clusters the five classes: danger, informative, mandatory, prohibitory, and warning.

Training Details. We use the same training setting and hyperparameters as in the experiment with the mini-ImageNet dataset.

Evaluation. Figure 5 shows that KG-NN outperforms CE by 0.8% on the source and by 7.1% on the target dataset. It can be seen that KG-NN exceeds the accuracy of SupCon by 55.0% on GTSRB and by 35.7% on CTSD. SupCon with its self-supervised loss needs large datasets to form a good embedding space, however, both datasets are quite small and from the special domain of road-sign-recognition. We do not compare against a GloVe embedding, as there are no instances for specific road signs and no clear procedure on how to generate these instances from a text corpus. Overall, KG-NN performs better and is more robust to unforeseen distribution shifts using the same amount of training data.

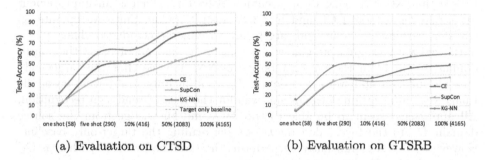

		CE	SupCon	KG-NN
GTSRB		96.1 +0.8%	41.9 +55.0%	**96.9**
CTSD		63.0 +7.1%	34.4 +35.7%	**70.1**

Fig. 5. Accuracy of the domain generalization task using GTSRB as the source and CTSD as the target domain. We compare KG-NN with the standard CE and SupCon, a version of our loss without auxiliary knowledge of a KG.

(a) Evaluation on CTSD	(b) Evaluation on GTSRB

Fig. 6. Comparison of KG-NN, SupCon, and CE on the test dataset of the target domain for five different amounts of target data: a) evaluates the NNs on the target domain; b) evaluates the same NNs on the initial source domain to reflect *catastrophic forgetting* phenomena.

4.2 Scenario 2 - Supervised Domain Adaptation

Supervised domain adaptation describes the task of transfer learning that adapts models learned on a source domain to a specific labeled target domain. We claim that an NN learned using an image-data-independent h_{KG} can adapt to new domains and new classes better as both domains use the same embedding space. For this experiment, we use the same settings described in Experiment 2. First, KG-NN, CE, and SupCon, are pre-trained on the source dataset. Second, we use the encoder networks of each NN and presume the pre-training on the target dataset. The NNs are retrained with different amounts of labeled target data. The one-shot (58) experiment uses 58 images, one image for each class of the CTSD target dataset. The five-shot (290) experiment uses 290 images, five images for each class of the CTSD. The 10% (416) experiment uses 416 images, 10% of images of the CTSD. The 50% (2083) experiment uses 2,083 images, 50% of images of the CTSD. The 100% (4165) experiment uses 4,165 images, 100% of images of the CTSD target dataset. Similar to the previous experiments, we use the *linear layer phase* to adopt the pre-trained encoder network to the target task. As shown in Fig. 6, all experiments are evaluated on the full CTSD target dataset and on the 25 common classes of the GTSRB source dataset.

Evaluating the approaches on the initial source domain, we find that all NN suffer from *catastrophic forgetting*, as depicted in Fig. 6b. If 100% of target data is used for training, the accuracy of CE drops from 96.1% to 49.5%, the accuracy of SupCon drops from 41.9% to 37.2%, and the accuracy of KG-NN drops from 96.9% to 60.7% on the source domain. This means that KG-NN is still the best performing model on the source domain, even after retraining on a target domain with an increased difference to CE from 0.8% to 11.2%. We think that the fixed embedding space between source and target domain helps to overcome the issue of *catastrophic forgetting*.

If we compare the approaches on the target domain as illustrated in Fig. 6a, we see that KG-NN achieves an accuracy of 88.1%, which is an improvement by 5.9% over standard CE and by 23.4% over SupCon. Since we operate on transfer learning, an additional target-only baseline is introduced. Thus, CE is initialized with weights pre-trained on ImageNet, instead of using the source domain to pre-train the parameters of the NN. We see that the target-only baseline suffers from fewer target data in D_T yielding only 53.1% accuracy as the ImageNet initialization does not suit well for the task of road sign recognition. All approaches seem to be able to transfer some knowledge from the source domain D_S to the target domain D_T outperforming the target-only baseline. However, KG-NN significantly outperforms the baseline by 35.0%, whereas CE improves by 29.1% and SupCon by 11.6%.

Interestingly, with less than five target images per class, which is fewer than 7% of target data, KG-NN surpasses the performance of the target-only baseline. We observe KG-NN always outperforms CE by approximately 10% of accuracy. When compared to SupCon, we see the accuracy difference even increases if more labeled target data is available. In the one-shot scenario, KG-NN outperforms CE by 12.2% of accuracy, in the five-shot-scenario by 13.8%, in the 10%-scenario by 11.2%, in the 50%-scenario by 10.7%, and on the full target dataset by 5.9%. In the one-shot scenario KG-NN outperforms SupCon by 10.3% of accuracy, in the five-shot-scenario by 25.4%, in the 10%-scenario by 25%, in the 50%-scenario by 31.6%, and on the full target dataset by 23.4%.

5 Related Work

Embedding spaces trained with the cross-entropy loss tend to be specialized embedding spaces for a particular domain. To reduce the high dependency on the training domain, pre-training methods that generate rich embedding spaces seem to be a promising research direction for CV and NLP. Most neuro-symbolic approaches only learn a transformation function, e.g., MLP, on top of a pre-trained h_v. We refer to these models as visual-semantic transformation models. Since the weights of the visual feature extractor are a really important part of robust object recognition, recent approaches have shown that learning a visual-semantic feature extractor from scratch improves generalization capabilities and makes the NN applicable to further downstream and transfer learning tasks [36]. We refer to these models as visual-semantic feature extractors.

Neural Networks Improved by Knowledge Graphs. Most of the works that combine KGs with NNs use WordNet [50], small-scale label [6,25] or scene [5] graphs as KG. However, the capacity of WordNet as a lexical database is limited. Large-scale KGs such as DBPedia [3] or ConceptNet [42] encode additional semantic information by using higher order relations between concepts. Although their applications are still sparse in the visual domain, there are a few works that have shown promising results. DBPedia is already used in the field of explainable AI [11,24], object detection [26], and visual question answering [49]; and ConceptNet is used for video classification [53] and zero-shot action recognition [10]. However, all approaches use the KG only as a post-validation step on a pre-trained visual feature extractor, while KG-NN learns the visual feature extractor by itself based on the KG.

Visual-Semantic Transformation Models are learned via a transformation function, e.g. MLP, from a pre-trained h_v into h_s. One of the first approaches that use h_s with NNs is the work from Mitchell et al. [29]. They use word embeddings derived from text corpus statistics to generate neural activity patterns, i.e. images. Instead of generating images from text, Palatucci et al. [34] learn a linear regression model to map neural activity patterns into word embedding space. In their work, they improve zero-shot learning by extrapolating the knowledge gathered from in the h_s related classes to novel classes. Socher et al. [40] present a model for zero-shot learning that learns a transformation function between an h_v space, obtained by an unsupervised feature extraction method, and an h_s, based on an NN-based language model. The authors trained a 2-layer NN with the MSE loss to transform the h_v into the word embedding of 8 classes. Frome et al. [9] introduce the deep visual-semantic embedding model DeViSE that extends the approach from 8 known and 2 unknown classes to 1000 known classes for the image model and up to 20,000 unknown classes. Therefore, they pre-train their visual feature extractor using ImageNet and their h_s based on the Word2Vec [27] language model, exposed to the text of a single online encyclopedia. In contrast to Socher et al. [40], DeVISE learns a linear transformation function between the h_v space and the h_s space using a combination of dot-product similarity and hinge rank loss since MSE distance fails in high dimensional space. Norouzi et al. [32] propose *convex combination of semantic embeddings* (ConSE), a simple framework for constructing a zero-shot learning classifier. ConSE uses a semantic word embedding model to reason about the predicted output scores of the NN-based image classifier. To predict unknown classes, it performs a convex combination of the classes in the h_s space, weighted by their predicted output scores of the NN. Similarly, Zhang et al. [55] introduce the *semantic similarity embedding* (SSE), which models target data instances as a mixture of seen class proportions. SSE builds a semantic space where each novel class could be represented as a probabilistic mixture of the projected source attribute vectors of the seen classes. Akata et al. [1] refer to their h_s space transformations as label embedding methods. They compared transformation functions from the h_v space to the attribute label embedding space, the hierarchy label embedding space, and the Word2Vec label embedding space, in which embedded classes can share features among themselves.

Visual-Semantic Feature Extractors: The approaches mentioned so far only learn a transformation from h_v to h_s. However, the parameters of the feature extractor are not affected by the auxiliary information. Thus, if the feature extractor cannot detect visual features due to the domain shift problem, the performance of the final prediction suffers. Instead of maximizing the likelihood on the output, some approaches maximize the energy (i.e. difference between the prediction and the excepted result) directly on the embedding space to learn the NN. Hadsell et al. [14] introduce the contrastive loss for a *siamese architecture* to learn a robust embedding space from unlabeled data. They show that their self-supervised energy-based method can learn a lighting and rotation-invariant embedding space. Recently, many approaches claim that training an embedding space in a self-supervised manner using the contrastive loss tends to find a more general and domain-invariant representation [4,16]. Furthermore, Tian et al. [45] show that learning an embedding space using the contrastive loss, followed by training a supervised linear classifier on top of this representation, outperforms state-of-the-art few-shot learning methods.

Joulin et al. [22] demonstrate that feature extractors trained to predict words in image captions can learn useful visual-semantic embedding spaces $h_{v(s)}$. Further, Radford et al. [36] proposed a simple and general pre-training of an NN with natural language supervision using a dataset of 400 million image-text pairs collected from the internet and the contrastive objective of Zhang et al. [54].

To the best of our knowledge, there is no work that learn a visual feature extractor using a KG or its embedding space h_{KG}. We choose to use prior knowledge encoded in a knowledge graph instead of using the unstructured knowledge of a language embedding as they are highly dependent on their text corpus, inconsistent, and do not incorporate expert knowledge.

6   Conclusion and Future Work

In this paper, we propose KG-NN, a knowledge graph-based approach that enables NN to learn more robust and controlled embedding spaces for transfer learning tasks. The core idea of our approach is to use domain-invariant knowledge represented in a KG, transform it into a vector space using knowledge graph embedding algorithms, and train an NN so that its embedding space is adapted to the domain-invariant embeddings given by the KG. Using our KG-based contrastive loss function, we force the NN to adapt its h_v space to the domain-invariant space h_{KG} given by the KG, thus forming $h_{v(KG)}$. Our experimental results show that NNs benefit from exploiting prior knowledge. As a result, it increases the accuracy on known and unknown domains and allows them to keep up with NNs trained with the cross-entropy loss despite requiring significantly less training data.

There are several directions of future work: First, identifying discriminative factors to best influence the domain-invariant space. Therefore, further investigations are needed to determine what knowledge is relevant and should be modeled in the KG to enable transfer learning. Second, analyzing how the prior knowledge can be modeled and represented best, e.g., via n-ary relations or hyper-relational graphs. Third, exploring various embedding techniques to operate on multi-modal information or Riemannian metrics to exploit hierarchical relations. And finally, evaluating different contrasting dimensions and knowledge infusion techniques could lead to further improvements.

We believe that the construction of task-specific knowledge graph embeddings and their combination with learned embeddings of NNs will help to build more interpretable, more robust, and more accurate machine learning models, while at the same time requiring less training data.

Acknowledgments. This publication was created as part of the research project "KI Delta Learning" (project number: 19A19013D) funded by the Federal Ministry for Economic Affairs and Energy (BMWi) on the basis of a decision by the German Bundestag.

References

1. Akata, Z., Perronnin, F., Harchaoui, Z., Schmid, C.: Label-embedding for image classification. IEEE Trans. Pattern Anal. Mach. Intell. **38**, 1425–1438 (2016)
2. van Assem, M., Isaac, A., von Ossenbruggen, J.: WordNet 3.0 in RDF (2010). http://semanticweb.cs.vu.nl/lod/wn30/
3. Auer, S., Bizer, C., Kobilarov, G., Lehmann, J., Cyganiak, R., Ives, Z.G.: DBpedia: a nucleus for a web of open data. In: ISWC (2007)
4. Chen, T., Kornblith, S., Norouzi, M., Hinton, G.E.: A simple framework for contrastive learning of visual representations. In: ICML (2020)
5. Chen, X., Li, L., Fei-Fei, L., Gupta, A.: Iterative visual reasoning beyond convolutions. In: CVPR (2018)
6. Chen, Z., Wei, X., Wang, P., Guo, Y.: Multi-label image recognition with graph convolutional networks. In: CVPR (2019)
7. D'Amour, A., et al.: Underspecification presents challenges for credibility in modern machine learning. CoRR (2020)
8. Dettmers, T., Minervini, P., Stenetorp, P., Riedel, S.: Convolutional 2D knowledge graph embeddings. In: AAAI (2018)
9. Frome, A., et al.: Devise: a deep visual-semantic embedding model. In: NIPS (2013)
10. Gao, J., Zhang, T., Xu, C.: I know the relationships: zero-shot action recognition via two-stream graph convolutional networks and knowledge graphs. In: AAAI (2019)
11. Geng, Y., Chen, J., Jiménez-Ruiz, E., Chen, H.: Human-centric transfer learning explanation via knowledge graph [extended abstract]. CoRR (2019)
12. Goodfellow, I.J., Bengio, Y., Courville, A.C.: Deep learning. In: Adaptive Computation and Machine Learning (2016)
13. Goodfellow, I.J., Shlens, J., Szegedy, C.: Explaining and harnessing adversarial examples. In: Bengio, Y., LeCun, Y. (eds.) ICLR (2015)

14. Hadsell, R., Chopra, S., LeCun, Y.: Dimensionality reduction by learning an invariant mapping. In: CVPR (2006)
15. Hastie, T., Friedman, J.H., Tibshirani, R.: The elements of statistical learning: data mining, inference, and prediction (2001)
16. He, K., Fan, H., Wu, Y., Xie, S., Girshick, R.B.: Momentum contrast for unsupervised visual representation learning. In: CVPR (2020)
17. He, K., Zhang, X., Ren, S., Sun, J.: Deep residual learning for image recognition. In: CVPR (2016)
18. Hendrycks, D., Basart, S., Mu, N., Kadavath, S., Wang, F., et al.: The many faces of robustness: a critical analysis of out-of-distribution generalization. CoRR (2020)
19. Hendrycks, D., Dietterich, T.G.: Benchmarking neural network robustness to common corruptions and perturbations. In: ICLR (2019)
20. Hendrycks, D., Zhao, K., Basart, S., Steinhardt, J., Song, D.: Natural adversarial examples. CoRR (2019)
21. Hogan, A., et al.: Knowledge graphs. CoRR (2020)
22. Joulin, A., van der Maaten, L., Jabri, A., Vasilache, N.: Learning visual features from large weakly supervised data. In: Leibe, B., Matas, J., Sebe, N., Welling, M. (eds.) ECCV 2016. LNCS, vol. 9911, pp. 67–84. Springer, Cham (2016). https://doi.org/10.1007/978-3-319-46478-7_5
23. Khosla, P., et al.: Supervised contrastive learning. In: NeurIPS (2020)
24. Lécué, F., Chen, J., Pan, J.Z., Chen, H.: Knowledge-based explanations for transfer learning. In: Studies on the Semantic Web (2020)
25. Lee, C., Fang, W., Yeh, C., Wang, Y.F.: Multi-label zero-shot learning with structured knowledge graphs. In: CVPR (2018)
26. Liu, Z., Jiang, Z., Wei, F.: OD-GCN object detection by knowledge graph with GCN. CoRR (2019)
27. Mikolov, T., Sutskever, I., Chen, K., Corrado, G.S., Dean, J.: Distributed representations of words and phrases and their compositionality. In: NIPS (2013)
28. Miller, G.A.: WordNet: a lexical database for English. ACM Commun. **38**, 39–41 (1995)
29. Mitchell, T.M., et al.: Predicting human brain activity associated with the meanings of nouns. Science **320**, 1191–1195 (2008)
30. Nguyen, D.Q., Nguyen, T.D., Nguyen, D.Q., Phung, D.Q.: A novel embedding model for knowledge base completion based on convolutional neural network. In: NAACL-HLT (2018)
31. Nickel, M., Rosasco, L., Poggio, T.A.: Holographic embeddings of knowledge graphs. In: Schuurmans, D., Wellman, M.P. (eds.) AAAI (2016)
32. Norouzi, M., et al.: Zero-shot learning by convex combination of semantic embeddings. In: ICLR (2014)
33. van den Oord, A., Li, Y., Vinyals, O.: Representation learning with contrastive predictive coding. CoRR (2018)
34. Palatucci, M., Pomerleau, D., Hinton, G.E., Mitchell, T.M.: Zero-shot learning with semantic output codes. In: NIPS (2009)
35. Pennington, J., Socher, R., Manning, C.D.: Glove: global vectors for word representation. In: EMNLP (2014)
36. Radford, A., et al.: Learning transferable visual models from natural language supervision. Image (2021)
37. Recht, B., Roelofs, R., Schmidt, L., Shankar, V.: Do ImageNet classifiers generalize to ImageNet? In: ICML (2019)
38. Ruder, S., Plank, B.: Learning to select data for transfer learning with bayesian optimization. In: EMNLP (2017)

39. Russakovsky, O., Deng, J., Su, H., et al.: ImageNet large scale visual recognition challenge. Int. J. Comput. Vis. **115**, 211–252 (2015)
40. Socher, R., Ganjoo, M., Manning, C.D., Ng, A.Y.: Zero-shot learning through cross-modal transfer. In: NIPS (2013)
41. Sohn, K.: Improved deep metric learning with multi-class n-pair loss objective. In: NIPS (2016)
42. Speer, R., Chin, J., Havasi, C.: ConceptNet 5.5: an open multilingual graph of general knowledge. In: AAAI (2017)
43. Stallkamp, J., Schlipsing, M., Salmen, J., Igel, C.: Man vs. computer: Benchmarking machine learning algorithms for traffic sign recognition. Neural Networks **32**, 323–332 (2012)
44. Tan, C., Sun, F., Kong, T., Zhang, W., Yang, C., Liu, C.: A survey on deep transfer learning. In: ICANN (2018)
45. Tian, Y., Wang, Y., Krishnan, D., Tenenbaum, J.B., Isola, P.: Rethinking few-shot image classification: a good embedding is all you need? In: Vedaldi, A., Bischof, H., Brox, T., Frahm, J.-M. (eds.) ECCV 2020. LNCS, vol. 12359, pp. 266–282. Springer, Cham (2020). https://doi.org/10.1007/978-3-030-58568-6_16
46. University, P.: About WordNet (2010). https://wordnet.princeton.edu
47. Vinyals, O., Blundell, C., Lillicrap, T., Kavukcuoglu, K., Wierstra, D.: Matching networks for one shot learning. In: NIPS (2016)
48. Wang, H., Ge, S., Lipton, Z., Xing, E.P.: Learning robust global representations by penalizing local predictive power. In: NeurIPS (2019)
49. Wang, P., Wu, Q., Shen, C., Dick, A.R., van den Hengel, A.: Explicit knowledge-based reasoning for visual question answering. In: IJCAI (2017)
50. Wang, X., Ye, Y., Gupta, A.: Zero-shot recognition via semantic embeddings and knowledge graphs. In: CVPR (2018)
51. Wilcke, W.X., Bloem, P., de Boer, V., van t Veer, R.H., van Harmelen, F.A.H.: End-to-end entity classification on multimodal knowledge graphs. CoRR (2020)
52. Yang, Y., Luo, H., Xu, H., Wu, F.: Towards real-time traffic sign detection and classification. IEEE Trans. Intell. Transp. Syst. **17**, 2022–2031 (2016)
53. Yuan, F., et al.: End-to-end video classification with knowledge graphs. CoRR (2017)
54. Zhang, Y., Jiang, H., Miura, Y., Manning, C.D., Langlotz, C.P.: Contrastive learning of medical visual representations from paired images and text. CoRR (2020)
55. Zhang, Z., Saligrama, V.: Zero-shot learning via semantic similarity embedding. In: ICCV (2015)

Controlled Query Evaluation over Prioritized Ontologies with Expressive Data Protection Policies

Gianluca Cima[1]([envelope])[iD], Domenico Lembo[2][iD], Lorenzo Marconi[2][iD],
Riccardo Rosati[2][iD], and Domenico Fabio Savo[3][iD]

[1] University of Bordeaux, CNRS, Bordeaux INP, LaBRI, Bordeaux, France
gianluca.cima@u-bordeoux.fr
[2] Sapienza Università di Roma, Rome, Italy
{lembo,marconi,rosati}@diag.uniroma1.it
[3] Università degli Studi di Bergamo, Bergamo, Italy
domenicofabio.savo@unibg.it

Abstract. We study information disclosure in Description Logic ontologies, in the spirit of Controlled Query Evaluation, where query answering is filtered through optimal censors maximizing answers while hiding data protected by a declarative policy. Previous works have considered limited forms of policy, typically constituted by conjunctive queries (CQs), whose answer must never be inferred by a user. Also, existing implementations adopt approximated notions of censors that might result too restrictive in the practice in terms of the amount of non-protected information returned to the users. In this paper we enrich the framework, by extending CQs in the policy with comparison predicates and introducing preferences between ontology predicates, which can be exploited to decide the portion of a secret that can be disclosed to a user, thus in principle augmenting the throughput of query answers. We show that answering CQs in our framework is first-order rewritable for *DL-Lite$_A$* ontologies and *safe* policies, and thus in AC^0 in data complexity. We also present some experiments on a popular benchmark, showing effectiveness and feasibility of our approach in a real-world scenario.

1 Introduction

In this paper, we study how to manage disclosure of sensitive information in Description Logic (DL) ontologies. This problem has been recently addressed in knowledge-based systems through Controlled Query Evaluation (CQE) [5,7–9,12], a declarative approach to data confidentiality preservation, originally investigated in the context of databases [4,14]. In a nutshell, CQE over ontologies involves specifying a data-protection policy as a set of queries whose answer must never be inferred by a user who

This work was partly supported by the ANR AI Chair INTENDED (ANR-19-CHIA-0014), by the EU within the H2020 Programme under the grant agreement 834228 (ERC Advanced Grant WhiteMec) and the grant agreement 825333 (MOSAICrOWN), by Regione Lombardia within the Call Hub Ricerca e Innovazione under the grant agreement 1175328 (WATCHMAN), and by the Italian MUR (Ministero dell'Università e della Ricerca) through the PRIN project HOPE (prot. 2017MMJJRE), and by Sapienza (project CQEinOBDM).

© Springer Nature Switzerland AG 2021
A. Hotho et al. (Eds.): ISWC 2021, LNCS 12922, pp. 374–391, 2021.
https://doi.org/10.1007/978-3-030-88361-4_22

is able to make standard reasoning and query answering over the ontology. To enforce privacy preservation, query answering is altered by a function called censor. Intuitively, optimal censors maximize answers to queries still guaranteeing that disclosed information cannot lead to answer queries in the policy.

Among various approaches, the one proposed in [6] has been shown to be particularly interesting from the practical point of view, since it allows for an effective reduction of conjunctive query answering under censors over *DL-Lite$_R$* ontologies to standard processing of conjunctive queries in Ontology-based Data Access (OBDA), where mappings connecting the ontology to a source database can filter the data acting as a censor. This approach is based on the notion of *IGA censor*. Intuitively, the IGA censor protects data by disclosing to the users the intersection of all inclusion-maximal subsets of the ground facts that are inferred by the ontology and that do not violate the policy (such subsets are returned by so-called optimal GA censors [6, 12]).

Example 1. Assume that an oil company wants to keep information on unproductive wildcat drilling confidential, since it does not want to disclose data about the failure of this high-risk exploration activity in new areas outside of known extraction fields[1]. Thus, no answer has to be returned to the query $\exists x.\mathsf{emptyWell}(x) \land \mathsf{type}(x, 'wildcat')$. Assume also that the terminological component of the ontology, i.e., the TBox, says that each empty well is a wellbore and it is maintained by someone (e.g., a sub-unit of the company), and also that everything having a type is maintained by someone (i.e., $\mathsf{emptyWell} \sqsubseteq \mathsf{wellbore}$, $\mathsf{emptyWell} \sqsubseteq \exists\mathsf{maintainedBy}$, $\exists\mathsf{type} \sqsubseteq \exists\mathsf{maintainedBy}$, in DL formulas), and consider an ontology ABox containing the facts $\mathsf{emptyWell}(e)$ and $\mathsf{type}(e, 'wildcat')$. Two optimal GA censors exist, one exposing to users the facts $\{\mathsf{emptyWell}(e), \mathsf{wellbore}(e)\}$, and the other accounting for $\{\mathsf{type}(e, 'wildcat'), \mathsf{wellbore}(e)\}$ (note that $\mathsf{wellbore}(e)$ is implied by the ontology). Thus, the IGA censor returns only the fact $\mathsf{wellbore}(e)$.   □

The use of the above approach in practice is however hampered by some limitations of the proposed framework. Namely, the policy considered in [6] allows only for the specification of conjunctive queries (CQs), thus ruling out many important data protection statements typical of real-world applications. The company of our example, for instance, might want to protect only data referring to facts occurred after a certain year, and this cannot be expressed through a CQ. Moreover, IGA censors might result too restrictive with respect to the amount of non-protected data disclosed to the user. In our example, the query $\exists x.\mathsf{maintainedBy}(e, x)$ is implied under both the GA censors (i.e., inferred by each ontology we obtain by coupling the TBox with the ABox returned by a GA censor), but it is not implied under the IGA censor. Thus, confidentiality protection through IGA censors might obfuscate too much information. At the same time, answering CQs by reasoning over all GA censors is intractable, as shown in [12], and randomly selecting one single censor is arbitrary without additional metadata.

However, in practical scenarios such metadata are often available, and may lead to prefer one censor to another, so that simply taking the intersection of the results of all censors would be unsatisfactory. For instance, the company of our example might consider it preferable to disclose $\mathsf{type}(e, 'wildcat')$ over $\mathsf{emptyWell}(e)$, but not acceptable disclosing both, according to the policy. This situation calls for new modeling tools.

---

[1] This example is inspired by the benchmark we use in the experiments.

In this paper we contribute to fill the previous gaps, by enriching the CQE framework of [6] to support prioritized ontologies and a more expressive policy language[2], thus allowing for a more flexible management of information disclosure, still guaranteeing feasibility of the approach. Our contributions can be summarized as follows:

- We consider ontologies specified in DL-$Lite_A$, which is more expressive than DL-$Lite_R$ studied in [6] and is one of the richest DLs of the DL-$Lite$ family, i.e., the logical underpinning of the OWL 2 profile OWL 2 QL[3].
- We extend the policy language by allowing for CQs with atoms using comparison predicates, in a controlled way.
- We allow for the presence of priority relations between ontology predicates, such as, e.g., type≻emptyWell, and exploit them to identify preferred optimal censors. To this aim, we first propose priority-based censor semantics for our framework, by adapting the well-known notions of Pareto and Global optimal repairs proposed in [15] in the context of Consistent Query Answering (CQA). To overcome intractability of query answering under such semantics, we provide a sound approximation of both the Pareto and Global censors, called DD censor, for which CQ answering in DL-$Lite_A$ is polynomial in data complexity.
- We exhibit a parametrized version of the DD censor enabling for first-order rewritable CQ answering in DL-$Lite_A$, which proves AC^0 data complexity.
- We show practical applicability of our approach through an experimental study over the NPD benchmark [11]. To this aim, we cable our rewriting technique in the method given in [6] that solves query answering under censors via a reduction to query processing in OBDA. Our experiments show that CQE under priorities is feasible in practice and that priorities are particularly effective in increasing the amount of data disclosed to the user, still guaranteeing confidentiality preservation.

Related Work. Previous works on CQE over ontologies have considered policies expressed as ground atoms [8], ontology axioms [5], or CQs [6,7,9,12], which, as said, we extend with the presence of comparison predicates. Query answering under censors as a form of skeptical reasoning, as we do in this paper, has been first investigated in [12], from the theoretical viewpoint. In [5] and [7] censors over DL ontologies have been studied under the indistinguishability perspective, explicitly requiring that the answer returned by a censor does not allow the user to distinguish the instances containing sensitive information from the ones with no secrets. As shown in [5], this property may also protect from attacks of users with some background knowledge, thus it is important for robust privacy-preservation. We remark that, as proved in the following, the censors we consider in this paper satisfy this property. Leveraging an indistinguishability-based notion of source policy compliance, reference [2] studies information disclosure in OBDA, but does not consider query answering, as we do in this paper.

To the best of our knowledge, this is the first paper considering CQE over prioritized ontologies. The priority-based CQE semantics we propose are adapted from the literature on CQA. More in detail, our DD censor has a correspondence with the grounded

---

[2] For the sake of presentation, we consider here CQE over ontologies. Our extensions and results apply straightforwardly to a privacy-protected OBDA framework [6].

[3] https://www.w3.org/TR/owl2-profiles/.

extension recently introduced in [3] through a transformation of the CQA problem into argumentation framework. Also, our rewritability result corresponds to an analogous finding mentioned in that paper. Besides the differences between the settings studied in the two papers, we remark that priorities considered in [3] are specified between ABox facts, whereas we here assume priorities between ontology predicates, maintaining this aspect at the intensional level, thus enriching the modeling abilities of the system designer. Furthermore, our treatment is tailored to CQE, and does not require transformation into a different problem, thus streamlining the technical aspects of the approach. Finally, the rewriting algorithm that we provide allows us to easily exploit the idea of [6] for solving CQE over ontologies through the use of off-the-shelf tools for OBDA.

Paper Organization. In Sect. 2 we provide some preliminaries. In Sect. 3 we present the CQE framework for ontologies and the new policy language considered in this paper. In Sect. 4 we introduce priority relations between ontology predicates and define Pareto and Global censors. In Sect. 5 we provide sound approximations of the Pareto and Global censors and give our query-rewriting algorithm. In Sect. 6, we present our experiments, and in Sect. 7 we conclude the paper.

2 Preliminaries

Description Logics (DLs) are decidable first-order (FO) languages using unary and binary predicates [1]. Unary predicates are called concepts, corresponding to classes in OWL, which denote sets of objects, whereas binary predicates can be either roles, called object properties in OWL, denoting relations between concepts, or attributes, called data properties in OWL, denoting relations between concepts and data-types. Hereinafter we assume to have the pairwise disjoint countably infinite alphabets Σ_O, Σ_I, Σ_V, and Σ_V, for ontology predicates, constants (a.k.a. individuals), values, and variables, respectively. Σ_O is in turn partitioned in three pairwise disjoint sets Σ_C, Σ_R, Σ_A, for names of concepts, a.k.a. atomic concepts, roles, a.k.a. atomic roles, and attributes, respectively. Furthermore, with $\Sigma_T = \Sigma_I \cup \Sigma_V \cup \Sigma_V$ we denote the alphabet of terms.

A *DL ontology* $\mathcal{O}$ is a set $\mathcal{T} \cup \mathcal{A}$, where $\mathcal{T}$ is the *TBox*, i.e., a finite set of assertions modeling intensional knowledge, and $\mathcal{A}$ is the *ABox*, i.e., a finite set of assertions specifying extensional knowledge. For us, an ABox is always a set of assertions of the form $A(a)$, $P(a,b)$, $U(a,v)$, where $A \in \Sigma_C$, $P \in \Sigma_R$, $U \in \Sigma_A$, $a, b \in \Sigma_I$, and $v \in \Sigma_V$. The set of concept, role, and attribute names occurring in $\mathcal{O}$ is the *signature* of $\mathcal{O}$, denoted $\Sigma_O(\mathcal{O})$. The semantics of $\mathcal{O}$ is given in terms of interpretations [1]. A *model* of $\mathcal{O}$ is an interpretation that satisfies all assertions in $\mathcal{T}$ and $\mathcal{A}$. $\mathcal{O}$ is *consistent* if it has at least one model, *inconsistent* otherwise. Then, $\mathcal{O}$ *entails* an FO sentence ϕ, i.e., a closed FO formula, if ϕ is true in every model of $\mathcal{O}$. Given a TBox $\mathcal{T}$, *an ABox* $\mathcal{A}$ *for* $\mathcal{T}$ contains only assertions over $\Sigma_O(\mathcal{T})$, Σ_I and Σ_V, and $\mathcal{A}$ is such that $\mathcal{T} \cup \mathcal{A}$ is consistent. In the following, given an ABox $\mathcal{A}$ for $\mathcal{T}$, we denote by $\text{cl}(\mathcal{T}, \mathcal{A})$ the set of all facts α constructible over the alphabets $\Sigma_O(\mathcal{T})$, Σ_I and Σ_V, such that $\mathcal{T} \cup \mathcal{A} \models \alpha$.

A *query* q *over a DL ontology* $\mathcal{O}$ is an FO formula $\phi(\vec{x})$ over $\Sigma_O(\mathcal{O}) \cup \Sigma_T$. The variables in $\vec{x}$ are the free variables of q, and the number of variables in $\vec{x}$ is the *arity* of q. The *evaluation of* q over a model $\mathcal{I}$ for $\mathcal{O}$ is the set of tuples of elements in the domain of $\mathcal{I}$ that assigned to the variables in $\vec{x}$ make the query true in $\mathcal{I}$.

An *atom* over $\Sigma_O \cup \Sigma_T$ is an expression of the form $A(t)$, $P(t_1, t_2)$ or $U(t_1, t_2)$ where $A \in \Sigma_C$, $P \in \Sigma_R$, $U \in \Sigma_A$ and t, t_1, t_2 are terms from Σ_T. A query q over $\mathcal{O}$ is a *conjunctive query (CQ)* if $\phi(\vec{x})$ is an expression of the form $\exists \vec{y}.S_1(\vec{x}, \vec{y}) \wedge \ldots \wedge S_n(\vec{x}, \vec{y})$, where $n \geq 1$, $\vec{y}$ are the existential variables, and each $S_i(\vec{x}, \vec{y})$ is an atom over $\Sigma_O(\mathcal{O}) \cup \Sigma_T$ with variables in $\vec{x} \cup \vec{y}$. Each variable in $\vec{x} \cup \vec{y}$ occurs in at least one atom of q. Boolean CQs (BCQs) are queries whose arity is zero (i.e., BCQs are sentences).

We will focus on the *DL-Lite$_A$* language, whose constructs are formed as follows:

$$B \longrightarrow A \mid \exists R \mid \exists U \qquad R \longrightarrow P \mid P^-$$

where $A \in \Sigma_C$, $P \in \Sigma_R$, P^- is the *inverse* of $P \in \Sigma_R$, and $U \in \Sigma_A$. B and R denote a *basic concept* and a *basic role*, respectively. The concept $\exists R$ and $\exists U$ are the domain of R and U, respectively. *DL-Lite$_A$* TBox assertions assume the following form:

$$
\begin{array}{lllll}
B_1 \sqsubseteq B_2 & R_1 \sqsubseteq R_2 & U_1 \sqsubseteq U_2 & \rho(U) \sqsubseteq F & \\
B_1 \sqsubseteq \neg B_2 & R_1 \sqsubseteq \neg R_2 & U_1 \sqsubseteq \neg U_2 & (\text{funct } R) & (\text{funct } U)
\end{array}
$$

where $\rho(U)$ denotes the range of an attribute U, i.e., the set of values to which U relates some object, and $F \subseteq \Sigma_V$ is a value-domain (e.g., integers, strings, etc.). A *DL-Lite$_A$* *TBox* $\mathcal{T}$ is a finite set of assertions of the above kind, such that each basic role R or attribute U that is functional in $\mathcal{T}$, i.e., (funct R) $\in \mathcal{T}$ or (funct U) $\in \mathcal{T}$, is never specialized, i.e., it (or its inverse, in the case of role) does not occur in assertions of the form $R' \sqsubseteq R$ or $U' \sqsubseteq U$. For the semantics of *DL-Lite$_A$*, we refer the reader to [13].

All our complexity results are given with respect to the size of the ABox only, i.e., they refer to data complexity. For the sake of exposition, in the following we deal with entailment of BCQs from DL ontologies. Our results can be straightforwardly extended to non-Boolean CQs, which we indeed consider in the experiments.

3   Framework for CQE in DLs

We now define the framework for CQE over DL ontologies. In this section we do not consider priorities between ontology predicates, which will be introduced in the next section. We start with the definition of *Boolean CQs with inequalities (BCQ$_{ineq}$)*. To this aim, we first define *inequality atoms* over Σ_T as expressions of the form $t_1 \, op \, t_2$ where $t_1, t_2 \in \Sigma_T$ and $op \in \{\neq, <, \leq, >, \geq\}$. Then, a *BCQ$_{ineq}$* q over an ontology $\mathcal{O}$, is a sentence of the form: $\exists \vec{y}.\alpha_1 \wedge \ldots \wedge \alpha_n \wedge \rho_1 \wedge \ldots \wedge \rho_m$, where $n \geq 1$, $m \geq 0$, every α_i is an atom over $\Sigma_O(\mathcal{O}) \cup \Sigma_T$, with variables in $\vec{y}$, and every ρ_i is an inequality atom over Σ_T with variables in $\vec{y}$. We denote as *Ineq(q)* the set of inequality atoms occurring in q, and as *Pos(q)* the Boolean CQ obtained from q by eliminating all the inequality atoms. We also assume that every variable x occurring in *Ineq(q)* occurs at least once in *Pos(q)*. The evaluation of q over an interpretation is given in the standard way, by assuming that $\{\neq, <, \leq, >, \geq\}$ are interpreted in the same way in every interpretation.

Given a DL TBox $\mathcal{T}$, *a policy* $\mathcal{P}$ *for* $\mathcal{T}$ is a set of denial assertions (or simply *denials*), i.e., formulas of the form $\forall \vec{x}.\phi(\vec{x}) \rightarrow \bot$ such that $\exists \vec{x}.\phi(\vec{x})$ is a *BCQ$_{ineq}$* over $\mathcal{T}$. We always assume that $\mathcal{T} \cup \mathcal{P}$ is consistent, i.e., there exists a model $\mathcal{I}$ of $\mathcal{T}$ such that all the formulas in $\mathcal{P}$ are satisfied. We point out that queries used in the previous definition are more expressive than formulas used in policies in previous works on CQE over ontologies (e.g., [7,9,12]). We also notice that reasoning over $\mathcal{T} \cup \mathcal{P}$ may be problematic from a computational viewpoint, even for a TBox expressed in a light DL. At the end of this section we will give a syntactic restriction on the interaction between $\mathcal{T}$ and $\mathcal{P}$ for the case in which $\mathcal{T}$ is a *DL-Lite$_A$* TBox. As we will show in the rest of the paper, this restriction is enough to obtain a setting with well-founded CQE semantics and efficient reasoning (namely query answering), amenable to implementation.

An $\mathcal{L}$ *CQE specification* $\mathcal{E}$ is a pair $\langle \mathcal{T}, \mathcal{P} \rangle$, where $\mathcal{T}$ is a TBox in the DL $\mathcal{L}$ and $\mathcal{P}$ a policy for $\mathcal{T}$ (we will omit $\mathcal{L}$ for definitions and results applying to any DL language).

Example 2. Consider the *DL-Lite$_A$* CQE specification $\mathcal{E} = \langle \mathcal{T}, \mathcal{P} \rangle$, where:

$\mathcal{T} = \{\exists \mathsf{doc}^- \sqsubseteq \mathsf{wellbore}\}$

$\mathcal{P} = \{\forall w, y, d.\mathsf{wellbore}(w) \wedge \mathsf{type}(w, \text{'wildcat'}) \wedge \mathsf{year}(w, y) \wedge \mathsf{doc}(d, w) \wedge y > 1980 \rightarrow \bot,$

$\quad \forall w, y.\mathsf{wellbore}(w) \wedge \mathsf{year}(w, y) \wedge \mathsf{doc}(d, w) \wedge y > 1992 \rightarrow \bot,$

$\quad \forall w, d.\mathsf{wellbore}(w) \wedge \mathsf{doc}(d, w) \wedge \mathsf{age}(w, \text{'Eocene'}) \rightarrow \bot\}$

In words, the TBox $\mathcal{T}$ sanctions that the documents are always about wellbores. The first denial in $\mathcal{P}$ declares confidential documents about wildcat wellbores that have been drilled after 1980. The second denial asserts that documents about wellbores drilled after 1992 have not to be disclosed. Finally, the last denial specifies that no document about wellbores that extract hydrocarbons from lithostratigraphic unit of Eocene era have to be divulged. □

A censor for $\mathcal{E}$ is a function disclosing only information that does not lead to violations of the policy $\mathcal{P}$. Below we provide a notion studied in [6,7,12].

Definition 1 (GA censor). *Let* $\mathcal{E} = \langle \mathcal{T}, \mathcal{P} \rangle$ *be a CQE specification. A Ground Atom (GA) censor for* $\mathcal{E}$ *is a function* $\mathsf{cens}(\cdot)$ *such that for each ABox* $\mathcal{A}$ *for* $\mathcal{T}$*, returns a set* $\mathsf{cens}(\mathcal{A}) \subseteq \mathsf{cl}(\mathcal{T}, \mathcal{A})$ *such that* $\mathcal{T} \cup \mathcal{P} \cup \mathsf{cens}(\mathcal{A})$ *is consistent*

Given two GA censors $\mathsf{cens}(\cdot)$ and $\mathsf{cens}'(\cdot)$ for a CQE specification $\mathcal{E} = \langle \mathcal{T}, \mathcal{P} \rangle$, we say that $\mathsf{cens}'(\cdot)$ is *more informative* than $\mathsf{cens}(\cdot)$ if: (i) $\mathsf{cens}(\mathcal{A}) \subseteq \mathsf{cens}'(\mathcal{A})$, for every ABox $\mathcal{A}$ for $\mathcal{T}$, and (ii) there exists an ABox $\mathcal{A}'$ for $\mathcal{T}$ such that $\mathsf{cens}(\mathcal{A}') \subset \mathsf{cens}'(\mathcal{A}')$.

We say that a GA censor $\mathsf{cens}(\cdot)$ for $\mathcal{E}$ is *optimal* if there does not exist a GA censor $\mathsf{cens}'(\cdot)$ for $\mathcal{E}$ such that $\mathsf{cens}'(\cdot)$ is more informative than $\mathsf{cens}(\cdot)$. We denote by $\mathsf{optGACens}(\mathcal{E})$ the set of all optimal GA censors for a CQE specification $\mathcal{E}$.

Example 3. Let $\mathcal{E}$ be as in Example 2, and let $\mathsf{cens}(\cdot)$ be the function such that, given an ABox $\mathcal{A}$ for $\mathcal{T}$, $\mathsf{cens}(\mathcal{A}) = \mathsf{cl}(\mathcal{T}, \mathcal{A}')$, where $\mathcal{A}'$ is the ABox obtained from $\mathcal{A}$ by adding the atom $\mathsf{wellbore}(w)$ and removing the atom $\mathsf{doc}(d, w)$ for each pair of individuals (d, w) such that $\mathcal{T} \cup \mathcal{A} \models \exists y.(\mathsf{wellbore}(w) \wedge \mathsf{type}(w, \text{'wildcat'}) \wedge \mathsf{year}(w, y) \wedge \mathsf{doc}(d, w) \wedge y > 1980) \vee (\mathsf{wellbore}(w) \wedge \mathsf{year}(w, y) \wedge \mathsf{doc}(d, w) \wedge y > 1992) \vee (\mathsf{wellbore}(w) \wedge \mathsf{doc}(d, w) \wedge \mathsf{age}(w, \text{'Eocene'}))$. One can easily verify that $\mathsf{cens} \in \mathsf{optGACens}(\mathcal{E})$. □

We now define query entailment over GA censors.

Definition 2. *Let* $\mathcal{E} = \langle \mathcal{T}, \mathcal{P} \rangle$ *be a CQE specification, q be a BCQ, and $\mathcal{A}$ be an ABox for* $\mathcal{T}$*. GA-Cens-Ent is the problem of deciding whether* $\mathcal{T} \cup \mathsf{cens}(\mathcal{A}) \models q$ *for each* $\mathsf{cens} \in \mathsf{optGACens}(\mathcal{E})$.

As shown in [12], the above problem is intractable even for light DLs such as *DL-Lite$_\mathcal{R}$* and $\mathcal{EL}_\perp$, and for a policy language less expressive than the one we consider in this paper. Towards the identification of a practical setting, in [6] the authors have proposed a sound approximation of GA censors, for which entailment of BCQs in *DL-Lite$_\mathcal{R}$* CQE specifications (with a policy denying CQs) has been shown to be reducible to standard BCQ entailment in OBDA.

Definition 3 (IGA censor). *Let $\mathcal{E} = \langle \mathcal{T}, \mathcal{P} \rangle$ be a CQE specification, the* intersection GA (IGA) censor *for $\mathcal{E}$ is the function* cens$_{IGA}(\cdot)$ *such that, for every ABox $\mathcal{A}$ for $\mathcal{T}$,* cens$_{IGA}(\mathcal{A}) = \bigcap_{\text{cens} \in \text{optGACens}(\mathcal{E})}$ cens$(\mathcal{A})$.

The IGA censor for a CQE specification $\mathcal{E}$ always exists [6]. Given a BCQ q and an ABox $\mathcal{A}$ for $\mathcal{T}$, IGA-Cens-Ent amounts to decide whether $\mathcal{T} \cup$ cens$_{IGA}(\mathcal{A}) \models q$. Obviously, IGA-Cens-Ent implies (i.e., it is a sound approximation of) GA-Cens-Ent.

Example 4. Consider the CQE specification $\mathcal{E}$ of Example 2 and Example 3, and the ABox $\mathcal{A} = \{\text{type}(o, \text{'wildcat'}), \text{year}(o, 1985), \text{doc}(d, o), \text{age}(o, \text{'Eocene'})\}$. One can verify that cens$_{IGA}(\mathcal{A}) = \{\text{wellbore}(o)\}$. □

As said in the introduction, to increase robustness of censors, literature on CQE has often looked at censors satisfying a property of instance indistinguishability [2,4,5,7]. Intuitively, a censor fulfilling such a property masks confidential information in such a way that a user cannot distinguish an instance actually containing data protected by the policy from an instance without such data, so that the incompleteness of the information of a possible attacker is increased. In our framework, this is formalized as follows.

Definition 4 (indistinguishability). *Let $\mathcal{E} = \langle \mathcal{T}, \mathcal{P} \rangle$ be a CQE specification and* cens$(\cdot)$ *be a censor for $\mathcal{E}$. We say that* cens$(\cdot)$ *satisfies the indistinguishability property if for every ABox $\mathcal{A}$ for $\mathcal{T}$, there exists an ABox $\mathcal{A}'$ for $\mathcal{T}$ (not necessarily distinct from $\mathcal{A}$) such that: (i)* cens$(\mathcal{A}) =$ cens$(\mathcal{A}')$, *and (ii) $\mathcal{T} \cup \mathcal{P} \cup \mathcal{A}'$ is consistent.*

It is not difficult to see that the following proposition holds.

Proposition 1. *For every CQE specification $\mathcal{E}$, both optimal GA censors and the IGA censor for $\mathcal{E}$ satisfy the indistinguishability property.*

We next provide with two definitions that will be useful in the following. Let $\mathcal{E} = \langle \mathcal{T}, \mathcal{P} \rangle$ be a CQE specification and $\mathcal{A}$ be an ABox for $\mathcal{T}$. We say that a set of ABox assertions $\mathcal{S} \subseteq$ cl$(\mathcal{T}, \mathcal{A})$ is a *secret* in $\mathcal{T} \cup \mathcal{P} \cup \mathcal{A}$, if $\mathcal{T} \cup \mathcal{P} \cup \mathcal{S}$ is inconsistent and for each assertion $\sigma \in \mathcal{S}$ we have that $\mathcal{T} \cup \mathcal{P} \cup \mathcal{S} \setminus \{\sigma\}$ is consistent. We denote with *secrets*$(\mathcal{T}, \mathcal{P}, \mathcal{A})$ the set of all secrets in $\mathcal{T} \cup \mathcal{P} \cup \mathcal{A}$, and, given an ABox assertion γ, with *inSecrets*$(\mathcal{T}, \mathcal{P}, \mathcal{A}, \gamma)$ the set of secrets $\mathcal{S} \in$ *secrets*$(\mathcal{T}, \mathcal{P}, \mathcal{A})$ such that $\gamma \in \mathcal{S}$.

As announced, we conclude this section by discussing the case of *DL-Lite$_A$* CQE specifications to provide a practical syntactic condition that we will exploit to obtain our main computational results. We say that a denial $\forall \vec{x}.\phi(\vec{x}) \rightarrow \perp$ is *safe* w.r.t. a *DL-Lite$_A$* TBox $\mathcal{T}$ if every variable x in *Ineq*$(\exists \vec{x}.\phi(\vec{x}))$ occurs in *Pos*$(\exists \vec{x}.\phi(\vec{x}))$ only in safe attribute range positions, i.e., in atoms of the form $U(t, x)$ such that U is an attribute and there exists no basic concept $B \neq \exists U$ such that $\mathcal{T} \models B \sqsubseteq \exists U$. Then, a policy $\mathcal{P}$ is safe w.r.t. $\mathcal{T}$, if $\mathcal{P}$ contains only denials that are safe w.r.t. $\mathcal{T}$, and a *DL-Lite$_A$* CQE specification $\mathcal{E} = \langle \mathcal{T}, \mathcal{P} \rangle$ is *safe* if $\mathcal{P}$ is safe w.r.t. $\mathcal{T}$. It is easy to see that the *DL-Lite$_A$* CQE specification of Example 2 (and throughout all examples of this paper) is safe.

4   Prioritized CQE Framework

Given a TBox $\mathcal{T}$, a priority relation $\succ$ over $\mathcal{T}$ is an acyclic binary relation over the signature of $\mathcal{T}$, i.e., $\succ \subseteq \Sigma_O(\mathcal{T}) \times \Sigma_O(\mathcal{T})$. A *prioritized* $\mathcal{L}$ *CQE specification* $\mathcal{E}_\succ$ is a triple $\langle \mathcal{T}, \mathcal{P}, \succ \rangle$, such that $\langle \mathcal{T}, \mathcal{P} \rangle$ is an $\mathcal{L}$ CQE specification.

Example 5. $\mathcal{E}_\succ = \langle \mathcal{T}, \mathcal{P}, \succ \rangle$, where $\mathcal{E} = \langle \mathcal{T}, \mathcal{P} \rangle$ is as in Example 2 and $\succ$ specifies that type$\succ$doc and year$\succ$doc, is a (safe) prioritized *DL-Lite$_A$* CQE specification. □

The definitions of GA censor, optimal GA censor, IGA censor, GA-Cens-Ent, and IGA-Cens-Ent apply also to a prioritized CQE specification (e.g., given one such specification $\mathcal{E}_\succ = \langle \mathcal{T}, \mathcal{P}, \succ \rangle$, cens($\cdot$) is a GA censor for $\mathcal{E}_\succ$ if it is a GA censor for the CQE specification $\mathcal{E} = \langle \mathcal{T}, \mathcal{P} \rangle$). We also use for prioritized CQE specifications the same notations introduced in Sect. 3 for CQE specifications, with the same meaning.

We now exploit the priority relation to define a preference criterion over censors. We consider two optimality notions introduced by [15] in the context of consistent query answering over databases, and recently adopted in [3] for repairing inconsistent prioritized DL ontologies. Whereas the priority relations considered in this paper are intentional, i.e., between ontology predicates, priorities considered in [3,15] are between (conflicting) facts. Intentional priorities however straightforwardly induce priorities over facts: given a TBox $\mathcal{T}$, a priority relation $\succ$ over $\mathcal{T}$, an ABox $\mathcal{A}$ for $\mathcal{T}$, and two assertions $S_1(\vec{n})$ and $S_2(\vec{m})$ in $\mathcal{A}$, we have that $S_1(\vec{n}) \succ S_2(\vec{m})$ if $S_1 \succ S_2$. Below we take the definitions of Pareto- and Global-optimal repair from [3] and adapt them to our framework.

Definition 5 (Pareto/Global censor). *Let* $\mathcal{E}_\succ = \langle \mathcal{T}, \mathcal{P}, \succ \rangle$ *be a prioritized CQE specification,* $\mathcal{A}$ *be an ABox for* $\mathcal{T}$*, and* cens($\cdot$) $\in$ optGACens($\mathcal{E}_\succ$)*. We say that an ABox* $\mathcal{A}' \subseteq$ cl($\mathcal{T}, \mathcal{A}$)*, such that* $\mathcal{A}' \neq$ cens($\mathcal{A}$) *and* $\mathcal{T} \cup \mathcal{P} \cup \mathcal{A}'$ *is consistent, is:*

- *a* Pareto *improvement of* cens($\mathcal{A}$) *w.r.t.* $\mathcal{E}_\succ$ *if there exists* $\gamma' \in \mathcal{A}' \setminus$ cens($\mathcal{A}$) *such that* $\gamma' \succ \gamma$ *for every* $\gamma \in$ cens($\mathcal{A}$) $\setminus \mathcal{A}'$ *and* $\{\gamma, \gamma'\} \subseteq \mathcal{S}$ *for some* $\mathcal{S} \subset$ secrets($\mathcal{T}, \mathcal{P}, \mathcal{A}$)*;*
- *a* Global *improvement of* cens($\mathcal{A}$) *w.r.t.* $\mathcal{E}_\succ$ *if for each* $\gamma \in$ cens($\mathcal{A}$) $\setminus \mathcal{A}'$ *there exists* $\gamma' \in \mathcal{A}' \setminus$ cens($\mathcal{A}$) *such that* $\gamma' \succ \gamma$ *and* $\{\gamma, \gamma'\} \subseteq \mathcal{S}$ *for some* $\mathcal{S} \in$ secrets($\mathcal{T}, \mathcal{P}, \mathcal{A}$)*.*

Then, cens($\cdot$) *is a* Pareto *(resp.* Global*) censor for* $\mathcal{E}_\succ$ *if there exists no other GA censor* cens'($\cdot$) *for* $\mathcal{E}_\succ$ *such that, for each ABox* $\mathcal{A}$ *for* $\mathcal{T}$*, either* cens'($\mathcal{A}$) $=$ cens($\mathcal{A}$) *or* cens'($\mathcal{A}$) *is a Pareto (resp. Global) improvement of* cens($\mathcal{A}$) *w.r.t.* $\mathcal{E}_\succ$*.*

We denote with PCens($\mathcal{E}_\succ$) (resp. GCens($\mathcal{E}_\succ$)) the set of all Pareto (resp. Global) censors for $\mathcal{E}_\succ$. It is easy to see that GCens($\mathcal{E}_\succ$) $\subseteq$ PCens($\mathcal{E}_\succ$) $\subseteq$ optGACens($\mathcal{E}_\succ$) for every $\mathcal{E}_\succ$, analogous to the containment between Global and Pareto repairs given in [15]. Also, if $\succ$ is empty, then PCens($\mathcal{E}_\succ$) $=$ GCens($\mathcal{E}_\succ$) $=$ optGACens($\mathcal{E}_\succ$). As done for GA censors, we define intersection-based versions of Pareto and Global censors. Namely, we call *Intersection Pareto (IP) censor* for $\mathcal{E}_\succ$ the function cens$_{IP}(\cdot)$ such that, for every ABox $\mathcal{A}$ for $\mathcal{T}$, cens$_{IP}(\mathcal{A}) = \bigcap_{\text{cens} \in \text{PCens}}$ cens($\mathcal{A}$), and *Intersection Global (IG) censor* for $\mathcal{E}_\succ$ the function cens$_{IG}(\cdot)$ such that, for every ABox $\mathcal{A}$ for $\mathcal{T}$, cens$_{IG}(\mathcal{A}) = \bigcap_{\text{cens} \in \text{GCens}}$ cens($\mathcal{A}$). Obviously, cens$_{IP}(\mathcal{A}) \subseteq$ cens$_{IG}(\mathcal{A})$ for each ABox $\mathcal{A}$ for $\mathcal{T}$. Also, if $\succ$ is empty, then, since PCens($\mathcal{E}_\succ$) $=$ GCens($\mathcal{E}_\succ$) $=$ optGACens($\mathcal{E}_\succ$), we have that cens$_{IP}(\cdot) =$ cens$_{IG}(\cdot) =$ cens$_{IGA}(\cdot)$.

Given an ABox $\mathcal{A}$ for $\mathcal{T}$ and a BCQ q, P-Cens-Ent (resp. G-Cens-Ent) is the problem of deciding whether $\mathcal{T} \cup \text{cens}(\mathcal{A}) \models q$ for each $\text{cens}(\cdot) \in \text{PCens}(\mathcal{E}_{\succ})$ (resp. $\text{cens}(\cdot) \in \text{GCens}(\mathcal{E}_{\succ})$), and IP-Cens-Ent (resp. IG-Cens-Ent) is the problem of deciding whether $\mathcal{T} \cup \text{cens}_{IP}(\mathcal{A}) \models q$ (resp. $\mathcal{T} \cup \text{cens}_{IG}(\mathcal{A}) \models q$). It is immediate to see that P-Cens-Ent implies G-Cens-Ent, and IP-Cens-Ent (resp. IG-Cens-Ent) implies P-Cens-Ent (resp. G-Cens-Ent). The following results immediately follow from [3].

Theorem 1. *Let $\mathcal{E}_{\succ} \langle \mathcal{T}, \mathcal{P}, \succ \rangle$ be a safe prioritized DL-Lite$_A$ CQE specification, $\mathcal{A}$ be an ABox for $\mathcal{T}$, and q be a BCQ. P-Cens-Ent and IP-Cens-Ent are coNP-hard in data complexity, whereas G-Cens-Ent and IG-Cens-Ent are Π_2^p-hard in data complexity.*

Results in Theorem 1 represent a clear obstacle to the use of the above forms of priority-based censors over real-world, large datasets. In the next section we will see how these censors can be suitably approximated for a practical use.

5   FO-rewritable Prioritized CQE in *DL-Lite$_A$*

In this section we first give a deterministic notion of priority-based censor (DD censor) and its parametrized sound approximation called k-DD censor. Then, we provide an algorithm that computes a non-redundant policy, i.e., such that the image of each policy assertion corresponds to a secret. This step is crucial in order to define our query rewriting technique, which shows that BCQ entailment under k-DD censors in *DL-Lite$_A$* is FO rewritable. The full rewriting algorithm is given in the last part of this section.

5.1   DD Censors and k-DD Censors

Theorem 1 clearly says that under Pareto or Global censors, or their intersection-based versions, entailment of BCQs is inherently non-deterministic. Towards the identification of a tractable approximation, we give below the notion of *deterministically disclosed (DD)* and *deterministically censored (DC)* atoms. Hereinafter, given a priority relation $\succ$, a fact α, and a set of facts $\mathcal{S}$, we write $\alpha \succ \mathcal{S}$ if there exists $\beta \in \mathcal{S}$ such that $\alpha \succ \beta$.

Definition 6. *Given a prioritized CQE specification $\mathcal{E}_{\succ} = \langle \mathcal{T}, \mathcal{P}, \succ \rangle$ and an ABox $\mathcal{A}$ for $\mathcal{T}$, we denote by $DD(\mathcal{E}_{\succ}, \mathcal{A})$ and $DC(\mathcal{E}_{\succ}, \mathcal{A})$ the inclusion-minimal subsets of $\text{cl}(\mathcal{T}, \mathcal{A})$ such that:*

$$DD(\mathcal{E}_{\succ}, \mathcal{A}) = \{\alpha \in \text{cl}(\mathcal{T}, \mathcal{A}) \mid \forall \mathcal{S} \in inSecrets(\mathcal{T}, \mathcal{P}, \mathcal{A}, \alpha) \text{ either } \alpha \succ (\mathcal{S} \setminus \{\alpha\})$$
$$\text{or } \mathcal{S} \cap DC(\mathcal{E}_{\succ}, \mathcal{A}) \neq \emptyset \}$$
$$DC(\mathcal{E}_{\succ}, \mathcal{A}) = \{\alpha \in \text{cl}(\mathcal{T}, \mathcal{A}) \mid \exists \mathcal{S} \in inSecrets(\mathcal{T}, \mathcal{P}, \mathcal{A}, \alpha) \text{ s.t. } \mathcal{S} \setminus DD(\mathcal{E}_{\succ}, \mathcal{A}) = \{\alpha\}\}$$

In words, a DD atom α is such that α does not occur in any secret, or, either, in each secret in which it occurs there is an atom β such that $\alpha \succ \beta$ or β is a DC atom. Instead, a DC atom is such that there is a secret where it is the only non-DD atom. It is immediate to verify that $DD(\mathcal{E}_{\succ}, \mathcal{A})$ and $DC(\mathcal{E}_{\succ}, \mathcal{A})$ are unique for a given pair $(\mathcal{E}_{\succ}, \mathcal{A})$.

Given a prioritized CQE specification $\mathcal{E}_{\succ} = \langle \mathcal{T}, \mathcal{P}, \succ \rangle$, we call DD *censor* for $\mathcal{E}_{\succ}$ the function $\text{cens}_{DD}(\cdot)$ such that, for each ABox $\mathcal{A}$ for $\mathcal{T}$, $\text{cens}_{DD}(\mathcal{A}) = DD(\mathcal{E}_{\succ}, \mathcal{A})$.

Example 6. Consider the safe prioritized $DL\text{-}Lite_A$ CQE specification $\mathcal{E}_\succ$ of Example 5 and the censor cens of Example 3. We have that cens coincides with the DD censor for $\mathcal{E}_\succ$. Moreover, for the ABox $\mathcal{A}$ of Example 4, $\mathrm{cens}(\mathcal{A}) = \{\mathsf{wellbore}(o), \mathsf{type}(o, \textit{'wildcat'}), \mathsf{year}(o, 1985), \mathsf{age}(o, \textit{'Eocene'})\}$. $\qquad\square$

The proposition below follows from the definition of DD censor[4].

Proposition 2. *Let $\mathcal{E}_\emptyset = \langle \mathcal{T}, \mathcal{P}, \emptyset \rangle$ be a prioritized CQE specification with an empty priority relation. The DD censor for $\mathcal{E}_\emptyset$ coincides with the IGA censor for $\mathcal{E}_\emptyset$.*

It is also easy to verify that the DD censor satisfies the property given in Definition 4.

Proposition 3. *For every prioritized CQE specification $\mathcal{E}_\succ$, the DD censor for $\mathcal{E}_\succ$ satisfies the indistinguishability property.*

We now establish the relationship between DD censors and the previously presented IP and IG censors.

Proposition 4. *Let $\mathcal{E}_\succ = \langle \mathcal{T}, \mathcal{P}, \succ \rangle$ be a prioritized CQE specification, and let $\mathrm{cens}_{IP}(\cdot)$ and $\mathrm{cens}_{IG}(\cdot)$ be the Intersection Pareto and Global censor for $\mathcal{E}_\succ$. Then, $DD(\mathcal{E}_\succ, \mathcal{A}) \subseteq \mathrm{cens}_{IP}(\mathcal{A}) \subseteq \mathrm{cens}_{IG}(\mathcal{A})$, for every ABox $\mathcal{A}$ for $\mathcal{T}$.*

BCQ entailment under DD censors is defined as usual. Namely, given a prioritized CQE specification $\mathcal{E}_\succ = \langle \mathcal{T}, \mathcal{P}, \succ \rangle$, an ABox $\mathcal{A}$ for $\mathcal{T}$, and a BCQ q, DD-Cens-Ent is the problem of deciding whether $\mathcal{T} \cup \mathrm{cens}_{DD}(\mathcal{A}) \models q$. From Proposition 4, it follows that DD-Cens-Ent implies IP-Cens-Ent (and consequently IG-Cens-Ent).

Given a prioritized CQE specification $\mathcal{E}_\succ = \langle \mathcal{T}, \mathcal{P}, \succ \rangle$, and an ABox $\mathcal{A}$ for $\mathcal{T}$, it is not difficult to see that $DD(\mathcal{E}_\succ, \mathcal{A})$ and $DC(\mathcal{E}_\succ, \mathcal{A})$ correspond to the least fixpoint of the equations:

$$DD_{i+1}(\mathcal{E}_\succ, \mathcal{A}) = \{\alpha \in \mathsf{cl}(\mathcal{T}, \mathcal{A}) \mid \forall \mathcal{S} \in inSecrets(\mathcal{T}, \mathcal{P}, \mathcal{A}, \alpha),$$
$$\alpha \succ (\mathcal{S} \setminus \{\alpha\}) \text{ or } \mathcal{S} \cap DC_i(\mathcal{E}_\succ, \mathcal{A}) \neq \emptyset \}$$
$$DC_{i+1}(\mathcal{E}_\succ, \mathcal{A}) = \{\alpha \in \mathsf{cl}(\mathcal{T}, \mathcal{A}) \mid \exists \mathcal{S} \in inSecrets(\mathcal{T}, \mathcal{P}, \mathcal{A}, \alpha) \text{ s.t.}$$
$$\mathcal{S} \setminus DD_i(\mathcal{E}_\succ, \mathcal{A}) = \{\alpha\}\}$$

where $DD_0(\mathcal{E}_\succ, \mathcal{A}) = DC_0(\mathcal{E}_\succ, \mathcal{A}) = \emptyset$. For safe prioritized $DL\text{-}Lite_A$ CQE specifications, computing such fixpoint is in P in the size of $\mathcal{A}$, and from the results in [3] it also follows that DD-Cens-Ent is P-hard in data complexity. By fixing a k, we can define a new censor $\mathrm{cens}DD_k(\cdot)$, which we call k-DD censor for $\mathcal{E}_\succ$, such that $\mathrm{cens}DD_k(\mathcal{A}) = DD_k(\mathcal{E}_\succ, \mathcal{A})$, for each ABox $\mathcal{A}$ for $\mathcal{T}$.

We next define BCQ entailment under k-DD censors, which is the problem that we study in the rest of the paper for safe prioritized $DL\text{-}Lite_A$ CQE specifications.

Definition 7. *Let $\mathcal{E}_\succ = \langle \mathcal{T}, \mathcal{P}, \succ \rangle$ be a prioritized $\mathcal{L}$ CQE specification, k be a positive integer, $\mathcal{A}$ be an ABox for $\mathcal{T}$, and q be a BCQ. kDD-Cens-Ent is the problem of deciding whether $\mathcal{T} \cup \mathrm{cens}DD_k(\mathcal{A}) \models q$.*

---

[4] A similar result is provided in [3, Theorem 38] in the context of CQA.

Since for every prioritized CQE specification $\mathcal{E}_\succ$, positive integer k, and ABox $\mathcal{A}$, $DD_k(\mathcal{E}_\succ, \mathcal{A}) \subseteq DD(\mathcal{E}_\succ, \mathcal{A})$, the k-DD censor for $\mathcal{E}_\succ$ constitutes a sound approximation of the DD censor for $\mathcal{E}_\succ$, and thus kDD-Cens-Ent implies DD-Cens-Ent. Moreover, it is immediate to verify that the k-DD censor preserves the indistinguishability property.

Example 7. For the specification $\mathcal{E}_\succ$ of Example 5 and the ABox $\mathcal{A}$ of Example 4, we have that $DD_1(\mathcal{E}_\succ, \mathcal{A}) = \{\text{wellbore}(o), \text{type}(o, \textit{'wildcat'}), \text{year}(o, 1985)\}$, while $DD_3(\mathcal{E}_\succ, \mathcal{A}) = \{\text{wellbore}(o), \text{type}(o, \textit{'wildcat'}), \text{year}(o, 1985), \text{age}(o, \textit{'Eocene'})\}$, which coincides with the DD-censor for $\mathcal{E}_\succ$. $\square$

5.2 Generating a Non-redundant Policy Specification

We now provide the algorithm PolicyRefine, which we use to produce a non-redundant policy specification. A specification of this kind enjoys the property that every image over the ABox of a BCQ_{ineq} q in a policy denial is a secret, where the image is a minimal set of facts inferring q. This property is crucial for the correctness of the query rewriting algorithm presented in Sect. 5.3. It is not difficult to see that in general a policy can be redundant. For example, consider the policy $\mathcal{P} = \{A(x) \wedge U(x, y) \wedge y < 20 \rightarrow \perp; U(x, y) \wedge y < 15 \rightarrow \perp\}$ and the ABox $\mathcal{A} = \{A(a), U(a, 12)\}$, the ABox $\mathcal{A}$ itself is an image of the query in the premise of the first denial, but it is not a secret, since $U(a, 12)$ alone is a secret. The technique we propose here extends the one discussed in [6], tailored to policy assertions denying CQs.

We start with some preliminary definitions. As said before, the symbol op represents a comparison operator in $\{=, \neq, >, \geq, <, \leq\}$. Given a set of sets of inequalities RC and a denial $\delta = \forall \vec{x}.\phi(\vec{x}) \rightarrow \perp$, we denote by $\tau(\delta, RC)$ the function that returns the *extended denial assertion* $\forall \vec{x}.\phi(\vec{x}) \wedge \neg(\pi(\vec{x})) \rightarrow \perp$, where $\pi(\vec{x})$ is the disjunction of conjunctions of inequalities

$$\bigvee_{Ineq \in RC} \left(\bigwedge_{t_1 op\, t_2 \in Ineq} t_1\, op\, t_2 \right)$$

In the rest of this section we call *non-extended denial*, or simply *denial*, a denial as defined in Sect. 3. Moreover, we call *extended policy* a set of extended denials and non-extended denials.

Given two set of inequalities $Ineq$ and $Ineq'$, we write $Ineq \models Ineq'$ to denote that every inequality in $Ineq'$ is implied by the inequalities in $Ineq$.

Definition 8. *Given an extended policy $\mathcal{P}$ and a non-extended denial δ in $\mathcal{P}$, we say that a set of inequalities $Ineq$ is a strict redundancy condition for δ in $\mathcal{P}$ if there exists $\delta' \in \mathcal{P}$ such that: (i) $\delta' \models \delta \cup Ineq$ and $\delta \cup Ineq \not\models \delta'$; (ii) there exists no set of inequalities $Ineq'$ such that $Ineq \models Ineq'$ and $\delta \models \delta' \cup Ineq'$ and $\delta' \cup Ineq' \not\models \delta$.*

We say that a set SRC of strict redundancy conditions for δ in $\mathcal{P}'$ is *complete* if, for every extended denial δ' in $\mathcal{P}'$, if there exists a set of inequalities $Ineq$ such that conditions (i) and (ii) of Definition 8 hold, then there exists a set $Ineq' \in SRC$ such that $Ineq \models Ineq'$.

Then, we say that an extended denial δ' is a *non-redundant representation of δ in $\mathcal{P}'$* if every minimal ABox $\mathcal{A}$ such that $\{\delta'\} \cup \mathcal{A}$ is inconsistent is also a minimal ABox such that $\mathcal{P}' \cup \mathcal{A}$ is inconsistent.

Algorithm 1. PolicyRefine

---

input: a policy $\mathcal{P}$;
output: an extended policy $\mathcal{P}'$ that is a non-redundant representation of $\mathcal{P}$;
1) $\mathcal{P}' \leftarrow \emptyset$;
2)   **foreach** denial $\delta \in \mathcal{P}$ **do**
3) $RC \leftarrow \emptyset$;
4)   **foreach** denial $\delta' \in \mathcal{P}$ such that $\delta \neq \delta'$ **do**
5)   **foreach** partition $Q_1, \ldots, Q_{k+1}$ of $Atoms(\delta)$ **do**
6)   **foreach** partition $Q'_1, \ldots, Q'_k$ of $PredAt(\delta')$
7)   **such that,** for each i s.t. $1 \leq i \leq k$,
8) $Q_i \cup Q'_i$ is a set of unifiable atoms **do**
9) $\sigma \leftarrow \bigcup_{1 \leq i \leq k} MGU(Q_i \cup Q'_i)$;
10)   **if** $\sigma(Atoms(\delta')) \not\models \sigma(Q_{k+1})$
11)   **then** $RC \leftarrow RC \cup \{\sigma\} \cup \sigma(CompAt(\delta'))$;
12) $\mathcal{P}' \leftarrow \mathcal{P}' \cup \{\tau(\delta, RC)\}$;
13) **return** $\mathcal{P}'$;

Definition 9. *We say that an extended policy $\mathcal{P}'$ is a* non-redundant representation *of an extended policy $\mathcal{P}$ if: (i) $\mathcal{P}'$ is equivalent to $\mathcal{P}$; and (ii) every $\delta \in \mathcal{P}'$ is such that there exists no strict redundancy condition for δ in $\mathcal{P}'$.*

We are now able to define the algorithm PolicyRefine (Figure 1). Given a policy $\mathcal{P}$, PolicyRefine($\mathcal{P}$) returns an extended policy $\mathcal{P}'$ that is a non-redundant representation of $\mathcal{P}$. To this aim, PolicyRefine identifies, for each denial δ in $\mathcal{P}$, a set of sets of inequalities RC that is a complete set of strict redundancy conditions for δ in $\mathcal{P}$, and then represents the denial δ by the extended denial $\tau(\delta, RC)$ in $\mathcal{P}'$. In the algorithm, $Atoms(\delta)$ denotes the set of all atoms occurring in the denial δ, $PredAt(\delta)$ denotes the set of standard predicate atoms, and $CompAt(\delta)$ denotes the set of comparison atoms. Moreover, $MGU(Q)$ denotes the most general unifier of the set of atoms Q.

The correctness of the algorithm is stated by the following theorem.

Theorem 2. *Let $\mathcal{P}$ be a policy and let $\mathcal{P}'$ be the extended policy returned by PolicyRefine($\mathcal{P}$). Then, $\mathcal{P}'$ is a non-redundant representation of $\mathcal{P}$.*

We finally notice that, given a *DL-Lite$_A$* TBox $\mathcal{T}$ and a policy $\mathcal{P}$ that is safe w.r.t. $\mathcal{T}$, before refining $\mathcal{P}$, in our procedure we have to reformulate it by using the algorithm PerfectRef($\mathcal{T}, \mathcal{P}$) of [13], which returns relevant policy assertions implied by $\mathcal{T}$ and $\mathcal{P}$[5].

Example 8. Let $\mathcal{T}$ and $\mathcal{P}$ be as in Example 2. One can verify that the set $\mathcal{P}' = $ PolicyRefine(PerfectRef($\mathcal{T}, \mathcal{P}$)) is constituted by the following denials:

$$\mathcal{P} = \{\forall w, y, d.\text{type}(w, \text{'wildcat'}) \land \text{year}(w, y) \land \text{doc}(d, w) \land 1980 < y \leq 1992 \rightarrow \bot,$$
$$\forall w, y.\text{year}(w, y) \land \text{doc}(d, w) \land y > 1992 \rightarrow \bot,$$
$$\forall w, d.\text{doc}(d, w) \land \text{age}(w, \text{'Eocene'}) \rightarrow \bot\}$$

$\square$

---

[5] Technically speaking, PerfectRef rewrites CQs. We here adopt a variant that rewrites the positive part of each BCQ_{ineq} in the premise of a policy assertion, which provides a correct reformulation under the safe policy assumption.

5.3 Query Rewriting Algorithm

We now give our query rewriting technique. In the following, without loss of generality, we assume that in each denial, the arguments of an atom are always variables different to one another (the presence of the same variable or of constants can be indeed expressed through equalities). First of all, given a *DL-Lite$_A$* TBox $\mathcal{T}$ and a policy $\mathcal{P}$ that is safe w.r.t. $\mathcal{T}$, we reformulate $\mathcal{P}$ by using the algorithm PerfectRef$(\mathcal{T}, \mathcal{P})$. Then, let α and β be two atoms. We say that β is compatible with α if there exists a mapping $\mu_{\alpha/\beta}$ of the variables occurring in β to the terms occurring in α such that $\mu(\beta) = \alpha$. Given an atom α and an FO formula Φ, we denote by compSet(α, Φ) the set of atoms of Φ that are compatible with α. Moreover, let α be an atom, let $\mathcal{Q}$ be a set of FO formulas, and let $\succ$ be a preference relation, we denote by notPreferred$(\alpha, \mathcal{Q}, \succ)$ the set of formulas $\Phi \in \mathcal{Q}$ such that there does not exist in Φ any atom β such that $\alpha \succ \beta$.

Let $\Phi = \exists \vec{x}. \alpha \wedge \beta_1 \wedge \ldots \wedge \beta_n$ be a query, we denote by allDD$_i(\Phi, \alpha)$ the FOL formula $\exists \vec{y}.\mathrm{DD}_i(\beta_1) \wedge \ldots \wedge \mathrm{DD}_i(\beta_n)$ where $\vec{y}$ are the variables in $\vec{x}$ that do not occur in α and by oneDC$_i(\Phi, \alpha)$ the FO formula $\mathrm{DC}_i(\beta_1) \vee \ldots \vee \mathrm{DC}_i(\beta_n)$ (of course, if $n = 0$ then allDD$_i(\Phi, \alpha) = true$ and oneDC$_i(\Phi, \alpha) = false$). Also, $\mathrm{DD}_0(\alpha) = \mathrm{DC}_0(\alpha) = false$, for each atom α. Moreover, we denote by $\mathcal{Q}_\mathcal{P}$ the set of queries returned by PolicyRefine(PerfectRef$(\mathcal{T}, \mathcal{P})$).

For an atom α and a natural number $i \geq 1$, we denote by $\mathrm{DD}_i(\alpha)$ the FO formula:

$$\alpha \wedge \left(\bigwedge_{\substack{\forall q_d \in \mathsf{notPreferred}_\succ (\alpha, \mathcal{Q}_\mathcal{P}), \\ \forall \beta \in \mathsf{compSet}(\alpha, q_d)}} \forall \vec{w}. \left(\neg \mu_{\alpha/\beta}(q_d) \vee \mathsf{oneDC}_{i-1}(\mu_{\alpha/\beta}(q_d), \alpha) \right) \right)$$

Where $\vec{w}$ contains all the variables in $\mu_{\alpha/\beta}(q_d)$ that do not occur in α.

For an atom α and a natural number $i \geq 1$, we denote by $\mathrm{DC}_i(\alpha)$ the FO formula:

$$\bigvee_{\substack{\forall q_d \in \mathsf{notPreferred}_\succ (\alpha, \mathcal{Q}_\mathcal{P}), \\ \forall \beta \in \mathsf{compSet}(\alpha, q_d)}} \exists \vec{v}. \mu_{\alpha/\beta}(q_d) \wedge \mathsf{allDD}_{i-1}(\mu_{\alpha/\beta}(q_d), \alpha)$$

Given a union of BCQs Q and a prioritized CQE specification $\mathcal{E}_\succ$, we define the FO query k-DDClosed$(Q, \mathcal{E}_\succ)$ as follows:

$$k\text{-DDClosed}(Q, \mathcal{E}_\succ) = \bigvee_{q \in Q} \left(\bigwedge_{\alpha \in q} \mathrm{DD}_k(\alpha) \right)$$

Given a *DL-Lite$_A$* TBox $\mathcal{T}$ and an FO query ϕ, we define expand$(\mathcal{T}, \phi)$ as the FO query obtained from ϕ by replacing every atom α occurring in ϕ with its "$\mathcal{T}$-expansion" expand$(\mathcal{T}, \alpha)$, where:

(i) if $\alpha = C(t)$, then expand$(\mathcal{T}, \alpha) = \bigvee_{\mathcal{T} \models D \sqsubseteq C} D(t) \vee \bigvee_{\mathcal{T} \models \exists R \sqsubseteq C}(\exists x. R(t, x)) \vee \bigvee_{\mathcal{T} \models \exists R^- \sqsubseteq C}(\exists x. R(x, t))$.

(ii) if $\alpha = R(t_1, t_2)$, then expand$(\mathcal{T}, \alpha) = \bigvee_{\mathcal{T} \models S \sqsubseteq R} S(t_1, t_2) \vee \bigvee_{\mathcal{T} \models \exists S^- \sqsubseteq R} S(t_2, t_1)$.

Finally, given a safe *DL-Lite$_A$* prioritized CQE specification $\mathcal{E}_\succ = \langle T, \mathcal{P}, \succ \rangle$, a positive integer k, and a BCQ q we define:

$$k\text{-DDRew}(\mathcal{E}_\succ, q) = \text{expand}(T, k\text{-DDClosed}(\text{PerfectRef}(T, q), \mathcal{E}_\succ)). \quad (1)$$

Notice that, for every odd i, $\text{DD}_i(\alpha) = \text{DD}_{i+1}(\alpha)$ (by definition), and thus $i\text{-DDRew}(\mathcal{E}_\succ, q) = (i{+}1)\text{-DDRew}(\mathcal{E}_\succ, q)$.

It is easy to see that $k\text{-DDRew}(\mathcal{E}_\succ, q)$ is an FO query. The following theorem states that, for safe prioritized *DL-Lite$_A$* CQE specifications, kDD-Cens-Ent can always be solved by checking whether $k\text{-DDRew}(\mathcal{E}_\succ, q)$ is entailed by the ABox, which amounts to evaluating such query over the ABox. In other terms, the problem is FO rewritable.

Theorem 3. *Let $\mathcal{E}_\succ = \langle T, \mathcal{P}, \succ \rangle$ be a safe prioritized DL-Lite$_A$ CQE specification, k be a positive integer, and $\text{cens}DD_k$ be the k-DD censor for $\mathcal{E}_\succ$. For every ABox $\mathcal{A}$ for T and BCQ q, $T \cup \text{cens}DD_k(\mathcal{A}) \models q$ iff $\mathcal{A} \models k\text{-DDRew}(\mathcal{E}_\succ, q)$.*

Proof. The proof is based on three crucial lemmas. The first recalls a property of the PerfectRef algorithm [13].

Lemma 1. *$T \cup \text{cens}DD_k(\mathcal{A}) \models q$ iff $\text{cens}DD_k(\mathcal{A}) \models \text{PerfectRef}(T, q)$.*

Then, we prove the following property.

Lemma 2. *Let Q be a union of BCQs. Then, $\text{cens}DD_k(\mathcal{A}) \models Q$ iff $\text{cl}(T, \mathcal{A}) \models k\text{-DDClosed}(Q, \mathcal{E}_\succ)$.*

Proof (sketch). First, we prove inductively the following property: For every i such that $0 \leq i \leq k$, and for every atom α, $\alpha \in \text{DD}_i(\mathcal{E}_\succ, \mathcal{A})$ iff $\text{cl}(T, \mathcal{A}) \models \text{DD}_k(\alpha)$ and $\alpha \in \text{DC}_i(\mathcal{E}_\succ, \mathcal{A})$ iff $\text{cl}(T, \mathcal{A}) \models \text{DC}_k(\alpha)$. The base case holds since $\text{DD}_0(\mathcal{E}_\succ, \mathcal{A}) = \text{DC}_0(\mathcal{E}_\succ, \mathcal{A}) = \emptyset$ and $\text{DD}_0(\alpha) = \text{DC}_0(\alpha) = \textit{false}$. The inductive case follows immediately from Theorem 2, Definition 6, and the definition of the formulas $\text{DD}_i(\alpha)$ and $\text{DC}_i(\alpha)$. Then, the thesis follows immediately from the previous property and the definition of $k\text{-DDClosed}(Q, \mathcal{E}_\succ)$. ∎

The next lemma directly follows from the definition of $\text{cl}(T, \mathcal{A})$ and $\text{expand}(T, \phi)$.

Lemma 3. *Let ϕ be a FO query. Then, $\text{cl}(T, \mathcal{A}) \models \phi$ iff $\mathcal{A} \models \text{expand}(T, \phi)$.*

Then, the theorem is an immediate consequence of the above lemmas. □

Example 9. Consider the safe prioritized CQE specification $\mathcal{E}_\succ = \langle T, \mathcal{P}, \succ \rangle$ of Example 5, and the BCQ $q = \exists x, y, z.\text{year}(x, y) \wedge \text{age}(x, z)$. We have that:

$$1\text{-DDRew}(\mathcal{E}_\succ, q) = \exists x, y, z.\text{year}(x, z) \wedge \text{age}(x, y) \wedge \forall w.(\neg(\text{doc}(w, x) \wedge \text{age}(x, y) \wedge$$
$$y = \text{`Eocene'}))$$

$$3\text{-DDRew}(\mathcal{E}_\succ, q) = \exists x, y, z.\text{year}(x, z) \wedge \text{age}(x, y) \wedge \forall w.(\neg(\text{doc}(w, x) \wedge \text{age}(x, y) \wedge$$
$$y = \text{`Eocene'}) \vee (\exists v, u.\text{type}(x, v) \wedge v = \text{`wildcat'} \wedge \text{year}(x, u) \wedge$$
$$\text{doc}(w, x) \wedge 1980 < u \leq 1992) \vee (\exists r.\text{year}(x, r) \wedge \text{doc}(w, x) \wedge$$
$$r > 1992))$$

Now, let $\mathcal{A}$ be the ABox of Example 4. It is easy to see that $\mathcal{A} \not\models 1\text{-DDRew}(\mathcal{E}_\succ, q)$, while $\mathcal{A} \models 3\text{-DDRew}(\mathcal{E}_\succ, q)$. □

The corollary below follows from Theorem 3 and the fact that evaluating an FO query over an ABox is in AC^0 in the size of the ABox (i.e., in data complexity).

Corollary 1. *kDD-Cens-Ent for safe prioritized DL-Lite$_A$ CQE specifications is in AC^0 in data complexity.*

Table 1. k-DD censor results for the six considered settings. $\emptyset, \emptyset$: empty policy and empty preference relation; $\mathcal{P}, \emptyset$: policy $\mathcal{P}$ and empty preference relation; $\mathcal{P}, \succ, i$: policy $\mathcal{P}$, preference relation $\succ$, and $k = i$, with $i \in \{1, 3, 5, 7\}$. In the time columns, "t.o." indicates a time out (30 min), and nK stands for $n \cdot 10^3$.

Setting	q_3 [5]		q_4 [4]		q_5 [6]		q_9 [5]		q_{12} [10]		q_{13} [7]		q_{14} [5]		q_{18} [9]		q_{44} [6]	
	#	time	#	time	#	time	#	time	#	time	#	time	#	time	#	time	#	time
$\emptyset, \emptyset$	910	207	1558	168	17254	585	1566	320	96671	5665	22541	811	141439	2553	339	1525	5078	221
$\mathcal{P}, \emptyset$	910	278	252	295	14797	825	416	331	13028	2876	9374	2861	62255	12372	311	1804	325	153
$\mathcal{P}, \succ, 1$	910	221	252	179	17254	612	416	216	96671	5933	22541	914	125656	4145	311	1384	325	112
$\mathcal{P}, \succ, 3$	910	249	521	1445	17254	749	1252	1148	96671	5378	22541	716	131791	15873	311	1416	4630	1952
$\mathcal{P}, \succ, 5$	910	242	566	8942	17254	723	1456	7715	96671	5219	22541	732	132127	1625K	311	4733	4630	522K
$\mathcal{P}, \succ, 7$	910	472	–	t.o.	17254	993	–	t.o.	96671	7691	22541	912	–	t.o.	311	5464	–	t.o.

6 Experiments

For our experiments, we used the NPD benchmark for OBDA [11], which models the Norwegian Petroleum Directorate's FactPages domain. The benchmark provides an OWL 2 QL version of the NPD TBox[6] comprising 1377 axioms (over 321 concepts, 135 roles, and 233 attributes), the NPD ABox expressed in RDF with a total of around 2 millions of instances, and a set of 30 SPARQL queries.

Following the approach of [6], we reduced query answering over prioritized CQE specifications under k-DD censors to query answering in OBDA. We recall that an OBDA instance is a pair $(\mathcal{J}, D)$, where $\mathcal{J} = \langle \mathcal{T}, \mathcal{M}, \mathcal{S} \rangle$ is an OBDA specification, with TBox $\mathcal{T}$, source schema $\mathcal{S}$, and mapping $\mathcal{M}$ between $\mathcal{T}$ and $\mathcal{S}$, and D is a database for $\mathcal{S}$ [13]. In the experiments, we proceeded as follows: we used the TBox $\mathcal{T}$ of the benchmark, generated the schema $\mathcal{S}$ comprising unary and binary tables corresponding to predicates of the signature of $\mathcal{T}$ (for a total of 689 tables), and produced a database D for $\mathcal{S}$ in which the extension of each table coincides with the extension of the corresponding predicate in the (RDF) ABox $\mathcal{A}$ of the benchmark.

For each of the settings considered in our experiments, i.e., pairs with a prioritized CQE specification $\mathcal{E}_\succ = \langle \mathcal{T}, \mathcal{P}, \succ \rangle$ and positive integer k, we produced a mapping $\mathcal{M}^k_{\mathcal{E}_\succ}$. More precisely, for each atomic concept A in $\mathcal{T}$, $\mathcal{M}^k_{\mathcal{E}_\succ}$ contains an assertion $\Phi(x) \rightsquigarrow A(x)$, where $\Phi(x)$ is the rewriting of the query $A(x)$ returned by k-DDRew, in which ontology predicates are substituted with the corresponding table symbol in $\mathcal{S}$. Analogously for atomic roles and attributes. Under this transformation, answering CQs under k-DD censor over $(\mathcal{E}_\succ, \mathcal{A})$ is equivalent to answering CQs over the OBDA instance $(\mathcal{J}, D)$, where $\mathcal{J} = \langle \mathcal{T}, \mathcal{M}^k_{\mathcal{E}_\succ}, \mathcal{S} \rangle$.

---

[6] http://sws.ifi.uio.no/vocab/npd-v2.

Exactly as done in [6], we executed the *conjunctive version* of 9 queries of the benchmark, i.e., q_3, q_4, q_5, q_9, q_{12}, q_{13}, q_{14}, q_{18}, and q_{44}.[7]

We analyzed six different settings. In the first one we set an empty policy (and, consequently, an empty priority relation), which corresponds to the case of standard query answering over the ontology. For the other settings, we specified a policy $\mathcal{P}$ constituted by the following denials:

$d_1 : \forall w, d, i.dateWellboreEntry(w, d) \wedge wellboreMaxInclation(w, i) \wedge$
$\quad wellboreType(w, \text{``}initial\text{''}) \wedge i \neq 6 \rightarrow \perp$

$d_2 : \forall c, w, d, y.coreForWellbore(c, w) \wedge wellboreCompletionYear(w, y) \wedge$
$\quad documentForWellbore(d, w) \wedge y \neq 1985 \rightarrow \perp$

$d_3 : \forall w, c, t, s.wellOperator(w, c) \wedge taskForCompany(t, c) \wedge$
$\quad wellboreCompletionYear(w, 1985) \wedge oilSampleTestForWellbore(s, w) \rightarrow \perp$

$d_4 : \forall w, l, d.explorationWellboreForLicence(w, l) \wedge documentForWellbore(d, w) \rightarrow \perp$

$d_5 : \forall f, p, l.Field(f) \wedge currentFieldOwner(f, p) \wedge ProductionLicence(p) \wedge$
$\quad licenseeForLicence(l, p) \rightarrow \perp$

$d_6 : \forall p, f.productionMonth(p, 1) \wedge productionForField(p, f) \rightarrow \perp$

By coupling $\mathcal{P}$ with the OWL 2 QL version of the NPD TBox we obtained a safe CQE specification. In the second setting, the prioritized CQE specification contains the policy $\mathcal{P}$ illustrated above, and an empty priority relation. Notice that, according to Proposition 2, this setting is similar to the full setting considered in [6], but with a different policy. All the other settings are intended to verify the effectiveness of providing a priority relation and filtering data with a k-DD censor. In each setting we used a different odd k with $1 \leq k \leq 7$, and considered the following priority relations, which, together with the denials in $\mathcal{P}$, generate challenging scenarios for our technique.

$$wellboreType \succ dateWellboreEntry,$$
$$coreForWellbore \succ documentForWellbore,$$
$$licenseeForLicence \succ currentFieldOwner,$$
$$wellboreCompletionYear \succ documentForWellbore,$$
$$wellboreCompletionYear \succ wellOperator,$$
$$oilSampleTestForWellbore \succ wellboreCompletionYear$$

We performed the experiments through the Java API of MASTRO system [10] for OBDA on a standard laptop with an Intel i7 @2.6 GHz processor and 16 GB of RAM.

Table 1 reports the result of our experiments. The column "#" under each query q_i displays the number of tuples in its evaluation, while the column "time" indicates the evaluation time in milliseconds. Finally, the length of each query, i.e., the number of atoms occurring in it, is indicated in square brackets near the query.

The values in the second row show that the policy $\mathcal{P}$ has an effect on query answering for eight of the nine queries (query q_3 is the only one not altered by the censor), hiding several answers with respect to the setting with no policy (with the only exception

---

[7] In [6], we have extracted the conjunctive component of each such query, which in NPD contains also aggregate operators.

of queries q_5, q_{18}, answers to queries are reduced by up to one third). By introducing the priority relation, already with $k = 1$, we recover a substantial portion of the original answers for query q_{14}, whereas for q_5, q_{12}, q_{13} the recovery is even total. Interestingly, the evaluation time slightly increases w.r.t. the setting without policy but it decreases w.r.t. the setting with the policy without a priority relation. This is due to the fact that, for each atom α, when we adopt a priority relation, $DD_1(\alpha)$ contains less conditions than the case with empty priority relation.

As for $k = 3$, we have a noticeable recovery of original answers for queries q_9 and q_{44}, a further increment for query q_{14}, and a small one for query q_4. In these cases the evaluation times are only slightly affected. When $k = 5$, for some queries we notice a worsening of the evaluation time, with only a limited recovery of the original answers in queries q_4, q_9, and q_{14}. With $k = 7$, query execution was feasible only for five queries, in particular those for which we already recovered all the original answers with a smaller k. For the remaining queries, we stopped the execution after 30 min.

We remark that in our experiments difficulties in executing queries have been encountered only for $k = 7$. However, the largest number (arguably, a considerable one) of original query answers has been recovered for $k = 1$ and $k = 3$, for which the associated evaluation times improve and worsen slightly, respectively, with respect to the setting with the policy without a priority relation.

7 Conclusions

Our experiments show applicability in the practice of our technique, and how priorities, besides being an important modeling feature for the designer, play an important role in increasing the amount of answers disclosed to the user, while still preserving confidentiality. An interesting direction for our research, leveraging the fact that priorities are specified between ontology predicates and not on facts, is investigating the problem of establishing at the intensional level the value for k which makes the k-DD censor coincide with the DD censor. We leave this aspect for future research.

References

1. Baader, F., Calvanese, D., McGuinness, D., Nardi, D., Patel-Schneider, P.F. (eds). The Description Logic Handbook: Theory, Implementation and Applications. 2nd edn, Cambridge University Press, Cambridge (2007)
2. Benedikt, M., Cuenca Grau, B., Kostylev, E.V.: Logical foundations of information disclosure in ontology-based data integration. AIJ **262**, 52–95 (2018)
3. Bienvenu, M., Bourgaux, C.: Querying and repairing inconsistent prioritized knowledge bases: complexity analysis and links with abstract argumentation. In: Proceedings of KR, pp. 141–151 (2020)
4. Biskup, J., Bonatti, P.A.: Controlled query evaluation for known policies by combining lying and refusal. AMAI **40**(1–2), 37–62 (2004)
5. Bonatti, P.A., Sauro, L.: A confidentiality model for ontologies. In: Alani, H., Kagal, L., Fokoue, A., Groth, P., Biemann, C., Parreira, J.X., Aroyo, L., Noy, N., Welty, C., Janowicz, K. (eds.) ISWC 2013. LNCS, vol. 8218, pp. 17–32. Springer, Heidelberg (2013). https://doi.org/10.1007/978-3-642-41335-3_2

6. Cima, G., Lembo, D., Marconi, L., Rosati, R., Savo, D.F.: Controlled query evaluation in ontology-based data access. In: Proceedings of ISWC, pp. 128–146 (2020)
7. Cima, G., Lembo, D., Rosati, R., Savo, D.F.: Controlled query evaluation in description logics through instance indistinguishability. In: Proceedings of IJCAI, pp. 1791–1797 (2020)
8. Cuenca Grau, B., Kharlamov, E., Kostylev, E.V., Zheleznyakov, D.: Controlled query evaluation over OWL 2 RL ontologies. In: Alani, H., Kagal, L., Fokoue, A., Groth, P., Biemann, C., Parreira, J.X., Aroyo, L., Noy, N., Welty, C., Janowicz, K. (eds.) ISWC 2013. LNCS, vol. 8218, pp. 49–65. Springer, Heidelberg (2013). https://doi.org/10.1007/978-3-642-41335-3_4
9. Cuenca Grau, B., Kharlamov, E., Kostylev, E.V., Zheleznyakov, D.: Controlled query evaluation for datalog and OWL 2 profile ontologies. In: Proceedings of IJCAI (2015)
10. De Giacomo, G., et al.: MASTRO: a reasoner for effective ontology-based data access. In: Proceedings of ORE (2012)
11. Lanti, D., Rezk, M., Xiao, G., Calvanese, D.: The NPD benchmark: reality check for OBDA systems. In: Proceedings of EDBT, pp. 617–628 (2015)
12. Lembo, D., Rosati, R., Savo, D.F.: Revisiting controlled query evaluation in description logics. In: Proceedings of IJCAI, pp. 1786–1792 (2019)
13. Poggi, A., Lembo, D., Calvanese, D., De Giacomo, G., Lenzerini, M., Rosati, R.:. Linking data to ontologies. Journal on Data Semantics X, pp. 133–173 (2008)
14. Sicherman, G.L., de Jonge, W., van de Riet, R.P.: Answering queries without revealing secrets. ACM Trans. Database Syst. 8(1), 41–59 (1983)
15. Staworko, S., Chomicki, J., Marcinkowski, J.: Prioritized repairing and consistent query answering in relational databases. AMAI 64(2–3), 209–246 (2012)

ProGS: Property Graph Shapes Language

Philipp Seifer[1][(✉)] ⓘ, Ralf Lämmel[1] ⓘ, and Steffen Staab[2,3] ⓘ

[1] The Software Languages Team, University of Koblenz-Landau, Koblenz, Germany
{pseifer,laemmel}@uni-koblenz.de
[2] Institute for Parallel and Distributed Systems, University of Stuttgart,
Stuttgart, Germany
steffen.staab@ipvs.uni-stuttgart.de
[3] Web and Internet Science Research Group, University of Southampton,
Southampton, England

Abstract. Knowledge graphs such as Wikidata are created by a diversity of contributors and a range of sources leaving them prone to two types of errors. The first type of error, falsity of facts, is addressed by property graphs through the representation of provenance and validity, making triples occur as first-order objects in subject position of metadata triples. The second type of error, violation of domain constraints, has not been addressed with regard to property graphs so far. In RDF representations, this error can be addressed by shape languages such as SHACL or ShEx, which allow for checking whether graphs are valid with respect to a set of domain constraints. Borrowing ideas from the syntax and semantics definitions of SHACL, we design a shape language for property graphs, ProGS, which allows for formulating shape constraints on property graphs including their specific constructs, such as edges with identities and key-value annotations to both nodes and edges. We define a formal semantics of ProGS, investigate the resulting complexity of validating property graphs against sets of ProGS shapes, compare with corresponding results for SHACL, and implement a prototypical validator that utilizes answer set programming.

Keywords: Property graphs · Graph validation · SHACL

1 Introduction

Knowledge graphs such as Wikidata [20] require a data model that allows for the representation of data annotations. While property graphs serve well as data models for representing such knowledge graphs, they lack sufficient means for validation against domain constraints, for instance required provenance annotations. The shapes constraint language SHACL [22] was introduced to allow for validating knowledge graphs that use the RDF data model [21]. Wikidata and other knowledge graphs, however, make use of triples in subject position to represent provenance metadata, such as references or dates, going beyond the capabilities of the RDF framework. Similar to extensions of RDF, such as RDF* [10] or aRDF [19], property graphs are a promising data model for meeting the modelling needs of annotated knowledge graphs. Recent property-graph data

© Springer Nature Switzerland AG 2021
A. Hotho et al. (Eds.): ISWC 2021, LNCS 12922, pp. 392–409, 2021.
https://doi.org/10.1007/978-3-030-88361-4_23

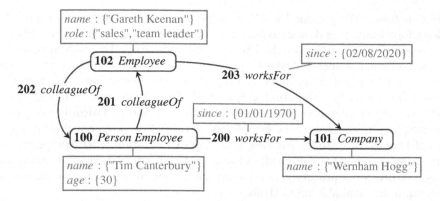

Fig. 1. Example property graph G_{office} showing employment relationships in G-CORE style: Nodes are depicted as rounded boxes. Each node has exactly one identifier, e.g., 100 or 101, and it has zero or more labels, e.g., *{Person, Employee}* or *{Company}*. Each edge has an identifier, e.g., 200, as well as zero or more labels, e.g., *{worksFor}*. Both nodes and edges may have a set of affiliated properties (key-value pairs shown in rectangular boxes), e.g., *{age : {30}}* or *{since : {01/01/1970}}*.

model (and query language) proposals include G-CORE [2] and the upcoming GQL standard [12], as well as the recently established openCypher standard [16]. They have attracted a lot of research interest and popularity in practical use-cases [18].

Property-graph models differ from RDF in substantial ways, featuring edges with identities (allowing multiple edges between nodes with the same labels) and property annotations (that is key-value annotations) on edges. A schema or shape-based validation language must account for these differences. While there exist efforts to formally define property graph schema languages [3,11], and some practical implementations support simple schemata [14] (e.g., uniqueness constraints) or even enable SHACL validation for RDF compatible subsets of the data graph [15], they do not allow for expressing shape constraints involving all elements of property graphs. In particular, existing approaches lack support for qualified number restrictions over edge identities, path expressions or the targeted validation of edges.

Consider the example graph G_{office} depicting employment relationships in Fig. 1. Some of the nodes and edges have property annotations. The edge with identity 200, for example, has the annotation *since* with values {01/01/1970}. One may wish to define *shapes* to require that all edges labelled *worksFor* have such metadata annotations. Shapes that constrain *Employee* or *Company* and their interrelationships will lead to recursive descriptions and thus require a corresponding semantics. Like [6], we adopt a model-based formal semantics based on the notion of (partial) assignments that map nodes and edges to sets of shape names and constitute the basis for a three-valued evaluation function.

Contributions. We present ProGS, a shape language for property graphs that allows for formulating domain constraints and that significantly extends SHACL to property graph data models. ProGS comprises property-graph specific features, including shapes for edges with identities, qualified number restrictions over such edges and constraints on properties and their values. We define the formal semantics for validating graphs with ProGS shapes, including cyclic, recursive shape references, based on the notion of partial faithful assignments inspired by [6]. We analyse the complexity of validating property graphs against sets of ProGS constraints. We show that ProGS validation is NP complete, thus remaining in the same complexity class as SHACL while increasing expressiveness. We provide a prototypical reference implementation relying on answer set programming, available on GitHub.

Outline. The remainder of this paper is structured as follows. Section 2 gives a short overview of property graph data models. In Sect. 3 we define the abstract syntax and semantics of ProGS, including assignment-based validation of graphs against a set of ProGS shapes. Section 4 analyses the complexity of the ProGS graph validation problem. Section 5 investigates implementation approaches for ProGS and introduces a prototypical implementation relying on an encoding of the validation problem as an answer set program. Section 6 discusses related work and Sect. 7 concludes the paper.

2   Foundations

Before providing a working definition of property graphs as the basis of ProGS, we compare existing property graph models to determine essential features. To this end, consider Table 1. We compare the property graph models underlying the graph query languages G-CORE [2], Cypher [9], Gremlin [4], and PGQL [17]; we also include the RDF [21] data model and RDF* [10] as a point of reference.

   We use the example depicted in Fig. 2, an excerpt from Wikidata, to illustrate the differences between property graphs, RDF and RDF*. The defining feature of property graphs are properties, that are key-value pairs, on edges and nodes. For example, *point in time* in Fig. 2 could be represented as such a property annotation for the edge labelled *nominated for*. Property keys are strings, while value domains vary between approaches, ranging from simple scalar values and strings to lists or maps of values. The key differences to RDF arise from the fact that edges in property graphs have identities. The edge *nominated for*, for example, would have a unique identity acting as a target for property annotations. While this is not possible in plain RDF, node properties can be simulated through edges to literal nodes. RDF* extends RDF by introducing triples that are first-order (first-order) objects, meaning they can occur in both subject and object position of other triples. This importantly subsumes edge properties, again through an encoding of literal nodes. While not using RDF*, Wikidata also allows for annotations on edges referencing other resources. This highlights the key difference between support for triples in subject position of arbitrary triples and property

Table 1. Comparison of feature support for common property graph models and RDF. (a) using triples with literals as objects (b) triples in subject position of triples with literals as objects.

	G-CORE	Cypher	Gremlin	PGQL	RDF*	RDF
Nodes as first-order objects	+	+	+	+	+	+
Node properties	+	+	+	+	+[a]	+[a]
Node labels	set	set	none	set	set (rdf:type)	set (rdf:type)
Edges as first-order objects	+	+	+	+	+	-
Triples as first-order objects	−	−	−	−	+	−
Edge properties	+	+	+	+	+[b]	−
Edge labels	set	single	single	set	single	single
Paths as first-order objects	+	−	−	−	−	−
Path properties	+	−	−	−	−	−
Path labels	set	−	−	−	−	−

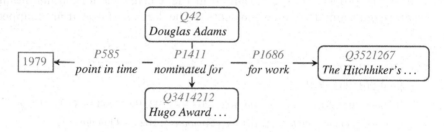

Fig. 2. Excerpt from Wikidata.

annotations: While *point in time* could be represented as a property annotation on the *nominated for* edge, *for work* could not.

There are some further differences between the various property graph models. Support for labels differs between approaches ranging from sets of labels on both nodes and edges (G-CORE, PGQL) to no support for node labels in Gremlin and single edge types in both Gremlin and Cypher. Finally, only G-CORE features paths as first-order objects, i.e., paths that can be annotated with property annotations and labels.

2.1 Definition of Property Graphs

The formalization of the property graph model we use as a basis for the definition of ProGS is based on the data model presented for G-CORE [2]. We do not consider first-class paths, and instead restrict the model to the core subset shared with other property graph models as discussed in the previous section. In terms of value domains in properties, we provide exemplary support for the types `string`, `int` and `date`, without loss of generality.

Let the set of labels $L = L_N \cup L_E$ where L_N is an infinite set of node labels and L_E an infinite set of edge labels. As a matter of convention, we use

CamelCase for all $l_N \in L_N$ and *camelCase* for all $l_E \in L_E$. Let K be an infinite set of property names (or keys) and V an infinite set of literal values from the union of sets in $T \in \{\texttt{int}, \texttt{string}, \texttt{date}\}$. We refer to elements of T as the type of the respective value. Let furthermore $\mathrm{FSET}(X)$ denote all finite subsets of a set X.

Definition 1 (Property Graph). *A property graph is a tuple $G = (N, E, \rho, \lambda, \sigma)$, where N denotes a set of node identifiers and E a set of edge identifiers, with $N \cap E = \emptyset$, $\rho : E \to (N \times N)$ is a total function, $\lambda : (N \cup E) \to \mathrm{FSET}(L)$ is a total function, $\sigma : (N \cup E) \times K \to \mathrm{FSET}(V)$ is a total function for which a finite set of tuples $(x, k) \in (N \cup E) \times K$ exists such that $\sigma(x, k) \neq \emptyset$.*

A property graph consists of a set of nodes $n \in N$ and edges $e \in E$, where ρ maps elements of E to pairs of nodes. The function λ maps nodes and edges to all assigned labels $l \in L$ and likewise the function σ maps pairs of nodes or edges, and property names to the property values assigned to them. The example in Fig. 3 shows the property graph visualized in Fig. 1 using the formal definition. Note that we omit infinitely many elements of the domain of σ that are mapped to $\emptyset$.

$$N = \{100, 101, 102\}$$
$$E = \{200, 201, 202, 203\}$$
$$\rho = \{200 \mapsto (100, 101), 201 \mapsto (100, 102), 202 \mapsto (102, 100), 203 \mapsto (102, 101)\}$$
$$\lambda = \{100 \mapsto \{Person, Employee\}, 101 \mapsto \{Company\}, 102 \mapsto \{Employee\},$$
$$200 \mapsto \{worksFor\}, 201 \mapsto \{colleagueOf\}, 202 \mapsto \{colleagueOf\}$$
$$203 \mapsto \{worksFor\}\}$$
$$\sigma = \{(100, name) \mapsto \{\text{"Tim Canterbury"}\}, (100, age) \mapsto \{30\},$$
$$(101, name) \mapsto \{\text{"Wernham Hogg"}\}, (102, name) \mapsto \{\text{"Gareth Keenan"}\},$$
$$(102, role) \mapsto \{\text{"sales", "team leader"}\}, (200, since) \mapsto \{01/01/1970\},$$
$$(203, since) \mapsto \{02/08/2020\}\}$$

Fig. 3. Formal model for the example property graph G_{office} rendered in Fig. 1.

3   Shapes for Property Graphs

Our shape language for property graph validation, called ProGS, has been inspired by SHACL [22], the W3C recommendation for writing and evaluating RDF graph validation constraints. More specifically, we base the ProGS shape language on the abstract syntax proposed by [6], which formalizes a syntactic core of SHACL. Corman et al. [6] also defined a formal semantics for this syntactic core that addresses recursion, in particular. We facilitate the understanding of differences between SHACL and ProGS by colour coding. Expressions that we borrow from SHACL will be displayed in black font, while novel expressions will be coded in blue font.

3.1   Requirements on a Property Graph Shapes Language

Requirements for our target language stem from the differences between the RDF and property graph data models, which we mentioned in Sect. 2. Table 2 explains how RDF may be mapped to the G-CORE property graph model. Based on this mapping we design ProGS to adopt language constructs from SHACL. The reader may note that this mapping includes some design decisions that are not unique, e.g., we interpret class instantiations as corresponding to G-CORE labellings of nodes. We follow a simplification of the third mapping $\mathcal{IM}_3$ discussed in [3], e.g., by excluding blank nodes.

Table 2. Sketching correspondences between the RDF and G-CORE graph models.

Description	RDF	G-CORE/ProGS
Node id i	IRI i	$i \in N$
Node n has label l	n rdf:type l.	$l \in \lambda(n)$
Node n has key k with value v	$n\,k\,v$.	$v \in \sigma(n, k)$
Edge id i	not available	$i \in E$
Edge label l, in triple $s\,p\,o$.	$s\,l\,o$	$l \in \lambda(p)$
Edge e has key k with value v	not available	$v \in \sigma(e, k)$
Triple $s\,p\,o$.	$s\,p\,o$.	$p \in \lambda(i), \rho(i) = (s, o)$

Edges in property graphs have identities necessitating two distinct kinds of shapes for nodes (R1) and for edges (R2) as well as two kinds of qualified number restrictions for nodes, counting edges (R3) and counting reachable nodes via some path (R4). Property annotations require dedicated constraints dealing with the set of values reachable via a specific key, for both nodes (R5) and edges (R6). The presence of properties must also be considered for constraints that include comparison operations (R7). Lastly, the existence of certain properties, or properties with certain values, also require new means of targeting nodes and edges in target queries (R8).

3.2   Definition of Shapes

Intuitively, a shape defines constraints on how certain nodes or edges in a graph are formed. As both nodes and edges in property graphs have identities, we define *node shapes* that apply to nodes and *edge shapes* that apply to edges. Each shape is a triple consisting of a shape name, a constraint, and a target query defining which nodes or which edges of a graph must conform to the shape, i.e., fulfil all of its constraints, for the graph to be considered in conformance with the shape.

Example 1. The node shape $_N\langle EmployeeShape, Person, Employee\rangle$ is a triple with the shape name *EmployeeShape*, the constraint *Person*, which requires that

$$[\![\bot]\!]_G = \emptyset$$
$$[\![n]\!]_G = \{n\}$$
$$[\![l_N]\!]_G = \{n \mid n \in N \land l_N \in \lambda(n)\}$$
$$[\![k]\!]_G = \{n \mid n \in N \land \sigma(n,k) \neq \emptyset\}$$
$$[\![k:v]\!]_G = \{n \mid n \in N \land v \in \sigma(n,k)\}$$

Fig. 4. Evaluation of target node queries.

each graph node assigned this shape has the label *Person*, and the target query *Employee*, meaning all nodes with the label *Employee* are targets of this shape. For the graph G_{office} in Fig. 1, node 100 conforms to this shape, whereas node 102 does not, lacking the *Employee* label. Given that at least one target node does not conform to the constraint, the entire graph does not conform to *EmployeeShape*.

As shown in the first example, we use $_N\langle s_N, \phi_N, q_N\rangle$ to indicate triples that are node shapes and use $_E\langle s_E, \phi_E, q_E\rangle$ to refer to triples that are edge shapes.

Before defining the components of shapes, we define the syntax of path expressions p in Eq. (1) in analogy to property path expressions defined in SHACL [22], which are in turn based on path expressions in the SPARQL query language. A path expression, when evaluated on a starting node, describes the set of nodes reachable from this node via paths that match the path expression.

$$p ::= l_E \mid p^- \mid p_1/p_2 \mid p_1\|p_2 \mid p* \mid p+ \mid ?p \tag{1}$$

Path expressions may include edge labels l_E, inverse paths p^-, path sequences p_1/p_2, alternate paths $p_1\|p_2$ and zero or more ($p*$), one or more ($p+$) and zero or one ($?p$) expressions. Note the minor difference to paths in RDF graphs, in that edges in property graphs may have multiple labels.

Example 2. The path *worksFor/worksFor$^-$* describes the set of all colleagues of a starting node n (including n itself), by first finding all employers of n (i.e., nodes reachable from n via an edge with label *worksFor*) and then all employees of those employers (i.e., nodes with incoming *worksFor* edges). For the graph G_{office} in Fig. 1 and starting node 100, the result of evaluating this path would be the same as evaluating *colleagueOf*$*$, namely the set $\{100, 102\}$.

Let the set of shapes $S = S_N \cup S_E$ consist of node and edge shapes and the set of shape names be called Names(S). A node shape is a tuple $_N\langle s_N, \phi_N, q_N\rangle$ consisting of a shape name $s_N \in$ Names(S_N), a node constraint ϕ_N and a query for target nodes q_N. A query for target nodes is either $\bot$, meaning the query has no targets, an explicitly targeted node $n \in N$, all nodes with label $l_N \in L_N$, all nodes with property $k \in K$ or possibly further constrained as $k : v$ by a concrete value $v \in V$. The syntax of target node queries q_N is summarized in Eq. (2). We write $[\![q_N]\!]_G$ for the evaluation of a target node query, which is defined in Fig. 4.

$$q_N ::= \bot \mid n \mid l_N \mid k \mid k:v \tag{2}$$

Example 3. The target query $q_N = Employee$ targets all nodes that are labelled with the label *Employee*. The set of targets when evaluating q_N on the example graph G_{office} in Fig. 1 is therefore $[\![q_N]\!]_{G_{\text{office}}} = \{100, 102\}$.

Node constraints ϕ_N essentially specify which outgoing or incoming edges, which labels, or which properties a targeted node must have. Assuming $s_N \in S_N$, $n \in N$, $l_N \in L_N$, $k \in K$, $i \in \mathbb{N}$, comparison operations $\odot$ for sets or singleton sets (e.g., $=$, $<$, $\subset$) and arbitrary value predicate functions $f : V \to \{0, 1\}$ such as ≥ 0, $\neq 19$, or type restrictions for a specific data type such as int, string or date, the syntax of node constraints ϕ_N is defined as in Eq. (3).

$$\phi_N ::= \top \mid s_N \mid n \mid l_N \mid \neg\phi_N \mid \phi_N^1 \wedge \phi_N^2 \mid \geq_i p.\phi_N \mid \odot(p_1, p_2)$$
$$\mid \geq_i k.f \mid \geq_i^{\leftarrow} \phi_E \mid \geq_i^{\rightarrow} \phi_E \mid \odot(p_1, k_1, p_2, k_2) \mid \odot(k_1, k_2) \tag{3}$$

A node constraint may be always satisfied ($\top$), reference another node shape with name s_N that must be satisfied, require a specific node identity n in this place or require a node label l_N. It may also be the negation $\neg\phi_N$ or conjunction $\phi_N^1 \wedge \phi_N^2$ of other node constraints. Furthermore, the constraint $\geq_i p.\phi_N$ requires i nodes that can be reached via path p to conform to ϕ_N. $\odot(p_1, p_2)$ is an arbitrary comparison operation between sets of node identities that can be reached via the two path expressions p_1 and p_2.

Example 4. Consider the shape $_N\langle s_1, \geq_1 colleagueOf.Person, Employee\rangle$ targeting all nodes with the label *Employee*. s_1 requires at least one path *colleagueOf*, i.e., an outgoing edge that has the label *colleagueOf*, to a node which has the label *Person*. For the graph in Fig. 1, node 102 satisfies this constraint, because the only node reachable via path *colleagueOf* is node 100, and *Person* $\in \lambda(100)$. With analogous reasoning, the constraint does not hold for node 100, because *Person* $\notin \lambda(102)$

The aforementioned constraints were essentially transferred from core constraint components of the SHACL language. Novel kinds of constraints are printed in blue font. A qualified number restriction $\geq_i k.f$ restricts the number of values matching the predicate f for the property k. The qualified number constraints $\geq_i^{\leftarrow} \phi_E$ and $\geq_i^{\rightarrow} \phi_E$ require i incoming or outgoing edges that conform to the given edge constraint ϕ_E (defined below). $\odot(p_1, k_1, p_2, k_2)$ compares the annotated sets of values for properties k_1 and k_2, reached via paths p_1 and p_2 and $\odot(k_1, k_2)$ does the same for the current node.

Example 5. Consider the shape $_N\langle s_2, \geq_2 role.\text{string} \wedge s_1, name :$ "Gareth Keenan"$\rangle$, which targets all nodes n where "Gareth Keenan" $\in \sigma(n, name)$. For the graph G_{office} in Fig. 1, node 102 is the only target. The constraint $\geq_2 role.\text{string} \wedge s_1$ requires that this node conforms to shape s_1 from Example 4, as well as that the *role* property has at least two elements of type string. From Example 4 it follows that 102 conforms to s_1. The property $\sigma(102, role)$ has two values {"sales","team leader"}, both of which are strings. Therefore, node 102 conforms to s_2. Since node 102 is the only target of s_2, G_{office} conforms to s_2 as well.

Edge shapes apply to edges and, just as a node shape, require specific labels or properties for all targeted edges. Similarly to how node shapes constrain outgoing and incoming edges, edge shapes may constrain the source or destination node of an edge.

An edge shape is a tuple $_E\langle s_E, \phi_E, q_E\rangle$ consisting of shape name $s_E \in$ Names(S_E), an edge constraint ϕ_E and a target edge query q_E. Edge target queries are defined analogously to node target queries in Eq. (4) and Fig. 5.

$$q_E ::= \perp \mid e \mid l_E \mid k \mid k : v \qquad (4)$$

Most constraint components of edge constraints ϕ_E are defined similarly to node constraints ϕ_N, albeit in terms of the respective edge identities e, edge labels l_E and edge shapes s_E. Unique to edge constraints are the constraints $\Leftarrow \phi_N$ and $\Rightarrow \phi_N$, which constrain source or destination nodes of an edge to conform to a node shape ϕ_N. The syntax of edge constraints ϕ_E is defined as in Eq. (5).

$$\phi_E ::= \top \mid s_E \mid e \mid l_E \mid \neg\phi_E \mid \phi_E^1 \wedge \phi_E^2 \mid \geqslant_i k.f \mid \Rightarrow \phi_N \mid \Leftarrow \phi_N \mid \odot (k_1, k_2) \qquad (5)$$

$$[\![\perp]\!]_G = \emptyset$$
$$[\![e]\!]_G = \{e\}$$
$$[\![l_E]\!]_G = \{e \mid e \in E \wedge l_E \in \lambda(e)\}$$
$$[\![k]\!]_G = \{e \mid e \in E \wedge \sigma(e, k) \neq \emptyset\}$$
$$[\![k : v]\!]_G = \{e \mid e \in E \wedge v \in \sigma(e, k)\}$$

Fig. 5. Evaluation of target edge queries.

Example 6. Consider $_E\langle s_3, \Leftarrow Person \wedge \geqslant_1 since.(\geq 01/01/2020), worksFor\rangle$ which targets edges with the label *worksFor*. For the two matching edges of graph G_office in Fig. 1, 200 and 203, only 200 fulfils the constraint $\Leftarrow Person$, since $Person \in \lambda(100)$ and $\rho(200) = (100, 101)$. That is, the source node of edge 200 has the label *Person*. Only edge 203 fulfils the constraint $\geqslant_1 since. \geq 01/01/2020$, because at least one element of $\sigma(203, since) = \{02/08/2020\}$ fulfils the given value predicate $\geq 01/01/2020$, because $02/08/2020 \geq 01/01/2020$. Neither edge fulfils s_3.

Example 7. There is a difference between a node constraint $\geqslant_3$ *colleagueOf.Person* and a node constraint $\geqslant_3^{\rightarrow}$ (*colleagueOf* $\wedge \Rightarrow Person$). In the first case, we require 3 distinct nodes with the label *Person*, reachable via edges that match *colleagueOf*. In the second case, we require 3 outgoing edges labelled *colleagueOf* with destination nodes labelled *Person*. The nodes in the second case are not required to be distinct. Indeed, a graph with a single node having three self-loops could potentially fulfil the second, but never the first constraint.

In addition to these core constraints, we define useful syntactic sugar for both node constraints ϕ_N and edge constraint ϕ_E as shown in Fig. 6. For target queries, both conjunction and disjunction can also be defined as syntactic sugar (we use ϕ and q to mean either a node or edge constraint and query, respectively). Any shape with target $q_1 \wedge q_2$ and constraint ϕ is equivalent to a shape with target q_1 and the constraint $(\phi \wedge \phi_{q_2}) \vee \neg\phi_{q_2}$, where ϕ_{q_2} is the constraint equivalent to the target query (i.e., validating exactly the targets). Any shape s with target $q_1 \vee q_2$ and constraint ϕ can be expressed via two utility shapes with target q_1 and constraint s and target q_2 and constraint s, as well as the shape s with target $\perp$ and constraint ϕ.

3.3 Shape Semantics

Our definition of ProGS allows shape names to occur in constraints, meaning recursive cycles of references to other shapes can arise. Therefore, we follow an approach defined for recursive SHACL [6] and define evaluation of shapes on the basis of *partial assignments* for graph nodes and edges to sets of shapes. Our approach then relies on validating a given assignment in polynomial time (e.g., by guessing an assignment).

We formally define assignments on the basis of atoms, such that for each atom that pairs the name of a node shape with a node $s_N(n)$ or the name of an edge shape with an edge $s_E(e)$ a truth value from $\{0, 0.5, 1\}$ may be assigned.

$$
\begin{aligned}
\perp &:= \neg\top & \exists^{\leftarrow}\phi_E &:= \geqslant_1^{\leftarrow} \phi_E \\
\leqslant_i^{\leftarrow} \phi_E &:= \neg \geqslant_{i+1}^{\leftarrow} \phi_E & \exists p.\phi_N &:= \geqslant_1 p.\phi_N \\
\leqslant_i p.\phi_N &:= \neg \geqslant_{i+1} p.\phi_N & \exists k.f &:= \geqslant_1 k.f \\
\leqslant_i k.f &:= \neg \geqslant_{i+1} k.f & \forall^{\leftarrow}\phi_E &:= \leqslant_0^{\leftarrow} \neg\phi_E \\
=_i^{\leftarrow} \phi_E &:= \geqslant_i^{\leftarrow} \phi_E \wedge \leqslant_i^{\leftarrow} \phi_E & \forall p.\phi_N &:= \leqslant_0 p.\neg\phi_N \\
=_i p.\phi_N &:= \geqslant_i p.\phi_N \wedge \leqslant_i p.\phi_N & \forall k.f &:= \leqslant_0 k.\neg f \\
=_i k.f &:= \geqslant_i k.f \wedge \leqslant_i k.f & \phi_1 \vee \phi_2 &:= \neg(\neg\phi_1 \wedge \neg\phi_2)
\end{aligned}
$$

Fig. 6. Syntactic sugar for constraints, where ϕ is placeholder for either ϕ_N or ϕ_E. Definitions for syntactic sugar related to $\geqslant_i^{\rightarrow} \phi_E$ are omitted, since they are analogous to $\geqslant_i^{\leftarrow} \phi_E$.

Definition 2 (Atoms). *For a property graph $G = (N, E, \rho, \lambda, \sigma)$ and a set of shapes $S = S_N \cup S_E$, the set* $\mathrm{atoms}(G, S) = \mathrm{atoms}_N(G, S_N) \cup \mathrm{atoms}_E(G, S_E)$ *where* $\mathrm{atoms}_N(G, S_N) = \{s_N(n) \mid s_N \in S_N \wedge n \in N\}$ *and* $\mathrm{atoms}_E(G, S_N) = \{s_E(e) \mid s_E \in S_E \wedge e \in E\}$ *is called the set of atoms of G and S.*

For the set of atoms of G and S, meaning essentially all tuples of shapes in S and nodes (or edges, respectively) in G, we define a partial assignment as a function Σ that maps for $x \in N \cup E$ all atoms $s(x) \in \mathrm{atoms}(G, S)$ to 1, if the shape s is assigned to x, to 0 if $\neg s$ is assigned to x, and to 0.5 otherwise.

$$[\![\top]\!]^{\Sigma,n,G} = 1$$

$$[\![s_N]\!]^{\Sigma,n,G} = \Sigma(s_N(n))$$

$$[\![n']\!]^{\Sigma,n,G} = [\,n' = n\,]$$

$$[\![l_N]\!]^{\Sigma,n,G} = [\,l_N \in \lambda(n)\,]$$

$$[\![\neg\phi_N]\!]^{\Sigma,n,G} = 1 - [\![\phi_N]\!]^{\Sigma,n,G}$$

$$[\![\phi_N^1 \wedge \phi_N^2]\!]^{\Sigma,n,G} = \min\{[\![\phi_N^1]\!]^{\Sigma,n,G}, [\![\phi_N^2]\!]^{\Sigma,n,G}\}$$

$$[\![\geqslant_i p.\phi_N]\!]^{\Sigma,n,G} = \begin{cases} 1 & |\{n_2 \mid n_2 \in [\![p]\!]^{\Sigma,n,G} \wedge [\![\phi_N]\!]^{\Sigma,n_2,G} = 1\}| \geq i \\ 0 & |[\![p]\!]^{\Sigma,n,G}| - \\ & |\{n_2 \mid n_2 \in [\![p]\!]^{\Sigma,n,G} \wedge [\![\phi_N]\!]^{\Sigma,n_2,G} = 0\}| < i \\ 0.5 & \text{otherwise} \end{cases}$$

$$[\![\odot\,(p_1, p_2)]\!]^{\Sigma,n,G} = [\,[\![p_1]\!]^{\Sigma,n,G} \odot [\![p_2]\!]^{\Sigma,n,G}\,]$$

$$[\![\geqslant_i^{\leftarrow} \phi_E]\!]^{\Sigma,n,G} = \begin{cases} 1 & |\{e \mid e \in E \wedge n_2 \in N \wedge \rho(e) = (n_2, n) \\ & \wedge [\![\phi_E]\!]^{\Sigma,e,G} = 1\}| \geq i \\ 0 & |\{e \mid e \in E \wedge n_2 \in N \wedge \rho(e) = (n_2, n)\}| - \\ & |\{e \mid e \in E \wedge n_2 \in N \wedge \rho(e) = (n_2, n) \\ & \wedge [\![\phi_E]\!]^{\Sigma,e,G} = 0\}| < i \\ 0.5 & \text{otherwise} \end{cases}$$

$$[\![\geqslant_i^{\rightarrow} \phi_E]\!]^{\Sigma,n,G} = \begin{cases} 1 & |\{e \mid e \in E \wedge n_2 \in N \wedge \rho(e) = (n, n_2) \\ & \wedge [\![\phi_E]\!]^{\Sigma,e,G} = 1\}| \geq i \\ 0 & |\{e \mid e \in E \wedge n_2 \in N \wedge \rho(e) = (n, n_2)\}| - \\ & |\{e \mid e \in E \wedge n_2 \in N \wedge \rho(e) = (n, n_2) \\ & \wedge [\![\phi_E]\!]^{\Sigma,e,G} = 0\}| < i \\ 0.5 & \text{otherwise} \end{cases}$$

$$[\![\geqslant_i k.f]\!]^{\Sigma,n,G} = [\,|\{v \mid v \in \sigma(n,k) \wedge f(v)\}| \geq i\,]$$

$$[\![\odot\,(p_1, k_1, p_2, k_2)]\!]^{\Sigma,n,G} = \begin{aligned}[\,\{v \mid n \in [\![p_1]\!]^{\Sigma,n,G}, v \in \sigma(n, k_1)\} \\ \odot \{v \mid n \in [\![p_2]\!]^{\Sigma,n,G}, v \in \sigma(n, k_2)\}\,]\end{aligned}$$

$$[\![\odot\,(k_1, k_2)]\!]^{\Sigma,n,G} = [\,\sigma(n, k_1) \odot \sigma(n, k_2)\,]$$

Fig. 7. Evaluation rules for node constraints over graph G with assignment Σ.

Definition 3 (Partial Assignment). *Let G be a property graph and S a set of shapes. A partial assignment Σ is a total function $\Sigma : \mathrm{atoms}(G, S) \to \{0, 0.5, 1\}$.*

Evaluating whether a node $n \in N$ of G satisfies a constraint ϕ_N, written $[\![\phi_N]\!]^{\Sigma,n,G}$ is defined in Fig. 7 and evaluating whether an edge $e \in E$ of G satisfies a constraint ϕ_E, written $[\![\phi_E]\!]^{\Sigma,e,G}$, is defined in Fig. 8. In the latter figure we omit cases that are trivially analogous to node shapes. In both figures, $[P]$ is similar to the Iverson bracket, such that $[P]$ evaluates to 1 (the constraint is satisfied) if P is true and 0 (the constraint is not satisfied) if P is false. Conditions for evaluation to 0.5 are given explicitly.

$$[\![s_E]\!]^{\Sigma,e,G} = \Sigma(s_E(e))$$
$$[\![e']\!]^{\Sigma,e,G} = [e' = e]$$
$$[\![l_E]\!]^{\Sigma,e,G} = [l_E \in \lambda(e)]$$
$$[\![\Rightarrow \phi_N]\!]^{\Sigma,e,G} = [\![\phi_N]\!]^{\Sigma,n_2,G} \text{ where } (n_1, n_2) = \rho(e)$$
$$[\![\Leftarrow \phi_N]\!]^{\Sigma,e,G} = [\![\phi_N]\!]^{\Sigma,n_1,G} \text{ where } (n_1, n_2) = \rho(e)$$

Fig. 8. Evaluation rules for edge constraints over graph G with assignment Σ (omitting some cases that are analogous to cases in Fig. 7).

$$[\![l_E]\!]^{\Sigma,n,G} = \{n_1 \mid e \in E \wedge (n, n_1) = \rho(e) \wedge l_E \in \lambda(e)\}$$
$$[\![p^-]\!]^{\Sigma,n,G} = \{n_2 \mid n \in [\![p]\!]^{\Sigma,n_2,G}\}$$
$$[\![p_1/p_2]\!]^{\Sigma,n,G} = \bigcup \{[\![p_2]\!]^{\Sigma,n_1,G} \mid n_1 \in [\![p_1]\!]^{\Sigma,n,G}\}$$
$$[\![p_1\|p_2]\!]^{\Sigma,n,G} = [\![p_1]\!]^{\Sigma,n,G} \cup [\![p_2]\!]^{\Sigma,n,G}$$
$$[\![p+]\!]^{\Sigma,n,G} = \begin{cases} \emptyset, & \text{if } [\![p]\!]^{\Sigma,n,G} = \emptyset \\ [\![p]\!]^{\Sigma,n,G} \cup [\![p/p+]\!]^{\Sigma,n,G}, & \text{otherwise} \end{cases}$$
$$[\![p*]\!]^{\Sigma,n,G} = \{n\} \cup [\![p+]\!]^{\Sigma,n,G}$$
$$[\![?p]\!]^{\Sigma,n,G} = \{n\} \cup [\![p]\!]^{\Sigma,n,G}$$

Fig. 9. Evaluation of path expressions.

The semantics of path expressions are defined in Fig. 9. We write $\{n_1, \ldots, n_i\} = [\![p]\!]^{\Sigma,n,G}$ for the evaluation of path p on graph G, such that nodes $n_1, \ldots, n_i$ can be reached via p from node n.

In order for a property graph G to be valid with respect to a set of shapes S, an assignment must exists which complies with all targets and constraints in S. Transferring terminology from [6] we call such an assignment *strictly faithful*.

Definition 4 (Strictly Faithful Assignment). *An assignment Σ for a property graph $G = (N, E, \rho, \lambda, \sigma)$ and a set of shapes S is strictly faithful, if and only if the following 4 properties hold (given shapes of the form $_N\langle s_N, \phi_N, q_N\rangle$ and $_E\langle s_E, \phi_E, q_E\rangle$):*

1. $\forall \ s_N(n) \in atoms(G, S) : \Sigma(s_N(n)) = [\![\phi_N]\!]^{\Sigma,n,G}$
2. $\forall \ s_E(e) \in atoms(G, S) : \Sigma(s_E(e)) = [\![\phi_E]\!]^{\Sigma,e,G}$
3. $\forall n \in [\![q_N]\!]_G : \Sigma(s_N(n)) = 1$
4. $\forall e \in [\![q_E]\!]_G : \Sigma(s_E(e)) = 1$

This means a strictly faithful assignment is an assignment, where all atoms are assigned exactly the result of constraint evaluation, all targets $n \in [\![q_N]\!]_G$ are assigned the respective shape s_N, and all targets $e \in [\![q_E]\!]_G$ are assigned the respective shape s_E. We define conformance of a graph with respect to a set of shapes on the basis of faithful assignments.

Definition 5 (Conformance). *A property graph $G = (N, E, \rho, \lambda, \sigma)$ conforms to a set of shapes S if and only if there exists at least one assignment Σ for G and S that is strictly faithful.*

3.4 Fulfilment of Requirements and Relationship to SHACL

As visualized by the colour coding of our definitions, the syntax of ProGS is an extension of the $\mathcal{L}$ language formalization of SHACL [6]. There are some exceptions arising from the existence of edges that have identities in property graphs. In fulfilment of requirements R3 and R4, ProGS allows qualifying the number of outgoing and incoming edges as well as reachable nodes, whereas SHACL only needs to be concerned with reachable nodes via some path.

Node shapes in SHACL may target all subjects or objects of an RDF property via `targetSubjectsOf` and `targetObjectsOf` expressions. In ProGS, these target queries are not required. Instead, fulfilling requirements R1 and R2, as well as R8, ProGS allows targeting of edges directly with specialized edge shapes. The respective source and destination nodes can then be constrained in these shapes via $\Leftarrow \phi_N$ and $\Rightarrow \phi_n$, respectively.

Finally, the handling of RDF literals in SHACL differs from constraints dealing with property annotations on nodes (R5 and R7) in ProGS. In addition, ProGS allows validating property annotations on edges (R6), which do not exist in RDF.

4 Complexity

We analyse the complexity of validating a property graph against a set of ProGS shapes. Before we define the validation problem VALID through the notion of faithfulness of assignments, we simplify the definition of faithful assignments with respect to target queries, by showing that it suffices to consider only cases where there is exactly one target node.

Proposition 1. *For a graph $G = (N, E, \rho, \lambda, \sigma)$ and a set of shapes $S = S_N \cup S_E$ with target nodes $n \in N$ for each $s_N \in S_N$ and target edges $e \in E$ for each $s_E \in S_E$, a graph G' and set of shapes S' can be constructed in linear time, such that G is valid against S if and only if G' is valid against S' and S' has a single target in G'.*

Proof (Sketch). Essentially, we construct edges from a new, single target node n_0 to previous target nodes and source nodes of target edges. Then we adapt constraints appropriately. Let $s_N^1, \ldots, s_N^n$ and $s_E^1, \ldots, s_E^n$ be shapes in S with targets $n_1^1, \ldots, n_1^m, \ldots, n_n^1, \ldots, n_n^m$ and targets $e_1^1, \ldots, e_1^m, \ldots, e_n^1, \ldots, e_n^m$. Extend G with a fresh node n_0 and fresh edges ne_i^j with $\rho(ne_i^j) = (n_0, n_i^j)$ for each target n_i^j as well as edges ee_i^j with $\rho(ee_i^j) = (n_0, n_1)$ where $(n_1, n_2) = \rho(e_i^j)$ for each target e_i^j. Then set all target queries for shapes in S to $\bot$ and introduce node shape s_{N_0} with target n_0 and constraint $\phi_{N_0} = \geqslant_1 ne_1^1.\phi_{s_N^1} \wedge \ldots \wedge \geqslant_1 ne_n^m.\phi_{s_N^n} \wedge \geqslant_1 ee_1^1. \geqslant_1 (e_1^1 \wedge \phi_{s_E^1}) \wedge \ldots \wedge \geqslant_1 ee_n^m. \geqslant_1 (e_n^m \wedge \phi_{s_E^n})$. □

On the basis of this transformation, we can redefine strictly faithful assignments.

Definition 6 (Strictly Faithful Assignment for Graphs with a Single Target Node). *Let s_{N_0} be the shape and n_0 the node constructed by Proposition 1 as the single target node. An assignment Σ for a graph $G = (N, E, \rho, \lambda, \sigma)$ and a set of shapes S is strictly faithful, if and only if:*

1. $\forall \; s_N(n) \in atoms(G, S) : \Sigma(s_N(n)) = \llbracket \phi_N \rrbracket^{\Sigma, n, G}$
2. $\forall \; s_E(e) \in atoms(G, S) : \Sigma(s_E(e)) = \llbracket \phi_E \rrbracket^{\Sigma, e, G}$
3. $\Sigma(s_{N_0}(n_0)) = 1$

The validation problem VALID for validation of property graphs with respect to a set of ProGS shapes is defined as follows.

Definition 7 (Validation). *The problem of validating a property graph G with respect to a set of shapes S (such that in S there is exactly one shape s_{N_0} with a target query different from $\perp$ that targets node n_0, which can be constructed via Proposition 1 for any graph and set of shapes) is defined as* $\text{VALID}(G, S, s_{N_0}(n_0))$.

We first show that VALID is in NP.

Theorem 1. *VALID is in NP.*

Proof (Sketch). In order to show that $\text{VALID}(G, S, s_{N_0}(n_0))$ is in NP, we first construct, in polynomial time, an instance $\text{VALID}(G', S', s_{N_0}(n_0))$ which is true if and only if $\text{VALID}(G, S, s_{N_0}(n_0))$ is true, and S' does not contain any path expressions (except for l_E) and each constraint in S' has at most one operator. We assume an oracle for a strictly faithful assignment of such an instance $\text{VALID}(G', S', s_{N_0}(n_0))$. Then we can, for each $s \in S'$, compute $\llbracket \phi_s \rrbracket^{\Sigma, n, G}$ for each $n \in N$ and $\llbracket \phi_s \rrbracket^{\Sigma, e, G}$ for each $e \in E$ in polynomial time in $|\Sigma| + |G'| + |S'|$. $\square$

The complete proof can be found in an extended version of this work[1]. We next derive NP-hardness from the NP-hardness of $\mathcal{L}$.

Corollary 1. *RDF graph validation with $\mathcal{L}$, which is equivalent to SHACL, is clearly reducible to ProGS validation over property graphs, since RDF graphs can be trivially represented in property graphs and constraints in $\mathcal{L}$ are a subset of ProGS constraints. According to [6], $\mathcal{L}$ is NP-hard. Therefore, ProGS is also NP-hard.*

Then we can also conclude that VALID for ProGS is NP-complete.

Corollary 2. *VALID is NP-complete, since it is both NP-hard (shown in Corollary 1) and in NP (shown in Theorem 1).*

We only consider the combined complexity here, even though graphs are typically significantly larger than sets of shapes. However, from this we infer that validation for a fixed set of shapes (data complexity) or a fixed graph (constraint complexity) are also NP-complete, since they are already NP-complete for $\mathcal{L}$ as shown in [6], and combined complexity of validation for ProGS is in NP.

---

[1] https://arxiv.org/abs/2107.05566.

5   Implementation

Drawing inspiration from an experimental feature of the SHaclEX [24] implementation of ShEx [23] and SHACL [22], we implement a prototypical validator for ProGS by encoding the validation problem as an answer set program. Answer set programming (ASP) allows for declarative implementations of NP-hard search problems, such as ProGS validation with faithful assignments. In particular, we rely on ASP for efficiently finding candidate assignments (in the worst-case considering all possible assignments), while deciding whether an assignment is faithful is a straightforward mapping of our validation semantics into another ASP model.

The implementation consists of three components: An encoding of property graphs and ProGS shapes, both of which are straight-forward and can be generated from non-ASP representations. A set of rules directly representing the validation semantics of ProGS (Sect. 3.3). And finally the search problem of finding faithful assignments. With these components, an ASP solver (our implementation relies on Clingo[2]) produces one (or more) faithful assignments for the graph and set of shapes (if any exist).

In addition to the ASP encoding, we also provide a surrounding set of tools, including a concrete syntax for ProGS shapes and a corresponding parser, as well as a tool for extracting and encoding Neo4j[3] instances. The graph encoding is based on the Neo4j JSON export format and therefore straight-forward to replicate for other property-graph stores. The tool suite is available on GitHub[4], including further documentation and examples. More details about the ASP encoding and a short demonstration can be found in the extended version of this work.

5.1   Towards Practical Implementations of ProGS

Our implementation is well-suited as a reference implementation, for experimenting with ProGS examples, and for validating smaller-sized graphs. For large-scale graphs, the explicit ASP encoding of the data graph may be too inefficient, both in terms of runtime and memory requirements. Instead, efficient validation demands an implementation operating directly on a specific property-graph store. Such an implementation could, for example, aim to replicate the resolution approach of an ASP solver for finding candidate assignments and evaluate the validation procedure directly on the graph. For simplified SHACL shapes that do not include recursive shape references, efficient validation approaches are well-known and widely used in real-world SHACL implementations. These approaches, operating on graph stores directly, could be applied for ProGS as well. Another alternative would be to adapt validation over SPARQL endpoints [5] for Cypher and ProGS instead. Indeed, neosemantics [15] relies on

---

[2] https://potassco.org/clingo/.
[3] https://neo4j.com/.
[4] https://github.com/softlang/progs.

Cypher for the validation of SHACL over RDF graphs encoded as property graphs. Such an approach, as is also shown by [5], can be extended to validate recursive shapes by inclusion of a SAT solver.

6   Related Work

There are a number of schema languages for property graphs in proprietary implementations of graph databases. For instance, the data definition language for Cypher [9] described in the Neo4j manual [14] allows for simple constraints regarding the existence or uniqueness of properties. For TigerGraph [7], a similar implementation exists. However, these systems lack a formal description, making their expressiveness, features and complexity hard to assess.

Only a small number of property-graph schema languages have been formally defined. In [11], the GraphQL [8] schema language is used to define restrictive property-graph schemas, where for each node label a GraphQL object type can be defined. This allows for constraining the existence of certain properties, edges, and properties on these edges via field definitions of the object types. The schemas are closely tied to node labels, meaning the approach does not allow for the validation of edges as individual entities, which is crucial for validating metadata annotations across an entire graph. The approach also omits other elements supported by ProGS, such as negation, qualified number restrictions and path expressions in number restrictions or equality constraints. Validation with constraints that are associated to labels can be emulated with ProGS target queries. Graph validation based on GraphQL was shown to be in AC_0.

[1] defines property graph schemas, also focusing on node and edge types on the basis of labels. In particular, schemas allow for restricting the data types of specific properties on nodes and edges, as well as the edges allowed between node types. More advanced constraints are mentioned, but not formally defined. In general, this approach only provides a small subset of the features of ProGS.

While shape-based validation approaches such as SHACL [22] and ShEx [23] exist for validating RDF graphs, to the best of our knowledge no shape-based validation language for property graphs has been formally defined until now. A syntactic construct for SHACL validation of RDF* (and other reification-based RDF extensions) has been proposed in an unofficial draft proposal [13], though no semantics has been specified. The `reifiableBy` construct allows constraining an edge via a node shape for provenance annotations. The approach is similar to our notion of edge shapes and our semantics can be applied, as long as graphs are restricted to property graphs (i.e., edge properties are restricted to a given set of value domains). Finally, there exists an extension for Neo4j which implements SHACL validation for RDF subsets of property graphs [15].

7   Concluding Remarks

We present ProGS, a shape language extending SHACL for validating property graphs. We define the semantics of this language based on the notion of faithfulness of partial assignments and are therefore able to support shape references and negation. Despite the addition of property-graph specific constructs, such as edge shapes that target edges with identities, the complexity of validating graphs against sets of ProGS shapes does not increase when compared to SHACL. The validation problem remains NP-complete.

As future work, we plan to investigate the satisfiability problem of ProGS shapes and then further utilize these results to define a validation approach for property-graph queries. We are also interested in extending ProGS with the unique features introduced by G-CORE, in particular first-class paths, and RDF*, in particular triples in object position of other triples.

References

1. Angles, R.: The property graph database model. In: Proceedings of International Workshop on Foundations of Data Management. CEUR, vol. 2100 (2018). http://ceur-ws.org/Vol-2100/paper26.pdf
2. Angles, R., et al.: G-CORE: a core for future graph query languages. In: Proceedings of SIGMOD, pp. 1421–1432. ACM (2018). https://doi.org/10.1145/3183713.3190654
3. Angles, R., Thakkar, H., Tomaszuk, D.: Mapping RDF databases to property graph databases. IEEE Access **8**, 86091–86110 (2020). https://doi.org/10.1109/ACCESS.2020.2993117
4. Apache: Gremlin Property Graph Model (2016). https://github.com/tinkerpop/blueprints/wiki/Property-Graph-Model
5. Corman, J., Florenzano, F., Reutter, J.L., Savković, O.: Validating SHACL constraints over a SPARQL endpoint. In: Ghidini, C., et al. (eds.) ISWC 2019. LNCS, vol. 11778, pp. 145–163. Springer, Cham (2019). https://doi.org/10.1007/978-3-030-30793-6_9
6. Corman, J., Reutter, J.L., Savković, O.: Semantics and validation of recursive SHACL. In: Vrandečić, D., et al. (eds.) ISWC 2018. LNCS, vol. 11136, pp. 318–336. Springer, Cham (2018). https://doi.org/10.1007/978-3-030-00671-6_19
7. Deutsch, A., Xu, Y., Wu, M., Lee, V.E.: TigerGraph: a native MPP graph database. CoRR abs/1901.08248 (2019)
8. Facebook: GraphQL Spec. (2018). https://graphql.github.io/graphql-spec/
9. Francis, N., et al.: Cypher: an evolving query language for property graphs. In: Proceedings of SIGMOD, pp. 1433–1445. ACM (2018). https://doi.org/10.1145/3183713.3190657
10. Hartig, O.: Rdf* and sparql*: an alternative approach to annotate statements in RDF. In: Proceedings of ISWC, Posters & Demonstrations and Industry Tracks. CEUR Workshop Proceedings, vol. 1963. CEUR-WS.org (2017). http://ceur-ws.org/Vol-1963/paper593.pdf
11. Hartig, O., Hidders, J.: Defining schemas for property graphs by using the graphql schema definition language. In: GRADES/NDA@SIGMOD/PODS, pp. 6:1–6:11. ACM (2019). https://doi.org/10.1145/3327964.3328495
12. ISO/IEC JTC1 SC32 WG3: GQL Standardization Project (2020). https://www.gqlstandards.org/
13. Knublauch, H.: DASH Reification Support for SHACL (2021). http://datashapes.org/reification.html
14. Neo4j: Neo4j Constraints (2020). https://neo4j.com/docs/cypher-manual/4.2/administration/constraints/

15. Neosemantics: Neo4j Neosemantics Validation (2020). https://neo4j.com/labs/neosemantics/4.0/validation/
16. openCypher: openCypher Project (2020). http://www.opencypher.org/
17. Oracle: PGQL 1.3 Specification (2020). https://pgql-lang.org/spec/1.3/
18. Seifer, P., Härtel, J., Leinberger, M., Lämmel, R., Staab, S.: Empirical study on the usage of graph query languages in open source Java projects. In: Proceedings of Software Language Engineering, pp. 152–166. ACM (2019). https://doi.org/10.1145/3357766.3359541
19. Udrea, O., Recupero, D.R., Subrahmanian, V.S.: Annotated RDF. ACM Trans. Comput. Log. **11**(2), 10:1–10:41 (2010). https://doi.org/10.1145/1656242.1656245
20. Vrandecic, D., Krötzsch, M.: Wikidata: a free collaborative knowledgebase. Commun. ACM **57**(10), 78–85 (2014). https://doi.org/10.1145/2629489
21. W3C: RDF Concepts and Abstract Syntax (2014). https://www.w3.org/TR/rdf11-concepts/
22. W3C: Shapes constraint language (SHACL) (2017). https://www.w3.org/TR/shacl/
23. W3C: Shapes expressions language (ShEx) (2019). http://shex.io/shex-semantics/
24. WESO: Shaclex (2021). https://github.com/weso/shaclex

Improving Knowledge Graph Embeddings with Ontological Reasoning

Nitisha Jain[1,2]([⊠]) [iD], Trung-Kien Tran[1], Mohamed H. Gad-Elrab[1] [iD],
and Daria Stepanova[1] [iD]

[1] Bosch Center for Artificial Intelligence, Renningen, Germany
{nitisha.jain,trung-kien.tran,mohamed.gad-elrab}@de.bosch.com
[2] Hasso Plattner Institute, University of Potsdam, Potsdam, Germany
nitisha.jain@hpi.de

Abstract. Knowledge graph (KG) embedding models have emerged as powerful means for KG completion. To learn the representation of KGs, entities and relations are projected in a low-dimensional vector space so that not only existing triples in the KG are preserved but also new triples can be predicted. Embedding models might learn a good representation of the input KG, but due to the nature of machine learning approaches, they often lose the semantics of entities and relations, which might lead to nonsensical predictions. To address this issue we propose to improve the accuracy of embeddings using ontological reasoning. More specifically, we present a novel iterative approach *ReasonKGE* that identifies dynamically via symbolic reasoning inconsistent predictions produced by a given embedding model and feeds them as negative samples for retraining this model. In order to address the scalability problem that arises when integrating ontological reasoning into the training process, we propose an advanced technique to generalize the inconsistent predictions to other semantically similar negative samples during retraining. Experimental results demonstrate the improvements in accuracy of facts produced by our method compared to the state-of-the-art.

1 Introduction

Motivation. Knowledge Graphs (KG) describe facts about a certain domain of interest by representing them using entities interconnected via relations. Prominent examples of large KGs are DBpedia [4], Yago [31], and WikiData [34]. KGs are widely used for natural question answering, web search and data analytics. Modern KGs store information about millions of facts, however, since they are typically constructed semi-automatically or using crowd-sourcing methods, KGs are often bound to be incomplete.

To address this issue, knowledge graph embedding methods have been proposed for the *knowledge completion* task, i.e. predicting links between entities. Embedding methods learn the representation of the input KG by projecting entities and relations in a low-dimensional vector space so that not only existing triples in the KG are preserved but also new triples can be predicted (see, e.g., [36] for overview of existing approaches). Typically, the training of KG embedding models aims at discerning between correct (positive) and incorrect (negative) triples. A completion model then associates a score with every input triple. The goal of the embedding models is to rank every positive triple higher than all its negative alternatives. Therefore, the quality of embedding models is heavily impacted by the generated negative triples. Since KGs store explicitly only positive triples, proper negative triple generation is acknowledged to be a challenging problem [11,21,39,40].

State-of-the-Art and Limitations. In the majority of existing methods the generation of negative triples is done either completely at random [9], relying on the (local) closed world assumption [27], or by exploiting the KG structure for the generation of likely true negative samples (e.g. [1,2,40]). However, these methods do not guarantee that the generated negative samples are actually incorrect ones. In [11] this issue is partially addressed by taking as negative examples precomputed triples that are inconsistent with the KG and the accompanied ontology. Since the generation of all such possible inconsistent triples as negative samples is clearly infeasible in practice, only a subset of them is precomputed, and hence certain important inconsistent triples might be missing in the set obtained in [11]. Furthermore, as embedding models rely purely on the data in the input KGs, they often lose the real semantics of entities and relations, and hence provide undesired predictions [37]. This calls for more goal-oriented approaches in which ontological reasoning is used to verify and improve the actual predictions made by embedding models.

Approach and Contributions. To address the presented shortcomings, in this work we propose an iterative method that dynamically identifies inconsistent predictions produced by a given embedding model via symbolic reasoning and feeds them as negative samples for retraining this model. We first start with any available negative sampling procedure (e.g., [21,40]) and train the embedding model as usual. Then, among predictions made by the model, we select those that cause inconsistency when being added to the KG, as negative samples for the next iteration of our method. To avoid predicting similar wrong triples, along with the inconsistent triples explicitly inferred by the embedding model, we also generate triples that are semantically similar via a *generalization procedure*. To address the scalability problem that arises when integrating ontological reasoning into the training process of embedding models, we consider ontologies in an extension of the Description Logic (DL) *DL-Lite* [3] so that consistency checking and the generalization procedure can be performed efficiently. Our method can support any embedding model, and with the increasing number of iterations it yields better embeddings that make less inconsistent predictions and achieve higher prediction accuracy w.r.t. standard metrics.

The salient contributions of our work can be summarized as follows.

- We introduce the *ReasonKGE* framework for exploiting ontological reasoning to improve existing embedding models by advancing their negative sampling.
- To efficiently filter inconsistent embedding-based predictions, we exploit the locality property of light-weight ontologies. Moreover, in the spirit of [32] we generalize the computed inconsistent facts to a set of other similar ones to be fed back to the embedding model as negative samples.
- The evaluation of the proposed method on a set of state-of-the-art KGs equipped with ontologies, demonstrates that ontological reasoning exploited in the suggested way indeed improves the existing embedding models with respect to the quality of fact prediction.

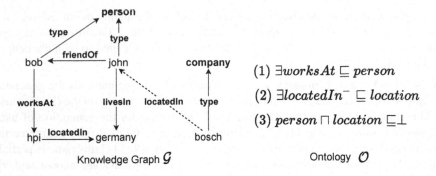

Fig. 1. Example knowledge graph with its ontology, where solid links correspond to the true facts, while the dashed one to a spurious predicted fact.

Organization. The rest of the paper is structured as follows. In Sect. 2 we present necessary background on KGs, ontologies and embedding models. In Sect. 3 our approach is described in detail, and then in Sect. 4 the results of our empirical evaluation are discussed. Finally, in Sect. 5 we present the related work, and conclude in Sect. 6. An extended version of this work[1] contains additional experimental details.

2   Preliminaries

We assume countable pairwise disjoint sets N_C, N_P and N_I of class names (*a.k.a.* types), property names (*a.k.a.* relations), and individuals (*a.k.a.* entities). We also assume the standard relation *rdf:type* (abbreviated as *type*) to be included in N_P. A *knowledge graph* (KG) $\mathcal{G}$ is a finite set of *triples* of the form $\langle s, p, o \rangle$, where $s \in N_I, p \in N_P, o \in N_I$, if $p \neq type$, and $o \in N_C$ otherwise. KGs typically follow Open World Assumption (OWA), meaning that they store only a fraction of positive facts. For instance, given the KG from Fig. 1 $\langle john, type, person \rangle$ and $\langle john, livesIn, germany \rangle$ are true KG facts; however, whether $\langle john, worksAt, bosch \rangle$ holds or not is unknown. Given a triple α, we denote by $\mathsf{Ent}(\alpha)$ a set of all entities occurring in α and extend this notation to a set of triples as $\mathsf{Ent}(\mathcal{G}) = \bigcup_{\alpha \in \mathcal{G}} \mathsf{Ent}(\alpha)$.

An ontology $\mathcal{O}$ (*a.k.a.* TBox) is a set of axioms expressed in a certain Description Logic (DL) [5]. In this work we focus on *DL-Lite$^{\mathcal{SU}}$*, i.e., extension of *DL-Lite* [3] with transitive roles and concept disjunctions. Classes C denoting sets of entities, and roles R denoting binary relations between entities, obey the following syntax:

$$C::=A \mid \exists R \mid A \sqcup B \mid A \sqcap B \mid \neg C$$
$$R::=P \mid P^-$$

Here, $A, B \in N_C$ are atomic classes and $P \in N_P$ is an atomic property (i.e., binary relation). An ontology $\mathcal{O}$ is a finite set of axioms of the form $C_1 \sqsubseteq C_2$, $R_1 \sqsubseteq R_2$, $R \circ R \sqsubseteq R$, reflecting the transitivity of the relation R. The summary of the DL syntax

---

[1] https://github.com/nitishajain/ReasonKGE.

Table 1. Syntax and semantics of the ontology language considered in this paper where A, R are a class name and property name, respectively; C and D are class expressions, P, S are property expressions, and a, b are entities.

DL syntax	OWL syntax	Semantics
R	R	$R^{\mathcal{I}} \subseteq \Delta^{\mathcal{I}} \times \Delta^{\mathcal{I}}$
R^-	ObjectInverseOf(R)	$\{\langle e, d\rangle \mid \langle d, e\rangle \in R^{\mathcal{I}}\}$
A	A	$A^{\mathcal{I}} \subseteq \Delta^{\mathcal{I}}$
$\top$	owl:Thing	$\Delta^{\mathcal{I}}$
$\bot$	owl:NoThing	$\emptyset$
$\neg C$	ObjectComplementOf(C)	$\Delta^{\mathcal{I}} \setminus C^{\mathcal{I}}$
$C \sqcap D$	ObjectIntersectionOf(C, D)	$C^{\mathcal{I}} \cap D^{\mathcal{I}}$
$C \sqcup D$	ObjectUnionOf(C, D)	$C^{\mathcal{I}} \cup D^{\mathcal{I}}$
$\exists P$	ObjectSomeValuesFrom(P, owl:Thing)	$\{d \mid \exists e \in \Delta^{\mathcal{I}}: \langle d, e\rangle \in P^{\mathcal{I}}\}$
$C \sqsubseteq D$	SubClassOf(C, D)	$C^{\mathcal{I}} \subseteq D^{\mathcal{I}}$
$P \sqsubseteq S$	SubObjectPropertyOf(P, S)	$P^{\mathcal{I}} \subseteq S^{\mathcal{I}}$
$P \circ P \sqsubseteq P$	TransitiveObjectProperty(P)	$P^{\mathcal{I}} \circ P^{\mathcal{I}} \subseteq P^{\mathcal{I}}$
$\langle a, type, c\rangle$	ClassAssertion(C, a)	$a^{\mathcal{I}} \in C^{\mathcal{I}}$
$\langle a, p, b\rangle$	ObjectPropertyAssertion(P, a, b)	$\langle a^{\mathcal{I}}, b^{\mathcal{I}}\rangle \in P^{\mathcal{I}}$

in $DL\text{-}Lite^{\mathcal{SU}}$ and its translation to OWL 2[2] is presented in Table 1. In the rest of the paper, we assume that all ontologies in this work are expressed in $DL\text{-}Lite^{\mathcal{SU}}$.

Our running example of a KG with an ontology given in Fig. 1 reflects the domain knowledge about people and their working places. The ontology states that (1) the domain of *worksAt* relation is *person*, (2) the range of *locatedIn* is *location*, and (3) *person* is disjoint with *location*.

Inconsistency and Explanations. The semantics of knowledge graphs and ontologies is defined using the direct model-theoretic semantics via interpretations [26]. An *interpretation* $\mathcal{I} = (\Delta^{\mathcal{I}}, \cdot^{\mathcal{I}})$ consists of a non-empty set $\Delta^{\mathcal{I}}$, the *domain* of $\mathcal{I}$, and an *interpretation function* $\cdot^{\mathcal{I}}$, that assigns to each $A \in N_C$ a subset $A^{\mathcal{I}} \subseteq \Delta^{\mathcal{I}}$, to each $R \in N_R$ a binary relation $R^{\mathcal{I}} \subseteq \Delta^{\mathcal{I}} \times \Delta^{\mathcal{I}}$, and to each $a \in N_I$ an element $a^{\mathcal{I}} \in \Delta^{\mathcal{I}}$. This assignment is extended to (complex) classes and roles as shown in Table 1.

An interpretation $\mathcal{I}$ *satisfies* an axiom α (written $\mathcal{I} \models \alpha$) if the corresponding condition in Table 1 holds. Given a KG $\mathcal{G}$ and an ontology $\mathcal{O}$, $\mathcal{I}$ is a *model* of $\mathcal{G} \cup \mathcal{O}$ (written $\mathcal{I} \models \mathcal{G} \cup \mathcal{O}$) if $\mathcal{I} \models \alpha$ for all axioms $\alpha \in \mathcal{G} \cup \mathcal{O}$. We say that $\mathcal{G} \cup \mathcal{O}$ *entails* an axiom α (written $\mathcal{G} \cup \mathcal{O} \models \alpha$), if every model of $\mathcal{G} \cup \mathcal{O}$ satisfies α. A KG $\mathcal{G}$ is *inconsistent* w.r.t. an ontology $\mathcal{O}$ if no model for $\mathcal{G} \cup \mathcal{O}$ exists. In this case, $\mathcal{G} \cup \mathcal{O}$ is inconsistent. Intuitively, $\mathcal{G} \cup \mathcal{O}$ is inconsistent when some facts of $\mathcal{G}$ contradict some axioms of $\mathcal{O}$.

Under the considered ontology language, KG inconsistency has a locality property, i.e., the problem of checking inconsistency for a KG (w.r.t. an ontology $\mathcal{O}$) can be reduced to checking inconsistency for separated KG *modules* (w.r.t. $\mathcal{O}$) [32].

---

[2] https://www.w3.org/TR/owl2-overview/.

Definition 1 (Modules). *Given a KG $\mathcal{G}$ and an entity $e \in \text{Ent}(\mathcal{G})$, the module of e w.r.t. $\mathcal{G}$ is defined as $\mathcal{M}(e, \mathcal{G}) = \{\alpha \mid \alpha \in \mathcal{G} \text{ and } e \text{ occurs in } \alpha\}$. We denote the set of all modules for individuals occurring in $\mathcal{G}$ as $\mathcal{M}_{\mathcal{G}} = \{\mathcal{M}(e, \mathcal{G}) \mid e \in \text{Ent}(\mathcal{G})\}$.*

Lemma 1 (Consistency Local Property). *Let $\mathcal{G}$ be a KG and $\mathcal{O}$ an ontology. Then $\mathcal{G} \cup \mathcal{O}$ is consistent iff $\mathcal{M}(a, \mathcal{G}) \cup \mathcal{O}$ is consistent for every $a \in \text{Ent}(\mathcal{G})$.*

An *explanation* for inconsistency of $\mathcal{G} \cup \mathcal{O}$ [20], denoted by $\mathcal{E} = \mathcal{E}_{\mathcal{G}} \cup \mathcal{E}_{\mathcal{O}}$ with $\mathcal{E}_{\mathcal{G}} \subseteq \mathcal{G}$ and $\mathcal{E}_{\mathcal{O}} \subseteq \mathcal{O}$, is a (subset-inclusion) smallest inconsistent subset of $\mathcal{G} \cup \mathcal{O}$.

Example 1. The KG from Fig. 1 with all facts including the dashed red one is inconsistent with the ontology $\mathcal{O}$, and a possible explanation for that is $\mathcal{E} = \mathcal{E}_{\mathcal{G}} \cup \mathcal{E}_{\mathcal{O}}$ with $\mathcal{E}_{\mathcal{G}} = \{\langle bosch, locatedIn, john \rangle, \langle john, type, person \rangle\}$ and $\mathcal{E}_{\mathcal{O}} = \{\exists locatedIn^{-} \sqsubseteq location, person \sqcap location \sqsubseteq \bot\}$.

KG Embeddings. KG embeddings (see [36] for overview) aim at representing all entities and relations in a continuous vector space, usually as vectors or matrices called *embeddings*. Embeddings can be used to estimate the likelihood of a triple to be true via a scoring function: $f : N_I \times N_P \times N_I \rightarrow \mathbb{R}$. Concrete scoring functions are defined based on various vector space assumptions. The likelihood that the respective assumptions of the embedding methods hold, should be higher for triples in the KG than for negative samples outside the KG. The learning process is done through minimizing the error induced from the assumptions given by their respective loss functions. Below we describe widely-used assumptions for KG embeddings:

(i) The translation-based assumption, *e.g.*, TransE [9] embeds entities and relations as vectors and assumes $\mathbf{v_s} + \mathbf{v_p} \approx \mathbf{v_o}$ for true triples, where $\mathbf{v_s}, \mathbf{v_p}, \mathbf{v_o}$ are vector embeddings for subject s, predicate p and object o, respectively. The models that rely on the translation assumption are generally optimised by minimizing the following ranking-based loss function

$$\sum_{\langle s_i, p_i, o_i \rangle \in S^+} \sum_{\langle s'_i, p_i, o'_i \rangle \in S^-} [\gamma - f(s_i, p_i, o_i) + f(s'_i, p_i, o'_i)]_+ \tag{1}$$

where $f(s, p, o) = -\|\mathbf{v_s} + \mathbf{v_p} - \mathbf{v_o}\|_1$, S^+ and S^- correspond to the sets of positive and negative training triples respectively, that are typically disjoint.

(ii) The linear map assumption, *e.g.*, ComplEx [33] embeds entities as vectors and relations as matrices. It assumes that for true triples, the linear mapping $\mathbf{M_p}$ of the subject embedding $\mathbf{v_s}$ is close to the object embedding $\mathbf{v_o}$: $\mathbf{v_s}\mathbf{M_p} \approx \mathbf{v_o}$. The loss function used for training the linear-map embedding models is given as follows:

$$\sum_{\langle s_i, p_i, o_i \rangle \in S^+} \sum_{\langle s'_i, p_i, o'_i \rangle \in S^-} l(1, f(s_i, p_i, o_i)) + l(-1, f(s'_i, p_i, o'_i))) \tag{2}$$

where $f(s, p, o) = \mathbf{v_s}\mathbf{M_p}\mathbf{v_o}$ and $l(\alpha, \beta) = log(1 - exp(-\alpha\beta))$.

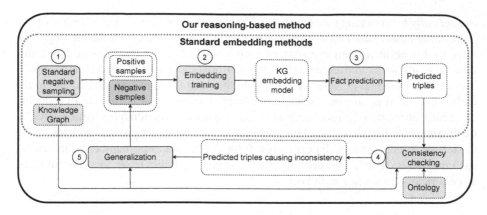

Fig. 2. Standard embedding pipeline (grey dotted frame) and our reasoning-based method (black frame) in a nutshell

3   Ontological Reasoning for Iterative Negative Sampling

While a variety of embedding models exist in the literature [36], one of the major challenges for them to perform accurate fact predictions is finding an effective way for generation of relevant negative samples [11,29,35]. Commonly used approaches for negative sampling randomly corrupt existing triples by perturbing their subject, predicate or object [9,13,30] or rely on the (local) closed world assumption (LCWA). Based on CWA all triples not present in the KG are assumed to be false, while LCWA is a variation of CWA, in which for every $\langle s, p, o \rangle$, only facts of the form $\langle s, p, o' \rangle \notin \mathcal{G}$ are assumed to be false. For instance, given the facts in Fig. 1, the corrupted negative triples obtained based on the LCWA could be $\langle john, livesIn, hpi \rangle$ or $\langle bob, worksAt, bosch \rangle$.

However, since KGs follow OWA, the standard sampling methods might often turn out to be sub-optimal, resulting in false positive negative samples [11]. For example, the corrupted triple $\langle bob, worksAt, bosch \rangle$ from above might actually be true in reality.

A natural method to avoid false positives and generate only relevant negative samples is by relying on ontologies with which KGs are typically equipped. A naive approach for that is to generate all facts that can be formed using relations and entities in $\mathcal{G}$ (i.e., construct the Herbrand base) and check which among the resulting candidates are inconsistent with $\mathcal{G} \cup \mathcal{O}$. As modern KGs store millions of facts, the described procedure is infeasible in practice. To still sample some inconsistent triples, in [11] facts $p(s, o) \in \mathcal{G}$ are corrupted by substituting s (resp. o) with s' (resp. o') s.t. s and s' (resp. o and o') belong to disjoint classes and the resulting corrupted triple is inconsistent. For example, given $\mathcal{G}$ and $\mathcal{O}$ in Fig. 1, from $\langle bob, worksAt, germany \rangle$ we can obtain $\alpha_1 = \langle germany, worksAt, germany \rangle$ or $\alpha_2 = \langle bob, worksAt, john \rangle$, as $person$ is disjoint with $location$. However, this method might fail to avoid the inconsistent triples that the model actually predicts. E.g., $\langle bosch, locatedIn, john \rangle$ is not generated by this method as a negative example, and the model can in principle still predict it.

Therefore, instead of pre–computing a static set of negative examples, we propose to iteratively generate and improve this set (and subsequently also the embedding model)

dynamically by computing a collection of negative samples in a guided fashion from embedding model based on its predictions that are inconsistent with the ontology. We refer to this negative sampling strategy as *dynamic sampling*. On the one hand, this intuitively allows us to overcome the computational challenge of generating all possible negative examples at once, but rather add the most relevant ones on demand to the embedding training process. On the other hand, this approach is capable of reducing frequently encountered errors (in terms of inconsistent predictions) for particularly difficult triples by directly incorporating feedback from incorrect predictions back to the model for further training. Indeed, when trained for increasing number of iterations, such method is capable of generating embeddings that predict fewer inconsistent facts, as empirically demonstrated in Sect. 4.

3.1   Approach Overview

Next we describe in more details the proposed framework referred to as *ReasonKGE*, whose main steps are depicted in Fig. 2. Given a KG, ontology and an embedding method, we aim at generating an enhanced KG embedding, which is trained for predicting facts that are consistent with the KG and the ontology at hand.

The input to our method (represented by blue dashed boxes) is the KG and the ontology, while the output (the red dashed box) is the set of negative samples that is incorporated during the iterative training and tuning of a KG embedding model in each iteration. As negative samples are obtained based on predictions made by an existing embedding, a baseline model is required in the first iteration. For this, in step (1) we obtain the negative samples with **standard negative sampling** using any of the existing methods [9, 11, 13, 30]. We then perform **embedding training** in step (2) to construct the initial KG embedding model.

This model is used for obtaining predictions and computing the set of negative samples for the next training iteration. Specifically, in step (3) the model is used for **fact prediction** as follows. For every triple in the training set, given its subject s and predicate p, we retrieve the top ranked object and obtain the fact $\langle s, p, o \rangle$ as the respective prediction. The same is done inversely for computing the top ranked subject given the object o and predicate p in the training set. Note that only triples that are not in the training set are considered as predictions. In step (4) we check whether the predicted triple complies with the ontology relying on the **consistency checking** procedure. In case the respective triple is found to be inconsistent, in step (5) we generalize it to other semantically similar triples using the **generalization** procedure to obtain an extended set of negative samples. Finally, the computed negative samples, both for subject and object predictions are fed back as input to the next iteration of the embedding training process. The detailed steps are presented in Algorithm 1 and explained in what follows.

3.2   Consistency Checking

The goal of the consistency checking procedure is to verify which predictions made by the embedding model in step (3) are inconsistent with the ontology $\mathcal{O}$ and the original KG $\mathcal{G}$. In principle, any reasoner capable of performing consistency checking effectively for ontologies in the considered $DL\text{-}Lite^{\mathcal{S}\sqcup}$ language can be used in this step. As

---

Algorithm 1: Training embedding models with negative samples using ontological reasoning

---

Input : Baseline embedding model **E**, a knowledge graph $\mathcal{G}$, and an ontology $\mathcal{O}$

```
/* Step 1 and Step 2                                      */
```
1 Train the baseline embedding model **E** for a certain number of epochs.
```
/* Retrain the baseline model with negative samples derived
   from reasoning                                         */
```
2 **Loop**
```
    /* Step 3                                             */
```
3   **foreach** *triple* $\alpha = \langle s, p, o \rangle \in \mathcal{G}$ **do**
4   Get a set Predictions(α) of predicted triples of the form $\langle s, p, \hat{o} \rangle$ and $\langle \hat{s}, p, o \rangle$ by giving $\langle s, p \rangle$ and $\langle p, o \rangle$ as inputs to **E** and obtaining predicted entities $\hat{o}$ and $\hat{s}$, respectively.
```
        /* Step 4                                         */
```
5   NegSamples(α) $\leftarrow \emptyset$
6   **foreach** *predicted triple* $\beta \in$ Predictions(α) **do**
7   Compute the relevant set Relv($\beta, \mathcal{G}$) of β w.r.t. $\mathcal{G}$.
8   **if** Relv($\beta, \mathcal{G}$) $\cup \mathcal{O}$ *is inconsistent* **then**
```
            /* Step 5                                     */
```
9   Compute explanations for inconsistency.
10   **foreach** *inconsistency explanation* $\mathcal{E}_{\mathcal{G}} \cup \mathcal{E}_{\mathcal{O}}$ **do**
11   Compute GeneralizedSamples(β) as defined in Definition 4.
12   NegSamples(α) $\leftarrow$ NegSamples(α) $\cup$ GeneralizedSamples(β)

13   Retrain **E** in which, for each training step that considers $\alpha \in \mathcal{G}$, NegSamples(α) is used as negative samples in the loss function, e.g. Equation 1 or Equation 2.

---

the task that we consider concerns verifying whether a particular triple causes inconsistency, for the target DL when performing the consistency check one does not need to account for the whole KG, but only a small subset of relevant facts. To this end, we define the *relevant sets* as follows.

Definition 2 (Relevant set). *Let $\mathcal{G}$ be a KG and α be a triple. The* relevant set $\mathsf{Relv}(\alpha, \mathcal{G})$ *of α w.r.t. $\mathcal{G}$ is defined as* $\mathsf{Relv}(\alpha, \mathcal{G}) = \{\alpha\} \cup \{\beta \in \mathcal{G} \,|\, \mathsf{Ent}(\beta) \cap \mathsf{Ent}(\alpha) \neq \emptyset\}$.

Example 2. For $\alpha = \langle bosch, locatedIn, john \rangle$ and $\mathcal{G}$ in Fig. 1, we have the following relevant set $\mathsf{Relv}(\alpha, \mathcal{G}) = \{\alpha\} \cup \{\langle john, livesIn, germany \rangle, \langle john, friendOf, bob \rangle, \langle john, type, person \rangle, \langle bosch, type, company \rangle\}$.

The following proposition allows us to reduce the consistency checking of $\alpha \cup \mathcal{G} \cup \mathcal{O}$ to the consistency checking of $\mathsf{Relv}(\alpha, \mathcal{G}) \cup \mathcal{O}$.

Proposition 1. *Let $\mathcal{G}$ be a knowledge graph, $\mathcal{O}$ an ontology such that $\mathcal{G} \cup \mathcal{O}$ is consistent, and α a triple. Then, $\alpha \cup \mathcal{G} \cup \mathcal{O}$ is consistent iff $\mathsf{Relv}(\alpha, \mathcal{G}) \cup \mathcal{O}$ is consistent.*

Proof. Since $\mathsf{Relv}(\alpha, \mathcal{G}) \subseteq \mathcal{G}$, we have $\alpha \cup \mathcal{G} \cup \mathcal{O}$ being consistent implies that $\mathsf{Relv}(\alpha, \mathcal{G}) \cup \mathcal{O}$ is also consistent. We start showing the remaining direction by assuming that $\mathsf{Relv}(\alpha, \mathcal{G}) \cup \mathcal{O}$ is consistent and then show that $\alpha \cup \mathcal{G} \cup \mathcal{O}$ is also consistent.

Let $\alpha = \langle s, p, o \rangle$, by Definition 2, we have $\mathsf{Relv}(\alpha, \mathcal{G}) = \mathcal{M}(s, \alpha \cup \mathcal{G}) \cup \mathcal{M}(o, \alpha \cup \mathcal{G})$. Since $\mathcal{G} \cup \mathcal{O}$ is consistent, by Lemma 1, we have $\mathcal{M}(e, \mathcal{G}) \cup \mathcal{O}$ is consistent for every entity in $\mathsf{Ent}(\mathcal{G}) \setminus \{s, o\}$. Since $e \notin \{s, o\}$, we have $\mathcal{M}(e, \mathcal{G}) = \mathcal{M}(e, \alpha \cup \mathcal{G})$, which implies $\mathcal{M}(e, \alpha \cup \mathcal{G}) \cup \mathcal{O}$ is consistent $(\star)$. From the assumption that $\mathsf{Relv}(\alpha, \mathcal{G}) \cup \mathcal{O}$ is consistent and $\mathsf{Relv}(\alpha, \mathcal{G}) = \mathcal{M}(s, \alpha \cup \mathcal{G}) \cup \mathcal{M}(o, \alpha \cup \mathcal{G})$, we obtain $\mathcal{M}(s, \alpha \cup \mathcal{G})$ and $\mathcal{M}(o, \alpha \cup \mathcal{G})$ are consistent w.r.t. $\mathcal{O}$ $(\dagger)$. From $(\star)$ and $(\dagger)$ we have $\alpha \cup \mathcal{G} \cup \mathcal{O}$ is consistent using Lemma 1. $\qquad\square$

Relying on Proposition 1, it is sufficient to check the consistency of a triple α with respect to $\mathcal{G} \cup \mathcal{O}$ using $\mathsf{Relv}(\alpha, \mathcal{G})$ rather than the whole KG. We make use of this property in step (4), and for every prediction produced by the embedding model, we first construct the relevant set for the respective prediction, and then perform the consistency check relying only on the corresponding relevant sets.

Example 3. Assume that the fact $\alpha = \langle bosch, locatedIn, john \rangle$ has been predicted by the embedding model in step (3). Then in the consistency checking step (4) we first construct the relevant set for α as $\mathsf{Relv}(\alpha, \mathcal{G})$ given in Example 2 and check the consistency of $\mathsf{Relv}(\alpha, \mathcal{G}) \cup \mathcal{O}$. Clearly, we have $\mathsf{Relv}(\alpha, \mathcal{G}) \cup \mathcal{O} = \{\langle bosch, locatedIn, john \rangle\} \cup \{\langle john, livesIn, germany \rangle, \langle john, type, person \rangle, \langle john, friendOf, bob \rangle, \langle bosch, type, company \rangle\} \cup \mathcal{O}$ is inconsistent, since $\langle bosch, locatedIn, john \rangle$ and $\{\exists locatedIn^- \sqsubseteq location\} \in \mathcal{O}$ imply that $\langle john, type, location \rangle$, which contradicts the fact that $\langle john, type, person \rangle \in \mathcal{G}$ and $person \sqcap location \sqsubseteq \bot \in \mathcal{O}$. Thus, we have that $\alpha \cup \mathcal{G} \cup \mathcal{O}$ is inconsistent by monotonicity. Proposition 1 further guarantees that it is sufficient to check the consistency of $\alpha \cup \mathcal{G} \cup \mathcal{O}$ this way.

3.3   Negative Sample Generalization

Given each triple of the input KG in the training step, one needs to sample not a single corrupted triple but a set of such triples to train the embedding model at hand. In other words, the inconsistent prediction needs to be *generalized* to obtain a set of similar inconsistent facts within the KG, which ideally have the same structure. Therefore, once an inconsistent prediction for a triple is identified, we proceed with detecting the inconsistency pattern from that prediction and relying on the respective pattern we generate other similar incorrect triples (in step 5 of our method). This allows us to compute sufficient number of negative samples for retraining the embedding model, and to give hints to the embedding model about the wrong patterns that it learned, subsequently avoiding the prediction of similar incorrect triples in next iterations.

A naive approach to obtain the generalized triples of an inconsistent predicted triple, e.g. $\langle s, p, \hat{o} \rangle$, is to replace $\hat{o}$ by another entity o in the input KG such that o has similar KG neighborhood as $\hat{o}$. However, it might happen that only a subset of triples containing $\hat{o}$ is inconsistent w.r.t. the ontology. Therefore, it is sufficient to find such o that it has similar triples as in that subset. This will increase the number of generalized triples as demonstrated in Example 4. To compute a subset of triples of $\hat{o}$ that is inconsistent w.r.t. the ontology, we compute explanations for the inconsistency of $\mathsf{Relv}(\langle s, p, \hat{o} \rangle, \mathcal{G}) \cup \mathcal{O}$.

Example 4. Consider the KG $\mathcal{G}$ and ontology $\mathcal{O}$ as in Fig. 1. Assume that $\alpha = \langle bosch, locatedIn, john \rangle$ is the predicted triple, i.e., the embedding model predicted *john* as the object entity for the given subject *bosch* and relation *locatedIn*. The explanation for inconsistency of $\mathsf{Relv}(\alpha, \mathcal{G}) \cup \mathcal{O}$ is $\mathcal{E} = \mathcal{E}_\mathcal{G} \cup \mathcal{E}_\mathcal{O}$, for which it holds that $\mathcal{E}_\mathcal{G} = \{\langle bosch, locatedIn, john \rangle, \langle john, type, person \rangle\}$ and $\mathcal{E}_\mathcal{O} = \{\exists located^- \sqsubseteq location, person \sqcap location \sqsubseteq \bot\}$. Note that there is no other entity in $\mathcal{G}$ that has similar triples as those for *john*. However, if we restrict to the triples in the explanation for inconsistency of $\mathsf{Relv}(\alpha, \mathcal{G}) \cup \mathcal{O}$, then *bob* has the same neighborhood triple $\langle bob, type, person \rangle$ as *john* (the predicted triple is ignored). Therefore, we can take $\langle bosch, locatedIn, bob \rangle$ as another negative sample, which together with $\mathcal{G}$ is clearly inconsistent w.r.t. $\mathcal{O}$.

To formally obtain generalized triples as in Example 4, we rely on the notion of *local type* of an entity [16, 17, 32] as follows.

Definition 3 (Local Types). *Let $\mathbf{T}$ be a set of triples and e an entity occurring in $\mathbf{T}$. Then, the local type of e w.r.t. $\mathbf{T}$, written as $\tau(e, \mathbf{T})$ or $\tau(e)$ when $\mathbf{T}$ is clear from the context, is defined as a tuple $\tau(e) = \langle \tau_i(e), \tau_c(e), \tau_o(e) \rangle$, where $\tau_i(e) = \{p \mid \langle s, p, e \rangle \in \mathcal{G}\}$, $\tau_c(e) = \{t \mid \langle e, type, t \rangle \in \mathcal{G}\}$, and $\tau_o(e) = \{p' \mid \langle e, p', o \rangle \in \mathcal{G}\}$. The local type $t = \langle t_i, t_c, t_o \rangle$ is smaller than or equal to the local type $t' = \langle t'_i, t'_c, t'_o \rangle$, written as $t \preceq t'$, iff $t_i \subseteq t'_i, t_c \subseteq t'_c$, and $t_o \subseteq t'_o$.*

Intuitively, a local type of an entity represents a set of types (τ_c) as well as the incoming relations (τ_i) and outgoing relations (τ_o) for that entity in a set of triples.

Example 5 (Example 4 continued). For *bob* in Fig. 1, we have the local type of *bob* w.r.t. $\mathcal{G}$ being $\tau(bob) = \langle \{friendOf\}, \{person\}, \{worksAt\} \rangle$. The local type of *john* w.r.t. $\mathcal{E}_\mathcal{G} \setminus \alpha$ is $\tau(john) = \langle \emptyset, \{person\}, \emptyset \rangle$ and it holds that $\tau(john) \preceq \tau(bob)$.

We now define the set of generalized samples of a given inconsistent predicted triple.

Definition 4 (Generalized Samples). *Let $\mathcal{G}$ be a KG, $\mathcal{O}$ an ontology, and $\alpha = \langle s, p, \hat{o} \rangle$ be a triple in which $\hat{o}$ is predicted by an embedding model given the subject entity s and relation p. Furthermore, let $\mathcal{E} = \mathcal{E}_\mathcal{G} \cup \mathcal{E}_\mathcal{O}$ be an inconsistency explanation of $\mathsf{Relv}(\alpha, \mathcal{G}) \cup \mathcal{O}$. Then, the set of generalized samples of α (w.r.t. $\hat{o}$, $\mathcal{E}$, and $\mathcal{G}$) is defined as $\mathsf{GeneralizedSamples}(\alpha, \hat{o}) = \{\langle s, p, o \rangle \mid \tau(\hat{o}, \mathcal{E}_\mathcal{G} \setminus \alpha) \preceq \tau(o, \mathcal{G})\}$. The generalized samples $\mathsf{GeneralizedSamples}(\beta, \hat{s})$ of $\beta = \langle \hat{s}, p, o \rangle$, in which $\hat{s}$ is predicted by an embedding model, is defined analogously. When it is clear from the context, we often write $\mathsf{GeneralizedSamples}(\alpha)$ without mentioning the corresponding entity.*

Example 6 (Example 5 continued). According to Definition 4 and the local types of *john* and *bob* computed in Example 5, we have $\mathsf{GeneralizedSamples}(\alpha) = \{\alpha\} \cup \{\langle bosch, LocatedIn, bob \rangle\}$.

The following Lemma guarantees that if a triple is inconsistent (together with the input KG) w.r.t. an ontology $\mathcal{O}$ then all generalized triples of that triple are also inconsistent.

Lemma 2. *Let $\mathcal{G}$ be a KG, $\mathcal{O}$ an ontology, α a triple such that $\mathsf{Relv}(\alpha, \mathcal{G}) \cup \mathcal{O}$ is inconsistent with an explanation $\mathcal{E} = \mathcal{E}_\mathcal{G} \cup \mathcal{E}_\mathcal{O}$, and $\mathsf{GeneralizedSamples}(\alpha)$ is the set of generalized triples of α w.r.t. $\mathcal{E}$, $\mathcal{G}$, and some entity occurring in α. Then, we have $\mathsf{Relv}(\beta, \mathcal{G}) \cup \mathcal{O}$ is inconsistent for every $\beta \in \mathsf{GeneralizedSamples}(\alpha)$.*

Table 2. Knowledge graph statistics.

	LUBM3U	Yago3-10	DBpedia15K
# Entities	127,645	123,182	12,842
# Predicates	28	37	279
# Training facts	621,516	1,079,040	69,320
# Validation facts	77,689	5,000	9,902
# Test facts	77,689	5,000	19,805
# TBox axioms	325	4,551	3,006

Proof (Sketch). W.l.o.g. let $\alpha = \langle s, p, \hat{o} \rangle$, GeneralizedSamples$(\alpha)$ is w.r.t. $\hat{o}$, and $\beta = \langle s, p, o \rangle$. Using the result in [32], one can show that if $\langle s, p, \hat{o} \rangle \in \mathcal{E}_{\mathcal{G}}$ then $\mathcal{E}_{\mathcal{G}}$ does not contain $\langle s', p, o \rangle$, where $s \neq s'$ due to the minimality of explanations. Together with the condition $\tau(\hat{o}) \preceq \tau(o)$, we can construct a homomorphism from Relv$(\alpha, \mathcal{G})$ to Relv$(\beta, \mathcal{G})$, which implies that Relv$(\beta, \mathcal{G}) \cup \mathcal{O}$ is inconsistent. $\qquad\square$

We now describe the details of step (5). For each predicted triple that is inconsistent w.r.t. the input KG and the ontology, we compute explanations for inconsistency, and for each such explanation, we obtain the generalized triples using Definition 4. These generalized triples are then used as negative samples to retrain the embedding model.

4 Experiments

We have implemented the proposed method in a prototype system *ReasonKGE* and evaluated its performance on the commonly used datasets enriched with ontologies. In this section, we present the results of the evaluation in terms of the impact of our method on the quality of fact predictions compared to the baselines.

4.1 Experimental Setup

Datasets. Among commonly used datasets for evaluating embedding models, we chose those datasets that are equipped with ontologies. More specifically, the following datasets with their respective ontologies have been selected.

- **LUBM3U:** A synthesized dataset derived from the Lehigh University Benchmark [18]. The ontology describing the university domain contains 325 axioms. The respective KG stores data for 3 universities.
- **Yago3-10:** A subset of the widely used Yago dataset. We use the ontology with 4551 axioms introduced in [31] based on Yago schema and class hierarchy.
- **DBpedia15K:** A subset of DBpedia KG proposed in [24]. We exploit the general DBpedia ontology enriched with axioms reflecting the disjointness of classes. The ontology comprises of 3006 axioms.

The statistics of the respective datasets is presented in Table 2.

Embedding Models. To demonstrate the benefits of the proposed iterative ontology-driven negative sampling, we apply our method over the following widely used embeddings: ComplEx [33] and TransE [9]. These models have been selected as prominent examples of translation-based and linear-map embeddings. While more recent embedding models exist in the literature, as shown in [29] classical embeddings are in fact very competitive when combined with effective parameter search. Thus, as baselines we have selected the most widely used and popular embedding models with the best parameters found using the LibKGE library [29].

We also consider another baseline [11] that incorporates background knowledge into the embedding models. We refer to such technique as *static sampling* because in contrast to our proposed *dynamic sampling* method, the approach from [11] generates the negative samples for all triples of the KG in the pre-processing step. Since the authors of [11] only mentioned that they utilized such ontology axioms as *Domain, Range, Functional,* and *Disjointness*, but have not described the exact procedure of how these have been exploited for generating negative samples, we have implemented such static sampling strategy based on our best knowledge, and present the details of the implementation in the extended version.[3]

Measures. We evaluate the performance of the embedding models in terms of the traditional metrics i.e. *MRR* and *Hits@k* in the filtered setting [9]. In addition, we also compute the proportion of inconsistent facts (*Inc@k*) ranked in the *top-k* predictions produced by the presented methods. The measure *Inc@k* intuitively reflects how well the model is capable of avoiding inconsistent predictions (the lower the better).

System Configuration. In the experiments, we used HermiT [15] as the reasoner and the explanation method in [20] to compute inconsistency explanations. We run *ReasonKGE* for multiple iterations. In every iteration, the model is trained for $n = 100$ epochs during which, for each subject and object of a triple, $m >= 1$ negative examples are generated. We exploit the optimal value of m tuned for the respective baseline model. In the first iteration, m negative samples are generated using the default random sampling strategy[4]. In the subsequent iterations, we use the trained model to obtain the top $k = 1$ subject and object predictions and compute the inconsistent negative samples to be used for the next iteration of the embedding training as described in Sect. 3. The number m of negative samples for the next iteration is dynamically computed based on the statistical mean of the size of the generalized samples sets as an indicator.

4.2 Results

The results of the conducted experiments illustrate the benefit of *ReasonKGE* in producing higher quality predictions with less inconsistencies compared to the baselines.

Link Prediction Quality. Table 3 reports the results for the link prediction task obtained by our method and the baselines. Both TransE and ComplEx were trained using the default random sampling strategy [9], the *static sampling* [11], and using *ReasonKGE* for 3 iterations. For fair comparison, the number of the training epochs was kept the same as for *ReasonKGE* in all cases (i.e., 300 epochs).

---

[3] Available at https://github.com/nitishajain/ReasonKGE.

[4] For each triple the subject (resp. object) is randomly perturbed to obtain m samples [9].

Table 3. Link prediction results

Model	KG	Default Training			Static Sampling			ReasonKGE		
		MRR	Hits@1	Hits@10	MRR	Hits@1	Hits@10	MRR	Hits@1	Hits@10
TransE	LUBM3U	0.119	0.069	0.214	0.125	**0.082**	0.213	**0.135**	0.079	**0.256**
	Yago3-10	0.226	0.044	0.537	0.351	0.183	0.621	**0.367**	**0.197**	**0.629**
	DBpedia15k	0.109	0.061	0.206	0.101	0.073	0.254	**0.118**	**0.101**	**0.299**
ComplEx	LUBM3U	0.159	0.119	0.242	0.181	0.136	0.276	**0.233**	**0.195**	**0.313**
	Yago3-10	0.482	0.400	0.643	0.515	0.431	0.665	**0.530**	**0.453**	**0.668**
	DBpedia15k	0.099	0.061	0.174	0.098	0.107	0.193	**0.115**	**0.125**	**0.221**

Table 4. Ratio of inconsistent predictions (the lower, the better).

Model	KG	Prediction	Default Training		Static Sampling		ReasonKGE	
			Inc@1	Inc@10	Inc@1	Inc@10	Inc@1	Inc@10
TransE	LUBM3U	subject	0.169	0.270	0.428	0.250	**0.037**	**0.133**
		object	0.095	0.097	0.212	0.104	**0.005**	**0.007**
	YAGO3-10	subject	**0.075**	0.280	0.629	0.492	**0.075**	**0.273**
		object	0.026	0.136	0.114	**0.089**	**0.020**	0.117
	DBpedia15K	subject	0.311	0.652	0.401	0.663	**0.217**	**0.585**
		object	0.413	0.538	0.428	0.544	**0.170**	**0.460**
ComplEx	LUBM3U	subject	0.041	0.097	0.177	0.136	**0.036**	**0.069**
		object	0.008	0.012	**0.003**	**0.007**	0.005	**0.007**
	YAGO3-10	subject	0.113	0.198	0.169	**0.128**	**0.071**	0.143
		object	0.037	0.115	0.065	0.084	**0.015**	**0.074**
	DBpedia15K	subject	0.488	0.667	0.436	0.695	**0.344**	**0.583**
		object	0.397	0.585	0.365	0.528	**0.318**	**0.533**

One can observe that reasoning-based sampling consistently achieves better results than random sampling for training all considered embeddings on all KGs. For the Yago3-10 dataset the improvements are the most significant, achieving more than 10% enhancement for all measures over TransE. This indicates the advantage of ontology-based reasoning for enhancing the existing KG embeddings.

The comparison of our dynamic sampling method against static sampling [11] presented in Table 3 reveals that *ReasonKGE* outperforms the *static sampling* approach in almost all cases, which illustrates the benefits of exploiting inconsistent predictions as negative samples dynamically using our method, as opposed to their pre-computation.

By keeping the same training configuration and total number of training epochs, we ensure that the reflected performance gains are not merely due to additional training steps, but rather a result of the proposed reasoning-based approach.

Consistency of Predictions. In Table 4, we measure the proportion of inconsistent facts that were obtained when retrieving *top-k* ($k = \{1, 10\}$) predictions for the triples in the test set. We report the inconsistency values both for the prediction of the *subject* and the *object* of the triple separately. From the results, we can observe that for all models in the majority of the cases *ReasonKGE* managed to reduce the ratio of inconsistent predictions over the test sets compared to the results of training the models using *default* random and *static* sampling. This illustrates that the proposed procedure is effective for improving embeddings with respect to the overall consistency of their predictions.

5   Related Work

Negative Sampling Strategies. The closest to our method is the work [11], in which ontologies are used to generate a selection of negative samples in the pre-processing step for training a certain embedding model. While we use this pre-processing based sampling as a baseline for comparison in Sect. 4, our method is different in that we do not generate all negative examples at once, but rather compute them iteratively on demand relying on the inconsistent predictions produced by the given embedding. The major advantage of the *ReasonKGE* method compared to [11] is the dynamic and adaptable nature of negative sample generation, wherein, the method is able to specifically target the weaknesses of the previously trained model by leveraging inconsistent predictions to derive negative samples, and use them for re-training of the model in next iterations. This is in contrast to the process of precomputing negative samples using ontology axioms as suggested in [11].

Another related method is concerned with type-constrained negative sampling [22]. Given a triple from the KG, the negative candidates (subjects or objects) are mined by constraining the entities to belong to the same type as that of the subject or object of the original triple. However, unlike our inconsistency-driven method, the typed-constrained sampling can generate false negatives. This sampling method can be in principle also used as the starting point for our method instead of the random sampling.

More distant random negative samplings generate false candidate triples based on the (local) closed world assumption [27]. Alternatives include Distributional Negative Sampling (DNS) [12] and its variation [2], where during training, given a positive triple, negative examples are generated by replacing it's entity with other similar entities. Unlike in our method, no ontological information is considered in these sampling strategies. The same holds for the triple perturbation or triple corruption approach [30].

Nearest Neighbor and *Near Miss sampling* [21] resp. exploit a pre-trained embedding model for generating negative samples by selecting triples that are close to the positive target triple in vector space. Intuitively, this strategy is supposed to help the model to learn to discriminate between positives and negatives that are very similar to each other. These approaches are similar to ours, in that the embedding training procedure itself is exploited for the generation of negative samples. However, in [21] no ontological knowledge is taken into account which is in contrast to our work.

Another research direction concerns making use of Generative Adversarial Networks (GANs) [10,35,39] for negative sampling. The work [1] presents structure-aware negative sampling (SANS), which utilizes the graph structure by selecting negative samples from a node's neighborhood. The NSCaching sampling method [40] suggests to sample negatives from a cache that can dynamically hold large-gradient samples. While in these works negative triples are updated dynamically like in our method, these approaches are totally different from ours, as they rely purely on the machine learning techniques, and do not consider any extra ontological knowledge. Thus, the proposals are rather complementary in nature.

Integration of Ontological Knowledge into KG Embeddings. Another relevant line of work concerns the integration of ontological knowledge directly into embedding models (e.g., [11,14,19,22,25,37,41]), which is typically done via changes in the loss function, rather than negative sampling.

For example, a related method *Embed2Reason (E2R)* has been proposed by Garg *et al.* [14]. *E2R* relies on the quantum logic, and injects ontology axioms via the loss function, by summing up the terms relevant for these axioms. However, it is unclear how this method captures the interaction among the axioms, which is often the reason for inconsistency. Since the available code of [14] only supports a limited set of axioms, i.e., `SubClassOf`, `SubPropertyOf`, `Domain`, `Range`, which are insufficient for generating inconsistencies, we could not perform a direct comparison of our method to *E2R*. Note that in general, our method is conceptually different from *E2R*. Indeed, in contrast to [14], we focus on ontology-driven targeted improvements of the negative sampling procedure with the goal of teaching a given embedding model to make only consistent predictions, and interactions among the axioms are key to our method. Moreover, our proposed approach can be built on top of any embedding model including [14], making the two methods rather complementary in nature.

The recent work [37] suggests to exploit ontological reasoning for verifying consistency of predictions made by a machine learning method (e.g., embedding or rule learning). However, instead of feeding inconsistent predictions back to the given embedding model, the authors propose to get rid of them and feed other consistent predictions along with the original KG as input to a further KG completion method. In [19] the ontology is explicitly included in the training data to jointly embed entities and concepts. By treating the ontology and KG in the same way, only very restricted ontological knowledge is accounted for.

Our work can be also positioned broadly within neural-symbolic methods, and we refer the reader to [6,38] for other less related neural-symbolic approaches.

Inconsistency in Ontologies. The problems of explaining and handling inconsistency in ontologies have been tackled in different settings [7,8,20,23,28,32]. However, typically these works focus on detecting inconsistency [8,20], scalable reasoning [28,32], or performing reasoning in the presence of such inconsistency [7,23] assuming that the KG is constructed and complete. In other words, these approaches deal purely with data cleaning rather than KG completion. In contrast, our method integrates the reasoning process into the embedding models to improve the accuracy of predicted triples.

6   Conclusion

We have presented a method for ontology-driven negative sampling that proceeds in an iterative fashion by providing at each iteration negative samples to the embedding model on demand from its inconsistent predictions along with their generalizations. The main takeaway message of this work is that targeted negative example generation is beneficial for training the model to predict consistent facts as witnessed by our empirical evaluation on state-of-the-art KGs equipped with ontologies.

While in this work we focused on ontologies in DL-Lite, our method can be adapted to support more expressive ontologies. In this case, the soundness will still be preserved, but the completeness of the generalized negative sampling step might not be theoretically guaranteed, i.e., not all possible similar negative samples will be obtained based on a given inconsistent prediction of the embedding model. In practice, this will likely have a small impact on the effectiveness of our method, since the majority of useful negative samples will anyway be generated.

There are several exciting directions for future work. First, integrating the developed negative sampling method into the combination of rule learning and embedding-based approaches [37] for KG completion is promising. Second, extending the proposed approach to target other more expressive ontology languages is a relevant future direction. Last but not least, adapting our method to jointly clean and complete KGs can be helpful for facilitating the automatic KG curation.

References

1. Ahrabian, K., Feizi, A., Salehi, Y., Hamilton, W.L., Bose, A.J.: Structure-aware negative sampling in knowledge graphs. EMNLP **2020**, 6093–6101 (2020)
2. Alam, M.M., Jabeen, H., Ali, M., Mohiuddin, K., Lehmann, J.: Affinity dependent negative sampling for knowledge graph embeddings. In: (DL4KG2020) - (ESWC 2020) (2020)
3. Artale, A., Calvanese, D., Kontchakov, R., Zakharyaschev, M.: The DL-Lite family and relations. CoRR abs/1401.3487 (2014)
4. Auer, S., Bizer, C., Kobilarov, G., Lehmann, J., Cyganiak, R., Ives, Z.G.: Dbpedia: a nucleus for a web of open data. In: ISWC, pp. 722–735 (2007)
5. Baader, F., Horrocks, I., Sattler, U.: Description logics. In: Hb on Ontology, pp. 21–43 (2009)
6. Bianchi, F., Rossiello, G., Costabello, L., Palmonari, M., Minervini, P.: Knowledge graph embeddings and explainable AI. In: Tiddi, I., Lécué, F., Hitzler, P. (eds.) KGs for XAI: Foundations, Applications and Challenges, vol. 47, pp. 49–72. IOS Press (2020)
7. Bienvenu, M.: A short survey on inconsistency handling in ontology-mediated query answering. Künstliche Intell. **34**(4), 443–451 (2020)
8. Bischof, S., Krötzsch, M., Polleres, A., Rudolph, S.: Schema-agnostic query rewriting in SPARQL 1.1. In: ISWC, pp. 584–600 (2014)
9. Bordes, A., Usunier, N., Garcia-Duran, A., Weston, J., Yakhnenko, O.: Translating embeddings for modeling multi-relational data. In: NeurIPS, pp. 2787–2795 (2013)
10. Cai, L., Wang, W.Y.: KBGAN: adversarial learning for knowledge graph embeddings. NAACL-HLT **2018**, 1470–1480 (2018)
11. d'Amato, C., Quatraro, N.F., Fanizzi, N.: Injecting background knowledge into embedding models for predictive tasks on knowledge graphs. In: ESWC, to appear (2021)
12. Dash, S., Gliozzo, A.: Distributional negative sampling for knowledge base completion. CoRR abs/1908.06178 (2019)
13. Dettmers, T., Minervini, P., Stenetorp, P., Riedel, S.: Convolutional 2D knowledge graph embeddings. In: AAAI, pp. 1811–1818 (2018)
14. Garg, D., Ikbal, S., Srivastava, S.K., Vishwakarma, H., Karanam, H.P., Subramaniam, L.V.: Quantum embedding of knowledge for reasoning. In: NeurIPS, pp. 5595–5605 (2019)
15. Glimm, B., Horrocks, I., Motik, B., Stoilos, G., Wang, Z.: Hermit: an OWL 2 reasoner. J. Autom. Reasoning **53**(3), 245–269 (2014)
16. Glimm, B., Kazakov, Y., Liebig, T., Tran, T.K., Vialard, V.: ISWC, pp. 180–195 (2014)
17. Glimm, B., Kazakov, Y., Tran, T.: Ontology materialization by abstraction refinement in horn SHOIF. In: AAAI, pp. 1114–1120 (2017)

18. Guo, Y., Pan, Z., Heflin, J.: LUBM: a benchmark for OWL knowledge base systems. J. Web Semant. **3**(2–3), 158–182 (2005)
19. Hao, J., Chen, M., Yu, W., Sun, Y., Wang, W.: Universal representation learning of knowledge bases by jointly embedding instances and ontological concepts. In: KDD, pp. 1709–1719 (2019)
20. Horridge, M., Parsia, B., Sattler, U.: Explaining inconsistencies in owl ontologies. In: Scalable Uncertainty Management, pp. 124–137 (2009)
21. Kotnis, B., Nastase, V.: Analysis of the impact of negative sampling on link prediction in knowledge graphs. CoRR abs/1708.06816 (2017). http://arxiv.org/abs/1708.06816
22. Krompaß, D., Baier, S., Tresp, V.: Type-constrained representation learning in knowledge graphs. In: ISWC, pp. 640–655 (2015)
23. Lembo, D., Lenzerini, M., Rosati, R., Ruzzi, M., Savo, D.F.: Inconsistency-tolerant query answering in ontology-based data access. J. Web Semant. **33**, 3–29 (2015)
24. Liu, Y., Li, H., Garcia-Duran, A., Niepert, M., Onoro-Rubio, D., Rosenblum, D.S.: MMKG: multi-modal knowledge graphs. In: ESWC, pp. 459–474 (2019)
25. Minervini, P., Demeester, T., Rocktäschel, T., Riedel, S.: Adversarial sets for regularising neural link predictors. In: UAI (2017)
26. Motik, B., Patel-Schneider, P.F., Grau, B.C.: OWL 2 web ontology language direct semantics (Second Edition). Tech. rep. (2012). https://www.w3.org/TR/owl-direct-semantics/
27. Nickel, M., Murphy, K., Tresp, V., Gabrilovich, E.: A review of relational machine learning for knowledge graphs. Proc. IEEE **104**(1), 11–33 (2016)
28. Paulheim, H., Gangemi, A.: Serving DBpedia with DOLCE – more than just adding a cherry on top. In: Arenas, M., et al. (eds.) ISWC 2015. LNCS, vol. 9366, pp. 180–196. Springer, Cham (2015). https://doi.org/10.1007/978-3-319-25007-6_11
29. Ruffinelli, D., Broscheit, S., Gemulla, R.: You CAN teach an old dog new tricks! on training knowledge graph embeddings. In: ICLR (2020)
30. Socher, R., Chen, D., Manning, C.D., Ng, A.Y.: Reasoning with neural tensor networks for knowledge base completion. In: NIPS. pp. 926–934 (2013)
31. Suchanek, F.M., Kasneci, G., Weikum, G.: Yago: a core of semantic knowledge. In: WWW (2007)
32. Tran, T., Gad-Elrab, M.H., Stepanova, D., Kharlamov, E., Strötgen, J.: Fast computation of explanations for inconsistency in large-scale KGS. In: WWW, vol. 2020, pp. 2613–2619 (2020)
33. Trouillon, T., Welbl, J., Riedel, S., Gaussier, É., Bouchard, G.: Complex embeddings for simple link prediction. In: ICML, pp. 2071–2080 (2016)
34. Vrandecic, D., Krötzsch, M.: Wikidata: a free collaborative knowledgebase. Commun. ACM **57**(10), 78–85 (2014)
35. Wang, P., Li, S., Pan, R.: Incorporating GAN for negative sampling in knowledge representation learning. In: AAAI, pp. 2005–2012 (2018)
36. Wang, Q., Mao, Z., Wang, B., Guo, L.: Knowledge graph embedding: a survey of approaches and applications. IEEE Trans. Knowl. Data Eng. **29**(12), 2724–2743 (2017)
37. Wiharja, K., Pan, J.Z., Kollingbaum, M.J., Deng, Y.: Schema aware iterative knowledge graph completion. J. Web Semant. **65**, 100616 (2020)
38. Zhang, J., Chen, B., Zhang, L., Ke, X., Ding, H.: Neural-symbolic reasoning on knowledge graphs. CoRR abs/2010.05446 (2020)
39. Zhang, Y., Yao, Q., Chen, L.: Efficient, simple and automated negative sampling for knowledge graph embedding. CoRR abs/2010.14227 (2020), https://arxiv.org/abs/2010.14227
40. Zhang, Y., Yao, Q., Shao, Y., Chen, L.: Nscaching: simple and efficient negative sampling for knowledge graph embedding. In: ICDE, pp. 614–625 (2019)
41. Ziegler, K., et al.: Injecting semantic background knowledge into neural networks using graph embeddings. In: 26th IEEE, WETICE, pp. 200–205 (2017)

Resources Track

CKGG: A Chinese Knowledge Graph for High-School Geography Education and Beyond

Yulin Shen, Ziheng Chen, Gong Cheng[✉], and Yuzhong Qu

State Key Laboratory for Novel Software Technology,
Nanjing University, Nanjing, China
{ylshen,chenziheng}@smail.nju.edu.cn, {gcheng,yzqu}@nju.edu.cn

Abstract. As part of a long-term research effort to provide students with better computer-aided education, we create CKGG, a Chinese knowledge graph for the geography domain at the high school level. Using GeoNames and Wikidata as a basis, we transform and integrate various kinds of geographical data in different formats from diverse sources, including gridded temperature data in NetCDF, precipitation data in HDF5, solar radiation data in AAIGrid, polygon data in GPKG, climate and ocean current data in images, and government data in tables. The current version of CKGG contains 1.5 billion triples and is accessible as Linked Data. We also publish a reified version for provenance tracking. We illustrate the potential application of CKGG with a prototype.

Keywords: Knowledge graph · Ontology · Geography

1 Introduction

Computers and artificial intelligence (AI) have fundamentally changed education. As part of a long-term research effort to provide students with better computer-aided and AI-powered education, in recent years we have been particularly focused on the geography subject in China's high-school education. Among others, we employed Semantic Web technology to enhance educational applications including question answering (QA) systems [7,9,17]. One lesson we learned from these research activities is that there is still a lack of high-quality knowledge graphs (KGs) that can cover the core geographical knowledge at the high-school level. Existing geographical KGs suffer from incompleteness or inaccuracy. For example, GeoNames[1] only covers basic geographical data such as location and administrative subdivision. Clinga [6] extracts rich geographical data such as climate from online encyclopedias, but the extracted KG is rather noisy. Indeed, for a QA system to answer high-school geographical questions such as those from [7], we need a KG providing rich and precise geographical knowledge (such as temperature and precipitation) for a large number of locations in the world.

---

[1] https://www.geonames.org/.

© Springer Nature Switzerland AG 2021
A. Hotho et al. (Eds.): ISWC 2021, LNCS 12922, pp. 429–445, 2021.
https://doi.org/10.1007/978-3-030-88361-4_25

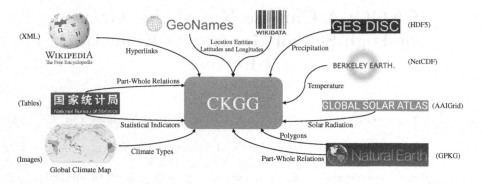

Fig. 1. Data sources integrated into CKGG.

Research Challenge. Despite the inadequacy of KGs, a variety of high-quality geographical data is publicly available in other formats on the Web, but their integration is a non-trivial task. For example, Berkeley Earth and GES DISC have published global temperature and precipitation data, respectively. Such data is in gridded NetCDF or HDF5 formats but is not directly associated with named geographical features (e.g., cities). More challenging examples include the global climate map used in China which is only available as an image. Transforming and integrating such highly heterogeneous data is complicated and labour-intensive.

Contributed Resource. To meet the challenge, we firstly constructed an ontology to cover the core concepts in a popular study guide for geography used in China's high schools. Using this ontology as the schema, we constructed the Chinese Knowledge Graph for Geography (CKGG) to cover the core geographical knowledge at the high-school level. Specifically, we collected and consolidated location entities from GeoNames and Wikidata [14]. Moreover, we used or developed a variety of NLP, math, and GIS tools to integrate heterogeneous data in grids, polygons, images, and tables from diverse sources to enrich location entities with valuable geographical properties including temperature, precipitation, solar radiation, part-whole relations, climate types, and statistical indicators, as depicted in Fig. 1. The ontology and all entities in CKGG are identified by permanent dereferenceable URIs in w3id.[2] The data is also available as RDF dump files on Zenodo. The source code for constructing CKGG and the VoID metadata about CKGG are available on GitHub.[3] All the resources are published under CC BY-SA 4.0. Below we summarize our contribution in the paper.

– We integrate Web data and construct CKGG containing 1.5 billion RDF triples and we publish it following Linked Data best practices. Our preliminary evaluation demonstrates the high quality of location entities in CKGG.

---

[2] https://w3id.org/ckgg/1.0/.

[3] https://github.com/nju-websoft/CKGG.

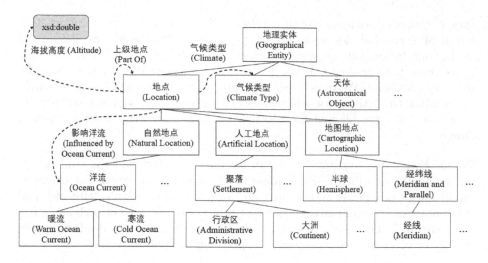

Fig. 2. A sample of the CKGG ontology.

- We present a prototype educational information system based on CKGG. It can be used to search and browse geographical knowledge in and related to CKGG. We also discuss the potential use of CKGG in question answering.

Outline. The remainder of the paper is organized as follows. We introduce the construction of the CKGG ontology in Sect. 2, describe the construction of CKGG in Sect. 3, and show its potential application in Sect. 4. Related work is discussed in Sect. 5. The paper is concluded in Sect. 6.

2 Schema of CKGG

This section describes the construction of an ontology as the schema of CKGG.

2.1 Construction of Ontology

We followed Ontology Development 101 [13] to construct *the CKGG ontology* as the schema of CKGG. In Fig. 2 we illustrate a part of it.

Step 1: Determine the domain and scope of the ontology. CKGG is expected to cover the core geographical knowledge at the high-school level. Since our current focus is on China's high-school education, the CKGG ontology is expected to cover the core concepts in major teaching/learning materials used in China. We selected one of the most popular study guides as the source of concepts.

Step 2: Consider reusing existing ontologies. In addition to the standard RDF and RDFS vocabularies such as `rdf:type` and `rdfs:label`, we considered reusing ontologies that are popular or highly relevant to our domain and scope. We selected two ontologies in the geographical domain: WGS84 Geo Positioning[4] and Clinga [6]. We reused two basic properties in WGS84 Geo Positioning representing the latitude (`wgs84_pos:lat`) and longitude (`wgs84_pos:long`) of a location, and we followed the hierarchy of administrative division types in Clinga.

Step 3: Enumerate important terms in the ontology. We read the study guide and manually identified a list of important concept-level terms. For example, important geographical concepts include "location", a location's "altitude" and "climate type", "ocean current", different types of ocean current such as "warm ocean current". Then we reviewed the identified terms and added a few missing ones, most of which were common concepts such as "public facility".

Step 4: Define the classes and the class hierarchy. We followed a top-down approach. We started with creating a single top-level class: `GeographicalEntity`. Then we specialized it by creating its subclasses such as `Location` (i.e., geographical feature) and `ClimateType`. We further categorized each class. For example, we categorized `Location` into `NaturalLocation`, `ArtificialLocation`, etc. We followed categorizations available in the study guide. For example, we categorized `OceanCurrent` into `WarmOceanCurrent` and `ColdOceanCurrent`.

Step 5: Define the properties of classes. After selecting classes from the list of terms, most of the remaining terms were properties. We attached each property to a class as its `rdfs:domain`. Most properties were attached to `Location` which is a central class in the ontology. For example, `altitude`, `climate`, and `influencedByOceanCurrent` are such properties. In particular, a `Location` can be part of another `Location`, represented by the property `partOf`. We specialized this property by creating its subproperties such as `inCountry`.

Step 6: Define the facets of the properties. We specified the value type or allowed values of each property by defining its `rdfs:range`. The range of a datatype property is an XML Schema datatype. For example, we defined the range of `altitude` as `xsd:double`. For some properties we defined a new datatype by enumerating its allowed values using `owl:oneOf`. For example, `technologyLevel` is chosen from {`very high`, `high`, `medium`, `low`, `very low`}. The range of an object property is a class. For example, `climate` and `influencedByOceanCurrent` relate `Location` to `ClimateType` and `OceanCurrent`, respectively.

Step 7: Create instances. We did not define instances in the ontology but only used it as the schema of CKGG. The creation of instances, i.e., the construction of CKGG, will be described in Sect. 3.

---

[4] `wgs84_pos`: http://www.w3.org/2003/01/geo/wgs84_pos#.

2.2 Statistics About Ontology

The constructed ontology is online: https://w3id.org/ckgg/1.0/ontology/. It contains 755 classes, 304 datatype properties, and 89 object properties. The maximum depth of a class in the class hierarchy is 10, and the maximum depth of a property in the property hierarchy is 3.

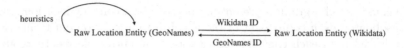

Fig. 3. Inter-source and intra-source matches between raw location entities.

3 Construction of CKGG

This section describes the construction of CKGG. Due to space limitations, we cannot address every detail of CKGG but will focus on its main content.

3.1 Location Entities

Collection of Location Entities. Location entities are central to CKGG. We collected *raw location entities* from GeoNames and Wikidata [14].

From GeoNames (accessed on 10/26/2020) we imported all the 12,051,898 geographical points as raw location entities. For Wikidata (accessed on 11/18/2020) we filtered its entities as follows. We only chose entities from the class of geographical entity (Q27096213), and we filtered out entities not having a well-formed value of coordinate location (P625) because later we relied on latitude and longitude for integrating data from other sources. Moreover, as our current focus is on China's education, we filtered out entities not having any Chinese label; this operation removed 94.65% of entities. The remaining 412,187 entities were imported as raw location entities.

Consolidation of Location Entities. Raw location entities might refer to the same real-world location entity. We identified both *inter-source matches* and *intra-source matches*, as depicted in Fig. 3. Specifically, we employed both Wikidata IDs (wkdt) attached to the entities in GeoNames and GeoNames IDs (P1566) attached to the entities in Wikidata to identify inter-source matches. Furthermore, we observed matches between raw location entities both imported from GeoNames. For example, both 1799960 and 1799962 in GeoNames refer to the Nanjing city in China. We identified such intra-source matches using the following heuristics: having at least one common Chinese name, having at least one common word in their English names (to reduce false positives derived from noisy Chinese names), belonging to the same administrative divisions, and located close to each other (≤ 10 km for P.PPL; ≤ 70 km otherwise).

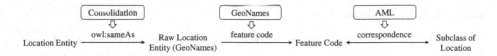

Fig. 4. Typing location entities with subclasses of `Location`.

We constructed a graph representing matches between raw location entities. We consolidated each component of the graph into a location entity in CKGG, and we linked it to each consolidated raw location entity via `owl:sameAs`. For example, the following four raw location entities were consolidated: 1799960 and 1799962 in GeoNames, Q16666 and Q28794795 in Wikidata.

There were 8,481,827 trivial components. We consolidated 3,710,324 non-trivial ones, most of which (98.6%) consisted of two raw location entities in an inter-source match. The largest component contained 20 raw location entities.

3.2   Essential Properties

For location entities, we considered type (`rdf:type`), label (`rdfs:label`), latitude (`wgs84_pos:lat`), and longitude (`wgs84_pos:long`) as essential properties.

Type. For each location entity, we assigned it as an instance of `Location`. Moreover, we identified a set of subclasses of `Location` in the CKGG ontology as its specific types. Specifically, we employed a state-of-the-art multilingual ontology matching tool, AgreementMakerLight (AML) [4], to compute correspondences between the hierarchy rooted at `Location` in the CKGG ontology (in Chinese) and the hierarchy of feature codes in GeoNames (in English), and we manually checked the computed correspondences. For each location entity, its specific types were identified by successively following: its raw location entities from GeoNames (if available), the feature codes of these raw location entities, and the corresponding classes of these feature codes. The process is depicted in Fig. 4.

Label. For each location entity, we kept all distinct Chinese names of its raw location entities from GeoNames and Wikidata, and kept the standard English names of its raw location entities from GeoNames. We converted traditional Chinese into simplified Chinese using OpenCC.[5]

Latitude and Longitude. For each location entity, we obtained a set of candidate latitude-longitude pairs from properties of its raw location entities: latitude/longitude in GeoNames, and P625 in Wikidata. We chose the latitude-longitude pair having the smallest total spherical distance from the other latitude-longitude pairs as the *canonical latitude and longitude* of this location entity.

---

[5] https://github.com/BYVoid/OpenCC.

3.3   Other Geographical Properties

For each location entity, we imported some useful properties of its raw location entities from GeoNames (e.g., altitude, population). Furthermore, we found other high-quality geographical data from different sources on the Web, but they were published in different formats. We transformed and integrated the following data into CKGG based on the essential properties of location entities.

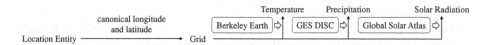

Fig. 5. Associating location entities with gridded temperature, precipitation, and solar radiation.

Fig. 6. Associating location entities with polygons.

Grids to KG. We collected monthly global average temperature data in NetCDF format from Berkeley Earth (accessed on 12/08/2020),[6] monthly global precipitation data in HDF5 format from GES DISC (accessed on 11/17/2020),[7] and daily global solar radiation data in AAIGrid format from Global Solar Atlas (accessed on 12/18/2020).[8] For solar radiation we converted daily totals into annual totals. We also augmented data as follows: for temperature we calculated annual averages based on monthly averages; for precipitation we calculated annual totals based on monthly totals.

To integrate the above data provided for each latitude-longitude grid, for each location entity we identified its grid based on its canonical latitude and longitude, and then added the monthly/annual average temperature, monthly/annual total precipitation, and annual total solar radiation in the grid as its properties. The process is depicted in Fig. 5.

Polygons to KG. For each location entity, we imported the lowest-level administrative divisions of its raw location entities from GeoNames and added them as values of its `partOf` property. To discover and add more part-whole relations, particularly those between locations other than administrative divisions, we exploited their polygon representations.

---

[6] http://berkeleyearth.lbl.gov/auto/Global/Gridded/Land_and_\penalty-\@MOcean_Alternate_LatLong1.nc.

[7] https://disc.gsfc.nasa.gov/datasets/GPM_3IMERGM_06/summary.

[8] https://api.globalsolaratlas.info/download/World/World_GHI_GISdata\penalty-\@M_LTAy_AvgDailyTotals_GlobalSolarAtlas-v2_AAIGRID.zip.

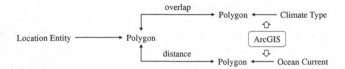

Fig. 7. Associating location entities with climate types and influence of ocean currents in map images.

Observe that a location is generally not a point but has an area. For each location entity, we associated it with a polygon. Specifically, we collected global polygon data in GPKG format from Natural Earth (accessed on 12/08/2020)[9] which contains links to Wikidata entities. For each location entity, its polygon was identified by successively following: its raw location entity from Wikidata (if available), and the corresponding polygon of this raw location entity. The process is depicted in Fig. 6.

We employed polygons to heuristically identify part-whole relations between location entities. For two location entities e_i and e_j associated with polygons $\texttt{plg}(e_i)$ and $\texttt{plg}(e_j)$, we added $\texttt{partOf}$ as e_i's property with value e_j if the following two conditions about their areas were satisfied:

$$\texttt{area}(\texttt{plg}(e_i)) < \texttt{area}(\texttt{plg}(e_j)) \quad \text{and} \quad \frac{\texttt{area}(\texttt{plg}(e_i) \cap \texttt{plg}(e_j))}{\texttt{area}(\texttt{plg}(e_i))} \geq 95\%. \quad (1)$$

Rather than requiring $\texttt{plg}(e_i) \subset \texttt{plg}(e_j)$, the second condition in Eq. (1) could tolerate noise in the collected polygon data. However, if e_i was not associated with any polygon, we could not use Eq. (1) but instead, we used e_i's canonical latitude and longitude to decide whether $e_i \in \texttt{plg}(e_j)$. This heuristic could be dangerous. For example, Wales was not associated with any polygon and would be considered as part of every polygon containing the canonical latitude and longitude of Wales. To avoid making such errors on important locations, we did not apply this heuristic to countries and first-level administrative divisions.

For each location entity, we also employed its polygon or its canonical latitude and longitude to calculate its distance from the nearest coastline based on the polygons of all coastlines. The distance was added as a property.

Images to KG. Unlike the popular Köppen climate classification available as structured data, the climate classification used in China's teaching/learning materials was only available as a map image. We employed ArcGIS to annotate the map and represent the distributions of climate types as polygons. For each location entity associated with a polygon, we identified its climate types by computing all its overlapping polygons of climate types. For each location entity not associated with any polygon, we computed all the polygons of climate types containing its canonical latitude and longitude. The process is depicted in Fig. 7.

---

[9] http://naciscdn.org/naturalearth/packages/natural_earth_vector.gpkg.zip.

Fig. 8. Associating administrative divisions with part-whole relations and statistical indicators in tables.

Similarly, the global distribution of ocean surface currents was only available as a map image (accessed on 12/18/2020).[10] We also employed ArcGIS to annotate the map and represent ocean currents as polygons. For each location entity e, we used its polygon or its canonical latitude and longitude to calculate its distance from each ocean current. We added `influencedByOceanCurrent` as e's property with all ocean currents as values such that their distances from e were smaller than 1,000 km. The process is depicted in Fig. 7.

Tables to KG. Observe that the part-whole relations obtained from GeoNames and polygons were incomplete. To enrich part-whole relations, particularly those about administrative divisions of China, we collected the official hierarchy of administrative divisions of China in tabular format from the website of National Bureau of Statistics of China (NBS, accessed on 01/12/2021).[11] To compute correspondences between the administrative divisions in CKGG and those at the top four levels of the official hierarchy, we processed the official hierarchy level by level in a top-down manner. For each level, we created an edge-weighted bipartite graph: nodes representing administrative divisions at this level and those in CKGG, and edges connecting administrative divisions having a common name. An edge was assigned a large (resp. small) weight if for the two incident administrative divisions there was a correspondence (resp. mismatch) between their ancestor administrative divisions at higher levels. We computed a maximum weight matching in this graph, from which we derived correspondences at this level. Based on the computed correspondences we enriched part-whole relations with the official hierarchy. The process is depicted in Fig. 8.

Also based on the above correspondences, we associated each administrative division of China with its official administrative division code in NBS. These codes helped us integrate many and various statistical indicators indexed by administrative division code in NBS. Specifically, we collected all statistical indicators about provincial-level administrative divisions of China in tabular format from NBS (accessed on 02/02/2021).[12] To compute correspondences between the properties in the CKGG ontology and the columns in NBS, we calculated the cosine similarity between their TF-IDF vectors and we manually checked the

---

[10] https://commons.wikimedia.org/wiki/File:Corrientes-oceanicas.png.
[11] http://www.stats.gov.cn/tjsj/tjbz/tjyqhdmhcxhfdm/2020/.
[12] https://data.stats.gov.cn/adv.htm?cn=E0103.

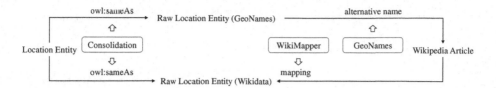

Fig. 9. Associating location entities with Wikipedia articles.

computed correspondences. We obtained ten correspondences including birth rate, crop yield, GDP per capita, and unemployment rate in the latest year. For each provincial-level administrative division of China, we added these latest statistical indicators as its properties by successively following: its corresponding administrative division in NBS, the administrative division code thereof, and its indexed statistical indicators. The process is depicted in Fig. 8.

3.4 Entity Ranking

To facilitate downstream tasks, we associated each location entity with a score representing its salience. Scores could be used to rank location entities in entity search, entity browsing, entity linking, etc. We defined the score of a location entity as the number of hyperlinks to its corresponding articles in Wikipedia.

For each location entity, we obtained its English and Chinese Wikipedia articles by two methods. The first method successively followed its raw location entity from GeoNames (if available), and the Wikipedia links in the alternative names of this raw location entity in GeoNames. The second method successively followed its raw location entity from Wikidata (if available), and the mappings to this raw location entity from Wikipedia article titles. The mappings were computed by WikiMapper.[13] We used precomputed mappings (accessed on 03/16/2021).[14] The process is depicted in Fig. 9.

From the XML dumps of English (accessed on 03/18/2021) and Chinese (accessed on 03/23/2021) versions of Wikipedia[15] we employed Annotated-WikiExtractor[16] to extract all hyperlinks to each of the above Wikipedia article. For each location entity, we associated it with the total number of hyperlinks to its English and Chinese Wikipedia articles as its ranking score.

3.5 Statistics About CKGG

CKGG is available as two sets of RDF dump files on Zenodo containing different versions of the KG: the *standard* version[17] and the *reified* version.[18] All entity

---

[13] https://github.com/jcklie/wikimapper.
[14] https://public.ukp.informatik.tu-darmstadt.de/wikimapper/.
[15] https://dumps.wikimedia.org/.
[16] https://github.com/jodaiber/Annotated-WikiExtractor.
[17] https://doi.org/10.5281/zenodo.4668711.
[18] https://doi.org/10.5281/zenodo.4678089.

URIs in the namespace https://w3id.org/ckgg/1.0/instances/ are dereference-able. The standard version contains 1.50B triples. It contains 12.19M location entities, each described by an average of 1.34 types and 121.45 other triples. In this version, for the convenience of downstream applications, we resolved conflicting property values based on predefined rules. For example, for each location entity we only kept its canonical latitude and longitude. The reified version contains 7.49B triples. For this version, we did not resolve conflicts but kept all property values associated with provenance information. Since CKGG is very large, we split it into a set of small dump files by partitioning the triples by properties. Users who are interested in only a few properties do not need to download all the dump files.

3.6   Quality of CKGG

It is difficult, if not impossible, to comprehensively evaluate the quality of a very large and integrated KG like CKGG. Observe that location entities are central to CKGG. Our evaluation was focused on their quality, including their coverage, consolidation, and part-whole relations.

Coverage of Location Entities. Recall that CKGG is expected to cover the core geographical knowledge at the high-school level. We manually identified 295 location entities mentioned in the study guide and checked CKGG's coverage of these entities. We successfully found 233 of them (79%) in CKGG. Among the uncovered ones: 42 (14%) were mainly complex entities (e.g., the drainage basin of the Yangtze River) and did not exist in GeoNames or Wikidata; 20 (7%) could be found in Wikidata but were filtered out due to their missing type, coordinate location, or Chinese label according to the filtering rules we used to collect location entities in Sect. 3.1. We would regard the former case as an open problem. For the latter case, including those entities in CKGG would not benefit downstream applications due to their missing essential properties.

Consolidation of Location Entities. We randomly sampled 100 small components containing two raw location entities and 200 large components containing three or more raw location entities which were consolidated based on inter-source and intra-source matches in Sect. 3.1. We manually checked all matches in each component. We confirmed the correctness of all matches in the sampled 100 small components, demonstrating the high quality of consolidation since small components occupied 98.6% of all non-trivial components. We found incorrect matches in 14 of the sampled 200 large components (7%): 8 (4%) were due to incorrect inter-source matches between GeoNames and Wikidata provided by these sources; only 6 (3%) were related to the heuristics we used to identify intra-source matches.

Part-Whole Relations Between Location Entities. In Sect. 3.3, for each location entity we used heuristics to identify its `partOf` properties based on its polygon or, if not available, based on its canonical latitude and longitude. For each case we randomly sampled and manually checked 100 `partOf` properties. We confirmed the correctness of all the sampled 200 `partOf` properties, demonstrating the high precision of `partOf` properties in CKGG.

4   Application of CKGG

To illustrate the potential application of CKGG, this section describes the implementation of a prototype educational information system based on CKGG, and also discusses the potential use of CKGG in QA systems.

4.1   Prototype: An Educational Information System

We have implemented a prototype educational information system[19] based on CKGG. Students, teachers, and other potential users can use the system to search and browse geographical knowledge in and related to CKGG.

Location Search. We stored and indexed CKGG in Virtuoso, based on which we provided two search functions: keyword search and proximity search. For keyword search, we relied on Virtuoso's full-text search (`bif:contains`) to find location entities matching an input keyword query. For proximity search, we relied on Virtuoso's spatial search (`bif:st_within`) to find location entities at most 30 km away from an input point on the map. Location entities were ranked by their associated scores computed in Sect. 3.4. Top-ranked location entities were presented, from which the user could select a location entity to browse.

Entity Browsing and Navigation. The browsing interface is illustrated in Fig. 10. On the left-hand side we visualized the location entity on the map provided by OpenStreetMap based on its polygon (if available) or canonical latitude and longitude. On the right-hand side we showed its types and properties. In particular, we employed Chart.js to visualize its monthly precipitation as bars and its monthly temperature as points. The user could navigate to its related entities by clicking its property values to further browse.

For example, by clicking the climate type of a location entity, the user could browse the definition of this climate type and its distribution on the map based on its polygon, as illustrated in Fig. 11. The user could further ask to show top-ranked location entities having this climate type on the map. A similar interface was implemented for browsing ocean currents.

---

[19] https://w3id.org/ckgg/1.0/demo/.

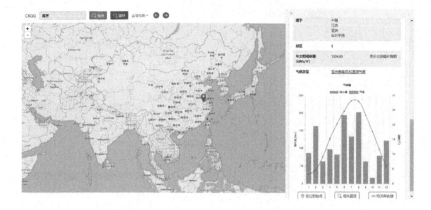

Fig. 10. Browse a location entity.

Fig. 11. Browse a climate type.

Question Search and Linking. We imported thousands of high-school geographical questions from existing datasets [7, 9], and we employed Apache Lucene to index all questions and support full-text search. Moreover, we employed LTP [1] to recognize mentions of locations in each question and then linked them to location entities in CKGG. When browsing a question, all the location entities mentioned in the question were highlighted, as illustrated in Fig. 12. The user could click a location entity to further browse. It could help the user better understand and answer this question. When browsing a location entity, the user could also ask to show all questions mentioning this location entity. It could help the user better understand this location.

4.2 Discussion: QA Systems

In recent years we have been working on QA systems for answering high-school geographical questions [7, 9, 17]. A question sampled from the GeoSQA

Fig. 12. Browse a group of questions.

下图示意某地区某月等温线分布，读图完成以下问题。

The figure below shows isotherms in some area in some month. Please answer the following question based on the figure.

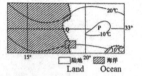
Land   Ocean

Natural language annotations of the image (provided by GeoSQA)
• 图中区域的经度位于15°和20°之间，纬度是33° The longitude of the area is between 15° and 20°, and the latitude is 33°.
• Q处位于大陆西岸 Location Q is at the west coast of the land.
• Q处纬度为33° The latitude of location Q is 33°.

Q地与北京气候相比较，一年中____

Comparing the climates of location Q and Beijing, we know that during a year

(A) 两地都雨热同期 Both places feature simultaneous high precipitation and high temperature.

(B) Q地气温较高的月份，北京的气温也较高 When location Q features high temperature, Beijing also features it.

(C) Q地受高压控制的季节，北京盛行偏南风 When location Q is influenced by high atmospheric pressure, south wind prevails in Beijing.

(D) Q地的多雨期与北京基本一致 The rainy periods of location Q and Beijing are basically the same.

Fig. 13. A high-school geographical question sampled from the GeoSQA dataset [7].

dataset [7] is illustrated in Fig. 13. Students in China's high schools would answer this question in the following steps. First, from the isotherms we infer that location Q is in the Southern Hemisphere. Then according to its latitude and longitude we know it is somewhere in South Africa. The west and east coasts of South Africa have different climate types. Note that location Q is at the west coast. Now we can obtain its climate type and compare it with Beijing to answer the question.

Current neural methods can hardly realize the above inference process, as suggested by the extensive experimental results reported in [7]. Symbolic methods are needed where CKGG would exhibit usefulness. For example, based on the latitude and longitude of location Q, we can identify the nearest town in CKGG (i.e., Vredenburg) and then retrieve its climate type, precipitation, and temperature data from CKGG. The obtained knowledge is clearly very useful for determining the correctness of the four options in the question.

Table 1. Comparison between KGs.

	CKGG	Clinga	CrowdGeoKG	GeoNames	Wikidata
Latitude and Longitude	✓	✓	✓	✓	✓
Altitude	✓	X	X	✓	✓
Polygon	✓	X	✓	X	✓
Part-Whole	✓	✓	X	✓	✓
Administrative Division	✓	✓	X	✓	✓
Climate	✓	✓	X	X	X
Temperature	✓	X	X	X	X
Precipitation	✓	X	X	X	X
Solar Radiation	✓	X	X	X	X
Statistical Indicator	✓	✓	X	X	✓

That said, current QA systems are still far away from answering such a question. For example, understanding the complex natural language description in the question is a great challenge. A hybrid neuro-symbolic method is demanded.

5   Related Work

Clinga [6] is one of the first Chinese KGs for the geography domain. It mainly extracted information from online encyclopedias. As a result, for many location entities some important properties are missing. For example, only 12% of the entities in Clinga have a latitude and a longitude, making it difficult to be integrated with other data sources. GeoKG [15] formalizes a geographical ontology but only populates it with a manually created small KG. By contrast, GeoNames provides latitudes and longitudes for a large number of location entities. We used it as a basis for integrating other data. CrowdGeoKG [2] is another geographical KG extracted from OpenStreetMap and Wikidata. However, the kinds of geographical knowledge covered by GeoNames and CrowdGeoKG are limited and insufficient for high-school education. For example, they lack temperature and precipitation data which are core concepts in high-school geography education and are needed for answering the question in Fig. 13.

Encyclopedic KGs such as Wikidata [14] and DBpedia [8] also contain many location entities. We imported location entities from Wikidata as a complement to GeoNames but still, there is a lack of domain-specific knowledge in Wikidata such as temperature and precipitation. We did not use DBpedia because we were concerned about the quality of the data it integrated. For example, in DBpedia, some triples describing the Yunnan Province mistakenly refer to the Baoshan District in Shanghai. Wikidata appeared better in this aspect.

Table 1 compares the above-mentioned KGs. By integrating a variety of domain-specific data from reliable sources, CKGG provides high-quality geographical knowledge and is more comprehensive than existing KGs. It provides latitudes, longitudes, climate, temperature, and precipitation data, all of which are very useful for answering high-school geographical questions such as the one in Fig. 13 as we discussed in Sect. 4.2.

6   Conclusion and Future Work

By transforming and integrating high-quality geographical data in different formats from diverse sources, we constructed and published CKGG. To the best of our knowledge, it is the most comprehensive geographical KG available on the Web. Although our original goal of constructing this KG was to cover the core geographical knowledge at the high-school level, the current CKGG has the potential to support a wider range of applications. Still, our work has the following limitations which we will address in the future.

Quality of CKGG. We have conducted a preliminary evaluation of CKGG. While the location entities were generally shown to be of high quality, a few errors were identified due to the original data sources and/or our integration methods. We will continue improving the quality of CKGG. In the meantime we will continue extending CKGG to cover broader kinds of geographical knowledge. Indeed, 655 classes and 353 properties defined in the CKGG ontology have not been populated in the current KG. For some properties we have not found any relevant and reliable data source to integrate. We will consider text mining, but accuracy rather than coverage will be our primary concern at all times.

Application of CKGG. We have discussed the potential use of CKGG in QA systems. At the time of writing we implemented two BERT-based QA systems [12,16] incorporating CKGG as domain knowledge. Their experimental results on the GeoSQA dataset [7] were not satisfying: we did not observe significant improvement by using CKGG. Indeed, most properties in the current KG have numerical values, which could not be effectively used by existing embedding-based QA models. Therefore, one possible solution is to further incorporate a rule engine to infer qualitative facts from numerical properties, which will be our future work. We will also explore novel hybrid neuro-symbolic methods.

We have also implemented an educational information system. We will continue extending its functions and evaluate its value for high-school education. Among others, we plan to employ entity summarization techniques [11] to generate an interactive summary for each location entity [10], and to generate comparative and connective summaries for multiple related location entities mentioned in a question [3,5].

Acknowledgements. This work was supported by the National Key Research and Development Program of China (2018YFB1005100).

References

1. Che, W., Feng, Y., Qin, L., Liu, T.: N-LTP: a open-source neural Chinese language technology platform with pretrained models. CoRR abs/2009.11616 (2020)
2. Chen, J., Deng, S., Chen, H.: CrowdGeoKG: crowdsourced geo-knowledge graph. In: Li, J., Zhou, M., Qi, G., Lao, N., Ruan, T., Du, J. (eds.) CCKS 2017. CCIS, vol. 784, pp. 165–172. Springer, Singapore (2017). https://doi.org/10.1007/978-981-10-7359-5_17
3. Cheng, G., Xu, D., Qu, Y.: Summarizing entity descriptions for effective and efficient human-centered entity linking. In: WWW 2015, pp. 184–194 (2015). https://doi.org/10.1145/2736277.2741094
4. Faria, D., Pesquita, C., Santos, E., Palmonari, M., Cruz, I.F., Couto, F.M.: The AgreementMakerLight ontology matching system. In: Meersman, R., et al. (eds.) OTM 2013. LNCS, vol. 8185, pp. 527–541. Springer, Heidelberg (2013). https://doi.org/10.1007/978-3-642-41030-7_38
5. Gunaratna, K., Yazdavar, A.H., Thirunarayan, K., Sheth, A.P., Cheng, G.: Relatedness-based multi-entity summarization. In: IJCAI 2017, pp. 1060–1066 (2017). https://doi.org/10.24963/ijcai.2017/147
6. Hu, W., et al.: Clinga: bringing Chinese physical and human geography in linked open data. In: Groth, P., et al. (eds.) ISWC 2016. LNCS, vol. 9982, pp. 104–112. Springer, Cham (2016). https://doi.org/10.1007/978-3-319-46547-0_11
7. Huang, Z., et al.: GeoSQA: a benchmark for scenario-based question answering in the geography domain at high school level. In: EMNLP-IJCNLP 2019, pp. 5865–5870 (2019). https://doi.org/10.18653/v1/D19-1597
8. Lehmann, J., et al.: DBpedia - a large-scale, multilingual knowledge base extracted from Wikipedia. Semant. Web 6(2), 167–195 (2015). https://doi.org/10.3233/SW-140134
9. Li, X., Sun, Y., Cheng, G.: TSQA: tabular scenario based question answering. In: AAAI 2021 (2021)
10. Liu, Q., Chen, Y., Cheng, G., Kharlamov, E., Li, J., Qu, Y.: Entity summarization with user feedback. In: Harth, A., et al. (eds.) ESWC 2020. LNCS, vol. 12123, pp. 376–392. Springer, Cham (2020). https://doi.org/10.1007/978-3-030-49461-2_22
11. Liu, Q., Cheng, G., Gunaratna, K., Qu, Y.: Entity summarization: state of the art and future challenges. J. Web Semant. 69, 100647 (2021). https://doi.org/10.1016/j.websem.2021.100647
12. Liu, W., et al.: K-BERT: enabling language representation with knowledge graph. In: AAAI 2020, pp. 2901–2908 (2020)
13. Noy, N.F., McGuinness, D.L.: Ontology development 101: a guide to creating your first ontology. Technical report, KSL-01-05, Stanford University (2001)
14. Vrandecic, D., Krötzsch, M.: Wikidata: a free collaborative knowledge base. Commun. ACM 57(10), 78–85 (2014). https://doi.org/10.1145/2629489
15. Wang, S., Zhang, X., Ye, P., Du, M., Lu, Y., Xue, H.: Geographic knowledge graph (GeoKG): a formalized geographic knowledge representation. ISPRS Int. J. Geo Inf. 8(4), 184 (2019). https://doi.org/10.3390/ijgi8040184
16. Yang, A., et al.: Enhancing pre-trained language representations with rich knowledge for machine reading comprehension. In: ACL 2019, vol. 1, pp. 2346–2357 (2019). https://doi.org/10.18653/v1/p19-1226
17. Zhang, Z., et al.: Towards answering geography questions in gaokao: a hybrid approach. In: Zhao, J., Harmelen, F., Tang, J., Han, X., Wang, Q., Li, X. (eds.) CCKS 2018. CCIS, vol. 957, pp. 1–13. Springer, Singapore (2019). https://doi.org/10.1007/978-981-13-3146-6_1

A High-Level Ontology Network for ICT Infrastructures

Oscar Corcho[1(✉)], David Chaves-Fraga[1], Jhon Toledo[1],
Julián Arenas-Guerrero[1], Carlos Badenes-Olmedo[1], Mingxue Wang[2],
Hu Peng[2], Nicholas Burrett[2], José Mora[2], and Puchao Zhang[2]

[1] Ontology Engineering Group, Universidad Politécnica de Madrid, Madrid, Spain
{ocorcho,dchaves,jatoledo,cbadenes}@fi.upm.es,
julian.arenas.guerrero@upm.es
[2] Huawei Research Ireland, Dublin, Ireland
{wangmingxue1,patrick.hupeng,nicholas.burrett,jose.mora,
zhangpuchao}@huawei.com

Abstract. The ICT infrastructures of medium and large organisations
that offer ICT services (infrastructure, platforms, software, applications,
etc.) are becoming increasingly complex. Nowadays, these environments
combine all sorts of hardware (e.g., CPUs, GPUs, storage elements, network equipment) and software (e.g., virtual machines, servers, microservices, services, products, AI models). Tracking, understanding and acting upon all the data produced in the context of such environments is
hence challenging. Configuration management databases have been so
far widely used to store and provide access to relevant information and
views on these components and on their relationships. However, different
databases are organised according to different schemas. Despite existing
efforts in standardising the main entities relevant for configuration management, there is not yet a core set of ontologies that describes these
environments homogeneously, and which can be easily extended when
new types of items appear. This paper presents an ontology network
created with the purpose of serving as an initial step towards an homogeneous representation of this domain, and which has been already used
to produce a knowledge graph for a large ICT company.

Keywords: Configuration management database · Ontology network ·
Knowledge graph

Resource type: Ontology
License: CC BY 4.0 International
DOI: 10.5281/zenodo.4701264
URL: http://w3id.org/devops-infra

1 Introduction

Most ICT organisations (IT service providers, cloud providers, telecom industry,
etc.) are witnessing, in recent years, the growing amount and interdependencies

© Springer Nature Switzerland AG 2021
A. Hotho et al. (Eds.): ISWC 2021, LNCS 12922, pp. 446–462, 2021.
https://doi.org/10.1007/978-3-030-88361-4_26

of hardware and software components that they need to handle as part of their infrastructure. Distinctions between hardware and software-related functionalities are sometimes blurring due to virtualisation: some hardware items may now be virtualised as software (e.g., virtual machines, DNSs). Terms like infrastructure as a service (IaaS), platform as a service (PaaS), software as a service (SaaS), etc., are now part of the ICT infrastructure jargon, and new terms are appearing (e.g., AI as a service -AIaaS-). This makes these environments increasingly difficult to track and understand.

Information about all these physical or virtual components has been traditionally handled in several types of (often loosely interconnected) databases: configuration management databases (CMDB), IT Service Management (ITSM) systems, IT Asset Management (ITAM) databases and tools, etc. The first group of databases (CMDBs) store and provide access to relevant information on these components and their relationships, providing organised views of configuration data and dynamic views on their functioning. These databases have evolved in recent years to reflect not only those components, but also the DevOps universe of technology and practices, including software configuration scripts, containers, cloud resources, etc. The second group (ITSM) is focused more exclusively on service management KPIs. The latter (ITAM) is usually more static and provide general information about the lifecycle of hardware components (purchase information, suppliers, disposal, etc.). There are many other types of products, tools and databases that provide support for other parts of the global ICT architecture of an organisation, following general architectural frameworks such as those identified in the Open Group Architecture Forum (TOGAF) [19].

Our work focuses on the description of the items and relationships normally covered under the umbrella of CMDBs and ITSMs, and the four major tasks that these systems and databases provide support to, according to the IT Infrastructure Library (ITIL) service management framework [2]:

- **Discovery**. Identify and catalogue the resources and groups of resources (also known collectively as configuration items) that are managed by the organisation or influence in the delivery of products and services.
- **Security**. Control that data can only be accessed and/or changed by those individuals or services that are authorised to do so.
- **Maintenance and Reporting**. Record, maintain, update and report the current status of all the handled resources (e.g., a server is up and running or idle, an IP address may be assigned or not).
- **Auditing and Recovery**. Verify that the data about all resources is accurate and identify causes of errors, so that remedial actions can be taken (by humans or by software). For instance, identify which systems may be affected by an outage and which groups of actions should be taken to repair its negative consequences.

Our expectation is that a set of ontologies focused around these main entities will allow organisations to have a global unified view of all of their resources, and provide better support for the aforementioned tasks, abstracting away from the characteristics of the underlying data sources. Knowledge graphs created according to these ontologies may also allow connecting the data commonly used in CMDBs and ISTMs with other data sources (product details from providers, product and service databases, CRM and ERP systems, etc.).

Contribution. The main contribution of our work is the development of **an ontology network that identifies and captures high-level entities (configuration items, resources and resource groups) that are common across configuration and IT Service management databases, together with the most common relationships among them.** This network is composed of a top-level ontology, describing general characteristics of all configuration items, and a set of 9 interconnected ontologies to represent: organisations, product and service descriptions, data centers, server infrastructure, network components and services, software, databases, hardware components and network security (including digital certificates). This ontology network results from the joint work of a team of ontology engineers and domain experts for approximately one year, following state-of-the-art ontology development practices. The resulting ontology network reflects the shared agreement on the core types of resources dealt with in this domain, and has been used as the basis for the creation of a knowledge graph related to the cloud and DevOps operations at a telecommunications company (Huawei). We expect this ontology network to serve as an initial step towards the standardisation of the main resources to be managed in the context of CMDBs and ISTMs in the future.

The remainder of this paper is structured as follows: Sect. 2 motivates our work with a typical use case related to disaster recovery for a cloud service provider. Section 3 describes our methodological approach for the development of a high-level network of ontologies in the area of configuration management and IT service management. Section 4 describes the ontology network, which consists of a top-level ontology and a set of 9 interconnected ontologies. Section 5 details how the ontology network has been used to drive the creation of a knowledge graph (KG) from Huawei's CMDB, using declarative RDB2RDF mappings and related technology, and how the KG can be exploited using SPARQL queries and a natural language question answering system, which is planned to be integrated in a chatbot. Section 6 presents some related work, pointing to previous efforts on the development of ontologies in this area, and their main limitations. And Sect. 7 outlines the main conclusions derived from the ontology development process and from the current set of ontologies, and describes future lines of work.

2   Motivational Example

Our work is motivated by the real-world challenges problems that a large cloud provider has to face in an increasingly demanding context where continuous integration and continuous deployment are more frequent and automated. As discussed in the introduction, the increase in the complexity of the underlying infrastructures and the runtime constraints imposed by DevOps practices increases the amount of problems and the costs associated to infrastructure maintenance and recovery operations. And this is expected to grow even more in the near future with the addition of AIOps [5] on top of current DevOps.

A typical example is the scenario where a sudden drop in performance (e.g., data throughput) is detected in the provision of a cloud-based product or service (e.g., in a video transmission application that uses a content delivery network). For this performance drop to be dealt with, site reliability engineers (SREs) need to inspect first the topology of services and microservices (e.g., object storage services, domain name services, elastic cloud servers) that are used by the product where the problem is detected. These services and microservices are running in specific servers and clusters and are based on a specific software module version, available in some software directory. At the same time, those servers (commonly virtual servers) are running on specific configurations of hardware items (including hardware servers, network cards, etc.) that are hosted in a data center. And this should be done independently of which specific types of infrastructures, hardware and software providers are being used.

By having a comprehensive view of all the components that are involved in this context, the SREs (usually in conjunction with AI algorithms prepared for that purpose) can perform the described actions with fewer and shorter queries and fewer actions, which is especially important when time is a pressing matter. Shorter queries and fewer actions implies less potential human errors, e.g. overlooking small groups of software or hardware elements as larger groups are generally more relevant.

3   Methodological Approach for Ontology Development

We have built the ontology network following the Linked Open Terms (LOT) methodology [17], whose main actors, activities and artefacts are depicted in Fig. 1. This methodology is rooted on NeOn methodology [18] and inspired by agile software development techniques, with sprints and iterations representing the main workflow organisation. In addition, the methodology focuses on the publication of the ontology according to Linked Data principles, together with all of its associated intermediate and final products (requirements, HTML documentation, etc.), so as to facilitate reuse.

The LOT methodology defines iterations over a basic workflow composed of the following activities: (1) ontological requirements specification; (2) ontology implementation; (3) ontology publication; and (4) ontology maintenance. In this section, we describe the process that we have followed, while Sect. 4 describes the final published outputs. We have used OnToology [1] connected to the GitHub repository of the ontology network (as discussed in Sect. 4) as the continuous integration environment to provide technological support during the ontology development process, making use of tools like Widoco [10] for ontology documentation and Oops! [15] for ontology evaluation.

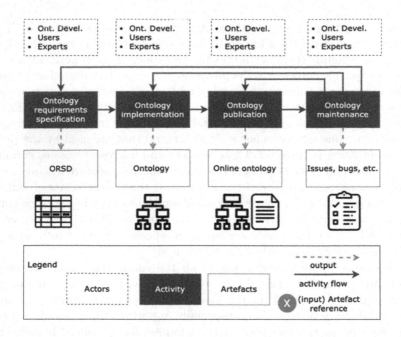

Fig. 1. LOT methodology basic workflow of processes [17]

3.1 Ontological Requirements Specification Process

The process of obtaining ontological requirements for the ontology network has been bootstrapped from three main types of sources:

- A set of competency questions related to the types of questions posed by our domain experts (site reliability engineers). This includes questions and requests such as "What is the current status of servers in a data center?", "Find the service topology for service X", etc. 31 questions and 88 facts have been collected, and are made available in the ontology network website and GitHub repository[1]. These have been further used for the validation and exploitation of the knowledge graph, as described in Sect. 5.2.
- The data model used by Huawei's Configuration Management and IT Service Management Database[2]. This data model was provided in SQL, and contains 82 tables that represent entities (e.g., Server, Software Module, Service, Data Center, etc.), 85 tables that represent relationships between entities (e.g., a service is running in one or serveral servers), and 59 tables representing views that connect different entities (e.g., lists of services and servers running in a data center).
- Several CSV files commonly used by domain experts from the AI-DevOps team at Huawei as additional intermediate views of specific entities from the

---

[1] https://github.com/oeg-upm/devops-infra.
[2] This data model is not available publicly for confidentiality reasons.

aforementioned database. Even though these CSV files are obtained using queries to the relational database, they do not follow exactly the same structure as the views in the data model.

All these resources come from several organisational departments inside a single company. During the ontology development process we have also checked further online resources describing database models used for this purpose [4,9] and contrasted with domain experts from other organisations so as to make sure that the design decisions were not biased towards the data models or practices used by a specific company.

The process has run during 10 iterations with domain experts. An initial set of requirements were proposed from the initial set of queries identified by domain experts and from the entities and attributes available in the data model and CSV structures. We used the spreadsheet-based structure available at https://github. com/oeg-upm/ORSD-template so as to determine the classes to be created, their associated data and object properties, the enumerations to be transformed into SKOS thesauri, and the SPARQL queries to be generated once the ontology implementation would be ready. From an initial set of 165 competency questions (121 facts and 44 questions), 119 (88 and 31 respectively) were kept. The final set of competency questions is available at the GitHub repository.

3.2 Ontology Implementation Process

The ontology implementation process has followed a traditional approach. Our team of ontology engineers, who were already involved in the ontology requirement specification process, analysed the requirements and divided them into modules for the ontology network, considering the different areas of specialisation that domain experts would normally have in an organisation offering cloud services (as described in Sect. 4). This organisation into modules is also created with the objective of facilitating the evolution of the ontology network in the future. It has been validated (and refined) with some of the domain experts that were involved in the requirement specification process. We created and discussed conceptual models with them, following the graphical representations proposed in CHOWLK[3], transformed them into OWL, edited further with Protégé and maintained the different versions of the OWL ontologies in GitHub.

In order to facilitate the governance process afterwards, a set of ontology development guidelines and principles have been considered and deployed in the top-level ontology (the so-called core ontology), which describes the most generic items of Configuration Item, Resource and Resource Group. General properties to be used for the description of any Configuration Item have been determined, including the use of `rdfs:label` for names, `dct:identifier` for identifiers, and specialisations of `dct:created` and `dct:modified` for the creation and update times. Although these properties are not available as attributes in all the data models examined for all resources, this provides an initial level of homogeneisation for these simple properties. Our main goal on the decision for the ontology

---

[3] https://chowlk.linkeddata.es.

This page contains the list of ontologies for the description of the DevOps infrastructure domain developed jointly by the Ontology Engineering Group (OEG) and Huawei Research Ireland.

Ontology	Serialization	License	Language	Links	Description
Core ontology ⓘ	rdf+xml html	CC-BY	en	🗂 Repository ⓘ Issues ≡ Requirements	Core ontology used for the whole ontology network, which defines the general concepts of Resource and Resource Groups
Organisation Ontology ⓘ	rdf+xml html	CC-BY	en	🗂 Repository ⓘ Issues ≡ Requirements	Ontology for describing organisational aspects of the DevOps infrastructure ...See more
Business Product ontology ⓘ	rdf+xml html	CC-BY	en	🗂 Repository ⓘ Issues ≡ Requirements	Business Product ontology, which defines the business offering of a company, including the offered services and microservices
Data Center ontology ⓘ	rdf+xml html	CC-BY	en	🗂 Repository ⓘ Issues ≡ Requirements	Data Center ontology, used to describe all characteristics related to data centers, and their interconnections with the resources from other ontologies in the network

Fig. 2. Excerpt from the landing page of the ontology network

modules to structure the ontology network was to have a reduced number of classes and properties (in the range of tens as a maximum) so as to make them more manageable and easily extensible in the future. Figure 3 provides a general conceptual view of the main classes and properties of the ontology network (more details for each module are provided in the corresponding HTML documentation of each of the ontologies in the network).

3.3   Ontology Publication

In terms of ontology publication, we have followed usual practices proposed for Linked Data publication for ontologies. This has been facilitated by the usage of our suite of tools for ontology publication and evaluation, as aforementioned (OnToology, Widoco and Oops!).

More specifically, the ontology network landing page is published at http://w3id.org/devops-infra, as shown in Fig. 2. It follows the layout commonly used for other ontology networks (ontology name and URI, serialisation, license, language, links to the GitHub repository, open issues and requirements, and a brief description). Thanks to the content negotiation capabilities provided by W3id, the ontologies are dereferenced in HTML and OWL (both in RDF/XML and Turtle serialisations) in their corresponding URIs, so that they can be easily imported by ontology editors.

The ontology network is also archived in Zenodo [6], following usual practices in Open Science.

3.4   Ontology Maintenance

Our setup is now prepared for the ontology maintenance phase for all ontologies, with the possibility of submitting issues (bugs, requests for additions, etc.) for each of the ontologies in the network, so as to facilitate discussions that may arise during future standardisation processes (as discussed in Sect. 7) or ontology usage by other organisations. Indeed, the creation of declarative mappings for the

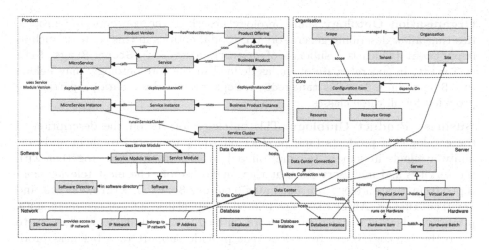

Fig. 3. High-level conceptual view of the main concepts and relationships in the ontology network

construction of Huawei's knowledge graph did already rise several issues (e.g., URI modifications and homogeneisation, common properties that were moved to the core ontology, etc.) that have been dealt with.

4 An Ontology Network for ICT Infrastructures

In this section we describe the current version of the implementation of this network of ontologies, and the main decisions taken during their development. Figure 3 shows an overview of the main concepts and relationships of our ontology network (except for the Certificate Ontology), as discussed in Sect. 3.2.

Core Ontology. The core ontology describes the most general concepts and properties that are used across the ontology network. Namely, it defines the concepts of Resource and ResourceGroup, as subclasses of the most general concept ConfigurationItem (the term that is commonly used in CMDBs), which describe any type of individual resource or group of resources that may need to be identified and managed in this context. Resources include databases, physical and virtual servers, data centers, different types of network equipment, services, microservices, products, etc. Besides the object properties that allow describing dependencies among resources and resource groups (dependsOn, which can be further specialised by the other ontologies in the network), relating a resource to a resource group (belongsToResourceGroup) and relating a resource group to another one (parentResourceGroup), this ontology proposes the use of other general data and object properties to ensure homogeneous descriptions of resources and resource groups across the ontology network, namely created, modified, version and status. When applicable, these properties are specialisations of the corresponding Dublin Core terms.

Organisation Ontology. This ontology describes the concepts and properties that allow describing general organisational entities in this context, such as Department (which is a subclass of org:Organization), Scope, Stage, Site or Tenant. In general, a Resource, as defined in the core ontology, may belong to a Scope and a Scope is managedBy a Department. Basic data properties are provided for all these classes.

Business Product Ontology. This ontology focuses on the description of the catalogue of products (and product offerings associated to them and normally available in some catalogue) offered by the organisation, together with the services and microservices that they make use of. The most relevant concepts from this ontology are BusinessProduct, Service, MicroService and ServiceCluster. All of these are related by specialisations of the dependsOn property, which is definied in the core ontology, so that it would be easy to trace the topology of microservices that provide support to a business product, for example (something relevant for the maintenance and troubleshooting operations). Besides these concepts that can be used to describe these general entities, their instances deployed in a specific infrastructure can be represented, with their corresponding properties.

Data Center Ontology. This is a central ontology in the ontology network, since the DataCenter concept is related to many other concepts defined in other ontologies, especially those in the server and network infrastructure ontologies, as well as in the hardware ontology. Indeed, a DataCenter is understood as an entity that hosts different types of resources, is locatedIn a Site, allowsConnectionVia a DataCenterConnection and offers different network-related elements (offersIPAddress, offersIPNetwork, offersNetworkSegment). As in the previous ontologies, multiple data properties are defined to describe further the core concepts of DataCenter and DataCenterConnection.

Server Infrastructure Ontology. This ontology defines all those concepts that are strongly related to the physical and virtual infrastructure of servers that are handled in this context. This includes the concept Server and its two main subclasses PhysicalServer and VirtualServer, which may be further extended to account for specific types of servers handled by an organisation. It also defines the HostImage and different types of HostConfiguration for virtual servers, and the concept of ServerLoadBalancer.

Network Infrastructure Ontology. This ontology describes the resources that are relevant for the configuration of the network infrastructure, including aspects like IPAddress and all of its subclasses for public and private IP addresses, IPNetwork, NetworkSegment, DNSDomain and its other related entities, FirewallCluster, PublicNATEntry and SSHChannel. All of these entities are interconnected with the corresponding object properties.

Software Ontology. This ontology describes in a general manner all those components that can be characterised as Software, including the software that can be used to deploy some service (`ServiceModule`). Any `Software` item may be available in a `SoftwareDirectory` and may be represented as a `File`. This ontology serves as a generic ontology for the description of software, and may be specialised by other ontologies if more details are needed.

Database Ontology. This ontology is also created as a general ontology to describe general concepts related to databases, such as the concepts of `Database`, `DatabaseInstance`, `DatabaseReplica` and `DatabaseScanReport`.

Hardware Ontology. This ontology is the one that allows relating the concepts managed by a CMDB with those normally handled by an IT Asset Management (ITAM) database. It allows describing pieces of hardware equipment such as `Disk`, `Frame`, `ServerHardware`, `NetworkCard`, etc. All of these items may have been purchased in a `HardwareBatch`, which acts as the main link to such an ITAM database.

Certificate Ontology. This ontology is focused on the description of aspects related to the management of digital certificates (including `DigitalCertificate` as well as `DigitalCertificateBundle`, `DigitalCertificateDeployment` and `DigitalCertificateSigningRequest`). All the data properties defined in this ontology are focused on describing the main characteristics of such certificates, as commonly understood in existing standards.

Finally, a set of thesauri have been generated in the form of SKOS concept schemes in those cases where specific codelists or simple taxonomies are required (e.g., status of any resource, types of tenants, types of hardware, etc.). In general, these have been derived initially from the set of enumerated columns appearing in the CMDB data model that we have used as one of the starting points, which have been conveniently cleaned and aligned with other existing enumerations from other providers, so as to provide a more comprehensive set of values. It is expected that these thesauri will evolve in the future when the ontology starts to be used by additional organisations.

5   Ontology Usage Scenarios

This section describes how we have used this ontology network as the basis for the creation of a knowledge graph related to the ICT infrastructure of a company like Huawei, based on its current CMDB and ITSM, already mentioned in Sect. 3 as one of the resources used for the requirements specification. This database has been developed in-house and is being used for storing and monitoring the current ICT infrastructure used by the company for service and product provisioning. It consists of several thousands of products and services, hundreds of data centers across the world, and millions of running services and microservices.

The ICT infrastructure of the company is maintained in a relational database that stores data from 82 different types of entities. The specific configuration of this database is generated from a JSON-based configuration file that provides support for simple taxonomies of resources and resource groups, and which specifies the main attributes (columns) that are considered for each of these resources and resource groups. Given the fact that this database can be considered as a legacy database, the schema has been evolving over time and there are sometimes different names for attributes that refer to the same types of properties (e.g., simple descriptions, labels for resources, etc.), unlike what is done in the ontology, where these should be homogeneous.

Furthermore, the design decisions behind the creation of the database have considered that it was useful, for extensibility purposes, to have different types of tables and views, as briefly discussed in Sect. 3.1: tables describing resources and resource groups, tables describing relationships among them (instead of making use of primary and foreign key relationships across tables, so as to facilitate the possibility of extensions and generating m:n relationships as the database evolves without impacting the design of the underlying tables, even though some performance metrics may be compromised) and tables that represent views. This JSON-based file is processed by an ad-hoc system and generates a SQL schema, which is the basis for the storage of all the data maintained by this CMDB and ISTM database.

5.1   Knowledge Graph Construction

Taking into account this rather unusual database structure (although common across Configuration Management Database models), the generation of the knowledge graph has still been based on state-of-the-art techniques for the generation of RDF-based knowledge graphs, more specifically the usage of RML mappings [8] that are initially expressed in YARRRML [11]. To this extent, and to facilitate the generation of these mappings, we have created a specific piece of software[4] that generates YARRRML mappings from the OWL ontology implementation, as a way to bootstrap this process for the knowledge engineer that is creating and maintaining mappings. The current set of mappings cover 41 concepts, 61 object properties and 91 data properties from the ontology network, which are associated to 41 entity tables and 38 relationship tables[5].

The KG creation process has been supported with tools from the Morph suite[6]. We opted for the materialisation of the RDF dataset and its storage in a Virtuoso triple store for the purpose of facilitating the integration of these technologies into the software stack of the teams involved at the company, since the integration of virtualised KG creation tools would have required further integration efforts with additional software development teams, which were out of the scope of our initial prototyping phase. However, virtualisation and query translation techniques are not discarded for the near future.

5.2   KG Exploitation Using a Question Answering System

Our competency questions have been transformed into SPARQL queries, showing some of the advantages of using a global view over the underlying data

---

[4] https://github.com/oeg-dataintegration/owl2rml.
[5] The mappings are maintained in a private repository, for confidentiality reasons.
[6] https://morph.oeg.fi.upm.es/.

(something that will be more clear when other types of databases from other organisations and CMDB and ISTM vendors are also transformed according to this ontology network). Furthermore, in order to show the range of possibilities that the KG provides and how it could be integrated in a DevOps chatbot that is being currently deployed at Huawei, we have developed a knowledge-graph based question answering (KGQA) system. A KGQA system allows exploring a KB using queries expressed in natural language, such as those used in some of the competency questions. Natural language questions are transformed into SPARQL queries that can be used to retrieve the desired data.

We have developed an unsupervised KGQA system, since we did not have annotated data for this domain, and we wanted to have a system that may be applied to other domains (or extensions of this domain) if needed. Five tasks have been traditionally identified in this process [7]: *question analysis, phrase mapping, disambiguation, query construction* and *distributed knowledge querying*. In the following, we briefly describe these steps and how we have approached them, illustrating them with a simple example. Assume the user inputs the question: "Where is hosted the instance of the cores_db database?".

In the *question analysis* task, techniques based on syntactic features are used to extract information about the question. We create n-grams and annotate the part-of-speech to retrieve the relevant phrases. 1-gram nouns and verbs are identified, since the rest of grammatical forms are not covered in the KG resources. The following phrases are considered from the input question: 'hosted', 'instance', 'cores_db database', 'hosted the instance', 'instance of the cores_db', 'instance of the cores_db database', 'hosted the instance of the cores_db' and 'hosted the instance of the cores_db database'.

In the *phrase mapping* task we search for resources that may correspond to phrases. Since there is potentially more than one term that can be related to KG resources (e.g. the words 'server', 'service', or 'deployment' can refer to devopsserver:Server), we avoid having to identify all those synonyms by projecting the resources into a vector space based on word embeddings. Entities, predicates and instances are directly retrieved from the SPARQL endpoint. One or more labels are automatically associated to each resource, since they will be used to obtain its vector representation. The labels are created from their URI, either by obtaining the value of some properties (e.g. skos:prefLabel, rdfs:label or skos:altLabel) or directly by parsing the URL using regular expressions (e.g. 'hardware network card' from http://w3id.org/devops-infra/hardware#NetworkCard). Our embedding space is built on top of the Fasttext model[7] using 300 dimensions to describe vectors for each resource, and they were stored in a Nearest Neighbour-based index to be able to perform searches taking into account the cosine distance.

This way we can identify the resources, and their distance, with respect to the phrases from the previous step. For the input example they are: devopsdb:Database (0,718), devopsdb:hostedInFrame (0,814), devopsserver:hostedBy (0,657), resource:database/Cores_DB (0,718), devopsdb:DatabaseInstance

---

[7] https://fasttext.cc.

(0,879), `devopsdb:DatabaseReplica` (0,900), `devopsdb:hasDatabaseInstance` (0,655), The purpose of the *disambiguation* task is to determine which of the previous resources are the right ones. Our approach is unsupervised, so we adapt a technique that measures the relevance of terms using density-based clustering techniques [3]. Resources and their distances are organized in a bidimensional space. Candidates that are close, i.e. resources whose distance between them is less than the standard deviation of the set, are grouped in the same cluster and their relevance depends on the absolute value of their distances. The closer the distance is to 0, the higher the relevance. In the above example, the most relevant resources are `devopsdb:hasDatabaseInstance`, `devopsserver:hostedBy` and `resource:database/Cores_DB`.

The *query construction* task creates the SPARQL query to retrieve data. This part also covers the construction of queries that require special operators such as comparatives and superlatives. Our approach is based on SQG [21], a modular SPARQL Query Generator that discovers a minimal subgraph based on uncertain lists of predicates and resources. The original source code[8] was extended to handle queries that restrict the type of resources (e.g. "'Core_DB' database" implies that the Core_DB resource type is 'Database', which allows to extend the original query to other resources of the same type); and to browse any SPARQL endpoint using configuration files without having to develop specific source code for that endpoint. The source code is publicly available[9]. In the example above, the generated SPARQL query is listed in 1.1.

Listing 1.1. SPARQL query to retrieve the location of a database instance

```
1  PREFIX devops: <https://w3id.org/devops-infra/>
2
3  SELECT DISTINCT ?server WHERE {
4      <http://database/Cores_DB> devops:database#hasDatabaseInstance  ?db .
5      ?db devops:server#hostedBy ?server
6  }
```

The final result of our query in a dummy database that we have created to demonstrate our work, for confidentiality reasons, is `resource:server/5`.

6   Related Work

As far as we were able to determine after the initial literature search at the beginning of this ontology development process, as well as during the identification of ontological resources to be reused, this is the first comprehensive and fully documented effort for the generation of an ontology network in this area, which is born with the objective of serving further standardisation and community-driven initiatives around this domain.

That said, we can mention some previous approaches reported in the literature, where ontologies for some specific types of infrastructure are reported. However, in all of these cases the ontology implementations are not available

---

[8] https://github.com/AskNowQA/SQG.
[9] https://github.com/oeg-upm/nlp2sparql.

anymore, nor is there any comprehensive documentation associated to those reported ontologies.

One of the seminal papers on the topic of ontologies for cloud computing is [20], from 2008, where the authors propose an organisation of the domain of cloud computing in five layers: firmware/hardware (HaaS), software kernel, cloud software infrastructure - including computational resources (IaaS), storage (DaaS) and communications (CaaS) -, cloud software environment (PaaS) and cloud application (SaaS). Although the title of this paper may suggest that an ontology or a network of ontologies had been produced as a result of this paper, the reality is that this paper only discusses the main characteristics of these layers and identifies some examples of different types of systems available at that time that would fit into each of these layers. However, no implementation in a formal ontology language is provided nor discussed, even though ontology languages like OWL already existed. Something similar happens with the work presented a bit later in [12], which does not provide an implementation either, or in [14], which only provides some snapshots of the corresponding implementation in the Protégé editor.

The Cloud Computing Ontology (CoCoOn), described in [22], focused on the computational resources part (IaaS) of the cloud software infrastructure identified in the aforementioned paper, and used it for a recommender system. Even though this ontology was implemented in OWL, it is not accessible anymore at the corresponding URL at the Australian W3C chapter pages, and therefore its reuse has not been possible in our development. The recommender is not available either. However, it was useful for the differentiation of some of our ontologies in the network (such as the server, hardware and network ontologies), and for the identification of some of the data and object properties that have been included in our ontologies for the classes in these ontologies.

Finally, the latest work that we have been able to find in this context is the one presented in [13], which is indeed closer to the type of work that we have performed, since it focuses on the representation of some of the entities that are commonly found in the CMDB databases, in the context of DevOps processes. This work claims the usage of OWL and SWRL for the implementation of the ontology, but does not describe the generated ontology in sufficient detail nor does it provide any link to the corresponding implementation.

7 Conclusions and Future Work

As discussed in the previous Section, a clear problem that we identified in this domain when starting the ontology development process was the lack of implementations of ontologies or common data models in this area, which may benefit from a comprehensive and systematic representation and publication of ontologies according to best practices in ontology implementation and publication. Indeed, the state of the art analysis has clearly revealed that only some partial efforts had been done in the past, and those did not result into a sustained effort afterwards for its maintenance.

Therefore, our aim has been to provide such a systematic approach that could lead into further standardisation work by putting together more organisations that have already shown interest in having common models for the representation of many of the types of entities and data that they are handling in this context.

In terms of impact, therefore, we consider that this work and its results can fill an important gap that has not been addressed sufficiently in the state of art. This would be as well a resource of interest for the Semantic Web community, in general, demonstrating how ontologies and semantic technologies can be used in an area where data heterogeneity exists and that could hence benefit from this type of approach.

We have not demonstrated yet any reuse of our ontology network, given that it has been only created recently. We expect, though, that there may be an interest in the context of standardisation and technical committees at IEEE and OASIS, as discussed earlier in this paper. As a result, we have already started contacting those that may be interested in this work, so as to show the potential advantages that such standardisation may bring in. Besides, the way in which the ontology network has been structured, together with the rich set of documentation provided for it, should facilitate such reuse and extensibility in the future, even for situations that have not been originally foreseen (product and service descriptions, root cause analysis, etc.).

The development has followed state-of-the-art practices in ontology development that we are applying in all of the ontology development projects that our group is involved in. This includes the LOT methodology and many of the ontology development support tools that we have been working on in the past years, and whose focus is to go further than just the implementation in OWL.

In terms of the availability, we cannot claim that our ontology network is yet completely FAIR compliant, especially considering that there is a strong debate in the state of the art on what the FAIR principles mean for ontologies (e.g., [16]), but we have at least followed what the community considers to be a good approach towards FAIRness: the ontology network is available in a permanent URI, thanks to w3id, it has an open license, all the resources are completely available online and in GitHub and archived in Zenodo (with a corresponding DOI). Indeed, at the time of writing, the usage of the FOOPS validator[10] provides a FAIRness score of 0.74.

References

1. Alobaid, A., Garijo, D., Poveda-Villalón, M., Santana-Perez, I., Fernández-Izquierdo, A., Corcho, O.: Automating ontology engineering support activities with OnToology. J. Web Semant. **57**, 100472 (2019)
2. AXELOS. ITIL Foundation: ITIL, 4th edn (2019)
3. Badenes-Olmedo, C., Redondo-García, J.L., Corcho, O.: Efficient clustering from distributions over topics. In: Proceedings of the Knowledge Capture Conference, K-CAP 2017. Association for Computing Machinery, New York (2017)

---

[10] https://foops.linkeddata.es/FAIR_validator.html.

4. BMC. Planning to populate BMC CMDB, version 20.08 (2020). https://docs.bmc. com/docs/ac2008/planning-to-populate-bmc-cmdb-929634733.html
5. Boasman-Patel, A., et al.: AIOps: a practical framework for AI driven operations in the telecom industry (2020). https://www.tmforum.org/resources/ whitepapers/ai-operations-a-practical-framework-for-ai-driven-operations-in-the-telecom-industry/
6. Corcho, O., et al.: DevOps infrastructure ontology network (2021). https://doi. org/10.5281/zenodo.4701264
7. Diefenbach, D., Lopez, V., Singh, K., Maret, P.: Core techniques of question answering systems over knowledge bases: a survey. Knowl. Inf. Syst. **55**(3), 529–569 (2018)
8. Dimou, A., Vander Sande, M., Colpaert, P., Verborgh, R., Mannens, E., Van de Walle, R.: RML: a generic language for integrated RDF mappings of heterogeneous data. In: LDOW (2014)
9. Distributed Management Task Force (DMTF) Inc., Configuration Management Database (CMDB) Federation Specification, version 1.0.1 (2010). https://www. dmtf.org/sites/default/files/standards/documents/dsp0252_1.0.1_0.pdf
10. Garijo, D.: WIDOCO: a wizard for documenting ontologies. In: d'Amato, C., et al. (eds.) ISWC 2017. LNCS, vol. 10588, pp. 94–102. Springer, Cham (2017). https:// doi.org/10.1007/978-3-319-68204-4_9
11. Heyvaert, P., De Meester, B., Dimou, A., Verborgh, R.: Declarative rules for linked data generation at your fingertips! In: Gangemi, A., et al. (eds.) ESWC 2018. LNCS, vol. 11155, pp. 213–217. Springer, Cham (2018). https://doi.org/10.1007/ 978-3-319-98192-5_40
12. Hoefer, C.N., Karagiannis, G.: Taxonomy of cloud computing services. In: 2010 IEEE Globecom Workshops, pp. 1345–1350 (2010)
13. McCarthy, M.A., Herger, L.M., Khan, S.M., Belgodere, B.M.: Composable DevOps: automated ontology based DevOps maturity analysis. In: 2015 IEEE International Conference on Services Computing, pp. 600–607, June 2015
14. Moscato, F., Aversa, R., Di Martino, B., Fortiş, T., Munteanu, V.: An analysis of mosaic ontology for cloud resources annotation. In: 2011 Federated Conference on Computer Science and Information Systems (FedCSIS), pp. 973–980 (2011)
15. Poveda-Villalón, M., Gómez-Pérez, A., Suárez-Figueroa, M.C.: OOPS! (OntOlogy pitfall scanner!): an on-line tool for ontology evaluation. Int. J. Semant. Web Inf. Syst. (IJSWIS) **10**(2), 7–34 (2014)
16. Poveda-Villalón, M., Espinoza-Arias, P., Garijo, D., Corcho, O.: Coming to terms with FAIR ontologies. In: Keet, C.M., Dumontier, M. (eds.) EKAW 2020. LNCS (LNAI), vol. 12387, pp. 255–270. Springer, Cham (2020). https://doi.org/10.1007/ 978-3-030-61244-3_18
17. Poveda-Villalón, M., Fernández-Izquierdo, A., Garcia-Castro, R.: Linked open terms (LOT) methodology (2019). https://doi.org/10.5281/zenodo.2539305
18. Suárez-Figueroa, M.C., Gómez-Pérez, A., Fernández-López, M.: The NeOn methodology for ontology engineering. In: Suárez-Figueroa, M.C., Gómez-Pérez, A., Motta, E., Gangemi, A. (eds.) Ontology Engineering in a Networked World, pp. 9–34. Springer, Heidelberg (2012). https://doi.org/10.1007/978-3-642-24794-1_2
19. The Open Group. The TOGAF standard, version 9.2 (2020). https://publications. opengroup.org/standards/togaf
20. Youseff, L., Butrico, M., Da Silva, D.: Toward a unified ontology of cloud computing. In: 2008 Grid Computing Environments Workshop, pp. 1–10 (2008)

21. Zafar, H., Napolitano, G., Lehmann, J.: Formal query generation for question answering over knowledge bases. In: Gangemi, A., et al. (eds.) ESWC 2018. LNCS, vol. 10843, pp. 714–728. Springer, Cham (2018). https://doi.org/10.1007/978-3-319-93417-4_46
22. Zhang, M., Ranjan, R., Haller, A., Georgakopoulos, D., Menzel, M., Nepal, S.: An ontology-based system for cloud infrastructure services' discovery. In: 8th International Conference on Collaborative Computing: Networking, Applications and Worksharing (CollaborateCom), pp. 524–530, October 2012

Chimera: A Bridge Between Big Data Analytics and Semantic Technologies

Matteo Belcao[1](✉), Emanuele Falzone[1](✉), Enea Bionda[2](✉),
and Emanuele Della Valle[1](✉)

[1] Politecnico di Milano, DEIB, Milan, Italy
matteo.belcao@mail.polimi.it,
{emanuele.falzone,emanuele.dellavalle}@polimi.it
[2] Ricerca sul Sistema Energetico - RSE S.p.A., Milan, Italy
enea.bionda@rse-web.it

Abstract. In the last decades, Knowledge Graph (KG) empowered analytics have been used to extract advanced insights from data. Several companies integrated legacy relational databases with semantic technologies using Ontology-Based Data Access (OBDA). In practice, this approach enables the analysts to write SPARQL queries both over KGs and SQL relational data sources by making transparent most of the implementation details. However, the volume of data is continuously increasing, and a growing number of companies are adopting distributed storage platforms and distributed computing engines. There is a gap between big data and semantic technologies. Ontop, one of the reference OBDA systems, is limited to legacy relational databases, and the compatibility with the big data analytics engine Apache Spark is still missing. This paper introduces Chimera, an open-source software suite that aims at filling such a gap. Chimera enables a new type of *round-tripping* data science pipelines. Data Scientists can query data stored in a data lake using SPARQL through Ontop and SparkSQL while saving the semantic results of such analysis back in the data lake. This new type of pipelines semantically enriches data from Spark before saving them back.

Keywords: Ontology based data access · Semantic technologies · Big data · Apache spark · Knowledge graph · Analytics

1 Introduction

The fast growth of the analytic sector of these years and the exponential increment of the data volumes lead to the massive adoption of new large-scale analytics engines to store and process large volumes of relational data. At the same time, semantic reasoning on domain ontologies allowed for gathering advanced insights on heterogeneous data.

Until nowadays, these two worlds were totally separated. As depicted in Fig. 1, the Knowledge Engineers (KEs) use the Web Ontology Language (OWL) to design Knowledge Graphs (KGs), which capture the knowledge of the domain experts, and store them in RDF Repositories. On the contrary, Data Engineers

© Springer Nature Switzerland AG 2021
A. Hotho et al. (Eds.): ISWC 2021, LNCS 12922, pp. 463–479, 2021.
https://doi.org/10.1007/978-3-030-88361-4_27

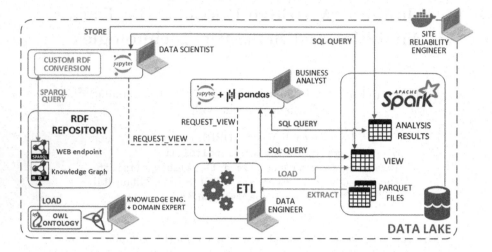

Fig. 1. The classical analytical pipeline involving manual ETL operations and custom SPARQL integration.

(DEs) ingest and store relational data in data lakes and create and maintain ETLs for Business Analysts (BAs) and Data Scientists (DS). DSs, who want to perform KG-empowered analytics, have to combine manually 1. semantic data, coming from SPARQL queries evaluated over KGs, and 2. relational data, coming from SQL queries performed over the data lake. The BAs need to read and analyze both the raw data in the data lake and DSs' analysis results. Furthermore, the Site Reliability Engineers (SREs) experience difficulty maintaining infrastructure efficiency, ensuring performance and scalability.

This scenario resembles several problems. First of all, the ETL tasks are problem-dependent: whenever a DS or a BA needs to perform a new analytical query, they ask DEs for a new ETL. Each ETL may require several days of work and many meetings between DEs and analysts. Moreover, the DSs have to persist their analysis results in the data lake to make them available for the BAs. Furthermore, only a combination of multiple tools can achieve such a result.

In the past decades, the scientific community focused on researching new methodologies to combine the advantages of relational databases and the reasoning capabilities offered by ontologies. The research effort led to the definition of the Ontology-Based Data Access (OBDA) paradigm [2,20]. OBDA offers users a conceptual layer that abstracts specific aspects related to the data source using a convenient query vocabulary. In this way, the OBDA paradigm lowers the complexity of data analysis tasks. It enables domain experts to create analytical queries without the need for advanced SQL knowledge or data professionals' help. DSs and BAs can write queries over an ontology that makes transparent the task of retrieving data from several tables and joining them.

Nowadays, among the OBDA systems [4,13,17] Ontop [3] is one of the first to be offered as a commercial solution[1]. Ontop's current scope is relational

---

[1] Ontop project: https://ontop-vkg.org, Ontopic company: https://ontopic.biz/.

databases. Several real-world users cannot benefit from Ontop to integrate data stored in data lakes that engines such as Apache Spark [23] can process.

The scientific literature documents several attempts to integrate Ontop in real large-scale analytics projects. Statoil [8] and Siemens Energy [9] implemented OBDA solutions for performing analytical queries in big data scenarios by using custom implementations of Ontop. Moreover, the University of New South Wales [22] developed a system for inferring diabetes on new potential patients using reasoning over their EHRs (E-Health Records) accessed via Ontop. However, a reusable framework is still missing.

In this paper, we present Chimera[2], a software suite that aims at better connecting the big data world with semantic technologies. It provides components for enabling KG-empowered analytics to scale to big data technologies, using Apache Spark [23] as a query processing engine for accessing the data stored in a data lake. The Chimera suite is composed of: 1. Ontop$_{Spark}$, an extended version of Ontop that allows formulating SPARQL queries over an Apache Spark cluster, and 2. PySPARQL, a python library that can materialize a SPARQL response as a Spark DataFrame or a GraphFrame.

Chimera introduces new possibilities for implementing *round-trip* data analysis pipelines. Those pipelines query the data lake with SPARQL to get a semantically enriched response by leveraging Ontop and materialize the responses as new Spark tables to query in another iteration (namely, *trip*). Notably, *round-trip* pipelines require to combine both Ontop$_{Spark}$ and PySPARQL. As a result, companies that already have Apache Spark as an analytical engine and would like to use ontologies to improve their analysis, but complain about the complexity of managing the integration of several tools, can integrate semantic technologies into their business processes.

The paper is structured as follows. Section 2 shows the most adopted OBDA technologies and their advancements in supporting big data technologies. Section 3 formalizes the requirements that we elicited, while Sect. 4 illustrates Chimera. Section 5 describes a running example that showcases the components' capabilities in an IoT scenario, and Sect. 6 illustrates a real industrial deployment of Chimera. Section 7 discusses related work. Finally, Sect. 8 concludes, discussing future developments and maintenance plans.

2   Ontology Based Data Access

The OBDA paradigm enables creating analytical SPARQL queries based on data physically stored in relational formats by writing queries over an ontology that makes transparent the task of retrieving data from several SQL tables.

The most successful OBDA systems are Mastro [4], UltraWrap [17], Morph-RDB [13], and Ontop. All of them support the connection over JDBC to legacy relational databases. Ontop and Mastro are also available as Protégé plugins.

Specifically, Ontop [3] is one of the first to be offered as a commercial solution. It enables to perform data integration by exposing relational databases as Virtual

---

[2] https://chimera-suite.github.io/.

Knowledge Graph (VKG) [21]. The VKG mechanism allows creating an RDF representation of relational data without allocating additional space. All the data remains in its original format and location. This approach enables Ontop to avoid triple materialization. It answers SPARQL queries by directly translating them into SQL queries over the data sources However, VKGs support is limited to ontologies expressed in OWL2QL. This expressivity does not forbid users to use more expressive OWL2 profiles. Users interested in doing so shall use another reasoner (e.g., Hermit) to materialize T-box and A-box inference. And they shall store the resulting KG in an RDF repository that supports SPARQL 1.1 Federation Queries[3]. In this way, the RDF repository SPARQL endpoint can answer queries that refer to the KG and the relational data accessed via OBDA using the VKG approach. As we will explain, Chimera requires identifying a subset of the KG's T-Box to use in Ontop as a *DB-descriptive ontology*.

Ontop supports all the W3C standards related to OBDA, and comes in different distributions. The most popular are the Protégé extension and the *Ontop-CLI*, which offers both a web and a terminal interface.

To perform the VKG translations, the Ontop engine needs a set of user-defined RDF-to-SQL mappings expressed in R2RML or in the Ontop mapping language [3]. R2RML is a W3C standard language for expressing bindings from SQL tuples to RDF triples, and Ontop already integrates the mapping engine. The other viable option is to write the mapping using the Ontop native mapping language, which has a more compact notation than R2RML. Each of such mappings consists of a source SQL query, and an RDF triple target with placeholders for the values of the attributes of the source query [2]. If the SQL mapping query involves aggregate operators (e.g., `AVG()`) with a `GROUP BY` clause, the endpoint automatically instantiates an intermediate view layer between the database and the Virtual Knowledge Graphs. However, the mappings involving an intermediate layer must have the data types explicitly stated.

Ontop needs three files to respond to SPARQL queries by building the corresponding VKGs: 1. an ontology file (usually .owl or .ttl) containing the ontological concepts in OWL2QL profile needed by the Ontop reasoner, 2. a configuration file for correctly instantiating a JDBC connection to the database, and 3. a mapping file for the RDF-to-SQL translation of the VKGs.

3   Requirements

This section presents our requirement analysis. The goal of Chimera is to build a general framework applicable to a variety of industrial scenarios. Chimera shall improve the support of KG-empowered analytical solutions to big data and enable the creation of *round-tripping* data pipelines. Therefore, Chimera has to be scalable and problem-agnostic to encourage the adoption of many companies.

The developed solution should fulfill the following requirements, which Table 1 maps to the respective actors:

R.1 Scalability: it must be possible to instantiate any component of the solution many times on different machines, according to the user's needs.

---

[3] https://www.w3.org/TR/sparql11-federated-query/.

R2 Generality and Abstraction: the solution must be problem-agnostic so that a broad set of industrial scenarios can benefit from it.

R3 Ease of Deployment: the solution must be available as a Docker image, enabling easy deployment and configuration with Docker.

R4 Industrial Adoption: The solution's deployment must be based on industrially supported software to ensure support, documentation, and updated over time.

R5 Notebooks support: several data analysis libraries are available for python hence the solution must allow executing and managing SPARQL queries from Jupyter notebooks.

R6 Standards Compliance: the solution must adhere to SPARQL 1.1 standards. The Knowledge Graph has to be modeled using OWL2 standards. The DB-descriptive ontology in Ontop must be in the OWL2QL profile. The mapping of SQL datatypes to XML Schema datatypes must be compliant with the W3C recommendations and support R2RML mapping language.

R7 Semantic access to data: the relational data must be exposed to the RDF world by adopting an OBDA approach. In particular, it must be possible to access both the starting relational tables and the results of the analyzes.

R8 Semantic results persisted: it must be possible to persist the results of the data analyzes, which are built upon SPARQL query results, in the data lake.

R9 Ease of configuration: The solution must be easy to configure. Furthermore, it must be easy to instantiate a notebook connection to both the SPARQL endpoint and the big data engine.

Table 1. Requirements matrix

Requirement	KE	BA	DS	DE	SRE
R1 Scalability	X	X	X	X	X
R2 Generality and Abstraction	X				X
R3 Ease of Deployment					X
R4 Industrial Adoption					X
R5 Notebooks support		X	X		
R6 Standards Compliance	X	X	X	X	
R7 Semantic access to data	X	X	X	X	
R8 Semantic results persisted	X		X		
R9 Ease of configuration	X			X	

4   Chimera

The requirements listed in Sect. 3 led to Chimera's design and development. Indeed, Chimera enables performing KG-empowered analysis using python notebooks: Ontop$_{Spark}$ allows running SPARQL queries over a Spark instance, while PySPARQL allows for managing a SPARQL result in Spark.

Section 4.1 illustrates the *round-tripping* analysis while depicting Chimera's infrastructure. Section 4.2 and Sect. 4.3 provide a detailed description of Ontop$_{Spark}$ and PySPARQL, respectively.

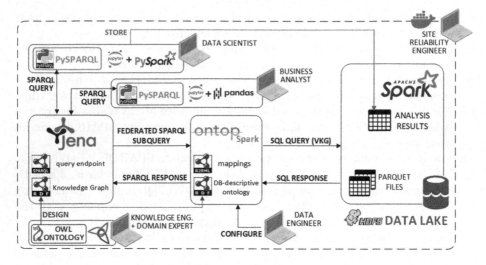

Fig. 2. The interaction between the components of the infrastructure.

4.1 Infrastructure

DSs and BAs can adopt the Chimera components into their data-science pipeline to perform KG-empowered analysis tasks. A reference deployment is available on GitHub[4] where users can find a series of docker-compose files that allows for easily integrating Chimera in existing big data infrastructures[5].

In particular, using Ontop$_{Spark}$ and PySPARQL, it is possible to accomplish what we have previously called *round-trip* analysis (R7). To better understand the *round-trip* process, it is crucial to know where the information sources are. Consider Fig. 2. The data lake is a Spark warehouse made of several Apache Parquet[6] files distributed on HDFS[7] and managed as Spark tables. Multiple servers assure the needed degree of parallelization (R1). A Spark Thrift Server exposes a JDBC endpoint that allows users to send SQL queries to the SparkSQL[8] engine, which, in turn, generates code to process the data in the data lake. On the other hand, the semantic data is stored according to the functionality it provides. Jena Fuseki[9] stores the Knowledge Graph and Ontop the DB-descriptive ontology. Notably, we chose HDFS and Jena Fuseki for our convenience, but Chimera users are free to choose alternatives. They can change HDFS in any other distributed file system as long as Apache Spark supports it (R4). Moreover, they can adopt any other RDF repository instead of Jena Fuseki, as long as it complies with SPARQL 1.1 (R2).

---

[4] https://github.com/chimera-suite/infrastructure.

[5] Chimera supports several Spark versions, starting from 2.4.0 to 3.1.1. Users can change the version by selecting the appropriate image tags.

[6] https://parquet.apache.org/.

[7] https://hadoop.apache.org/.

[8] https://spark.apache.org/sql/.

[9] https://jena.apache.org/documentation/fuseki2/.

The DSs can write their analytical SPARQL queries on notebooks (R5) using PySPARQL, which sends them to Jena Fuseki. The query part inside the SERVICE clause, known as *federated query*, is resolved by Ontop$_{Spark}$ using the OBDA approach, which retrieves the data from Spark and translates the SQL responses into RDF triples using the R2RML mapping file (R6) and the DB-descriptive ontology. Once the triples are back from Ontop$_{Spark}$, Jena Fuseki has to enrich them by using the Knowledge Graph and send back the results to the notebook (R7). At this point, the result is available to the user in the form of Spark DataFrame or GraphFrame, which can be further analyzed using the notebook and, if necessary, persisted in the data lake (R8) by executing a PySPARQL function. The materialization task ends the *round-trip* circle. The DSs can start a new analysis iteration if needed.

DSs and BAs can also issue SPARQL queries to the Fuseki or the Ontop$_{Spark}$ endpoints (R2), but, in this way, they lose the opportunity to materialize the data in new Spark tables, hence to use the available data science libraries.

The following two sections detail Ontop$_{Spark}$ and PySPARQL showing their architecture and explaining how to employ them for KG-empowered analysis.

4.2 Ontop$_{Spark}$

The Ontop$_{Spark}$ extension enables Ontop to perform OBDA on relational data using Apache Spark. Given in input the mappings between RDF statements and SparkSQL queries, it is possible to submit SPARQL queries (R6) to the Ontop endpoint and obtain a response from SparkSQL based on the tables that form the data lake (R7). The integration of a distributed data processing engine such as Apache Spark allows exploiting the Ontop data integration capabilities at its maximum potential because it brings all the advantages of parallel and distributed computation to the task of answering a SPARQL query.

Ontop$_{Spark}$ performs SparkSQL queries by interacting with the Spark Thrift Server through standard JDBC calls. For this extension, we decided to use a third-party JDBC driver[10]. The extension work mainly consists of implementing seven Java classes, which we inserted inside the Ontop source code in the *ontop-rdb* package that contains all the extensions for the supported relational databases. First of all, we implemented the *SparkSQLDBMetadataProvider* that reads the database metadata by interacting with the JDBC driver. It was hard to implement because none of the drivers we explored have full support for all standard JDBC calls. In the end, it has been necessary to retrieve the default schema and the metadata. Other relevant implemented classes are the *Spark-SQLDBTypeFactory* and the *SparkSQLDBFunctionSymbolFactory*. The first one has been tested to be compliant with the W3C recommendations[11](R6), while the second one translates SPARQL functions into SparkSQL functions.

Ontop$_{Spark}$ was developed according to the Ontop official guidelines[12] (R4) to ease the integration in the original codebase and is available under the Apache

---

[10] https://repo1.maven.org/maven2/org/apache/hive/hive-jdbc/.

[11] https://www.w3.org/2001/sw/rdb2rdf/wiki.

[12] https://ontop-vkg.org/dev/db-adapter.html#required-implementations.

License 2.0. Furthermore, it supports R2RML (R9) mappings and all the W3C standards related to OBDA of the Ontop project [2] (R6).

Ontop$_{Spark}$ is available in two different packages, namely *Ontop$_{Spark}$-Protege* and *Ontop$_{Spark}$-CLI*. The first one is an extension that allows building ontologies and mappings using the graphical interface of Protégé (R2, R4), while the second exposes a SPARQL endpoint (web GUI or CLI) used for industrial deployment (R4). We use the *Ontop$_{Spark}$-CLI* package for building a Docker image (R1, R3) that is freely available on DockerHub[13]. To complete the project and make it readily available to the adopters, we have also created a GitHub repository[14] containing the Ontop$_{Spark}$ source code and documentation.

4.3 PySPARQL

The `PySPARQL` module allows the users to query a SPARQL endpoint and process the response inside Apache Spark (R7). `PySPARQL` leverages `pyspark`[15] to manage Spark DataFrames, and uses well known libraries such as `SPARQLWrapper`[16] and `rdflib`[17] to handle the communication with a SPARQL endpoint and manage the result, respectively (R6). We tested the module with multiple Spark versions. `PySPARQL` is available on PyPi[18], and interested readers can access its code, tests, and a comprehensive documentation on its public git repository[19]. It is released under Apache License 2.0. Hereafter, we briefly discuss how it works. You can find a concrete code example in Sect. 5.

`PySPARQL` takes in input a SPARQL query as a python string and executes the query against the configured SPARQL endpoint. The library retrieves the results and materializes them inside the configured Spark Session. Users shall specify the endpoint configuration at initialization time and change it during the program execution (R9). In particular, the output type directly depends on the SPARQL query type. `SELECT` queries return Spark DataFrames in which the columns directly correspond to the variables declared in the SPARQL query (R2). However, `PySPARQL` does not convert the value types. The users can then process the DataFrame inside Spark and, if necessary, save the DataFrame as a Spark table (R8). `CONSTRUCT` queries return either a DataFrame or a Graph-Frame depending on what the user chooses to materialize. In both cases the data resemble the constructed graph (R2). In particular, `PySPARQL` can materialize three types of DataFrame:

- TiplesDataFrame: it contains the triples of the constructed graph. It has three columns corresponding to `?subject` , `?object` and `?predicate` .

---

[13] https://hub.docker.com/r/chimerasuite/ontop.
[14] https://github.com/chimera-suite/OntopSpark.
[15] https://spark.apache.org/docs/3.0.1/api/python/.
[16] https://sparqlwrapper.readthedocs.io/.
[17] https://rdflib.readthedocs.io/.
[18] https://pypi.org/project/PySPARQL/.
[19] https://github.com/chimera-suite/PySPARQL.

- VertexDataFrame: it contains the literals associated with each vertex of the constructed graph. It has an ID column reporting the Internationalized Resource Identifier (IRI) of the vertex and a variable number of columns. Each column represents the IRI of the predicate that relates the vertex to a literal.
- EdgesDataFrame: it contains the relationships between vertexes. It has three columns reporting to source vertex, relationship, and target vertex IRIs.

The VextexDataFrame and EdgesDataFrame are combined to construct a GraphFrame. The user can choose the preferred output type, and the materialization happens at runtime (R1). The users can then process the results inside Spark and, optionally, save the DataFrame inside a Spark table (R8).

At the time of writing, PySPARQL only supports SELECT and CONSTRUCT queries. However, we plan to support ASK and DESCRIBE queries in a future release. PySPARQL is included in the Chimera Jupyter notebook (R5), published on Dockerhub[20] (R3).

5 Running Example

This section presents a minimal use-case of IoT anomaly detection using an extended version of the Stanford pizza ontology[21] [12]. Section 5.1 introduces the scenario, while Sect. 5.2 shows how to handle Chimera to make a *round-tripping* analysis pipeline. We published an extended version of this section as a tutorial on GitHub[22].

5.1 Scenario

PizzaInternational is a restaurant chain with many locations worldwide. To achieve a high-quality standard in all the restaurants, PizzaInternational installed new advanced ovens that integrate IoT sensors. Consequently, to accommodate the growing volumes of data produced by the ovens, they updated the IT infrastructure. It now resembles the one depicted in Fig. 2. The ovens' observations, such as temperature and cooking time, are stored in a data lake built upon HDFS and Apache Spark. As it often happens in Industry 4.0 projects, multiple Spark tables contain information about the observations of the pizzas cooked in the restaurants. Moreover, those tables have a different schema. A Spark JDBC endpoint, exposed by the Apache Thrift Server, allows users to query the data lake using SparkSQL queries.

A knowledge engineer team selected the Pizza Ontology and asked Peppo, a famous Neapolitan pizza chef, to add the optimal cooking parameters. Figure 3 illustrates a portion of the pizza Knowledge Graph. Each kind of pizza has its temperature and cooking time annotations. For example, according to Peppo's

---

[20] https://hub.docker.com/r/chimerasuite/jupyter-notebook.
[21] https://protege.stanford.edu/ontologies/pizza/pizza.owl.
[22] https://github.com/chimera-suite/use-case.

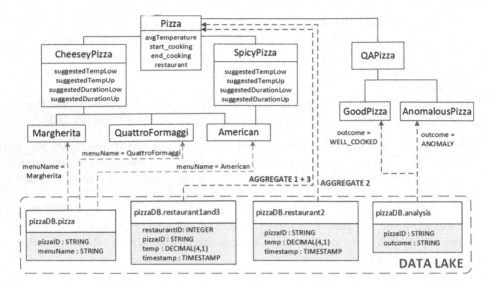

Fig. 3. Portion of the pizza ontology. The mappings are the dashed coloured lines.

experience, restaurants shall cook a *CheeseyPizza* at low temperatures to avoid burning the cheese. In contrast, they can cook a *SpicyPizza* with higher temperatures, but for a shorter period. As a consequence, some pizzas have cooking suggestions inherited from multiple classes of pizzas. For instance, an *American* pizza is both a *CheeseyPizza* and a *SpicyPizza*. It is correct to cook it adhering to both the *CheeseyPizza* and *SpicyPizza* cooking suggestions. Consequently, precise small ranges of cooking temperatures and duration should be satisfied to obtain a "WELL COOKED" *American* pizza, both from a *CheeseyPizza* and *SpicyPizza* perspective. The team stored the resulting Knowledge Graph in Apache Jena and exposed a SPARQL endpoint using Fuseki.

Being PizzaInternational a data-driven company, the executives are interested in exploiting the collected data to check the cooking performance across all the restaurants. Given such a requirement, the central branch's DSs have decided to make an explorative analysis of the cooking quality across all the restaurants and save those results inside Spark tables for the BAs, who needs to create a report for the executives showing which are the most critical restaurants. In the following section, we discuss how the adoption of Chimera can ease such a result.

5.2 Solution

The first part of this section shows how to configure the pipeline and write a notebook that sends analytical SPARQL queries to Jena Fuseki using PySPARQL. The last part shows how to persist a Spark DataFrame in the data lake and retrieve it again on a second iteration plotting data in a notebook.

```
mappingId    temperature-example
target       :{pizzaID} :temperature {temperature}^^xsd:decimal .
source       SELECT pizzaID, AVG(temp) AS temperature
             FROM pizzaDB.restaurant2 GROUP BY pizzaID
```

Listing 1.1. Example of Ontop aggregate mapping.

```
SELECT ?pizzaID ?outcome
WHERE {
  ?pizzaType :suggestedTempLow ?tempLow; :suggestedDurationLow ?durLow;
             :suggestedTempUp ?tempUp; :suggestedDurationUp ?durUp .
  SERVICE <http://ontop:8080/sparql> {
        ?pizzaID a ?pizzaType; :temperature ?avgTemp;
        ?pizzaID :start_cooking ?start; :end_cooking ?end. }
  BIND ((?end-?start) AS ?cookDuration)
  BIND( IF ((?avgTemp >= ?tempLow && ?avgTemp <= ?tempUp) &&
            (?cookDuration >= ?durLow && ?cookDuration <= ?durUp)
            ,"WELL_COOKED","ANOMALY") AS ?outcome) }
```

Listing 1.2. SPARQL query and results storage in a Spark table

To use Ontop$_{Spark}$, the DEs, together with the KEs, have to define some configuration files. In particular, they have to create a DB-descriptive ontology for describing the Spark tables data and to define the mappings between SQL and RDF that the Ontop reasoner will process to create the VKGs. Since the restaurants' table schemas are different, there is a need for multiple mappings. For example, in Fig. 3, the mapping *AGGREGATE 1+3* is different from *AGGREGATE 2*. For this example, we choose to use the Ontop native mapping language. Listing 1.1 shows a mapping that transforms a SQL aggregation, which returns the average cooking temperatures for each pizza in an assertion of the observed temperature for each pizza.

The way that Ontop manages this particular mapping deserves special attention: if the SQL statement involves aggregate operators such as `Count()` and `AVG()` with a `GROUP BY` clause, the Ontop automatically instantiates an intermediate view layer between the database and the VKGs.

The DSs, who are familiar with notebooks and python, use `PySPARQL` to express the analytical query in SPARQL and retrieve the results as a Spark DataFrame. This approach ensures flexibility because they can use any python data science library while benefitting from Peppo's experience captured in the KG. Using the code in Listings 1.2 and 1.3, the DSs retrieve the anomalous pizzas and store the results in a Spark table.

Notably, Ontop$_{Spark}$ answers the part of the query inside the `SERVICE` clause using the VKG approach. It retrieves the tuples stored in the Spark tables by making SparkSQL queries and translating the results into instances and assertions using the SQL-to-RDF mappings. Also, the KG stored in Jena Fuseki enriches the Ontop$_{Spark}$ result by adding semantic information. In the exam-

```
wrapper = PySPARQLWrapper(spark_session, fuseki_url)
resultDF = wrapper.query(query).dataFrame
resultDF.write.mode("overwrite").saveAsTable("pizzadb.analysis")
```

Listing 1.3. SPARQL query and results storage in a Spark table

```
SELECT (COUNT(?anomalous)/(COUNT(?pizzaChecked)) as ?count) ?
    restaurant
WHERE {
    SERVICE <http://ontop:8080/sparql> {
        {?anomalous a :AnomalousPizza; :restaurant ?restaurant.}
        UNION
        {?pizzaChecked a :QAPizza; :restaurant ?restaurant.} }
} GROUP BY ?restaurant
```

Listing 1.4. SPARQL query in the notebook for finding the anomalous pizzas

ple depicted in Listing 1.2, the *federated query* retrieves the pizza instances from Spark tables with average temperatures and starting/ending cooking times. Moreover, the remaining part of the query uses the KG to express the decision rules in the `BIND` clause to determine the pizza quality outcome. Furthermore, in the example, the `:American` pizzas instances are both `:CheeseyPizza` and `:SpicyPizza`, so it is correct to cook them according to the optimal parameters asserted for both the classes. Consequently, some `:American` pizzas are `"WELL COOKED"` for the `:CheeseyPizza` class but not for the `:SpicyPizza` class and vice versa. Completed the analysis, the DSs can use the code depicted in Listing 1.3 to publish the results as a Spark table for the BAs.

The BAs are interested in creating a histogram that shows the most critical restaurants. In this case, they need both the DSs results from the first *round-trip* iteration and the original restaurants' data, which relates pizzas to restaurants. Spark tables store both the information. Listing 1.4 shows the `PySPARQL` code that executes the SPARQL query that retrieves the anomalous pizzas for each restaurant. It refers to the pizzas' quality concepts present in the KG.

Fuseki and Ontop$_{Spark}$ manage the query procedure as in the previous example. However, this time the BAs does not store the results in a Spark table. They use a *barplot* to prepare the visualization in Fig. 4 for the executives.

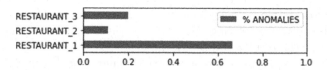

Fig. 4. The % of anomalous pizzas for each restaurant

6   Real World Deployment

Ricerca sul Sistema Energetico S.p.A.[23] (RSE) is the largest Italian public company for industrial research in the energy sector. They used Chimera to develop a solution [1] for monitoring the cables' energy workloads in the Milan city's Unareti[24] distribution network.

RSE developed a KG containing around 7 million triples representing Milan's metropolitan area. It used the methodology presented in [18] and the vocabulary specified in the IEC 61968/61970 and 62325-A standards, which the energy sector calls the Common Information Model (CIM) [19]. The KG stores the network topology and all the information about the various pieces of electrical equipment. From a bird view, nodes represent thousands of power providers, consumers, switches, breakers, etc., whereas links represent tens of thousands of conducting equipment connecting them.

Moreover, RSE collected a power load dataset containing more than 300 million time-series entries, stored it in Amazon S3, and uses the managed Spark offered by Databricks[25] as a data analytics platform.

RSE adopted Chimera because it was searching for a solution able to reduce the friction between big data and semantic technologies. In particular, RSE stated the following two requirements: 1. Let the DS team make analytical predictions in Databricks by querying both the Knowledge Graph and the big data repository. 2. Let the KE team make SPARQL queries to access the CIM network graph and retrieve the results of the Data Scientists' analysis.

Thanks to the current deployment of Chimera, RSE DSs and KEs can now build complex *round-tripping* data analysis pipelines. RSE's DSs can use PySPARQL in Databricks notebooks to write analytical SPARQL queries that use Ontop$_{Spark}$ to access both the KG and the time-series stored in Databricks. Moreover, they can save the resulting DataFrames as Spark tables so that RSE's KEs can leverage them in another round of analysis.

7   Related Work

The literature reports several attempts to applying distributed big data processing technologies to improve SPARQL queries' analytical capabilities.

Optique [6], a project funded by the European Commission's Seventh Framework Program (FP7), was the first successful endeavor to create an OBDA system designed for big data scenarios. The Optique underlying architecture mainly uses 1. Ontop, which manages the OBDA data access using R2RML mappings, and 2. Exareme [5], which acts as a back-end query execution component handling large-scale data processing tasks. Unfortunately, Exareme is more a research prototype than an industry-adopted software. Furthermore, it lacks the parallelization capabilities of a big data processing engine such as Apache

---

[23] http://www.rse-web.it/.
[24] https://www.unareti.it/.
[25] https://databricks.com/.

Spark [23]. Differently from Optique, Chimera opts for notebook centrality and proposes PySPARQL as a bridge between SPARQL and Spark. Other OBDA systems such as Mastro [4], UltraWrap [17], and Morph-RDB [13] are not involved in relevant projects supporting Apache Spark.

Ontop$_{Spark}$ uses a relatively small KG to access massive volumes of data not initially designed for being translated as RDF triples using the OBDA approach. To be noticed that Ontop$_{Spark}$ is not a distributed RDF datastore based on Apache Spark; thus, we have excluded from our comparison systems like SHARD [14] and PigSPARQL [15]. The more recent SPARQLGX [7] and S2RDF [16] distributed SPARQL evaluators, despite using Apache Spark as a query engine and a mapping mechanism called Virtual Partitioning, store data in Spark tables with a rigid structure that is similar to an RDF triplestore.

Semantic ANalytics StAck (SANSA) [10] is a scalable big data engine for RDF processing that uses Apache Spark and Flink as query engines. In particular, they developed Squerall [11], an OBDA tool that allows querying several SQL databases by using Spark as a wrapper for making SPARQL-to-SQL conversions. We have identified SANSA as Chimera's main competitor, as the latter tool claims to offer the same features. In building Chimera, we bid on extending Ontop because of its broad and active GitHub community and the recent start of a commercial offering. We hope to benefit from an OBDA engine that will mature update after update.

To demonstrate the differences between the two solutions, we ran a series of tests[26]. The comparison dataset has been taken from the official Sansa-stack repo[27] and comprises five CSV files inspired by the BSBM[28] benchmark. We used the nine original testing queries of SANSA (Q1 to Q10, Q9 not available) plus two additional SPARQL queries to highlight the differences between Ontop$_{Spark}$ and Squerall. Since Ontop$_{Spark}$ needs an Ontology for running, we needed to adjust the SANSA's mappings accordingly.

Figure 5 demonstrates that the query execution times are comparable (we run each query 10 times). The differences between the two solutions are probably related to design implementation choices. Ontop$_{Spark}$ was unable to execute the query Q6 (missing implementation of the *regex()* function) and Q10 because the query made by Squerall violates the RDF entailment regime of SPARQL; it asks for triples whose subject is a literal. However, thanks to the integrated reasoner and the full compliance with the RDF syntax and OWL2QL standard, Ontop$_{Spark}$ has been able to execute query Q(?s ?p), which retrieves all the subjects and predicates given a fixed object, and query Q(?s ?p ?o), which retrieves the full RDF materialization of the dataset under OWL2QL *entailment regime*. The queries achieved an average execution time of 12.7 sec for Q(?s ?p) and 183 sec for Q(?s ?p ?o), respectively. It was not possible to execute the two queries mentioned above with Squerall.

---

[26] https://github.com/chimera-suite/OntopSpark-evaluation.

[27] https://github.com/SANSA-Stack/SANSA-Stack/tree/develop/sansa-query/
sansa-query-spark/src/test/resources/datalake.

[28] http://wifo5-03.informatik.uni-mannheim.de/bizer/berlinsparqlbenchmark/.

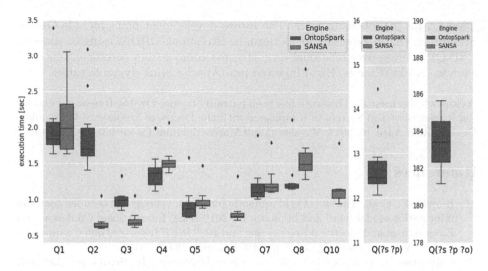

Fig. 5. Query execution times comparison wrt. Squerall(SANSA)

8   Conclusions and Future Work

This paper presents Chimera[29], an open-source software suite for KG-empowered analytics tasks in big data scenarios. Chimera allows querying a Spark data lake with SPARQL using Ontop$_{Spark}$ to get a semantically enriched response by leveraging reasoning on a KG. Also, python notebook users can leverage PySPARQL to automatically get the SPARQL query response converted in a Spark DataFrame/GraphFrame, which can be further analyzed using the notebook and persisted into Spark on need. Even if they are two separated components, the synergy between them enables building *round-tripping* pipelines where semantic technologies enrich data going back and forth from Spark.

To provide evidence of the benefits of Chimera, we presented two scenarios where the integration of big data technologies with an OBDA approach helps solving analytical problems. In particular, we presented a running example that demonstrates the technology in a relevant environment showing how to perform *round-trip* analysis using Chimera. Moreover, we presented a real-world deployment, which proves the usage of Chimera in an operational environment.

All the Chimera's components are available on GitHub[30]: Ontop$_{Spark}$ (we opened a pull request[31] and merged the code into Ontop) and PySPARQL. We also published the Docker images of Ontop$_{Spark}$ and Chimera Jupyter notebook, which integrates PySPARQL, on Dockerhub[32]. Thanks to RSE co-founding and Politecnico di Milano's resources, we are committed to maintain ad improve

---

[29] https://chimera-suite.github.io/.
[30] https://github.com/chimera-suite.
[31] https://github.com/ontop/ontop/pull/422.
[32] https://hub.docker.com/u/chimerasuite.

Chimera for the following years. The future development plans include Ontop-Stream, an Ontop extension for performing Streaming-OBDA, using continuous RSP-QL queries, over relational data streams coming from heterogeneous data sources (Kafka, Kinesis, Hive) ingested into Apache Flink dynamic tables.

Acknowledgements. This work has been partially financed by the Research Fund for the Italian Electrical System in compliance with the Decree of Minister of Economical Development April 16, 2018. We also thank Marco Balduini for initiating Chimera.

References

1. Bionda, E., et al.: The smart grid semantic platform: synergy between iec common information model (cim) and big data. In: 2019 IEEE International Conference on Environment and Electrical Engineering and 2019 IEEE Industrial and Commercial Power Systems Europe (EEEIC/I&CPS Europe). IEEE (2019)
2. Calvanese, D., et al.: OBDA with the ontop framework. In: SEBD, pp. 296–303. Curran Associates, Inc. (2015)
3. Calvanese, D., et al.: Ontop: answering SPARQL queries over relational databases. Semant. Web **8**(3), 471–487 (2017)
4. Calvanese, D., et al.: The MASTRO system for ontology-based data access. Semant. Web **2**(1), 43–53 (2011)
5. Chronis, Y., et al.: A relational approach to complex dataflows. In: EDBT/ICDT Workshops. CEUR Workshop Proceedings, vol. 1558. CEUR-WS.org (2016)
6. Giese, M., et al.: Optique: zooming in on big data. Computer **48**(3), 60–67 (2015)
7. Graux, D., Jachiet, L., Genevès, P., Layaïda, N.: SPARQLGX: efficient distributed evaluation of SPARQL with apache spark. In: Groth, P., et al. (eds.) ISWC 2016. LNCS, vol. 9982, pp. 80–87. Springer, Cham (2016). https://doi.org/10.1007/978-3-319-46547-0_9
8. Kharlamov, E., et al.: Ontology based data access in statoil. J. Web Semant. **44**, 3–36 (2017)
9. Kharlamov, E., et al.: Semantic access to streaming and static data at siemens. J. Web Semant. **44**, 54–74 (2017)
10. Lehmann, J., et al.: Distributed semantic analytics using the SANSA stack. In: d'Amato, C., et al. (eds.) ISWC 2017. LNCS, vol. 10588, pp. 147–155. Springer, Cham (2017). https://doi.org/10.1007/978-3-319-68204-4_15
11. Mami, M.N., Graux, D., Scerri, S., Jabeen, H., Auer, S., Lehmann, J.: Squerall: virtual ontology-based access to heterogeneous and large data sources. In: Ghidini, C., et al. (eds.) ISWC 2019. LNCS, vol. 11779, pp. 229–245. Springer, Cham (2019). https://doi.org/10.1007/978-3-030-30796-7_15
12. Noy, N.F., McGuinness, D.L., et al.: Ontology development 101: A guide to creating your first ontology (2001)
13. Priyatna, F., Corcho, Ó., Sequeda, J.F.: Formalisation and experiences of r2rml-based SPARQL to SQL query translation using morph. In: WWW, pp. 479–490. ACM (2014)
14. Rohloff, K., Schantz, R.E.: High-performance, massively scalable distributed systems using the mapreduce software framework: the SHARD triple-store. In: PSI EtA, p. 4. ACM (2010)
15. Schätzle, A., Przyjaciel-Zablocki, M., Lausen, G.: Pigsparql: mapping SPARQL to pig latin. In: SWIM, p. 4. ACM (2011)

16. Schätzle, A., Przyjaciel-Zablocki, M., Skilevic, S., Lausen, G.: S2RDF: RDF querying with SPARQL on spark. Proc. VLDB Endow. **9**(10), 804–815 (2016)
17. Sequeda, J.F., Miranker, D.P.: Ultrawrap: SPARQL execution on relational data. J. Web Semant. **22**, 19–39 (2013)
18. Suárez-Figueroa, M.C., Gómez-Pérez, A., Motta, E., Gangemi, A. (eds.): Ontology Engineering in a Networked World. Springer, Heidelberg (2012). https://doi.org/10.1007/978-3-642-24794-1
19. Uslar, M., Specht, M., Rohjans, S., Trefke, J., González, J.M.: The Common Information Model CIM: IEC 61968/61970 and 62325-A practical introduction to the CIM. Springer Science & Business Media (2012)
20. Xiao, G., Calvanese, D., Kontchakov, R., Lembo, D., Poggi, A., Rosati, R., Zakharyaschev, M.: Ontology-based data access: a survey. In: IJCAI, pp. 5511–5519. ijcai.org (2018)
21. Xiao, G., Ding, L., Cogrel, B., Calvanese, D.: Virtual knowledge graphs: an overview of systems and use cases. Data Intell. **1**(3), 201–223 (2019)
22. Yu, H., Liaw, S., Taggart, J., Khorzoughi, A.R.: Using ontologies to identify patients with diabetes in electronic health records. In: International Semantic Web Conference (Posters & Demos). CEUR Workshop Proceedings, vol. 1035, pp. 77–80. CEUR-WS.org (2013)
23. Zaharia, M., et al.: Apache spark: a unified engine for big data processing. Commun. ACM **59**(11), 56–65 (2016)

Scalable Transformation of Big Geospatial Data into Linked Data

George Mandilaras[(✉)] and Manolis Koubarakis[(✉)]

Department of Informatics and Telecommunications, National and Kapodistrian
University of Athens, Athens, Greece
{gmandi,koubarak}@di.uoa.gr

Abstract. In the era of big data, a vast amount of geospatial data has
become available originating from a large diversity of sources. In most
cases, this data does not follow the linked data paradigm and the existing
transformation tools have been proved ineffective due to the large volume
and velocity of geospatial data. This is because none of the existing tools
can utilize effectively the processing power of clusters of computers. We
present the system GeoTriples-Spark which is able to massively transform
big geospatial data into RDF graphs using Apache Spark. We evaluate
GeoTriple-Spark's performance and scalability in standalone and distributed environments and show that it exhibits superior performance
and scalability when compared to all of its competitors.

1 Introduction

A vast amount of geospatial data is now available on the Web, originating from
a large diversity of sources like crowd-sourced projects (e.g., OpenStreetMap[1]),
geospatial search engines like Google Maps, data hubs like the ESRI Open
Data Hub[2] and Earth observation programs such as Copernicus[3]. As a result,
researchers and practitioners working in Semantic Technologies have started
transforming this big geospatial data into linked data, interlinking it with other
data sources and further populating the Linked Open Data Cloud[4]. The project
LinkedGeoData [3] was the first project to do this by collecting information from
OpenStreetMap and converting it into linked data. Furthermore, projects such
as TELEIOS [20], LEO [9], MELODIES [8] and Copernicus App Lab [4] have
published several geospatial datasets that are Earth observation products, like
CORINE Land Cover and the Urban Atlas[5]. This methodology has also been
followed in the development of geospatial knowledge graphs like YAGO2geo [17],

---

[1] https://www.openstreetmap.org/.
[2] https://hub.arcgis.com/search.
[3] https://www.copernicus.eu/.
[4] https://lod-cloud.net/.
[5] http://kr.di.uoa.gr/#datasets.

The present work was funded by the European Union's Horizon 2020 research and
innovation project under grant agreement No 825258.

A. Hotho et al. (Eds.): ISWC 2021, LNCS 12922, pp. 480–495, 2021.
https://doi.org/10.1007/978-3-030-88361-4_28

which extends YAGO2 [13] with precise geospatial information originated from multiple official government sources.

In many cases, geospatial data comes in large volumes and with high velocity. For example, this is the case in Earth observation programs such as Copernicus. Up to 2019 the Copernicus Open Access Hub[6] had published approximately 13 million Earth observation products, with a publication rate of over 30,500 products per day[7]. The size of such Earth observation products depends on the resolution of the image, and it can vary from a few megabytes (MB) to multiple gigabytes (GB). Data of such large scale requires special techniques and tools in order to process it efficiently. Despite the bulk of work on storage and querying of big RDF graphs [2,16], the scalable transformation of big geospatial data into linked data has been overlooked so far. The present paper attempts to close this gap.

Transforming geospatial data into linked data, enables users to leverage the power of ontologies for modeling the domain. Furthermore, users can interlink their data with other linked geospatial data using tools like the temporal and geospatial extension of Silk [31], RADON [30] or GIA.nt [27], pose GeoSPARQL queries by storing it into spatially-enabled triple stores such as Strabon [19] or GraphDB[8], and visualize it using visualization tools like Sextant [26]. One of the activities in the research project ExtremeEarth[9] [18] is to publish data extracted from Copernicus imagery into RDF graphs, so as to interlink it with other geospatial sources (e.g., in-situ observations), and provide it as linked open data [24]. At the moment though, there is no existing tool able to deal with the large scale of Copernicus data, and for this reason, we developed a new version of the tool GeoTriples [21] able to transform big geospatial data into linked data. In more details, the contributions of this paper are the following:

- We design and implement the system *GeoTriples-Spark*[10],[11], which is a new version of GeoTriples that runs on top of Apache Spark and enables the transformation of big geospatial data into linked data. GeoTriples-Spark is an open source project, licensed under the Apache license version 2.0.
- We evaluate our system using datasets of varying input sizes, in different scenarios, and compare its performance with its main competitors: GeoTriples-Hadoop [21] and the Spark-based implementation of TripleGeo [28]. We show that, in most cases, GeoTriples-Spark decreases the transformation time by approximately 40%. We also show that GeoTriples-Spark can transform terabytes of data in a reasonable amount of time when no other system has been proven to be able to do so.

---

[6] https://scihub.copernicus.eu/.
[7] https://scihub.copernicus.eu/twiki/do/view/SciHubWebPortal/AnnualReport2019.
[8] https://graphdb.ontotext.com/.
[9] http://earthanalytics.eu/.
[10] https://github.com/LinkedEOData/GeoTriples.
[11] https://zenodo.org/record/4899793.

To enable the reproduction of our experiments, all the relevant data and code is available in the repository of GeoTriples-Spark[12].

The structure of the rest of the paper is as follows. Section 2 discusses related work. Section 3 introduces the tool GeoTriples and its main components. In Sect. 4 we present GeoTriples-Spark, and in Sect. 5 we evaluate it against other systems. In Sect. 6 we sum up and present directions for future work.

2   Related Work

Geospatial data can exist in raster or vector forms. Raster data refers to images where each pixel is associated with a specific location and its colour may indicate a metric or a class. A well-known format for storing raster data is GeoTIFF, which is an industry-standard for images from GIS and satellite remote sensing applications. Vector data are made up of vertices and edges and are composed of three basic geometry types: points, lines and polygons. They are commonly available in formats such as ESRI shapefile, GeoJSON, KML and GML documents and in spatially-enabled RDBMS like PostGIS. CSV files can also store geospatial information, by containing complex geometric types expressed as Well Known Text[13] (WKT), a text markup language for representing vector geometries. In this work, we focus exclusively on vector data.

Two are the main approaches for the transformation of relational and non-relational data into RDF graphs: direct mapping and using mapping languages. Direct mapping[14] is a straightforward approach to map relational data into RDF. In direct mapping, the tables of the relational database become the classes, the column names are mapped into RDF properties that represent the relation between subject and object, the subjects of triples are formed using the primary key of each tuple, and the objects of triples are formed using the values for the rest of the columns of the table. In this approach, the generated triples are dictated by the initial schema of the relational data. Alternatively, the transformation using mapping languages allows us to define a set of mapping rules that indicate how to map the input data into RDF triples. There are two well-known mapping languages: *R2RML*[15] and *RML*[16] [11]. R2RML is also a W3C recommendation and it is used for expressing customized mappings to map relational databases into RDF graphs. RML is a more generic mapping language that can express rules able to map data from semi-structured (like XML and JSON) and structured formats into RDF graphs. Both mapping languages are very rich and enable the manipulation of the input data in numerous ways.

Historically, the first tool for transforming geospatial data into RDF was GEOMETRYtoRDF [23] which enabled users to transform data stored in spatially-enabled RDBMS into RDF graphs. GEOMETRYtoRDF mapped the

---

[12] https://github.com/LinkedEOData/GeoTriples/tree/master/data.

[13] https://www.ogc.org/standards/wkt-crs.

[14] https://www.w3.org/TR/rdb-direct-mapping/.

[15] https://www.w3.org/TR/r2rml/.

[16] https://rml.io/.

geometrical data into GML files which were then transformed into RDF triples using the open source libraries GeoTools[17] and Apache Jena[18]. Even though this project is no longer maintained, its code-base was the basis for the development of tool TripleGeo which is discussed below.

A different approach appears in [10] which shows how R2RML can be combined with a spatially-enabled relational database in order to transform geospatial data into RDF. However, the transformation of other geospatial data sources for vector data e.g., shapefiles is not discussed.

The closest existing tool to GeoTriples is *TripleGeo*[19] [28,29] which was developed in the project GeoKnow[20]. Similarly to GeoTriples, TripleGeo is a tool for transforming geospatial features from various sources into RDF graphs. TripleGeo supports the transformation of structured data (ESRI shapefiles, CSV, GeoJSON and GPX) or semi-structured data (XML, GML and KML), as well as from spatially-enabled DBMSs and of less standard formats such as Open-StreetMap data and certain INSPIRE data and metadata. Furthermore, recently in the project SLIPO[21], TripleGeo was further extended with several novel features and specific functionalities to efficiently support the transformation of large datasets containing Points of Interest (POIs). This was achieved by extending TripleGeo to run on top of Apache Spark. However, it was designed to run only in standalone mode and not in distributed environments, so it cannot utilize the processing power of clusters of computers. Therefore, TripleGeo cannot be used for the transformation of very big geospatial data that requires more than a single machine to process it.

We close this related work section by point out that there are applications where the data owners might not be willing to transform their geospatial data into RDF, but still want to use Semantic Technologies in their application. In this case, one cannot adopt the transformation-into-RDF paradigm of this paper, but can instead use the geospatial ontology-based data access paradigm pioneered by Ontop-spatial [5]. For example, [6] shows that you can leave geospatial data in their original vector or raster formats and still be able to query them using GeoSPARQL and the system Ontop-spatial[22].

3   GeoTriples

GeoTriples [21,22] is an open source tool developed by our team[23] in the National and Kapodistrian University of Athens, for the transformation of geospatial data into linked geospatial data. GeoTriples currently supports the transformation of spatially-enabled databases (PostGIS and MonetDB), ESRI shapefiles, XML

---

[17] https://geotools.org/.
[18] https://jena.apache.org/documentation/io/streaming-io.html.
[19] https://github.com/SLIPO-EU/TripleGeo.
[20] http://geoknow.eu/Welcome.html.
[21] http://slipo.eu/.
[22] http://ontop-spatial.di.uoa.gr/.
[23] http://ai.di.uoa.gr/.

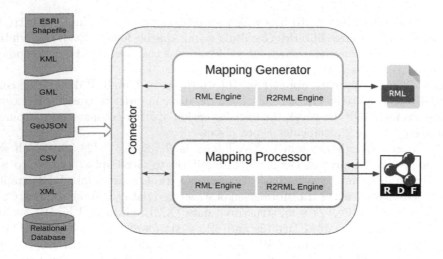

Fig. 1. The system architecture of GeoTriples

documents (hence GML documents), KML, GeoJSON and CSV documents. The produced graph is by default compliant with the GeoSPARQL vocabulary and can be manifested in any of the popular RDF syntaxes such as Turtle, RDF/XML, Notation3 or N-Triples.

GeoTriples consists of two components: a mapping generator that, given an input file, it generates a mapping file containing the mapping rules, and a mapping processor that applies the mapping rules in order to map each instance of the input data into the corresponding RDF triples. Additionally, the first component of GeoTriples is a connector that provides an abstraction layer and allows the other components to transparently access the input data regardless of the format of the source. Figure 1 displays a simplified diagram of GeoTriples system architecture.

The execution of GeoTriples comprises three steps. In the first step, we use the mapping generator to create a mapping file containing the mapping rules. Then, as a second optional step, the user can edit the mapping file so the produced triples will adopt any vocabulary or ontology she wants. Finally, the last step follows the transformation of the input file, in which the mapping processor applies the mapping rules to map the input data into RDF triples.

The mappings produced by the mapping generator consist of two triples maps: one for handling non-geometric (thematic) data, and one related to the geospatial data. The triples map that handles the thematic information defines a logical table that contains the attributes of the input data source and a unique identifier for the generated instances. Combined with a URI template, the unique identifier is used to produce the subjects of the produced triples. For each attribute of the input data, GeoTriples generates a term map that defines an RDF predicate according to the name of the attribute and a predicate-object map. The triples map that handles the geospatial information defines a logical table with a unique identifier similar to the thematic one. The logical table contains term maps that indicate the serialization of the geometric information according to the WKT representation, and the generation of all the necessary attributes for producing a GeoSPARQL compliant RDF graph. Hence, if the input is an ESRI shapefile, GeoTriples constructs RML mappings with transformations that invoke GeoSPARQL/stSPARQL extension functions. If the input is a relational database, GeoTriples constructs SQL queries that utilize the appropriate spatial functions of the Open Geospatial Consortium[24] standard [12] to generate the information required.

At the beginning of the transformation, GeoTriples parses the input mappings and extracts the content of the logical table using the appropriate way (e.g., a SELECT query). If the subject map is a template-valued term map or a column-valued term map, the related columns are extracted and stored in memory. Then, the processor iterates over all predicate-object maps, and for each one, it extracts all template- and column-valued term maps. These term maps are cached in memory along with the position that they appear in. Afterwards, the processor extracts all the features that are referenced by the term maps that appear in the subject, predicate and object positions for the current predicate map and iterates over the results. For each predicate and object value in the result row, a new RDF triple is constructed.

4   GeoTriples-Spark

Apache Spark[25] [34] is an open source, distributed, general-purpose, cluster computing framework that uses a *master/worker* architecture. There is a *Driver* process that is responsible to split the job into tasks, to schedule them to run on *Executors* and to coordinate the overall execution. Executors are distributed agents that execute tasks in parallel or sequentially. At the core of Apache Spark is the notion of data abstraction as a distributed collection of objects, known as *Resilient Distributed Datasets* (RDDs) [33]. RDDs allow the user to apply a series of transformations (i.e., map, filters, etc.), creating a lineage graph that will not be executed before calling an action (i.e., count, write to file, etc.). All transformations and actions are performed in parallel, as each Executor is assigned with a portion of the overall data known as partition and the execution of the transformation linkage graph runs inside a task.

GeoTriples-Spark is a new version of GeoTriples that runs on top of Apache Spark and enables the massive transformation of big geospatial data into RDF graphs. The input big geospatial data can be provided as multiple separate files which will be transformed concurrently or as a big single file. Currently, GeoTriples-Spark supports the transformation of CSV, GeoJSON and ESRI shapefiles and it can run in any standalone or distributed environment that supports the execution of Apache Spark jobs. Figure 2 displays the architecture of GeoTriples-Spark.

---

[24] https://www.ogc.org/standards/sfs.
[25] https://spark.apache.org/.

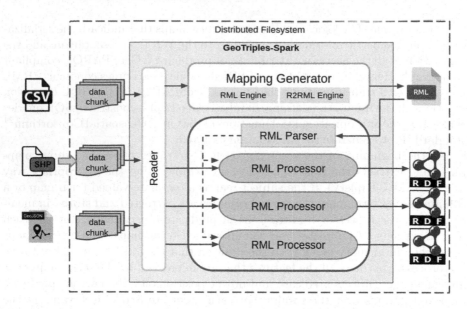

Fig. 2. The GeoTriples-Spark architecture

The mapping generator is the same as the one in the original GeoTriples system. However, the mapping processor is new and makes effective use of Apache Spark as we explain below.

The first component of GeoTriples-Spark is the Reader, which employs the appropriate libraries in order to load the input data into an Apache Spark `Dataset`, which is a distributed immutable collection of data organized into named columns. When a dataset is stored in a distributed filesystem (like HDFS), it is split into multiple chunks of constant size. When GeoTriples-Spark starts, the Reader loads these data chunks into partitions, which will be transformed as individual units in parallel. Users can change the default number of partitions in order to increase parallelization, but this can invoke data shuffling. To load ESRI shapefiles and GeoJSON, we use the library *GeoSpark*[26] [32] which is a cluster computing framework that extends Apache Spark with spatial computations. After initializing the `Dataset`, a new column is inserted containing a monotonically increasing unique index which will be combined with a URI template to form the subjects of produced triples. This is the default way of constructing subjects, but the user can overwrite it by editing the mapping file. Moreover, this generated index is not consecutive, as this would require to have counted all the records of the input data, which would add an overhead to the execution. Additionally, before the transformation starts, the Reader also loads and extracts the mapping rules from the mapping file, and broadcasts them so they will be available in all nodes.

---

[26] http://geospark.datasyslab.org/.

The transformation starts with a Map phase where for each partition, an RML processor is initialized, responsible for transforming all the records of the input partitions into RDF triples. Each RML processor iterates over all the records of its input partition and applies the mapping rules extracted by the mapping file, generating the corresponding triples. Note that, in most cases, the size of the produced triples exceeds the size of the initial dataset, which is sensible due to the nature of RDF triples. Hence, we avoid performing a Reduce and collect the produced triples into a single node, as this can overwhelm the targeted node and lead to memory errors. Consequently, after the transformation, the triples of each partition are stored in an individual file, thus the produced triples are stored into multiple files, one for each partition. Therefore, the whole procedure is a highly parallelized one as each process works individually from the rest and it simply loads its corresponding partitions, applies the mapping rules and stores the generated triples in a file.

Note that except for the broadcast of the mapping rules, there is no need for further data shuffling during the whole procedure as each partition already contains all the necessary information to perform the transformation. Additionally, when the produced triples of a record are generated, they are directly written in the target file. Consequently, the whole procedure is memory friendly, as it needs to maintain in the memory neither the initial data nor the produced triples. This makes GeoTriples-Spark highly scalable and able to transform a large amount of data with minimum memory requirements.

The parallelization of the whole procedure is based on the number of partitions and available resources (i.e., the physical processing units). More partitions mean the more parallelized the whole procedure can be (according to the number of the concurrently executed threads), but it also means that each process will have to transform a smaller chunk of data, as the initial dataset will have been divided into more partitions of fewer records. The number of partitions is determined by the size and the format of the source, and by the configuration settings of the filesystem, but it can also be configured by the user. However, increasing the initial number of partitions can invoke data shuffling, which in a distributed cluster can invoke network and disk I/O, which in its turn can affect negatively the performance of the system.

The transformation of CSV and GeoJSON documents is very similar. These filetypes are considered text files, and therefore they are directly loaded as multiple partitions by Spark, as they are distributedly stored across the cluster. The geometry feature in CSV files is expected to be in WKT and hence it does not require any further processing. Regarding GeoJSON, the system loads them as simple JSON files that follow the GeoJSON specification of RFC 7946[27]. In GeoJSON, the information is stored as a collection of geometric features consisting of the geometries and the thematic properties. The geometries are specified by the type (e.g., Point, LineString, Polygon, etc.) and by a list of coordinates, and the thematic properties are defined by a set of key-value pairs. So, using Spark's API, we load the properties of the geometric features into an Apache

---

[27] https://tools.ietf.org/html/rfc7946.

Spark `Dataset`, and then we extract and transform the geometries into WKT, which we add to the `Dataset`. Finally the partition-wise transformation of the `Dataset` into RDF triples follows.

The case of ESRI shapefiles is a bit more complicated. As mentioned, we load ESRI shapefiles using GeoSpark, whose shapefile reader always loads the input shapefile into a single partition[28]. Since shapefiles are composed of multiple files, in order to load them, we first need to merge all the related component files into one. This is happening because all the related component files must be located in the same node to utilize the shapefile index and the related attributes. Loading shapefiles from distributed filesystems is a well-known problem and it has been studied extensively in [1]. Hence, if users want to parallelize the transformation of a single shapefile, they must repartition the loaded data in order to redistribute it into multiple partitions. This will probably invoke data shuffling which may have a negative effect on the performance. However, shapefiles are typically small, and actually, there is a 2 GB size limit for any of its component files[29]. Additionally, it is very common to store geospatial data as multiple shapefiles. Thus, we have enabled GeoTriples-Spark to be able to transform multiple shapefiles concurrently, by loading them as individual partitions that will be transformed in parallel.

5   Evaluation

For the evaluation of GeoTriples-Spark, we compare it with three competitors systems: the centralized version of GeoTriples, the Hadoop-based implementation of GeoTriples[30] and the Spark-based implementation of TripleGeo[31] which we refer to as TripleGeo-Spark. The following experiments concern the performance of the systems against varying input sizes, the scalability of GeoTriples-Spark and also its performance regarding the transformation of very big geospatial data into RDF. For the comparison with GeoTriples-Hadoop using shapefiles, we reproduce the same experiments presented in [21], while for the comparison using CSV files we perform large-scale experiments with bigger datasets.

For the experiments, we used three different environments, a Hadoop cluster, a standalone machine that runs Apache Spark, and a large-scale cluster that runs the Hospworks [15] platform. The main module of Hopsworks is Hops[32] , which is a next generation distribution of Apache Hadoop, using a new implementation of HDFS called HopsFS [25]. Since TripleGeo is designed to run only in standalone mode, it can neither read the configuration file nor write the output triples in a distributed filesystem. As a result, TripleGeo can run neither in Hopsworks

---

[28] https://github.com/DataSystemsLab/GeoSpark/issues/356.

[29] https://desktop.arcgis.com/en/arcmap/latest/manage-data/shapefiles/
geoprocessing-considerations-for-shapefile-output.htm.

[30] https://github.com/dimitrianos/GeoTriples-Hadoop.

[31] https://github.com/SLIPO-EU/TripleGeo/tree/master/src/eu/slipo/athenarc/
triplegeo/partitioning.

[32] https://github.com/hopshadoop/hops.

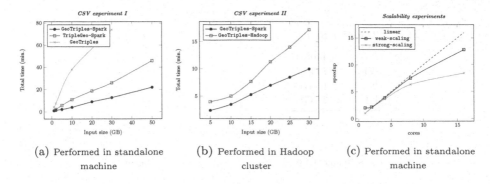

Fig. 3. CSV experiments

nor in the Hadoop cluster. Therefore, we compare the Spark- and Hadoop-based implementations of GeoTriples in the Hadoop cluster, and we compare the Spark-based implementations of GeoTriples and TripleGeo in the standalone machine. Last, we use the Hospworks cluster to perform large-scale experiments.

The Hadoop cluster consists of four nodes with 8 cores each with Intel(R) Xeon(R) E5-2650 v3 CPU at 2.30 GHz and 8 GB of memory. The standalone machine contains 32 virtual cores[33] at 2.20 GHz and 128 GB of memory. The large-scale cluster is a very powerful cluster provided to us by the company Logical Clocks[34], containing approximately 1000 CPU cores at 2.40 GHz, 12TB of RAM and 1PB of storage. Some of the data used in the experiments are from the Global Administrative Areas dataset[35] (GADM) while the rest are extracts of the OpenStreetMap project that are publicly available from the company GEOFABRIK[36]. Moreover, we further edit and replicate the datasets, in order to increase the input size. To enable the reproduction of the experiments, all the datasets are available in the repository of GeoTriples-Spark.

Figures 3a and 3b show the performance of GeoTriples-Spark for varying input CSV file sizes against the Hadoop-based implementation of GeoTriples and the Spark-based implementation of TripleGeo. In the experiment of Fig. 3a, both GeoTriples-Spark and TripleGeo-Spark, load the input data as 32 partitions which are transformed concurrently by 32 tasks. In the experiment of Fig. 3b, we did not change the initial number of loaded partitions of the datasets, as it would invoke network I/O which we wanted to avoid. In both experiments of Fig. 3, GeoTriples-Spark outperforms its competitors and we can also observe that as the size of input data increases, the effectiveness of GeoTriples-Spark becomes even clearer, particularly for the last datasets where the execution time decreases up to 47% compared to TripleGeo-Spark and 42% compared to GeoTriples-Hadoop. The results are similar when using GeoJSON documents as input.

---

[33] The system uses hyper-threading hence it has 16 physical cores.
[34] https://www.logicalclocks.com/.
[35] https://gadm.org/.
[36] http://download.geofabrik.de/.

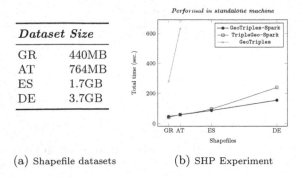

Dataset	Size
GR	440MB
AT	764MB
ES	1.7GB
DE	3.7GB

(a) Shapefile datasets   (b) SHP Experiment

Fig. 4. ESRI shapefiles experiments: Transformation of big shapefiles

This difference in the performance of the two systems derives from their implementation differences. First of all, GeoTriples-Spark uses an extended RML processor, while the transformation of TripleGeo-Spark is based on StreamRDF of Apache Jena. Furthermore, the execution of GeoTriples-Spark is very straightforward as it simply reads the input data, performs the transformation by applying the mapping rules, and stores the produced triples directly in the files. All of these steps are performed natively using Apache Spark's API. On the other hand, TripleGeo-Spark performs partition-wise transformation, and stores the results after transforming batches of input records, maintaining intermediate results in memory. Moreover, the writing procedure is not implemented natively using Spark's interface, but using Jena's StreamRDF writers. Last but not least, TripleGeo-Spark computes and outputs extra attributes derived from geometries, like the area of polygons and the length of lines. This adds an extra overhead in the execution, as such computations are expensive especially for big geometries.

Figure 3c depicts the scalability experiments with regards to *strong* and *weak* scaling[37]. In *strong scaling*, we examine how the overall computational time of the job scales as we increase the number of available processing cores. In *weak scaling*, we examine the speedup while increasing both the job size and the number of processing elements. In the strong scaling experiment, the size of the job is 15 GB, while in the weak scaling, the input size is equivalent to the number of active cores (i.e., 2 cores → 2 GB, 4 cores → 4 GB). In weak scaling, we can observe that the execution is almost linear but we can notice that there is a small deceleration as the number of cores increases. We observe similar in the strong scaling experiment. The main reason for this is because the Executors read and write in the same disk, hence more active cores lead to bigger latencies in disk I/O.

---

[37] https://www.kth.se/blogs/pdc/2018/11/scalability-strong-and-weak-scaling/.

Table 1. ESRI Shapefile experiments: Transformation of multiple shapefiles of varying sizes

Dataset	Size (MB)	Times loaded	GeoTriples-Spark (sec.)	GeoTriples-Hadoop (sec.)
Andorra	888	15	345	370
Australia	247	60	382	499
Ukraine	2	1000	428	1002

For the experiments with ESRI shapefiles, we evaluate the performance of GeoTriples-Spark in two kinds of experiments. In the first experiment, we compare the performance of GeoTriples-Spark and TripleGeo-Spark in the transformation of big ESRI shapefiles. The shapefiles are displayed in Table 4a and contain information of the road system of four countries (Greece, Austria, Spain and Germany) originated from OSM. In most cases, ESRI shapefiles are relatively small because they are compressed database files. So, to create bigger ones, we merge multiple shapefiles into one. The largest shapefile we use (i.e., *DE*) contains the whole road-system of Germany and it was created by merging the shapefiles of the road-system of the states of Germany. In these experiments, both tools repartition the input data into 32 partitions which are all transformed in parallel. The results are presented in Fig. 4b. Both systems perform well and quite similarly, but in the last and largest dataset, GeoTriples-Spark outperforms TripleGeo-Spark, as it requires 62.5% of the time TripleGeo-Spark needs to transform it. This performance benefit becomes even more distinctive as we increase the size of the input.

In the second experiment, we examine and compare the performance of the Spark- and Hadoop-based implementations of GeoTriples regarding the transformation of multiple shapefiles concurrently. Similarly to GeoTriples-Spark, GeoTriples-Hadoop loads the data of a shapefile into a single mapper, but in contrast with the Spark implementation, GeoTriples-Hadoop cannot re-distribute the load to other mappers, as it is mentioned in [21]. Therefore, GeoTriples-Hadoop is good for transforming multiple shapefiles where each one is assigned to a different mapper, but it is incapable of transforming shapefiles where their size exceeds the available memory of mappers. In this experiment, we load three different shapefiles of varying sizes multiple times, in order to evaluate how the two systems perform when the goal is to transform multiple small (Ukraine), medium (Australia) and large files (Andorra). The results are displayed in Table 1 and we can see that both tools perform similarly regarding the big and the medium shapefiles, with GeoTriples-Spark performing slightly better. However, we observe a significant difference in the last dataset where GeoTriples-Spark is superior as it requires less than 50% of the time GeoTriples-Hadoop needs.

Let us now present our large-scale experiments shown in Tables 2 and 3. For the experiments with CSV documents, we constructed a dataset of size up to 250 GB, which we load multiple times. Likewise, for the experiments with

Table 2. Large-scale experiments with CSV documents

Dataset	Times loaded	Input Size	#Executors	Output Size	Total time (in minutes)
100 GB.csv	1	100 GB	41	840.1 GB	3.3
250 GB.csv	1	250 GB	60	2.1 TB	6.6
250 GB.csv	2	500 GB	65	4.1 TB	13
250 GB.csv	4	**1 TB**	70	8.3 TB	26
250 GB.csv	8	**2 TB**	80	16.6 TB	50

Table 3. Large-scale experiments with ESRI shapefiles

Dataset	Times loaded	Input Size	#Executors	Output Size	Total time (in minutes)
AT	153	100 GB	20	427.7 GB	4.3
AT	381	250 GB	30	1068.6 GB	9.9
DE	136	500 GB	15	2.5 TB	17
DE	258	**1 TB**	27	5.1 TB	34

ESRI shapefiles, we load the AT and DE shapefiles multiple times. The memory requirements of each Executor are the minimum, as neither the input data nor the generated triples are cached in memory. Furthermore, there is no need for large Spark execution memory[38] since there is little to none data shuffling. So, in these experiments, we equipped each Executor with 2 GB of memory. In the end, we managed to transform 2TB of CSV input in less than an hour and 1TB consisting of multiple shapefiles in less than half an hour.

An important issue that arises with very large input files is the size of the output files, as this is approximately eight times bigger than the initial input. To solve this issue, we are streaming the produced triples directly in a distributed geospatial triple store we are currently developing [7], instead of writing them on the disk. This will facilitate access to the produced graphs and will enable us to pose GeoSPARQL queries efficiently.

To ensure the quality of the output and to verify that the produced graphs are the expected ones, we performed limited quality control. To do this, we stored the produced graph of the smallest of the large-scale experiments in a spatially-enabled triple store and the initial data into a spatially enabled database. Then we posed a series of queries to both stores and we validated the correctness of the results using a Geographic Information Systems (GIS). This way we confirmed that neither the geometries nor the thematic information has altered in any way by the transformation. Additionally, we also deduced that all the necessary links/predicates of the graph were generated, as otherwise, it would have not produced the correct results.

---
[38] https://spark.apache.org/docs/latest/tuning.html.

6   Summary and Future Work

In this work, we presented GeoTriples-Spark, which is a new version of GeoTriples, able to transform big geospatial data into RDF. We also evaluated its performance against the original version of GeoTriples, the Spark-based implementation of TripleGeo and GeoTriples-Hadoop. GeoTriples-Spark not only outperforms its competitors, but we also show that it is capable of transforming up to terabytes of input data, in a reasonable amount of time. GeoTriples-Spark is used in the project ExtremeEarth in order to transform data extracted from satellite images into linked data.

In a use case scenario of ExtremeEarth [24], we first download satellite images that cover areas in the Polar regions. Then, using deep learning techniques, we extract information and store it as multiple shapefiles. Then, we transform these multiple shapefiles into RDF concurrently using GeoTriples-Spark and interlink them with other geospatial datasets containing in-situ observations. Finally, we store the produced triples into a distributed geospatial RDF store which is currently under development by our group. The goal is to be able to run the whole pipeline in real-time. GeoTriples-Spark is designed especially for such use cases where one needs to transform multiple CSV files or shapefiles concurrently in an efficient way.

As for future work, we plan to extend GeoTriples-Spark in order to be able to transform data from other geospatial sources like big KML and GML documents, and from systems that are built on top of Hadoop, like Apache Hive[39] and Apache Accumulo[40]. Moreover, we plan to extend both GeoTriples and GeoTriples-Spark to support the GeoSPARQL+ [14] vocabulary, which enables handling raster geospatial data.

References

1. Abdul, J., Alkathiri, M., Potdar, M.B.: Geospatial Hadoop (GS-Hadoop) an efficient mapreduce based engine for distributed processing of shapefiles. In: ICACCA (2016)
2. Ali, W., Saleem, M., Yao, B., Hogan, A., Ngomo, A.N.: A Survey of RDF Stores & SPARQL Engines for Querying Knowledge Graphs. CoRR (2021)
3. Auer, S., Lehmann, J., Hellmann, S.: LinkedGeoData: adding a spatial dimension to the web of data. In: ISWC (2009)
4. Bereta, K., et al.: The copernicus app lab project: easy access to copernicus data. In: EDBT (2019)
5. Bereta, K., Koubarakis, M.: Ontop of geospatial databases. In: ISWC (2016)
6. Bereta, K., Koubarakis, M.: Creating virtual semantic graphs on top of big data from space. In: BiDS (2017)
7. Bilidas, D., Ioannidis, T., Mamoulis, N., Koubarakis, M.: Efficient storage and querying for big linked geospatial data: the system Strabo 2. Manuscript in preparation (2021)

---

[39] https://hive.apache.org/.
[40] https://accumulo.apache.org/.

8. Blower, J., Clifford, D., Goncalves, P., Koubarakis, M.: The MELODIES project: integrating diverse data using linked data and cloud computing. In: BiDS (2014)
9. Burgstaller, S., et al.: LEOpatra: a mobile application for smart fertilization based on Linked Data. In: HAICTA (2017)
10. Chentout, K., Vaisman, A.A.: Adding spatial support to R2RML mappings. In: OTM Workshops (2013)
11. Dimou, A., Sande, M.V., Colpaert, P., Verborgh, R., Mannens, E., de Walle, R.V.: RML: a generic language for integrated RDF mappings of heterogeneous data. In: LDOW (2014)
12. Herring, J.R.: OpenGIS Implementation Standard for Geographic information - Simple feature access - Part 2: SQL option. Open Geospatial Consortium standard (2010). http://portal.opengeospatial.org/files/?artifact_id=25354
13. Hoffart, J., Suchanek, F.M., Berberich, K., Weikum, G.: YAGO2: A Spatially and Temporally Enhanced Knowledge Base from Wikipedia (2013)
14. Homburg, T., Staab, S., Janke, D.: GeoSPARQL+: syntax, semantics and system for integrated querying of graph, raster and vector data. In: Pan, J.Z., et al. (eds.) ISWC 2020. LNCS, vol. 12506, pp. 258–275. Springer, Cham (2020). https://doi.org/10.1007/978-3-030-62419-4_15
15. Ismail, M., Gebremeskel, E., Kakantousis, T., Berthou, G., Dowling, J.: Hopsworks: improving user experience and development on hadoop with scalable. ICDCS, strongly consistent metadata. In: 2017 IEEE 37th International Conference on Distributed Computing Systems (ICDCS) (2017)
16. Kaoudi, Z., Manolescu, I., Zampetakis, S.: Cloud-Based RDF Data Management (2020)
17. Karalis, N., Mandilaras, G.M., Koubarakis, M.: Extending the YAGO2 knowledge graph with precise geospatial knowledge. In: ISWC (2019)
18. Koubarakis, M., et al.: From copernicus big data to extreme earth analytics. In: EDBT (2019)
19. Kyzirakos, K., et al.: The spatiotemporal RDF store strabon. In: SSTD (2013)
20. Kyzirakos, K., et al.: Wildfire monitoring using satellite images, ontologies and Linked Geospatial Data. J. Web Semant. **24**, 18–26 (2014)
21. Kyzirakos, K., et al.: GeoTriples: transforming geospatial data into RDF graphs using R2RML and RML mappings. J. Web Semant. **52**, 16–32 (2018)
22. Kyzirakos, K., Vlachopoulos, I., Savva, D., Manegold, S., Koubarakis, M.: GeoTriples: a tool for publishing geospatial data as RDF graphs using R2RML mappings. In: ISWC Posters (2014)
23. de León, A., Saquicela, V., Vilches, L.M., Villazón-Terrazas, B., Priyatna, F., Corcho, O.: Geographical linked data: a spanish use case. In: I-SEMANTICS (2010)
24. Mandilaras, G., Pantazi, D.A., Koubarakis, M., Hughes, N., Everett, A., Kiærbech, A.: Ice monitoring with extremeearth. In: LASCAR (2020)
25. Niazi, S., Ismail, M., Haridi, S., Dowling, J., Grohsschmiedt, S., Ronström, M.: HopsFS: scaling hierarchical file system metadata using NewSQL databases. In: FAST (2017)
26. Nikolaou, C., et al.: Sextant: visualizing time-evolving linked geospatial data. J. Web Semant. **35**, 35–52 (2015)
27. Papadakis, G.A., Mandilaras, G., Nikos, M., Koubarakis, M.: Progressive, holistic geospatial interlinking. In: Web Conference (2021)
28. Patroumpas, K., Alexakis, M., Giannopoulos, G., Athanasiou, S.: TripleGeo: an ETL Tool for transforming geospatial data into RDF triples. In: EDBT/ICDT (2014)

29. Patroumpas, K., Skoutas, D., Mandilaras, G.M., Giannopoulos, G., Athanasiou, S.: Exposing points of interest as linked geospatial data. In: SSTD (2019)
30. Sherif, M.A., Dreßler, K., Smeros, P., Ngomo, A.N.: Radon - rapid discovery of topological relations. In: AAAI (2017)
31. Smeros, P., Koubarakis, M.: Discovering spatial and temporal links among RDF data. In: LDOW (2016)
32. Yu, J., Wu, J., Sarwat, M.: GeoSpark: a cluster computing framework for processing large-scale spatial data. In: SIGSPATIAL (2015)
33. Zaharia, M., et al.: Resilient distributed datasets: a fault-tolerant abstraction for in-memory cluster computing. In: USENIX (2012)
34. Zaharia, M., et al.: Apache spark: a unified engine for big data processing. Commun. ACM **59**(11), 56–65 (2016)

AgroLD: A Knowledge Graph
for the Plant Sciences

Pierre Larmande[1,2,3](✉) [iD] and Konstantin Todorov[3] [iD]

[1] DIADE, IRD, Univ. Montpellier, CIRAD, Montpellier, France
pierre.larmande@ird.fr
[2] French Institute of Bioinformatics (IFB)—South Green Bioinformatics Platform,
Bioversity, CIRAD, INRAE, IRD, Montpellier, France
[3] LIRMM, CNRS, Univ. Montpellier, Montpellier, France
todorov@lirmm.fr

Abstract. Recent advances in sequencing technologies and high-throughput phenotyping have revolutionized the analysis in the field of the plant sciences. However, there is an urgent need to effectively integrate and assimilate complementary information to understand the biological system in its entirety. We have developed AgroLD, a knowledge graph that exploits Semantic Web technologies to integrate information on plant species and in this way facilitate the formulation and validation of new scientific hypotheses. AgroLD contains around 900M triples created by annotating and integrating more than 100 datasets coming from 15 data sources. Our objective is to offer a domain specific knowledge platform to answer complex biological and plant sciences questions related to the implication of genes in, for instance, plant disease resistance or adaptative responses to climate change. In this paper, we present results of the project, which focused on genomics, proteomics and phenomics. We present the AgroLD pipeline for lifting the data, the open source tools developed for these purposes, as well as the web application allowing to explore the data.

Keywords: Knowledge graph · Linked data · Plant sciences

1 Introduction

The understanding of genotype-phenotype interactions, which stand for the regulation of gene expression conferring a phenotype, is one of the most critical research areas in agronomy. However, these interactions are complex to identify because they are expressed at different molecular levels in the plant and are strongly influenced by environmental factors. The new challenges consist in identifying these interactions between various molecular entities involved in the expression of the phenotype, which, we believe, can only be addressed by integrating information from different levels in a global model using a systemic approach in order to understand the real functioning of the biological system. Recent high-throughput technologies such as Next Generation Sequencing, which

© Springer Nature Switzerland AG 2021
A. Hotho et al. (Eds.): ISWC 2021, LNCS 12922, pp. 496–510, 2021.
https://doi.org/10.1007/978-3-030-88361-4_29

allow DNA to be sequenced much more rapidly than previous methods, can only partially capture these dynamics of interactions [1]. Similarly, high-throughput phenotyping, which allows to produce a large amount of experimental data in various environmental conditions, lack in filling the gap with genomics data because of missing links in the data. Even if these new technologies allow to go further and further in obtaining new data, the current limitations and challenges are mainly at the level of data integration and data analysis. Moreover, a methodology to standardize and share data according to the FAIR (Findable, Accessible, Interoperable, Reusable) principles should allow to group data efficiently, and thus contribute to the improvement of the biological knowledge [2]. Indeed, it appears that this knowledge is still fragmented and this fragmentation hinders the elucidation of the molecular mechanisms that govern the expression of complex phenotypes [3].

The question is, therefore, how to structure and manage the complexity of biological data in order to extract knowledge that can be used to identify the molecular mechanisms controlling the expression of plant phenotypes. Our hypothesis is that weaving these data and disparate information into a knowledge graph (KG) would enable the formulation and validation of research hypotheses that would link genotype to phenotype, hence unlocking the potential of the currently available decentralized scientific data.

We have developed AgroLD (for Agronomy Linked Data) [4],[1] a FAIR knowledge graph powered by Semantic Web technologies as a structure to integrate data, to enable knowledge sharing and to allow information retrieval at scale. It is designed to integrate available information on various plant model species in the agronomic domain such as rice, arabidopsis and wheat, to name a few. The online documentation[2] shows the complete list of species with the total number of related protein entities. Among the contributions of the project is the development of the AgroLD schema, which combines newly created concepts/properties with concepts/properties imported from various ontologies from the biology field. Because life sciences and bioinformatics produce a large plethora of specific data formats, specific open source tools for data conversion to the Resource Description Framework (RDF) following the AgroLD schema have been developed and discusses in this paper. These different steps have led to the construction of several graphs on plant molecular interactions, which have been interlinked to form the AgroLD KG. We present these tools, together with a data fusion approach that allows for the construction of the pivotal AgroLD graph. Finally, we introduce an exploratory search engine that allows to browse the knowledge graph.

---

[1] www.agrold.org.

[2] http://www.agrold.org/documentation.jsp.

2 Related Work

In the last decade, many initiatives emerged in the biomedical and bioinformatics fields aiming at providing integrated environments to formulate scientific hypotheses about the role of genes in the expression of phenotypes or the emergence of diseases. Among them, we cite Bio2RDF [27], EBI RDF [28], Uniprot RDF [29], WikiPathways [30], OpenPhacts [31] and PubChemRDF [32]. Moreover, we can mention the BioHackathon[3] [33] which gather multidisciplinary scientists to solve biomedical and bioinformatics issues in data integration and knowledge representation. Since 15 years, the BioHackathon produces tools, ontologies [34] and guidelines [35] for RDF modelling and conversion. Recently, the DisGeNET [36] RDF platform and the Monarch Initiative [37] were created for human biology data. OntoForce[4] developed a new tool named DISQOVER for data discovery in life sciences. However, to the best of our knowledge, there was no equivalent in the plant sciences field before the AgroLD platform [4] was launched in 2015. In a related topic, KNETMINER [38] is a graph database for plant molecular network that has been developed with Neo4J and provides also a subset of its datasets through a SPARQL endpoint. Both KNETMINER and AgroLD have the same purpose and target the same scientific community. However, KNETMINER offers limited access to its features in its free version, while AgroLD has the advantage of being open and FAIR.

3 The AgroLD Knowledge Graph

3.1 Overview

AgroLD is built in phases spanning vast aspects of plant molecular interactions. The current phase (second phase) covers information on genes, proteins, predictions of homologous genes, metabolic pathways, plant phenotype and genetic studies. At this stage, we have integrated data from several resources such as Ensembl plants [5], UniProtKB [6], Gene Ontology Annotation [7]. The choice of these sources has been guided by the biological community, as they are widely used and have a strong impact on the user's confidence. We have also integrated resources developed by the local SouthGreen platform [8] such as TropGeneDB [9], a tropical plant genetics database, OryGenesDB [10], a rice genomics database, GreenPhylDB [11], a comparative genomics database for tropical plants, OryzaTagLine [12], a rice phenotype database and SniPlay [23], a rice genomic variation database. These resources bring together experimental data produced by researcher groups in Montpellier and the South of France. The online documentation provides an overview of the integrated data sources (See Footnote 2).

The conceptual framework of AgroLD is based on well-established ontologies in the plant field such as Gene Ontology [14], Plant Ontology [15] or Plant

---

[3] http://www.biohackathon.org.
[4] https://www.ontoforce.com.

Trait Ontology [16]. Furthermore, we developed a dedicated schema[5] that creates links between the imported ontologies and introduces new classes and properties. The online documentation (See Footnote 2) shows the complete list of the used ontologies. The majority of these ontologies are hosted by the OBO Foundry project [17].

In the following, we describe the components of the knowledge graph and the process of its construction.

3.2   Statistics

As of today, AgroLD contains more than 900 Millions triples resulting of the integration of roughly 100 datasets gathered in 33 named graphs. Table 1 gives a summary of all number of features. Table 3 gives an overview of available resources and tools. All datasets are available in Zenodo under the Creative Commons Attribution 4.0 International license (CC-BY 4.0). Each resource can contain several datasets, for instances, one dataset per species or per data type. Combining all ontologies and datasets imported, AgroLD graph gather 383 classes and 793 properties. Among the pipelines developed to lift up the datasets, we focused also on connecting our datasets with others. The property *rdfs:seeAlso* reach the total number of almost 80 millions of outbound links making the AgroLD graph correctly linked with other datasets in the LOD. Besides, we paid attention to increasing the number of semantic annotations with imported ontologies, which increased the number of links between datasets making the overall graph denser. We created more than 14 million semantic links linking entities to ontological classes. Finally, our data linking strategy (see next section) allowed us to create around 160,000 *owl:sameAs* links between entities (Table 2).

Table 1. Features of the AgroLD knowledge graph.

Features	Number of features
Datasets	100
Graphs	20
Triples	933,663,219
Classes	383
Properties	793
rdfs:seeAlso	79,696,972
owl:sameAs	166,551
Semantic annotations	14,652,812

3.3   AgroLD Integration Pipelines

Our contributions focus, among other things, on the development of various RDF conversion workflows for large agronomic datasets. Although several generic tools

---

[5] https://github.com/SouthGreenPlatform/AgroLD_ETL/tree/master/model.

Table 2. Data sources integrated in AgroLD. Ontologies are referenced as GO = gene ontology, PO = plant ontology, TO = plant trait ontology, EO = plant environment ontology, SO = sequence ontology, CO = crop ontology (plant specific traits)

Data sources	Nb of datasets	File format	Ontology used	Nb of triples
Oryzabase	2	TSV	GO,PO,TO	347 K
GO Associations	2	GAF	GO	6,440 K
Genome Hub	7	GFF	GO, SO	12,233 K
Gramene	6	Custom flat file	All	159 K
Ensembl	34	GFF	All	808,874 K
UniprotKB	2	Uniprot	GO, PO	60,034 K
Oryza Tag Line	2	Custom flat file	PO, TO, CO	282 K
TropGeneDB	2	Custom flat file	PO, TO, CO	20 K
GreenPhylDB	2	Custom flat file	GO, PO	3,627 K
SNiPlay	1	HapMap, VCF	GO	16,204 K
Q-TARO	2	TSV	PO, TO	20 K
MSU	2	Custom flat file	PO, TO	2,068 K
RiceNetDB	6	Custom flat file	PO, TO	5,879 K
RapDB	3	GFF	PO, TO	1,026 K
PlantTftDB	12	Custom flat file	PO, TO	86 K
Interpro	1	Custom flat file	PO, TO	196 K
CEGResources	2	GFF	PO, TO	1,031 K
OBO ontologies	12	OWL		15,131 k
TOTAL	100			**934,342 M**

exist within the Semantic Web community, including Datalift [21], Tarql [22], RML.io [23], none of them were adapted to take into account the complexity of data formats in the biological domain (e.g. VCF format [18]) or even the complexity of the information they could contain. A simple example illustrates this complexity through the GFF (Generic Feature Format) [19], which represents genomic data in a TSV type format (file with tabs as separators). It contains a column with key = value type information, of variable length and having different information depending on the data source. In this case, the transformation needs to be adapted according to the data source. Furthermore, the large volume of data was a limiting factor for the above-mentioned tools. In this context, we developed RDF conversion tools adapted to a large range of genomics data standards such as GFF [19], Gene Ontology Annotation File (GAF) [24], Variant Call Format [18] and we are currently working on packaging these ETL tools in an API[6]. These data standards represent a first step, as they are indeed the most widely used in the community. However, we plan to develop more tools as we will integrate new data standards.

---

[6] https://github.com/SouthGreenPlatform/AgroLD_ETL.

Table 3. Links to AgroLD resource and tools

Name of resource or tool and description, URL
Data
AgroLD datasets, https://doi.org/10.5281/zenodo.4694518   **List of graphs**, http://www.agrold.org/documentation.jsp   **List of ontologies**, http://www.agrold.org/documentation.jsp   **AgroLD vocabulary**,   https://github.com/SouthGreenPlatform/AgroLD_ETL/tree/master/model   **AgroLD SPARQL Endpoint**, http://agrold.southgreen.fr/sparql   **Example queries**, http://www.agrold.org/sparqleditor.jsp   **Use case queries**, https://github.com/pierrelarmande/ISWC-use-case
Tools
Web application, https://github.com/SouthGreenPlatform/AgroLD_webapp   **RDF conversion pipelines** (GFF2RDF, GAF2RDF, VCF2RDF, Datasets),   https://github.com/SouthGreenPlatform/AgroLD_ETL

3.4 The AgroLD Schema

In order to match the different data types and properties, we developed a schema that associates the classes and properties identified in AgroLD with corresponding ontologies. Figure 1 shows an overview of the AgroLD ontology including these mappings. For instance, the *Protein class*[7] is associated with the *SO polypeptide class*[8] with the *owl:equivalentClass* property. Similar mappings have been done for the properties. For example, the *has_function* property is linked with properties from the *RO ontology*,[9] with *owl:equivalentProperty*. When an equivalent property did not exist, we associated it with the higher level property with *rdfs:subPropertyOf*. For example, the property *has_trait*[10], linking entities with TO terms is associated with a more generic property from RO: *causally related to*[11]. So far, 55 mappings have been manually identified.

3.5 URI Design

In the transformation pipelines, RDF graphs share a common namespace and are named according to the corresponding data sources. Entities in RDF graphs are linked by the common URI principle. In general, we build URIs by referring to Identifiers.org [19] which provides design patterns for each registered source. For instance, genes integrated from Ensembl Plants are identified by the base URI.[12] When they are not provided by Identifiers.org, new URIs are constructed

---

[7] http://www.southgreen.fr/agrold/vocabulary/Protein.
[8] http://purl.obolibrary.org/obo/SO_000010.
[9] http://purl.obolibrary.org/obo/RO_0000085.
[10] http://www.southgreen.fr/agrold/vocabulary/has_trait.
[11] http://purl.obolibrary.org/obo/RO_0002410.
[12] http://identifiers.org/ensembl.plant/{Entity_ID}.

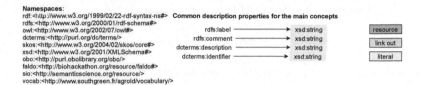

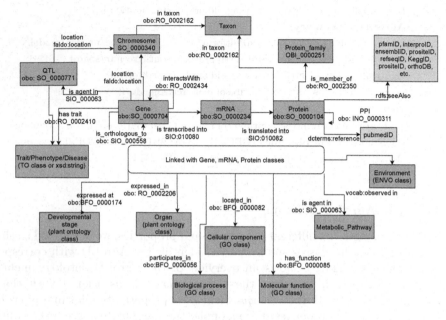

Note: Some classes and properties have been omitted from the graph model or the sake of clarity

Fig. 1. Overview of the AgroLD schema

and in this case URIs take the form.[13] In addition, the properties linking the entities are constructed as form.[14]

In order to link identical entities from different data sources, we used the approach based on URI pattern matching. Its principle is to scan the URIs in order to look for similar patterns in the terminal part of the URI (i.e. Entity_ID). In addition, we also followed the common URI approach which recommends to use the same URI pattern for two identical entities. Therefore, for the same entity, this allowed us to aggregate information from different RDF graphs. In addition, we used cross-reference links by transforming them to URIs and linking the resource to the *rdfs* predicate `seeAlso`. This significantly increases the number of outbound links by reaching almost 80 million links, making AgroLD better integrated with other data sources. In the future, we plan to implement a similarity entity profile approach to identify matches between entities with different URIs.

---

[13] http://www.southgreen.fr/agrold/resource/{Entity_ID}.
[14] http://www.southgreen.fr/agrold/vocabulary/{property}.

4   Challenges in Creating the AgroLD Graph

The process of creating a knowledge graph is complex and challenging. In this section, we will present some of the challenges we had to address and in particular those related to managing the heterogeneity of the datasets and their sizes, aligning the entities and assessing the data quality.

Concerning **data heterogeneity**, the main problem was the variety of the data formats which we solved by having RDF as unified format. We proposed several pipelines that were able to handle this variety and manage the size of the datasets. Indeed, as discussed in Sect. 3.3, in the majority of cases, we preferred developing our own solutions instead of using generic tools to manage better the complexity or the size of the datasets. Another problem was the heterogeneity of the genomic coordinates (i.e. different naming of the chromosome identifier, missing information, etc.). We solved it by choosing a unique representation and transforming all coordinates in URIs patterns following the FALDO ontology representation [34].

Concerning the **entity linking** problem (i.e. same entities having different names or identifiers), we managed to only partially solve this problem, by using pattern matching in URIs, or database cross-links to identify mappings between entities. Indeed, in the case where entities have a different namespace URI (e.g. namespace1:identifier1 and namespace2:identifier1), we search patterns matching in the URIs and create a new URI doing the mapping between them. In the case when entities have different URIs with no matching patterns but having synonym properties (i.e. skos:altLabel, skos:prefLabel, skos:synonym or specific ones), we search matches with these properties and the URIs patterns. For entities that do not contain the above information, we adopt a more global approach based on properties and values analysis. However it is an open challenge that we are currently working on.

Concerning the processes followed for **data quality assessment**, pre-processing quality assessments such as input file format, raw line and missing value check were developed for the resources used by the ETL pipeline. Then, the produced triples were validated for syntax with built-in libraries (e.g. with RDFlib). Further assessments include counting the number of entities (e.g. genes, proteins, chromosomes, etc.) and checking the presence/absence of properties with sets of SPARQL queries. More complex quality assessment such as type restriction on properties is planned in the future.

5   Data Access and Applications

The AgroLD KG is available for access via a SPARQL enpoint[15]. However, although the SPARQL language is efficient to build queries, regarding access to RDF data, it remains difficult to handle for our main users, which are mainly

---

[15] http://agrold.southgreen.fr/sparql.

biologists with little or no background in formal query languages. Therefore, we propose a web application implementing various elements of a semantic search systems, such as pattern-based querying, graphical visualization, information retrieval tools.[16]

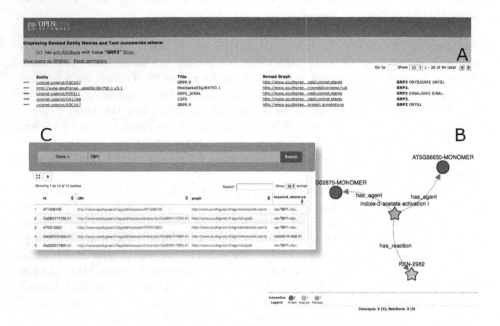

Fig. 2. Overview of AgroLD Web interfaces. (A) displays the Faceted search interface. (B) displays results from the KnetMaps tool. (C) displays results from the advanced search interface.

Hence, the AgroLD platform provides three entry points, as described in [4]:

- *Quick Search* is a faceted search plugin made available by Virtuoso that allows users to search by keywords and browse AgroLD content by navigating through links. Figure 2A shows the result of a keyword search. In this example a user submitted the *GRP2* keyword which stands for a gene name. Results are ranked according to the number of occurrences found in various fields of the entities.
- *Advanced Search* is an interface allowing specific searches by class of entities such as filtering by Gene, Protein, Pathway and having an aggregation engine for external resources (Fig. 2C). The Advanced Search form is based on a RESTFul API. The purpose of this interface is to provide a tool to query the knowledge graph while hiding the technical aspects of SPARQL querying. The interest of coupling the AgroLD RESTFul API and this interface is to be

---

[16] http://www.agrold.org.

able to interactively combine searches with external services API such as for instance Pubmed or EMBL APIs. Moreover, this is made possible through the user interface and also programmatically. As shown in Fig. 2C, the users begin by entering one or several keywords and select which type of entity they want to retrieve. In this example, we selected the type *Gene* and the keyword *TBP1*. The results are presented in the form of a table which can be sorted and explored. Moreover, results could be visualised as a graph as shown in Fig. 2B. This tool was adapted from KnetMaps [39].

- *The SPARQL Editor* is a query editor that provides an interactive environment for formulating SPARQL queries. We developed the editor based on the YASQE and YASR [26] tools and adapted them for our system. In addition, we proposed a list of modular and customizable query patterns according to the users' needs that can be automatically executed through the editor. Figure 3 shows the SPARQL Editor. The editor is divided in three areas. The main area on the top left corresponds to the query area. Thanks to the YASQE tool, proposing several code editing functions, the code syntax is highlighted and checked for errors. Furthermore, users can load their own queries stored in a file in order to run batch queries and save their results in various file formats. It is also possible to build up queries by using query patterns. In this case, the users can select one of the dozen query patterns shown on the right. The query appears in the left-hand area within the query text box. Users can read the code of the query and see differently colored pieces of code according to the type of variable, string fields and SPARQL syntax. Hence, users can directly modify the code. There is also a text box above the query box that allows users to modify the value of the string parameter and by clicking on the *apply* button, it modifies the string value of the query. Finally, the results are displayed at the bottom of the editor as a table (by default), but they can also be displayed in JSON or graph-based formats. Each column can be sorted and text filters can be applied to search among the results. Data can be downloaded as a CSV file.

6   Use-Case Scenarios

A better understanding of genotype-phenotype relationships requires the integration of biological information of various kinds. However, this information is often dispersed in several databases on the Internet each with different data models, scales or distinct means of access. For biologists, it is difficult to search relevant information in these databases as the mass of information can be incomplete and hard to manage. These problems are particularly relevant in the context of genetic association analyses or GWAS (Genome Wide Association Studies), which allow to associate large regions of the genome (locus) with a phenotypic trait (trait). GWAS loci often include several hundred genes that need to be analysed in order to identify only a fraction of the genes associated with the trait under study. At some point, each scientist will have to choose which genes to investigate further in the laboratory.

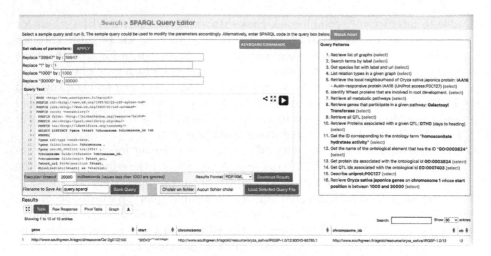

Fig. 3. The SPARQL query editor. The Query patterns frame allows to select a query from a natural language question. The Query text frame allows to visualize and modify the SPARQL query. The results frame displays results returned from the query.

In order to show how AgroLD can help in this type of analysis, we took the results published in [40] and tried to reproduce the experiments. The paper studies the key genes that are responsible of the panicle architecture in rice. The authors outlined, based on a manual literature review, a list of 319 candidate genes known to regulate the plant architecture. The aim of our use-case study is to reproduce these results automatically.

The authors of [40] identified numerous GWAS loci combining several trait associations all along the chromosomes and studied chromosome 4, which was associated with ten panicle and yield traits. We found less associations with the query Q1[17] in AgroLD. Indeed, only five phenotypic traits loci associated to "panicle" trait name were retrieved.

Next, the authors identified 20 candidate genes distributed along chromosome 4. By building a second query Q2, which retrieve the genes available for chromosome 4 and using a filter on "panicle", we obtained 15 genes results.

Finally, the authors narrowed down the genomic region of chromosome 4 between 30 Megabases and 32 Megabases. They identified five candidates genes namely OsKS3, OsKS1, OsKS2, OsMADS31 and NAL1. On our side, querying the same genomic region with similar filters (Q3), we obtained only one gene: NAL1. However, using a less restrictive query (Q4), we obtained 81 genes results including the five candidates identified by the authors.

By comparing our results to the ones in the paper, we can first argue that the authors have a larger GWAS/QTL datasets than AgroLD currently has integrated. Thus, they get more genomic regions associated with phenotypic

---

[17] Example Use case, available from: https://github.com/pierrelarmande/ISWC-use-case.

trait than we get in Q1. Second, they have a better selection of candidate genes for a given genomic region. Even if AgroLD contains a large number of genes (81 genes) for the same genomic region, the final result is smaller when genes are filtered by the name of the trait. After checking, we observed that this value is absent in the majority of cases. The authors extracted this information from the manual review of scientific papers.

7   Conclusion and Future Work

Data in the agronomic domain are highly heterogeneous and dispersed. For plant scientists to make informed decisions in their daily work it is critical to integrate information at different scales. Semantic Web technologies play a pivotal role in data integration and knowledge management. The biomedical domain provides a good example to follow by capitalizing on previous experience and addressing lessons learned. To build on this line of research in the agronomy field, we have developed the AgroLD KG. The knowledge base exploits the power of seamless data integration offered by RDF. It contains more than 900 Millions triples resulting of the integration of roughly 100 datasets gathered in 33 named graphs. However, it coverage with respect to the species and the data sources are expected to grow with the subsequent releases. To our knowledge, AgroLD is one of the first initiatives taken to bring Semantic Web practices to the agronomic domain, playing a complimentary role in the integrative approaches adopted by the community.

AgroLD is being actively developed based on feedback from domain experts. It also benefits from the support of the SouthGreen Bioinformatics Platform since its beginning in 2015 by providing IT support and infrastructure to host data and web applications. SouthGreen is one of the core platforms of the French Elixir-EU node, thus will provide a long lasting support for AgroLD. AgroLD is strongly linked to several use-cases of the D2KAB project[18] (National Research Agency funded project) to demonstrate the benefits of linked data to discover gene-phenotype interactions. With the achievement of the second phase, user feedback reveals some limitations and challenges on the current version. Thus, a number of issues are a matter of ongoing or future work.

On the one hand, the KG coverage has to be extended to a larger number of biological entities (e.g. miRNA) and relations (e.g. co-expression, regulation and interaction networks) in order to capture a broader view of the molecular interactions. For instance, we need to integrate information on gene expression and gene regulatory networks. On the other hand, the ETL process for KG creation is mostly based on domain specific approaches thus limiting its re-usability. We will investigate approaches using declarative functions for its creation.

Methods for knowledge augmentation need to be applied and adapted to our data. Indeed, we have observed that certain information remains hidden in the RDF literal contents, such as biological entities or relationships between

---

[18] https://d2kab.mystrikingly.com/.

them, while a wealth of related knowledge is available in external sources. We currently developing methods to extract information embedded in unstructured data such as the text fields from the KG or from external web documents and scientific publications and bring this information under a structured form to the knowledge base. Finally, we are in the process of extending state-of-art data linking techniques by considering the specificities of the biological domain.

References

1. Kemble, H., Nghe, P., Tenaillon, O.: Recent insights into the genotype-phenotype relationship from massively parallel genetic assays. Evol. Appl. **12**(9), 1721–1742 (2019)
2. Wilkinson, M.D., Dumontier, M., Aalbersberg, I.J., Appleton, G., Axton, M., Baak, A., et al.: The FAIR guiding principles for scientific data management and stewardship. Sci. Data **3**, 1–9 (2016)
3. Weighill, D., et al.: Multi-phenotype association decomposition: unraveling complex gene-phenotype relationships. Front. Genet. **10**, 417 (2019). https://doi.org/10.3389/fgene.2019.00417
4. Venkatesan, A., Tagny Ngompe, G., Hassouni, N.E., Chentli, I., Guignon, V., Jonquet, C., et al.: Agronomic linked data (AgroLD): a knowledge-based system to enable integrative biology in agronomy. PLoS ONE **13**, 17 (2018)
5. Bolser, D., Staines, D.M., Pritchard, E., Kersey, P.: Ensembl plants: integrating tools for visualizing, mining, and analyzing plant genomics data. Methods Mol. Biol. Clifton NJ **1374**, 115–40 (2016)
6. The UniProt consortium: UniProt: a worldwide hub of protein knowledge. Nucleic Acids Res. **47**, D506–0515 (2018)
7. Huntley, R.P., Sawford, T., Mutowo-Meullenet, P., Shypitsyna, A., Bonilla, C., Martin, M.J., et al.: The GOA database: gene ontology annotation updates for 2015. Nucleic Acids Res. **43**, D1057-1063 (2015)
8. South green collaborators: the south green portal: a comprehensive resource for tropical and mediterranean crop genomics south green collaborators. Curr. Plant Biol. **78**, 6–9 (2016)
9. Hamelin, C., Sempere, G., Jouffe, V., Ruiz, M.: TropGeneDB, the multi-tropical crop information system updated and extended. Nucleic Acids Res. **41**, D1172–D1175 (2013)
10. Droc, G., Périn, C., Fromentin, S., Larmande, P.: OryGenesDB 2008 update: database interoperability for functional genomics of rice. Nucleic Acids Res. **37**, D992-995 (2009)
11. Valentin, G., Abdel, T., Gaëtan, D., Jean-François, D., Matthieu, C., Mathieu, R.: GreenPhylDB v5: a comparative pangenomic database for plant genomes. Nucleic Acids Res. (2020)
12. Larmande, P., Gay, C., Lorieux, M., Périn, C., Bouniol, M., Droc, G., et al.: Oryza tag line, a phenotypic mutant database for the genoplante rice insertion line library. Nucleic Acids Res. **36**, D1022-1027 (2008)
13. Dereeper, A., Homa, F., Andres, G., Sempere, G., Sarah, G., Hueber, Y., et al.: SNiPlay3: a web-based application for exploration and large scale analyses of genomic variations. Nucleic Acids Res. **43**, W295-300 (2015)
14. Gene Ontology Consortium: The Gene Ontology Resource: 20 years and still GOing strong. Nucleic Acids Res. **47**, D330–0338 (2019)

15. Plant, T., Consortium, O.: The plant ontology consortium and plant ontologies. Compt. Funct. Genomics. **3**, 137–142 (2002)

16. Cooper, L., Meier, A., Laporte, M.A., Elser, J.L., Mungall, C., Sinn, B.T., et al.: The planteome database: an integrated resource for reference ontologies, plant genomics and phenomics. Nucleic Acids Res. **46**, D1168–D1180 (2018)

17. Smith, B., Ashburner, M., Rosse, C., Bard, J., Bug, W., Ceusters, W., et al.: The OBO foundry: coordinated evolution of ontologies to support biomedical data integration. Nat. Biotech. **25**, 1251–1255 (2007)

18. Genome project Consortium. Variant Call Format (VCF). http://samtools.github.io/hts-specs/. Accessed 4 Apr 2021

19. The formal specification of GFF3. http://www.sequenceontology.org. Accessed 4 Apr 2021

20. Laibe, C., Wimalaratne, S., Juty, N., Le Novère, N., Hermjakob, H.: Identifiers.org: integration tool for heterogeneous datasets. Dils 2014 **14** (2014)

21. Scharffe, F., Atemezing, G., Troncy, R., Gandon, F., Villata, S., Bucher, B., et al.: Enabling linked data publication with the Datalift platform. In: AAAI (2012)

22. Tarql: SPARQL for Tables. https://tarql.github.io. Accessed 4 Apr 2021

23. Dimou, A., Sande, M.V., Colpaert, P., Verborgh, R., Mannens, E., Van De Walle, R.: RML: a generic language for integrated RDF mappings of heterogeneous data. In: CEUR Workshop Proceedings (2014)

24. The Gene Ontology Consortium. Gene Annotation File (GAF) specification [Internet]. http://geneontology.org/page/go-annotation-file-format-20. Accessed 4 Apr 2021

25. Heim, P., Hellmann, S., Lehmann, J., Lohmann, S., Stegemann, T.: RelFinder: revealing relationships in RDF knowledge bases. In: Chua, T.S., Kompatsiaris, Y., Mérialdo, B., Haas, W., Thallinger, G., Bailer, W. (eds.) SAMT 2009. LNCS, vol. 5887, pp. 182–187. Springer, Heidelberg (2009). https://doi.org/10.1007/978-3-642-10543-2_21

26. Rietveld, L., Hoekstra, R.: The YASGUI family of SPARQL clients. Semant. Web J. (2015)

27. Belleau, F., Tourigny, N., Good, B., Morissette, J.: Bio2RDF: towards a mashup to build bioinformatics knowledge systems. J. Biomed. Inform. **41**(5), 706–716 (2008)

28. Jupp, S., Malone, J., Bolleman, J., Brandizi, M., Davies, M., Garcia, L., et al.: The EBI RDF platform: linked open data for the life sciences. Bioinformatics **30**, 1–2 (2014)

29. Redaschi, N., Consortium, U.: UniProt in RDF: tackling data integration and distributed annotation with the semantic web. In: Nature Proceedings [Internet] (2009). https://doi.org/10.1038/npre.2009.3193.1

30. Waagmeester, A., et al.: Using the semantic web for rapid integration of WikiPathways with other biological online data resources. PLoS Comput. Biol. **12**(6), e1004989 (2016)

31. Chichester, C., Digles, D., Siebes, R., Loizou, A., Groth, P., Harland, L.: Drug discovery FAQs: workflows for answering multidomain drug discovery questions. Drug Discov. Today **20**(4), 399–405 (2015)

32. Fu, G., Batchelor, C., Dumontier, M., Hastings, J., Willighagen, E., Bolton, E.: PubChemRDF: towards the semantic annotation of PubChem compound and substance databases. J. Cheminf. **7**(1), 1–15 (2015). https://doi.org/10.1186/s13321-015-0084-4

33. Aoki-Kinoshita, K., et al.: Implementation of linked data in the life sciences at BioHackathon 2011. J. Biomed. Semant. **6**(3), 1–3 (2015). https://doi.org/10.1186/2041-1480-6-3

34. Bolleman, J.T., Mungall, C.J., et al.: FALDO: a semantic standard for describing the location of nucleotide and protein feature annotation. J. Biomed. Semant. **13**(7), 39 (2016). https://doi.org/10.1186/s13326-016-0067-z
35. DBCLS guidelines for RDFizing databases. https://github.com/dbcls/rdfizing-db-guidelines. Accessed 4 Apr 2021
36. Piñero, J., et al.: The DisGeNET knowledge platform for disease genomics: 2019 update. Nucleic Acids Res. (2019)
37. Mungall, C.J., et al.: The monarch initiative: an integrative data and analytic platform connecting phenotypes to genotypes across species. Nucleic Acids Res. **48**, D704–D715 (2019)
38. Hassani-Pak, K, et al.: KnetMiner: a comprehensive approach for supporting evidence-based gene discovery and complex trait analysis across species. Plant Biotechnol. J. (2021)
39. Singh, A., Rawlings, C.J., Hassani-Pak, K.: KnetMaps: a BioJS component to visualize biological knowledge networks. F1000Res. **7**, 1651 (2018)
40. Crowell, S., Korniliev, P., Falcão, A., et al.: Genome-wide association and high-resolution phenotyping link Oryza sativa panicle traits to numerous trait-specific QTL clusters. Nat. Commun. **7**, 10527 (2016). https://doi.org/10.1038/ncomms10527

LiterallyWikidata - A Benchmark for Knowledge Graph Completion Using Literals

Genet Asefa Gesese[1,2](✉), Mehwish Alam[1,2](✉), and Harald Sack[1,2](✉)

[1] FIZ Karlsruhe – Leibniz Institute for Information Infrastructure,
Eggenstein-Leopoldshafen, Germany
{genetasefa.gesese,mehwish.alam,harald.sack}@fiz-karlsruhe.de
[2] Karlsruhe Institute of Technology, Institute AIFB, Karlsruhe, Germany

Abstract. In order to transform a Knowledge Graph (KG) into a low dimensional vector space, it is beneficial to preserve as much semantics as possible from the different components of the KG. Hence, some link prediction approaches have been proposed so far which leverage literals in addition to the commonly used links between entities. However, the procedures followed to create the existing datasets do not pay attention to literals. Therefore, this study presents a set of KG completion benchmark datasets extracted from Wikidata and Wikipedia, named LiterallyWikidata. It has been prepared with the main focus on providing benchmark datasets for multimodal KG Embedding (KGE) models, specifically for models using numeric and/or text literals. Hence, the benchmark is novel as compared to the existing datasets in terms of properly handling literals for those multimodal KGE models. LiterallyWikidata contains three datasets which vary both in size and structure. Benchmarking experiments on the task of link prediction have been conducted on LiterallyWikidata with extensively tuned unimodal/multimodal KGE models. The datasets are available at https://doi.org/10.5281/zenodo.4701190.

Keywords: Knowledge graph completion · Knowledge graph embedding · Link prediction · Literals · Benchmark dataset

1 Introduction

Knowledge Graphs (KGs) are composed of structured information describing facts about a particular domain through entities and interrelations between them. Recently, KGs have become crucial to improve diverse real-world applications mainly in the areas of Natural Language Processing (NLP) such as question answering, named entity disambiguation, information extraction, and etc. [9, 38]. Due to the Open World Assumption, KGs are never complete, i.e., there are always some facts missing. In order to solve this problem, different KG embedding models have been proposed for automated KG Completion (KGC). Most of these models are based on the tasks such as link prediction, triple classification, and entity classification/typing. Some of these embedding models make

© Springer Nature Switzerland AG 2021
A. Hotho et al. (Eds.): ISWC 2021, LNCS 12922, pp. 511–527, 2021.
https://doi.org/10.1007/978-3-030-88361-4_30

use of only relational triples (triples with object properties), such as TransE
[6], DistMult [43], ConVE [10], RotatE [34], and etc. On the other hand, some
models such as LiteralE [21], KBLRN [13], MTKGNN [35], and MKBE [27]
use relational triples together with attributive triples (i.e., triples with datatype
properties which take literals as values) and images of entities (refer to [15] for
more details).

The performance of various KGE approaches, mainly link prediction models,
has been evaluated using some commonly known KGC datasets. Most of these
datasets except CoDEx [29], are outdated and easy for link prediction tasks such
as FB15K [6] and FB15K-237 [36] which are subsets of the no longer maintained
KG Freebase [5]. Moreover, attributive triples have not been handled properly in
any of the current datasets. For instance, in CoDEx-M [29], it is not possible to
find a single datatype property in Wikidata with numerical literal values for some
of the entities. Apart from numerical properties, the major existing datasets also
contain a significant number of entities for which there is no textual description
available. For instance, in CoDEx among the total number of 77,951 entities,
17,276 of them do not have textual descriptions in English, i.e., they are not
represented in English Wikipedia. Hence, in those studies which combine KG
and textual entity descriptions for representation learning (such as DKRL [41])
it is common to filter out these entities in order to train the embedding models.
This indicates that a high-quality benchmark that covers both relational and
attributive triples is required to evaluate the performance of the state-of-the-art
KGC models.

Therefore, in this work a KGC benchmark **LiterallyWikidata** which properly combines attributive triples with relational triples by taking into account
the aforementioned concerns is presented. **LiterallyWikidata** consists of a set
of KGC datasets extracted from Wikidata and Wikipedia. In addition to Github,
all of the datasets are made available also on Zenodo under Creative Commons
Attribution 4.0 International license to ensure long-term findability through a
persistent identifier[1].

The contributions of this work are summarized as follows:

- **Datasets: LiterallyWikidata** which is a benchmark containing three subsets of Wikidata varying in size and structure is introduced. Each of these subsets contains both relational and attributive triples along with entity types.
- **Automatic dataset creation pipeline**: As compared to the way the current benchmarks are created, for instance, CoDEx, the pipeline used in this
  work requires very little human intervention. In CoDEx, the first step taken
  was defining a set of initial classes in some specific domains whereas in our
  pipeline it is not required for the domains and initial classes to be predefined.
  Moreover, it is possible to adapt the pipeline to create new datasets with
  newer Wikidata dumps.
- **Benchmarking**: Extensive KGC experiments have been conducted on **LiterallyWikidata** for selected embedding models with and without attributive
  triples on the task of link prediction.

---

[1] The details including the DOI are given under the reference [14].

– **Review of existing link prediction datasets**: A review of the existing KGC datasets in terms of their sources, domain, and support for literals has been conducted and presented in Table 1.

The rest of the paper is organized as follows: Sect. 2 discusses the existing KGC frameworks/datasets followed by Sect. 3, where a detailed description of the procedure followed to generate the LiterallyWikidata datasets is presented. Section 4 demonstrates the comparison between existing datasets and Literally-Wikidata whereas Sect. 5 presents benchmarking experiments on the generated datasets with uni/multimodal KGE models. Finally, concluding remarks along with directions for future work are stated in Sect. 6.

2   Related Work

A summary of the recent and the most common existing KGC benchmarks, specifically link prediction datasets, is given in Table 1. The sources of the majority of these datasets are Freebase [5], WordNet [25], YAGO [33], Wikidata [37], and NELL [8].

Freebase Extracts. FB15K and FB15K-237 are among the most popular datasets to evaluate KGC models. Even though the original releases of both datasets do not include any attributive triples, they have been extended with textual and numerical attributes [21,40,41]. However, different studies [10,15,29] have claimed that FB15K does not possess the required qualities to be actually used as a benchmark, i.e., it contains multiple inverse relations. On the other hand, in FB15K-237 which is a subset of FB15K without inverse relations, all validation and test triples containing entity pairs directly linked in the training set have been removed. Moreover, FB15K-237 contains a significant amount of triples with skewed relations towards either some head or tail entities [29] (see Sect. 4 for more details).

WordNet Extracts. Among the WordNet datasets, WN18 [6] and WN18RR [10] are the most popular ones. Both datasets are smaller in size and domain-specific as compared to the other datasets such as FB15K-237. Besides, the original releases do not contain any numerical attributive triples.

YAGO Extracts. YAGO3-10 [10] is the widely used dataset among those extracted from YAGO. It is a dataset that contains only relational triples from YAGO3 [23] mostly about locations and people. The dataset has been extended with numerical attributes, textual entity descriptions, and entity images in [27] and only with numerical attributes in [21]. Most of all, as discussed in [1], YAGO3-10 has a significant number of triples with two duplicate relations *isAffiliatedTo* and *playsFor* which makes the dataset easy for a link prediction task.

Wikidata (and Wikipedia) Extracts. Wikidata-authors [30] is a domain-specific dataset containing relational triples from Wikidata where the head entities are persons who are authors or writers. Apart from having a narrow scope and a small set of triples (i.e., 86,376), this dataset doesn't have any attributive triples. CoDEx [29] is a recent KGC benchmark extracted from Wikidata and Wikipedia. The relational triples in this dataset are from Wikidata and the attributive triples have been provided as auxiliary information taken from both Wikidata and Wikipedia. The auxiliary information contains Wikidata labels, descriptions of entities and relations along with Wikipedia page extracts for entities. This dataset does not include any numeric attribute and if we try to extract them from Wikidata, there are only limited number of entities in the dataset which have numeric attributes. Moreover, in CoDEx the set of triples already contain classes and this may decrease the level of difficulty of the dataset for tasks other than link prediction and triple classification that involve classes, i.e., entity typing/classification.

Others. There are other datasets such as NELL-995 [42] and MovieLens [27] (see Table 1 for more details). NELL-995 is a dataset extracted from the 995th iteration of NELL [8]. Due to the fact that the triples in NELL-995 are nonsensical or overly generic, the dataset is not suitable to be used as a KGC benchmark [29]. Moreover, the dataset does not have any attributive triples. MovieLens [27] is a dataset about movies where relational triples, numerical attributes, and textual attributes are from ML100K [17] and images are movie posters from TMDB[2]. This dataset contains few entities, relations, and triples as compared to the widely used KGC datasets, such as FB15K-237. Moreover, not all of the entities have textual attributes. Another very recently released benchmark is Kgbench [4] which could be used for both node classification and link prediction. However, baseline results are only provided for node classification task because the datasets are generated primarily for that particular task. Kgbench provides a set of different domain-specific datasets and in each dataset the source for the multimodality are mainly images and hence, numeric literals are available only for a limited number of entities whereas LiterallyWikidata is a collection of domain-generic datasets with every entity having some numeric literals.

In general, the existing KGC benchmarks do not give proper emphasis to attributive triples, i.e., attributes are treated as auxiliary information. Consequently, the attributive triples are either way unbalanced, less in number, or have few unique attributes. Therefore, in this work, a new KGC benchmark called **LiterallyWikidata** is presented which properly handles literals, specifically, numerical attributes and textual descriptions.

3   Dataset Creation

In this section, the procedure followed to create the LiterallyWikidata benchmark is discussed in detail. First, attributive triples with numerical literals are extracted from the Wikidata full dump from 07 September, 2020[3]. Then, relational triples are retrieved from the dump for the entities with the attributive triples. Once the triples are extracted, duplicate triples are filtered out and different datasets varying in size and structure are generated, namely, **LitWD1K**,

---

[2] https://www.themoviedb.org/.
[3] https://dumps.wikimedia.org/wikidatawiki/.

Table 1. Existing KGC datasets for the task of link prediction.

Dataset	Sources	Domain: Specific (•) Generic (⋆)	Attributive triples: Text (•), Numerical (⋆), Image (✓)	
			Original	Extended
CoDEx [29]	Wikidata [37], Wikipedia	⋆	•	
Wikidata-authors [30]	Wikidata	•		
FB15K [6]	Freebase	⋆		• [41] ⋆[40] ⋆[21]
FB15K-237 [36]				⋆[21] • [21]
FB15k-237-OWE [31]			•	
FB20K [41]			•	
FB13 [32]				
FB5M [39]				
FB24K [22]				
FB15K-401 [43]				
WN18 [6]	WordNet [25]	•		
WN18RR [10]				
WN11 [32]				
YAGO3-10 [10]	YAGO	⋆		⋆[21] • ⋆ ✓ [27]
YAGO37 [16]				
YG58K [40]				⋆[40]
NELL-995 [42] and other Nell varieties [26]	NELL [8]			
MovieLens [27]	ML 100K [17], TMDB^a	•	• ⋆ ✓	
UMLS [20]	UMLS [24]			
kinship [20]	Alyawarra kinship [19]			
Nations [20]	Nations Project [28]			
Countries [7]	Countries data^b			
Family [11,12]	Families [18]			

^a https://www.themoviedb.org/.
^b https://github.com/mledoze/countries.

LitWD19K, and **LitWD48K**. Finally, each of the datasets is divided into training, validation, and testing triples. Note that classes explicitly have not been considered as entities in this framework in order to enable the adaptability of the datasets for tasks other than link prediction such as entity type prediction. Classes in Wikidata are those items which occur either as the value/object in an instance-of (P31) statement/triple or they are subject or value/object in a subclass-of (P279) statement. In the subsequent sections, the steps taken to generate the datasets are discussed in detail, i.e., i) extracting attributive triples, ii) extracting relational triples, and iii) filtering the triples.

3.1   Extracting Attributive Triples

Note that in this phase the main focus is on extracting attributive triples with datatype properties taking numerical values. Therefore, the first step is identifying those data type properties in Wikidata. The Wikidata properties which are typed with any of the three Wikimedia datatypes *Wikimedia:Time*, *Wikimedia:GlobeCoordinate*, and *Wikimedia:Quantity* are considered, in this work, as properties taking numeric values.

Wikimedia:Time. Those properties which take *point in time* values, such as P569 (date of birth) are categorized as *Wikimedia:Time* properties.

Wikimedia:GlobeCoordinate. The values of *Wikimedia:GlobeCoordinate* typed properties such as P625 (coordinate location), are geographic coordinates given as latitude-longitude pairs. We have separated these pairs by attaching the postfix "longtiude" and "latitude" to the ID of the properties. For instance, the triple

   `<Q100000 P62''Point(5.7678 50.8283)"^^geo`[4]`:wktLiteral .>`

is transformed into the following two triples:

   `<Q100000 P625_Longtiude ''5.7678"^^xsd`[5]`:double .>` and
   `<Q100000 P625_Latitude ''50.8283"^^xsd:double .>`

Note that some entities have multiple values per property. For such entities, splitting their corresponding triples might create a logical problem, i.e., it would be difficult to associate longitude and latitude values once the triples are split. Therefore, only one triple per <*entity, property*> pair has been randomly selected before splitting.

Wikimedia:Quantity. Properties of wikimedia type *Wikimedia:Quantity* take quantities representing decimal numbers, such as P2049 (width). In the case of these properties, for every <*entity, property*> pair statements ranked as "preferred" are retrieved if there are any. Otherwise, all statements which are ranked as "Normal" are extracted. In Wikidata, such statements have units associated with their values. These units might be either SI units or non-SI units. Those values with non-SI units are normalized to their corresponding SI unit whenever possible. There are still properties with more than one unit after normalization. These units are either not normalizable or are outliers. For each statement with a non-normalizable unit, the unit is attached to the ID of the property as a postfix. For example, the property P3362 (Operating Income) takes currencies such as Q4916 (Euro), Q4917 (United States Dollar), and Q25224 (Pound sterling), as units that could not be converted to one base unit and thus, they will be combined with the property ID as in P3362_Q4916, P3362_Q4917, and P3362_Q25224 respectively. For each property, units that occur less than 1% of the time are considered outliers and are removed.

---

[4] http://www.opengis.net/ont/geosparql#.
[5] http://www.w3.org/2001/XMLSchema#.

Note that the extracted triples with the aforementioned data type properties do not include those entities which satisfy at least one of the following conditions:

- The entities do not have site-links at least to the English Wikipedia. This step is required in order to support those link prediction models which leverage textual descriptions of entities.
- The entities have types only from the set of subclasses of the class Q17379835 (Wikimedia page outside the main knowledge tree). This is imposed in order to keep only those entities which describe real-world concepts.

3.2   Extracting Relational Triples

As mentioned in Sect. 1, those triples with properties of Wikibase type *wikibase:Item* are referred to as relational triples in this paper. Once the entities with numerical literals are obtained as discussed above in Sect. 3.1, the next step is to extract relational triples for these entities. At this phase, we address both inverse properties and symmetric properties as follows:

- **Inverse properties:** Given two inverse properties p_1 and p_2 connected with the property P1696 (inverse property) where the frequency of p_1 is greater than or equal to that of p_2, the subject and object entities of those triples with p_2 have been swapped and p_2 is replaced with p_1.
- **Symmetric Properties:** In these relational triples, every relation, except P1889 (different from) whose head-tail pairs overlap with its tail-head pairs at least 50% of the time is considered as symmetric and hence, for each pair of redundant triples belonging to this relation, only one of them is kept. The property P1889 (different from) has been removed due to the fact that it occurs in a significantly high number of triples but the semantic information captured in this property is not that much beneficial for KG embedding approaches to learn better KG representation.

3.3   Filtering the Triples

Taking as inputs the extracted attributive and relational triples, the goal in this phase is to create three datasets that vary in structure and size to be used for different purposes. The smallest dataset could be used for debugging and testing KGE models with and without literals whereas the medium size dataset would suit for evaluating KGE approaches on multiple tasks in general. On the other hand, the largest dataset could be used for few-shot evaluations in addition to general evaluations for KGEs. In this section, these datasets are referred to as small, medium, and large. The following three steps are applied to create these datasets:

Seeding Entities. The top N entities with the highest number of datatype properties are considered as seed entities. The value of N is $200,000$ for the small and large datasets and $50,000$ for the medium datasets. Different values have been tried out for N and those particular values are chosen because they suit well to generate appropriate-sized datasets.

Extending the Seed Entities. At this phase, fractions of the relational triples are taken by extending the seed entities with their **one-hop** entities for the small and large datasets and with their **two-hop** neighbors for the medium dataset.

Creating k-cores. The size of the triples extracted using the steps discussed so far is huge as it is from the entire Wikidata dump. Hence, the relational triples have been further filtered into $k - cores$, i.e., maximal-subgraphs G' of a given graph G where each node in the sub-graphs has at least a degree of k [3]. The value of k is 15 for the small and medium datasets and 6 for the large datasets. Note that the values for k are determined by taking into consideration both the size and structure of the datasets to be generated. The value of k is less for the largest dataset as compared to the others because this dataset is intended to be used for few-shot evaluations. In case of few-shot evaluations, it would be possible to see the advantages of literals in learning representations for entities occurring in few structured triples. Once the k-cores are created, some triples have been removed from each of the k-cores due to the following factors:

- Either the head or the tail entity doesn't have a summary section on the corresponding English Wikipedia page or the section contains less than 3 non-stop words.
- All entities having exactly the same Wikipedia pages for various reasons have been excluded in order to avoid having meaningless descriptions.
- Relations (object properties) with more than 50% subject-object overlap have been considered as duplicates and only one of them is kept.
- Relations occurring less than 3 times have been removed to ensure that every relation has a chance to appear in the training, validation, and test sets.
- Attributes (data properties) skewed 100% of the time towards a single (head) entity have been excluded.

In the subsequent sections, the created small, medium, and large datasets are referred to as LitWD1K, LitWD19K, and LitWD48K respectively. The statistics and analysis of these datasets are presented in Table 2. Each of these datasets has been split into 90/5/5 train/valid/test sets. While splitting the datasets, we have ensured that the entities which occur in validation and test sets also occur in the respective training sets. Moreover, the test sets do not contain any relation which is 100% skewed towards a single head or tail entity. LitWD48K contains more than double the number of entities in LitWD19K. However, both datasets have almost the same number of structured triples. This is due to the way the datasets are created, i.e., LitWD19K is based on two-hop whereas LitWD48K is based on one-hop as discussed above. Table 2 also presents a summary of the analysis of the datasets in terms of graph connectivity, diameter, and density.

3.4   Textual Information

In addition to the relational and attributive (numerical) triples discussed in Sect. 3.2 and Sect. 3.1, textual information about the entities and relations has also been extracted. The textual information includes **Wikidata labels**,

Table 2. Dataset Statistics and Analysis

		LitWD1K	LitWD19K	LitWD48K
Statistics	#Entities	1,533	18,986	47,998
	#Relations	47	182	257
	#Attributes	81	151	291
	#StruTriples	29,017	288,933	336,745
	#AttrTriples	10,988	63,951	324,418
	#Train	26,115	260,039	303,117
	#Test	1,451	14,447	16,838
	#Valid	1,451	14,447	16,838
Analysis	Connectivity	Yes	Yes	No^a
	Diameter	5	7	8^b
	Density	0.01235	0.0008	0.00014

^{a} LitWD48K contains 3 connected components and the largest component contains 47,994 entities.
^{b} The diameter of the largest component of LitWD48K is 8.

aliases, and **descriptions of entities, relations, and attributes**. Moreover, for each entity, the **summary** sections of the corresponding English, German, Russian, and Chinese Wikipedia pages have been extracted. The statistics of the text literals for each dataset are given in Table 3.

Table 3. Short and long text literals extracted from Wikidta and Wikipedia for entities, relations and attributes. The values are presented in percentage.

	Wikipedia summary				Wikidata (entity/relation/attrb) (en)		
	en	de	ru	zh	Labels	Aliases	Descriptions
LitWD1K	100	78	72	66	100/100/100	38/83/81	95/98/100
LitWD19K	100	80	65	39	100/100/100	44/87/81	99/99/100
LitWD48K	100	88	75	29	100/100/100	47/87/79	99/99/100

3.5 Domain of the Datasets

Since the pipeline developed in this study to create LiterallyWikidata framework does not require pre-defining the domains or classes of entities or relations, the created datasets are generic and their domains could be identified only after they are created. Based on the types/classes of entities, People, Geography, Entertainment, Transportation, Sport, Travel, Business, and Research are among the domains covered in LiterallyWikidata. The classes/types of the entities are also released along with the datasets.

4   Comparison with Existing Datasets

Link prediction benchmark datasets are usually characterized based on the nature of the relations such as symmetricity, inversion, skeweness, and cartesian product (fixed-set). Link prediction with symmetric/inverse/cartesian product relations is easy and does not require a complex embedding model [1,29]. It could also be done with simple rule based approaches. Here, the comparison will be with two existing datasets, FB15K-237 as the most popular extension of FB15K and CoDEx-M as the most recent dataset extracted from Wikidata. In order to make a fair comparison, the LitWD19K dataset is chosen to be compared against these datasets as it is comparable to both in terms of size.

Skeweness. As reported in CoDEx [29], 15.98% and 1.26% of test triples in FB15K-237 and CoDEx-M contain relations which are skewed 50% or more toward a single head or tail entity. In our case, as it has already been mentioned above, while splitting the LiterallyWikidata datasets we have made sure to exclude any relation which is 100% skewed towards a single head or tail entity in each of the datasets. However, for a fair comparison with the numbers reported in CoDEx [29], we also consider skewed relations as relations which are skewed 50% or more (instead of 100%) towards a single head or tail entity and find 6.48% of the test sets of LitWD19K to contain such skewed relations. This number does not have much of an impact as its coverage of the test set is low and also as already mentioned, none of the relations are 100% skewed.

Symmetricity. 4.01% of the triples in CoDEx-M contain symmetric relations [29]. In case of FB15K-237, every validation and test triple containing entity pairs that are directly linked in the training set were removed, which leads to deleting any symmetric relations from its test/validation sets. LitWD19K does not contain any symmetric relation in the entire dataset not only test/valid sets.

Inversion. Similar to the existing datasets FB15K-237 and CoDEx-M, LitWD19K also do not contain any inverse relations (see Sect. 3.2 for more details).

Cartesian Product or Fixed-set Relations. As reported in [29], about 12.7% of test triples in FB15K-237 contain fixed-set relations, i.e., relations which connect entities to fixed sets of values. On the other hand, both CoDEx-M and our dataset (LitWD19K) do not contain any such kind of relation.

5   Benchmarking Experiments on Link Prediction

In this section, the benchmarking experiments conducted on the link prediction task are discussed. The chosen KGE approaches, the model selection strategy, and the obtained results are presented. Note that there are properties in the LiterallyWikidata datasets which take date values. In order to treat those date values as numeric literals, for the experiments, the values are converted to decimals. This allows leveraging the semantics present in all parts of the date values, i.e., the year, the month, the days, and so on.

5.1 KGE Models

In this study, the models DistMult-LiteralE, DistMult, and ComplEx have been chosen to conduct the benchmarking experiments. The model DistMult-LiteralE was selected because the main focus of this study lies in providing benchmark datasets for KGE with literals whereas the other models DistMult and ComplEx are included to show the comparisons with and without literals. For more details on KGEs with literals please refer to [15]. **DistMult** scores a given triple using a diagonal bilinear interaction function between the head and tail entity embeddings and the relation embeddings - $f(h, t, r) = h^T diag(r)t$. This model can only deal with symmetric relations due to the fact that $f(h, t, r) = f(r, t, h)$. **ComplEx** is an extension of DistMult, which uses complex-valued embeddings in order to better handle asymmetric relations. Its scoring function is defined as - $f(h, t, r) = Re(h^T diag(r)\bar{t})$ where $Re(.)$ is the real part and $\bar{t}$ is the conjugate of t. **DistMultLiteral** extends DistMult by modifying the scoring function f such that the entity embeddings of h and t are replaced with their respective literal enriched representations h^{lit} and t^{lit}.

5.2 Model Selection

As it has been demonstrated in [2], in addition to a model's architecture, the combination of the training approach and the loss function used also plays an important role to determine a model's performance. Hence, we used a pytorch-based configurable KGE framework **Pykeen**[6] to search from a large range of hyperparameters listed in Table 4. First, around 70 different combinations of datasets, models, training approaches, losses, regularizers and optimizers (for example, **LitWD1K + DistMult + LCWA + CEL + LP + Adam**) were defined as configurations. Then, for each of these configurations, **random search** has been used to perform the hyper-parameter optimizations over all other hyper-parameters in order to select the best models. The details on the training approaches, losses, and search strategies are given as follows:

Training Approaches and Loss Functions. The models have been trained based on the sLCWA (Stochastic Local Closed World Assumption) and LCWA (Local Closed World Assumption) approaches. The sLCWA training approach has been used with UNS (Uniform Negative Sampler) to generate negative samples. The loss functions Cross Entropy Loss (CEL) and Binary Cross Entropy Loss (BCEL) are used together with LCWA whereas BCEL and Margin Ranking Loss (MRL) are used with sLCWA. In order to learn more about these training approaches and losses refer to [2].

Search Strategies. For each configuration with LitWD1K, a maximum of 100 trials are generated within a bound of 24 h for DistMult and DistMultLiteral, and 36 h for ComplEx. During each trial, the model is trained for 1000 epochs. On the other hand, for LitWD19K and LitWD48K a maximum of 100 trials are

---

[6] https://pykeen.readthedocs.io/en/latest/.

Table 4. Hyper-parameter search space

Hyper-parameter	Range
Embedding dimension	{64,128,256}
Initialization	{Xavier}
Optimizers[a]	{Adam, Adadgrad}
Regulaizer	{None, L1, L2}
Weight for L1 and L2	[0.01, 1.0)
Learning Rate (log scale)	[0.001, 0.1)
Batch size	{128, 256, 512, 1024}
Input dropout[b]	{0,0.1,0.2,0.3,0.4,0.5}
Training Approach[c]	
sLCWA	
Loss	{BCEL, MRL}
Number of Negatives	{1, 2, ... , 100}
Margin for MRL	{0.5, 1.5, ... , 9.5}
LCWA	
Loss	{BCEL, CEL}
Label Smoothing (log scale)	[0.001, 1.0)

[a] We evaluated both Adam & Adagrad using DistMult & DistMultLiteral on LitWD1K and using DistMult on LitWD19K & LitWD48K(sLCWA). The result indicates that Adagrad performs better than Adam on the smallest dataset whereas Adam is better on the larger ones. Hence, for that reason and also due to the fact that Adam is known for addressing the problem of decreasing learning rate in Adagrad, for the two larger datasets, we sticked to Adam for the rest of the experiments in order to reduce computational cost.

[b] The input dropout range is applied to DistMultLiteral

[c] We have evaluated both sLCWA & LCWA using DistMult & DistMultLiteral on all the three datasets and learned that LCWA performs better at all times. Hence, we used only LCWA for the rest of the experiments.

generated within 48 h for DistMult and DistMultLiteral, and 60 h for ComplEx. Every trial is run for a maximum of 500 epochs where early stopping is performed by evaluating the model every 25 epochs with a patience of 50 epochs on the validation set using MRR. Finally, for each dataset and embedding model pair (e.g., LitWD1K+DistMult), the best configuration is chosen based on the evaluation result on the validation set. Then, evaluation is carried out using the test set by retraining the selected models on each dataset for 1000 epochs. In order to make sure that the results reported are consistent, the retraining is done three times for all models on LitWD1K and for DistMult on LitWD19K and since we find the results to be very close, we run the retraining only once for the rest of the experiments.

The experiments with LitWD1K and LitWD19K are run on TITAN X (Pascal) 12 GB whereas those on LitWD48K are run on NVIDIA Tesla V100S-PCIE-32GB. The optimal hyperparameter values for each of the models on all the datasets are provided along with the datasets on Github[7].

5.3 Results

The results of the experiments on link prediction are presented in Table 5. Three different comparisons can be made from the results, i.e., i) unimodal vs. multimodal, ii) between uni-modals, and ii) proposed datasets vs. existing datasets.

- **Unimodal vs. Multi-modal:** Here, we compare DistMult with DistMut-Literal because DistMutLiteral is a multimodal KGE that extends DistMult. As it is seen in the results, for all of the three datasets DistMultLiteral outperforms DistMult w.r.t. almost all metrics. This indicates that making use of literals (numeric literals) improves entity representations.
- **Unimodal vs. Unimodal:** When comparing the unimodals, ComplEx, and DistMult, we see that ComplEx performs better than DistMult on the largest dataset LitWD48K. On the other two datasets, the results of the two models are comparable.
- **Proposed datasets vs. Existing datasets:** In order to show the level of difficulty of the proposed datasets, here we compare the results of the two unimodals on LitWD19K and the existing datasets FB15K-237 and CoDEx-M. For both ComplEx and DistMult, w.r.t. all metrics, the results on LitWD19K are worse than those on FB15K-237 and CoDEx-M.

Table 5. Results of link prediction

Dataset		Model	MRR	Hits@1	Hits@10
Ours	LitWD1K	DistMult	0.419	0.283	0.697
		ComplEx	0.413	0.28	0.673
		DistMultLiteral	**0.431**	**0.297**	**0.703**
	LitWD19K	DistMult	0.195	0.138	0.308
		ComplEx	0.181	0.122	0.296
		DistMultLiteral	**0.245**	**0.168**	**0.399**
	LitWD48K	DistMult	0.261	0.195	0.4
		ComplEx	0.277	**0.207**	0.428
		DistMultLiteral	**0.279**	0.204	**0.434**
Existing*	FB15K-237	DistMult	0.343	0.250	0.531
		ComplEx	0.348	0.253	0.536
	CoDEx-M	ComplEx	0.337	0.262	0.476

* The results are copied from LibKGE (https://github.com/uma-pi1/kge.)

---

[7] https://github.com/GenetAsefa/LiterallyWikidata.

6   Conclusion and Future Work

This study presents LiterallyWikidata which is a set of KGC datasets extracted from Wikidata and Wikipedia with a special focus on literals. The existing datasets FB15K-237 (popular) and CoDEx (recent) are both valuable datasets for link prediction with unimodal KGC models. However,we have shown that LiterallyWikidata is appropriate for both unimodal and multimodal link prediction tasks. Besides, directions for future work on LiterallyWikidata are indicated as follows:

- **More tasks**: Using the datasets with other tasks such as triple classification.
- **More Experiments**: Conducting experiments with text literals and also by fusing relational triples, numeric literals, short text literals (aliases and labels), and long text literals all together. Moreover, experiments with more varieties of KGE models will be performed.
- **Detailed analysis**: Conducting further analysis on the datasets in terms of compositionality will be undertaken, so as to explore its use for models which leverage paths.
- **Studying data bias**: Bias in training data is one of the crucial aspects of Machine Learning that needs to be carefully addressed. Since Wikidata is one of the crowd-sourced KGs, it is susceptible to biases. These biases in Wikidata reflect the real-world and hence, LiterallyWikidata may as well be biased. However, the current version of the dataset is not yet de-biased. We are currently investigating whether de-biasing should be done and what methods exist for such purpose.

We hope that the release of LiterallyWikidata fosters research on more sophisticated KGE models that exploit the additional semantics provided with literals.

References

1. Akrami, F., Saeef, M.S., Zhang, Q., Hu, W., Li, C.: Realistic re-evaluation of knowledge graph completion methods: An experimental study. In: Proceedings of the ACM SIGMOD International Conference on Management of Data (2020)
2. Ali, M., et al.: Bringing light into the dark: a large-scale evaluation of knowledge graph embedding models under a unified framework. arXiv preprint arXiv:2006.13365 (2020)
3. Batagelj, V., Zaveršnik, M.: Fast algorithms for determining (generalized) core groups in social networks. Adv. Data Anal. Classif. **5**(2), 129–145 (2011)
4. van Berkel, L., de Boer, V.: kgbench: A collection of knowledge graph datasets for evaluating relational and multimodal machine learning. In: ESWC (2021)
5. Bollacker, K., Evans, C., Paritosh, P., Sturge, T., Taylor, J.: Freebase: a collaboratively created graph database for structuring human knowledge. In: Proceedings of the ACM SIGMOD international conference on Management of data (2008)

6. Bordes, A., Usunier, N., Garcia-Duran, A., Weston, J., Yakhnenko, O.: Translating embeddings for modeling multi-relational data. In: NIPS (2013)
7. Bouchard, G., Singh, S., Trouillon, T.: On approximate reasoning capabilities of low-rank vector spaces. In: AAAI Spring Symposia (2015)
8. Carlson, A., Betteridge, J., Kisiel, B., Settles, B., Hruschka, E.R., Mitchell, T.M.: Toward an architecture for never-ending language learning. In: Proceedings of the Twenty-Fourth AAAI Conference on Artificial Intelligence. AAAI Press (2010)
9. Daza, D., Cochez, M., Groth, P.: Inductive entity representations from text via link prediction. In: Proceedings of the Web Conference 2021, pp. 798–808 (2021)
10. Dettmers, T., Minervini, P., Stenetorp, P., Riedel, S.: Convolutional 2d knowledge graph embeddings. In: Thirty-Second AAAI Conference on Artificial Intelligence (2018)
11. García-Durán, A., Bordes, A., Usunier, N.: Effective blending of two and three-way interactions for modeling multi-relational data. In: Calders, T., Esposito, F., Hüllermeier, E., Meo, R. (eds.) ECML PKDD 2014. LNCS (LNAI), vol. 8724, pp. 434–449. Springer, Heidelberg (2014). https://doi.org/10.1007/978-3-662-44848-9_28
12. García-Durán, A., Bordes, A., Usunier, N.: Composing relationships with translations. In: Proceedings of the Conference on Empirical Methods in Natural Language Processing, pp. 286–290. Association for Computational Linguistics (2015)
13. García-Durán, A., Niepert, M.: KBLRN: End-to-end learning of knowledge base representations with latent, relational, and numerical features. In: Globerson, A., Silva, R. (eds.) Proceedings of the Thirty-Fourth Conference on Uncertainty in Artificial Intelligence, pp. 372–381. AUAI Press (2018)
14. Gesese, G.A., Alam, M., Sack, H.: LiterallyWikidata - A Benchmark for Knowledge Graph Completion using Literals April 2021. https://doi.org/10.5281/zenodo.4701190
15. Gesese, G.A., Biswas, R., Alam, M., Sack, H.: A survey on knowledge graph embeddings with literals: Which model links better literal-ly?. arXiv preprint arXiv:1910.12507 (2019)
16. Guo, S., Wang, Q., Wang, L., Wang, B., Guo, L.: Knowledge graph embedding with iterative guidance from soft rules. In: Proceedings of the Thirty-Second AAAI Conference on Artificial Intelligence (2018)
17. Harper, F.M., Konstan, J.A.: The movielens datasets: history and context. ACM Trans. Interact. Intell. Syst. 5(4), 1–19 (2015)
18. Hinton, G.E., et al.: Learning distributed representations of concepts. In: Proceedings of the Eighth Annual Conference of the Cognitive Science Society, vol. 1, p. 12. Amherst (1986)
19. Kemp, C., Tenenbaum, J.B., Griffiths, T.L., Yamada, T., Ueda, N.: Learning systems of concepts with an infinite relational model. In: Proceedings of the 21st National Conference on Artificial Intelligence, vol. 1, pp. 381–388. AAAI 2006, AAAI Press (2006)
20. Kok, S., Domingos, P.: Statistical predicate invention. In: Proceedings of the 24th International Conference on Machine Learning. Association for Computing Machinery (2007)
21. Kristiadi, A., Khan, M.A., Lukovnikov, D., Lehmann, J., Fischer, A.: Incorporating literals into knowledge graph embeddings. In: Ghidini, C., et al. (eds.) ISWC 2019. LNCS, vol. 11778, pp. 347–363. Springer, Cham (2019). https://doi.org/10.1007/978-3-030-30793-6_20

22. Lin, Y., Liu, Z., Sun, M.: Knowledge representation learning with entities, attributes and relations. In: Proceedings of the Twenty-Fifth International Joint Conference on Artificial Intelligence IJCAI 2016, pp. 2866–2872. AAAI Press (2016)
23. Mahdisoltani, F., Biega, J., Suchanek, F.M.: Yago3: A knowledge base from multilingual wikipedias. In: CIDR (2015)
24. McCray, A.: An upper-level ontology for the biomedical domain. Comp. Funct. Genomics **4**, 80–84 (2003)
25. Miller, G.A.: Wordnet: a lexical database for english. Commun. ACM **38**, 39–41 (1995)
26. Mitchell, T., et al.: Never-ending learning. Commun. ACM **61**(5), 103–115 (2018)
27. Pezeshkpour, P., Chen, L., Singh, S.: Embedding multimodal relational data for knowledge base completion. In: Proceedings of the 2018 Conference on Empirical Methods in Natural Language Processing, pp. 3208–3218. Association for Computational Linguistics October-November 2018
28. Rummel, R.J.: Dimensionality of nations project: Attributes of nations and behavior of nation dyads, pp. 1950–1965, 16 February 1992
29. Safavi, T., Koutra, D.: CoDEx: A comprehensive knowledge graph completion benchmark. In: Proceedings of the 2020 Conference on Empirical Methods in Natural Language Processing (EMNLP), November 2020
30. Safavi, T., Koutra, D., Meij, E.: Improving the utility of knowledge graph embeddings with calibration. arXiv preprint arXiv:2004.01168 (2020)
31. Shah, H., Villmow, J., Ulges, A., Schwanecke, U., Shafait, F.: An open-world extension to knowledge graph completion models. In: AAAI (2019)
32. Socher, R., Chen, D., Manning, C.D., Ng, A.Y.: Reasoning with neural tensor networks for knowledge base completion. In: Proceedings of the 26th International Conference on Neural Information Processing Systems, vol. 1 (2013)
33. Suchanek, F.M., Kasneci, G., Weikum, G.: Yago: A core of semantic knowledge. In: 16th International Conference on the World Wide Web, pp. 697–706 (2007)
34. Sun, Z., Deng, Z.H., Nie, J.Y., Tang, J.: Rotate: knowledge graph embedding by relational rotation in complex space. In: International Conference on Learning Representations (2019)
35. Tay, Y., Tuan, L.A., Phan, M.C., Hui, S.C.: Multi-task neural network for non-discrete attribute prediction in knowledge graphs. In: Proceedings of the 2017 ACM on Conference on Information and Knowledge Management. pp. 1029–1038. Association for Computing Machinery (2017)
36. Toutanova, K., Chen, D.: Observed versus latent features for knowledge base and text inference. In: Proceedings of the 3rd Workshop on Continuous Vector Space Models and their Compositionality (2015)
37. Vrandečić, D., Krötzsch, M.: Wikidata: a free collaborative knowledgebase. Commun. ACM **57**(10), 78–85 (2014)
38. Wang, Q., Mao, Z., Wang, B., Guo, L.: Knowledge graph embedding: a survey of approaches and applications. IEEE Trans. Knowl. Data Eng. **29**(12), 2724–2743 (2017)
39. Wang, Z., Zhang, J., Feng, J., Chen, Z.: Knowledge graph embedding by translating on hyperplanes. In: Proceedings of the Twenty-Eighth AAAI Conference on Artificial Intelligence AAAI 2014, pp. 1112–1119. AAAI Press (2014)
40. Wu, Y., Wang, Z.: Knowledge graph embedding with numeric attributes of entities. In: Proceedings of The Third Workshop on Representation Learning for NLP, pp. 132–136. Association for Computational Linguistics (2018)

41. Xie, R., Liu, Z., Jia, J., Luan, H., Sun, M.: Representation learning of knowledge graphs with entity descriptions. In: AAAI (2016)
42. Xiong, W., Hoang, T., Wang, W.Y.: DeepPath: A reinforcement learning method for knowledge graph reasoning. In: Proceedings of the Conference on Empirical Methods in Natural Language Processing (EMNLP) (2017)
43. Yang, B., Yih, W.t., He, X., Gao, J., Deng, L.: Embedding entities and relations for learning and inference in knowledge bases. In: International Conference on Learning Representations (ICLR) (2015)

A Framework for Quality Assessment of Semantic Annotations of Tabular Data

Roberto Avogadro[1], Marco Cremaschi[1]([✉]), Ernesto Jiménez-Ruiz[2,3],
and Anisa Rula[4]

[1] University of Milano - Bicocca, Milano, Italy
{roberto.avogadro,marco.cremaschi}@unimib.it
[2] City, University of London, London, UK
ernesto.jimenez-ruiz@city.ac.uk
[3] University of Oslo, Oslo, Norway
[4] University of Brescia, Brescia, Italy
anisa.rula@unibs.it

Abstract. Much information is conveyed within tables, which can be semantically annotated by humans or (semi)automatic approaches. Nevertheless, many applications cannot take full advantage of semantic annotations because of the low quality. A few methodologies exist for the quality assessment of semantic annotation of tabular data, but they do not automatically assess the quality as a multidimensional concept through different quality dimensions. The quality dimensions are implemented in STILTool 2, a web application to automate the quality assessment of the annotations. The evaluation is carried out by comparing the quality of semantic annotations with gold standards. The work presented here has been applied to at least three use cases. The results show that our approach can give us hints about the quality issues and how to address them.

Keywords: Data quality · Semantic annotations · Tabular data · Semantic table interpretation

Resource type	Software Framework
Website	https://bitbucket.org/disco_unimib/stiltool/
Permanent URL	http://doi.org/10.5281/zenodo.4704645.

1 Introduction

Much information is conveyed within tables. A prominent example is the large set of relational databases or tabular data present on the Web. To size the spread of tabular data, 2.5M tables have been identified within the Common Crawl repository [12]. The current snapshot of Wikipedia contains more than 3.23M tables from more than 520k Wikipedia articles [7]. The tables may contain high-value

© Springer Nature Switzerland AG 2021
A. Hotho et al. (Eds.): ISWC 2021, LNCS 12922, pp. 528–545, 2021.
https://doi.org/10.1007/978-3-030-88361-4_31

data, but they can be challenging to understand both for humans and machines due to the lack of contextual information or metadata. In order to solve this problem, several techniques have been proposed in the state-of-the-art, whose aim is the semantic annotation of tabular data using information extracted from a Knowledge Graph (KG) (e.g., DBpedia[1]). However, modelling and constructing semantically annotated datasets poses different quality issues due to: (i) the automatic procedures which are often error-prone; (ii) the autonomous information providers who are not aware of the final usage of the dataset; (iii) the schema-last approach which allows to first publish the data and optionally creates the schema. These may create several concerns with regard to the quality of the annotations.

There already exist some approaches which are focused on the quality assessment of the datasets [4,19]. Besides conceptual and theoretical considerations, several tools and methodologies for practical assessment are proposed [4,18]. However, most of these approaches are focused on the quality assessment of datasets and not on the quality assessment of the process used to transform tabular data to their semantic representation. Instead, a few approaches are proposed for the quality assessment of the mappings generated by the mapping languages such as R2RML [5,6,11,14,16]. As explained by the authors in [5], the root cause of the low quality of datasets is often due to the problems encountered during the mapping phase, such as inconsistencies with the KG schema. Inspired by the approaches proposed for the quality assessment of mapping languages, we think that an approach proposed for the quality assessment of the annotation process would be of benefit for the consumption of the semantic annotations.

To better understand the quality issues in a semantic annotation process but, at the same time, their root causes, we provide an open-source framework within the STILTool system [1], named STILTool 2. First, we need to measure and assess the quality of the steps belonging to the semantic annotation process through several quality dimensions. There are different possible ways to assess semantic table annotations, either employing a gold standard or not. As explained in [15] the assessment through gold standards may present advantages (e.g., highly reliable results) and disadvantages (e.g., costly to produce). While other frameworks such as Luzzu [4] implement only metrics that do not use a gold standard, our framework STILTool 2 has the advantage that its architectural design choices allow the implementation of metrics that require or not a gold standard. Second, we aim to guide the users to understand the real causes of the detected quality issues. STILTool 2 is not only able to assess the quality metrics on semantic annotations similarly to Luzzu, but it also provides hints on the possible quality issues in the process of semantic annotation. The insights gained from such assessment are useful to inform users about particular problems and help identify which stage of the annotation process must be improved.

In this work, we make the following contributions:

- we provide a methodology that can be used to characterise the levels of quality for a semantically annotated dataset;

---

[1] https://wiki.dbpedia.org/.

- we introduce our (open-source) quality assessment framework to be adopted by the SemTab 2021 challenge [9,10];
- we evaluate our approach empirically;
- we briefly present three use cases where STILTool 2 can be used.

The rest of the paper is organised as follows: an overview of the semantic annotation steps is given in Sect. 2. The approach for the assessment of quality metrics for each step of the semantic annotation is detailed in Sect. 3. Details of the architectural and implementation choices are discussed in Sect. 4. Evaluation is provided in Sect. 5. Related work on the assessment of quality metrics is discussed in Sect. 6. Finally, we conclude and suggest planned extensions of our framework in Sect. 7.

2   Semantic Annotation Tasks

In order to produce the annotation of tabular data, it is necessary to take two elements as input: *(i)* a *well-formed and normalised* relational table T (*i.e.*, a table with headers and simple values, thus excluding nested and figure-like tables), as the one in Fig. 1, and *(ii)* a *KG* which describes real world entities in the domain of interest (*i.e.*, a set of concepts, datatypes, predicates/properties, instances, and the relations among them), as the example in Fig. 2. The table in Fig. 1 is extracted from T2Dv2 gold standards[2]. The output returned is a semantically annotated table, as shown in Fig. 3.

Name	Coordinates	Height	Range
Mont Blanc	45°49′57″N 06°51′52″E	4808	Mont Blanc massif
Lyskamm	45°55′20″N 07°50′08″E	4527	Pennine Alps
Monte Cervino	45°58′35″N 07°39′31″E	4478	Pennine Alps

Fig. 1. Example of a well-formed relational table T, with labels that are used in this paper.

We can identify three types of annotations of tabular data [9]: *(i)* Column-Type Annotation (CTA), *(ii)* Columns-Property Annotation (CPA) and *(iii)* Cell-Entity Annotation (CEA). These tasks can be performed by humans or by automatic or semi-automatic approaches. The *CTA* expects the prediction of the semantic types (*i.e.*, KG classes or concepts) for every given table column c_j in a table T, *i.e.*, $CTA(T, c_j, KG) = st_1, ..., st_a$. The *CEA* requires the prediction of the entity or entities (*i.e.*, instances) that a cell $(i,j) \in T$ represents, *i.e.*,

---

[2] http://webdatacommons.org/webtables/goldstandardV2.html table index: 1431124 4_0_7604843865524657408, 49801939_0_6964113429298874283.

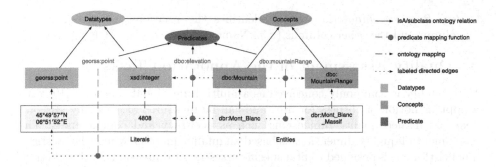

Fig. 2. A sample of Knowledge Graph.

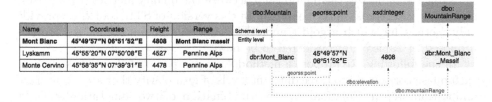

Fig. 3. Example of an annotated table.

$CEA(T, (i, j), KG) = e_1, ..., e_b$. Finally, the *CPA* expects as output a set of KG properties that represent the relationship between the elements of the input columns c_j and c_k, *i.e.*, $CPA(T, c_j, c_k, KG) = p_1, ..., p_c$. Note that CTA (resp. CEA) focuses on categorical columns (resp. cells) that can be represented with a KG class (resp. KG entity) [10].

To obtain the three types of annotation described above, various processes have been defined in the state-of-the-art, which we can summarise in these steps:

(i) Semantic classification of columns, which considers the content of the cells of each column c_j to mark a column as *Literal column (L-column)* if values in cells are elements of a datatype (*e.g.*, strings, numbers, dates such as 4808, 10/04/1983), or as *Named-Entity column (NE-column)* if values are elements of a concept (*e.g.*, Mountain, Mountain Range such as Mont_Blanc, Mont_Blanc_massif);

(ii) Detection of the subject column (S-column), which has the goal of identifying, among the NE-columns, the column that all the others are referring to (*e.g.*, the Name column in Fig. 3);

(iii) Concept, entity and datatype annotation, which pairs NE-columns with concepts extracted from the KG by first linking cell entities to KG and then inferring the column concept st (*e.g.*, the column Name is associated with Mountain in DBpedia[3]), and L-columns with a datatype dt in the KG (*e.g.*, the column Coordinates is of type `georss:point`); and

---

[3] http://dbpedia.org/resource/Mountain.

(iv) Property annotation, which identifies the relations p between the S-column and the other columns (*e.g.*, Name `dbo:elevation` Height).

3 Quality Assessment of the Annotation Tasks

Data quality is commonly conceived as a multi-dimensional construct [19] with a popular notion of "fitness for use" and can be measured along many abstract concepts named quality dimensions such as accuracy and completeness. The assessment of quality dimensions is based on quality metrics, where the metric is a heuristic that is designed to fit a specific assessment dimension. In this Section, we provide quality metrics and their relations with the annotation steps, which should help to detect possible quality issues in the semantic annotations.

Table 1 summarizes the relationship between the quality metrics (in the rows) and annotation steps (in the columns). In this version of STILTool 2, we provide only metrics for which a gold standard is required. Therefore, all the metrics proposed in Table 7 are considered to be new.

In the following, we propose a methodology composed of three phases where each phase correspond to three different levels of granularity that are: *(i)* a single annotation step in isolation, *(ii)* the combination of two annotation steps at instance level (*e.g.*, CEA and CPA), and *(iii)* the combination of two annotation steps at schema level (*e.g.*, CTA and CPA). For each step, there is a set of metrics applied for capturing the quality issues. Metrics can be further aggregated to produce a single quality score. To each metric we assign a weight according to its importance with respect to the annotation steps. For simplicity, we assign a default weight of 1.0 to all metrics.

Table 1. Relationship between quality metrics and the semantic annotation steps.

Metric	Abbr	Annotation steps			
		Concept annotation	Entity annotation	Datatype annotation	Property Annotation
Concept and datatype completeness	CM1	Y		Y	
Property completeness	CM3				Y
Entity completeness	CM2		Y		
Entity candidate coverage	EC		Y		
Type specificity	TS	Y			
Link completeness	LC		Y	Y	Y
Link accuracy	AC		Y	Y	Y
Abstract link completeness	ALC	Y			Y
Abstract link accuracy	ALA	Y			Y

3.1 Phase I: Quality Assessment of the Single Annotation Step

In this first phase, we focus on assessing the quality in terms of completeness and consistency of the single annotation steps.

Completeness Dimension refers to the degree to which all required information is present in a particular dataset [19].

Concept and Datatype Completeness returns the number of the non missing concepts and datatypes in the semantic annotation with respect to the gold standard. The two annotation steps which can generate issues related to this quality metric are: concept and datatype annotation.

Property Completeness returns the number of the non missing properties in the semantic annotation with respect to the gold standard. The annotation step which can generate issues related to this quality metric is: property annotation. In the example of Fig. 3 the table is annotated with concepts: dbo:Mountain, dbo:MountainRange; properties: georss:point, dbo:elevation, dbo:mounta inRange; and datatypes: georss:point, xsd:integer. Suppose that the values of the coordinates column are not present in the KG but location names are such as Haute-Savoie which in turn is not present in the table. Therefore, it is not possible to annotate the property for the column *Coordinates* since its values are not available in the KG. As such, the metric, completeness of properties will identify two properties out of three.

Entity Completeness returns the number of the non missing entities in the semantic annotation with respect to the gold standard. The annotation step which can generate issues related to this quality metric is: entity annotation. In the example of Fig. 3 the table is annotated with entities such as dbr:Mont_Blanc in the NE-columns. Suppose that for disambiguation reasons, the Lyskamm mountain cannot find an entity in the KG. Therefore, it is not possible to indicate an entity for that value, as such, the metric completeness of entities will identify two entities out of three.

Entity Candidate Coverage returns the number of correct candidate entities with respect to the gold standard. The annotation step which can generate issues related to this quality metric is: entity annotation. For example, consider the table in Fig. 3, retrieving all the entities candidates for the cells belonging to NE-columns *Name* and *Range* columns. Suppose that the candidates of the cells "Mont Blanc", "Lyskamm" and "Pennine Alps" contain the correct entities from the candidate list obtained by our approach. In this case, the metric will return a coverage of 60%, meaning that only three cells out of five obtained the correct entity in the list of the candidates returned. This metric is also an indication of the upper threshold of the precision of our approach, *i.e.*, whatever we do in the next steps of the selection of the entity, we will never get a precision higher than the coverage score.

Consistency Dimension means that a knowledge base is free of (logical/formal) contradictions with respect to particular knowledge representation and inference mechanisms [19].

Type Specificity returns the number of "specific/generic" types with respect to the gold standard. The annotation step which can generate issues related to this quality metric is: concept annotation. In particular, this metric will not only identify a boolean of correct and wrong concepts but will identify *good* concepts too. These concepts are in a subclass or superclass relationship with the correct concept (also referred to as perfect concept), that is, they are *descendent* and *ancestor* concepts, respectively. For example consider Fig. 3 and suppose our approach annotates the column *Name* with dbo:NaturalPlace and *Range* with dbo:MountainRange. In this case, we will have one ancestor annotation and one perfect annotation.

3.2   Phase II: Quality Assessment of the Combined Annotation Steps at Instance Level

In this second phase, we focus on assessing the quality in terms of interlinking completeness and accuracy of the combined annotation tasks of CEA and CPA.

Interlinking Dimension refers to the degree to which entities are linked to each other within a data source or among two or more data sources [19]. We are interested to measure the completeness and the accuracy of links (*i.e.*, RDF triples) because the combination of the elements in the triples such as pairs of two entities or, an entity and its property, may provide us additional insights about the coverage or accuracy.

Link Completeness returns the number of the non missing triples in the semantic annotation with respect to the gold standard. The annotation steps which can generate issues related to this quality metric are: entity and property annotation. Referring to Fig. 3, we only have one subject column and the others are either Literal or NE-columns, therefore, the total number of possible triples generated by this table of dimension 3×3 (without considering the subject) is nine. Suppose that our approach generates eight out of nine triples, thus the metric will return 89% of completeness.

Link Accuracy returns the number of correct triples in the semantic annotation with respect to the gold standard. The annotation steps which can generate issues related to this quality metric are: entity and property annotation. While completeness focus on the number of missing triples returned, this metric assesses if all the three elements (subject, property and object) of the triple are correct. Suppose a triple returned from the annotation in Fig. 3 where only the subject is correct <dbr:Mont_Blanc,dbo:mountainRange,dbr:Mont_Blanc_Massif> thus, the triple is considered not accurate which will be penalized by assigning a score of zero. While the metrics of completeness and accuracy in **Phase I** indicate the single elements of this triple to be correct, the link accuracy metric captures the errors due to the combination of the elements in a triple.

3.3   Phase III: Quality Assessment of the Combined Annotation Steps at Schema Level

In the third phase we focus on assessing the quality in terms of interlinking completeness and accuracy of the combined annotation tasks of CTA and CPA.

Types Interlinking Dimension refers to the degree to which types are linked to each other through a property. Interlinking aspects can be influenced by the combination of types and property annotation tasks. For example, if two columns are to be annotated with the types A and B in CTA and with the property R in CPA, this combined annotation can be represented as an abstract triple $<A,R,B>$. We are interested to measure the completeness and the accuracy of links which refer to (abstract) RDF triples.

Abstract Link Completeness returns the number of the non missing (abstract) triples in the semantic annotation with respect to the gold standard. As shown in Table 1, the annotation steps which can generate issues related to this quality metric are: concept and property annotation. This metric is similarly calculated as the link completeness metric in **Phase II** where each entity has at maximum one type assigned.

Abstract Link Accuracy returns the numbers of correct (abstract) triples in the semantic annotation with respect to the gold standard. As shown in Table 1, the annotation steps which can generate issues related to this quality metric are concept and property annotation. For example, if we consider the (abstract) triple $<$dbo:NaturalPlace, dbo:locatedInArea, dbo:MountainRange$>$ generated by the annotation, the metric will identify it as not correct with respect to the gold standard, although the elements separately can be correct (*e.g.*, dbo:MountainRange and dbo:NaturalPlace are both ancestors)

4   System Overview and Implementation

Figure 4 shows the general architecture of STILTool 2[4]. The tool is developed with the Django framework[5] in Python, and exploits a MongoDB[6] database as data repository. Three main layers can be identified. Within the *view*, three main components have been implemented. The first component allows to view the list, and manage, the gold standards. The second component allows the management of semantic annotations. The third component of the view allows the visualisation of the loaded tables. For each table, the tool visualises the analysis related to the evaluation metrics (*e.g.*, Accuracy, Recall, F measure) and the quality dimensions described in the previous sections. In the second level, the *controller*, the methods (creation, reading, updating and deletion) for managing the gold standards and the semantic annotations have been implemented. Two components, on the other hand, allow the calculation of quality and evaluation metrics. The controller also allows the query of external KGs (*i.e.*, DBpedia and Wikidata) necessary to calculate quality metrics. In the last level, the *model*, it is possible to identify the representations in the form of an object (ORM) of the entities present in the database.

---

[4] https://stiltool.disco.unimib.it/.
[5] https://www.djangoproject.com/.
[6] https://www.mongodb.com/.

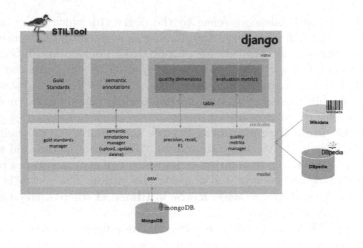

Fig. 4. Architecture of STILTool 2.

The tool is available through a Git repository[7]. The tool has been encapsulated in a Docker container, with an image on Docker Hub[8], to facilitate the deployment and scalability by replication using HAProxy[9]. HAProxy an open-source software that provides a load balancer and proxy server for TCP and HTTP-based applications that spreads requests across multiple servers. It is written in C and has a reputation for being fast and efficient (in terms of processor and memory usage).

The management of messages is performed by using Task Queues (*i.e.*, Celery Workers[10]). Figure 5 shows two screenshots of the application. The first (left) displays information on metrics, while the second (right) displays statistics on the most common errors.

Fig. 5. Screenshots of the STILTool 2.

---

[7] https://bitbucket.org/disco_unimib/stiltool/.

[8] https://hub.docker.com/repository/docker/cremarco/stiltool.

[9] http://www.haproxy.org/.

[10] https://docs.celeryproject.org/en/latest/userguide/workers.html.

5 Evaluation and Use Cases

The main aim of STILTool 2 is to assess semantically annotated datasets included in different real-world use cases. To shed light on the state of the semantically annotated datasets, we consider the datasets from the SemTab 2020 challenge [10][11]. Specifically, the real-world datasets involved in the challenge represent the multiple kinds of dirty data one finds in practice. We have also selected for the same datasets different annotations proposed by the tools[10] that participated in the challenge.

In the following, we present our experimental setup, including the datasets and their annotations. After that, we give an overview of the quality assessment of the different annotations and provide some insights from the results. With the above considerations in mind, we aim to answer the following questions:

- What are the results of the quality metrics for each annotation provided by a different tool?
- Can we say something about the errors related to the quality assessment result?
- How is the quality evaluation influenced by the KG used?

5.1 Gold Standards

Several approaches on the tabular data annotation have been proposed over the past years. To validate these approaches, several gold standards have also been proposed. Among these, it is possible to mention T2Dv2[12], LimayeAll [13], Limaye200 [21] and Zhang2020 [20]. Furthermore, in the last period, semantic annotation has received an ever-increasing interest within the scientific community. This interest is also shown by the birth of some international challenges, such as "SemTab"[13], already in its second version. The target KG in 2019 was DBpedia [9], while in 2020 was Wikidata [10]. A new gold standard, Tough Tables (2T) [2], was also introduced during SemTab 2020 Round4. In the context of the SemTab 2020 challenge, the table corpora are significantly large with thousands of tables and cells to annotate (*cf.* Table 3).

The approaches of the tabular data annotation only consider one gold standard at a time, meaning that a new gold standard can be uploaded, and the same table can be evaluated on different gold standards separately. In the current gold standards, the tables are annotated using the elements (*i.e.*, entities, classes, properties) coming from the same KG. However, STILTool is agnostic to the use of one or more Knowledge Graphs (KGs) (Table 2).

5.2 Results

We evaluate the proposed approach using the above annotated datasets by different tools. We carry out two set of experiments. Table 4 analyses the semantic

---

[11] https://www.cs.ox.ac.uk/isg/challenges/sem-tab/2020/index.html.
[12] http://webdatacommons.org/webtables/goldstandardV2.html.
[13] http://www.cs.ox.ac.uk/isg/challenges/sem-tab/.

Table 2. Characteristics of the Gold Standards.

	Table	Columns				Rows				Columns			Concepts	Pred.
		Total	Min	Max	Avg	Total	Min	Max	Avg	S	NE	L		
T2Dv2	234	1157	1	13	4	27966	5	585	119	231	-	-	39	154
Limaye200	200	919	2	11	4	4036	3	102	20	200	504	216	84	-
SemTab2019	14966	75429	1	38	92	515302	1	1533	631	14966	22883	52546	22176	17084
SemTab2020	131648	534892	1	8	23	1401463	2	15477	62	131468	156595	378297	191069	402636

Table 3. Overview of the SemTab 2020 table corpus in each round.

	Round1	Round2	Round3	Round4	
				Standard	Tough Table
Tables	34K	12K	63K	22K	180
Cells to annotate	985K	283K	768K	951K	105K
Unique cells to annotate	264K	138K	378K	516K	23K
Average cell length	20	21	20	14	11

annotation tool Mantistable on two different datasets: SemTab2019 Round4 on DBpedia and SemTab 2020 Round4 on Wikidata - Standard (*i.e.*, without Tough Table). The three metrics considered in the table refer to schema, property and entity completeness (*cf.* Table 1), respectively, with respect to the annotation tasks and the gold standard provided in the SemTab challenge. Mantistable indicates a high quality when DBpedia is used while the quality decreases for the cases of Wikidata which may be explained by the fact that the DBpedia dataset is smaller and less complex than Wikidata and as such the research of correct candidate entities and their disambiguation is easier.

Table 4. Overview of the metrics obtained by Mantistable in Round4 of Semtab 2019 and SemTab 2020.

Approach	Round4					
	DBpedia			Wikidata (Standard)		
	CM1	CM2	CM3	CM1	CM2	CM3
Mantistable	0.99	0.998	0.331	0.579	0.702	0.685

Table 5 shows the approaches assessed according to the completeness metrics. In this case, the two KG used are SemTab 2020 Round4 on Wikidata - Standard and SemTab 2020 Round4 on Wikidata - Tough Table, but since the latter does not cover the CPA, thus we cannot provide CM3. The results shown in the table for the metrics CM1 and CM2 are higher for Round4 - Standard than Round4 - Tough Table. In particular, we notice this huge difference on CM2, which indicates that the entity annotation task performed on Round4 - Tough Table is more difficult to be performed since the dataset itself is complex. We notice that on the best four scores for Round4 - Standard on metric CM1 are by the approaches *SSL, LinkingPark, MTab4Wikidata, bbw* while the worst is from *Kepler-aSI*. In Round4 - Tough Table the best scores on metric CM1 is *SSL, MTab4Wikidata, LexMa, AMALGAM* and the worst continues to be *Kepler-aSI*. The first approach SSL remains constant while some others get worse, and some that were not having high scores in the Round4 - Standard are getting higher scores in Round4 - Tough Table. Overall, we may conclude that some approaches remain almost constant (high/low score) in both Round4 - Standard and Round4 - Tough Table and another group although have a high score on Round4 - Standard get worse either on CM1 or in CM2 in Round4 - Tough Table, *i.e.*, this indication of low quality on instance or schema level will need two different directions of improvements.

Table 5. Overview of the metrics calculated for the different SemTab 2020 approaches in Round4.

Approach	Round4				
	Standard			Tough Table	
	CM1	CM2	CM3	CM1	CM2
AMALGAM	0.993	0.954	-	0.991	0.412
bbw	0.999	0.989	0.999	0.483	0.869
dagobah	0.998	0.998	0.998	0.924	0.379
JenTab	0.998	0.996	0.998	0.876	0.527
Kepler-aSI	0.23	0.016	-	0	0.001
LexMa	-	0.864	-	0.998	0.585
LinkingPark	1.0	1.0	0.993	0.994	0.998
MTab4Wikidata	0.999	1.0	1.0	1.0	0.998
SSL	1.0	1.0	1.0	1.0	0.99

Table 6 shows the quality assessment according to the metrics of Phase II and Phase III of the approach, in particular, Interlinking Completeness and Accuracy Completeness of triples and (abstract) triples. As we may notice, completeness is higher than accuracy which is an indication that while the retrieved entities, properties and types are almost the same as indicated by the gold standard the correctly retrieved entities, properties and types are less.

Table 6. Overview of the metrics calculated on CEA and CTA triples for the different SemTab 2020 approaches in Round4.

Approach	Round4			
	Standard CEA triples		Standard CTA triples	
	LC	AC	ALC	ALA
Mantistable	0.698	0.685	0.491	0.475
bbw	0.975	0.941	0.996	0.912
dagobah	0.993	0.966	0.998	0.908
JenTab	0.989	0.949	0.992	0.792
LinkingPark	0.997	0.939	0.957	0.799
MTab4Wikidata	0.996	0.982	0.997	0.924
SSL	0.885	0.808	0.998	0.889

Table 7 shows the results for the Type Specificity (TS) metric provided by the different approaches. It considers how many times the perfect annotation has been identified. In case when the perfect annotation is not retrieved, it looks for the first ancestor or first descendent; otherwise, the type is classified as an error. The results of this metric show that in most cases the problem is not the most specific or generic type but most of the approaches get the wrong types. These cases are due to a wrong identification of the type or the type was not found.

Table 7. Overview of the metrics calculated on type specificity (TS) for the different SemTab 2020 approaches in Round4.

Approach	Round4							
	Standard				Tough Table			
	perfect	ancestor	descendent	error	perfect	ancestor	descendent	error
Mantistable	0.56	0.003	0.005	0.425	0.304	0	0.113	0.583
AMALGAM	0.833	0.023	0.009	0.135	0.515	0.004	0.15	0.331
bbw	0.966	0.018	0.002	0.014	0.289	0.072	0.078	0.561
dagobah	0.944	0.039	0.001	0.016	0.511	0.228	0.043	0.219
JenTab	0.894	0.043	0.004	0.059	0.502	0.08	0.041	0.378
Kepler-aSI	0.147	0.007	0.006	0.84	0	0	0	1.0
LinkingPark	0.913	0.055	0.005	0.027	0.58	0.093	0.067	0.261
MTab4Wikidata	0.963	0.018	0.012	0.008	0.617	0.033	0.146	0.204
SSL	0.927	0.024	0.002	0.047	0.27	0.043	0.102	0.585

Table 8 shows the Entity Candidate Coverage metric obtained only by the Mantistable approach because the data about the candidate entities were not available for the other approaches. As shown from the results, the Round4 - Tough Table has a coverage value of 0.748 because of its complexity, while

Round4 - Standard has almost a total coverage. This value in Round4 - Tough Table indicates that the next steps of the STI annotation process will not improve the results. Therefore, this metric serve as an upper limit and thus will influence our decision on proceeding or not with the subsequent steps of the STI process *i.e.*, we learn a priori that if we run all the other steps we will get an equal or even a worse score. Thus this metric may save time and resources.

Table 8. Entity Coverage metrics calculated on Mantistable approach.

Approach	Round4	
	Standard	Tough Table
	EC	EC
Mantistable	0.989	0.748

Flexibility. Our approach is flexible since it evaluates different types of metrics according to cells, columns or rows.

Correctness of Metrics. In order to test the correctness of implemented metrics, we have implemented unit tests and in cases of small datasets we have checked the result obtained by our approach manually.

5.3   Use Cases

The proposed quality assessment framework may be used in many use cases. These includes the following three scenarios:

Comparison and Evaluation of Semantic Table Interpretation (STI) Approaches. The framework can be used for comparing different STI approaches. The functionalities of the previous version of STILTool have been defined as part of the SemTab 2020 challenge. The organizers of this challenge have expressed their intention to adopt STILTool 2 as part of the next challenge, SemTab 2021.

Integration and Quality Assessment of Product Data. In this scenario it is required to integrate product data by first annotating them. The semantic annotations are the main driver for the integration of product datasets. One of the key features of the integration process is the data fusion task. Consider two different semantically annotated datasets containing product data and their properties, as well as a set of hierarchies of types connected to entities. The data fusion process produces a third, final dataset, containing consolidated descriptions of the linked product data. This process depends on the quality of the input data, therefore, it requires a mechanism for data quality check. We use STILTool 2 to check the quality of each input dataset against the gold standard. If the two datasets are annotated using two different KGs then STILTool 2 will take as input two different gold standards. To assure the quality of the fusion process we need to have annotations with high quality.

Natural Language Generation of RDF Triples. A considerable amount of data, presented in a structured, tabular form, is available on the Web nowadays. For the informational content of such data to be made accessible and understandable to *all* users, its translation into natural language can be a valid solution. Table summarisation is the process of obtaining a summary of the tabular data in such a way as to describe the complex information it conveys. This summary can be generated concerning the interest and information needs of the user. In this scenario, it is evident the importance of the high quality of annotations. Considering the table in Fig. 1, an incorrect annotation relating to the first cell (Mont Blanc) would completely distort the sentence's meaning; for instance, a sentence relating to Mont Blanc on the moon[14] could be generated, conveying utterly incorrect information. In this scenario, deep learning models, particularly Neural Machine Translation models, are used for sentence generation. In this case, STILTool 2 can be used to measure the quality of the annotated datasets. For example, the evaluation of the WebNlg 2017 dataset which should use triples extracted from DBpedia, allowed us to identify some properties not currently present within this KG.

5.4   Limitations

As described in the previous sections, STILTool allows measuring the quality of a dataset by using gold standards, but data quality is commonly conceived as "fitness for use" for a specific application or real-world cases, meaning it will be subjective. For example, there are cases where the same tabular data can be annotated differently, depending on the user's needs and related design choices (*e.g.*, use of different vocabularies). Gold standards can be used to fit a particular (potentially narrow, but controlled) view of the task by making certain assumptions with a specific purpose in mind. However, to create semantic table annotation approaches that can satisfy real-world needs, it is necessary to consider the output to achieve (*i.e.*, in term of annotations), so we need controlled and predefined scenarios to get specific insights and evaluate the approaches. The desired output can then be described through a gold standard, partial gold standard, or silver standard, which can be used for enabling a fully automated evaluation. The generality is guaranteed since STILTool allows the use of different gold standards, both those defined in the state-of-the-art and those defined by users, to satisfy real-world needs.

Regarding the second limitation, which is related to approaches tailored to a specific type of semantic table annotation, STILTool considers all the annotation tasks described in Sect. 2. In particular, the Columns-Property Annotation task involves identifying a subject column to define the relationships between the subject column and the other columns in the form of properties. However, in the

---

[14] https://en.wikipedia.org/wiki/Mont_Blanc_(Moon).

current version our tool considers all the steps and there may be some limitations for other semantic annotation tools that address only some of the tasks (*e.g.*, apply CPA without identifying subject columns). In future versions of the tool, it will be possible to evaluate annotations of tables without subject columns or with more than one subject column, to introduce greater generalisation and therefore consider more real-world cases.

6 Related Work

In this work, we propose quality assessment metrics for semantically enriched tabular data as a result of an STI process and its annotations. Different approaches have been proposed to assess the quality of knowledge graphs. The approaches of quality assessment can be distinguished in those applied to the quality of datasets [4, 19] and mapping definitions [6] which can be further classified into i) manual, ii) semi−automatic and iii) automatic. In particular, the work in [19] focuses on the definitions and formalisation of quality assessment metrics for knowledge graphs. In a more recent work, [4] proposes the formalisation of the quality metrics from the practical and implementation point of view. In [8], the authors evaluate the quality assessment of crawled datasets containing around 12M RDF triples. The main aim was to discuss common problems found in RDF datasets, and possible solutions. The authors also provide suggestions on how publishers can improve their data, so that consumers can find "high-quality" datasets. However, these approaches do not provide any quality metrics for the transformation process.

A number of works have been published on the quality assessment of RDF mapping languages [5, 6, 11, 14, 16]. The existing literature tends to focus on a particular subset of quality metrics. Randles et al. [16] propose a framework to assess and improve the quality of R2RML mapping language. The quality metrics are provided in SHACL which require additional knowledge on writing them. The work in [11] propose an extension of the quality assessment framework, Luzzu [3], which is mainly used for the quality assessment of the RDF datasets by introducing four quality metrics for the quality assessment of mappings. The authors in [14] propose a tool for the quality assessment of mappings. In [6], the authors assess mapping definitions from semistructured data to RDF by proposing an incremental, iterative and uniform validation workflow where violation might arise from incorrect usage of schemas, in addition, they suggest mapping refinements based on the results of these quality assessments. The authors have extended RDFUnit to also cover the validation of mappings against its vocabularies and ontologies. Dimou et al. [5] demonstrate that assessing an RDF dataset requires a considerable measure of time, therefore it cannot be often executed, and when that happens, the violations' root is not detected. On the other hand, assessing the RDF mappings requires essentially less time and the violations' root can be detected. There is (to the best of our knowledge) no study to support the quality assessment of the STI process and its annotations.

7 Conclusions and Future Work

STILTool 2 aims to perform a quality assessment of semantic annotations of tabular data. To the best of our knowledge, our proposal is one of the most comprehensive frameworks to support the evaluation of the semantic annotation process. STILT2 can be used in evaluation and comparison over the different tasks of semantic annotation. The modularity of STILTool 2 allows us to implement and extend with other quality metrics, which can operate in one of the phases as defined in Sect. 3. The framework has been published with an open-source licence in order to be used by the whole community. STILTool 2 will be adopted by the organisers of SemTab 2021 to support the evaluation campaign. SemTab participants will also potentially benefit from the use of the framework.

In the future, we plan to maintain and extend the tool with additional quality metrics such as Correct Object/Datatype Property Values. Another direction is to analyse the root causes by not only visualising the aggregated scores of quality but highlighting the quality issues in the annotations. We also plan to introduce estimated quality metrics that may need a partial gold standard and indicate the quality score for the whole dataset. If a gold standard is not available, our goal is to store versions of different annotations applied on the same dataset to analyse their evolution. One key point in the evolution analysis is the computation of quality metrics between different versions to detect the quality issues [17].

References

1. Cremaschi, M., Siano, A., Avogadro, R., Jimenez-Ruiz, E., Maurino, A.: STILTool: a semantic table interpretation evaLuation tool. In: Harth, A., et al. (eds.) ESWC 2020. LNCS, vol. 12124, pp. 61–66. Springer, Cham (2020). https://doi.org/10.1007/978-3-030-62327-2_11
2. Cutrona, V., Bianchi, F., Jiménez-Ruiz, E., Palmonari, M.: Tough tables: carefully evaluating entity linking for tabular data. In: Pan, J.Z., et al. (eds.) ISWC 2020. LNCS, vol. 12507, pp. 328–343. Springer, Cham (2020). https://doi.org/10.1007/978-3-030-62466-8_21
3. Debattista, J., Auer, S., Lange, C.: Luzzu-a methodology and framework for linked data quality assessment. JDIQ 8(1) (2016)
4. Debattista, J., Lange, C., Auer, S., Cortis, D.: Evaluating the quality of the LOD cloud: an empirical investigation. SWJ 9(6), 859–901 (2018)
5. Dimou, A., et al.: DBpedia mappings quality assessment. In: Poster & Demo at ISWC, vol. 1690. CEUR (2016)
6. Dimou, A., et al.: Assessing and refining mappings to RDF to improve dataset quality. In: Arenas, M., et al. (eds.) ISWC 2015. LNCS, vol. 9367, pp. 133–149. Springer, Cham (2015). https://doi.org/10.1007/978-3-319-25010-6_8
7. Fetahu, B., Anand, A., Koutraki, M.: TableNet: an approach for determining fine-grained relations for Wikipedia tables. In: WWW 2019, pp. 2736–2742. ACM (2019)
8. Hogan, A., Umbrich, J., Harth, A., Cyganiak, R., Polleres, A., Decker, S.: An empirical survey of linked data conformance. JWS 14, 14–44 (2012)

9. Jiménez-Ruiz, E., Hassanzadeh, O., Efthymiou, V., Chen, J., Srinivas, K.: SemTab 2019: resources to benchmark tabular data to knowledge graph matching systems. In: Harth, A., et al. (eds.) ESWC 2020. LNCS, vol. 12123, pp. 514–530. Springer, Cham (2020). https://doi.org/10.1007/978-3-030-49461-2_30
10. Jimenéz-Ruiz, E., Hassanzadeh, O., Efthymiou, V., Chen, J., Srinivas, K., Cutrona, V.: Results of SemTab 2020. In: Proceedings of the Semantic Web Challenge on Tabular Data to Knowledge Graph Matching, vol. 2775, pp. 1–8 (2020)
11. Junior, A.C., Debattista, J., O'Sullivan, D.: Assessing the quality of R2RML mappings. In: Joint Proceedings of the 1st Sem4Tra and the 1st AMAR at SEMANTiCS 2019), vol. 2447. CEUR (2019)
12. Lehmberg, O., Ritze, D., Meusel, R., Bizer, C.: A large public corpus of web tables containing time and context metadata. In: WWW 2016, pp. 75–76. ACM (2016)
13. Limaye, G., Sarawagi, S., Chakrabarti, S.: Annotating and searching web tables using entities, types and relationships. VLDB **3**(1–2), 1338–1347 (2010)
14. Moreau, B., Serrano-Alvarado, P.: Assessing the quality of RDF mappings with EvaMap. In: Harth, A., et al. (eds.) ESWC 2020. LNCS, vol. 12124, pp. 164–167. Springer, Cham (2020). https://doi.org/10.1007/978-3-030-62327-2_28
15. Paulheim, H.: Knowledge graph refinement: a survey of approaches and evaluation methods. Semant. Web **8**(3), 489–508 (2017)
16. Randles, A., Junior, A.C., O'Sullivan, D.: Towards a vocabulary for mapping quality assessment. In: The 15th OM at (ISWC 2020), vol. 2788, pp. 241–242 (2020)
17. Rashid, M., Torchiano, M., Rizzo, G., Mihindukulasooriya, N., Corcho, O.: A quality assessment approach for evolving knowledge bases. SWJ **10**(2), 349–383 (2019)
18. Sejdiu, G., Rula, A., Lehmann, J., Jabeen, H.: A scalable framework for quality assessment of RDF datasets. In: Ghidini, C., et al. (eds.) ISWC 2019. LNCS, vol. 11779, pp. 261–276. Springer, Cham (2019). https://doi.org/10.1007/978-3-030-30796-7_17
19. Zaveri, A., Rula, A., Maurino, A., Pietrobon, R., Lehmann, J., Auer, S.: Quality assessment for linked data: a survey. SWJ **7**(1), 63–93 (2016)
20. Zhang, S., Meij, E., Balog, K., Reinanda, R.: Novel entity discovery from web tables. In: WWW 2020, pp. 1298–1308. ACM (2020)
21. Zhang, Z.: Effective and efficient semantic table interpretation using tableminer+. SWJ **8**(6), 921–957 (2017)

EduCOR: An Educational and Career-Oriented Recommendation Ontology

Eleni Ilkou[1](✉)[iD], Hasan Abu-Rasheed[3][iD], Mohammadreza Tavakoli[1,2][iD],
Sherzod Hakimov[2][iD], Gábor Kismihók[2][iD], Sören Auer[2][iD],
and Wolfgang Nejdl[1][iD]

[1] L3S Research Center, Leibniz University Hannover, Hanover, Germany
{ilkou,tavakoli,nejdl}@l3s.de
[2] TIB – Leibniz Information Centre for Science and Technology, Hannover, Germany
{sherzod.hakimov,gabor.kismihok,auer}@tib.eu
[3] WBS&WM Institute, University of Siegen, Siegen, Germany
hasan.abu.rasheed@uni-siegen.de

Abstract. With the increased dependence on online learning platforms and educational resource repositories, a unified representation of digital learning resources becomes essential to support a dynamic and multi-source learning experience. We introduce the EduCOR ontology, an educational, career-oriented ontology that provides a foundation for representing online learning resources for personalised learning systems. The ontology is designed to enable learning material repositories to offer learning path recommendations, which correspond to the user's learning goals and preferences, academic and psychological parameters, and labour-market skills. We present the multiple patterns that compose the EduCOR ontology, highlighting its cross-domain applicability and integrability with other ontologies. A demonstration of the proposed ontology on the real-life learning platform eDoer is discussed as a use case. We evaluate the EduCOR ontology using both gold standard and task-based approaches. The comparison of EduCOR to three gold schemata, and its application in two use-cases, shows its coverage and adaptability to multiple OER repositories, which allows generating user-centric and labour-market oriented recommendations.

Resource: https://tibonto.github.io/educor/.

Keywords: Ontology · Educational resources · OER · Education · Labour market · Skill · Learning path · User profile · Personalised recommendation

1 Introduction

In recent years, digital education is increasingly relying on Educational Resources (ERs) and Open Educational Resources (OER). These ERs are available in many

A. Hotho et al. (Eds.): ISWC 2021, LNCS 12922, pp. 546–562, 2021.
https://doi.org/10.1007/978-3-030-88361-4_32

different formats, such as videos, slide decks, audio recordings from lectures, digital textbooks, or simple web pages. Furthermore, ERs and OERs usually come with low-quality metadata [33], and they are isolated from other, content-wise similar ERs. That is one of the crucial reasons for lacking high-quality services, such as recommendation and search services, based on OERs [32]. Therefore, it is not surprising that the Semantic Web (SW) community shows increased interest in organising and classifying ERs, and enhancing the metadata in publicly available ER and OER [13,25]. Although many schemata and vocabularies were suggested in the past for the educational domain, only a few of them are still available online and can accommodate particularities of OERs, and related personalised recommendation systems' features. Furthermore, recent works revealed the increased interest in educational Knowledge Graphs [10,20], which, however, often lack an underlying ontology or schema [5]. Commercial products seem to follow a similar direction, as they usually do not use or do not publish their underlying knowledge schema[1]. Additionally, surveys in e-learning have shown that an ontology helps to achieve personalised recommendation systems [17,31]. Moreover, there is an increased interest on the education side to enrich current tools with Artificial Intelligence to achieve Smart Education. In this line, ontologies offer a wide variety of benefits for Smart Tutoring Systems [28]. In addition, the SW has a significant focus on question answering and (learning) recommendation systems. The latter is evolving rapidly to offer interoperability, explainability, and user privacy while providing personalised learning recommendations [1,6].

On the broader community side, there is strong evidence of the everyday usage of online learning. Societies put enormous effort into the digital transformation of education, such as the Digital Educational Plan of the European Union[2], on matching work and relevant skills, and on executing skill development in online learning platforms [11]. These online learning platforms are used daily by millions of learners, especially during the COVID-19 pandemic, when education has been pushed towards online environments worldwide. Consequently, a need for lifelong learning tools emerged that could assist people in career changes, (re)skilling, or (re)entering the labour market after a period of unemployment. This trend is visible in the last decade through an increased public interest in online learning supportive platforms, such Coursera [9] for lifelong learning, or Khan Academy[3] for school education. These platforms usually contain ERs in video format and assessments to validate learners' knowledge, yet they also indicate new challenges by shifting learning towards personalised recommendations.

However, this personalisation agenda of education requires novel ways to model learning processes, especially in complex learning environments. This is

---

[1] An example is the Mathspace https://mathspace.co, a math education platform that offers personalised learning based on a Knowledge Graph. However, its knowledge schema is not publicly available.

[2] https://ec.europa.eu/education/education-in-the-eu/digital-education-action-plan_en.

[3] https://www.khanacademy.org.

especially challenging when the ingredients of the learning process are originated from the angles of education (learning content and instruction), the labour market (learning context), and individual needs of learners (learning objectives). Ontologies engineered by the SW community can play a crucial role here. While there are plenty of works available, both as e-learning and occupational ontologies, no model is available currently to connect these two domains.

Therefore, following both SW and broader community interest, we developed the Education and Career-Oriented Recommendation Ontology, the EduCOR ontology. This syntactic formalism describes ERs, skills, and the user profile in rich metadata. It creates the bridge between the demanding and constantly changing needs of the labour market and the educational domain. EduCOR provides both the basis of an educational Knowledge Graph, and serves as a potential framework for personalised, OER recommendation systems. To the best of our knowledge, the EduCOR ontology is breaking new ground on modelling ERs for a personalised recommendation system based on the learner's learning path and user profile. Moreover, EduCOR fills an essential gap in connecting personalised learning recommendation systems, educational data and skills with the labour market, making it a vital schema for future applications.

2 EduCOR Ontology

The EduCOR ontology is proposed to organise different domain ERs and OERs under a common ontology, link to the labour market, and offer personalised recommendation systems in the e-learning domain. A general cross-domain educational ontology should serve different purposes. Given this multidisciplinary interest and diversity of applications, there is a need for semantic representation under a unified framework that can accommodate associations between entities and attributes. We performed a requirement analysis for e-learning platforms to host personalised recommendations by reviewing the literature and an existing e-learning system. As a result, we identified the key components around which we constructed our ontology.

2.1 Ontology Composition

Our ontology introduces the necessary classes and properties to construct an e-learning environment that supports personalised recommendations. Before developing our ontology, we examined state-of-the-art related works, open standards, and best practices.

Since our goal was to create a general ontology, we limited our conceptual work to high-level, fundamental constructs. Consequently, we examined a series of open standards related to educational content, and we critically choose those that offer a wide coverage over the narrower focused ones. Thus, we adopted the widely used IEEE LOM Standard[4] and LRMI Standard[5]. Furthermore, we

---

[4] https://standards.ieee.org/standard/1484_12_1-2020.html.
[5] https://www.dublincore.org/specifications/dublin-core/dces.

reuse parts from the Curriculum Course Syllabus Ontology (CCSO) [24] and schema.org[6]. Furthermore, our ontology is aligned with FAIR principles [37]. Our data are assigned globally unique and persistent identifiers, and they are described with rich metadata, which is accessible and retrievable as it is demonstrated in the ontology page[7]. We use OWL for the ontology representation, and we reuse vocabularies that follow FAIR principles and include references to them. We describe the scope of our data and have them published under the licence CC0 1.0 Universell (CC0 1.0) Public Domain Dedication[8], and it has the canonical citation: "E. Ilkou et al.: EduCOR: An Educational and Career-Oriented Recommendation Ontology. April 2021. https://github.com/tibonto/educor".

Before finalising our design, we had an expert evaluation phase, where we received feedback from domain and ontology experts. The ontology also offers classes as plug-in points, where other ontologies can be mapped for more specific utilisation. Such an example is the 'Learning Preference' that could host a thorough analysis as it is presented by Ciloglugil and Inceoglu [8]. In Fig. 1, we present a conceptual overview of the classes in EduCOR ontology with connections to a domain ontology and job ontology. A comprehensive presentation of each class's object and data properties can be found on the ontology page.

2.2 Patterns

EduCOR consists of independent modules that can be combined to create the complete schema of the ontology. We also refer to the modules as patterns. Based on our requirement analysis, we identified the key components of a personalised learning recommendation system. Taking these components as the central theme of each module presentation, we created the additional patterns, respectively. The patterns EduCOR identifies are the following: *Educational Resource, Knowledge Topic, Skill, Learning Path, Test, Recommendation, User Profile*. Each pattern stands alone and can be added to another ontology, used as a single pattern separated from the EduCOR ontology, if an application does or does not need it accordingly. In Fig. 1, the classes of each pattern are represented in different colours.

In the *Educational Resource* pattern in Fig. 1 pattern (A), the 'Educational Resource' class represents the learning material or learning object. It can have multiple types that are covered by the 'Multimedia Data' class. The 'Education Resource' also has a 'Quality Indicator', reflecting any quality measure required by the hosting content repository. Learners' different access requirements are covered through the 'Accessibility' class, which represents the access rights and methods of the learning material.

Each 'Educational Resource' refers to a specific 'Knowledge Topic' in *Knowledge Topic* pattern (D). Knowledge Topics represent specific themes in a partic-

---

[6] https://schema.org/.
[7] http://ontology.tib.eu/educor.
[8] https://creativecommons.org/publicdomain/zero/1.0/deed.de.

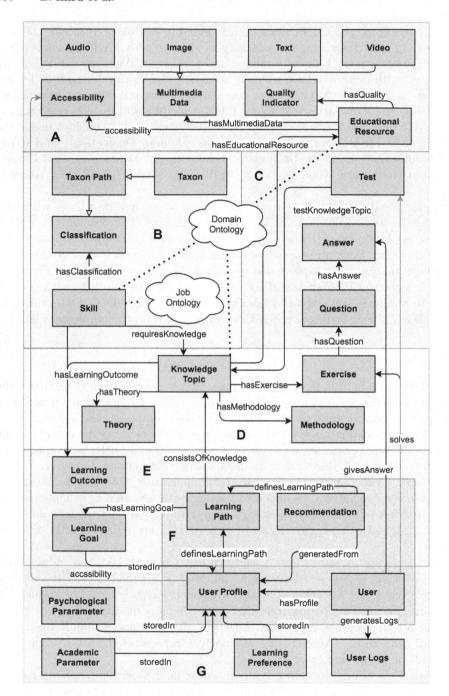

Fig. 1. An overview of the EduCOR ontology classes. Each pattern of the ontology is highlighted individually, **A**: Educational resource pattern, **B**: Skill pattern, **C**: Knowledge topic pattern, **D**: Test pattern, **E**: Learning path pattern, **F**: Recommendation Pattern, **G**: User profile pattern.

ular domain of knowledge, such as the "Quadratic Equations" in the "Mathematics" domain. A 'Knowledge Topic' has a 'Theory' and an 'Exercise' content, which the learner experiences through a specific 'Methodology'. The 'Exercise' class is connected to both the *Knowledge Topic* and *Test* patterns.

In *Test* pattern (C), the 'Test' class represents the learning assessment procedure. It is composed of one or more 'Exercises', which in turn have questions and corresponding answers. A 'Test' can be composed of exercises that belong to many knowledge topics, skills, and domains.

Knowledge Topics are the requirements of achieving a target 'Skill'. The 'Skill' class, in *Skill* pattern (B), is the link between knowledge topics and the labour market job ontology.

Mastering a targeted 'Skill' and 'Knowledge Topic' can happen through their unique 'Learning Outcome'. Such 'Learning Outcome' results from the recommended 'Learning Path', in *Learning Path* pattern (E). The 'Learning Path' represents the sequence of knowledge topics needed to reach a user-defined 'Learning Goal' through the intermediate 'Learning Outcomes' of each 'Knowledge Topic' in the recommended 'Learning Path'.

The 'Recommendation' class, in *Recommendation* pattern (F), is designed to cover a range of recommended item-types based on the use-case requirements. A 'Recommendation' is directly generated from the 'User Profile', in pattern (G), which is the means of modelling the 'User' in the proposed ontology.

We design the *User Profile* to cover the interest, intention and behavioural aspects defined in [16]. Those are represented by the classes 'Learning Preference', 'Learning Goal', 'Academic Parameter', and 'Psychological Parameter'. The 'Academic Parameter' captures the learner's performance, such as test scores, while the 'Psychological Parameter' reflects the state-of-mind of the learner, such as being tired. This focus on the psychological state is due to its influence on the overall learning process and performance. The 'User Profile' is also linked to the 'Accessibility' class. The latter could describe user accessibility, content access rights, and user privacy issues.

3   Use Case Scenario

We describe a general and a specific use case. In a general use case, an OER repository owner could utilise the EduCOR ontology to model the learning materials in their repository. The repository serves learners through a standard search and information retrieval functionality. In the future, it could be possible to integrate an automatic decision-support system with minimum to zero adjustments of the repository structure.

We also used our ontology in specific use case, in the development of eDoer[9] platform, an open learning recommender system prototype, focusing on Data Science related jobs [34–36]. Since eDoer aims to empower learners through open, personalised learning and curriculum recommendations based on labour market

---

[9] http://edoer.eu.

information and OERs, the following components have been deployed using the EduCOR ontology: 1) we used the *Skill* pattern to bridge between jobs and their required qualities, 2) we applied the *Knowledge Topic* pattern to decompose each skill into relevant learning components, 3) the *Learning Path* pattern was used to create a path for learners which includes a sequence of knowledge topics towards their learning goals (i.e. target job or skills), 4) to store the required learning resources into our system, we applied the *Educational Resource* pattern, 5) in the process of building a personalised learning content recommender engine, we benefited from *Recommendation* and *User Profile* patterns to offer the most relevant learning items (i.e. knowledge topics and learning materials) to learners based on their learning goals, learning preferences, and their current knowledge level, and 6) the *Test* pattern was used to offer assessment services in order to help learners to monitor their progress towards their learning goals.

Therefore, on the eDoer platform, learners can set their target job, and the system will provide them with a list of skills they need to master for that particular job. Learners are offered to select one or more of those skills and set them as learning objectives. Moreover, learners can search through other existing skills and add different learning goals. They can also set their learning preferences, such as the type of learning materials and the length of content, which results in personalised learning content recommendations. The generated learning path includes the target skills and the necessary knowledge topics covered for each skill. Subsequently, users receive OERs for each knowledge topic, which can be viewed, rated, and changed. Based on the users' feedback (i.e. ratings) on each of the recommendations, eDoer updates the users' preferences to capture any changes in user preferences. Moreover, there are various assessments available both on skill and knowledge topic levels that provide means to monitor the learning process[10]. Up to now, we evaluated eDoer in the context of a *Business Analytics* course at the *University of Amsterdam*. This evaluation revealed that 24 students out of 97, who worked with our system voluntarily, achieved higher course grades than those that did not.

4   Evaluation

Several evaluation methods have been introduced in the literature on ontology development. A recent survey [21] classified evaluation methods under five main approaches: 1) Gold-standard based, 2) Corpus-based or data-driven, 3) Task-based of Application-based, 4) Criteria-based, and 5) Evaluation by humans.

To ensure objectivity when evaluating EduCOR, we decided to use inductive methods following [4,27] to select the most relevant evaluation criteria for our proposed ontology. Therefore, based on [2,12], we focus on coverage and adaptability as key performance indicators (KPIs) of the EduCOR ontology. In the context of ER representation for learning-material repositories, the coverage is defined as the ability to describe learning materials by classes. Adaptability is defined as the potential to represent multiple repositories homogeneously. Based

---

[10] You can watch a demo of eDoer here: https://youtu.be/5PRcUgNa7tA.

on these two KPIs, we conduct the gold-standard and task-based evaluation approaches. The gold-standard valuation is meant to compare EduCOR directly to other repository schemata, while the task-based evaluation is meant to validate its performance in real-world use cases. We also evaluated the proposed ontology design with experts in the ontology development domain to validate its structure and classes qualitatively.

4.1 Gold Standard-Based Evaluation

To measure EduCOR's coverage and adaptability towards other existing ontologies, we selected three well-established repositories for ER resources, namely Merlot[11], SkilsCommons[12], and OERCommons[13]. We chose these repositories due to their richness in metadata that describes ERs and OERs. This, in turn, enabled extracting a comprehensive schema that can be used for the evaluation. Since those repositories' APIs are not open, we conducted a thorough analysis of repositories' schemas based on the information on their websites, user guides, and the use of hosted materials and resources. We extracted the overall class representations of the three schemas. Ultimately, these schemas are accepted as gold standards, against which the EduCOR ontology is compared. The comparison is conducted through four steps: 1) the extraction of the gold standard repositories, 2) analyzing class names and their meanings, 3) mapping EduCOR classes to the underlying schema of each repository, and 4) calculating the coverage score for each gold standard repository. Repository schemata and the four steps of comparison are elaborated in detail on EduCOR's resource page.

The mapping process refers to identifying classes in gold standard repositories that are also represented in EduCOR. Since mapping is dependent on the clear definition of a schema's own vocabulary, it may lead to a subjective evaluation. Therefore, we conducted this mapping as a multi-fold process, in which four different developers assessed the meaning of the classes in the proposed ontology and the compared schema. Once the mapping process was conducted, we sought a tangible representation of the coverage and adaptability metrics. To accomplish this task, we followed the work of [2] to calculate the recall based on the definition from the information-retrieval domain to represent the coverage of EduCOR. In this adaption, we defined the true positive value as the number of classes covered by EduCOR and existing in the gold schema. In contrast, the false negative value was defined by the number of classes in the schema that EduCOR did not cover. The calculated recall values are given in Table 1. They indicate the ability of the EduCOR ontology to represent data in the selected repositories with a coverage level of more than 83%. Suppose a class is not directly mapped to EduCOR. In that case, repository owners can either represent it with a different (but similar) class or datatype property from EduCOR or add it explicitly to their own schema. In other words, false negative values of the recall do not hinder adopting EduCOR as a comprehensive foundation of an ER or OER repository.

---

[11] https://www.merlot.org.
[12] https://www.skillscommons.org.
[13] https://www.oercommons.org.

Table 1. Recall values of EduCOR as calculated for each gold schema

	OER-Commons	SkillsCommons	Merlot
EduCOR ontology	0.833	0.857	0.875

To evaluate adaptability, we refer to the definition as mentioned earlier of this measure in the context of ER repositories. Here we qualitatively assess the ability of EduCOR to represent three different repositories, which have distinct differences in focus when representing the ERs and OERs. Examples of those differences include the emphasis of Merlot on user roles, the links in SkillsCommons between ERs and industrial occupations, and the focus on educational and evaluation standards in OER-Commons. Despite those differences, our proposed ontology homogeneously represented them all, with high recall values. Moreover, EduCOR ontology provides other repositories with additional features in learning material representation, user modelling and learning recommendations. This can be seen from linking ERs and OERs to the labour market through the 'Skill' class, the inclusion of 'Psychological Parameter' in the user profile, and through the 'Recommendation' and 'Learning Path' classes that enable a personalized learning experience.

4.2   Task-Based Evaluation

In this step of the ontology evaluation, we defined specific tasks and evaluated EduCOR's ability to fulfil them. For the task-based evaluation, we followed the approach of Chari et al. [4], where competency questions are defined to reflect the main contributions of EduCOR, based on a sample use case that is expected to be executed by a potential user of the ontology. Such a use case is described as a general use case in Sect. 3. This use case was designed to manifest the contributions of EduCOR in representing ERs and OERs from multiple repositories and enabling user-centric, job market-oriented learning recommendations. From the previous use case, we define three main tasks that EduCOR should fulfill:

1. Adaptable representation of OERs from multiple sources.
2. Consideration of labour market skills in the learning path.
3. User-centred design, considering learner's academic and psychological needs within the user profile.

To evaluate EduCOR's ability of performing these tasks, the following set of questions were designed:

- Q1: How to retrieve OERs from multiple sources for a learning goal?
- Q2: How can a personalized OER difficulty be chosen for the user?
- Q3: How to provide an OER to a user with a specific access mode?
- Q4: How to retrieve required OERs for a certain job skill?
- Q5: What is required to generate a personalized learning path?

– Q6: How to personalize a learning recommendation based on a user's psychological state?

The first question Q1 reflects the adaptability metric in the evaluation of the ontology. Questions Q2 and Q3 focus on the personalisation of the retrieved material towards specific user needs, such as the difficulty levels and accessibility modes. Those questions represent the richness in data-type properties, which scaffolds the personalisation of retrieved or recommended ERs and OERs. Q4 evaluates links that the ontology draws between the ERs and the labour market needs. This allows the ER repository developer to support the users with career-oriented recommendations. Q5 and Q6 evaluate the user-centricity of the ontology. They assess the representation of the user's academic and psychological parameters in a recommendation or the retrieval of ERs. These parameters are important as they reflect the user's status, mentally and academically, which allows the recommendations to be more tailored towards their actual needs from the ERs. These competency questions are directed to the EduCOR ontology through SPARQL queries, where their answers are retrieved from any available data associated with the ontology. A sample SPARQL query is provided in Listing 1.1. The full description of queries and their answers are accessible on the documentation web page.

Listing 1.1. SPARQL query to answer the competency question Q2

```
1   PREFIX ec: <https://github.com/tibonto/educor#>
2   PREFIX dc: <http://purl.org/dcx/lrmi-vocabs/alignmentType/>
3
4   SELECT *
5   WHERE {
6       ?test              ec:testKnowledgeTopic    ?knowResource.
7       ?knowResource      ec:difficulty            ?difficulty.
8       ?user              ec:solves                ?test.
9       ?user              ec:hasProfile            ?userProfile.
10      ?acadParam         ec:storedIn              ?userProfile.
11      ?acadParam         dc:educationalLevel      ?currentLevel.
12  }
```

5   Related Work

Ontology development for the educational domain is not a new task. Many ontologies have been developed in the last years related to education systems and learning materials [31]. However, we find a series of issues that dated published ontologies have, such as maintainability, online availability, metadata, and their quality[14]. The biggest challenge is that most of the relevant works are not publicly available anymore. Another critical factor to consider is that

---

[14] An example is the Medical Educational Resource Aggregator https://bioportal.bioontology.org/ontologies/MERA.

the main interest in educational domain ontologies comes from educators and non-technical personnel. Therefore, the majority of these ontologies focus on educational perspectives rather than rich metadata.

In the plethora of educational and e-learning ontologies, we find the majority of ontologies in the domain of application or task-specific. Only a small minority were developed to describe the learning domain and learner data [30]. This creates a challenge in adopting such ontologies to general settings and applications. Such an example could be the recent work in ontology-based curriculum mapping by Zouri and Ferworn [38], which is focused on creating a core ontology for curricula and courses in higher education institutions. Such an ontology raises significant challenges when trying to fit in a general purpose e-learning environment as they cannot be mapped accurately to another domain. General domain educational ontologies are closely related to our goal; hence, we focus our analysis there.

Koutsomitropoulos and Solomou [26] create an ontology-based on the IEEE LOM standard and SKOS for OER repositories. They propose an enhancement of the ER's metadata, and they link to thesauri dataset. However, they offer no personalised content capabilities. Recently Chimalakonda and Nori [7] suggested "an ontology based modelling framework for design of educational technologies". Similar to their model, we include context and domain-specific ontology to our design and add the "GoalsOntology" as 'Learning Goal' in our system. However, in contrast to their framework, our design offers personalised recommendation features.

Another related domain in the literature are personalised recommendation systems. Bulathwela et al. [3] propose an OER recommendation system based on learner background knowledge and content but without an underlying ontology. However, recent reviews show the growing significance of personalisation and recommendation systems in e-learning models, and ontologies are proven to be useful in this respect [17]. Jando et al. [22] show that most techniques use such an ontology to accomplish personalisation, such as the work in [18,23]. A review by Tarus et al. [31] presents the state-of-the-art for "ontology-based recommenders in e-learning". It points out the gained popularity of e-learning resource-recommendations and "their ability to personalise learner profiles based on the learner's characteristics, such as background knowledge, learning style, learning paths and knowledge level". It is noticeable from the state-of-the-art that despite the variety of ontology-based recommender systems in the last years, only the most recent works have developed the ontology in OWL or RDF and offer metadata descriptions. Moreover, the vast majority of publications use an ontology as a tool that provides information to a recommendation algorithm rather than integrating recommendation requirements in the ontology itself. We address this issue in EduCOR by integrating a recommendation class with the overall representation of ERs and user profile.

In terms of connecting the labour market representation with an educational ontology, one of the most related approaches is the "Ontology-based personalised course recommendation framework" by Ibrahim et al. [19], which uses a course, a student and a job ontology to recommend courses and jobs. Inspired by their design, we divided the student ontology into *User Profile* and *Skill* patterns, offering personalisation capabilities, such as the 'Learning Preference' class.

Table 2. Table comparison of the related work compared to EduCOR

Paper	FAIR	Evaluation	Data availability	Personalisation	Reuse of vocabularies
[7]	No	Yes	Yes	Goals (Learning goals)	No
[18]	No	No	No	Learning preferences, Learning style, Learner characteristics, Knowledge level, Learning activities	W3C recommendation ontology
[19]	No	Yes	No	Education information, Job related skills	No
[23]	No	No	No	Learning Style, Learning pathways	IEEE LOM
[26]	No	Yes	No	Datatype properties	IEEE LOM, thesauri, SKOS
[29]	No	Yes	No	Accessibility, Activities, Health conditions	No
[38]	No	No	No	Learning pathways	No
Ours	Yes	Yes	Yes	Learning Goal, Learning pathways, Accessibility, Learning preferences, Psychological parameter, Academic parameter, Recommendation, Datatype properties	IEEE LOM, CCSO, DCMI, SKOS, schema.org

User modelling plays an essential role in ontology-based recommendations [17] since the information about the user is vital to personalise the recommendation itself. Eke et al. [14] present a comprehensive review on user modelling and argue that ontologies are the best solution to unify the user profile representation. Gao et al. [16] categorise user modelling approaches under three main classes: behavioral modelling, interest modelling and intention modelling. They show that personalisation is based on these three pillars. User profiling and content modelling are both considered inputs to a filtering algorithm, such as a recommendation system, to generate a personalised output. The content of user profiles has also been witnessing increased attention in recent years. This is also influenced by the ability to transfer the user profiles among multiple applications and domains [14]. In the educational domain, not only the academic parameters are essential in generating personalised recommendations, but also the psychological parameters, as pointed out by Fatahi [15]. This importance is shown in their adaptive e-learning environment study, where they showed enhanced student performance when receiving personalised recommendations.

Students in their study also showed more attraction to the personalised system, since it "can understand their emotional state better". Further, the authors in Skillen et al. [29] developed an ontological representation of users, putting a focus on their psychological health conditions alongside their learning-related preferences and activities. We found these previous approaches necessary in the educational field. Therefore, we expanded and complemented this set of ontological user profiling works by proposing a hybrid representation in EduCOR. As a result, in our *User Profile* pattern, static and dynamic parameters represent the learner's both academic and psychological aspects.

Table 2 shows a summary of the comparison between EduCOR and those mentioned above related educational ontologies. From this summary, one can notice that EduCOR exceeds state of the art. It is aligned with the FAIR data principles and provides richer personalisation features, both in classes and datatype properties, compared to related ontologies. Furthermore, EduCOR extends these works by embedding the 'Recommendation' and 'Skill' classes in a unified representation, offering stronger links between the ERs and personalised recommendations.

6 Discussion and Future Steps

EduCOR is a publicly available, findable, registered[15], and lightweight ontology that can host ERs and OERs, personalised recommendation system features, and user profiles. It is created to address the gap between the educational domain, the labour market, and personalised learning. EduCOR can be used as a whole or as parts via the patterns introduced in Sect. 2. It is a semantically enhanced ontology that is adaptable. Therefore, EduCOR can be used in different educational domains, such as Computer Science, to support online learning platforms and personalised education systems. EduCOR is enriched with the necessary vocabulary and rich metadata to be general enough to be used in different settings. We leverage and maintain compatibility with existing educational repositories related to Massive Open Online Courses (MOOC) and OERs, as shown in Sect. 4. Moreover, we expand on them to include personalised representational primitives needed for modelling the components of a recommendation system.

However, EduCOR does not provide data specific to an application domain, and expert intervention may be necessary to seamlessly align the domain-specific ontology to the EduCOR ontology. Also, EduCOR does not offer automatic mapping of courses and curricula to its ontology. Although, this can happen by identifying courses, or chapters' learning objectives, and classifying them in skill categories with corresponding knowledge topics. An automatic alignment system for domain and task-specific ontologies mapping to EduCOR ontology is also part of future efforts.

We have implemented the basic ER and OER components that are necessary to link with the labour market and offer personalised learning. However, some

---

[15] You can find EduCOR's presentation at http://ontology.tib.eu/educor and on our GitHub page at https://github.com/tibonto/educor.

aspects of OERs, and the recommendation system might need more thorough analysis. We foresee EduCOR extensions to include further analysis of some classes. The quality indicators could extend to summarize the resource multimedia and metadata quality with user's feedback ratings. Another extension could be the analysis of learning preferences, which could further link to special education coverage. Also, the accessibility analysis could expand to offer additional representations in our system, by covering user accessibility, preferences, and content access rights. In this line, we could additionally focus on the user's privacy, which at the moment boils down to each developer's implementation plan to decide how to implement This work will additionally aim to assist in the user privacy and profile restrictions alignment with our ontology.

In future work, we plan to publish an Open Educational Knowledge Graph, connecting educational resources with the labour market while offering personalised recommendation features by combining ERs from multiple sources. Upon identifying the appropriate content and repositories, we wish to gather the requirements and publish the Knowledge Graph based on the EduCOR ontology. Therefore, we foresee a sustainability plan for the following years as we plan to use the EduCOR ontology as the basis of our future work. We are committed to its maintenance and extensibility to address future challenges and meet future requirements.

7   Conclusion

We have built an open-source, free access ontology to model educational resources, personalised learning recommendations, user profiles, and labour market skills. We argued that this interdisciplinary attempt is vital both for the SW, educators and the broader community. Our requirement analysis came from reviewing the literature and an existing e-learning system that revealed the key components of a perspective system around which we built our ontology. We presented our design and ontological components, which adopt open community standards and FAIR data principles. We evaluated EduCOR with gold-standard and task-based approaches and showed that the EduCOR ontology achieves high coverage of multiple OER repositories. Through a carefully crafted set of competency questions, we evaluated the capabilities of EduCOR in assisting the system designers in e-learning based recommendation systems to determine the necessary elements for their design. We believe our ontology can be a beneficial tool for system designers as they implement personalised features in their recommendation system. We are committed to continuing this line of work towards supporting future requirements that would extend our ontology.

Acknowledgements. We would like to thank Dr. Javad Chamanara for setting up the ontology page. This work was partially funded by the European Union's Horizon 2020 research and innovation program under the Marie Skłodowska-Curie project Knowgraphs (grant agreement ID: 860801), the European Research Council for the project ScienceGRAPH (grant agreement ID: 819536) and the ERASMUS+ Key Action 204 Higher Education project OSCAR (grant agreement ID: 2020-1-DE01-KA203-005713).

References

1. Barria-Pineda, J., Akhuseyinoglu, K., Brusilovsky, P.: Explaining need-based educational recommendations using interactive open learner models. In: Adjunct Publication of the 27th Conference on User Modeling, Adaptation and Personalization, pp. 273–277 (2019)
2. Brewster, C., Alani, H., Dasmahapatra, S., Wilks, Y.: Data driven ontology evaluation (2004)
3. Bulathwela, S., Pérez-Ortiz, M., Yilmaz, E., Shawe-Taylor, J.: TrueLearn: a family of Bayesian algorithms to match lifelong learners to open educational resources. In: The Thirty-Fourth AAAI Conference on Artificial Intelligence, AAAI, pp. 565–573. AAAI Press (2020)
4. Chari, S., Seneviratne, O., Gruen, D.M., Foreman, M.A., Das, A.K., McGuinness, D.L.: Explanation ontology: a model of explanations for user-centered AI. In: Pan, J.Z., et al. (eds.) ISWC 2020. LNCS, vol. 12507, pp. 228–243. Springer, Cham (2020). https://doi.org/10.1007/978-3-030-62466-8_15
5. Chen, P., Lu, Y., Zheng, V.W., Chen, X., Yang, B.: KnowEdu: a system to construct knowledge graph for education. IEEE Access 6, 31553–31563 (2018)
6. Chicaiza, J., Piedra, N., Lopez-Vargas, J., Tovar-Caro, E.: Recommendation of open educational resources. an approach based on linked open data. In: 2017 IEEE Global Engineering Education Conference (EDUCON), pp. 1316–1321. IEEE (2017)
7. Chimalakonda, S., Nori, K.V.: An ontology based modeling framework for design of educational technologies. Smart Learn. Environ. 7(1), 1–24 (2020). https://doi.org/10.1186/s40561-020-00135-6
8. Ciloglugil, B., Inceoglu, M.M.: A learner ontology based on learning style models for adaptive E-learning. In: Gervasi, O., et al. (eds.) ICCSA 2018. LNCS, vol. 10961, pp. 199–212. Springer, Cham (2018). https://doi.org/10.1007/978-3-319-95165-2_14
9. Coursera: Coursera — build skills with online courses from top institutions (2012). https://www.coursera.org/
10. Dang, F., Tang, J., Li, S.: MOOC-KG: a MOOC knowledge graph for cross-platform online learning resources. In: 2019 IEEE 9th International Conference on Electronics Information and Emergency Communication (ICEIEC), pp. 1–8. IEEE (2019)
11. Davies, H., Lehdonvirta, V., Margaryan, A., Albert, J., Larke, L.: Developing and matching skills in the online platform economy: findings on new forms of digital work and learning from Cedefop's CrowdLearn study (2020)
12. Degbelo, A.: A snapshot of ontology evaluation criteria and strategies. In: Proceedings of the 13th International Conference on Semantic Systems, SEMANTICS 2017, Amsterdam, The Netherlands, 11–14 September 2017, pp. 1–8. ACM (2017)
13. Durán, C.G., Ramírez, C.M.: Integration of open educational resources using semantic platform. IEEE Access (2021)
14. Eke, C.I., Norman, A.A., Shuib, L., Nweke, H.F.: A survey of user profiling: state-of-the-art, challenges, and solutions. IEEE Access 7, 144907–144924 (2019)
15. Fatahi, S.: An experimental study on an adaptive e-learning environment based on learner's personality and emotion. Educ. Inf. Technol. 24(4), 2225–2241 (2019)
16. Gao, M., Liu, K., Wu, Z.: Personalisation in web computing and informatics: theories, techniques, applications, and future research. Inf. Syst. Frontiers 12(5), 607–629 (2010)

17. George, G., Lal, A.M.: Review of ontology-based recommender systems in e-learning. Comput. Educ. **142** (2019)
18. Harrathi, M., Touzani, N., Braham, R.: A hybrid knowlegde-based approach for recommending massive learning activities. In: 14th IEEE/ACS International Conference on Computer Systems and Applications, AICCSA 2017, Hammamet, Tunisia, 30 October–3 November 2017, pp. 49–54. IEEE Computer Society (2017)
19. Ibrahim, M.E., Yang, Y., Ndzi, D.L., Yang, G., Al-Maliki, M.: Ontology-based personalized course recommendation framework. IEEE Access **7**, 5180–5199 (2018)
20. Ilkou, E., Signer, B.: A technology-enhanced smart learning environment based on the combination of knowledge graphs and learning paths. In: Proceedings of the 12th International Conference on Computer Supported Education, CSEDU 2020, Prague, Czech Republic, 2–4 May 2020, vol. 2, pp. 461–468. SCITEPRESS (2020)
21. Ivanova, T., Popov, M.: Ontology evaluation and multilingualism. In: Proceedings of the 21st International Conference on Computer Systems and Technologies 2020, CompSysTech 2020, pp. 215–222. Association for Computing Machinery, New York (2020)
22. Jando, E., Hidayanto, A.N., Prabowo, H., Warnars, H.L.H.S., et al.: Personalized e-learning model: a systematic literature review. In: 2017 International Conference on Information Management and Technology (ICIMTech), pp. 238–243. IEEE (2017)
23. Jeevamol, J., Renumol, V.G.: An ontology-based hybrid e-learning content recommender system for alleviating the cold-start problem. Educ. Inf. Technol. **26**(4), 4993–5022 (2021). https://doi.org/10.1007/s10639-021-10508-0
24. Katis, E., Kondylakis, H., Agathangelos, G., Vassilakis, K.: Developing an ontology for curriculum and syllabus. In: Gangemi, A., et al. (eds.) ESWC 2018. LNCS, vol. 11155, pp. 55–59. Springer, Cham (2018). https://doi.org/10.1007/978-3-319-98192-5_11
25. Koutsomitropoulos, D., Andriopoulos, A., Likothanassis, S.: Semantic classification and indexing of open educational resources with word embeddings and ontologies. Cybern. Inf. Technol. **20**(5), 95–116 (2020)
26. Koutsomitropoulos, D.A., Solomou, G.D.: A learning object ontology repository to support annotation and discovery of educational resources using semantic thesauri. IFLA J. **44**(1), 4–22 (2018)
27. Li, N., Motta, E., d'Aquin, M.: Ontology summarization: an analysis and an evaluation, vol. 666 (2010)
28. Salem, A.M., Nikitaeva, A.Y.: Knowledge engineering paradigms for smart education and learning systems. In: 42nd International Convention on Information and Communication Technology, Electronics and Microelectronics, MIPRO 2019, Opatija, Croatia, 20–24 May 2019, pp. 1571–1574. IEEE (2019)
29. Skillen, K., Chen, L., Nugent, C.D., Donnelly, M.P., Burns, W., Solheim, I.: Ontological user modelling and semantic rule-based reasoning for personalisation of help-on-demand services in pervasive environments. Future Gener. Comput. Syst. **34**, 97–109 (2014)
30. Stancin, K., Poscic, P., Jaksic, D.: Ontologies in education - state of the art. Educ. Inf. Technol. **25**(6), 5301–5320 (2020)
31. Tarus, J.K., Niu, Z., Mustafa, G.: Knowledge-based recommendation: a review of ontology-based recommender systems for e-learning. Artif. Intell. Rev. **50**(1), 21–48 (2017). https://doi.org/10.1007/s10462-017-9539-5
32. Tavakoli, M., Elias, M., Kismihók, G., Auer, S.: Quality prediction of open educational resources a metadata-based approach. In: 2020 IEEE 20th International Conference on Advanced Learning Technologies (ICALT), pp. 29–31. IEEE (2020)

33. Tavakoli, M., Elias, M., Kismihók, G., Auer, S.: Metadata analysis of open educational resources. In: LAK21: 11th International Learning Analytics and Knowledge Conference, pp. 626–631 (2021)
34. Tavakoli, M., Faraji, A., Mol, S.T., Kismihók, G.: OER recommendations to support career development. In: 2020 IEEE Frontiers in Education Conference (FIE), pp. 1–5. IEEE (2020)
35. Tavakoli, M., Hakimov, S., Ewerth, R., Kismihók, G.: A recommender system for open educational videos based on skill requirements. In: 2020 IEEE 20th International Conference on Advanced Learning Technologies (ICALT), pp. 1–5. IEEE (2020)
36. Tavakoli, M., Mol, S.T., Kismihók, G.: Labour market information driven, personalized, OER recommendation system for lifelong learners. In: International Conference on Computer Supported Education (CSEDU) (2020)
37. Wilkinson, M.D., et al.: The fair guiding principles for scientific data management and stewardship. Sci. Data **3**(1), 1–9 (2016)
38. Zouri, M., Ferworn, A.: An ontology-based approach for curriculum mapping in higher education. In: 11th IEEE Annual Computing and Communication Workshop and Conference, CCWC 2021, Las Vegas, NV, USA, 27–30 January 2021, pp. 141–147. IEEE (2021)

The Punya Platform: Building Mobile Research Apps with Linked Data and Semantic Features

Evan W. Patton[1]([envelope]) [ID], William Van Woensel[2] [ID], Oshani Seneviratne[3] [ID],
Giuseppe Loseto[4] [ID], Floriano Scioscia[4] [ID], and Lalana Kagal[1] [ID]

[1] Massachusetts Institute of Technology, Cambridge, MA 02143, USA
{ewpatton,lkagal}@mit.edu
[2] Dalhousie University, Halifax, NS B3H 4R2, Canada
william.van.woensel@dal.ca
[3] Rensselaer Polytechnic Institute, Troy, NY 12180, USA
senevo@rpi.edu
[4] Polytechnic University of Bari, 70125 Bari, BA, Italy
{giuseppe.loseto,floriano.scioscia}@poliba.it

Abstract. Modern smartphones offer advanced sensing, connectivity, and processing capabilities for data acquisition, processing, and generation: but it can be difficult and costly to develop mobile research apps that leverage these features. Nevertheless, in life sciences and other scientific domains, there often exists a need to develop advanced mobile apps that go beyond simple questionnaires: ranging from sensor data collection and processing to self-management tools for chronic patients in healthcare. We present Punya, an open source, web-based platform based on MIT App Inventor that simplifies building Linked Data-enabled, advanced mobile apps that exploit smartphone capabilities. We posit that its integration with Linked Data facilitates the development of complex application and business rules, communication with heterogeneous online services, and interaction with the Internet of Things (IoT) data sources using the smartphone hardware. To that end, Punya includes an embedded semantic rule engine, integration with GraphQL and SPARQL to access remote graph data, and support for IoT devices using Bluetooth Low Energy and Linked Data Platform Constrained Application Protocol (LDP-CoAP). Moreover, Punya supports generating Linked Data descriptions of collected data. The platform includes built-in tutorials to quickly build apps using these different technologies. In this paper, we present a short discussion of the Punya platform, its current adoption that includes over 500 active users as well as the larger app-building MIT App Inventor community of which it is a part, and future development directions that would greatly benefit Semantic Web and Linked Data application developers as well as researchers who leverage Linked Open Data resources for their research.

Resource: http://punya.mit.edu

Keywords: Mobile app development · Research apps · Linked Data · Semantic rules · Internet of Things · GraphQL · Rapid prototyping

© Springer Nature Switzerland AG 2021
A. Hotho et al. (Eds.): ISWC 2021, LNCS 12922, pp. 563–579, 2021.
https://doi.org/10.1007/978-3-030-88361-4_33

1 Introduction

Scientific research apps rarely leverage the advanced sensing, interaction, and computing capabilities of smartphones. A recent survey [34] found that most smartphone apps in psychological studies do not use smartphone features such as sensors and complex analytical methods. Instead, they are limited to porting existing interfaces to mobile screens to offer mobility (e.g., ad-hoc interactions) via the smartphone. Indeed, it is difficult and time-consuming to integrate an app with peripheral sensors, link to online data sources, and offer complex decision logic. One has to deal with heterogeneous services, protocols and schemas, as well as build complex application and business rules. This results in high software development costs. Since researchers usually rely on one-shot grant funding to develop (and maintain) research apps, and often operate in exploratory settings where app requirements may change over time, they may lack funds to cover costly software development projects [16].

Prior experiences by the authors have demonstrated this: Praino, Scioscia *et al.* [43] developed a mobile patient diary for Systemic Sclerosis patients to annotate the evolution of symptoms via scientifically validated questionnaires, on-device camera, and wearable devices. However, due to difficulty achieving secure mobile communication with electronic health records (EHR), data was not sent: instead, a summary report was generated and communicated to physicians. Moreover, due to heterogeneous and proprietary device protocols, manually customized modules were needed for different types of wearables. Van Woensel *et al.* [55] developed an intelligent mobile diary for Atrial Fibrillation (AFib) patients to enter daily symptoms and vitals, offering local decision support for time-sensitive health feedback. However, a reasoning system had to be manually ported to the device for decision support; and, due to similar reasons as [43], the app could only integrate with a single, off-the-shelf peripheral device.

These experiences highlight the need for an easy to use, open source, platform for developing research apps that provides mechanisms to access peripheral sensors, link to online data sources, and use decision logic.

In addition, we propose that Linked Data (LD) and Semantic Web (SW) technology will help democratize the development of research apps, as it affords creators the following:

- SPARQL [42], GraphQL [19] and Linked Data Platform (LDP) [52] queries and requests, in terms of a domain ontology, to access online data and services; which avoids dealing with discordant schemas and protocols.
- Semantic Web of Things (SWoT) [46] offers methods and tools that generate a unifying layer, in terms of a domain ontology, across heterogeneous IoT device services that hides manufacturer-specific protocols.
- Well-established semantic formalisms, such as OWL [33], SWRL [22], and N3 [5], offer the tools and techniques to define and execute complex processing, application, and decision logic to implement Expert System features.
- Collected and processed research data can be annotated with relevant ontologies and uploaded to a semantic repository or SOLID pod [47].

– Auto-generating wire-frame Linked Data forms from domain ontologies, with fields connected to ontology terms, to avoid boilerplate view-controller code.

In general, relying on re-usable, well-known domain ontologies, standards and tools, avoids re-inventing the wheel in the form of yet another custom data model, online/device service schemas and proprietary protocols; and the downstream efforts required by consumers to support and implement them. The Punya platform [28] is an end-user development environment built on MIT App Inventor [57], a web-based platform that offers a drag-and-drop interface for easily building interfaces and application logic. Punya expands on MIT App Inventor by adding LD & SW affordances to support research apps.

Punya was originally conceived in 2013 as a way to support relief efforts during humanitarian crises, e.g. conflicts in countries as South Sudan, Iraq, and Yemen and the Central African Republic, and Typhoon Haiyan in the Philippines. The goal was to enable relief workers to quickly put together mobile apps, which could be customized to the language/cultural/technical requirements of the specific region and crisis, to aid co-ordination of relief efforts, and to provide information to key decision makers. However, we realized that it was useful for much more than disaster management and started exploring its use in ecology, tracking air pollution, personal health management and other areas.

2   Related Work

Apple ResearchKit [4] is a software framework for apps that let medical researchers gather study data through surveys, forms, and activities, and supports integration with the HealthKit [3] and CareKit [2] frameworks to gather data from peripheral health devices. These 'kits' allow researchers to gather informed consent, create surveys, visualize trends in the data and conduct active evaluations. While ResearchKit is excellent at creating survey-based research apps with customized workflows, it currently lies beyond its purview to connect to existing, online health data sources, or implement complex application and processing logic; nor does it afford the general advances of relying on semantic ontologies. Also, since ResearchKit is rooted in the iOS framework, building an app that uses ResearchKit will require knowledge of the underlying framework—one needs to install the XCode IDE and manually add many code snippets to tie together a ResearchKit app—this increases the learning curve and is not ideal for researchers looking to rapidly build study applications. In contrast, the Punya platform provides a convenient drag-and-drop environment for researchers to quickly prototype their ideas and easily access Linked Data resources through its in-built Semantic Web capabilities.

Node-RED [37] provides a browser-based editor to wire up event-based applications quickly, and it is popular in applications that use IoT components [7]. A Node-RED application can be run on a web server, Raspberry Pi, Arduino, or on an Android device using an emulator. However, Node-RED rather focuses on setting up data flows including IoT devices and online services, as opposed to the prototyping of general (research) apps, outfitted with a fully-fledged UI and leveraging Linked Data and Semantic Web features as outlined before.

For many types of consumer-facing applications, designers can utilize prototyping tools to ensure high fidelity and adaptability in the final application delivered to their target userbase. For example, Qualtrics [45] is a simple-to-use, web-based survey tool to conduct survey research, evaluations, and other data collection activities. Designers, with no prior experience, are able to use its research suite to build surveys, send surveys and analyze responses. Some other popular prototyping tools include InVision [23], Marvel [31], MockPlus [35], and Proto.io [44]. These tools allow their users to collaborate, research and test their ideas on the cloud-based digital platform, and even integrate with several third-party workflow products and services, where designers can import mockups from Sketch or Photoshop easily. Several of these products have companion apps for mobile platforms such as iOS and Android, enabling designers to create mockups natively on the devices. However, regarding the development of research apps, none of these tools allow going beyond relatively simple survey-based applications, which do not leverage Linked Open Data nor open-source and free-for-unrestricted-use software.

Other frameworks, such as Apache Cordova[1] or React Native[2], focus on web-first principles—i.e., using web technologies for mobile app development. As another example, Progressive Web Apps (PWAs)[3] are single-page web applications that present as native applications, if the mobile platform supports it. These approaches are useful for developing cross-platform apps using a single code base, especially for developers comfortable with JavaScript and web APIs. However, these technologies may be unapproachable for researchers who need to develop apps and who are not trained as software engineers.

3   Punya Components for Semantic Research Apps

The Punya platform builds on MIT App Inventor, providing a suite of additional components that enrich the platform for building semantically-enabled, research-oriented mobile apps. Briefly, the MIT App Inventor interface allows app creators to visually compose one or more screens of an application by dragging and dropping user interface elements into a mock phone screen (called the *Designer*). The behavior of the app is scripted in a visual programming language built on the Google Blockly framework (called the *Blocks Editor*).[4] Apps can be tested in real time using an app called the Companion (Punya provides its own version). Once an app is complete, it can be compiled into a app package (currently Android only) for distribution, such as through the Google Play Store. In this section, we discuss a subset of these components, starting with the core LD support (Sect. 3.1) and then elaborating on Semantic Web of Things, online LD access, and Expert System features (Sects. 3.2–3.4).

---

[1] https://cordova.apache.org/.
[2] https://reactnative.dev/.
[3] https://web.dev/progressive-web-apps/.
[4] https://developers.google.com/blockly.

3.1 Linked Data Elements

One strength of Punya is its ability to integrate with LD resources as we have previously discussed [28,29]. We briefly summarize each component and discuss how they can be used specifically for building LD-enabled research applications.

- **LinkedData** component wraps a Jena [13] Model object, and, in line with the building block-based design paradigm of App Inventor, offers a block-based interface to an RDF graph, allowing the update and retrieval of RDF data. The component supports reading and writing graph data on the web using SPARQL, and on local storage by serializing the graph as Turtle. An important feature of the `LinkedData` component is its ability to convert the contents of a `LinkedDataForm` into an RDF graph, and, inversely, populating these forms with RDF data. Using this functionality, app developers can use the LinkedData component as a general data store for application content and similarly use the content to drive the user interface.
- **LinkedDataForm** provides the ability to annotate components with `InverseProperty`, `ObjectType`, `PropertyURI`, and `SubjectIdentifier` fields, which can be filled using an autocomplete feature. This allows laying out LD-aware components, similar to HTML `form` elements with RDFa [1]. The contents of the form can then be used to construct RDF graphs based on the form fields and their annotations. `LinkedDataForms` can be nested to create arbitrarily complex UIs and ensuing RDF graph structures.
- **LinkedDataListPicker** is an LD-enhanced version of the App Inventor `ListPicker` component. It populates its list by evaluating a SPARQL query against a remote endpoint. The labels for the entities are retrieved using the well-known properties *rdfs:label*, *skos:prefLabel*, *foaf:name*, and *dc:title*.
- **Linked Data Form Generator** is a feature of Punya developed by WeiHua Li [29] that allows auto-generating a wire-frame `LinkedDataForm` from a given RDFS or OWL ontology. Researchers can then build an app quickly from best-in-class ontologies for their domain(s) and greatly reduce the amount of manual development.

3.2 Semantic Web of Things

The *Semantic Web of Things* (SWoT) vision [46] integrates knowledge representation and reasoning techniques from the Semantic Web into Internet of Things (IoT) architectures. SWoT enables new classes of smart applications that augment real-world objects, locations, and events with machine-understandable data, annotated with a domain ontology, using mobile and pervasive devices such as smartphones, wearables, and IoT sensors. Currently, Punya supports *Linked Data Platform for the Constrained Application Protocol* (*LDP-CoAP*), a SWoT protocol that enables lightweight, LD-based resource dissemination and discovery in dynamic ad-hoc contexts. Moreover, developers can use App Inventor support for Bluetooth Low Energy (BLE) that allows for low-energy consumption of mobile services.

- **LDP-CoAP Web of Things protocol** is grounded on the LDP W3C Recommendation [52] as reference format and guidelines for managing collections of Linked Data resources on the Web. However, LDP only defines resource management primitives for HTTP, leaving out Web of Things (WoT) scenarios where more lightweight application protocols are required. CoAP [9] is an application-level protocol for machine-to-machine (M2M) communications, based on a loosely coupled stateless client/server model. LDP-CoAP [30] defines an adaptation of the LDP specification for CoAP, which allows publishing Linked Data on the WoT while preserving all LDP features and capabilities. Using the LdpCoapClient Punya component, a mobile app can expose data, collected via embedded sensors or peripheral devices, as RDF resources to other parties through an LDP-CoAP server. In particular, the component supports the GET, PUT, POST and DELETE CoAP methods to request, create, update and remove LDP Resources, which can be organized in hierarchical relationships by means of LDP Containers. To discover RDF resources exposed by external devices, a key feature in dynamic SWoT contexts, the Punya LDP-CoAP component supports the Constrained RESTful Environments (CoRE) Link Format protocol and its discovery functionality [48].
- **Bluetooth Low Energy.** Introduced in 2010, BLE aims to overcome the limitations of the traditional Bluetooth technology in regards to energy consumption and device interoperability. In particular, BLE allows low-energy communication with remote devices (e.g., BLE beacons) in terms of standard-compliant services (e.g., heart rate, blood pressure services). This facilitates the development of smart, energy-efficient mobile apps that monitor personal and contextual data using different types of peripherals and sensors. The App Inventor BLE extension, BluetoothLE,[5] provides standards-based Profiles and Services to connect to a range of BLE-enabled peripheral devices, such as health and fitness monitors, environmental sensors, and more. To that end, BluetoothLE includes a range of functions for advertising and discovering services, connecting remote devices, and communicating with them.

3.3   Online Data Access

Most use cases in Sect. 4 illustrate the need for integration with remote data sources for research apps. To that end, we have introduced two new features in Punya. The first is support for GraphQL, which can be used to query a number of graph-based data sources (e.g., Facebook) that would otherwise be opaque silos. The second is support for SPARQL in the blocks language, which makes it easier to construct syntactically valid SPARQL queries. We briefly describe each of these features and how they can be used.

- **GraphQL** is a declarative language for querying graph data, originally developed at Facebook and open sourced in 2015 [18]. A number of large companies offer GraphQL endpoints for querying their data. To facilitate unlocking these

---

[5] http://iot.appinventor.mit.edu/#/bluetoothle/bluetoothleintro.

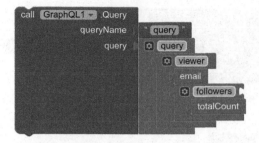

Fig. 1. An example of a GraphQL query for user email and number of followers using the dynamically generated GraphQL blocks.

silos, we have included a GraphQL component [14]. The GraphQL component leverages the introspective nature of the GraphQL language to generate blocks for the types supported by the endpoint. This allows for dynamically building queries while developing the app. GraphQL can be used, for example, to query the social graph of a research study participant, for social research. Figure 1 shows an example of how one might construct a GraphQL query requesting the number of followers of a user via a social network. The blocks are dynamically created by examining the server's schema and shown in context when hovering the cursor over the type names.

– **Writing SPARQL:** Previously, Punya required app developers to programmatically construct SPARQL queries using the built-in text block capabilities. It is possible, for example, to store query templates as file assets in the application. These queries can then be read into memory, and substitutions applied before executing the query against an endpoint. The new version of Punya provides built-in SPARQL blocks inspired by [10]. The SPARQL block functionality performs appropriate type checking on the connections to prevent the construction of syntactically invalid queries. An example SPARQL query to check for drug-drug interactions is shown in Fig. 2.

3.4 Ruleset Construction and Evaluation

Mobile rule engine features allow developers to deploy complex semantic reasoning locally on the smartphone. In general, this can be utilized to realize a form of edge computing [51]—improving response times, reducing bandwidth and need for continuous connectivity, increasing privacy protection and, in some cases, removing the need for online services for storage and processing support.

Of course, important considerations with regards to local processing include performance, scalability, and battery consumption. Patton *et al.* [40] performed a study on battery use during OWL reasoning, comparing battery consumption of 4G, 3G, and WiFi radio. The authors found that it takes less energy to reason on several ontologies using Apache Jena [13] compared to requesting the results from an external source via the 3G or 4G. Although Bobed *et al.* [8] and Kazakov

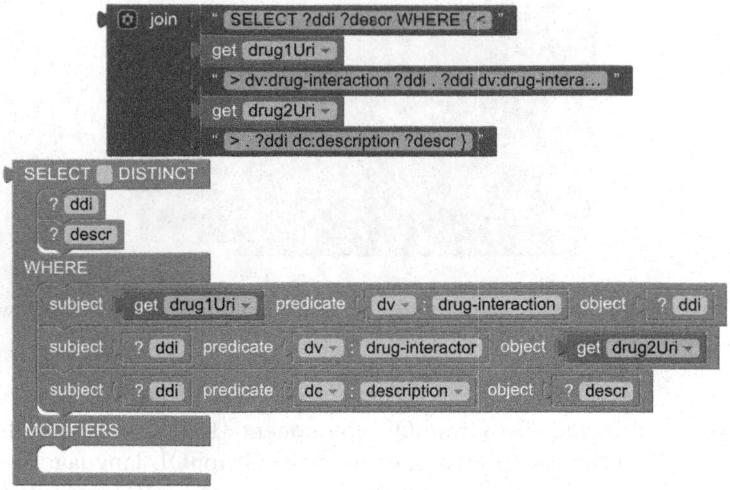

Fig. 2. An example SPARQL query to check DrugBank for drug interactions. Top: Old style; Bottom: New style.

et al. [24] found orders of magnitude difference between reasoning on PC and Android, they also showed promising trends: reasoners on the Android RunTime (ART), which features ahead-of-time compilation, were around two times faster than in Dalvik [8]. In prior work, the same team also found a performance increase of around 30% between Android devices only one-year apart [58]. Van Woensel *et al.* [54] found acceptable performance for Apache Jena on Android for OWL ontologies comprising 500 statements or less. As these studies indicate the feasibility of local reasoning on smartphones, we added to Punya the `Reasoner` component: supporting rule-based reasoning using RDFS, a subset of OWL, or even custom rulesets added by the developers using `Ruleblock`'s.

- **Reasoner** is a component newly added to the Punya platform. It uses the Jena [13] rule-based reasoner to make inferences over the RDF graph provided by a `LinkedData` component. Jena provides built-in rules for RDFS and subsets of OWL, and custom rules can be provided from files or via `RuleBlock`'s (see below). Rule evaluation occurs on a background thread for performance reasons. Reasoning begins when the app invokes the reasoner's `Run` method, and an event, `ReasoningComplete`, is fired when the reasoning has completed and results are available.
- **Writing Rulesets** dynamically based on user input is facilitated by a set of blocks for the language to make syntactically correct rules. These `Ruleblocks` reuse blocks from the SPARQL functionality (see above), e.g., the triple pattern and variable declaration blocks. The `Ruleblocks` provide support to model both forward chaining and backward chaining (Fig. 3). Forward rules can be used to generate backward rules by binding variables in the body, which will hold for the backward rules.

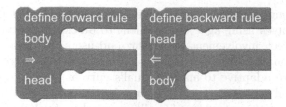

Fig. 3. Blocks to define forward and backward chaining rules.

4 Use Cases and Functionality

We briefly introduce five research-oriented scenarios that rely on mobile apps for data collection, analysis, and interpretation. Following the use cases, we categorize the distinct features of these apps, and show how the Punya components in Sect. 3 were used to address their functional requirements. A more detailed description of how these apps were built and the Punya application code for these research use cases are available at http://punya.mit.edu/#use-cases.

4.1 Use Cases

1. **Sleep Apnea Diary.** Mobile patient diaries are apps used by chronic patients to record medications, symptoms, and vitals—they provide a convenient way for patients to keep track of their health data, and, when they are integrated into Electronic Health Records (EHR), communicate health data to clinicians for longitudinal follow-up. Clinical decision support (CDS) tools, added to the EHR system, can issue recommendations to help with diagnosis and treatment. In many cases, however, it would be opportune for a patient diary to directly provide decision support: for urgent patient health issues, when wireless connectivity is lacking, or when secure integration with an EHR system is non-existent. Sleep Apnea, for example, has an estimated prevalence from 3% to nearly 50% depending on age group and sex [27], with a gold-standard diagnosis involving polysomnography [32], a comprehensive test which involves monitoring heart, lung, and brain activity, breathing patterns, and blood oxygen levels. However, more simple home sleep apnea testing may be used to indicate the diagnosis in symptomatic patients [27]. An app, running locally on the user's device and outfitted with mobile decision support (Sect. 3.4), can directly analyze the user's health, based on user input and sensor data, and issue health recommendations—in this case, a possible diagnosis of sleep apnea.
2. **Diabetes Prevention and Intervention App.** Diabetes is a chronic health condition that affects approximately 10.5% of the United States population [15]. People with diabetes are typically advised to engage in several self-management behaviors to improve their health outcomes, including healthy dieting and exercise—this is known to require personalized educational material and multitudes of data on suitable foods and types of exercise. Yet,

sustained, long-term behavior change remains challenging [11]. A possible solution involves using agile development to quickly prototype mobile apps, with the direct involvement of patient end-users, to design a mobile app that is personalized to their requirements and needs. In general, interventions that are adaptive to an individual's current psychological, social, and environmental context, are arguably in a better position to address behavior change than static or 'one-size-fits-all' approaches. Such a bespoke, context-sensitive, and data-intensive approach, requires a mobile development platform that facilitates end-user development, including patients and researchers, and allows easy integration with context-gathering sensors (Sect. 3.2) and online data sources (Sect. 3.3), such as the FoodKG [21], Ontology of Physical Activity [25], the Diabetes Mellitus Treatment Ontology [17], and large scale biomedical data repositories such as Bio2RDF [6].

3. **Remote Monitoring for Healthy Aging.** The elderly ($\geq$ 65 years old) population is expected to grow from about 725 million to approximately 1.8 billion in the next 40 years, with prevalence jumping from nearly 10% to 18% [53]. Healthy, active aging is a global challenge for the next decades from healthcare, technological and social standpoints. Many research projects have been studying *Ambient-Assisted Living* (AAL) to support healthy aging through automated activity recognition, psychophysical well-being monitoring, and injury prevention [36]. AAL relies on an array of information and communication technologies, deployed in "smart" environments outfitted with camera systems and mobile and wearable sensors, to assess the subject's condition, activate timely assistance requests to caregivers, and provide feedback and support. In AAL, smartphones often play the role of cluster heads, reading data from a variety of sensors embedded in the smartphone, such as accelerometers, gyroscopes, and orientation sensors; wearable sensors setup in typical Body Area Network (BAN) configurations [20]; and devices deployed in the room, communicating through short-range wireless links (e.g., using BLE, Sect. 3.2). In this paradigm, mobile processing capabilities are exploited to collect, integrate and enrich collected data, and run lightweight data preprocessing and mining procedures. Additionally, the mobile phone can act as a gateway towards a back-end infrastructure where larger volumes of information can be stored and analyzed (e.g., using SWoT protocols like LDP-CoAP, Sect. 3.2).

4. **Provenance of Sensor Networks.** Capturing provenance metadata in the field during deployment, calibration, maintenance, and removal of sensor platforms, is vital to helping scientists analyze and understand sensor data back. Kinkead et al. [26] discuss a research tool, in the form of a mobile app, to collect metadata about which sensor platforms were deployed where and when, as part of a larger inter-institutional effort to study water and ecosystem quality around Lake George, NY, USA. Rather than using traditional paper-based metadata collection, the mobile app facilitated real-time gathering and communication of metadata in an efficient, error-free, and standardized way: using the device's camera to identify the sensor using their QR code, and GPS to automatically identify the sensor's location. In doing so, the app allowed

accurate downstream statistical analysis based on properly calibrated and positioned sensors. The quick prototyping of such research apps by non-IT professionals (in this case, ecologists) requires an end-user development platform with a minimal learning curve. Using Punya,[6] the ecologists were able to develop the app in a matter of weeks [26]—moreover, the researchers believed that the platform could be similarly utilized to rapidly prototype observation-based mobile apps in other fields.

5. **Experience Sampling Methodologies.** Experience sampling methodologies (ESM) are utilized to build a picture of user behavior over time, relying on automated sensor input and manual user entry. For instance, Shih [50] developed a mobile app featuring ESM to study the contextual factors that influence people's privacy preferences regarding mobile apps: such as frequently visited places, specific time slots, who is around, and activities people are engaged in. As another example, Ecological Momentary Assessments (EMA) are a type of ESM that is essential to perform reliable, psychology- and healthcare-related assessments in the patient's natural environment, as they minimize recall bias and maximize the real-world validity of observations [49]—with the current ubiquity of smartphones, mobile apps have become excellent tools to perform EMA [34]. To build a complete and accurate picture of user behavior, developing ESM apps require integrating data from many different sensors and apps. Moreover, an advanced use case of ESM involves collecting detailed information on the user's social interactions, and social networks may be leveraged to automatically collect this type of information (Sect. 3.3).

4.2 Common Features

Each of these use cases brings its own requirements. We observe that, in many cases, these functional requirements are shared across apps. We briefly discuss each of these requirements, and outline how researchers can realize them within a mobile app using Punya.

– **Reading and Writing LD.** Mobile apps addressing each of the use cases above leverage Punya's ability to read and write LD (Sect. 3.3). In all cases, this data may be stored locally on the device, using a `LinkedData` model (Sect. 3.1), to support down-stream local decision-making (use case 1), realize context-sensitivity (use cases 2 and 5), perform pre-processing and data mining (use case 3), or merely for offline storage (use case 4). Subsequently, the data can be uploaded to a remote data store (e.g., EHR), when connectivity is available, to allow for remote storage, processing, and decision-making (e.g., [56]). In [26], provenance data related to sensor platform deployments are captured on-site, and then uploaded to a remote data store when connec-

---

[6] The authors mention App Inventor, but several Punya LD components were used.

tivity is restored. Moreover, in order to aid patients in behavior change, such as healthy dieting, use case 2 relies on reading online, large-scale LD from online data sources such as the FoodKG [21], Ontology of Physical Activity [25], the Diabetes Mellitus Treatment Ontology [17], and Bio2RDF [6].

- **Reasoning over LD.** Use cases 1 and 2 utilize the Punya reasoning components (Sect. 3.4) to write `Ruleset` blocks and apply the `Reasoner` to analyze self-reported health data, issue health recommendations, and implement context sensitivity. Use case 3 can apply either simple data mining algorithms or rule-based reasoning to perform a local pre-processing of data, required to enable edge computing scenarios and reduce both response times and bandwidth usage while increasing privacy compared to traditional centralized approaches. Moreover, in use case 4, one could also utilize the `Reasoner` to validate metadata when it is collected, e.g., to ensure that a sensor platform is still in an undeployed state at the time the app is deployed [26].

- **Integrating Sensor Data.** All use cases make use of Punya's wide array of sensor components (e.g., `BarcodeScanner`, `Pedometer`, `LocationSensor`) to achieve their goals. Some examples include: collecting health-related sensor data to aid in diagnosis (use case 1), the psychological, social, and environmental context for effective behavior change (use case 2) and accurate experience sampling (use case 5), embedded and peripheral sensor data for AAL (use case 3); and to aid in collecting sensor provenance metadata (use case 4). Data can also be annotated according to widespread modeling approaches, per the LDP guidelines, and shared via WoT protocols (use case 3). By exploiting LDP-CoAP, external data sources can be discovered at run-time and accessed, and annotated data generated by the app can be published as LDP Resources organized in containers to aggregate them, e.g., by type (OWL class), provenance (user, area, etc.), or time slot.

- **Accessing non-RDF Graph Data.** Use case 5 presents a scenario where information about study participants' social graphs and activities are relevant to privacy preferences [50] and ecological momentary assessments [49]. Understanding social graphs can be done using the `GraphQL` component to query a social network with appropriate authorization. Combined with some environmental sensing, one could imagine an ESM app that asks questions about a social relationship based on proximity to friends and family. Likewise, vocabularies like Friend Of a Friend (FOAF) [12] could also be used, assuming that participants publish their own FOAF profiles or use another platform that does so on their behalf.

- **Tracking Provenance.** Every use case could benefit from gathering provenance at the point of data collection: sensor data provided by the mobile app platform, such as time (`Clock`), location (`LocationSensor`), and ownership of the device, all can supply provenance metadata. For example, if the grand vision that one day EHR encompass in-situ patient data on a fine-grained time scale (e.g., to the second or minute), then healthcare professionals will want to know how the data were collected, by whom, and how trustworthy those data are based on their sources. In use case 4, for example, provenance about the sensors (e.g., manufacturer, date of manufacture, model numbers, calibration data) may all prove valuable in the long run, and this information can be captured with Punya and serialized to RDF for future use.

5   Learning Materials

Punya, hosted at http://punya.appinventor.mit.edu, includes a suite of built-in tutorials for learning how to build Linked Data-aware mobile apps inspired by the use cases presented in Sect. 4. Some of these new built-in instructional materials are based on a tutorial session previously presented at ISWC 2020 [41]. For example, the RdfNotepad[7] tutorial teaches the basics of using the LinkedDataForm to construct and edit RDF graphs and reading and writing of RDF using the LinkedData component. Those interested in rule-based expert systems can explore the Sleep Apnea tutorial[8] discussed in Sect. 1. Integration of mobile app sensors and the Semantic Web of Things can be explored as part of a tutorial on LDP-CoAP.[9]

6   Usage and Community Engagement

Over 5,000 app creators have used the Punya platform since its debut in 2014. However, because the framework by design does not embed any tracking information within apps, we are unaware of whether the resulting apps have been published in mobile app stores or otherwise widely distributed. Punya has been presented as a tutorial at two meetings of the International Semantic Web Conference, once in 2015 at Lehigh University and once virtually in 2020. In the year ending March 31, 2021, there were 529 active users, of which 31 made use of the Linked Data features exclusive to Punya (Fig. 4).

Because Punya is built on MIT App Inventor, developers can tap into a large community of app developers worldwide (1,967 active community members in the 30 days ending April 1, 2021, and almost 900,000 yearly active users).[10] There is also a rich community of extension developers around MIT App Inventor, with over 3,000 extensions published [39]. Creators of Linked Data apps using Punya can leverage these extensions to further enrich their applications. Some popular extensions include the BluetoothLE extension for IoT connectivity and machine learning extensions using Tensorflow.js.

---

[7] http://punya.appinventor.mit.edu/?repo=RdfNotepad.
[8] http://punya.appinventor.mit.edu/?repo=SleepApnea.
[9] http://punya.appinventor.mit.edu/?repo=LdpCoapTutorial.
[10] https://community.appinventor.mit.edu.

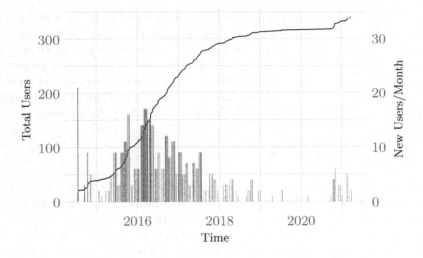

Fig. 4. Growth of users leveraging Linked Data components in Punya

7   Conclusion and Future Work

Punya is an open source[11] platform that can be used for building semantically aware research apps. A ready-to-use development environment with interactive tutorials is available online at http://punya.appinventor.mit.edu. For those interested in offline use or use without a Google account, it is possible to build and host a local copy following the instructions in the GitHub repository. Punya provides a rich suite of components for researchers to develop data-collection and expert-system type applications. Its integration of novel technologies like LDP-CoAP opens new possibilities for integrating with the Semantic Web of Things. App developers using Punya can also tap into a worldwide network of others building mobile apps via the MIT App Inventor community. We have provided a suite of tutorials to get researchers and Linked Data practitioners up to speed and building apps quickly. All the resources related to Punya, including use cases, sample apps, and tutorials, can be accessed at http://punya.mit.edu.

A continuous avenue of future work involves the integration of Semantic Web technology to further facilitate research app development—*e.g.*, we currently target an ontology-based layer on top of the `BluetoothLE` components to abstract from the relatively low-level BLE protocol. Recently, MIT App Inventor released a version that supports Apple's iOS operating system. A future iteration of Punya will build on this new platform to allow researchers to quickly prototype *cross-platform* Linked Data and Semantic Web apps. We are also looking to make the platform smarter with respect to energy consumption, aiming to move computation to either the device or server based on smart predictions [38]. We are actively building more example apps and establishing future partnerships to leverage the ease of app development with Punya to developing countries.

---

[11] Apache Licensed, see https://github.com/mit-dig/punya.

References

1. Adida, B., Birbeck, M., McCarron, S., Herman, I.: RDFa Core 1.1 - Third Edition). W3C Recommendation, World Wide Web Consortium, March 2015. https://www.w3.org/TR/rdfa-core/
2. Apple Inc.: CareKit. https://developer.apple.com/carekit
3. Apple Inc.: HealthKit. https://developer.apple.com/health-fitness/
4. Apple Inc.: ResearchKit. http://researchkit.org/
5. Arndt, D., Van Woensel, W.: Notation 3 (N3) Community Group (2018). https://www.w3.org/community/n3-dev/
6. Belleau, F., Nolin, M.A., Tourigny, N., Rigault, P., Morissette, J.: Bio2RDF: towards a mashup to build bioinformatics knowledge systems. J. Biomed. Inform. **41**(5), 706–716 (2008)
7. Blackstock, M., Lea, R.: Toward a distributed data flow platform for the web of things (distributed node-red). In: Proceedings of the 5th International Workshop on Web of Things, pp. 34–39 (2014)
8. Bobed, C., Yus, R., Bobillo, F., Mena, E.: Semantic reasoning on mobile devices: do androids dream of efficient reasoners? Web Semant. Sci. Services Agents World Wide Web **35**, 167–183 (2015)
9. Bormann, C., Castellani, A.P., Shelby, Z.: CoAP: an application protocol for billions of tiny internet nodes. IEEE Internet Comput. **16**(2), 62–67 (2012)
10. Bottoni, P., Ceriani, M.: Sparql playground: a block programming tool to experiment with sparql. In: VOILA@ ISWC, p. 103 (2015)
11. Bouton, M.E.: Why behavior change is difficult to sustain. Prev. Med. **68**, 29–36 (2014)
12. Brickley, D., Miller, L.: FOAF vocabulary specification 0.91 (2007)
13. Carroll, J.J., Dickinson, I., Dollin, C., Reynolds, D., Seaborne, A., Wilkinson, K.: Jena: implementing the semantic web recommendations. In: Proceedings of 13th International World Wide Web Conference Papers & Posters, pp. 74–83 (2004)
14. Cen, L., Patton, E.W.: Block affordances for graphql in mit app inventor. CoolThink@ JC, p. 147 (2019)
15. Centers for Disease Control and Prevention, U.S. Department of Health and Human Services, National Diabetes Statistics Report, Atlanta (2020)
16. Dominguez Veiga, J.J., Ward, T.: Data collection requirements for mobile connected health: an end user development approach. In: Proceedings of the 1st International Workshop on Mobile Development, pp. 23–30 (2016)
17. El-Sappagh, S., Kwak, D., Ali, F., Kwak, K.S.: DMTO: a realistic ontology for standard diabetes mellitus treatment. J. Biomed. Semant. **9**(1), 1–30 (2018)
18. Facebook Inc.: GraphQL: a data query language. https://engineering.fb.com/2015/09/14/core-data/graphql-a-data-query-language
19. Hartig, O., Pérez, J.: Semantics and complexity of GraphQL. In: Proceedings of the 2018 World Wide Web Conference, pp. 1155–1164 (2018)
20. Hasan, K., Biswas, K., Ahmed, K., Nafi, N.S., Islam, M.S.: A comprehensive review of wireless body area network. J. Netw. Comput. Appl. **143**, 178–198 (2019)
21. Haussmann, S., et al.: FoodKG: a semantics-driven knowledge graph for food recommendation. In: Ghidini, C., et al. (eds.) ISWC 2019. LNCS, vol. 11779, pp. 146–162. Springer, Cham (2019). https://doi.org/10.1007/978-3-030-30796-7_10
22. Horrocks, I., Patel-Schneider, P.F., Boley, H., Tabet, S., Grosof, B., Dean, M., et al.: SWRL: a semantic web rule language combining OWL and RuleML. W3C Member Submission **21**(79), 1–31 (2004)

23. InVision Inc.: InVision. https://www.invisionapp.com
24. Kazakov, Y., Klinov, P.: Experimenting with ELK reasoner on android. In: Proceedings of 2nd International Workshop on OWL Reasoner Evaluation, pp. 68–74 (2013)
25. Kim, H., Mentzer, J., Taira, R.: Developing a physical activity ontology to support the interoperability of physical activity data. J. Med. Internet Res. **21**(4), e12776 (2019)
26. Kinkead, L., Pinheiro, P., McGuinness, D.L.: Automating the collection of semantic sensor network metadata in the field with mobile applications. In: Proceedings of 1st International Workshop on Mobile Deployment of Semantic Technologies, pp. 32–43 (2015)
27. Laratta, C.R., Ayas, N.T., Povitz, M., Pendharkar, S.R.: Diagnosis and treatment of obstructive sleep apnea in adults. CMAJ **189**(48), E1481–E1488 (2017)
28. Li, W., Seneviratne, O., Patton, E.W., Kagal, L.: A semantic platform for developing data-intensive mobile apps. In: Proceedings of 13th International Conference on Semantic Computing (ICSC), pp. 71–78. IEEE (2019)
29. Li, W.J.: Helping the helpers: a toolkit for mobile humanitarian assistance apps. Master's thesis, Massachusetts Institute of Technology (2016)
30. Loseto, G., Ieva, S., Gramegna, F., Ruta, M., Scioscia, F., Di Sciascio, E.: Linked data (in low-resource) platforms: a mapping for constrained application protocol. In: Groth, P., et al. (eds.) ISWC 2016. LNCS, vol. 9982, pp. 131–139. Springer, Cham (2016). https://doi.org/10.1007/978-3-319-46547-0_14
31. Marvel Inc.: Marvel. https://marvelapp.com
32. Mayo Clinic: Polysomnography (sleep study). https://www.mayoclinic.org/tests-procedures/polysomnography/about/pac-20394877
33. McGuinness, D.L., Van Harmelen, F., et al.: OWL web ontology language overview. W3C Recommendation **10**(2) (2004)
34. Miralles, I., et al.: Smartphone apps for the treatment of mental disorders: systematic review. JMIR Mhealth Uhealth **8**(4), e14897 (2020)
35. MockPlus Inc.: MockPlus. https://www.mockplus.com
36. Nilsson, M.Y., Andersson, S., Magnusson, L., Hanson, E.: Ambient assisted living technology-mediated interventions for older people and their informal carers in the context of healthy ageing: a scoping review. Health Sci. Rep. **4**(1), e225 (2021)
37. Node-RED community: Node-RED: Low-code programming for event-driven applications. https://nodered.org
38. Patton, E.W.: Energy aware reasoning agents for the mobile semantic web. Ph.D. thesis, RPI (2016)
39. Patton, E.W.: A look at component usage in MIT App Inventor (2020). http://appinventor.mit.edu/blogs/evan/2020/12/20/component-usage-mit-app-inventor. Accessed 01 Apr 2021
40. Patton, E.W., McGuinness, D.L.: A power consumption benchmark for reasoners on mobile devices. In: Mika, P., et al. (eds.) ISWC 2014. LNCS, vol. 8796, pp. 409–424. Springer, Cham (2014). https://doi.org/10.1007/978-3-319-11964-9_26
41. Patton, E.W., Scioscia, F., Van Woensel, W.: Building mobile semantic web apps with Punya. In: Proceedings of ISWC 2020 Tutorials (2020)
42. Pérez, J., Arenas, M., Gutierrez, C.: Semantics and complexity of SPARQL. ACM Trans. Database Syst. (TODS) **34**(3), 1–45 (2009)
43. Praino, E., et al.: SScEntry: a personal disease diary app for Systemic Sclerosis patients. Ann. Rheum. Dis. **79**, 558–559 (2020). eULAR 2020 European eCongress of Rheumatology

44. Proto.io Inc.: Proto.io: Prototyping for all. https://proto.io
45. Qualtrics Inc.: Qualtrics: XM OS - Experience Design and Improvement. https://www.qualtrics.com
46. Ruta, M., Scioscia, F., Di Sciascio, E.: Enabling the semantic web of things: framework and architecture. In: 2012 IEEE Sixth International Conference on Semantic Computing, pp. 345–347. IEEE (2012)
47. Sambra, A., et al.: Solid: a platform for decentralized social applications based on linked data. Technical report, MIT CSAIL & Qatar Computing Research Institute (2016)
48. Shelby, Z.: Constrained RESTful Environments (CoRE) Link Format. RFC 6690, Internet Engineering Task Force, August 2012
49. Shiffman, S., Stone, A.A., Hufford, M.R.: Ecological momentary assessment. Annu. Rev. Clin. Psychol. **4**, 1–32 (2008)
50. Shih, F.: Exploring mobile privacy in context. Ph.D. thesis, MIT (2015)
51. Sittón-Candanedo, I., Alonso, R.S., Corchado, J.M., Rodríguez-González, S., Casado-Vara, R.: A review of edge computing reference architectures and a new global edge proposal. Futur. Gener. Comput. Syst. **99**, 278–294 (2019)
52. Steve Speicher and John Arwe and Ashok Malhotra: Linked Data Platform 1.0. https://www.w3.org/TR/ldp
53. United Nations Department of Economic and Social Affairs: World Population Prospects 2019. https://population.un.org/wpp/
54. Van Woensel, W., Abidi, S.: Benchmarking semantic reasoning on mobile platforms: towards optimization using OWL2 RL. Semantic Web **10**(4), 637–663 (2019)
55. Van Woensel, W., Roy, P., Abidi, S., Abidi, S.: A mobile and intelligent patient diary for chronic disease self-management. In: Studies in Health Technology and Informatics, vol. 216 (2015)
56. Wilkinson, M., Vandervalk, B., McCarthy, L.: The semantic automated discovery and integration (SADI) web service design-pattern, API and reference implementation. Nat. Preced. 1 (2011)
57. Wolber, D., Abelson, H., Friedman, M.: Democratizing computing with app inventor. GetMobile: Mob. Comput. Commun. **18**(4), 53–58 (2015)
58. Yus, R., Bobed, C., Esteban, G., Bobillo, F., Mena, E.: Android goes semantic: DL reasoners on smartphones. In: Proceedings of 2nd International Workshop on OWL Reasoner Evaluation, pp. 46–52 (2013)

BEEO: Semantic Support
for Event-Based Data Analytics

Michele Ciavotta, Vincenzo Cutrona, Flavio De Paoli, Matteo Palmonari,
and Blerina Spahiu$^{(\boxtimes)}$

University of Milano-Bicocca, Milan, Italy
{michele.ciavotta,vincenzo.cutrona,flavio.depaoli,matteo.palmonari,
blerina.spahiu}@unimib.it

Abstract. Recent developments in data analysis and machine learning
support novel data-driven operations. Event data provide social and environmental context, thus, such data may become essential for the workflow of data analytic pipelines. In this paper, we introduce our Business
Event Exchange Ontology (BEEO), based on Schema.org that enables
data integration and analytics for event data. BEEO is available under
Apache 2.0 license on GitHub, and is seeing adoption among both its
creator companies and other product and service companies. We present
and discuss the ontology development drivers and process, its structure,
and its usage in different real use cases.

Resource Type: Ontology
License: Apache 2.0
DOI: https://doi.org/10.5281/zenodo.4695281
Repository: https://github.com/UNIMIBInside/Business-Event-Ex
change-Ontology

Keywords: Event data · Business events · Custom events · API ·
Ontology · Data analytics

1 Introduction

Events can be defined as changes happening at a given time and in a given
(physical or virtual) environment, where some actors take part showing some
action features [13]. Since events and the data traces they generate describe the
behavior of humans and machines, event data are becoming essential in everyday
applications in multiple domains. Examples of events that are tracked and used
by computer applications include clicks on Web pages, changes in product prices,
marketing campaigns, log records of software applications, and health check-up
records. Leveraging event data to derive insights is crucial to make effective
decisions in several contexts, e.g., for advertising, human and computing resource
planning, price strategies, therapy prescriptions and so on.

© Springer Nature Switzerland AG 2021
A. Hotho et al. (Eds.): ISWC 2021, LNCS 12922, pp. 580–596, 2021.
https://doi.org/10.1007/978-3-030-88361-4_34

With the increasing uptake of data-driven decision making and automation in the industry, often powered by data analytics and machine learning, event-based analytics is providing a unique opportunity to develop and optimize data-driven business services in a vast variety of business domains. Many examples of these services can be found in the large number of companies operating in the eCommerce, Retail, Customer Relationship Management (CRM) and Digital Marketing industries. These companies collect large amounts of data about customers at different touch points across the so-called consumer journey (from need recognition to purchase and customer support) [9]. All these companies are part of a complex value constellation, where their data-driven business-to-consumer and business-to-business services generate high business value.

Consider, for example, a company running a CRM application, which serves a client company launching a promotional campaign. Upon campaign launch, the number of customers' requests served by the CRM company are likely to peak, requiring supplementary resources to be timely allocated. As another example, consider resource planning at retail. Foot traffic is known to increase after events like paydays, holidays, or promos for specific products. In event-based data analytics, companies that have data tracking their own Key Performance Indicators (KPIs), e.g., served requests in CRM, foot traffic count in retail, need to enrich their records with event data so as to train predictive models to estimate the impact of events on their own KPIs and act accordingly (e.g., improve resource planning). Similar services have been developed in a production environment as part of the EW-Shopp EU project,[1] whose goal was to develop technologies to facilitate, with the help of semantics, the creation of these services, with specific attention to the simplification of the event-based data enrichment processes required to support weather and event-based data analytics [4].

In these contexts, the semantics is a key factor because usually event data are not generated internally, but originate from third parties. In the CRM example, the company launching the campaign would generate the data, while the CRM company would use them. Similar scenarios occur in the retail case. Event data exchange across parties is relevant to the domain of event-based data analytics, which explains why supporting semantic interoperability in this context is compelling to streamline the development of data-driven services. Semantic vocabularies and ontologies to define events have been developed. In particular, event modeling has been significantly investigated in the past [1,8,17], but often proposing event ontologies that provide complex representations (e.g., nested descriptions) [1], which, although useful in specific domain contexts, may result too complicated to support the practical tasks of event-based data enrichment (served well by flatter representations). The representation of event data is also very relevant for representing event data on the web and, in fact, Schema.org provides a vocabulary to describe events[2] that achieve a good trade-off between richness and simplicity. A question is, therefore, whether Schema.org covers business needs addressed in the depicted event-based analytics scenario.

---

[1] https://www.ew-shopp.eu/.
[2] https://schema.org/Event.

Stemming from this question, in this paper, we present a Business Event Exchange Ontology (BEEO) that addresses the need of harmonizing the description of events provided or used by EW-Shopp partners to enrich information about proprietary data describing a business phenomenon of interest. As a matter of fact, none of the existing ontologies or vocabularies fully covers the aspects that emerged from the requirements analysis carried on within the project, and Schema.org is the resource covering most of the necessary general concepts. BEEO is, in fact, an extension of the Schema.org vocabulary that covers event representation relevant to support data analytics in several domains such as eCommerce, Retail, CRM and Digital Marketing industries. We publish BEEO in Turtle format under a public license to support further extensions. In addition, as a consequence of the requirements collected from business partners, we have developed JSON-LD-based[3] APIs to support event-data exchange based on the proposed ontology. We found JSON-LD to be appreciated also by practitioners working in the industry who are not familiar with pure RDF-based technology. The ontology as well as the APIs have been agreed upon by software engineers of different companies and tested in real business environments. For example, a data enrichment service has been developed for ASIA,[4] a semantic table annotation application that supports data enrichment at scale [3].

The contributions made in this paper can be summarized as follows: (i) we present the methodology used to design and publish BEEO; (ii) we make the ontology available under an open license; (iii) we present the APIs developed to support event data exchange and usage; and (iv) we show different use cases where this can be applied, one of which is explained more in detail.

This paper is organized as follows: In the next Sect. 2 we discuss the requirements and adopted methodology; Then in Sect. 3 a detailed description of BEEO is provided; Sect. 4 presents the API along with an example of use; Sect. 5 compares BEEO with other event models; Finally, Sect. 6 draws some conclusions and outlines future work.

2   Requirements and Methodology

For the development of the ontology, we applied common techniques recommended by well-established ontology development methods [14]. We used a bottom-up approach by identifying the scope and user group of the ontology, requirements, and ontological and non-ontological resources.

2.1   Requirements

The primary resources used during the development of the ontology were company data provided by the industrial partners of the EW-Shopp project to be harmonized to allow for further processing with the tools developed during the

---

[3] https://json-ld.org/.
[4] https://github.com/UNIMIBInside/asia-backend.

project. In the following, we provide a brief description of each business case and discuss the general requirements for the ontology. Technical requirements on the API to access and use the ontology will be discussed in Sect. 4. Table 1 reports examples of interactions (queries/responses) that the ontology-mediated API should support for each business case.[5]

Brand Performance Insights. Ceneje[6] provides an ecommerce search engine and a comparison-shopping platform to make users' shopping experience smarter, and to provide their business-to-business partners with deep insights into consumer past behavior and predictions on future behavior. Ceneje collects information about users' searches and clicks on vendors' offers (performance indicators of the advertised products) and analyzes their evolution at different levels of aggregation (SKU, brand, category, vendor, price). Such data need to be enriched with business events data, tagged for different category, brand, and marketing segments, to support a predictive service that estimates how the market reacts to certain business events (e.g., price changes, marketing campaigns, new product introductions) to add real value in the decision-making process. Examples of data challenges concern the representation of concepts around the notion of *price changes* and the possibility to support internal identifiers for products, which may be different from the official ones. Other concepts, such as *SKU, EAN code* or *seller* are already present in shared vocabularies like Schema.org.

Weather and Event-Aware Business Intelligence for the Optimization of Campaigns and Human Resources. BigBang[7] is a retailer company in the segment of Consumer Electronics and Home Appliances with on-line and 18 physical stores. The stores importance can be measured by the number of visitors or/and employees on the floor. Running a prediction service to help decision-makers in optimizing sales-force and marketing communication planning with estimations of the daily number of visitors requires company data (e.g., number of on-line and in-person visitors) to be enriched with internal business events (e.g., marketing campaigns grouped by channel), and external events (e.g., suppliers' marketing campaigns). Specific data requirements in this case concern the representation of the *marketing channels* and *price discount* concepts that are not present in shared vocabularies or ontologies.

Workforce and Campaign Management Optimization. Browsetel/CDE[8] provides clients with services for Customer support, CRM and Customer Engagement Management. The primary goal is to optimize the system resources (the number of agents working in a campaign that serves specific topics of the client). In order to predict interaction traffic, historical data recorded by the system and weather and (custom) event data from external sources have to be integrated.

---

[5] More details are available at https://github.com/UNIMIBInside/Business-Event-Exchange-Ontology.
[6] https://www.ceneje.si/.
[7] https://www.bigbang.si/.
[8] https://www.cde.si/.

Custom events are generated by clients (e.g., the launch of a new product on the market) and used by the support service to optimize the workforce (e.g., predict the number of agents needed on the floor). Examples of data challenges are the representations of the *source* (e.g., the client) and the *size* (e.g., the potential customers involved) of an event.

Event and Weather-Aware Foot Traffic Predictions and Analytics. Measurence[9] provides retailers with devices to sense and count people in and around their physical location and services that exploits such information to support retailers' decision making about the best time for marketing campaigns. The use of business events is crucial to enrich the collected data, understand the past customer flows, and enable for reliable predictions for future marketing events. The data challenge here is to distinguish between the number of people interested (e.g., registered attendees) and attending (e.g., actual participants) an event. Even this simple pair of concepts are surprisingly not represented in generic vocabularies such as Schema.org.

General Requirements. The data provided by the above companies were analyzed to determine the scope and requirements for the ontology. The analysis led to the identification of the major concerns that the ontology should address. The overall requirement was to support the integration of all data provided by at least one data provider modeled in different ways under a single representation schema.

Events were classified by their size, type, and context to enable a more efficient integration. Starting from the general concept of event, the main requirement that emerged was the need to capture the concept of marketing event. For the use in the project business cases, a lightweight specification of the ontology as a vocabulary is sufficient (properties, classification schemes, etc.), even if an OWL specification may be desired but not strictly required. A requirement that was strongly supported by the industrial partners was to reuse existing ontologies as often as possible, to reduce effort and promote the use of integrated data. For the design of BEEO, we considered all the above requirements as MUST[10].

2.2   Methodology

We developed BEEO by following one of the most recent ontology design methodologies based on agile and simplified design [15]; in particular, this methodology proposes a cycle consisting of the following three phases:

P1 Collection of domain information with the help of domain experts, definition of usage scenarios and test cases, definition of a modelet (ontology piece) based on these principles and meeting the usage requirements, definition of test cases, and release of the modelet;

---

[9] https://www.measurence.com/.
[10] According to the MoSCoW prioritization technique - RFC2119.

Table 1. Intuitive query and response for each business case

Business Case	Intuitive Query & Response
Brand Performance Insights	QUERY: Given a table containing data about users queries for products, retrieve all events (from products price history) that describe the change in price in a selected temporal span (days) - API request: `/events/2021-01-01?query=event.measure.priceChange>10`
	RESPONSE: From the requirements, all data about events that present a change in price greater than 10% for a given product are retrieved and stored inside the `eventArray`. For each event, types and properties from the BEEO ontology are used, e.g., the type `beeo:Measure` is used to represent the change in price for the product on the given date.
Weather and Event-aware Business Intelligence for the Optimization of Campaigns and Human Resources	QUERY: Given a table containing data about user visits in online and physical stores in a selected temporal span (for instance 10 days), retrieve all recorded marketing events for a certain channel that took place in that period - API request: `/events/2021-01-01+9?query=event.channelCode=xcodeA32_3`
	RESPONSE: All event data regarding channel xcodeA32_3 and related to marketing events scheduled between 01-01-2021 and 01-10-2021 are retrieved and stored inside the `eventArray`. For each event, types and properties from the BEEO ontology are used, e.g., the type `beeo:channelCode` is used to represent the code associated with a certain channel.
Workforce & Campaign Management Optimization	QUERY: To build a dataset with user interaction data, retrieve all events about new product launch that occurred in the 30-day time interval - API request: `/events/2021-01-01+29?query=event.category.description=product%20launch`
	RESPONSE: All events that (i) belong to a category (`beeo:Category`) with a description matching the query "product launch" and (i) occurred between 01-01-2021 and 01-30-2021 (29 days) are returned to the caller. Each event returns the "attendingAudience" information of type *beeo:Measure* that will be used to study the resulting interactions with users.
Event and Weather-aware Foot Traffic Predictions and Analytics	QUERY: Given a table with information about user visiting a showroom in Milan (Italy) with postal code 20131, retrieve data about the interested audience for events occurred over a 6-day time span - API request: `/events/2021-05-05+5?query=event.location.addressCountry=ITA&event.location.postalCode=20131`
	RESPONSE: All the events occurred in Milan in the considered time period are returned by the API to the caller. Among the various pieces of information, the one that is used to enrich the caller's data set is "InterestedAudience" of type *beeo:Measure*

P2 Integration of the test cases with the current ontology;

P3 Refactoring of the current ontology. The methodology also includes in its sub-steps several recommendations: usage of a glossary (terms to be considered) for the definition of the test cases, reuse of ontology design patterns and existing ontologies, keep the modelets and the ontology simple and close to the requirements specified in the test set, best practices for entity names.

The work to design BEEO has been, therefore, organized in the following phases (we include references to the above-mentioned methodology).

1. (P1) State-of-the-art: a comprehensive review of the literature and available tools. This preliminary study allowed us to identify the recurrent patterns for modeling events, and rank ontologies by popularity and completeness. To this we added the analysis of event descriptions in Schema.org. The outcome of this phase is that Schema.org is the most popular event ontology and the one that best covers the collected requirements. This ontology provides, in fact, several patterns for modeling events and related information (a guideline recommended in the adopted methodology).

2. (P1) Sample event data collections: the current definition of BEEO started by collecting event data samples from partners to identify the main concepts and data of interest for each partner.

3. (P1) Schema alignment: sample tables have been compared to identify common concepts (properties for the description of events), and preliminary data type definition.

4. (P1) Use and test cases definition: the usage of ontology-compliant event descriptions, with consequent test cases, is well defined in EW-Shopp: it consists in the enrichment of corporate data with custom event data relevant for their analysis.
5. (P1) Definition of guidelines for the ontology definition: based on the state-of-the-art review and the analysis of samples of partners' event data, we have derived a set of guidelines that have inspired the definition of the ontology.
6. Ontology definition: Schema.org has been adopted as starting ontology to define mappings where possible and add new concepts to comply the EW-Shopp needs. The main advantage is to keep compliance with existing tools and systems that already adopt Schema.org as reference ontology. This definition phase has followed the following sub-steps:

   6.1 (P2) definition of the subset of Schema.org of interest based on the vocabulary used in the sample schemas;
   6.2 (P2-P3) for each event data source: mapping of each data schemas to Schema.org and extension of the ontology with the source properties not covered by Schema.org;
   6.3 (P3) refactoring of the ontology and finalization of the first version.

Based on the initial use cases that support event-based analytics workflows in the industry, and on the previous steps of the adopted methodology, we have drawn the following guidelines to drive the design of the ontology:

- Harmonization reusing shared ontologies. To make the ontology valuable and extensible beyond the specific data preparation and analytics workflows supported in the project, we use the terminology of existing ontologies to harmonize the terminology used to describe events.
- Limited nesting of event descriptions. After the semantic enrichment step, event data appear in the columns of a table that contains the enriched data; as a consequence, when used in the analytical modeling steps, the event descriptions are flattened into a table; the event ontology should, therefore, natively support the enrichment step.
- Intuitive rendering of properties as table attributes in event descriptions. Because of (2), the column headers should intuitively describe the content of the columns; while searching for harmonizing the terminology used to describe the event (i.e., reducing the number of different terms used to describe similar properties of the events) the terminology must make the data still understandable by users who will work with them in the analytical modeling steps of the workflow. As a consequence, some of the terminology used by partners to describe their events should be preserved in the ontology.
- Polymorphic property usage and heuristic specifications of domains and ranges. We found that the reasons that motivated the polymorphic property usage and the heuristic specification of domains and range (i.e., as a recommendation more than as a normative specification) also applies to the context where this event ontology is used. For example, the event ontology is primarily used to specify the meaning of properties used in data exchanged

Fig. 1. Main types used in BEEO and their mutual relations.

using the JSON-LD format. Instead, when event data appear in an enriched dataset, events are either modeled in JSON or in a tabular format; in the first case, JSON-LD is fully JSON compliant; in the second case, ontology types do not appear while property names are column headers.

The resulting ontology is property-driven, which means that the primary goal is to harmonize the properties already used to describe events. When data are collected as JSON data, JSON-LD can be used to reuse the ontology properties; when data are collected as or factored into a table, properties can provide a header for each column. For this reason, we mostly specified the properties of the ontology, identifying a minimal number of types that are relevant as they are used as types of subjects or objects (values) for these properties. We found this agile methodology for data-driven vocabulary creation quite useful and applied it *as-is* in other projects as well (e.g., to model the vocabulary of a fantasy football knowledge graph).

3   Ontology Description

The BEEO ontology is built upon Schema.org, rather than upon other existing ontologies for two reasons: (i) the uptake of Schema.org in domains and communities related to eCommerce, digital marketing, etc., and (ii) was found convincing for our partners as it covered all the use cases.

Following the adoption of Schema.org as the reference ontology, we identified, among the available properties, those that can be mapped onto the ones in use by data providers. For those that do not represent the concepts of interest, we introduced new properties as specialization of existing Schema.org properties, so to keep the highest possible compliance. Table 2 reports the properties taken from Schema.org (with **schema** prefix and highlighted with orange background), and the ones introduced by EW-Shopp (with **beeo** prefix and highlighted with yellow background). The "notes" column reports the relations between the property specified in a row and Schema.org properties: the phrase "derived from a type" means that the type is specified among the domains of the property, and *subproperty of* is used to specify the superproperty connected to the new property.

The ontology is specified in RDF. Figure 1 reports the main types used in the ontology and their mutual relations. The color convention is consistent with the one introduced in Table 2: dark orange is for types and properties specified in Schema.org, yellow for types and properties introduced in BEEO, green for data types, and purple for a generic URI type (considered equivalent to Thing) and the property from SKOS ontology. We omit the prefixes of all types and properties that are either reused from Schema.org or based on xsd:types (i.e., Time and DateTime). Properties that are not shown in the figure are those that either have data types as ranges (e.g., integers, floats, etc.), with the only exception of time-related information that is central for event representation, or have literal values or describe more detailed information (e.g., postal addresses).

The ontology has the following characteristics:

- It is based on an extension of Schema.org ontology.
- As Schema.org, it uses polymorphic properties and heuristic domain/range specifications (with includesDomain and includesRange); these features make it difficult to depict multiple domain and range specifications in Fig. 1 (we represent multiple range specifications as single nodes with more labels separated by the | symbol and only report main types used as ranges).
- The main types considered in the ontology are derived from Schema.org and are listed among the most frequently used types.[11] These types are:
  - schema:Event, which is the type associated with all events;
  - schema:Product, which is the type associated with products;
  - schema:Place, which is the type associated with locations;
- Additional types used in the ontology are:
  - beeo:MarketingEvent, which is the only new type introduced in the ontology, and is defined as subclass of schema:Event;
  - skos:Concept, which is defined as the possible type for a property schema:category, which is introduced to associate a category with an event; the type schema:CategoryCode is pending in the Schema.org definition and has not been used in domains similar to the ones addressed in EW-Shopp so far; for this reason we reused a type defined in SKOS,[12] a W3C-recommended language to define simple categorization systems;
  - schema:PostalAddress, which is used because it is the recommended value for the schema:address property that is attributed to locations (instances of schema:Place); in practice, a postal address is a placeholder used to aggregate more specific address information specified using a number of properties; leveraging the non-normative specification of domains and ranges in Schema.org, we also consider descriptions where these properties (e.g., schema:postalCode) are directly referred to places without using an instance of postal address as intermediary.
  - Schema.org does not provide properties to describe measures of every event aspect, e.g., it provides properties to capture the number of registered attendees, but not the number of actual attendees that participated in an event; we introduced dedicated properties to describe these measures; in this case, we preferred to keep the terminology as close as possible to the one used by the partners; however, we linked these properties to Schema.org by specifying their superproperties in Schema.org.

---

[11] https://schema.org/docs/gs.html#schemaorg_types.

[12] https://www.w3.org/TR/2008/WD-skos-reference-20080829/skos.html.

The recommended version of BEEO is based on the Schema.org modeling approach, with heuristic specifications of domains and ranges. However, we also provide an OWL version of the ontology, especially to support visualization and editing with ontology editors. In Schema.org, properties are used in a polymorphic fashion: a property can be used either as ObjectProperty or as DataTypeProperty. In the OWL version, properties are classified as ObjectProperty or DataTypeProperty based on their preferred usage. Domain and range restrictions are introduced only for properties where only one class/datatype was specified as value of the domainIncludes and rangeIncludes properties. Users willing to extend the ontology can look at the recommended types specified in Schema.org in the annotation properties.

All data, and, in particular, textual data are represented using Unicode UTF-8 character encoding to support interoperability across languages at the alphabet level. In total, the Business Event Exchange Ontology has 53 classes (52 from Schema.org and one defined within EW-Shopp (beeo:MarketingEvent)) and 40 properties (27 from Schema.org and 13 defined within EW-Shopp).

4 BEEO API and Use Cases

From the analysis of the use cases described in Sect. 2.1 emerged the need to provide access to the event registries with a shared API that can provide machine-readable descriptions of event properties. The use of the popular format JSON, along with JSON-LD to support identifiers exchanging, was identified as the preferred format to simplify the use of the ontology and event descriptions.

In the remainder of this section, we first describe the API to access a generic event registry designed according to BEEO, and then discuss an example of use from the EW-Shopp partners.

4.1 BEEO API

Implementation of BEEO is realized by offering an Event API to the user. The API will enable the user to manipulate the event data, which are stored in an Event DB, and fetch them according to the proposed model. Within the suggested API implement action, the number of methods is optimized to the ones, (i) reflecting the actual needs of a typical user, and (ii) keeping the manipulations as simple as possible. A typical scenario in event-based data analytics is to fetch all events under certain constraints (e.g., related to one product) in a given time window.

The BEEO API specification is publicly available.[13] This API is build following best practices[14] and is based on a reduced set of calls (GET event/{date[+N]}, POST event, and POST events) and a simple format in JSON-LD. REST APIs are one of the most common web services available as they allow various clients

---

[13] https://app.swaggerhub.com/apis/EW-Shopp/Business-Event-Exchange-Ontology-API/2.2.0.

[14] https://json-ld.org/spec/latest/json-ld-api-best-practices/.

Table 2. Business event exchange ontology properties

Name	Range	Description	Notes
		BEEO definition (properties that describe instances of schema:Event)	
schema:identifier	URI|Text	An identifier of an item	schema:Thing
schema:name	Text	The name of the item.	schema:Thing
schema:description	Text	A description of the item.	schema:Thing
beeo:source	Text	A description of event source	
beeo:channelCode	Text	A code associated with a channel in a marketing event	beeo:MarketingEvent
beeo:channelDescription	Text	A description associated with a channel in a marketing event	
schema:startDate	Date|DateTime	The start date (and time) of the item	schema:Event
schema:endDate	Date|DateTime	The end date (and time) of the item	schema:Event
schema:category	URI	A category for an item	schema:Thing (subproperty of schema:about; rec. range is skos:Concept)
beeo:quantity	xsd:int	A number identifying a generic quantity	Subproperty of beeo:simpleMeasure
beeo:quantyUnitId	URI|Text	The specification of the unit in which a quantity is measured	Subproperty of schema:identifier
beeo:interestedAudience	xsd:int	Number of interested/registered people	Subproperty of beeo:simpleMeasure
beeo:attendingAudience	xsd:int	Number of event attendees	Subproperty of beeo:simpleMeasure
beeo:priceChanged	Boolean	Specify if the product price has been changed	Subproperty of beeo:booleanMeasure
schema:discount	Text|Boolean	Any discount applied (to an Order)	schema:Order
beeo:priceChange	xsd:float	Price change in %	Subproperty of beeo:simpleMeasure
schema:price	xsd:float	The offer price of a product, or of a price component when attached to PriceSpecification and its subtypes.	schema:Offer
beeo:product	URI|Product	The product the event refers to (only for events about products)	Subproperty of schema:about
schema:location	Text|Place|PostalAddress	The location of an event, or where an action takes place.	schema:Event
beeo:simpleMeasure	xsd:float|xsd:int	A generic measure.	Subproperty of schema:value
beeo:booleanMeasure	xsd:float|xsd:int	A measure that assigns a boolean value	Subproperty of schema:value
		Classification definition	
schema:description	Text	A description of the item.	schema:Thing
		Product definition (properties that describe instances of schema:Product)	
schema:gtin13	Text	The GTIN-13 code of the product, or the product subject of an offer.	schema:Product
schema:description	Text	A description of the item.	schema:Thing
schema:seller	URI	An entity which offers/sells/ leases/lends/loans the services or goods. A seller may be a provider.	schema:BuyAction or schema:Offer or schema:Order
schema:sku	Text	A merchant-specific identifier for a product or service, or the product to which the offer refers.	schema:Product or schema:Offer
beeo:catalogId	Text	Specify the identifier	Subproperty of schema:identifier
schema:description	Text	A description of the item.	schema:Thing
schema:category	URI	Specified as subproperty of schema:about; range is skos:Concept	schema:Product or schema:Thing
		Location definition (properties that describe instances of schema:Place and PostalAddress)	
schema:name	Text	The name of the item.	schema:Thing
schema:description	Text	A description of the item.	schema:Thing
schema:addressLocality	Text	The name of the locality	schema:PostalAddress
schema:addressCountry	Country|Text	The country (also formatted as ISO 3166-1 alpha-2)	schema:PostalAddress
schema:latitude	Number|Text	The latitude of a location.	schema:GeoCoordinates
schema:longitude	Number|Text	The longitude of a location.	schema:GeoCoordinates
schema:addressRegion	Text	The region. E.g., CA.	schema:PostalAddress
schema:streetAddress	Text	The street address.	schema:PostalAddress
schema:postalCode	Text	The postal code. E.g., 94043	schema:PostalAddress
schema:address	Text|PostalAddress	The address, possibly specified as a structured PostalAddress specification.	schema:Place or schema:Person or schema:Organization or schema:GeoShape or schema:GeoCoordinates

(browsers, apps, etc.,) to communicate with a server. The GET event purpose is to get a list of events starting from a certain date and spanning over N days. N is given as an optional parameter with the default value equal to "0". The Path parameter date[+N] represents a date in ISO 8601 format to which is optionally concatenated (by means of the + operator) the information on the number of days $(0 < N \leq 99)$ making up the time interval within which the events to be obtained have begun. For example, the following dates are valid: 2016-04-06T10:10:09Z+5, 2016-04-06+9, 2016-04-06, 2016-04-06+10, 2016-04-06+10:01. Successful responses return the retrieved data (Listing 1.1), while specific error responses are implemented to handle standard HTTP error response codes.

Listing 1.1. Successful pull of event data.

```
1   {
2       "@context": {
3           "@version": 1.1,
4           "@base": "http://inside.disco.unimib.it/BEEO/",
5           "schema": "http://schema.org/",
6           "beeo": "http://inside.disco.unimib.it/BEEO/ontology/",
7           "beed": "http://inside.disco.unimib.it/BEEO/data/rdf",
8           "xsd": "http://www.w3.org/2001/XMLSchema#",
9           "lang": "@language",
10          "text": "@value",
11          "identifier": "@id",
12          "eventArray": {
13              "@id": "beeo:eventArray",
14              "@type": "@id",
15              "@container": "@set",
16              "@context": { "@base": "/rdf/event/" }
17          },
18          "name": {
19              "@id": "schema:name",
20              "@language": "en"
21          },
22                          [...] MISSING CONTENT [...]
23          "location": {
24              "@type": "beeo:PostalAddress",
25              "addressLocality": "Mountain␣View",
26              "addressCountry": "USA",
27              "addressRegion": "CA",
28              "streetAddress": "1600␣Amphitheatre␣Pkwy",
29              "postalCode": 94043
30          }
31      }
32  }
```

A large number of schemas can optionally be used; among them: IntegerMeasure, AudienceMeasure, PriceMeasure, PostalAddress, LangString, Place, Product, EventsArray, Seller, Category, Context, Event.

4.2   Use Case

We demonstrate the usage of the ontology in one of the business cases described in Sect. 2, where the exchange of third-party event data is more crucial and now operational, making the use of semantics for event data more relevant.

Workforce and Campaign Management Optimization. Browsetel and CDE are developing and selling the COCOS Customer Engagement Platform (COCOS CEP) Omni-channel communication solution to SME clients and large enterprises. Prediction of optimal resources and correct timing for placing campaign calls has always been a challenge within the Contact Center. The optimal number of agents depends on the predicted traffic of inbound/outbound calls and on the success rate of the outbound calls. Plenty of different parameters influence the overall success of marketing campaigns and resource optimization. When the prediction system considers not only internal criteria based on contact center call history, but also external factors, the prediction models can be significantly improved. The Contact Center has been always working in conjunction with clients' departments where their customers are supported by automated chatbots and/or human agents. Activities on the clients' side affect the overall behavior at the Contact Center, therefore, when an event occurs (e.g., the launch of a new product on the market, or a change of a service offered by a client) the Contact Center should be notified in advance, and the workforce management tool should be able to support the managers to define the needed number of active agents. The use of **BEEO** and of the event API has the objective of simplifying the notification process by the clients, which can exploit event API to provide the Contact Center with their events, and the workforce management tool to consume events with to feed the training process of predictive models.

To optimize its Workforce and Campaign Management process the company used the following inputs: (i) Contact center historical data (recorded interactions between contact center customers and agents), (ii) Weather Data (collected from the ECMWF[15] available Weather Resources), and (iii) events (referred to as Custom Events) collected from the COCOS CEP Business Clients. To enable the management of the Custom Events, the company used the Event API and upgraded its COCOS Campaign Management tool. The Event API has been added to the system in order to enable the COCOS CEP Business Client to directly insert its own events into the system. Thus, enabling the prediction of non-standard events influences the system load. The event ontology supports sharp definitions of events by setting, among others, the source of the event (beeo:source) with a category (schema:category) and associated quantity (beeo:quantity) to size the event (e.g., the number of customers that will be affected by the new version of a service). Such semantic event descriptions are used to enrich the historical Contact Center data, which records the (anonymized) interactions between customers and agents, as well as results of the Contact Center campaigns.

For example, Fig. 2 reports predictions (lines) and actual data (blocks) about the success rate of outbound calls and shows that predictions that also consider events are more accurate than predictions based on other factors (e.g., only

---

[15] https://www.ecmwf.int/en/forecasts.

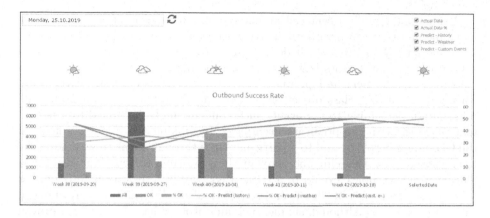

Fig. 2. Use case: predictions vs. actual data.

weather). Events have shown to be key factors to improve the reliability of predictions in this[16] and other similar tasks.[17]

5   Related Work

Event ontology is a shared, formal and explicit specification of an event class system model that exists in real world objectively [13]. Even though there is a number of ontologies suitable for representing events, they were created to serve different purposes. Event ontologies are used in different domains [16], including museums and libraries to describe historical events (e.g. wars, or births) as well as events in the histories of the objects being described (e.g. changes of ownership, or restoration) [5], ABC for modelling archive or digital resources [12], scholarly events for scientific communication channels [6], event logs from databases [2], for biological processes [11], journalism [10], etc.

An overview and a comparison of existing event models is provided in [17]. The main aim is to review different choices that might be used to represent events and build an interlingua model to resolve interoperability problems. This is solved by providing a set of axioms that express mappings between existing event ontologies. The result of this work is LODE,[18] an OWL ontology for representing and Linking Open Descriptions of Events licensed under the Creative Commons License. The ontology defines classes and properties to describe historical events as linked data, mappings to other event-related vocabularies and ontologies (e.g., OWL-Time).

---

[16] https://www.ew-shopp.eu/solution/cocos-cep-worforce-campaign-management-optimization/.

[17] https://www.ew-shopp.eu/solutions/.

[18] http://linkedevents.org/ontology/.

Event Ontology[19] is centered around events that occur at a certain place and time and that can involve the participation of a number of physical objects both animate and inanimate. It defines one main concept Event that may have a location, a time, factors (e.g., a musical instrument), active agents (e.g., an instrument performer) and products (e.g., the performed sound). Events are considered as a first class object or "token", acting like a hook for additional information pertaining to the event. Such concept might be linked to a particular place through the predicate *event:place* by linking the Event ontology to the Geonames ontology, and to a particular time through event:time, linking the Event ontology to the Timeline ontology. It is possible to represent also information about complex events in a structured way by breaking it into simpler subevents, where each of which can carry part of the information pertaining to the complex whole. Although simple, such an ontology has already been proven useful in a wide range of context, e.g., talks in a conference, descriptions of concerts, or chords being played in a Jazz piece (when used with the Timeline ontology), festivals, etc.

EventsML-G2[20] is a data model and format specified in XML-Schema for collecting and distributing event information. It is part of NewsML-G2, a data model and format to exchange text, images, video, audio news and event or sports data among news agencies. EventsML-G2 is defined as a standard for conveying event information in a news industry environment, but can be used also for publishing all facts about a specific event by a news provider, storing facts about knowledgeable events in archives, adding information regarding the coverage of an event by a news provider. EventsML-G2 is defined by IPTC, a body for developing and publishing Industry Standards for the exchange of news data of all common media types.

LODE and Event Ontology have been adopted by large communities of users and are quite abstract. While the NewsML-G2 standard is adopted by different news agencies, it is not clear if the EventsML-G2 vocabulary is frequently used. In addition this standard is known in the news domain but not adopted in domains addressed by this paper.

GoodRelations[21] is a powerful vocabulary that is used for publishing business-related goods and services. It finds applications in different use cases such as information about products and services exchange, pricing, payment options, other terms and conditions, store locations and their opening hours, and many other aspects of e-commerce, between networks of computer systems [7].

In [8] authors propose to extend an event ontology by firstly, classifying the types of events (e.g., natural events and artificial events). The approach attempts to construct event classifications based on two ontological views: component structures (knowledge representation of events) and semantic functions of events (which imply the logical and ontological semantics of events for reasoning). Secondly, event relations (e.g., causal relations and next-event relations)

---

[19] http://motools.sourceforge.net/event/event.122.html.
[20] https://iptc.org/standards/eventsml-g2.
[21] http://www.heppnetz.de/ontologies/goodrelations/v1.html.

captures the differences between instances and classes of events. The semantic functions of events were analyzed in expressive logical formulas that would allow to infer logical conclusions from event occurrences.

The Rich Event Ontology goal is to provide a unified representation of events [1]. The main reference ontology encompasses 161 classes and 553 axioms. Including the lexical resource ontologies and the linking models into counts brings the totals to 3,065 classes and 60,531 axioms, as well as 16,005 individuals representing the vocabulary (unique lemmas) of events. Authors provide different use cases, how users could benefit from such ontology. Despite, the authors claim that the ontology will be available, but at the time of writing it is not available and freely used.

6   Conclusions and Future Work

In this paper, we have presented BEEO, an extension of Schema.org that enables data integration and analytics with event data. The ontology is available under a public license and can be freely used, reused, and further extended. Based on BEEO, an API has been developed to support event-data exchange. The ontology and the respective API have been created and tested in real business environments.

Requirements have been collected from the real business cases developed in the EW-Shopp EU project to provide shared terminology and common tools to support tailored services in various contexts with different goals. The development of BEEO was required to overcome the limits of existing vocabularies like Schema.org, and proved to be effective to model key aspects in the marketing domain. Each partner has implemented a private version of the API to upload and retrieve events according to BEEO data model. In this way, partners were able to use the open-source tools provided by the projects to develop, test, and successfully deploy their services. Such a development model can be replicated by new users, either business companies or research institutions, to augment their data with events.

In BEEO we do not yet have classes or properties that cover specific concepts thus a future direction is to increase the expressivity of the ontology to support such specific-level semantics.

Acknowledgements. This research has been supported in part by EU H2020 projects EW-Shopp - Grant n. 732590, and EuBusinessGraph - Grant n. 732003.

References

1. Brown, S.W., Bonial, C., Obrst, L., Palmer, M.: The rich event ontology. In: Proceedings of the Events and Stories in the News Workshop, pp. 87–97 (2017)
2. Calvanese, D., Montali, M., Syamsiyah, A., van der Aalst, W.M.P.: Ontology-driven extraction of event logs from relational databases. In: Reichert, M., Reijers, H.A. (eds.) BPM 2015. LNBIP, vol. 256, pp. 140–153. Springer, Cham (2016). https://doi.org/10.1007/978-3-319-42887-1_12

3. Cutrona, V., Ciavotta, M., De Paoli, F., Palmonari, M.: ASIA: a tool for assisted semantic interpretation and annotation of tabular data. In: ISWC Satellites, pp. 209–212 (2019)
4. Cutrona, V., et al.: Semantically-enabled optimization of digital marketing campaigns. In: Ghidini, C., et al. (eds.) ISWC 2019. LNCS, vol. 11779, pp. 345–362. Springer, Cham (2019). https://doi.org/10.1007/978-3-030-30796-7_22
5. Doerr, M.: The cidoc conceptual reference module: an ontological approach to semantic interoperability of metadata. AI Mag. **24**(3), 75–75 (2003)
6. Fathalla, S., Vahdati, S., Auer, S., Lange, C.: The scientific events ontology of the openresearch. org curation platform. In: Proceedings of the 34th ACM/SIGAPP Symposium on Applied Computing, pp. 2311–2313 (2019)
7. Hepp, M.: GoodRelations: an ontology for describing products and services offers on the web. In: Gangemi, A., Euzenat, J. (eds.) EKAW 2008. LNCS (LNAI), vol. 5268, pp. 329–346. Springer, Heidelberg (2008). https://doi.org/10.1007/978-3-540-87696-0_29
8. Kaneiwa, K., Iwazume, M., Fukuda, K.: An upper ontology for event classifications and relations. In: Orgun, M.A., Thornton, J. (eds.) AI 2007. LNCS (LNAI), vol. 4830, pp. 394–403. Springer, Heidelberg (2007). https://doi.org/10.1007/978-3-540-76928-6_41
9. Kietzmann, J., Paschen, J., Treen, E.: Artificial intelligence in advertising: How marketers can leverage artificial intelligence along the consumer journey. J. Advert. Res. **58**(3), 263–267 (2018)
10. Kowalczuk, E., Lawrynowicz, A.: The reporting event ontology design pattern and its extension to report news events. Adv. Ontol. Des. Patterns **32**, 105–117 (2017)
11. Kushida, T., Takagi, T., Fukuda, K.I.: Event ontology: a pathway-centric ontology for biological processes. In: Biocomputing 2006, pp. 152–163. World Scientific (2006)
12. Lagoze, C., Hunter, J.: The ABC ontology and model. In: International Conference on Dublin Core and Metadata Applications, pp. 160–176 (2001)
13. Liu, W., Liu, Z., Fu, J., Hu, R., Zhong, Z.: Extending owl for modeling event-oriented ontology. In: 2010 International Conference on Complex, Intelligent and Software Intensive Systems, pp. 581–586. IEEE (2010)
14. Noy, N.F., McGuinness, D.L., et al.: Ontology development 101: a guide to creating your first ontology (2001)
15. Peroni, S.: A simplified agile methodology for ontology development. In: Dragoni, M., Poveda-Villalón, M., Jimenez-Ruiz, E. (eds.) OWLED/ORE -2016. LNCS, vol. 10161, pp. 55–69. Springer, Cham (2017). https://doi.org/10.1007/978-3-319-54627-8_5
16. Rodrigues, F.H., Abel, M.: What to consider about events: a survey on the ontology of occurrents. Appl. Ontol. **14**(4), 343–378 (2019)
17. Shaw, R., Troncy, R., Hardman, L.: LODE: linking open descriptions of events. In: Gómez-Pérez, A., Yu, Y., Ding, Y. (eds.) ASWC 2009. LNCS, vol. 5926, pp. 153–167. Springer, Heidelberg (2009). https://doi.org/10.1007/978-3-642-10871-6_11

Rail Topology Ontology: A Rail Infrastructure Base Ontology

Stefan Bischof$^{(\boxtimes)}$ and Gottfried Schenner

Siemens AG Österreich, Vienna, Austria
{bischof.stefan,gottfried.schenner}@siemens.com

Abstract. Engineering projects for railway infrastructure typically involve many subsystems which need consistent views of the planned and built infrastructure and its underlying topology. Consistency is typically ensured by exchanging and verifying data between tools using XML-based data formats and UML-based object-oriented models. A tighter alignment of these data representations via a common topology model could decrease the development effort of railway infrastructure engineering tools. A common semantic model is also a prerequisite for the successful adoption of railway knowledge graphs. Based on the RailTopoModel standard, we developed the Rail Topology Ontology as a model to represent core features of railway infrastructures in a standard-compliant manner. This paper describes the ontology and its development method, and discusses its suitability for integrating data of railway engineering systems and other sources in a knowledge graph.

With the Rail Topology Ontology, software engineers and knowledge scientists have a standard-based ontology for representing railway topologies to integrate disconnected data sources. We use the Rail Topology Ontology for our rail knowledge graph and plan to extend it by rail infrastructure ontologies derived from existing data exchange standards, since many such standards use the same base model as the presented ontology, viz., RailTopoModel.

Keywords: Rail Topology · Rail infrastructure · Rail network · Network reachability · Ontology · Industrial knowledge graph

Resource Type: Ontology
Resource URI: https://w3id.org/rail/topo#

1 Introduction

Rail infrastructure is the basis for a significant share of person and freight transportation volume and is considered essential to reach climate goals.[1]

---

[1] https://uic.org/com/enews/article/norway-railways-essential-to-achieve-climate-goals.

© Springer Nature Switzerland AG 2021
A. Hotho et al. (Eds.): ISWC 2021, LNCS 12922, pp. 597–612, 2021.
https://doi.org/10.1007/978-3-030-88361-4_35

Throughout the lifecycle of rail infrastructure, different systems must work together to ensure safe and reliable transport: track vacancy detection, signalling, interlocking, route setting, freight logistics management, timetables, scheduling, ticketing and passenger systems for journey planning and live passenger information. Besides these operational systems, there are tools for engineering the infrastructure as well as systems to assess and monitor the condition of all the various parts of the infrastructure: field devices and the operational systems that control them. To ensure safety and reliability, all these systems need *consistent* models of the rail infrastructure they depend on.

Consistency of rail infrastructure data is currently achieved by the implementation of many, often proprietary, data exchange interfaces. Railway infrastructure managers and software vendors intend to reduce the effort of data import and export interfaces by standardizing data exchange formats.

However, data exchange is often not a sufficient approach. On the one hand, new use cases profit from an up-to-date integrated view of the data residing in application-specific databases. Such use cases include asset management, predictive maintenance or global consistency checking. On the other hand, software providers can reduce development effort by relying on standard data models both by reusing domain knowledge of software engineers and omitting the implementation of many proprietary interfaces.

Regardless of the concrete data integration approach, a widely accepted common data model is necessary. Such a common data model is especially useful in an industrial knowledge graph, where data is already represented as RDF/OWL. Additionally, data integration is typically easier to handle in a system using semantic web technologies than in systems based on UML data models and relational databases.

Requirements. Our ontology engineering process is guided by three types of requirements: competency questions, functional requirements, and adherence to data exchange standards and best practices. The following extends our previously published requirements [5].

To support railway infrastructure engineering, we chose the following two competency questions:

1. If a train runs from A to B on the railway network, which infrastructure elements (including their orientation) will be traversed?
2. What are the possible paths between A and B on the railway network?

We have the following functional requirements regarding modelling the railway domain and adherence to existing data exchange standards: (i) represent the (logical) topology of a railway network, (ii) contain the main infrastructure elements found in every railway network, such as tracks, switches and signals, (iii) the (logical) position and orientation of these infrastructure elements in the railway network must be defined and (iv) express logical aggregation, for example, to denote to which station a signal or switch belongs.

When designing and publishing the railway ontology, we intend to increase adoption by following ontology engineering best practices. Specifically, the ontology should be vendor-independent, easily reusable and openly available. The concepts of the ontology must be well documented (especially important in engineering as it must be clear which concepts of the real world correspond to concepts of the ontology) and the ontology should be *minimal*, in the sense that it should contain no aspects not related to the topology of railway networks.

While we aim to stay inside the OWL 2 profiles for efficient reasoning (we are specifically interested in OWL 2 RL for terminological reasoning) modelling the domain accurately is more important. A more expressive ontology serves also as a more accurate basis for secondary uses. For example, tools to automatically create SHACL shapes for validity checking (e.g., Astrea [8]) or to automatically create REST APIs (e.g., OBA [11]) do not depend on OWL 2 profiles and can exploit more expressive input ontologies.

Since no previously published ontology fulfils all these requirements, we created the Rail Topology Ontology (RTO). In this paper, we present the RTO and describe our approach to develop and publish it.

The rest of this paper is structured as follows: Sect. 2 sets our work in context to existing related work. Section 3 gives an overview of the RTO and describes the ontology development approach. Section 4 assesses the ontology with respect to the given competency questions and requirements. Section 5 concludes our work, summarizes the paper and gives an outlook on future work.

2   Related Work

Transportation Ontologies. Several ontologies containing railway-related concepts have been published in the past. Typically, the concepts and level of detail are determined by the envisioned use case of the ontology. For example, OTN, a general ontology of transportation networks, contains some railway concepts at a level of detail sufficient to describe transportation between railway stations [16]. OTN is also an example of a reusable ontology, as it has been included in the smart-city ontology km4city [3]. Daniele and Pires [9] describe an ontological approach to logistics. Katsumi and Fox [14] survey ontologies for transportation research. Although ontologies for transportation research often also contain railway concepts, they lack the necessary detail to describe the topology of a railway network at the operating level (e.g., switches, tracks, signals).

Data Integration Ontologies. Heterogeneous data in railway system typically arise in two ways. Either different subsystems of the railway system have a slightly different view of the overall system, or there exist country- and vendor-specific views of the same subsystem. For historic reasons, railway signalling is very country-specific, especially in the European Union. Therefore, many ontologies for integrating railway data have been developed by EU-funded research projects and during European initiatives like SHIFT2Rail[2] and its predecessors. As one of the first projects, the InteGRail project [19] developed ontologies to integrate the major railway subsystems and provide a coherent view of the

---

[2] https://shift2rail.org/.

data. The RaCoOn ontology [21] was developed to demonstrate ontology-based data integration of different subsystems and was used in the European Capacity4Rail[3] project. The recent ST4RT [7] project leverages Shift2Rail Interoperability Framework components to improve interoperability. Their prototype implementations include travel and ticketing applications. These ontologies typically focus on the interoperability and mapping aspect and not on modelling the topology of the railway network. Additionally, some ontologies were no longer available online and maintained.

Railway Infrastructure and Signalling Ontologies. Some ontologies have been developed especially for the formal verification of railway infrastructure. These ontologies typically model the railway network in sufficient detail and allow reasoning about the topology of the network. Examples of this class of ontologies are the RI* ontology [15] and the RAISO ontology [2]. In principle, these ontologies might answer our competency questions. However, these ontologies are not available online and not aligned to relevant railway standards.

Existing Standards and Data Formats. The RailTopoModel (RTM) is a (UML-based) model of railway infrastructure that has been standardized as IRS30100 (International Railway Standard) by the UIC (Union internationale des chemins de fer/international union of railways) [22]. RailML is an XML-based standard way to exchange railway data. The topological core of RailML is based on the RTM [13]. EULYNX[4] standardizes interfaces and elements of signalling systems and is also based on RTM. Similarly, IFC Rail[5] for building information systems is also aligned with RTM. We selected RTM in its most recent version 1.1[6] as the base resource for our ontology.

3   Rail Topology Ontology

For developing the Rail Topology Ontology, we followed the NeOn methodology [20]. In an extensive literature search (documented in the previous section) we found no suitable ontology to satisfy our requirements. We implemented scenario 2 of the NeON methodology: "Re-engineering Non-Ontological Resources".

The three activities of the first phase of Scenario 2 of the NeON methodology are search, assessment and selection of an appropriate non-ontological resource. The results of the first two activities are described in the previous section. Based on our requirements, we selected RTM 1.1 as the main resource in the third activity.

3.1   Resource Engineering

The second phase, the resource engineering process, consists of the three activities reverse engineering, resource transformation and ontology forward engineering. The result of this phase is the RTO ontology.

---

[3] http://www.capacity4rail.eu/.
[4] https://www.eulynx.eu/.
[5] https://www.buildingsmart.org/standards/rooms/railway/ifc-rail-project/.
[6] https://uic.org/rail-system/railtopomodel.

Reverse Engineering. We manually analysed the RTM specification and the UML model before approaching the subsequent activities.

Resource Transformation. For transforming the RTM UML model to OWL 2 we adapt the approach of Zedlitz and Luttenberger [25] to our requirements. The following list summarizes our conversion of UML modelling features to OWL 2:

UML classes are converted to OWL classes. UML generalizations are mapped to subclass axioms. Sibling classes (classes with the same direct superclass) are defined as disjoint.

UML attributes are converted to asymmetric, irreflexive OWL data properties with a single class or a union of classes as domain and one data type in the range.

UML data types are converted to the corresponding XML Schema data types for primitive UML types, and to OWL custom data types for UML enumerations.

UML associations are converted to OWL asymmetric, irreflexive object properties with a single class or a union of classes as domain and one class as the range.

UML aggregations are converted in the same way as associations. Their additional UML defined constraint – UML aggregations must be acyclic since instances must not aggregate themselves – is not expressed

UML compositions are also converted like aggregations, but they are additionally defined as inverse functional.

UML multiplicities on ends of UML associations, aggregations and compositions come in (only) three shapes in RTM:

0..* is ignored in the conversion.
1..* is converted to an existential restriction.
1 is converted to existential restriction and a (qualified) maximum cardinality constraint.

UML Multiplicity Elements, which are annotations on the ends of UML associations, are not considered by Zedlitz and Luttenberger [25]. There exists only one instance of such an element in RTM: the range of the UML association elementParts from OrderedCollection to NetElement is specified as {ordered}. Intuitively, an OrderedCollection relates to an *ordered* list of NetElements. The graph data model of RDF provides no canonical representation of ordered lists; ontology engineers have to choose between several modelling patterns. Most prominent, since they are defined by the RDF Schema specification [6], are the different RDF containers (rdf:Bag, rdf:Seq and rdf:Alt) and RDF collections. For RTO, we combine RDF collections with the standard "unordered" mapping of associations to allow simple unordered retrieval while at the same time keeping the information about the order. Additionally, the Turtle serialization [1] provides an intuitive shorthand syntax for RDF collections using parentheses.

The class, object and data property URIs are solely derived from the class, association and attribute names, respectively. This allows straightforward transformation of data, other models and user knowledge from RTM. However, we

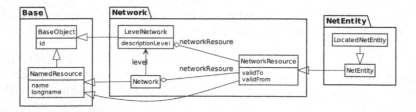

Fig. 1. Schematic overview of the Base, Network and NetEntity packages

have to (semi-automatically) ensure that this policy creates no inconsistencies. In several cases multiple associations (attributes) were merged into a single object (data) property. In every one of these cases the range of the property is a single class. The domain is then defined as a union of classes.

Mapping to Upper Ontology. The upcoming part 14 of the ISO 15926 standard[7], currently a working draft [24], serves as an upper ontology for the RTO. Originally, ISO 15926 aimed at integration of lifecycle data of oil and gas plants. Later the scope widened, and the standard was positioned as a generic industrial upper ontology. Part 14 formalizes the ISO standards concepts in an OWL 2 ontology.

We manually mapped all RTO top-level classes and some subclasses as well as some object properties to respective classes and object properties of the upper ontology.

Ontology Forward Engineering. In this last activity, we define the additional object property reaches to simplify reachability queries necessary for answering the competency questions. We give a more detailed explanation of this property in Sect. 3.3.

3.2   Overview of the Rail Topology Ontology

This section gives an overview of RTM and RTO. For details on the RTM classes we refer the reader to IRS 30100 standard [22] and the RTM 1.1 specification (see footnote 6).

RTM describes its UML class model in six different packages. We describe the ontology using the same package structure only for didactic reasons, as OWL has no "package" construct.

Figure 1 visualizes the three smallest packages: Base, Network and NetEntity.

The Base package provides the BaseObject to denote objects/instances which are identifiable by some id. NamedResource is the base class for all instances which can be named. name and longname are defined as subproperties of rdfs:label and rdfs:comment, respectively.

The Network package provides concepts to describe rail Networks at different levels of detail. One Network can have multiple LevelNetworks, each describing the

---

[7] Once standardized, available at https://standards.iso.org/iso/15926/part14.

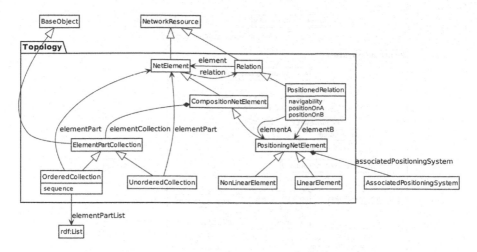

Fig. 2. Schematic overview of the Topology package

Network at the given descriptionLevel. The recommended description levels are 'macro', 'meso' and 'micro'. Informally, a macro LevelNetwork represents nodes (e.g. railway stations) and lines, a meso LevelNetwork additionally represents the tracks between nodes, and a micro LevelNetwork represents the railway network in detail, i.e., the topology as defined by switches, tracks and crossings.

The NetEntity package includes the base class for NetEntities, which are rail infrastructure entities. LocatedNetEntities can be located on the rail network using the Locate package. The core topology ontology does not contain specific subclasses (e.g. signals, level crossings...) of Netentities. These must be provided by additional ontologies, if required.

The Topology package, shown in Fig. 2, is used to define the topology of a railway network. The NetElement subclasses define segments of the rail network. PositionedRelations define the connection and navigability between NetElements using the properties navigability, positionOnA and positionOnB. For example, a PositionedRelation with positionOnA 0, positionOnB 1 and navigability "AB" expresses that movement of a train is only possible from A to B between the 0-end of the elementA and the 1-end of the elementB of the PositionedRelation.

The CompositionNetElement class aggregates NetElements using the Element-PartCollections. The modelling of the {ordered} association end of the element-Part association allows users to retrieve the element parts of OrderedCollections and UnorderedCollection in a uniform (unordered) manner.

Ordered access is possible via the object property elementPartList, which links the OrderedCollection to an RDF collection. The following listing shows the Turtle serialization of an OrderedCollection oc1 with its parts ne2, ne1 and ne3, in that order:

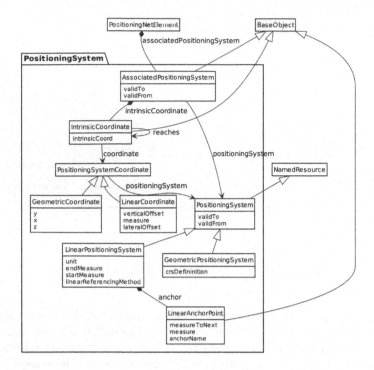

Fig. 3. Schematic overview of the PositioningSystem package

```
<ocl> a topo:OrderedCollection ;
  topo:sequence 1 ;
  topo:elementPartList ( <ne2>   <ne1>   <ne3> ) ;
  topo:elementPart       <ne1>, <ne2>, <ne3> .
```

Figure 3 shows the classes for describing positioning systems. Positioning systems are either GPS-based or linear positioning systems that are typically used in line-based railway positioning. PositioningNetElements from the Topology package are assigned positions via the AssociatedPositioningSystem class.

The Location package (Fig. 4) establishes the connection between the NetEntity instances and the topology defined by the NetElements. Again, for the details, we refer to the RTO and RTM documentation. The main purpose of the Location package is to assign either a linear location or a spot location to a NetEntity by relating it to concepts of the Topology and PositioningSystem packages. The applicationDirection property defines in which direction a NetEntity is active, e.g., a railway signal with application direction "normal" is only relevant for train movement if the train is moving from 0 to 1 on the corresponding NetElement of the signal.

Compatibility with RailTopoModel 1.1. The ontology was built to be compatible with the UML model of RTM 1.1 to simplify the transition between RTM and RTO. This simplifies not only the transition between RTM and RTO for human

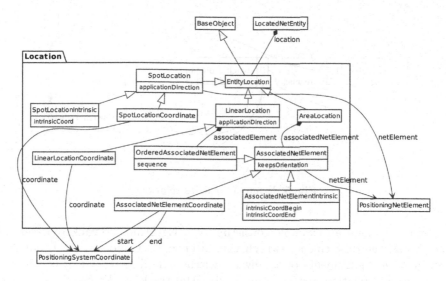

Fig. 4. Schematic overview of the Location package

users, but also simplifies the development of ontologies based on standards which are themselves based on RTM. Contrary to the RTM UML model, all object properties derived from UML associations were defined in singular form instead of the plural used for associations with a maximum cardinality greater than 1 in the RTM UML model. Since object properties link a subject to a single object entity and not collections of entities, their names should be singular.

3.3 Directed Reachability

Answering reachability queries–i.e., determining which infrastructure elements are reachable by a train moving through the rail network–constitute an important application of the topology ontology. On the micro level of a railway topology, it is often necessary to compute reachability without changing direction. We call this *directed reachability*. Directed reachability can only be defined for LinearElements, because by traversing a NonLinearElement we lose the information about the orientation of the train on the element. Unfortunately, writing a SPARQL query to obtain directly reachable LinearElements is non-trivial, since we have to consider the different (local) orientations of the topology elements.

In principle, a train can traverse a LinearElement in two directions. In RTM nomenclature, this corresponds to moving from the beginning (IntrinsicCoordinate 0) of a LinearElement to the end (IntrinsicCoordinate 1) or, vice versa. We therefore can define *directed reachability* with a relation reaches between Intrinsic-Coordinates. Informally, `:ic1 :reaches :ic2` expresses that a train leaving a LinearElement at IntrinsicCoordinate `:ic1` can reach the IntrinsicCoordinate `:ic2` without changing direction.

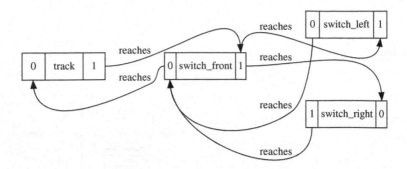

Fig. 5. Example: reaches relation

Figure 5 shows an example consisting of a NetElement **track** representing a track and the NetElements **switch_tip**, **switch_left** and **switch_right** representing the NetElements of a railway switch. The directed edges correspond to the **reaches** relation, e.g., a train leaving the track at the coordinate 1 can reach the left and right branches of the switch. A train entering the switch over the left/right branch can only reach the track, but not the other branch of the switch. The **reaches** relation has the following noteworthy properties:

- The directions 0/1 are local directions. There is no direct relation to a global direction of the overall rail network or line. Therefore, it is possible for the reaches relation to directly go from a IntrinsicCoordinate 0 to a IntrinsicCoordinate 1, and vice versa (see example).
- If the underlying rail network is acyclic, the reaches relation consists of two unconnected subgraphs. Each subgraph is a directed acyclic graph and corresponds to one possible train direction.

Deriving Directed Reachability with SPARQL. In the following, we describe how to derive the **reaches** object property using SPARQL 1.1. SPARQL 1.1 property path expressions can compute undirected reachability of RTO instances. However, directed reachability requires a complicated SPARQL query, taking into account the navigability of the PositionedRelations as well as considering the local direction of the NetElements. The example SPARQL 1.1 **CONSTRUCT** query in Listing 1 computes the **reaches** object property. The **VALUES** clauses handle the different orientations of the two LinearElements and the PositionedRelation. The materialized **reaches** object property can then be used for more complicated queries like determining the order of elements or the paths between elements.

Listing 2 shows an example SPARQL query to use the **reaches** property in a SPARQL property path expression to retrieve the transitively reachable LinearElements when leaving the LinearElement named **"switch_front"** at its end 1. For the example given in Fig. 5 the SPARQL query would return **"switch_left"** and **"switch_right"** as bindings for the variable **?targetlabel**.

Still, some graph properties are hard or impossible (number of paths between two elements) to express in SPARQL. In these cases the reaches object property

Listing 1. Example SPARQL 1.1 query to compute directed reachability for LinearElements

```
PREFIX : <https://w3id.org/rail/topo#>
CONSTRUCT {
  ?icSource :reaches ?icTarget
}
WHERE {
  ?nr a :PositionedRelation ; # PositionedRelation -> NetElements
      ?elemSource ?neSource ; ?posOnSource ?usageSource ;
      ?elemTarget ?neTarget ; ?posOnTarget ?usageTarget .

  # Ensure navigability of PositionedRelation
  { ?nr :navigability "Both" } UNION { ?nr :navigability ?navSingle }

  # Navigate from linear NetElements to intrinsic coordinates
  ?neSource a :LinearElement ;
    :associatedPositioningSystem/:intrinsicCoordinate ?icSource .
  ?neTarget a :LinearElement ;
    :associatedPositioningSystem/:intrinsicCoordinate ?icTarget .

  # IntrinsicCoordinate -> numeric coordinate
  ?icSource :intrinsicCoord ?iccSource .
  ?icTarget :intrinsicCoord ?iccTarget .

  # Leave source NetElement at end 0 or 1
  VALUES (?usageSource ?iccSource ) {
         (1          1.0 )
         (0          0.0 ) }

  # Traverse over target NetElement from end 0 or 1 to the other end
  VALUES (?usageTarget ?iccTarget) {
         (0          1.0)
         (1          0.0) }

  # navigate NetRelation ?nr either A -> B or B -> A
  VALUES (?elemSource ?elemTarget ?posOnSource ?posOnTarget ?navSingle) {
         (:elementA  :elementB  :positionOnA :positionOnB "AB")  # A -> B
         (:elementB  :elementA  :positionOnB :positionOnA "BA") } # B -> A
}
```

can be converted to a graph representation suitable for a graph library like networkx[8], which provides standard graph algorithms.

3.4 Ontology Publication

We publish the RTO under the weak copyleft Mozilla Public License Version 2.0. The ontology and documentation is available under a permanent URL from W3ID http://w3id.org/rail/topo. Additionally, the ontology is indexed by Linked Open Vocabularies [23].[9] The ontology contains metadata annotations for the ontology itself, as well as classes and properties. The ontology documentation was partly generated by WIDOCO [10]. The tool also helped publishing the ontology and its documentation following existing best practices: depending on the agent (standard HTTP browser, ontology editing tool) and the used

---

[8] https://networkx.org.

[9] https://lov.linkeddata.es/dataset/lov/vocabs/rto.

Listing 2. Example query retrieve reachable target NetElements in direction 1.0 of the ?source LinearElement

```
PREFIX topo: <https://w3id.org/rail/topo#>
SELECT ?source ?targetlabel
WHERE {
  ?source a topo:LinearElement ; topo:name "switch_front" ;
      topo:associatedPositioningSystem/topo:intrinsicCoordinate ?ic .

  ?ic topo:intrinsicCoord 1.0 ;
      topo:reaches+/^topo:intrinsicCoordinate/
        ^topo:associatedPositioningSystem/topo:name ?targetlabel.
}
```

HTTP Accept header, either the documentation or the ontology (in JSON-LD, RDF/XML, N-Triples or Turtle format) is served to the client.

4   Ontology Assessment and Discussion

In this section we discuss the ontology's suitability to address the requirements stated in Sect. 1, give arguments on potential adoption and outline a use case scenario.

Requirements. Both competency questions ask for paths and elements on these paths. RDF and the RTO model can express all the information needed to answer these questions. Although standard SPARQL cannot return paths including the traversed "edges" and "nodes", custom software can be used to retrieve the necessary information from RTO instance data.

We now discuss whether and to what extent RTO fulfils the functional requirements: (i) The topology package of RTO represents the logical topology of a rail infrastructure network. (ii) The main infrastructure elements can be represented by using the LocatedNetEntity class. Following RTM, we deliberately abstained from explicitly modelling infrastructure elements in RTO. If more fine-grained classes for different infrastructure elements (for example the mentioned tracks, switches and signals) are needed, extensions of that class will be necessary. (iii) Modelling position and orientation of infrastructure elements is a core functionality of RTO. (iv) Aggregation of networks at different levels of abstraction is also a core feature of RTO.

The resulting ontology is vendor-independent since it is based on the international standard RTM 1.1. By following best practices for publishing ontologies, the resource is openly available and should be easy to reuse.

Expressivity. The ontology is contained in OWL 2 DL but not contained in any of the OWL 2 Profiles QL, RL or EL. The following OWL 2 features used in the UML conversion are not contained in the OWL 2 profiles:

- Union of classes in `rdfs:domain` due to merging of object and data properties with the same name. The alternative of differentiating individual associations and attributes by more precise and verbose naming, for example based on association and domain class name, makes the model more cumbersome to handle: SPARQL queries become harder to read and write due to increased length and, more importantly, users would hardly accept more complicated object and data property names than the ones they know from RTM.

- Existential restriction resulting from the conversion of the UML cardinalities. There is no alternative way to express a (minimum) cardinality of 1 in the three OWL 2 Profiles. However, cardinalities are necessary and useful in many scenarios (for example for the mentioned tools for automatic SHACL shapes or REST API creation).
- Definition of custom data types from the mapping of UML enumerations and their use in the range of data properties.
- The use of finite data types such as Boolean, float or double, which is forbidden in OWL 2 QL. RTO inherits these data types from RTM. The remedy of falling back to xsd:string is considered infeasible since it would severely limit data validation (for example via SHACL).

When selecting a reasoner for RTO data, users must be aware of these limitations.

Use Case. We use the RTO in our in-house rail knowledge graph. Its main data sources are different rail infrastructure engineering tools. The knowledge graph provides global access to the otherwise disconnected engineering data.

To set this isolated data into a spatial and network context, we integrate data supplied by the European Union Agency for Railways (ERA) with their EU-wide rail infrastructure database "Registers of Infrastructure" (RINF)[10]. Rail infrastructure managers of all EU countries are obligated to provide data about their infrastructure, which is then published by RINF. With RTO, we can access data of these sources using one common model independent of the source data.

General. To base the ontology on an existing standard avoids "reinventing the wheel" and allows a subject-matter expert for the existing standard to identify the common concepts easily. Also, it is unrealistic to expect that a newly created railway ontology without any relation to existing standards will be adopted by the community.

On the other hand, as the standard is based on UML the model–especially the class hierarchy and naming conventions–might feel unfamiliar to knowledge engineers used to OWL ontologies.

Although the RTM way of modelling the railway topology might not be intuitive for the non railway expert, it has been well documented why the complexity is necessary [12]. A basic knowledge of the railway domain is necessary to use the ontology effectively. Other aspects like the use of the Location package can be overwhelming for the beginner. This is one of the reasons why we will try to

---

[10] https://www.era.europa.eu/registers_en#rinf.

accompany the ontology with corresponding SPARQL queries and instance data to illustrate the use of the ontology.

Deriving the ontology from an existing standard enables easier data exchange with existing systems. As the existing standard is based on UML, data exchange is not entirely without effort because of the required mapping between the RTM UML model and the corresponding XML schema (RailML) for serialization. This additional mapping complexity would not exist in standards directly based on RDF/OWL.

For sustainability of the ontology, we maintain the RTO internally through its use in our internal rail knowledge graph. In this knowledge graph, we integrate and provide access to data from several rail infrastructure data sources. The RTO serves as a core schema for this integration. Externally, we further develop the RTO within the new RailML semantic modelling working group.

5   Summary and Future Work

With the RTO we address the first of our previously identified challenges in creating a rail knowledge graph [4]: the lack of a standard ontology for rail infrastructure engineering. We believe that standard modular ontologies are a prerequisite for the adoption of semantic technologies in industry. Also, we have experienced in the past that the lack of standard (UML) data models created a lot of inefficiencies and effort for data integration, even when the data models were only slightly incompatible. This ontology should foster collaboration between the semantic web community and the railway community.

Specializations of the LocatedNetEntity class with different types of rail infrastructure elements are necessary. These include switches, signals and tracks on the micro level and operating points, lines and section of lines on the macro level. Due to the tight alignment to RTM, the RTO can be a good basis for the development of more specialized rail infrastructure ontologies derived from standard specifications based on RTM, specifically for developing ontologies derived from RailML, EULYNX or IFC Rail. This approach helps to accelerate ontology development and to integrate data of these different formats. Furthermore, the ontology could serve as a starting point for mapping between railway infrastructure ontologies. In the new RailML ontology working group, we are working on a RailML-based infrastructure ontology.

When integrating data in a knowledge graph, instance linking (or alignment) is another important task. The RTO topology data have special challenges concerning this task. To accommodate a broad range of use cases, RTM (and thus RTO) leaves a lot of modelling freedom, which makes instance alignment harder. We are investigating different approaches to this problem and for improving the data integration process.

Acknowledgements. We thank the anonymous reviewers for their constructive feedback. For authoring the ontology and documentation we used Protégé 5.5 [17], Widoco [10] and the OOPS! ontology scanner [18]. To prepare the figures in this paper we used PlantUML and Graphviz.

References

1. Beckett, D., Berners-Lee, T., Prud'hommeaux, E., Carothers, G. (eds.): RDF 1.1 Turtle. W3C Recommendation (2014). https://www.w3.org/TR/turtle/
2. Bellini, P., Nesi, P., Zaza, I.: RAISO: railway infrastructures and signaling ontology for configuration management, verification and validation. In: 10th International Conference on Semantic Computing, pp. 350–353. IEEE (2016). https://doi.org/10.1109/ICSC.2016.94
3. Bellini, P., Benigni, M., Billero, R., Nesi, P., Rauch, N.: Km4city ontology building vs data harvesting and cleaning for smart-city services. J. Vis. Lang. Comput. **25**(6), 827–839 (2014). https://doi.org/10.1016/j.jvlc.2014.10.023
4. Bischof, S., Schenner, G.: Challenges of constructing a railway knowledge graph. In: The Semantic Web: ESWC 2019 Satellite Events, pp. 253–256 (2019). https://doi.org/10.1007/978-3-030-32327-1_44
5. Bischof, S., Schenner, G.: Towards a railway topology ontology to integrate and query rail data silos. In: Proceedings of the Demos and Industry Tracks of the 19th International Semantic Web Conference (ISWC 2020). No. 2721 in CEUR Workshop Proceedings, CEUR-WS.org (2020). http://ceur-ws.org/Vol-2721/paper588.pdf
6. Brickley, D., Guha, R. (eds.): RDF Schema 1.1. W3C Recommendation (2014). https://www.w3.org/TR/rdf-schema/
7. Carenini, A., Comerio, M., Celino, I.: Semantic-enhanced national access points to multimodal transportation data. In: ISWC 2018 Posters & Demonstrations, Industry and Blue Sky Ideas Tracks. No. 2180 in CEUR Workshop Proceedings, CEUR-WS.org (2018). http://ceur-ws.org/Vol-2180/paper-09.pdf
8. Cimmino, A., Fernández-Izquierdo, A., García-Castro, R.: Astrea: automatic generation of SHACL shapes from ontologies. In: Harth, A., et al. (eds.) ESWC 2020. LNCS, vol. 12123, pp. 497–513. Springer, Cham (2020). https://doi.org/10.1007/978-3-030-49461-2_29
9. Daniele, L., Pires, L.F.: An ontological approach to logistics. In: Enterprise Interoperability, Research and Applications in the Service-Oriented Ecosystem, IWEI, vol. 13, pp. 199–213 (2013). https://doi.org/10.1002/9781118846995
10. Garijo, D.: WIDOCO: a wizard for documenting ontologies. In: d'Amato, C., et al. (eds.) ISWC 2017. LNCS, vol. 10588, pp. 94–102. Springer, Cham (2017). https://doi.org/10.1007/978-3-319-68204-4_9
11. Garijo, D., Osorio, M.: OBA: an ontology-based framework for creating REST APIs for knowledge graphs. In: Pan, J.Z., et al. (eds.) ISWC 2020. LNCS, vol. 12507, pp. 48–64. Springer, Cham (2020). https://doi.org/10.1007/978-3-030-62466-8_4
12. Gély, L., Dessagne, G., Pesneau, P., Vanderbeck, F.: A multi scalable model based on a connexity graph representation. Computers in Railways XII, vol. 1, pp. 193–204 (2010). https://doi.org/10.2495/CR100191
13. Hlubuček, A.: RailTopoModel and RailML 3 in overall context. Acta Polytechnica CTU Proc. **11**, 16–21 (2017). https://doi.org/10.14311/APP.2017.11.0016
14. Katsumi, M., Fox, M.: Ontologies for transportation research: a survey. Transp. Res. Part C-Emerg. Technol. **89**, 53–82 (2018). https://doi.org/10.1002/9781118846995.ch21
15. Lodemann, M., Luttenberger, N., Schulz, E.: Semantic computing for railway infrastructure verification. In: 7th International Conference on Semantic Computing, pp. 371–376. IEEE (2013). https://doi.org/10.1109/ICSC.2013.69

16. Lorenz, B., Ohlbach, II.J., Yang, L.: Ontology of transportation networks. Project deliverable, REWERSE project (2005). http://rewerse.net/deliverables/m18/a1-d4.pdf

17. Musen, M.A.: The protégé project: a look back and a look forward. AI Matters **1**(4), 4–12 (2015). https://doi.org/10.1145/2757001.2757003

18. Poveda-Villalón, M., Gómez-Pérez, A., Suárez-Figueroa, M.C.: OOPS! (OntOlogy pitfall scanner!): an on-line tool for ontology evaluation. Int. J. Semant. Web Inf. Syst. (IJSWIS) **10**(2), 7–34 (2014). https://doi.org/10.4018/ijswis.2014040102

19. Shingler, R., Fadin, G., Umiliacchi, P.: From RCM to predictive maintenance: the integrail approach. In: 4th International Conference on Railway Condition Monitoring. IET (2008). https://doi.org/10.1049/ic:20080324

20. Suárez-Figueroa, M.C., Gómez-Pérez, A., Fernández-López, M.: The NeOn methodology for ontology engineering. In: Suárez-Figueroa, M.C., Gómez-Pérez, A., Motta, E., Gangemi, A. (eds.) Ontology Engineering in a Networked World, pp. 9–34. Springer, Heidelberg (2012). https://doi.org/10.1007/978-3-642-24794-1_2

21. Tutcher, J., Easton, J.M., Roberts, C.: Enabling data integration in the rail industry using RDF and OWL: the RaCoOn ontology. ASCE-ASME J. Risk Uncertain. Eng. Syst. Part A: Civil Eng. **3**(2) (2015). https://doi.org/10.1061/AJRUA6.0000859

22. UIC: RailTopoModel - railway infrastructure topological model. Standard, International Railway Solution IRS 30100:2016, International Union of Railway (UIC) (2016)

23. Vandenbussche, P.Y., Atemezing, G.A., Poveda-Villalón, M., Vatant, B.: Linked open vocabularies (LOV): a gateway to reusable semantic vocabularies on the web. Semant. Web J. **8**(3), 437–452 (2016). https://doi.org/10.3233/SW-160213

24. Walther, D., et al.: Industrial automation systems and integration-integration of life-cycle data for process plants including oil and gas production facilities-part 14: industrial top-level ontology. Deliverable, READI project (2020). https://readi-jip.org/wp-content/uploads/2020/10/ISO_15926-14_2020-09-READI-Deliverable.pdf. Working Draft (WD) Proposal for ISO 15926-14:2020(E)

25. Zedlitz, J., Luttenberger, N.: Conceptual modelling in UML and OWL-2. Int. J. Adv. Softw. **7**(1 & 2), 182–196 (2014). http://www.iariajournals.org/software/

In-Use Track

Mapping Manuscript Migrations on the Semantic Web: A Semantic Portal and Linked Open Data Service for Premodern Manuscript Research

Eero Hyvönen[1,2(✉)], Esko Ikkala[1], Mikko Koho[1,2], Jouni Tuominen[1,2], Toby Burrows[3], Lynn Ransom[4], and Hanno Wijsman[5]

[1] Semantic Computing Research Group (SeCo), Aalto University, Espoo, Finland
`eero.hyvonen@aalto.fi`
[2] HELDIG – Helsinki Centre for Digital Humanities, University of Helsinki, Helsinki, Finland
`mikko.koho@helsinki.fi`
[3] Oxford e-Research Centre, University of Oxford, Oxford, UK
[4] Schoenberg Institute for Manuscript Studies, University of Pennsylvania, Philadelphia, USA
[5] Institut de recherche et d'histoire des textes, Aubervilliers, France

Abstract. This paper presents the *Mapping Manuscript Migrations* (MMM) system in use for modeling, aggregating, publishing, and studying heterogeneous, distributed premodern manuscript databases on the Semantic Web. A general "Sampo model" is applied to publishing and using linked data in Digital Humanities (DH) research and to creating the MMM system that includes a semantic portal and a Linked Open Data (LOD) service. The idea is to provide the manuscript data publishers with a novel collaborative way to enrich their contents with related data of the other providers and by reasoning. For the end user, the MMM Portal facilitates semantic faceted search and exploration of the data, integrated seamlessly with data analytic tools for solving research problems in manuscript studies. In addition, the SPARQL endpoint of the LOD service can be used with external tools for customized use in DH research and applications. The MMM services are available online, based on metadata of over 220 000 manuscripts from the Schoenberg Database of Manuscripts of the Schoenberg Institute for Manuscript Studies (University of Pennsylvania), the Medieval Manuscripts in Oxford Libraries, and Bibale of Institut de recherche et d'histoire des textes in Paris. Evaluation of the MMM Portal suggests that the system is useful in manuscript studies and outperforms current systems online in searching, exploring, and analyzing data.

Keywords: Manuscripts · Semantic portals · Linked data · Digital humanities

1 Introduction

The study of premodern manuscripts, i.e., books and documents produced before the age of print, is an essential element in understanding our shared intellectual and cultural heritages across time and geographies [6]. Manuscripts, unlike printed books, are unique witness to the times in which they were produced. Whereas a printed copy of a text exists in multiple identical copies, the textual contents of premodern manuscripts reflect specific circumstances of production that cannot be reproduced in other copies

© Springer Nature Switzerland AG 2021
A. Hotho et al. (Eds.): ISWC 2021, LNCS 12922, pp. 615–630, 2021.
https://doi.org/10.1007/978-3-030-88361-4_36

of the same text or textual groupings. Over the centuries, manuscripts have been bought and sold, stolen and lost, and broken up and rebound. Hundreds of thousands of European premodern manuscripts have survived until the present day.

Consider. e.g., the Christian Bible, repeatedly copied, translated, revised, and disseminated in a variety of formats until the 13th century when the book started to look something like the modern standardized Bible with chapter and verse divisions contained in a single volume in two-column format in a hand-holdable size. This process began with manuscripts resembling the Dead Sea Scrolls. Another example is Marco Polo's (1254–1324) original text *The Travels of Marco Polo* that he dictated in a prison to a fellow inmate. The original copy of his words has not been found, but a total of about 150 copies in various languages and produced at different times throughout the Middle Ages are known to exist in different collections.

Over the last twenty years there has been a proliferation of digital data relating to premodern manuscripts, including catalogues, specialist databases, and numerous collections of digital images[1]. The databases may contain metadata about the manuscripts, and also transliterated texts extracted from them, possibly with translations. However, there is little in the way of having a coherent, *interoperable digital infrastructure for the manuscript data* for Digital Humanities (DH) research [9,23]. As a result, cross-collection discovery and analysis requires the time-consuming exploration of numerous disparate resources. To mitigate this problem, this paper introduces the Mapping Manuscript Migrations (MMM) system, an outcome of the MMM project[2] [4]. MMM is a data publishing framework including a semantic portal demonstrator and a Linked Open Data (LOD) service for manuscript studies. The model supports several user groups: 1) The data publishers are provided with a collaborative model for harmonizing, enriching, and publishing their content in a shared knowledge graph hosted by a LOD server. 2) Collection managers and curators are facilitated with a semantic portal for accessing the enriched collections in order to develop and maintain their own collections. 3) Manuscript researchers are provided with a semantic portal for exploring, visualizing, and analyzing the data with seamlessly integrated data-analytic tooling without technical expertise. The researchers can also use the SPARQL endpoint and other APIs of the framework directly for custom-made analyses. 4) The APIs can be used by system developers for creating new applications on top of the data service. The MMM Portal[3] and LOD service[4] are in pilot use on the Semantic Web since 2020.

In the following, we first introduce the data and data model of MMM. After this the "Sampo model" for publishing and using data in DH is presented and applied to the MMM case study to create the MMM Portal and data service. Using the MMM Portal and the LOD service for studying the manuscripts are discussed with examples, including a presentation of the implementation. Finally, evaluation of the usability of the portal is discussed, contributions of the paper are summarized in relation to related works, and lessons learned are summarized. This paper concerns the MMM system from a LOD publishing and portal design perspectives, complementing our earlier papers on

---

[1] Using, e.g., IIIF: https://iiif.io.
[2] https://seco.cs.aalto.fi/projects/mmm/.
[3] https://mappingmanuscriptmigrations.org.
[4] https://www.ldf.fi/dataset/mmm.

the MMM project in general [4], on MMM data modeling and data transformations [18], tooling for implementing the portal interface [17], and on evaluating the system with end users [5].

2   Modeling Manuscript Data

MMM Data. The MMM knowledge graph (KG) aggregates data from three databases in which different data models and data base systems were used. Furthermore, the data contained in the databases was different in nature, including, e.g., both records of manuscripts and observations about them, such as transfers of custody in auctions.

1. **Bibale**[5]. The Bibale data comes from the Institute for Research and History of Texts (IRHT). The 55 000 Bibale database records belong to one of eight object types: manuscripts, works, persons, bindings, collections, ownership marks, texts, and sources.
2. **Schoenberg Database of Manuscripts (SDBM)**[6]. Entries in the SDBM use up to 36 fields to record data from observations of manuscripts found in published and unpublished sources. The data is in a MySQL relational database and contains over 250 000 records focusing on provenance-related manuscript histories.
3. **Medieval Manuscripts in Oxford Libraries (MMOL)**[7]. The MMOL dataset in MMM covers 10 272 manuscripts represented in TEI format[8].

Each of the source datasets 1–3 has its own preconditions and goals, and thus follows its own data modeling conventions. Therefore, a unified data model for harmonizing the datasets was needed as well as a pipeline for transforming the datasets into the harmonized model including aligning the data values used in the metadata elements, such as historical people and places. For this purpose a set of shared ontologies was selected, such as the Getty Thesaurus of Geographic Names[9] (TGN), and both automatic and semi-automatic tools were used in the data transformation process.

A major challenge for the data harmonization was that the databases contain data that is semantically different in nature. Bibale and MMOL contain traditional metadata about the manuscripts, e.g., who is the author, when the text was written, and the shelf mark of the document. In contrast, SDBM focuses on provenance metadata about the object, e.g., who has owned the manuscript in different times, where has it been, and what has happened to it during the centuries. Actually, the fundamental question "what is a manuscript" is not easy to answer based on the entries in different databases. The different concepts related to a manuscripts as physical units (e.g., manuscript group, volume, item, part, fragment) are inconsistently used or missing, often even within a single database. Creating a comprehensive model covering all this variation of information is a challenge from a data modeling perspective.

---

[5] The current web service is described in http://bibale.irht.cnrs.fr.
[6] See https://sdbm.library.upenn.edu for details about the SDBM data and the web service.
[7] See https://medieval.bodleian.ox.ac.uk for a catalogue of Western manuscripts at the Bodleian Libraries and selected Oxford colleges.
[8] https://tei-c.org.
[9] https://www.getty.edu/research/tools/vocabularies/tgn/.

MMM Data Model. When dealing with premodern manuscripts, it is important to be able to make the distinction between the abstract "distinct intellectual or artistic creation" behind a manuscript (*work*, in terms of the Functional Requirements for Bibliographic Records (FRBR) model[10] [20,27]), "the specific intellectual or artistic form that a work takes each time it is realized" (*expression* in FRBR), say a translation, and the "the physical embodiment of an expression of a work" (manifestation in FRBR). The manifestation represents all the physical objects that bear the same characteristics, in respect to both intellectual content and physical form, i.e., *items* in FRBR terminology.

The harmonizing MMM data model as well as the data harmonization pipeline is presented in detail in [18]. The model is a result of thorough discussions between manuscript researchers and computer scientists in the MMM project and is based on FRRBoo and CIDOC CRM[11]. The final model has 16 main classes for describing manuscripts and related intellectual property, seven classes for describing collections, and nine classes for representing transactions and manuscript observations with some 40 properties in between. For the purposes of this paper, focusing on using the MMM Portal on top of the data service, it is sufficient to consider the classes represented in Table 1, based on the Erlangen CIDOC CRM[12] and FRBRoo[13] namespaces. This is because the MMM Portal is based on searching instances of these classes and on performing data-analyses on subsets of the instances of these classes. These instances are characterized in terms of sets of properties whose values are represented as facets, such as places in a meronymy, in the faceted search engines of the MMM Portal. Table 2 summarizes the facet properties pertaining to the classes of Table 1. The most complex class is Manuscript whose instances may have 22 different properties.

Table 1. Main classes of the MMM knowledge graph whose instances are searched for in the MMM Portal.

Class	# of inst.	URI	Meaning
Manuscript	222 605	frbroo:F4_Manifestation_Singleton	Physical manuscript objects
Work	435 428	frbroo:F1_Work	Intellectual manuscript contents
Event	937 158	crm:E5_Event	Events related to the manuscripts
Actor	56 685	crm:E39_Actor	People and institutions
Place	5077	crm:E52_Place	Places related to manuscripts and actors

3   Application of the Sampo Model to the MMM System

The Sampo model [15] is a consolidated set of principles listed is Table 3 for collaborative publishing and using of LOD on the Semantic Web. The model has been developed gradually and tested in a dozen of online cultural heritage "Sampo" portals in 2002–2021

---

[10] https://www.ifla.org/publications/functional-requirements-for-bibliographic-records.
[11] http://www.cidoc-crm.org/.
[12] crm = http://erlangen-crm.org/current/.
[13] frbroo = http://erlangen-crm.org/efrbroo/.

Table 2. Properties and property paths for the main classes of the MMM Portal in Table 1 that are used as facets in the MMM Portal.

Class	#	Properties (facets)
Manuscript	22	Manuscript, Author, Work, Production place, Production data, Note, Language, Owner, Collection, Transfer of custody place, Transfer of custody date, Last known location, Material, Height, Width, Folios, Lines, Columns, Miniatures, Decorated initials, Historiated initials, Source
Work	6	Title, Possible author, Language, Manuscript production date, Collection, Source
Event	5	Type, Manuscript/Collection, Date, Place, Source
Actor	6	Name, Type, Birth/formation date, Death/dissolution date, Activity location, Source
Place	3	Name, Parent place, Source

Table 3. Sampo model principles P1–P6

P1. Support collaborative data creation and publishing
P2. Use a shared open ontology infrastructure
P3. Provide multiple perspectives to the same data
P4. Standardize portal usage by a simple filter-analyze two-step cycle
P5. Support data analysis and knowledge discovery in addition to data exploration
P6. Make clear distinction between the LOD service and the user interface (UI)

that have had up to millions of end users[14]. The model is based on standards and best practices of W3C for Linked Data publishing [11, 12] supporting FAIR principles[15].

The Sampo model concerns only publishing data, not issues of maintaining linked data. It is assumed that there is a separate pipeline that creates the linked data in a SPARQL endpoint. This section shows how the principles P1–P6 were applied to the MMM system.

P1. Support Collaborative Data Creation and Publishing. The Sampo model is based on the idea of collaborative content creation, where data is aggregated, harmonized, and interlinked from multiple data silos in a global data service, based on a shared ontology infrastructure. The local data is enriched with each other by linking and by reasoning, based on Semantic Web standards[16]. This is arguably a win-win model for data publishers to join and, especially, for the end users of the enriched data.

Figure 1 depicts the overall publication model of the MMM system. The three datasets are transformed (T1–T3 in the figure) into the unified harmonizing data model used in the MMM Linked Data Service that is depicted in the middle of the figure. The data service can be used in external applications via the SPARQL endpoint (on the left), and the data is also documented and can be studied using publishing tools (on the right).

P2. Use a Shared Open Ontology Infrastructure. In MMM the key idea is to enrich data from the three databases with each other, as the same manuscripts, persons, places,

---

[14] See https://seco.cs.aalto.fi/applications/sampo/ for more info about the Sampo portals.

[15] https://www.go-fair.org/fair-principles/.

[16] https://www.w3.org/standards/semanticweb/.

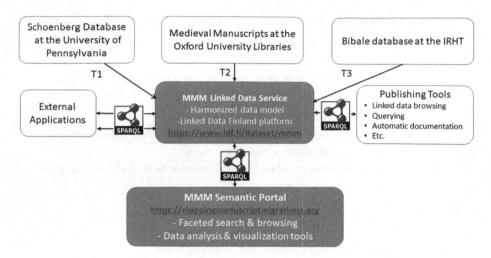

Fig. 1. MMM publishing model

and other entities can be mentioned in all of them. The key elements of the underlying ontology infrastructure are the data model of Sect. 2 and a set of domain ontologies, such as TGN and an ontology of historical people, that are used for populating the instances of the data model classes.

P3. Provide Multiple Perspectives to the Same Data. Sampo model fosters the idea that on top of the LOD service different *application perspectives* to the data can be created by re-using the data service, without modifying the data, which is typically costly. In each perspective, the result set can be studied through a set of visualizations, e.g., as a table, using a chart, or on maps. Furthermore, each instance to be searched for in the perspectives has a homepage aggregating data about it with the possibility of providing visualizations of the individual and its relations.

The perspectives are provided on the landing page of the Sampo system, and enrich each other by data linking. By selecting one of them the corresponding application is opened. The landing page of the MMM Portal depicted in Fig. 2 offering five perspectives for digging into the data: Manuscripts, Works, Events, Actors, and Places.

P4. Standardize Portal Usage by a Simple Filter-Analyze Two-Step Cycle. The application perspectives can be used by a two-step cycle for research: Firstly, the focus of interest, the target group, is filtered out using faceted semantic search [30,31]. Secondly, the target group is visualized or analyzed by using ready-to-use DH tools of the application perspectives. This idea was inspired by the research method used in prosopographical research [32][17].

In the MMM Portal each application perspective enables the user to filter out instances of the core class of the perspective (cf. Table 1). After this, the filtered

---

[17] Prosopography is a method that is used to study groups of people through their biographical data. The goal of prosopography is to find connections, trends, and patterns from these groups.

Fig. 2. MMM Portal landing page

instances can be explored and browsed for close reading, or data-analytic tools can be applied to the filtered result set for distant reading [24, 28].

The facets in each perspective are the same as the properties of the corresponding classes in Table 2. For example, Fig. 3 depicts the Manuscripts perspective that the user has selected on the landing page. The user has made three clicks on the facets on the left: *Place of production* = France; *Production date* = 1100–1200; *Language* = Greek. The 12 results found are shown as a table on the right, paginated in groups of ten manuscripts. The table columns correspond to the facets and the metadata involved. Notice that some facets, such as *Place of production* based on the Getty Thesaurus of Geographical Names (TGN), are hierarchical. By selecting *France*, all provinces, cities villages etc. within France are automatically included in the search—the user does not need to know more about the placenames in France. This is arguable useful even if the semantic problems of representing historical places are challenging in many ways due to, e.g., temporal changes [16, 29]. In our case study, Bibale data was originally based on references to the contemporary GeoNames[18] gazetteer, but in SDBM and MMOL data TGN was already used as the main place authority. To align the gazetteers, a mapping from GeoNames to TGN was created as there was none available.

P5. Support Data Analysis and Knowledge Discovery in Addition to Data Exploration. The model aims, as discussed in [14], not only at data publishing with search and data exploration [22], but also to data analysis and knowledge discovery with seamlessly integrated tooling for finding, analysing, and even solving research problems in interactive ways, based on AI techniques.

---

[18] https://geonames.org.

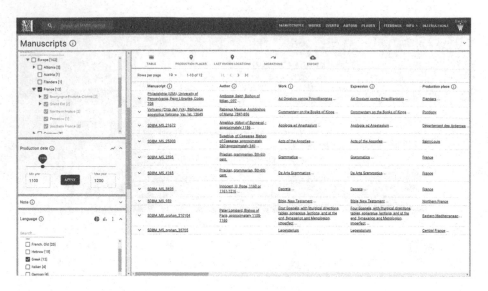

Fig. 3. Manuscripts perspective in the MMM Portal

In MMM, reasoning is to used to enrich the data by rules based on SPARQL CON-STRUCT and SPARQL path expressions in a pre-processing phase. For example, reasoning was used for determining the last known locations of the manuscripts based on provenance data. On the data analysis and knowledge discovery side, it is possible to create alternative data analytic visualizations, represented as separate tabs, for the result set in addition to the table view illustrated in Fig. 3. For example, in the case of the Manuscripts perspective, there are the following tabs available in addition to the default TABLE view: 1) PRODUCTION PLACES tab shows the results on a map based on their place of production. 2) LAST KNOWN LOCATIONS tab shows the last known location of the manuscripts in the same vein. 3) MIGRATIONS tab shows how the filtered manuscripts have migrated from the place of production to the last know location. This is illustrated in Fig. 4 for the 8575 manuscripts owned by the well-known collector Sir Thomas Phillipps (1792–1872). This visualization is an answer to one of the original research question in manuscript studies set when starting the MMM project [3].

In addition to analyzing and visualizing the results on tabs, the facets provide buttons for visualizing the statistics of the results along the facet dimensions. For example, the *Production date* facet provides a button for showing the Phillipps manuscripts distribution along a timeline and the *Owner* facet a button for visualizing the distribution of former and current owners of the manuscripts in the result set as a pie chart.

In addition to studying result sets, each instance in the result set is associated with an information "homepage" that contains an aggregated description on the instance and how it is related to other instances. For example, Sir Thomas Phillipps can be found as a person instance in the Actors perspective with the following metadata fields on his homepage as a table: full name, birth and death dates, locations of activities, works created by the person (none in the case of Thomas Phillipps), manuscripts related to

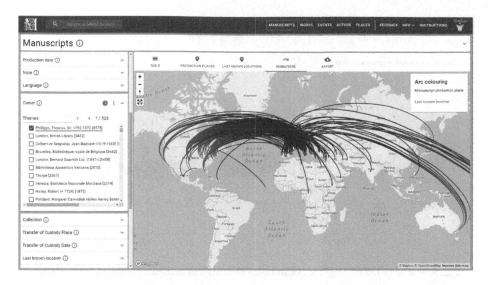

Fig. 4. Migrations of manuscripts owned by Sir Thomas Phillipps (1792–1872) from the place of production (blue end of an arc) to the last known location (red end of the arc) (Color figure online)

the person, and roles of the person in the data (collection owner, manuscript owner, and selling agent for Sir Thomas). Also the URI and the class of the instance are shown.

P6. Make Clear Distinction Between the LOD Service and the User Interface (UI). The architecture in Fig. 1 makes a clear distinction between the MMM Linked Data Service and the user interface, i.e., MMM Semantic Portal, based on only the standard SPARQL API. The MMM knowledge graph is available on the Linked Data Finland (LDF) platform [13], providing a home page for the dataset and its graphs[19], and a public SPARQL endpoint[20]. The homepage provides information, such as schema documentation automatically generated by the platform (using the LODE service[21] [25]), sample SPARQL queries, and metadata using *SPARQL Service Description*[22] and *Vocabulary of Interlinked Datasets (VoID)*[23]. The LDF platform also provides the user with dereferencing of URIs for both human users and machines, and a generic RDF browser for technical users, which opens when a URI is visited directly with a web browser. The data is also available as a data dump on the Zenodo repository[24] with a canonical citation [19].

---

[19] The home page of the KG: https://www.ldf.fi/dataset/mmm.
[20] The public SPARQL endpoint: http://ldf.fi/mmm/sparql.
[21] https://essepuntato.it/lode/.
[22] https://www.w3.org/TR/sparql11-service-description/.
[23] https://www.w3.org/TR/void/.
[24] https://zenodo.org/record/4440464.

4   Using the Data Service

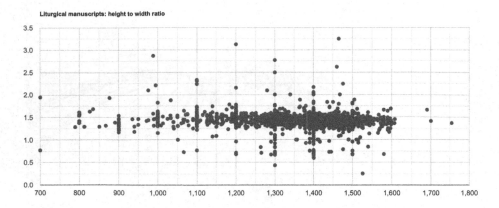

Fig. 5. Visualization of height to width ratios of liturgical manuscripts through SPARQL

In addition to using the MMM Portal, the MMM LOD service can be used directly via the SPARQL endpoint. This expands the possibilities for running complex research questions against the data. For example, the question "What are the ratios of height to width in liturgical manuscripts[25] produced between 700AD and 1800AD?" can be addressed through a SPARQL query[26], but not through the MMM Portal interface. The ratios calculated for 4 030 liturgical manuscripts are shown in Fig. 5 where the x-axis represents the year of production 700–1800 and y-axis the ratio. Most manuscripts have a ratio between 1.25 and 1.6, while ratios of less than 1.0 are only found for a small number of manuscripts which are wider than they are tall. The types of manuscripts covered are missals, breviaries, antiphonals, and graduals.

Manuscripts often have production dates in the form of an estimated range, such as "1200–1300", since the exact date is unknown. This query uses the earliest date in the range. It also averages the dates when a manuscript has more than one estimated production range, usually because of differences between the source datasets or because of multiple records for the same manuscript in the Schoenberg Database. Averaging is also used when a manuscript has more than one set of height and width measurements, for similar reasons. The query can also be adjusted to show ratios for each specific sub-type of liturgical manuscripts, as well as for other types of manuscripts.

To illustrate how the SPARQL endpoint is programmatically used by the MMM Portal for implementing faceted search coupled with data analytic tools, the relatively short query[27] for creating the migrations visualization in Fig. 4 is listed below:

---

[25] Liturgical manuscripts are retrieved using string comparison on the work labels as there is no classification of manuscript types in the data sources.

[26] The SPARQL query can be seen and run at: https://api.triplydb.com/s/czV6XZJx8.

[27] The SPARQL query can be seen and run at: https://api.triplydb.com/s/91ZiMF51i.

```
PREFIX skos: <http://www.w3.org/2004/02/skos/core#>
PREFIX geo: <http://www.w3.org/2003/01/geo/wgs84_pos#>
PREFIX crm: <http://erlangen-crm.org/current/>
PREFIX mmm-schema: <http://ldf.fi/schema/mmm/>
PREFIX mmm-actor: <http://ldf.fi/mmm/actor/>

SELECT DISTINCT
?arc_id ?from_id ?from_prefLabel ?from_lat ?from_long
?to_id ?to_prefLabel ?to_lat ?to_long
(COUNT(DISTINCT ?manuscript) as ?instanceCount)
WHERE {
    ?manuscript crm:P51_has_former_or_current_owner
        mmm-actor:bodley_person_73979081 ; # Sir Thomas Phillipps
        ^crm:P108_has_produced/crm:P7_took_place_at ?from_id ;
        mmm-schema:last_known_location ?to_id .
    ?from_id skos:prefLabel ?from_prefLabel ;
            geo:lat ?from_lat ;
            geo:long ?from_long .
    ?to_id skos:prefLabel ?to_prefLabel ;
        geo:lat ?to_lat ;
        geo:long ?to_long .
    BIND(IRI(CONCAT(STR(?from_id), "-", REPLACE(STR(?to_id),
    "http://ldf.fi/mmm/place/", ""))) as ?arc_id)
    FILTER(?from_id != ?to_id) # ignore manuscripts that have stayed put
}
GROUP BY ?arc_id ?from_id ?from_prefLabel ?from_lat ?from_long
?to_id ?to_prefLabel ?to_lat ?to_long
ORDER BY desc(?instanceCount)
```

The query fetches all unique arcs from place of production to last known location, and counts how many manuscripts have travelled that route. The number of manuscripts is used for scaling the width of the arcs in the interactive visualization. Manuscripts are limited to those owned by Sir Thomas Phillipps at some point of time. Here the benefits of the LOD approach implemented in the MMM data conversion pipeline can be clearly seen: the Bibale[28], SDBM[29], and MMOL[30] records for Sir Thomas have been merged into one MMM record[31], and all references in the data have been corrected to point to this unified record.

Due to missing data, only place of production and last known location are used in the query. If there were more complete and harmonized data in the source databases about the locations and dates of the manuscripts throughout their histories, the query could be expanded for visualizing the full details of the movement of a limited group of individual manuscripts as series of arcs numbered in chronological order.

Experiences in using the MMM data service by SPARQL are discussed in more depth in [2].

5   Implementation: MMM Portal and Data Service

MMM Portal. The user interface of the MMM Portal is implemented as a web-based application[32], written purely in JavaScript. The general architecture, provided

---

[28] http://bibale.irht.cnrs.fr/933.

[29] https://sdbm.library.upenn.edu/names/7182.

[30] https://medieval.bodleian.ox.ac.uk/catalog/person_73979081.

[31] http://ldf.fi/mmm/actor/bodley_person_73979081.

[32] https://github.com/SemanticComputing/mmm-web-app.

by the Sampo-UI framework [17], is presented in Fig. 6. The application consists of a NodeJS[33] backend build with Express framework[34] (top right) and a client based on React[35] and Redux[36] (top left). The client makes use of base maps from external map services (bottom left). The MMM Data Service is shown on the bottom right corner.

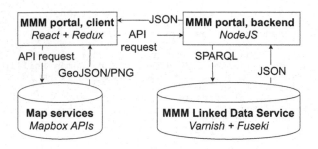

Fig. 6. MMM Portal architecture

MMM Linked Data Service. The MMM knowledge graph is published on the Linked Data Finland platform, which is powered by a combination of Fuseki SPARQL server[37] for storing the primary data[38] and a Varnish Cache web application accelerator[39] for routing URIs, content negotiation, and caching.

Deployment. The portal and the data service implementation are based on a microservice architecture, using Docker containers[40]. Each individual component (MMM Portal, Varnish, Fuseki) is run in its own dedicated container, making the deployment of the services easy due to installation of software dependencies in isolated environments, enhancing the portability of the services.

Currently, we use as an underlying technical infrastructure a combination of the OpenShift container cloud[41] (MMM Portal, Varnish) and virtual machines on the OpenStack cloud platform[42] (Fuseki), provided by the CSC – IT Center for Science, Finland. By using containers, the services can be migrated to another computing environment in a straightforward way, and third parties can re-use and run the services on their own. The container architecture also allows for horizontal scaling for high availability, by starting new container replicas based on demand.

---

[33] https://nodejs.org/en/.

[34] https://expressjs.com.

[35] https://reactjs.org.

[36] https://redux.js.org.

[37] https://jena.apache.org/documentation/fuseki2/.

[38] https://github.com/mapping-manuscript-migrations/mmm-fuseki.

[39] https://varnish-cache.org.

[40] https://www.docker.com.

[41] https://www.openshift.com.

[42] https://www.openstack.org.

6   Discussion

Evaluation. Usability of the MMM Portal based on the Sampo model has been evaluated by researchers in manuscript studies in [5]. The overall conclusion of the evaluation report was that "the MMM portal is an excellent tool, and very easy to use". However, the testers also made several suggestions for further development related to usability and noted that it is not easy to differentiate the challenges between the quality of the underlying data and portal design. According to [3] the evaluation showed that the portal performed significantly better than the original current interfaces and was capable of fully answering most of the original 25 research questions about manuscript history and provenance set in the beginning of the project. Also using the MMM Linked Data service has been deemed useful as discussed in [2]. The manuscript researchers now have a flexible way to access their enriched data and, for example, the researchers at the Schoenberg Institute started to arrange weekly "SPARQL Wednesdays" for learning more about the technology and the data. The ability to find interesting knowledge from the MMM Portal has been noted also by R. Engels in [7].

Thus far the MMM Portal has been used by 8400 distinct users from Hong Kong (18 %), US (17 %), UK (9 %), France (7 %), Italy (6 %), and from other countries (131 countries in total), according to Google Analytics.

Related Work. There are various online resources for studying manuscripts, in addition to the databases of our research, such as *e-codices – Virtual Manuscript Library of Switzerland*[43], *vHMML*[44] initiative of the Hill Museum & Manuscript Library, *METAscripta*[45], *Biblissima*[46] [8], and *Digital Scriptorium*[47]. These aggregate manuscript information from multiple sources and make the information accessible from a single user interface. Metadata about manuscripts is harmonized to some extent, for search purposes, but the provenance metadata is shallow or it doesn't exist. Instead of metadata, many of these systems focus on delivering high quality images of manuscripts to manuscript scholars and other interested users. The *Digitized Medieval Manuscripts*[48] project is producing a map of manuscript repositories around the world.

Challenges in connecting data from manuscript collections are discussed in [1] along with an overview of existing quantitative research on aggregated manuscript data. There are some existing Semantic Web approaches for harmonizing manuscript collections, of which most are based on CIDOC CRM and FRBRoo. Modeling rare and unique documents like manuscripts using CIDOC CRM and FRBRoo has been studied in [20], and we have used the insights of the study to guide the modeling work. Zhitomirsky et al. [33] have modelled a catalog of post-medieval Hebrew manuscripts as Linked Data using, e.g. FRBRoo, and provided a decomposition analysis of the data, and built prototype user interfaces for the data.

---

[43] http://www.e-codices.unifr.ch/en.
[44] https://www.vhmml.org.
[45] https://metascripta.org.
[46] https://biblissima.fr.
[47] https://digital-scriptorium.org.
[48] https://digitizedmedievalmanuscripts.org.

The ideas behind the Sampo model have been explored and developed before in different contexts. For example, the notion of collaborative content creation by data linking is a fundamental idea behind the Linked Open Data Cloud movement[49] and has been developed also in various other settings, e.g., in ResearchSpace[50]. The idea of providing multiple analyses and visualizations to a set of filtered search results has been used in other portals, such as the ePistolarium[51] [26] for epistolary data, and using multiple perspectives have been studied as an approach in decision making [21]. Faceted search [10,30,31], also know as "view-based search" and "dynamic ontologies", is a well-known paradigm for explorative search and browsing [22] in computer science and information retrieval, based on S. R. Ranganathan's original ideas of faceted classification in Library Science in the 1930's. The two step usage model is used in prosopographical research [32] (without the faceted search component). The novelty of the Sampo model lies in combining several ideas and operationalizing them for developing applications in Digital Humanities, and for delivering the solutions related to user interfaces for re-use in the open source Sampo-UI framework [17].

Lessons Learned. The premodern manuscript data turned out in many ways more challenging from a data modeling and technical perspectives than expected. Defining the very concept of "the manuscript" itself raised many ontological modeling questions, since manuscripts can be just fragments of a whole, can be separated into parts, copied, annotated, and united to others over time. Also the data from three sources was very heterogeneous and represented both documents and their provenance. A major goal of the MMM project was to map manuscript migrations in spatio-temporal spaces using maps and timelines, but references to locations in many cases are missing, the mentions refer to historical places that may not exist on modern maps or may have changed over hundreds of years of history, and initially many placenames mentioned were not even geocoded. The data are often incomplete, uncertain, and imprecise in many ways. The amount of data is also large, hundreds of thousands of records, which set efficiency challenges for the technical solutions.

The project started by creating a list of Digital Humanities research questions relating to manuscript histories, and continued by trying to figure out what kind of data model and data are needed to solve them. In spite of the challenges related to the data, the Linked Open Data approach and Sampo model turned out to be successful in the helping the researchers in solving their research question, and managed in our mind to set a new norm for the state-of-the-art for supporting DH research in manuscript studies for further research.

Acknowledgements. Thanks to Antoine Brix, Doug Emery, Mitch Fraas, Benjamin Heller, David Lewis, Synnøve Myking, Kevin Page, Pierre-Louis Pinault, Guillaume Porte, Emma Thomson, Athanasios Velios, Pip Willcox and other members of the project team for discussions and collaboration. Our work was funded by the Trans-Atlantic Platform under its Digging into Data Challenge https://diggingintodata.org for 2017–2019. The project was led by the University of Oxford, in partnership with the University of Pennsylvania, Aalto University and

---

[49] https://lod-cloud.net.

[50] https://www.researchspace.org.

[51] http://ckcc.huygens.knaw.nl.

Helsinki Centre for Digital Humanities (HELDIG) at the University of Helsinki, and the Institut de recherche et d'histoire des textes (IRHT). The technical development presented in this paper was funded mainly by the Academy of Finland. CSC – IT Center for Science provided computational resources for the project.

References

1. Burrows, T.: Connecting medieval and renaissance manuscript collections. Open Libr. Humanit. **4**(2) (2018). https://doi.org/10.16995/olh.269
2. Burrows, T., Cleaver, L., Emery, D., Koho, M., Ransom, L., Thomson, E.: Using SPARQL to investigate the research potential of an aggregated linked open data dataset: the Mapping Manuscript Migrations project. DH Benelux (2021)
3. Burrows, T., et al.: Mapping Manuscript Migrations: Digging into data for researching the history and provenance of medieval and renaissance manuscripts (white paper), August 2020. https://diggingintodata.org/file/1281/download?token=x59u8fFQ
4. Burrows, T., Hyvönen, E., Ransom, L., Wijsman, H.: Mapping Manuscript Migrations. Digging into data for the history and provenance of medieval and renaissance manuscripts. Manuscript Studies J. Schoenberg Institute Manuscript Studies **3**(1), 249–252 (2018)
5. Burrows, T., Pinto, N.B., Cazals, M., Gaudin, A., Wijsman, H.: Evaluating a semantic portal for the "Mapping Manuscript Migrations" project. DigItalia **2**, 178–185 (2020). http://digitalia.sbn.it/article/view/2643
6. Clemens, R., Graham, T.: Introduction to Manuscript Studies. Cornell University Press, Ithaca (2007)
7. Engels, R.: Digital scholarship and medieval manuscripts: access, technologies and potential. In: Payer, B.A., Wall, A. (eds.) Illuminating Life: Manuscript Pages of the Middle Ages. The University of Guelph (2020)
8. Frunzeanu, E., Robineau, R., MacDonald, E.: Biblissima's choices of tools and methodology for interoperability purposes = Biblissima: selección de herramientas y de metodología para fomentar la interoperabilidad. CIAN-Revista de Historia de las Universidades **19**, 115–132 (2016). https://doi.org/10.20318/cian.2016.3146
9. Gardiner, E., Musto, R.G.: The Digital Humanities: A Primer for Students and Scholars. Cambridge University Press, New York (2015). https://doi.org/10.1017/CBO9781139003865
10. Hearst, M.: Design recommendations for hierarchical faceted search interfaces. In: ACM SIGIR Workshop on Faceted Search, Seattle, WA, pp. 1–5 (2006)
11. Heath, T., Bizer, C.: Linked Data: Evolving the Web into a Global Data Space, 1st edn. Synthesis Lectures on the Semantic Web: Theory and Technology. Morgan & Claypool (2011). http://linkeddatabook.com/editions/1.0/
12. Hyvönen, E.: Publishing and Using Cultural Heritage Linked Data on the Semantic Web. Synthesis Lectures on the Semantic Web: Theory and Technology. Morgan & Claypool, Palo Alto (2012)
13. Hyvönen, E., Tuominen, J., Alonen, M., Mäkelä, E.: Linked Data Finland: a 7-star model and platform for publishing and re-using linked datasets. In: Presutti, V., Blomqvist, E., Troncy, R., Sack, H., Papadakis, I., Tordai, A. (eds.) ESWC 2014. LNCS, vol. 8798, pp. 226–230. Springer, Cham (2014). https://doi.org/10.1007/978-3-319-11955-7_24
14. Hyvönen, E.: Using the semantic web in digital humanities: shift from data publishing to data-analysis and serendipitous knowledge discovery. Semantic Web **11**(1), 187–193 (2020). https://doi.org/10.3233/SW-190386
15. Hyvönen, E.: Digital humanities on the Semantic Web: Sampo model and portal series (2021, submitted). https://seco.cs.aalto.fi/publications/2021/hyvonen-sampo-model-2021.pdf

16. Hyvönen, E., Tuominen, J., Kauppinen, T., Väätäinen, J.: Representing and utilizing changing historical places as an ontology time series. In: Ashish, N., Sheth, A. (eds.) Geospatial Semantics and Semantic Web: Foundations, Algorithms, and Applications, pp. 1–25. Springer, Boston (2011). https://doi.org/10.1007/978-1-4419-9446-2_1

17. Ikkala, E., Hyvönen, E., Rantala, H., Koho, M.: Sampo-UI: A full stack JavaScript framework for developing semantic portal user interfaces. Semantic Web - Interoperability, Usability, Applicability (2021, in press). http://www.semantic-web-journal.net/

18. Koho, M., et al.: Harmonizing and publishing heterogeneous pre-modern manuscript metadata as linked open data. J. Assoc. Inf. Sci. Technol. (JASIST) 1–18 (2021). https://doi.org/10.1002/asi.24499

19. Koho, M., et al.: Mapping Manuscript Migrations knowledge graph (2021). https://doi.org/10.5281/zenodo.4440464

20. Le Boef, P.: Modeling rare and unique documents: using FRBRoo/CIDOC CRM. J. Arch. Organ. 10(2), 96–106 (2012). https://doi.org/10.1080/15332748.2012.709164

21. Linstone, H.A.: Multiple perspectives: concept, applications, and user guidelines. Syst. Pract. 2(3), 307–331 (1989). https://doi.org/10.1007/BF01059977

22. Marchionini, G.: Exploratory search: from finding to understanding. Commun. ACM 49(4), 41–46 (2006). https://doi.org/10.1145/1121949.1121979

23. McCarty, W.: Humanities Computing. Palgrave, London (2005)

24. Moretti, F.: Distant Reading. Verso Books (2013)

25. Peroni, S., Shotton, D., Vitali, F.: The live OWL documentation environment: a tool for the automatic generation of ontology documentation. In: ten Teije, A., et al. (eds.) EKAW 2012. LNCS (LNAI), vol. 7603, pp. 398–412. Springer, Heidelberg (2012). https://doi.org/10.1007/978-3-642-33876-2_35

26. Ravenek, W., van den Heuvel, C., Gerritsen, G.: The ePistolarium: Origins and techniques. In: van Hessen, A., Odijk, J. (eds.) CLARIN in the Low Countries, pp. 317–323. Ubiquity Press (2017). 10.5334/bbi

27. Riva, P., Doerr, M., Žumer, M.: FRBRoo: enabling a common view of information from memory institutions. Int. Cataloguing Bibliographic Control 38(2), 30–34 (2009)

28. Shultz, K.: What is distant reading? New York Times, 24 June 2011

29. Southall, H., Mostern, R., Berman, M.L.: On historical gazetteers. Int. J. Humanit. Arts Comput. 5(2), 127–145 (2011)

30. Tunkelang, D.: Faceted search. Synth. Lect. Inf. Concepts Retr. Serv. 1(1), 1–80 (2009)

31. Tzitzikas, Y., Manolis, N., Papadakos, P.: Faceted exploration of RDF/S datasets: a survey. J. Intell. Inf. Syst. 48(2), 329–364 (2017)

32. Verboven, K., Carlier, M., Dumolyn, J.: A short manual to the art of prosopography. In: Prosopography Approaches and Applications. A handbook, pp. 35–70. Unit for Prosopographical Research (Linacre College) (2007). 1854/8212

33. Zhitomirsky-Geffet, M., Prebor, G.: Toward an ontopedia for historical Hebrew manuscripts. Front. Digital Humanit. 3, 3 (2016). https://doi.org/10.3389/fdigh.2016.00003

Wikibase as an Infrastructure for Knowledge Graphs: The EU Knowledge Graph

Dennis Diefenbach[1,2]([✉])([iD]), Max De Wilde[3]([✉])([iD]), and Samantha Alipio[4]

[1] The QA Company, Saint-Etienne, France
dennis.diefenbach@univ-st-etienne.fr
[2] Université de Lyon, CNRS UMR 5516 Laboratoire Hubert Curien, Lyon, France
[3] Université libre de Bruxelles, Brussels, Belgium
max.de.wilde@ulb.be
[4] Wikimedia Deutschland, Berlin, Germany

Abstract. Knowledge graphs are being deployed in many enterprises and institutions. An easy-to-use, well-designed infrastructure for such knowledge graphs is not obvious. After the success of Wikidata, many institutions are looking at the software infrastructure behind it, namely Wikibase.

In this paper we introduce Wikibase, describe its different software components and the tools that have emerged around it. In particular, we detail how Wikibase is used as the infrastructure behind the "EU Knowledge Graph", which is deployed at the European Commission. This graph mainly integrates projects funded by the European Union, and is used to make these projects visible to and easily accessible by citizens with no technical background.

Moreover, we explain how this deployment compares to a more classical approach to building RDF knowledge graphs, and point to other projects that are using Wikibase as an underlying infrastructure.

Keywords: Knowledge graph · Wikibase · EU Knowledge Graph

1 Introduction

Wikibase[1] is the software that runs Wikidata[2] [12]. Wikidata evolved into a central hub on the web of data and one of the largest existing knowledge graphs, with 93 million items maintained by a community effort. Since its launch, an impressive 1.3 billion edits have been made by 20 000+ active users.[3] Today, Wikidata contains information about a wide range of topics such as people, taxons, countries, chemical compounds, astronomical objects, and more. This

---

[1] https://wikiba.se.
[2] https://www.wikidata.org.
[3] https://www.wikidata.org/wiki/Wikidata:Statistics.

© Springer Nature Switzerland AG 2021
A. Hotho et al. (Eds.): ISWC 2021, LNCS 12922, pp. 631–647, 2021.
https://doi.org/10.1007/978-3-030-88361-4_37

information is linked to other key data repositories maintained by institutions such as Eurostat, the German National Library, the BBC, and many others, using 6 000+ external identifiers.[4] The knowledge from Wikidata is used by search engines such as Google Search, and smart assistants including Siri, Alexa, and Google Assistant in order to provide more structured results. While one of the main success factors of Wikidata is its community of editors, the software behind it also plays an important role. It enables the numerous editors to modify a substantial data repository in a scalable, multilingual, collaborative effort.

Because of the success of Wikidata, many projects and institutions are looking into Wikibase, the software that runs Wikidata. Their objective is mainly to reuse the software to construct domain-specific knowledge graphs. Besides this success, two main factors make Wikibase attractive: 1) the fact that it is a well-maintained open source software, and 2) the fact that there is a rich ecosystem of users and tools around it. Moreover, Wikimedia Deutschland (WMDE), the maintainer of Wikibase, has made considerable investments toward optimising the use of the software outside of Wikidata or other Wikimedia projects. Since 2019, Wikibase has had a separate product roadmap[5] and its own driving strategy based on the diverse needs of the many institutions, researchers, and individuals who depend upon the software for their projects.

In this paper, we show how Wikibase can be used as the infrastructure of a knowledge graph. While Wikibase as a standalone piece of software has been available for several years, there are not many production systems using it. We detail how Wikibase is used to host the infrastructure of a knowledge graph at the European Commission called "The EU Knowledge Graph".[6] This graph contains heterogeneous data items such as countries, buildings, and projects funded by the European Union. It is used to serve multiple services such as the Kohesio website[7] that aims to make projects funded by the EU easily accessible by citizens. Several bots help to enrich the data and to keep it up-to-date. Beside the EU Knowledge Graph, we point to other relevant Wikibase deployments.

The paper is organized as follows. In Sect. 2, we list some notable knowledge graphs and describe how they are deployed. In Sect. 3, we describe Wikibase and how it can be used to set up a local knowledge graph. In Sect. 4, we describe the instance that we deployed at the European Commission, including how the data is ingested, what is the current content, how it is maintained using bots, what services are offered for public consumption, and finally Kohesio, the service that is mainly served by it. In Sect. 5, we provide a short comparison between a typical approach to deploying knowledge graphs and our approach using a Wikibase instance. In Sect. 6, we present other projects that are also using Wikibase. We conclude and point to future work in Sect. 7.

---

[4] The exact number is growing every day and can be tracked at https://w.wiki/3BSZ.
[5] https://www.wikidata.org/wiki/Wikidata:Development_plan#Wikibase_ecosystem.
[6] https://linkedopendata.eu.
[7] https://kohesio.eu.

2   Related Work

Knowledge graphs [6] are data structures that are well-suited to store heterogeneous information. Many enterprises and institutions create knowledge
graphs. Generally, one distinguishes between Open Knowledge Graphs, which
are intended to share knowledge with the general public, and Enterprise Knowledge Graphs, which are used to store and model internal or restricted knowledge.

Domain-specific Open Knowledge Graphs include, for example, the Sci-
Graph[8] [3] which aims to aggregate metadata about the publications of Springer
Nature. Recently, a knowledge graph about companies has been constructed with
the aim of discovering aggressive tax planning strategies[9] [8]. Europeana[10] [4],
a platform that aggregates the digitised collections of more than 3 000 institutions across Europe, releases its collections as an RDF graph.[11] The common
pattern behind these knowledge graphs is that they generally are constructed
by: (1) defining an underlying RDF data model, (2) integrating heterogeneous
information across different data sources using this model and (3) exposing it
using a triplestore.

Enterprise Knowledge Graphs are deployed at Google,[12] Airbnb,[13] Amazon,[14] LinkedIn,[15] etc. Since these graphs are not public, the technology stacks
used to create and maintain them are largely unknown.

The tool closest to Wikibase is Semantic MediaWiki[16] [7], which also allows
the integration and editing of knowledge in a collaborative effort. The main
difference is that Semantic MediaWiki is developed for visualizing and using
data within the wiki itself. Wikibase, on the other hand, has been developed to
collaboratively create and maintain knowledge which then can be consumed by
external applications.

3   Wikibase

In this section, we describe the different technological components that make up
the core of Wikibase. It is important to understand that "Wikibase" is often used
to refer to different things. We use the term Wikibase for all services and software
components included in the Wikibase Docker container,[17] which is generally
seen as the standard way to deploy a local Wikibase instance. All components
described in this section are summarized in Fig. 1.

---

[8] https://www.springernature.com/gp/researchers/scigraph.
[9] http://taxgraph.informatik.uni-mannheim.de.
[10] https://www.europeana.eu.
[11] https://pro.europeana.eu/page/linked-open-data.
[12] https://blog.google/products/search/introducing-knowledge-graph-things-not/.
[13] https://medium.com/airbnb-engineering/scaling-knowledge-access-and-retrieval-
at-airbnb-665b6ba21e95.
[14] https://www.amazon.science/blog/building-product-graphs-automatically.
[15] https://engineering.linkedin.com/blog/2016/10/building-the-linkedin-knowledge-
graph.
[16] https://www.semantic-mediawiki.org.
[17] https://github.com/wmde/wikibase-docker.

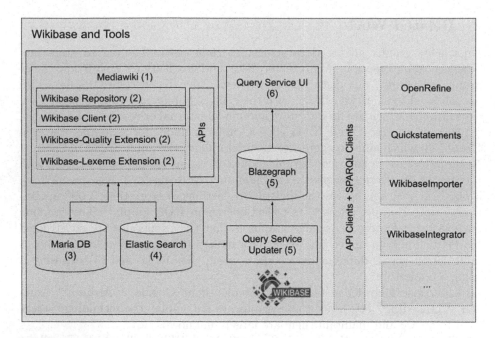

Fig. 1. Architecture of Wikibase. On the left, the core Wikibase infrastructure; on the right, the services that are constructed around it using the different MediaWiki APIs and SPARQL clients. In yellow, we have highlighted the places where the data is stored. The arrows indicate the direction of the data flows. (Color figure online)

3.1 Wikibase Infrastructure

The Wikibase infrastructure consists of the following software components:

- MediaWiki, a wiki engine that is mainly known as the software running Wikipedia. MediaWiki started in 2002 and is continuously developed by the Wikimedia Foundation. It is mainly written in PHP and there is a vibrant ecosystem of extensions around it, i.e. components that allow the customization of how a MediaWiki installation looks and works. Today, there are more than 1 800 extensions available.
- Wikibase itself includes several of these extensions. The main extensions are the Wikibase Repository[18] and the Wikibase Client.[19] While MediaWiki was originally designed to store unstructured data, the Wikibase extensions modify it for use as a structured data repository and improve the user-friendliness of its interface. There are two more extensions that play an important role in Wikidata but which are not included in the Wikibase Docker file: the Wikibase Quality Extension[20] and the Wikibase Lexemes extension.[21] The first

---

[18] https://www.mediawiki.org/wiki/Extension:Wikibase_Repository.

[19] https://www.mediawiki.org/wiki/Extension:Wikibase_Client.

[20] https://www.mediawiki.org/wiki/Extension:Wikibase_Quality_Extensions.

[21] https://www.mediawiki.org/wiki/Extension:WikibaseLexeme.

was designed to enable Wikibase users to define ontological constraints and detect if they are not respected at the data level. This includes, for example, the definition of domain and range constraints. The goal of the second extension is to allow the modeling of lexical entities such as words and phrases. The first extension is very useful for managing knowledge graphs and is used in the EU Knowledge Graph. The Lexemes extension, on the other hand, is not used. All these extensions are developed and maintained by WMDE and written in PHP.

- All the data is stored natively in a MariaDB[22] relational database. This includes the user management, permission management, the full log of the change history, the pages, and more.[23] The above-mentioned extensions also store data in this database, including the item list, the properties, and the changes.[24]
- The core Wikibase infrastructure includes an Elasticsearch instance. This instance is responsible for the "search-as-you-type" completion that is used to search and edit the data. Moreover, it is used for full-text search over all labels and descriptions.
- While the data is stored in a relational database, it is also exported into a triplestore which is a Blazegraph derivative maintained by the Wikimedia Foundation. Wikibase does not only provide the triplestore but tightly integrates it into the rest of the infrastructure so that changes in the relational database are directly reflected in the triplestore. A process called updater monitors the changes and reflects them in the triplestore at an interval of 10 s.
- The final Wikibase component is the SPARQL user interface. This offers a user interface for editing SPARQL, querying the data, and exporting the results in various formats (JSON, CSV/TSV, HTML...). It also offers different widgets for rendering the result sets in graphs, charts, maps, and more.

All of these software components make up the core infrastructure of Wikibase. The complexity is hidden inside a Docker container that is provided by WMDE, which allows for simple set up of a local Wikibase instance. While the Docker container considerably reduces the effort needed to maintain such an instance, it is still crucial to understand all components and how they interact in order to run, maintain, and customize the instance.

3.2 Tools

Around the Wikibase core infrastructure, there is a rich number of additional tools. These can be either MediaWiki extensions or external tools that are connected to MediaWiki through its APIs. In particular, there are client libraries

---

wrapped around the Wikibase API[25] for different programming languages. The most notable include Pywikibot[26] for Python, the Wikidata Toolkit[27] for Java, and the wikibase-javascript-api[28] for JavaScript.

One particular type of tools are Bots,[29] i.e. programs that edit the data in a Wikibase without human intervention. Since Wikibase is the software used by Wikidata, every tool developed for Wikidata can in theory be used also for a custom Wikibase instance, although some adaptation might be necessary. A publicly maintained list of tools around Wikidata can be found at https://www.wikidata.org/wiki/Wikidata:Tools.

Some popular tools that are used in combination with a local Wikibase instance are:

- OpenRefine[30] [11], a tool for working with messy data: cleaning it, transforming it from one format into another, and extending it with web services and external data. OpenRefine provides a native Wikidata reconciliation service that can be extended to other Wikibase instances.[31]
- WikibaseImport,[32] a Wikimedia extension for importing entities from Wikidata into a local Wikibase.
- QuickStatements,[33] a tool to import and edit data in a Wikibase using a simplified, non-programmatic language.
- WikibaseIntegrator,[34] a Python library for creating bots on top of Wikibase.
- WikibaseManifest,[35] an extension that provides an API endpoint allowing automated configuration discovery. The endpoint returns important metadata about the local Wikibase and can be used to configure external tools.
- EntitySchema,[36] an extension for storing Shape Expression (ShEx) Schemas on wiki pages. ShEx [9] is a language for validating and describing RDF.

4   The EU Knowledge Graph

As described above, it is relatively straightforward to set up an empty Wikibase instance with many services that are offered out of the box. In this section, we describe the workflow that we followed to build the EU Knowledge Graph which is available at https://linkedopendata.eu. This includes how we initialized the graph, how we ingest data, how we maintain it, which services we provide, and which services rely on it.

---

[25] https://www.mediawiki.org/wiki/Wikibase/API.
[26] https://www.mediawiki.org/wiki/Manual:Pywikibot.
[27] https://www.mediawiki.org/wiki/Wikidata_Toolkit.
[28] https://github.com/wikimedia/wikibase-javascript-api.
[29] https://www.wikidata.org/wiki/Wikidata:Bots.
[30] https://openrefine.org/.
[31] https://github.com/wetneb/openrefine-wikibase/.
[32] https://github.com/Wikidata/WikibaseImport.
[33] https://www.wikidata.org/wiki/Help:QuickStatements.
[34] https://github.com/LeMyst/WikibaseIntegrator.
[35] https://www.mediawiki.org/wiki/Extension:WikibaseManifest.
[36] https://www.mediawiki.org/wiki/Extension:EntitySchema.

4.1   Creating Seed Entities and Relations

While a Wikibase instance is usually intended to ingest knowledge that is not contained in Wikidata, the latter still generally provides entities and properties that are relevant to model domain-specific knowledge. Therefore, as a first step, we identified entities in Wikidata that are relevant for the European Commission. This includes concepts like the European Union, member states, capital cities, heads of states, European institutions, and more. We imported these entities directly into our local installation using the WikibaseSync[37] tool developed during the course of the project. The tool creates two properties in the Wikibase (external identifiers) and generates, for each item and property imported from Wikidata, a corresponding entity in the local Wikibase instance.

The two external identifiers keep track of the correspondence between the items and relations in the Wikibase and in Wikidata (in particular these can be used to translate a SPARQL query over Wikidata to one over Wikibase). This first step enables the reuse of many items and properties from Wikidata that can be further used to model domain-specific knowledge. In general, we followed the policy to always reuse items and relations from Wikidata whenever possible, i.e. we introduced new items and relations in the Wikibase only if they were not preexisting in Wikidata.

4.2   A Typical Data Import

In this section, we describe a typical data import workflow. As an example, we detail how we imported data about the buildings that are occupied by the European Commission in Brussels. This includes the following steps:

– **Data collection**: All information about the buildings is made available through an API. A snippet is shown in Fig. 2.
– **Modeling**: To model this piece of data, we need the concepts of building and office, as well as properties like address, opening hours, and occupant. Whenever possible, we take Wikidata entities/properties or reuse existing entities/properties in the Wikibase. In particular, the following concepts already exist in Wikidata and were imported into the Wikibase using the WikibaseSync tool:

- Building (Q41176 in Wikidata; Q8636 in the Wikibase)
- Office (Q182060 in Wikidata; Q244596 in the Wikibase)
- the property occupant (P466 in Wikidata; P641 in the Wikibase)
- and some more...

Note that by ingesting Wikidata knowledge, we know for example that a "building" is called "Gebäude" in German, that "office" is a subclass of a "workplace", and that "phone number" is also expressed as "telephone number". In particular, this means that part of the knowledge is created by people outside the European Commission. In more specific domains, a close interaction with domain experts might be necessary to correctly understand and model the data.

---

[37] https://github.com/the-qa-company/WikibaseSync.

```
1    {
2        "type": "OFFICES",
3        "code": "BU25",
4        "name": "Beaulieu 25",
5        "photoLink": "BU25.jpg",
6        "occupants": "CNECT",
7        "contactList": {
8            "contacts": [
9                {
10                   "name": "Réception",
11                   "phone": "+32229 53818"
12               }
13           ]
14       },
15       "buildingAddress": {
16           "streetAddress": "Avenue de Beaulieu 25",
17           "gpsCoordinates": {
18               "latitude": 50.814347,
19               "longitude": 4.412298
20           }
21       }
22   }
```

Fig. 2. Snippet of the JSON API response describing buildings occupied by the European Commission.

- **Attention to identifiers**: When importing data, we make sure to always insert external identifiers so we can easily link the newly ingested data to the original data repository. For the particular building in Fig. 2 for example, we want to use the code "BU25" as an external identifier.
- **Linking**: Some entities are already present in the Wikibase, such as the occupant "CNECT" which is the Directorate-General (DG) of the European Commission for Communications Networks, Content, and Technology. The most common strategy that we use is a simple key linking, using external identifiers provided in Wikidata and/or the Wikibase instance. We take advantage of the fact that Wikidata has become established as a reference point for many datasets. The more than 6 000 external identifiers make this possible.
- **Import**: Finally, we import the data itself based on the chosen data model. The import is performed with Pywikibot.[38] The entity corresponding to the initial JSON snippet[39] is shown in Fig. 3.

---

[38] https://www.mediawiki.org/wiki/Manual:Pywikibot.
[39] https://linkedopendata.eu/entity/Q242372.

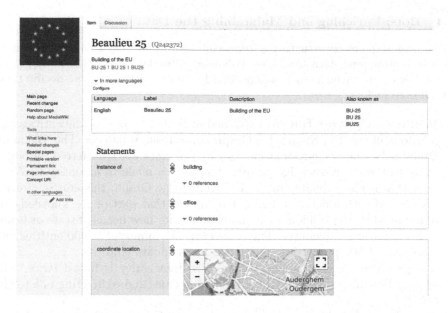

Fig. 3. View of the BU25 building in the EU Knowledge Graph.

4.3 Current Content

The current content of the EU Knowledge Graph has been imported as described above. It includes:

- institutions of the European Union (like the European Parliament and the Council of the European Union);
- countries of the world, and in particular member states of the European Union (like Hungary and Italy);
- capital cities of European countries (like Athens and Tallinn);
- DGs of the European Commission (like DG CNECT and DG REGIO);
- buildings, canteens, cafeterias and car parks of the European Commission;
- the largest part of the graph is composed of 705 108 projects[40] and 112 688 beneficiaries[41] of projects funded by the European Union under Cohesion Policy. This data has been aggregated from more than 40 Excel and CSV sheets provided in a non-standardized format by the member states of the European Union. These files describe the projects funded on a national or regional level, following EU regulations.

To date, the whole dataset comprises 96 million triples and 1 845 properties.

---

[40] Like https://linkedopendata.eu/entity/Q77409.
[41] Like https://linkedopendata.eu/entity/Q2529763.

4.4 Bots: Enriching and Maintaining the Data

Important steps in constructing a knowledge graph include data enrichment as well as maintaining data freshness. Following Wikidata practices, we deployed a number of bots which work independently and each focus on a specific task. These bots include:

- **Wikidata Updater Bot**: As explained in Sect. 4.1, some of the entities and relations of the EU Knowledge Graph come from Wikidata. The Wikidata Updater Bot makes sure that changes in Wikidata are transferred automatically to the EU Knowledge Graph. If an edit is made to an entity in Wikidata that is also available in the EU Knowledge Graph, this edit is directly transferred with a delay of 5 min. This means that part of the knowledge is maintained by the Wikidata Community, e.g. for new heads of state or heads of government of a country. There are currently almost 130 000 entities and more than 1 800 properties maintained by Wikidata editors.
- **Merger Bot**: It can happen that a Wikidata entity is linked twice. The Merger Bot takes care of merging the two entities and redirecting one to the other.
- **Translator Bot**: An important element for the European Commission is that the knowledge can be made available in multiple languages. The Translator Bot translates specific entities from one language to another. This bot relies on machine translation provided by the eTransation tool.[42]
- **Geocoding Bot**: This bot is responsible for inferring geographic coordinates from the postal code. For example, if a project includes only a postal code, the corresponding geographic coordinates are inferred with Nominatim.[43]
- **Beneficiary Linker Bot**: One key piece of information for funded projects is the beneficiary. However, this often consists of a simple string. The objective of the Linker Bot is to detect if the beneficiary is also available as an entity in Wikidata and attempt to link it. The project https://linkedopendata.eu/entity/Q77409 for instance indicates as a beneficiary "PARAFIA ŚW. ŁUKASZA EWANGELISTY W LIPNICY WIELKIEJ". The Linker Bot, based on machine learning, identifies the following Wikidata entity as a match: https://www.wikidata.org/entity/Q11811090. This allows us to enrich the data and to provide links to external sources. In this case, we are able to infer that the beneficiary is a parish of the Roman Catholic Archdiocese of Kraków whose website is http://www.parafia-lipnicawielka.pl/.
- **Beneficiary Classifier Bot**: This bot is responsible for classifying beneficiaries into public and private entities. This information is important for decision makers and for understanding how the money is spent.
- **NUTS Bot**: This bot is responsible for inferring the NUTS3[44] statistical region in which a project is contained from its geographic coordinates.

---

[42] https://ec.europa.eu/cefdigital/wiki/display/CEFDIGITAL/eTranslation.
[43] https://nominatim.openstreetmap.org.
[44] https://ec.europa.eu/eurostat/web/nuts/background.

Fig. 4. Query displaying all projects in France funded by the EU under Cohesion Policy, using the query service available at https://query.linkedopendata.eu.

4.5 Services

While it is important to collect and maintain the knowledge, it is also crucial to make it easily consumable. Besides the user-friendly interface of Wikibase, we offer three ways to consume the data:

1. Data Exports: we provide full dumps of the data after the Wikidata fashion. The dumps are available at https://data.linkedopendata.eu. Moreover, we provide CSV/Excel exports of specific parts of the data for people not familiar with RDF.
2. Query Service: the standard query service of the Wikibase is available at https://query.linkedopendata.eu. Like Wikidata, it allows for the retrieval and visualisation of information. A screenshot is displayed in Fig. 4.
3. Question Answering Service: we offer QAnswer [2] as a question answering service. It enables access to data in the knowledge graph via natural language queries. The service is available at https://qa.linkedopendata.eu and is shown in Fig. 5.

4.6 Kohesio

Currently, the EU Knowledge Graph is mainly used as the data repository of the Kohesio project available at https://kohesio.eu (see Fig. 6). Kohesio aims to collect the data of projects funded in the frame of the EU Cohesion Policy, which supports tens of thousands of projects across Europe annually. This is done through funding programmes whose management is shared between national and regional authorities on the one hand, and the European Commission on the other hand. Kohesio is still under development and is scheduled to be launched officially during the first quarter of 2022.

Fig. 5. Question answering service https://qa.linkedopendata.eu for the question "projects in the Loire department with a budget higher than 100 000 euros".

The projects are imported from several files published by the member states, aligned into a common data model, and enriched with additional information using bots. All data used by the website is extracted from the EU Knowledge Graph via SPARQL queries, exposed as REST APIs.[45]

5   Comparing Classical Approach vs Wikibase

In this section, we compare at a high level the differences between a classical RDF knowledge graph deployment and a Wikibase deployment. By a classical RDF deployment, we mean a knowledge graph that is constructed and maintained as described in Sect. 2: (1) defining an underlying RDF data model, (2) integrating heterogeneous information across different data sources using the model, and (3) exposing it using a triplestore. We summarize the differences in Table 1.

In a classical deployment, Semantic Web technologies are central. This allows, for example, the usage of reasoning and RDF-related technologies like SHACL, which is not the case for Wikibase as it does not natively store the data as RDF but only exposes it in this format. Despite this difference, the Wikibase community runs into problems that are similar to those encountered in the Semantic Web community. They address some of these issues in a different way, such as the Wikibase Quality Extensions mentioned above.

One of the drawbacks of Wikibase is that it does not allow the reuse of external RDF vocabularies. Entities and properties will always be QIDs and PIDs.

---

[45] Most of the code is published as open source at https://github.com/ec-doris.

Fig. 6. Kohesio interface showing projects around Europe about "incubators".

The only available workaround is to create items and properties in Wikibase, and indicate using a custom property that they are equivalent to some RDF vocabulary. Moreover, the data model of Wikibase is more restrictive than the general RDF data model. For example, blank nodes are not allowed and the datatype of the object of a property must be defined at creation time. It is therefore not possible to define a property that has both URIs and literals as objects. The data model is also more rigid because it restricts to one specific model for reification, namely n-ary [5]. This implies that it is not possible to easily import an RDF dataset into Wikibase. Additionally, a limitation of Wikibase is that the SPARQL endpoint is read-only, making it impossible to insert or update data via SPARQL. All data has to be ingested using the APIs of Wikibase.

The main advantage of Wikibase is that it offers a series of services out of the box. These include: built-in visualizations in the SPARQL endpoint (like in Fig. 4), an automatic full-text search as well as a search-as-you-type functionality over the items and properties, and a simple interface to edit the data even by non-expert users. All these functionalities can also be offered in classical RDF deployments, but need special infrastructure. Another important feature is full tracking of changes. It is therefore always possible to see who contributed to the knowledge. This is important in scenarios were multiple people edit the data. We are not aware of a solution that achieves this functionality in a classical deployment.

In general, one can say that a classical deployment allows full flexibility but requires a lot of specific infrastructure to provide functionalities like data visualisation, editing, etc. Conversely, Wikibase is more rigid but provides many out-of-the-box services, as well as a deep integration into a well-established ecosystem.

Table 1. Classical RDF infrastructure vs Wikibase

	Classical approach	Wikibase
RDF support	Full support	The information can be dumped as RDF but is not natively in this format. RDF data is hard to ingest
Reuse of external vocabularies and ontologies	Full support	One cannot use external vocabularies directly, but only align them with new properties in the Wikibase
Scalability	Depending on the underlying triplestore	Ingesting large datasets is time-consuming but some projects are trying to address this issue[a] [10]
Updating queries	Relying on SPARQL	Not possible over SPARQL, since the endpoint is read-only. Only through the Wikibase APIs
Data model	Flexible	Rigid. For example, the reification model is fixed but well established
Visualisation	A particular software has to be installed[b]	Out-of-the-box
Editing the data	A plugin is needed	Out-of-the-box
Search	A plugin is needed	Out-of-the-box with Elasticsearch
Track changes	Unclear	Out-of-the-box
Recent changes	Unclear	Out-of-the-box

[a]Like https://github.com/UB-Mannheim/RaiseWikibase.
[b]Such as the Virtuoso Faceted Browser

6 In-use Wikibase Instances

Besides the EU Knowledge Graph, there are several Wikibase instances used by different institutions and communities. These deployments are either in a testing, pilot, or production phase. On a voluntary basis, it is possible to register a Wikibase instance in the Wikibase Registry.[46] Here are some notable projects:

- L'Agence bibliographique de l'enseignement supérieur (ABES) and the Bibliothèque nationale de France (BnF) are currently building a shared platform for collaboratively creating and maintaining reference data about entities (persons, corporate bodies, places, concepts, creative works, etc.) which will be initially used by the Bibliothèque nationale de France and all the French Higher Education Libraries, and in a second phase by other cultural institutions (archives, museums). Its initial deployment is planned for 2023.

[46] https://wikibase-registry.wmflabs.org (the full list of instances can be accessed at https://tinyurl.com/y8xun3wy).

- The Enslaved.org project [13], available at https://enslaved.org/, aims to track the movements and details of people in the historical slave trade. The main objective of the project is to allow students, researchers, and the general public to search over numerous databases in order to reconstruct the lives of individuals who were part of the slave trade. The Enslaved.org project uses Wikibase as the main infrastructure to integrate the data from heterogeneous sources. The instance is available at https://lod.enslaved.org. QuickStatements is mainly used to clean, ingest, and model the data. The project was released in December, 2020.
- The Deutsche Nationalbibliothek[47] (DNB) is running a multi-year pilot to provide their Integrated Authority File (GND) with an alternative website. The objective is to make the free structured authority data easier to access and interoperable, and Wikibase is seen as a user-friendly solution to host and maintain the GND containing more than 9 million items. QuickStatements and Wikidata Integrator have been tested to ingest the data into the Wikibase, although a quicker custom application is now being developed. Besides the instance containing the actual authority files, a second Wikibase instance will provide all rules and regulations as structured data items and properties. This will help improve the usability of the documentation and the quality of the data processed in the first instance via shared schemas. The pilot started in 2019 and is planned to go live in 2023.
- The Archives of Luxembourg are experimenting with Wikibase to integrate data from 8 different GLAM[48] institutions (like the Archives Nationales de Luxembourg and the Bibliothèque nationale de Luxembourg). These institutions will publish their catalogue in the CIDOC Conceptual Reference Model (CRM), an extensible ontology for concepts and information in the cultural heritage domain. This data can then be ingested into a Wikibase and synchronised across institutions.
- Factgrid[49] is run by the Gotha Research Centre Germany at the University of Erfurt. It started out as a project to track the activities of the Illuminati, but it is now a collaborative, multilingual digital humanities project that collects historical research data. It uses Wikibase and has over 150 active community members.
- Wikimedia Commons uses Wikibase to enhance over 57 million CC0 media files with structured data.[50] Wikibase users can easily link entities within their instance to relevant images on Commons. A SPARQL endpoint is also provided.[51]
- Rhizome[52] is dedicated to the preservation and promotion of digital art and was among the earliest adopters of Wikibase in 2015. Wikibase's flexible data

---

[47] https://www.dnb.de.
[48] Galleries, libraries, archives, and museums.
[49] https://database.factgrid.de/wiki/Main_Page.
[50] https://commons.wikimedia.org/wiki/Commons:Structured_data.
[51] https://wcqs-beta.wmflabs.org.
[52] https://rhizome.org/art/artbase/.

model is used to describe a unique catalog of internet artworks with specialized preservation metadata.

– The Centre for Historical Research and Documentation on War and Contemporary Society (CegeSoma[53]) in Belgium launched a pilot Wikibase instance in the context of the ADOCHS project[54] to evaluate its added value for the management of names authority files. In the context of her PhD [1], Chardonnens explored several options and documented all configuration choices on her blog Linking the Past.[55] Based on this successful experiment, a new project about members of the Resistance is about to start.

7 Conclusion and Future Work

In this paper, we have presented how Wikibase can be used as an infrastructure for knowledge graphs. We have shown that while Wikibase is not as flexible as a traditional RDF deployment, it offers many out-of-the-box services that are either necessary or convenient for deploying a knowledge graph infrastructure. One of the biggest advantages is that it allows non-expert users to directly access the knowledge graph. Moreover, it deeply integrates into an ecosystem of tools and libraries that are widely used (mainly for Wikidata).

Wikibase development in the near-term will be focused around two core areas. The first is improving the installation, setup, and maintenance experience for Wikibase administrators. This includes – but is not limited to – establishing a regular, predictable release cycle; improving documentation around software installation and updating; creating an improved deployment pipeline for the software; and publishing improved Docker images. The second development focus for Wikibase is around the concept of federation. In the Wikibase context, federation refers to enabling different Wikibases to link their content (e.g. entities), query across instances, or share ontologies. Most often, Wikibase projects express a desire to enhance their local instance by linking with the vast amount of general-purpose knowledge on Wikidata. For this reason, WMDE will continue its earlier work[56] by making it possible to access and reuse Wikidata's properties in combination with a local data model. These efforts will lay the groundwork for more robust sharing and linking of data between Wikibases.

Acknowledgements. We would like to thank: Anne Thollard who initiated the Kohesio project and drove the use case internally at the European Commission; the team at DG REGIO for their support as domain experts and their precious advice; the team at DG CNECT for their initiative in investigating such an innovative approach and the technical deployments of the Kohesio user interface; DIGIT for following the project and giving feedback, in particular the helpful discussions with Ivo Velitchkov; Georgina

---

[53] https://www.cegesoma.be.

[54] https://adochs.arch.be.

[55] https://linkingthepast.org.

[56] https://doc.wikimedia.org/Wikibase/master/php/md_docs_components_repo-federated-properties.html.

Burnett and Jens Ohlig who coordinated the relationship between Wikimedia Deutschland and the European Commission. Finally we would like to thank the whole team of WMDE for providing great open source software, as well as the Wikidata editors for all the knowledge that they are providing every day!

References

1. Chardonnens, A.: La gestion des données d'autorité archivistiques dans le cadre du Web de données. Ph.D. thesis, Université libre de Bruxelles (2020)
2. Diefenbach, D., Both, A., Singh, K., Maret, P.: Towards a question answering system over the semantic web. Semantic Web **11**(3), 421–439 (2020)
3. Hammond, T., Pasin, M., Theodoridis, E.: Data integration and disintegration: managing springer nature scigraph with SHACL and OWL. In: ISWC (2017)
4. Haslhofer, B., Isaac, A.: data. europeana. eu: the europeana linked open data pilot. In: International Conference on Dublin Core and Metadata Applications, pp. 94–104 (2011)
5. Hernández, D., Hogan, A., Krötzsch, M.: Reifying RDF: what works well with wikidata? SSWS@ ISWC **1457**, 32–47 (2015)
6. Hogan, A., et al.: Knowledge Graphs (2021)
7. Krötzsch, M., Vrandečić, D., Völkel, M.: Semantic MediaWiki. In: Cruz, I., et al. (eds.) ISWC 2006. LNCS, vol. 4273, pp. 935–942. Springer, Heidelberg (2006). https://doi.org/10.1007/11926078_68
8. Lüdemann, N., Shiba, A., Thymianis, N., Heist, N., Ludwig, C., Paulheim, H.: A knowledge graph for assessing agressive tax planning strategies. In: Pan, J.Z., et al. (eds.) ISWC 2020. LNCS, vol. 12507, pp. 395–410. Springer, Cham (2020). https://doi.org/10.1007/978-3-030-62466-8_25
9. Prud'hommeaux, E., Labra Gayo, J.E., Solbrig, H.: Shape expressions: an RDF validation and transformation language. In: ISWC, pp. 32–40 (2014)
10. Shigapov, R., Mechnich, J., Schumm, I.: Raisewikibase: fast inserts into the BERD instance (2021)
11. Verborgh, R., De Wilde, M.: Using OpenRefine. Packt Publishing Ltd (2013)
12. Vrandečić, D., Krötzsch, M.: Wikidata: a free collaborative knowledgebase. Commun. ACM **57**(10), 78–85 (2014)
13. Zhou, L., et al.: The enslaved dataset: a real-world complex ontology alignment benchmark using wikibase. In: CIKM, pp. 3197–3204 (2020)

Leveraging Semantic Technologies for Digital Interoperability in the European Railway Domain

Julián Andrés Rojas[1]([📧]) [iD], Marina Aguado[2], Polymnia Vasilopoulou[2],
Ivo Velitchkov[3], Dylan Van Assche[1]([📧]) [iD], Pieter Colpaert[1]([📧]) [iD],
and Ruben Verborgh[1]([📧]) [iD]

[1] IDLab, Department of Electronics and Information Systems,
Ghent University – imec, Technologiepark-Zwijnaarde 122, 9052 Ghent, Belgium
{julianandres.rojasmelendez,dylan.vanassche,
pieter.colpaert,ruben.verborgh}@ugent.be
[2] European Union Agency for Railways, Lille, France
[3] DG DIGIT, Brussels, Belgium

Abstract. The European Union Agency for Railways is an European authority, tasked with the provision of a legal and technical framework to support harmonized and safe cross-border railway operations throughout the EU. So far, the agency relied on traditional application-centric approaches to support the data exchange among multiple actors interacting within the railway domain. This lead however, to isolated digital environments that consequently added barriers to digital interoperability while increasing the cost of maintenance and innovation. In this work, we show how Semantic Web technologies are leveraged to create a semantic layer for data integration across the base registries maintained by the agency. We validate the usefulness of this approach by supporting route compatibility checks, a highly demanded use case in this domain, which was not available over the agency's registries before. Our contributions include (i) an official ontology for the railway infrastructure and authorized vehicle types, including 28 reference datasets; (ii) a reusable Knowledge Graph describing the European railway infrastructure; (iii) a cost-efficient system architecture that enables high-flexibility for use case development; and (iv) an open source and RDF native Web application to support route compatibility checks. This work demonstrates how data-centric system design, powered by Semantic Web technologies and Linked Data principles, provides a framework to achieve data interoperability and unlock new and innovative use cases and applications. Based on the results obtained during this work, ERA officially decided to make Semantic Web and Linked Data-based approaches, the default setting for any future development of the data, registers and specifications under the agency's remit for data exchange mandated by the EU legal framework. The next steps, which are already underway, include further developing and bringing these solutions to a production-ready state.

© Springer Nature Switzerland AG 2021
A. Hotho et al. (Eds.): ISWC 2021, LNCS 12922, pp. 648–664, 2021.
https://doi.org/10.1007/978-3-030-88361-4_38

1   Introduction

The establishment of an interoperable European railway area without frontiers, while guaranteeing railway operation safety, is the prime objective of the European Union Agency for Railways (ERA) [7]. Since 2019 ERA became the European authority[1] for cross-border rail traffic in Europe, mandated under the European Union (EU) law, to devise the technical and legal framework for supporting harmonised and safe cross-border railway operations.

The European railway ecosystem presents a particularly challenging scenario for interoperability, not only regarding physical aspects (e.g., infrastructure, energy systems, etc.) but also digital ones (e.g., information). Multiple organisations, such as Infrastructure Managers (IMs)[2] and Railway Undertakings (RUs)[3] [6], need to interact and exchange information to ensure safe cross-border railway operations. These organisations rely on different information management systems from multiple vendors, that are often incompatible with each other. To increase digital interoperability among heterogeneous data and information systems, ERA supports and maintains a set of base registries,[4] in the form of relational databases, where organisations input and access the different aspects of the information they manage and require.

However, following such traditional approach lead to isolated digital environments that consequently added barriers to digital interoperability. Tightly coupling base registries to the applications that operate over them, triggered the proliferation of overlapping and difficult to manage data models hidden inside application code, which also increased maintenance and innovation costs. Moreover, stakeholder organisations such as IMs, have to report the same information multiple times for different registries, increasing the probability of data inconsistency issues, while adding more costs to IMs due to duplicated efforts.

To address these issues, we propose a digital interoperability strategy for ERA, that adheres to the Linked Data principles[5] [19] and relies on standard Semantic Web [1] technologies. We built the foundations to establish a *semantic layer* for data integration within the agency, initially spanning three different base registries[6]:, Register of Infrastructure (RINF), Register of Authorized Types

---

[1] ERA is the European authority for cross-border rail traffic in Europe: https://www.era.europa.eu/content/era-becomes-european-authority-cross-border-rail-traffic-europe_en.

[2] An Infrastructure Manager is defined as any body or firm responsible in particular for establishing, managing and maintaining railway infrastructure, including traffic management, control-command and signalling.

[3] A Railway Undertaking is defined as any public or private licensed undertaking, the principal business of which is to provide services for the transport of goods and/or passengers by rail with a requirement that the undertaking ensure traction.

[4] *"A base registry is a trusted and authoritative source of information which can and should be digitally reused by others, where one organisation is responsible and accountable for the collection, use, updating and preservation of information."* [24].

[5] Principles of Linked Data: https://www.w3.org/DesignIssues/LinkedData.html.

[6] Base registries of ERA: https://www.era.europa.eu/registers_en.

of Vehicles (ERATV) and the Centralized Virtual Vehicle Register (ECVVR). We validate the usefulness of the approach by reusing the produced semantic data to support route compatibility checks (RCC), a highly-demanded use case in the railway domain. The RCC use case is stipulated and specified in EU regulations 2016/797 and 2019/773 [8,10] and was so far, unsupported by ERA due to interoperability issues among base registries. Additionally, we show the flexibility of graph-based data models, by integrating an additional external data source that complements the resulting Knowledge Graph.

The contributions of this paper include (i) an ontology,[7] modelling railway infrastructure aspects, rolling stock and authorized vehicle types, and 28 independently managed reference datasets; (ii) a public and reusable RDF Knowledge Graph[8] with 13.8 million triples about the European railway infrastructure and more than 800 thousand rolling stocks; (iii) a cost-efficient system architecture that enables high-flexibility for use case support; and (iv) an open source and RDF native Web application[9] to support and process RCC queries.

This work demonstrates how data-centric system design, powered by Semantic Web technologies, provides a framework to achieve data interoperability and unlock innovative use cases and applications. The results of the work presented in this paper had a strong impact on ERA,[10] which decided on making Semantic Web technologies the default setting for any future development of data, registers and specifications, under the agency's remit, for data exchange mandated by the EU legal framework. The next steps, which are already underway, include further extending the ontology with additional aspects, aligned with the requirements of the railway domain and evolving the system architecture towards a production-ready solution, fully integrated with the data management workflows of ERA.

The remainder of this paper is organized as follows: Sect. 2 presents an overview of related work in the context of modelling approaches and interoperability for the railway domain. Section 3 describes the data sources and the RCC use case requirements. Section 4 gives an overview and description of our proposed solution architecture. Section 5 discusses advantages and limitations of the approach and Sect. 6 presents our conclusions and perspectives for future work.

2   Related Work

In this section, we present different (semantic) data models to describe the railway domain focusing on different aspects of the domain and motivated by different use cases. Also existing related work applying semantic technologies in the railway domain. We studied these models, aiming on reusing as much as possible their embedded domain-specific knowledge (e.g. definitions, categorizations, naming conventions, etc.), during the creation of ERA's ontology.

---

[7] http://era.ilabt.imec.be/era-vocabulary/index-en.html.

[8] http://era.ilabt.imec.be/.

[9] http://era.ilabt.imec.be/test/compatibility-check-demo/.

[10] ERA's roadmap for Linked Data mainstreaming: https://www.era.europa.eu/sites/default/files/agency/docs/decision/decision_n250_annex1_linked_data_en.pdf.

Multiple domain data models were proposed (some still under active development), to bridge the interoperability challenges by uniformly describing the different technical aspects related to the railway domain. However, most lack semantic definitions that promote/guarantee the use of persistent identifiers across data sources, hindering interoperability when exchanging data across organizations. Available models range from company-specific to industrial consortium-driven standardization efforts. For example, the *Informatie Model Spoor*,[11] developed by the Dutch IM ProRail, provides an XML Schema-based model with integrated functional and geographic information about the railway infrastructure. IMSpoorXML is currently used within ProRail and is under active maintenance and development. The International Railway Standard IRS:30100 RailTopoModel[12] [22] was developed under the patronage of the International Union of Railways (UIC) and provides a systemic UML-based model for describing the topological aspects of railway infrastructure. It relies on the *connexity graph* mathematical concept [16] to describe the interconnection of the different railway network elements. Implementations of RailTopoModel include RailML[13] [21] and the EULYNX[14] initiative, both currently developed by industrial consortiums.

The use of semantic technologies, for modelling the railway domain is not new. In 2011, the EU project InteGRail created an ontology integrating the major railway sub-systems, to achieve higher levels of performance in terms of capacity, average speed and punctuality, safety and the optimised usage of resources in railway systems [28]. Smart Rail is another EU project that applied semantic technologies for modelling organizational aspects of the railway domain. It produced an ontology[15], focused on modelling stakeholders and physical resources of the railway infrastructure. RaCoOn (Rail Core Ontologies) is a set of domain ontologies that model areas of the rail domain commonly used in railway data exchange [26]. A study of how Linked Data was applied in the British railway domain, highlights the reduction of costs as a consequence of more efficient data flows, and hints towards the need for increasing adoption from industry [23]. More recently, Bischof et al. [2] outlined the requirements and challenges to define an open standard ontology for railway topologies based on existing standards. None of these approaches evolved beyond academic exercises and the produced ontologies are currently unmaintained or no longer available. In contrast, one of the main goals of ERA, as an European authority for the domain, is to provide a fully supported and open reference ontology not only for internal data management operations but targeting also its adoption and extension by the stakeholders of the railway domain, as an asset that supports their own use cases.

---

[11] https://confluence.rigd-loxia.nl/display/IMSP/IMSpoor+Publicatie+Home.

[12] http://www.railtopomodel.org/en/download/irs30100-apr16-7594BCA1524E14224
D0.html?file=files/download/RailTopoModel/180416_uic_irs30100.pdf.

[13] https://wiki3.railml.org/wiki/Main_Page.

[14] https://dataprep.eulynx.eu/2020-10/index.htm.

[15] https://ontology.tno.nl/smart-rail/.

3 Data Sources and Use Case

In this section, we outline the different data sources reused by our proposed solution and describe the RCC use case as the main motivator for this work.

3.1 ERA's Base Registries

Our approach considers, so far, 3 of the base registries[16] maintained by ERA, namely the Register of Infrastructure (RINF), the Register of Authorized Types of Vehicles (ERATV) and the Centralized Virtual Vehicle Register (ECVVR). These registries contain overlapping conceptual definitions, represented as properties of different types of entities, which are locked within their respective data silos. Next, we give a brief description for each of these registries.

Register of Infrastructure. The European Register of Infrastructure (RINF) was introduced following Article 35 of the EU regulation 2008/57/EC [4]. RINF contains the main features of fixed installations related to subsystems of infrastructure, energy and parts of control-command and signaling. It publishes performance and technical characteristics mainly related to interfaces with rolling stock and operation. It is maintained as a relational database and its content is provided by different European IMs, by means of a predefined XML Schema.[17]

Register of Authorized Types of Vehicles. The European Register of Authorized Types of Vehicles (ERATV) is introduced by Article 5 of the EU regulation 2011/665/EU [5]. It aims to publish and keep an up-to-date set of authorized types of vehicles including information that references the technical specifications for each parameter. ERATV is maintained as a relational database populated through a Web application by multiple authorizing organizations. It also provides additional information for a certain vehicle type, such as manufacturing country, manufacturer, category and different physical and operational parameters.

Centralized Virtual Vehicle Register. The European Centralised Virtual Vehicle Register (ECVVR) is a base registry maintained by ERA, in accordance with the EU regulation 2018/1614 [9]. ECVVR defines a decentralized architecture for information search and retrieval of rolling stock data, where each Member State hosts and publishes their own national vehicle registry(ies), accessible through Web-based interfaces.

3.2 External Data Source

There are known limitations for ERA's base registries, as is the case of RINF and the limited granularity it gives over the railway topology. RINF provides a

---

[16] https://www.era.europa.eu/registers_en.
[17] https://www.era.europa.eu/sites/default/files/registers/docs/rinf_schema_en.xsd.

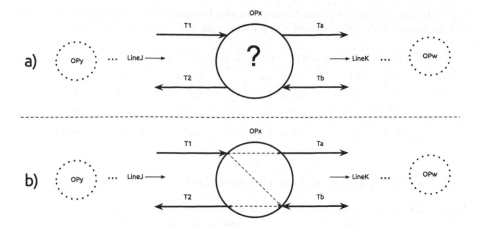

Fig. 1. a) a schematic diagram of an operational point where its internal connections are unknown; b) how this information can be completed from data provided in Table 1.

view over the railway infrastructure, commonly referred to as meso-level view,[18] where complex topological structures inside stations, junctions, switches, etc., are abstracted into single nodes in the network graph. Route calculations over this limited view, may wrongfully assume certain direction changes, not possible in the real world. Calculating end-to-end routes with high accuracy, requires further data about the connectivity within each network node. This connectivity issue currently stands as one of the main challenges, for an accurate and reliable data source description of the European railway infrastructure topology. For this reason, we also consider an external data source, provided by the Dutch IM ProRail, which provides an additional topological description for addressing this issue limited to the region of Utrecht in The Netherlands.

Connectivity Data in the Utrecht Area. The Dutch IM ProRail, provided us with an additional data source for exploring an alternative solution for the lack of real information about the internal connectivity inside network nodes (also called operational points). It consists of a table that groups all the different permutations of incoming and outgoing tracks for a set of operational points, and states if they are connected or not.

The operational point OPx (Fig. 1) has two incoming tracks ($T1$ and $T2$) from OPy and belonging to the national line $LineJ$. We know these are incoming tracks thanks to the logical direction defined for $LineJ$, despite $T1$ being a bidirectional track. OPx also has two outgoing tracks (Ta, Tb), going towards OPw and belonging to another national line $LineK$. Based on this information, we establish the correct connectivity that reflects real-world behavior.

---

[18] See Sect. 1.6 of [22] for a description of railway vie levels.

Table 1. All the possible permutations between incoming and outgoing tracks of OPx, plus a column that states if there is a possible connection between two pairs of tracks.

IN_Line	IN_OP	IN_Track	OP	OUT_Track	OUT_OP	OUT_Line	Connected
LineJ	OPy	T1	OPx	Ta	OPw	LineK	**True**
LineJ	OPy	T1	OPx	Tb	OPw	LineK	**True**
LineJ	OPy	T2	OPx	Ta	OPw	LineK	**False**
LineJ	OPy	T2	OPx	Tb	OPw	LineK	**True**

3.3 Use Case: Route Compatibility Check

Article 23 (point b) of the European regulation 2016/797 stipulates [8] that: *"Before a railway undertaking uses a vehicle in the area of use specified in its authorisation for placing on the market, it shall check: ...(b) that the vehicle is compatible with the route on the basis of the infrastructure register, the relevant TSIs or any relevant information to be provided by the infrastructure manager free of charge and within a reasonable period of time, where such a register does not exist or is incomplete".*

The specific procedures for assessing if a certain vehicle is compatible with a certain route, are further specified by the Annex D1 of the EU regulation 2019/773 [10]. These specifications directly refer to specific data properties within RINF and ERATV, of 22 different technical aspects that need to be compared to determine if there is technical compatibility. This specification already highlights a clear need for interoperability at least between RINF and ERATV, which we address with the proposed ontology and derived Knowledge Graph.

To determine if a certain vehicle type is compatible with a certain route, is necessary to first find possible routes through the railway infrastructure, which involves a very particular type of queries, namely graph pathfinding queires. The standard query language for RDF graphs (SPARQL) does not support finding complex relation paths between RDF entities [17]. The Property Paths querying syntax, introduced in SPARQL 1.1, only allows for testing path existence but falls short on counting and retrieving the actual paths between two nodes [25], which is crucial for the RCC use case. Currently there exist non-standard extensions to SPARQL (e.g. Stardog path queries[19]) that address this limitation they are not widely supported across RDF graph databases. We consider this limitation in our proposed architecture and propose an alternative solution (see Sect. 4.2) to non-standard SPARQL extensions and according to the current Web standards to prevent vendor lock-in issues.

4 Proposed Solution

Considering the interoperability obstacles that exist among the base registries maintained by ERA, we propose and design a solution architecture, capable of

---

[19] https://docs.stardog.com/archive/7.5.0/query-stardog/path-queries.

creating a semantic interoperability layer for data integration over them. Moreover, we exploit the inherent flexibility of graph-based data models to also include an external data source, that enriches the resulting Knowledge Graph (KG) and addresses intrinsic limitations of the original base registries. The proposed architecture relies on an ontology, defined to cover, but not limited to, the explicit interoperability requirements brought forth by the RCC use case. The architecture implements an ETL (Extract Transform Load)-based pipeline that relies on a fully declarative approach for the KG generation process, and leverages fundamental Web principles such as caching, to reduce computational infrastructure costs while maintaining a high querying flexibility.

In this section, we present a description of the main architectural components of our proposed solution. We describe the proposed ontology and give a full overview of the solution architecture, which includes a fully functional application to support route compatibility (checks available online[20]).

4.1 The ERA Vocabulary

Our proposed ontology, the ERA Vocabulary,[21] was created in a collaborative effort with domain experts from ERA, ProRail, SNCF and Semantic Web experts from DG DIGIT and IDLab-imec. The ERA Vocabulary provides unique identifiers and semantic definitions for concepts and properties, common to the railway domain. We make available online its documentation, using Widoco [15] as a template generator, and the source files in a public GitHub repository.[22]

Following Semantic Web best practices, the ontology reuses external ontologies such as OGC GeoSPARQL, Schema.org and the EU publications office authority table[23] for country definitions. It defines a layered model (see Fig. 2), inspired from RINF's relational model, where the topological and functional aspects of the railway infrastructure are defined by independent entity types. The *abstraction* layer defines logical entities form the network topology graph, with *era:NodePorts* acting as nodes and both *era:MicroLinks* and *era:InternalNodeLinks* acting as edges. The *implementation* layer, represents concrete and functional objects in the real world, such as tracks, operational points (stations, switches, etc.) and vehicles (types). The link between these two layers is given by the *era:MicroNode - era:OperationalPoint* and *era:MicroLink - era:Track* relationships. Additionally, 28 reference datasets[24] were extracted from the base registries and defined as SKOS controlled vocabularies. They contain definitions for different domain-related technical aspects, which are envisioned to be independently managed by relevant authorities.

---

[20] http://era.ilabt.imec.be/test/compatibility-check-demo/.
[21] http://era.ilabt.imec.be/era-vocabulary/index-en.html.
[22] https://github.com/julianrojas87/era-vocabulary/tree/master.
[23] http://publications.europa.eu/resource/authority/country.
[24] http://era.ilabt.imec.be/era-vocabulary/era-skos#.

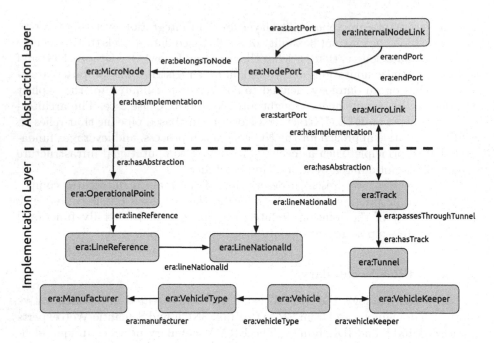

Fig. 2. Layered data model of the ERA Vocabulary.

4.2   Architecture Overview

Our proposed solution architecture is composed by 4 main modules (see Fig. 3), namely the *Data Sources*, *KG Generation*, *KG Querying* and *User Application* modules. The *Data Sources* module represents the considered data sources (previously described in Sect. 3). The components from the *KG Generation* module, access the data sources to produce the RDF triples that compose the ERA KG. The ERA KG is published and made available for querying by the *KG Querying* module, which provides the necessary interfaces for the *User Application* module to support specific use cases. Next, we provide a description and the rationale behind these modules.

KG Generation. The KG generation process in our solution follows an ETL-based approach and uses the RML[13] technology stack for declaratively generating the RDF triples of the ERA Knowledge Graph. RML was selected for handling heterogeneous data sources, which in our case are relational DBs and CSV files, but XML Schema-based data sources (e.g., RailML) are also envisioned as a next step. The steps followed in this process are:

1. Definition of RML rules[25] in YARRRML [20] syntax.
2. Translation of YARRRML rules to RML using the yarrrml-parser[26].

---

[25] https://github.com/julianrojas87/era-data-mappings.
[26] https://github.com/RMLio/yarrrml-parser.

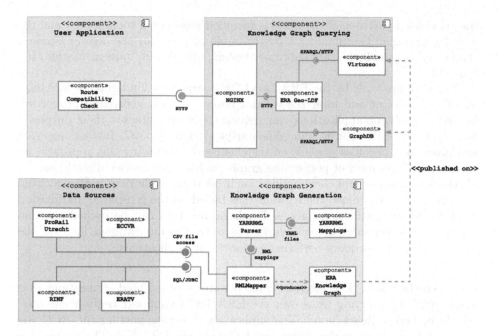

Fig. 3. Overview of the proposed solution architecture for semantic data interoperability across ERA's base registries.

3. Production of RDF data via the RMLMapper[27], according to the set of given RML rules.
4. Publishing of the resulting KG in a triple store. At the time of writing the ERA KG, had a total of 13.8 million triples, which we also make available as a raw data dump.[28]

KG Querying. We published the ERA KG in two different triple stores (GraphDB[29] and Virtuoso[30]) to prove that our proposed solution is vendor-independent. This module includes one of the core components of the architecture: the ERA Geo-LDF, which is implemented as a Node.js application.[31] The main purpose of this component is exposing a Linked Data and Hypermedia-based API over the ERA KG. It builds on the Linked Data Fragments [27] approach to provide metadata annotated fragments (tiles) of the ERA KG, based on a predefined geospatial pattern. It follows the slippy maps specification,[32] where

---

[27] https://github.com/RMLio/rmlmapper-java.
[28] https://drive.google.com/file/d/1KofPzYx2ovgAz85rLuO5J98SEs2BjWbO/view?usp =sharing.
[29] http://era.ilabt.imec.be/sparql.
[30] https://linked.ec-dataplatform.eu/sparql?default-graph-uri=https%3A%2F%2Flink ed.ec-dataplatform.eu\%2Fera.
[31] https://github.com/julianrojas87/era-ldf/.
[32] https://wiki.openstreetmap.org/wiki/Slippy_map_tilenames.

the grid-based partition of the world is specified based on a zoom level z and the x and y cartesian coordinates. A live example of a tile for the area of Brussels can be accessed on http://era.ilabt.imec.be/ldf/sparql-tiles/implementation/10/524/343.

The tiles are built by the ERA Geo-LDF component via template SPARQL queries that select and filter the entities based on their geospatial properties. In this way, client applications can request relevant data for their purposes, and since the API returns unmodified triples from the KG, further querying and processing becomes possible on the client-side. Following this approach, we address the limitation of performing graph pathfinding queries directly on the SPARQL endpoints. Our client application implements a shortest-path algorithm and proceeds to download the relevant tiles based on the geospatial information given by origin-destination queries. Furthermore, tiles can be cached both on client- and server-side, which reduces the overall computational load on the server and improves query performance for client applications.

User Application. This module represents any user-oriented applications that would perform querying tasks over the ERA KG to support a given use case. We developed a React-based Web application[33] for supporting the RCC use case and demonstrating data interoperability via the ERA KG. The application allows users to select an origin-destination pairs of operational points (visible in map-based UI) to calculate one or more routes between them. Once selected, it proceeds to download the relevant KG tile fragments and perform the pathfinding process. It handles RDF triples natively and implements the A* [18] and Yen's [29] algorithms for graph shortest path and top-k shortest path calculations respectively. Once a route is found, users may select a vehicle (type) to assess technical compatibility. Currently, the application evaluates compatibility for 15 different parameters of both track sections and vehicle (types). Users can also visualize the internal connectivity of operational points that form part of a calculated route, by means of a schematic diagram that shows the possible internal connections defined in the ERA KG. This feature is particularly interesting for operational points around the city of Utrecht in The Netherlands, considering the additional data source from ProRail (Sect. 3), that was integrated into the KG.

5 Discussion

The implementation of our proposed solution allowed us to achieve semantic interoperability over the considered data sources, which stood as independent and disconnected data silos before. Our architecture relies entirely on semantic web technologies and tools, starting from the KG generation and ending with an RDF native Web application that supports the addressed RCC use case.

---

[33] https://github.com/julianrojas87/era-compatibility-check

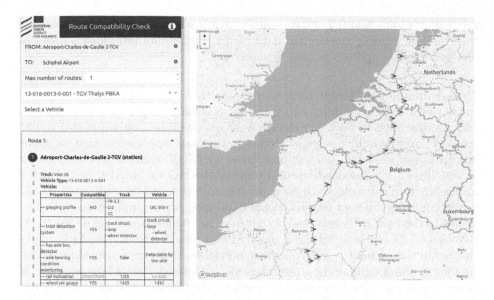

Fig. 4. The RCC Web application: a route calculated from the Charles de Gaulle airport in Paris to the Schipol airport in Amsterdam. On the lower left panel, the results of the compatibility check process for the TGV Thalys PBKA vehicle type.

5.1   Solution Features

Next we outline the main features of our proposed solution:

Fully Declarative KG Generation. One key feature of our proposed solution relates to the ERA KG generation process, which is accomplished following a fully declarative approach. In other words, no pre-processing steps nor dedicated software/scripts are required to generate the RDF triples of the ERA KG. The KG generation rules are defined as RML mapping rules, which are executed by an existing and general purpose engine, that follows the given rules to produce the desired RDF triples. This feature has an important value from a data governance perspective, considering that no additional ad hoc software needs to be maintained. The RML mapping rules become the central resource for the ERA KG generation process, which can be adjusted or extended to include additional data sources, with significantly less effort compared to developing and maintaining additional software for every new data source to be included in the ERA KG. Furthermore, the mappings can be reused and adapted by IMs to produce their own internal KGs.

KG Enrichment Flexibility. We were also able to explore and alternative solution to integrate additional data originated directly from an IM, to address the missing connectivity issue of the railway infrastructure. This approach demonstrated the flexibility that graph-based data models hold, considering that adding additional data sources requires significantly less effort, than for example, altering a relational data model, potentially introducing breaking changes for the applications that depend on it.

Cost-Efficient KG Publishing and Querying. Our architecture design was made, with data publishing and querying cost-efficiency as a guiding principle. As described in Sect. 4.2, the ERA KG is published on triple stores with support for SPARQL querying. However, the user application that supports the RCC use case does not perform direct SPARQL queries over these triple stores. Instead, it downloads specific parts of the KG via an API, over which it applies its business logic. Such an approach is no different to traditional REST-based application design over relational databases, where applications are given access to data via APIs only, and do not have unbounded querying access to the database(s) [3,14]. In contrast to most API implementations, the APIs implemented in this architecture, follow the hypermedia constraints defined by REST, providing self-describing data responses via hypermedia metadata controls. In other words, the API data responses include additional metadata that describe how it can be used by client applications to retrieve more relevant data for a particular query. Such descriptions enable the creation of smarter and more autonomous client applications, avoiding the need of hard-coding the application according to specific API interfaces.

More importantly, the API design in this architecture has been done to maximize the cacheability of API responses. By following a geospatial fragmentation approach, which suits the RCC use case, the API publishes fragments of the ERA KG that can be cached both on client- and server-side. This further reduces the computational cost on the triple stores, which only need to process once the query for a given fragment. A client application that requested a certain data fragment does not need to request it again (client cache) and has full flexibility to perform any type of further processing on the data it contains. When another client application needs access to the same type of data, it can rely on server-side cached API responses which also improve overall application performance.

Shortest Path Querying Over an RDF KG. The ability to indirectly support calculation of path finding queries, is an important feature of our architectural design. Our approach not only enables solving this particular type of queries, but also opens the door for clients to implement any pathfinding algorithm, and further customize them to better suit their requirements. Such level of specialization of algorithms is not always possible to be defined through general purpose query languages or it could potentially result in highly inefficient queries.

5.2   Limitations and Open Challenges

The identified limitations of our approach include:

Performance of Long-Distance Queries. One of the main limitations of our proposed solution is related to the trade-off between server computational cost and query performance, that is introduced when shifting query processing tasks to the client. This is particularly visible when dealing with long distance route calculations, due to the increasing amount of data fragments that needs to be fetched and processed by the client. Different alternatives could be explored to address this limitation:

Server-Side Route Planning Engine: This is the most common approach followed by route planning solutions. It requires setting a dedicated engine (e.g., postGIS-based system[34]), which imports the whole topology graph and then is capable of executing a route planning algorithm over it. The drawbacks of this approach include the considerable increase of computational load for the server and less flexibility for client applications to select and tailor the algorithms for their own needs. But more importantly, available solutions do not support RDF data out of the box, which introduces an additional burden for the architecture by having to convert and keep in sync the ERA KG towards the required format of the route planning engine.

Non-standard Graph Database: Another alternative is to replace the standard RDF triple store by a graph database that has support for route plan querying (e.g. Stardog[35] or Neo4J[36] both with RDF support). Again the drawbacks of this approach are related to scalability and application flexibility, but they also may lead to vendor-locking issues, since they rely on non-standard solutions.

Speed-up Techniques: The application of speed-up techniques for shortest path algorithms, such as Contraction Hierarchies [12] or Multilevel Dijkstra [11], stands as a possible solution. These techniques rely on preprocessing steps that create summarizations of the graph topology, allowing to quickly compute long-distance path queries. They have been applied mostly to road networks graphs, where hierarchies of roads (highway, road, residential street, etc.) can be used to create summaries for long distances. In principle, they could also be applied to the railway topology graph. The drawbacks of these approaches are related to the introduction of additional complexity for creating the graph summaries that need to be managed and kept in sync with the original KG. However, they could still allow full flexibility for client applications to perform any business logic, since the summaries are only additional data that does not change the original RDF triples of the ERA KG.

KG Based on Stale Sources. The KG generation process is periodically performed over stale versions of the base registry relational DBs. To accurately

---

[34] https://pgrouting.org/.

[35] https://docs.stardog.com/archive/7.5.0/query-stardog/path-queries.

[36] https://neo4j.com/docs/graph-data-science/current/algorithms/dijkstra-source-target/.

reflect the real state of the railway network, is necessary to capture in *real-time* the changes introduced into the source DBs, and immediately reflect them in the ERA KG. Other use cases such as signaling and interlocking, require precise and accurate data to guarantee safe vehicle operations. Approaches such as Linked Data Event Streams,[37] remain to be investigated to support this requirements.

Hardcoded Compatibility Check Rules. The compatibility check rules, were directly implemented into the source code of the RCC client application. This constitutes a limitation, given that it makes it more difficult to maintain and evolve the rules. Also, it makes the rules to be indistinguishable from the application, hindering their potential reusability in other use cases. Alternatives to address this issue could explore the use of Notation3 or SHACL Rules to declaratively define the RCC rules, which can be then independently managed and published for applications such as the RCC client to consume and evaluate.

6   Conclusion and Future Work

The most important achievement of this work, is the strong impact it had on the decision taken by ERA[38] to make Semantic Web technologies the default setting for any future development of data, registers and specifications under the agency's remit. Considering ERA's position as a European authority this decision could potentially influence the different stakeholders in the railway domain to take similar paths.

The results obtained from this work, demonstrated with a practical approach, how Semantic Web technologies enable higher data interoperability. Data integration is achieved at the *data level* (data-centric) instead of being locked into application-specific business logic (application-centric), opening the door for new and innovative use cases. We were able to create a semantic interoperability layer over the different considered data sources, which requires significantly less effort to be created and managed, compared to developing ad-hoc applications and 1-to-1 interfaces between different information systems. Furthermore, this work also demonstrated that Semantic Web technologies can be used to create functional Web applications based on modern and developer-friendly frameworks such as React with little additional effort from a development perspective and in a reasonable time frame.

The choice of architecture design made for this prototype leverages HTTP caching mechanisms to achieve higher scalability while providing full querying flexibility to client applications. This is demonstrated by the ability of the RCC client application to perform route planning calculations over the ERA KG, which are not supported by standard RDF triple stores. Yet, this approach

---

[37] https://w3id.org/ldes/specification.

[38] https://www.era.europa.eu/sites/default/files/agency/docs/decision/decision_n250_annex1_linked_data_en.pdf.

establishes a trade-off between scalability and flexibility vs. performance. Further optimizations are required to achieve production-level performance without losing the benefits of the proposed solution architecture.

In the future, we aim to explore how more granular descriptions of the railways topology can be integrated to increase the reliability of the ERA KG. From an architectural perspective, stream-processing and KG virtualization approaches may be studied to support cases with higher requirements on up-to-date data.

Acknowledgements. The authors would like to extend their gratitude to ProRail, SNCF, BANE NOR, EIM, UIP, CEDEX, RailML, EULYNX, the Publications Office of the EU and the ELISE action team for providing us with their invaluable data, expertise and feedback to make this work possible.

References

1. Berners-Lee, T., Hendler, J., Lassila, O.: The semantic web. Sci. Am. **284**(5), 34–43 (2001)
2. Bischof, S., Schenner, G.: Towards a railway topology ontology to integrate and query rail data silos. In: SEMWEB (2020)
3. Chaudhuri, S., Weikum, G.: Rethinking database system architecture: Towards a self-tuning RISC-style database system. In: Proceedings of the 26th International Conference on Very Large Data Bases, VLDB 2000, pp. 1–10. Morgan Kaufmann Publishers Inc., San Francisco (2000)
4. Council of European Union: Council regulation (EU) no 2008/57 (2008). https://eur-lex.europa.eu/legal-content/EN/TXT/?uri=celex%3A32008L0057
5. Council of European Union: Council regulation (EU) no 2011/65 (2011). https://eur-lex.europa.eu/legal-content/EN/TXT/?uri=celex%3A32011L0065
6. Council of European Union: Council regulation (EU) no 2012/34 (2016). https://eur-lex.europa.eu/legal-content/EN/TXT/?uri=CELEX%3A32012L0034
7. Council of European Union: Council regulation (EU) no 2016/796 (2016). https://eur-lex.europa.eu/legal-content/EN/TXT/?uri=CELEX%3A32016R0796
8. Council of European Union: Council regulation (EU) no 2016/797 (2016). https://eur-lex.europa.eu/legal-content/EN/TXT/?uri=CELEX%3A32016L0797
9. Council of European Union: Council regulation (EU) no 2018/1614 (2018). https://eur-lex.europa.eu/legal-content/EN/TXT/?uri=uriserv:OJ.L_.2018.268.01.0053.01.ENG&toc=OJ:L:2018:268:TOC
10. Council of European Union: Council regulation (EU) no 2019/773 (2019). https://eur-lex.europa.eu/eli/reg_impl/2019/773/oj
11. Delling, D., Goldberg, A., Pajor, T., Werneck, R.F.: Customizable route planning in road networks. Transp. Sci. **51**, 566–591 (2017)
12. Dibbelt, J., Strasser, B., Wagner, D.: Customizable contraction hierarchies. ACM J. Exp. Algorithmics **21**, 1–49 (2016)
13. Dimou, A., Vander Sande, M., Colpaert, P., Verborgh, R., Mannens, E., Van de Walle, R.: RML: a generic language for integrated RDF mappings of heterogeneous data. In: Proceedings of the 7th Workshop on Linked Data on the Web. CEUR Workshop Proceedings, vol. 1184, April 2014
14. Fielding, R.T., Taylor, R.N.: Principled design of the modern web architecture. ACM Trans. Internet Technol. **2**(2), 115–150 (2002)

15. Garijo, D., et al.: Zack-83: dgarijo/Widoco: WIDOCO 1.4.15_1 (pre-release): Namespace prefixes fixes and WebVowl update, December 2020
16. Gély, L., Dessagne, G., Pesneau, P., Vanderbeck, F.: A multi scalable model based on a connexity graph representation. WIT Trans. Built Environ. **114**, 193–204 (2010)
17. Gubichev, A., Neumann, T.: Path query processing on very large RDF graphs. In: WebDB (2011)
18. Hart, P.E., Nilsson, N.J., Raphael, B.: A formal basis for the heuristic determination of minimum cost paths. IEEE Trans. Syst. Sci. Cybern. **4**(2), 100–107 (1968)
19. Heath, T., Bizer, C.: Linked Data: Evolving the Web into a Global Data Space (2011). http://linkeddatabook.com/editions/1.0/
20. Heyvaert, P., De Meester, B., Dimou, A., Verborgh, R.: Declarative rules for linked data generation at your fingertips! In: Gangemi, A., et al. (eds.) ESWC 2018. LNCS, vol. 11155, pp. 213–217. Springer, Cham (2018). https://doi.org/10.1007/978-3-319-98192-5_40
21. Hlubuček, A.: Railtopomodel and railML 3 in overall context. Acta Polytechnica CTU Proceedings **11**, 16 (2017). https://doi.org/10.14311/APP.2017.11.0016
22. RailTopoModel - Railway Infrastructure Topological Model. Standard, International Union of Railways, Paris, FR (2016)
23. Morris, C., Easton, J., Roberts, C.: Applications of linked data in the rail domain. In: 2014 IEEE International Conference on Big Data (Big Data), pp. 35–41 (2014)
24. Publications Office of the European Union: New European interoperability framework: promoting seamless services and data flows for European public administrations (2017). https://ec.europa.eu/isa2/sites/default/files/eif_brochure_final.pdf
25. Savenkov, V., Mehmood, Q., Umbrich, J., Polleres, A.: Counting to k or how sparql1.1 property paths can be extended to top-k path queries. In: Proceedings of the 13th International Conference on Semantic Systems, Semantics 2017, pp. 97–103. Association for Computing Machinery, New York (2017)
26. Tutcher, J., Easton, J., Roberts, C.: Enabling data integration in the rail industry using RDF and OWL: the RaCoOn ontology. ASCE-ASME J. Risk Uncertainty Eng. Syst. Part A: Civil Eng. **3**, F4015001 (2017)
27. Verborgh, R., Vander Sande, M., Colpaert, P., Coppens, S., Mannens, E., Van de Walle, R.: Web-scale querying through Linked Data Fragments. In: Bizer, C., Heath, T., Auer, S., Berners-Lee, T. (eds.) Proceedings of the 7th Workshop on Linked Data on the Web. CEUR Workshop Proceedings, vol. 1184, April 2014
28. Verstichel, S., et al.: Efficient data integration in the railway domain through an ontology-based methodology. Transp. Res. Part C Emerging Technol. **19**(4), 617–643 (2011)
29. Yen, J.Y.: Finding the k shortest loopless paths in a network. Manage. Sci. **17**(11), 712–716 (1971)

Use of Semantic Technologies to Inform Progress Toward Zero-Carbon Economy

Stefano Germano[1]([✉])(iD), Carla Saunders[2](iD), Ian Horrocks[1](iD),
and Rick Lupton[2](iD)

[1] Department of Computer Science, University of Oxford, Oxford, UK
{stefano.germano,ian.horrocks}@cs.ox.ac.uk
[2] Department of Mechanical Engineering, University of Bath, Bath, UK
{cs2537,R.C.Lupton}@bath.ac.uk

Abstract. To investigate the effect of possible changes to decarbonise the economy, a detailed picture of the current production system is needed. Material/energy flow analysis (MEFA) allows for building such a model. There are, however, prohibitive barriers to the integration and use of the diverse datasets necessary for a system-wide yet technically-detailed MEFA study. Herein we describe a methodology exploiting Semantic Web technologies to integrate and reason on top of this diverse production system data. We designed an ontology to model the structure of our data, and developed a declarative logic-based approach to address the many challenges arising from data integration and usage in this context. Further, this system is designed for easy access to the needed data in terms relevant for additional modelling and to be applied by non-experts, allowing for a wide use of our methodology. Our experiments with UK production data confirm the usefulness of this methodology through a case study based on the UK production system.

Keywords: Semantic technology · Resource efficiency · Rule-based approach · Data integration · Material Flow Analysis · Ontology · Decision Support System

1 Introduction

A whole-systems understanding of production systems is essential to navigating the necessary rapid transition to a zero-carbon economy. Identifying opportunities and monitoring progress relies on having access to data about the production and consumption of physical resources (materials, products, energy, etc.) and their associated environmental impacts. However, due to the economy-wide yet detailed nature of these questions, they cannot be answered from single datasets collected by one entity, but must instead be based on many pieces of

This work was supported by the EPSRC project UK FIRES (EP/S019111/1), the SIRIUS Centre for Scalable Data Access (Research Council of Norway, project no.: 237889), and Samsung Research UK.

A. Hotho et al. (Eds.): ISWC 2021, LNCS 12922, pp. 665–681, 2021.
https://doi.org/10.1007/978-3-030-88361-4_39

data from different international and national organisations, individual companies, and academic research.

This data is incomplete, and defined using inconsistent categorisations of the types of resource and activities. It is thus challenging to obtain the clear, complete and robust picture that is needed of how our economies are functioning and could change [20]. In addition, the lack of well-defined data models for this type of data is limiting to data reuse and holding back academic research [9,19]. While progress has been made in developing shared data models [8,11,17,18] and data catalogues [14,16], which improve access to and reuse of relevant datasets, they do not yet confront the fundamental challenge of resolving conflicts where individual datasets are defined in inconsistent ways.

Semantic Web technologies are well placed to help with these types of problem, but there are some key challenges to their application. The knowledge representation and reasoning side requires complex modelling and expressive logic-based languages, due to the heterogeneity of the data. Furthermore, any solution must be accessible by people without specialised knowledge of Semantic Web technologies, requiring care in selecting an appropriate model and designing and implementing suitable technical solutions.

In this paper, we propose and develop a solution using a domain ontology and the RDFox triple store to efficiently implement Datalog rules integrating diverse data points into a consistent structure. This forms part of the "Physical Resources Observatory" (PRObs) system, being developed within the *UK FIRES* research programme[1], where it supports a wider research agenda on resource efficiency and decarbonisation in UK industrial strategy.

2   The Need for Monitoring the Physical Economy

Understanding how we produce and consume physical resources is fundamental to understanding the impacts human activity has, and how we can operate more efficiently. The following examples illustrate a range of uses for this knowledge.

Example 1 (Innovation in material efficiency). About half of industrial CO_2 emissions are due to production of just five major bulk materials [1]. Reducing scrap created during manufacturing processes would reduce overall demand for materials and hence emissions. But identifying the potential savings and opportunities for new manufacturing processes requires an understanding of how and where scrap is currently produced in the supply chain.

Example 2 (Reuse of building components). Components of buildings could be reused when the building is no longer needed [2], which would reduce emissions from recycling and production. But doing this requires knowledge of what components are available in existing buildings, which is generally not known directly. By monitoring materials going into construction and from demolition, the current composition of the building stock can be estimated.

---

[1] https://ukfires.org.

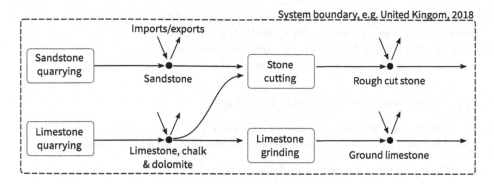

Fig. 1. MEFA system showing rock processing stages in the UK. Processes are shown by boxes. The arrows represent flows. The types of materials are shown by dots, with the vertical flows representing trade flows across the system boundary.

Example 3 (Supply constraints). Biomass is in demand for low-carbon energy supply and as a low-carbon building material, but supply is limited [6]. Reconciling this requires a whole-system view of total quantities of materials produced, together with all uses.

Since all the important characteristics of these systems cannot generally be measured directly, models are used to fill gaps and reconcile conflicts in data. Information is sparse, meaning that every piece of relevant data is valuable to confirm or improve our understanding of the system.

2.1 Material/Energy Flow Analysis

Although the general challenges of data access apply to a broader range of sustainability assessment methods, our focus is on system-level issues studied through Material/Energy Flow Analysis (MEFA). This is a systematic approach to understanding the flows (movements) and stocks (accumulations) of material within a system, typically defined by a spatial area (such as a country) and a time period (such as a year). It gives a clearer technological understanding of the system than economic models of the economy, and the principles of conservation of mass and energy allow for checking and reconciliation of the model [3]. Essentially an MEFA is an abstract representation of a system in terms of *processes*, *stocks*, and *flows*. A process is a part of the system where material/energy is transformed, transported or stored. A stock is the accumulation of material within a process. A flow represents the transfer of material/energy between processes, or between a process within the system and the surrounding environment. The system of processes and flows can be seen as a bipartite directed graph [17], as in Fig. 1.

Once the system is defined in this way, the available data can be mapped onto the relevant parts of the system. The MEFA approach is then essentially a constrained optimisation problem to find the size of the flows, subject to the constraints set by conservation of mass/energy and the known technical characteristics of the processes, while matching as closely as possible the known data [4]. This paper focuses on the first step: finding and querying the available data in a form that can act as an input to the subsequent model solving stage.

2.2   Use Cases and Research Problems

To guide the development of the PRObs system, we identified use cases from the literature and from needs of researchers within the *UK FIRES* project.

Use Case 1 (Data Integration Including "System Context"). It is important that resource data can be associated with its "system context" [20], so it can be linked into a MEFA system and integrated with other data. For example, government statistics on material production should not be viewed simply as a table of numbers, but each value should be associated with the region and time period for which it was measured, and explicitly linked to the edge(s) in a system diagram like Fig. 1 to which it relates. However, datasets vary in the completeness and format of this metadata. A general data model for resource data has been proposed [16] which is largely sufficient to meet these requirements. The main barrier to allow its use with Semantic Technologies is the formalisation into a proper ontology which exploits the characteristics of this data model.

Use Case 2 (Access Diverse Data in a Consistent and Flexible Structure). Different data sources classify their information in different ways, and these classifications may evolve over time. Long-term time-series data are critical to understand the dynamics of past and future resource use, so it is important to be able to convert data published in different classification systems into one consistent set of categories. Differences in the measurement units also need to be harmonised.

Even if data were already reported in fully-consistent classification systems, there is still a need to alter the structure, since some data is more detailed than is needed for modelling the system. For example, production statistics provide information on pharmaceuticals at a high level of detail which is unnecessary and should be aggregated for a model focused on high-mass materials.

To enable flexible queries at the desired level of detail to be answered, a system is needed which can take account of the hierarchical structure of processes and materials/goods classification to aggregate data as needed. Aggregation must avoid double-counting values where data already exists at different levels of the hierarchy, and deal with missing values, which occur frequently in statistics due to confidentiality concerns or other lack of coverage.

Use Case 3 (Tracking the Provenance and Uncertainty of Data). Confidence in modelling results increases when data can be validated against independent sources. Different datasets are more or less credible, depending on their source and measurement methodology. During aggregation, uncertainty may increase due to missing data or dependence on lower-quality datasets. It is important to track the providence of values returned by queries, so they can be given a suitable measure of uncertainty, and independent data for validation can be identified.

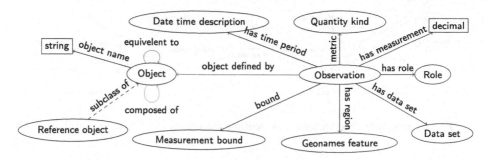

Fig. 2. The core concepts and relations in the PRObs ontology.

Use Case 4 (Streamline Usage of Semantic Web Tools for Domain Experts). The PRObs system is intended to be used to support MEFA modelling by domain experts unfamiliar with semantic web technologies. As such, they should be supported to enter information (e.g. about materials of interest and their hierarchical structure) and retrieve results without becoming experts in RDF and complex SPARQL queries. Because defining the system is subjective (a different definition could be chosen for different modelling goals), users should be supported in clearly documenting their choices. It should be possible to use the system as far as possible on typical researchers' computers without many cores and RAM, and integrate with typical modelling workflows involving e.g. Python notebooks.

The rest of this paper addresses these use cases as follows:

Use case 1: An ontology, building on an existing data model for the domain, for describing specific data points and their relationships (Sect. 3)

Use cases 2 & 3: Datalog rules/algorithms to infer new information and convert data between different classification systems (Sect. 4).

Use case 4: A system wrapping the RDFox implementation with Python packages to ease application by domain experts (Sect. 5).

3 The PRObs Ontology

To allow quantified data points on resource use to be expressed in RDF, we build on the data model proposed by Pauliuk et al. [16]. This describes three components of a data point: value, metadata, and "system location". The value can be a simple numerical value with associated physical units, or could account for uncertain values by defining probability distributions or bounds. The metadata includes provenance information. The system location is the component specific to MEFA: it associates the data point with its context, as in Use Case 1 above.

To represent this in RDF, we introduce the concept of an *Observation* to represent an individual data point and its value, linked to its system location (Fig. 2). We then introduce concepts describing types of materials/goods, and

Fig. 3. Example observations representing data from the Prodcom database.

how they are related. Full details are available in Ref. [7] and the online documentation[2]. The ontology links to several external vocabularies: *PROV*[3] for data provenance, *QUDT*[4] for physical units, *Geonames*[5] for spatial regions, and *OWL-Time*[6] for time.

Example 4 (Stone, sand and gravel example). To explain the ontology, we use a small subset of a model of the UK production system as a running example. This example describes the production of "crushed stone" and "sand & gravel". To illustrate the way that data can be expressed at a coarser or finer level of detail, three sub-types of "crushed stone" are distinguished, and all these materials are collectively described as "aggregates". Two datasets are used in the example: "Prodcom" provides statistics on the production of manufactured goods, while "BGS" refers to the British Geological Survey Minerals Yearbook. Full details are available online[7]. This example features in Figs. 3, 4 and 5, described below.

3.1 Observations

An *Observation* represents a single data point. Every *Observation* is associated with the geospatial location and time period for which it was measured (defined using terms from the *Geonames* and *OWL-Time* vocabularies). Figure 3 shows how two example data points from the Prodcom database are represented, describing equivalent data for the United Kingdom recorded in different years.

The system context (i.e. the edge(s) in a system diagram like Fig. 1 to which the data relates) is defined by a *Role*, *Process* and/or *Object*. *Object* refers generically to any type of thing, including materials, goods and substances, but also non-material things that can flow through the system such as energy and services. *Process* refers to a type of activity. *Role* defines which element of the MEFA system is being measured. For simplicity all examples in this paper use the role "sold production", i.e. the total production of an *Object*.

---

[2] https://ukfires.github.io/probs-ontology.
[3] http://www.w3.org/TR/prov-o.
[4] http://qudt.org/2.1/vocab/citation.
[5] https://www.geonames.org/ontology.
[6] https://www.w3.org/TR/owl-time.
[7] Ref. [12], viewable at https://ukfires.github.io/probs-ISWC2021-example.

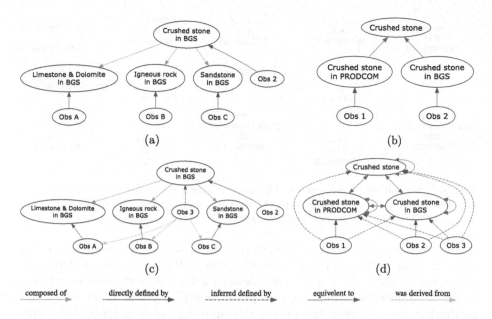

Fig. 4. Composition (a) and equivalence (b) of objects from Example 4, with only original observations shown. In (c–d) new inferred observations are included.

The way in which the data is measured is defined by the *Metric* (e.g. mass or volume), represented using the *QuantityKind* concepts from the *QUDT* vocabulary. Since conversions between alternative physical units for a given *Metric* are lossless and well-defined (e.g. to convert kilograms to tonnes), we normalise all values to a single reference unit for each metric type. The value is described by the *measurement* property. The presence of data whose value has been redacted (e.g. for confidentiality) is represented by an *Observation* with no *measurement*.

3.2   Composition and Equivalence of Objects

The next set of relations in Fig. 2 describes the relationships between *Objects*, allowing data from different sources at different levels of detail to linked.

Composition. When an *Object* can be broken down into several smaller categories, the *composite* object is linked to the *component* objects via the *objectComposedOf* object property. This relationship is stronger than simply a part-whole relationship. The *components* are implied to be *Mutually Exclusive, Collectively Exhaustive* (MECE) with respect to the *composite*; i.e. there are no other *components* of the *composite* parent which are not explicitly mentioned.

This allows *compatible* observations of the *components* to be aggregated to infer new observations for the *composite*. Observations are *compatible* if they share the same *Role, Region, Time Period,* and *Metric*. If any *components* are

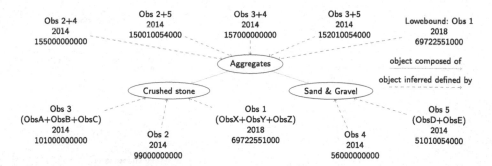

Fig. 5. Composition of *Aggregates*. The observations of *Crushed stone* are those in Fig. 4d. Those at the top arise from the different combinations of *components*. The *TimePeriod* is shown in square brackets, above the *measurement*.

missing measurement values, the result is only a lower bound, and if any *components* have multiple conflicting *compatible* observations (e.g. from independent data sources), there are multiple possible aggregated values that can be inferred.

In the running example, data on production of *Crushed stone* is reported in Prodcom as a single category, but the equivalent data in BGS is also split into three smaller categories. Figure 4a shows how the *component* and *composite Object*s are related. The three observations *Obs A*, *Obs B*, and *Obs C* are *compatible* and can be aggregated to infer a new observation (*Obs 3*) for the composite object *Crushed stone in BGS*, as shown in Fig. 4c. We use the relations *objectDirectlyDefinedBy* and *objectInferredDefinedBy* to denote, respectively, the observations we load directly from the datasets, and those we infer using equivalence or composition. They are subclasses of *objectDefinedBy*.

Equivalence. Different *Object* instances may be used in different datasets which in fact refer to the same type of thing. The matching instances are linked by the *objectEquivalentTo* relation, which is an equivalence relation (it is reflexive, symmetric, and transitive). When an *Observation* is linked to an *Object*, it should also be linked to any *Object* that is equivalent to the original (i.e. equivalent objects share the same observations).

In the running example, there are two dataset-specific *Object* instances for "crushed stone". To easily refer to these, a *ReferenceObject* is defined which gives the canonical representation of several equivalent individuals. In Fig. 4b, there is a *ReferenceObject* called simply *Crushed stone* which is equivalent to both the dataset specific instances. Figure 4d shows that both the original direct observations (*Obs 1* and *Obs 2*) and the inferred observation generated by composition (*Obs 3*) are propagated to the equivalent objects. In this way, the original data can be accessed via alternative terms.

Further Example of Composition and Equivalence. Figure 5 shows more complex cases of composition. The object *Crushed stone* and the object *Sand & Gravel* have 4 observations that are all *compatible* with each other (*Obs 2–5*). They are combined in all possible ways, generating 4 observations (shown in the upper part of the figure). On the other hand, the observation *Obs 1* of the object *Crushed stone* is not *compatible* with any observation of the object *Sand & Gravel*, being defined for a different time period, so it generates a lower bound observation. If this lower bound observation is used to generate other observations, then they will also be lower bound observations.

Classification Systems. While not every dataset is linked to well-defined classification systems for *Objects*, there are several important systems in use, for example for international trade data. In these cases the classification system has been used to create the composition and equivalence relations described above.

4   Reasoning with the PRObs Ontology

The ontology described in the previous section provides a data model for *Observations*, allowing data from sources in diverse formats to be integrated together with the necessary system context (Use case 1). However, if different data points have been defined using different classification systems, they cannot yet be easily and transparently retrieved for reuse in new analyses (Use case 2 & 3). New information needs to be inferred from the raw data using rules that implement the semantics of MEFA systems. Generally, this involves converting data between different definitions of time, location, activity, and object type. In this section, we describe our approach to this, focusing specifically on converting definitions of object types, since this is the most pressing issue in the use of the system so far.

We decided to use the Datalog language with stratified negation and aggregates to perform these computations. This allows the complex behaviours required to be expressed in simple rules, while benefiting from the efficient solvers available for evaluating Datalog programs. Although more expressive/complex logic-based language exist, they are not likely to work in our scenario due to the large amount of data and the huge number of combinations that arise from their evaluation.

4.1   Equivalence and Composition

Equivalence. As described in Sect. 3, equivalent objects are linked by the :objectEquivalentTo object property. These objects should share the same observations (Fig. 4d). Although this may seem trivial, it has several subtleties reflected in the Datalog rule we used:

```
1  [?Obs , :objectInferredDefinedBy , ?O1] :-
2          [?O1 , :objectEquivalentTo , ?O2] ,
3          FILTER(?O1 != ?O2) ,
4          [?Obs , :objectDefinedBy , ?O2] ,
5          NOT [?Obs , :objectDirectlyDefinedBy , ?O1] .
```

Rule set 1.1. Equivalence propagation

Propagation of observations has several advantages over duplication; for instance, it allows saving memory and to have more consistent answers. In rule 1.1 we identify the equivalent objects ?O1 and O2 (line 2), avoiding the reflexive links (line 3), and for each observation of ?O2 (line 4), that is not a direct observation of ?O1 (line 5), we add it as a new inferred observation of ?O1.

This rule may seem overcomplicated for the simple task of sharing the observations among equivalent objects, but it is required to avoid unwanted behaviours. Given that :objectEquivalentTo is an equivalence relation, negation as failure is required to avoid deriving :objectInferredDefinedBy relations for objects that are already defined by direct observations. Figure 4 shows an example of the correct behaviour needed in this case; a naive definition of this rule would have derived that two additional :objectInferredDefinedBy relations from *Obs 1* and *Obs 2* to *Crushed stone in Prodcom* and *Crushed stone in BGS* respectively.

Composition. If an object is composed of multiple *component* objects, we want to create new inferred aggregated observations derived from all combinations of *compatible* observations of the *components*, as explained in Sect. 3.2. Although this type of computation is not possible in Datalog in general, we found the peculiar characteristics of our problem do allow a solution. To confirm this, we designed and implemented an "algorithm" called PCSC, discussed below.

If each object always had only one observation, then we could have used the aggregation feature of Datalog to infer the composed observations, but, as Fig. 5 shows, in general this is not the case. Finding all possible results requires aggregating values from the Cartesian product of an unbounded number of facts, but Datalog, as most logic-based languages, does not include an operator for this.

Moreover, since what we are computing is inherently recursive, we cannot achieve it using stratified rules. Aggregation and negation-as-failure are non-monotonic extensions of Datalog [5], but a simple stratification condition ensures a monotonic behaviour. Languages with non-monotonic operators are known to be much harder to evaluate, and thus not suitable for applications involving large amounts of data that may be involved in a combinatorial explosion.[8]

PCSC "Algorithm". The main idea behind PCSC is to avoid the unboundedness over the branches of the :objectComposedOf relation by building a tree (T) that transposes the breadth of the composition hierarchy into the depth of T. This solves the aggregation issue mentioned in Sect. 4.1. In particular, starting from a root node that represents the *composite*, after choosing an order among its *components*, we iteratively add as children the *Observations* of each *component*. Figure 6a shows the T constructed from the example shown in Fig. 4c.

---

[8] A detailed explanation of the reasons to prefer monotonic reasoning over a non-monotonic one is beyond the scope of this paper, but we want to point out that in the context of this paper we are running specific calculations over our data while non-monotonic approaches are typically designed to solve combinatorial problems.

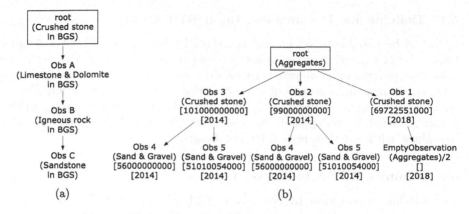

Fig. 6. Examples of trees build by the PCSC "algorithm". (a) and (b) show the trees corresponding to the examples in Fig. 4c and Fig. 5, respectively.

After building the tree T of the *composite* object O, aggregating the *measurement* in each path from the root to a leaf produces the new inferred observations of O.

To handle the case where some *components* have missing or 'not *compatible*' *Observations*, we add an *EmptyObservation* for each 'missing node' in T. The *EmptyObservations* do not affect the *measurement* value of the inferred observations, and are useful to identify the *lower bound* observations. The tree T constructed from the example shown in Fig. 5 is shown in Fig. 6b.

To compute the new aggregated inferred observations using stratified programs, we create a copy of all the classes and properties involved in the composition into a different named graph, and then use them to infer the information about the new observations. Because in our specific scenario we know in advance how many iterations are needed to derive all possible inferred observations, we can use a multi-step approach to derive all the inferred observations even for multi-level hierarchies of composed objects. This solves the monotonic behaviour issue mentioned in Sect. 4.1. To illustrate this, in the example we first derive *Obs3* for *Crushed stone in BGS* from its *components* (Fig. 4c), and which is then used in turn to derive the inferred observations of *Aggregates* (Fig. 5).

We designed and implemented several improvements, both from the conceptual and the technical sides, to make this "algorithm" work with a large amount of data. The complete version also derives additional relations capturing the provenance of the inferred observations. The full code can be found in the ontology repository.

5 System Implementation

Our system consists of a frontend interface for defining and documenting system definitions as input RDF data, and a backend implementation based on RDFox.

5.1   Defining and Documenting Input RDF Data

It should be possible to set up and use the PRObs system without a detailed knowledge of semantic web technologies (Use Case 4). To achieve this, we adopt a literate programming approach to produce code (RDF) and documentation (HTML) from a single source, by extending the Sphinx documentation system[9] with domain-specific extensions[10]. This allows for full documentation-writing features, including concept indices, cross-references, text formatting, and bibliographies, within Python executable notebooks.

5.2   Running RDFox to Answer Queries

The PRObs system runs RDFox scripts to load the input data and answer queries, supported by Python utilities to embed this within a testing or analysis workflow. The input data consists of system definitions in RDF as described above, with external datasets provided in the form of tabular data files and mapping scripts which are read during processing by RDFox.

RDFox was originally developed at the University of Oxford and is now being commercialised by a spin-out company, Oxford Semantic Technologies[11]. RDFox supports the RDF graph data model, the OWL 2 RL ontology language and the SPARQL query language. Rules in RDFox can be represented using a powerful extension to the Datalog language allowing, e.g. the use of much of SPARQL in rule bodies [15]. RDFox has a small memory footprint, is very efficient in its use of memory to store RDF triples, and exploits modern multi-core architectures for fast parallel reasoning. RDFox reasons by materialising all the triples implied by the data and rules, which allows for fast query answering [13]. RDFox has a scripting language which can sequentially run commands covering all features of the system[12], and exposes a REST API, which includes a SPARQL endpoint.

PRObs Ontology and RDFox Scripts. The ontology (Sect. 3) and the RDFox scripts implementing the rules and algorithm (Sect. 4) are published online (See footnote 4). To streamline use in a MEFA analysis, we have developed Python wrappers that assist with setting up the RDFox scripts to load the relevant datasets, and running RDFox as part of a wider workflow to answer queries retrieving relevant *Observations* for input to subsequent modelling and analysis steps. A utility called `rdfox_runner` provides generic support for interacting with RDFox processes[13].

Our current pipeline is shown in Fig. 7. We first run some preprocessing steps to transform the data and the ontology into a format that is more compatible with RDFox. Then we load the datasets and the ontologies, and we run the 'Conversion' phase to convert the data into RDF, enrich them with new information

---

[9] https://www.sphinx-doc.org.
[10] https://github.com/ricklupton/sphinx_probs_rdf.
[11] https://www.oxfordsemantic.tech.
[12] https://docs.oxfordsemantic.tech/command-line-reference.html.
[13] https://github.com/ricklupton/rdfox_runner.

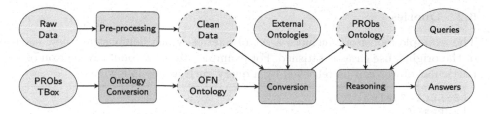

Fig. 7. Back-end pipeline. The rectangles represent the steps of our pipeline (green for Python scripts and blue for RDFox scripts). The ellipses represent inputs and outputs (dashed for internal results). (Color figure online)

(for instance, the new inferred *Observations* from equivalence and composition), and save them. Finally, in the 'Reasoning' phase the whole PRObs Ontology is loaded and a SPARQL endpoint is exposed to answer queries over it.

6   Case Study and Evaluation

To illustrate the use of the system, we describe a case study of mapping flows through the UK production system.

6.1   Case Study: UK Production System

This case study forms part of the ongoing research within the *UK FIRES* programme, motivated by seeking opportunities for innovation in manufacturing processes. The goal is to obtain a detailed understanding of how supply chains are dependent on different manufacturing processes, and where scrap is currently arising within the system, in order to quantify the benefits of innovation in different areas. To this end, a MEFA model is used to define the structure of supply chains and estimate the pattern of flows through the system which best matches the available measurements. The role of the PRObs ontology described here is to provide access to data from a diverse set of external datasets in a coherent structure aligned to the required inputs of the optimisation model.

Since there is no standard system definition of UK manufacturing supply chains at the level of technical detail required for this analysis, a major element of the project is to describe a suitable set of *Processes* and *Objects* to which the available data can be mapped, and which describe entities of relevance to the study's research questions. These are defined and documented using the system described in Sect. 5.1. Figure 1 illustrates a very small extract of the MEFA system; the whole project includes 701 processes and 617 object types. The datasets used include Prodcom and Comtrade. As mentioned in Sect. 3, a working example of a small extract of the case study system is available online (See footnote 9).

6.2   Queries

The example repository includes a set of queries which demonstrate how each of the original use cases is satisfied. For example, all data about production of a particular object can be retrieved by a query such as the following:

```
 1  SELECT ?Value
 2  WHERE {
 3      ?Observation  :objectDefinedBy
 4                  [ a :ReferenceObject ;
 5                    :objectName "Crushed stone" ] ;
 6              :hasRegion [gn:name "Great Britain"] ;
 7              :hasTimePeriod
 8                  [ time:unitType time:unitYear ;
 9                    time:year "2014"^^xsd:gYear ] ;
10              :hasRole :SoldProduction ;
11              :metric quantitykind:Mass ;
12              :measurement ?Value .
13  }
```

In the full case study dataset and model, we use similar queries to access data linked to the processes and objects forming the MEFA model, enabling data from different sources to be transparently and easily linked into the modelling process.

Due to the use of concepts from the ontology and the Datalog rules, the queries are straightforward, easy to read and fast to evaluate.

7   Related Work

The data model proposed by Pauliuk et al. [16] provided the starting point for the ontology described here. A key difference is that the original data model focused on describing results already in the form of a modelled, consistent MEFA system, whereas we aim to represent raw data about the system. Because of this, the PRObs ontology includes additional concepts such as the "sold production" role which do not map one-to-one to the *flows* described by the original data model. On the other hand, the original data model include some other data types such as ratios and metrics which are out of scope of the PRObs ontology.

The existing implementation of the data model does not yet aim to deal with the issues discussed here about harmonising individual data points between datasets based on composition and equivalence of object types. It allows for key-word searching, but the specified materials within each dataset are not standardised or consistent. A search for "steel" returns 75 data sets, but, for example, two sources use "iron ore" and "iron ore, in ground" respectively to mean the same thing. Our system provides a way to formally link these datasets.

Within the broader field of sustainability assessment, several efforts have been made to apply semantic web technologies for Life Cycle Assessment (LCA) in particular. Kuczenski et al. [11] describe the history of ontology development for LCA, and present an overall ontology for LCA based on previous "ontology design patterns" [10,21]. They demonstrate how multiple LCA datasets can be catalogued and analysed using this metadata. While the ontology design patterns have elements of overlap with the ontology presented here, especially with regard to "spatio-temporal scope" of processes, their concepts are tightly bound to the LCA modelling approach. More recently, the BONSAI project [8] has been developing a broader ontology which aims to catalogue a range of datasets relevant to sustainability assessment. They acknowledge the problems of working with actual data points defined with differing terminology, but also stop short of harmonising individual data points.

8   Conclusion

We presented a novel solution to integrate and reason on different production system data using Semantic Technologies. We introduced an ontology based on a general data model for resource data, and we presented an original technique to generate new information about related objects. Finally, we provided some details about the implementation of our method and its effectiveness.

The proposed solution is the basis of the "Physical Resources Observatory", which has been developed and applied initially to support analysis within the UK FIRES research programme. However, this approach applies generally to MEFA-type analysis, and the ontology and data integration approach are currently being applied in a further project to study worldwide petrochemicals emissions. The core ontology is a starting point for more specific additions, and further development of concepts needed for flexible data visualisation is underway.

Applying Semantic Web technologies in this context has raised interesting challenges. Through the integration of existing ontologies and the adoption of logic-based approaches, we have been able to tackle a rather demanding knowledge integration and completion task and automate many of the processes that have been performed manually so far. However, we have also seen that such technologies can pose a significant obstacle for those without a specialised background. To mitigate this we developed a customised set of solutions, which we found simplifies the information retrieval process even for non-experts.

Acknowledgements. We would like to acknowledge the support of José Azevedo and Christopher Cleaver, whose work on the UK production system case study has provided essential context for the development of this work, and the Oxford Semantic Technologies team for their support.

References

1. Allwood, J.M., Ashby, M.F., Gutowski, T.G., Worrell, E.: Material efficiency: a white paper. Resour. Conserv. Recycl. **55**(3), 362–381 (2011). https://doi.org/10.1016/j.resconrec.2010.11.002

2. Arora, M., Raspall, F., Cheah, L., Silva, A.: Buildings and the circular economy: estimating urban mining, recovery and reuse potential of building components. Resour. Conserv. Recycl. **154**, 104581 (2020). https://doi.org/10.1016/j.resconrec. 2019.104581

3. Brunner, P.H., Rechberger, H.: Practical Handbook of Material Flow Analysis. CRC/Lewis, Boca Raton (2004)

4. Cencic, O.: Nonlinear data reconciliation in material flow analysis with software STAN. Sustain. Environ. Res. **26**(6), 291–298 (2016). https://doi.org/10.1016/j. serj.2016.06.002

5. Ceri, S., Gottlob, G., Tanca, L.: Logic Programming and Databases. Surveys in Computer Science. Springer, Heidelberg (1990). https://www.worldcat.org/oclc/ 20595273

6. Committee on Climate Change: Biomass in a low-carbon economy. Technical report, CCC (2018). https://www.theccc.org.uk/wp-content/uploads/2018/ 11/Biomass-in-a-low-carbon-economy-CCC-2018.pdf

7. Germano, S., Saunders, C., Lupton, R.: ukfires/probs-ontology: probs-ontology v1.5.2, July 2021. https://doi.org/10.5281/zenodo.5052739

8. Ghose, A., Hose, K., Lissandrini, M., Weidema, B.P.: An open source dataset and ontology for product footprinting. In: Hitzler, P., et al. (eds.) ESWC 2019. LNCS, vol. 11762, pp. 75–79. Springer, Cham (2019). https://doi.org/10.1007/978-3-030-32327-1_15

9. Hertwich, E., et al.: Nullius in verba: advancing data transparency in industrial ecology. J. Ind. Ecol. (2018). https://doi.org/10.1111/jiec.12738

10. Janowicz, K., et al.: A minimal ontology pattern for life cycle assessment data. In: Proceedings of the Workshop on Ontology and Semantic Web Patterns (6th Edition), Wop 2015 (2015)

11. Kuczenski, B., Davis, C.B., Rivela, B., Janowicz, K.: Semantic catalogs for life cycle assessment data. J. Clean. Prod. **137**, 1109–1117 (2016). https://doi.org/10. 1016/j.jclepro.2016.07.216

12. Lupton, R., Germano, S., Saunders, C.: ukfires/probs-ISWC2021-example: initial release for ISWC2021 paper, April 2021. https://doi.org/10.5281/zenodo.5052758

13. Motik, B., Nenov, Y., Piro, R.E.F., Horrocks, I.: Incremental update of datalog materialisation: the backward/forward algorithm. In: Proceedings of the Twenty-Ninth AAAI Conference on Artificial Intelligence, Austin, Texas, USA, 25–30 January 2015, pp. 1560–1568. AAAI Press (2015)

14. Myers, R.J., Fishman, T., Reck, B.K., Graedel, T.E.: Unified materials information system (UMIS): an integrated material stocks and flows data structure. J. Ind. Ecolo. (2018). https://doi.org/10.1111/jiec.12730

15. Nenov, Y., Piro, R., Motik, B., Horrocks, I., Wu, Z., Banerjee, J.: RDFox: a highly-scalable RDF store. In: Arenas, M., et al. (eds.) ISWC 2015. LNCS, vol. 9367, pp. 3–20. Springer, Cham (2015). https://doi.org/10.1007/978-3-319-25010-6_1

16. Pauliuk, S., Heeren, N., Hasan, M.M., Müller, D.B.: A general data model for socioeconomic metabolism and its implementation in an industrial ecology data commons prototype. J. Ind. Ecol. (2019). https://doi.org/10.1111/jiec.12890

17. Pauliuk, S., Majeau-Bettez, G., Müller, D.B.: A general system structure and accounting framework for socioeconomic metabolism. J. Ind. Ecol. **19**(5), 728–741 (2015). https://doi.org/10.1111/jiec.12306

18. Pauliuk, S., Majeau-Bettez, G., Müller, D.B., Hertwich, E.G.: Toward a practical ontology for socioeconomic metabolism. J. Ind. Ecol. **20**(6), 1260–1272 (2016). https://doi.org/10.1111/jiec.12386

19. Pauliuk, S., Majeau-Bettez, G., Mutel, C.L., Steubing, B., Stadler, K.: Lifting industrial ecology modeling to a new level of quality and transparency: a call for more transparent publications and a collaborative open source software framework. J. Ind. Ecol. **19**(6), 937–949 (2015). https://doi.org/10.1111/jiec.12316
20. Petavratzi, E., et al.: A roadmap towards monitoring the physical economy. Technical report, MinFuture Team, November 2018. https://minfuture.eu/downloads/D5.3_Roadmap.pdf
21. Yan, B., et al.: An ontology for specifying spatiotemporal scopes in life cycle assessment. In: Diversity++@ ISWC, pp. 25–30 (2015)

Towards Semantic Interoperability in Historical Research: Documenting Research Data and Knowledge with *Synthesis*

Pavlos Fafalios[1]([🖂]) [iD], Konstantina Konsolaki[1], Lida Charami[1],
Kostas Petrakis[1], Manos Paterakis[1], Dimitris Angelakis[1],
Yannis Tzitzikas[1,2] [iD], Chrysoula Bekiari[1], and Martin Doerr[1]

[1] Centre for Cultural Informatics and Information Systems Laboratory, FORTH-ICS,
Heraklion, Greece
{fafalios,konsolak,lida,cpetrakis,paterakis,agelakis,tzitzik,
bekiari,martin}@ics.forth.gr
[2] Computer Science Department, University of Crete, Heraklion, Greece

Abstract. A vast area of research in historical science concerns the documentation and study of artefacts and related evidence. Current practice mostly uses spreadsheets or simple relational databases to organise the information as rows with multiple columns of related attributes. This form offers itself for data analysis and scholarly interpretation, however it also poses problems including i) the difficulty for collaborative but controlled documentation by a large number of users, ii) the lack of representation of the details from which the documented relations are inferred, iii) the difficulty to extend the underlying data structures as well as to combine and integrate data from multiple and diverse information sources, and iv) the limitation to reuse the data beyond the context of a particular research activity. To support historians to cope with these problems, in this paper we describe the *Synthesis* documentation system and its use by a large number of historians in the context of an ongoing research project in the field of History of Art. The system is Web-based and collaborative, and makes use of existing standards for information documentation and publication (CIDOC-CRM, RDF), focusing on semantic interoperability and the production of data of high value and long-term validity.

Keywords: Historical research · Documentation · Digital humanities · Semantic interoperability

1 Introduction

Historical science is the field that describes, examines, and questions a sequence of past events, and investigates the patterns of cause and effect that are related to them. A vast area of research in this field concerns the discovery, collection, organisation, presentation, and interpretation of information about historical events. This includes either the *digitization* (and then *curation*) of archival

© Springer Nature Switzerland AG 2021
A. Hotho et al. (Eds.): ISWC 2021, LNCS 12922, pp. 682–698, 2021.
https://doi.org/10.1007/978-3-030-88361-4_40

sources, like in [5,14] for the case of Maritime History, or the detailed *documentation* of cultural artefacts and related evidence [1], with the latter being the focus of this paper.

Although computing in historical research has developed enormously over the last years, with Semantic Web technologies starting playing a significant and ever increasing role [9], information management problems still exist and are still vast and very varied. Current practice mostly uses spreadsheets or simple relational databases to organise the information as rows with multiple columns of related attributes.[1] This form offers itself for data analysis and scholarly interpretation, however it also poses problems including i) the difficulty for collaborative but controlled documentation by a large number of historians of different research groups, ii) the lack of representation of the details from which the documented relations are inferred, important for the long-term validity of the research results, iii) the difficulty to combine and integrate information extracted from multiple and diverse information sources documented by more than one researcher, iv) the difficulty to easily extend the existing data structures on demand for enabling the incorporation of additional information of historical interest (not originally thought), v) the difficulty of third parties to understand and re-use the documented data, resulting in the production of data with limited longevity that lacks semantic interoperability.

To try coping with these problems, in this paper we present the *Synthesis* documentation system and its use by a large number of historians in the context of a European research project (ERC) of History of Art, called RICONTRANS. *Synthesis* utilises XML technology, offering flexibility in terms of versioning, workflow management and data model extension, and focuses on semantic interoperability by making use of existing standards for data modelling and publication, in particular the formal ontology (ISO standard) CIDOC-CRM [2] and RDF. The aim is the production of data with high value, longevity, and long-term validity that can be (re)used beyond a particular research activity.

We show how the documentation process is performed by researchers working in the RICONTRANS project, the data model used, the functionality and user interface offered by *Synthesis*, as well as how the documented data is transformed to a rich semantic network of linked data (an RDF knowledge graph). We also discuss lessons learned from our collaboration with historians of RICONTRANS as well as future work related to data dissemination and exploitation.

The rest of this paper is organised as follows: Sect. 2 describes the context of this work, the requirements and the corresponding challenges. Section 3 details how the *Synthesis* system is used for data documentation in historical research. Section 4 presents the user interface of *Synthesis* and provides usage statistics. Section 5 discusses lessons learned and future data exploitation. Finally, Sect. 6 concludes the paper and discusses interesting directions for future work.

---

[1] We have witnessed this through our participation in a large number of projects in the fields of cultural heritage and digital humanities, and our collaboration with researchers in these fields.

2   Context, Requirements and Challenges

2.1   The RICONTRANS Project

RICONTRANS[2] is an ongoing European research project in the field of History of Art consisting of research groups in Greece, Serbia, Romania, Bulgaria, and Russia [4]. The project investigates the transnational phenomenon of artefact transfer and the various aspects of the reception of these objects in the host societies, in different historical periods and circumstances. The focus is on Russian religious artefacts brought to the Balkans the period 16th–20th centuries, which are now preserved in monasteries, churches or museum collections.

In particular, the project aims to i) map the phenomenon in its long history by identifying preserved objects in the region; ii) follow the paths through which these art objects were brought to the Balkans and the Eastern Mediterranean; iii) identify and classify the mediums of their transfer; iv) analyse the dynamics and the various moving factors (religious, political, ideological) of this process; v) study, analyse and classify these objects according to their iconographic and artistic particularities; vi) inquire into the aesthetic, ideological, political, and social factors which shaped the context of the reception of the transferred objects in the various social, cultural and religious environments; and vii) investigate their influence on the visual culture of the host societies.

2.2   Data Management Requirements and Challenges

To achieve these objectives, art historians and other researchers of RICON-TRANS first need to collect primary and secondary sources, such as archival sources, old books and newspapers, oral history sources, that provide information about Russian artefacts and their transfers to the Balkans. The collected information, as well as the knowledge derived by the analysis of the sources, must then be documented in detail and stored in a database in a form that allows its effective exploitation for both current and future research.

Specifically, the database should contain information about *art objects* (such as icons, triptychs, crosses and censers), *object transfers* (from/to location, purpose of transfer, etc.), *historical figures* (involved in transfers), *locations* (such as cities, villages, monasteries, churches and museums), as well as *related events* (such as the ordination of archbishop, or the erection of a church). It must also provide metadata information about the collected *sources*, since this is important for tracking provenance information about the research findings (and thus ensure their long-term validity). Finally, it must allow including (and documenting) *digital files* such as images of art objects, or scans of documents.

To enable the construction of such a database, we need to cope with the below main data management challenges:

---

[2] RICONTRANS - *Visual Culture, Piety and Propaganda: Transfer and Reception of Russian Religious Art in the Balkans and the Eastern Mediterranean (16th - early 20th c.)*. ERC Consolidator Grant (ID: 818791). 1 May 2019–30 April 2024. https://ricontrans-project.eu/.

– How to support *collaborative* data entry, documentation and curation by a large number of researchers belonging to different research teams that are spread across the world? How to provide to all researchers a common and secure place for storing and accessing their data internally and releasing parts of it to a wider audience when they want to do so?

– How to balance between documentation *richness* and database *usability*? How to support researchers in providing detailed information about the documented entities, as well as additional metadata/provenance information, in a structured but straightforward way?

– How to facilitate easy *extension* of the database schema for allowing documenting new type of information about the documented entities? In ongoing research projects where new data sources might become available at any time, frequent updates of the database schema are unavoidable.

– How to *control* the data entry process for certain pieces of documented information so that a *common terminology* is used across researchers performing the documentation? This is very important for enabling effective information integration and data exploration.

– How to facilitate *future exploitation/reuse* of the database by others (beyond the particular research project)? How to enable easy integration of the data with other relevant data provided by other researchers? How to ensure the long-term validity and longevity of the data?

3   Data Documentation with *Synthesis*

We provide an overview of the system (Sect. 3.1), detail its data model and the supported types of documentation fields (Sect. 3.2), and discuss how the data is transformed to a semantic network, i.e., an RDF knowledge graph (Sect. 3.3).

3.1   System Overview

Synthesis is a Web-based system for the collaborative documentation of information and knowledge in the fields of cultural heritage and digital humanities. It utilises XML technology and a multi-layer architecture, offering high *flexibility* and *extensibility* (in terms of data structures and data types), as well as *sustainability* (each documented entity, such as an object or object transfer, is stored as an XML document readable by both humans and machines). Its database server is *eXist-db*[3], a native XML database. Also, *Synthesis* is *multilingual*, supporting the parallel use of multiple languages for documentation, and supports *versioning* of the documented information.

The system supports four roles of users: i) *system administrator*, responsible for the whole system, with rights to create new 'organisations' (groups); ii) *organisation administrator*, responsible for the documentation process of a particular organisation, with rights to create new editors and guests for this organisation; iii) *editor*, belonging to a specific organisation, with rights to create and document entities for this organisation; iv) *guest*, belonging to a specific organisation,

---

[3] http://exist-db.org/.

with rights to only view the documented entities of a specific organisation. As we detail below, in *Synthesis* users create and document *entities* belonging to a set of pre-configured *entity types*. Users of role 'editor' can only edit entities created by themselves, can provide edit access to other users, and can view only the entities created by editors belonging to the same organisation. However, the management of rights can be easily adjusted for any specific need. For example, one or more editors can be configured to have edit access to all entities because, for instance, they have the responsibility to make corrections.

Synthesis has embedded processes for transforming the data stored in the XML documents to an ontology-based RDF dataset (knowledge graph), thus supporting the creation of a knowledge base (KB) of integrated data. Contrary to approaches that support users in creating a KB from the beginning, such as ResearchSpace [12] or WissKi [15], *Synthesis* decouples data entry (made by the research team) from the ontology-based integration and creation of the KB (a process supported by data engineers). The main reasons behind this decision are the following (inspired by [3]):

- Versioning in a KB is difficult; individual contributions, alternatives, corrections, etc., all in the same *pool of valid knowledge* can hardly be regarded as a standard procedure. We consider a KB as an ideal tool for integrating the *latest stage of knowledge* acquired through diverse processes.
- We regard as very different a KB of facts believed together as true, versus managing, coordinating and consolidating the knowledge acquisition process of a large research team. This requires a document structure such as XML, for making local versioning, workflow management, provenance tracing, and exchanging documents between team members easy.
- Decoupling data entry from KB creation allows the straightforward production of different KB versions, considering different ontologies or different versions of the same ontology. This only requires creating and maintaining the schema mappings that transform the documented data to RDF.

3.2   Data Model

The data model used by *Synthesis* is carefully designed for a given application domain (History of Art, in our case), with a particular focus on *semantic interoperability* [2,13]. This notion is defined as the ability of computer systems to exchange data with unambiguous, shared meaning. *Synthesis* achieves this by a) linking each element of its data model to a domain ontology, b) allowing users to add metadata about the data, and c) allowing users to link a term to a controlled (shared) vocabulary or thesaurus of terms (more below).

A user in *Synthesis* can create and start documenting *entities* organised in *entity types*. Each *entity type* has its own data structure (*schema*). A *schema* is XML-based, containing a set of *fields* organised in an hierarchical (tree-like) structure. The leaves in this tree-like structure are the *documentation fields* that are to be filled by the users. Figure 1 shows a small part of the schema of the entity type 'Object', as configured for the RICONTRANS project.

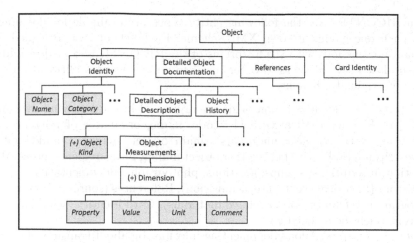

Fig. 1. A part of the schema of the entity type Object.

The schema of each entity type is carefully designed to be fully compatible with the CIDOC Conceptual Reference Model (CRM).[4] CIDOC-CRM is a high-level, event-centric ontology (ISO standard) of human activity, things and events happening in spacetime, providing definitions and a formal structure for describing the implicit and explicit concepts and relationships used in cultural heritage documentation [2]. This means that there is a mapping between the schema of an entity type and CIDOC-CRM, allowing the straightforward transformation of the data to a semantic network (RDF graph) that is compatible with CIDOC-CRM. For example, Fig. 2 shows how an *Object Measurement* (as documented for an object; cf. Fig. 1) is mapped to CIDOC-CRM.

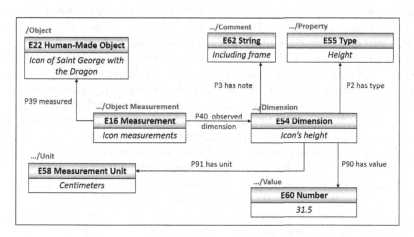

Fig. 2. Mapping of object measurement to CIDOC-CRM.

---

[4] http://www.cidoc-crm.org/, https://www.iso.org/standard/57832.html.

In RICONTRANS, the following entity types are available for documentation, each one having its own XML schema. Each schema was designed after extensive discussions with the historians of the RICONTRANS project and has been updated several times in order to allow documenting additional information, not originally thought.

- *Objects*: The documentation fields are organised in the following categories: Object Identity (indicative fields: code, name, originator of reference, collection, category, basic material(s), main object image), Detailed Object Description (indicative fields: other object names, measurements, object decoration, inscriptions, stamps, locations, photographic documentation), Object History (historical events, use, acquisition), References (source references, bibliographic references, other related materials), Card Identity (scientific supervisor, scientific associates).
- *Object Transfers*: Allows documenting information about transfers of objects. Indicative fields: transfer name/title, transfer date, transferred object, from location, to location, description, transfer purpose, person(s) involved, based on (link to source(s), source passage(s), bibliography).
- *Routes*: Allows grouping a set of object transfers based on a particular object, type of objects, or other criteria. Indicative fields: route name, object transfers, creation information (author, date).
- *Archival Sources*: Allows documenting information about archival sources used to obtain information about an entity of interest (e.g., about an object, object transfer, historical figure, etc.). Indicative fields: title, subject area, short description, category, type, collection, series, file, language.
- *Books*: Allows documenting information about (old) books used to obtain information about an entity of interest. Indicative fields: title, author(s), type, subject area, repository, language, publisher, publication date.
- *Newspapers and Periodical/Reviews*: Allows documenting information about (old) newspapers and periodical/reviews. Indicative fields: title, type, subject area, author, language, editor, publisher, publication date.
- *Oral History Sources*: Allows documenting information about oral history sources, like an oral testimony or interview. Indicative fields: title, subject area, description, language, interview date, interviewer, interviewee.
- *Web Sources*: Allows documenting information about web sources providing historical information about one or more entities of interest. Indicative fields: URI, web page title, subject area, content language, text.
- *Bibliography*: Allows documenting information about bibliographic references related to the project. Indicative fields: type, title, author(s), publisher, publication date/place, conference title, volume and issue number, language.
- *Source Passages*: Allows documenting information about a specific source passage that provides important information for an entity of interest (e.g., an object transfer). Indicative fields: title, subject area, topic, origin (source or bibliography), source passage text, translation, commentary.
- *Collection of Source Passages*: Allows grouping a set of source passages, e.g., based on an object, source, etc. Indicative fields: title, subject, short description, source passage(s).

- *Researcher Comments*: Allows documenting information about research results, e.g., the findings of observing the inscriptions of an icon. Indicative fields: researcher, title, about (object, transfer, route, historical figure), description, date, based on (type of research), conclusion, property of analysis, outcome of analysis, method of analysis, date of analysis.
- *Historical Figures*: Allows documenting information about historical persons, like a bishop, patriarch, etc. Indicative fields: name, role, service, birth place, ethnicity, life period, activity period, references.
- *Collections*: Allows documenting information about collections of objects, e.g., museum collections. Indicative fields: code number, subject, originator of reference, description.
- *Events*: Allows documenting information about historical events, such as a prince reception, an archbishop ordination, or the erection of a church. Indicative fields: name, time of event, location, description, references.
- *Locations*: Allows documenting information about locations, such as cities, villages, monasteries, churches and museums. Indicative fields: name, location type, geopolitical hierarchy, coordinates.
- *Persons*: Allows documenting information about persons (not historical), such as the researchers participating in the project, a photographer, etc. Indicative fields: name, name in native language, role, member of, description.
- *Organisations*: Allows documenting information about organisations, such as museums, libraries, ephorates, etc. Indicative fields: name, type, pursuit (field), location, contact information, description.
- *Digital Objects*: Allows documenting metadata information about the uploaded digital objects like photos. Indicative fields: title, type, short description, file, rights, creation date, creator.

Types of Documentation Fields. Each documentation field in *Synthesis* has a particular type which specifies the type of value that it can receive. The supported types are the following:

- *Link to entity*. The user can select another entity that is documented in the system. The entity can belong to one or more (pre-defined) entity types. The fields *Originator of Reference* (link to Organisation) and *Current Location* (link to Location) of an object are examples of this field type.
- *Link to vocabulary term*. The user can select a term from a static or dynamic vocabulary. A dynamic vocabulary allows users to directly create a new term (which is then added in the vocabulary), while a static vocabulary limits the options to a specific set of terms. An example of a static vocabulary is the *Category* of an object and an example of a dynamic vocabulary is the *Publisher Name* of a book. Both static and dynamic vocabularies can be managed through an administration page in *Synthesis*.
- *Link to thesaurus term*. The user can select a term from a thesaurus of terms which is managed through the THEMAS thesaurus management system. THEMAS[5] is an open source Web-based system for creating, managing

---

[5] https://www.ics.forth.gr/isl/themas-thesaurus-management-system.

and administering multi-faceted and multilingual thesauri according to the principles of ISO standards 25964-1 and 25964-2. THEMAS offers an API which allows its connection with *Synthesis*.

- *Unformatted free text*. The user can provide a piece of text that is usually small in size and that cannot be formatted. Examples of fields of such type are the fields *Object Name* and *Object Code* of the entity type Object.
- *Formatted free text*. The user can provide a piece of text that is usually long in size and which can be formatted. The field *Transfer Description* of an Object Transfer is an example of this type.
- *Number*. The user can provide a numeric value, e.g., an integer number. The field *Dimension Value* of an object measurement is an example of this type.
- *Time expression*. The user can provide a date range in an accepted format relevant to the documentation of historical information, such as *decade of 1970, ca. 1920, 1st half 4th century, 1500 BCE, 3rd century - 5th century*).[6] Restricting the accepted value types of a date range is important for enabling comparisons and effective data exploration. An example of a documentation field of this type is the field *Creation/Production Date* of an object.
- *Location coordinates*. The user can select a point or polygon on a map and the field will be automatically filled with the corresponding coordinates.
- *Location ID*. The system offers the capability to query external geolocation services, in particular Getty Thesaurus of Geographic Names (TGN)[7] or Geonames[8], and get the unique ID and the coordinates of a location.
- *Digital file(s)*. The user can upload one or more digital files of a given file type, e.g., image or document.

A field can also be defined as 'multiple', which means that the user can create multiple instances of it. In case a multiple field is not a leaf, the whole structure (having the field as root) is duplicated. An example of such a multiple field is the *Dimension* field of the object schema (shown in Fig. 1), allowing to add multiple dimensions for a measurement, such as height and width.

The total number of documentation fields in all entity types that link to other entities is currently 158, showcasing the high connectivity of the documented entities. The number of distinct vocabularies is currently 113, while the number of documentation fields in all entity types that link to vocabulary terms is 244, with objects having the highest number of such fields (123, in total). Also, there are two fields that link to a thesaurus in THEMAS: the field *object kind* (of objects and object transfers) and the field *topic* (of objects and source passages).

3.3   Data Transformation (for Knowledge Graph Production)

For transforming the documented data to a rich semantic network of interconnected data (an RDF knowledge graph), we make use of the X3ML framework

---

[6] The full list of the accepted time expressions is available at: https://isl.ics.forth.gr/FeXML_ricontrans/HelpPage_en.html.
[7] http://www.getty.edu/research/tools/vocabularies/tgn/.
[8] https://www.geonames.org/.

and the X3ML mapping definition language [8], a declarative, XML-based language that supports the cognitive process of schema mapping definition. X3ML separates schema mappings from the generation of proper resource identifiers (URIs), so it distinguishes between activities carried out by the domain experts and data engineers, who know the data, from activities carried out by the IT experts who implement data transformation.

Given our target domain ontology (CIDOC-CRM), we need to create one mapping file for each schema of *Synthesis*, i.e., for each entity type. In general, the definition of the mappings from the source schemas to the target ontology is a time-consuming process that can require many revisions as long as the data engineer better understands the data or changes are made to the schemas of the entity types. This process is supported by 3M Editor [8], an X3ML mapping management system suitable for creating and handling the mapping files. It offers a user interface and a variety of actions that help experts manage their schema mappings collaboratively. For technical details about the data transformation process and the tools X3ML and 3M Editor, the reader can refer to [8].

The hierarchies of terms created in THEMAS are represented in RDF using SKOS (Simple Knowledge Organization System[9]), while the vocabularies maintained in *Synthesis* are represented using the class *E55 Type* of CIDOC-CRM.

The transformation of the data to a CIDOC-CRM compliant semantic network increases their value and their long term validity, facilitates integration with other CIDOC-CRM compliant datasets, and enables their advanced querying, analysis and exploration (more about the latter in Sect. 5).

4   User Interface and Usage Statistics

We present the web interface of *Synthesis* (Sect. 4.1), describe how the documentation process is performed (Sect. 4.2), and provide usage statistics (Sect. 4.3).

4.1   The *Synthesis* Web Interface

The interface of *Synthesis* is Web-based and quite simple. After a successful user login, the homepage contains a left menu showing all the supported entity types, grouped in categories (Fig. 3). For each entity type, the user is shown a table with all entities that belong to the selected type and that are currently documented in *Synthesis*, as shown in Fig. 3 for the entity type 'Object'. For each entity, the table shows some basic information which is configurable for each different entity type. For example, for an entity of type Object the table shows its *name*, its *originator of reference* (the organisation responsible for the object), its *current location*, an *image*, the *creator* of the documentation entity (i.e., the researcher who takes care of the object's documentation), the card *status* (unpublished, pending, published; allows tracking the status of the entity's documentation card), and its *ID* (automatically assigned by the system).

---

[9] https://www.w3.org/TR/skos-reference/.

The user can *filter* the entities shown in the table by writing some text in an input field that exists above the table (cf. Fig. 3). In this case, the table shows only those entities for which any of the characteristics shown in the table match the input text. Also, the system offers a *search* functionality, which allows keyword-based searching within the entity's documentation fields, as well as an *advanced search* functionality which allows searching based on values on specific fields, such as searching for object transfers having the value 'donation' as purpose of transfer and the date 'within 18th century' as the transfer date. Advanced search also provides the option to save a query in order to use it in the future (either from the same user or from other users).

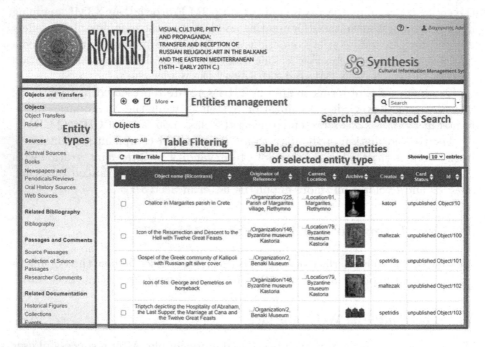

Fig. 3. The user interface of *Synthesis* displaying the supported entity types and the table of documented entities of type 'Object'.

From the web page of a particular entity type, the user has the following options: i) create a new entity for documentation, ii) view the documentation card of one of the entities that appear in the table, iii) edit one of the entities (its documentation card), iv) request for publishing one or more entities (which means that the documentation of these entities has been completed and no more editing is required), v) create a new version of an entity, vi) view the existing versions of an entity, vii) delete one or more entities, viii) create a copy of an entity (for documenting a similar entity), ix) give edit rights for one or more entities to another user account, x) export the schema of the entity type, xi) export the data of one or more entities in XML or RDF format, xii) import an XML of a documented entity.

Regarding the export of data to RDF, the exported data will be CIDOC-CRM compliant if there is an X3ML mapping file for the corresponding entity type. If there is no such mapping file, a naive (ontology-agnostic) schema is used for transforming the data to RDF.

For certain entity types, the user can select one or more entities and display them on a map. In RICONTRANS, this option is currently available for the entity types *Location*, *Object* (showing the current location of the selected objects; as shown in Fig. 4), *Object Transfer* (showing lines connecting the starting and ending locations of the selected transfers), and *Route* (showing sets of object transfers). The information to show for each point in the map is configurable per entity type.

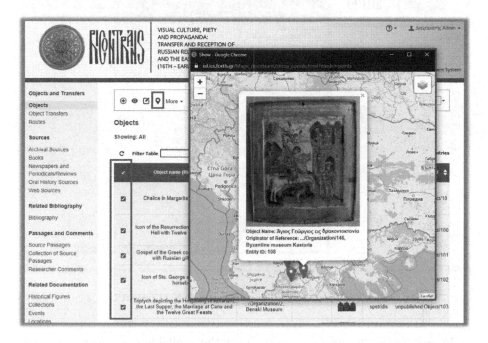

Fig. 4. Displaying a set of objects in a map.

4.2 Entity Documentation

The documentation of entities is performed in a dedicated environment called FeXML, which communicates with *Synthesis* and supports the creation and editing of XML documents. FeXML is activated when the user a) creates a new entity for documentation, b) selects to view one of the documented entities (its *documentation card*), or c) selects to edit one of the documented entities (e.g., for continuing its documentation, correcting a field value, etc.).

Figure 5 shows an example of the documentation card of an entity of type 'Historical Figure', as shown in FeXML in view mode. The documented information is shown in a tree-like structure, where the root of the tree is the name of the entity type and the leaves are the documentation fields. The user can expand or collapse fields on-demand, in order to facilitate its navigation to the documentation fields. By default, when the documentation card of an entity is viewed, FeXML shows as expanded only the filled fields. In the bottom of the documentation card, the user is also shown with all the entity's associations with other documented entities (those the entity references and those the entity is referenced by).

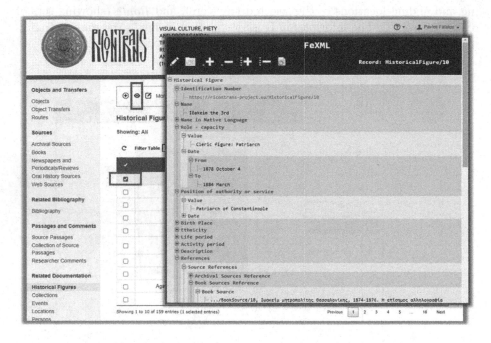

Fig. 5. Viewing the documentation card of an entity.

In edit mode, the user can start filling the available documentation fields. Figure 6 shows examples on how the user can fill information for different types of fields. Also, there is a button on the top of the FeXML window which allows users to see all the accepted time expressions, as well as a button which opens an XML Map showing the full hierarchy of the fields (for facilitating navigation especially when the documentation card is very lengthy, like in the case of objects).

Finally, the management of the vocabularies is performed through a dedicated page accessible through the administration menu of *Synthesis*. This menu option is only shown to user accounts that have the rights to edit the vocabularies. The user can select a vocabulary and *add* new terms, *edit* or *delete* existing terms, as well as *export* the whole vocabulary or *import* a vocabulary from a text file.

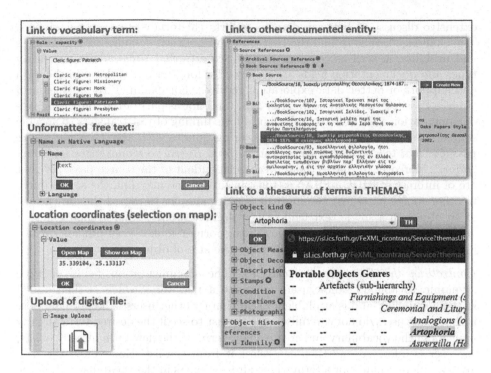

Fig. 6. Examples of documentation fields of different types.

4.3   Usage Statistics

The system is currently being used by 40 users (historians, art historians, philologists, and students in these fields) belonging to 10 institutions in 5 countries. The current (as of July 2, 2021) number of documented entities per entity type is: 1,089 objects, 368 object transfers, 93 routes, 150 archival sources, 45 books, 98 newspapers and periodicals/reviews, 3 oral history sources, 59 web sources, 309 bibliographic items, 533 source passages, 3 collections of source passages, 203 historical figures, 155 collections, 33 events, 491 locations, 98 persons, 394 organisations, and 1,138 digital objects.

5   Lessons Learned and Future Data Exploitation

Collaborating with historians in the context of RICONTRANS gave us the unique chance to learn how domain experts in this area work, what their questions are, what data is important for them to document, and most importantly, what difficulties they face in terms of data management. Below we provide some lessons learned from this collaboration:

Selection of Entity Types and Design of Schemas. The decision on the entity types to support as well as on the documentation fields of each type requires extensive discussions between domain experts (historians) and data engineers. The challenge here is to find the best trade-off between documentation richness and usability, as well as convince domain experts that some additional entity types and documentation fields are required for long-term usefulness of the data and support of better data exploration services. For example, the inclusion of 'Source Passages' as a different entity type, and not as part of the sources, makes documentation a bit more complex but allows linking object transfers to specific source passages and thus supports answering queries such as: *"Give me source passages that talk about transfers of icons from Russia to monasteries in Mount Athos."* Moreover, it makes the sources independent of the source passages that are of interest in RICONTRANS (thus, in future one may link the same source to other source passages). Similarly, it is much simpler to record the dimensions of an object in a single text field (e.g., "15 cm × 20 cm") than breaking it to 3 fields (*property, value, unit*). However, the former makes very difficult, if not impossible, to make comparisons between the size of objects.

Controlling the Dynamic Vocabularies. The documentation fields of type 'dynamic vocabulary' allow users to create a new term which is then added in the vocabulary and is available for selection by other users. The problem here is that some users do not carefully check the list to see if the desired term already appears in the vocabulary and create a new term. If the new term already exists, the user is informed and then can select it from the list. However, if the user gives a different name for a term which already exists in the vocabulary, then the new term is included in the vocabulary. This results in vocabularies containing multiple terms that refer to the same concept, making their future exploitation difficult. For instance, in a search system one might search for all events of a particular category (type) but do not get back all relevant events because the same category has been included in the vocabulary multiple times with different names/labels. Thereby, there is a need for curating the dynamic vocabularies frequently, which is time consuming and may require the curator to contact other users for understanding the meaning of some specific terms.

Understanding the Tree-Like Structure of the Documentation Fields. Many users seem to get confused with the tree-like structure of the documentation fields, which sometimes results in data entry errors. For example, the same field 'Name' exists in multiple positions in the hierarchy of the fields, e.g., "Object/.../Object History/Event/Name", "Object/.../Object History/Use/Name", "Object/.../Object History/Acquisition/Name". To solve this problem we renamed many fields so that their meaning is clear (e.g., from "Name" to "Event Name").

Data Dissemination and Exploitation. The project is currently in the data entry phase where users gather and document information about entities of interest. Apart from the study of the documented data for historical research, part of the data will be made publicly available. The current plan for dissemination and exploitation comprises three main services: 1) *map visualization*, 2) *data publication*, and 3) *semantic network exploration*.

Map Visualisation. Part of the data, such as objects and object transfers, will be visualised on a Web-accessible map application. This will allow historians and other interested parties to explore the data in an interactive environment and learn about the historical routes of several religious artefacts brought to the Balkans the period 16th to 20th centuries.

Data Publication. Part of the data, such an object of high interest and its transfers, will be presented in web pages. The information shown in the web pages will be directly linked to the data in *Synthesis*, which means that updates in *Synthesis* will be directly reflected in the web pages.

Semantic Network Exploration. The CIDOC-CRM compliant semantic network (RDF graph), derived from the data transformation process (cf. Sect. 3.3), can support the advanced exploration of the documented data and the answer of complex information needs. The user-friendly exploration of such a network can be performed through two main general access methods: i) *keyword search*, where the user submits a free text query and gets back a ranked list of results that are relevant to the query terms (e.g., [6,11]), and ii) *interactive access*, where the user explores the data through intuitive interactions with a data access system, e.g., using a *faceted search* interface [16] or *assistive query building* (like in [12] and [7]). Our plan is to make use of an assistive query building interface which will support users in finding answers to information needs that require exploiting the rich associations among the entities and their characteristics, such as *"find me objects of type 'icon' transferred from Russia to monasteries in Greece as a donation"*, or *"find me sources passages that talk about donations of icons transferred to Greece before the 18th century."*

6   Conclusion

We have presented the use of the *Synthesis* system for data documentation and management in the context of a large-scale research project in the field of History of Art, called RICONTRANS. The system is Web-based, collaborative and makes use of established standards (CIDOC-CRM, RDF) for information documentation and publication, facilitating data integration and reuse, and focusing on the production of data with high value, long term validity and longevity.

Synthesis provides full-fledged support for the complete knowledge production life-cycle in historical research. It is currently used by a large number of historians for the documentation of data about religious artefacts, their transfers, sources of information like archival and oral history sources, and other involved entities, such as historical figures and locations.

An interesting direction for future work is the application of information extraction techniques that can facilitate or accelerate data entry, such as the use of named entity extraction [10] for semi-automatically filling the 'referenced information' fields of source passages (referenced persons, locations, dates, etc.).

Acknowledgements. This work has received funding from the European Union's Horizon 2020 research and innovation programme under i) the Marie Sklodowska-Curie grant agreement No 890861 (Project "ReKnow"), and ii) the European Research Council (ERC) grant agreement No 818791 (Project "RICONTRANS").

References

1. Bekiari, C., Doerr, M., Angelakis, D., Karagianni, F.: Building comprehensive management systems for cultural-historical information. In: Proceedings of the 42nd Annual Conference on Computer Applications and Quantitative Methods in Archaeology, pp. 227–234. Archaeopress, Oxford (2014)
2. Doerr, M.: The CIDOC conceptual reference module: an ontological approach to semantic interoperability of metadata. AI Mag. **24**(3), 75 (2003)
3. Doerr, M., Iorizzo, D.: The dream of a global knowledge network-a new approach. J. Comput. Cult. Herit. (JOCCH) **1**(1), 1–23 (2008)
4. Dumitran, A., et al.: The Ricontrans project. Museikon. J. Relig. Art Culture/Revue d'art et de culture religieuse **3**(3), 189–189 (2019)
5. Fafalios, P., et al.: FAST CAT: collaborative data entry and curation for semantic interoperability in digital humanities. ACM J. Comput. Cult. Herit. **14**(4) (2021). https://doi.org/10.1145/3461460
6. Kadilierakis, G., Fafalios, P., Papadakos, P., Tzitzikas, Y.: Keyword search over RDF using document-centric information retrieval systems. In: Harth, A., et al. (eds.) ESWC 2020. LNCS, vol. 12123, pp. 121–137. Springer, Cham (2020). https://doi.org/10.1007/978-3-030-49461-2_8
7. Kritsotakis, V., Roussakis, Y., Patkos, T., Theodoridou, M.: Assistive query building for semantic data. In: SEMANTICS Posters&Demos (2018)
8. Marketakis, Y., et al.: X3ML mapping framework for information integration in cultural heritage and beyond. Int. J. Digit. Libr. **18**(4), 301–319 (2016). https://doi.org/10.1007/s00799-016-0179-1
9. Meroño-Peñuela, A., et al.: Semantic technologies for historical research: a survey. Semantic Web **6**(6), 539–564 (2015)
10. Mountantonakis, M., Tzitzikas, Y.: LODsyndesisIE: entity extraction from text and enrichment using hundreds of linked datasets. In: Harth, A., et al. (eds.) ESWC 2020. LNCS, vol. 12124, pp. 168–174. Springer, Cham (2020). https://doi.org/10.1007/978-3-030-62327-2_29
11. Nikas, C., Kadilierakis, G., Fafalios, P., Tzitzikas, Y.: Keyword search over RDF: is a single perspective enough? Big Data Cogn. Comput. **4**(3), 22 (2020)
12. Oldman, D., Tanase, D.: Reshaping the knowledge graph by connecting researchers, data and practices in ResearchSpace. In: Vrandečić, D., et al. (eds.) ISWC 2018. LNCS, vol. 11137, pp. 325–340. Springer, Cham (2018). https://doi.org/10.1007/978-3-030-00668-6_20
13. Ouksel, A.M., Sheth, A.: Semantic interoperability in global information systems. ACM Sigmod Record **28**(1), 5–12 (1999)
14. Petrakis, K., et al.: Digitizing, curating and visualizing archival sources of maritime history: the case of ship logbooks of the nineteenth and twentieth centuries. Drassana **28**, 60–87 (2021)
15. Scholz, M., Goerz, G.: WissKI: a virtual research environment for cultural heritage. In: ECAI 2012, pp. 1017–1018. IOS Press (2012)
16. Tzitzikas, Y., Manolis, N., Papadakos, P.: Faceted exploration of RDF/S datasets: a survey. J. Intell. Inf. Syst. **48**(2), 329–364 (2016). https://doi.org/10.1007/s10844-016-0413-8

On Constructing Enterprise Knowledge Graphs Under Quality and Availability Constraints

Matthew Kujawinski[1]([✉])[ID], Christophe Guéret[1][ID], Chandan Kumar[3], Brennan Woods[3], Pavel Klinov[2], and Evren Sirin[2]

[1] Accenture Labs, San Jose, USA
{matthew.kujawinski,christophe.gueret}@accenture.com
[2] Stardog, Arlington, USA
{pavel,evren}@stardog.com
[3] Accenture, Dublin, Ireland
{chandan.w.kumar,brennan.woods}@accenture.com

Abstract. Knowledge graph technologies have proven their applicability and usefulness to integrate data silos and answer questions spanning over the different sources. However the integration of data can pose some risks and challenges (security, audit needs, quality control, ...). In this paper we abstract from two client use-cases, one in the banking domain and one in the pharmaceutical domain, to highlight those risks/challenges and propose a generic approach to address them. This approach leverages Semantic web technologies and is implemented using Stardog.

Keywords: Data integration · SHACL · Knowledge graphs

1 Introduction

Combining different data silos into an Enterprise Knowledge Graph (EKG) delivering a 360 degrees view of the data held across those silos is becoming a key asset for several major industries. Be it to better track information about customer across different departments or integrate data from a factory line [7], knowledge graphs provide a streamlined access to data and enable advanced querying capabilities [6].

Beyond the common need of creating a knowledge graph from data found in different silos, Stardog and Accenture found some specific requirements when working on client projects. We hereby report in particular about the needs emerging from two use-cases, one applied to a banking client and the other applied to a pharmaceutical company.

This paper aims at presenting the approach to tackle the requirements and give some example information from the use cases, under the limits of what the clients agreements make it possible for us to disclose. To be more specific, we consider the contribution of this paper as follows:

© Springer Nature Switzerland AG 2021
A. Hotho et al. (Eds.): ISWC 2021, LNCS 12922, pp. 699–713, 2021.
https://doi.org/10.1007/978-3-030-88361-4_41

Paper Main Contributions

- The synthesis of requirements expressed from different industrial deployments of knowledge graphs and the proposal for a generic architecture for addressing them;
- The implementation report of the architecture and its usage for two different client case-studies currently in production stage;
- Some lessons learned and suggestions for future work on Semantic Web technologies and standards which could contribute to better addressing the highlighted challenges.

The remainder of this paper first overviews related work in Sect. 3 to discuss how current best practices and known approaches address our requirements detailed in Sect. 2. The implementation we have of the approach we recommend is then described in Sect. 4 and our example use cases in Sect. 5. We finally conclude on our lessons learned and offer suggestions for further work in Sect. 6.

2 Platform Requirements

The general requirement expressed is the integration of data from different sources in order to solve business intelligence needs spanning over several of those sources. These specific requirements emerging, at least partially, from the two concrete EKG deployments presented in this paper and some others highlight some specific business needs sometimes overlooked by the Semantic Web research community. More specifically we have identified and faced additional constraints around security and entitlements (Requirement 1 - R1), graph preservation (R2), data availability (R3) and quality (R4):

R1. Security and entitlements: Creating an integrated knowledge representation can represent a significant risk for cyber attacks as all the information that would otherwise be found in different sources, each having to be attacked one after the other, is now readily available from one source only and already semantically integrated. This key feature of an EKG could turn into a major flaw under the wrong usage context. Besides the cyber-threat risk, combining data can also lead to a risk of infraction against regulations such as the European GDPR by creating Personally Identifiable Information (PII) data when connecting information otherwise acceptable when consumed separately. In order to mitigate both risks we need to ensure that entitlements to the original data sources are not superseded by the graph: someone not having access to a data found in a particular silo should not have access to this data once integrated into the EKG.

R2. Graph preservation: Businesses using an EKG for activities relevant to regulatory frameworks (for instance, GDPR) may be asked to produce a copy of the graph at a particular point in time. Those time-stamped archives of the production data need to be archived and preserved for a couple of years in order to enable audit enquiries. To a lesser extent, the software preservation of the tools used to query the data should also be considered.

R3. Data availability: The two case studies reported on in this paper depend on the availability of data close to being the live equivalent of the data sources. We also found out cases where the data from the source was deemed too sensitive to be exported to disk via traditional ETL processes and had to be queried live from the source only, and then be consumed only in-memory.

R4. Knowledge Graph Data Quality: The data acquired from the different sources is expected to come as inconsistent because of known issues, and should otherwise be treated with caution in order to avoid mistakes during the construction of the EKG. As the aim for constructing this graph is to enable answering business questions spanning over several sources it is critical that the information surfaced is as accurate as possible. This last requirement comes in a possible opposition to the previous one, R3, as the data needs to be as fresh as possible and yet undergo a verification step to check that no erroneous information might be consumed by end-users. For example, each clinical study should have a single stage information such as Phase I or Phase II indicating the current phase. If the information about clinical study is duplicated in multiple data sources there can be discrepancies about the current stage. We would like to detect and correct these errors before the information is shown to end users.

The Semantic Web research community, the W3C and the industry ecosystem all together proposed solutions addressing some of those requirements. Our work and contribution consisted in identifying the standards best fit for each task and connect things together in a sound pipeline. In the following section we review the relevant technologies and related work.

3   Related Work and Technologies

The approach described in this paper relates to different interests of the Semantic Web research community. We hereafter name relevant work in the domain of secure data access, preservation, knowledge graph construction, and data quality control.

Security and Entitlements (R1)

The data access for our platform had to be easy and secured. In terms of ease of access, consuming the data from a knowledge graph can be done with languages such as SPARQL, GraphQL or Gremlin but all those require getting familiar with the specific aspects. The specifications for Linked Data Platform[1] and Linked Data API[2] offers a level of simplifications by enriching the options for de-referencability. GRLC [8], for instance, implements the latter to wrap SPARQL queries into more intuitive RESTful API calls. But neither of these tackle the aspect of security and entitlements. In fact, in terms of security, and

---

[1] https://www.w3.org/TR/ldp/.
[2] https://github.com/UKGovLD/linked-data-api.

as noted in the requirement R1, we need to ensure that the level of access granted at the data source level is reflected at the EKG level. So the result of the queries is expected to differ based on the credentials of the client emitting those queries.

As explained in details by Kirrane *et al.* in [5], there is now a large variety of access control models and standards which have been proposed and applied to Linked Data. Our work can be seen as fitting in the Role Based Access Control (RBAC) model by controlling the access to different named graphs based on the roles associated to the credentials of the user.

Graph Preservation (R2)

Because of its Web-based and dynamic nature, the preservation of Linked Data represents a challenge [1]. We can highlight here the role of the Memento protocol [10] to enable the access to historical descriptions of resource descriptions, however the focus of our approach is closer to saving static dumps of entire graphs. The objective for our use-case is to freeze the knowledge graph in time to eventually later on re-play what consuming application would have had access to. In this respect, HDT [2] is a more relevant work enabling storing large graphs in a compressed and queriable way.

Data Availability (R3)

The Semantic Web community has been active proposing architectures to transform silos into Knowledge graphs. Acknowledging the strong presence of RDBMS systems R2RML came in early and is featured in Sequeda *et al.* "pay as you go" methodology [9] for building EKGs using an Ontology-based Data Access approach. R2RML is a technology part of the virtualization of Knowledge graphs [11] which contrary to rigid one-way mass ETL process introduces flexibility and dynamism in data access. Beyond R2RML, platforms such as Metaphactory [4] and Stardog[3] show how many more types of data sources can be virtualized with the same benefits.

KG Data Quality (R4)

The integration of data from different silos is likely to cause inconsistencies as with the example given earlier for the requirement R4. Assessing data quality has several dimensions [12] including, for instance, looking at the overall shape of the graph to find inconsistencies in it [3] but what is of interest to us here is not to check for quality in terms of potential value. Our focus is on detecting constraint violation with respect to how the data is expected to be shaped. One of the latest addition to the family of Semantic Web standards, SHACL, comes in handy there.

Close to our needs, Metaphactory [4] uses SHACL to control the quality of the data as it goes though the federated query layer "Ephedra" of the platform.

---

[3] https://www.stardog.com/categories/virtualization/.

This approach does not however tackle R4 as we expressed it because we need to identify errors before they get a chance to be consumed by downstream clients applications.

The architecture presented here in this paper builds upon and takes inspiration from this state of the art to stitch together a pipeline addressing the four requirements in scope. We hereafter report on the generic pipeline architecture and our implementation leveraging the capabilities of the knowledge integration platform Stardog.

4   Architecture and Implementation

The solution architecture is comprised of three main parts: data ingestion, reasoning, and API enabled querying. Our clients choose Stardog over other vendors largely because of its virtualization capabilities. We then moved on to implementing the other requirements with Stardog and external tools the platform natively integrates with. We would however like to highlight that those requirements expressed in the introduction and the pipeline we report on in this paper go beyond our specific use-cases and could be re-implemented by other vendors.

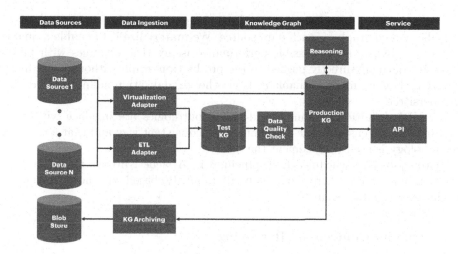

Fig. 1. The overall architecture and data flow

Figure 1 shows this architecture in term of functional blocks. One particularity to note is the materialization of some of the virtualized sources via a staging/production DB whilst some others are directly consumed live from the production DB. We hereafter go into the details of the implementation of each of those functional blocks and motivate our design choices.

4.1 Data Ingestion

The first set of functional parts of the pipeline concern the virtualization of the data sources. We use two parallel approaches to be able to tackle possible varied complexities in using the data sources: one is based on using native adapters from Stardog and the other leverages Apache Nifi as a tightly coupled ETL approach.

Virtualization adapter is one of the virtualization adapter supported by Stardog. We use the language SMS[4] in order to be able to cover for the full range of possible data sources, beyond the limitation to relational databases from R2RML. An SMS file is created to define a mapping from the data source to the knowledge graph.

ETL Adapter is there for cases where virtualization is not available or SMS is not expressive enough. We use Apache NiFi as a fall back option to turn the source data into triples.

Archiving of a named graph inside the production DB is done before a new version of this named graph is preserved along with metadata indicating when it had been used. This allows for auditing of previous data when looking for historical information. Highly sensitive data sources are by default excluded from this process to comply with not persisting the data they serve.

Data from all sources is sent first to a designated testing database under a specific named graph for each data source. We materialize it to enable a quality check and bypass some possible performance issues. Data sources with highly sensitive data are directly pushed to the production graph without being materialized, they are made available as-is via the virtualization adapter and do not get persisted.

A URI definition document and global ontologies are in place within the organization to ensure URIs are minted in a consistent way and that a common terminology is used to document the data.

Cron jobs and scheduled ETL pipelines in Apache NiFi are used to refresh data regularly, anywhere from daily to monthly based on the frequency of updates in the data sources.

4.2 Quality Control and Reasoning

It is important to validate the data and also allow for expressing inferred connections between data brought together in the knowledge graph. We implemented a balanced approach that capitalized on the benefits of Semantic Web technology without sacrificing data quality.

Quality check is a module looking at the data in the testing database and validating it against a set of shapes expressed in SHACL. Based on the report, the data is pushed into production or an alarm is raised. Checking SHACL

---

[4] https://docs.stardog.com/virtual-graphs/mapping-data-sources#sms2-stardog-mapping-syntax-2.

constraints is implemented via SPARQL queries and thus can handle both materialized and virtualized data. The former is more efficient since more optimizations are available, e.g. validating many RDF nodes at once with more complex queries. For the latter, Stardog uses a two-step procedure internally which first generates SPARQL queries for SHACL constraints and then rewrites them to SQL using the mappings. That process is transparent to the user. It has performance overhead which can be mitigated by using Stardog cache nodes[5].

Reasoning is done by Stardog's built-in reasoner which performs inferences on the data based on the ontology. Notably, reasoning in Stardog is based on query rewriting, not materialization, and thus is agnostic to whether the data is virtualized or ETL'ed. Reasoning also allows creating a level of abstraction between client applications and data sources so that queries do not break when data source schemas change.

Ontologies are edited using Protégé and maintained as dedicated assets ingested by the platform. Data is validated using the SHACL shapes and against the ontology terms, meaning all data is associated with a validated ontology in the production graph.

4.3 Data Usage

The last functional part of our architecture is around the data access. Here we need to cater to different kinds of access via APIs and end-user tools but most importantly do so whilst keeping an eye on R1 about data access. As highlighted in the introduction, missing on controlling for entitlements to the data sources could lead to security and privacy risks.

The architecture shows only API under service layer as a representative catch-all for accessing data in Stardog. However, the architecture supports all components listed below for real-world implementation:

Data API we wrap SPARQL queries, and other Stardog-specific query tooling such as path finding, into an API for easier user consumption without requiring end-users to write and test their own SPARQL, or GraphQL, queries;

BI integration following a need expressed to have a view over the content of the graph via business intelligence tools (for example, Tableau[6]), we leverage Stardog's ability to expose the graph as a set of relational tables which can be queried with SQL;[7]

Graph browsing is the third piece offering a browsing interface for the graph for stake-holders not able to use the APIs, the relational view, or SPARQL.

---

[5] Cache nodes are nodes in the Stardog cluster which transparently cache (and periodically refresh) virtualized data: https://docs.stardog.com/cluster/operating-the-cluster/cache-management.

[6] https://www.tableau.com/.

[7] https://docs.stardog.com/query-stardog/bi-tools-and-sql-queries.

We implement this functionality by deploying Stardog Explorer[8], the latest addition to the family of Stardog products.

In order to ensure entitlements are checked via *all* the data access interfaces we implemented a restriction based on named graphs. Each of the data sources in the pipeline is identified with an IRI in the EKG. The access rules for each named graph are defined to align with those of the data source. Stardog's Named Graph Security mechanism[9] ensures that every query gets to see only named graphs which the current user has access to. Internally, all access methods: API calls, GraphQL queries, SQL queries, etc., are compiled into SPARQL so that check cannot be bypassed.

The remaining part is user authentication for which we use Kerberos and LDAP. The full approach is depicted in Fig. 2.

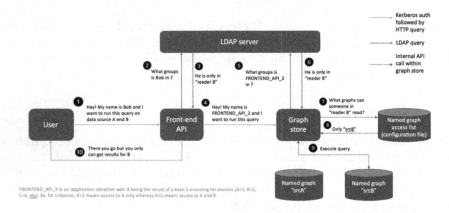

Fig. 2. Approach to handle entitlements by combining named-graph access rules, Kerberos for the authentication and an LDAP directory for listing groups

It is important to note here that API calls are identified the same way as human users in the systems and need to use their own credentials. In order to pass along the entitlements of a user into the API call, we associate each user with a group name in the LDAP directory for which the graph store then handles authorization. Each API call proceeds as follows:

- The user identifies itself to the front-end API ❶;
- The front-end queries the LDAP directory for the list of groups the requester is in ❷ and gets a response ❸;
- Based on the response the API call is authenticated as a user matching a list of groups ❹. For this to work, a set of users called "FRONTEND_API_X" is created for each possible group combination X where X is a base 10 number (Group A = 1, Group B = 2, Group C = 4, ...);

---

[8] https://www.stardog.com/blog/stardog-explorer-early-access-release/.
[9] https://docs.stardog.com/operating-stardog/security/named-graph-security.

- The graph store executes a query ❺ similar to ❶ and gets a response in ❻ (also aligning with ❷);
- The server then refers internally to the named graph security configuration to check which named graphs can be consumed by the user ❼, and gets a response in ❽;
- The query is finally executed against the allowed graphs ❾ and the results are returned back to the user in ❿.

5   Use-Cases

Accenture and Stardog deployed the above architecture in production in two different places. The first one, a major financial services company in need for tracking the flow of PII data across its systems. The second, a major pharmaceutical company that wants to provide a unified view of its disconnected data sources to its employees. We found those two relevant to report on as they both share the need for the four above stated requirements yet with different focus points. For example, the auditing need is more important for the financial context than it is for the internal R&D of the medical deployment.

5.1   Financial Services Use-Case

A Data Center of Excellence (CoE) sits within a large financial services company providing centralized data services to the various lines of business throughout the company. Consumers of the CoE's data services have asked for more transparency into the impacts and dependencies of changes that affect infrastructure components, applications, and sensitive PII data elements. However, providing that information to the data consumers presents two sets of challenges: ensuring seamless data source integration and resolving unique data consumer requirements.

The types of data required by the data consumers consists of infrastructure components, data elements, and business processes, etc. and each type of data resides in a separate data source. Additionally, each data consumer has their own unique set of data requirements that the CoE's solution must meet. Each data source has its own security controls, access permissions, data models, and data quality standards. For example, the data source containing infrastructure data grants end-user permissions only for the specific columns within a specific table that the end-user requested access. Additionally, while the infrastructure data source contained information about PII data, that data is not consistently formatted or held to the same data quality standards as the data source containing information about all data elements. So, those two sources can't be simply joined together. Regarding the data consumers, each one provides the CoE with their own set of requirements for the solution. This means there are many consumers with different questions and requirements about the same data. So, the data model for the knowledge graph solution needs to be general enough to support all consumers while not over generalizing at risk of misrepresenting, or losing the intended meaning, of the underlying data sources.

If we summarise based on the requirements stated in Sect. 2, we have:

- **R1**: the data consumers can only view data in the graph that comes from sources they have already been granted access;
- **R2**: each version of the graph must be persisted for future audit needs;
- **R3**: some data consumers will use the graph for activities which are time dependent (*e.g.* track changes);
- **R4**: quality checks are crucial for mitigating errors when integrating data sources which may provide conflicting data about the same entity.

Our knowledge graph solution models the data from all sources via a unified graph schema based on the schemas of the underlying data sources. Data from each source is then brought into the knowledge graph based on the described architecture, either through virtualization or standard ETL pipelines, in accordance with the unified graph schema. The schema is based on an ontology designed by the CoE for this use case and ensures support for the unique use cases of each consumer, while maintaining the intended meaning of the underlying data sources. As depicted in Fig. 1, the solution is comprised of four distinct layers: data source layer, data ingestion layer, knowledge graph layer, and API/presentation layer.

In the data source layer we currently connect to two data sources (containing information on infrastructure and data elements respectively), with plans to expand to connecting to at least four additional sources (adding information about the company's business processes, change records, risk assessments, and a taxonomy repository).

The data ingestion layer includes two distinct methods of bringing data into the knowledge graph: data virtualization and ingestion by ETL pipelines. Our solution utilized data virtualization for connecting to data sources containing PII data, where the data was not permitted to leave its originating data source. For all other sources, Apache NiFi is used for creating and executing ETL pipelines on a scheduled basis. These pipelines would get data required by the consumers of the knowledge graph, apply transformations, and load the data into the knowledge graph based on the unified schema. Data is loaded into the knowledge graph as triples within a named graph that indicates from which data sources the data originates.

There are currently about 6.8 million triples loaded into the knowledge graph and the plan is to scale that to 15+ million triples over the coming months by connecting to the previously mentioned data sources. The triples in the knowledge graph are made available to data consumer via API endpoints which trigger SPARQL queries on the knowledge graph. Since all triples in the knowledge graph are assigned to a specific named graph based on the underlying data source, SPARQL queries are only executed over named graphs which the user has permissions to view. This feature provides an additional layer of security in the knowledge graph layer, and helps prevent exposing PII data that must be contained solely to its named graph.

The CoE's requirements for the knowledge graph solution are driven by the requirements of the data consumers. There are currently three main data consumers who's use cases and requirements drove the current solution and the long-term plan is to make the solution available to all lines of business in the company. The three data consumers use cases dealt with change management and how changes affect sensitive data elements which reside on infrastructure that the consumers owned. In the following examples, a change is defined as an alteration to a piece of infrastructure, software/code, data store, or business process.

- When planned or unplanned changes occur, what are the infrastructure components and data elements that are impacted and who is responsible for those components and data elements.
- For a given line of business, who is responsible for each PII data element, where does that data exist, where does that data originate from, where is that data being distributed to, and what security controls exist for that data (such as encryption).

The three main data consumers are actively using our solution in favor of the previous solution. Our solution has been perceived as an improvement by providing more clarity to users as they interpret the information presented by the solution about their infrastructure components and data elements. For example, there are many different types of infrastructure components such as networks, SANs, virtual servers, etc. with many instances of each type of component, and our solution more clearly shows how these components are dependent on one another. Additionally, our solution more clearly explains where PII data originates from outside of the user's consumer group, whereas the previous solution did not reliably identify where PII data existed.

Our solution meets the requirements of the CoE and the data consumers by implementing the following features:

- Provides complete data lineage across all target infrastructure
- Identifies ownership (both individual personnel and lines of business) of all target infrastructure
- Enforces security controls in all layers of solution architecture:
  - Data Source Layer: Each data source has its own security controls, so users with access to the knowledge graph solution also go through the data approval process for each data source that is used by their consumer group.
  - Ingestion Layer: Only approved members of the CoE can execute ETL pipelines
  - Knowledge Graph Layer: Named graphs categorize triples by source system and Role-Based Access Controls (RBAC) are implemented for granting permissions to users based on the source system requirements of their line of business.
  - API/Presentation Layer: Users only have the ability to execute queries that their role has permissions to execute query. User and role information

is passed in tandem with the query, so users will receive different results for the same query depending on what data they have permissions to view.

5.2   Pharmaceutical Use Case

In one of the world's largest pharmaceutical companies each Research and Development lab has their own data systems and processes that are specialized to the lab's needs which is typical for companies of this size. This results in proliferation of copies of data which quickly gets out of date. For example, it is difficult for someone in oncology to see if there is any related data within the vaccine lab.

We have used the architecture described above to provide a unified view over multiple data sources so researchers, clinicians, analysts and data scientists within the organization can access the information they need in a single location. The data sources range from structured relational databases to semi-structured data sources such as MongoDb and Elastic Search.

There are currently 5 data sources that has been mapped to RDF using SMS mappings. Each data source is materialized via a NiFi workflow to a distinct named graph (so that the graph represents the triplified view of the relational source). The central entity in the knowledge graph is the concept of a project. Projects are linked to information on genes, assays, targets and activities in several internal and external databases. The materialization process unifies the different naming and identifier schemes used across data sources to provide a unified view. There current contents of the knowledge graph contain many different entity types such as projects (8.4K), people (2.9K), clinical studies (47.8K), genes (5.6K) and chemical compounds (14.1M) for a total of about 100M triples. The plan is to increase the number of data sources integrated to 11 later this year that will increase the size of the knowledge graph to 500 million triples.

Data validation is an important requirement especially because some of the data sources are created from unstructured documents using automated NLP techniques. Technical publications, internal documents and various other kinds of unstructured documents are processed by an NLP pipeline that extracts structure content and saves the results in the knowledge graph. The automated extraction process might introduce inaccurate information. In addition, there might be inconsistencies between structured data sources when they have overlapping information. At the beginning of the project simple SPARQL queries have been used for quality checks and over time these queries have been migrated to shape constraints in SHACL.

The main use case for the knowledge graph is to power a Google-like environment for the employees in the R&D division to search the data and traverse the graph and entities based on context and knowledge. Access to detailed information about past projects makes it possible to see connections that would have been invisible before. R&D decisions can be based on all the relevant data rather than relying on tribal knowledge and personal experience.

To recall our list of requirements stated in Sect. 2, here is how those map to this specific use-case:

- **R1**: is less complex than in the financial case, but controls need to be introduced nonetheless to restrict the access to the graph;
- **R2**: the graph should be persisted in order to trace back the thought process leading to a particular trial being conducted;
- **R3**: in order to support the R&D process the data needs to be aggregated from a variety of sources and be up to date all the time;
- **R4**: quality checks are important to mitigate the errors the NLP pipeline can be reasonably expected to make.

The next steps is to go beyond search and explore use case and provide an API end point for data scientists and researchers to the data from the knowledge graph within their own projects and not have to rely on the search interface. One potential data science project is using the characteristics of particular gene targets to predict if a trial will be successful.

6   Conclusion

In this paper we described the implementation of a knowledge graph architecture and discussed how it is applied for two separate use cases: tracking the flow of PII data across many infrastructure components within a financial services company and providing pharmaceutical company employees with a unified view of disconnected data sources. The role of Semantic Web technologies is critical to the success of both use cases. We modeled disconnected data in unified schemas, used data virtualization and materialization to create knowledge graph instances, made the data available to many end-users via authenticated APIs, and leveraged shape-checking standards (SHACL) to keep an eye on the quality of the data.

In our experience data virtualization is a successful approach to integrating siloed data. It does, however, impose certain restrictions on data processing tasks, such as SHACL or querying. Not all of SPARQL can be translated into a query language supported by some upstream data source in the organization. That is true, for example, for arbitrary property paths or SPARQL extensions, like full-text search or path finding queries. In practice, such issues can usually be avoided by using less expressive queries (like fixed-length paths expressed as SPARQL BGPs) or by doing less computation in the upstream system and thus bringing more intermediate query results to Stardog (i.e. at performance cost). When none of these compromises is acceptable, it is always possible to use Stardog cache nodes to transparently cache and refresh virtualized data inside the Stardog cluster[10].

The implemented architecture is not limited to the two described industries and can be applied to use cases in other domains that require connecting siloed data sources containing sensitive data such as manufacturing, energy production,

---

[10] https://docs.stardog.com/cluster/operating-the-cluster/cache-management.

or healthcare. In future work, we would like to see updates on R2RML for non-relational data, as well as authentication support for LDP. Those two aspects limit the capabilities we can offer using standards, or require more custom code to be implemented, and their development could be leveraged by both our implementation and the broader Semantic Web community. Within our architecture we will seek to improve SPARQL query performance over a partially virtualized knowledge graph.

References

1. Batsakis, S., et al.: PRELIDA D3.1 State of the art assessment on Linked Data and Digital Preservation. European Commission (2014)
2. Fernández, J.D., Martínez-Prieto, M.A., Gutiérrez, C., Polleres, A., Arias, M.: Binary RDF representation for publication and exchange (HDT). J. Web Semant. **19**, 22–41 (2013). http://dblp.uni-trier.de/db/journals/ws/ws19.html#FernandezMGPA13
3. Guéret, C., Groth, P., Stadler, C., Lehmann, J.: Linked data quality assessment through network analysis. In: Proceedings of the 10th International Semantic Web Conference (ISWC 2011) (2011)
4. Haase, P., Herzig, D.M., Kozlov, A., Nikolov, A., Trame, J.: Metaphactory: a platform for knowledge graph management. Semantic Web **10**(6), 1109–1125 (2019). https://doi.org/10.3233/SW-190360
5. Kirrane, S., Mileo, A., Decker, S.: Access control and the resource description framework: a survey. Semantic Web **8**(2), 311–352 (2017). https://doi.org/10.3233/SW-160236
6. Li, X., Lyu, M., Wang, Z., Chen, C.H., Zheng, P.: Exploiting knowledge graphs in industrial products and services: a survey of key aspects, challenges, and future perspectives. Comput. Ind. **129**(March) (2021). https://doi.org/10.1016/j.compind.2021.103449
7. Mehdi, A., Kharlamov, E., Stepanova, D., Loesch, F., Grangel-González, I.: Towards semantic integration of bosch manufacturing data. In: Suárez-Figueroa, M.C., Cheng, G., Gentile, A.L., Guéret, C., Keet, C.M., Bernstein, A. (eds.) ISWC Satellites. CEUR Workshop Proceedings, vol. 2456, pp. 303–304. CEUR-WS.org (2019). http://dblp.uni-trier.de/db/conf/semweb/iswc2019p.html#MehdiK0LG19
8. Meroño-Peñuela, A., Hoekstra, R.: grlc makes GitHub taste like linked data APIs. In: Sack, H., Rizzo, G., Steinmetz, N., Mladenić, D., Auer, S., Lange, C. (eds.) ESWC 2016. LNCS, vol. 9989, pp. 342–353. Springer, Cham (2016). https://doi.org/10.1007/978-3-319-47602-5_48
9. Sequeda, J.F., Briggs, W.J., Miranker, D.P., Heideman, W.P.: A pay-as-you-go methodology to design and build enterprise knowledge graphs from relational databases. In: Ghidini, C., et al. (eds.) ISWC 2019. LNCS, vol. 11779, pp. 526–545. Springer, Cham (2019). https://doi.org/10.1007/978-3-030-30796-7_32
10. Van de Sompel, H., Nelson, M.L., Sanderson, R., Balakireva, L.L., Ainsworth, S., Shankar, H.: Memento: Time Travel for the Web (2009). arXiv:0911.1112

11. Xiao, G., Ding, L., Cogrel, B., Calvanese, D.: Virtual knowledge graphs: an overview of systems and use cases. Data Intell. **1**(3), 201–223 (2019). https://doi.org/10.1162/dint_a_00011
12. Zaveri, A., Rula, A., Maurino, A., Pietrobon, R., Lehmann, J., Auer, S.: Quality assessment methodologies for linked open data: a systematic literature review and conceptual framework. Semantic Web **1**, 33 (2012). http://www.semantic-web-journal.net/sites/default/files/DQ_Survey.pdf

Reconciling and Using Historical Person Registers as Linked Open Data in the AcademySampo Portal and Data Service

Petri Leskinen[1]([⊠]) [iD] and Eero Hyvönen[1,2] [iD]

[1] Semantic Computing Research Group (SeCo), Aalto University, Espoo, Finland
{petri.leskinen,eero.hyvonen}@aalto.fi
[2] HELDIG – Helsinki Centre for Digital Humanities, University of Helsinki, Helsinki, Finland
http://seco.cs.aalto.fi, http://heldig.fi

Abstract. This paper presents a method for extracting and reassembling a genealogical network automatically from a biographical register of historical people. The method is applied to a dataset of short textual biographies about all 28 000 Finnish and Swedish academic people educated in 1640–1899 in Finland. The aim is to connect and disambiguate the relatives mentioned in the biographies in order to build a continuous, genealogical network, which can be used in Digital Humanities for data and network analysis of historical academic people and their lives. An artificial neural network approach is presented for solving a supervised learning task to disambiguate relatives mentioned in the register descriptions using basic biographical information enhanced with an ontology of vocations and additional occasionally sparse genealogical information. Evaluation results of the record linkage are promising and provide novel insights into the problem of historical people register reconciliation. The outcome of the work has been used in practise as part of the in-use AcademySampo portal and linked open data service, a new member in the Sampo series of cultural heritage applications for Digital Humanities.

Keywords: Data reconciling · Biographies · Linked data · Digital humanities

1   Introduction

A key idea of Linked Data is to enrich datasets by integrating complementary local information sources in an interoperable way into a global knowledge graph. This involves harmonization of local data models used, as well as aligning the concepts and entities used in populating the local data models. The latter problem has been addressed traditionally in the field of *record linkage (RL)* [7,13,36], where the goal is to find matching data records between heterogeneous databases. For example, how to match person records in different registers, which may contain data about same persons, but where the data is represented using different metadata schemas and notational conventions? Using RL, richer global descriptions of persons can be

© Springer Nature Switzerland AG 2021
A. Hotho et al. (Eds.): ISWC 2021, LNCS 12922, pp. 714–730, 2021.
https://doi.org/10.1007/978-3-030-88361-4_42

created based on fusing local datasets. In addition, RL facilitates data enrichment by linking together local datasets that use different vocabularies and identifiers for representing same resources, such as persons.

This paper concerns the problem of entity reconciliation and RL of people in historical person registers. As a case study, academic people and their relatives extracted automatically from the textual biographical descriptions of the Royal Academy of Turku and University of Helsinki are considered. The primary data contains some 28 000 short biographical descriptions of people in 1640–1899, covering virtually all university students in Finland during this time period. This data contains not only the 1) the explicit set of students recorded but also 2) the implicit set of persons mentioned in the short biography record texts of (1), such as relatives and prominent historical persons. The task is to construct a knowledge graph of all persons referred to in the data (1)–(2) in order to study the characteristics of the underlying academic network.

As a solution approach, a probabilistic RL solution for linking person records is presented and tested with promising evaluation results. In our method, RL is based on the attributes of an actor, such as the name, life years, and vocations relating to her/his life. The key novel idea here is to enrich these attributes with genealogical information, i.e., information about the names and lifespans of actors' relatives. Integrating local person registers into a single global *knowledge graph (KG)* facilitates biographical and prosopographical research based on enriched data. For this purpose, the aligned enriched person data has been used as a basis for a new in-use semantic portal and data service, *AcademySampo – Finnish Academic People 1640–1899 on the Semantic Web*[1]. The linked data model, data extraction, and data service of AcademySampo are described in [25], while in this paper the focus is on describing data reconciling and linking methods used, as well as on illustrating how the data service and semantic portal are actually used. More details on using the system (in Finnish) are available in [17].

This paper is structured as follows: We first present related works, the primary data of our study, and how it has been transformed into Linked Data. After this, the method of reconciling mentions of person in person registries is explained, and evaluation results in our case study are presented. In conclusion, contributions of the paper are discussed, and directions for further research are pointed out.

2   Related Work

The RL field is presented in [3,13,36]. Several nation-wide projects are underway on integrating person registries. For example, the Norwegian Historical Population Register (HPR) is pursuing to cover the country's whole population in 1800–1964, based on combining church records and census data [32]. The Links

---

[1] The portal and its linked open data service, including a SPARQL endpoint, was released on February 5, 2021. More information about AcademySampo can be found on the project homepage: https://seco.cs.aalto.fi/projects/yo-matrikkelit/.

project[2] in the Netherlands aims to reconstruct all nineteenth and early twentieth century families in the Netherlands based on civil certificates.

The problem of reconciling person records is evident in genealogical research. For example, in [26] Machine Learning has been applied to automatic construction of family trees from person records. Antolie et al. [2] present a case study of integrating Canadian World War I data from three sources: soldier records, casualty records, and census data. Here more traditional crafted RL processes were used, and using the data in research is demonstrated. Also Cunningham [8] concerns military person data. Here World War I military service records have been integrated with a census data, and the integrated data is used for data analysis. In Ivie et al. [19] the RL process is enhanced with the available genealogical data, e.g., information about spouses and children, to achieve a higher accuracy. Also Pixton et al. [27] utilize the genealogical information and apply a neural network for RL. Representing and analyzing biographical data has grown into a new research and application field, reported, e.g., in the Biographical Data in Digital World workshops BD2015 [4], BD2017 [11], and BD2019. In [23], analytic visualizations were created based on U.S. Legislator registry data, and the Six Degrees of Francis Bacon system[3] [22,34] utilizes data of the Oxford Dictionary of National Biography. Extracting Linked Data from texts has been studied in several works, such as [12]. In [10], language technology was applied for extracting entities and relations in RDF using Dutch biographies in the BiographyNet, as part of the larger NewsReader project [29].

Our own earlier works related to the topic include reconciling biographees and their relatives in the BiographySampo semantic portal [15,24]. Here genealogical statistics, e.g., average ages of becoming a parent or getting married were extracted from the source data, and person's life years are estimated according to that distribution. References to World War II soldiers were reconciled for data linking in the WarSampo portal and knowledge graph [14,21]. Unlike in these projects, in this paper a neural network model is trained to learn the classification rules from the existing ground truth linkage.

3   Knowledge Graph of Historical Academic Persons

This section presents the data used in our study: the Finnish university student registries "Ylioppilasmatrikkeli" containing short biographical descriptions.

3.1   Primary Data Sources

The student registry datasets in our focus are based on original handwritten university enrollment documents. In an earlier project, the documents have been transliterated manually into textual form and extended with information from

---

[2] Cf. the project homepage https://iisg.amsterdam/en/hsn/projects/links and research papers at https://iisg.amsterdam/en/hsn/projects/links/links-publications.

[3] http://www.sixdegreesoffrancisbacon.com.

other sources about later life events of the biographees. It has been estimated that ten man years of manual work of archivists was needed to accomplish this.

Our work concerns two main parts of the student registry: the database covering the years 1640–1852[4] available in Finnish and Swedish, and the registry of 1853–1899[5] for the next years. The records contain short biographical descriptions of 28 000 students of the University of Helsinki[6], originally the Royal Academy of Turku[7] in Finland. These student registries cover a significant part of the history of Finland and the Finnish university institution, since the University of Helsinki was the only university in the country during the time frame in focus. The data is widely used by genealogists and historians. There are lots of mentions of relatives as well as of prominent related persons in the biographical descriptions. Generally, the data is divided into four parts: the students (*D1640*) in 1640–1852 register and their relatives (*R1640*) and likewise the students (*D1853*) and their relatives (*R1853*) in the later register.

A key challenge in transforming this kind of data into Linked Data for data-analysis is how to reconcile mentions of people in the records and their biographical texts. For example, the data contains records of ten students with the same name *Johan Wegelius*. In addition, eight of them have a vocation related to clergy—more than half of the students who studied before the year 1780 worked as priests after their graduation.[8] In the textual descriptions of the students, there are 72 mentions of spouses or mothers with the name *Maria Johansdotter*. Furthermore, there are variations in how the names are written because the data has been collected from multiple sources by different archivists, when it was extended by additional information about the later lives of the students. For example, the name *Sofia Dorotea Cedercreutz* can also be written as *Sophia Dorothea Cedercreutz*.

3.2 Extracting Information from Text

A comprehensive description about the data conversion as well as about the used data model is presented in an earlier article [25]. For example, an extract of the registry entry for *Anders Israel Cajander*[9] is depicted in Fig. 1. The description starts with the date or year of enrollment, in this case *11.2.1830*. After that there is the full name and a unique database identifier followed by the place and time of birth (Leppävirralla 24.2.1811). Next there is a Finnish abbreviation *Vht* meaning parents; in the example case the father is Zachris Johan Cajander and the mother Gustava Karolina Neiglick. After that there are two lists of events, one related to studies and academic career, and other describing the later career

---

[4] https://ylioppilasmatrikkeli.helsinki.fi.

[5] https://ylioppilasmatrikkeli.helsinki.fi/1853-1899.

[6] https://en.wikipedia.org/wiki/University_of_Helsinki.

[7] https://en.wikipedia.org/wiki/Royal_Academy_of_Turku.

[8] This statistical result was obtained after we used the reconciled data in AcademySampo for data analysis.

[9] https://ylioppilasmatrikkeli.helsinki.fi/henkilo.php?id=14689.

of the biographee. At the end of the first paragraph, a person's death is marked with the symbol † and burial with ‡; the person in the example died in Wyborg on December 18th, 1901 († Viipurissa 18.12.1901).

11.2.1830 Anders Israel Cajander 14689. * Leppävirralla 24.2.1811. Vht: Savon alisen kihlakunnan kruununvouti *Zachris Johan Cajander* (†1862) ja *Gustava Karolina Neiglick*. Kuopion triviaalikoulun oppilas 4.2.1822 – 22.6.1826 (betyg). Viipurin lukion oppilas 17.9.1827 – 1.7.1829. Ylioppilas Helsingissä 11.2.1830 (arvosana approbatur cum laude äänimäärällä 14). Viipurilaisen osakunnan jäsen 12.2.1830 *12/2 1830 \ Anders Israel Cajander \ 24/2 1811 \ KronoFogden Zachr. Joh. Cajander i Randasalmi \ Leppävirta \ [med betyg] fr. Gymn. i Wiborg \ Uttog betyg d. 12/10 1833 för att ingå vid Rättegångsverken.* Merkitty oikeustieteellisen tiedekunnan nimikirjaan 9.10.1832. Savokarjalaisen osakunnan perustajajäsen 1833 *Anders Israël Cajander.* Tuomarintutkinto 10.12.1833. Vaasan hovioikeuden auskultantti 24.12.1833. — Varatuomari 1837. Kihlakunnantuomarin arvonimi 1847. Äyräpään tuomiokunnan tuomari 1857, Jääsken tuomiokunnan 1870, Rannan tuomiokunnan 1877, ero 1891. Hovioikeudenasessorin arvonimi 1868. Laamannin arvonimi 1870. Valtiopäivämies 1872. †Viipurissa 18.12.1901.

Pso: 1841 *Fredrika Emelie Schildt* (†1892).
Veli: Räisälän kappalainen *Gustaf Adolf Cajander* 15376 (yo 1835, †1882).
Veli: kirjailija *Zakarias Cajander* 16147 (yo 1843, †1895).
Lanko: lääninmetsänhoitajan apulainen *Berndt Vilhelm Kristoffer Schildt* 14968 (yo 1832, †1892).

Fig. 1. Partial extract from a register entry text for *Anders Israel Cajander*

After the life time description, there are possible fields for relatives. In the example case, the spouse is mentioned first as Pso: 1841 Fredrika Emelie Schildt where *Pso* is a Finnish abbreviation for *puoliso* (spouse). There are three relatives who also have an entry in the register, i.e., two brothers (Veli: Gustaf Adolf Cajander and Veli: Zakarias Cajander) and a brother-in-law (Lanko: Berndt Vilhelm Kristoffer Schildt). The author of the *D1640* dataset, Yrjö Kotivuori, has manually added links from the description texts to the mentioned people also found in the register, like the three relatives in the example case. These links also contain linkage to the relatives in the *D1853* dataset.

3.3   Available Information

The previous person example was from the *D1640* data. However, the provided data in *D1853* differs in some aspects. For instance, *D1853* only mentions a person's parents and spouses, never children or any other relatives, and the people are not interlinked. Abbreviations are used generally for, e.g., vocations, which was taken into consideration in the data conversion by using specific lists of abbreviations.

Generally, the record linkage consists of the following partial tasks: 1) linkage from *R1640* to *D1640*, 2) linkage from *R1853* to *D1853*, 3) linkage from *R1853* to *D1640*, and 4) disambiguation of *R1640* and 5) *R1853* data. Table 1 shows an analysis of the known positive sample pairs in the both datasets. Here column *source* refers to the relative, and *target* to the corresponding student entry. The rows show how many of the example pairs of particular data field are available, altogether the data contains 4285 training pairs. One can notice that for the six uppermost properties, e.g., preferred label, gender, death, vocation, child, and spouse are available for both the source and target records. On the other hand, the data fields indicating the place of death, year of birth, names of mother or father, as well as the alternative labels are usually not available. The column *common* indicates the number of cases where both the source and the target entries have the particular data field and *same* the number of entries where the source and the target values are equal.

This table clearly indicates which properties should be considered crucial in decision making. Notice that some attributes that are usually significant for a general case of RL, such as places of birth and death, are not chosen in this particular case study.

Table 1. Available data fields in the training data

	Data 1640–1852				Data 1853–1899			
	Source	Target	Common	Same	Source	Target	Common	Same
Preferable label	4285	4285	4285	3979	698	698	698	517
Gender	4283	4284	4283	4283	698	698	698	688
Year of death	4229	4208	4192	4141	135	352	134	130
Vocation	4281	4270	4270	940	600	567	543	365
Child	4285	4284	4284	3211	430	341	340	2
Spouse	4285	4273	4273	–	698	687	687	2
Place of death	2	3494	2	2	–	348	–	–
Year of birth	–	2906	–	–	–	351	–	–
Mother	–	3475	–	–	–	349	–	–
Father	–	3478	–	–	–	348	–	–
Alternative label	–	1761	–	–	30	165	29	22

4   Method: Linking Person Records

This section describes the chosen formats for comparing two person registry entries. Generally, the input format for data comparison consists of numeric difference or similarity values between the data points of the two records, not the data of the records as it is. We first introduce the chosen input formats for data in different domains, e.g., for names and for vocations of the actors and the relatives. Finally, the architecture of the network model as well as the training setting are introduced.

4.1   Person Names

Person names in the datasets consist of a preferred and possibly alternative labels. Each label includes a family name and a sequence of given names. For the classifier input we considered four different variations of a label with a maximum of three first given names, only 0.4% of people entries have more than three given names. The classifier input is in a matrix format where the entry elements are statistical values calculated from the dataset. Each family and given name gets a *rarity* value so that first the frequency of the appearances for each name is counted and the ranks are mapped into the numeric range [0.0, 1.0]: the most common names get a near-zero and the rarest values closer to 1.0 in order to distinguish the rare names.

Figure 2 depicts an example of a name comparison matrix, in this case the family names of two person entries. The rows and columns mutually correspond to the data of two names that are compared. The uppermost row (0.000, 0.808, 0.983, ...) consists of the rarity values for the first, and likewise the leftmost column (0.000, 0.987, 0.991, 0.100, ...) for the second entry. The other values inside the matrix are Jaro-Winkler similarity values [35] between the name strings so that e.g., perfectly matching names get the value 1.0.

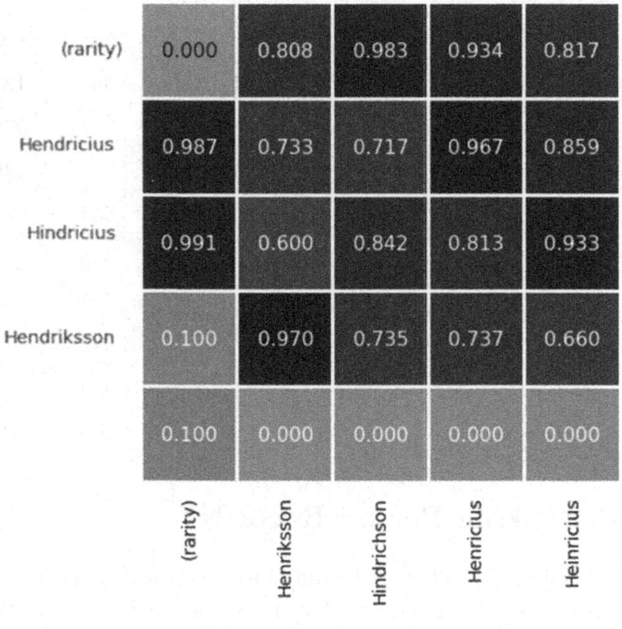

(rarity)	0.000	0.808	0.983	0.934	0.817
Hendricius	0.987	0.733	0.717	0.967	0.859
Hindricius	0.991	0.600	0.842	0.813	0.933
Hendriksson	0.100	0.970	0.735	0.737	0.660
	0.100	0.000	0.000	0.000	0.000
	(rarity)	Henriksson	Hindrichson	Henricius	Heinricius

Fig. 2. Example of a matrix for comparing family names

4.2 Vocations

The vocations are the titles extracted from the source data. These titles often consists of a place name and a related profession, e.g., *Bishop of Turku* or *Bishop of Porvoo*. To enrich the data the vocations are linked to the hierarchical AMMO [20] ontology of historical occupations. Statistical values are used here like with the name entries. A *rarity* value is calculated for each title following the same principle as with the titles. In addition to that, a value of co-occurrences between two titles is calculated.

Figure 3 depicts an example of a vocation comparison matrix. The value in the leftmost upper corner (0.455) is the Jaccard index [31] between the two sets of vocations. Similarly to the name matrix, the rows and columns correspond to the vocation in two dataset entries with the rarity values on the uppermost row (0.909, 0.804, 0.249...) and leftmost columns. The rarity values are in a descending order so that the rarest vocations appear first on the lists. The other values filling the rest of the matrix are the co-occurrence values. In the data matrix, the co-occurrence value for a pair *(Law Reader, Mayor)* is 0.985, while the pair *(Court Attorney, Mayor)* has a value 0.250 indicating that this pair co-occurs in the data more frequently. The zero-valued elements on the right indicate that one of the title sets has less than the reserved seven data fields.

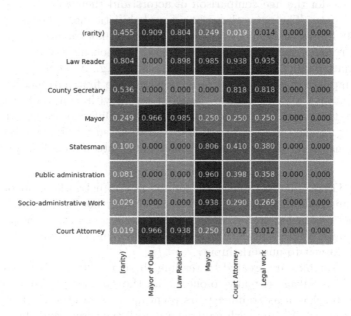

Fig. 3. Matrix for comparing the vocations

4.3   Years of Birth and Death, Gender

The difference in actor's and relatives' birth and death years and their genders were also input to the network. The years use a precision of one year due to the format used in source data: the birth and death of the actor is usually known with a precision of a day, while in the case of relatives only the precision of a year is used. The actual difference is years is mapped into a near-zero range by using the arctan function. Gender was indexed using value −1.0 for female, 1.0 for male, and 0.0 for the rare cases where the gender was not known.

4.4   Relative Information

The information of the relatives consists of details about the children and spouses of an actor, and basic information about her/his parents. The relative information uses the same matrix format as for the names, lifetime information, and vocations of the actor. It has reserved space for three children and three spouses, according to analyzing the data. In the data more than 99% have three or less spouses, and 95% three or less children.

4.5   Network Model

The used network model is depicted in Fig. 4. It is a multi-input network based on the Keras functional API [6]. The network has eight inputs out of which six for the given and family names of the two actors, their spouses, and their children, one for the age comparison of actors and their relatives, and one for the actors' titles. The network acts as a probabilistic classifier and the output is $\bar{y} \approx [0.0, 1.0]$ for matching entries and $\bar{y} \approx [1.0, 0.0]$ for not matching pairs. For a binary decision these values are filtered by choosing the positive matches when the latter value exceeds a chosen threshold, e.g., $\lambda = 0.9$.

Some inputs are in a matrix format, which are first flattened[10], and after that run through a Dense[11] layer. Dropout layers with a ratio of 25% are used to prevent the overfit to the training data [30]. Different inputs of the same domain (e.g., names and years) are first concatenated[12] to one another. After a layer of Dense network the network concatenates into the final output.

Training Data. The training data for the neural network could be input by either as an single data entry or in several smaller batches of data. We chose to feed the data in batches utilizing the Keras Data Generator Sequence [1] as described by A. Amidi and S. Amidi[13] due to the amount of data preprocessing from RDF format to numeric input.

Positive samples are created by reading the manually marked matches from the data. This linkage is many-to-one, so all the samples pointing to the same target can be chosen as training pairs pointing to each other. Finally, positive sample data is augmented with pairs where both the target and the source refer to the same resource.

The easiest way to gather the negative samples is to pick random pairs from the data. However, we chose to sample pairs that are likely to have some similar data values to improve the decision making. The dataset contains relations indicating, e.g., that two persons are siblings, cousins, or namesakes. Close relatives often have same similar characteristics, like family name or nearby years of birth.

---

[10] https://keras.io/api/layers/reshaping_layers/flatten/.
[11] https://keras.io/api/layers/core_layers/dense/.
[12] https://keras.io/api/layers/merging_layers/concatenate/.
[13] https://stanford.edu/~shervine/blog/keras-how-to-generate-data-on-the-fly.

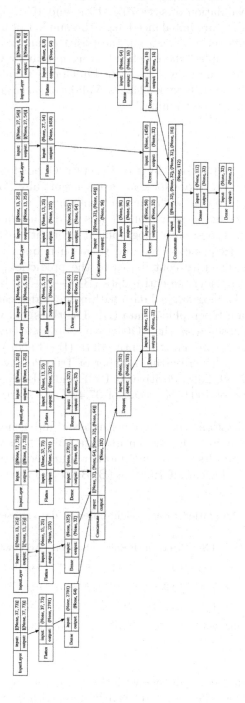

Fig. 4. Classifier model structure

Model Training. For the training the data was split into separate sets for training, testing, and validation of sizes 70%, 15%, and 15%, respectively. The classes in the training data are imbalanced, e.g., the number of negative samples ($N_n \approx 200000$) is significantly larger than the positive samples ($N_p \approx 13000$). Therefore the positive samples where defined to have a larger weight than the negative ones [5,33]. The training was performed in Google Colab, and the training with 100 epochs using a GPU took 4242.2 s. Validation accuracy of more than 99.6% was achieved during the training.

4.6 Evaluation

The results were analyzed closely by the Receiver Operating Characteristic (ROC) curve (Fig. 5) and by taking look at the details of False Positive and False Negative classifications. To deal with the data imbalance, a validation set with equal amount of positive and negative sample was used. The classifier input was divided by four different types: basic biographical information (B), genealogical information (G), name frequencies (N), and vocation frequencies (V). To analyze how much each data entry contributes to the prediction, evaluation was performed for four times using the entire data (B+G+N+V), biographical and genealogical data (B+G), biographical data with name and vocation frequencies (B+N+V), and the plain biographical data (B). The threshold value λ for optimal performance was chosen from the ROC curve coordinates by the point closest to the upper left corner [9]. For the entire data (B+G+N+V) the threshold value was $\lambda = 90.01\%$ and the resulting number of True Positives (TP) is 2035, True Negatives (TN) 2089, False Positives (FP) 0, and False Negatives (FN) 54 with measures precision of 100.00%, recall of 97.42%, F_1-score of 98.69%, and accuracy of 98.71%.

In the ROC visualization, the curve with basic and genealogical (B+G) almost emerges with the curve for the entire data (B+G+N+V). Also Table 2 shows how close these results are to one another. Furthermore, the validation results without the genealogical information (B, B+N+V) show lower accuracy.

Table 2. Validation results using different data subsets

Data Subset	TP	FP	FN	TN	Precision	Recall	F_1-score	Accuracy	AUC	λ
B+G+N+V	2035	0	54	2089	100.00%	97.42%	98.69%	98.71%	99.98%	90.01%
B+G	2007	1	82	2088	99.95%	96.07%	97.97%	98.01%	99.97%	84.06%
B+N+V	2011	150	78	1939	93.06%	96.27%	94.64%	94.54%	98.47%	16.86%
B	587	12	1502	2077	98.00%	28.10%	43.68%	63.76%	97.48%	92.15%

Full Disambiguation. Record linkage with the real dataset was a many-to-one task, e.g. many records in the source set can be merged into one in the target data. When applying the model to the real dataset first blocking strategies [7]

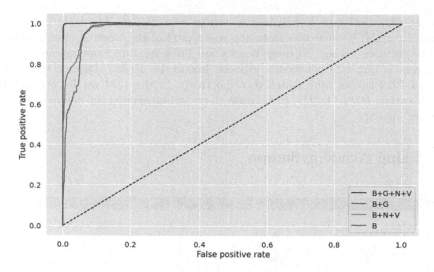

Fig. 5. ROC curve

where applied to reduce the number of comparisons. For instance, candidate pairs of different gender or mismatching life years when known, could be omitted from candidate pairs. Likewise, candidates mentioned in a same register entry text e.g. siblings or different spouses could be omitted—same person is never mentioned twice in one text entry. Some preliminary disambiguation was performed already during the data conversion, e.g., aligning spouses of a person, if the names had a high string similarity. The iterative process was run for several times because merging two person records furthermore can lead to finding more matches also among the relatives. To achieve a high precision and to minimize the number of false positive classification a high threshold values ($\lambda \geq 0.9$) were used.

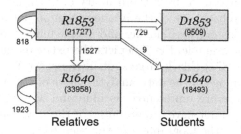

Fig. 6. Number of matches between the datasets

Figure 6 depicts the number of records in each part of the dataset and the numbers of matches detected within them. The number of records before the RL are in parenthesis. For example, 729 of the records in *R1853* were merged into *D1853*, 1527 into *R1640*, and 9 records into *D1640*. The latter number is relatively small because this matching was a part of the existing manual linkage by the dataset author, so these results are links missing from manual linkage or errors in our data conversion process. Inside the *R1853* dataset, 818 and in *R1640* 1923 entries were matched, respectively. Notice that we did not link the records from *R1640* to *D1640* because the existing manual linkage made by the dataset author.

5 Using AcademySampo

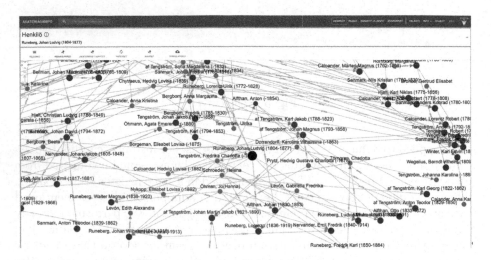

Fig. 7. Family relations of J. L. Runeberg (1804–1877) visualized in AcademySampo (Color figure online)

The people KG extracted from the primary data turned out be richly inter-linked and forms the backbone of the AcademySampo portal and LOD service. Academic circles in history were smaller and people tended to marry within their own social class. For example, Fig. 7 depicts the extracted family relations of J. L. Runeberg (1804–1877) (black large spot in the centre), the Finnish national poet, as visualized in one of the data-analytic views of the AcademySampo portal. Men in the figure are represented as blue and women as red spots. Most women in the data do not have a data entry of their own in the databases but are only mentioned in the biographies of the men because women were allowed to sign in universities only in the late 19th century. There are only 521 female academics out of 28 000 in the data.

The relations shown include both mentioned and inferred relations, such as brother in law, based on reasoning. Here is an example[14] of a SPARQL query that finds children of the same parent and concludes whether they are brothers

---

[14] https://api.triplydb.com/s/IE4w29n0T.

or sisters based on the gender. Using AcademySampo portal and the SPARQL endpoint for historical research is discussed in more detail in [17].

Deployment. The AcademySampo KG was published on the Linked Data Finland platform[15] [16] powered by Fuseki SPARQL server[16] and Varnish Cache web application accelerator[17] for routing URIs, content negotiation, and caching. The portal user interface was implemented by the Sampo-UI framework [18]. AcademySampo system is based on Docker microservice architecture containers[18]. By using containers, the services can be migrated to another computing environment easily, and third parties can re-use and run the services on their own. The architecture also allows for horizontal scaling for high availability, by starting new container replicas on demand. The portal has had 4600 distinct users during its first four months according to Google Analytics.

6 Discussion

The work described in this article shows that using genealogical information in RL is useful and can improve significantly the accuracy in person name reconciliation. This argument was tested and evaluated in detail in a case study using the AcademySampo datasets with promising results. We anticipate that similar results can be obtained in related use cases using other datasets. In the AcademySampo project, the genealogical information has been used also when linking the records with Wikidata for semantic data enrichment.

When analysing the resulting matched pairs some weak cases needing separate handling where found. Historically, patronymic family names, e.g., *Johansdotter (Daughter of Johan)* have been common for women. However, the chosen Jaro-Winkler similarity may not be optimal to always disambiguate between cases like *Jöransdotter* and *Johansdotter*. Likewise, the classifier made some false results with the vocation of a farmer. Farmer was a common vocation in the 17th–19th century Finland, but yet rare in data records of academic people, for which reason we had put some excess weight on it in the classifying system.

This paper presented a method for reconciling person names mentioned in biographical texts of other people. The method was applied to creating a semantic KG of people that is used for studying and analyzing academic networks of people. For this purpose, the AcademySampo portal has been created, but also the underlying Linked Open Data service can be used for custom-made data-analyses using, e.g., YASGUI[19] [28] and SPARQL or Python scripting in Google Colab[20] or Jupyter[21] notebooks, and for developing new applications [17].

---

[15] https://www.ldf.fi/dataset/yoma.
[16] https://jena.apache.org/documentation/fuseki2/.
[17] https://varnish-cache.org.
[18] https://www.docker.com.
[19] https://yasgui.triply.cc.
[20] https://colab.research.google.com/notebooks/intro.ipynb.
[21] https://jupyter.org.

Acknowledgements. Thanks to Yrjö Kotivuori and Veli-Matti Autio for their seminal work in creating the original databases used in our work, and for making the data openly available. Discussions with Heikki Rantala, Esko Ikkala, Mikko Koho, and Jouni Tuominen are acknowledged. This work is part of the EU project InTaVia: In/Tangible European Heritage (https://intavia.eu/), and is related to the EU COST action Nexus Linguarum (https://nexuslinguarum.eu/the-action) on linguistic data science. CSC – IT Center for Science provided computational resources for the work.

References

1. Keras Documentation, Sequence. https://www.tensorflow.org/api_docs/python/tf/keras/utils/Sequence. Accessed 10 Dec 2020
2. Antonie, L., Gadgil, H., Grewal, G., Inwood, K.: Historical data integration, a study of WWI Canadian soldiers. In: 2016 IEEE 16th International Conference on Data Mining Workshops (ICDMW), pp. 186–193. IEEE (2016)
3. Barlaug, N., Gulla, J.A.: Neural networks for entity matching. arXiv preprint arXiv:2010.11075 (2020)
4. ter Braake, S., Anstke Fokkens, R.S., Declerck, T., Wandl-Vogt, E. (eds.): BD2015, Biographical Data in a Digital World 2015. CEUR Workshop Proceedings, vol. 1399 (2015). http://ceur-ws.org/Vol-1272/
5. Brownlee, J.: Machine Learning Mastery: How to Develop a Cost-Sensitive Neural Network for Imbalanced Classification. https://machinelearningmastery.com/cost-sensitive-neural-network-for-imbalanced-classification/. Accessed 10 Dec 2020
6. Chollet, F.: Keras, The Functional API. https://keras.io/guides/functional_api/. Accessed 10 Dec 2020
7. Christen, P.: Data Matching: Concepts and Techniques for Record Linkage, Entity Resolution, and Duplicate Detection. Springer, Heidelberg (2012). https://doi.org/10.1007/978-3-642-31164-2
8. Cunningham, A.: After "it's over over there": using record linkage to enable the reconstruction of World War I veterans' demography from soldiers' experiences to civilian populations. Historical Methods: J. Quant. Interdisc. Hist. **51**, 1–27 (2018)
9. Fawcett, T.: An introduction to ROC analysis. Pattern Recogn. Lett. **27**(8), 861–874 (2006)
10. Fokkens, A., et al.: BiographyNet: extracting relations between people and events. In: Europa baut auf Biographien, pp. 193–224. New Academic Press, Wien (2017)
11. Fokkens, A., ter Braake, S., Sluijter, R., Arthur, P., Wandl-Vogt, E. (eds.): BD2017 Biographical Data in a Digital World 2015. CEUR Workshop Proceedings, vol. 1399 (2017). http://ceur-ws.org/Vol-2119/
12. Gangemi, A., Presutti, V., Recupero, D.R., Nuzzolese, A.G., Draicchio, F., Mongiovì, M.: Semantic web machine reading with FRED. Semantic Web **8**, 873–893 (2017)
13. Gu, L., Baxter, R., Vickers, D., Rainsford, C.: Record linkage: current practice and future directions. CSIRO Mathematical and Information Sciences (2003). cMIS Technical Report No. 03/83
14. Heino, E., et al.: Named entity linking in a complex domain: case second world war history. In: Gracia, J., Bond, F., McCrae, J.P., Buitelaar, P., Chiarcos, C., Hellmann, S. (eds.) LDK 2017. LNCS (LNAI), vol. 10318, pp. 120–133. Springer, Cham (2017). https://doi.org/10.1007/978-3-319-59888-8_10

15. Hyvönen, E., et al.: BiographySampo – publishing and enriching biographies on the semantic web for digital humanities research. In: Hitzler, P., et al. (eds.) ESWC 2019. LNCS, vol. 11503, pp. 574–589. Springer, Cham (2019). https://doi.org/10.1007/978-3-030-21348-0_37

16. Hyvönen, E., Tuominen, J., Alonen, M., Mäkelä, E.: Linked data Finland: a 7-star model and platform for publishing and re-using linked datasets. In: Presutti, V., Blomqvist, E., Troncy, R., Sack, H., Papadakis, I., Tordai, A. (eds.) ESWC 2014. LNCS, vol. 8798, pp. 226–230. Springer, Cham (2014). https://doi.org/10.1007/978-3-319-11955-7_24

17. Hyvönen, E., Leskinen, P., Rantala, H., Ikkala, E., Tuominen, J.: Akatemiasampo-portaali ja -datapalvelu henkilöiden ja henkilöryhmien historialliseen tutkimuk-seen (academysampo portal and data service for biographical and prosopo-graphical research). Informaatiotutkimus (2021, in press). https://seco.cs.aalto.fi/publications/2021/hyvonen-et-al-akatemiasampo-2021.pdf

18. Ikkala, E., Hyvönen, E., Rantala, H., Koho, M.: Sampo-UI: A full stack JavaScript framework for developing semantic portal user interfaces. Semantic Web (2021, accepted). http://www.semantic-web-journal.net/

19. Ivie, S., Pixton, B., Giraud-Carrier, C.: Metric-based data mining model for genealogical record linkage. In: 2007 IEEE International Conference on Information Reuse and Integration, pp. 538–543. IEEE (2007)

20. Koho, M., Gasbarra, L., Tuominen, J., Rantala, H., Jokipii, I., Hyvönen, E.: AMMO ontology of Finnish historical occupations. In: Proceedings of the First International Workshop on Open Data and Ontologies for Cultural Heritage (ODOCH 2019), vol. 2375, pp. 91–96. CEUR Workshop Proceedings, June 2019. http://ceur-ws.org/Vol-2375/

21. Koho, M., Leskinen, P., Hyvönen, E.: Integrating historical person registers as linked open data in the WarSampo knowledge graph. In: Blomqvist, E., et al. (eds.) SEMANTICS 2020. LNCS, vol. 12378, pp. 118–126. Springer, Cham (2020). https://doi.org/10.1007/978-3-030-59833-4_8

22. Langmead, A., Otis, J., Warren, C., Weingart, S., Zilinski, L.: Towards interoper-able network ontologies for the digital humanities. Int. J. Humanit. Arts Comput. 10(1), 22–35 (2016)

23. Larson, R.: Bringing lives to light: biography in context. Final Project Report, Uni-versity of Berkeley (2010). http://metadata.berkeley.edu/Biography_Final_Report.pdf

24. Leskinen, P., Hyvönen, E.: Extracting genealogical networks of linked data from biographical texts. In: Hitzler, P., et al. (eds.) ESWC 2019. LNCS, vol. 11762, pp. 121–125. Springer, Cham (2019). https://doi.org/10.1007/978-3-030-32327-1_24

25. Leskinen, P., Hyvönen, E.: Linked open data service about historical Finnish aca-demic people in 1640–1899. In: DHN 2020 Digital Humanities in the Nordic Coun-tries. Proceedings of the Digital Humanities in the Nordic Countries 5th Confer-ence, vol. 2612, pp. 284–292. CEUR Workshop Proceedings, October 2020. http://ceur-ws.org/Vol-2612/short14.pdf

26. Malmi, E., Gionis, A., Solin, A.: Computationally inferred genealogical networks uncover long-term trends in assortative mating. arXiv (2018). arXiv:1802.06055 [cs.SI]

27. Pixton, B., Giraud-Carrier, C.: Using structured neural networks for record linkage. In: Proceedings of the Sixth Annual Workshop on Technology for Family History and Genealogical Research (2006)

28. Rietveld, L., Hoekstra, R.: The YASGUI family of SPARQL clients. Semantic Web 8(3), 373–383 (2017). https://doi.org/10.3233/SW-150197

29. Rospocher, M., et al.: Building event-centric knowledge graphs from news. Web Semantics **37**, 132–151 (2016)
30. Srivastava, N., Hinton, G., Krizhevsky, A., Sutskever, I., Salakhutdinov, R.: Dropout: a simple way to prevent neural networks from overfitting. J. Mach. Learn. Res. **15**(1), 1929–1958 (2014)
31. Tan, P.N., Steinbach, M., Kumar, V.: Introduction to data mining, 1st edn (2005)
32. Thorvaldsen, G., Andersen, T., Sommerseth, H.L.: Record linkage in the historical population register for Norway. In: Bloothooft, G., Christen, P., Mandemakers, K., Schraagen, M. (eds.) Population Reconstruction, pp. 155–171. Springer, Cham (2015). https://doi.org/10.1007/978-3-319-19884-2_8
33. Wang, S., Liu, W., Wu, J., Cao, L., Meng, Q., Kennedy, P.J.: Training deep neural networks on imbalanced data sets. In: 2016 International Joint Conference on Neural Networks (IJCNN), pp. 4368–4374. IEEE (2016)
34. Warren, C., Shore, D., Otis, J., Wang, L., Finegold, M., Shalizi, C.: Six degrees of Francis Bacon: a statistical method for reconstructing large historical social networks. Digit. Humanit. Q. **10**(3) (2016)
35. Winkler, W.E.: String comparator metrics and enhanced decision rules in the fellegi-sunter model of record linkage (1990)
36. Winkler, W.E.: Overview of record linkage and current research directions. Technical report, U.S. Census Bureau (2006)

Author Index